# NEW WEBSTER'S EXPANDED DICTIONARY

edited by
R.F. Patterson, M.A., D. Litt.

## 1993 EDITION

*New Expanded Webster's Dictionary* is not associated with, or published by, the original publishers of Webster's Dictionary or their successors.

Custom Manufactured for

SUNOCO

Distributed by:
Contract Marketing, Inc.
235 West Boylston Street
West Boylston, Massachusetts 01583
(508) 835-9000

Cover Design 1993 by
Barbara Baron


Published by:
P.S.I. & Associates, Inc.
U.S.A.



Manufactured in The United States of America
1 2 3 4 5 6 7 8 9 10 - 93 92 90 89

# New Expanded Webster's Dictionary

All entries are arranged in alphabetical order and appear in bold faced type. Following each entry are related words, derivations, and meanings. Each bold entry also includes a special simplified syllabic pronunciation help. Each entry also displays a symbol indicating the specific part of speech.

## ABBREVIATIONS USED IN THIS DICTIONARY

| | | |
|---|---|---|
| *a.* adjective. | *n.pl.* noun plural. | *pret.* preterit. |
| *adu* adverb. | *p.a.* participial adjective. | *pron.* pronoun. |
| *conj.* conjunction. | *pl.* plural. | *vi.* verb intransitive. |
| *int.* interjection. | *pp.* past participle. | *vt.* verb transitive. |
| *n.* noun. | *prep.* preposition. | |

## GUIDE TO PRONUNCIATION

ch, *ch*ain; g, *g*o; ng, si*ng*; ŦH, *th*en; th, *th*in; w, *w*ig; wh, *wh*ig; ah, azure;
fāte, fär, fat, fąll; mē, met, her; pīne, pin; nōte, not, möve;
tūbe, tub, bṳll; oil, pound.

# Computer Terms and Definitions

The following is a list of some of the common terms, along with their definitions, used by the computer industry that are unique to that field.

**Basic:** A high-level interactive programming language that comes with most computers. Basic is relatively easy to learn to use if you want to try your hand at writing your own computer programs.

**Bit:** The smallest unit of information that the computer recognizes. A bit is represented in the computer by the presence or absence of an electronic pulse represented by humans as a zero or one.

**Byte:** A group of bits (usually 8 or 16) which stand for a single letter or number in the computer. Each byte is stored in its own address/location in memory.

**CAD/CAM:** Short for Computer-Aided-Design and Computer-Aided-Manufacturing—encompassing almost every computer-related design, manufacturing and business function.

**Cassette:** The cheapest and slowest way to store information when the computer's off. Cassettes transfer 30-120 bytes (characters) per second. That's slow.

**Chip (Silicon):** A microprocessor that is the complete computer on a single chip of silicon.

**COBOL:** Common Business Oriented Language—High-level programming language used for business applications.

**CP/M:** Control Program/Microcomputer. One of several "operating systems" for computers.

**CPU:** Abbreviation for Central Processing Unit. The portion of a computer, sometimes called the brain, that controls the interpretation/execution of the programs and processing instructions.

**CRT:** Abbreviation for Cathode Ray Tube. Another name for a picture tube, monitor or video display terminal (VDT).

**Data base:** Program that files information—names, addresses, amounts owed. Some programs allow the user to sort the information alphabetically, by zip code, etc.

**Disk drive:** A memory storage device that operates something like a record player, using removable, flexible diskettes (also called floppies or disks)

**DOS:** Disk Operating System. One of the most popular "operating systems" for computers.

**File:** A collection of organized records the computer treats as a unit.

**Floppy Disk:** Single flexible magnetic disk (about the size of a 45-RPM record) that is used with small computers and word processors.

**Hardware:** The physical components of a computer system.

**IC:** The abbreviation for Integrated Circuit. The small electronic components that work together on circuit boards to perform a designated task. These components are usually referred to as chips.

**I/O:** The abbreviation for Input/Output.

**Interface:** A circuit board (also called a card) that electronically connects a computer to its accessories via a cable.

**K:** One thousand (actually 1,024), usually referring to memory. A 64K computer has 64,000 (actually 65,536) characters of random access memory. One double-spaced, typed page needs about 2K of memory.

**Kilobyte (K):** Approximately one thousand bytes. This refers to the amount of computer memory in a system. For example: 512K memory equals approximately 512,000 bytes.

**Languages:** Programming languages. They include: Basic, COBOL, Pascal (business), Fortran (scientific), Forth.

**LASER:** Acronym for Light Amplification by Stimulated Emission of Radiation. A device that produces a very narrow beam of coherent light. Lasers are used to produce ultra high resolution images on advanced typesetting systems such as the CG 9600 and Scanner 2000.

**Mainframes:** Largest, fastest, and most expensive class of computers.

**Megabyte (MB):** Approximately one million bytes or one thousand kilobytes. Often used to measure disk, tape, or larger computer storage capacity. For example: 30 MB hard disk drive.

**Microcomputers:** Smallest and least expensive class of computers containing microprocessors on silicon chips.

**Microprocessor:** The miniature, integrated electronic circuit in the CPU that executes the instructions of a program task.

**MODEM:** The acronym for MOdulator/DEModulator. A device that uses a telephone hook-up to convert computer signals so that data can be sent or received over telephone lines.

**Module:** Set of logically related program statements.

**Monitor:** Video display that gives a higher quality picture than a TV set. Typical size is 12 inches diagonal. Monochrome monitors are available in green, amber, or white displays. Some have non-glare faces. Color monitors are either composite color (so-so for reading words and numbers, fine for graphics and games), or RGB (red-green-blue). Display quality depends heavily on quality of the computer signal.

**Operating system:** A program or procedure that tells the computer how to operate. The computer you buy determines the operating system you get or have to buy. To operate a computer with disk drives, you need DOS (pronounced doss), a disk operating system.

**Pascal:** Structured high-level programming language.

**Peripheral:** An input/output device directed from a controller or computer. Examples: disk drives, printers.

**Program:** Step-by-step set of instructions that directs the computer to perform certain operations to solve a problem preparing for the execution.

**Programmer:** Person trained to design, code and test computer programs.

**RAM:** Random Access Memory. The memory the computer uses to store data. The more the better. Most personal computers store up to 64K bytes (64,000 characters). You lose what's stored in RAM when the computer is turned off, which is why you need a cassette recorder or disk drive.

**ROM:** Read only memory. ROM provides permanent storage of the computer's operating system and the Basic programming language, and can't be altered. It isn't lost when the computer is off. Caution: some computer makers advertise "total memory" meaning RAM and ROM added up, while most just list RAM, which is more meaningful.

**Semiconductor (Silicon):** A crystalline substance that conducts electric current when it has been "doped" with chemical impurities shot into the lattice-like structure of the crystal.

**Software:** A term used to describe the programs, instructions and applications of a computer system.

**System:** Organized set of related components established to perform a certain task.

**Terminal:** The peripheral device used to enter or extract data from the computer. It is sometimes referred to as the workstation or human interface. It usally consists of a CRT and keyboard. Sometimes called a monitor.

**Word Processing:** Computer-based system for inputting, editing, storing and printing of documents.

# A

**A,** the indefinite article, used before a consonant. *See* AN.
**Aaron's-beard,** ā'ronz-bërd, *n*. A name of several plants.
**Aback,** a-bak', *adv*. Backwards; by surprise.
**Abacus,** ab'a-kus, *n*.; pl. **-ci,** or **-cuses.** A square slab forming the crowning of a column.
**Abaft,** a-bäft', *adv*. or *prep*. On or towards the aft or hinder part of a ship.
**Abandon,** a-ban'dun, *vt*. To forsake entirely; to desert.
**Abandoned,** a-ban'dund, *p.a*. Depraved.
**Abandonment,** a-ban'dun-ment, *n*. A total desertion.
**Abase,** a-bās', *vt*. (abasing, abased). To bring low; degrade; disgrace.
**Abasement,** a-bās'ment, *n*. State of being abased; degradation.
**Abash,** a-bash', *vt*. To put to confusion; to make ashamed.
**Abate,** a-bāt', *vt*. (abating, abated). To lessen. *vi*. To become less.
**Abatement,** a-bāt'ment, *n*. Act of abating; a mitigation; deduction.
**Abattis, Abatis,** ab'a-tis or ab-a-tē', *n*.; pl. the same. A fortification consisting of felled trees with the smaller branches cut off.
**Abattoir,** a-ba-twär', *n*. A public slaughterhouse.
**Abbacy,** ab'a-si, *n*.; pl. **-cies.** The dignity, rights, and privileges of an abbot.
**Abbé,** ab-ā, *n*. An inferior R. Catholic ecclesiastic with no benefice.
**Abbess,** ab'es, *n*. A female superior of a nunnery.
**Abbey,** ab'i, *n*.; pl. **-eys.** A monastery, or convent.
**Abbot,** ab'ut, *n*. The male superior of an abbey.
**Abbreviate,** ab-brē'vi-āt, *vt*. To shorten.
**Abbreviation,** ab-brē'vi-ā''shon, *n*. A shortening; contraction.
**Abbreviator,** ab-brē'vi-ā-tėr, *n*. One who abbreviates or abridges.
**Abdicate,** ab'di-kāt, *vt*. (abdicating, abdicated). To resign voluntarily; to relinquish. *vi*. To resign power.
**Abdication,** ab-di-kā'shon, *n*. Act of abdicating an office.
**Abdomen,** ab-dō'men, *n*. The lower belly.
**Abdominal,** ab-dom'in-al, *a*. Pertaining to the lower belly.
**Abduct,** ab-dukt', *vt*. To entice or lead away wrongly.
**Abduction,** ab-duk'shon, *n*. The felonious carrying off a man's daughter, wife, etc.
**Abeam,** a-bēm', *adv*. or *pred.a*. At right angles to the length of a ship.
**Abed,** a-bed', *adv*. On or in bed.
**Aberrant,** ab-e'rant, *a*. Wandering from; deviating from an established rule.
**Aberration,** ab-e-rā'shon, *n*. A wandering from; alienation of the mind.
**Abet,** a-bet', *vt*. (abetting, abetted). To urge on; to encourage. (Chiefly in a bad sense.)
**Abetment,** a-bet'ment, *n*. Act of abetting.
**Abetter, Abettor,** a-bet'ėr, *n*. One who abets.
**Abeyance,** a-bā'ans, *n*. Temporary extinction. (With *in* before it.)
**Abhor,** ab-hor', *vt*. (abhorring, abhorred). To shrink from with horror; to loathe, detest.
**Abhorrence,** ab-hor'rens, *n*. Detestation.
**Abhorrent,** ab-hor'rent, *a*. Hating; inconsistent with. (With *to*).
**Abide,** a-bīd, *vi*. (abiding, abode or abided). To stay in a place; to dwell.—*vt*. To wait for; to endure.
**Abiding,** a-bīd'ing, *p.a*. Permanent.
**Abigail,** ab'i-gāl, *n*. A familiar name for a waiting woman or lady's-maid.
**Ability,** a-bil'li-ti, *n*. Power to do anything; talent; skill; in *pl*. the powers of the mind.
**Abiogenesis,** ab'i-ō-jen''e-sis, *n*. The doctrine that living matter may be produced by not-living matter.
**Abiogenetic,** ab'i-o-jen-et''ik, *a*. Pertaining to abiogenesis.
**Abject,** ab'jekt, *a*. Mean; despicable.
**Abjuration,** ab-jū-rā'shon, *n*. Act of abjuring; oath taken for that end.
**Abjure,** ab-jūr', *vt*. (abjuring, abjured). To renounce upon oath; to reject.
**Ablative,** ab'lat-iv, *a*. or *n*. Applied to a case of nouns in Latin and other languages.
**Ablaze,** a-blāz', *adv*. On fire; in a blaze.
**Able,** ā'bl, *a*. Having power sufficient; capable; skilful.
**Ablution,** ab-lū'shon, *n*. A washing away from; a purification by water.
**Ably,** ā'bli, *adv*. With ability.
**Abnegate,** ab'nē-gāt, *vt*. To deny; to renounce.
**Abnegation,** ab-nē-gā'shon, *n*. A denial.
**Abnormal,** ab-norm'al, *a*. Deviating from a fixed rule; irregular.
**Aboard,** a-bōrd', *adv*. or *prep*. On board; in a ship or vessel.
**Abode,** a-bōd', *n*. Residence; habitation.
**Abolish,** a-bol'ish, *vt*. To destroy; to abrogate.
**Abolition,** ab-ō-li'shon, *n*. Act of abolishing; state of being abolished.
**Abolitionist,** ab-ō-li'shon-ist, *n*. One who seeks to abolish anything, especially slavery.
**Abominable,** a-bom'in-a-bl, *a*. Loathsome.
**Abominably,** a-bom'in-a-bli, *adv*. Odiously.
**Abominate,** a-bom'in-āt, *vt*. (abominating, abominated). To hate extremely; to abhor.
**Abomination,** a-bom'in-ā''shon, *n*. Hatred; object of hatred; loathsomeness.
**Aboriginal,** ab-ō-rij'in-al, *a*. Primitive.
**Aborigines,** ab-ō-rij'in-ēz, *n.pl*. The original inhabitants of a country.
**Abort,** a-bort', *vi*. To miscarry in giving birth.
**Abortion,** a-bor'shon, *n*. A miscarriage.
**Abortive,** a-bort'iv, *a*. Immature; causing abortion; coming to nought.
**Abortively,** a-bort'iv-li, *adv*. Immaturely.
**Abound,** a-bound', *vi*. To be, or have, in great plenty.
**Abounding,** a-bound'ing, *p.a*. In great plenty; prevalent.
**About,** a-bout', *prep*. Around; near to; relating to; engaged in.—*adv*. Around; round; nearly; here and there.
**Above,** a-buv', *prep*. To or in a higher place than; superior to; more than; beyond; before.—*adv*. To or in a higher place; chiefly.
**Above-board,** a-buv'bōrd, *adv*. Without concealment or deception.
**Abrade,** a-brād', *vt*. (abrading, abraded). To scrape off; to waste by friction.
**Abrasion,** ab-rā'zhon, *n*. A rubbing off; substance worn off by rubbing.
**Abreast,** a-brest', *adv*. In a line; side by side.
**Abridge,** a-brij', *vt*. To shorten; to condense.
**Abridgment,** a-brij'ment, *n*. An epitome; a summary.
**Abroach,** a-brōch', *adv*. In a posture to flow out; set afloat; ready to be diffused.
**Abroad,** a-brad', *adv*. At large; away from home; in a foreign country.
**Abrogate,** ab'rō-gāt, *vt*. (abrogating, abrogated). To repeal; to make void.
**Abrogation,** ab-rō-gā'shon, *n*. Act of abrogating; a repeal; annulment.
**Abrupt,** ab-rupt', *a*. Broken off; steep; sudden; unceremonious.
**Abruptly,** ab-rupt'li, *adv*. Suddenly; unceremoniously.
**Abruptness,** ab-rupt'nes, *n*. Suddenness; unceremonious haste.
**Abscess,** ab'ses, *n*. A gathering of purulent matter in some part of the body.
**Abscind,** ab-sind', *vt*. To cut off.
**Abscission,** ab-si'zhon, *n*. The act of cutting off; severance; removal.
**Abscond,** ab-skond', *vi*. To hide oneself; to fly

from justice.
**Absence,** ab'sens, *n.* State of being absent; inattention to things present.
**Absent,** ab'sent, *a.* Being away from; not present; wanting in attention.
**Absent,** ab-sent', *vt.* To keep away from. (With refl. pron.)
**Absentee,** ab-sen-tē', *n.* One who absents himself.
**Absenteeism,** ab-sen-tē'izm, *n.* State or habit of an absentee.
**Absently,** ab'sent-li, *adv.* With absence of mind.
**Absinthe,** ab'sinth, *n.* A liqueur consisting of spirit flavored with wormwood.
**Absolute,** ab'sō-lūt, *a.* Unlimited; unconditional; certain; despotic.
**Absolutely,** ab'sō-lūt-li, *adv.* Unconditionally; peremptorily.
**Absoluteness,** ab'sō-lūt-nes, *n.* State or quality of being absolute.
**Absolution,** ab-sō-lū'shon, *n.* A loosing from guilt, or its punishment.
**Absolutism,** ab'sō-lūt-izm, *n.* The principles of absolute government.
**Absolve,** ab-solv', *vt.* To free from, as from guilt or punishment; acquit; pardon.
**Absorb,** ab-sorb', *vt.* To drink in; to engross.
**Absorbable,** ab-sorb'a-bl, *a.* That may be absorbed or swallowed up.
**Absorbent,** ab-sorb'ent, *a.* Imbibing; swallowing.—*n.* That which absorbs.
**Absorption,** ab-sorp'shon, *n.* Act or process of imbibing or swallowing up.
**Abstain,** ab-stān', *vi.* To keep back from; to refrain; to forbear.
**Abstemious,** ab-stē'mi-us, *a.* Sparing in food or drink; temperate; sober.
**Absterge,** ab-stėrj', *vt.* To rub or wipe off; to cleanse.
**Abstergent,** ab-stėrj'ent, *a.* Having absterging properties.—*n.* Whatever absterges.
**Abstinence,** ab'sti-nens, *n.* A keeping from the indulgence of the appetites, especially from intoxicating liquors.
**Abstinent,** ab'sti-nent, *a.* Abstaining from; refraining from indulgence.
**Abstinently,** ab'sti-nent-li, *adv.* With abstinence.
**Abstract,** ab-strakt', *vt.* To draw from; to separate and consider by itself; to epitomize.
**Abstract,** ab'strakt, *a.* Existing in the mind only; not concrete; general in language or in reasoning.—*n.* A summary; an abridgment.
**Abstracted,** ab-strakt'ed, *a.* Absent in mind.
**Abstractedly,** ab-strakt'ed-li, *adv.* In an absent manner.
**Abstraction,** ab-strak'shon, *n.* Act of abstracting; deep thought; absence of mind.
**Abstractive,** ab-strakt'iv, *a.* Having the power or quality of abstracting.
**Abstractly,** ab-strakt'li, *adv.* Separately; absolutely.
**Abstruse,** ab-strūs', *a.* Difficult of comprehension; profound in meaning; obscure.
**Absurd,** ab-sėrd', *a.* Contrary to reason or common sense; ridiculous.
**Absurdity,** ab-sėrd'i-ti, *n.* Quality of being absurd; that which is absurd.
**Absurdly,** ab-sėrd'li, *adv.* In an absurd manner; against common sense; ridiculously.
**Abundance,** a-bun'dans, *n.* Plenteousness; copiousness; wealth.
**Abundant,** a-bun'dant, *a.* Abounding; plentiful; ample.
**Abundantly,** a-bun'dant-li, *adv.* Fully; amply; plentifully.
**Abuse,** a-būz', *vt.* (abusing, abused). To turn from the proper use; to ill-use; to deceive; to vilify; to violate.
**Abuse,** a-būs', *n.* Misuse; bad language addressed to a person; insulting words; violation.
**Abusive,** a-būs'iv, *a.* Practicing abuse; containing abuse; insulting.
**Abut,** a-but', *vi.* (abutting, abutted). To border; to meet. (With *upon*.)
**Abutment,** a-but'ment, *n.* That which abuts; solid support for the extremity of a bridge, arch, etc.
**Abyss,** a-bis', *n.* A bottomless gulf; a deep pit or mass of waters; hell.
**Acacia,** a-kā'shi-a, *n.* A genus of ornamental plants, yielding catechu, gum-arabic, etc.
**Academic, Academical,** ak-a-dem'ik, ak-a-dem'ik-al, *a.* Belonging to an academy or university.
**Academician,** ak'a-dē-mi''shi-an, *n.* A member of an academy.
**Academy,** a-kad'ē-mi, *n.* A seminary of arts or sciences; a society of persons for the cultivation of arts and sciences.
**Acajou,** ak'a-jö, *n.* A heavy red mahogany.
**Acanthus,** a-kan'thus, *n.* A prickly plant, the model of the foliage of the Corinthian order.
**Acaridan,** a-kar'i-dan, *n.* A mite, tick, or allied animal.
**Accede,** ak-sēd', *vi.* (acceding, acceded). To assent to; to comply with.
**Accelerate,** ak-sel'lė-rāt, *vt.* (accelerating, accelerated). To hasten; to quicken the speed of.
**Acceleration,** ak-sel'lė-rā''shon, *n.* Act of accelerating; increase of velocity.
**Accelerative,** ak-sel'lė-rāt-iv, *a.* Adding to velocity; accelerating.
**Accent,** ak'sent, *n.* A tone or modulation of the voice; stress of the voice on a syllable or word; the mark which indicates this stress; manner of speaking.
**Accent,** ak-sent', *vt.* To express or note the accent of.
**Accented,** ak-sent'ed, *p.a.* Uttered or marked with accent.
**Accentual,** ak-sent'ū-al, *a.* Pertaining to accent.
**Accentuate,** ak-sent'ū-āt, *vt.* (accentuating, accentuated). To mark or pronounce with an accent or accents; to emphasize.
**Accentuation,** ak-sent'ū-ā''shon, *n.* Act of marking with the proper accents.
**Accept,** ak-sept', *vt.* To receive; to admit; to promise to pay, by attaching one's signature.
**Acceptability,** ak-sept'a-bil''li-ti, *n.* Quality of being acceptable.
**Acceptable,** ak-sept'a-bl, *a.* That may be accepted; pleasing; gratifying.
**Acceptably,** ak-sept'a-bli, *adv.* In an acceptable manner.
**Acceptance,** ak-sept'ans, *n.* Reception; reception with approbation; a bill of exchange accepted.
**Acceptation,** ak-sep-tā'shon, *n.* Kind reception; meaning in which a word is understood.
**Accepter, Acceptor,** ak-sept'ėr, ak-sept'or, *n.* A person who accepts.
**Access,** ak'ses, *n.* Approach; admission; means of approach; increase.
**Accessary,** ak'ses-a-ri. *See* ACCESSORY.
**Accessibility,** ak-ses'i-bil''li-ti, *n.* Quality of being accessible.
**Accessible,** ak-ses'i-bl, *a.* Easy of approach; affable.
**Accessibly,** ak-ses'i-bli, *adv.* So as to be accessible.
**Accession,** ak-se'shon, *n.* The act of acceding; augmentation; succession to a throne.
**Accessorial,** ak-ses-sō'ri-al, *a.* Pertaining to an accessory.
**Accessory,** ak'ses-sō-ri, *a.* Additional, contributing to.—*n.* An accomplice; an adjunct.
**Accidence,** ak'si-dens, *n.* The changes which inflected parts of speech undergo; a work exhibiting such changes.
**Accident,** ak'si-dent, *n.* Quality of a being not essential to it; an unfortunate event occurring casually.
**Accidental,** ak-si-dent'al, *a.* Happening by chance; not necessarily belonging to.—*n.* A property or thing not essential.
**Accidentally,** ak-si-dent'al-li, *adv.* By accident or chance; casually.
**Acclaim,** ak-klām', *n.* Acclamation.—*vt.* To ap-

plaud; to declare by acclamation.
**Acclamation,** ak-kla-mā'shon, *n.* A shout of applause, assent, or approbation.
**Acclimatize,** ak-klī'mat-īz, *vt.* To habituate to a climate different from the native one.
**Acclivity,** ak-kliv'i-ti, *n.* A rise, as of a hill, viewed from below; ascent.
**Accolade,** ak-kō-lād', *n.* A ceremony used in conferring knighthood, usually a blow on the shoulder with the flat of a sword.
**Accommodate,** ak-kom'mō-dāt, *vt.* (accommodating, accommodated). To make suitable; to adjust; to furnish with.
**Accommodating,** ak-kom'mō-dāt-ing, *p.a.* Obliging; complying.
**Accommodation,** ak-kom'mō-dā''shon, *n.* Act of accommodating; a convenience; lodgings; loan.
**Accompaniment,** ak-kum'pa-ni-ment, *n.* That which accompanies; the subordinate part or parts, in music.
**Accompany,** ak-kum'pa-ni, *vt.* (accompanying, accompanied). To go with; to associate with; to perform music along with.
**Accomplice,** ak-kom'plis, *n.* An associate, especially in a crime.
**Accomplish,** ak-kom'plish, *vt.* To fulfil; to execute fully; to perfect.
**Accomplishable,** ak-kom'plish-a-bl, *a.* That may be accomplished.
**Accomplished,** ak-kom'plisht, *p.a.* Elegant; having a finished education.
**Accomplishment,** ak-kom'plish-ment, *n.* Fulfilment; acquirement; embellishment.
**Accord,** ak-kord', *n.* Harmony; agreement; will.—*vt.* To make to agree; to grant, or concede.—*vi.* To agree; to be in correspondence.
**Accordance,** ak-kord'ans, *n.* Agreement; conformity; harmony.
**Accordant,** ak-kord'ant, *a.* Corresponding; consonant; agreeable.
**According,** ak-kord'ing, *p.a.* Agreeing; harmonizing; agreeable.
**Accordingly,** ak-kord'ing-li, *adv.* Agreeably; consequently.
**Accordion,** ak-kord'i-on, *n.* A small melodious, keyed wind-instrument.
**Accost,** ak-kost', *vt.* To speak to first; to address.
**Accouchement,** ak-kösh'mont. *n.* Delivery in child-bed.
**Accoucheur,** ak-kö-shėr', *n.* A man who assists women in child-birth.
**Account,** ak-kount', *n.* A reckoning; a register of facts relating to money; narration; advantage; end; importance.—*vt.* To reckon; to consider; to deem; to value.—*vi.* To give or render reasons; to explain (with *for*).
**Accountability,** ak-kount'a-bil''li-ti, *n.* State of being accountable; liability.
**Accountable,** ak-kount'a-bl, *a.* Liable to be called to account; amenable.
**Accountably,** ak-kount'a-bli, *adv.* In an accountable manner.
**Accountant,** ak-kount'ant, *n.* One skilled or employed in accounts; one whose profession is to examine accounts.
**Accountantship,** ak-kount'ant-ship, *n.* The office or duties of an accountant.
**Accoutre,** ak-kö'tėr, *vt.* (accoutring, accoutred). To furnish with a military dress and arms.
**Accoutrements,** ak-kö'tėr-ments, *n.pl.* Military dress and arms; dress.
**Accredit,** ak-kred'it, *vt.* To give credit or authority to; to receive, as an envoy; to bring into vogue, as a word.
**Accredited,** ak-kred'it-ed, *p.a.* Authorized; sanctioned.
**Accresce,** ak-kres', *vi.* To accrue.
**Accrescent,** ak-kres'ent, *a.* Increasing.
**Accretion,** ak-krē'shon, *n.* A growing to, or increase by natural growth.
**Accretive,** ak-krēt'iv, *a.* Increasing by growth.
**Accrue,** ak-krö', *vi.* (accruing, accrued). To arise or come; to be added.
**Accumulate,** ak-kū'mū-lāt, *vt.* (accumulating, accumulated). To heap up; to amass.—*vi.* To increase.
**Accumulation,** ak-kū'mū-lā''shon, *n.* Act of accumulating; a heap; a collection.
**Accumulative,** ak-kū'mū-lāt-iv, *a.* That accumulates, or is accumulated.
**Accumulator,** ak-kū'mū-lāt-ėr, *n.* A kind of battery which stores electric energy.
**Accuracy,** ak'kū-rā-si, *n.* State of being accurate; precision; exactness.
**Accurate,** ak'kū-rāt, *a.* Done with care; exact; without error.
**Accurately,** ak'kū-rāt-li, *adv.* Exactly.
**Accursed,** ak-kėrs'ed, *a.* Lying under a curse; doomed; wicked.
**Accusable,** ak-kūz'a-bl, *a.* That may be accused.
**Accusation,** ak-kū-zā'shon, *n.* Act of accusing; impeachment; that of which one is accused.
**Accusative,** ak-kūz'at-iv, *a.* or *n.* A case in grammar, in English the objective.
**Accuse,** ak-kūz', *vt.* (accusing, accused). To charge with a crime; to impeach; to censure.
**Accused,** ak-kūzd', *n.* A person charged with a crime or offense.
**Accuser,** ak-kūz'ėr, *n.* One who accuses.
**Accustom,** ak-kus'tum, *vt.* To inure to a custom; to make familiar with by use.
**Accustomed,** ak-kus'tumd, *p.a.* Familiar by custom; usual; often practised.
**Ace,** ās, *n.* A unit; a single point on cards or dice; a distinguished airman, who has destroyed many enemy planes.
**Acephalous,** a-sef'al-us, *a.* Without a head.
**Acerbity,** a-sėrb'i-ti, *n.* Sourness; bitterness or severity of language.
**Acetic,** a-set'ik, *a.* Relating to vinegar; sour.
**Acetify,** a-set'i-fī, *vt.* or *i.* (acetifying, acetified). To turn into acid or vinegar.
**Acetous,** as-ēt'us, *a.* Having the quality of vinegar; sour; acid.
**Acetylene,** a-set'i-lēn, *n.* A gas used for lighting houses, &c.
**Ache,** āk, *vi.* (aching, ached). To be in pain; to be distressed.—*n.* Continued pain.
**Achieve,** a-chēv, *vt.* (achieving, achieved). To bring to an end; to accomplish; to obtain by effort.
**Achievement,** a-chēv'ment, *n.* Act of achieving; exploit; an escutcheon.
**Aching,** āk'ing, *p.a.* Being in continued pain.—*n.* Pain.
**Achromatic,** ak-rō-mat'ik, *a.* Free from color.
**Acid,** as'id, *a.* Sharp, or sour to the taste.—*n.* A sour substance; a substance that with certain other substances forms salts.
**Acidifiable,** as-id'i-fī-a-bl, *a.* Capable of being acidified.
**Acidification,** as-id'i-fi-kā''shon, *n.* The act or process of acidifying.
**Acidifier,** as-id'i-fī-ėr, *n.* A principle whose presence is necessary for acidity.
**Acidify,** as-id'i-fī, *vt.* (acidifying, acidified). To make acid; to convert into an acid.
**Acidity,** as-id'i-ti, *n.* Sourness.
**Acidulate,** as-id'ū-lāt, *vt.* To make moderately acid.
**Acidulous,** as-id'ū-lus, *a.* Slightly acid.
**Acknowledge,** ak-nol'lej, *vt.* (acknowledging, acknowledged). To own the knowledge of; to avow; to own or confess.
**Acknowledgment,** ak-nol'lej-ment, *n.* Act of acknowledging; recognition.
**Acme,** ak'mē, *n.* The top or highest point.
**Acolyte,** ak'ol-īt, *n.* One of the lowest order in the Roman church; an attendant.
**Aconite,** ak'on-īt, *n.* The herb wolf's-bane.
**Acorn,** ā'korn, *n.* The fruit of the oak.
**Acotyledon,** a-kot'il-ē''don, *n.* A plant whose seeds have no seed-lobes.
**Acotyledonous,** a-kot'il-ē''don-us, *a.* Having no seed-lobes.
**Acoustic,** a-kous'tik, *a.* Pertaining to the sense of

hearing, or to the doctrine of sounds.
**Acoustics**, a-kous'tiks, *n*. The science of sound.
**Acquaint**, ak-kwānt', *vt*. To make to know; to make familiar; to inform.
**Acquaintance**, ak-kwānt'ans, *n*. Familiar knowledge; intimacy; a person well known.
**Acquaintanceship**, ak-kwānt'ans-ship, *n*. State of being acquainted.
**Acquiesce**, ak-kwi-es', *vi*. (acquiescing, acquiesced). To rest satisfied; to admit without opposition; to comply.
**Acquiescence**, ak-kwi-es'ens, *n*. Assent.
**Acquiescent**, ak-kwi-es'ent, *a*. Resting satisfied; submitting.
**Acquirable**, ak-kwīr'a-bl, *a*. That may be acquired.
**Acquire**, ak-kwīr', *vt*. (acquiring, acquired). To obtain; to procure.
**Acquirement**, ak-kwīr'ment, *n*. Act of acquiring; the thing acquired; attainment.
**Acquisition**, ak-kwi-zi'shon, *n*. Act of acquiring; the thing acquired; gain.
**Acquisitive**, ak-kwiz'it-iv, *a*. Prone or eager to acquire.
**Acquit**, ak-kwit', *vt*. (acquitting, acquitted). To set free from a charge or blame; to absolve; to bear or conduct (with refl. pron.).
**Acquittal**, ak-kwit'al, *n*. A setting free from a charge; a judicial discharge.
**Acquittance**, ak-kwit'ans, *n*. Discharge or release from a debt.
**Acre**, ā'kėr, *n*. A quantity of land, containing 4840 square yards.
**Acreage**, ā'kėr-āj, *n*. A number of acres in a piece of land.
**Acred**, ā'kėrd, *a*. Possessing acres or landed property.
**Acrid**, ak'rid, *a*. Sharp; hot or biting to the taste; corroding; harsh.
**Acridity**, ak-rid'i-ti, *n*. Acrid quality.
**Acrimonious**, ak-ri-mō'ni-us, *a*. Full of acrimony; severe; sarcastic.
**Acrimoniously**, ak-ri-mō'ni-us-li, *adv*. With sharpness or acrimony.
**Acrimony**, ak'ri-mo-ni, *n*. Sharpness; harshness; severity.
**Acrobat**, ak'rō-bat, *n*. A rope-dancer; one who practices vaulting, tumbling, etc.
**Acrobatic**, ak'rō-bat-ik, *a*. Pertaining to an acrobat or his performance.
**Acrocephalic**, ak'rō-se-fal''ik, *a*. High-skulled.
**Acrogen**, ak'rō-jen, *n*. A plant increasing by extension of the stem at the top.
**Acrogenous**, a-kroj'en-us, *a*. Pertaining to acrogens.
**Acropolis**, a-krop'o-lis, *n*. The citadel of a Greek city, as of Athens.
**Across**, a-kros', *prep*. or *adv*. From side to side; transversely; crosswise.
**Acrostic**, a-kros'tik, *n*. A composition in verse, in which the first (or other) letters of the lines form the name of a person, etc.
**Act**, akt, *vi*. To be in action; to exert power; to conduct oneself.—*vt*. To do; to perform, as an assumed part; to counterfeit.—*n*. A deed; power, or the effect of power, put forth; a state of reality; a part of a play; law, as an act of parliament.
**Acting**, akt'ing, *n*. Action; mode of performing a part of a play.
**Actinia**, ak-tin'i-a, *n*.; pl. **-iae.** A sea-anemone.
**Actinic**, ak-tin'ik, *a*. Pertaining to actinism.
**Actinism**, ak'tin-izm, *n*. The chemical action of the sun's rays.
**Action**, ak'shon, *n*. A deed; operation; a series of events; gesture; a suit or process; an engagement, battle.
**Actionable**, ak'shon-a-bl, *a*. Furnishing ground for an action at law.
**Active**, ak'tiv, *a*. That acts or is in action; busy; quick; denoting action.
**Actively**, ak'tiv-li, *adv*. In an active manner.
**Activity**, ak-tiv'i-ti, *n*. Quality of being active; agility; nimbleness.
**Actor**, akt'ėr, *n*. One who acts; an active agent; a stage-player.
**Actress**, akt'res, *n*. A female stage-player.
**Actual**, ak'tū-al, *a*. Existing in act; real; certain; positive.
**Actuality**, ak-tū-al'li-ti, *n*. State of being actual; reality.
**Actually**, ak'tū-al-li, *adv*. In fact; really.
**Actuary**, ak'tū-a-ri, *n*. A registrar or clerk; a specially able accountant.
**Actuate**, ak'tū-āt, *vt*. (actuating, actuated). To put into action; to incite.
**Aculeate**, a-kū'lē-āt, *a*. Having prickles or sharp points.
**Acumen**, a-kū'men, *n*. Sharpness of perception; sagacity.
**Acupressure**, ak-ū-pre'shūr, *n*. The stopping of hemorrhage from arteries, in surgical operations, by needles or wires.
**Acute**, a-kūt', *a*. Sharpened; sharp; ending in a sharp point; penetrating; having nice sensibility; sharp in sound.
**Acutely**, a-kūt'li, *adv*. Sharply.
**Acuteness**, a-kūt'nes, *n*. Sharpness; shrewdness; faculty of nice perception.
**Adage**, ad'āj, *n*. A proverb; a maxim.
**Adagio**, a-da'jō, *a*. and *adv*. In *music*, slow; with grace.—*n*. A slow movement.
**Adamant**, ad'a-mant, *n*. Any substance of impenetrable hardness; the diamond.
**Adamantine**, ad-a-mant'in, *a*. Made of adamant; very hard.
**Adam's-apple**, ad'amz-ap'l, *n*. The prominence on the forepart of the throat.
**Adapt**, a-dapt', *vt*. To fit; to adjust; to suit.
**Adaptability**, a-dapt'a-bil''li-ti, *n*. Capability of being adapted.
**Adaptable**, a-dapt'a-bl, *a*. That may be adapted.
**Adaptation**, a-dap-tā'shon, *n*. Act of adapting; the result of adapting.
**Add**, ad, *vt*. To join to; to annex; to say further.
**Addendum**, ad-den'dum, *n*.; pl. **-da.** A thing to be added; an appendix.
**Adder**, ad'ėr, *n*. A venomous serpent.
**Addict**, ad-dikt', *vt*. To apply habitually; generally in a bad sense, with refl. pron.
**Addicted**, ad-dikt'ed, *p.a*. Habitually given to a practice; inclined; prone.
**Addiction**, ad-dik'shon, *n*. The state of being addicted; devotion.
**Addition**, ad-di'shon, *n*. Act of adding; the thing added; increase.
**Additional**, ad-di'shon-al, *a*. Added on.
**Additive**, ad'it-iv, *a*. That is to be or may be added.
**Addle**, ad'l, *a*. Rotten; barren.—*vt*. (addling, addled). To make corrupt or barren.
**Addle-headed**, ad'l-hed-ed, *a*. Having barren brains; of weak intellect.
**Address**, ad-dres', *vt*. To direct; to apply to by words or writing; to speak to; to apply (oneself); to write a name and destination on.—*n*. Verbal or written application; speech or discourse to a person; tact; courtship (generally in *plural*); direction of a letter.
**Addressee**, ad-dres'ē, *n*. One addressed.
**Adduce**, ad-dūs', *vt*. (adducing, adduced). To bring forward; to cite.
**Adducible**, ad-dūs'i-bl, *a*. That may be adduced.
**Adductor**, ad-dukt'ėr, *n*. A muscle which draws one part to another.
**Adenoid**, ad'en-oid, *a*. Glandular.—*n.pl.* Gland-like morbid growths in the throat behind the soft palate.
**Adept**, a-dept', *n*. One fully skilled in any art.—*a*. Well skilled; completely versed or acquainted.
**Adequacy**, ad'ē-kwa-si, *n*. State or quality of being adequate.
**Adequate**, ad'ē-kwāt, *a*. Equal to; proportionate; fully sufficient.
**Adequately**, ad'ē-kwāt-li, *adv*. In an adequate manner.

**Adhere,** ad-hēr', *vi.* (adhering, adhered). To stick; to cling; to remain firm.
**Adherence,** ad-hēr'ens, *n.* State of adhering; attachment; fidelity.
**Adherent,** ad-hēr'ent, *a.* Sticking to; united with.—*n.* A follower; a partisan.
**Adhesion,** ad-hē'zhon, *n.* Act or state of sticking to; adherence.
**Adhesive,** ad-hē'siv, *a.* Apt or tending to adhere; sticky; tenacious.
**Adhibit,** ad-hib'it, *vt.* To attach (one's signature).
**Adhortatory,** ad-hor'ta-tō-ri, *a.* Containing counsel or warning.
**Adieu,** a-dū', *interj.* Farewell.—*n.*; pl. **-us** or **-ux.** A farewell.
**Adipose,** ad'i-pōs, *a.* Consisting of or resembling fat; fatty.
**Adit,** ad'it, *n.* An approach; the horizontal opening into a mine.
**Adjacence, Adjacency,** ad-jā'sens, ad-jā'sen-si, *n.* State of lying close or contiguous.
**Adjacent,** ad-jā'sent, *a.* Lying near; adjoining; contiguous; neighboring.
**Adjectival,** ad'jek-tiv-al, *a.* Belonging to or like an adjective.
**Adjective,** ad'jek-tiv, *n.* A word used with a noun, to express some quality or circumstance.
**Adjoin,** ad-join', *vt.* To join to.—*vi.* To lie or be next; to be contiguous.
**Adjoining,** ad-join'ing, *p.a.* Adjacent.
**Adjourn,** ad-jėrn', *vt.* To put off to a future day; to postpone.—*vi.* To leave off for a future meeting.
**Adjournment,** ad-jėrn'ment, *n.* Act of adjourning; interval during which a public body defers business.
**Adjudge,** ad-juj', *vt.* To decree judicially; to decide.
**Adjudicate,** ad-jū'di-kāt, *vt.* To adjudge; to determine judicially.
**Adjudication,** ad-jū'di-kā''shon, *n.* Judicial sentence; judgment or decision.
**Adjudicator,** ad-jū'di-kāt-or, *n.* One who adjudicates.
**Adjunct,** ad'jungkt, *n.* A thing (or person) joined to another.—*a.* United with.
**Adjuration,** ad-jū-rā'shon, *n.* Act of adjuring; an oath or solemn charge.
**Adjure,** ad-jūr', *vt.* (adjuring, adjured). To charge on oath; to charge earnestly and solemnly.
**Adjust,** ad-just', *vt.* To rectify; to make exact; to regulate; to adapt; to settle.
**Adjustable,** ad-just'a-bl, *a.* That may or can be adjusted.
**Adjustment,** ad-just'ment, *n.* Act of adjusting; arrangement; settlement.
**Adjutancy,** ad'jū-tan-si, *n.* Office of an adjutant.
**Adjutant,** ad'jū-tant, *n.* An officer who assists a commanding officer; a large species of bird allied to the stork.
**Admeasure,** ad-me'zhūr, *vt.* To ascertain the size or capacity of.
**Admeasurement,** ad-me'zhūr-ment, *n.* Act of admeasuring; dimensions.
**Adminicle,** ad-min'i-kl, *n.* Support; aid.
**Administer,** ad-min'is-tėr, *vt.* To manage; to dispense; to distribute.
**Administration,** ad-min'is-trā''shon, *n.* Management; executive part of a government.
**Administrative,** ad-min'is-trāt-iv, *a.* That administers.
**Administrator,** ad-min-is-trāt'or, *n.* One who manages an intestate estate.
**Admirable,** ad'mi-ra-bl, *a.* Worthy of admiration; excellent.
**Admirably,** ad'mi-ra-bli, *adv.* In an admirable manner.
**Admiral,** ad'mi-ral, *n.* The chief commander of a fleet or navy.
**Admiralty,** ad'mi-ral-ti, *n.* A board of officials for administering naval affairs; the official buildings of this board.
**Admiration,** ad-mi-rā'shon, *n.* Wonder mingled with delight; esteem.
**Admire,** ad-mīr', *vt.* (admiring, admired). To regard with delight or affection.
**Admirer,** ad-mīr'ėr, *n.* One who admires; a lover.
**Admiringly,** ad-mīr'ing-li, *adv.* With admiration.
**Admissibility,** ad-mis'i-bil''li-ti, *n.* Quality of being admissible.
**Admissible,** ad-mis'i-bl, *a.* That may be admitted.
**Admission,** ad-mi'shon, *n.* Admittance; access; introduction; concession.
**Admit,** ad-mit', *vt.* (admitting, admitted). To allow to enter; to grant; to concede.
**Admittance,** ad-mit'ans, *n.* Permission to enter; entrance; allowance.
**Admixture,** ad-miks'tūr, *n.* That which is mixed with something else; a mixing.
**Admonish,** ad-mon'ish, *vt.* To warn; to reprove solemnly or quietly; to exhort.
**Admonisher,** ad-mon'ish-ėr, *n.* One who admonishes.
**Admonition,** ad-mō-ni'shon, *n.* Gentle or solemn reproof; instruction; caution.
**Admonitory,** ad-mon'i-tō-ri, *a.* Containing admonition.
**Ado,** a-dö', *n.* Stir; bustle; difficulty.
**Adobe,** a-dō'be, *n.* A sun-dried brick.
**Adolescence,** ad-ō-les'ens, *n.* A growing up to manhood; the age of youth.
**Adolescent,** ad-ō-les'ent, *a.* Advancing to manhood.
**Adopt,** a-dopt', *vt.* To take and treat as a child, giving a title to the rights of a child; to embrace.
**Adoption,** a-dop'shon, *n.* Act of adopting; state of being adopted.
**Adoptive,** a-dopt'iv, *a.* Adopting or adopted.
**Adorable,** a-dōr'a-bl, *a.* Worthy to be adored.
**Adorably,** a-dōr'a-bli, *adv.* In a manner worthy of adoration.
**Adoration,** a-dōr-ā'shon, *n.* Worship paid to God; profound reverence.
**Adore,** a-dōr', *vt.* (adoring, adored). To address in prayer; to worship with reverence and awe; to love intensely.
**Adorer,** a-dōr'ėr, *n.* One who adores.
**Adoringly,** a-dōr'ing-li, *adv.* With adoration.
**Adorn,** a-dorn', *vt.* To deck with ornaments; to embellish; to beautify.
**Adown,** a-doun', *prep.* Down; towards the lower part of.—*adv.* Down; on the ground.
**Adrift,** a-drift', *adv.* Floating at random; at the mercy of any impulse.
**Adroit,** a-droit', *a.* Dexterous; skilful; ready.
**Adroitly,** a-droit'li, *adv.* With dexterity.
**Adroitness,** a-droit'nes, *n.* Dexterity.
**Adscititious,** ad'si-ti''shus, *a.* Additional; not requisite.
**Adstriction,** ad-strik'shon, *n.* A binding fast.
**Adulation,** ad-ū-lā'shon, *n.* Servile flattery; excessive praise.
**Adulatory,** ad'ū-lā-tō-ri, *a.* Flattering; praising excessively or servilely.
**Adult,** a-dult', *a.* Grown to maturity.—*n.* A person grown to manhood.
**Adulterate,** a-dul'tėr-āt, *vt.* (adulterating, adulterated). To change to a worse state by mixing; to contaminate with base matter.
**Adulterate,** a-dul'tėr'āt, *a.* Adulterated.
**Adulterated,** a-dul'tėr-āt-ed, *p.a.* Debased by admixture.
**Adulteration,** a-dul'tėr-ā''shon, *n.* Act of adulterating, or state of being adulterated.
**Adulterer,** a-dul'tėr-ėr, *n.* A man guilty of adultery.
**Adulteress,** a-dul'tėr-es, *n.* A woman guilty of adultery.
**Adulterine,** a-dul'tėr-īn, *a.* Proceeding from adulterous commerce; spurious.
**Adulterous,** a-dul'tėr-us, *a.* Guilty of adultery; pertaining to adultery.
**Adulterously,** a-dul'tėr-us-li, *adv.* In an adulterous manner.
**Adultery,** a-dul'tė-ri, *n.* Unfaithfulness to the

A

marriage-bed.
**Adumbrate,** ad-um'brāt, *vt.* (adumbrating, adumbrated). To give a faint shadow of; to shadow out; to describe faintly.
**Adumbration,** ad-um-brā'shon, *n.* Act of adumbrating; a faint sketch.
**Adust,** a-dust', *a.* Burnt up; scorched.
**Advance,** ad-vans', *vt.* (advancing, advanced). To put forward; to promote; (in *commerce*) to pay beforehand; to supply.—*vi.* To go forward; to be promoted.—*n.* A going forward; preferment; first hint or step; rise in value; a giving beforehand.
**Advanced,** ad-vanst', *p.a.* In the van of intellectual or religious progress.
**Advancement,** ad-vans'ment, *n.* Act of moving forward; improvement.
**Advantage,** ad-van'tāj, *n.* Favorable state; superiority; gain—*vt.* (advantaging, advantaged). To benefit; to promote.
**Advantageous,** ad-van-tāj'us, *a.* Profitable; beneficial; useful.
**Advantageously,** ad-van-tāj'us-li, *adv.* In an advantageous manner.
**Advent,** ad'vent, *n.* Arrival; the coming of Christ; the four weeks before Christmas.
**Adventitious,** ad-ven-ti'shi-us, *a.* Accidental; casual; accessory; foreign.
**Adventure,** ad-ven'tūr, *n.* Hazardous enterprise; a bold undertaking.—*vt.* To risk or hazard.—*vi.* To dare; to venture.
**Adventurer,** ad-ven'tūr-ėr, *n.* One who risks, hazards, or braves.
**Adventuress,** ad-ven'tūr-es, *n.* A female adventurer.
**Adventurous,** ad-ven'tūr-us, *a.* Prone to incur hazard; daring; full of hazard.
**Adventurously,** ad-ven'tūr-us-li, *adv.* In a manner to incur hazard.
**Adverb,** ad'vėrb, *n.* A word which modifies a verb, adjective, or another adverb.
**Adverbial,** ad-vėrb'i-al, *a.* Pertaining to an adverb.
**Adverbially,** ad-vėrb'i-al-li, *adv.* In the manner of an adverb.
**Adversary,** ad'vėr-sa-ri, *n.* An enemy; an antagonist.
**Adversative,** ad-vėrs'at-iv, *a.* Noting or causing opposition.—*n.* A word denoting opposition.
**Adverse,** ad'vėrs, *a.* Hostile; unprosperous.
**Adversely,** ad-vėrs'li, *adv.* In an adverse manner.
**Adversity,** ad-vėrs'i-ti, *n.* Misfortune; affliction; calamity; distress.
**Advert,** ad-vėrt', *vi.* To refer or allude to; to regard. (With *to*.)
**Advertence,** ad-vėrt'ens, *n.* Regard; attention; heedfulness.
**Advertent,** ad-vėrt'ent, *a.* Attentive.
**Advertise,** ad-vėr-tīz', *vt.* (advertising, advertised). To inform; to announce; to publish a notice of.
**Advertisement,** ad-vėr'tiz-ment, *n.* Information; public notice.
**Advertiser,** ad-vėr-tīz'ėr, *n.* One who advertises.
**Advertising,** ad-vėr-tīz'ing, *p.a.* Containing or furnishing advertisements.
**Advice,** ad-vīs', *n.* Opinion offered; counsel; information.
**Advisable,** ad-vīs'a-bl, *a.* Fitting or proper to be done; expedient; fit.
**Advise,** ad-vīz', *vt.* (advising, advised). To counsel; to warn; to inform.—*vi.* To deliberate or consider.
**Advised,** ad-vīzd', *p.a.* Cautious; done with advice.
**Advisedly,** ad-vīz'ed-li, *adv.* With deliberation or advice.
**Adviser,** ad-vīz'ėr, *n.* One who advises.
**Advocacy,** ad'vō-kā-si, *n.* Act of pleading for; defence; vindication.
**Advocate,** ad'vō-kāt, *n.* One who pleads for another; an intercessor.—*vt.* (advocating, advocated). To plead in favor of; to vindicate.
**Advocateship,** ad'vō-kāt-ship, *n.* The office or duty of an advocate.
**Adze,** adz, *n.* A kind of axe, with the edge at right angles to the handle.
**Aedile,** ē'dīl, *n.* A Roman magistrate who had the care of public buildings, etc.
**Aegis,** ē'jis, *n.* A shield; protection.
**Aeolian,** ē-ō'li-an, *a.* Pertaining to Aeolus, the god of the winds; played upon by the wind.
**Aerate,** ā'ėr-āt, *vt.* (aerating, aerated). To put air into; to combine with carbonic acid.
**Aeration,** ā-ėr-ā'shon, *n.* Impregnation of a liquid with carbonic acid gas.
**Aerial,** ā-ē'ri-al, *a.* Belonging to the air; high; lofty.—*n.* The overhead structure of a wireless station, used for transmitting and receiving electrical oscillations.
**Aerie,** ē'rē, *n.* The nest of a bird of prey; a brood of such birds.
**Aerify,** ā'ėr-i-fī, *vt.* (aerifying, aerified). To infuse air into.
**Aerolite,** ā'ėr-ō-līt, *n.* A meteoric stone; a meteorite.
**Aerology,** ā-ėr-ol'o-ji, *n.* The science of atmospheric phenomena.
**Aerometer,** ā-ėr-om'et-ėr, *n.* An instrument for finding the density of air and gases.
**Aerometry,** ā-ėr-om'et-ri, *n.* The science of measuring the density of air and gases.
**Aeronaut,** ā-ėr-ō-nat, *n.* One who sails or floats in the air.
**Aeronautic,** ā'ėr-ō-nat''ik, *a.* Pertaining to aerial sailing.
**Aeronautics,** ā'ėr-ō-nat''iks, *n.* The science or art of flying in aircraft.
**Aerostatic,** ā'ėr-ō-stat''ik, *a.* Pertaining to aerostatics.
**Aerostatics,** ā'ėr-ō-stat''iks, *n.* The science which treats of air in a state of rest.
**Aesculapian,** es-kū-lā'pi-an, *a.* Pertaining to Aesculapius, the god of medicine.
**Aesthetic, Aesthetical,** ēs-thet'ik, ēs-thet'ik-al, or es-, *a.* Pertaining to aesthetics.
**Aesthetics,** ēs-thet'iks, or es-, *n.* The science of the beautiful; the philosophy of taste.
**Afar,** a-fär', *adv.* At, to, or from a distance.
**Affability,** af-fa-bil'i-ti, *n.* Courteousness; civility; urbanity.
**Affable,** af'fa-bl, *a.* Easy to be spoken to; courteous; accessible.
**Affably,** af'fa-bli, *adv.* In an affable manner.
**Affair,** af-fār', *n.* That which is to do, or which is done; business.
**Affect,** af-fekt', *vt.* To act upon; to move the feelings of; to aim at; to pretend.
**Affectation,** af-fek-tā'shon, *n.* False pretense; an artificial air put on by a person.
**Affected,** af-fekt'ed, *p.a.* Inclined to; full of affectation; assumed artificially.
**Affectedly,** af-fekt'ed-li, *adv.* In an affected manner; feignedly.
**Affecting,** af-fekt'ing, *p.a.* Pathetic; tender; exciting.
**Affectingly,** af-fekt'ing-li, *adv.* In an affecting manner.
**Affection,** af-fek'shon, *n.* The state of being affected; fondness; love.
**Affectionate,** af-fek'shon-āt, *a.* Tender; loving; fond.
**Affectionately,** af-fek'shon-āt-li, *adv.* Fondly.
**Affectioned,** af-fek'shond, *a.* Inclined.
**Affeer,** af-fēr', *vt.* To assess or settle, as an arbitrary fine.
**Afferent,** af'fėr-ent, *a.* Carrying to or inwards.
**Affiance,** af-fī'ans, *n.* Faith pledged; marriage contract; reliance.—*vt.* (affiancing, affianced). To pledge one's faith to; to betroth.
**Affianced,** af-fī'anst, *p.a.* Betrothed.
**Affidavit,** af-fi-dā'vit, *n.* A written declaration upon oath.
**Affiliate,** af-fil'li-āt, *vt.* (affiliating, affiliated). To adopt; to assign to a father; to unite to a chief society or body.

**Affiliation,** af-fil'li-ā''shon, *n.* Act of affiliating; association.
**Affinity,** af-fin'i-ti, *n.* Relation by marriage; resemblance; chemical attraction.
**Affirm,** af-fėrm', *vt.* To assert; to declare; to ratify.—*vi.* To declare solemnly.
**Affirmable,** af-fėrm'a-bl, *a.* That may be affirmed.
**Affirmation,** af-fėrm-ā'shon, *n.* Act of affirming; declaration; ratification.
**Affirmative,** af-fėrm'at-iv, *a.* That affirms; positive.—*n.* That which expresses assent.
**Affirmatively,** af-fėrm'at-iv-li, *adv.* In an affirmative manner.
**Affix,** af-fiks', *vt.* To fasten to; to subjoin.—*n.* af-'fiks. A syllable or letter added to a word.
**Afflatus,** af-flā'tus, *n.* Inspiration.
**Afflict,** af-flikt', *vt.* To distress; to grieve; to harass.
**Affluence,** af'flū-ens, *n.* A flowing to; abundance; opulence; wealth.
**Affluent,** af'flū-ent, *a.* Flowing to; wealthy; abundant.—*n.* A river that flows into another river.
**Afflux,** af'fluks, *n.* A flowing to; that which flows to.
**Afford,** af-fōrd', *vt.* To yield; to supply; to be able to give, grant, buy, or expend.
**Afforest,** af-for'est, *vt.* To convert into forest.
**Affranchise,** af-fran'chiz, *vt.* To make free.
**Affray,** af-frā', *n.* A tumult; brawl.
**Affront,** af-frunt', *vt.* To insult; to offend.—*n.* Open defiance; insult.
**Afield,** a-fēld', *adv.* To or in the field.
**Afloat,** a-flōt', *adv.* or *a.* Floating; in circulation (as a rumor).
**Afoot,** a-fut', *adv.* On foot, in action.
**Aforehand,** a-fōr'hand, *adv.* Beforehand; before.
**Aforementioned,** a-fōr'men-shond, *a.* Mentioned before.
**Aforenamed,** a-fōr'nāmd, *a.* Named before.
**Aforesaid,** a-fōr'sād, *a.* Said before.
**Afraid,** a-frād', *a.* Struck with fear; fearful.
**Afresh,** a-fresh', *adv.* Anew; again.
**African,** af'rik-an, *a.* Belonging to Africa.—*n.* A native of Africa.
**Afrikander,** af'rik-an-dėr, *n.* A native of South Africa, born of white, especially of Dutch, parents.
**Aft,** äft, *a.* or *adv.* Abaft; astern.
**After,** äft'ėr, *a.* Later in time; subsequent.—*prep.* Later in time than; behind; according to; in imitation of.—*adv.* Later in time.
**Afterbirth,** äft'ėr-bėrth, *n.* That which is expelled from the uterus after the birth of a child.
**Aftermath,** äft'ėr-math, *n.* A second crop of grass in the same season; consequences; results.
**Aftermost,** äft'ėr-most, *a.* Hindmost.
**Afternoon,** äft'ėr-nön, *n.* The part of the day which follows noon.
**Afterpiece,** äft'ėr-pēs, *n.* A piece performed after a play; a farce.
**Afterthought,** äft'ėr-that, *n.* Reflection after an act.
**Afterward, Afterwards,** äft'ėr-wėrd, äft'ėr-wėrdz, *adv.* In subsequent time.
**Again,** a-gen', *adv.* Once more; further.
**Against,** a-genst', *prep.* In opposition to; in expectation of.
**Agape,** a-gāp', *a.* With the mouth wide open.
**Agate,** ag'āt, *n.* A semi-pellucid mineral.
**Age,** āj, *n.* A period of time; an epoch; number of years during which a person has lived; decline of life; oldness; legal maturity.—*vi.*and *t.* (aging, aged). To grow or make old; to show signs of advancing age.
**Aged,** āj'ed, *a.* Old; having a certain age.
**Agency,** ā'jen-si, *n.* Instrumentality; office or business of an agent.
**Agenda,** a-jen'da, *n.pl.* Memoranda; business to be transacted at a meeting.
**Agent,** ā'jent, *n.* One who acts; a deputy; an active cause or power.
**Agglomerate,** ag-glom'mė-rāt, *vt.* To gather into a mass.—*vi.* To grow into a mass.
**Agglomeration,** ag-glom'mė-rā''shon, *n.* Act of agglomerating; heap.
**Agglutinant,** ag-glū'tin-ant, *n.* Any viscous or gluey substance.
**Agglutinate,** ag-glū'tin-āt, *vt.* To glue to; to cause to adhere.
**Agglutination,** ag-glū'tin-ā''shon, *n.* Act of agglutinating; in *philology*, the loose combination of roots to form words.
**Aggrandize,** ag'gran-dīz, *vt.* To make great; to magnify.
**Aggrandizement,** ag'gran-dīz-ment, *n.* Act of aggrandizing; augmentation.
**Aggravate,** ag'gra-vāt, *vt.* (aggravating, aggravated). To intensify; to exasperate.
**Aggravating,** ag'gra-vāt'ing, *p.a.* Making worse; provoking.
**Aggravation,** ag-gra-vā'shon, *n.* Act of aggravating; provocation.
**Aggregate,** ag'grē-gāt, *vt.* To bring together; to heap up.—*a.* Formed of parts collected.—*n.* A sum, mass, or assemblage of particulars.
**Aggregately,** ag'grē-gāt-li, *adv.* Collectively.
**Aggregation,** ag-grē-gā'shon, *n.* Act of aggregating; an aggregate or collection.
**Aggression,** ag-gre'shon, *n.* The first act of hostility; attack.
**Aggressive,** ag-gres'iv, *a.* Taking the first step against; prone to encroachment.
**Aggressor,** ag-gres'or, *n.* The person who commences hostilities.
**Aggrieve,** ag-grēv', *vt.* To pain, oppress, or injure.
**Aghast,** a-gast', *a.* or *adv.* Amazed; stupefied. Also *agast.*
**Agile,** aj'il, *a.* Ready to act; nimble.
**Agility,** a-jil'i-ti, *n.* Nimbleness; activity.
**Agio,** ā'ji-ō, *n.* The difference in value between paper and metallic money.
**Agitate,** aj'it-āt, *vt.* (agitating, agitated). To put in violent motion; to shake briskly; to excite; to consider; to discuss.
**Agitated,** aj'it-āt-ed, *p.a.* Disturbed.
**Agitation,** aj-it-ā'shon, *n.* Excitement; emotion; discussion.
**Agitator,** aj'it-āt-or, *n.* One who excites discontent, sedition, or revolt.
**Aglet,** ag'let, *n.* A point or tag at the ends of fringes or of lace.
**Agnate,** ag'nāt, *a.* Related by the father's side.
**Agnomen,** ag-nō'men, *n.* An additional name or epithet conferred on a person.
**Agnostic,** ag-nos'tik, *n.* One who disclaims any knowledge of God or of anything but material phenomena.—*a.* Pertaining to agnostics or their doctrines.
**Agnosticism,** ag-nos'ti-sizm, *n.* The doctrines or belief of agnostics.
**Ago,** a-gō, *adv.* or *a.* Past; gone.
**Agog,** a-gog', *adv.* In eager excitement.
**Agoing,** a-gō'ing, *adv.* In motion.
**Agonize,** ag'ō-nīz, *vi.* (agonizing, agonized). To writhe with extreme pain.—*vt.* To distress with extreme pain; to torture.
**Agonizing,** ag'ō-nīz-ing, *p.a.* Giving extreme pain.
**Agonizingly,** ag'ō-nīz-ing-li, *adv.* With extreme anguish.
**Agony,** ag'ō-ni, *n.* Extreme pain of body or mind; anguish; the pangs of death.
**Agora,** ag'o-ra, *n.* A public assembly in ancient Greece; the marketplace.
**Agrarian,** a-grā'ri-an, *a.* Relating to lands.
**Agrarianism,** a-grā'ri-an-izm, *n.* The principles of those who favor an equal division of lands.
**Agree,** a-grē', *vi.* (agreeing, agreed). To be in concord; to correspond; to suit.
**Agreeable,** a-grē'a-bl, *a.* Suitable to; pleasing; grateful.
**Agreeableness,** a-grē'a-bl-nes, *n.* Quality of being agreeable; suitableness.

A

**Agreeably,** a-grē'a-bli, *adv.* In an agreeable manner; conformably.
**Agreement,** a-grē'ment, *n.* Harmony, conformity; stipulation.
**Agrestic,** a-gres'tik, *a.* Rural; rustic.
**Agricultural,** ag-ri-kul'tūr-al, *a.* Pertaining to agriculture.
**Agriculture,** ag'ri-kul-tūr, *n.* The art or science of cultivating the ground.
**Agriculturist,** ag-ri-kul'tūr-ist, *n.* One skilled in agriculture.
**Aground,** a-ground', *adv.* Stranded.
**Ague,** ā'gū, *n.* An intermittent fever, with cold fits and shivering.
**Agued,** ā'gūd, *p.a.* Having a fit of ague.
**Aguish,** ā'gū-ish, *a.* Having the qualities of an ague; shivering.
**Ah,** ä, *interj.* Expressing surprise, pity, etc.
**Aha,** ä-hä', *interj.* Expressing triumph or contempt.
**Ahead,** a-hed', *adv.* Before; onward.
**Ahoy,** a-hoi', *exclam.* A sea-term used in hailing.
**Aid,** ād, *vt.* To help; to relieve.—*n.* Help; assistance; a helper.
**Aide-de-camp,** ād-de-konp, *n.*; pl. **Aides-de-camp.** An officer attendant on a general.
**AIDS,** ādz, *n.* Acquired Immune Deficiency Syndrome. A breakdown of the human body's immune system.
**Aigret, Aigrette,** ā'gret, ā-gret', *n.* A plume or ornament for the head composed of feathers or precious stones.
**Aiguille,** ā'gwil, *n.* A needle-like pointed rock or mountain mass, or mass of ice.
**Ail,** āl, *vt.* To pain; to affect with uneasiness.—*vi.* To be in pain or trouble.
**Ailment,** āl'ment, *n.* Pain; disease.
**Aim,** ām, *vi.* To point with a missive weapon; to intend; to endeavor.—*vt.* To level or direct as a firearm.—*n.* That which is aimed at; direction; purpose; drift.
**Aimless,** ām'les, *a.* Without aim.
**Air,** ār, *n.* The fluid which we breathe; a light breeze; a tune; mien; *pl.* affected manner.—*vt.* To expose to the air; to ventilate; to dry.
**Air-bladder,** ār'blad-dėr, *n.* The bladder of a fish containing air.
**Aircraft,** ār-kraft, *n.* A general name for craft designed for the navigation of the air, such as airplanes, airships or balloons.
**Air-cushion,** ār'kush-on, *n.* An inflated bag of air-tight cloth or indiarubber.
**Airgraph,** ār'graf, *n.* A letter reproduced as a micro-film, sent home by air, and enlarged before delivery to the addressee.
**Air-gun,** ār'gun, *n.* A gun to discharge bullets by means of condensed air.
**Airily,** ār'i-li, *adj.* In an airy manner.
**Airiness,** ār'i-nes, *n.* Openness; gaiety.
**Airing,** ār'ing, *n.* An exposure to the air or to a fire; an excursion in the open air.
**Airplane,** ār'o-plān, *n.* A heavier-than-air power-driven flying-machine having one or two pairs of wings (monoplane or biplano) which support it owing to the reaction of the air.
**Airport,** ār'pōrt, *n.* An area for landing airplanes, usually having customs houses, servicing facilities, etc.
**Air-pump,** ār'pump, *n.* A machine for pumping the air out of a vessel.
**Air-shaft,** ār'shaft, *n.* A passage for air into a mine.
**Air-tight,** ār'tīt, *a.* So tight or compact as not to let air pass.
**Airy,** ā'ri, *a.* Open to the free air; high in air; light; thin; vain; gay.
**Aisle,** īl, *n.* A wing or side of a church; a passage in a church.
**Ajar,** a-jär', *adv.* Partly open, as a door.
**Akee,** a-kē', *n.* The fruit of a W. African tree, now common in the W. Indies, etc.
**Akimbo,** a-kim'bō, *pred.a.* or *adv.* With the elbow outwards and the hand on the hip.
**Akin,** a-kin', *a.* Of kin; related to; partaking of the same properties.
**Alabaster,** al'a-bas-tėr, *n.* A soft marble-like mineral.—*a.* Made of alabaster.
**Alacrity,** a-lak'ri-ti, *n.* Liveliness; cheerful readiness; promptitude.
**Alamode,** ä-lä-mōd', *adv.* According to fashion.
**Alarm,** a-lärm', *n.* A call to arms; sudden surprise; fright; a notice of danger.—*vt.* To give notice of danger; to disturb.
**Alarm clock,** a-lärm' klok, *n.* A clock which can be set to awaken sleepers at a given time by ringing a small gong.
**Alarming,** a-lärm'ing, *p.a.* Terrifying.
**Alarmingly,** a-lärm'ing-li, *adv.* So as to excite apprehension.
**Alarmist,** a-lärm'ist, *n.* One prone to excite alarm.—*a.* Exciting unnecessary alarm.
**Alarum,** a-lär'um, *n.* Alarm. (Poet.)
**Alas,** a-las', *interj.* Expressing grief, pity, etc.
**Alb,** alb, *n.* A long robe of white linen.
**Albata,** al-bā'ta, *n.* German silver.
**Albatross,** al'ba-tros, *n.* An aquatic bird of southern seas, the largest sea-bird known.
**Albeit,** al'bē'it, *adv.* Be it so; although.
**Albino,** al-bī'nō, *n.* A person with abnormally white skin and hair, and pink eyes.
**Album,** al'bum, *n.* A book for autographs, sketches, etc.
**Albumen,** al-bū'men, *n.* The white of an egg; a substance of the same kind found in animals and vegetables.
**Albuminous,** al-bū'min-us, *a.* Pertaining to or having the properties of albumen.
**Alburnum,** al-bėr'num, *n.* Sap-wood of a tree.
**Alchemist,** al'kem-ist, *n.* One who practiced alchemy.
**Alchemy,** al'ke-mi, *n.* An obsolete science, aiming at changing metals into gold, etc.
**Alcohol,** al'kō-hol, *n.* Pure spirit of a highly intoxicating nature.
**Alcoholic,** al-kō-hol'ik, *a.* Pertaining to alcohol.
**Alcoholism,** al'kō-hol-izm, *n.* The condition of habitual drunkards.
**Alcove,** al'kov, *n.* A recess.
**Aldehyde,** al'dē-hīd, *n.* A colorless liquid produced by oxidation of alcohol.
**Alder,** al'dėr, *n.* A tree generally growing in moist land.
**Alderman,** al'dėr-man, *n.*; pl. **-men.** A magistrate of a town.
**Ale,** āl, *n.* A fermented malt liquor; beer.
**Alee,** a-lē', *adv.* On the lee side of a vessel.
**Alembic,** a-lem'bik, *n.* A vessel used in chemical distillation.
**Alert,** a-lėrt', *a.* Vigilant; quick; prompt.—*n.* An air-raid warning.
**Alertness,** a-lėrt'nes, *n.* Briskness; activity.
**Alexandrine,** al'legz-an''drin, *n.* A line with six stresses.
**Alga,** al'ga, *n.*; pl. **-gae,** A sea-weed.
**Algebra,** al'je-bra, *n.* The science of computing by symbols.
**Algebraic, Algebraical,** al-jē-brā'ik, al-jē-brā'ik-al, *a.* Pertaining to algebra.
**Algebraically,** al-jē-brā'ik-al-li, *adv.* By algebraic process.
**Algebraist,** al'jē-brā-ist, *n.* One versed in algebra.
**Alias,** ā'li-as, *adv.* Otherwise.—*n.*; pl. **-ses,** An assumed name.
**Alibi,** al'i-bī, *n.* The plea of a person who, charged with a crime, alleges that he was elsewhere when the crime was committed.
**Alien,** āl'yen, *a.* Foreign; estranged from.—*n.* A foreigner.
**Alienable,** āl'yen-a-bl, *a.* That may be alienated or transferred to another.
**Alienate,** āl'yen-āt, *vt.* (alienating, alienated). To transfer to another; to estrange.
**Alienation,** āl'yen-ā'shon, *n.* Act of alienating.
**Alight,** a-līt', *vi.* To get down; to settle on.
**Alike,** a-līk', *a.* Like; similar.—*adv.* In the same

manner, form, or degree.
**Aliment,** al'i-ment, *n.* Nourishment; food.
**Alimental,** al-i-ment'al, *a.* Nourishing.
**Alimentary,** al-i-ment'a-ri, *a.* Pertaining to aliment or food.
**Alimony,** al'i-mo-ni, *n.* Allowance to a woman legally separated from her husband.
**Aliped,** al'i-ped, *n.* A wing-footed animal.
**Aliquot,** al'i-kwot, *a.* A part of a number which divides the whole without remainder.
**Alive,** a-līv', *a.* Living; lively; susceptible.
**Alkalescent,** al-ka-les'ent, *a.* Slightly alkaline.
**Alkali,** al'ka-li, *n.*; pl. **-ies** or **-is.** A substance, as potash and soda, which neutralizes acids and unites with oil or fat to form soap.
**Alkaline,** al'ka-līn, *a.* Having the properties of an alkali.
**Alkaloid,** al'ka-loid, *n.* A substance resembling an alkali, or having alkaline properties.
**Alkoran,** al-kō'ran, *n.* The Koran.
**All,** al, *a.* Every part; every one.—*n.* The whole; everything.—*adv.* Wholly; entirely.
**Allah,** al'la, *n.* The Arabic name of God.
**Allay,** al-lā', *vt.* To repress; to assuage.
**Allegation,** al-lē-gā'shon, *n.* Affirmation; declaration.
**Allege,** al-lej', *vt.* (alleging, alleged). To adduce; to assert; to plead in excuse.
**Allegiance,** al-lē'ji-ans, *n.* Loyalty.
**Allegoric, Allegorical,** al-li-gor'ik, al-li-gor'ik-al, *a.* Pertaining to allegory; figurative.
**Allegorically,** al-lē-gor'ik-al-li, *adv.* By way of allegory.
**Allegorist,** al'li-gō-rist, *n.* One who allegorizes.
**Allegorize,** al'li-gō-rīz, *vt.* To turn into allegory.—*vi.* To use allegory.
**Allegory,** al'li-gō-ri, *n.* A speech or discourse which conveys a meaning different from the literal one.
**Allegro,** al-lā'grō. A word denoting a brisk sprightly movement.
**Alleluiah,** al-lē-lū'ya, *n.* Praise to Jehovah; a word used to express pious joy.
**Allergic,** a-ler'jik, *a.* Possessing allergy.
**Allergy,** al'er-je, *n.* A state of the body in which the cells are specially sensitive to certain substances, usually proteins.
**Alleviate,** al-lē'vi-āt, *vt.* (alleviating, alleviated). To make light; to assuage.
**Alleviation,** al-lē-vi-ā'shon, *n.* Act of alleviating; mitigation.
**Alley,** al'i, *n.* A narrow walk or passage.
**All-fools' Day,** al'fölz'dā, *n.* 1st April.
**All-hallow, All-hallows,** al-hal'lō, al-hal'lōz, *n.* All-Saints' Day.
**Alliance,** al-lī'ans, *n.* State of being allied; confederacy; league.
**Allied,** al-līd', *p.a.* United by treaty.
**Alligation,** al-li-gā'shon, *n.* Act of tying together; a rule of arithmetic.
**Alligator,** al'li-gā-tor, *n.* The American crocodile.
**Alliteration,** al-lit-ėr-ā'shon, *n.* The repetition of a letter at the beginning of two or more words in close succession.
**Alliterative,** al-lit'ėr-at-iv, *a.* Pertaining to alliteration.
**Allocate,** al'lō-kāt, *vt.* (allocating, allocated). To distribute; to assign to each his share.
**Allocation,** al-lō-kā'shon, *n.* Distribution; assignment.
**Allocution,** al-lō-kū'shon, *n.* The act or manner of speaking; a formal address.
**Allodial,** al-lō'di-al, *a.* Held independent of a lord paramount.
**Allodium,** al-lō'di-um, *n.* Freehold estate.
**Allomorphism,** al-lo-mor'fizm, *n.* Difference of form, with sameness of substance.
**Allopathic,** al-lō-path'ik, *a.* Pertaining to allopathy.
**Allopathy,** al-lop'a-thi, *n.* The ordinary mode of curing diseases, by using medicines which produce a condition contrary to that of the disease.
**Allot,** al-lot', *vt.* (allotting, allotted). To give by lot; to apportion.
**Allotment,** al-lot'ment, *n.* Act of allotting; a share allotted.
**Allotrophy,** al-lot'ro-pi, *n.* The capability of substances of existing in more than one form.
**Allow,** al-lou', *vt.* To grant; to admit; to abate; to bestow, as compensation.
**Allowable,** al-lou'a-bl, *a.* That may be allowed.
**Allowably,** al-lou'a-bli, *adv.* In an allowable manner.
**Allowance,** al-lou'ans, *n.* Act of allowing; that which is allowed; abatement.
**Alloy,** al-loi', *vt.* To mix with baser metals; to abate by mixture.—*n.* A baser metal mixed with a finer; a metallic compound.
**All Saints' Day,** al'sānts dā, *n.* 1st November.
**All Souls' Day,** al'sōlz dā, *n.* 2nd November.
**All-spice,** al-spīs, *n.* Pimento or Jamaica pepper, supposed to combine many different flavors.
**Allude,** al-lūd', *vi.* (alluding, alluded). To refer to; to hint at.
**Allure,** al-lūr', *vt.* (alluring, allured). To draw by some lure; to entice; to decoy.
**Allurement,** al-lūr'ment, *n.* That which allures; temptation; enticement.
**Alluring,** al-lūr'ing, *p.a.* Attractive.
**Alluringly,** al-lūr'ing-li, *adv.* In an alluring manner.
**Allusion,** al-lū'zhon, *n.* The act of alluding; a hint; a reference.
**Allusive, Allusory,** al-lū'siv, al-lū'so-ri, *a.* Containing allusion.
**Alluvial,** al-lū'vi-al, *a.* Deposited by water.
**Alluvion,** al-lū'vi-on, *n.* Land added to a property by soil washed up by the sea or a river.
**Alluvium,** al-lū'vi-um, *n.*; pl. **-via.** Soil deposited by the action of water.
**Ally,** al-lī', *vt.* (allying, allied). To unite by friendship, marriage, or treaty; to associate. *n.* One related by marriage or other tie; an associate.
**Almanac,** al'ma-nak, *n.* A calendar of days, weeks, and months, etc.
**Almightiness,** al-mī'ti-nes, *n.* Omnipotence.
**Almighty,** al-mī'ti, *a.* Omnipotent.—*n.* God.
**Almond,** ä'mund, *n.* The nut of the almond-tree; *pl.* the tonsils of the throat.
**Almoner,** al'mon-ėr, *n.* A dispenser of alms.
**Almonry,** al'mon-ri, *n.* The place where alms are distributed.
**Almost,** al'most, *adv.* Nearly; well-nigh; for the greatest part.
**Alms,** ämz, *n.pl.* A charitable gift.
**Aloe,** al'ō, *n.* A succulent plant; *pl.* a bitter purgative medicine.
**Aloetic,** al-ō-et'ik, *a.* Pertaining to aloes.
**Aloft,** a-loft', *adv.* In the sky; on high.
**Alone,** a-lōn', *a.* Solitary.—*adv.* Separately.
**Along,** a-long', *adv.* Lengthwise; forward.—*prep.* By the side of; lengthwise.
**Aloof,** a-löf', *adv.* At a distance; apart.
**Aloud,** a-loud', *adv.* Loudly.
**Alp,** alp, *n.* A high mountain.
**Alpaca,** al-pak'a, *n.* A Peruvian animal, with long, soft, and woolly hair; cloth made of its hair, or a similar cloth.
**Alpenstock,** al'pen-stok, *n.* A long stick shod with iron, used in climbing mountains.
**Alpha,** al'fa, *n.* The first letter in the Greek alphabet; the first or beginning.
**Alphabet,** al'fa-bet, *n.* The letters of a language arranged in the customary order.
**Alphabetical,** al-fa-bet'ik-al, *a.* In the order of an alphabet.
**Alphabetically,** al-fa-bet'ik-al-li, *adv.* In an alphabetical manner or order.
**Alpine,** al'pīn, *a.* Pertaining to high mountains.
**Already,** al-red'i, *adv.* Before or by this time; even now.
**Also,** al'sō, *adv.* Likewise; in the same manner, further.
**Altar,** al'tėr, *n.* An elevated place on which sacrifices were offered; the communion table.
**Altar-cloth,** al'tėr-kloth, *n.* A cloth to lay upon an

A

altar in churches.
**Altar-piece**, al'tėr-pēs, *n*. A painting placed over the altar in a church.
**Alter**, al'tėr, *vt*. To make some change in; to vary.—*vt*. To vary.
**Alterable**, al'tėr-a-bl, *a*. That may alter, or be altered.
**Alteration**, al-tėr-ā'shon, *n*. Partial change or variation.
**Alterative**, al'tėr-at-iv, *a*. Causing alteration.—*n*. A medicine which induces a change in the habit or constitution.
**Altercate**, al'tėr-kāt, *vi*. (altercating, altercated). To dispute; to wrangle.
**Altercation**, al-tėr-kā'shon, *n*. Heated dispute; wrangle.
**Alternate**, al-tėr'nāt, *a*. Being by turns.—*vt*. (alternating, alternated). To cause to follow by turns; to interchange.—*vi*. To happen or act by turns.
**Alternately**, al-tėrn'āt-li, *adv*. By turns.
**Alternation**, al-tėrn-ā'shon, *n*. Reciprocal succession; interchange.
**Alternative**, al-tėrn'at-iv, *n*. A choice of two things.
**Alternatively**, al-tėrn'at-iv-li, *adv*. In the manner of alternatives.
**Although**, al'THō', *conj*. Be it so; admit all that.
**Altitude**, al'ti-tūd, *n*. Height; eminence; elevation.
**Alto**, al'tō, *a*. High.—*n*. In *music*, contralto.
**Altogether**, al-tö-geTH'ėr, *adv*. Wholly; entirely; without exception.
**Alto-rilievo** (or **-re-**), al'tō-rē-lyā''vō, re-lyā'', *n*. High relief: a term in sculpture.
**Altruism**, al'trö-izm, *n*. Devotion to others or to humanity; the opposite of selfishness.
**Altruistic**, al-trö-ist'ik, *a*. Pertaining or relating to altruism.
**Alum**, al'um, *n*. An astringent salt of great use in medicine and the arts.
**Alumina**, al-ū'min-a, *n*. The oxide of aluminium; the chief ingredient of clay.
**Aluminum**, **a-lu-mi-num**, *n*. A very light metal of a silvery white color.
**Alumnus**, a-lum'nus, *n*.; pl. **-ni**. A pupil; a graduate of a university.
**Alveolar**, **Alveolate**, al-vē'o-lėr, al-vē'o-lāt, *a*. Containing sockets; resembling a honeycomb.
**Alvine**, al'vin, *a*. Belonging to the lower belly.
**Always**, al'wāz, *adv*. At all times; continually.
**Am**, am. The first person singular, present tense, indicative mood, of the verb *to be*.
**Amain**, a-mān', *adv*. Vigorously.
**Amalgam**, a-mal'gam, *n*. A compound of quicksilver with another metal; a compound.
**Amalgamate**, a-mal'gam-āt, *vt*. To mix, as quicksilver with another metal.—*vi*. To unite in an amalgam; to blend.
**Amalgamation**, a-mal'gam-ā''shon, *n*. The act or operation of amalgamating.
**Amanuensis**, a-man'ū-en''sis, *n*.; pl. **-ses**. One who writes what another dictates.
**Amaranth**, am'a-ranth, *n*. The unfading flower; a color inclining to purple.
**Amaranthine**, am-a-ran'thin, *a*. Unfading.
**Amaryllis**, am-a-ril'lis, *n*. Lily-asphodel.
**Amass**, a-mas', *vt*. To form into a mass; to accumulate; to heap up.
**Amateur**, am-a-tūr', *n*. A lover of any art or science, not a professor.
**Amatory**, am'a-tō-ri, *a*. Relating to love; causing love; amorous.
**Amaze**, a-māz', *vt*. (amazing, amazed). To astonish; to bewilder.
**Amazedly**, a-māz'ed-li, *adv*. With amazement.
**Amazement**, a-māz'ment, *n*. Wonder; perplexity.
**Amazing**, a-māz'ing, *p.a*. Very wonderful.
**Amazingly**, a-māz'ing-li, *adv*. In an astonishing degree.
**Amazon**, am'a-zon, *n*. A warlike or masculine woman; a virago.
**Amazonian**, am-a-zō'ni-an, *a*. Relating to the Amazons.
**Ambassador**, am-bas'sa-dor, *n*. A representative of a sovereign or state at a foreign court.
**Ambassadress**, am-bas'sa-dres, *n*. The wife of an ambassador.
**Amber**, am'bėr, *n*. A mineralized pale-yellow resin of extinct pine-trees.
**Ambergris**, am'bėr-grēs, *n*. A fragrant, solid, opaque, ash-colored substance, obtained from the spermaceti whale.
**Ambidexter**, am-bi-deks'tėr, *n*. One who uses both hands with equal facility.
**Ambidextrous**, am-bi-deks'trus, *a*. Using both hands alike.
**Ambient**, am'bi-ent, *a*. Encompassing.
**Ambiguity**, am-bi-gū'i-ti, *n*. Doubtfulness of signification.
**Ambiguous**, am-big'ū-us, *a*. Of uncertain signification; doubtful.
**Ambiguously**, am-big'ū-us-li, *adv*. In an ambiguous manner.
**Ambit**, am'bit, *n*. Compass; scope.
**Ambition**, am-bi'shon, *n*. Desire of preferment or power.
**Ambitious**, am-bi'shus, *a*. Aspiring.
**Ambitiously**, am-bi'shus-li, *adv*. In an ambitious manner.
**Amble**, am'bl, *vi*. (ambling, ambled). To move, as a horse, by lifting the two legs on each side alternately; to go between a walk and a trot.—*n*. A peculiar motion of a horse; a pace between a walk and a trot.
**Ambler**, am'blėr, *n*. A horse which ambles.
**Ambrosia**, am-brō'zhi-a, *n*. The imaginary food of the gods, which conferred immortality.
**Ambrosial**, am-brō'zhi-al, *a*. Of the nature of ambrosia; fragrant; delicious.
**Ambulance**, am'bū-lans, *n*. An itinerant hospital; a wagon for the sick or wounded.
**Ambulatory**, am'bū-lā-tō-ri, *a*. Movable.—*n*. A part of a building to walk in.
**Ambuscade**, am-bus-kād', *n*. The act or place of lying in wait in order to surprise; the troops lying in wait; ambush.
**Ambush**, am'bush, *n*. Ambuscade.
**Ameliorate**, a-mēl'yor-āt, *vt*. To make better.
**Amelioration**, a-mēl'yor-ā''shon, *n*. A making better; improvement.
**Amen**, ā-men', *adv*. So be it.
**Amenable**, a-mēn'a-bl, *a*. Accountable; responsible.
**Amend**, a-mend', *vt*. To correct; to improve.—*vi*. To grow better.
**Amendment**, a-mend'ment, *n*. A change for the better; correction; reformation.
**Amends**, a-mendz', *n.pl*. Compensation; satisfaction; recompense.
**Amenity**, a-men'i-ti, *n*. Pleasantness; agreeableness of situation.
**Amerce**, a-mėrs', *vt*. (amercing, amerced). To punish by fine.
**Amerceable**, a-mėrs'a-bl, *a*. Liable to amercement.
**Amercement**, a-mėrs'ment, *n*. A pecuniary penalty inflicted on an offender.
**American**, a-me'ri-kan, *n*. A native of America.—*a*. Pertaining to America.
**Americanism**, a-me'ri-kan-izm, *n*. An American idiom or custom.
**Amethyst**, am'ē-thist, *n*. A variety of quartz, a precious stone of a violet or purple color.
**Amethystine**, a-mē-thist'in, *a*. Pertaining to or resembling amethyst.
**Amiability**, ā'mi-a-bil''i-ti, *n*. Sweetness of temper.
**Amiable**, ā'mi-a-bl, *a*. Lovable; sweet-tempered.
**Amiably**, ā'mi-a-bli, *adv*. In an amiable manner.
**Amianth**, **Amianthus**, am'i-anth, am-i-an'-thus, *n*. Mountain-flax, flexible asbestos.
**Amicable**, am'ik-a-bl, *a*. Friendly; kind.
**Amicably**, am'ik-a-bli, *adv*. In a friendly manner.
**Amice**, am'is, *n*. A cloth worn by priests about the shoulders.
**Amid**, **Amidst**, a-mid', a-midst', *prep*. In the

midst of; enveloped with.
**Amidships,** a-mid'ships, *adv.* or *pred.a.* In or towards the middle of a ship.
**Amiss,** a-mis', *a.* In error; improper.—*adv.* In a faulty manner; improperly.
**Amity,** am'i-ti, *n.* Friendship; harmony.
**Ammeter,** am'met-ėr, *n.* An instrument for measuring an electric current (in AMPERES).
**Ammonia,** am-mō'ni-a, *n.* Volatile alkali.
**Ammoniac, Ammoniacal,** am-mō'ni-ak, am-mo-nī'ak-al, *a.* Pertaining to ammonia.
**Ammoniac,** am-mō'ni-ak, *n.* A gum obtained from a plant.
**Ammonite,** am'mon-īt, *n.* The fossil shell of extinct cuttle-fishes.
**Ammunition,** am-mu-ni'shon, *n.* Military projectiles; formerly military stores generally.
**Amnesty,** am'nes-ti, *n.* A general pardon of offenses against a government.
**Amnion,** am'ni-on, *n.* The innermost membrane surrounding the fetus of mammals, birds, and reptiles.
**Amoeba,** a-mē'ba, *n.*; pl. **-bae.** A microscopic animal commonly found in fresh water.
**Amoebean,** am-ē-bē'an, *a.* Exhibiting persons speaking alternately (an amoebean poem).
**Among, Amongst,** a-mung', a-mungst', *prep.* Amidst; throughout; of the number.
**Amorous,** am'or-us, *a.* Inclined to love; enamored; fond; relating to love.
**Amorously,** am'or-us-li, *adv.* In an amorous manner.
**Amorphous,** a-mor'fus, *a.* Without shape; of irregular shape.
**Amount,** a-mount', *vi.* To mount up to; to result in.—*n.* The sum total; effect or result.
**Amour,** a-mör', *n.* A love intrigue.
**Ampere,** am-pār', *n.* The unit in measuring the strength of an electric current.
**Amphibian,** am-fib'i-an, *n.*; pl. **Amphibia,** am-fib'i-a. An animal capable of living both in water and on land; an animal that has both lungs and gills.
**Amphibious,** am-fib'i-us, *a.* Able to live under water and on land.
**Amphibology,** am-fi-bol'o-ji, *n.* Speech susceptible of two interpretations.
**Amphibrach,** am'fi-brak, *n.* A poetical foot of three syllables, the first and third short, and the second long.
**Amphitheater,** am-fi-thē'a-tėr, *n.* An edifice of an oval form, with rows of seats all round, rising higher as they recede from the area.
**Ample,** am'pl, *a.* Spacious; copious; rich.
**Ampleness,** am'pl-nes, *n.* Spaciousness; abundance.
**Amplification,** am'pli-fi-kā''shon, *n.* Act of amplifying; enlargement; discussion.
**Amplifier,** am'pli-fī-ėr, *n.* One who or that which amplifies or enlarges.
**Amplify,** am'plif-ī, *vt.* (amplifying, amplified). To enlarge; to treat copiously.—*vi.* To speak copiously; to be diffuse.
**Amplitude,** am'pli-tūd, *n.* Ampleness; extent; abundance.
**Amply,** am'pli, *adv.* Largely; liberally; fully; copiously.
**Amputate,** am'pū-tāt, *vt.* (amputating, amputated). To cut off, as a limb.
**Amputation,** am-pū-tā'shon, *n.* Act of amputating.
**Amuck,** a-muk', *n.* or *adv.* Only in phrase *to run amuck,* to rush about frantically, to attack all and sundry.
**Amulet,** am'ū-let, *n.* A charm against evils or witchcraft.
**Amuse,** a-mūz', *vt.* (amusing, amused). To entertain; to beguile.
**Amusement,** a-mūz'ment, *n.* Diversion; entertainment.
**Amusing,** a-mūz'ing, *a.* Giving amusement; diverting.
**Amusingly,** a-mūz'ing-li, *adv.* In an amusing manner.
**Amygdalate,** a-mig'da-lāt, *n.* Milk of almonds.
**Amygdaloid,** a-mig'da-loid, *n.* A kind of igneous rock, containing cavities filled with various minerals.
**Amyl,** am'il, *n.* A hypothetical radical said to exist in many substances.
**Amyloid,** am'il-oid, *a.* Resembling or of the nature of starch.—*n.* A starchy substance.
**An,** an, *a.* The indefinite article, used before words beginning with a vowel-sound.
**Anabaptist,** an-a-bap'tist, *n.* One who maintains that adults only should be baptized.
**Anachronism,** an-ak'ron-izm, *n.* An error in chronology.
**Anaconda,** an-a-kon'da, *n.* A large species of serpent tribe.
**Anacreontic,** a-nak'rē-on''tik, *a.* Pertaining to Anacreon; noting a kind of verse or measure; amatory.
**Anagram,** an'a-gram, *n.* A transposition of the letters of a name or sentence, by which a new word or sentence is formed.
**Anal,** ā'nal, *a.* Pertaining to the anus.
**Analogical,** an-a-loj'ik-al, *a.* According to analogy.
**Analogous,** an-al'og-us, *a.* Having analogy; corresponding.
**Analogy,** an-al'o-ji, *n.* Likeness; similarity.
**Analysis,** an-al'i-sis, *n.*; pl. **-ses.** A resolution of a thing into its elements; synopsis.
**Analyst,** an'a-list, *n.* One who analyses.
**Analytic, Analytical,** an-a-lit'ik, an-a-lit'ik-al, *a.* Pertaining to analysis.
**Analytically,** an-a-lit'ik-al-li, *adv.* In the manner of analysis.
**Analytics,** an-a-lit'iks, *n.* The science of analysis.
**Analyze,** an'a-līz, *vt.* (analyzing, analyzed) To subject to analysis; to resolve into its elements.
**Anapest,** an'a-pest, *n.* A poetical foot of three syllables, the first two short, the last long.
**Anapestic,** an-a-pes'tik, *a.* Pertaining to an anapest; consisting of anapests.
**Anarchic, Anarchical,** an-ärk'ik, an-ärk'ik-al, *a.* Without rule or government.
**Anarchist,** an'ärk-ist, *n.* An author or promoter of anarchy; one who opposes all existing systems of government.
**Anarchy,** an'är-ki, *n.* State of being without rule; political confusion.
**Anathema,** a-nath'e-ma, *n.* An ecclesiastical denunciation; curse.
**Anathematize,** a-nath'e-mat-īz, *vt.* (anathematizing, anathematized). To pronounce an anathema against; to excommunicate.
**Anatomical,** an-a-tom'ik-al, *a.* Relating to anatomy.
**Anatomist,** a-nat'ō-mist, *n.* One skilled in anatomy.
**Anatomize,** a-nat'ō-mīz, *vt.* (anatomizing, anatomized). To cut up or dissect.
**Anatomy,** a-nat'ō-mi, *n.* The art of dissection; doctrine of the structure of the body learned by dissection.
**Ancestor,** an'ses-tėr, *n.* A progenitor; forefather.
**Ancestral,** an-ses'tral, *a.* Relating or belonging to ancestors.
**Ancestry,** an'ses-tri, *n.* Lineage; descent.
**Anchor,** ang'kėr, *n.* An iron instrument for holding a ship at rest in water. *vt.* To hold fast by an anchor.—*vi.* To cast anchor.
**Anchorage,** ang'kėr-āj, *n.* A place where a ship can anchor; duty on ships for anchoring.
**Anchorite,** ang'kō-rīt, *n.* A hermit.
**Anchovy,** an-chō'vi, *n.* A small fish of the herring kind, furnishing a fine sauce.
**Ancient,** ān'shent, *a.* That happened in former times; old, antique.
**Anciently,** ān'shent-li, *adv.* In old times.
**Ancientness,** ān'shent-nes, *n.* Antiquity.
**Ancillary,** an'sil-la-ri, *a.* Pertaining to a maidservant; subservient or subordinate.

**And,** and, *conj.* A particle which connects words and sentences together.
**Andante,** an-dan'te, *a.* In *music,* with slow, graceful movement.
**Andiron,** and'ī-ėrn, *n.* A metallic support for logs of wood burned on an open hearth.
**Anecdote,** an'ek-dōt, *n.* A short story.
**Anecdotical,** an-ek-dot'ik-al, *a.* Pertaining to an anecdote.
**Anele,** a-nēl', *vt.* To give extreme unction.
**Anemometer,** an-e-mom'et-ėr, *n.* An instrument for measuring the force of the wind.
**Anemia,** a-nē'mi-a, *n.* Bloodlessness.
**Anemone,** a-nem'o-nē, *n.* Wind-flower, a genus of plants.
**Anent,** a-nent', *prep.* About; regarding.
**Aneroid,** an'ē-roid, *a.* Dispensing with fluid, said of a kind of barometer.
**Anesthetic,** an-es-thet'ik, *a.* Producing insensibility.—*n.* A substance, as chloroform, which produces insensibility.
**Aneurysm,** an'ū-rizm, *n.* Dilatation of an artery.
**Aneurysmal,** an-ū-riz'mal, *a.* Pertaining to an aneurysm.
**Anew,** a-nū', *adv.* On new; fresh.
**Angel,** ān'jel, *n.* A divine messenger; a spirit; an old English gold coin worth ten shillings.
**Angelic, Angelical,** an-jel'ik, an-jel'ik-al, *a.* Belonging to or resembling an angel.
**Angelically,** an-jel'ik-al-li, *adv.* Like an angel.
**Anger,** ang'gėr, *n.* A violent passion, excited by real or supposed injury; resentment.—*vt.* To excite anger; to irritate.
**Angina,** an-ji'na, *n.* Angina pectoris, a fatal disease characterized by paroxysms of intense pain and a feeling of constriction in the chest.
**Angle,** ang'gl, *n.* The inclination of two lines which meet in a point but have different directions; a corner.
**Angle,** ang'gl, *n.* A fishing-hook, or hook with line and rod.—*vi.* (angling, angled). To fish with an angle.
**Angler,** ang'glėr, *n.* One that fishes with an angle.
**Anglican,** ang'glik-an, *a.* Pertaining to England, or to the English Church.
**Anglicism,** ang'gli-sizm, *n.* An English idiom.
**Anglicize,** ang'gli-sīz, *vt.* To make English.
**Anglomania,** ang-glō-mā'ni-a, *n.* Excessive attachment to English people, customs, etc.
**Anglophobia,** ang-glō-fō'bi-a, *n.* Excessive hatred of English people, customs, etc.
**Anglo-Saxon,** ang-glō-sak'son, *n.* One of the English race; the English language in its first stage.—*a.* Pertaining to the Anglo-Saxons, or their language.
**Angrily,** ang'gri-li, *adv.* In an angry manner.
**Angry,** ang'gri, *a.* Affected with anger; provoked; wrathful; resentful.
**Anguish,** ang'gwish, *n.* Extreme pain, either of body or mind; agony; grief.
**Angular,** ang'gū-lėr, *a.* Having an angle; stiff.
**Angularity,** ang-gū-la'ri-ti, *n.* Quality of being angular.
**Anile,** an'īl, *a.* Aged; imbecile.
**Aniline,** an'i-lin, *n.* A substance obtained from coal-tar, used in dyeing.
**Anility,** a-nil'i-ti, *n.* State of being anile.
**Animadversion,** an'i-mad-vėr''shon, *n.* Censure; criticism.
**Animadvert,** an'i-mad-vėrt'', *vi.* To criticise; to censure (with *upon*).
**Animal,** an'i-mal, *n.* A living being having sensation and voluntary motion; a quadruped.—*a.* Belonging to animals; gross.
**Animalcular,** ani-mal'kūl-ėr, *a.* Pertaining to animalcules.
**Animalcule,** an-i-mal'kūl, *n.* A minute animal seen by means of a microscope.
**Animalism,** an'i-mal-izm, *n.* Sensuality.
**Animate,** an'i-māt, *vt.* (animating, animated). To give natural life to; to enliven.
**Animated,** an'i-māt-ed, *p.a.* Lively; living.
**Animism,** an'i-mizm, *n.* The belief that natural phenomena are due to spirits, and that inanimate objects have spirits.
**Animosity,** an-i-mos'i-ti, *n.* Violent hatred; active enmity; malignity.
**Animus,** an'i-mus, *n.* Intention; hostile spirit.
**Anise,** an'is, *n.* An aromatic plant, the seeds of which are used in making cordials.
**Aniseed,** an'i-sēd, *n.* The seed of the anise.
**Ankle,** ang'kl, *n.* The joint which connects the foot with the leg.
**Anna,** an'na, *n.* In Indian coin worth 1½*d.*
**Annalist,** an'nal-ist, *n.* A writer of annals.
**Annals,** an'nalz, *n.pl.* A record of events under the years in which they happened.
**Anneal,** an'nēl', *vt.* To temper glass or metals by heat; to fix colors laid on glass.
**Annelid,** an'ne-lid, *n.* An invertebrate animal whose body is formed of numerous small rings, as the worm, leech, etc.
**Annex,** an-neks', *vt.* To unite at the end; to subjoin; to take possession of.
**Annexation,** an-neks-ā'shon, *n.* Act of annexing.
**Annihilable,** an-nī'hil-a-bl, *a.* That may be annihilated.
**Annihilate,** an-nī'hil-āt, *vt.* (annihilating, annihilated). To reduce to nothing; to destroy the existence of.
**Anniversary,** an-ni-vėrs'a-ri, *n.* A day on which some event is annually celebrated.
**Annotate,** an'nō-tāt, *vt.* (annotating, annotated). To write notes upon.
**Annotation,** an-nō-tā'shon, *n.* A remark on some passage of a book, etc.
**Annotator,** an'nō-tāt-ėr, *n.* A writer of notes.
**Announce,** an-nouns', *vt.* (announcing, announced). To declare; to proclaim.
**Announcement,** an-nouns'ment, *n.* Declaration.
**Annoy,** an-noi', *vt.* To hurt; to molest; to vex.
**Annoyance,** an-noi'ans, *n.* Act of annoying; state of being annoyed.
**Annual,** an'nū-al, *a.* Yearly; lasting a year.—*n.* A plant whose root dies yearly; a book published yearly.
**Annually,** an'nū-al-li, *adv.* Yearly.
**Annuitant,** an-nū'it-ant, *n.* One who receives an annuity.
**Annuity,** an-nū'i-ti, *n.* A sum of money payable yearly, etc.
**Annual,** annul', *vt.* (annulling, annulled). To make void or of no effect; to repeal.
**Annular,** an'nū-lėr, *a.* Having the form of a ring; pertaining to a ring.
**Annulment,** an-nul'ment, *n.* Act of annulling.
**Annulose,** an'nū-lōs, *a.* Having a body composed of rings; applied to annelids.
**Annunciation,** an-nun'si-ā''shon, *n.* The angel's salutation to the Virgin Mary, and its anniversary, the 25th of March.
**Anode,** an'ōd, *n.* The positive pole of a voltaic current.
**Anodyne,** an'ō-din, *n.* Any medicine which allays or mitigates pain.—*a.* Assuaging pain.
**Anoint,** a-noint', *vt.* To rub over with oil; to consecrate by unction.
**Anointed,** a-noint'ed, *n.* The Messiah.
**Anomalous,** a-nom'a-lus, *a.* Deviating from common rule.
**Anomaly,** a-nom'a-li, *n.* Irregularity; deviation from common rule.
**Anon,** a-non', *adv.* Immediately.
**Anonymous,** a-non'im-us, *a.* Nameless; without the real name of the author.
**Anonymously,** a-non'im-us-li, *adv.* Without a name.
**Another,** an-uTH'ėr, *a.* Not the same; different; any other.
**Anserine,** an'sėr-īn, *a.* Relating to the goose.
**Answer,** an'sėr, *vt.* To reply to; to satisfy; to suit.—*vi.* To reply; to be accountable; to succeed.—*n.* A reply; a solution.
**Answerable,** an'sėr-a-bl, *a.* That may be answered; accountable; suitable.

**Answerably**, an'sėr-a-bli, *adv*. In due proportion; suitably.
**Ant**, ant, *n*. An emmet; a pismire.
**Antagonism**, an-tag'ō-nizm, *n*. Opposition; contest.
**Antagonist**, an-tag'ō-nist, *n*. One who struggles with another in combat; an opponent; that which acts in opposition.
**Antagonistic**, an-tag'ō-nist''ik, *a*. Opposing in combat; contending against.
**Antarctic**, ant-ärk'tik, *a*. Relating to the south pole, or to the region near it.
**Antecedent**, an-tē-sē'dent, *a*. Going before; prior.—*n*. That which goes before; the noun to which a relative refers; *pl*. a man's previous history, etc.
**Antechamber**, an'tē-chām-bėr, *n*. An apartment leading into a chief apartment.
**Antedate**, an'tē-dāt, *n*. Prior date.—*vt*. To date before the true time.
**Antediluvian**, an'tē-di-lū''vi-an, *a*. Before the flood.—*n*. One who lived before the flood.
**Antelope**, an'tē-lōp, *n*. An animal resembling the deer, but with hollow, unbranched horns.
**Antemeridian**, an'tē-mē-rid''i-an, *a*. Before midday; pertaining to the forenoon.
**Antemundane**, an-tē-mun'dān, *a*. Before the creation of the world.
**Antenna**, an-ten'na, *n*.; pl. **Antennae**, an-ten'nē. The feeler of an insect; an aerial.
**Antenuptial**, an-tē-nup'shi-al, *a*. Before nuptials or marriage.
**Antepenult**, an'tē-pē-nult'', *n*. The last syllable of a word except two.
**Antepenultimate**, an'tē-pē-nul''ti-māt, *a*. Pertaining to the antepenult.—*n*. Antepenult.
**Anterior**, an-tē'ri-ėr, *a*. Before; prior; in front.
**Anteroom**, an'tē-röm, *n*. A room in front of a principal apartment.
**Anthem**, an'them, *n*. A sacred song sung in alternate parts; a piece of Scripture set to music.
**Anther**, an'thėr, *n*. The summit of the stamen in a flower, containing the pollen.
**Anthological**, an-tho-loj'ik-al, *a*. Pertaining to anthology.
**Anthology**, an-thol'o-ji, *n*. A collection of poems.
**Anthracite**, an'thra-sīt, *n*. A hard, compact coal which burns almost without flame.
**Anthropoid**, an'thrō-poid, *a*. Resembling man: applied to the higher apes.
**Anthropology**, an-thrō-pol'o-ji, *n*. The science of man and mankind; the study of the physical and mental constitution of man.
**Anthropomorphism**, an-thrō'pō-mor''fizm, *n*. The representation of a deity in human form, or with human attributes.
**Anthropophagi**, an-thrō-pof'a-ji, *n.pl*. Man-eaters; cannibals.
**Anthropophagy**, an-thrō-pof'a-ji, *n*. Cannibalism.
**Anti-aircraft**, an'ti-âr-kraft, *a*. Used in defense against attacks from the air, as guns, searchlights, etc.
**Antic**, an'tik, *a*. Grotesque; fantastic.—*n*. A buffoon; buffoonery.
**Antichrist**, an'ti-krīst, *n*. The great adversary of Christ.
**Antichristian**, an-ti-kris'ti-an, *a*. Pertaining to Antichrist.
**Anticipate**, an-tis'-i-pāt, *vt*. (anticipating, anticipated). To forestall; to foretaste; to preclude; to expect.
**Anticipation**, an-tis'i-pā''shon, *n*. Act of anticipating; foretaste, expectation.
**Anti-climax**, an-ti-klī'maks, *n*. A sentence in which the ideas become less striking at the close.
**Anticlinal**, an-ti-klī'nal, *a*. Marking inclination in opposite directions.
**Anticyclone**, an'ti-sī-klōn, *n*. An opposite state of atmospheric or meteorological conditions to what exists in a cyclone.
**Antidotal**, an'ti-dōt-al, *a*. Acting as an antidote.
**Antidote**, an'ti-dōt, *n*. A remedy for poison or any evil.
**Anti-macassar**, an'ti-ma-kas''är, *n*. A movable covering for chairs, sofas, etc.
**Antimonial**, an-ti-mō'ni-al, *a*. Pertaining to antimony.
**Antimony**, an'ti-mo-ni, *n*. A brittle, white-colored metal, used in the arts and in medicine.
**Antinomian**, an-ti-nō'mi-an, *n*. One who opposes the moral law.
**Antipathy**, an-tip'a-thi, *n*. Instinctive aversion; dislike; opposition.
**Antiphlogistic**, an'ti-flo-jis''tik, *a*. Counteracting inflammation.
**Antiphon**, an'ti-fōn, *n*. The chant or alternate singing in choirs of cathedrals.
**Antiphrasis**, an-tif'ra-sis, *n*. The use of words in a sense opposite to the proper one.
**Antipodal**, an-tip'od-al, *a*. Pertaining to the antipodes.
**Antipodes**, an-tip'o-dēz, *n.pl*. Those who live on opposite sides of the globe; the opposite side of the globe.
**Antipope**, an'ti-pōp, *n*. An opposition pope.
**Antipyrin**, an-ti-pī'rin, *n*. A drug used to reduce fever and relieve pain.
**Antiquarian**, an-ti-kwā'ri-an, *a*. Pertaining to antiquaries.—*n*. One versed in antiquities.
**Antiquarianism**, an-ti-kwā'ri-an-izm, *n*. Love or knowledge of antiquities.
**Antiquary**, an'ti-kwa-ri, *n*. One versed in antiquities.
**Antiquated**, an'ti-kwāt-ed, *a*. Grown old; obsolete.
**Antique**, an-tēk', *a*. Old; of genuine antiquity.—*n*. Anything very old; an ancient relic.
**Antiquity**, an-tik'wi-ti, *n*. Ancient times; great age; *pl*. remains of ancient times.
**Antiseptic**, an-ti-sep'tik, *a*. Counteracting putrefaction.—*n*. A substance which resists or corrects putrefaction.
**Antistrophe**, an-tis'tro-fi, *n*. The stanza of an ode, succeeding the strophe.
**Antithesis**, an-tith'e-sis, *n*.; pl. **-theses.** Opposition of thoughts or words; contrast.
**Antithetical**, an-ti-thet'ik-al, *a*. Pertaining to antithesis.
**Antitype**, an'ti-tīp, *n*. That which is shadowed out by a type or emblem.
**Antitypical**, an-ti-tip'ik-al, *a*. Pertaining to an antitype; explaining the type.
**Antler**, ant'lėr, *n*. A branch of a stag's horn.
**Antonym**, ant'ō-nim, *n*. A word of directly contrary signification to another: the opposite of a synonym.
**Anus**, ā'nus, *n*. The opening of the body by which excrement is expelled.
**Anvil**, an'vil, *n*. An iron block on which smiths hammer and shape their work.
**Anxiety**, ang-zī'e-ti, *n*. State of being anxious; concern.
**Anxious**, angk'shus, *a*. Suffering mental distress; solicitous; concerned.
**Anxiously**, angk'shus-li, *adv*. In an anxious manner.
**Anxiousness**, angk'shus-nes, *n*. Anxiety.
**Any**, en'i, *a*. One indefinitely; whatever; some.—*adv*. At all; in any degree.
**Anzac**, an'zak, *n*. The Australian New Zealand Army Corps; an Australasian Expeditionary soldier.
**Aorist**, ā'or-ist, *n*. An indefinite past tense in the Greek verb.
**Aorta**, ā-ort'a, *n*. The great artery which rises up from the left ventricle of the heart.
**Aortal, Aortic**, ā-ort'al, ā-ort'ik, *a*. Pertaining to the aorta or great artery.
**Apace**, a-pās', *adv*. Quick; fast; speedily.
**Apart**, a-pärt', *adv*. Separately; aside.
**Apartment**, a-pärt'ment, *n*. A room.
**Apathetic**, ap-a-thet'ik, *a*. Void of feeling; free from passion; indifferent.
**Apathy**, ap'a-thi, *n*. Want of feeling; insensibility;

indifference.
**Ape,** āp, *n.* A monkey; an imitator.—*vt.* (aping, aped). To imitate servilely; to mimic.
**Aperient,** a-pē'ri-ent, *a.* Mildly purgative.—*n.* A laxative; a mild purgative.
**Aperture,** ap'ėr-tūr, *n.* An opening; a hole.
**Apex,** ā'peks, *n.*; pl. **-exes** and **-ices.** The summit of anything.
**Aphaeresis, Apheresis,** a-fē're-sis, *n.* The taking of a letter or syllable from the beginning of a word.
**Aphelion,** a-fē'li-on, *n.*; pl. **-lia.** The point of a planet's orbit farthest from the sun.
**Aphorism,** af-or-izm, *n.* A precept expressed in few words; a maxim.
**Apiary,** ā'pi-a-ri, *n.* A place where bees are kept.
**Apiece,** a-pēs', *adv.* In a separate share; to each; noting the share of each.
**Apish,** āp'ish, *a.* Resembling an ape.
**Aplomb,** a-plong, *n.* Self-possession.
**Apocalypse,** a-pok'a-lips, *n.* Revelation; the last book of the New Testament.
**Apocalyptic,** a-pok'a-lip''tik, *a.* Pertaining to the Apocalypse.
**Apocope,** a-pok'ō-pē, *n.* The cutting off of the last letter or syllable of a word.
**Apocrypha,** a-pok'ri-fa, *n.pl.* Certain books whose authenticity as inspired writings is not generally admitted.
**Apocryphal,** a-pok'ri-fal, *a.* Pertaining to the Apocrypha; not canonical; fictitious.
**Apogee,** ap'ō-jē, *n.* The point in the moon's orbit farthest from the earth.
**Apologetic,** a-pol'ō-jet''ik, *a.* Containing apology; defending; excusing.
**Apologetics,** a-pol'ō-jet''iks, *n.pl.* The branch of theology which defends Christianity.
**Apologist,** a-pol'ō-jist, *n.* One who apologizes; an excuser, or defender.
**Apologize,** a-pol'ō-jīz, *vi.* (apologizing, apologized). To make an apology.
**Apologue,** ap'o-log, *n.* A moral fable.
**Apology,** a-pol'ō-ji, *n.* That which is said in defense; vindication; excuse.
**Apophthegm, Apothegm,** ap'o-them, *n.* A terse, pointed saying.
**Apoplectic,** ap-o-plek'tik, *a.* Pertaining to apoplexy.
**Apoplexy,** ap'ō-plek'si, *n.* A sudden privation of sense and voluntary motion.
**Apostasy,** a-pos'ta-si, *n.* Departure from one's faith; desertion of a party.
**Apostate,** a-pos'tāt, *n.* One who renounces his religion or his party.—*a.* False; traitorous.
**Apostatize,** a-pos'ta-tīz, *vi.* To abandon one's religion or party.
**Aposteme,** ap'os-tēm, *n.* An abscess.
**Apostle,** a-pos'l, *n.* One sent to preach the gospel; one of the twelve disciples.
**Apostleship,** a-pos'l-ship, *n.* Office of an apostle.
**Apostolic, Apostolical,** ap-os-tol'ik, ap-os-tol'ikal, *a.* Pertaining to an apostle.
**Apostrophe,** a-pos'tro-fē, *n.* An addressing of the absent or the dead as if present; a mark (') indicating contraction of a word, or the possessive case.
**Apostrophize,** a-pos'trof-īz, *vi.* To make an apostrophe.—*vt.* To address by apostrophe.
**Apothecary,** a-poth'e-ka-ri, *n.* One who prepares and sells drugs or medicines.
**Apothegm,** ap'o-them, *n.* *See* APOPHTHEGM.
**Apotheosis,** ap-o-thē'ō-sis or -thē-ō'sis, *n.* A deification; a placing among the gods.
**Appal,** ap-pal', *vt.* (appalling, appalled). To depress with fear; to dismay.
**Appalling,** ap-pal'ing, *a.* Causing dread or terror.
**Appanage,** ap'pan-āj, *n.* Lands or revenue settled on the younger son of a ruler; an adjunct; appendage.
**Apparatus,** ap-pa-rā'tus, *n.*; pl. **-tus,** or **-tuses,** Set of instruments or utensils for performing any operation.
**Apparel,** ap-pa'rel, *n.* Equipment; clothing. *vt.* (apparelling, apparelled). To dress; to array.
**Apparent,** ap-pā'rent, *a.* That may be seen; evident; seeming, not real.
**Apparently,** ap-pā'rent-li, *adv.* Openly; seemingly.
**Apparition,** ap-pa-ri'shon, *n.* An appearance; a specter; a ghost or phantom.
**Appeal,** ap-pēl', *vi.* To call; to refer to a superior court; to have recourse.—*vt.* To remove to a superior court.—*n.* The removal of a cause to a higher tribunal; a reference to another.
**Appear,** ap-pēr', *vi.* To be or become visible; to seem.
**Appearance,** ap-pēr'ans, *n.* Act of coming into sight; semblance; likelihood.
**Appeasable,** ap-pēz'a-bl, *a.* That may be appeased.
**Appease,** ap-pēz', *vt.* (appeasing, appeased). To pacify; to tranquilize.
**Appellant,** ap-pel'ant, *n.* One who appeals.
**Appellate,** ap-pel'āt, *a.* Pertaining to appeals.
**Appellation,** ap-pel-ā'shon, *n.* Name; title.
**Appellative,** ap-pel'at-iv, *a.* Naming; designating.—*n.* A name; an appellation.
**Append,** ap-pend', *vt.* To add; to annex.
**Appendage,** ap-pend'āj, *n.* Something added; a subordinate part.
**Appendant,** ap-pend'ant, *a.* Annexed.—*n.* Something subordinate or incidental.
**Appendix,** ap-pen'diks, *n.*; pl. **-ixes** or **-ices.** An adjunct or appendage; a supplement; a narrow tube with blind end leading out of intestine.
**Appertain,** ap-pėr-tān', *vi.* To belong; to relate.
**Appetence, Appetency,** ap'pē-tens, ap'pē-ten-si, *n.* Desire; sensual appetite.
**Appetite,** ap'pē-tīt, *n.* A desire or relish for food or other sensual gratifications.
**Appetize,** ap'pē-tīz, *vt.* (appetizing, appetized). To give an appetite to; to whet the appetite.
**Appetizer,** ap'pē-tīz-ėr, *n.* That which appetizes.
**Applaud,** ap-plad', *vt.* To praise by clapping the hands, etc.; to extol.
**Applause,** ap-plaz', *n.* Praise loudly expressed; acclamation.
**Apple,** ap'l, *n.* The fruit of the apple-tree; the pupil of the eye.
**Appliance,** ap-plī'ans, *n.* Act of applying; thing applied; article of equipment.
**Applicability,** ap'pli-ka-bil''li-ti, *n.* Quality of being applicable.
**Applicable,** ap'pli-ka-bl, *a.* That may be applied; suitable.
**Applicably,** ap'pli-ka-bli, *adv.* In an applicable manner.
**Applicant,** ap'pli-kant, *n.* One who applies.
**Application,** ap-pli-kā'shon, *n.* Act of applying; request; close study; assiduity; the thing applied.
**Apply,** ap-plī, *vt.* (applying, applied). To fasten or attach; to use; to employ with assiduity.—*vi.* To suit; to solicit; to have recourse to.
**Appoint,** ap-point', *vt.* To fix; to allot; to nominate; to equip.—*vi.* To determine.
**Appointment,** ap-point'ment, *n.* Act of appointing; office held; arrangement; decree; *pl* equipments.
**Apportion,** ap-pōr'shon, *vt.* To portion out; to assign in just proportion.
**Apportioner,** ap-pōr'shon-ėr, *n.* One who apportions.
**Apportionment,** ap-pōr'shon-ment, *n.* Act of apportioning.
**Apposite,** ap'pō-zit, *a.* Suitable; applicable; pat.
**Appositely,** ap'pō-zit-li, *adv.* Suitably.
**Appositeness,** ap'pō-zit-nes, *n.* Fitness.
**Apposition,** ap-pō-zi'shon, *n.* In *grammar,* the relation of one noun to another, when it explains its meaning, while agreeing in case.
**Appraise,** ap-prāz', *vt.* (appraising, appraised). To fix or set a price on; to estimate.
**Appraisement,** ap-prāz'ment, *n.* Valuation.
**Appraiser,** ap-prāz'ėr, *n.* One who values; a valu-

ator.
**Appreciable**, ap-prē'shi-a-bl, *a*. That may be appreciated.
**Appreciate**, ap-prē'shi-āt, *vt*. (appreciating, appreciated). To value; to estimate justly.
**Appreciation**, ap-prē'shi-ā''shon, *n*. Act of appreciating; a just valuation.
**Apprehend**, ap-prē-hend', *vt*. To take hold of; to arrest; to conceive; to fear.—*vi*. To think; to imagine.
**Apprehensible**, ap-prē-hen'si-bl, *a*. That may be apprehended or conceived.
**Apprehension**, ap-prē-hen'shon, *n*. Seizure; faculty of conceiving ideas; dread.
**Apprehensive**, ap-prē-hen'siv, *a*. Fearful; suspicious.
**Apprentice**, ap-pren'tis, *n*. One who is indentured to a master to learn a trade, an art, etc.—*vi*. To bind as an apprentice.
**Apprenticeship**, ap-pren'tis-ship, *n*. The term an apprentice serves; state or condition of an apprentice.
**Apprise**, ap-prīz', *vt*. (apprising, apprised). To inform; to make known of.
**Approach**, ap-prōch', *vi*. To come near; to approximate.—*vt*. To come near to; to resemble.—*n*. Act of drawing near; an avenue; access.
**Approachable**, ap-prōch'a-bl, *a*. That may be approached.
**Approbation**, ap-prō-bā'shon, *n*. Approval; attestation; a liking.
**Appropriable**, ap-prō'pri-a-bl, *a*. That may be appropriated.
**Appropriate**, ap-prō'pri-āt, *vt*. (appropriating, appropriated). To take to oneself as one's own; to set apart for.—*a*. Set apart for a particular use or person; suitable; adapted.
**Appropriately**, ap-prō'pri-āt-li, *adv*. In an appropriate manner.
**Appropriateness**, ap-prō'pri-āt-nes, *n*. Peculiar fitness.
**Appropriation**, ap-prō'pri-ā''shon, *n*. Act of appropriating; application to special use.
**Approvable**, ap-prov'a-bl, *a*. That may be approved.
**Approval**, ap-pröv'al, *n*. Approbation.
**Approve**, ap-pröv', *vt*. (approving, approved). To deem good; to like; to sanction.—*vi*. To feel or express approbation (with *of*).
**Approver**, ap-pröv'ėr, *n*. One who approves.
**Approximate**, ap-prok'si-māt, *a*. Near; approaching.—*vt*. (approximating, approximated). To bring near.—*vi*. To come near; to approach.
**Approximately**, ap-prok'si-māt-li, *adv*. Nearly.
**Approximation**, ap-prok'si-mā''shon, *n*. Act of approximating; approach.
**Appurtenance**, ap-pėr'ten-ans, *n*. That which pertains to; an appendage.
**Apricot**, ā'pri-kot, *n*. Stone-fruit, resembling the peach.
**April**, ā'pril, *n*. The fourth month of the year.
**Apron**, ā'prun, *n*. A cloth, or piece of leather, worn in front to protect the clothes.
**Apropos**, ap'rō-pō, *adv*. To the purpose; opportunely.
**Apsis**, ap'sis, *n*.; pl. **-sides**, -si-dēz. One of the two points in a planet's orbit which mark its greatest and least distance from the body round which it revolves.
**Apt**, apt, *a*. Suitable; liable; ready.
**Apterous**, ap'tėr-us, *a*. Destitute of wings.
**Apteryx**, ap'tė-riks, *n*. A bird of New Zealand, with rudimentary wings, and no tail.
**Aptitude**, ap'ti-tūd, *n*. Fitness; readiness.
**Aptly**, apt'li, *adv*. In an apt manner.
**Aptness**, apt'nes, *n*. Aptitude.
**Aqua**, ak'wa, *n*. Water.
**Aqua fortis**, ak'wa for-tis, *n*. Weak and impure nitric acid.
**Aquarium**, a-kwā'ri-um, *n*.; pl. **-iums** or **-ia**. A vessel or tank for aquatic plants and animals; a collection of such vessels.
**Aquarius**, a-kwā'ri-us, *n*. The water-bearer, a sign in the zodiac.
**Aquatic**, a-kwat'ik, *a*. Living or growing in water.—*n*. A plant which grows in water; *pl*. sports or exercises in water.
**Aquatint**, ak'wa-tint, *n*. A method of etching which gives effects resembling drawing in water-colors or Indian ink.
**Aqueduct**, ak'wē-dukt, *n*. A conduit made for conveying water.
**Aqueous**, ā'kwē-us, *a*. Watery.
**Aquiline**, ak'wil-īn, *a*. Belonging to the eagle; hooked like the beak of an eagle.
**Arab**, a'rab, *n*. A native of Arabia; a street urchin; an Arabian horse.
**Arabesque**, ar'ab-esk, *n*. A species of ornamentation consisting of fanciful figures and floral forms.
**Arabian**, a-rā'bi-an, *a*. Pertaining to Arabia.—*n*. A native of Arabia.
**Arabic**, a'rab-ik, *a*. Belonging to Arabia.—*n*. The language of the Arabians.
**Arable**, a'ra-bl, *a*. Fit for farming.
**Arachnida**, a-rak'ni-da, *n.pl*. A class of annulose wingless animals, such as spiders.
**Aramaic**, **Aramean**, a-ra-mā'ik, a-ra-mē'an, *a*. Pertaining to the languages, etc., of the Syrians and Chaldeans.
**Araucaria**, ar-a-kā'ri-a, *n*. A coniferous prickly tree, the monkey-puzzle.
**Arbiter**, är'bit-ėr, *n*. A person appointed by parties in controversy to decide their differences; an umpire.
**Arbitrament**, är-bit'ra-ment, *n*. Decision.
**Arbitrarily**, är'bi-tra-ri-li, *adv*. By will only; despotically.
**Arbitrary**, är'bi-tra-ri, *a*. Depending on one's will; despotic.
**Arbitrate**, är'bi-trāt, *vi*. (arbitrating, arbitrated). To act as an arbiter; to decide.
**Arbitration**, är-bi-trā'shon, *n*. The act of arbitrating.
**Arbitrator**, är'bi-trāt-ėr, *n*. A person chosen to decide a dispute; umpire.
**Arbor**, är'bėr, *n*. A bower; a shelter in a garden, formed of trees, etc.
**Arboreous**, är-bō'rē-us, *a*. Belonging to trees.
**Arborescence**, är-bor-es'sens, *n*. The state of being arborescent.
**Arborescent**, är-bor-es'sent, *a*. Growing like a tree; becoming woody.
**Arboretum**, är-bo-rē'tum, *n*. A place where trees are cultivated for scientific purposes.
**Arboriculture**, är-bo'ri-kul''tūr, *n*. The art of cultivating trees and shrubs.
**Arbutus**, är'bū-tus, *n*. An evergreen shrub, with berries like the strawberry.
**Arc**, ärk, *n*. A part of a circle or curve.
**Arcade**, är-kād', *n*. A walk arched above; an arched gallery; a covered passage containing shops.
**Arcadian**, är-kā'di-an, *a*. Pertaining to Arcadia.
**Arcanum**, är-kān'um, *n*.; pl. **-na**. Mystery.
**Arch**, ärch, *a*. Chief; cunning; sly; roguish.
**Arch**, ärch, *n*. A concave structure supported by its own curve; a vault.—*vt*. To cover with an arch; to form with a curve.
**Archeological**, är-kē-ō-loj'ik-al, *a*. Relating to archeology.
**Archeologist**, är-kē-ol'o-jist, *n*. One versed in archeology.
**Archeology**, är-kē-ol'o-ji, *n*. The science of antiquities; knowledge of ancient art.
**Archaic**, är-kā'ik, *a*. Antiquated; obsolete.
**Archaism**, är'kā-izm, *n*. Obsolete word or expression.
**Archangel**, ärk-ān'jel, *n*. An angel of the highest order.
**Archangelic**, ärk-an-jel'ik, *a*. Belonging to archangels.
**Archbishop**, ärch-bish'up, *n*. A chief bishop; a bishop who superintends other bishops, his suf-

fragans, in his province.
**Archbishopric,** ärch-bish'up-rik, *n.* The province of an archbishop.
**Archdeacon,** ärch-dē'kn, *n.* A church dignitary next in rank below a bishop.
**Archdeaconry,** ärch-dē'kn-ri, *n.* The office or residence of an archdeacon.
**Archdeaconship,** ärch-dē'kn-ship, *n.* The office of an archdeacon.
**Archduke,** ärch-dūk', *n.* Formerly a title of princes of the House of Austria.
**Archer,** ärch'ėr, *n.* A bowman; one who shoots with a bow and arrow.
**Archery,** ärch'ė-ri, *n.* The practice, art, or skill of archers.
**Archetype,** är'kē-tīp, *n.* The original model from which a thing is made.
**Archidiaconal,** är'ki-dī-ak''on-al, *a.* Pertaining to an archdeacon.
**Archiepiscopal,** är'ki-ē-pis''kō-pal, *a.* Belonging to an archbishop.
**Archipelago,** är-ki-pel'a-gō, *n.* The Aegean Sea; a sea abounding in small islands.
**Architect,** är'ki-tekt, *n.* One who plans buildings, etc.; a contriver.
**Architectural,** är-ki-tek'tūr-al, *a.* Pertaining to architecture.
**Architecture,** är'ki-tek-tūr, *n.* The art or science of building; structure.
**Architrave,** är'ki-trāv, *n.* In *architecture*, the part of an entablature resting on a column.
**Archive,** är'kīv, *n.* A record; generally *pl.*, records of a kingdom, city, family, etc.
**Archly,** ärch'li, *adv.* Shrewdly; roguishly.
**Archness,** ärch'nes, *n.* Roguishness.
**Archon,** är'kon, *n.* One of the chief magistrates of ancient Athens.
**Archway,** ärch'wā, *n.* A way or passage under an arch.
**Arctic,** ärk'tik, *a.* Pertaining to the regions about the north pole; frigid; cold.
**Ardency,** är'den-si, *n.* Ardor; eagerness.
**Ardent,** är'dent, *a.* Burning; fervent; eager.
**Ardently,** är'dent-li, *adv.* With ardour.
**Ardor,** är'dėr, *n.* Warmth; fervency; eagerness.
**Ardous,** är'dū-us, *a.* Difficult; laborios.
**Ardously,** är'dū-us-li, *adv.* In an arduos manner; with effort.
**Are,** är. The plural pres. indic. of the verb *to be*.
**Area,** ā'rē-a, *n.* Any open surface; superficial contents; any inclosed space.
**Arena,** a-rē'na, *n.* An open space of ground, strewed with sand or saw-dust, for combatants; any place of public contest.
**Arenaceous,** a-rē-nā'shus, *a.* Sandy.
**Areopagus,** ar-ē-op'a-gus, *n.* The supreme court of ancient Athens, held on a hill of this name.
**Argent,** är'jent, *a.* Silvery; like silver.
**Argil,** är'jil, *n.* White clay; potter's earth.
**Argillaceous,** är-jil-lā'shus, *a.* Clayey.
**Argon,** är'gon, *n.* A gas existing in the atmosphere in very small quantities; an inert chemical element.
**Argonaut,** är'go-nat, *n.* One who sailed in the ship *Argo* in quest of the golden fleece.
**Argue,** är'gū, *vi.* (arguing, argued). To offer reasons; to dispute.—*vt.* To show reasons for; to discuss.
**Argument,** är'gū-ment, *n.* A reason offered; a plea; subject of a discourse; heads of contents; controversy.
**Argumentation,** är-gū-ment-ā''shon, *n.* Act, art, or process of arguing.
**Argumentative,** är-gū-ment'at-iv, *a.* Consisting of or prone to argument.
**Argus,** är'gus, *n.* A fabulous being with a hundred eyes; a watchful person.
**Arian,** ā'ri-an, *a.* Pertaining to Arius, who denied the divinity of Christ.—*n.* One who adheres to the doctrines of Arius.
**Arianism,** ā'ri-an-izm, *n.* The doctrines of the Arians.
**Arid,** a'rid, *a.* Dry; dried; parched.
**Aridity,** a-rid'i-ti, *n.* Dryness.
**Aries,** ā'ri-ēz, *n.* The Ram, the first of the twelve signs of the zodiac.
**Aright,** a-rīt', *adv.* Rightly; justly.
**Arise,** a-rīz', *vi.* (arising, pret. arose, pp. arisen). To rise up; to proceed from.
**Aristocracy,** a-ris-tok'ra-si, *n.* Government by the nobility; the nobility.
**Aristocrat,** a'ris-to-krat, *n.* A noble; one who favors aristocracy.
**Aristocratic,** a-ris-to-krat'ik, *a.* Pertaining to aristocracy.
**Aristocratically,** a-ris-to-krat'ik-al-li, *adv.* In an aristocratic manner.
**Aristotelian,** a-ris-to-tē'li-an, *a.* Pertaining to Aristotle, or to his philosophy.
**Arithmetic,** a-rith'met-ik, *n.* The science of numbering; the art of computation.
**Arithmetical,** a-rith-met'ik-al, *a.* Pertaining to arithmetic.
**Arithmetically,** a-rith-met'ik-al-li, *adv.* By means of arithmetic.
**Arithmetician,** a-rith'me-ti''shan, *n.* One skilled in arithmetic.
**Ark,** ärk, *n.* A chest; a large floating vessel.
**Arm,** ärm, *n.* The limb from the shoulder to the hand; anything extending from a main body; a weapon; *pl.* war; armor; armorial bearings.—*vt.* To furnish with arms; to fortify.—*vi.* To take up arms.
**Armada,** är-mā'da, *n.* A fleet of armed ships; a squadron.
**Armadillo,** är-ma-dil'lō, *n.* A quadruped of the southwestern U.S. with a hard bony shell.
**Armament,** ärm'a-ment, *n.* A force armed for war; war-munitions of a ship.
**Armenian,** är-mē'ni-an, *a.* Pertaining to Armenia.—*n.* A native of Armenia; the language of the country.
**Arminian,** är-min'i-an, *a.* Pertaining to Arminius.—*n.* A Protestant who denies the doctrine of predestination.
**Arminianism,** är-min'i-an-izm, *n.* The peculiar doctrines of the Arminians.
**Armipotent,** är-mip'ō-tent, *a.* Powerful in arms.
**Armistice,** är'mis-tis, *n.* A cessation of hostilities for a short time; a truce.
**Armlet,** ärm'let, *n.* A bracelet.
**Armorial,** är-mō'ri-al, *a.* Belonging to armour, or to the arms of a family.
**Armoric,** är-mo'rik, *a.* Pertaining to Brittany.—*n.* The language of Brittany.
**Armor,** ärm'ėr, *n.* Defensive arms.
**Armorer,** ärm'ėr-ėr, *n.* One who makes or has the care of arms.
**Armory,** ärm'e-ri, *n.* A repository of arms.
**Armpit,** ärm'pit, *n.* The hollow place under the shoulder.
**Army,** är'mi, *n.* A body of men armed for war; a great number.
**Aroma,** a-rō'ma, *n.* Perfume; the fragrant principle in plants, etc.
**Aromatic,** a-rō-mat'ik, *a.* Fragrant; spicy.—*n.* A fragrant plant or drug.
**Around,** a-round', *prep.* About; on all sides of; encircling.—*adv.* On every side.
**Arouse,** a-rouz', *vt.* (arousing, aroused). To rouse; to stir up.
**Arquebus, Arquebuse,** är'kwē-bus, *n.* An old-fashioned hand-gun.
**Arrack,** a'rak, *n.* A spirituous liquor distilled in the E. Indies from rice, etc.
**Arraign,** a-rān', *vt.* To indict; to censure.
**Arraigner,** a-rān'ėr, *n.* One who arraigns.
**Arraignment,** a-rān'ment, *n.* Act of arraigning; accusation.
**Arrange,** a-rānj', *vt.* (arranging, arranged). To put in order; to classify.
**Arrangement,** a-rānj'ment, *n.* Orderly disposition; adjustment; classification.
**Arrant,** a'rant, *a.* Downright; thorough.
**Arras,** a'ras, *n.* Tapestry.
**Array,** a-rā', *n.* Order; order of battle; apparel.—

*v.t.* To draw up in order; to adorn.
**Arrear,** a-rēr', *n.* That which remains unpaid. Generally in plural.
**Arrest,** a-rest', *vt.* To stop; to apprehend.—*n.* A seizure by warrant; stoppage.
**Arrival,** a-rīv'al, *n.* Act of coming to a place; persons or things arriving.
**Arrive,** a-rīv', *vi.* (arriving, arrived). To come; to reach; to attain.
**Arrogance,** a'rō-gans, *n.* Assumption; haughtiness; insolent bearing.
**Arrogant,** a'rō-gant, *a.* Assuming; haughty.
**Arrogantly,** a'rō-gant-li, *adv.* In an arrogant manner.
**Arrogate,** a'rō-gāt, *vt.* (arrogating, arrogated). To claim unduly; to assume.
**Arrow,** a'rō, *n.* A straight-pointed weapon, to be discharged from a bow.
**Arrow-headed,** a'rō-hed-ed, *a.* Shaped like the head of an arrow.
**Arrowroot,** a'rō-röt, *n.* A W. Indian plant; the starch of the plant, a medicinal food.
**Arrowy,** a'rō-i, *a.* Of or like arrows.
**Arsenal,** är'sē-nal, *n.* A public establishment where ammunition and guns are manufactured or stored.
**Arsenic,** är'sen-ik, *n.* A virulent mineral poison; an oxide of a brittle metal, called also arsenic.
**Arsenical,** är-sen'ik-al, *a.* Consisting of or containing arsenic.
**Arson,** är'son, *n.* The malicious setting on fire of a house, etc.
**Art,** ärt, *v.* The second person, present indicative of the verb *to be.*
**Art,** ärt, *n.* Practical skill; a system of rules for certain actions; cunning; profession of a painter, etc.
**Arterial,** är-tē'ri-al, *a.* Pertaining to an artery or the arteries.
**Artery,** är'te-ri, *n.* A tube which conveys blood from the heart.
**Artesian,** är-tē'zi-an, *a.* Designating a well made by boring till water is reached.
**Artful,** ärt'ful, *a.* Full of art; skilful; crafty.
**Artfully,** ärt'ful-li, *adv.* With art.
**Artfulness,** ärt'ful-nes, *n.* Craft; address.
**Arthritis,** är-thrī'tis, *n.* Gout.
**Artichoke,** är'ti-chōk, *n.* An esculent plant somewhat resembling a thistle.
**Article,** är'ti-kl, *n.* A separate item; stipulation; a particular commodity; a part of speech used before nouns, as *the.*—*vt.* To bind by articles.—*vi.* To stipulate.
**Articulate,** är-tik'ū-lāt, *a.* Distinct; clear.—*vi.* To utter distinct sounds, syllables, or words.—*vt.* To speak distinctly.
**Articulately,** är-tik'ū-lāt-li, *adv.* Distinctly.
**Articulation,** är-tik'ū-lā''shon, *n.* Juncture of bones; joint; distinct utterance.
**Artifice,** ärt'i-fis, *n.* An artful device; fraud; stratagem.
**Artificer,** är-tif'is-ėr, *n.* A contriver; a mechanic.
**Artificial,** ärt-i-fi'shal, *a.* Made by art; not natural.
**Artificially,** ärt-i-fi'shal-li, *adv.* In an artificial manner.
**Artillery,** är-til'lė-ri, *n.* Cannon; the troops who manage them; gunnery.
**Artisan,** ärt'i-zan, *n.* One trained to manual dexterity; a mechanic.
**Artist,** ärt'ist, *n.* One skilled in some art, especially the fine arts, as painting, etc.
**Artiste,** är-tēst, *n.* One skilled in some art not one of the fine arts, as singing, dancing.
**Artistic,** är-tist'ik, *a.* Conformed to art.
**Artistically,** är-tist'ik-al-li, *adv.* In an artistic manner.
**Artless,** ärt'les, *a.* Wanting art; unaffected.
**Artlessly,** ärt'les-li, *adv.* In an artless manner.
**Artlessness,** ärt'les-nes, *n.* Quality of being artless; simplicity.
**Aryan,** är-i-an or ā'ri-an, *a.* Indo-European; belonging to the Hindus, Persians, and most Europeans (except Turks, Hungarians, Finns, etc.), and to their languages.
**As,** az, *adv.* and *conj.* Like; even; equally; while; since; for example.
**Asbestos,** as-bes'tos, *n.* A mineral fibrous substance which is incombustible.
**Ascend,** as-send', *vi.* To rise; to go backward in order of time.—*vt.* To move upward upon; to climb.
**Ascendancy, Ascendency,** as-send'an-si, as-send'en-si, *n.* Controlling power; sway.
**Ascendant,** as-send'ant, *a.* Rising; superior; predominant.—*n.* Ascendancy; superiority.
**Ascension,** as-sen'shon, *n.* Act of ascending.
**Ascent,** as-sent', *n.* Rise; a mounting upward; the means of ascending.
**Ascertain,** as-sėr-tān', *vt.* To make certain; to find out.
**Ascertainable,** as-sėr-tān'a-bl, *a.* That may be ascertained.
**Ascetic,** as-set'ik, *a.* Unduly rigid in devotion.—*n.* One rigidly austere.
**Asceticism,** as-set'i-sizm, *n.* State or practice of ascetics.
**Ascribable,** as-krīb'a-bl, *a.* That may be ascribed.
**Ascribe,** as-krīb', *vt.* (ascribing, ascribed). To attribute; to assign.
**Ascription,** as-krip'shon, *n.* Act of ascribing; the thing ascribed.
**Asdic,** as'dik, *n.* A kind of hydrophone for detecting submarines (*A*llied *S*ubmarine *D*etection *I*nvestigation *C*ommittee).
**Aseptic,** a-sep'tik, *a.* Not liable to putrefy.
**Ash,** ash, *n.* A well-known timber tree.
**Ashamed,** a-shāmd', *a.* Affected by shame.
**Ashen,** ash'en, *a.* Pertaining to ash; made of ash.
**Ashes,** ash'ez, *n.pl.* The dust produced by combustion; the remains of a dead body.
**Ashlar, Ashler,** ash'lėr, *n.* A facing of dressed stones on a wall; hewn stone.
**Ashore,** a-shōr', *adv.* or *pred.a.* On shore.
**Ash-Wednesday,** ash-wenz'dā, *n.* The first day of Lent, so called from a custom of sprinkling ashes on the head.
**Ashy,** ash'i, *a.* Resembling or composed of ashes.
**Asiatic,** ā-shi-at'ik, *a.* Belonging to Asia.—*n.* A native of Asia.
**Aside,** a-sīd', *adv.* On one side; apart; at a small distance.
**Asinine,** as'i-nīn, *a.* Belonging to or resembling the ass.
**Ask,** ask, *vt.* To request; to question; to invite.—*vi.* To request or petition; to make inquiry.
**Askance, Askant,** a-skans', a-skant', *adv.* Awry; obliquely.
**Askew,** a-skū', *adv.* or *pred.a.* Awry.
**Aslant,** a-slant', *pred.a.* or *adv.* On slant; obliquely; not perpendicularly.
**Asleep,** a-slēp', *pred.a.* or *adv.* Sleeping; at rest.
**Aslope,** a-slōp', *pred.a.* or *adv.* On slope; obliquely.
**Asp,** asp, *n.* A small venomous serpent of Egypt.
**Asparagus,** as-pa'ra-gus, *n.* A well-known esculent plant.
**Aspect,** as'pekt, *n.* Appearance; situation.
**Aspen,** asp'en, *n.* A species of the poplar.
**Asperity,** as-pe'ri-ti, *n.* Roughness; harshness.
**Asperse,** as-pėrs', *vt.* (aspersing, aspersed). To calumniate; to slander.
**Aspersion,** as-pėr'shon, *n.* Calumny.
**Asphalt,** as-falt', *n.* A bituminous, hard substance, used for pavement, etc.
**Asphaltic,** as-falt'ik, *a.* Pertaining to asphalt.
**Asphodel,** as'fō-del, *n.* A kind of lily.
**Asphyxia,** as-fik'si-a, *n.* Suspended animation from suffocation, etc.
**Asphyxiate,** as-fik'si-āt, *vt.* To bring to a state of asphyxia.
**Aspirant,** as-pīr'ant, *n.* A candidate.
**Aspirate,** as'pi-rāt, *vt.* (aspirating, aspirated). To pronounce with an audible breath; to add an *h*-sound to.—*n.* An aspirated letter.

**Aspiration,** as-pi-rā'shon, *n.* Ardent desire; an aspirated sound.
**Aspire,** as-pīr', *vi.* (aspiring, aspired). To aim at high things; to soar.
**Asquint,** a-skwint', *adv.* Out of the corner or angle of the eye; obliquely.
**Ass,** as, *n.* A well-known animal skin to the horse; a dolt.
**Assagai,** as'sa-gā, *n.* A Kaffir throwing spear; a species of javelin. Also *Assegai.*
**Assail,** as-sāl', *vt.* To attack; to assault.
**Assailable,** as-sāl'a-bl, *a.* That may be assailed.
**Assailant,** as-sāl'ant, *n.* One who assails.
**Assassin,** as-sas'sin, *n.* One who kills, or attempts to kill, by surprise or secretly.
**Assassinate,** as-sas'sin-āt, *vt.* (assassinating, assassinated). To murder by surprise or secretly.
**Assassination,** as-sas'sin-ā''shon, *n.* Act of murdering by surprise.
**Assault,** as-salt', *n.* An attack; a storming.—*vt.* To assail; to storm.
**Assaulter,** as-salt'ėr, *n.* One who assaults.
**Assay,** as-sā', *n.* Proof; trial; determination of the quantity of metal in an ore or alloy.—*vt.* To try; to ascertain the purity or alloy of.—*vi.* To try or endeavor.
**Assayer,** as-sā'ėr, *n.* One who assays.
**Assaying,** as-sā'ing, *n.* Act of ascertaining the purity of the precious metals.
**Assemblage,** as-sem'blāj, *n.* A collection of individuals or things.
**Assemble,** as-sem'bl, *vt.* (assembling, assembled). To bring together.—*vi.* To come together.
**Assembly,** as-sem'bli, *n.* An assemblage; a convocation.
**Assent,** as-sent', *n.* Act of agreeing to anything; consent.—*vi.* To agree; to yield.
**Assert,** as-sėrt', *vt.* To affirm; to maintain; to vindicate.
**Assertion,** as-sėr'shon, *n.* Act of asserting.
**Assertive,** as-sėrt'iv, *a.* Affirming confidently; peremptory.
**Assess,** as-ses', *vt.* To fix a charge to be paid upon; to rate.
**Assessable,** as-ses'a-bl, *a.* That may be assessed.
**Assessment,** as-ses'ment, *n.* Act of assessing; the sum levied; a tax.
**Assessor,** as-ses'ėr, *n.* A legal adviser who assists a magistrate or judge.
**Assets,** as'sets, *n.pl.* Goods available to pay debts.
**Asseverate,** as-sev'ė-rāt, *vt.* (asseverating, asseverated). To declare seriously or solemnly; to protest.
**Asseveration,** as-sev'ė-rā''shon, *n.* Positive and solemn declaration.
**Assiduity,** as-si-dū'i-ti, *n.* Close application; diligence.
**Assiduous,** as-sid'ū-us, *a.* Constantly diligent.
**Assign,** as-sīn', *vt.* To designate; to allot; to make over to another.—*n.* A person to whom property or any right may be or is transferred.
**Assignable,** as-sīn'a-bl, *a.* That may be assigned.
**Assignation,** as-sig-nā'shon, *n.* An appointment to meet, as of lovers; a making over by transfer of title.
**Assignee,** as-sī-nē', *n.* One to whom an assignment is made.
**Assigner,** as-sīn'ėr, *n.* One who assigns.
**Assignment,** as-sīn'ment, *n.* Act of assigning; thing assigned; a writ of transfer.
**Assimilate,** as-sim'il-āt, *vt.* (assimilating, assimilated). To make like to; to digest.—*vi.* To become similar or of the same substance.
**Assimilation,** as-sim'il-ā''shon, *n.* Act of assimilating.
**Assist,** as-sist', *vt.* To help.—*vi.* To lend help; to contribute.
**Assistance,** as-sist'ans, *n.* Help; aid.
**Assistant,** as-sist'ant, *n.* One who assists.
**Associable,** as-sō'shi-a-bl, *a.* Companionable.
**Associate,** as-sō'shi-āt, *vt.* (associating, associated). To join in company with; to combine.—*vi.* To keep company with.—*n.* A companion; friend.
**Association,** as-sō'si-ā''shon, *n.* Act of associating; union; confederacy; one of the two principal varieties of football, played by eleven men a side, with a round ball, handling (except by the goalkeeper) being forbidden.
**Assoil,** as-soil', *vt.* To release; to absolve.
**Assonance,** as'sō-nans, *n.* Resemblance of sounds.
**Assort,** as-sort', *vt.* To sort; to arrange.—*vi.* To suit; to agree.
**Assortment,** as-sort'ment, *n.* Act of assorting; quantity of things assorted; variety.
**Assuage,** as-swāj', *vt.* (assuaging, assuaged). To allay; to calm.—*vi.* To abate or subside.
**Assuagement,** as-swāj'ment, *n.* Mitigation.
**Assume,** as-sūm', *vt.* (assuming, assumed). To take for granted; to usurp.—*vi.* To claim more than is due; to be arrogant.
**Assuming,** as-sūm'ing, *a.* Arrogant.
**Assumption,** as-sum'shon, *n.* Act of assuming; the thing assumed; the taking up of any person into heaven.
**Assurance,** a-shör'ans, *n.* Act of assuring; secure confidence; impudence; positive declaration; insurance.
**Assure,** a-shör', *vt.* (assuring, assured). To make sure; to confirm; to insure.
**Assuredly,** a-shör'ed-li, *adv.* Certainly.
**Assuredness,** a-shör'ed-nes, *n.* State of being assured.
**Assurer,** a-shör'ėr, *n.* One who assures or insures.
**Assyrian,** as-sir'i-an, *a.* Pertaining to Assyria or its inhabitants.—*n.* A native of Assyria; the language of the Assyrians.
**Astatic,** a-stat'ik, *a.* Being without polarity, as a magnetic needle.
**Aster,** as'tėr, *n.* A genus of composite plants, with flowers somewhat like stars.
**Asterisk,** as'tė-risk, *n.* The figure of a star, thus *, used in printing.
**Astern,** a-stėrn', *adv.* In or at the hinder part of a ship.
**Asteroid,** as'tėr-oid, *n.* A small planet.
**Asthma,** as'ma or as'thma, *n.* A disorder of respiration, characterized by difficulty of breathing, cough, and expectoration.
**Asthmatic,** as-mat'ik, *a.* Pertaining to asthma; affected by asthma.
**Astigmatism,** a-stig'mat-izm, *n.* A malformation of the eye, in which rays of light do not properly converge to one point.
**Astir,** a-stėr', *adv.* or *pred.a.* On stir; active.
**Astonish,** as-ton'ish, *vt.* To surprise; to astound.
**Astonishing,** as-ton'ish-ing, *a.* Marvellous.
**Astonishment,** as-ton'ish-ment, *n.* Amazement.
**Astound,** as-tound', *vt.* To astonish; to stun; to strike dumb with amazement.
**Astounding,** as-tound'ing, *a.* Adapted to astonish; most astonishing.
**Astraddle,** a-strad'l, *adv.* or *pred.a.* Astride.
**Astragal,** as'tra-gal, *n.* A moulding surrounding the top or bottom of a column.
**Astrakhan,** as'tra-kan, *n.* A rough kind of cloth with a curled pile.
**Astral,** as'tral, *a.* Belonging to the stars.
**Astray,** a-strā', *adv.* or *pred.a.* Straying.
**Astrict,** as-trikt', *vt.* To contract; to limit.
**Astriction,** as-trik'shon, *n.* Contraction.
**Astride,** a-strīd', *adv.* or *pred.a.* With the legs apart or across a thing.
**Astringency,** as-trinj'en-si, *n.* Power of contracting, or of giving firmness.
**Astringent,** as-trinj'ent, *a.* Contracting tissues of the body; strengthening.—*n.* A medicine which contracts and strengthens.
**Astrolabe,** as'trō-lāb, *n.* An old instrument for taking the altitude at sea.
**Astrologer,** as-trol'o-jėr, *n.* One versed in astrology.
**Astrological,** as-trō-loj'ik-al, *a.* Pertaining to as-

trology.
**Astrology,** as-trol'o-ji, *n.* The pretended art of foretelling future events from the stars.
**Astronomer,** as-tron'ō-mėr, *n.* One versed in astronomy.
**Astronomical,** as-trō-nom'ik-al, *a.* Pertaining to astronomy.
**Astronomy,** as-tron'o-mi, *n.* The science of the heavenly bodies.
**Astrut,** a-strut', *adv.* or *pred.a.* In a strutting manner.
**Astute,** as-tūt', *a.* Shrewd; crafty.
**Astutely,** as-tūt'li, *adv.* Shrewdly.
**Astuteness,** as-tūt'nes, *n.* Shrewdness.
**Asunder,** a-sun'dėr, *adv.* or *pred.a.* Apart; into parts; in a divided state.
**Asylum,** a-sī'lum, *n.* A place of refuge; an institution for the care or relief of the unfortunate.
**Asyndeton,** a-sin'de-ton, *n.* The dispensing with conjunctions in speech.
**At,** at, *prep.* Denoting presence or nearness; in a state of; employed in, on, or with; with direction towards.
**Atavism,** at'a-vizm, *n.* The resemblance of offspring to a remote ancestor.
**Atelier,** ä-tl-yā, *n.* A workshop; a studio.
**Athanasian,** ath-a-nā'si-an, *a.* Pertaining to Athanasius or to his creed.
**Atheism,** ā'thē-izm, *n.* The disbelief in the existence of a God.
**Atheist,** ā'thē-ist, *n.* One who disbelieves the existence of a God.
**Atheistic, Atheistical,** ā-thē-ist'ik, ā-thē-ist'ik-al, *a.* Pertaining to atheism.
**Athenaeum,** ath-e-nē'um, *n.* An establishment connected with literature, science, or art.
**Athenian,** a-thēn'i-an, *a.* Pertaining to Athens.—*n.* A native of Athens.
**Athirst,** a-thėrst', *pred.a.* Thirsty.
**Athlete,** ath-lēt', *n.* One skilled in exercises of agility or strength.
**Athletic,** ath-let'ik, *a.* Pertaining to an athlete; strong; robust; vigorous.
**Athleticism,** ath-let'i-sizm, *n.* The practice of athletics.
**Athletics,** ath-let'iks, *n.pl.* Athletic exercises.
**Athwart,** a-thwart', *prep.* Across; from side to side.—*adv.* Crossly; wrong.
**Atlantean,** at-lan-tē'an, *a.* Gigantic.
**Atlantic,** at-lan'tik, *a.* Pertaining to the ocean between Europe, Africa, and America.—*n.* This ocean.
**Atlas,** at'las, *n.* A collection of maps.
**Atmosphere,** at'mos-fēr, *n.* The mass of gas around the earth; air; pervading influence.
**Atmospheric,** at-mos-fe'rik, *a.* Pertaining to the atmosphere.—*n.* (plural). In wireless telegraphy, disturbances produced in the receiving circuits by electrical action in the atmosphere or in the earth's crust.
**Atoll,** a-tol', *n.* A ring-shaped coral island.
**Atom,** a'tom, *n.* A minute particle of matter; anything extremely small.
**Atomic,** a-tom'ik, *a.* Pertaining to or consisting of atoms.
**Atomic bomb,** a-tom'ik bom, *n.* A bomb in which the splitting of atoms causes vast heating and explosion on a catastrophic scale.
**Atomism,** at'om-izm, *n.* Atomic philosophy; the doctrine that atoms of themselves formed the universe.
**Atone,** a-tōn', *vi.* (atoning, atoned). To make satisfaction.—*vt.* To expiate.
**Atonement,** a-tōn'ment, *n.* Reconciliation; satisfaction.
**Atrabilious,** at-ra-bil'i-us, *a.* Melancholic or hypochondriacal. Also *Atrabiliar, Atrabilarious.*
**Atrip,** a-trip', *adv.* or *pred.a.* Just raised from the ground, as an anchor.
**Atrocious,** a-trō'shus, *a.* Extremely cruel or wicked; flagitious.
**Atrociously,** a-trō'shus-li, *adv.* In an atrocious manner.
**Atrocity,** a-tros'i-ti, *n.* Horrible wickedness.
**Atrophy,** at'rō-fi, *n.* A wasting away; emaciation.
**Attach,** at-tach', *vt.* To affix; to connect; to arrest; to win.—*vi.* To adhere.
**Attaché,** at-ta-shā', *n.* One attached to the suite of an ambassador. **Attaché case,** *n.* A small oblong case of leather or fiber, for carrying documents, books, etc.
**Attachment,** at-tach'ment, *n.* State of being attached; fidelity; tender regard.
**Attack,** at-tak', *vt.* To assault; to assail.—*n.* An assault; seizure by a disease.
**Attain,** at-tān', *vi.* To come or arrive.—*vt.* To reach; to gain; to obtain.
**Attainable,** at-tān'a-bl, *a.* That may be attained.
**Attainder,** at-tān'dėr, *n.* Extinction of civil rights, in consequence of a capital crime.
**Attainment,** at-tān'ment, *n.* Act of attaining; acquirement; accomplishment.
**Attaint,** at-tānt', *vt.* To affect with attainder.
**Attar,** at'tär, *n.* An essential oil made from roses, forming a valuable perfume.
**Attemper,** at-tem'pėr, *vt.* To temper; to modify; to accommodate.
**Attempt,** at-temt', *vt.* To try to do; to make an effort upon.—*n.* An essay; enterprise.
**Attend,** at-tend', *vt.* To wait on; to accompany or be present at.—*vi.* To pay regard; to hearken; to wait.
**Attendance,** at-tend'ans, *n.* Act of attending; service; retinue.
**Attendant,** at-tend'ant, *a.* Accompanying, as subordinate.—*n.* One who waits on, is present, or accompanies.
**Attention,** at-ten'shon, *n.* Act of attending; heed; courtesy.
**Attentive,** at-tent'iv, *a.* Heedful.
**Attentively,** at-tent'iv-li, *adv.* With attention.
**Attentiveness,** at-tent'iv-nes, *n.* State of being attentive; heedfulness.
**Attenuate,** at-ten'ū-āt, *vt.* (attenuating, attenuated). To make slender or thin (as liquids).—*vi.* To diminish.
**Attenuation,** at-ten'ū-ā''shon, *n.* Act of attenuating; thinness; slenderness.
**Attest,** at-test', *vt.* To bear witness to; to certify; to call to witness.
**Attestation,** at-test-ā'shon, *n.* Testimony.
**Attic,** at'tik, *a.* Pertaining to Attica or to Athens; pure; elegant in style or language.—*n.* The dialect of Attica or Athens; the uppermost story of a building; garret.
**Attire,** at-tīr', *vt.* (attiring, attired). To dress; to array.—*n.* Dress.
**Attitude,** at'ti-tūd, *n.* Posture.
**Attitudinize,** at-ti-tūd'in-īz, *vi.* To assume affected attitudes or airs.
**Attorney,** at-tėr'ni, *n.* One who acts in place of another; one who practices in law-courts.
**Attract,** at-trakt', *vt.* To draw to; to entice.
**Attractable,** at-trakt'a-bl, *a.* That may be attracted.
**Attraction,** at-trak'shon, *n.* Act of attracting; allurement; charm.
**Attractive,** at-trakt'iv, *a.* Having the power of attracting; enticing.
**Attractively,** at-trakt'iv-li, *adv.* In an attractive manner.
**Attributable,** at-trib'ūt-a-bl, *a.* That may be attributed.
**Attribute,** at-trib'ūt, *vt.* (attributing, attributed). To ascribe; to impute.—*n.* at'tri-būt. Inherent property; characteristic; an adjectival word or clause.
**Attribution,** at-tri-bū'shon, *n.* Act of attributing, or the quality ascribed.
**Attributive,** at-trib'ūt-iv, *a.* That attributes.—*n.* That which is attributed.
**Attrition,** at-tri'shon, *n.* Act of wearing, or state of being worn, by rubbing.
**Attune,** at-tūn', *vt.* (attuning, attuned). To put in tune; to adjust to another sound.
**Auburn,** a'bėrn, *a.* Reddish-brown.

**Auction,** ak'shon, *n.* A public sale in which the article falls to the highest bidder.
**Auctioneer,** ak-shon-ēr', *n.* The person who sells at auction.
**Audacious,** a-dā'shus, *a.* Daring; impudent.
**Audacity,** a-das'i-ti, *n.* Daring; reprehensible boldness; impudence.
**Audible,** a'di-bl, *a.* That may be heard.
**Audibly,** a'di-bli, *adv.* In an audible manner.
**Audience,** a'di-ens, *n.* Act of hearing; an assembly of hearers; admittance to a hearing; ceremonial interview.
**Audit,** a'dit, *n.* An official examination of accounts.—*vt.* To examine and adjust, as accounts.
**Auditor,** a'dit-ėr, *n.* One who examines and adjusts accounts.
**Auditorship,** a'dit-ėr-ship, *n.* The office of auditor.
**Auditory,** a'di-tō-ri, *a.* Pertaining to the sense or organs of hearing.—*n.* An audience; an auditorium.
**Augean,** a-jē'an, *a.* Pertaining to Augeas, King of Elis, in Greece, whose stable for 3000 oxen, uncleaned for thirty years, was cleaned by Hercules in one day.
**Auger,** a'gėr, *n.* An instrument for boring holes.
**Aught,** at, *n.* Anything; any part; a whit.
**Augment,** ag-ment', *vt.* To make larger; to add to.—*vi.* To grow larger.
**Augment,** ag'ment, *n.* Increase; a prefix to a word.
**Augmentable,** ag-ment'a-bl, *a.* Capable of augmentation.
**Augmentation,** ag-ment-ā'shon, *n.* Act of augmenting; increase; addition.
**Augmentative,** ag-ment'at-iv, *a.* Having the quality of augmenting.—*n.* A word formed to express greatness.
**Augur,** a'gėr, *n.* One who foretold the future by observing the flight of birds; a soothsayer.—*vi.* To predict; to bode.—*vt.* To predict or foretell.
**Augury,** a'gū-ri, *n.* Omen; prediction.
**August,** a-gust', *a.* Grand; majestic; awful.
**August,** a'gust, *n.* The eighth month of the year.
**Augustan,** a-gust'an, *a.* Pertaining to Augustus, or to his reign; classic.
**Augustness,** a-gust'nes, *n.* Quality of being august; dignity of mien.
**Auk,** ak, *n.* A swimming bird found in the British seas, with very short wings.
**Aunt,** änt, *n.* The sister of one's father or mother.
**Aureate,** a-rē'āt, *a.* Golden.
**Aurelia,** a-rē'li-a, *n.* The chrysalis of an insect.
**Aureola, Aureole,** a-rē'o-la, a'rē-ōl, *n.* An illumination represented as surrounding a holy person, as Christ; a halo.
**Auricle,** a'ri-kl, *n.* The external ear; either of the two ear-like cavities over the two ventricles of the heart.
**Auricula,** a-rik'ū-la, *n.* Species of primrose.
**Auricular,** a-rik'ū-lėr, *a.* Pertaining to the ear; confidential.
**Auriferous,** a-rif'ėr-us, *a.* Yielding gold.
**Aurist,** a'rist, *n.* One skilled in disorders of the ear.
**Aurochs,** a'roks, *n.* A species of wild ox, once abundant in Europe.
**Aurora,** a-rō'ra, *n.* The dawn; the goddess of the dawn.
**Aurora Borealis,** a-rō'ra bō-rē-ā'lis, *n.* The northern lights or streamers.—**Aurora Australis,** a similar phenomenon in the S. hemisphere.
**Auscultation,** as-kul-tā'shon, *n.* A method of discovering diseases of the lungs, etc., by listening for the sounds arising there.
**Auspice,** a'spis, *n.* Augury from birds; protection; influence.
**Auspicious,** a-spi'shus, *a.* Fortunate; propitious.
**Auspiciously,** a-spi'shus-li, *adv.* Prosperously; favorably.
**Austere,** a-stēr', *a.* Rigid; sour; stern; severe.
**Austerely,** a-stēr'li, *adv.* In an austere manner.
**Austerity,** a-ste'ri-ti, *n.* Severity of manners or life; rigor.
**Austral,** as'tral, *a.* Southern.
**Autarky,** a'tar-ki, *n.* Self sufficiency; economic independence.
**Authentic,** a-then'tik, *a.* Genuine; authoritative.
**Authentically,** a-then'tik-al-li, *adv.* In an authentic manner.
**Authenticate,** a-then'ti-kāt, *vt.* To render or prove authentic.
**Authentication,** a-then'ti-kā''shon, *n.* Act of authenticating; confirmation.
**Authenticity,** a-then-tis'i-ti, *n.* Quality of being authentic; genuineness.
**Author,** a'thėr, *n.* One who creates; an originator; the writer of a book, etc.
**Authoress,** a'thėr-es, *n.* A female author.
**Authoritative,** a-tho'ri-tā-tiv, *a.* Having due authority; peremptory.
**Authoritatively,** a-tho'ri-tā-tiv-li, *adv.* In an authoritative manner.
**Authority,** a-tho'ri-ti, *n.* Legal power or right; influence conferred by character or station; person in power; testimony; credibility; precedent.
**Authorize,** a'thor-īz, *vt.* (authorizing, authorized). To give authority to; to make legal; to sanction.
**Authorship,** a'thėr-ship, *n.* Quality or state of being an author.
**Autobiographical,** a-tō-bī'ō-graf''ik-al, *a.* Pertaining to or containing autobiography.
**Autobiography,** a'tō-bī-og''ra-fi, *n.* Memoirs of a person written by himself.
**Autocracy,** a-tok'ra-si, *n.* Absolute government by one man.
**Autocrat,** a'tō-krat, *n.* An absolute prince or sovereign.
**Auto-de-fe,** au'tō-de-fā'', *n.*; pl. **Autos-de-fe.** The burning of heretics by authority of the Inquisition. **Auto-da-fe,** ou'tō-dä-fā'', is the Portuguese form.
**Autogiro,** a-tō-jī'rō, *n.* Trade name for a type of aircraft with rotating blades hinged at one end to a vertical shaft.
**Autograph,** a'tō-graf, *n.* A person's own handwriting; signature.
**Automatic,** a-tō-mat'ik.—*a.* Self-acting; moving spontaneously.—*n.* A pistol which is reloaded by force of the recoil.
**Automaton,** a-tom'a-ton, *n.*; pl. **-ta.** A self-moving machine, or one which moves by invisible machinery.
**Automobile,** a'tō-mō-bēl'', *n.* A motor-car or similar vehicle.
**Autonomy,** a-ton'o-mi, *n.* The power or right of self-government.
**Autopsy,** a'top-si, *n.* Personal observation; post-mortem examination.
**Autumn,** a'tum, *n.* The third season of the year, between summer and winter.
**Autumnal,** a-tum'nal, *a.* Belonging or peculiar to autumn.
**Auxiliary,** ag-zil'i-a-ri, *a.* Aiding.—*n.* One who aids; a verb which helps to form the moods and tenses of other verbs; *pl.* foreign troops employed in war.
**Avail,** a-vāl', *vt.* To profit; to promote.—*vi.* To be of use; to answer the purpose.—*n.* Advantage; use.
**Available,** a-vāl'a-bl, *a.* That may be used; attainable.
**Avalanche,** av'a-lansh, *n.* A large body of snow or ice sliding down a mountain.
**Avarice,** av'a-ris, *n.* Covetousness.
**Avaricious,** av-a-ri'shus, *a.* Covetous; greedy of gain; niggardly.
**Avariciously,** av-a-ri'shus-li, *adv.* In an avaricious manner.
**Avast,** a-väst', *exclam.* Hold! stop! (Nautical.)
**Avatar,** av-a-tär', *n.* A descent of a Hindu deity; a remarkable appearance of any kind.
**Avaunt,** a-vant', *exclam.* Hence! begone!
**Ave,** ā'vē, *n.* Hail; an abbreviation of the Ave-Maria, or Hail-Mary.

**Avenge,** a-venj', *vt.* (avenging, avenged). To vindicate; to take satisfaction for.
**Avenger,** a-venj'ėr, *n.* One who avenges.
**Avenue,** av'e-nū, *n.* An approach to; an alley of trees leading to a house, etc.
**Aver,** a-vėr', *vt.* (averring, averred). To declare positively; to assert.
**Average,** av'ėr-āj, *n.* Medium; mean proportion.—*a.* Medial; containing a mean proportion.—*vt.* To find the mean of.—*vi.* To form a mean.
**Averment,** a-vėr'ment, *n.* Affirmation; declaration.
**Averruncator,** av-e-rung'kāt-ėr, *n.* Shears for pruning trees.
**Averse,** a-vėrs', *a.* Disinclined; not favorable.
**Averseness,** a-vėrs'nes, *n.* Aversion.
**Aversion,** a-vėr'shon, *n.* Dislike; antipathy.
**Avert,** a-vėrt', *vt.* To turn aside or away from; to keep off or prevent.
**Aviary,** ā-vi-a-ri, *n.* A place for keeping birds.
**Aviation,** ā'vi-ā-shon, *n.* Aerial navigation by machines heavier than air.
**Avidity,** a-vid'i-ti, *n.* Eager desire; greediness; strong appetite.
**Avizandum,** av-i-zan'dum, *n.* In Scotland, the private consideration by a judge of a case which has been heard in court.
**Avocation,** av-ō-kā'shon, *n.* Business; occupation.
**Avoid,** a-void', *vt.* To shun; to evade; to make void.
**Avoidable,** a-void'-a-bl, *a.* That may be avoided.
**Avoidance,** a-void'ans, *n.* Act of avoiding; the state of being vacant.
**Avoirdupois,** av'ėr-dū-poiz'', *n.* or *a.* A system of weight, in which a pound contains sixteen ounces.
**Avouch,** a-vouch', *vt.* To affirm; to avow.
**Avow,** a-vou', *vt.* To declare with confidence; to confess frankly.
**Avowable,** a-vou'a-bl, *a.* That may be avowed.
**Avowal,** a-vou'al, *n.* An open declaration; frank acknowledgment.
**Avowedly,** a-vou'ed-li, *adv.* In an open manner; with frank acknowledgment.
**Await,** a-wāt', *vt.* To wait for; to expect; to be in store for.
**Awake,** a-wāk', *vt.* (awaking, pret. woke, awaked, pp. awaked). To rouse from sleep or from a state of inaction.—*vi.* To cease from sleep; to rouse oneself.—*a.* Not sleeping; vigilant.
**Awaken,** a-wāk'n, *vt.* and *i.* To awake.
**Awakening,** a-wāk'n-ing, *n.* Act of awaking.
**Award,** a-ward', *vt.* To adjudge.—*vi.* To make an award.—*n.* A judgment; decision of arbitrators.
**Aware,** a-wār', *a.* Informed; conscious.
**Away,** a-wā', *adv.* Absent; at a distance; in motion from; by degrees; in continuance.—*exclam.* Begone!
**Awe,** a, *n.* Fear; fear mingled with reverence.—*vt.* (awing, awed). To strike with fear and reverence.
**Aweary,** a-we'ri, *pred.a.* Weary; tired.
**Aweigh,** a-wā', *adv.* or *pred.a.* Atrip.
**Awful,** a'ful, *a.* Filling with awe; terrible.
**Awfully,** a'ful-li, *adv.* In an awful manner.
**Awfulness,** a'ful-nes, *n.* Quality or state of being awful.
**Awhile,** a-whīl', *adv.* For some time.
**Awkward,** ak'wėrd, *a.* Inexpert; inelegant.
**Awkwardly,** ak'wėrd-li, *adv.* In a bungling manner; inelegantly.
**Awl,** al, *n.* A pointed iron instrument for piercing small holes in leather.
**Awn,** an, *n.* The beard of corn or grass.
**Awned,** and, *a.* Furnished with an awn.
**Awning,** an'ing, *n.* A cover of canvas, etc., to shelter from the sun or wind.
**Awry,** a-rī, *pred.a.* or *adv.* Twisted toward one side; distorted; asquint.
**Axe,** aks, *n.* An instrument for hewing and chopping.
**Axial,** aks'i-al, *a.* Pertaining to an axis.
**Axilla,** aks-il'la, *n.* The arm-pit.
**Axiom,** aks'i-om, *n.* A self-evident truth; an established principle.
**Axiomatic,** aks'i-ō-mat''ik, *a.* Pertaining to an axiom.
**Axiomatically,** aks'i-ō-mat''ik-al-li, *adv.* By the use of axioms.
**Axis,** aks'is, *n.*; pl. **Axes,** aks'ēz. The straight line, real or imaginary, passing through a body, on which it revolves.
**Axle, Axle-tree,** aks'l, aks'l-trē, *n.* The pole on which a wheel turns.
**Ay, Aye,** ī, *adv.* Yea; yes.—*n.* An affirmative vote.
**Ayah,** ā'yä, *n.* A native Indian waiting woman.
**Aye,** ā, *adv.* Always; ever; continually.
**Azalea,** a-zā'lē-a, *n.* The generic name of certain showy plants of the heath family.
**Azimuth,** az'i-muth, *n.* An arc of the horizon between the meridian of a place and a vertical circle.
**Azoic,** a-zō'ik, *a.* Destitute of organic life.
**Azote,** az'ōt, *n.* Nitrogen.
**Azure,** ā'zhūr, *a.* Sky-colored.—*n.* The fine blue color of the sky; the sky.

# B

**Baa,** bä, *n.* The cry of a sheep.—*vi.* To cry or bleat as sheep.
**Babble,** bab'bl, *vi.* (babbling, babbled). To talk idly; to prate.—*vt.* To utter idly.—*n.* Idle talk; murmur, as of a stream.
**Babblement,** bab'bl-ment, *n.* Babble.
**Babbler,** bab'bl-ėr, *n.* One who babbles.
**Babe,** bāb, *n.* An infant; a young child.
**Babel,** bā'bel, *n.* Confusion; disorder.
**Baboon,** ba-bön', *n.* A large kind of monkey.
**Baby,** bā'bi, *n.* A babe; a young child.—*a.* Pertaining to a baby.
**Baby-farmer,** bā'bi-fär-mėr, *n.* One who makes a trade of rearing infants.
**Babylonian, Babylonish,** ba-bi-lōn'i-an, ba-bi-lōn'ish, *a.* Pertaining to Babylon.
**Baccarat,** bak-ka-rä, *n.* A game of cards played by any number and a banker.
**Bacchanal,** bak'ka-nal, *n.* A votary of Bacchus; a revel.—*a.* Characterized by intemperate drinking.
**Bacchanalia,** bak-a-nā'li-a, *n.pl.* Feasts in honor of Bacchus.
**Bacchanalian,** bak-ka-nā'li-an, *a.* Bacchanal.—*n.* A reveller; a votary of Bacchus.
**Bachelor,** bach'el-ėr, *n.* An unmarried man; one who has taken the university degree below that of Master or Doctor.
**Bachelorhood, Bachelorship,** bach'el-ėr-hud, bach'el-ėr-ship, *n.* The state of being a bachelor.
**Bacillus,** ba-sil'lus, *n.*; pl. **-illi.** A microscopic organism which causes disease.
**Back,** bak, *n.* The hinder part of the body in man and the upper part in beasts; the hinder part.—*vt.* To support; to cause to recede; to endorse.—*vi.* To move back.—*adv.* To the rear; to a former state; in return.
**Backbite,** bak'bīt, *vt.* To speak evil of secretly.
**Backbone,** bak'bōn, *n.* The spine; strength.
**Back-door,** bak'dōr, *n.* A door in the back part of a building.
**Backer,** bak'ėr, *n.* One who backs or supports another in a contest.
**Backgammon,** bak-gam'mon, *n.* A game played by two persons on a board, with men and dice.
**Background,** bak'ground, *n.* The part of a picture represented as farthest away; a situation little noticed.
**Backhand, Backhanded,** bak'hand, bak'hand-ed, *a.* With the hand turned backward; indirect.
**Backslide,** bak-slīd', *vt.* To apostatize; to relapse.

**Backslider,** bak-slīd'ėr, *n.* An apostate.
**Backward, Backwards,** bak'wėrd, bak'wėrdz, *adv.* With the back forwards; towards past times; back; from better to worse.
**Backward,** bak'wėrd, *a.* Lagging behind; reluctant; late; dull.
**Backwardly,** bak'wėrd-li, *adv.* In a backward manner; unwillingly.
**Backwardness,** bak'wėrd-nes, *n.* Unwillingness; reluctance; dilatoriness.
**Backwoods,** bak'wụdz, *n.pl.* Outlying forest districts.
**Bacon,** bā'kn, *n.* Swine's flesh cured and dried.
**Bacteriology,** bak-tē'ri-ol''o-ji, *n.* The doctrine or study of bacteria.
**Bacterium,** bak-tē'ri-um, *n.*; pl. **-ia.** A disease germ.
**Bad,** bad, *a.* Not good; wicked; immoral; injurious; incompetent.
**Badge,** baj, *n.* A mark or cognizance worn.
**Badger,** baj'ėr, *n.* A burrowing quadruped, nocturnal in habits.—*vt.* To worry; to pester.
**Badinage,** bä'di-näzh, *n.* Raillery; banter.
**Badly,** bad'li, *adv.* In a bad manner.
**Badminton,** bad'min-ton, *n.* A game like lawn-tennis played with shuttlecocks.
**Baffle,** baf'fl, *vt.* (baffling, baffled). To elude; to frustrate; to defeat.
**Bag,** bag, *n.* A sack; what is contained in a bag; a certain quantity of a commodity.—*vt.* (bagging, bagged). To put into a bag; to distend.—*vi.* To swell like a full bag.
**Bagatelle,** bag-a-tel', *n.* A trifle; a game somewhat like billiards.
**Baggage,** bag'āj, *n.* The necessaries of an army; luggage; lumber.
**Bagging,** bag'ing, *p.n.* The cloth for bags.
**Bagnio,** ban'yō, *n.* A bath; brothel; prison.
**Bagpipe,** bag'pīp, *n.* A musical wind-instrument.
**Bail,** bāl, *vt.* To liberate from custody on security for reappearance; to free (a boat) from water; to bale.—*n.* Security given for release; the person who gives such security.
**Bailable,** bāl'a-bl, *a.* That may be bailed.
**Bailie, Baillie,** bā'li, *n.* A magistrate in Scotland, corresponding to an alderman.
**Bailiff,** bā'lif, *n.* A subordinate civil officer; a steward.
**Bailiwick,** bā'li-wik, *n.* The extent or limit of a bailiff's jurisdiction.
**Bait,** bāt, *n.* A substance used to allure fish, etc.; an enticement.—*vt.* To furnish with a lure; to give food and drink to a beast when traveling; to harass; to annoy.—*vi.* To take refreshment on a journey.
**Baize,** bāz, *n.* A coarse woolen stuff with a long nap.
**Bake,** bāk, *vt.* (baking, baked). To heat, dry, and harden by fire or the sun's rays; to cook in an oven.—*vi.* To do the work of making bread; to be baked.
**Bakelite,** bāk'l-īt, *n.* Trade name for a hard, insoluble, infusible substance derived by heat treatment from phenol and formaldehyde.
**Baker,** bāk'ėr, *n.* One whose occupation is to bake bread, etc.
**Bakery,** bāk'ė-ri, *n.* A place for baking.
**Baking,** bāk'ing, *p.n.* The action of the verb *to bake;* the quantity baked at once.
**Bakshish,** bak'shēsh, *n.* A gratuity of money.
**Balance,** bal'ans, *n.* A pair of scales; equilibrium; surplus; difference of two sums; the sum due on an account.—*vt.* (balancing, balanced). To bring to an equilibrium; to weigh, as reasons; to settle, as an account.—*vi.* To be in equilibrium; to be equal when added up; to hesitate.
**Balance-sheet,** bal'ans-shēt, *n.* A statement of assets and liabilities.
**Balcony,** bal'ko-ni, *n.* A platform projecting from a window.
**Bald,** bald, *a.* Wanting hair; unadorned; bare; paltry.
**Baldachin,** bal'da-kin, *n.* A canopy held over the pope; a canopy over an altar or throne.
**Balderdash,** bal'dėr-dash, *n.* Senseless prate; jargon.
**Baldly,** bald'li, *adv.* Nakedly; meanly.
**Baldness,** bald'nes, *n.* State of being bald; inelegance of style; want of ornament.
**Baldrick, Baldric,** bald'rik, *n.* A broad belt worn diagonally across the body.
**Bale,** bāl, *n.* A bundle or package of goods.—*vt.* (baling, baled). To make up in a bale; to free from water; to bail. **Bale out,** *vi.* To leave aircraft by parachute.
**Baleen,** ba-lēn', *n.* The whalebone of commerce.
**Baleful,** bāl'ful, *a.* Calamitous; deadly.
**Balk,** bak, *n.* A ridge of land left unploughed; a great beam; a barrier; a disappointment.—*vt.* To baffle; to disappoint.
**Ball,** bal, *n.* A round body; a globe; a bullet; an entertainment of dancing.—*vi.* To form, as snow, into balls, as on horses' hoofs.
**Ballad,** bal'lad, *n.* A short narrative poem; a popular song.
**Ballade,** ba-läd', *n.* A poem of three stanzas of eight lines and an envoy of four lines.
**Ballast,** bal'last, *n.* Heavy matter carried in a ship to keep it steady; that which confers steadiness.—*vt.* To load with ballast; to make or keep steady.
**Ball-cock,** bal'kok, *n.* A kind of self-acting stopcock, used in cisterns.
**Ballet,** bal'lā, *n.* A theatrical dance.
**Ballista,** bal-lis'ta, *n.* A military engine used by the ancients for throwing stones.
**Ballistic,** bal-lis'tik, *a.* Pertaining to projectiles.—*n.pl.* The science of projectiles in motion.
**Balloon,** bal-lön', *n.* A spherical hollow body; a large bag filled with a gas which makes it rise and float in the air.
**Ballot,** bal'lot, *n.* A ball, paper, etc., used for voting in private; the system of voting by such means.—*vi.* To vote by ballot.
**Balm,** bäm, *n.* Balsam; that which heals or soothes; the name of several aromatic plants.—*vt.* To anoint with balm; to soothe.
**Balmoral,** bal-mo'ral, *n.* A kind of Scottish bonnet.
**Balmy,** bäm'i, *a.* Aromatic; soothing.
**Balsam,** bal'sam, *n.* An oily, aromatic substance got from trees; a soothing ointment.
**Balsamic,** bal- or bal-sam'ik, *a.* Balmy; mitigating.
**Baluster,** bal'us-tėr, *n.* A small column or pillar, used for balustrades.
**Balustrade,** bal-us-trād', *n.* A row of balusters joined by a rail.
**Bamboo,** bam-bö', *n.* A tropical plant of the reed kind.
**Bamboozle,** bam-bö'zl, *vt.* (bamboozling, bamboozled). To hoax; to humbug; to perplex.
**Ban,** ban, *n.* A public proclamation; curse; excommunication; *pl.* proclamation of marriage.—*vt.* (banning, banned). To curse.
**Banal,** ban'al, or ba-nal', *a.* Hackneyed; vulgar.
**Banality,** ba-nal'i-ti, *n.* State of being banal.
**Banana,** ba-nä'na, *n.* A plant allied to the plantain, with soft luscious fruit.
**Band,** band, *n.* That which binds; a bond; a fillet; a company; a body of musicians.—*vt.* To bind together; to unite in a troop or confederacy.—*vi.* To unite in a band.
**Bandage,** band'āj, *n.* A band; a cloth for a wound, etc.—*vt.* (bandaging, bandaged). To bind with a bandage.
**Bandbox,** band'boks, *n.* A slight box for caps, bonnets, etc.
**Banded,** band'ed, *p.a.* United in a band.
**Banderole,** ban'de-rōl, *n.* A little flag.
**Bandit,** ban'dit, *n.*; pl. **-itti, -its.** An outlaw; a robber; a highwayman.
**Bandog,** ban'dog, *n.* A large fierce dog, usually kept chained.
**Bandolier,** ban-dō-lēr', *n.* A shoulder-belt for carrying cartridges.

**Bandrol,** band'rōl, *n.* Same as *Banderole.*
**Bandy,** ban'di, *n.* A bent club for striking a ball; a play at ball with such a club.—*vt.* (bandying, bandied). To strike to and fro; to exchange (compliments, etc.).
**Bandy-legged,** ban'di-legd, *a.* Having crooked legs.
**Bane,** bān, *n.* That which causes hurt or death; ruin; poison; mischief.
**Baneful,** bān'ful, *a.* Pernicious; poisonous.
**Bang,** bang, *vt.* To thump; to treat with violence.—*n.* A heavy blow.
**Bangle,** bang'gl, *n.* An ornamental ring worn upon the arms and ankles.
**Banian,** ban'yan, *n. See* BANYAN.
**Banish,** ban'ish, *vt.* To drive away; to exile.
**Banishment,** ban'ish-ment, *n.* Act of banishing; exile.
**Banister,** ban'is-tėr, *n.* A baluster.
**Banjo,** ban'jō, *n.* A six-stringed musical instrument.
**Bank,** bangk, *n.* Ground rising from the side of a river, lake, etc.; any heap piled up; a bench of rowers; place where money is deposited; a banking company.—*vt.* To fortify with a bank; to deposit in a bank.
**Banker,** bangk'ėr, *n.* One who deals in money.
**Banking,** bangk'ing, *p.n.* The business of a banker.
**Bank-note,** bangk'nōt, *n.* A promissory note issued by a banking company.
**Bankrupt,** bangk'rupt, *n.* One who cannot pay his debts.—*a.* Unable to pay debts.
**Bankruptcy,** bangk'rupt-si, *n.* State of being a bankrupt; failure in trade.
**Bank-stock,** bangk'stok, *n.* A share or shares in the capital stock of a bank.
**Banner,** ban'nėr, *n.* A flag bearing a device or national emblem; a standard.
**Banquet,** bang'kwet, *n.* A feast; a sumptuous entertainment.—*vt.* To treat with a feast.—*vi.* To feast.
**Banshee,** ban'shē, *n.* An Irish fairy believed to attach herself to a house or family.
**Bantam,** ban'tam, *n.* A small breed of domestic fowl with feathered shanks.
**Banter,** ban'tėr, *vt.* To attack with jocularity; to rally.—*n.* Raillery; pleasantry.
**Bantling,** bant'ling, *n.* An infant.
**Banyan,** ban'yan, *n.* An Indian tree of the fig genus.
**Baptism,** bap'tizm, *n.* An immersing in or sprinkling with water, as a religious ceremony.
**Baptismal,** bap-tiz'mal, *a.* Pertaining to baptism.
**Baptist,** bap'tist, *n.* One of those Protestants who believe in adult baptism by immersion.
**Baptistery,** bap'tis-te-ri, *n.* A place where baptisms take place.
**Baptize,** bap-tīz', *vt.* (baptizing, baptized). To administer baptism to; to christen.
**Bar,** bär, *n.* A bolt; obstacle; a long piece of wood or metal; inclosure in an inn or court; a tribunal; body of barristers; obstruction at the mouth of a river; a counter where liquors are served.—*vt.* (barring, barred). To secure; to hinder; to prohibit; to except.
**Barb,** bärb, *n.* The points which stand backward in an arrow, hook, etc.; a Barbary horse.—*vt.* To furnish with barbs or points.
**Barbarian,** bär-bā'ri-an, *a.* Belonging to savages; uncivilized.—*n.* A savage.
**Barbarism,** bär'bär-izm, *n.* Barbarity; an impropriety of speech.
**Barbarity,** bär-ba'ri-ti, *n.* The state or qualities of a barbarian; ferociousness.
**Barbarize,** bär'bär-īz, *vt.* (barbarizing, barbarized). To make barbarous.
**Barbarous,** bär'bär-us, *a.* In a state of barbarism; cruel; inhuman.
**Barbarously,** bär'bär-us-li, *adv.* In a savage, cruel, or inhuman manner.
**Barbecue,** bär-be-kū, *n.* A hog, etc., roasted whole; a feast in the open air.—*vt.* To dress and roast whole.
**Barbed,** bärbd, *a.* Jagged with hooks or points.
**Barbel,** bär'bel, *n.* A fish having on its upper jaw four beard-like appendages.
**Barber,** bär'bėr, *n.* One who shaves beards and dresses hair.
**Barberry,** bär'be-ri, *n.* A thorny shrub bearing red berries.
**Barbette,** bär-bet', *n.* A platform from which cannon may be fired over the parapet instead of through an embrasure; circular armored platform for guns in warships.
**Barbican,** bär'bi-kan, *n.* An outer-work defending a castle, etc.
**Barcarolle,** bär'ka-rōl, *n.* A melody sung by Venetian gondoliers.
**Bard,** bärd, *n.* A Celtic minstrel; a poet.
**Bardic,** bärd'ik, *a.* Pertaining to bards.
**Bare,** bār, *a.* Uncovered; empty; scanty; worn.—*vt.* (baring, bared). To make naked.
**Barebacked,** bār'bakt, *a.* Unsaddled.
**Barefaced,** bār'fāst, *a.* Shameless; glaring.
**Barefoot,** bār'fut, *a.* or *adv.* With the feet bare.
**Barely,** bār'li, *adv.* Nakedly; scarcely.
**Bargain,** bär'gin, *n.* A contract; a gainful transaction; a thing bought or sold.—*vi.* To make a bargain.—*vt.* To sell.
**Bargainer,** bär'gin-ėr, *n.* One who makes a bargain.
**Barge,** bärj, *n.* A boat of pleasure or state; a flat-bottomed boat of burden.
**Bargee,** bärj-ē', *n.* One of a barge's crew.
**Bargeman,** bärj'man, *n.* The man who manages a barge.
**Barilla,** ba-ril'la, *n.* An impure soda obtained by burning several species of plants.
**Bar-iron,** bär'ī-ėrn, *n.* Iron in bars.
**Baritone,** ba'ri-tōn, *a.* Having a voice ranging between tenor and bass.—*n.* A male voice between tenor and bass.
**Bark,** bärk, *n.* The outer rind of a tree; a barque; the noise made by a dog, wolf, etc.—*vt.* To strip bark off; to treat with bark; to make the cry of dogs, etc.
**Barley,** bär'li, *n.* A species of grain used especially for making malt.
**Barley-corn,** bär'li-korn, *n.* A grain of barley; the third part of an inch.
**Barley-sugar,** bär-li-shug'ėr, *n.* Sugar boiled till it is brittle and candied.
**Barm,** bärm, *n.* Yeast.
**Barmaid,** bär'mād, *n.* A woman who tends a bar where liquors are sold.
**Barmy,** bärm'i, *a.* Containing barm; light-headed; made.
**Barn,** bärn, *n.* A building for grain, hay, etc.
**Barnacle,** bär'na-kl, *n.* A shell-fish, often found on ships' bottoms; a species of goose.
**Barnacles,** bär'na-klz, *n.pl.* An instrument put on a horse's nose; a pair of spectacles.
**Barograph,** ba'rō-graf, *n.* An instrument for recording changes in the atmosphere.
**Barometer,** ba-rom'et-ėr, *n.* An instrument for measuring the weight of the atmosphere.
**Barometric,** ba-rō-met'rik, *a.* Pertaining or relating to the barometer.
**Barometrically,** ba-rō-met'rik-al-li, *adv.* by means of a barometer.
**Barouche,** ba-rösh', *n.* A four-wheeled carriage with a collapsible top.
**Barque,** bärk, *n.* A sailing vessel; a three-masted ship, the mizzen-mast without yards.
**Barrack,** ba'rak, *n.* A building for soldiers, especially in garrison (generally in *pl.*).
**Barrage,** bar'aj, *n.* The discharge of artillery in such a manner as to keep a selected zone under continuous fire.
**Barrator,** ba'rat-ėr, *n.* One who excites law suits.
**Barratry,** ba'ra-tri, *n.* The practice of a barrator; fraud by a shipmaster.
**Barrel,** ba'rel, *n.* A round wooden cask; the quantity which a barrel holds; a hollow cylinder.—*vt.*

B

(barreling, barreled). To pack in a barrel.
**Barreled,** ba'reld, *a.* Having a barrel or barrels.
**Barren,** ba'ren, *a.* Sterile; unfruitful; unsuggestive.
**Barrenness,** ba'ren-nes, *n.* The state or quality of being barren.
**Barricade,** ba-ri-kād', *n.* A temporary fortification to obstruct an enemy; a barrier.—*vt.* To obstruct; to bar.
**Barrier,** ba'ri-ėr, *n.* Fence; obstruction.
**Barrister,** ba'ris-tėr, *n.* A counselor at law; a lawyer whose profession is to speak in court on behalf of clients.
**Barrow,** ba'rō, *n.* A small hand or wheel carriage; a sepulchral mound.
**Barter,** bär'tėr, *vi.* To traffic by exchange.—*vt.* To exchange in commerce.—*n.* Traffic by exchange.
**Bartizan,** bär'ti-zan, *n.* A small overhanging turret with apertures to shoot through.
**Baryta, Barytes,** ba-rī'ta, ba-rī'tēz, *n.* The heaviest of the alkaline earths.
**Basalt,** ba-zalt', *n.* A dark volcanic rock, often found in columnar form.
**Bascule,** bas'kūl, *n.* An arrangement in bridges by which one part balances another.
**Base,** bās, *a.* Low in value or station; worthless; despicable.—*n.* Foundation; lower side; support; chief ingredient of a compound; the gravest part in music.—*vt.* (basing, based). To place on a basis; to found.
**Base-ball,** bās'bal, *n.* The national game of the U.S.A. played with bat and ball by two sides of nine men each.
**Base-born,** bās'born, *a.* Illegitimate.
**Baseless,** bās'les, *a.* Without base; groundless.
**Base-line,** bās'līn, *n.* A line taken as a base of operations.
**Basely,** bās'li, *adv.* In a base manner.
**Basement,** bās'ment, *n.* The ground floor of a building.
**Baseness,** bās'nes, *n.* Lowness; meanness; vileness.
**Bash,** bash, *vt.* To beat violently.
**Bashaw,** ba-shä', *n.* A pasha; a proud, overbearing person.
**Bashful,** bash'fụl, *a.* Modest; wanting confidence.
**Bashfully,** bash'ful-li, *adv.* In a shy manner.
**Bashfulness,** bash'ful-nes, *n.* Quality of being bashful; extreme modesty.
**Basic,** bās'ik, *a.* Relating to a base.
**Basil,** baz'il, *n.* An aromatic pot-herb.
**Basilica,** ba-sil'i-ka, *n.* An ancient Roman public hall; a church in imitation thereof.
**Basilisk,** baz'il-isk, *n.* A fabulous serpent, lizard, or cockatrice; a genus of crested lizards; an old kind of cannon.
**Basin,** bā'sn, *n.* A broad circular dish; a reservoir; a dock; tract of country drained by a river.
**Basis,** bās'is, *n.*; pl. **-ses.** A base; foundation; groundwork.
**Bask,** bask, *vt.* To lie in warmth, or in the sun; to enjoy ease and prosperity.—*vt.* To warm by exposure to heat.
**Basket,** bas'ket, *n.* A domestic vessel made of twigs, etc.; the contents of a basket.—*vt.* To put in a basket.
**Bas-relief,** bas'rē-lēf, or bä', *n.* Low relief; sculpture in which the figures do not stand out prominently.
**Bass,** bās, *n.* The American linden; a mat made of bast; a fish allied to the perch.
**Bass,** bās, *n.* The lowest part in musical harmony; the lowest male voice.
**Basset,** bas'set, *n.* The outcrop of a stratum.
**Bassinet,** bas'si-net, *n.* A wicker cradle; a type of perambulator.
**Bassoon,** bas-sön', *n.* A musical wind-instrument which serves for a bass.
**Bass-relief,** bäs'rē-lēf, *n.* Bas-relief.
**Bast,** bast, *n.* The inner bark of the lime tree.
**Bastard,** bas'tėrd, *n.* An illegitimate child.—*a.* Illegitimate; not genuine.
**Bastardize,** bas'tėrd-īz, *vt.* (bastardizing, bastardized). To prove to be a bastard.
**Bastardy,** bas'tėrd-i, *n.* The state of being a bastard.
**Baste,** bāst, *vt.* (basting, basted). To beat with a stick; to drip fat or butter on meat while roasting; to sew with temporary stitches.
**Bastinado,** bas-ti-nā'dō, *n.* A beating with a cudgel on the soles of the feet.—*vt.* To beat thus.
**Bastion,** bas'ti-on, *n.* A large mass of earth or masonry standing out from a rampart.
**Bat,** bat, *n.* A flying mammal, like a mouse; a heavy stick; a club used to strike the ball in cricket, etc.—*vi.* (batting, batted). To play with a bat.
**Batch,** bach, *n.* Quantity of bread baked at one time; a quantity.
**Bate,** bāt, *vt.* (bating, bated). To abate.
**Bath,** bäth, *n.* Place to bathe in; immersion in water, etc.; a Jewish measure.
**Bath-brick,** bäth'brik, *n.* A brick of siliceous earth for cleaning knives, etc.
**Bath-chair,** bäth'chãr, *n.* A wheeled chair for invalids.
**Bathe,** bāTH, *vt.* (bathing, bathed). To immerse in water, etc.—*vi.* To take a bath.
**Bathometer,** ba-thom'et-ėr, *n.* An apparatus for taking soundings.
**Bathos,** bā'thos, *n.* A ludicrous sinking in writing or speech; anti-climax.
**Batist, Batiste,** ba-tēst', *n.* A kind of cambric.
**Batman,** bat'man, *n.* An officer's servant.
**Baton,** ba'ton, *n.* A staff; a truncheon; a badge of office carried by field-marshals.
**Battalion,** bat-ta'li-on, *n.* A body of infantry, consisting of from 300 to 1000 men.
**Batten,** bat'n, *n.* A piece of wood from 1 to 7 inches broad, and from 1/2 to 2 1/2 thick; a plank.—*vt.* To fasten with battens; to fatten.
**Batter,** bat'tėr, *vt.* To beat with violence; to wear by hard usage.—*n.* A mixture beaten together with some liquid.
**Battering-ram,** bat'tėr-ing-ram, *n.* An ancient engine for battering down walls.
**Battery,** bat'tė-ri, *n.* A number of cannon prepared for field operations; a parapet covering guns; an apparatus for originating an electric current; a violent assault.
**Battle,** bat'l, *n.* Encounter of two armies; a combat.—*vi.* (battling, battled). To contend in fight.
**Battle-axe,** bat'l-aks, *n.* An axe anciently used as a weapon of war.
**Battledore,** bat'l-dōr, *n.* An instrument to strike a ball or shuttlecock.
**Battlement,** bat'l-ment, *n.* A parapet with openings to discharge missiles through.
**Battue,** bat'tu, *n.* The shooting of game that is driven towards the sportsmen.
**Bauble,** ba'bl, *n.* A trifling piece of finery; a gewgaw.
**Bawd,** bad, *n.* A procurer or procuress; a pimp.
**Bawdy,** ba'di, *a.* Obscene; unchaste.
**Bawl,** bal, *vi.* To shout; to clamor.
**Bay,** bā, *a.* Reddish-brown.—*n.* An arm of the sea; the laurel tree; a laurel-crown, fame (generally in *pl.*); a deep-toned bark of a dog.—*vi.* To bark.—*vt.* To bark at; to follow with barking. **At bay,** so pressed by enemies as to be compelled to face them.
**Bayadere,** bā-ya-dēr', *n.* In the East Indies, a professional dancing girl.
**Bayonet,** bā'on-et, *n.* A dagger-like weapon fixed to a rifle.—*vt.* (bayoneting, bayoneted). To stab with a bayonet.
**Bay-rum,** bā'rum, *n.* A spirituous liquor containing the oil of the bayberry of Jamaica.
**Bay-window,** bā'win-dō, *n.* A projecting window which forms a recess within.
**Bazaar,** ba-zär', *n.* A place of sale; a sale of articles for a charitable purpose.
**Bdellium,** del'li-um, *n.* An aromatic gum-resin.

**Be**, bē, *vi. substantive* (being, been; pres. am, art, is, are; pret. was, wast or wert, were). To exist; to become; to remain.
**Beach**, bēch, *n*. The shore of the sea.—*vt*. To run (a vessel) on a beach.
**Beached**, bēcht, *p.a.* Having a beach; stranded.
**Beacon**, bē'kn, *n*. A light to direct seamen; a signal of danger.—*vt*. To afford light, as a beacon; to light up.
**Bead**, bēd, *n*. A little ball strung on a thread, any small globular body; a small molding.
**Beadle**, bē'dl, *n*. A messenger or crier of a court; a petty officer in a parish, church, university, etc.
**Bead-roll**, bēd'rōl, *n*. A list of persons to be prayed for.
**Beadsman**, bēdz'man, *n*. One who prays for others; a privileged beggar.
**Beagle**, bē'gl, *n*. A small hunting dog.
**Beak**, bēk, *n*. The bill of a bird; anything like a bird's beak.
**Beaked**, bēkt, *a*. Having a beak.
**Beaker**, bēk'ėr, *n*. A large drinking-cup.
**Beam**, bēm, *n*. A main timber in a building; part of a balance which sustains the scales; pole of a carriage; a ray of light.—*vt*. To send forth, as beams; to emit.—*vi*. To shine.
**Beaming**, bēm'ing, *a*. Emitting beams or rays; radiant; expressing joy in the face.
**Beamy**, bēm'i, *a*. Emitting beams or rays; radiant; shining.
**Bean**, bēn, *n*. A name of several kinds of pulse.
**Bear**, bār, *vt*. (bearing, pret. bore, pp. borne). To carry; to suffer; to produce; to have; to permit; to behave (oneself).—*vi*. To suffer; to be patient; to produce; to take effect; to be situated as to the point of the compass; to refer (with *upon*).
**Bear**, bār, *n*. A large carnivorous plantigrade quadruped; one of two constellations, the Greater and Lesser; an uncouth person; one who tries to bring down the price of stock.
**Bearable**, bār'a-bl, *a*. That can be borne.
**Beard**, bērd, *n*. The hair on the chin, etc.; the awn of corn.—*vt*. To defy to the face.
**Bearded**, bērd'ed, *a*. Having a beard.
**Beardless**, bērd'les, *a*. Without a beard.
**Bearer**, bār'ėr, *n*. One who bears; one who carries a letter, etc.; a support.
**Bear-garden**, bār'gär-dn, *n*. A place where bears were kept; a place of disorder.
**Bearing**, bār'ing, *n*. A carrying; deportment; mien; relation; tendency.
**Bearing-rein**, bār'ing-rān, *n*. The rein by which a horse's head is held up.
**Bearish**, bār'ish, *a*. Partaking of the qualities of a bear.
**Beast**, bēst, *n*. Any four-footed animal; a brutal man.
**Beastly**, bēst'li, *a*. Brutal; filthy; bestial.
**Beat**, bēt, *vt*. (beating, pret. beat, pp. beat, beaten). To strike repeatedly; to overcome; to crush; to harass.—*vi*. To throb, as a pulse; to sail against the wind.—*n*. A stroke; a pulsation; a course frequently trodden.
**Beater**, bēt'ėr, *n*. One who beats; that which beats; one who rouses game from coverts.
**Beatific**, bē-a-tif'ik, *a*. Blessing or making happy.
**Beatification**, bē-at'i-fi-kā''shon, *n*. Act of beatifying; a kind of canonization.
**Beatify**, bē-at'i-fī, *vt*. (beatifying, beatified). To make happy; to declare a person blessed.
**Beating**, bēt'ing, *n*. Act of striking; chastisement by blows; a conquering; defeat.
**Beatitude**, bē-at'i-tūd, *n*. Blessedness; bliss; one of the declarations of blessedness to particular virtues made by Christ.
**Beau**, bō, *n*.; pl. **-aux** or **-aus**, bōz. A man fond of fine dress; a gallant; a lover.
**Beau-ideal**, bō-ī-dē'al, *n*. An imagined standard of perfection.
**Beauteous**, bū'tē-us, *a*. Beautiful; fair.
**Beautiful**, bū'ti-ful, *a*. Full of beauty; lovely.—*n*. That which possesses beauty.
**Beautifully**, bū'ti-ful-li, *adv*. In a beautiful manner.
**Beautify**, bū'ti-fī, *vt*. (beautifying, beautified). To make beautiful; to adorn.—*vi*. To become beautiful.
**Beauty**, bū'ti, *n*. Loveliness; elegance; grace; a beautiful woman.
**Beauty-spot**, bū'ti-spot, *n*. A patch placed on the face to heighten beauty.
**Beaver**, bē'vėr, *n*. A rodent quadruped; beaver-fur, or a hat made of it; the face-guard of a helmet; a visor.—*a*. Made of beaver, or of its fur.
**Beavered**, bē'vėrd, *a*. Having a visor.
**Bebeeru**, bē-bē'rö, *n*. A tree of British Guiana, called also *green-heart*.
**Becalm**, bē-käm', *vt*. To make calm.
**Because**, bē-kaz'. By cause; on this account that.
**Beccafico**, bek-a-fē'kō, *n*. A bird resembling the nightingale; the garden-warbler.
**Bechamel**, besh'a-mel, *n*. A fine white sauce thickened with cream.
**Beck**, bek, *n*. A sign with the hand or head.—*vi*. To make a sign or nod.—*vt*. To notify by a sign or nod.
**Beckon**, bek'n, *vi*. To make a sign by nodding, etc.—*vt*. To make a sign to.
**Becloud**, bē-kloud', *vt*. To cloud; to obscure.
**Become**, bē-kum', *vi*. (becoming, pp. become, pret. became). To come to be; to change to.—*vt*. To suit; to add grace to; to be worthy of.
**Becoming**, bē-kum'ing, *a*. Fit; graceful.
**Becomingly**, bē-kum'ing-li, *adv*. In a becoming or proper manner.
**Bed**, bed, *n*. Something to sleep or rest on; the channel of a river; place where anything is deposited; a layer; a stratum.—*vt*. (bedding, bedded). To lay in a bed; to sow; to stratify.—*vi*. To go to bed.
**Bedaub**, bē-dab', *vt*. To daub over; to besmear.
**Bedchamber**, bed'chām-bėr, *n*. An apartment for a bed.
**Bedding**, bed'ing, *n*. The materials of a bed.
**Bedeck**, bē-dek', *vt*. To deck; to adorn.
**Bedesman**, bēdz'man, *n*. A beadsman.
**Bedew**, bē-dū', *vt*. To moisten, as with dew.
**Bedight**, bē-dīt', *vt*. To array; to dress.
**Bedim**, bē-dim', *vt*. To make dim.
**Bedizen**, bē-dī'zn, *vt*. To adorn gaudily.
**Bedlam**, bed'lam, *n*. A madhouse; a place of uproar.—*a*. Belonging to a madhouse.
**Bedouin**, bed'ö-in, *n*. A nomadic Arab living in tents in Arabia, Syria, Egypt, etc.
**Bedraggle**, bē-drag'l, *vt*. To soil by drawing along on mud.
**Bedrid, Bedridden**, bed'rid, bed'rid-n, *a*. Confined to bed by age or infirmity.
**Bedroom**, bed'röm, *n*. A sleeping apartment.
**Bedrop**, bē-drop', *vt*. (bedropping, bedropped). To sprinkle, as with drops.
**Bedstead**, bed'sted, *n*. A frame for supporting a bed.
**Bee**, bē, *n*. The insect that makes honey.
**Beech**, bēch, *n*. A large smooth-barked tree yielding a hard timber and nuts.
**Beechen**, bēch'en, *a*. Consisting of the wood or bark of the beech.
**Beef**, bēf, *n*. The flesh of an ox, bull, or cow.—*a*. Consisting of such flesh.
**Beef-eater**, bēf'ēt-ėr, *n*. A yeoman of the royal guard of England.
**Beef-tea**, bēf'tē, *n*. A soup made from beef.
**Beef-wood**, bēf'wụd, *n*. The wood of some Australian trees.
**Bee-line**, bē'līn, *n*. The direct line between two places.
**Beer**, bēr, *n*. A fermented alcoholic liquor made from barley and hops.
**Bees'-wax**, bēz'waks, *n*. The wax collected by bees, of which their cells are made.
**Bees'-wing**, bēz'wing, *n*. A film in port-wines showing age and quality.
**Beet**, bēt, *n*. A vegetable with thick, fleshy roots, yielding sugar.

**Beetle,** bē'tl, *n.* A coleopterous insect; a heavy wooden mallet.—*vi.* (beetling, beetled). To jut; to hang over.
**Beetle-browed,** bē'tl-broud, *a.* Having prominent brows.
**Beetling,** bē'tl-ing, *a.* Jutting; overhanging.
**Beeves,** bēvz, *n.pl.* of beef. Cattle; black cattle.
**Befall,** bē-fal', *vt.* To happen to.—*vi.* To happen.
**Befit,** bē-fit', *vt.* To suit; to become.
**Befitting,** bē-fit'ing, *a.* Suitable.
**Befog,** bē-fog', *vt.* (befogging, befogged). To involve in fog; to confuse.
**Befool,** bē-föl', *vt.* To fool; to delude.
**Before,** bē-fōr', *prep.* In front of; in presence of; earlier than; in preference to.—*adv.* In time preceding; further; onward; in front.
**Beforehand,** bē-fōr'hand, *a.* In good pecuniary circumstances.—*adv.* In advance.
**Befoul,** bē-foul', *vt.* To make foul.
**Befriend,** bē-frend', *vt.* To act as a friend to.
**Beg,** beg, *vt.* (begging, begged). To ask in charity; to ask earnestly; to take for granted.—*vi.* To ask or live upon alms.
**Beget,** bē-get', *vt.* (begetting, pp. begot, begotten, pret. begot). To procreate; to produce.
**Begetter,** bē-get'ėr, *n.* One who begets.
**Beggar,** beg'gėr, *n.* One who begs.—*vt.* To impoverish.
**Beggarliness,** beg'gėr-li-nes, *n.* Meanness; extreme poverty.
**Beggarly,** beg'gėr-li, *a.* Like a beggar; poor.—*adv.* Meanly; despicably.
**Beggary,** beg'gė-ri, *n.* Extreme indigence.
**Begin,** bē-gin', *vi.* (pp. begun, pret. began). To take rise; to do the first act; to commence.—*vt.* To enter on; to originate.
**Beginner,** bē-gin'ėr, *n.* One who begins; a novice.
**Beginning,** bē-gin'ing, *n.* The first cause, act, or state; origin; commencement.
**Begird,** bē-gėrd', *vt.* To gird round about; to bind.
**Begone,** bē-gon', *interj.* Get you gone! go away!
**Begonia,** bē-gō'ni-a, *n.* A showy tropical plant much cultivated in hothouses.
**Begrudge,** bē-gruj', *vt.* To envy the possession of.
**Beguile,** bē-gīl', *vt.* (beguiling, beguilded). To practice guile on; to dupe; to while away.
**Beguilement,** bē-gīl'ment, *n.* Act of beguiling.
**Beguiler,** bē-gīl'ėr, *n.* One who or that which beguiles.
**Begum,** bē'gum, *n.* An Indian lady of rank.
**Behalf,** bē-haf', *n.* Interest; support.
**Behave,** bē-hāv', *vt.* (behaving, behaved). To conduct (oneself).—*vi.* To act; to conduct oneself.
**Behavior,** bē-hāv'i-ėr, *n.* Conduct; deportment.
**Behead,** bē-hed', *vt.* To cut off the head of.
**Behemoth,** bē-hē'moth, *n.* A huge beast mentioned in the Book of Job and supposed to be an elephant or hippopotamus.
**Behest,** bē-hest', *n.* Command; precept.
**Behind,** bē-hīnd', *prep.* In the rear of; remaining after; inferior to.—*adv.* In the rear; backwards; remaining.
**Behindhand,** bē-hīnd'hand, *adv.* or *pred.a.* Backwards; in arroars.
**Behold,** bē-hōld', *vt.* (beholding, beheld). To look upon; to regard with attention.—*vi.* To look; to fix the mind.
**Beholden,** bē-hōld'n, *a.* Obliged; indebted.
**Behoof,** bē-höf', *n.* Behalf; profit.
**Behove,** bē-höv', *vt.* (behoving, behoved). To be meet or necessary for (used impersonally).
**Beige,** bāzh, *n.* A fabric made of unbleached or undyed wool; a greyish-brown color.
**Being,** bē'ing, *n.* Existence; a creature.
**Belabor,** bē-lā'bėr, *vt.* To beat soundly; to thump.
**Belated,** bē-lāt'ed, *p.a.* Made late; benighted.
**Belay,** bē-lā', *vt.* *Nautical,* to fasten by winding round something.
**Belch,** belch, *vt.* To eject, as wind from the stomach; to cast forth violently.—*vi.* To eject wind from the stomach; to issue out, as by eructation.—*n.* Eructation.
**Beldam,** bel'dam, *n.* An old woman; a hag.
**Beleaguer,** bē-lē'gėr, *vt.* To surround with an army; to blockade; to besiege.
**Belemnite,** bel'em-nīt, *n.* A dart-shaped fossil common in the chalk formation.
**Belfry,** bel'fri, *n.* A bell-tower; place where a bell is hung.
**Belial,** bē'li-al, *n.* An evil spirit; Satan.
**Belie,** bē-lī', *vt.* (belying, belied). To represent falsely; to be in contradiction to; to fail to equal.
**Belief,** bē-lēf' *n.* Assent of the mind; persuasion; creed; opinion.
**Believe,** bē-lēv', *vt.* (believing, believed). To give belief to; to credit; to expect with confidence.—*vi.* To have a firm persuasion.
**Believer,** bē-lēv'ėr, *n.* One who believes.
**Belittle,** bē-lit'l, *vt.* To make smaller; to speak disparagingly of.
**Bell,** bel, *n.* A metallic vessel used for giving sounds by being struck; anything in form of a bell.—*vi.* To flower.—*vt.* To put a bell on.
**Belladonna,** bel-la-don'na, *n.* A European plant yielding a powerful medicine.
**Belle,** bel, *n.* A lady of great beauty.
**Belles-lettres,** bel-let'tr, *n.pl.* Polite literature, including poetry, rhetoric, history, etc.
**Bell-founder,** bel'found-ėr, *n.* A man who casts bells.
**Bellicose,** bel'li-kōs, *a.* Warlike; pugnacious.
**Bellied,** bel'lid, *a.* Swelled in the middle.
**Belligerent,** bel-lij'ėr-ent, *a.* Waging war.—*n.* A nation or state waging war.
**Bell-metal,** bel'me-tal, *n.* A mixture of copper and tin, used for bells.
**Bellow,** bel'ō, *vi.* To make a hollow loud noise, as a bull; to roar.—*n.* A roar.
**Bellows,** bel'ōz, *n.sing.* and *pl.* An instrument for blowing fires, supplying wind to organ-pipes, etc.
**Bell-ringer,** bel'ring-ėr, *n.* One whose business is to ring a church or other bell.
**Bell-wether,** bel'weTH-ėr, *n.* A sheep which leads the flock with a bell on his neck.
**Belly,** bel'li, *n.* That part of the body which contains the bowels.—*vt.* and *i.* (bellying, bellied). To swell, bulge.
**Belly-band,** bel'li-band, *n.* A band that goes round the belly of a horse.
**Belong,** bē-long', *vi.* To be the property; to appertain; to be connected; to have original residence.
**Belonging,** bē-long'ing, *n.* That which pertains to one: generally in *pl.*
**Beloved,** bē-luvd', bē-luv'ed, *a.* Greatly loved.
**Below,** bē-lō', *prep.* Under in place; beneath; unworthy of.—*adv.* In a lower place; beneath; on earth; in hell.
**Belt,** belt, *n.* A girdle; a band.—*vt.* To encircle.
**Beltane,** bel'tān, *n.* An ancient festival on 1st May (Scotland) or 21st June (Ireland).
**Belted,** belt'ed, *a.* Having a belt.
**Belvedere,** bel've-dēr, *n.* An open erection on the top of a house; a summer-house.
**Bemire,** bē-mīr', *vt.* (bemiring, bemired). To drag in or cover with mire.
**Bemoan,** bē-mōn', *vt.* To lament; bewail.
**Bemused,** bē-muzd', *a.* Muddled; stupefied.
**Ben,** ben, *n.* A mountain peak.
**Bench,** bensh, *n.* A long seat; seat of justice; body of judges.—*vt.* To furnish with benches.
**Bencher,** bensh'ėr, *n.* A senior barrister in an inn of court.
**Bend,** bend, *vt.* (pp. and pret. bent and bended). To curve; to direct to a certain point; to subdue.—*vi.* To become crooked; to lean or turn; to yield.—*n.* A curve.
**Beneath,** bē-nēth', *prep.* Under; lower in place, rank, dignity, etc.; unworthy of.—*adv.* In a lower place; below.
**Benediction,** ben-ē-dik'shon, *n.* Act of blessing; invocation of happiness.
**Benefaction,** ben-ē-fak'shon, *n.* The doing of a benefit; a benefit conferred.
**Benefactor,** ben-ē-fak'tėr, *n.* He who confers a

benefit.
**Benefactress,** ben-ē-fak'tres, *n.* A female who confers a benefit.
**Benefice,** ben'ē-fis, *n.* An ecclesiastical living.
**Beneficed,** ben'ē-fist, *p.a.* Possessed of a benefice or church preferment.
**Beneficence,** bē-nef'i-sens, *n.* Active goodness.
**Beneficent,** bē-nef'i-sent, *a.* Kind; bountiful.
**Beneficently,** bē-nef'i-sent-li, *adv.* In a beneficent manner.
**Beneficial,** ben-ē-fi'shal, *a.* Conferring benefit.
**Beneficially,** ben-ē-fi'shal-li, *adv.* Helpfully.
**Beneficiary,** ben-ē-fi'shi-a-ri, *n.* A person who is benefited or assisted.
**Benefit,** ben'ē-fit, *n.* An act of kindness; a favor; advantage.—*vt.* To do a service to.—*vi.* To gain advantage.
**Benevolence,** bē-nev'ō-lens, *n.* Kindness; active love of mankind.
**Benevolent,** bē-nev'ō-lent, *a.* Kind; charitable.
**Benevolently,** bē-nev'ō-lent-li, *adv.* In a kind manner; with good-will.
**Bengalee, Bengali,** ben-gal-ē', *n.* The language of Bengal; a native of Bengal.
**Benight,** bē-nīt', *vt.* To involve in night; to overwhelm in moral darkness or ignorance.
**Benign,** bē-nīn', *a.* Gracious; kind; mild.
**Benignant,** bē-nig'nant, *a.* Gracious; favorable.
**Benignantly,** bē-nig'nant-li, *adv.* In a benignant manner.
**Benignity,** bē-nig'ni-ti, *n.* Kindness; graciousness; beneficence.
**Benignly,** bē-nīn'li, *adv.* Graciously.
**Benison,** ben'i-zn, *n.* A blessing, benediction.
**Bent,** bent, pret. and pp. of *bend.*—*n.* Bias of mind; inclination; a wiry grass; a wild piece of land.
**Benumb,** bē-num', *vt.* To deprive of sensation; to make torpid; to stupefy.
**Benzene,** ben'zēn, *n.* A liquid used to remove grease spots, etc.
**Benzoin, Benzoine,** ben-zō'in or ben'zoin, *n.* A fragrant resinous juice.
**Benzole, Benzoline,** ben'zōl, ben'zō-lin. Same as *Benzene.*
**Bepraise,** bē-prāz', *vt.* To praise greatly or extravagantly.
**Bequeath,** bē-kwēTH', *vt.* To leave by will; to hand down.
**Bequest,** bē-kwest', *n.* A legacy.
**Bere,** bēr, *n.* A species of barley.
**Bereave,** bē-rēv', *vt.* (bereaving, pp. and pret. bereaved and bereft). To deprive of.
**Bereavement,** bē-rēv'ment, *n.* Act of bereaving; state of being bereft.
**Beret,** be'ri, *n.* A close-fitting round woolen cap.
**Beretta.** *See* BIRETTA.
**Bergamot,** bėrg'a-mot, *n.* A species of pear; perfume from the fruit of the lime; a coarse tapestry.
**Beri-beri,** ber'i-ber'i, *n.* A dangerous disease endemic in parts of India and Ceylon, characterized by paralysis, difficult breathing, and other symptoms.
**Berlin,** bėr'lin or bėr-lin', *n.* A four-wheeled vehicle; a wool for fancy work.
**Berry,** be'ri, *n.* A pulpy fruit containing many seeds.
**Berserker,** bėr'sėr-kėr, *n.* A furious Scandinavian warrior of heathen times.
**Berth,** bėrth, *n.* A station in which a ship lies; a place for sleeping in a ship, etc.—*vt.* To allot a berth to.
**Beryl,** be'ril, *n.* A hard greenish mineral.
**Beseech,** bē-sēch', *vt.* (beseeching, besought). To entreat; to solicit.
**Beseechingly,** bē-sēch'ing-li, *adv.* In a beseeching manner.
**Beseem,** bē-sēm', *vt.* To become; to be fit.
**Beseeming,** bē-sēm'ing, *a.* Becoming.
**Beset,** bē-set', *vt.* (besetting, beset). To surround; to press on all sides.
**Besetting,** bē-set'ing, *a.* Habitually assailing.
**Beshrew,** bē-shrö', *vt.* To wish a curse to.
**Beside, Besides,** bē-sīd', bē-sīdz', *prep.* By the side of; near; over and above; distinct from.—*adv.* Moreover; in addition.
**Besiege,** bē-sēj', *vt.* (besieging, besieged). To lay siege to; to beset.
**Besieger,** bē-sēj'ėr, *n.* One who besieges.
**Besmear,** bē-smēr', *vt.* To smear; to soil.
**Besom,** bē'zum, *n.* A brush of twigs; a broom.
**Besot,** bē-sot', *vt.* (besotting, besotted). To make sottish.
**Besotted,** bē-sot'ed, *p.a.* Make sottish; stupid.
**Bespangle,** bē-spang'gl, *vt.* To adorn with spangles.
**Bespatter,** bē-spat'tėr, *vt.* To spatter over.
**Bespeak,** bē-spēk', *vt.* (pp. bespoke, bespoken, pret. bespoke). To speak for beforehand; to indicate.
**Bespread,** bē-spred', *vt.* To spread over.
**Besprinkle,** bē-spring'kl, *vt.* To sprinkle over.
**Bessemer-steel,** bes'e-mėr-stēl, *n.* Steel made directly from molten cast-iron by driving through it air to carry off impurities.
**Best,** best, *a.superl.* Most good; having good qualities in the highest degree; exceeding all.—*n.* The utmost; highest endeavor.—*adv.* In the highest degree; beyond all others.
**Bestead,** bē-sted', *pp.* or *a.* Placed, circumstanced; with *ill,* etc.
**Bestial,** bes'ti-al, *a.* Belonging to a beast; brutish; vile.
**Bestiality,** bes-ti-al'i-ti, *n.* The quality of being bestial; brutal conduct.
**Bestially,** bes'ti-al-li, *adv.* Brutally.
**Bestiary,** bes'ti-a-ri, *n.* A book of the middle ages treating fancifully of beasts.
**Bestir,** bē-stėr', *vt.* To stir up; to put into brisk action. (Usually with *refl.* pron.)
**Bestow,** bē-stō', *vt.* To lay up; to give; to confer; to dispose of; to apply.
**Bestowal,** bē-stō'al, *n.* Act of bestowing; disposal.
**Bestower,** bē-stō'ėr, *n.* One who bestows; a giver; a disposer.
**Bestraddle,** bē-strad'dl, *vt.* To bestride.
**Bestrew,** bē-strö', *vt.* To scatter over.
**Bestride,** bē-strīd', *vt.* (pp. bestrid, bestridden, pret. bestrid, bestrode). To stride over; to place a leg on each side of.
**Bestud,** bē-stud', *vt.* To set with studs; to adorn with bosses.
**Bet,** bet, *n.* A wager; that which is pledged in a contest.—*vt.* (betting, betted). To wager.
**Betake,** bē-tāk', *vt.* To apply (oneself); to have recourse to.
**Bethink,** bē-thingk', *vt.* To call to mind; to recollect.
**Betide,** bē-tīd', *vt.* (pp. betid, pret. betid, betided). To happen to; to befall.—*vi.* To happen.
**Betimes,** bē-tīmz', *adv.* Seasonably; early.
**Betoken,** bē-tō'kn, *vt.* To portend; to signify.
**Betray,** bē-trā', *vt* To disclose treacherously; to entrap.
**Betrayal,** bē-trā'al, *n.* Act of betraying.
**Betrayer,** bē-trā'ėr, *n.* One who betrays.
**Betroth,** bē-trōTH', *vt.* To affiance; to pledge to marriage.
**Betrothal,** bē-trōTH'al, *n.* Mutual contract of marriage.
**Better,** bet'tėr, *a.comp.* More good; improved.—*adv.* More excellently; in a higher degree.—*vt.* To make better; to advance.—*n.* A superior (generally in *pl.*).
**Bettor,** bet'ėr, *n.* One who bets.
**Between,** bē-twēn', *prep.* In the middle; from one to another of; belonging to two.
**Betwixt,** bē-twikst', *prep.* Between.
**Bevel,** be'vel, *n.* An instrument for taking angles; an angle not a right angle.—*a.* Slant; oblique.—*vt.* (beveling, beveled). To cut to a bevel angle.
**Beverage,** bev'ėr-āj, *n.* Drink; liquor.
**Bevy,** be'vi, *n.* A flock of birds; a company of females.
**Bewail,** bē-wāl', *vt.* To lament.—*vi.* To utter deep

B

grief.
**Beware,** bē-wār′, *vi.* To take care (with *of*).
**Bewilder,** bē-wil′dėr, *vt.* To confuse; to perplex.
**Bewilderment,** bē-wil′dėr-ment, *n.* State of being bewildered.
**Bewitch,** bē-wich′, *vt.* To enchant; to fascinate; to overpower by charms.
**Bewitchery,** bē-wich′ėr-i, *n.* Fascination.
**Bewitching,** bē-wich′ing, *p.a.* Fascinating; captivating.
**Bewitchingly,** bē-wich′ing-li, *adv.* In a fascinating manner.
**Bewitchment,** bē-wich′ment, *n.* Fascination.
**Bewray,** bē-rā′, *vt.* To betray.
**Bey,** bā, *n.* A Turkish governor.
**Beyond,** bē-yond′, *prep.* On the further side of; farther onward than; out of the reach of; above.—*adv.* At a distance.
**Bezel,** bez′el, *n.* The part of a ring which holds the stone.
**Bezique,** be-zēk′, *n.* A game at cards.
**Bhang,** bang, *n.* A narcotic drug prepared from an Indian hemp.
**Biangular,** bī-ang′gū-lėr, *a.* Having two angles.
**Bias,** bī′as, *n.*; pl. **-ses.** Weight on one side; a leaning of the mind; bent.—*vt.* To incline to one side; to prejudice.
**Biased, Biassed,** bī′ast, *p.a.* Prejudiced.
**Bib,** bib, *n.* A cloth worn by children over the breast.
**Bibber,** bib′ėr, *n.* A drinker; a tippler.
**Bible,** bī′bl, *n.* The Holy Scriptures.
**Biblical,** bib′lik-al, *a.* Pertaining to the Bible.
**Biblically,** bib′lik-al-li, *adv.* In accordance with the Bible.
**Biblicist,** bib′li-sist, *n.* One skilled in biblical knowledge.
**Bibliographical,** bib′li-ō-graf″ik-al, *a.* Pertaining to bibliography.
**Bibliography,** bib-li-og′ra-fi, *n.* A history of books and their editions; list of books by one author or on one subject.
**Bibliomania,** bib′li-ō-mā″ni-a, *n.* A rage for possessing rare books.
**Bibliophile,** bib′li-ō-fīl, *n.* A lover of books.
**Bibliopolist,** bib-li-op′ol-ist, *n.* A bookseller.
**Bibulous,** bib′ū-lus, *a.* Spongy; addicted to intoxicants.
**Bicarbonate,** bī-kär′bon-āt, *n.* A carbonate containing two equivalents of carbonic acid to one of a base.
**Bicentenary,** bī-sen′te-na-ri, *n.* Two hundred years.
**Biceps,** bī′seps, *n.* A muscle of the arm and of the thigh.
**Bicker,** bik′ėr, *vt.* To skirmish; to quarrel.
**Bicycle,** bī′si-kl, *n.* A two-wheeled vehicle propelled by the rider.
**Bicyclist,** bī′sik-list, *n.* One who rides a bicycle.
**Bid,** bid, *vt.* (bidding, pp. bid, bidden, pret. bid, bade). To ask; to order; to offer.—*n.* An offer, as at an auction.
**Biddable,** bid′a-bl, *a.* Obedient; docile.
**Bidding,** bid′ing, *n.* Invitation; order; offer.
**Bide,** bīd, *vi.* (biding, bode). To dwell; to remain.—*vt.* To endure; to abide.
**Bidental,** bī-dent′al, *a.* Having two teeth.
**Bidet,** bi-det′ or bē-dā, *n.* A baggage horse.
**Biennial,** bī-en′ni-al, *a.* Continuing for two years; taking place once in two years.—*n.* A plant which lives two years.
**Biennially,** bī-en′ni-al-li, *adv.* Once in two years; at the return of two years.
**Bier,** bēr, *n.* A carriage or frame for conveying a corpse to the grave.
**Bifid,** bī′fid, *a.* Cleft into two parts; forked.
**Bifurcate,** bī-fėr′kāt, *a.* Forked.
**Big,** big, *a.* Great; large; pregnant; arrogant.
**Bigamist,** big′am-ist, *n.* One who has two wives or husbands at once.
**Bigamy,** big′a-mi, *n.* The crime of having two wives or husbands at once.
**Bigg,** big, *n.* A variety of winter barley.
**Bight,** bīt, *n.* A small bay; a loop.
**Bigness,** big′nes, *n.* Quality of being big; size.
**Bigot,** big′ot, *n.* A person obstinately wedded to a particular creed.
**Bigoted,** big′ot-ed, *a.* Obstinately attached to some creed.
**Bigotry,** big′ot-ri, *n.* Blind zeal in favor of a creed, party, sect, or opinion.
**Bijou,** bē-zhö′, *n.*; pl. **-joux,** -zhö. A trinket; a jewel.
**Bilander,** bī′lan-dėr, *n.* A Dutch two-masted vessel.
**Bilateral,** bī-lat′ėr-al, *a.* Two-sided.
**Bilberry,** bil′be-ri, *n.* The whortleberry or blaeberry.
**Bilbo,** bil′bō, *n.* A rapier; a sword.
**Bilboes,** bil′bōz, *n.pl.* A sort of stocks for offenders on board of ships.
**Bile,** bīl, *n.* A yellowish bitter liquid secreted in the liver; spleen; anger.
**Bilge,** bilj, *n.* The protuberant part of a cask; the breadth of a ship's bottom.—*vi.* (bilging, bilged). To leak in the bilge.
**Bilge-water,** bilj′wa-tėr, *n.* Water on the bilge or bottom of a ship.
**Biliary,** bil′i-a-ri, *a.* Belonging to the bile.
**Bilingual,** bī-lin′gwal, *a.* In two languages.
**Bilious,** bil′i-us, *a.* Affected by bile.
**Biliteral,** bī-lit′ėr-al, *a.* Consisting of two letters.
**Bilk,** bilk, *vt.* To defraud; to elude.
**Bill,** bil, *n.* The beak of a bird; anything resembling a bird's beak; an instrument for pruning, etc.; a military weapon now obsolete; an account of money due; draught of a proposed new law; a placard.—*vi.* To join bills, as doves; to fondle.—*vt.* To announce by bill; to stick bills on.
**Billet,** bil′et, *n.* A small note in writing; a ticket directing soldiers where to lodge; a situation; a stick of wood.—*vt.* To quarter, as soldiers.—*vi.* To be quartered.
**Billet-doux,** bil-e-dö′, *n.* A love-letter.
**Billiards,** bil′yėrdz, *n.pl.* A game played on a table with balls and cues.
**Billingsgate,** bil′lingz-gāt, *n.* Foul language.
**Billion,** bil′yon, *n.* A million of millions.
**Billow,** bil′lō, *n.* A great wave of the sea.—*vi.* To roll in large waves.
**Billowy,** bil′lō-i, *a.* Swelling into large waves.
**Bimanous,** bī′man-us, *a.* Having two hands.
**Bimensal,** bī-men′sal, *a.* Occurring every two months.
**Bimetallism,** bī-met′al-izm, *n.* A system of currency which recognizes silver and gold as legal tender to any amount.
**Bimetallist,** bī-met′al-ist, *n.* One who favors bimetallism.
**Bimonthly,** bī-munth′li, *a.* Occurring every two months.
**Bin,** bin, *n.* A receptacle for corn, etc.; a partition in a wine-cellar.
**Binary,** bī′na-ri, *a.* Twofold.
**Bind,** bīnd, *vt.* (binding, bound). To tie; to confine; to oblige; to cover (a book); to render costive; to make firm.—*vi.* To grow hard; to be obligatory.
**Binder,** bīnd′ėr, *n.* One who binds books or sheaves; a bandage.
**Binding,** bīnd′ing, *p.n.* Act of binding; the cover and sewing, etc., of a book.
**Bind-weed,** bīnd′wēd, *n.* Convolvulus.
**Bing,** bing, *n.* A large heap.
**Binnacle,** bin′a-kl, *n.* A case in which a ship's compass is kept.
**Binocular,** bī-nok′ū-lėr, *a.* Adapted for both eyes.—*n.* A small telescope for using with both eyes at once.
**Binomial,** bī-nō′mi-al, *a.* or *n.* An algebraic expression consisting of two terms.
**Biochemistry,** bī-ō-kem′ist-ri, *n.* The study of the chemistry of living things.
**Biogenesis,** bī-ō-jen′e-sis, *n.* The doctrine that living organisms can spring only from living parents.
**Biographer,** bī-og′ra-fėr, *n.* A writer of biography.

**Biographical,** bī-ō-graf'ik-al, *a.* Pertaining to biography.
**Biography,** bī-og'ra-fi, *n.* An account of one's life and character.
**Biologist,** bī-ol'o-jist, *n.* One skilled in biology.
**Biology,** bī-ol'o-ji, *n.* The science of life.
**Bioplasm,** bī'ō-plazm, *n.* The germinal matter in plants and animals.
**Bipartite,** bī-pärt'īt, *a.* Having two parts.
**Biped,** bī'ped, *n.* An animal with two feet.
**Birch,** bėrch, *n.* A tree having small leaves, white bark, and a fragrant odor.
**Birch, Birchen,** bėrch, bėrch'en, *a.* Made of birch; consisting of birch.
**Bird,** bėrd, *n.* One of the feathered race.
**Bird-lime,** bėrd'līm, *n.* A viscous substance used to catch birds.
**Bird's-eye,** bėrdz'ī, *a.* Seen as by a flying bird; wide and rapid.—*n.* A finely cut tobacco.
**Bireme,** bī'rēm, *n.* An ancient Greek or Roman vessel with two banks of oars.
**Biretta, Beretta,** bi-ret'ta, be-ret'ta, *n.* A square cap worn by ecclesiastics.
**Birth,** bėrth, *n.* Act of bearing or coming into life; extraction.
**Birthday,** bėrth'dā, *n.* The day on which a person is born, or its anniversary.
**Birthplace,** bėrth'plās, *n.* Place where one is born.
**Birthright,** bėrth'rīt, *n.* Any right to which a person is entitled by birth.
**Biscuit,** bis'ket, *n.* Hard bread made into cakes; unglazed porcelain.
**Bisect,** bī-sekt', *vt.* To cut into two equal parts.
**Bisection,** bī-sek'shon, *n.* Act of bisecting; division into two equal parts.
**Bishop,** bish'up, *n.* Head of a diocese; a piece in chess which moves diagonally.
**Bishopric,** bish'up-rik, *n.* Office of a bishop; a diocese.
**Bismuth,** bis'muth, *n.* A brittle yellowish or reddish-white metal.
**Bison,** bī'zon, *n.* A quadruped of the ox family; the American buffalo.
**Bisque,** bisk, *n.* Unglazed white porcelain; odds given at tennis, etc.
**Bit,** bit, *n.* A morsel; fragment; the metal part of a bridle inserted in a horse's mouth; a boring tool.—*vt.* (bitting, bitted). To put the bit in the mouth.
**Bitch,** bich, *n.* A female dog; a name of reproach for a woman.
**Bite,** bīt, *vt.* (biting, pp. bit, bitten, pret. bit). To crush or sever with the teeth; to cause to smart; to wound by reproach, etc.; to corrode.—*n.* Act of biting; wound made by biting; a mouthful.
**Biting,** bīt'ing, *p.a.* Sharp; severe; sarcastic.
**Bitingly,** bīt'ing-li, *adv.* In a biting or sarcastic manner.
**Bitter,** bit'ėr, *a.* Sharp to the taste; severe; painful; calamitous; distressing.
**Bittern,** bit'ėrn, *n.* A bird of the heron kind.
**Bitterness,** bit'ėr-nes, *n.* Quality of being bitter; hatred; deep distress.
**Bitters,** bit'ėrz, *n.pl.* A liquor in which bitter herbs or roots are steeped.
**Bitumen,** bi-tū'men, *n.* A mineral, pitchy, inflammable substance.
**Bituminous,** bi-tū'min-us, *a.* Having the qualities of or containing bitumen.
**Bivalve,** bī'valv, *n.* A molluscous, bivalvular animal.
**Bivalve, Bivalvular,** bī'valv, bī-valv'ū-lėr, *a.* Having two shells which open and shut, as the oyster.
**Bivouac,** bi'vö-ak, *n.* Encampment of soldiers for the night in the open air.—*vi.* (bivouacking, bivouacked). To encamp during the night without covering.
**Biweekly,** bī-wēk'li, *a.* Occurring every two weeks.
**Bizarre,** bi-zär', *a.* Odd; fantastical.
**Blab,** blab, *vt.* (blabbing, blabbed). To tell indiscreetly.—*vi.* To talk indiscreetly.
**Black,** blak, *a.* Destitute of light; dark; gloomy; sullen; astrocious; wicked.—*n.* The darkest color; a negro.—*vt.* To make black.
**Blackamoor,** blak'a-mör, *n.* A negro.
**Black-ball,** blak'bal, *n.* A composition for blacking shoes; a ball used as a negative in voting.—*vt.* To reject by private voting.
**Blackberry,** blak'be-ri, *n.* A plant of the bramble kind, and its fruit.
**Blackbird,** blak'bėrd, *n.* A species of thrush.
**Blackboard,** blak'bōrd, *n.* A board for writing on with chalk for instruction.
**Black-cap,** blak'kap, *n.* A British song-bird.
**Blackcock,** blak'kok, *n.* A species of grouse.
**Blacken,** blak'n, *vt.* To make black; to defame.—*vi.* To grow black or dark.
**Black-friar,** blak'frī-ėr, *n.* A friar of the Dominican order.
**Blackguard,** blak'gärd or bla'gärd, *n.* A scoundrel.—*vt.* To revile in scurrilous language.
**Blackguardly,** blak'gärd-li or bla'gärd-li, *a.* Rascally; villainous.
**Blacking,** blak'ing, *n.* A substance used for blacking shoes.
**Black-lead,** blak'led, *n.* A dark mineral substance used for pencils; plumbago.
**Black-leg,** *n.* A swindler; one who works during a strike.
**Black-letter,** blak'let-tėr, *n.* The old English letter or character.
**Black-list,** blak-list, *n.* A list of bankrupts.
**Black-mail,** blak'māl, *n.* Money paid for protection; extortion by intimidation.
**Black-market,** blak-mär'ket, *n.* Illegal dealing in goods or currencies which are scarce or controlled.
**Black-out,** blak'out, *n.* In war-time, the period between dusk and dawn during which no light must be visible through windows and doors.
**Black-sheep,** blak'shēp, *n.* One whose conduct is discreditable.
**Blacksmith,** blak'smith, *n.* A smith who works in iron.
**Blackthorn,** blak'thorn, *n.* The sloe.
**Bladder,** blad'ėr, *n.* A thin sac in animals containing the urine, bile, etc.; a blister; anything like the animal bladder.
**Bladder-wrack,** blad'ėr-rak, *n.* A common large kind of seaweed.
**Blade,** blād, *n.* A leaf; cutting part of a sword, knife, etc.; flat part of an oar.
**Blaeberry,** blā'be-ri, *n.* The bilberry.
**Blamable,** blām'a-bl, *a.* Deserving of blame.
**Blame,** blām, *vt.* (blaming, blamed). To censure; to reprimand.—*n.* Censure; fault.
**Blameless,** blām'les, *a.* Free from blame.
**Blanch,** blansh, *vt.* To make white.—*vi.* To grow white; to bleach.
**Blanc-mange,** bla-mängzh', *n.* A dish of arrowroot or maize-flour boiled with milk.
**Bland,** bland, *a.* Mild; soothing; gentle.
**Blandish,** bland'ish, *vt.* To soothe; to caress; to flatter.
**Blandishment,** bland'ish-ment, *n.* Soft words; artful caresses; flattery.
**Blank,** blangk, *a.* White; pale; void; void of writing; without rhyme.—*n.* A white unwritten paper; a void space; the white mark which a shot is to hit.
**Blanket,** blang'ket, *n.* A woolen covering for a bed, horses, etc.
**Blanketing,** blang'ket-ing, *n.* Cloth for blankets.
**Blankly,** blangk'li, *adv.* In a blank manner; with paleness or confusion.
**Blank-verse,** blangk'vėrs, *n.* Ten-syllabled line without rhyme.
**Blare,** blār, *vi.* (blaring, blared). To give forth a loud sound.—*vt.* To sound loudly; to proclaim noisily.—*n.* Sound like that of a trumpet; roar.
**Blarney,** blär'ni, *n.* Excessively complimentary language; gammon.—*vt.* To flatter.

B

**Blasé**, blä-zā, *a*. Satiated; used up; bored.
**Blaspheme**, blas-fēm', *vt*. (blaspheming, blasphemed). To speak irreverently of, as of God; to speak evil of.—*vi*. To utter blasphemy.
**Blasphemer**, blas-fēm'ėr, *n*. One who blasphemes.
**Blasphemous**, blas'fēm-us, *a*. Impiously irreverent.
**Blasphemy**, blas'fēm-i, *n*. Profane speaking; an indignity offered to God.
**Blast**, blast, *n*. A gust of wind; sound of a wind-instrument; violent explosion of gunpowder; pernicious influence, as of wind; blight.—*vt*. To blight; to strike with some sudden plague, etc.; to destroy; to blow up by gunpowder.—*vi*. To wither; to be blighted.
**Blatant**, blā'tant, *a*. Bellowing; noisy.
**Blaze**, blāz, *n*. A flame; brilliance; a bursting out; a white spot.—*vi*. (blazing, blazed). To flame; to send forth a bright light.—*vt*. To noise abroad; to proclaim.
**Blazer**, blāz'ėr, *n*. A bright-colored coat suited for sports.
**Blazon**, blāz'on, *vt*. To display; to adorn; to explain in heraldic terms.—*n*. A coat of arms; description of coats of arms.
**Blazoner**, blāz'on-ėr, *n*. A herald.
**Blazonry**, blāz'on-ri, *n*. The art of explaining coats of arms in proper terms.
**Bleach**, blēch, *vt*. To make white or whiter.—*vi*. To grow white.
**Bleacher**, blēch'ėr, *n*. One whose occupation is to whiten cloth.
**Bleachery**, blēch'ėri-i, *n*. A place for bleaching.
**Bleak**, blēk, *a*. Exposed; chill; dreary.
**Blear**, blēr, *a*. Sore; dimmed, as the eyes.—*vt*. To dim or impair.
**Blear-eyed**, blēr'īd, *a*. Having sore eyes; having the eyes dim with rheum.
**Bleat**, blēt, *vi*. To cry as a sheep.—*n*. The cry of a sheep.
**Bleed**, blēd, *vi*. (bleeding, bled). To emit blood; to die by slaughter; to feel agony, as from bleeding; to drop, as blood.—*vt*. To take blood from; to extort money from.
**Bleeding**, blēd'ing, *n*. A discharge of blood; the operation of letting blood; the drawing of sap from a tree.
**Blemish**, blem'ish, *vt*. To mar; to tarnish.—*n*. A mark of imperfection; dishonor.
**Blench**, blensh, *vi*. To shrink; to flinch.
**Blend**, blend, *vt*. To mix together.—*vi*. To be mixed.—*n*. A mixture.
**Blenheim**, blen'em, *n*. A spaniel.
**Blenny**, blen'ni, *n*. A small sea fish.
**Bless**, bles, *vt*. (blessing, blessed or blest). To make happy; to wish happiness to; to consecrate.
**Blessed**, bles'ed, *a*. Happy; prosperous; holy and happy; happy in heaven.
**Blessedness**, bles'ed-nes, *n*. Sanctity; joy.
**Blessing**, bles'ing, *n*. A prayer imploring happiness upon; piece of good fortune.
**Blest**, blest, *a*. Blessed; cheering
**Blight**, blīt, *n*. That which withers up; mildew.—*vt*. To wither up; to corrupt with mildew; to frustrate.
**Blind**, blīnd, *a*. Destitute of sight; wanting discernment; having no outlet.—*n*. A screen; something to mislead; a pretext.—*vt*. To make blind; to obstruct the view.
**Blindfold**, blīnd'fōld, *a*. Having the eyes covered.—*vt*. To cover the eyes of.
**Blindly**, blīnd'li, *adv*. Heedlessly.
**Blindness**, blīnd'nes, *n*. Want of sight or discernment; ignorance.
**Blind-worm**, blīnd'wėrm, *n*. A small harmless reptile; the slow-worm.
**Blink**, blingk, *vi*. To wink; to twinkle.—*vt*. To shut the eyes upon; to avoid.—*n*. A twinkle; a glimpse or glance.
**Blinker**, bling'kėr, *n*. A flap to prevent a horse from seeing sideways.
**Bliss**, blis, *n*. Blessedness; perfect happiness.
**Blissful**, blis'ful, *a*. Full of bliss.
**Blister**, blis'tėr, *n*. A thin bladder on the skin; a pustule; something to raise a blister.—*vi*. To rise in blisters.—*vt*. To raise a blister or blisters on; to apply a blister to.
**Blister-fly**, blis'tėr-flī, *n*. The Spanish fly, used in raising a blister.
**Blistery**, blis'tėr-i, *a*. Full of blisters.
**Blithe**, blīTH, *a*. Joyful; gay; mirthful.
**Blithely**, blīTH'li, *adv*. In a blithe manner.
**Blithesome**, blīTH'som, *a*. Gay; merry.
**Blitz**, blitz, *n*. A concentrated attack by air.
**Blizzard**, bliz'ėrd, *n*. A violent snow-storm, with high wind and intense cold.
**Bloat**, blōt, *vt*. To make turgid; to cure by salting and smoking.—*vi*. To grow turgid.
**Bloated**, blōt'ed, *p.a*. Inflated; overgrown.
**Bloater**, blōt'ėr, *n*. A smoke-dried herring.
**Blob**, blob, *n*. A small globe of liquid.
**Block**, blok, *n*. A heavy piece of wood or stone; a lump of solid matter; piece of wood in which a pulley is placed; a mass of buildings; an obstacle; a stupid person.—*vt*. To shut up; to obstruct; to form into blocks.
**Blockade**, blok-ād', *n*. A close siege by troops or ships.—*vt*. (blockading, blockaded). To besiege closely.
**Blockhead**, blok'hed, *n*. A stupid fellow.
**Block-house**, blok'hous, *n*. A building used for defense, chiefly of timber.
**Blockish**, blok'ish, *a*. Stupid; dull.
**Block-tin**, blok'tin, *n*. Tin cast into blocks.
**Blond, Blonde**, blond, *a*. Of a fair complexion.—*n*. A person of fair complexion.
**Blood**, blud, *n*. The fluid which circulates in animals; kindred; high birth; the juice of fruits.—*a*. Pertaining to blood; of a superior breed.—*vt*. To bleed; to stain with blood; to inure to blood.
**Blood-heat**, blud'hēt, *n*. The heat of the human blood, about 98° Fah.
**Blood-horse**, blud'hors, *n*. A horse of the purest breed.
**Blood-hound**, blud'hound, *n*. A hound of remarkably acute smell.
**Bloodily**, blud'i-li, *adv*. Cruelly.
**Bloodiness**, blud'i-nes, *n*. State of being bloody; disposition to shed blood.
**Bloodless**, blud'les, *a*. Without blood; without shedding blood.
**Blood-money**, blud'mu-ni, *n*. Money earned by the shedding of blood or murder.
**Bloodshed**, blud'shed, *n*. The shedding of blood; slaughter.
**Blood-shot**, blud'shot, *a*. Inflamed.
**Blood-stone**, blud'stōn, *n*. A greenish stone with red spots.
**Blood-sucker**, blud'suk-ėr, *n*. Any animal that sucks blood; an extortioner.
**Bloodthirsty**, blud'thėrs-ti, *a*. Eager to shed blood.
**Blood-vessel**, blud'ves-sel, *n*. An artery or a vein.
**bloody**, blud'i, *a*. Stained with blood; cruel; given to the shedding of blood.
**Bloody flux**, blud'i-fluks, *n*. The dysentery.
**Bloom**, blōm, *n*. A blossom; a flower; state of youth; native flush on the cheek; the powdery coating on plums, etc.; a lump of puddled iron.—*vi*. To blossom; to flourish; to show the freshness of youth.
**Bloomy**, blōm'i, *a*. Full of bloom.
**Blossom**, blos'om, *n*. The flower of a plant.—*vi*. To bloom; to flower; to flourish.
**Blot**, blot, *vt*. (blotted, blotting). To spot; to stain; to cancel (with *out*); to dry.—*n*. A spot or stain; an obliteration.
**Blotch**, bloch, *n*. Pustule upon the skin; an eruption; a confused patch of color.
**Blotchy**, block'i, *a*. Having blotches.
**Blotter**, blot'ėr, *n*. One who blots; a piece of blotting-paper.
**Blotting-paper**, blot'ing-pā-pėr, *n*. Unsized paper, serving to absorb ink.

B

**Blouse,** blouz, *n.* A light loose upper garment.
**Blow,** blō, *vi.* (blowing, pp. blown, pret. blew). To make a current of air; to emit air or breath; to pant; to sound by being blown; to bloom; to flourish.—*vt.* To impel by wind; to inflate; to sound by the breath; to infect with the eggs of flies.—*n.* A blast; a blossoming; bloom; a stroke; a calamitous event.
**Blower,** blō'ėr, *n.* One who blows; a contrivance to increase the draught of a chimney.
**Blowpipe,** blō'pīp, *n.* A tube by which a current of air is driven through a flame.
**Blowze,** blouz, *n.* A ruddy, fat-faced woman.
**Blowzy,** blouz'i, *a.* Fat and ruddy.
**Blubber,** blub'bėr, *n.* The fat of whales and other large sea-animals; the sea-nettle.—*vi.* To weep in a noisy manner.
**Blucher,** bluch'ėr or blö'kėr, *n.* A strong half-boot.
**Bludgeon,** blud'jon, *n.* A short club with one end loaded.
**Blue,** blü, *n.* The color which the sky exhibits; (*pl.*) depression, the dumps.—*a.* Of a blue color; sky-colored.—*vt.* (bluing, blued). To dye of a blue color.
**Bluebell,** blü'bel, *n.* The wild hyacinth (in England), the harebell (in Scotland).
**Blue-book,** blü'buk, *n.* A name applied to British government official reports and other papers.
**Blue-jacket,** blü'jak-et, *n.* A sailor.
**Blue-pill,** blü'pil, *n.* Mercurial pill.
**Blue-print,** blü'print, *n.* A print obtained by the action of light on prepared paper over which a transparent drawing is laid. The exposed part of the paper becomes covered with Prussian blue, and the drawing is shown in white.
**Blue-stocking,** blü'stok-ing, *n.* A learned and pedantic lady.
**Blue-stone,** blü'stōn, *n.* Sulphate of copper.
**Bluff,** bluf, *a.* Steep; blustering; burly; hearty.—*n.* A steep projecting bank.—*vt.* and *i.* To impose on by a show of boldness or strength.
**Bluish,** blü'ish, *a.* Blue in a small degree.
**Blunder,** blun'dėr, *vi.* To err stupidly; to stumble.—*vt.* To confound.—*n.* A gross mistake; error.
**Blunderbuss,** blun'dėr-bus, *n.* A short gun with a large bore.
**Blunt,** blunt, *a.* Dull on the edge or point; not sharp; dull in understanding; unceremonious.—*vt.* To make blunt or dull.
**Bluntly,** blunt'li, *adv.* In a blunt manner.
**Bluntness,** blunt'nes, *n.* Dullness of edge or point; rude sincerity or plainness.
**Blur,** blėr, *n.* A stain; a blot.—*vt.* (blurring, blurred). To stain; to obscure; to render indistinct.
**Blurb,** blėrb, *n.* A brief epitome or eulogy of a book, often printed on its jacket.
**Blurt,** blėrt, *vt.* To utter suddenly or unadvisedly.
**Blush,** blush, *vi.* To redden in the face; to bear a blooming red color.—*n.* A red color caused by shame, confusion, etc.; sudden appearance or glance.
**Blushing,** blush'ing, *a.* Reddening in the cheeks or face; roseate.
**Bluster,** blus'tėr, *vi.* To roar like wind; to swagger.—*n.* A violent gust of wind; swagger.
**Blusterer,** blus'tėr-ėr, *n.* A swaggerer.
**Blustering,** blus'tėr-ing, *a.* Noisy; windy.
**Boa,** bō'a, *n.* A genus of large serpents without fangs and venom; a long piece of fur, etc., worn round the neck.
**Boar,** bōr, *n.* The male of swine.
**Board,** bōrd, *n.* A piece of timber broad and thin; a table; food; persons seated round a table; a council; the deck of a ship; a thick stiff paper.—*vt.* To cover with boards; to supply with food; to place as a boarder; to enter a ship by force.—*vi.* To live in a house at a certain rate.
**Boarder,** bōrd'ėr, *n.* One who receives food and lodging at a stated charge; one who boards a ship in action.
**Boarding,** bōrd'ing, *n.* Act of one who boards; boards collectively.
**Boarding-house,** bōrd'ing-hous, *n.* A house where board and lodging is furnished.
**Boarding-school,** bōrd'ing-sköl, *n.* A school which supplies board as well as tuition.
**Board-school,** bōrd'sköl, *n.* A school under the management of a school-board.
**Boarish,** bōr'ish, *a.* Like a boar; swinish.
**Boast,** bōst, *vi.* To brag; to talk ostentatiously.—*vt.* To brag of; to magnify.—*n.* A vaunting; the cause of boasting.
**Boaster,** bōst'ėr, *n.* One who boasts.
**Boastful,** bōst'ful, *a.* Given to boasting.
**Boastingly,** bōst'ing-li, *adv.* In an ostentatious manner; with boasting.
**Boat,** bōt, *n.* A small open vessel, usually impelled by oars; a small ship.—*vt.* To transport in a boat.—*vi.* To go in a boat.
**Boatman,** bōt'man, *n.* One who manages a boat.
**Boatswain,** bō'sn, *n.* A ship's officer who has charge of boats, sails, etc.
**Bob,** bob, *n.* A pendant; something that plays loosely; a short jerking motion; a docked tail; (slang) a shilling.—*vt.* (bobbing, bobbed). To move with a short jerking motion.—*vi.* To play backward and forward, or loosely.
**Bobbin,** bob'in, *n.* A small pin of wood to wind the thread on in weaving lace, etc.
**Bobbinet,** bob-in-et', *n.* A machine-made cotton net.
**Boche,** bosh, *n.* A German.
**Bode,** bōd, *vt.* (boding, boded). To portend; to be the omen of.—*vi.* To presage.
**Bodice,** bod'is, *n.* Something worn round the waist; a corset.
**Bodied,** bo'did, *a.* Having a body.
**Bodiless,** bo'di-les, *a.* Having no body.
**Bodily,** bo'di-li, *a.* Relating to the body; actual.—*adv.* Corporeally; entirely.
**Bodkin,** bod'kin, *n.* An instrument for piercing holes; a kind of large needle.
**Body,** bo'di, *n.* The trunk of an animal; main part; matter; a person; a system; strength; reality; any solid figure.—*vt.* (bodying, bodied). To give a body to; to embody (with *forth*).
**Body-guard,** bo'di-gärd, *n.* The guard that protects or defends the person.
**Boer,** bör, *n.* A Dutch colonist of S. Africa.
**Bog,** bog, *n.* A quagmire; a morass.—*vt.* (bogging, bogged). To whelm, as in mud.
**Bogey, Bogy,** bō'gi, *n.* A goblin.
**Boggle,** bog'l, *i* (boggling, boggled). To stop; to hesitate; to waver.
**Boggling,** bog'l-ing, *a.* Hesitating; bungling.
**Boggy,** bog'i, *a.* Containing bogs.
**Bogie, Bogey,** bō'gi, *n.* A four-wheeled truck supporting the front of a locomotive.
**Bogus,** bō'gus, *a.* Counterfeit; sham.
**Bohea,** bō-hē', *n.* A special kind of black tea.
**Bohemian,** bō-hē'mi-an, *n.* A native of Bohemia; a gypsy; an artist who leads an unconventional life.
**Boil,** boil, *vi.* To bubble from the action of heat; to seethe; to be cooked by boiling; to be in a state of agitation.—*vt.* To heat to a boiling state; to prepare by boiling.—*n.* A sore swelling or tumor.
**Boiler,** boil'ėr, *n.* One who boils; a vessel in which a thing is boiled, or steam generated.
**Boisterous,** bois'tėr-us, *a.* Stormy; noisy.
**Boisterously,** bois'tėr-us-li, *adv.* In a boisterous manner.
**Bold,** bōld, *a.* Daring; courageous; impudent; steep and abrupt.
**Boldly,** bōld'li, *adv.* In a bold manner.
**Boldness,** bōld'nes, *n.* Quality of being bold; intrepidity; assurance.
**Bole,** bōl, *n.* The body or stem of a tree; a kind of fine clay.
**Bolero,** bō-lär'ō, *n.* A Spanish dance.
**Boll,** bōl, *n.* A pod; an old Scottish dry measure of 6 bushels.—*vi.* To form into a pericarp.

**Bolshevik,** bol'shev-ik, *n.* The Russian name for the majority party in the 1903 split of the Social Democrats; revolutionists; extreme Socialists.
**Bolster,** bōl'stėr, *n.* A long pillow; a pad.—*vt.* To support with a bolster; to hold up; to maintain.
**Bolt,** bōlt, *n.* An arrow; a thunderbolt; a bar of a door; anything which fastens or secures.—*vi.* To leave suddenly.—*vt.* To fasten; to swallow hurriedly; to sift.
**Bolter,** bōlt'ėr, *n.* A machine for separating bran from flour.
**Bolt-upright,** bōlt'up-rīt, *a.* Perfectly upright.
**Bomb,** bom, *n.* An iron shell filled with explosive material.
**Bombard,** bom-bärd', *vt.* To attack with shot and shell.—*n.* An old short cannon.
**Bombardier,** bom-bärd-ēr', *n.* A non-commissioned officer who serves artillery.
**Bombardment,** bom-bärd'ment, *n.* The act of bombarding.
**Bombardon,** bom-bär'don, *n.* A large grave-toned trumpet.
**Bombast,** bom'bast, *n.* High-sounding words.
**Bombastic,** bom-bast'ik, *a.* Inflated; turgid.
**Bombastically,** bom-bas'tik-al-li, *adv.* In a bombastic or inflated manner.
**Bombazine, Bombasine,** bom-ba-zēn', *n.* A twilled fabric, with the warp silk and the weft worsted.
**Bona fide,** bō'na fī'dē, *adv.* and *a.* With good faith.
**Bon-bon,** bong-bong, *n.* A sweetmeat.
**Bond,** bond, *n.* That which binds; obligation; state of being bonded; a writing by which a person binds himself; in *pl.* chains; imprisonment.—*a.* In a servile state.—*vt.* To grant a bond in security for money; to store till duty is paid.
**Bondage,** bond'āj, *n.* Slavery; thraldom.
**Bonded,** bond'ed, *a.* Secured by bond; under a bond to pay duty; containing goods liable to duties.
**Bonder,** bon'dėr, *n.* One who bonds; one who deposits goods in a bonded warehouse.
**Bond-holder,** bond'hōld-ėr, *n.* A person who holds a bond for money lent.
**Bondman, Bondsman,** bond'man, bondz'man, *n.* A man slave.
**Bone,** bōn, *n.* A hard substance, forming the framework of an animal; something made of bone.—*vt.* (boning, boned). To take out bones from.
**Boned,** bōnd, *a.* Having bones; deprived of bones.
**Bonfire,** bon'fīr, *n.* A large fire in the open air expressive of joy.
**Bon-mot,** bong-mō, *n.* A witticism.
**Bonne,** bon, *n.* A French nursemaid.
**Bonnet,** bon'net, *n.* A dress for the head.
**Bonny,** bon'ni, *a.* Beautiful; blithe.
**Bonus,** bō'nus, *n.* A premium; extra dividend to shareholders.
**Bony,** bōn'i, *a.* Pertaining to or consisting of bones; full of bones; stout; strong.
**Bonze,** bonz, *n.* A Buddhist priest.
**Booby,** bö'bi, *n.* A dunce; a water-bird.
**Book,** buk, *n.* A printed or written literary work; a volume; division of a literary work.—*vt.* To enter in a book.
**Booking-office,** buk'ing-of-is, *n.* An office where passengers receive tickets, etc.
**Bookish,** buk'ish, *a.* Given to books or reading; fond of study.
**Book-keeper,** buk'kēp-ėr, *n.* One who keeps the accounts of a business house.
**Booklet,** buk'let, *n.* A little book.
**Book-maker,** buk'māk-ėr, *n.* One who compiles books; one who bets systematically.
**Bookseller,** buk'sel-ėr, *n.* One who sells books.
**Bookworm,** bük'wėrm, *n.* A worm that eats holes in books; a close student of books.
**Boom,** böm, *n.* A long pole to extend the bottom of a sail; a chain or bar across a river or mouth of a harbor; a hollow roar; briskness in commerce.—*vi.* To make a humming sound; to roar, as waves or cannon.
**Boomerang,** böm'e-rang, *n.* An Australian missile of hard wood, which can return to hit an object behind the thrower.
**Boon,** bön, *n.* Answer to a prayer; a favor, gift, or grant.—*a.* Merry; pleasant.
**Boor,** bör, *n.* A rustic; an ill-mannered or illiterate fellow.
**Boorish,** bör'ish, *a.* Clownish; rustic.
**Boose, Booze,** böz, *vi.* To drink largely.
**Boosy, Boozy,** bö'zi, *a.* A little intoxicated.
**Boot,** böt, *vt.* To benefit; to put on boots.—*n.* Profit; a covering for the foot and leg; *pl.* a male servant in a hotel.
**Booted,** böt'ed, *a.* Having boots on.
**Booth,** böᴛʜ, *n.* A temporary shed.
**Boot-jack,** böt'jak, *n.* An instrument for drawing off boots.
**Bootless,** böt'les, *a.* Unavailing; without boots.
**Boot-tree, Boot-last,** böt'trē, böt'last, *n.* An instrument for stretching a boot.
**Booty,** bö'ti, *n.* Spoil; plunder.
**Boracic,** bō-ras'ik, *a.* Relating to borax.
**Borax,** bō'raks, *n.* A salt found crude, or prepared from boracic acid and soda.
**Border,** bor'dėr, *n.* The outer edge of anything; boundary; margin.—*vi.* To approach near; to touch at the confines; to be contiguous.—*vt.* To surround with a border.
**Borderer,** bor'dėr-ėr, *n.* One who dwells on a border.
**Bore,** bōr, *vt.* (boring, bored). To make a hole in; to weary.—*vi.* To pierce.—*n.* The hole made by boring; the diameter of a round hole; a person or thing that wearies; a sudden rise of the tide in certain estuaries.
**Boreal,** bō'rē-al, *a.* Northern.
**Boreas,** bō'rē-as, *n.* The north wind.
**Borer,** bōr'ėr, *n.* One who or that which bores.
**Boric,** bō'rik, *a.* Same as *Boracic.*
**Born,** born, *pp.* of *bear,* to bring forth.
**Borne,** bōrn, *pp.* of *bear,* to carry.
**Borough,** bu'rō, *n.* A town with a municipal government.
**Borrow,** bo'rō, *vt.* To ask or receive as a loan; to appropriate.
**Borrower,** bo'rō-ėr, *n.* One who borrows.
**Bort,** bort, *n.* Fragments of diamonds.
**Boscage, Boskage,** bos'kāj, *n.* A mass of growing trees, groves, or thickets.
**Bosh,** bosh, *n.* Nonsense.
**Bosky,** bosk'i, *a.* Woody or bushy.
**Bosom,** bö'zum, *n.* The breast; the seat of the affections.—*vt.* To conceal.—*a.* Much beloved; confidential.
**Boss,** bos, *n.* A knob; an ornamental projection; a master.
**Bossy,** bos'i, *a.* Ornamented with bosses.
**Botanic, Botanical,** bō-tan'ik, bō-tan'ik-al, *a.* Pertaining to botany.
**Botanist,** bot'an-ist, *n.* One skilled in botany.
**Botanize,** bot'an-īz, *vi.* (botanizing, botanized). To study botany.
**Botany,** bot'a-ni, *n.* The science which treats of plants.
**Botch,** boch, *n.* A swelling on the skin; a clumsy patch; bungled work.—*vt.* To mend or perform clumsily.
**Botcher,** boch'ėr, *n.* One who botches.
**Botchy,** boch'i, *a.* Marked with botches.
**Both,** bōth, *a.* and *pron.* The two, taken by themselves; the pair.—*conj.* As well; on the one side.
**Bother,** boᴛʜ'ėr, *vt.* To annoy.—*vi.* To trouble oneself.—*n.* A trouble, vexation.
**Botheration,** boᴛʜ-ėr-ā'shon, *n.* The act of bothering; state of being bothered.
**Bothersome,** boᴛʜ'ėr-sum, *a.* Causing trouble.
**Bothie, Bothy,** both'i, *n.* In Scotland, a farm building for servants.
**Bott, Bot,** bot, *n.* A maggot found in the intestines of horses, etc.: generally in *pl.*
**Bottle,** bot'l, *n.* A narrow-mouthed vessel of glass, leather, etc., for liquor; the contents of a

bottle.—*vt.* (bottling, bottled). To put into a bottle or bottles.
**Bottle-nose,** bot'l-nōz, *n.* A kind of whale.
**Bottom,** bot'tom, *n.* The lowest part; the ground under water; foundation; a valley; native strength; a ship; dregs.—*vt.* To found or build upon.
**Bottomless,** bot'tom-les, *a.* Without a bottom; fathomless.
**Bottomry,** bot'tom-ri, *n.* The act of borrowing money on a ship.
**Boudoir,** bö-dwar', *n.* A lady's private room.
**Bough,** bou, *n.* A branch of a tree.
**Bougie,** bö-zhē, *n.* A wax-taper; a medical instrument.
**Bouilli,** bö-yē, *n.* Boiled or stewed meat.
**Boulder,** bōl'dėr, *n.* A large roundish stone.
**Boulevard,** böl-vär, *n.* A wide street planted with trees.
**Bounce,** bouns, *vi.* (bouncing, bounced). To spring or rush out suddenly; to thump; to boast or bully.—*n.* A strong sudden thump; a rebound; a boast.
**Bouncer,** bouns'ėr, *n.* A boaster; a liar.
**Bouncing,** bouns'ing, *p.a.* Big; strong; boasting.
**Bound,** bound, *n.* A boundary; a leap.—*vt.* To limit; to restrain.—*vi.* To leap; to rebound.—*p.a.* Obliged; sure.—*a.* Ready; destined.
**Boundary,** bound'a-ri, *n.* A mark designating a limit; border.
**Bounden,** bound'en, *a.* Obligatory.
**Bounder,** boun'dėr, *n.* A loud-mannered and vulgar person.
**Boundless,** bound'les, *a.* Unlimited.
**Bounteous,** boun'tē-us, *a.* Liberal; bountiful.
**Bounteously,** boun'tē-us-li, *adv.* Liberally; generously; largely.
**Bountiful,** boun'ti-ful, *a.* Munificent; generous.
**Bounty,** boun'ti, *n.* Liberality; generosity; a gratuity; premium to encourage trade.
**Bouquet,** bö-kā', *n.* A bunch of flowers; a nosegay; an agreeable aromatic odor.
**Bourgeois,** bur-jō', *n.* A small printing type.
**Bourgeois,** börzh-wa̤, *n.* A citizen; a man of middle rank.
**Bourgeoisie,** börzh-wa-zē, *n.* The middle classes, especially those dependent on trade.
**Bourn,** bōrn, *n.* A bound; a limit.
**Bourse,** börs, *n.* An exchange; a merchants' meeting-place for business.
**Bout,** bout, *n.* As much of an action as is performed at one time; turn; debauch.
**Bovine,** bō'vīn, *a.* Pertaining to oxen.
**Bow,** bou, *vt.* To bend; to bend the head or body in token of respect; to depress.—*vi.* To bend; to make a reverence; to yield.—*n.* A bending of the head or body, in token of respect; the rounding part of a ship's side forward.
**Bow,** bō, *n.* An instrument to shoot arrows; the rainbow; a curve; a fiddlestick; an ornamental knot.
**Bowdlerize,** bōd'lėr-īz, *vt.* To expurgate.
**Bowed,** bōd, *p.a.* Bent like a bow.
**Bowel,** bou'el, *n.* One of the intestines; *pl.* the intestines; the seat of pity; compassion.
**Bower,** bou'ėr, *n.* An anchor carried at the bow; a shady recess; an arbor.
**Bowry,** bou'ėr-i, *a.* Containing bowers; leafy.
**Bowie-knife,** bō'i-nīf, *n.* A knife from 10 to 15 inches long and about 2 inches broad.
**Bowl,** bōl, *n.* A large roundish cup; a ball, of wood, etc.; used for rolling on a level plat of ground; *pl.* the game played with such bowls.—*vi.* To play with bowls; to deliver a ball at cricket; to move rapidly.—*vt.* To roll as a bowl; to deliver (a ball) at cricket, etc.
**Bow-legged,** bō'legd, *a.* With crooked legs.
**Bowler,** bōl'ėr, *n.* One who bowls; a round-shaped felt hat.
**Bowline,** bō'līn, *n.* A rope to make a sail stand towards the bow to catch the wind.
**Bowling,** bōl'ing, *n.* Act or art of playing with bowls; art or style of a bowler.
**Bowling-green,** bōl'ing-grēn, *n.* A level piece of ground for bowling.
**Bowman,** bō'man, *n.* An archer.
**Bowshot,** bō'shot, *n.* The distance which an arrow flies when shot from a bow.
**Bowsprit,** bō'sprit, *n.* A large spar which projects over the bow of a ship.
**Bow-window,** bō'win-dō, *n.* A bay-window.
**Box,** boks, *n.* A case of wood, metal, etc.; quantity that a case contains; a seat in a playhouse, etc.; driver's seat on a coach; a sportsman's house; a blow on the ear; a tree or shrub, yielding a hard wood.—*vt.* To put in a box; to strike with the hand.—*vi.* To fight with the fists.
**Boxen,** boks'en, *a.* Made of boxwood.
**Boxer,** boks'ėr, *n.* One who boxes; a pugilist.
**Boxing,** boks'ing, *n.* The act or art of fighting with the fists; pugilism.
**Boxwood,** boks'wud, *n.* The hard-grained wood of the box-tree; the plant itself.
**Boy,** boi, *n.* A male child; a lad.
**Boycott,** boi'kot, *vt.* To combine in refusing to have dealings with.
**Boyhood,** boi'hud, *n.* The state of a boy.
**Boyish,** boi'ish, *a.* Like a boy; puerile.
**Boy Scout,** boi skout, *n.* A member of an organization founded in England in 1908 by Lord Baden-Powell with the object of promoting good citizenship.
**Brace,** brās, *n.* That which holds; a bandage; a couple.—*vt.* (bracing, braced). To tighten; to strain up; to strengthen.
**Bracelet,** brās'let, *n.* An ornament for the wrist.
**Brachial,** brā'ki-al, *a.* Belonging to the arm.
**Bracing,** brās'ing, *a.* Invigorating.
**Bracken,** brak'en, *n.* A kind of large fern.
**Bracket,** brak'et, *n.* A support for something fixed to a wall; a mark in printing to enclose words, etc.—*vt.* To place within or connect by brackets.
**Bracketing,** brak'et-ing. *n.* A series of brackets for the support of something.
**Brackish,** brak'ish, *a.* Salt; saltish.
**Bract,** brakt, *n.* An irregularly developed leaf at the base of a flower.
**Brad,** brad, *n.* A small nail with no head.
**Brae,** brā, *n.* A slope; an acclivity.
**Brag,** brag, *vi.* (bragging, bragged). To bluster; to talk big.—*n.* A boast.
**Braggadocio,** brag-a-dō'shi-ō, *n.* A boasting fellow; boastful words.
**Braggart,** brag'ärt, *a.* Boastful.—*n.* A boaster.
**Brahman, Brahmin,** brä'man, brä'min, *n.* A Hindu of the sacerdotal caste.
**Brahmanism, Brahminism,** brä'man-izm, brä'min-izm, *n.* The religion of the Brahmans.
**Braid,** brād, *vt.* To weave, knit, or wreathe; to intertwine.—*n.* A narrow woven band of silk, cotton, etc.; something braided.
**Braided,** brād'ed, *a.* Edged with braid.
**Brail,** brāl, *n.* A small rope attached to sails.—*vt.* To haul in by means of brails (with *up*).
**Braille,** brāl, *n.* A system of reading with raised letters for the blind.
**Brain,** brān, The nervous matter within the skull; seat of sensation and of the intellect; the understanding.—*vt.* To dash out the brains of.
**Brainless,** brān'les, *a.* Silly; thoughtless.
**Brain-sick,** brān'sik, *a.* Disordered in the understanding; crazed.
**Braise, Braize,** brāz, *vt.* (braising, braised). To cook with herbs, etc., in a close pan.
**Brake,** brāk, *n.* A place overgrown with brushwood, etc.; a thicket; the bracken; an instrument to break flax; a harrow for breaking clods; a contrivance for retarding the motion of wheels; a large wagonette.
**Braky,** brāk'i, *a.* Full of brakes; thorny.
**Bramble,** bram'bl, *n.* A prickly shrub of the rose family; its berry.
**Bran,** bran, *n.* The husks of ground corn.
**Branch,** bransh, *n.* The shoot of a tree or plant; the offshoot of anything, as of a river, family,

etc.; a limb.—*vi.* To spread in branches.—*vt.* To divide or form into branches.
**Branchy,** bransh'i, *a.* Full of branches.
**Brand,** brand, *n.* A burning piece of wood; a sword; a mark made with a hot iron; a note of infamy; a trade-mark; a kind or quality.—*vt.* To mark with a hot iron; to stigmatize as infamous.
**Brandish,** brand'ish, *vt.* To shake, wave, or flourish.—*n.* A waving; a flourish.
**Brandling,** brand'ling, *n.* The parr of the salmon; a small red worm.
**Brand-new, Bran-new,** brand'nū, bran'nū, *a.* Quite new.
**Brandy,** bran'di, *n.* An ardent spirit distilled from wine.
**Brangle,** brang'gl, *n.* A squabble; a wrangle.—*vi.* (brangling, brangled). To wrangle.
**Brank,** brangk, *n.* Buckwheat.
**Brash,** brash, *n.* A confused heap of fragments; small fragments of crushed ice.
**Brasier,** brā'zhėr, *n.* One who works in brass; a pan for holding coals.
**Brass,** bras, *n.* A yellow alloy of copper and zinc; a utensil, etc., made of brass; impudence.
**Brassard,** bras'ard, *n.* A badge worn on the arm; an armlet.
**Brassy,** bras'i, *a.* Made of brass; like brass.
**Brat,** brat, *n.* A child, so called in contempt.
**Brattice,** brat'is, *n.* A partition in coal-mines for ventilation; a fence round machinery.
**Bravado,** bra-vā'dō, *n.* A boast or brag; would-be boldness.
**Brave,** brāv, *a.* Daring; bold; valiant; noble.—*n.* A daring person; a savage warrior.—*vt.* (braving, braved). To challenge; to defy; to encounter with courage.
**Bravely,** brāv'li, *adv.* Courageously.
**Bravery,** brāv'ė-ri, *n.* Courage; heroism.
**Bravo,** brä'vō, *n.* A bandit; an assassin.—*interj.* Well done!
**Brawl,** bral, *vi.* To quarrel noisily.—*n.* A noisy quarrel; uproar.
**Brawler,** bral'er, *n.* A noisy fellow.
**Brawling,** bral'ing, *p.a.* Quarrelsome.
**Brawn,** bran, *n.* The flesh of a boar; the muscular part of the body; muscle.
**Brawny,** bran'i, *a.* Muscular; fleshy.
**Bray,** brā, *vt.* To beat or grind small.—*vi.* To make a loud harsh sound, as an ass.—*n.* The cry of an ass.
**Braze,** brāz, *vt.* (brazing, brazed). To cover with brass; to solder with brass.
**Brazen,** brāz'n, *a.* Made of brass; impudent.—*vt.* To behave with insolence (with *it*).
**Brazen-faced,** brāz'n-fāst, *a.* Impudent; bold to excess; shameless.
**Brazier,** brā'zi-ėr, *n.* *See* BRASIER.
**Breach,** brēch, *n.* The act of breaking, or state of being broken; infringement; quarrel.—*vt.* To make a breach or opening in.
**Bread,** bred, *n.* Food made of flour or meal baked; food; sustenance.
**Bread-corn,** bred'korn, *n.* Corn of which bread is made.
**Breadfruit-tree,** bred'fröt-trē, *n.* A tree of the Pacific Islands, producing a fruit which forms a substitute for bread.
**Breadstuff,** bred'stuf, *n.* Bread-corn; that from which bread is made.
**Breadth,** bredth, *n.* The measure across any plane surface; width; liberality.
**Break,** brāk, *vt.* (breaking, pret. broke, pp. broke, broken). To sever by fracture; to rend; to open; to tame; to make bankrupt; to discard; to interrupt; to dissolve any union; to tell with discretion.—*vi.* To come to pieces; to burst; to burst forth; to dawn; to become bankrupt; to decline in vigor; to change in tone.—*n.* An opening; breach; pause; the dawn; a brake for vehicles; a large wagonette.
**Breakage,** brāk'āj, *n.* A breaking; damage by breaking; allowance for things broken.
**Break-down,** brāk'doun, *n.* An accident; a downfall; a lively dance.
**Breaker,** brāk'ėr, *n.* One who or that which breaks; a rock; a wave broken by rocks.
**Breakfast,** brek'fast, *n.* The first meal in the day.—*vi.* To eat the first meal in the day.—*vt.* To furnish with breakfast.
**Break-neck,** brāk'nek, *a.* Steep and dangerous; dangerously fast.
**Break-up,** brāk'up, *n.* Disruption; dissolution.
**Breakwater,** brāk'wa-tėr, *n.* A mole to break the force of the waves.
**Bream,** brēm, *n.* A fish.—*vt.* To clean a ship's bottom by means of fire.
**Breast,** brest, *n.* The fore part of the body, between the neck and the belly; the heart; the conscience; the affections.—*vt.* To bear the breast against; to meet in front.
**Breast-bone,** brest'bōn, *n.* The bone of the breast.
**Breast-knot,** brest'not, *n.* A knot of ribbons worn on the breast.
**Breastplate,** brest'plāt, *n.* Armor for the breast.
**Breath,** breth, *n.* The air drawn into and expelled from the lungs; life; a single respiration; pause; a gentle breeze.
**Breathe,** brēTH, *vi.* (breathing, breathed). To draw into the eject air from the lungs; to live; to take breath; to rest.—*vt.* To inspire and exhale; to infuse; to utter softly or in private; to suffer to take breath.
**Breathing,** brēTH'ing, *n.* Respiration; inspiration; breathing-pace; an aspirate.
**Breathless,** breth'les, *a.* Being out of breath; spent with labor; dead.
**Breccia,** brech'i-a, *n.* A compound of fragments of rock united by a matrix or cement.
**Bred,** bred, *pp.* of *breed.*
**Breech,** brēch, *n.* The lower part of the body behind; the hinder part of a gun, etc.—*vt.* To put into breeches.
**Breeches,** brēch'ez, *n.pl.* A garment worn by men on the legs.
**Breed,** brēd, *vt.* (breeding, bred). To bring up; to educate; to engender; to bring forth; to occasion; to rear, as live stock.—*vi.* To produce offspring; to be with young; to be produced.—*n.* Offspring; kind; a brood.
**Breeder,** brēd'ėr, *n.* One that breeds.
**Breeding,** brēd'ing, *n.* The raising of a breed or breeds; education; deportment.
**Breeze,** brēz, *n.* A light wind.
**Breezy,** brēz'i, *a.* Subject to breezes; airy.
**Bren gun,** bren gun, *n.* A light machine-gun, fired from a bipod or tripod, and capable of firing 120 rounds a minute.
**Brethren,** breTH'ren, *n.pl.* of *brother.*
**Breton,** bret'on, *a.* Relating to Brittany.—*n.* The native language of Brittany.
**Brettice,** bret'is, *n.* *See* BRATTICE.
**Breve,** brēv, *n.* A written mandate; a note of time equal to four minims.
**Brevet,** brev'et, *n.* A commission entitling an officer to rank above his actual rank or pay.—*a.* Taking rank by brevet.
**Breviary,** brē'vi-a-ri, *n.* A book containing the daily service of the R. Catholic Church.
**Brevier,** brē-vēr', *n.* A small printing type.
**Brevity,** bre'vi-ti, *n.* Shortness; conciseness.
**Brew,** brö, *vt.* To prepare, as ale or beer, from malt, etc.; to concoct; to plot.—*vi.* To make beer; to be forming.—*n.* The mixture formed by brewing.
**Brewage,** brö'āj, *n.* Drink brewed.
**Brewer,** brö'ėr, *n.* One who brews.
**Brewery,** brö'ė-ri, *n.* A house where brewing is carried on.
**Brewing,** brö'ing, *n.* The act of making beer; the quantity brewed at once.
**Briar,** brī'ar, *n.* The root of the white heath, used extensively in the manufacture of tobacco-pipes.
**Bribe,** brīb, *n.* A gift to corrupt the conduct or

judgment.—*vt.* (bribing, bribed). To gain over by bribes.
**Briber,** brīb'ėr, *n.* One who gives bribes.
**Bribery,** brīb'ė-ri, *n.* The act or practice of giving or taking bribes.
**Bric-à-brac,** brik-a-brak, *n.* Articles of interest or value from rarity, antiquity, etc.
**Brick,** brik, *n.* A rectangular mass of burned clay, used in building, etc.; a loaf shaped like a brick.—*a.* Made of brick.—*vt.* To lay with bricks.
**Brickbat,** brik'bat, *n.* A piece of a brick.
**Brick-field,** brik'fēld, *n.* A field or yard where bricks are made.
**Brick-kiln,** brik'kiln, *n.* A kiln or furnace in which bricks are burned.
**Bricklayer,** brik'lā-ėr, *n.* One who builds with bricks.
**Brickwork,** brik'wėrk, *n.* Built work of bricks; place where bricks are made.
**Bridal,** brīd'al, *n.* A wedding-feast; a wedding.—*a.* Belonging to a bride or to a wedding.
**Bride,** brīd, *n.* A woman about to be or newly married.
**Brides-cake,** brīdz'kāk, *n.* The cake made for a wedding.
**Bridegroom,** brīd'gröm, *n.* A man about to be or newly married.
**Bride's-maid,** brīdz'mād, *n.* A woman who attends on a bride at her wedding.
**Bridewell,** brīd'wel, *n.* A house of hard labor for offenders.
**Bridge,** brij, *n.* A structure across a river, etc., to furnish a passage; the upper part of the nose.—*vt.* (bridging, bridged). To build a bridge over.
**Bridge,** brij, *n.* A game of cards resembling whist.
**Bridgehead,** brij'hed, *n.* Defensive work protecting approach to a bridge on side nearest to the enemy.
**Bridle,** brī'dl, *n.* The part of harness with which a horse is governed; a curb; a check.—*vt.* (bridling, bridled). To put a bridle on; to restrain.—*vi.* To hold up the head and draw in the chin.
**Brief,** brēf, *a.* Short; concise.—*n.* A short writing; a writ or precept; an abridgment of a client's case.
**Briefless,** brēf'les, *a.* Having no brief.
**Briefly,** brēf'li, *adv.* Concisely.
**Brier,** brī'ėr, *n.* A prickly shrub, species of the rose.
**Briery,** brī'ėr-i, *a.* Full of briers; rough.
**Brig,** brig, *n.* A vessel with two masts, square-rigged.
**Brigade,** bri-gād', *n.* A body of troops consisting of several battalions. **Brigade-major,** *n.* The principal staff-officer of a brigadier, usually a captain in rank.
**Brigadier,** bri-ga-dėr', *n.* The officer who commands a brigade.
**Brigand,** bri'gand, *n.* A freebooter.
**Brigandage,** bri'gand-āj, *n.* The practice of brigands; highway robbery; plunder.
**Brigantine,** brig'an-tīn, *n.* A light swift vessel, two-masted and square-rigged.
**Bright,** brīt, *a.* Clear; shining; glittering; acute; witty; lively; cheerful.
**Brighten,** brīt'n, *vt.* To make bright or brighter.—*vi.* To become bright; to clear up.
**Brightly,** brīt'li, *adv.* With luster; cheerfully.
**Brill,** bril, *n.* A fish allied to the turbot.
**Brilliance, Brilliancy,** bril'yans, bril'yan-si, *n.* State of being brilliant; splendor.
**Brilliant,** bril'yant, *a.* Shining; sparkling; splendid; of great talents.—*n.* A diamond of the finest cut; a small printing type.
**Brilliantly,** bril'yant-li, *adv.* Splendidly.
**Brim,** brim, *n.* The rim of anything; the upper edge of the mouth of a vessel.—*vi.* (brimming, brimmed). To be full to the brim.
**Brimful,** brim'ful, *a.* Full to the brim.
**Brimmer,** brim'ėr, *n.* A bowl full to the top.
**Brimstone,** brim'stōn, *n.* Sulphur.
**Brindled,** brind'ld, *a.* Marked with brown streaks.
**Brine,** brīn, *n.* Salt water; the sea.
**Bring,** bring, *vt.* (bringing, brought). To lead or cause to come; to fetch; to produce; to attract; to prevail upon.
**Bringer,** bring'ėr, *n.* One who brings.
**Brink,** bringk, *n.* The edge of a steep place.
**Briny,** brīn'i, *a.* Pertaining to brine.
**Briquette,** bri-ket', *n.* A lump of fuel, in the form of a brick, made from coal-dust.
**Brisk,** brisk, *a.* Lively; bright; effervescing.
**Brisket,** brisk'et, *n.* The breast of an animal, or that part next to the ribs.
**Briskly,** brisk'li, *adv.* Actively; vigorously.
**Bristle,** bris'l, *n.* A stiff hair of swine; stiff hair of any kind.—*vt.* (bristling, bristled). To erect in bristles.—*vi.* To stand erect, as bristles; to show anger, etc.
**Bristly,** bris'li, *a.* Thick set with bristles.
**Britannia-metal,** bri-tan'i-a-met-al, *n.* An alloy of tin, with copper and antimony.
**Britannic,** bri-tan'ik, *a.* Pertaining to Britain.
**British,** brit'ish, *a.* Pertaining to Britain or its inhabitants.
**Briton,** brit'on, *n.* A native of Britain.
**Brittle,** brit'l, *a.* Apt to break; not tough or tenacious.—*vt.* To cut up a deer.
**Broach,** brōch, *n.* A spit; a brooch.—*vt.* To pierce, as with a spit; to tap; to open up; to publish first.
**Broacher,** brōch'ėr, *n.* One who broaches; a spit.
**Broad,** brad, *a.* Having extent from side to side; wide; unrestricted; indelicate.
**Broadcasting,** brad'kast-ing, *n.* In wireless telegraphy, a system by which listeners provided with suitable receivers can hear items of music and speech transmitted at definite wavelengths from certain central stations.
**Broaden,** brad'n, *vi.* To grow broad.—*vt.* To make broad.
**Broadside,** brad'sīd, *n.* A discharge of all the guns on one side of a ship; a sheet of paper printed on one side.
**Broadsword,** brad'sōrd, *n.* A sword with a broad blade and a cutting edge.
**Brocade,** brō-kād', *n.* A silk or satin stuff variegated with gold and silver.
**Brocaded,** brō-kād'ed, *a.* Worked like brocade; dressed in brocade.
**Brocard,** bro-kärd', *n.* A law maxim; a canon.
**Broccoli,** brok'o-li, *n.* A kind of cauliflower.
**Brochure,** brō-shör', *n.* A pamphlet.
**Brock,** brok, *n.* A badger.
**Brocket,** brok'et, *n.* A stag in its second year.
**Brogue,** brōg, *n.* A shoe or raw hide; the pronunciation of English peculiar to the Irish.
**Broider,** broid'ėr, *vt.* To embroider.
**Broil,** broil, *n.* A brawl; a noisy quarrel.—*vt.* To cook over a fire; to subject to strong heat.—*vi.* To be subjected to heat; to be greatly heated.
**Broken,** brōk'n, *a.* Subdued; bankrupt.
**Broker,** brō'kėr, *n.* An agent who buys and sells for others; a pawn-broker.
**Brokerage,** bro'kėr-āj, *n.* The business of a broker; the pay or commission of a broker.
**Bromide,** brō'mid, *n.* A compound of bromine with another element.
**Bromine,** brō'mīn or brō'min, *n.* A simple non-metallic element with a rank odor.
**Bronchial,** brong'ki-al, *a.* Belonging to the tubes branching from the windpipe through the lungs.
**Bronchitis,** brong-kī'tis, *n.* Inflammation of the bronchial tubes.
**Bronze,** bronz, *n.* An alloy of copper and tin; a color to imitate bronze; a figure made of bronze.—*vt.* (bronzing, bronzed). To make appear on the surface like bronze.
**Bronzed,** bronzd, *p.a.* Made to resemble bronze.
**Brooch,** brōch, *n.* An ornamental pin or buckle used to fasten dress.
**Brood,** bröd, *vi.* To sit on eggs; to ponder anxiously (with *over* or *on*).—*n.* That which is bred;

B

birds of one hatching; offspring.
**Brook,** bruk, *n.* A natural stream smaller than a river.—*vt.* To bear; to endure.
**Brooklet,** bruk'let, *n.* A small brook.
**Broom,** bröm, *n.* A shrub with yellow flowers and angular branches; a brush.
**Broomy,** bröm'i, *a.* Full of broom.
**Broth,** broth, *n.* Liquor in which flesh, or some other substance, has been boiled.
**Brothel,** broth'el, *n.* A house of ill-fame.
**Brother,** bruTH'ėr, *n.*; pl. **Brothers, Brethren,** bruTH'ėrz, breTH'ren. A male born of the same parents; an associate; a fellow-creature.
**Brotherhood,** bruTH'ėr-hud, *n.* The state or quality of being a brother; an association.
**Brotherly,** bruTH'ėr-li, *a.* Like a brother.
**Brougham,** bröm or brö'am, *n.* A one-horse close carriage.
**Brow,** brou, *n.* The ridge over the eye; the forehead; the edge of a steep place.
**Browbeat,** brou'bēt, *vt.* To bear down with stern looks or arrogant speech.
**Brown,** broun, *a.* Of a dusky color, inclining to red.—*n.* A color resulting from the mixture of red, black, and yellow.—*vt.* To make brown.
**Brownie,** brou'ni, *n.* A domestic spirit of benevolent character; a junior Girl Guide, between the ages of 8 and 11.
**Brownish,** broun'ish, *a.* Somewhat brown.
**Brown-study,** broun'stu-di, *n.* Deep meditation; reverie.
**Browse,** brouz, *vt.* (browsing, browsed). To pasture or feed upon.—*vi.* To crop and eat food.
**Bruin,** brö'in, *n.* A familiar name of a bear.
**Bruise,** bröz, *vt.* (bruising, bruised). To crush; to make a contusion on.—*n.* A contusion; a hurt from a blow.
**Bruiser,** bröz'ėr, *n.* A boxer; a prize-fighter.
**Bruit,** bröt, *n.* Report; rumor.—*vt.* To noise abroad.
**Brumal,** brö'mal, *a.* Belonging to winter.
**Brunette,** brö-net', *n.* A woman with a brownish or dark complexion.
**Brunt,** brunt, *n.* The heat of battle; onset; shock.
**Brush,** brush, *n.* An instrument to clean by rubbing or sweeping; a painter's large pencil; a skirmish; a thicket; the tail of a fox.—*vt.* To sweep, rub, or paint with a brush; to touch lightly in passing.—*vi.* To move nimbly or in haste; to skim.
**Brushwood,** brush'wud, *n.* Small trees and shrubs growing together.
**Brushy,** brush'i, *a.* Rough; shaggy.
**Brusque,** brusk, *a.* Abrupt in manner; rude.
**Brussels-sprouts,** brus'elz-sprouts, *n.pl.* A variety of cabbage.
**Brutal,** bröt'al, *a.* Cruel; ferocious.
**Brutality,** bröt-al'i-ti, *n.* Quality of being brutal; savageness; cruelty.
**Brutalize,** bröt-al-īz, *vt.* (brutalizing, brutalized). To make brutal.—*vi.* To become brutal.
**Brutally,** bröt'al-li, *adv.* In a brutal manner.
**Brute,** bröt, *a.* Senseless; bestial; uncivilized.—*n.* A beast; a brutal person.
**Brutish,** bröt'ish, *a.* Brutal; grossly sensual.
**Bubble,** bub'bl, *n.* A small vesicle of fluid inflated with air; a vain project; a swindle.—*vi.* (bubbling, bubbled). To rise in bubbles.—*vt.* To cheat; to swindle.
**Bubo,** bū'bō, *n.*; pl. **-oes.** A swelling or abscess in a glandular part of the body.
**Bubonic,** bū-bon'ik, *a.* Pertaining to bubo.
**Buccaneer,** buk-a-nēr', *n.* A pirate.
**Buccaneering,** buk-a-nēr'ing, *n.* The employment of buccaneers.
**Buck,** buk, *n.* The male of deer, goats, etc.; a gay young fellow; a lye for steeping clothes in.—*vt.* To steep in lye.—*vi.* To leap, as a horse, so as to dismount the rider.
**Bucket,** buk'et, *n.* A vessel in which water is drawn or carried.
**Buck-jumper,** buk'jump-ėr, *n.* A horse that bucks so as to dismount its rider.
**Buckle,** buk'l, *n.* An instrument to fasten straps, etc.—*vt.* (buckling, buckled). To fasten with a buckle; to bend or warp.—*vi.* To apply with vigor (with *to*).
**Buckler,** buk'lėr, *n.* A small round shield.—*vt.* To shield; to defend.
**Buckram,** buk'ram, *n.* A coarse linen cloth stiffened with glue.—*a.* Stiff; formal.
**Buck-shot,** buk'shot, *n.* A large kind of shot used for killing large game.
**Buckthorn,** buk'thorn, *n.* A shrub bearing a purging berry, also used in dyeing.
**Buckwheat,** buk'whēt, *n.* A plant bearing small seeds which are ground into meal.
**Bucolic,** bū-kol'ik, *a.* Pastoral.—*n.* A pastoral poem.
**Bud,** bud, *n.* The first shoot of a leaf, etc.; a germ.—*vi.* (budding, budded). To put forth buds or germs; to begin to grow.—*vt.* To graft by inserting a bud.
**Buddhism,** bud'izm, *n.* The religion founded in India by Buddha.
**Buddhist,** bud'ist, *n.* One who adheres to Buddhism.
**Budding,** bud'ing, *n.* A mode of grafting buds.
**Budge,** buj, *vt.* (budging, budged). To move; to stir.
**Budgerigar,** bud'jer-ē-gär'', *n.* The grass or zebra parakeet; the Australian love-bird.
**Budget,** buj'et, *n.* A little sack with its contents; a stock; the annual statement respecting the British finances.
**Buff,** buf, *n.* Leather prepared from the skin of the buffalo, elk, etc.; a dull light yellow.—*a.* Light yellow; made of buff.
**Buffalo,** buf'fa-lō, *n.* A species of ox, larger than the common ox; the American bison.
**Buffer,** buf'ėr, *n.* An apparatus for deadening concussion.
**Buffet,** buf'et, *n.* A cupboard for wine, glasses, etc.; a place for refreshments (pron. bu-fe).
**Buffet,** buf'et, *n.* A blow; a slap.—*vt.* To beat; to box; to contend against.
**Buffo,** buf'fō, *n.* A comic actor in an opera.
**Buffoon,** buf-fön', *n.* One who makes sport by low jests and antic gestures; a droll.
**Buffoonery,** buf-fön'ė-ri, *n.* The arts and practices of a buffoon.
**Bug,** bug, *n.* A name for various insects, particularly one infesting houses and inflicting severe bites.
**Bugbear,** bug'bār, *n.* Something real or imaginary that causes terror.
**Buggy,** bug'i, *n.* A light one-horse carriage.
**Bugle,** bū'gl, *n.* A hunting-horn; a military instrument of music; a long glass bead, commonly black.
**Bugler,** bū'glėr, *n.* A soldier who conveys officers' commands by sounding a bugle.
**Buhl,** böl, *n.* Unburnished gold or brass used for inlaying; articles so ornamented.
**Build,** bild, *vt.* (building, built). To construct; to raise on a foundation; to establish.—*vi.* To form a structure.—*n.* Construction; make; form.
**Builder,** bild'ėr, *n.* One who builds.
**Building,** bild'ing, *n.* The art of constructing edifices; an edifice.
**Bulb,** bulb, *n.* A round root; a round protuberance.
**Bulbous,** bulb'us, *a.* Pertaining to a bulb; swelling out.
**Bulbul,** bul'bul, *n.* The Persian nightingale.
**Bulge,** bulj, *n.* A swelling; bilge.—*vi.* (bulging, bulged). To swell out; to be protuberant.
**Bulk,** bulk, *n.* Magnitude; the majority; extent.
**Bulky,** bulk'i, *a.* Of great bulk.
**Bull,** bul, *n.* The male of cattle; a sign of the zodiac; one who raises the price of stock; a letter or edict of the pope; a ludicrous contradiction in language.
**Bullace,** bul'ās, *n.* A British wild plum.
**Bull-baiting,** bul'bāt-ing, *n.* The practice of baiting or attacking bulls with dogs.
**Bull-dog,** bul'dog, *n.* A species of dog.

**Bulldozer,** bul'dōz-ėr, *n.* A machine provided with a blade for spreading and levelling material.
**Bullet,** bul'et, *n.* A small ball; a conical projectile generally of lead intended to be discharged from small-arms.
**Bulletin,** bul'e-tin, *n.* An official report.
**Bull-fight,** bul'fīt, *n.* A combat between armed men and bulls in a closed arena.
**Bullfinch,** bul'finsh, *n.* A British song-bird.
**Bull-frog,** bul'frog, *n.* A large species of frog in N. America, with a loud bass voice.
**Bullion,** bul'yon, *n.* Uncoined gold or silver.
**Bullock,** bul'ok, *n.* An ox or castrated bull.
**Bull's-eye,** bulz'ī, *n.* A circular opening for light or air; the centre of a target.
**Bull-trout,** bul'trout, *n.* A large species of trout.
**Bully,** bul'i, *n.* An overbearing quarrelsome fellow.—*vt.* (bullying, bullied). To insult and overbear.—*vi.* To bluster or domineer.
**Bulrush,** bul'rush, *n.* A large, strong kind of rush.
**Bulwark,** bul'wėrk, *n.* A bastion; a fortification; a means of defense or safety.
**Bumbailiff,** bum-bā'lif, *n.* An under-bailiff.
**Bumble-bee,** bum'bl-bē, *n.* A large bee.
**Bum-boat,** bum'bōt, *n.* A small boat for carrying provisions to a ship.
**Bump,** bump, *n.* A heavy blow, or the noise of it; a lump produced by a blow.—*vi.* To make a loud, heavy, or hollow noise.—*vt.* To strike heavily against.
**Bumper,** bump'ėr, *n.* A cup or glass filled to the brim; something completely filled.
**Bumpkin,** bump'kin, *n.* An awkward rustic; a lout.
**Bumptious,** bump'shus, *a.* Self-assertive.
**Bun,** bun, *n.* A kind of cake or sweet bread.
**Bunch,** bunsh, *n.* A knob or lump; a cluster.—*vi.* To swell out in a protuberance; to cluster.
**Bunchy,** bunsh'i, *a.* Like a bunch.
**Bundle,** bun'dl, *n.* A number of things bound together; a package.—*vt.* (bundling, bundled). To tie in a bundle; to dispose of hurriedly.—*vi.* To depart hurriedly (with *off*).
**Bung,** bung, *n.* The stopper of a cask.—*vt.* To stop with a bung; to close up.
**Bungalow,** bung'ga-lō, *n.* A single-storied house.
**Bungle,** bung'gl, *vi.* (bungling, bungled). To perform in a clumsy manner.—*vt.* To make or mend clumsily; to manage awkwardly.—*n.* A clumsy performance.
**Bungler,** bung'gl-ėr, *n.* A clumsy workman.
**Bungling,** bung'gl-ing, *p.a.* Clumsy; awkwardly done.
**Bunk,** bungk, *n.* A wooden box serving as a seat and bed; a sleeping berth.
**Bunker,** bung'kėr, *n.* A large bin or receptacle; a sandy hollow on a golf course.
**Bunkum, Buncombe,** bung'kum, *n.* Talking for talking's sake; mere words.
**Bunting,** bunt'ing, *n.* A bird allied to finches and sparrows; stuff of which flags are made; flags.
**Bunyon, Bunion,** bun'yon, *n.* An excrescence on some of the joints of the feet.
**Buoy,** boi, *n.* A floating mark to point out shoals, etc.; something to keep a person or thing up in the water.—*vt.* To keep afloat; to bear up.—*vi.* To float.
**Buoyancy,** boi'an-si, *n.* The quality of being buoyant; vivacity; cheerfulness.
**Buoyant,** boi'ant, *a.* Floating; light; elastic.
**Bur,** bėr, *n.* The rough prickly head of the burdock, chestnut, etc. *See* Burr.
**Burden, Burthen,** bėr'dn, bėr'THn, *n.* That which is borne; load; freight; that which is oppressive; chorus of a song; that which is often repeated.—*vt.* To load; to oppress.
**Burdensome,** bėr'dn-sum, *a.* Heavy; oppressive.
**Burdock,** bėr'dok, *n.* A plant with a rough prickly head.
**Bureau,** bū-rō', *n.*; pl. **-eaux,** -rōz, or **-eaus.** A writing table with drawers; an office or court; a government office.
**Bureaucracy,** bū-rō'kra-si, *n.* Centralized administration of a country, through regularly graded officials; such officials collectively.
**Burgeon,** bėr'jon, *n.* A bud, shoot, sprout.
**Burgess,** bėr'jes, *n.* An inhabitant, freeman, or parliamentary representative of a borough.
**Burglar,** bėrg'lėr, *n.* One who robs a house by night.
**Burglarious,** bėrg-lā'ri-us, *a.* Pertaining to burglary.
**Burglary,** bėrg'la-ri, *n.* Act of nocturnal house-breaking.
**Burgundy,** bėr'gun-di, *n.* A kind of wine, so called from Burgundy in France.
**Burial,** be'ri-al, *n.* Act of burying; interment.
**Burin,** bū'rin, *n.* A tool for engraving.
**Burlesque,** bėr-lesk', *a.* Tending to excite laughter.—*n.* A composition tending to excite laughter; caricature.—*vt.* (burlesquing, burlesqued). To turn into ridicule; to make ludicrous.
**Burly,** bėr'li, *a.* Great in size; boisterous.
**Burmese,** bur'mēz, *a.* Pertaining to Burma.—*n.* An inhabitant or inhabitants of Burma; their language.
**Burn,** bėrn, *vt.* (burning, burnt or burned). To consume with fire; to scorch; to inflame; to harden by fire.—*vi.* To be on fire; to be inflamed with desire; to rage fiercely.—*n.* A hurt caused by fire; a rivulet.
**Burner,** bėrn'ėr, *n.* One who burns; that which gives out light or flame.
**Burning,** bėrn'ing, *p.a.* Fiery; vehement.
**Burning-glass,** bėrn'ing-glas, *n.* A glass which collects the rays of the sun into a focus, producing an intense heat.
**Burnish,** bėr'nish, *vt.* To polish.—*vi.* To grow bright or glossy.—*n.* Gloss; luster.
**Burnt-offering,** bėrnt'of-fėr-ing, *n.* A sacrifice burnt on an altar.
**Burr,** bėr, *n.* A guttural sounding of the letter *r*; a rough or projecting ridge; bur.
**Burrow,** bu'rō, *n.* A hole in the earth made by rabbits, etc.—*vi.* To excavate a hole underground; to hide.
**Burst,** bėrst, *vi.* (bursting, burst). To fly or break open; to rush forth; to come with violence.—*vt.* To break by force; to open suddenly.—*n.* A violent disruption; a rupture.
**Burthen,** bėr'THn. *See* Burden.
**Bury,** be'ri, *vt.* (burying, buried). To put into a grave; to overwhelm; to hide.
**Bus,** bus, *n.*; pl. **Buses.** An omnibus.
**Busby,** buz'bi, *n.* A military head-dress.
**Bush,** bush, *n.* A shrub with branches; a thicket; the backwoods of Australia; a lining of hard metal in the nave of a wheel, etc.—*vi.* To grow bushy.
**Bushel,** bush'el, *n.* A dry measure containing eight gallons or four pecks.
**Bushy,** bush'i, *a.* Full of bushes; like a bush.
**Busily,** bi'zi-li, *adv.* In a busy manner.
**Business,** biz'nes, *n.* Occupation; concern; trade.—*a.* Pertaining to traffic, trade, etc.
**Busk,** busk, *n.* A piece of steel or whalebone worn in corsets.—*vt.* To equip; dress.
**Buskin,** bus'kin, *n.* A kind of half boot; the high shoe worn by ancient tragedians.
**Buskined,** bus'kind, *a.* Wearing buskins.
**Buss,** bus, *n.* A kiss.—*vt.* To kiss.
**Bust,** bust, *n.* The chest and thorax; a sculptured figure of the head and shoulders.
**Bustard,** bus'tėrd, *n.* A large heavy bird of the order of runners.
**Bustle,** bus'l, *vi.* (bustling, bustled). To hurry and be busy.—*n.* Hurry; tumult; a pad formerly worn by ladies at the back below the waist.
**Busy,** bi'zi, *a.* Occupied; actively engaged; officious.—*vt.* (busying, busied). To make or keep busy.
**Busy-body,** bi'zi-bo-di, *n.* An officious meddling person.

B

**But**, but, *conj. prep. adv.* Except; unless; only; however; nevertheless.
**Butcher**, buch'ėr, *n.* One who kills animals for market; one who sells meat; one who delights in bloody deeds.—*vt.* To kill animals for food; to slaughter cruelly.
**Butchery**, buch'ėr-i, *n.* A slaughter-house; massacre.
**Butler**, but'lėr, *n.* A male servant who has the care of wines, etc.
**Butt**, but, *n.* The end of a thing; a mark to be shot at; the person at whom ridicule, etc., is directed; a cask holding 126 gallons of wine.—*vi.* To thrust the head forward.—*vt.* To strike with the head or horns.
**Butter**, but'tėr, *n.* An oily substance obtained from cream by churning; any substance resembling butter.—*vt.* To spread with butter; to flatter grossly.
**Butter-cup**, but'tėr-kup, *n.* A wild yellow cup-shaped flower.
**Butterfly**, but'tėr-flī, *n.* The name of a group of winged insects.
**Buttermilk**, but'ėr-milk, *n.* The milk that remains after the butter is separated.
**Buttery**, but'tėr-i, *n.* An apartment where provisions are kept.—*a.* Like butter; smeared with butter.
**Buttock**, but'tok, *n.* The protuberant part of the body behind; the rump.
**Button**, but'n, *n.* A knob to fasten the parts of dress; a knob or stud; *pl.* a page-boy.—*vt.* To fasten with buttons.
**Button-hole**, but'n-hōl, *n.* A hole for a button; a flower for putting in this.—*vt.* To detain in conversation against one's will.
**Buttress**, but'tres, *n.* A projecting support for a wall; a prop.—*vt.* To support by a buttress; to prop.
**Buxom**, buks'um, *a.* Gay; brisk; wanton.
**Buy**, bī, *vt.* (buying, bought). To acquire by payment; to purchase; to bribe.—*vi.* To negotiate or treat about a purchase.
**Buyer**, bī'ėr, *n.* One who buys.
**Buzz**, buz, *vi.* To hum, as bees; to whisper.—*vt.* To whisper.—*n.* The noise of bees; a confused humming noise.
**Buzzard**, buz'ėrd, *n.* A species of hawk; a blockhead.
**By**, bī, *prep.* Used to denote the instrument, agent, or manner; at; near; beside; through or with; in; for; according to; at the rate of; not later than.—*adv.* Near; passing. In *composition*, secondary, side.
**By-and-by**, bī-and-bī, In the near future.
**Bye**, bī, *n.* A term in certain games; e.g. in cricket an odd or side run; the odd man in a game where the players pair off in couples.
**By-gone**, bī'gon, *a.* Past; gone by.
**By-law**, bī'la, *n.* A local law of a city, society, etc.; an accessory law.
**By-path**, bī'path, *n.* A private or side path.
**By-play**, bī'plā, *n.* Action carried on aside, and commonly in dumb-show.
**Byre**, bīr, *n.* A cow-house.
**By-stander**, bī'stand-ėr, *n.* One who stands near; a spectator; a mere looker-on.
**By-the-by**, (or **bye**), bī-THē-bī. By the way; in passing.
**By-way**, bī'wā, *n.* A private or obscure way.
**By-word**, bī'wėrd, *n.* A common saying; a proverb.
**Byzantine**, biz-an'tīn or biz', *a.* Pertaining to Byzantium or Constantinople and the Greek Empire of which it was the capital.

# C

**Cab**, kab, *n.* A covered one-horse carriage.
**Cabal**, ka-bal', *n.* An intrigue; persons united in some intrigue.—*vi.* (caballing, caballed). To combine in plotting.
**Caballer**, ka-bal'ėr, *n.* An intriguer.
**Cabaret**, kab'a-ret, ka-ba-rā, *n.* A tavern; a restaurant in which singing and dancing performances are given.
**Cabbage**, kab'āj, *n.* A culinary vegetable.—*vt.* (cabbaging, cabbaged). To purloin, especially pieces of cloth.
**Cabbage-rose**, kab'āj-rōz, *n.* A species of rose; called also *Provence rose.*
**Cabbala, Cabala**, kab'a-la, *n.* A mysterious tradition among Jewish rabbins.
**Cabby**, kab'i, *n.* A cabman.
**Caber**, kā'bėr, *n.* In Highland games, a long undressed stem of a tree, used for tossing as a feat of strength.
**Cabin**, kab'in, *n.* A hut; an apartment in a ship.—*vt.* To confine, as in a cabin.
**Cabinet**, kab'in-et, *n.* A closet; a small room; a set of drawers for curiosities; the ministers of state.
**Cabinet-maker**, kab'in-et-māk-ėr, *n.* One who makes articles of furniture.
**Cable**, kā'bl, *n.* The strong rope or chain to hold a ship at anchor; a large rope or chain; a submarine telegraph wire.—*vt.* (cabling, cabled). To furnish with a cable; to send by ocean telegraph.
**Cablegram**, kā'bl-gram, *n.* A message sent by an oceanic telegraph cable.
**Cabman**, kab'man, *n.* The driver of a cab.
**Cacao**, ka-kā'ō, *n.* The chocolate-tree.
**Cachalot**, kash'a-lot, *n.* The sperm-whale.
**Cachinnation**, kak-in-nā'shon, *n.* Loud or immoderate laughter.
**Cackle**, kak'l, *vi.* (cackling, cackled). To make the noise of a goose or hen; to chatter.—*n.* The noise of a hen, etc.; idle talk.
**Cacophony**, ka-kof'ō-ni, *n.* Unpleasant vocal sound; a discord.
**Cactus**, kak'tus, *n.*; pl. **-tuses** or **-ti.** A spiny shrub of numerous species.
**Cad**, kad, *n.* A mean, vulgar fellow.
**Cadaverous**, ka-dav'ėr-us, *a.* Resembling a dead human body; pale; ghastly.
**Caddie**, kad'i, *n.* A golfer's attendant.
**Caddy**, kad'i, *n.* A small box for tea.
**Cadence**, kā'dens, *n.* A fall of the voice at the end of a sentence; rhythm; the close of a musical passage or phrase.
**Cadet**, ka-det', *n.* A younger brother; a young man in a military school.
**Cadge**, kaj, *vt.* and *i.* (cadging, cadged). To carry about for sale; to go about begging.
**Cadger**, kaj'ėr, *n.* An itinerant hawker.
**Cadmium**, kad'mi-um, *n.* A whitish metal.
**Caduceus**, ka-dū'sē-us, *n.* Mercury's rod.
**Caesura**, sē-zū'ra, *n.* A pause in a verse.
**Café**, kaf-ā, *n.* A coffee-house; a restaurant.
**Cafeteria**, kaf-e-tēr'i-a, *n.* A restaurant in which customers serve themselves.
**Caffeine**, ka-fē'in, *n.* A slightly bitter alkaloid found in coffee, tea, etc.
**Cage**, kāj, *n.* An inclosure of wire, etc., for birds and beasts.—*vt.* (caging, caged). To confine in a cage.
**Cairn**, kārn, *n.* A rounded heap of stones.
**Cairngorm**, kārn'gorm, *n.* A yellow or brown rock-crystal found in Scotland.
**Caisson**, kās'son, *n.* An ammunition chest; a structure to raise sunken vessels; a structure used in laying foundations in deep water.
**Caitiff**, kā'tif, *n.* A mean villain; a despicable knave.
**Cajole**, ka-jōl', *vt.* (cajoling, cajoled). To coax; to court; to deceive by flattery.
**Cajolery**, ka-jōl'ė-ri, *n.* Flattery.
**Cake**, kāk, *n.* A composition of flour, butter, sugar, etc., baked; a mass of matter concreted.—*vt.* (caking, caked). To form into a cake or mass.—*vi.* To form into a hard mass.
**Calabash**, kal'a-bash, *n.* A gourd shell dried.
**Calamitous**, ka-lam'it-us, *a.* Miserable; afflictive.

**Calamity,** ka-lam'i-ti, *n.* Misfortune; disaster.
**Calash,** ka-lash', *n.* A light carriage with low wheels and a hood; a kind of head-dress for ladies.
**Calcareous,** kal-kā'rē-us, *a.* Of the nature of lime or chalk; containing lime.
**Calcination,** kal-sin-ā'shon, *n.* Act or operation of calcining.
**Calcine,** kal-sīn', *vt.* (calcining, calcined). To reduce to a powder by fire.—*vi.* To be converted by heat into a powder.
**Calculable,** kal'kū-la-bl, *a.* That may be calculated.
**Calculate,** kal'kū-lāt, *vt.* (calculating, calculated). To compute; to adjust; to make suitable.—*vi.* To make a computation.
**Calculating,** kal'kū-lāt-ing, *p.a.* Scheming.
**Calculation,** kal-kū-lā'shon, *n.* Estimate.
**Calculator,** kal'kū-lāt-ėr, *n.* One who calculates.
**Calculus,** kal'kū-lus, *n.*; pl. **-li.** The stone in the bladder, kidneys, etc.; a method of calculation in mathematics.
**Caldron,** kal'dron, *n.* A large kettle or boiler.
**Caledonian,** kal-i-dō'ni-an, *a.* Pertaining to Scotland.—*n.* A Scot.
**Calendar,** ka'len-dėr, *n.* A register of the months and days of the year; an almanac.
**Calender,** ka'len-dėr, *n.* A machine for smoothing and glazing cloth.—*vt.* To press between rollers to make smooth, glossy, wavy, etc.
**Calends,** ka'lendz, *n.pl.* Among the Romans, the first day of each month.
**Calf,** käf, *n.*; pl. **Calves,** kävz. The young of the cow; a kind of leather; the fleshy part of the leg below the knee.
**Caliber,** ka'li-bėr, *n.* Diameter of the bore of a gun; extent of mental qualities; a sort or kind.
**Calico,** ka'li-kō, *n.* Cotton cloth.
**Calipers,** *See* CALLIPERS.
**Caliph,** kā'lif, *n.* A title given to the successors of Mohammed.
**Calk,** kak, *vt. See* CAULK.
**Calkin, Calker,** kak'in, kak'ėr, *n.* The part of a horse-shoe bent downwards and pointed.
**Call,** kal, *vt.* To name; to style; to summon; to ask, or command to come; to appoint; to appeal to; to utter aloud; to awaken.—*vi.* To utter a loud sound; to make a short visit.—*n.* A vocal utterance; summons; demand; divine vocation; a short visit.
**Calligraphy,** kal-lig'ra-fi, *n.* The art of beautiful writing; penmanship.
**Calling,** kal'ing, *n.* Vocation; profession.
**Callipers,** kal'i-pėrz, *n.pl.* Compasses for measuring caliber.
**Callisthenics,** kal-is-then'iks, *n.* Exercise for health, strength, or grace of movement.
**Callosity,** ka-los'i-ti, *n.* Hardness of skin; horny hardness.
**Callous,** kal'us, *a.* Hardened; unfeeling; obdurate.
**Callow,** kal'ō, *a.* Destitute of feathers; unfledged.
**Calm,** käm, *a.* Still; free from wind; peaceable; composed.—*n.* Absence of wind; tranquillity.—*vt.* To make calm; to still; to assuage.—*vi.* To become calm.
**Calmly,** käm'li, *adv.* In a calm manner.
**Calmness,** käm'nes, *n.* Quietness; composure.
**Calomel,** ka'lō-mel, *n.* A preparation of mercury, much used in medicine.
**Caloric,** ka-lo'rik, *n.* The principle or simple element of heat; heat.
**Calorific,** ka-lo-rif'ik, *a.* Causing heat.
**Calotype,** ka'lō-tīp, *n.* A process of photography.
**Caltrop,** kal'trop, *n.* An iron ball with iron points to wound horses' feet.
**Calumet,** kal'ū-met, *n.* The North American Indians' pipe of peace.
**Calumniate,** ka-lum'ni-āt, *vt.* (calumniating, calumniated). To defame maliciously; to slander.—*vi.* To utter calumnies.
**Calumniation,** ka-lum'ni-ā''shon, *n.* False and malicious accusation.
**Calumniator,** ka-lum'ni-āt-ėr, *n.* One who calumniates.
**Calumnious,** ka-lum'ni-us, *a.* Partaking of calumny.
**Calumniously,** ka-lum'ni-us-li, *adv.* Slanderously.
**Calumny,** ka'lum-ni, *n.* False and malicious defamation; backbiting.
**Calvary,** kal'va-ri, *n.* A place of skulls, particularly the place where Christ was crucified.
**Calve,** käv, *vi.* (calving, calved). To give birth to a calf.
**Calvinism,** kal'vin-izm, *n.* The theological tenets of Calvin.
**Calvinist,** kal'vin-ist, *n.* One who embraces the doctrines of Calvin.
**Calvinistic,** kal-vin-is'tik, *a.* Pertaining to Calvin, or to his tenets.
**Calyx,** kā-liks, *n.*; pl. **-yces** or **-yxes.** The outer covering of a flower; the flower-cup.
**Cam,** kam, *n.* A projection on a wheel to give alternating motion to another wheel, etc.
**Camber,** kam'bėr, *n.* A convexity upon an upper surface, as a ship's deck, a bridge, a road, a beam.
**Cambrian,** kam'bri-an, *a.* Pertaining to Wales.—*n.* A Welshman.
**Cambric,** kām'brik, *n.* A fine white linen.
**Camel,** kam'el, *n.* A large ruminant hoofed quadruped used in Asia and Africa for carrying burdens.
**Camellia,** ka-mel'i-a or ka-mēl'ya, *n.* A genus of beautiful shrubs of the tea family.
**Camelopard,** kam-el'ō-pärd, *n.* The giraffe.
**Cameo,** kam'ē-ō, *n.* A stone or shell of different colored layers cut in relief.
**Camera,** kam'ė-ra, *n.* An arched roof; a council chamber; an apparatus for taking photographs.
**Camlet,** kam'let, *n.* A stuff of various mixtures of wool, silk, hair, etc.
**Camomile,** kam'ō-mīl, *n.* A bitter medicinal plant.
**Camouflage,** kam-ö-fläzh, *n.* The art of disguising; especially the art of disguising material in warfare.
**Camp,** kamp, *n.* The ground on which an army pitch their tents; an encampment.—*vi.* To pitch a camp; to encamp.
**Campaign,** kam-pān', *n.* The time an army keeps the field every year, during a war; its operations.—*vi.* To serve in a campaign.
**Campaigner,** kam-pān'ėr, *n.* An old soldier; a veteran.
**Campanile,** kam-pa-nē'lā or kam'pa-nīl, *n.*; pl. **-ili** or **-iles.** A bell-tower.
**Campanology,** kam-pa-nol'o-ji, *n.* The art or principles of ringing bells.
**Camphor,** kam'fėr, *n.* A whitish, bitter, strong-smelling substance used in medicine.
**Camphorate,** kam'fėr-āt, *vt.* (camphorating, camphorated). To impregnate with camphor.
**Campion,** kam'pi-on, *n.* A popular name of certain plants of the Pink family.
**Can,** kan, *n.* A cup or vessel for liquors.
**Can,** kan, *vi.* (pret. could). To be able; to have sufficient moral or physical power.
**Canal,** ka-nal', *n.* A channel; an artificial water-course for boats; a duct of the body.
**Canard,** ka-när or ka-närd', *n.* An absurd story; a false rumor.
**Canary,** ka-nā'ri, *n.* Wine made in the Canary Isles; a finch from the Canary Isles.
**Cancel,** kan'sel, *vt.* (cancelling, cancelled). To obliterate; to revoke; to set aside.—*n.* Act of cancelling.
**Cancer,** kan'sėr, *n.* One of the signs of the zodiac; a malignant growth in the body.
**Cancerous,** kan'sėr-us, *a.* Having the qualities of a cancer.
**Candelabrum,** kan-de-lā'brum, *n.*; pl. **-ra.** A branched ornamental candlestick.
**Candid,** kan'did, *a.* Sincere; ingenuous.

**Candidate,** kan'di-dāt, *n.* One who proposes himself, or is proposed, for some office; one who aspires after preferment.
**Candied,** kan'did, *a.* Preserved with sugar, or incrusted with it.
**Candle,** kan'dl, *n.* A cylindrical body of tallow, wax, etc., surrounding a wick, and used for giving light.
**Candlemas,** kan'dl-mas, *n.* A church festival on 2nd February, in honor of the purification of the Virgin Mary.
**Candlestick,** kan'dl-stik, *n.* An instrument to hold a candle.
**Candor,** kan'dėr, *n.* Frankness; sincerity.
**Candy,** kan'di, *vt.* (candying, candied). To conserve with sugar; to form into crystals.—*vi.* To take on the form of candied sugar.—*n.* Crystallized sugar; a sweetmeat.
**Cane,** kān, *n.* A reed; a walking-stick.—*vt.* (caning, caned). To beat with a cane.
**Canine,** ka'nīn, *a.* Pertaining to dogs.
**Caning,** kān'ing, *n.* A beating with a cane.
**Canister,** kan'is-tėr, *n.* A small box for tea, coffee, etc.; a case containing shot which bursts on being discharged.
**Canker,** kang'kėr, *n.* A malignant ulcer; a disease of trees; a disease in horses' feet; something that gnaws or corrodes.—*vt.* and *i.* To corrode or corrupt.
**Cankerous,** kang'kėr-us, *a.* Corroding.
**Canker-worm,** kang'kėr-wėrm, *n.* A worm destructive to trees or plants.
**Cannel-coal, Candle-coal,** kan'el-kōl, kan'dl-kōl, *n.* A coal which burns readily and brightly, used in making gas.
**Cannibal,** kan'ni-bal, *n.* A savage who eats human flesh.—*a.* Relating to cannibalism.
**Cannibalism,** kan'ni-bal-izm, *n.* The eating human flesh by mankind.
**Cannon,** kan'un, *n.* A great gun; the striking of a ball on two other balls successively.—*vi.* To strike with rebounding collision; to make a cannon at billiards.
**Cannonade,** kan-un-ād', *n.* An attack with cannon.—*vt.* (cannonading, cannonaded). To attack with cannon; to batter with cannonshot.
**Cannot,** kan'not. The negative of *can.*
**Canny, Cannie,** kan'i, *a.* Cautious; wary.
**Canoe,** ka-nö', *n.* A boat made of the trunk of a tree, or of bark or skins; a light boat propelled by paddles.
**Canon,** kan'on, *n.* A rule of doctrine or discipline; a law in general; the genuine books of the Holy Scriptures; a member of the cathedral chapter; a catalogue of saints canonized; a formula; a large kind of printing type.
**Canon, Canyon,** kan'yun, *n.* A long and narrow mountain gorge.
**Canonical,** kan-on'ik-al, *a.* According to the canon; ecclesiastical.
**Canonicals,** kan-on'ik-alz, *n.pl.* The full dress of the clergy worn when they officiate.
**Canonist,** kan'on-ist, *n.* One versed in canon or ecclesiastical law.
**Canonization,** kan'on-īz-ā''shon, *n.* Act of canonizing; state of being canonized.
**Canonize,** kan'on-īz, *vt.* (canonizing, canonized). To enroll in the canon as a saint.
**Canonry, Canonship,** kan'on-ri, kan'on-ship, *n.* The office of a canon in a cathedral or collegiate church.
**Canopy,** kan'ō-pi, *n.* A covering over a throne, bed, or person's head, etc.—*vt.* (canopying, canopied). To cover with a canopy.
**Cant,** kant, *vi.* To speak in a whining tone; to sham piety.—*vt.* To tilt up; to bevel.—*n.* A whining hypocritical manner of speech; jargon; slang; inclination from a perpendicular or horizontal line; a toss or jerk.—*a.* Of the nature of cant or slang.
**Cantankerous,** kan-tang'kėr-us, *a.* Ill-natured; cross; contentious.
**Cantata,** kan-tä'ta, *n.* A short musical composition in the form of an oratorio.
**Cantatrice,** kan-ta-trē'chā, *n.* A female singer.
**Canteen,** kan-tēn', *n.* A vessel used by soldiers for carrying liquor; a place in barracks where provisions, etc., are sold.
**Canter,** kan'tėr, *n.* A moderate gallop.—*vi.* To move in a moderate gallop.
**Cantharides,** kan-tha'ri-dēz, *n.pl.* Spanish flies, used to raise a blister.
**Canticle,** kan'ti-kl, *n.* A song; a passage of Scripture for chanting; in *pl.* the Song of Solomon.
**Cantilever,** kan'ti-lēv-ėr, *n.* A bracket to carry moldings, eaves, balconies, etc.; one of two long arms projecting toward each other from opposite banks or piers, used in bridgemaking.
**Cantle,** kan'tl, *n.* A corner; a piece; the hind part of a saddle.
**Canto,** kan'tō, *n.* A division of a poem; the treble part of a musical composition.
**Canton,** kan'ton, *n.* A division of territory or its inhabitants.—*vt.* To divide into cantons; to allot separate quarters to different parts of an army. (In *milit. lan.* pron. kan-tön'.)
**Cantonal,** kan'ton-al, *a.* Pertaining to a canton.
**Cantonment,** kan-ton'ment, *n.* A part of a town occupied by troops; a military town.
**Canvas,** kan'vas, *n.* A coarse cloth; sailcloth; sails of ships; cloth for painting on; a painting.
**Canvass,** kan'vas, *vt.* To scrutinize; to solicit the votes of.—*vi.* To solicit votes or interest; to use efforts to obtain.—*n.* Scrutiny; solicitation of votes.
**Canvasser,** kan'vas-ėr, *n.* One who solicits votes, etc.
**Canzonet,** kan-zō-net', *n.* A little song.
**Caoutchouc,** kou'chök or kö'chök, *n.* India-rubber; a very elastic gum.
**Cap,** kap, *n.* A covering for the head; something used as a cover; a top piece.—*vt.* (capping, capped). To put a cap on; to complete; to crown; to excel.
**Capability,** kā-pa-bil'i-ti, *n.* Quality of being capable.
**Capable,** kā'pa-bl, *a.* Having sufficient skill or power; competent; susceptible.
**Capacious,** ka-pā'shus, *a.* Wide; large; comprehensive.
**Capacitate,** ka-pas'i-tāt, *vt.* To make able; to qualify.
**Capacity,** ka-pas'i-ti, *n.* Power of holding; extent of space; ability; state.
**Cap-a-pie,** kap-a-pē', *adv.* From head to foot.
**Caparison,** ka-pa'ri-son, *n.* A covering laid over the saddle of a horse; clothing.—*vt.* To cover with a cloth; to dress richly.
**Cape,** kāp, *n.* The point of a neck of land extending into the sea; a loose cloak hung from the shoulders.
**Caper,** kā'pėr, *vi.* To prance; to spring.—*n.* A skip, spring, jump; the flower-bud of the caper-bush, much used for pickling.
**Capillary,** ka-pil'la-ri, or kap'il-la-ri, *a.* Resembling a hair; having a bore of very small diameter.—*n.* A tube with a very small bore; a fine vessel or canal in an animal body.
**Capital,** kap'it-al, *a.* First in importance; metropolitan; affecting the head; punishable with death.—*n.* The uppermost part of a column; the chief city; the stock of a bank, tradesman, etc.; a large letter or type.
**Capitalist,** kap'it-al-ist, *n.* A man who has a capital or wealth.
**Capitalize,** kap'it-al-īz, *vt.* (capitalizing, capitalized). To convert into capital.
**Capitally,** kap'it-al-i, *adv.* In a capital manner; so as to involve life.
**Capitation,** kap-it-ā'shon, *n.* Numeration by heads or individuals.
**Capitol,** kap'it-ol, *n.* The temple of Jupiter in Rome; a citadel; a state-house.
**Capitular, Capitulary,** ka-pit'ū-lėr, ka-pit'ū-la-ri, *n.* An act passed in an ecclesiastical chapter; body of laws or statutes of a chapter; the mem-

ber of a chapter.
**Capitular,** ka-pit'ū-lėr, *a.* Belonging to a chapter or capitulary.
**Capitulate,** ka-pit'ū-lāt, *vi.* (capitulating, capitulated). To surrender on conditions.
**Capitulation,** ka-pit'ū-lā''shon, *n.* Surrender on certain conditions.
**Capon,** kā'pon, *n.* A young castrated cock.
**Caprice,** ka-prēs', *n.* A freak; a sudden or unreasonable change of opinion or humor.
**Capricious,** ka-pri'shus, *a.* Full of caprice.
**Capriciously,** ka-pri'shus-li, *adv.* In a capricious manner; whimsically.
**Capricorn,** ka'pri-korn, *n.* The he-goat, one of the signs of the zodiac; the southern tropic.
**Capsicum,** kap'si-kum, *n.* The generic name of some tropical plants yielding chilies and cayenne pepper.
**Capsizal,** kap-sīz'al, *n.* The act of capsizing.
**Capsize,** kap-sīz', *vt.* (capsizing, capsized). To upset or overturn.
**Capstan,** kap'stan, *n.* An apparatus in ships to raise great weights, weigh anchors, etc.
**Capsular,** kap'sūl-ėr, *a.* Pertaining to a capsule; hollow like a capsule.
**Capsule,** kap'sūl, *n.* A dry, many-seeded seed-vessel; an envelope for drugs.
**Captain,** kap'tin, *n.* A head officer; the commander of a ship, troop of horse, or company of infantry; a leader.
**Captaincy,** kap'tin-si, *n.* The rank, post, or commission of a captain.
**Caption,** kap'shon, *n.* Seizure; arrest; heading or short title of a division of a book, or of a scene in a cinematograph film.
**Captious,** kap'shus, *a.* Ready to find fault; carping.
**Captiously,** kap'shus-li, *adv.* In a captious manner.
**Captivate,** kap'ti-vāt, *vt.* (captivating, captivated). To take captive; to fascinate.
**Captive,** kap'tiv, *n.* One taken in war; one ensnared by love, beauty, etc.—*a.* Make prisoner; kept in bondage.
**Captivity,** kap-tiv'i-ti, *n.* State or condition of being a captive; slavery.
**Captor,** kap'tėr, *n.* One who captures.
**Capture,** kap'tūr, *n.* Act of taking; the thing taken.—*vt.* (capturing, captured). To take by force or stratagem.
**Capuchin,** ka-pū-shēn', *n.* A Franciscan monk; a cloak with a hood.
**Car,** kär, *n.* A chariot; a vehicle in pageants; a railway or tramway carriage.
**Caracole,** ka'ra-kōl, *n.* A half-turn which a horseman makes.—*vi.* (caracoling, caracoled). To move in a caracole; to wheel.
**Carafe,** ka'raf, *n.* A glass water-bottle.
**Caramel,** ka'ra-mel, *n.* Burnt sugar, used to color spirits.
**Carat,** ka'rat, *n.* A weight of four grains, for weighing diamonds, etc.; a word employed to denote the fineness of gold, pure gold being of twenty-four carats.
**Caravan,** ka'ra-van, *n.* A company of travelers associated together for safety; a large close carriage.
**Caravanserai,** ka-ra-van'se-ri, *n.* A house in the East, where caravans rest at night.
**Caraway,** ka'ra-wā, *n.* A biennial, aromatic plant whose seeds are used in baking, etc.
**Carbide,** kär'bīd, *n.* A compound of carbon with a metal.
**Carbine,** kär'bīn, *n.* A short-barreled rifle used by cavalry, police, etc.
**Carbolic,** kär-bol'ik, *a.* An antiseptic and disinfecting acid obtained from coal-tar.
**Carbon,** kär'bon, *n.* Pure charcoal; an elementary substance, bright and brittle.
**Carbonaceous,** kär-bon-ā'shus, *a.* Pertaining to or containing carbon.
**Carbonate,** kär'bon-āt, *n.* A salt formed by the union of carbonic acid with a base.
**Carbonic,** kär-bon'ik, *a.* Pertaining to carbon, or obtained from it.
**Carboniferous,** kär-bon-if'ėr-us, *a.* Producing or containing carbon.
**Carbonize,** kär'bon-īz, *vt.* (carbonizing, carbonized). To convert into carbon.
**Carboy,** kär'boi, *n.* A globular bottle protected by a wicker covering.
**Carbuncle,** kär'bung-kl, *n.* A fiery red precious stone; an inflammatory tumor.
**Carbureted,** kär'bū-ret-ed, *a.* Combined with carbon.
**Carburetor,** kär'bū-ret-ėr, *n.* A device for vaporizing the light oil fuel used in the engines of motor-cars, airplanes, etc.
**Carcanet,** kär'ka-net, *n.* A jeweled collar.
**Carcass,** kär'kas, *a.* A dead body; anything decayed; a framework; a kind of bomb.
**Card,** kärd, *n.* A piece of pasteboard with figures, used in games; a piece of pasteboard containing a person's name, etc.; a printed invitation; a note; the dial of a compass; a large comb for wool or flax.—*vt.* To comb wool, flax, hemp, etc.
**Cardamom,** kär'da-mum, *n.* The aromatic capsule of various plants of the ginger family.
**Cardboard,** kärd'bōrd, *n.* A stiff kind of paper or pasteboard for making cards, etc.
**Carder,** kärd'ėr, *n.* One who cards wool.
**Cardiac,** kär'di-ak, *a.* Pertaining to the heart; stimulating.—*n.* A cordial.
**Cardigan,** kär'di-gan, *n.* A knitted waistcoat.
**Cardinal,** kär'din-al, *a.* Chief; fundamental.—*n.* A dignitary in the Roman Catholic Church next to the pope; a lady's short cloak.
**Cardinalate, Cardinalship,** kär'din-al-āt, kär'din-al-ship, *n.* The office, rank, or dignity of a cardinal.
**Care,** kār, *n.* Solicitude; attention; object of watchful regard.—*vi.* (caring, cared). To be solicitous; to be inclined; to have regard.
**Careen,** ka-rēn', *vt.* To lay (a ship) on one side, for the purpose of repairing.—*vi.* To incline to one side.
**Career,** ka-rēr', *n.* A race; course of action.—*vi.* To move or run rapidly.
**Careful,** kār'ful, *a.* Solicitous; cautious.
**Carefully,** kāār-ful-li, *adv.* In a careful manner.
**Carefulness,** kāār'ful-nes, *n.* Quality of being careful.
**Careless,** kār'les, *a.* Heedless; incautious.
**Carelessly,** kār'les-li, *adv.* In a careless way.
**Carelessness,** kār'les-nes, *n.* Quality of being careless.
**Caress,** ka-res', *vt.* To fondle; to embrace affectionately.—*n.* An act of endearment.
**Caressingly,** ka-res'ing-li, *adv.* In a caressing manner.
**Caret,** kā'ret, *n.* In writing, this mark, ʌ, noting insertion.
**Care-taker,** kār'tā-kėr, *n.* A person put in charge of a house, farm, or the like.
**Cargo,** kär'gō, *n.* The freight of a ship.
**Cariboo, Caribou,** ka'ri-bö, *n.* An American variety of the reindeer.
**Caricature,** ka-ri-kä-tūr', *n.* A portrait or description so exaggerated as to excite ridicule.—*vt.* (caricaturing, caricatured). To represent by caricature.
**Caries,** kā'ri-ēz, *n.* Ulceration of a bone.
**Carillon,** ka'ril-lon, *n.* A chime of bells; simple air adapted to a set of bells.
**Carious,** kā'ri-us, *a.* Ulcerated; decayed.
**Cark,** kärk, *n.* Anxiety.—*vi.* To be anxious.
**Carl, Carle,** kärl, *n.* A robust hardy man.
**Carman,** kär'man, *n.* A man who drives a car.
**Carminative,** kär'min-āt-iv, *n.* A medicine for flatulence, etc.
**Carmine,** kär'mīn, *n.* A bright crimson color.
**Carnage,** kär'nāj, *n.* Great slaughter in war; massacre; butchery.
**Carnal,** kär'nal, *a.* Fleshly; sensual.
**Carnality,** kär-nal'i-ti, *n.* Sensuality.

**Carnally,** kär'nal-li, *adv.* In a carnal manner; according to the flesh.
**Carnation,** kär-nā'shon, *n.* Flesh-color; a sweet-scented plant with pink flowers.
**Carnelian,** kär-nē'li-an, *n.* A red or flesh-colored stone, a variety of chalcedony.
**Carnival,** kär'ni-val, *n.* A festival during the week before Lent; a revel.
**Carnivora,** kär-niv'ō-ra, *n.pl.* Animals that feed on flesh.
**Carnivorous,** kär-niv'ō-rus, *a.* Feeding on flesh.
**Carob,** ka'rob, *n.* A tree with sweet nutritious pods called locust-beans.
**Carol,** ka'rol, *n.* A song of joy or devotion; a warble.—*vi.* (caroling, caroled). To sing; to warble.—*vt.* To celebrate in song.
**Carotid,** ka-rot'id, *a.* Pertaining to the two great arteries in the neck conveying the blood to the head.
**Carousal,** ka-rouz'al, *n.* A noisy revel.
**Carouse,** ka-rouz', *vi.* (carousing, caroused). To drink freely with noisy jollity.—*n.* A drinking bout.
**Carp,** kärp, *vi.* To cavil; to find fault.—*n.* A voracious fish, found in rivers and ponds.
**Carpenter,** kär'pen-tėr, *n.* One who works in timber.
**Carpentry,** kär'pen-tri, *n.* The trade, art, or work of a carpenter.
**Carpet,** kär'pet, *n.* A woven fabric for covering floors, etc.—*vt.* To cover with a carpet.
**Carpet-bag,** kär'pet-bag, *n.* A traveling bag made of the same material as carpets.
**Carpet-bagger,** kär'pet-bag-ėr, *n.* An outsider who takes part in political affairs.
**Carpeting,** kär'pet-ing, *n.* Cloth for carpets; carpets in general.
**Carping,** kärp'ing, *a.* Caviling.
**Carriage,** ka'rij, *n.* Act of carrying; that which carries; a vehicle; conveyance; price of carrying; behavior; demeanor.
**Carrier,** ka'ri-ėr, *n.* One who carries for hire.
**Carrion,** ka'ri-on, *n.* Dead and putrefying flesh.—*a.* Relating to putrefying carcasses; feeding on carrion.
**Carrot,** ka'rot, *n.* A yellowish or reddish esculent root of a tapering form.
**Carroty,** ka'rot-i, *a.* Like a carrot in color.
**Carry,** ka'ri, *vt.* (carrying, carried). To bear, convey, or transport; to gain; to capture; to import; to behave.—*vi.* To convey; to propel.—*n.* Onward motion.
**Cart,** kärt, *n.* A carriage of burden with two wheels.—*vt.* To carry or place on a cart.
**Cartage,** kärt'āj, *n.* Act of carrying in a cart; the price paid for carting.
**Carte,** kärt, *n.* A card; a bill of fare.
**Carte-blanche,** kärt-blänsh, *n.* A blank paper; unconditional terms.
**Cartel,** kär'tel, *n.* A challenge; an agreement for the exchange of prisoners.
**Carter,** kärt'ėr, *n.* One who drives a cart.
**Cartilage,** kär'ti-lāj, *n.* Gristle; an elastic substance from which bone is formed.
**Cartilaginous,** kär-ti-laj'in-us, *a.* Pertaining to or resembling a cartilage.
**Cartography,** kär-tog'ra-fi, *n.* The art or practice of drawing up charts.
**Cartoon,** kär-tön', *n.* A drawing for a fresco or tapestry; a pictorial sketch relating to a prevalent topic.
**Cartouch,** kär-tösh', *n.* A cartridge or cartridge-box; a sculptured ornament.
**Cartridge,** kär'trij, *n.* A case containing the charge of a gun or any firearm.
**Cartridge-paper,** kär'trij-pā-pėr, *n.* Thick paper, of which cartridges were made.
**Cartulary,** kär'tū-la-ri, *n.* See CHARTULARY.
**Carve,** kärv, *vt.* (carving, carved). To cut; to engrave; to shape by cutting.—*vi.* To cut up meat; to sculpture.
**Carver,** kärv'ėr, *n.* One who carves; a large table-knife for carving.
**Carving,** kärv'ing, *n.* The act or art of cutting meat or sculpturing figures; sculpture.
**Caryatid,** ka'ri-at-id, *n.*; pl. **-ids** or **-ides.** A figure of a woman serving as a column.
**Cascade,** kas'kād, *n.* A waterfall.
**Case,** kās, *n.* That which contains; a box; a receptacle; covering; an event; condition; a suit in court; a form in the inflection of nouns, etc.—*vt.* (casing, cased). To cover with a case; to put in a case.
**Case-harden,** kās'härd-n, *vt.* To harden on the outside, as iron.
**Casein, Caseine,** kā'sē-in, *n.* That ingredient in milk which forms curd and cheese.
**Casemate,** kās'māt, *n.* A bomb-proof vault.
**Casement,** kāz'ment, *n.* A case for a window.
**Caseous,** kā'sē-us, *a.* Pertaining to cheese.
**Casern,** ka-zėrn', *n.* Small barracks.
**Case-shot,** kās'shot, *n.* Shot, old iron, etc., put in cases to be discharged from cannon.
**Cash,** kash, *n.* Money; ready money; coin.—*vt.* To turn into money.
**Cashier,** kash-ēr', *n.* One who has charge of money.—*vt.* To deprive of office; to dismiss; to break.
**Cashmere,** kash'mēr, *n.* A rich kind of shawl; a fine woolen stuff.
**Casing,** kās'ing, *n.* Act of putting in a case; a covering.
**Casino,** ka-sē'nō, *n.* A public dancing, singing, or gaming saloon.
**Cask,** kask, *n.* A vessel for containing liquors.
**Casket,** kask'et, *n.* A small chest for jewels.
**Casque,** kask, *n.* A head-piece; a helmet.
**Cassava,** kas-sā'va or sä'va, *n.* A tropical shrub yielding a nutritious starch formed into tapioca, etc.
**Casserole,** kas'e-rōl, *n.* A sauce-pan; a kind of stew.
**Cassia,** kash'i-a, *n.* A sweet spice; wild cinnamon; a plant which yields senna.
**Cassimere,** kas'si-mēr, *n.* A twilled woolen cloth.
**Cassock,** kas'ok, *n.* A close garment worn by clergymen under the surplice.
**Cassowary,** kas'sō-wa-ri, *n.* A running bird allied to the ostrich.
**Cast,** kast, *vt.* (casting, cast). To throw; to impel; to throw off; to let fall; to condemn; to compute; to model; to found; to scatter (seed); to bring forth immaturely.—*vi.* To revolve in the mind; to contrive (with *about*); to warp.—*n.* A throw; the thing thrown; manner of throwing; distance passed by a thing thrown; a squint; form; a tinge; manner; that which is formed from a mould; the actors to whom the parts of a play are assigned.
**Castanet,** kas'ta-net, *n.* Small pieces of wood or ivory struck together in dancing.
**Castaway,** kast'a-wā, *n.* A person abandoned; a reprobate.
**Caste,** kast, *n.* A distinct hereditary order among the Hindus; a class of society.
**Castellated,** kas'tel-lāt-ed, *a.* Adorned with turrets and battlements.
**Caster,** kast'ėr, *n.* A founder; one employed in shoveling; a castor.
**Castigate,** kas'ti-gāt, *vt.* (castigating, castigated). To chastise; to punish by stripes.
**Castigation,** kas-ti-gā'shon, *n.* Chastisement.
**Castigator,** kas'ti-gāt-ėr, *n.* One who corrects.
**Casting,** kast'ing, *n.* Act of casting; that which is cast in a mold.
**Cast-iron,** kast'ī-ėrn, *n.* Iron which has been cast into pigs or molds.
**Castle,** kas'l, *n.* A fortified building; a large and imposing mansion; a piece in chess.
**Castled,** kas'ld, *a.* Furnished with castles; castellated.
**Cast-off,** kast'of, *a.* Laid aside; rejected.
**Castor,** kas'tėr, *n.* A small cruet; a small wheel on the leg of a table, etc.
**Castor-oil,** kas'tėr-oil, *n.* A medicinal oil obtained from a tropical plant.

**Castrametation,** kas'tra-me-tā''shon, *n.* The art or act of planning a camp.
**Castrate,** kas'trāt, *vt.* (castrating, castrated). To geld; to emasculate; to expurgate.
**Castration,** kas-trā'shon, *n.* Act of castrating.
**Cast-steel,** kast'stēl, *n.* Steel melted and cast into ingots and rolled into bars.
**Casual,** ka'zhū-al, *a.* Happening by chance; occasional; contingent.
**Casually,** ka'zhū-al-li, *adv.* In a casual manner; by chance.
**Casualty,** ka'zhū-al-ti, *n.* Accident, especially one resulting in death or injury; death or injury caused by enemy action.
**Casuistic,** ka-zū-ist'ik, *a.* Relating to cases of conscience or conduct.
**Casuistry,** ka'zū-is-tri, *n.* The science of determining cases of conscience; sophistry.
**Cat,** kat, *n.* A domestic animal of the feline tribe; a strong tackle; a double tripod; an instrument for flogging.
**Catachresis,** kat-a-krē'sis, *n.* The wresting of a word from its true sense.
**Cataclysm,** kat'a-klizm, *n.* A deluge; a sudden overwhelming catastrophe.
**Catacomb,** ka'ta-kōm, *n.* A subterranean place for the burial of the dead.
**Catafalque,** kat'a-falk, *n.* A temporary structure representing a tomb.
**Catalectic,** kat-a-lek'tik, *a.* Incomplete.
**Catalepsy,** ka'ta-leps-i, *n.* A nervous affection suspending motion and sensation.
**Cataleptic,** ka-ta-lep'tik, *a.* Pertaining to catalepsy.
**Catalogue,** ka'ta-log, *n.* A list; a register.—*vt.* (cataloguing, catalogued). To make a list of.
**Catamaran,** kat'a-ma-ran'', *n.* A kind of raft; a cross-grained woman.
**Cataplasm,** ka'ta-plazm, *n.* A poultice.
**Catapult,** kat'a-pult, *n.* An apparatus for throwing stones, etc.
**Cataract,** kat'a-rakt, *n.* A great waterfall; a disease of the eye.
**Catarrh,** ka-tär', *n.* A flow of mucus from the nose, etc.; a cold.
**Catarrhal,** ka-tär'al, *a.* Pertaining to or produced by catarrh.
**Catastrophe,** ka-tas'trō-fē, *n.* Calamity or disaster; final event.
**Catch,** kach, *vt.* (catching, caught). To lay hold on; to stop the falling of; to grasp; to entangle; to receive by contagion; to be seized with; to get.—*vi.* To lay hold; to be contagious.—*n.* Act of seizing; anything that takes hold; a sudden advantage taken; something desirable; a capture; a song.
**Catching,** kach'ing, *a.* Infectious; charming.
**Catch-penny,** kach'pen-ni, *n.* A thing of little value intended to gain money in market.
**Catch-word,** kach'wėrd, *n.* A word under the last line of a page, repeated at the top of the next; the last word of a preceding speaker.
**Cate,** kāt, *n.* Rich food; a delicacy: generally in *pl.*
**Catechetic,** ka-tē-ket'ik, *a.* Relating to a catechism or catechisms.
**Catechetically,** ka-tē-ket'ik-al-li, *adv.* In a catechetic manner.
**Catechise,** ka'tē-kīz, *vt.* (catechising, catechised). To instruct by question and answer; to question.
**Catechism,** ka'tē-kizm, *n.* A manual of instruction by questions and answers, especially in religion.
**Catechist,** ka'tē-kist, *n.* One who catechises.
**Catechu,** kat'ē-shū, *n.* An astringent vegetable extract.
**Catechumen,** ka-tē-kū'men, *n.* One who is being instructed in the first rudiments of Christianity.
**Categorical,** ka-tē-go'ri-kal, *a.* Pertaining to a category; absolute; positive.
**Categorically,** ka-tē-go'ri-kal-li, *adv.* Absolutely; directly; positively.
**Category,** kat'ē-go-ri, *n.* One of the highest classes to which objects of thought can be referred; class; a general head.
**Catena,** ka-tē'na, *n.* A chain; series of extracts, arguments, etc.
**Catenation,** kat-ē-nā'shon, *n.* Connection; union of parts; concatenation.
**Cater,** kā'tėr, *vi.* To buy or procure provisions, food, entertainment, etc.
**Caterer,** kā'tėr-ėr, *n.* One who caters.
**Cateress,** kā'tėr-es, *n.* A woman who caters.
**Caterpillar,** kat'ėr-pil-ėr, *n.* The hairy worm-like grub of butterflies and moths; a traction device consisting of an endless chain encircling the wheels of the tractor.
**Caterwaul,** kat'ėr-wal, *vi.* To cry as cats.
**Catgut,** kat'gut, *n.* The intestines of a cat; intestines made into strings for musical instruments, etc.; a kind of linen or canvas.
**Cathartic,** ka-thär'tik, *a.* Purging.—*n.* A medicine that purges.
**Cat-head,** kat'hed, *n.* A projecting beam with tackle for lifting the anchor.
**Cathedra,** ka-thē'dra or kath'e-dra, *n.* The throne or seat of a bishop.
**Cathedral,** ka-thē'dral, *n.* The principal church in a diocese.
**Catheter,** kath'e-tėr, *n.* A tubular instrument, to be introduced into the bladder.
**Cathode,** kath'ōd, *n.* The negative pole of an electric current.
**Catholic,** ka'thol-ik, *a.* Universal; liberal; pertaining to the universal Church; pertaining to the Roman Catholic Church.—*n.* A member of the universal Christian Church; an adherent of the Roman Catholic Church.
**Catholicism,** ka-thol'i-sizm, *a.* Adherence to the Catholic Church; adherence to the Roman Catholic Church; the Roman Catholic religion.
**Catkin,** kat'kin, *n.* The blossom of the willow, birch, etc., resembling a cat's tail.
**Catmint, Catnip,** kat'mint, kat'nip, *n.* A strong-scented labiate plant.
**Catoptrics,** kat-op'triks, *n.* The part of optics treating of vision by reflected light.
**Cat's-eye,** kats'ī, *n.* A variety of chalcedony.
**Cat's-paw,** kats'pa, *n.* A light breeze; a dupe; a tool.
**Cattle,** kat'tl, *n.pl.* Domestic quadrupeds serving for tillage or food; bovine animals.
**Caucus,** ka'kus, *n.* A private committee to manage election matters.
**Caudal,** ka'dal, *a.* Pertaining to a tail.
**Caul,** kal, *n.* A net for the hair; a membrane investing some part of the intestines.
**Cauliflower,** ka'li-flou-ėr, *n.* A variety of cabbage.
**Caulk,** kak, *vt.* To drive oakum into the seams of (a ship) to prevent leaking.
**Causal,** kaz'al, *a.* Implying cause.
**Causality,** kaz-al'i-ti, *n.* The agency of a cause.
**Causation,** kaz-ā'shon, *n.* The act or agency by which an effect is produced.
**Causative,** kaz'a-tiv, *a.* That expresses a cause or reason that effects.
**Cause,** kaz, *n.* That which produces an effect; reason; origin; sake; purpose; a suit in court; that which a person or party espouses.—*vt.* (causing, caused). To effect; to bring about.
**Causeless,** kaz'les, *a.* Having no cause.
**Causeway, Causey,** kaz'wā, kaz'i, *n.* A raised road; a paved way.
**Caustic,** kas'tik, *a.* Burning; corroding; cutting.—*n.* A substance which burns the flesh.
**Caustically,** kas'tik-al-li, *adv.* In a caustic manner; severely.
**Causticity,** kas-tis'i-ti, *n.* Quality of being caustic; severity; cutting remarks.
**Cautelous,** ka'tel-us, *a.* Cautious; wary.
**Cauterization,** ka'tėr-īz-ā''shon, *n.* Act of cauterizing.
**Cauterize,** ka'tėr-īz, *vt.* To burn with caustics, or hot iron, as morbid flesh.
**Caution,** ka'shon, *n.* Care; wariness; warning;

pledge.—*vt*. To warn.
**Cautionary,** ka'shon-a-ri, *a*. Containing caution; given as a pledge.
**Cautious,** ka'shus, *a*. Using caution; wary; circumspect; prudent.
**Cautiously,** ka'shus-li, *adv*. With caution.
**Cavalcade,** kä'val-kād, *n*. A procession of persons on horseback.
**Cavalier,** ka-va-lēr', *n*. A horseman; a gay military man; a beau.—*a*. Gay; brave; haughty; supercilious.
**Cavalierly,** ka-va-lēr'li, *adv*. Haughtily.
**Cavalry,** ka'val-ri, *n*. A body of troops mounted.
**Cave,** kāv, *n*. A hollow place in the earth; a den.
**Caveat,** kā'vē-at, *n*. A warning; a process to stop proceedings in a court.
**Cavern,** ka'vėrn, *n*. A large cave.
**Cavernous,** ka'vėrn-us, *a*. Hollow; full of caverns.
**Caviare, Caviar,** ka-vi-är', *n*. The roe of the sturgeon salted and prepared for food.
**Cavil,** ka'vil, *vi*. (caviling, caviled). To carp; to find fault with insufficient reason.—*n*. A captious objection.
**Caviler,** ka'vil-ėr, *n*. One who cavils.
**Cavity,** ka'vi-ti, *n*. A hollow place.
**Caw,** ka, *vi*. To cry like a crow, rook, or raven.—*n*. The cry of the rook or crow.
**Cayenne,** kā-en', *n*. A pepper made from capsicum seeds.
**Cease,** sēs, *vi*. (ceasing, ceased). To leave off; to fail; to stop; to become extinct.—*vt*. To put a stop to.
**Ceaseless,** sēs'les, *a*. Incessant; perpetual.
**Ceaselessly,** sēs'les-li, *adv*. Incessantly.
**Cedar,** sē'dėr, *n*. A large coniferous tree.—*a*. Made of cedar; belonging to cedar.
**Cede,** sēd, *vt*. (ceding, ceded). To give up; to surrender.—*vi*. To yeild; to lapse.
**Cedilla,** sē-dil'la, *n*. A mark under *c* (thus ç), to show that it is to be sounded like *s*.
**Ceil,** sēl, *vt*. To cover the inner roof of a building; to cover with a ceiling.
**Ceiling,** sēl'ing, *n*. The upper inside surface of a room.
**Celandine,** sel'an-dīn, *n*. A British poppy or ranunculus.
**Celebrant,** sel'ē-brant, *n*. One who performs a public religious rite.
**Celebrate,** sel'ē-brāt, *vt*. (celebrating, celebrated). To honor by solemn rites; to praise; to commemorate.
**Celebrated,** se'lē-brāt-ed, *a*. Famous.
**Celebration,** se-lē-brā'shon, *n*. The act of celebrating; ceremonious performance.
**Celebrity,** se-leb'ri-ti, *n*. Fame; eminence.
**Celerity,** sē-le'ri-ti, *n*. Speed; quickness.
**Celery,** se'le-ri, *n*. An umbelliferous plant cultivated for the table.
**Celestial,** sē-les'ti-al, *a*. Heavenly; pertaining to heaven.—*n*. An inhabitant of heaven.
**Celibacy,** se'li-ba-si, *n*. The unmarried state; a single life.
**Celibate,** se'li-bāt, *n*. One who intentionally remains unmarried.—*a*. Unmarried.
**Cell,** sel, *n*. A small room; a cave; a small mass of protoplasm forming the structural unit in animal tissues.
**Cellar** sel'lėr, *n*. An apartment underground used for storage.
**Cellophane,** sel'ō-fān, *n*. Trade name for a thin, waterproof solidification of viscose, much used for wrapping.
**Cellular,** sel'ū-lėr, *a*. Consisting of cells.
**Celluloid,** sel'lū-loid, *n*. An artificial substitute for ivory, bone, coral, etc.
**Cellulose,** sel'lū-lōs, *n*. The substance of which the permanent cell membranes of plants are always composed, in many respects allied to starch.
**Celt,** selt, *n*. One of a race of Western Europe; a prehistoric cutting instrument.
**Celtic,** selt'ik, *a*. Pertaining to the Celts.—*n*. Their language.
**Cement,** sē-ment', *n*. An adhesive substance which unites bodies; mortar; bond of union.—*vt*. To unite closely.—*vi*. To unite and cohere.
**Cementation,** sē-ment-ā'shon, *n*. Act of cementing.
**Cemetery,** se'mē-te-ri, *n*. A burial-place.
**Cenobite,** sē'nō-bīt, *n*. One of a religious order living in common.
**Cenotaph,** sen'ō-taf, *n*. A monument to one who is buried elsewhere.
**Censer,** sens'ėr, *n*. A vase or pan in which incense is burned.
**Censor,** sen'sėr, *n*. One who examines manuscripts, etc., before they are published; one who censures; in war-time, an official who controls the public press, etc., and who also supervises private correspondence.
**Censorious,** sen-sō'ri-us, *a*. Addicted to censure.
**Censorship,** sen'sėr-ship, *n*. The office or dignity of a censor.
**Censurable,** sen'shūr-a-bl, *a*. Blamable.
**Censurably,** sen'shūr-a-bli, *adv*. In a manner worthy of blame.
**Censure,** sen'shūr, *n*. Severe judgment; reproof.—*vt*. (censuring, censured). To judge unfavorably of; to blame.
**Census,** sen'sus, *n*. An enumeration of the inhabitants of a country.
**Cent,** sent, *n*. A hundred; a copper coin in America, etc.; the hundredth part of a dollar. *Per cent*, a certain rate by the hundred.
**Centage,** sent'āj, *n*. Rate by the hundred.
**Cental,** sen'tal, *n*. A weight of 100 lbs.
**Centaur,** sen'tar, *n*. A fabulous being, half man and half horse.
**Centenarian,** sen-ten-ā'ri-an, *n*. A person a hundred years old.
**Centennial,** sen-ten'ni-al, *a*. Consisting of a hundred years; happening every hundred years.
**Center,** sen'tėr, *n*. The middle point; a nucleus.—*vt*. (centering, centered). To fix on a center; to collect to a point.—*vi*. To be collected to a point; to have as a center.
**Center-board,** sen'tėr-bōrd, *n*. A movable keel in yachts.
**Centesimal,** sen-tes'i-mal, *a*. The hundredth.—*n*. The hundredth part.
**Centigrade,** sen'ti-grād, *a*. Divided into a hundred degrees.
**Centimeter,** sen'ti-mē-tėr, *n*. The hundredth part of a meter, about two-fifths of an inch.
**Centipede,** sen'ti-pēd, *n*. An insect having a great number of feet.
**Cento,** sen'tō, *n*. A composition, literary or musical, formed by selections from different authors or composers.
**Central,** sen'tral, *a*. Placed in the center; relating to the center.
**Centralization,** sen'tral-īz-ā'shon, *n*. Act of centralizing.
**Centralize,** sen'tral-īz, *vt*. (centralizing, centralized). To render central; to concentrate.
**Centrally,** sen'tral-li, *adv*. In a central manner.
**Centric, Centrical,** sen'trik, sen'trik-al, *a*. Placed in the center; central; middle.
**Centrifugal,** sen-trif'ū-gal, *a*. Tending to fly from a center.
**Centripetal,** sen-trip'et-al, *a*. Tending toward the center.
**Centuple,** sen'tū-pl, *a*. Hundredfold.
**Centurion,** sen-tū'ri-on, *n*. Among the Romans the captain of a hundred men.
**Century,** sen'tū-ri, *n*. A hundred; the period of a hundred years.
**Cephalic,** se-fal'ik, *a*. Pertaining to the head.
**Ceramic,** se-ram'ik, *a*. Pertaining to the manufacture of porcelain and earthenware.
**Cerate,** sē'rāt, *n*. A thick ointment, composed of wax and oil.
**Cere,** sēr, *n*. The wax-like skin that covers the base of the bill in some birds.—*vt*. (cering, cered). To wax or cover with wax.
**Cereal,** sē'rē-al, *a*. Pertaining to corn.—*n*.

A grain plant.
**Cerebral,** se'rē-bral, *a.* Pertaining to the brain.
**Cerebration,** se-rē-brā'shon, *n.* Action of the brain, conscious or unconscious.
**Cerecloth, Cerement,** sēr'kloth, sēr'ment, *n.* Cloth dipped in melted wax, used in embalming; *pl.* grave-clothes.
**Ceremonial,** se-rē-mō'ni-al, *a.* Relating to ceremony.—*n.* Sacred rite; outward form.
**Ceremonious,** se-rē-mō'ni-us, *a.* Formal.
**Ceremony,** se'rē-mō-ni, *n.* Outward rite; form; observance; formality.
**Cerise,** se-rēz', *n.* Cherry-color.
**Certain,** sėr'tān, *a.* Sure; undeniable; decided; particular; some; one.
**Certainly,** sėr'tān-li, *adv.* Without doubt.
**Certainty,** sėr'tān-ti, *n.* A fixed or real state; truth; fact; regularity.
**Certificate,** sėr-tif'i-kāt, *n.* A written testimony; a credential.
**Certifier,** sėr'ti-fī-ėr, *n.* One who certifies.
**Certify,** sėr'ti-fī, *vt.* (certifying, certified). To give certain information; to testify to in writing.
**Cerulean,** sē-rū'lē-an, *a.* Sky-colored.
**Cerumen,** sē-rū'mēn, *n.* The wax or yellow matter secreted by the ear.
**Ceruse,** sē'rūz, *n.* White-lead; a cosmetic prepared from white-lead.
**Cervine,** sėr'vīn, *a.* Pertaining to deer.
**Cess,** ses, *n.* A rate or tax.—*vt.* To rate, or impose a tax on.
**Cessation,** ses-ā'shon, *n.* Stoppage.
**Cession,** se'shon, *n.* Surrender; a yielding up.
**Cesspool,** ses'pöl, *n.* A receptacle for sewage.
**Cestus,** ses'tus, *n.* The girdle of Venus; a loaded boxing-glove.
**Cesura,** sē-zū'ra, *n.* *See* CAESURA.
**Cetaceous,** sē-tā'shus, *a.* Pertaining to animals of the whale kind.
**Chafe,** chāf, *vt.* (chafing, chafed). To make warm by rubbing; to fret by rubbing; to enrage.—*vi.* To be fretted by friction; to rage.—*n.* A heat; a fretting.
**Chafer,** chāf'ėr, *n.* A beetle that eats roots, leaves, and young shoots.
**Chaff,** chaf, *n.* The husk of corn and grasses; banter.—*vt.* To banter.
**Chaffy,** chaf'i, *a.* Full of chaff; light.
**Chagrin,** sha-grēn', *n.* Ill-humor; vexation.—*vt.* To vex; to mortify.
**Chain,** chān, *n.* A series of links; a line of things connected; that which binds; a line formed of links, 66 feet long; (*pl.*) bondage; slavery.—*vt.* To bind with a chain; to confine.
**Chain-pump,** chān'pump, *n.* A pump consisting of an endless chain equipped with buckets, etc.
**Chain-shot,** chān'shot, *n.* Two cannon-balls connected by a chain.
**Chair,** chār, *n.* A movable seat; an official seat; professorship.—*vt.* To place or carry in a chair.
**Chairman,** chār'man, *n.* The presiding officer of an assembly; a president.
**Chairmanship,** chār'man-ship, *n.* The office of a chairman.
**Chaise,** shāz, *n.* A light horse carriage.
**Chalcedony,** kal-sed'ō-ni, *n.* A variety of quartz, having a whitish color.
**Chaldaic, Chaldean, Chaldee,** kal-dā'ik, kal-dē'an, kal'dē, *a.* Pertaining to Chaldea.—*n.* The language of the Chaldeans.
**Chaldron,** chäl'dron, *n.* A measure of coals, consisting of 36 bushels.
**Chalice,** cha'lis, *n.* A drinking-cup.
**Chalk,** chak, *n.* A white calcareous earth or carbonate of lime.—*vt.* To mark with chalk.
**Chalky,** chak'i, *a.* Resembling chalk; consisting of or containing chalk.
**Challenge,** chal'lenj, *n.* A summons to fight; a calling in question; an exception taken.—*vt.* (challenging, challenged). To summon to a fight; to defy; to call in question; to object to.
**Challengeable,** chal'lenj-a-bl, *a.* That may be challenged.
**Challenger,** chal'lenj-ėr, *n.* One who challenges.
**Chalybeate,** ka-lib'ē-āt, *a.* Impregnated with particles of iron.—*n.* A liquid into which iron or steel enters.
**Chamber,** chām'bėr, *n.* An apartment; an office; a hall of justice or legislation; a legislative body.
**Chambered,** chām'bėrd, *a.* Having chambers; shut up in a chamber.
**Chamberlain,** chām'bėr-lān, *n.* One who has charge of the chambers of a monarch or noble; an officer of state; a city treasurer; a steward.
**Chamber-maid,** chām'bėr-mād, *n.* A female servant who has the care of chambers.
**Chameleon,** ka-mē'lē-on, *n.* A species of lizard, whose color changes.
**Chamfer,** cham'fėr, *n.* A small furrow in wood, etc.; a bevel.—*vt.* To cut a chamfer in; to bevel.
**Chamois,** sham'i or sham'wa, *n.* A species of antelope; a soft leather.
**Chamomile,** ka'mō-mīl, *n.* *See* CAMOMILE.
**Champ,** champ, *vt.* To devour with violent action of the teeth; to bite the bit, as a horse.—*vi.* To keep biting.
**Champagne,** sham-pān', *n.* A kind of brisk sparkling wine.
**Champaign,** sham'pān, *a.* Open; level.—*n.* A flat open country.
**Champion,** cham'pi-on, *n.* A combatant for another, or for a cause; a hero; one victorious in contest.—*vt.* To fight for.
**Championship,** cham'pi-on-ship, *n.* State of being a champion; support of a cause.
**Chance,** chans, *n.* That which happens; accident; possibility of an occurrence; opportunity.—*vi.* (chancing, chanced). To happen.—*a.* Happening by chance; casual.
**Chancel,** chan'sel, *n.* That part of a church where the altar is placed.
**Chancellor,** chan'sel-lėr, *n.* A high judicial officer who presides over a court of chancery, etc.; a presiding official.
**Chancellorship,** chan'sel-lėr-ship, *n.* The office of a chancellor.
**Chancery,** chan'se-ri, *n.* A court of public affairs; in England, a division of the High Court of Justice.
**Chancre,** shang'kėr, *n.* An ulcer which arises from the venereal virus.
**Chandelier,** shan-dē-lēr', *n.* A frame with branches for candles or lamps.
**Chandler,** chand'lėr, *n.* A maker and seller of candles; a retail dealer.
**Chandlery,** chand'lė-ri, *n.* Goods sold by a chandler.
**Change,** chānj, *vt.* (changing, changed). To cause to turn from one state to another; to substitute; to give one kind of money for another.—*vt.* To be altered.—*n.* Variation; small money.
**Changeable,** chānj'a-bl, *a.* Subject to alteration; fickle; wavering.
**Changeably,** chānj'a-bli, *adv.* Inconstantly.
**Changeful,** chānj'ful, *a.* Full of change; inconstant; mutable; fickle; uncertain.
**Changeling,** chānj'ling, *n.* A child substituted for another; a fool; one apt to change.
**Changer,** chānj'er, *n.* One who changes.
**Channel,** chan'nel, *n.* A water-course; a narrow sea; means of passing or transmitting.—*vt.* (channelling, channelled). To form into a channel; to groove.
**Channelled,** chan'neld, *a.* Grooved longitudinally.
**Chant,** chant, *vt.* and *i.* To sing; to sing after the manner of a chant.—*n.* Song; a kind of sacred music; a part of church srvice.
**Chanter,** chant'ėr, *n.* A singer; a bagpipe tube with finger-holes.
**Chanticleer,** chan'ti-klēr, *n.* A cock.
**Chantry,** chant'ri, *n.* A chapel where priests sing or say mass for the souls of others.
**Chaos,** kā'os, *n.* Confused mass; disorder.
**Chaotic,** kā-ot'ik, *a.* Pertaining to chaos.

**Chap,** chap, *vt.* (chapping, chapped). To cause to crack.—*vt.* To open in slits.—*n.* A crack in the skin; the jaw; a young fellow.
**Chapel,** chap'el, *n.* A place of worship; a church; a sanctuary.
**Chaperon,** sha'pe-rōn, *n.* A married lady who attends a young lady to public places.—*vt.* To act as chaperon to.
**Chap-fallen,** chap'faln, *a.* Dejected.
**Chapiter,** chap'i-tėr, *n.* The head of a column.
**Chaplain,** chap'lān, *n.* A clergyman of the army, navy, court, etc.
**Chaplaincy,** chap'lān-si, *n.* The office of a chaplain.
**Chaplet,** chap'let, *n.* A garland or wreath; a string of beads; a rosary.
**Chapman,** chap'man, *n*; pl. **-men.** A dealer; a hawker or peddler.
**Chapter,** chap'tėr, *n.* Division of a book; a society of clergymen belonging to a cathedral or collegiate church; an organized branch of some fratrnity.
**Char,** chär, *vt.* (charring, charred). To reduce to a carbon by burning; to burn slightly.—*n.* A charred body; a lake fish or the salmon kind.
**Char-à-banc,** shar'a-ban, *n.* A vehicle with transverse seats facing forwards, now usually motor-driven.
**Character,** ka'rak-tėr, *n.* A mark engraved; a letter or figure; manner of writing; distinctive qualities of a person or thing; certificate of qualifications; a person in fiction or drama; a peculiar person.
**Characteristic,** ka'rak-tėr-is''tik, *a.* Constituting character; marking distinctive qualities.—*n.* That which constitutes character.
**Characterize,** ka'rak-tėr-īz, *vt.* To give a character to; to designate.
**Charade,** sha-räd', *n.* A species of riddle upon the syllables of a word.
**Charcoal,** chär'kōl, *n.* Coal made by charring wood; the residue of animal, vegetable, and many mineral substances, when heated to redness in close vessls.
**Chare,** chăr, *n.* A single job; a day's work.—*vi.* (charing, chared). To work by the day; to do small jobs.
**Charge,** chärj, *vt.* (charging, charged). To load; to put a price on; to entrust; to impute, as a debt or crime; to command; to confide; to attack.—*vi.* To make a charge or onset.—*n.* That which is laid on; that which loads a rifle, etc.; an assault or onset; order; instruction; person or thing committed to another's care; accusation; cost.
**Chargeable,** chärj'a-bl, *a.* That may be charged.
**Chargé d'affaires,** shär-zhā dä-fār, *n.* One who transacts diplomatic business in place of an ambassador.
**Charger,** chärj'ėr, *n.* A large dish; a warhorse.
**Charily,** chā'ri-li, *adv.* Carefully; frugally.
**Chariot,** cha'ri-ot, *n.* A stately carriage with four wheels.
**Charioteer,** cha'ri-ot-ēr'', *n.* The person who drives or conducts a chariot.
**Charitable,** cha'rit-a-bl, *a.* Liberal to the poor; pertaining to charity; indulgent.
**Charitably,** cha'rit-a-bli, *adv.* In a charitable manner; kindly; liberally.
**Charity,** cha'ri-ti, *n.* A disposition to relieve the wants of others; benevolence; alms; a charitable institution.
**Charlatan,** shär'la-tan, *n.* A quack.
**Charm,** chärm, *n.* A spell; fascination; a locket, etc.—*vt.* To enthrall; to delight.
**Charmer,** chärm'ėr, *n.* One who charms.
**Charming,** chärm'ing, *a.* Enchanting.
**Charnel-house,** chär'nel-hous, *n.* A place for bones of the dead.
**Chart,** chärt, *n.* A map; delineation of coasts, etc.; tabulated facts.
**Charter,** chär'tėr, *n.* A writing given as evidence of a grant, contract, etc.—*vt.* To establish by charter; to hire or to let (a ship).
**Chartered,** chär'tėrd, *a.* Granted by charter; privileged.
**Chartulary,** kär'tū-la-ri, *n.* A collection of charters; a register, as of a monastery.
**Char-woman,** chär'wum-un, *n.* A woman hired for odd work, or for single days.
**Chary,** chā'ri, *a.* Careful; wary; frugal.
**Chase,** chās, *vt.* (chasing, chased). To pursue; to hunt; to enchase; to cut into the form of a screw.—*n.* Pursuit; hunt; that which is pursued; a printer's frame.
**Chaser,** chās'ėr, *n.* One who chases; a gun at the bow or stern of a ship; an enchaser.
**Chasm,** kazm, *n.* A wide opening; an abyss.
**Chaste,** chāst, *a.* Free from impure desires; undefiled; pure in taste and style.
**Chasten,** chās'n, *vt.* To afflict in order to reclaim; to chastise; to correct.
**Chastise,** chas-tīz', *vt.* (chastising, chastised). To correct by punishment.
**Chastisement,** chas'tiz-ment, *n.* Correction.
**Chastity,** chas'ti-ti, *n.* Purity of the body, mind, language, or style.
**Chasuble,** chas'ū-bl, *n.* A priest's uppermost vestment when celebrating the eucharist.
**Chat,** chat, *vi.* (chatting, chatter).—To talk familiarly.—*n.* Familiar talk; a small song-bird.
**Château,** shä'tō, *n.* A castle; a country seat.
**Chatelaine,** shat'ė-lān, *n.* A chain with keys, etc., worn at a lady's waist.
**Chattel,** chat'el, *n.* Any article of movable goods; in law, all goods except such as have the nature of freehold.
**Chatter,** chat'ėr, *vi.* To make a noise by repeated clashing of the teeth; to jabber.—*n.* Sounds like those of a magpie or monkey; idle talk.
**Chatter-box,** chat'ėr-boks, *n.* One that talks incessantly: applied chiefly to children.
**Chatterer,** chat'ėr-ėr, *n.* A prater; a bird that makes a chattering sound.
**Chatty,** chat'i, *a.* Talkative.
**Chauffeur,** shō'fėr, *n.* A person regularly employed to drive a private motor-car.
**Chauvinism,** shō'vin-izm, *n.* Absurdly exaggerated patriotism or military enthusiasm.
**Cheap,** chēp, *a.* Of a low price; common; not respected.
**Cheapen,** chēp'n, *vt.* To beat down in price; to depreciate.
**Cheaply,** chēp'li, *adv.* At a small price.
**Cheapness,** chēp'nes, *n.* State or quality of being cheap; lowness in price.
**Cheat,** chēt, *vt.* To defraud; to deceive.—*n.* A deceitful act; a swindler.
**Check,** chek, *vt.* To stop; to curb; to chide; to compare with corresponding evidence.—*vi.* To stop; to clash or interfere.—*n.* An attack made on the king in chess; a stop; control; a counterfoil; a token; a cheque; cloth with a square pattern.
**Checker,** chek'ėr, *n.* One who checks. *See* CHEQUER.
**Checkmate,** chek'māt, *n.* A move in chess which ends the game; defeat.—*vt.* To give checkmate to; to frustrate; to defeat.
**Cheddar,** ched'ėr, *n.* A rich English cheese.
**Cheek,** chēk, *n.* The side of the face below the eyes on each side; impudence.
**Cheep,** chēp, *vi.* and *t.* To pule; to chirp.—*n.* A chirp.
**Cheer,** chēr, *n.* Expression of countenance; gaiety; viands; a shout of joy.—*vt.* To brighten the countenance of; to gladden; to applaud.—*vi.* To grow cheerful.
**Cheerful,** chēr'ful, *a.* Gay; sprightly; willing.
**Cheerily,** chēr'i-li, *adv.* With cheerfulness.
**Cheering,** chēr'ing, *a.* Encouraging.
**Cheerless,** chēr'les, *a.* Gloomy; dejected.
**Cheery,** chēr'i, *a.* Blithe; sprightly; promoting cheerfulness.
**Cheese,** chēz, *n.* Coagulated milk pressed into a firm mass, and used as food; anything in the form of cheese.
**Chef,** shef, *n.* A head cook.

**Chemical,** kem'ik-al, *a.* Pertaining to chemistry.
**Chemically,** kem'ik-al-li, *adv.* By chemical process or operation.
**Chemise,** she-mēz', *n.* An under garment worn by women.
**Chemist,** kem'ist, *n.* One versed in chemistry.
**Chemistry,** kem'ist-ri, *n.* The science which treats of the properties and nature of elementary substances.
**Cherish,** che'rish, *vt.* To treat with tenderness; to encourage.
**Cheroot,** shē-röt', *n.* A kind of cigar with both ends cut square off.
**Cherry,** che'ri, *n.* A tree and its fruit, of the plum family.—*a.* Like a cherry in color.
**Cherub,** che'rub, *n.*; pl. **-ubs** and **-ubim.** An angel of the second order; a beautiful child.
**Cherubic,** cher'rū'bik, *a.* Angelic.
**Chess,** ches, *n.* A game played by two, with 16 pieces each on a board of 64 squares.
**Chess-board,** ches'bōrd, *n.* The checkered board used in the game of chess.
**Chess-man,** ches'man, *n.* A piece used in the game of chess.
**Chest,** chest, *n.* A large close box; the part of the body containing the heart, lungs, etc.—*vt.* To reposit in a chest.
**Chestnut,** ches'nut, *n.* A kind of tree; its fruit or nut; a stale joke or anecdote.—*a.* Of the color of a chestnut; reddish-brown.
**Chevalier,** she'va-lēr, *n.* A horseman; a knight.
**Chevron,** shev'run, *n.* A heraldic figure representing two rafters of a house meeting at the top; similar mark on uniform, worn by an N.C.O.
**Chew,** chö, *vt.* To grind with the teeth; to masticate.
**Chic,** shēk, *n.* Easy elegance; smartness.
**Chicane, Chicanery,** shi-kān', shi-kān'é-ri, *n.* Trickery; artifice.—*Chicane, vt.* (chicaning, chicaned). To use chicane or artifices.
**Chick, Chicken,** chik, chik'en, *n.* The young of various birds; a child.
**Chicken-hearted,** chik'en-härt-ed, *a.* Timid; fearful; cowardly.
**Chicken-pox,** chik'en-poks, *n.* An eruptive disease, generally appearing in children.
**Chickweed,** chik'wēd, *n.* A weed of which chickens and birds are fond.
**Chicory,** chik'o-ri, *n.* A common English plant, often used to mix with coffee.
**Chide,** chīd, *vt.* and *i.* (chiding, pret. chid, pp. chid, chidden). To reprove; to scold.
**Chief,** chēf, *a.* Being at the head; first; leading.—*n.* A principal person; a leader.
**Chiefly,** chēf'li, *adv.* Mainly; especially.
**Chieftain,** chēf'tān, *n.* A chief; the head of a troop, army, or clan.
**Chiffonir,** shif'fon-ēr, *n.* A small side-board.
**Chilblain,** chil'blān, *n.* A blain or sore produced on the hands or feet by cold.
**Child,** chīld, *n.*; pl. **Children.** An infant; one very young; a son or daughter; offspring.
**Child-bearing,** chīld'bār-ing, *n.* The act of bringing forth children.
**Childbed,** chīld'bed, *n.* The state of a woman in labor.
**Childbirth,** chīld'bėrth, *n.* The act of bringing forth a child; travail; labor.
**Childe,** chīld, *n.* A noble youth; a squire.
**Childhood,** chīld'hud, *n.* State of a child.
**Childish,** chīld'ish, *a.* Like a child; trifling.
**Childless,** chīld'les, *a.* Destitute of children.
**Childlike,** chīld'līk, *a.* Like a child; innocent.
**Chill,** chil, *n.* A shivering with cold; a cold fit; that which checks or disheartens.—*a.* Cold; tending to cause shivering; dispiriting.—*vt.* To make cold; to discourage.
**Chilling,** chil'ing, *a.* Causing to shiver; tending to repress enthusiasm.
**Chilly,** chil'i, *a.* Moderately chill.
**Chime,** chīm, *n.* A set of bells tuned to each other; their sound; harmony; the brim of a cask.—*vi.* (chiming, chimed). To sound in consonance; to agree.—*vt.* To cause to sound in harmony; to cause to sound.
**Chimera,** ki-mē'ra, *n.* a fire-breathing monster of fable; a vain or idle fancy.
**Chimere,** shi-mēr', *n.* A bishop's upper robe, to which the lawn sleeves are attached.
**Chimerical,** ki-me'rik-al, *a.* Wildly or vainly conceived.
**Chimney,** chim'nē, *n.* The funnel through which the smoke is conveyed; a flue; a glass funnel for a lamp, etc.
**Chimney-piece,** chim'nē-pēs, *n.* An ornamental structure round a fireplace.
**Chimpanzee,** chim'pan-zē, *n.* A large W. African ape.
**Chin,** chin, *n.* The lower part of the face; the point of the under jaw.
**China,** chī'na, *n.* A species of fine porcelain.
**Chinchilla,** chin-chil'la, *n.* A genus of S. American rodent animals; their fur.
**Chinese,** chī-nēz', *n. sing.* and *pl.* A native of China; the language of China.
**Chink,** chingk, *n.* A narrow opening; a cleft; a sharp metallic sound; money.—*vi.* To crack; to make a sound as by the collision of coins.—*vt.* To jingle, as coins.
**Chinky,** chingk'i, *a.* Full of fissures.
**Chintz,** chints, *n.* Cotton cloth printed with colored designs.
**Chip,** chip, *n.* A fragment; a small piece.—*vt.* (chipping, chipped). To cut into chips; to cut off chips.—*vi.* To fly off in small pieces.
**Chirography,** kī-rog'ra-fi, *n.* Handwriting; fortune-telling by examination of the hand.
**Chiromancy,** kī'rō-man-si, *n.* Palmistry.
**Chiropodist,** kīr-op'od-ist, *n.* One who extracts corns, removes bunions, etc.
**Chirp,** chėrp, *vi.* To make the lively noise of small birds.—*n.* A short, shrill note of birds.
**Chirrup,** chi'rup, *vi.* To chirp.
**Chisel,** chiz'el, *n.* A cutting tool, used in woodwork, masonry, sculpture, etc.—*vt.* (chiselling, chiselled). To cut, gouge, or engrave with a chisel.
**Chit,** chit, *n.* A note; an order or pass.
**Chit-chat,** chit'chat, *n.* Prattle.
**Chivalric, Chivalrous,** shi'val-rik, shi'val-rus, *a.* Pertaining to chivalry; gallant.
**Chivalry,** shi'val-ri, *n.* Knighthood; customs pertaining to the orders of knighthood; heroic defense of life and honor.
**Chive,** chīv, *n.* Same as *Cive.*
**Chloral,** klō'ral, *n.* An oily liquid produced from chlorine and alcohol; a narcotic.
**Chloric,** klō'rik, *a.* Pertaining to chlorine.
**Chloride,** klō'rid, *n.* A compound of chlorine and some other substance.
**Chlorine,** klō'rīn, *n.* A gaseous substance obtained from common salt, used in bleaching and disinfecting.
**Chlorodyne,** klō'rō-dīn, *n.* An anodyne, containing morphia, chloroform, and prussic acid.
**Chloroform,** klō'rō-form, *n.* A volatile thin liquid, used as an anesthetic.
**Chlorophyll,** klō'rō-fil, *n.* The green coloring matter of plants.
**Chocolate,** cho'kō-lāt, *n.* A preparation from the kernels of the cacao-nut.—*a.* Dark, glossy brown.
**Choice,** chois, *n.* Act of choosing; option; the thing chosen; best part of anything; the object of choice.—*a.* Select; precious.
**Choir,** kwīr, *n.* A body of singers in a church; part of a church set apart for the singers.
**Choke,** chōk, *vt.* (choking, choked). To strangle by compressing the throat of; to block up; to stiffle.—*vi.* To be suffocated; to be blocked up.
**Choke-damp** chōk'damp, *n.* Carbonic acid gas; a suffocating vapor in coal-mines, etc.
**Choler,** ko'lėr, *n.* Anger; wrath.
**Cholera,** ko'lė-ra, *n.* A disease accompanied by purging and vomiting.

C

**Choleric,** ko'lė-rik, *a.* Irascible; peevish.
**Choose,** chöz, *vt.* (choosing, pret. chose, pp. chosen). To take by preference.—*vi.* To make choice; to prefer.
**Chooser,** chöz'ėr, *n.* One who chooses.
**Chop,** chop, *vt.* (chopping, chopped). To cut into small pieces; to barter or exchange.—*vi.* To change; to turn suddenly.—*n.* A piece chopped off; a small piece of meat; a crack or cleft; a turn or change; the jaw; the mouth.
**Chop-fallen,** chop'fal-en, *a.* Dejected.
**Choppy,** chop'i, *a.* Full of clefts; having short abrupt waves.
**Chopsticks,** chop'stiks, *n.* Two sticks of wood, ivory, etc., used by the Chinese in eating.
**Choral,** kō'ral, *a.* Belonging to a choir.
**Chord,** kord, *n.* String of a musical instrument; the simultaneous combination of different sounds; a straight line joining the ends of the arc of a circle or curve.
**Chorister,** ko'rist-ėr, *n.* A singer in a choir.
**Chorus,** kō'rus, *n.* A company of singers; a piece performed by a company in concert; verses of a song in which the company join the singer; any union of voices in general.
**Chosen,** chōz'n, *a.* Select; eminent.
**Chough,** chuf, *n.* A bird of the crow family.
**Chouse,** chous, *vt.* (choosing, choused). To cheat; to trick.—*n.* A trick; imposition.
**Chrism,** krizm, *n.* Consecrated oil.
**CHRIST,** krīst, *n.* THE ANOINTED; the Messiah; the Saviour.
**Christen,** kris'n, *vt.* To baptize; to name.
**Christendom,** kris'n-dum, *n.* The countries inhabited by Christians; the whole body of Christians.
**Christening,** kris'n-ing, *n.* Baptism.
**Christian,** kris'ti-an, *n.* A professed follower of Christ.—*a.* Pertaining to Christ or Christianity.
**Christianity,** kris-ti-an'i-ti, *n.* The religion of Christians.
**Christianize,** kris'ti-an-īz, *vt.* (christianizing, christianized). To convert to Christianity.
**Christmas,** kris'mas, *n.* The festival of Christ's nativity, observed annually on 25th December.—*a.* Belonging to Christmas time.
**Chromatic,** kō-mat'ik, *a.* Relating to color; proceeding by semitones.
**Chrome, Chromium,** krōm, krō'mi-um, *n.* A steel-gray, hard metal, from which colored preparations are made.
**Chromic,** krōm'ik, *a.* Pertaining to chrome.
**Chronic,** kron'ik, *a.* Continuing a long time; lingering; continuous.
**Chronicle,** kron'i-kl, *n.* An historical account of events in order of time.—*vt.* (chronicling, chronicled). To record.
**Chronicler,** kron'i-klėr, *n.* An historian.
**Chronological,** kron-ō-loj'ik-al, *a.* Relating to chronology; in order of time.
**Chronologist,** kro-nol'o-jist, *n.* One who studies or is versed in chronology.
**Chronology,** kro-nol'o-ji, *n.* Arrangement of events according to their dates.
**Chronometer,** kro-nom'et-ėr, *n.* An instrument that measures time.
**Chrysalis,** kris'a-lis, *n.*; pl. **-ides** or **-ises.** The form of certain insects before they arrive at their winged state.
**Chrysanthemum,** kri-san'thē-mum, *n.* The name of numerous composite plants.
**Chrysoberyl,** kris'o-be-ril, *n.* A yellowish-green gem.
**Chrysolite,** kris'ō-līt, *n.* A gem of a yellowish or greenish color.
**Chrysoprase,** kris'o-präz, *n.* A yellowish-green mineral, a variety of chalcedony.
**Chub,** chub, *n.* A small river fish of the carp family.
**Chubby,** chub'i, *a.* Round or full-cheeked; plump; having a large fat face.
**Chuck,** chuk, *vi.* To make the noise of a hen.—*vt.* To call, as a hen her chickens; to tap under the chin; to throw with quick motion; to pitch.—*n.* The call of a hen; a slight blow under the chin; a short throw.
**Chuckle,** chuk'l, *vi.* (chuckling, chuckled). To laugh in the throat; to feel inward triumph or exultation.—*n.* A short and suppressed laugh in the throat.
**Chum,** chum, *n.* A sharer of one's rooms; an intimate friend.
**Chunk,** chungk, *n.* A short, thick piece.
**Church,** chėrch, *n.* A house consecrated to the worship of God among Christians; the collective body of Christians; a particular body of Christians; the body of clergy; eccelesiastical authority.—*vt.* To give or receive a service in church, as after childbirth.
**Churching,** chėrch'ing, *n.* The offering of thanks in church, as after childbirth.
**Churchman,** chėrch'man, *n.* An ecclesiastic; an adherent of the Church.
**Churchwarden,** chėrch-war'den, *n.* An official who manages the affairs of the church, and represents parish interests; a clay tobacco-pipe with a long stem.
**Churchyard,** chėrch'yärd, *n.* The ground adjoining the church, in which the dead are buried.
**Churl,** chėrl, *n.* A rude, ill-bred man; a rustic laborer; a miser.
**Churlish,** chėrl'ish, *a.* Surly; sullen.
**Churn,** chėrn, *n.* a vessel in which butter is made.—*vt.* To agitate cream for making butter; to shake with violence.
**Chyle,** kīl, *n.* A milky fluid separated from aliments in the intestines and entering the blood.
**Chyme,** kīm, *n.* The pulp of partially digested food before the chyle is extracted.
**Cicatrix, Cicatrice,** si-kā'triks, sik'a-tris, *n.* A scar; a mark of a wound or ulcer.
**Cicatrize,** si'ka-trīz, *vt.* (cicatrizing, cicatrized). To induce the formation of a scar.—*vi.* To heal or be healed; to skin over.
**Cicely,** sis'e-li, *n.* An umbelliferous plant.
**Cicerone,** chi-che-rō'ne, sis-e-rōne, *n.* A guide.
**Cider,** sī'dėr, *n.* A fermented drink prepared from the juice of apples.
**Cigar,** si-gär', *n.* A roll of tobacco for smoking.
**Cigarette,** sig-a-ret', *n.* A little cut tobacco rolled up in rice paper, used for smoking.
**Cilia,** sil'i-a, *n.pl.*. Minute hairs on plants or animals.
**Ciliary,** sil'i-a-ri, *a.* Belonging to or of the nature of eyelashes.
**Cimmerian,** sim-mē'ri-an, *a.* Pertaining to the fabulous Cimmerians, who dwelt in perpetual darkness; extremely dark.
**Cinchona,** sin-kō'na, *n.* A genus of S. American trees whose bark yields quinine; Peruvian bark.
**Cincture,** singk'tūr, *n.* A girdle.
**Cinder,** sin'der, *n.* A burned coal; an ember; a piece of dross or slag.
**Cinema,** sin'e-ma, *n.* A picture-house or theater for the exhibition of moving pictures.
**Cinematograph,** sin-e-mat'o-graf, *n.* A machine for projecting on a screen a series of photographs of changing scenes and moving objects, so as to produce the illusion of continuous motion.
**Cinerary,** si'ne-ra-ri, *a.* Pertaining to ashes.
**Çingalese,** sing'ga-lēz, *a.* Pertaining to Ceylon.
**Cinnabar,** sin'na-bär, *n.* Red sulphide of mercury; vermilion.
**Cinnamon,** sin'na-mon, *n.* The inner bark of a tree, a native of Ceylon; a spice.
**Cipher,** sī'fėr, *n.* The figure 0 or nothing; any numeral; a person or thing of no importance; a device; a secret writing.—*vi.* To use figures.—*vt.* To write in secret characters.
**Circle,** sėr'kl, *n.* A plane figure contained by a curved line, every point of which is equally distant from a point within the figure, called the center; the curved line itself; a ring; enclosure; a class; a coterie.—*vt.* (circling, circled). To

move round; to enclose.—*vi.* To move circularly.
**Circlet,** sėr'klet, *n.* A little circle; a chaplet.
**Circuit,** sėr'kit, *n.* Act of going round; space measured by travelling round; the journey of judges to hold courts; the district visited by judges; path of an electric current.
**Circuitous,** sėr-kū'it-us, *a.* Going in a circuit; round about; not direct.
**Circular,** sėr'kū-lėr, *a.* Round; addressed to a number of persons.—*n.* A paper addressed to a number of persons.
**Circulate,** sėr'kū-lāt, *vi.* (circulating, circulated). To move in a circle; to have currency.—*vt.* To spread; to give currency to.
**Circulating,** sėr'kū-lāt-ing, *a.* That circulates; repeating, as figures in decimals.
**Circulation,** sėr-kū-lā'shon, *n.* Act of circulating; diffusion; currency.
**Circumambient,** sėr-kum-am'bi-ent, *a.* Surrounding; encompassing.
**Circumcise,** sėr'kum-sīz, *vt.* (circumcising, circumcised). To cut off the foreskin, according to Jewish and Mohammedan law.
**Circumcision,** sėr-kum-si'zhon, *n.* The act of circumcising.
**Circumference,** sėr-kum'fė-rens, *n.* The bounding line of a circle.
**Circumflex,** sėr'kum-fleks, *n.* An accent on long vowels, generally marked thus (ˆ).
**Circumfuse,** sėr-kum-fūz', *vt.* To pour round; to spread round.
**Circumjacent,** sėr-kum-jā'sent, *a.* Lying round about.
**Circumlocution,** sėr-kum'lō-kū''shon, *n.* A roundabout mode of speaking.
**Circumlocutory,** sėr-kum-lok'ū-to-ri, *a.* Pertaining to circumlocution; periphrastic.
**Circumnavigate,** sėr-kum-na'vi-gāt, *vt.* To sail round.
**Circumnavigation,** sėr-kum-na'vi-gā''shon, *n.* Act of circumnavigating.
**Circumnavigator,** sėr-kum-na'vi-gāt-ėr, *n.* One who sails round.
**Circumscribe,** sėr'kum-skrīb, *vt.* To draw a line round; to limit; to restrict.
**Circumspect,** sėr'kum-spekt, *a.* Watchful on all sides; wary; thoughtful.
**Circumspection,** sėr-kum-spek'shon, *n.* Watchfulness; deliberation; wariness.
**Circumstance,** sėr'kum-stans, *n.* Something attending, or relative to a main fact or case; event; (*pl.*) state of affairs; condition.
**Circumstantial,** sėr-kum-stan'shal, *a.* Consisting in or pertaining to circumstances; attending; detailed.
**Circumstantiate,** sėr-kum-stan'shi-āt, *vt.* To confirm by circumstances.
**Circumvallation,** sėr-kum'val-lā''shon, *n.* The act of surrounding with fortifications; a line of field fortifications.
**Circumvent,** sėr-kum-vent', *vt.* To encompass; to outwit.
**Circumvention,** sėr-kum-ven'shon, *n.* Outwitting; overreaching.
**Circumvolution,** sėr-kum'vō-lū''shon, *n.* Act of turning or rolling round.
**Circus,** sėr'kus, *n.*; pl. **-ses.** Among the Romans, a place for horse-races; a place for feats of horsemanship and acrobatic displays.
**Cirrus,** sir'rus, *n.*; pl. **Cirri.** A tendril; a light fleecy cloud at a high elevation.
**Cist,** sist, *n.* A prehistoric place of interment formed of flat stones.
**Cistern,** sis'tėrn, *n.* An artificial receptacle for water, etc.; a natural reservoir.
**Citable,** sīt'a-bl, *a.* That may be cited.
**Citadel,** si'ta-del, *n.* A fortress in or near a city.
**Citation,** sī-tā'shon, *n.* Quotation; a summons.
**Cite,** sīt, *vt.* (citing, cited). To summon to appear in a court; to quote; to adduce.
**Citizen,** si'ti-zen, *n.* An inhabitant of a city; one who has full municipal and political privileges.—*a.* Having the qualities of a citizen.
**Citizenship,** si'ti-zen-ship, *n.* State of being vested with the rights of a citizen.
**Citric,** sit'rik, *a.* Belonging to citrons, or to lemons or limes.
**Citrine,** sit'rīn, *n.* A yellow pellucid variety of quartz.
**Citron,** sit'ron, *n.* The fruit of the citron tree, a large species of lemon; the tree itself.
**City,** si'ti, *n.* A large town; a borough or town corporate; the inhabitants of a city.
**Cive,** sīv, *n.* A small species of leek.
**Civet,** si'vet, *n.* A perfume taken from the anal glands of the civet-cat.
**Civet-cat,** si'vet-kat, *n.* A carnivorous animal, native of N. Africa and Asia.
**Civic,** si'vik, *a.* Pertaining to a city or citizen; relating to civil affairs.
**Civil,** si'vil, *a.* Relating to the government of a city or state; polite; political; lay; legislative, not military; intestine, not foreign.
**Civilian,** si-vil'i-an, *n.* One skilled in the civil law; one engaged in civil, not military or clerical pursuits.
**Civility,** si-vil'i-ti, *n.* Quality of being civil; good breeding; (*pl.*) acts of politeness.
**Civilization,** si'vil-iz-a''shon, *n.* Act of civilizing, or the state of being civilized.
**Civilize,** si'vil-īz, *vt.* (civilizing, civilized). To reclaim from a savage state.
**Civilized,** si'vil-īzd, *a.* Having civilization; refined.
**Clack,** klak, *n.* A sharp, abrupt noise; continual or excessive talk; an instrument that clacks.—*vi.* To make a sudden, sharp noise; to talk incessantly.
**Clad,** klad, pp. of *clothe.*
**Claim,** klām, *vt.* To ask; to demand as due.—*n.* A demand as of right; a title to something in the possession of another; a pretension.
**Claimable,** klām'a-bl, *a.* That may be claimed.
**Claimant,** klām'ant, *n.* One who claims.
**Clairvoyance,** klār-voi'ans, *n.* A power attributed to a mesmerised person, by which he discerns objects concealed from sight, etc.
**Clam,** klam, *vt.* (clamming, clammed). To smear with viscous matter.—*n.* A clamp; a bivalve shell-fish.
**Clamant,** klam'ant, *a.* Crying aloud; urgent.
**Clamber,** klam'bėr, *vi.* To climb with difficulty, or with hands and feet.
**Clammy,** klam'i, *a.* Sticky; adhesive.
**Clamor,** klam'ėr, *n.* Loud and continued noise; uproar.—*vi.* To call aloud; to make importunate demands.
**Clamp,** klamp, *n.* A piece of timber or iron, used to strengthen or fasten; a heavy footstep.—*vt.* To fasten or strengthen with clamps; to tread heavily.
**Clan,** klan, *n.* A family; a tribe; a sect.
**Clandestine,** klan-des'tin, *a.* Secret; underhand.
**Clang,** klang, *vt.* or *i.* To make a sharp sound, as by striking metallic substances.—*n.* A loud sound made by striking together metallic bodies.
**Clangor,** klang'gėr, *n.* A clang; a ringing sound.
**Clank,** klangk, *n.* The loud sound made by the collison of metallic bodies.—*vi.* or *t.* To sound or cause to sound with a clank.
**Clannish,** klan'ish, *a.* Devoted to the members of one's own clan and illiberal to others.
**Clansman,** klanz'man, *n.* One belonging to the same clan.
**Clap,** klap, *vt.* (clapping, clapped or clapt). To strike together so as to make a noise; to strike with something broad; to shut hastily; to pat.—*vi.* To move together suddenly with noise; to strike the hands together in applause.—*n.* A noise made by sudden collision; a sudden explosive sound; a striking of hands in applause.
**Clapper,** klap'ėr, *n.* He or that which claps; the tongue of a bell.
**Claptrap,** klap'trap, *n.* Words used merely to gain applause.—*a.* Showy in sentiment.

**Claret,** kla'ret, *n.* A French red wine.—*a.* Of the color of claret wine.
**Clarification,** kla'ri-fi-kā''shon, *n.* The clearing of liquids by chemical means.
**Clarifier,** kla'ri-fī-ėr, *n.* That which clarifies.
**Clarify,** kla'ri-fī, *vt.* (clarifying, clarified). To purify; to make clear.—*vi.* To become clear, pure, or fine.
**Clarion,** kla'ri-on, *n.* A kind of trumpet with a shrill tone.
**Clarionet, Clarinet,** kla'ri-on-et, kla'rin-et, *n.* A musical wind instrument of wood.
**Clary,** klā'r, *n.* A plant of the sage genus.
**Clash,** klash, *vi.* To make a noise by collision; to meet in opposition; to interfere.—*vt.* To strike noisily together.—*n.* Noisy collision; opposition.
**Clasp,** klasp, *n.* An embrace; a hook for fastening; a catch; a bar added to a military medal to commemorate a particular battle or campaign.—*vt.* To fasten together with a clasp; to inclose in the hand; to embrace closely.
**Clasper,** klasp'ėr, *n.* One who or that which clasps; the tendril of a vine.
**Clasp-knife,** klasp'nīf, *n.* A knife the blade of which folds into the handle.
**Class,** klas, *n.* A rank of persons or things; an order; a group.—*vt.* To arrange in classes.
**Classic,** klas'ik, *a.* Of the first rank; standard in literary quality; pertaining to Greek and Roman antiquity; pure in style.—*n.* An author of the first rank; a Greek or Roman author of this character; a work of the first rank.
**Classical,** klas'ik-al, *a.* Pertaining to writers of the first rank; pertaining to ancient Greece or Rome; correct; refined (taste, style, etc.).
**Classicism,** klas'i-sizm, *n.* A classic idiom or style.
**Classicist,** klas'i-sist, *n.* One versed in the classics; one imbued with classicism.
**Classification,** klas'i-fi-kā''shon, *n.* Act of forming into a class or classes.
**Classify,** klas'i-fī, *vt.* (classifying, classified). To distribute into classes.
**Clatter,** klat'tėr, *vi.* To make repeated rattling noises; to talk fast and idly.—*vt.* To cause to rattle.—*n.* A rattling, confused noise.
**Clause,** klaz, *n.* A member of a sentence; a distinct part of a contract, will, etc.
**Claustrophobia,** klas'trō-fo''bė-a, *n.* Morbid fear of confined spaces.
**Clavicle,** klav'i-kl, *n.* The collar-bone.
**Clavier,** klav'i-ėr, *n.* The key-board of the pianoforte, etc.
**Claw,** kla, *n.* The sharp hooked nail of an animal; that which resembles a claw.—*vt.* To scrape, scratch, or tear.
**Clay,** klā, *n.* A tenacious kind of earth; earth in general; the body.—*vt.* To cover with clay; to purify and whiten with clay, as sugar.
**Clayey,** klā'ē, *a.* Partaking of clay; like clay.
**Claymore,** klā'mōr, *n.* A large two-edged sword; a basket-hilted broadsword.
**Clean,** klēn, *a.* Free from dirt; pure.—*adv.* Quite; fully.—*vt.* To purify; to cleanse.
**Cleanliness,** klen'li-nes, *n.* State of being cleanly; purity.
**Cleanly,** klen'li, *a.* Clean in habits; neat.—*adv.* In a clean manner; neatly.
Ckeabbessm klēn'nes, *n.* Freedom from dirt; purity; innocence.
**Cleanse,** klenz, *vt.* (cleansing, cleansed). To make clean or pure; to free from guilt.
**Cleanser,** klenz'ėr, *n.* One who or that which cleanses.
**Clear,** klēr, *a.* Bright; shining; open; fair; plain; shrill; cheerful; acute; free from debt; free from guilt; exempt.—*adv.* Manifestly; quite; indicating entire separation.—*vt.* To make clear; to free from obstructions or obscurity; to cleanse; to justify; to make gain as profit; to prepare, as waste land, for tillage or pasture; to leap over; to pay customs on a cargo.—*vi.* To become clear; to become fair; to exchange checks.
**Clearance,** klēr'ans, *n.* Act of clearing; a certificate that a ship has been cleared at the custom-house.
**Clearer,** klēr'ėr, *n.* One who or that which clears.
**Clear-headed,** klēr'hed-ed, *a.* Having a clear understanding.
**Clearing,** klēr'ing, *n.* Act of making clear; act of distributing the proceeds of traffic passing over several railways; among bankers, the act of exchanging drafts on each other's houses; a tract of land cleared of wood.
**Clearly,** klēr'li, *adv.* In a clear manner.
**Clear-story, Clere-story,** klēr'stō-ri, *n.* The upper story of a cathedral or church.
**Cleat,** klēt, *n.* A piece of wood or iron in a ship to fasten ropes upon; a wedge.
**Cleavable,** klēv'a-bl, *a.* That may be cloven.
**Cleavage,** klēv'āj, *n.* The act or manner of cleaving.
**Cleave,** klēv, *vi.* (pret. clave, cleaved, pp. cleaved). To stick; to adhere.
**Cleave,** klēv, *vt.* (pret. clove, cleaved, cleft, pp. cloven, cleaved, cleft). To split; to sever.—*vi.* To part asunder.
**Cleaver,** klēv'ėr, *n.* One who cleaves; that which cleaves; a butcher's axe.
**Cleek,** klēk, *n.* A large hook; an iron-headed club used in golf.
**Clef,** klef, *n.* A character prefixed to a staff in music to determine the pitch.
**Cleft,** kleft, *n.* A crevice; a fissure.
**Cleg,** kleg, *n.* A gadfly; a horse-fly.
**Clematis,** klem'a-tis, *n.* The generic name of woody climbing plants.
**Clemency,** kle'men-si, *n.* Mercifulness; mildness; tenderness.
**Clement,** kle'ment, *a.* Mild; humane.
**Clench,** klensh, *vt.* To secure; to confirm; to grasp.
**Clepsydra,** klep'si-dra, *n.* A water-clock.
**Clergy,** klėr'ji, *n.pl.* The body or order of men set apart to the service of God, in the Christian church.
**Clergyman,** klėr'ji-man, *n.* A man in holy orders; a minister of the gospel.
**Cleric,** kle'rik, *a.* Clerical.—*n.* A clergyman.
**Clerical,** kle'rik-al, *n.* Pertaining to the clergy, or to a clerk.
**Clericalism,** kle'rik-al-izm, *n.* Clerical power to influence; sacerdotalism.
**Clerk,** klärk, *n.* A clergyman; one who reads the responses in church; one who is employed under another as a writer.
**Clerkship,** klärk'ship, *n.* The office or business of a clerk.
**Clever,** kle'vėr, *a.* Adroit; talented; excuted with ability.
**Cleverness,** kle'vėr-nes, *n.* Quality of being clever; smartness; skill.
**Cliché,** klē'shā, *n.* A hackneyed phrase.
**Click,** klik, *vi.* To make a small sharp noise, or a succession of such sounds.—*n.* A small sharp sound.
**Client,** klī'ent, *n.* A person under patronage; one who employs a lawyer.
**Clientele,** klī'en-tēl, *n.* One's clients collectively.
**Cliff,** klif, *n.* A precipice; a steep rock.
**Cliffy,** klif'i, *a.* Having cliffs; craggy.
**Climacteric,** kli-mak-te'rik, *n.* A critical period in human life.
**Climate,** klī'māt, *n.* The condition of a country in respect of temperature, dryness, wind, etc.
**Climatic,** klī-mat'ik, *a.* Pertaining to a climate; limited by a climate.
**Climax,** klī'maks, *n.* A figure of rhetoric, in which the language gradually rises in strength and dignity; culmination; acme.
**Climb,** klīm, *vi.* To creep up step by step; to ascend.—*vt.* To ascent.
**Climber,** klīm'ėr, *n.* One who climbs; a plant that rises on a support.
**Clime,** klīm, *n.* A region of the earth.
**Clinch,** klinsh, *vt.* To rivet; to clench; to make

conclusive.—*n.* A catch; a pun.
**Clincher,** klinsh'ėr, *n.* A kind of nail; a conclusive argument.
**Cling,** kling, *vi.* (clinging, clung). To hang by twining round; to adhere closely.
**Clinic, Clinical,** klin'ik, klin'ik-al, *a.* Pertaining to a sick-bed.—*n.* One confined to bed.
**Clink,** klingk, *vt.* To cause to ring or jingle.—*vi.* To ring.—*n.* A sound made by the collision of small sonorous bodies.
**Clinker,** klingk'ėr, *n.* A partially vitrified brick; a mass of incombustible slag.
**Clinometer,** klīn-om'et-ėr, *n.* An instrument for measuring the dip of rock strata.
**Clip,** klip, *vt.* (clipping, clipped). To shear; to trim with scissors; to cut short.—*n.* Act or product of sheep-shearing.
**Clipper,** klip'ėr, *n.* One who clips; a sharp fast-sailing vessel.
**Clipping,** klip'ing, *n.* The act of cutting off; a piece separated by clipping.
**Clique,** klēk, *n.* A party; a coterie; a set.
**Cloak,** klōk, *n.* A loose outer garment; a disguise; a pretext.—*vt.* To cover with a cloak; to hide; to veil.
**Clock,** klok, *n.* An instrument which measures time.
**Clock-work,** klok'wėrk, *n.* The machinery of a clock; well-adjusted mechanism.
**Clod,** klod, *n.* A lump of earth; a stupid fellow.—*vt.* (clodding, clodded). To pelt with clods.
**Clodhopper,** klod'hop-ėr, *n.* A clown, dolt.
**Clog,** klog, *vt.* (clogging, clogged). To hinder; to impede; to trammel.—*vi.* To be loaded.—*n.* Hindrance; a shoe with a wooden sole.
**Cloister,** klois'tėr, *n.* A monastery or nunnery; an arcade round an open court.—*vt.* To shut up in a cloister; to immure.
**Close,** klōz, *vt.* (closing, closed). To shut; to finish.—*vi.* To come close together; to end; to grapple; to come to an agreement.—*n.* End.
**Close,** klōs, *a.* Shut fast; tight; dense; near; stingy; trusty; intense; without ventilation; disposed to keep secrets.—*adv.* Tightly; in contact, or very near.—*n.* An inclosed place; precinct of a cathedral.
**Close-fisted,** klōs'fist-ed, *a.* Niggardly.
**Closely,** klōs'li, *adv.* In a close manner.
**Closet,** kloz'et, *n.* A small private apartment.—*vt.* To take into a private apartment.
**Closing,** klōz'ing, *p.a.* That concludes.
**Closure,** klōz'ūr, *n.* The act of closing; the act of ending a parliamentary debate.
**Clot,** klot, *n.* A mass of soft or fluid matter concreted.—*vi.* (clotting, clotted). To become thick; to coagulate.
**Cloth,** kloth, *n.* A woven material or fabric; the covering of a table; the clerical profession.
**Clothe,** klōᴛʜ, *vt.* (clothing, clothed or clad). To put clothes on; to cover or spread over.
**Clothes,** klōᴛʜz, *n.pl.* of *cloth.* Garments for the body; blankets, etc., on a bed.
**Clothes-horse,** klōᴛʜz'hors, *n.* A frame to hang clothes on.
**Clothier,** klōᴛʜ'i-ėr, *n.* A maker or seller of cloths or clothes.
**Cloud,** kloud, *n.* A collection of visible vapor, suspended in the air; something similar to this; what obscures, threatens, etc.; a great multitude, a mass.—*vt.* To obscure; to darken; to sully; to make to appear sullen.—*vi.* To grow cloudy.
**Cloudiness,** kloud'i-nes, *n.* State of being cloudy; gloom.
**Cloudless,** kloud'les, *a.* Without a cloud; clear.
**Cloudlet,** kloud'let, *n.* A little cloud.
**Cloudy,** kloud'i, *a.* Overcast with clouds; dark; not easily understood; indicating gloom.
**Clout,** klout, *n.* A patch of cloth, leather, etc.; a rag; a blow.—*vt.* To patch; to join clumsily.
**Clove,** klōv, *n.* The dried spicy bud of an East Indian tree; the tree itself; a small bulb in a compound bulb, as in garlic.
**Cloven-footed, Cloven-hoofed,** klōv'n-fut-ed, klōv'n-höft, *a.* Having the foot or hoof divided into two parts, as the ox.
**Clove-pink,** klōv'pingk, *n.* A species of carnation with an odor like that of cloves.
**Clover,** klō'vėr, *n.* A leguminous plant with three-lobed leaves.
**Clown,** kloun, *n.* An awkward country fellow; a lout; a professional jester.
**Clownish,** kloun'ish, *a.* Coarse; rude.
**Cloy,** kloi, *vt.* To glut; to fill to loathing.
**Club,** klub, *n.* A cudgel; a card of the suit marked with trefoils; a staff with a heavy head for driving the ball in golf, etc.; an association for some common object; the meeting-place of such an association.—*vt.* To beat with a club.—*vi.* To join for some common object.
**Clubbable,** klub'a-bl, *a.* Having the qualities tht fit a man for a club; social.
**Club-footed,** klub'fut-ed, *a.* Having short, crooked, or deformed feet.
**Club-house,** klub'hous, *n.* A house where a club meets.
**Club-law,** klub'la, *n.* Government by violence; the law of brute force.
**Club-room,** klub'röm, *n.* The apartment in which a club meets.
**Cluck,** kluk, *vi.* To make the noise of the hen when calling chickens.—*n.* Such a sound.
**Clue,** klö, *n.* A ball of thread; a thread serving to guide; something helping to unravel a mystery.
**Clump,** klump, *n.* A lump; a cluster of trees or shrubs.
**Clumsily,** klum'zi-li, *adv.* In a clumsy manner.
**Clumsiness,** klum'zi-nes, *n.* Quality of being clumsy.
**Clumsy,** klum'zi, *a.* Unwieldy; ungainly; rude in make.
**Cluster,** klus'tėr, *n.* A bunch, as of grapes; a knot; a small crowd.—*vi.* To be or to keep close together; to grow in bunches; to collect in masses.—*vt.* To collect into a body.
**Clutch,** kluch, *vt.* To seize hold of; to grasp.—*n.* A grasp; talon; a merciless hand; something that holds fast.
**Clutter,** klut'tėr, *n.* A confused noise; a bustle.—*vt.* To crowd together in disorder.—*vi.* To make a bustle.
**Clyster,** klis'tėr, *n.* An injection to cleanse the bowels, etc.
**Coach,** kōch, *n.* A large four-wheeled close vehicle; a tutor.—*vi.* To ride in a coach; to tutor.
**Coach-box,** kōch'boks, *n.* The seat on which the driver of a coach sits.
**Coachman,** kōch'man, *n.* The person who drives a coach.
**Coadjutor,** kō-ad-jū'tėr, *n.* An assistant; a colleague.
**Coadjutrix,** kō-ad-jū'triks, *n.* A female assistant.
**Coagent,** kō-ā'jent, *n.* A fellow-agent; an assistant or associate in an act.
**Coagulable,** kō-ag'ū-la-bl, *a.* Capable of being coagulated.
**Coagulate,** kō-ag'ū-lāt, *vt.* (coagulating, coagulated). To change from a fluid into a fixed state.—*vi.* To curdle; to congeal.
**Coagulation,** kō-ag'ū-lā''shon, *n.* Act of coagulating; mass coagulated.
**Coal,** kōl, *n.* Any combustible substance in a state of ignition; charcoal; a solid, black, fossil substance used as fuel.—*vt.* or *i.* To supply with coals; to take in coals.
**Coal-black,** kōl'blak, *a.* Black as coal.
**Coalesce,** kō-al-es', *vi.* (coalescing, coalesced). To grow together; to unite.
**Coalescence,** kō-al-es'ens, *n.* Act of coalescing; state of being united; union.
**Coalescent,** kō-al-es'ent, *a.* Coalescing.
**Coalition,** kō-al-i'shon, *n.* Act of coalescing; union of persons, parties, etc., into one body; alliance; confederation.
**Coal-mine,** kōl'mīn, *n.* A mine or pit containing mineral coal.

**Coal-pit,** kōl'pit, *n.* A pit where coal is dug.
**Coal-tar,** kōl'tär, *n.* A thick, black liquid condensed in the distillation of gas from coal.
**Coaly,** kōl'i, *a.* Like coal; containing coal.
**Coarse,** kōrs, *a.* Rude; not refined; crude; inelegant; gross.
**Coarsely,** kōrs'li, *adv.* In a coarse manner.
**Coast,** kōst, *n.* The sea-shore; the country near the sea.—*vi.* To sail along a shore; to sail from port to port.
**Coat,** kōt, *n.* An upper garment; vesture, as indicating office; hair or fur covering of animals; a layer; a covering; that on which ensigns armorial are portrayed.—*vt.* To cover; to spread over.
**Coating,** kōt'ing, *n.* A covering; a thin external layer; cloth for coats.
**Coax,** kōks, *vt.* To wheedle; to persuade by fondling and flattering.
**Coaxer,** kōks'ėr, *n.* A wheedler.
**Cob,** kob, *n.* A round knob; the head of clover or wheat; a smallish thick-set horse; a male swan.
**Cobalt,** kō'balt, *n.* A mineral of grayish color, and a metal obtained from it yielding a permanent blue; the blue itself.
**Cobble,** kob'l, *vt.* (cobbling, cobbled). To mend coarsely, as shoes; to botch.—*n.* A roundish stone.
**Cobbler,** kob'l-ėr, *n.* A mender of shoes; a clumsy workman; a cooling beverage.
**Coble,** kō'bl, *n.* A flattish-bottomed boat.
**Cobra, Cobra-de-capello,** kob'ra, kob'ra-de-kapel'lō, *n.* A hooded venomous snake.
**Cobweb,** kob'web, *n.* A spider's net; something flimsy.
**Coca,** kō'ka, *n.* The dried leaf of a S. American plant which gives power of enduring fatigue.
**Cocaine,** kō'ka-in, *n.* The active principle of coca, used as a local anesthetic.
**Cochineal,** ko'chi-nēl, *n.* An insect which forms a scarlet dye; a dye-stuff consisting of the bodies of these insects.
**Cock** kok, *n.* The male of the domestic fowl; the male of other birds; a vane; a person or thing having resemblance to a cock; a chief man; a tap for drawing off liquids; the hammer of a gun; a small pile of hay.—*vt.* To set erect; to set on the head with an air of pertness; to draw back the cock of a gun.
**Cockatoo,** kok-a-tö', *n.* A crested bird of the parrot family.
**Cockle,** kok'l, *n.* A weed that chokes corn; a small shell-fish.—*vi.* or *t.* To wrinkle; to shrink.
**Cock-loft,** kok'loft, *n.* A small loft close under a roof.
**Cockney,** kok'nė, *n.* An effeminate citizen; a native of London.—*a.* Pertaining to a cockney.
**Cockroach,** kok'rōch, *n.* The black beetle.
**Cock's-comb,** koks'kōm, *n.* The comb of a cock; a plant. *See* COXCOMB.
**Cocktail,** kok'tāl, *n.* A species of beetle; a half-bred horse; a short drink or appetizer, usually consisting of gin, bitters, and some flavoring, and often iced.
**Coco, Cocoa,** kō'kō, *n.* A tropical palm-tree.
**Cocoa,** kō'kō, *n.* The seed of the cacao prepared for a beverage; the beverage itself.
**Coco-nut, Cocoa-nut,** kō'kō-nut, *n.* The fruit of the coco palm.
**Cocoon,** kō'kön', *n.* The silky case in which the silkworm involves itself when still a larva; the envelope of other larvae.
**Cod,** kod, *n.* A species of sea fish allied to the haddock; a husk; a pod.
**Coddle,** kod'l, *vt.* (coddling, coddled). To fondle.
**Code,** kōd, *n.* A digest of laws; a collection of rules; a system of signals, etc.
**Codicil,** ko'di-sil, *n.* A writing by way of supplement to a will.
**Codification,** kōd'i-fi-kā''shon, *n.* Act or process of reducing laws to a code.
**Codify,** kōd'i-fī, *vt.* (codifying, codified). To reduce to a code.
**Codling, Codlin,** kod'ling, kod'lin, *n.* A variety of cooking apple.
**Codling,** kod'ling, *n.* A young codfish.
**Cod-liver oil,** kod'li-vėr oil, *n.* A medicinal oil obtained from the livers of the cod.
**Coefficient,** kō-ef-fi'shent, *a.* Jointly efficient; co-operating.—*n.* That which co-operates; a number or quantity that multiplies or measures another.
**Coequal,** kō-ē'kwal, *a.* Jointly equal.—*n.* One who is equal to another.
**Coerce,** kō-ėrs', *vt.* (coercing, coerced). To restrain by force; to compel.
**Coercion,** kō-ėr'shon, *n.* Act of coercing; restraint; compulsion.
**Coercive,** kō-ėrs'iv, *a.* That has power to coerce; constraining; compulsory.
**Coessential,** kō-es-sen'shal, *a.* One in essence; partaking of the same essence.
**Coeternal,** kō-ē-tėr'nal, *a.* Equally eternal with another.
**Coeval,** kō-ē'val, *a.* Of the same age; contemporary.—*n.* One of the same age.
**Coexecutor,** kō-eks-ek'ū-tėr, *n.* A joint executor.
**Coexist,** kō-egz-ist', *vi.* To live at the same time with another.
**Coexistence,** kō-egz-ist'ens, *n.* Existence at the same time with another.
**Coexistent,** kō-egz-ist'ent, *a.* Existing at the same time with another.
**Coextend,** kō-eks-tend', *vi.* To extend through the same space or duration with another.
**Coextensive,** kō-eks-ten'siv, *a.* Equally extensive.
**Coffee,** kof'i, *n.* A tree and its fruit or berries; a beverage made from the seeds.
**Coffee-house,** kof'i-hous, *n.* A house where coffee and refreshments are supplied.
**Coffee-room,** kof'i-röm, *n.* A public room in an inn where coffee, etc., is supplied.
**Coffer,** kof'ėr, *n.* A chest for holding gold, jewels, etc.
**Coffer-dam,** kof'ėr-dam, *n.* A case of piling, water-tight, serving to exclude water in laying the foundations of piers, bridges, etc.
**Coffin,** kof'fin, *n.* The chest in which a dead human body is buried.—*vt.* To inclose in a coffin.
**Cog,** kog, *n.* The tooth of a wheel.—*vt.* (cogging, cogged). To furnish with cogs; to trick, deceive; to manipulate dice unfairly.—*vi.* To cheat; to lie.
**Cogency,** kō'jen-si, *n.* Force; persuading power.
**Cogent,** kō'jent, *a.* Forcible; convincing.
**Cogently,** kō'jent-li, *adv.* In a cogent manner.
**Cogitate,** ko'jit-āt, *vi.* (cogitating, cogitated). To ponder; to meditate.
**Cogitation,** ko'jit-ā'shon, *n.* Act of thinking much or deeply; reflection.
**Cogitative,** ko'jit-āt-iv, *a.* Having the power of thinking; given to thought.
**Cognac,** kō'nyak, *n.* A kind of brandy.
**Cognate,** kog'nāt, *a.* Born of the same stock; akin; of the same nature.
**Cognition,** kog-ni'shon, *n.* Knowledge from personal view or experience.
**Cognizable,** kog'niz-a-bl, *a.* That may be known; that may be tried and determined.
**Cognizance,** kog'niz-ans, *n.* Knowledge; judicial notice; trial, or right to try; a badge.
Cognizant, kog'niz-ant, *a.* Having knowledge of.
**Cognomen,** kog-nō'men, *n.* A name added to a family name; a surname.
**Cohabit,** kō-hab'it, *vi.* To dwell together; to live as husband and wife, though not married.
**Cohabitation,** kō-hab'it-ā''shon, *n.* Act or state of cohabiting.
**Coheir,** kō-ār', *n.* A joint heir.
**Coheiress,** kō-ār'es, *n.* A joint heiress.
**Cohere,** kō-hēr', *vi.* (cohering, cohered). To stick together; to be consistent.
**Coherence, Coherency,** kō-hēr'ens, kō-hēr'-en-si, *n.* The state of being coherent; cohesion; congruity.
**Coherent,** kō-hēr'ent, *a.* Sticking together; consistent.
**Coherently,** kō-hēr'ent-li, *adv.* In a coherent man-

ner.
**Cohesion,** kō-hē'zhon, *n.* Act of sticking together; the attraction by which bodies are kept together; coherence.
**Cohesive,** kō-hē'siv, *a.* That has the power of cohering; tending to unite in a mass.
**Cohort,** kō'hort, *n.* A company of soldiers, among the Romans the tenth part of a legion.
**Coif,** koif, *n.* A kind of caul or cap.—*vt.* To cover or dress with a coif.
**Coiffure,** koif'ūr, *n.* Mode of dressing the hair in women.
**Coil,** koil, *vt.* To wind into a ring.—*n.* A ring or rings into which a rope, etc., is wound.
**Coin,** koin, *n.* A piece of metal stamped, as money; that which serves for payment.—*vt.* To stamp and convert metal into money; to mint; to invent; to fabricate.
**Coinage,** koin'āj, *n.* The act or art of coining; coined money; fabrication.
**Coincide,** kō-in-sīd', *vi.* (coinciding, coincided). To agree in position; to happen at the same time; to concur.
**Coincidence,** kō-in'si-dens, *n.* Concurrence; agreement.
**Coincident,** kō-in'si-dent, *a.* Having coincidence; concurrent; corresponding.
**Coiner,** koin'ėr, *n.* One who coins; a minter; a forger; an inventor.
**Coition,** kō-i'shon, *n.* Sexual intercourse.
**Coke** kōk, *n.* Coal charred and deprived of gas.—*vt.* (coking, coked). To turn into coke.
**Cola,** kō'la, *n.* An African tree with nuts containing much caffeine and yielding an invigorating beverage.
**Colander,** ko'lan-dėr, *n.* A strainer; sieve.
**Cold,** kōld, *a.* Not hot; chill; indifferent; reserved; stoical; unaffecting.—*n.* Absence of heat; sensation produced by the escape of heat; an ailment occasioned by cold.
**Cold-blooded,** kōld'blud-ed, *a.* Having cold blood; without sensibility or feeling.
**Coldish,** kōld'ish, *a.* Somewhat cold.
**Coldly,** kōld'li, *adv.* In a cold manner.
**Coldness,** kōld'nes, *n.* Want of heat; unconcern; frigidity of temper; reserve.
**Cole,** kōl, *n.* A kind of cabbage.
**Colewort,** kōl'wėrt, *n.* A species of cabbage.
**Colic,** kol'ik, *n.* A painful affection of the intestines.
**Colitis,** kō-lī'tis, *n.* Inflammation of the large intestine, especially of its mucous membrane.
**Collaborator,** kol-la'bo-rāt-ėr, *n.* An associate in literary or scientific labor.
**Collapse,** kol-laps', *n.* A wasting of the body; a sudden and complete failure.—*vi.* (collapsing, collapsed). To fall together, as the sides of a vessel; to break down.
**Collar,** kol'ėr, *n.* A part of dress that surrounds the neck; something worn round the neck.—*vt.* To seize by the collar; to put a collar on; to roll up and bind with a cord.
**Collar-bone,** kol'ėr-bōn, *n.* Each of the two bones of the neck.
**Collate,** kol-lāt', *vt.* (collating, collated). To lay together and compare, as books, etc.; to place in a benefice; to gather and place in order.—*vi.* To place in a benefice.
**Collateral,** kol-lat'ėr-al, *a.* Placed side by side; running parallel; descending from the same stock, but not one from the other; connected.—*n.* A kinsman.
**Collation,** kol-lā'shon, *n.* Act of collating; that which is collated; a light repast.
**Collator,** ko-lāt'ėr, *n.* One who collates.
**Colleague,** kol'lēg, *n.* An associate in office.
**Collect,** kol-lekt', *vt.* To bring together; to gain by information; to infer or deduce.—*vi.* To run together; to accumulate.
**Collect,** kol'ekt, *n.* A short comprehensive prayer; a short prayer adapted to a particular occasion.
**Collected,** kol-lekt'ed, *p.a.* Cool; self-possessed.
**Collectedly,** kol-kekt'ed-li, *adv.* In a collected state or manner.
**Collection,** kol-kek'shon, *n.* Act of collecting; that which is collected.
**Collective,** kol-lekt'iv, *a.* Gathered into a mass; congregated; united.
**Collectively,** kol-lekt'iv-li, *adv.* In a collected state; in a mass or body.
**Collectivism,** kol-lek'tiv-izm, *n.* The doctrine that the state should own or control the land and all means of production.
**Collector,** kol-lekt'ėr , *n.* One who collects; one who collects customs or taxes.
**College,** kol'lej, *n.* A society of men, invested with certain powers, engaged in some common pursuit; a seminary of the higher learning; the building occupied for such purposes.
**Collegian,** kol-lē'ji-an, *n.* A member of a college; a student.
**Collegiate,** kol-lē'ji-āt, *a.* Pertaining to a college.
**Collide,** kol-līd', *vi.* (colliding, collided). To strike against each other; to meet in opposition.
**Collie,** kol'i, *n.* A dog common in Scotland, much used for sheep.
**Collier,** kol'yėr, *n.* A ship that carries coals.
**Collimate,** kol'li-māt, *vt.* To adjust to the proper line of sight.
**Collingual,** kol-ling'gwal, *a.* Speaking the same language.
**Collision,** kol-li'zhon, *n.* Act of striking together; state of contrariety; conflict.
**Collocate,** kol'lō-kāt, *vt.* To place; to set; to station.
**Collocation,** kol-lō-kā'shon, *n.* Act of collocating; disposition.
**Collodion,** kol-lō'di-on, *n.* A solution of guncotton in ether, forming a thin film.
**Colloid,** kol'loid, *a.* Like glue or jelly; *chem.* applied to uncrystallizable liquids.
**Collop,** kol'lop, *n.* A slice of meat.
**Colloquial,** kol-lō'kwi-al, *a.* Pertaining to common conversation or discourse.
**Colloquialism,** kol-lō'kwi-al-izm, *n.* A colloquial form of expression.
**Colloquy,** kol'lō-kwi, *n.* A speaking together; mutual discourse; dialogue.
**Collude, 'kol-lūd',** *vi.* (colluding, colluded). To conspire in a fraud; to connive.
**Collusion,** kol-lū'zhon, *n.* Fraud by concert.
**Collusive,** kol-lū'siv, *a.* Fraudulently concerted.
**Colocynth,** kol'ō-sinth, *n.* A kind of gourd and a purgative got from it.
**Colon,** kō'lon, *n.* A mark of punctuation, thus (:); the largest of the intestines.
**Colonel,** kėr'nel, *n.* The chief commander of a regiment of troops.
**Colonelcy,** kėr'nel-si, *n.* The office, rank, or commission of a colonel.
**Colonial,** ko-lō'ni-al, *a.* Pertaining to a colony.—*n.* A person belonging to a colony.
**Colonialism,** ko-lō'ni-al-izm, *n.* A phrase, idiom, or practice peculiar to a colony.
**Colonist,** ko'lon-ist, *n.* An inhabitant of a colony.
**Colonization,** ko'lon-īz-ā''shon, *n.* Act of colonizing, or state of being colonized.
**Colonize,** ko'lon-īz, *vt.* (colonizing, colonized). To establish a colony in; to migrate to and settle in as inhabitants.
**Colonnade,** ko-lon-ād', *n.* A range of columns placed at regular intervals.
**Colony,** ko'lō-ni, *n.* A body of people transplanted from their mother country to inhabit some distant place; the country colonized.
**Colophon,** ko'lo-fōn, *n.* An inscription or device formerly on the last page of a book, now usually in its preliminary pages.
**Color,** kul'ėr, *n.* That which gives bodies different appearances independently of form; a pigment; complexion; appearance to the mind; pretense; (*pl.*) a flag.—*vt.* To give some kind of color to; to give a specious appearance to; to exaggerate in representation.—*vi.* To show color; to blush.
**Colorable,** kul'ėr-a-bl, *a.* Designed to cover or

conceal; specious; plausible.
**Color-blindness,** kul'ėr-blīnd-nes, *n.* Inability to distinguish colors.
**Colored,** kul'ėrd, *a.* Tinged; having a specious appearance; of a dark skin.
**Coloring,** kul'ėr-ing, *n.* Act of giving a color; color applied; a specious appearance; fair artificial representation.
**Colorist,** kul'ėr-ist, *n.* One who colors; a painter who excels in coloring.
**Colorless,** kul'ėr-les, *a.* Destitute of color.
**Colossal,** kō-los'al, *a.* Huge; gigantic.
**Colossus,** kō-los'us, *n.*; *pl.* **-lossi.** A statue of gigantic size.
**Colporteur,** kol'pōr-tėr, *n.* One who travels for the sale or distribution of moral books, etc.
**Colt,** kōlt, *n.* A young male of the horse kind; a young foolish fellow.
**Coltish,** kōlt'ish, *a.* Like a colt; wanton; gay.
**Columbine,** ko'lum-bīn, *n.* A plant of the buttercup family; the female companion of Harlequin in pantomimes.
**Columbium,** kō-lum'bi-um, *n.* A rare metal.
**Column,** ko'lum, *n.* A pillar; a formation of troops, narrow in front, and deep from front to rear; a perpendicular section of a page; a perpendicular line of figures.
**Columnar,** ko-lum'nėr, *a.* Formed in columns; having the form of columns.
**Colure,** kō-lūr', *n.* Either of two great circles of the heavens, passing through the solstitial and the equinoctial points of the ecliptic.
**Coma,** kō'ma, *n.* Deep sleep; stupor; the hair-like envelope round the nucleus of a comet.
**Comatose,** kō'ma-tōs, *a.* Pertaining to coma; lethargic.
**Comb,** kōm, *n.* An instrument for separating hair, wool, etc.; the crest of a cock; honeycomb.—*vt.* To separate and adjust with a comb.
**Combat,** kom'bat, *vi.* To fight; to act in opposition.—*vt.* To oppose; to resist.—*n.* A fighting; an engagement; a duel.
**Combatable,** kom-bat'a-bl, *a.* That may be combated, disputed, or opposed.
**Combatant,** kom'bat-ant, *a.* Contending.—*n.* One who combats.
**Combative,** kom'bat-iv, *a.* Disposed to combat.
**Combinable,** kom-bīn'a-bl, *a.* Capable of combining.
**Combination,** kom-bin-ā'shon, *n.* Act of combining; state of being combined; union; confederacy; (*pl.*) a close-fitting undergarment.
**Combine,** kom-bīn', *vt.* (combining, combined). To cause to unite; to join.—*vi.* To come into union; to coalesce; to league together.—kom'bīn, *n.* A union.
**Combined,** kom-bīnd', *a.* United closely; produced by combination.
**Combustible,** kom-bust'i-bl, *a.* Capable of catching fire; inflammable.—*n.* A substance easily set on fire.
**Combustion,** kom-bust'shon, *n.* A burning; chemical combination, attended with heat and light.
**Come,** kum, *vi.* (coming, pret. came, pp. come). To move hitherward; to draw nigh; to arrive; to happen; to appear; to rise; to result.
**Comedian,** ko-mē'di-an, *n.* An actor in or writer of comedies.
**Comedy,** ko'mē-di, *n.* A drama of the lighter kind.
**Comeliness,** kum'li-nes, *n.* The quality of being comely; good looks.
**Comely,** kum'li, *a.* Good-looking; handsome; becoming.
**Comestible,** kom'es-ti-bl, *n.* An eatable.
**Comet,** kom'et, *n.* A heavenly body having a luminous tail or train.
**Cometary,** kom'et-a-ri, *a.* Pertaining to or like a comet.
**Comfit,** kum'fit, *n.* A sweetmeat.
**Comfort,** kum'fėrt, *vt.* To console; to gladden.—*n.* Consolation; relief; moderate enjoyment.
**Comfortable,** kum'fėrt-a-bl, *a.* Enjoying or giving comfort.
**Comfortably,** kum'fėrt-a-bli, *adv.* In a comfortable manner.
**Comforter,** kum'fėrt-ėr, *n.* One who comforts; the Holy Spirit; a woollen scarf.
**Comfortless,** kum'fėrt-les, *a.* Destitute of comfort; forlorn; wretched.
**Comic,** kom'ik, *a.* Relating to comedy; comical.
**Comical,** kom'ik-al, *a.* Raising mirth; funny.
**Comically,** kom'ik-al-li, *adv.* In a comical manner.
**Coming,** kum'ing, *p.a.* Future.—*n.* Approach.
**Comity,** ko'mi-ti, *n.* Courtesy; civility.
**Comma,** kom'ma, *n.* A mark of punctuation, thus (,); an interval in music.
**Command,** kom-mand', *vt.* To order; to govern; to have at one's disposal.—*vi.* To have chief power.—*n.* Order; control; power of overlooking; power of defending.
**Commandant,** kom-man-dant', *n.* A commanding officer of a place or forces.
**Commander,** kom-mand'ėr, *n.* One who commands; an officer in the navy, between a lieutenant-commander and captain.
**Commandery,** kom-man'dėr-i, *n.* Among certain knights and religious orders, a district under a member called a commander.
**Commanding,** kom-mand'ing, *a.* Exercising command; overlooking a wide view.
**Commandment,** kom-mand'ment, *n.* A command; a precept of the moral law.
**Commando,** kom-man'dō, *n.* A member of a body of troops specially trained and selected for hazardous enterprises.
**Commemorable,** kom-mem'o-ra-bl, *a.* Worthy to be commemorated.
**Commemorate,** kom-mem'o-rāt, *vt.* To call to remembrance by a solemn act; to celebrate with honor and solemnity.
**Commemoration,** kom-mem'o-rā''shon, *n.* Solemn celebration.
**Commemorative,** kom-mem'o-rāt-iv, *a.* Tending to preserve in remembrance.
**Commence,** kom-mens', *vi.* (commencing; commenced). To take the first step; to begin to be.—*vt.* To begin; to originate.
**Commencement,** kom-mens'ment, *n.* Beginning; rise; origin; first existence.
**Commend,** kom-mend', *vt.* To commit to the care of; to recommend; to praise.
**Commendation,** kom-men-dā'shon, *n.* Praise; recommendation; compliments.
**Commendatory,** kom-mend'a-to-ri, *a.* That serves to commend; containing praise.
**Commensal,** kom-men'sal, *n.* One that eats at the same table; one living with another.
**Commensurable,** kom-men'sūr-a-bl, *a.* Having a common measure.
**Commensurate,** kom-men'sūr-āt, *a.* Proportional; having equal measure.
**Commensurately,** kom-men'sūr-āt-li, *adv.* Correspondingly; adequately.
**Comment,** kom-ment', *vi.* To make remarks or criticisms.—*vt.* To annotate.—*n.* kom'-ment. An explanatory note; criticism.
**Commentary,** kom'ment-a-ri, *n.* Book of comments; an historical narrative.
**Commentator,** kom'ment-āt-ėr, *n.* One who writes annotations; an expositor.
**Commerce,** kom'mėrs, *n.* Exchange of goods by barter or purchase; trade; intercourse.
**Commercial,** kom-mėr'shal, *a.* Pertaining to commerce; trading; mercantile.
**Commercially,** kom-mėr'shal-li, *adv.* In a commercial manner or view.
**Commination,** kom-mi-nā'shon, *n.* A threat; recital of God's threatenings on stated days.
**Comminatory,** kom-mi'na-to-ri, *a.* Threatening.
**Commingle,** kom-ming'gl, *vt.* To blend.—*vi.* To unite together.
**Comminute,** kom'mi-nūt, *vt.* To make small or fine; to pulverize.
**Comminution,** kom-mi-nū'shon, *n.* Act of comminuting; pulverization.

**Commiserate,** kom-miz'ė-rāt, *vt.* (commiserating, commiserated). To pity; to condole with.
**Commiseration,** kom-miz'ė-rā''shon, *n.* Act of commiserating; pity.
**Commissariat,** kom-mis-sā'ri-at, *n.* The department of an army which supplies provisions, etc.; the officers in this department.
**Commissary,** kom'mis-sa-ri, *n.* A delegate; an officer of a bishop; an officer who has the charge of furnishing provisions, clothing, etc., for an army.
**Commission,** kom-mi'shon, *n.* Trust; warrant; a written document, investing one with an office; allowance made to an agent, etc., for transacting business; a body of men joined in an office or trust, or their appointment; perpetration.—*vt.* To appoint; to depute.
**Commissionaire,** kom-mi-shon-ār', *n.* A porter or messenger.
**Commissioned,** kom-mi'shond, *a.* Furnished with a commission.
**Commissioner,** kom-mi'shon'ėr, *n.* One commissioned to perform some office.
**Commissure,** kom'mis-sūr, *n.* A joint or seam; juncture.
**Commit,** kom-mit', *vt.* (committing, committed). To intrust; to consign; to send to prison; to perpetrate; to endanger or compromise (oneself).
**Commitment,** kom'mit'ment, *n.* The act of committing; a sending to prison.
**Committal,** kom-mit'al, *n.* The act of committing in the various senses of the verb.
**Committee,** kom-mit'tē, *n.* A body of persons appointed to manage any matter.
**Commix,** kom-miks', *vt.* To blend; to mix.
**Commixture,** kom-miks'tūr, *n.* Act of mixing together; compound.
**Commode,** kom-mōd', *n.* A kind of small sideboard; a lady's head-dress; a night-stool.
**Commodious,** kom-mō'di-us, *a.* Convenient; spacious and suitable.
**Commodity,** kom-mo'di-ti, *n.* Something useful; any article of commerce; (*pl.*) goods;; merchandise.
**Commodore,** kom'mo-dōr, *n.* A captain in the navy who is discharging duties rather more important than those usually assigned to a captain.
**Common,** kom'mon, *a.* Having no separate owner; general; usual; of no rank; of little value,—*n.* An open public ground; *pl.* the untitled people; the lower House of Parliament; food at a common table; food in general.
**Commonage,** kom'mon-āj, *n.* The right of pasturing on a common.
**Commonalty, Commonality,** kom'on-al-ti, kom-on-al'i-ti, *n.* The common people.
**Commoner,** kom'on-ėr, *n.* One of the common people; a member of the House of Commons; a student of Oxford, not dependent for support on the foundation.
**Commonly,** kom'mon-li, *adv.* Usually.
**Commonplace,** kom'mon-plās, *n.* A usual topic; a trite saying.—*a.* Ordinary; trite.
**Common sense,** kom'mon sens, *n.* Sound practical judgment.
**Commonweal,** kom'mon-wēl, *n.* A commonwealth; the state.
**Commonwealth,** kom'mon-welth, *n.* The public good; the state; body politic; a form of government; a republic.
**Commotion,** kom-mō'shon, *n.* Violent agitation; tumultuous disorder.
**Commune,** kom-mūn', *vi.* (communing, communed). To confer; to meditate.
**Commune,** kom'mūn, *n.* A small administrative district in France; a socialist body which ruled over Paris in 1871.
**Communicable,** kom-mū'ni-ka-bl, *a.* Capable of being imparted to another.
**Communicant,** kom-mū'ni-kant, *n.* One who communicates; a partaker of the Lord's supper.
**Communicate,** kom-mū'ni-kāt, *vt.* (communicating, communicated). To cause to be common to others; to impart, as news, disease, etc.; to bestow; to reveal.—*vi.* To share with others; to partake of the Lord's supper; to have intercourse; to correspond.
**Communion,** kom-mūn'yon, *n.* A mutual participation in anything; mutual intercourse; condord; celebration of the Lord's supper.
**Communism,** kom'mūn-izm, *n.* The doctrine of a community of property.
**Communist,** kom'mūn-ist, *n.* One who holds the doctrines of communism.
**Community,** kom-mū'ni-ti, *n.* Mutual participation; the public; a society of persons under the same laws.
**Commutability,** kom-mūt'a-bil''i-ti, *n.* Quality of being commutable.
**Commutable,** kom-mūt'a-bl, *a.* That may be exchanged; convertible into money.
**Commutation,** kom-mū-tā'shon, *n.* Exchange; change; substitution of a less for a greater penalty.
**Commute,** kom-mūt', *vt.* (commuting, commuted). To exchange; to put one thing for another.
**Compact,** kom-pakt', *a.* Closely united; solid; dense; brief.—*vt.* To consolidate; to unite firmly.—*n.* kom'pakt. An agreement; a contract.
**Compactly,** kom-pakt'li, *adv.* Closely; densely; tersely.
**Companion,** kom-pan'yon, *n.* A comrade; an associate; one of the third rank in an order of knighthood; a raised cover to the cabin stair of a merchant vessel.
**Companionable,** kom-pan'yon-a-bl, *a.* Fitted to be an agreeable companion; sociable.
**Companionship,** kom-pan'yon-ship, *n.* Fellowship; association.
**Company,** kum'pa-ni, *n.* Companionship; an assembly of persons; partners in a firm; a division of a battalion, consisting of four platoons, and commanded by a major or mounted captain, with a captain as second-in-command; the crew of a ship.—*vi.* To associate with.
**Comparable,** kom'pa-ra-bl, *a.* That may be compared; being of equal regard.
**Comparably,** kom'pa-ra-bli, *adv.* By comparison; so as to be compared.
**Comparative,** kom-pa'ra-tiv, *a.* Estimated by comparison; not positive or absolute.
**Comparatively,** kom-pa'ra-tiv-li, *adv.* By comparison.
**Compare,** kom-pār', *vt.* (comparing, compared). To bring together and examine the relations between; to estimate one by another; to inflect in the degrees of comparison.—*vi.* To hold comparison.
**Comparison,** kom-pa'ri-son, *n.* Act of comparing; state of being compared; relation; the formation of an adjective in its degrees of signification; a simile.
**Compartment,** kom-pärt'ment, *n.* A division or part of a general design.
**Compass,** kum'pas, *n.* A round; a circuit; limit; extent; range; an instrument for directing the course of ships; an instrument for describing circles (often in *pl.*).—*vt.* To pass round; to inclose; to obtain; to contrive.
**Compassable,** kum'pas-a-bl, *a.* Capable of being accomplished.
**Compassion,** kom-pa'shon, *n.* Fellow-suffering; pity; sympathy.
**Compassionate,** kom-pa'shon-āt, *a.* Ready to pity; sympathizing.—*vt.* To pity.
**Compassionately,** kom-pa'shon-āt-li, *adv.* With compassion; mercifully.
**Compatibility,** kom-pat'i-bil''i-ti, *n.* Quality of being compatible.
**Compatible,** kom-pat'i-bl, *a.* Consistent; suitable; not incongruous.
**Compatibly,** kom-pat'i-bli, *adv.* Fitly.
**Compatriot,** kom-pā'tri-ot, *n.* One of the same

C

country.
**Compeer,** kom-pēr', *n.* An equal; an associate.
**Compel,** kom-pel', *vt.* (compelling, compelled). To drive; to urge; to necessitate.
**Compellable,** kom-pel'a-bl, *a.* That may be compelled.
**Compellation,** kom-pel-lā'shon, *n.* An addressing; a ceremonious appellation.
**Compendium,** kom-pen'di-um, *n.* An abridgment; a summary; an epitome.
**Compensate,** kom-pens'āt, *vi.* (compensating, compensated). To give equal value to; to make amends for; to requite.—*vt.* To make amends; to supply an equivalent.
**Compensation,** kom-pens-ā'shon, *n.* Act of compensating; recompense.
**Compensatory,** kom-pens'ā-to-ri, *a.* Serving for compensation; making amends.
**Compete,** kom-pēt', *vi.* (competing, competed). To strive for the same thing as another; to contend.
**Competence, Competency,** kom'pē-tens, kom'pē-ten-si, *n.* Suitableness; sufficiency; legal capacity or right.
**Competent,** kom'pē-tent, *a.* Suitable, sufficient; qualified; having adequate right.
**Competently,** kom'pē-tent-li, *adv.* Sufficiently; adequately.
**Competition,** kom-pē-ti'shon, *n.* Contest for the same object; rivalry.
**Competitive,** kom-pet'it-iv, *a.* Relating to competition; carried out by competition.
**Competitor,** kom-pet'it-ėr, *n.* One who competes; a rival; an opponent.
**Compilation,** kom-pi-lā'shon, *n.* Act of compiling; that which is compiled; a work made up of parts from various authors.
**Compile,** kom-pīl', *vt.* (compiling, compiled). To gather from various sources; to draw up by collecting parts from different authors.
**Compiler,** kom-pīl'ėr, *n.* One who compiles.
**Complacence, Complacency,** kom-plā'sens, kom-plā'sen-si, *n.* A feeling of quiet satisfaction; complaisance.
**Complacent,** kom-plā'sent, *a.* Showing complacency; complaisant.
**Complacently,** kom-plā'sent-li, *adv.* In a complacent manner; softly.
**Complain,** kom-plān', *vi.* to express grief or distress; to lament; to express dissatisfaction; to make a formal accusation.
**Complainant,** kom-plān'ant, *n.* One who complains; a plaintiff.
**Complaint,** kom-plānt', *n.* Expression of grief, censure, etc.; accusation; malady.
**Complaisance,** kom'plā-zans, *n.* A pleasing deportment; courtesy; urbanity.
**Complaisant,** kom'plā-zant, *a.* Pleasing in manners; desirous to please; courteous.
**Complaisantly,** kom'plā-zant-li, *adv.* With complaisance.
**Complement,** kom'plē-ment, *n.* That which fills up; full quantity or number.
**Complementary,** kom-plē-ment'a-ri, *a.* Completing; supplying a deficiency.
**Complete,** kom-plēt', *a.* Having no deficiency; finished; total; absolute.—*vt.* (completing, completed). To make complete; to finish; to fulfil.
**Completely,** kom-plēt'li, *adv.* Fully.
**Completeness,** kom-plēt'nes, *n.* State of being complete; perfection.
**Completion,** kom-plē'shon, *n.* Act of completing; state of being complete; fulfilment; accomplishment.
**Complex,** kom'pleks, *a.* Of various parts; involved; composite.—*n.* A series of emotionally accentuated ideas in a repressed state.
**Complexion,** kom-plek'shon, *n.* The color of the face; general appearance.
**Complexional,** kom-plek'shon-al, *a.* Pertaining to complexion.
**Complexity,** kom-pleks'i-ti, *n.* State of being complex; intricacy.
**Compliance,** kom-plī'ans, *n.* Submission; consent.
**Compliant,** kom-plī'ant, *a.* Yielding; bending; submissive; obliging.
**Complicacy,** kom'pli-ka-si, *n.* A state of being complex or intricate.
**Complicate,** kom'pli-kāt, *vt.* (complicating, complicated). To make complex or intricate; to entangle.
**Complicated,** kom'pli-kāt-ed, *p.a.* Involved; intricate.
**Complication,** kom-pli-kā'shon, *n.* That which consists of many things involved; entanglement; intricacy.
**Complicity,** kom-plis'i-ti, *n.* State or condition of being an accomplice.
**Compliment,** kom'pli-ment, *n.* Act or expression of civility or regard; delicate flattery; a favor bestowed.—*vt.* To pay a compliment to; to congratulate; to praise.
**Complimentary,** kom-pli-ment'a-ri, *a.* Containing compliment; flattering.
**Compline,** kom'plīn, *n.* In the Roman Catholic church, the last service at night.
**Complot,** kom'plot, *n.* A joint plot.—*vt.* and *i.* To plot together.
**Comply,** kom-plī', *vi.* (complying, complied). To yield; to assent; to acquiesce.
**Component,** kom-pōn'ent, *a.* Composing; forming an element of a compound.—*n.* A constituent part; ingredient.
**Comport,** kom-pōrt', *vi.* To agree; to suit.—*vt.* To bear or carry (oneself); to behave.
**Compose,** kom-pōz', *vt.* (composing, composed). To form by uniting; to constitute; to write; to calm; to set types in printing.
**Composed,** kom-pōzd', *p.a.* Calm; sedate.
**Composer,** kom-pōz'ėr, *n.* An author, especially a musical author.
**Composite,** kom'po-zīt or -zit, *a.* Compound; noting a rich order of architecture; noting plants whose flowers are arranged in dense heads.
**Composition,** kom-pō-zi'shon, *n.* Act of composing; a mixture; a literary or musical work; arrangement; agreement to receive or pay part of a debt in place of the whole; the part paid; act of setting types.
**Compositor,** kom-poz'it-ėr, *n.* On who sets types.
**Compost,** kom'pōst, *n.* A mixture for manure.
**Composure,** kom-pō'zhūr, *n.* A settled frame of mind; calmness; tranquillity.
**Compound,** kom-pound', *vt.* and *i.* To put together; to mix; to adjust; to discharge a debt by paying a part.—*a.* kom'pound. Composed of two or more ingredients, words, or parts.—*n.* A mass composed of two or more elements; inclosure in which houses stand.
**Compounder,** kom-pound'ėr, *n.* One who compounds.
**Comprehend,** kom-prē-hend', *vt.* To embrace within limits; to understand.
**Comprehensible,** kom-prē-hens'i-bl, *a.* That may be comprehended; intelligible.
**Comprehension,** kom-prē-hen'shon, *n.* Act of comprehending; power of comprehending; understanding.
**Comprehensive,** kom-prē-hens'iv, *a.* Comprising much; capacious; able to understand.
**Comprehensively,** kom-prē-hens'iv-li, *adv.* In a comprehensive manner.
**Compress,** kom-pres', *vt.* To press together; to squeeze; to condense.—*n.* kom'pres. A soft mass or bandage used in surgery.
**Compressed,** kom-prest', *p.a.* Pressed together; flattened; condensed.
**Compressibility,** kom-pres'i-bil''i-ti, *n.* The quality of being compressible.
**Compressible,** kom-pres'i-bl, *a.* Capable of being compressed.
**Compression,** kom-pre'shon, *n.* Act of compressing; state of being compressed.
**Comprise,** kom-prīz, *vt.* (comprising, comprised). To embrace; to contain; to inclose.

**Compromise,** kom'prō-mīz, *n*. An amicable agreement to settle differences; mutual concession.—*vi*. To settle by mutual concessions; to involve; to endanger the interests of.
**Comptroller,** kon-trōl'ėr, *n*. A controller; an officer who examines the accounts of collectors of public money.
**Compulsion,** kom-pul'shon, *n*. Act of compelling; state of being compelled; force.
**Compulsive,** kom-pul'siv, *a*. Having power to compel.
**Compulsory,** kom-pul'so-ri, *a*. Constraining; coercive; obligatory.
**Compunction,** kom-pungk'shon, *n*. Remorse; contrition.
**Compunctious,** kom-pungk'shus, *a*. Implying or feeling compunction.
**Compurgation,** kom-pėr-gā'shon, *n*. Act of justifying a man by the oath of others.
**Compurgator,** kom-pėr'gāt-ėr, *n*. One who swears to another's innocence.
**Computable,** kom-pūt'a-bl, *a*. Capable of being computed.
**Computation,** kom-pū-tā'shon, *n*. Act or process of computing; reckoning.
**Compute,** kom-pūt', *vt*. (computing, computed). To count; to estimate.
**Comrade,** kom'rād, *n*. A mate; a companion; an associate.
**Comradeship,** kom'rād-ship, *n*. State of being a comrade or comrades.
**Con,** kon, *vt*. (conning, conned). To learn; to fix in the mind; to peruse carefully; to direct the steering of (a ship).
**Concatenate,** kon-ka'tē-nāt, *vt*. To link together; to unite in a series.
**Concave,** kon'kāv, *a*. Hollow, as the inner surface of a sphere; opposed to convex.—*n*. A hollow; an arch or vault.
**Concavity,** kon-kav'i-ti, *n*. Hollowness; a concave surface.
**Conceal,** kon-sēl', *vt*. To hide; to secrete; to disguise.
**Concealable,** kon-sēl'a-bl, *a*. That may be concealed.
**Concealment,** kon-sēl'ment, *n*. Act of concealing; state of being concealed; a hiding-place.
**Concede,** kon-sēd', *vt*. (conceding, conceded). To yield; to grant.—*vi*. To make concession.
**Conceit,** kon-sēt', *n*. Conception; fancy; self-flattering opinion; vanity.
**Conceited,** kon-sēt'ed, *a*. Vain; egotistical.
**Conceivable,** kon-sēv'a-bl, *a*. That may be imagined or understood.
**Conceivably,** kon-sēv'a-bli, *adv*. In a conceivable or intelligible manner.
**Conceive,** kon-sēv', *vt*. (conceiving, conceived). To form in the womb; to take into the mind; to comprehend.—*vi*. To become pregnant; to have or form an idea.
**Concentrate,** kon'sen-trāt, *vt*. (concentrating, concentrated). To bring together; to direct to one object; to condense.
**Concentration,** kon-sen-trā'shon, *n*. Act of concentrating; state of being concentrated.
**Concentrative,** kon-sen'trāt-iv, *a*. Tending to concentrate.
**Concentric,** kon-sen'trik, *a*. Having a common center.
**Concept,** kon'sept, *n*. An object conceived by the mind; a general notion of a class of objects.
**Conception,** kon-sep'shon, *n*. Act of conceiving; state of being conceived; thing conceived; image in the mind; mental faculty which originates ideas.
**Conceptualist,** kon-sep'tū-al-ist, *n*. One who holds that the mind can give independent existence to general conceptions.
**Concern,** kon-sėrn', *vt*. To belong to; to affect the interest of; to make anxious.—*n*. That which relates to one; affair; care; anxiety; a commercial establishment.
**Concerned,** kon-sėrnd', *a*. Interested; anxious.
**Concerning,** kon-sėrn'ing, *prep*. Having relation to; respecting.
**Concernment,** kon-sėrn'ment, *n*. Affair; concern; solicitude.
**Concert,** kon-sėrt', *vt*. To plan together; to contrive.—*n*. kon'sėrt. Agreement in a design; harmony; performance of a company of players, singers, etc.
**Concerted,** kon-sėrt'ed, *p.a*. Mutually contrived; done in concert.
**Concertina,** kon-sėrt-ē'na, *n*. A musical instrument of the accordion species.
**Concerto,** kon-chär'tō, *n*. A musical composition for one principal instrument, with accompaniments for a full orchestra.
**Concession,** kon-se'shon, *n*. Act of conceding; the thing yielded; a grant.
**Concessive,** kon-ses'iv, *a*. Implying concession.
**Conch,** kongk, *n*. A marine shell.
**Conchoidal,** kong-koi'dal, *a*. With curves like shells.
**Conchology,** kong-kol'o-ji, *n*. The doctrine or science of shells.
**Conciliate,** kon-si'li-āt, *vt*. (conciliating, conciliated). To bring to friendliness; to win the favor or consent; to reconcile; to propitiate.
**Conciliation,** kon-si'li-ā''shon, *n*. Act of gaining favor or affection.
**Conciliator,** kon-si'li-āt-ėr, *n*. One who conciliates or reconciles.
**Conciliatory,** kon-si'li-a-to-ri, *a*. Tending to conciliate; pacific.
**Concise,** kon-sīs', *a*. Brief; abridged; comprehensive.
**Concisely,** kon-sīs'li, *adv*. Briefly.
**Conciseness,** kon-sīs'nes, *n*. Brevity.
**Concision,** kon-si'zhon, *n*. A cutting off; conciseness.
**Conclave,** kon'klāv, *n*. A private apartment; the assembly of cardinals for the election of a pope; a close assembly.
**Conclude,** kon-klūd', *vt*. (concluding, concluded). To end; to decide; to deduce.—*vi*. To end; to form a final judgment.
**Conclusion,** kon-klū'zhon, *n*. Act of concluding; that which is concluded; inference; consequence; final decision; end.
**Conclusive,** kon-klū'siv, *a*. That concludes or determines; final; convincing.
**Conclusively,** kon-klū'siv-li, *adv*. Decisively; with final determination.
**Concoct,** kon-kokt', *vt*. To devise; to plot.
**Concoction,** kon-kok'shon, *n*. Act of concocting; a mixture or preparation.
**Concomitance, Concomitancy,** kon-kom'i-tans, kon-kom'i-tan-si, *n*. A being together or in connection with another thing.
**Concomitant,** kon-kom'it-ant, *a*. Accompanying; concurrent.—*n*. An accompaniment; a connected circumstance.
**Concord,** kong'kord, *n*. Union in feelings, opinions, etc.; harmony; agreement of words in construction.
**Concordance,** kon-kord'ans, *n*. Agreement; index of the principal words of a book.
**Concordant,** kon-kord'ant, *a*. Agreeing together; correspondent; harmonious.
**Concordat,** kon-kord'at, *n*. An agreement made by a sovereign with the pope relative to ecclesiastical matters.
**Concourse,** kong'kōrs, *n*. Confluence; an assembly; crowd.
**Concrete,** kon'krēt, *a*. Composed of particles united in one mass; congealed; existing in a subject; not abstract.—*n*. A mass formed by concretion; a hard mass formed of lime, sand, etc.—*vi*. kon-krēt' (concreting, concreted). To unite in a mass; to become solid.
**Concretion,** kon-krē'shon, *n*. Act of concreting; state of being concreted; a mass concreted.
**Concubinage,** kon-kū'bin-āj, *n*. The living together as husband and wife without being married.

**Concubine,** kong'kū-bīn, *n.* A woman who cohabits with a man; a mistress.
**Concupiscence,** kon-kū'pis-ens, *n.* Lust.
**Concupiscent,** kon-kū'pis-ent, *a.* Lustful.
**Concur,** kon-kėr', *vi.* (concurring, concurred). To unite; to agree; to assent.
**Concurrence,** kon-ku'rens, *n.* Act of concurring; union; joint action.
**Concurrent,** kon-ku'rent, *a.* Acting together.—*n.* That which concurs; joint cause.
**Concurrently,** kon-ku'rent-li, *adv.* With concurrence; unitedly.
**Concussion,** kon-ku'shon, *n.* A violent shock.
**Concussive,** kon-kus'iv, *a.* Having the power or quality of shaking; agitating.
**Condemn,** kon-dem', *vt.* To pronounce to be wrong; to censure; to sentence.
**Condemnation,** kon-dem-nā'shon, *n.* Act of condemning; state of being condemned; sentence; cause of blame.
**Condemnatory,** kon-dem'na-to-ri, *a.* Condemning; bearing condemnation.
**Condensable,** kon-dens'a-bl, *a.* Capable of being condensed.
**Condensation,** kon-dens-ā'shon, *n.* Act of condensing; state of being condensed.
**Condense,** kon-dens', *vt.* (condensing, condensed). To reduce in compass; to reduce from a gaseous to a liquid or solid state.—*vi.* To become dense; to grow thick.
**Condenser,** kon-dens'ėr, *n.* One who or that which condenses; a vessel in which vapors are reduced to liquid by coldness; a chamber in which steam in condensed; an instrument for storing an electric charge.
**Condescend,** kon-dē-send', *vi.* To descend from the privileges of superior rank; to deign.
**Condescending,** kon-dē-send'ing, *a.* Yielding to inferiors; patronizing.
**Condescension,** kon-de-sen'shon, *n.* Act of condescending; courtesy; complaisance.
**Condign,** kon-dīn', *a.* Deserved; suitable.
**Condiment,** kon'di-ment, *n.* Seasoning; relish.
**Condition,** kon-di'shon, *n.* State; case; external circumstances; temper; stipulation.
**Conditional,** kon-di'shon-al, *a.* Depending on conditions; not absolute.
**Conditionally,** kon-di'shon-al-li, *adv.* With certain limitatons.
**Conditioned,** kon-di'shond, *a.* Having a certain condition, state, or qualities.
**Condole,** kon-dōl', *vi.* (condoling, condoled). To grieve with another; to sympathize.
**Condolement,** kon-dōl'ment, *n.* Sympathetic grief; sorrow with others.
**Condolence,** kon-dōl'ens, *n.* Act of condoling; expression of sympathy.
**Condone,** kon-dōn', *vt.* (condoning, condoned). To pardon; to imply forgiveness of.
**Condor,** kon'dor, *n.* A S. American vulture.
**Conduce,** kon-dūs', *vi.* (conducing, conduced). To lead; to tend; to contribute.
**Conducive,** kon-dūs'iv, *a.* Having a tendency to promote.
**Conduct,** kon'dukt, *n.* Personal behavior; management; escort.—*vt.* kon-dukt'. To lead or guide; to escort; to manage; to behave (oneself); to transmit, as heat, etc.
**Conductible,** kon-dukt'i-bl, *a.* That may be conducted.
**Conduction,** kon-duk'shon, *n.* Property by which bodies transmit heat or electricity.
**Conductive,** kon-dukt'iv, *a.* Having the physical property of conducting.
**Conductor,** kon-dukt'ėr, *n.* A leader; a director; a body that transmits heat, electricity, etc.
**Conductress,** kon-duk'tres, *n.* A female conductor.
**Conduit,** kon'dit or kun'dit, *n.* A channel or pipe to convey water, etc., or to drain off filth; a channel or passage.
**Cone,** kōn, *n.* A solid body having a circle for its base, and tapering to a point; the fruit of firs, pine-trees, etc.
**Confabulate,** kon-fab'ū-lāt, *vi.* (confabulating, confabulated). To talk familiarly.
**Confabulation,** kon-fab'ū-lā''shon, *n.* Easy conversation; familiar talk.
**Confection,** kon-fek'shon, *n.* A mixture; a sweetmeat.
**Confectioner,** kon-fek'shon-ėr, *n.* One who makes or sells sweetmeats.
**Confectionery,** kon-fek'shon-ė-ri, *n.* Sweetmeats in general; confections.
**Confederacy,** kon-fe'de-ra-si, *n.* A confederation; the parties united by a league.
**Confederate,** kon-fe'de-rāt, *a.* Allied by treaty.—*n.* One united with others in a league.—*vt.* and *i.* (confederating, confederated). To unite in a league.
**Confederation,** kon-fe'de-rā''shon, *n.* A league; alliance, particularly of states, etc.
**Confer,** kon-fėr', *vi.* (conferring, conferred). To consult together.—*vt.* To give or bestow.
**Conference,** kon'fėr-ens, *n.* A meeting for consultation, or for the adjustment of differences; bestowal.
**Confess,** kon-fes', *vt.* To own, as a crime, debt, etc.; to admit; publicly to declare adherence to; to hear a confession, as a priest.—*vi.* To make confession.
**Confessedly,** kon-fes'ed-li, *adv.* Avowedly.
**Confession,** kon-fe'shon, *n.* Act of confessing; that which is confessed; a formulary of articles of faith; a creed.
**Confessional,** kon-fe'shon-al, *n.* The place where a priest sits to hear confessions.
**Confessor,** kon-fes'ėr, *n.* One who confesses; a priest who hears confession.
**Confetti,** kon-fet'i, *n.* Small pieces of colored paper thrown at each other by revellers at carnivals, or at the bride and groom by wedding guests.
**Confidant,** kon'fi-dant, *n.m.*; **Confidante,** kon-fi-dant', *n.f.* A confidential friend.
**Confide,** kon-fīd', *vi.* (confiding, confided). To trust wholly; to have firm faith (with *in*).—*vt.* To intrust; to commit to the charge of.
**Confidence,** kon'fi-dens, *n.* Firm belief or trust; self-reliance; boldness; assurance; a secret.
**Confident,** kon'fi-dent, *a.* Having confidence; trusting; assured; dogmatical.
**Confidential,** kon-fi-den'shal, *a.* Enjoying confidence; trusty; private; secret.
**Confidentially,** kon-fi-den'shal-li, *adv.* In confidence.
**Confidently,** kon'fi-dent-li, *adv.* In a confident manner; positively.
**Confiding,** kon-fīd'ing, *a.* Trusting; reposing confidence.
**Configuration,** kon-fig'ūr-ā''shon, *n.* External form; contour.
**Confinable,** kon-fīn'a-bl, *a.* That may be confined.
**Confine,** kon'fīn, *n.* Boundary; territory near the end; border (generally in *pl.*).—*vt.* kon-fīn' (confining, confined). To restrain; to limit; to shut up; to imprison.—**To be confined,** to be in childbed.
**Confined,** kon-fīnd', *a.* Limited; secluded; close.
**Confinement,** kon-fīn'ment, *n.* Imprisonment; seclusion; childbirth.
**Confirm,** kon-fėrm', *vt.* To make firm or more firm; to establish; to make certain; to administer the rite of confirmation to.
**Confirmation,** kon-fėrm-ā'shon, *n.* Act of confirming; additional evidence; ratification; the laying on of a bishop's hands in the rite of admission to the privileges of a Christian.
**Confirmative,** kon-fėr'ma-tiv, *a.* Tending to confirm or establish; confirmatory.
**Confirmatory,** kon-fėrm'ā-to-ri, *a.* That serves to confirm.
**Confirmed,** kon-fėrmd', *a.* Fixed; settled in certain habits, state of health, etc.
**Confiscable,** kon-fis'ka-bl, *a.* That may be confis-

cated; liable to forfeiture.
**Confiscate,** kon'fis-kāt, *vt.* (confiscating, confiscated). To seize as forfeited to the public treasury.
**Confiscation,** kon-fis-kā'shon, *n.* Act of confiscating.
**Confiscator,** kon'fis- or kon-fis'kāt-ėr, *n.* One who confiscates.
**Conflagration,** kon-fla-grā'shon, *n.* A great fire.
**Conflict,** kon'flikt, *n.* a struggle; clashing of views or statements.—*vi.* kon-flikt'. To meet in opposition; to be antagonistic.
**Conflicting,** kon-flikt'ing, *a.* Contradictory.
**Confluence,** kon'flū-ens, *n.* A flowing together; meeting, or place of meeting, of rivers; a concourse; a crowd.
**Confluent,** kon'flū-ent, *a.* Flowing together; running into each other; united.
**Conflux,** kon'fluks, *n.* A flowing together; a concourse; a crowd.
**Conform,** kon-form', *vt.* To cause to be of the same form; to adapt.—*vi.* To comply.
**Conformable,** kon-for'ma-bl, *a.* In harmony or conformity; suitable; compliant; *geol.* lying in parallel planes.
**Conformably,** kon-for'ma-bli, *adv.* Suitably.
**Conformation,** kon-for-mā'shon, *n.* The act of conforming; structure; configuration.
**Conformist,** kon-for'mist, *n.* One who conforms; one who complies with the worship of the established church.
**Conformity,** kon-for'mi-ti, *n.* Agreement; resemblance; compliance with.
**Confound,** kon-found', *vt.* To confuse; to astound; to overthrow; to mistake.
**Confounded,** kon-foun'ded, *a.* Excessive; odious; detestable; reprehensible.
**Confoundedly,** kon-foun'ded-li, *adv.* Shamefully; odiously; detestably.
**Confraternity,** kon-fra-tėr'ni-ti, *n.* A brotherhood; a society or body of men.
**Confrère,** kong-frār, *n.* A colleague.
**Confront,** kon-frunt', *vt.* To face; to oppose; to bring into the presence of; to set together for comparison.
**Confucian,** kon-fū'shi-an, *a.* and *n.* Pertaining to, or a follower of, Confucius, the famous Chinese philosopher.
**Confuse,** kon-fūz', *vt.* (confusing, confused). To mix without order; to derange; to confound; to disconcert.
**Confused,** kon-fūzd', *p.a.* Perplexed; disconcerted.
**Confusedly,** kon-fūz'ed-li, *adv.* In a confused manner.
**Confusion,** kon-fū'zhon, *n.* Disorder; embarrassment.
**Confutable,** kon-fūt'a-bl, *a.* That may be confuted.
**Confutation,** kon-fūt-ā'shon, *n.* Act of confuting; refutation; overthrow.
**Confute,** kon-fūt', *vt.* (confuting, confuted). To prove to be false; to refute.
**Congé,** kon'jē, *n.* Leave to depart; leavetaking; a bow. Also the form **Congee** (kon'jē), and sometimes as a verb: to take leave; to make a bow (congeeing, congeed).
**Congeal,** kon-jēl', *vt.* To freeze; to coagulate.—*vi.* To pass from a fluid to a solid state.
**Congelation,** kon-jēl-ā'shon, *n.* Act or process of congealing; mass congealed.
**Congener,** kon'je-nėr, *n.* One of the same origin or kind.
**Congenial,** kon-jē'ni-al, *a.* Of like taste or disposition; kindly; adapted.
**Congeniality,** kon-jē'ni-al''i-ti, *n.* Natural affinity; suitableness.
**Congenital,** kon-jen'it-al, *a.* Pertaining to an individual from his birth.
**Conger,** kong'gėr, *n.* The sea-eel.
**Congeries,** kon-jē'ri-ēz, *n.* A heap or pile; a collection of several bodies in one mass.
**Congest,** kon-jest', *vt.* and *i.* To accumulate to excess, as blood, population, etc.
**Congestion,** kon-jest'shon, *n.* Excessive accumulation; undue fullness of blood-vessels in an organ.
**Conglobate,** kon-glōb'āt, *a.* Formed into a globe.—*vt.* To form into a ball.
**Conglobation,** kon-glōb-ā'shon, *n.* Act of forming into a ball; a round body.
**Conglomerate,** kon-glom'ėr-āt, *a.* Gathered into a ball; composed of fragments of rock cemented together.—*n.* A rock composed of pebbles cemented together.—*vt.* To gather into a ball or round mass.
**Congratulate,** kon-grat'ū-lāt, *vt.* (congratulating, congratulated). To express sympathy to in good fortune; to felicitate.
**Congratulation,** kon-grat'ū-lā''shon, *n.* Act of congratulating; expression of sympathetic joy at another's good fortune.
**Congratulator,** kon-grat'ū-lāt-ėr, *n.* One who offers congratulations.
**Congratulatory,** kon-grat'ū-lā-to-ri, *a.* Expressing congratulation.
**Congregate,** kong'grē-gāt, *vt.* (congregating, congregated). To collect together.—*vi.* To come together; to assemble.
**Congregation,** kong-grē-gā'shon, *n.* Act of congregating; an assembly; an assembly met for divine worhip.
**Congregational,** kong-grē-gā'shon-al, *a.* Pertaining to a congregation, or to the Congregationalists.
**Congregationalist,** kong-grē-gā'shon-al-ist, *n.* One who adheres to the system in which each separate congregation or church forms an independent body.
**Congress,** kong'gres, *n.* An assembly; a meeting of ambassaors, etc., for the settlement of affairs between different nations; the legislature of the United States.
**Congressional,** kon-gre'shon-al, *a.* Pertaining to a congress.
**Congreve,** kong'grēv, *n.* A kind of lucifer match.—**Congreve rocket,** an iron rocket for use in war.
**Congruence, Congruency,** kong'gru-ens, kong'gru-en-si, *n.* Accordance; consistency.
**Congruent,** kong'grü-ent, *a.* Suitable; agreeing; correspondent.
**Congruity,** kon-gru'i-ti, *n.* Suitableness; accordance; consistency.
**Congruous,** kong'grü-us, *a.* Accordant; suitable; consistent.
**Conic, Conical,** kon'ik, kon'ik-al, *a.* Having the form of a cone; pertaining to a cone.
**Conically,** kon'ik-al-li, *adv.* In the form of a cone.
**Conics,** kon'iks, *n.* That part of geometry which treats of the cone.
**Coniferous,** kōn-if'ėr-us, *a.* Bearing cones, as the pine, fir, etc.
**Conjecturable,** kon-jek'tūr-a-bl, *a.* That may be conjectured or guessed.
**Conjectural,** kon-jek'tūr-al, *a.* Depending on conjecture.
**Conjecture,** kon-jek'tūr, *n.* Supposition; opinion without proof; surmise.—*vt.* (conjecturing, conjectured). To judge by guess; to surmise.—*vi.* To form conjectures.
**Conjoin,** kon-join', *vt.* To join together; to unite; to associate.
**Conjoint,** kon-joint', *a.* United; connected; associated.
**Conjointly,** kon-joint'li, *adv.* Jointly.
**Conjugal,** kon'jū-gal, *a.* Pertaining to marriage; connubial.
**Conjugally,** kon'jū-gal-li, *adv.* Matrimonially; connubially.
**Conjugate,** kon'jū-gāt, *vt.* (conjugating, conjugated). To join together; to inflect (a verb) through its several forms.—*a.* Joined in pairs; kindred in origin and meaning.
**Conjugation,** kon-jū-gā'shon, *n.* The act of conjugating; the inflection of verbs; a class of verbs

C

similarly conjugated.
**Conjunct,** kon-jungkt', *a.* Conjoined; concurrent.
**Conjunction,** kon-jungk'shon, *n.* Act of joining; state of being joined; connection; a connecting word.
**Conjuctive,** kon-jungk'tiv, *a.* Serving to unite; subjunctive.
**Conjuncture,** kon-jungk'tūr, *n.* A combination of important events; a crisis.
**Conjuration,** kon-jū-rā'shon, *n.* The act of conjuring; an incantation; a spell.
**Conjure,** kon-jūr', *vt.* (conjuring, conjured). To call upon solemnly; to beseech.
**Conjure,** kon'jėr, *vt.* (conjuring, conjured). To summon up by enchantments.—*vi.* To practice the arts of a conjurer.
**Conjurer, Conjuror,** kun'jėr-ėr, *n.* An enchanter; one who practises legerdemain.
**Connate,** kon'nāt, *a.* Born with another; being of the same birth; united in origin.
**Connatural,** kon-na'tūr-al, *a.* Connected by nature; innate; congenital.
**Connect,** kon-nekt', *vt.* To conjoin; to combine; to associate.—*vi.* To unite or cohere together; to have a close relation.
**Connectedly,** kon-nekt'ed-li, *adv.* In a connected manner.
**Connection,** kon-nek'shon, *n.* Act of connecting; state of being connected; a relation by blood or marriage; relationship.
**Connective,** kon-nekt'iv, *a.* Having the power of connecting; tending to connect.—*n.* A word that connects other words and sentences; a conjunction.
**Connector,** kon-nekt'ėr, *n.* One who or that which connects.
**Connivance,** kon-nīv'ans, *n.* Voluntary blindness to an act; pretended ignorance.
**Connive,** kon-nīv', *vi.* (conniving, connived). To wink; to pretend ignorance or blindness; to forbear to see (with *at*).
**Conniver,** kon-nīv'ėr, *n.* One who connives.
**Connoisseur,** kon'i-sūr, *n.* A judge of any art, particularly painting and sculpture.
**Connotation,** kon-ō-tā'shon, *n.* That which constitutes the meaning of a word.
**Connote,** kon-nōt', *vt.* (connoting, connoted). To include in the meaning; to imply.
**Connubial,** kon-nū'bi-al, *a.* Pertaining to marriage; conjugal; matrimonial.
**Conoild,** kōn'oid, *n.* A body resembling a cone.—*a.* Resembling a cone. Also *conoidal.*
**Conquer,** kong'kėr, *vt.* To gain by force; to vanquish; to subjugate; to surmount,—*vi.* To overcome; to gain the victory.
**Conquerable,** kong'kėr-a-bl, *a.* That may be conquered or subdued.
**Conqueror,** kong'kėr-ėr, *n.* A victor.
**Conquest,** kong'kwest, *n.* Act of conquering; that which is conquered; a gaining by struggle.
**Conscience,** kon'shens, *n.* Internal knowledge or judgment of right and wrong; the moral sense; morality.
**Conscientious,** kon-shi-en'shus, *a.* Regulated by conscience; scrupulous.
**Conscientiously,** kon-shi-en'shus-li, *adv.* In a conscientious manner.
**Conscionable,** kon'shon-a-bl, *a.* Reasonable.
**Conscious,** kon'shus, *a.* Knowing in one's own mind; knowing by sensation or perception; aware; sensible; self-conscious.
**Consciously,** kon'shus-li, *adv.* In a conscious manner.
**Consciousness,** kon'shus-nes, *n.* State of being conscious; perception of what passes in one's own mind; sense of guilt or innocence.
**Conscript,** kon'skript, *a.* Registered; enrolled.—*n.* One compulsorily enrolled to serve in the army or navy.
**Conscription,** kon-skrip'shon, *n.* A compulsory enrolment for military or naval service.
**Consecrate,** kon'sē-kr āt, *vt.* (consecrating, consecrated). To appropriate to sacred uses; to dedicate to God.—*a.* Sacred; consecrated.
**Consecration,** kon-sē-krā'shon, *n.* Act of consecrating; ordination of a bishop.
**Consecutive,** kon-sek'ū-tiv, *a.* Following in regular order; following logically.
**Consecutively,** kon-sek'ū-tiv-li, *adv.* In a consecutive manner.
**Consent,** kon-sent', *n.* Agreement to what is proposed; concurrence; compliance.—*vi.* To be of the same mind; to assent; to comply.
**Consentient,** kon-sen'shi-ent, *a.* Consenting; agreeing; accordant.
**Consequence,** kon'sē-kwens, *n.* That which follows as a result; inference; importance.
**Consequent,** kon'sē-kwent, *a.* Following, as the natural effect, or by inference.—*n.* Effect; result; inference.
**Consequential,** kon-sē-kwen'shal, *a.* Following as the effect; pompous.
**Consequentially,** kon-sē-kwen'shal-li, *adv.* By consequence; pompously.
**Consequently,** kon'sė-kwent-li, *adv.* By consequence; therefore.
**Conservancy,** kon-sėrv'an-si, *n.* Conservation; preservation; official supervision.
**Conservation,** kon-sėrv-ā'shon, *n.* Preservation; the keeping of a thing entire.
**Conservatism,** kon-sėrv'at-izm, *n.* The political principles of Conservatives.
**Conservative,** kon-sėrv'at-iv, *a.* Preservative; adhering to existing institutions.—*n.* One opposed to political changes of a radical nature; a Tory.
**Conservatoire,** kong-sėr-vä-twär, *n.* A public establishment for the study of music.
**Conservator,** kon-sėrv-āt-ėr, *n.* A preserver; a custodian; a guardian.
**Conservatory,** kon-sėrv'a-to-ri, *n.* A greenhouse for exotics.
**Conserve,** kon-sėrv', *vt.* (conserving, conserved). To keep in a sound state; to candy or pickle.—*n.* kon'sėrv. That which is conserved, particularly fruits.
**Consider,** kon-si'dėr, *vt.* To fix the mind on; to ponder; to have respect to; to regard to be.—*vi.* To think seriously; to ponder.
**Considerable,** kon-si'dėr-a-bl, *a.* Worthy of consideration; moderately large.
**Considerably,** kon-si'dėr-a-bli, *adv.* In a considerable degree.
**Considerate,** kon-si'dėr-āt, *a.* Given to consideration; mindful of others; deliberate.
**Considerately,** kon-si'dėr-āt-li, *adv.* In a considerate manner.
**Consideration,** kon-si'dėr-ā''shon, *n.* Mental view; serious deliberation; importance; motive of action; an equivalent.
**Considering,** kon-si'dėr-ing, *prep.* Taking into account; making allowance for.
**Consign,** kon-sīn', *vt.* To deliver over to another by agreement; to intrust; to commit; to deposit.
**Consignee,** kon-sīn-ē', *n.* The person to whom goods are consigned.
**Consignment,** kon-sīn'ment, *n.* Act of consigning; the thing consigned.
**Consignor,** kon-sī'nor, *n.* The person who consigns.
**Consist,** kon-sist', *vi.* To be in a fixed state; to be comprised; to be made up; to be compatible; to agree.
**Consistence, Consistency,** kon-sis'tens, kon-sis'ten-si, *n.* A degree of density; firmness or coherence, harmony; agreement.
**Consistent,** kon-sis'tent, *a.* Fixed; firm; not contradictory; compatible.
**Consistently,** kon-sis'tent-li, *adv.* In a consistent manner.
**Consistorial,** kon-sis-tō'ri-al, *a.* Pertaining or relating to a consistory.
**Consistory,** kon'sis-to-ri, *n.* A spiritual court; the court of a diocesan bishop; college of cardinals.
**Consociation,** kon-sō'shi-ā''shon, *n.* Association; alliance; fellowship.

**Consolable,** kon-sōl'a-bl, *a.* That may be consoled or comforted.
**Consolation,** kon-sōl-ā'shon, *n.* A solace; alleviation of misery; what helps to cheer; what gives comfort.
**Consolatory,** kon-sol'a-to-ri, *a.* Tending to give solace; assuaging grief.
**Console,** kon-sōl', *vt.* (consoling, consoled). To comfort; to soothe; to cheer.
**Console,** kon'sōl, *n.* A bracket to support a cornice, vase, etc.
**Consolidate,** kon-sol'id-āt, *vt.* (consolidating, consolidated). To make solid or firm; to unite into one; to compact.—*vi.* To grow firm and solid.
**Consolidation,** kon-sol'id-ā''shon, *n.* Act of consolidating; state of being consolidated.
**Consonance,** kon'sō-nans, *n.* Concord; agreement; consistency.
**Consonant,** kon'sō-nant, *a.* Having agreement; accordant; consistent.—*n.* A letter always sounded with a vowel.
**Consonantal,** kon-sō-nant'al, *a.* Partaking of the nature of a consonant.
**Consort,** kon'sort, *n.* A partner; a wife or husband; a companion.—*vi.* kon-sort'. To associate; to accord.
**Conspectus,** kon-spek'tus, *n.* A comprehensive view of a subject; abstract or sketch.
**Conspicuous,** kon-spik'ū-us, *a.* Standing clearly in view; manifest; distinguished.
**Conspicuously,** kon-spik'ū-us-li, *adv.* In a conspicuous manner.
**Conspiracy,** kon-spi'ra-si, *n.* A plot; a treasonable combination.
**Conspirator,** kon-spi'rāt-ėr, *n.* One who engages in a plot or conspiracy.
**Conspire,** kon-spīr', *vi.* (conspiring, conspired). To plot; to combine for some evil purpose; to tend to one end.
**Constable,** kun'sta-bl, *n.* An officer of the peace; policeman.
**Constabulary,** kon-stab'ū-la-ri, *a.* Pertaining to constables.—*n.* The body of constables in a city, county, etc.
**Constancy,** kon'stan-si, *n.* Uniformity; steadfastness; lasting affection.
**Constant,** kon'stant, *a.* Steadfast; perpetual; assiduous; resolute.—*n.* That which remains unchanged; a fixed quantity.
**Constantly,** kon'stant-li, *adv.* In a constant manner
**Constellation,** kon-stel-lā'shon, *n.* A group of fixed stars; an assemblage of splendors or excellences.
**Consternation,** kon-stėr-nā'shon, *n.* Prostration of the mind by terror, dismay, etc.
**Constipate,** kon'sti-pāt, *vt.* (constipating, constipated). To make costive.
**Constipation,** kon-sti-pā'shon, *n.* Costiveness.
**Constituency,** kon-stit'ū-en-si, *n.* The body of constituents.
**Constituent,** kon-stit'ū-ent, *a.* Forming; existing as an essential part.—*n.* An elector; an essential part.
**Constitute,** kon'sti-tūt, *vt.* (constituting, constituted). To set up or establish; to compose; to appoint; to make and empower.
**Constitution,** kon-sti-tū'shon, *n.* The particular frame or character of the body or mind; established form of government; a system of fundamental laws; a particular law.
**Constitutional,** kon-sti-tū'shon-al, *a.* Adherent in the human constitution; consistent with the civil constitution; legal.—*n.* A walk for the sake of health.
**Constitutionalism,** kon-sti-tū'shon-al-izm, *n.* The theory of constitutional role; adherence to a constitution.
**Constitutionalist, Constitutionist,** kon-sti-tū'shon-al-ist, kon-sti-tū'shon-ist, *n.* An adherent to the constitution.
**Constitutionally,** kon-sti-tū'shon-al-li, *adv.* In consistency with the constitution.
**Constitutive,** kon'sti-tūt-iv, *a.* That constitutes; having power to enact, establish, etc.
**Constrain,** kon-strān', *vt.* To urge by force; to necessitate; to restrain.
**Constrainable,** kon-strān'a-bl, *a.* That may be constrained.
**Constrained,** kon-strānd', *a.* With a certain constraint or want of freedom; forced.
**Constraint,** kon-strānt', *n.* Necessity; reserve; restraint.
**Constrict,** kon-strikt', *vt.* To draw together; to contract.
**Constriction,** kon-strik'shon, *n.* Contraction.
**Constrictive,** kon-strik'tiv, *a.* Tending to contract or compress.
**Constrictor,** kon-strik'tėr, *n.* That which constricts; a muscle that closes an orifice; a serpent which crushes its prey.
**Construct,** kon-strukt', *vt.* To build; to frame with contrivance; to devise.
**Construction,** kon-struk'shon, *n.* Structure; arrangement of words in a sentence; sense; interpretation.
**Constructional,** kon-struk'shon-al, *a.* Pertaining to construction.
**Constructive,** kon-strukt'iv, *a.* Having ability to construct; created or deduced by construction; inferred.
**Constructively,** kon-strukt'iv-li, *adv.* In a constructive manner; by fair inference.
**Construe,** kon'strū, *vt.* (construing, construed). To arrange words so as to discover the sense of a sentence; to interpret.
**Consubstantial,** kon-sub-stan'shal, *a.* Having the same substance; co-essential.
**Consubstantiality,** kon-sub-stan'shi-al''i-ti, *n.* Participation of the same nature.
**Consubstantiation,** kon-sub-stan'shi-ā''shon, *n.* The doctrine of the presence of the body and blood of Christ in the sacramental elements.
**Consuetude,** kon'swē-tūd, *n.* Custom.
**Consul,** kon'sul, *n.* One of the two chief magistrates of ancient Rome; a person appointed by government to reside in a foreign country, and protect the commercial interests of his own country.
**Consular,** kon'sūl-ėr, *a.* Pertaining to a consul.
**Consulate,** kon'sūl-āt, *n.* The office, jurisdiction, or residence of a consul.
**Consulship,** kon'sul-ship, *n.* The office of a consul, or the term of his office.
**Consult,** kon-sult', *vi.* To seek the opinion of another; to deliberate in common; to consider.—*vt.* To ask advice of; to refer to for information; to have regard to.
**Consultation,** kon-sult-ā'shon, *n.* Act of consulting; a meeting for deliberation.
**Consulter,** kon-sult'ėr, *n.* One who consults.
**Consulting,** kon-sult'ing, *a.* Giving advice; used for consultations.
**Consumable,** kon-sūm'a-bl, *a.* That may be consumed.
**Consume,** kon-sūm', *vt.* (consuming, consumed). To reduce to nothing; to burn up; to squander.—*vi.* To waste away slowly; to be exhausted.
**Consumer,** kon-sūm'ėr, *n.* One who consumes.
**Consummate,** kon'sum-āt, *vt.* To finish; to perfect.—*a.* kon-sum'āt. Complete; perfect.
**Consummately,** kon-sum'āt-li, *adv.* Completely; perfectly.
**Consummation,** kon-sum-ā'shon, *n.* Act of consummating; end; perfection.
**Consumption,** kon-sum'shon, *n.* Act of consuming; quantity consumed; a gradual wasting away of the body; phthisis.
**Consumptive,** kon-sum'tiv, *a.* Affected with or inclined to consumption or phthisis.
**Contact,** kon'takt, *n.* A touching together; close union or juncture of bodies.
**Contagion,** kon-tā'jon, *n.* Communication of a disease by contact; poisonous emanation; infection.
**Contagious,** kon-tā'jus, *a.* Caught or communi-

cated by contact; infectious.
**Contagiously,** kon-tā'jus-li, *adv*. In a contagious manner; by contagion.
**Contain,** kon-tān', *vt*. To hold; to be able to hold; to comprise; to restrain.
**Containable,** kon-tān'a-bl, *a*. That may be contained or comprised.
**Container,** kon-tā'nėr, *n*. That which contains.
**Contaminate,** kon-tam'in-āt, *vt*. To corrupt; to taint; to vitiate.
**Contamination,** kon-tam'in-ā''shon, *n*. Pollution; defilement; taint.
**Contemn,** kon-tem', *vt*. To despise; to scorn.
**Contemner,** kon-tem'ėr, *n*. One who contemns; a despiser; a scorner.
**Contemplate,** kon'tem-plāt, *vt*. To view with continued attention; to meditate on; to design; to purpose.—*vi*. To study; to meditate.
**Contemplation,** kon-tem-plā'shon, *n*. Act of contemplating; meditation.
**Contemplative,** kon-tem'plāt-iv, *a*. Given to contemplation; thoughtful.
**Contemporaneous,** kon-tem'pō-rā''nē-us, *a*. Living or being at the same time.
**Contemporaneously,** kon-tem'pō-rā''nē-us-li, *adv*. At the same time.
**Contemporary,** kon-tem'pō-ra-ri, *a*. Living or occurring at the same time.—*n*. One who lives at the same time with another.
**Contempt,** kon-temt', *n*. Act of contemning; scorn; disregard; disobedience to the rules; etc., of a court.
**Contemptible,** kon-tem'ti-bl, *a*. Worthy of contempt; despicable; vile; mean.
**Contemptibly,** kon-tem'ti-bli, *adv*. In a contemptible manner; meanly.
**Contemptuous,** kon-tem'tū-us, *a*. Manifesting contempt; scornful; insolent.
**Contemptuously,** kon-tem'tū-us-li, *adv*. In a contemptuous manner.
**Contend,** kon-tend', *vi*. To strive; to vie; to dispute; to wrangle.
**Contender,** kon-tend'ėr, *n*. One who contends.
**Content,** kon-tent', *a*. Easy in mind; satisfied.—*vt*. To satisfy the mind of; to please or gratify.—*n*. State of being contented; contentment. Kontent' or kon'tent, things contained in a vessel, book, etc.: in these senses *pl*.; capacity; space occupied: in these senses *sing*.
**Contented,** kon-tent'ed, *a*. Satisfied; easy in mind.
**Contentedly,** kon-tent'ed-li, *adv*. In a contented manner.
**Contention,** kon-ten'shon, *n*. Struggle; quarrel; debate; emulation.
**Contentious,** kon-ten'shus, *a*. Quarrelsome.
**Contentment,** kon-tent'ment, *n*. State of being contended; satisfaction; content.
**Conterminous, conterminal,** kon-tėr'min-us, kon-tėr'min-al, *a*. Having the same bounds; contiguous.
**Contest,** kon-test', *vt*. To call in question; to strive for.—*vi*. To strive; to contend; to emulate.—*n*. kon'test. Struggle for victory; encounter; debate; competition.
**Contestable,** kon-test'a-bl, *a*. That may be contested; disputable; controvertible.
**Context,** kon'tekst, *n*. The parts which precede or follow a passage quoted.
**Contexture,** kon-teks'tūr, *n*. The interweaving of several parts into one body; disposition of parts; texture.
**Contiguity,** kon-ti-gū'i-ti, *n*. State of being contiguous; proximity.
**Contiguous,** kon-tig'ū-us, *a*. Touching one another; in contact; adjacent.
**Contiguously,** kon-tig'ū-us-li, *adv*. In a contiguous manner or position.
**Continence, Continency,** kon'ti-nens, kona-ti-nen-si, *n*. Restraint of the desires and passions; chastity; temperance.
**Continent,** kon'ti-nent, *a*. Chaste; moderate.—*n*. A connected tract of land of great extent; the mainland of Europe.
**Continental,** kon-ti-nent'al, *a*. Pertaining to a continent, particularly Europe.
**Continently,** kon'ti-nent-li, *adv*. In a continent manner; chastely.
**Contingence, Contingency,** kon-tin'jens, kon-tin'jen-si, *n*. Quality of being contingent; an event which may occur; chance; juncture.
**Contingent,** kon-tin'jent, *a*. Happening by chance; incidental; dependent upon an uncertainty.—*n*. A contingency; a quota; a quota of troops or a joint enterprise.
**Contingently,** kon-ten'jent-li, *adv*. Accidentally; dependently.
**Continual,** kon-tin'ū-al, *a*. Not intermitting; uninterrupted; often repeated.
**Continually,** kon-tin'ū-al-li, *adv*. Constantly; always.
**Continuance,** kon-tin'ū-ans, *n*. Permanence in one state; duration.
**Continuation,** kon-tin'ū-ā''shon, *n*. Succession; extension; prolongation.
**Continuator,** kon-tin'ū-āt-ėr, *n*. One who continues anything begun by another.
**Continue,** kon-tin'ū, *vi*. (continuing, continued). To remain in a state or place; to be durable; to persevere; to be steadfast.—*vt*. To prolong; to extend; to persevere in.
**Continuity,** kon-ti-nū'i-ti, *n*. Close union of parts; unbroken texture; cohesion.
**Continuous,** kon-tin'ū-us, *a*. Joined together closely; conjoined; continued.
**Continuously,** kon-tin'ū-us-li, *adv*. Without interruption.
**Contort,** kon-tort', *vt*. To twist; to writhe; to draw or pull awry.
**Contortion,** kon-tor'shon, *n*. A twisting.
**Contortionist,** kon-tor'shon-ist, *n*. An acrobat who practices contortions of the body.
**Contour,** kontör', *n*. The line that bounds a body; outline.
**Contour-map,** kon-tör' map, *n*. A map showing elevations about sea-level by curves (*contour lines*) drawn through places of equal elevation.
**Contraband,** kon'tra-band, *n*. Illegal traffic; smuggling.—*a*. Prohibited.
**Contrabandist,** kon'tra-band-ist, *n*. One who deals in contraband goods; a smuggler.
**Contract,** kon-trakt', *vt*. To draw together; to cause to shrink; to reduce; to betroth; to bring on; to incur.—*vi*. To shrink up; to make a mutual agreement.—*n*. kon'trakt. Agreement; bond; the writing which contains stipulations; betrothment.
**Contracted,** kon-trakt'ed, *a*. Limited; narrow; mean.
**Contractedly,** kon-trakt'ed-li, *adv*. In a contracted manner.
**Contractibility,** kon-trakt'i-bil''i-ti, *n*. Capability of being contracted.
**Contractible,** kon-trakt'i-bl, *a*. Capable of contraction.
**Contractile,** kon-trakt'īl, *a*. Having the power of contracting, as living fibers.
**Contraction,** kon-trak'shon, *n*. Shrinking; shortening; abbreviation.
**Contractor,** kon-trakt'ėr, *n*. One who contracts to perform any work or service, or to furnish supplies, at a certain price or rate.
**Contradict,** kon-tra-dikt', *vt*. To assert to be the contrary; to deny; to oppose.
**Contradiction,** kon-tra-dik'shon, *n*. A contrary assertion; inconsistency with itself.
**Contradictorily,** kon-tra-dik'to-ri-li, *adv*. In a contradictory manner.
**Contradictory,** kon-tra-dik'to-ri, *a*. Implying contradiction; inconsistent.
**Contradistinction,** kon'tra-dis-tingk''shon, *n*. Distinction by opposites.
**Contradistinctive,** kon'tra-dis-tingkt''iv, *a*. Disinguishing by contrast.
**Contradistinguish,** kon'tra-dis-tin''gwish, *vt*. To distinguish by opposite qualities.

**Contralto,** kon-tral'tō, *n.* The lowest voice of a woman or boy.
**Contraposition,** kon'tra-pō-zi'shon, *n.* A placing over against; opposite position.
**Contrapuntal,** kon-tra-punt'al, *a.* Pertaining to counterpoint.
**Contrapuntist,** kon-tra-punt'ist, *n.* One skilled in counterpoint.
**Contrariety,** kon-tra-rī'e-ti, *n.* Opposition; repugnance; inconsistency.
**Contrarily,** kon'tra-ri-li, *adv.* In a contrary manner; on the other hand.
**Contrariwise,** kon'tra-ri-wīz, *adv.* On the contrary; on the other hand.
**Contrary,** kon'tra-ri, *a.* Opposite; repugnant; inconsistent.—*adv.* In an opposite manner; in opposition.—*n.* A thing that is contrary.
**Contrast,** kon-trast', *vt.* To set in opposition; to show the difference or heighten the effect.—*vi.* To stand in contrast to.—*n.* kon'trast. Opposition or comparison of things; a person or thing strikingly different.
**Contravene,** kon-tra-vēn', *vt.* (contravening, contravened). To oppose; to trangress.
**Contravention,** kon-tra-ven'shon, *n.* Transgression; violation.
**Contretemps,** kong-tr-tong, *n.* An unexpected and untoward accident.
**Contribute,** kon-trib'ūt, *vt.* (contributing, contributed). To give in common with others.—*vi.* To give a part; to conduce.
**Contribution,** kon-tri-bū'shon, *n.* Act of contributing; that which is contributed; an article sent to a periodical, etc.
**Contributive,** kon-trib'ūt-iy, *a.* Tending to contribute; lending aid to promote.
**Contributor,** kon-trib'ūt-ėr, *n.* One who contributes; a writer to a periodical.
**Contributory,** kon-trib'ū-to-ri, *a.* Contributing to the same end.
**Contrite,** kon'trīt, *a.* Broken-hearted for sin; penitent.
**Contrition,** kon-tri'shon, *n.* Grief of heart for sin.
**Contrivable,** kon-trīv'a-bl, *a.* That may be contrived, invented, or devised.
**Contrivance,** kon-trīv'ans, *n.* Scheme; invention; artifice.
**Contrive,** kon-trīv', *vt.* (contriving, contrived). To invent; to devise.—*vi.* To form or design.
**Contriver,** kon-trīv'ėr, *n.* Inventor; schemer.
**Control,** kon-trōl', *n.* Restraint; superintendence; authority.—*vt.* (controlling, controlled). To restrain; to regulate.
**Controllable,** kon-trōl'a-bl, *a.* That may be controlled; subject to command.
**Controller,** kon-trōl'ėr, *n.* An officer who checks the accounts of collectors of public moneys.
**Controlment,** kon-trōl'ment, *n.* Power or act of controlling; control; restraint.
**Controversial,** kon-trō-vėr'shal, *a.* Relating to controversy.
**Controversialist,** kon-trō-vėr'shal-ist, *n.* One who carries on a controversy.
**Controversy,** kon'trō-vėr-si, *n.* A disputation, particularly in writing; litigation.
**Controvert,** kon'trō-vėrt, *vt.* To dispute by reasoning; to attempt to disprove or confute.
**Controvertible,** kon-trō-vėrt'i-bl, *a.* That may be controverted.
**Controvertibly,** kon-trō-vėrt'i-bli, *adv.* In a controvertible manner.
**Contumacious,** kon-tū-mā'shus, *a.* Opposing rightful authority; obstinate.
**Contumaciously,** kon-tū-mā'shus-li, *adv.* Obstinately; stubbornly.
**Contumacy,** kon'tū-mā-si, *n.* Resistance to authority; perverseness.
**Contumelious,** kon-tū-mē'li-us, *a.* Contemptuous; insolent; proudly rude.
**Contumely,** kon'tū-me-li, *n.* Haughty insolence; contemptuous language.
**Contuse,** kon-tūz', *vt.* (contusing, contused). To bruise; to injure without breaking the skin or substance.
**Contusion,** kon-tū'zhon, *n.* A severe bruise; injury without breaking of the skin.
**Conundrum,** kō-nun'drum, *n.* A sort of riddle turning on some odd resemblance between things quite unlike.
**Convalesce,** kon-va-les', *vi.* (convalescing, convalesced). To recover health.
**Convalescence,** kon-va-les'ens, *n.* The state of one convalescent; gradual recovery after illness.
**Convalescent,** kon-va-les'ent, *a.* Recovering health after sickness.—*n.* One recovering from sickness.
**Convenable,** kon-vēn'-bl, *a.* That may be convened or assembled.
**Convene,** kon-vēn', *vi.* (convening, convened). To assemble.—*vt.* To cause to assemble; to convoke.
**Convener,** kon-vēn'ėr, *n.* One who calls an assembly together.
**Convenience, Conveniency,** kon-vė'ni-ens, kon-vē'ni-en-si, *n.* Ease; comfort; suitable opportunity; an appliance or utensil.
**Convenient,** kon-vė'ni-ent, *a.* Suitable; adapted; opportune.
**Conveniently,** kon-vė'ni-ent-li, *adv.* Suitably; with ease.
**Convent,** kon'vent, *n.* A body of monks or nuns; a monastery; a nunnery.
**Conventicle,** kon-ven'ti-kl, *n.* A secret meeting; a meeting of religious dissenters; their meeting-place.
**Convention,** kon-ven'shon, *n.* An assembly; an agreement; recognized social custom.
**Conventional,** kon-ven'shon-al, *a.* Formed by agreement; tacitly understood; resting on mere usage.
**Conventionalism,** kon-ven'shon-al-izm, *n.* Arbitrary custom; a conventional phrase, ceremony, etc.
**Conventionally,** kon-ven'shon-al-li, *adv.* In a conventional manner.
**Conventual,** kon-ven'tū-al, *a.* Belonging to a convent.—*n.* A monk or nun.
**Converge,** kon-vėrj', *vi.* (converging, converged). To tend to the same point; to approach in position or character.
**Convergence, Convergency,** kon-vėrj'ens, kon-vėrj'en-si, *n.* Tendency to one point.
**Convergent,** kon-vėrj'ent, *a.* Tending to one point or object; approaching.
**Conversant,** kon'vėrs-ant, *a.* Having intercourse or familiarity; versed in; proficient; occupied or concerned.
**Conversation,** kon-vėr-sā'shon, *n.* Familiar intercourse; easy talk.
**Conversational,** kon-vėr-sā'shon-al, *a.* Pertaining to conversation.
**Converse,** kon-vėrs', *vi.* (conversing, conversed). To hold intercourse; to talk familiarly; to commune.—*n.* kon'vėrs. Conversation; familiarity; something forming a counterpart.—*a.* Put the opposite or reverse way.
**Conversely,** kon'vėrs-li, *adv.* In a converse manner; with inversion of order.
**Conversion,** kon-vėr'shon, *n.* Change from one state, religion, or party to another; interchange of terms in logic.
**Convert,** kon-vėrt', *vt.* and *i.* To change from one state, use, religion, or party to another; to turn from a bad life to a good; to interchange conversely.—*n.* kon'vėrt. One who has changed his opinion, practice, or religion.
**Convertibility,** kon-vėrt'i-bil''i-ti, *n.* Condition or quality of being convertible.
**Convertible,** kon-vėrt'i-bl, *a.* Transformable; interchangeable.
**Convertibly,** kon-vėrt'i-bli, *adv.* With interchange of terms.
**Convex,** kon'veks, *a.* Rising on the exterior surface into a round form: opposed to *concave*.
**Convexity,** kon-veks'i-ti, *n.* State of being convex;

C

roundness.
**Convexly,** kon'veks-li, *adv*. In a convex form.
**Convey,** kon-vā, *vt*. To transport; to deliver; to impart.
**Conveyable,** kon-vā'a-bl, *a*. That may be conveyed.
**Conveyance,** kon-vā'ans, *n*. Act or means of conveying; a carriage; transference; a deed which transfers property.
**Conveyancer,** kon-vā'ans-ėr, *n*. One who draws deeds by which property is transferred.
**Conveyer,** kon-vā'ėr, *n*. One who or that which conveys.
**Convict,** kon-vikt', *vt*. To prove or decide to be guilty—*n*. kon'vikt. A person found guilty; one undergoing penal servitude.
**Conviction,** kon-vik'shon, *n*. Act of finding a person guilty; strong belief; state of being sensible of wrong-doing.
**Convince,** kon-vins', *vt*. (convincing, convinced). To persuade by argument; to satisfy by evidence or proof.
**Convincingly,** kon-vins'ing-li, *adv*. In a convincing manner.
**Convivial,** kon-vi'vi-al, *a*. Festive; festal; jovial; social.
**Conviviality,** kon-vi'vi-al''i-ti, *n*. Convivial disposition; mirth at an entertainment.
**Convocation,** kon-vō-kā'shon, *n*. Act of convoking; an assembly, particularly of clergy or heads of a university.
**Convoke,** kon-vōk', *vt*. (convoking, convoked). To call together; to summon to meet.
**Convolute, Convoluted,** kon'vō-lūt, kon'-vō-lūt-ed, *a*. Rolled on itself; presenting convolutions.
**Convolution,** kon-vō-lū'shon, *n*. Act of rolling together or on itself; a winding; a spiral.
**Convolve,** kon-volv', *vt*. To roll together or on itself; to coil up.
**Convolvulus,** kon-volv'ū-lus, *n*. Bind-weed; a genus of slender twining plants.
**Convoy,** kon-voi', *vt*. To accompany for defense; to escort.—*n*. kon'voi. A protecting force; escort.
**Convulse,** kon-vuls', *vt*. (convulsing, convulsed). To contract violently, as the muscles; to affect by irregular spasms; to disturb.
**Convulsion,** kon-vul'shon, *n*. A violent involuntary contraction of the muscles; a violent irregular motion; disturbance.
**Convulsive,** kon-vuls'iv, *a*. Tending to convulse; spasmodic; agitating.
**Cony, Coney,** kō'ni, *n*. A rabbit; simpleton.
**Coo,** kö, *vi*. (cooing, cooed). To make a low sound, as doves; to act in a loving manner.
**Cook,** kuk, *vt*. To prepare food by fire or heat; to concoct; to tamper with.—*n*. One who prepares victuals for the table.
**Cookery,** kuk'ė-ri, *n*. The art of preparing victuals for the table.
**Cool,** köl, *a*. Moderately cold; dispassionate; self-possessed; impudent.—*n*. A moderate degree or state of cold.—*vt*. To make cool; to moderate; to calm; to render indifferent.—*vi*. To lose heat, ardor, affection, etc.
**Cooler,** köl'ėr, *n*. That which cools; anything which abates heat or excitement.
**Cool-headed,** köl'hed-ed, *a*. Having a temper not easily excited.
**Coolie,** kö'li, *n*. An Oriental porter.
**Coolly,** köl'li, *adv*. In a cool or indifferent manner; with calm assurance.
**Coolness,** köl'nes, *n*. Moderate degree of cold; indifference; calm assurance.
**Coop,** köp, *n*. A barrel or cask; a box for poultry, etc.—*vt*. To confine in a coop; to shut up in a narrow compass.
**Cooper,** kö'pėr, *n*. One who makes barrels.—*vt*. and *i*. To do the work of a cooper.
**Cooperage,** kö'pėr-āj, *n*. The work of a cooper; workshop of a cooper.
**Co-operate,** kō-op'ėr-āt, *vi*. To act with another; to concur in producing the same effect.
**Co-operation,** kō-op'ėr-ā''shon, *n*. Act of co-operating; concurrent effort or labor.
**Co-operative,** kō-op'ėr-āt-iv, *a*. Operating jointly to the same end.
**Co-operator,** kō-op'ėr-āt-ėr, *n*. One who co-operates.
**Co-ordinate,** kō-or'din-āt, *a*. Holding the same rank or degree.—*vt*. To arrange in due order.
**Co-ordination,** kō-or'din-ā''shon, *n*. State of being co-ordinate; act of co-ordinating.
**Coot,** köt, *n*. A black wading bird.
**Copal,** kō-pal', *n*. The juice of certain trees, used as a varnish.
**Coparcener,** kō-pär'sen-ėr, *n*. One who has an equal portion of an inheritance.
**Copartner,** kō-pärt'nėr, *n*. An associate.
**Cope,** kōp, *n*. A sacerdotal cloak; the arch of the sky; the roof of a house; the arch over a door, etc.—*vt*. (coping, coped). To cover, as with a cope; to strive, or contend; to oppose with success (with *with*).
**Copernican,** kō-pėr'ni-kan, *a*. Pertaining to Copernicus, or to his astronomical system.
**Copestone,** kōp'stōn, *n*. Head or top stone; hence, what finishes off.
**Copier, Copyist,** ko'pi-ėr, ko'pi-ist, *n*. One who copies; a transcriber; an imitator.
**Coping,** kōp'ing, *n*. The covering course of a wall, parapet, etc.
**Copious,** kō'pi-us, *a*. Abundant; exuberant; diffuse.
**Copiously,** kō'pi-us-li, *adv*. Abundantly.
**Copper,** kop'ėr, *n*. A reddish colored ductile and malleable metal; a large boiler; a copper coin.—*a*. Consisting of or resembling copper.—*vt*. To cover with sheets of copper.
**Copperas,** kop'ėr-as, *n*. Green vitriol or sulphate or iron.
**Copperplate,** kop'ėr-plāt, *n*. A plate of polished copper, on which designs are engraved; a print from a copperplate.
**Coppersmith,** kop'ėr-smith, *n*. One who works in copper.
**Coppery,** kop-ėr-i, *a*. Mixed with or made of copper; like copper in taste, smell, etc.
**Coppice, Copse,** kop'is, kops, *n*. A wood of small growth; a thicket.
**Coprolite,** kop'ro-lit, *n*. The petrified dung of extinct animals.
**Coptic,** kop'tik, *a*. Pertaining to the descendants of the ancient Egyptians, called *Copts*.—*n*. The language of the Copts.
**Copula,** kop'ū-la, *n*. The word which unites the subject and predicate of a proposition, part of *to be*; a bond; a link.
**Copulate,** kop'ū-lāt, *vi*. (copulating, copulated). To come together, as different sexes.
**Copulation,** kop-ū-lā'shon, *n*. Coition.
**Copulative,** kop'ū-lāt-iv, *a*. That unites.—*n*. A conjunction.
**Copy,** ko'pi, *n*. An imitation; a transcript; a pattern; a single example of a book, etc.; matter to be set up in type.—*vt*. (copying copied). To imitate; to transcribe.
**Copyist,** ko'pi-ist, *n*. A transcriber; imitator.
**Copyright,** kop'i-rīt, *n*. The exclusive right to print or produce, given for a limited number of years to an author, artist, etc., or his assignee.—*a*. Relating to, or protected by copyright.—*vt*. To secure by copyright.
**Coquet,** kō-ket', *vi*. (coquetting, coquetted). To trifle in love; to endeavor to excite admiration from vanity.
**Coquetry,** kō'ket-ri, *n*. The arts of a coquette; trifling in love.
**Coquette,** kō-ket', *n*. A vain, trifling woman; a flirt.
**Coquettish,** kō-ket'ish, *a*. Practicing coquetry.
**Coracle,** kor'a-kl, *n*. A boat made of wickerwork covered with leather or oil-cloth.
**Coral,** ko'ral, *n*. A hard calcareous substance found in the ocean; a piece of coral.—*a*. Made of coral; resembling coral.

**Coralliferous,** ko-ral-if'ėr-us, *a.* Producing or containing coral.
**Coralline,** ko'ral-īn, *a.* Consisting of, like, or containing coral.—*n.* A sea-weed; an orange-red color; a coral zoophyte.
**Coralloid,** ko'ral-oid, *a.* Having the form of coral; branching like coral.
**Corbel,** kor'bel, *n.* A piece projecting from a wall as a support.—*vt.* (corbelling, corbelled). To support on corbels; to provide with corbels.
**Cord,** kord, *n.* A small rope; a band; a sinew; a pile of wood, 8 feet long, 4 high, and 4 broad.—*vi.* To bind with a cord.
**Cordage,** kord'āj, *n.* Cords collectively; the ropes used in the rigging of a ship.
**Cordate,** kor'dāt, *a.* Heart-shaped.
**Cordelier,** kord'el-ēr, *n.* A Franciscan friar.
**Cordial,** kor'di-al, *a.* Hearty; heartfelt; invigorating.—*n.* A medicine or beverage which increases strength; anything that gladdens or exhilarates.
**Cordiality,** kor-di-al'i-ti, *n.* Heartiness; sincerity.
**Cordially,** kor'di-al-li, *adv.* Heartily.
**Cordite,** kor'dīt, *n.* A smokeless explosive introduced in 1889.
**Cordon,** kor'don, *n.* A line of military posts; a ribbon worn across the breast by knights.
**Cordovan,** kor'dō-van, *n.* Spanish leather.
**Corduroy,** kor-dė-roi', *n.* A thick cotton stuff corded or ribbed.
**Core,** kōr, *n.* The heart or inner part; the central part of fruit.
**Co-respondent,** kō-rē-spond'ent, *n.* A joint respondent; a man charged with adultery in a divorce case.
**Corf,** korf, *n.*; pl. **Corves.** A basket used in mines.
**Corgi,** kor'ji, *n.* A small Welsh breed of dog.
**Coriander,** ko-ri-an'dėr, *n.* A plant which produces aromatic seeds.
**Corinthian,** ko-rin'thi-an, *a.* Pertaining to Corinth; denoting an order in architecture, distinguished by fluted columns and ornamental capitals.—*n.* A gay fellow.
**Cork,** kork, *n.* The bark of a species of oak; the tree itself; a stopple made of cork.—*vt.* To stop with a cork.
**Corked,** korkt, *a.* Stopped with a cork; tasting of cork; blackened with burnt cork.
**Corky,** kork'i, *a.* Consisting of or like cork.
**Cormorant,** kor'mō-rant, *n.* A large voracious sea-bird; a glutton.
**Corn,** korn, *n.* Grain; the seeds of plants which grow in ears, and are made into bread; a horny excresence on a toe or foot.—*vt.* To preserve with salt in grains; to granulate.
**Corn-crake,** korn'krāk, *n.* The landrail.
**Cornea,** kor'nē-a, *n.* The horny transparent membrane in the fore part of the eye.
**Corned,** korned, *a.* Cured by salting.
**Cornelian,** kor-nē'li-an. Same as *Carnelian.*
**Corneous,** kor'nē-us, *a.* Horny; hard.
**Corner,** kor'nėr, *n.* A projecting extremity; angle; a secret or retired place; a nook.—*vt.* To buy up the whole stock of a commodity.
**Corner-stone,** kor'nėr-stōn, *n.* The stone which lies at the corner of two walls, and unites them; the principal stone.
**Cornet,** kor'net, *n.* A sort of trumpet; formerly a cavalry officer, of the lowest commissioned rank, who bore the standard.
**Cornice,** kor'nis, *n.* A molded projection crowning a part; uppermost molding of a pediment, room, etc.
**Cornish,** korn'ish, *a.* Pertaining to Cornwall.—*n.* The language of Cornwall.
**Cornucopia,** kor-nū-kō'pi-a, *n.* The representation of a horn filled with fruit, flowers, and grain, a symbol of plenty and peace.
**Cornuted,** kor-nūt'ed, *a.* Horned.
**Corny,** kor'ni, *a.* Producing corn; containing corn; tasting of corn or malt.
**Corolla,** ko-rol'la, *n.* The inner covering of a flower.
**Corollary,** ko'rol-la-ri, ko-rol'a-ri, *n.* Something added to a proposition demonstrated; an inference, deduction.
**Coronal,** ko'rō-nal, *a.* Belonging to the crown of the head.—*n.* A crown, garland.
**Coronation,** ko-rō-nā'shon, *n.* Act or solemnity of crowning a sovereign.
**Coroner,** ko'rō-nēr, *n.* An officer who holds a court of inquiry in a case of sudden death.
**Coronet,** ko'rō-net, *n.* A small crown worn by peers and peeresses; an ornamental headdress; something that surmounts.
**Corporal,** kor'po-ral, *n.* A non-commissioned officer ranking below a sergeant.—*a.* Belonging or relating to the body; material.
**Corporally,** kor'po-ral-li, *adv.* Bodily.
**Corporate,** kor'po-rāt, *a.* Formed into a legal body, and empowered to act in legal processes as an individual.
**Corporately,** kor'po-rāt-li, *adv.* In a corporate capacity.
**Corporation,** kor-po-rā'shon, *n.* A body corporate, empowered to act as an individual; the human body or frame.
**Corporeal,** kor-pō'rē-al, *a.* Having a body; material; opposed to spiritual.
**Corporeally,** kor-pō'rē-al-li, *adv.* In a bodily form or manner.
**Corps,** kōr, *n.*; pl. **Corps,** kōrz. A body of troops. *Army Corps.* Two or more divisions.
**Corpse,** korps, *n.* The dead body of a human being; a carcass; remains.
**Corpulence, Corpulency,** kor'pū-lens, kor'-pū-len-si, *n.* The state of being corpulent; excessive fatness.
**Corpulent,** kor'pū-lent, *a.* Having a gross or fleshy body; very fat; stout; lusty.
**Corpuscle,** kor'pus-l, *n.* A minute particle or physical atom; a minute animal cell.
**Corpuscular,** kor-pus'kū-lėr, *a.* Pertaining to corpuscles.
**Corral,** kor-räl', *n.* A pen for cattle; an inclosure formed by wagons; a stockade for capturing elephants.
**Correct,** ko-rekt', *a.* Right; accurate; exact.—*vt.* To make right; to chastise; to counteract.
**Correction,** ko-rek'shon, *n.* Act of correcting; state of being corrected; discipline; chastisement; counteraction.
**Correctional,** ko-rek'shon-al, *a.* Tending or pertaining to correction.
**Corrective,** ko-rekt'iv, *a.* Having the power to correct; tending to rectify.—*n.* That which corrects; restriction.
**Correctly,** ko-rekt'li, *adv.* Exactly; accurately.
**Correctness,** ko-rekt'nes, *n.* Freedom from faults or errors; accuracy; exactness.
**Corrector,** ko-rekt'ėr, *n.* One who or that which corrects.
**Correlate,** kor'ē-lāt, *n.* A correlative.—*vi.* (correlating, correlated). To be reciprocally related.—*vt.* To place in reciprocal relation; to determine the relations between.
**Correlation,** ko-rē-lā'shon, *n.* Reciprocal relation.
**Correlative,** ko-rel'at-iv, *a.* Having a mutual relation, as father and son.—*n.* One who or that which stands in reciprocal relation.
**Correspond,** ko-rē-spond', *vi.* To answer one to another; to be congruous; to fit; to hold intercourse by letters.
**Correspondence,** ko-rē-spond'ens, *n.* Act or state of corresponding; fitness; congruity; intercourse by letters; the letters interchanged.
**Correspondent,** ko-rē-spond'ent, *a.* Corresponding; suitable; congruous.—*n.* One who has intercourse by letters.
**Corresponding,** ko-rē-spond'ing, *a.* Answering; agreeing; suiting.
**Correspondingly,** ko-rē-spond'ing-li, *adv.* In a corresponding manner.
**Corridor,** ko'ri-dōr, *n.* A passage in a building, or round a court.

C

**Corrigenda,** ko-ri-jen'da, *n.pl.* Things to be corrected.
**Corrigible,** ko'ri-ji-bl, *a.* That may be corrected or reformed; punishable.
**Corrival,** ko-rī'val, *n.* A competitor.
**Corroborant,** ko-rob'ō-rant, *a.* Strengthening.
**Corroborate,** ko-rob'ō-rāt, *vt.* (corroborating, corroborated). To strengthen; to confirm.
**Corroboration,** ko-rob'ō-rā''shon, *n.* Act of corroborating; confirmation.
**Corroborative,** ko-rob'ō-rāt-iv, *a.* Tending to strengthen or confirm.
**Corrode,** ko-rōd', *vt.* (corroding, corroded). To eat or wear away by degrees; to prey upon; to poison, blight, canker.
**Corrodent,** ko-rō'dent, *a.* Having the power of corroding.—*n.* A substance that corrodes.
**Corrodible,** ko-rōd'i-bl, *a.* That may be corroded.
**Corrosion,** ko-rō'zhon, *n.* Action of corroding; state of being corroded.
**Corrosive,** ko-rōs'iv, *a.* Having the power of corroding; vexing; blighting.—*n.* That which has the quality of corroding.
**Corrugate,** ko'rū-gāt, *vt.* To wrinkle; to contract into folds or furrows.
**Corrugated,** ko'rū-gāt-ed, *a.* Wrinkled; having prominent ridges and grooves.
**Corrugation,** ko-rū-gā'shon, *n.* A wrinkling; contraction into wrinkles.
**Corrupt,** ko-rupt', *vt.* To make putrid; to deprave; to taint; to bribe; to infect with errors.—*vi.* To become putrid or vitiated.—*a.* Tainted; depraved; infected with errors.
**Corrupter,** ko-rupt'ėr, *n.* One who or that which corrupts.
**Corruptibility,** ko-rupt'i-bil''i-ti, *n.* The possibility of being corrupted.
**Corruptible,** ko-rupt'i-bl, *a.* That may be corrupted; subject to decay, destruction, etc.
**Corruptibly,** ko-rupt'i-bli, *adv.* In such a manner as to be corrupted.
**Corruption,** ko-rup'shon, *n.* Act or process of corrupting; depravity; pollution; taint of blood; bribe-taking; bribery.
**Corruptive,** ko-rupt'iv, *a.* Having the quality of corrupting or vitiating.
**Corruptly,** ko-rupt'li, *adv.* In a corrupt manner; with corruption; viciously.
**Corsair,** kor'sār, *n.* A pirate; a piratical vessel.
**Corse,** kors, *n.* A corpse (a poetical word).
**Corselet, Corslet,** kors'let, *n.* A cuirass to cover the body.
**Corset,** kor'set, *n.* An article of dress laced closely round the body; stays.
**Cortège,** kor'tāzh, *n.* A train of attendants.
**Cortes,** kor'tes, *n.pl.* The legislative assembly of Spain and of Portugal.
**Cortex,** kor'teks, *n.* The bark of a tree; a membrane enveloping part of the body.
**Cortical,** kor'tik-al, *a.* Belonging to, consisting of, or resembling bark; belonging to the external covering.
**Coruscant,** ko-rus'kant, *a.* Flashing.
**Coruscate,** ko-rus'kāt, *vi.* (coruscating, coruscated). To flash intermittently; to glitter.
**Coruscation,** ko-rus-kā'shon, *n.* A glittering or flashing; a quick vibration of light; intellectual brilliancy.
**Corvette,** kor-vet', *n.* A sloop of war with only one tier of guns; a small vessel used for escort duty.
**Corvine,** kor'vīn, *a.* Pertaining to the crow.
**Corymb,** kō'rimb, *n.* A form of inflorescence in which the blossoms form a mass with a convex or level top.
**Coryphaeus,** ko-ri-fē'us, *n.*; p. **-aei**. The leader of the chorus; the chief of a company.
**Cosh,** kosh, *n.* A bludgeon; a flexible tube filled with some heavy substance for use as a weapon.
**Cosmetic,** koz-met'ik, *a.* Improving beauty.—*n.* An application to improve the complexion.
**Cosmic, Cosmical,** koz'mik, koz'mik-al, *a.* Relating to the whole frame of the universe.
**Cosmic rays,** koz-mik rāz', *n.pl.* Penetrating radiation of shorter wavelength than X-rays, believed to reach the earth from outer space.
**Cosmogony,** koz-mog'on-i, *n.* The origin, or doctrine of the origin, of the universe.
**Cosmographer,** koz-mog'ra-fėr, *n.* One versed in cosmography.
**Cosmography,** koz-mog'ra-fi, *n.* A description of the world; the science of the construction of the universe.
**Cosmology,** koz-mol'o-ji, *n.* The science of the world or universe; cosmogony.
**Cosmopolitan, Cosmopolite,** koz-mō-pol'i-tan, koz-mop'o-līt, *n.* One who is at home in every place.—*a.* Free from local prejudices; common to all the world.
**Cosmopolitanism, Cosmopolitism,** koz-mō-pol'i-tan-izm, koz-mop'o-līt-izm, *n.* The state of being a cosmopolitan; disregard of local prejudices, etc.
**Cosmos,** koz'mos, *n.* The universe; the system of order and harmony in creation.
**Cost,** kost, *vt.* (costing, cost). To be bought for; to require to be laid out or borne.—*n.* That which is paid for anything; expenditure; loss; (*pl.*) expenses of a lawsuit.
**Costal,** kos'tal, *a.* Pertaining to the ribs.
**Costard,** kos'tärd, *n.* A large apple.
**Coster, Costermonger,** kos-tėr, kos'tėr-mung-gėr, *n.* A hawker of fruit or vegetables.
**Costive,** kos'tiv, *a.* Having the bowels bound; constipated.
**Costliness,** kost'li-nes, *n.* State of being costly; expensiveness; sumptuousness.
**Costly,** kost'li, *a.* Of a high price; valuable, precious; dear; sumptuous.
**Costmary,** kost'ma-ri, *n.* A perennial fragrant plant, a native of S. Europe.
**Costume,** kos'tūm, *n.* An established mode of dress; garb; attire.
**Costumier,** kos-tū'mi-ėr, *n.* One who prepares costumes; one who deals in costumes.
**Co-surety,** kō-shūr'ti, *n.* A joint surety; one who is surety with another.
**Cosy,** kō'zi, *a.* Snug; comfortable.—*n.* Padded covering put over a teapot to keep in the heat after the tea has been infused.
**Cot,** kot, *n.* A small house; a hut; a small bed.
**Cote,** kōt, *n.* A shelter for animals (as a dove-*cote*); a sheepfold; a cottage or hut.
**Coterie,** kō'te-rē, *n.* A circle of familiar friends who meet for social or literary intercourse; an exclusive society; a clique.
**Cothurnus,** kō-thėr'nus, *n.* A buskin; a highlaced shoe, such as was worn by tragic actors; tragedy.
**Cotidal,** kō-tīd'al, *a.* Marking an equality of tide.
**Cotillion,** ko-til'yon, *n.* A brisk dance; a kind of quadrille.
**Cottage,** kot'tāj, *n.* A cot; a small country or suburban house.
**Cottager,** kot-tāj-ėr, *n.* One who lives in a cottage.
**Cottar, Cotter,** kot'ėr, *n.* A cottager; a farm-servant.
**Cotton,** kot'tn, *n.* A soft, downy substance in the pods of several plants; cloth made of cotton.—*a.* Pertaining to, or consisting of, cotton.—*vi.* To agree; to become friendly.
**Cotton-wood,** kot'tn-wụd, *n.* A large tree of the poplar kind.
**Cotton-wool,** kot'tn-wụl, *n.* Cotton in the raw state.
**Cottony,** kot'tn-i, *a.* Soft like cotton; downy.
**Cotyledon,** kot-i-lē'don, *n.* The seed-leaf, or first leaf or leaves, of the embryo plant.
**Couch,** kouch, *vi.* To lie down; to bend down; to lie close and concealed.—*vt.* To lay down; to place upon a bed; to comprise; to express; to fix a spear in rest; to depress a cataract in the eye.—*n.* A bed; a place for rest and ease.
**Couchant,** kouch'ant, *a.* Lying down.
**Cougar,** kö'gär, *n.* A large carnivorous quadruped of the cat kind; the puma.

**Cough,** kof, *n.* A violent convulsive effort of the lungs to throw off offending matter.—*vi.* To make a violent effort, with noise, to expel the airs from the lungs, and throw off any offensive matter.—*vt.* To expel from the lungs by a violent effort with noise; to expectorate.
**Could,** kud, *pret.* of *can.* Was able.
**Coulter,** kōl'tėr, *n.* The blade of a plow that cuts the earth in advance of the share.
**Council,** koun'sil, *n.* An assembly for consultation; a body of men designated to advise a sovereign or chief magistrate; a convocation.
**Counsel,** koun'sel, *n.* Deliberation; consultation; advice; design; a barrister.—*vt.* (counselling, counselled). To advise; to warn.
**Counsellable,** koun'sel-a-bl, *a.* That may be counselled; willing to receive counsel.
**Counsellor,** koun'sel-ėr, *n.* A person who gives counsel; an adviser; a barrister.
**Count,** kount, *vt.* To enumerate; to compute; to consider; to judge.—*vi.* To reckon; to rely; to be reckoned.—*n.* Reckoning; a particular charge in an indictment; a continental title of nobility, equivalent to the English earl.
**Countable,** kount'a-bl, *a.* That may be numbered.
**Countenance,** koun'ten-ans, *n.* The human face; air; aspect; favor; encouragement.—*vt.* To favor; to encourage; to vindicate.
**Counter,** kount'ėr, *n.* One who or that which counts; anything used to reckon, as in games; a shop table.—*adv.* Contrary; in an opposite direction.—*a.* Adverse; opposing.
**Counteract,** koun-tėr-akt', *vt.* To act in opposition to; to render ineffectual.
**Counteraction,** koun'tėr-ak-shon, *n.* Action in opposition; hindrance.
**Counteractive,** koun'tėr-akt-iv, *a.* Tending to counteract.—*n.* That which counteracts.
**Counterbalance,** koun-tėr-bal'ans, *vt.* To weigh against with an equal weight; to act against with equal power.—*n.* Equal weight, power, or agency, acting in opposition.
**Countercharm,** koun'tėr-chärm, *n.* That which can oppose the effect of a charm.
**Countercheck,** koun-tėr-chek', *vt.* To oppose by some obstacle; to check.—*n.* Check; check that controls another check.
**Counterfeit,** koun'tėr-fit, *vt.* and *i.* To forge; to copy; to feign.—*a.* Made in imitation; fraudulent.—*n.* An imposter; a forgery.
**Counterfeiter,** koun'tėr-fit-ėr, *n.* A forger.
**Counterfoil,** koun'tėr—foil, *n.* A portion of a document retained as a check.
**Counter-irritant,** koun'tėr-i-rit-ant, *n.* An irritant employed to relieve another irritation or inflammation.
**Countermand,** koun'tėr-mand', *vt.* To annul or revoke a former command.—*n.* A contrary order; revocation of a former order.
**Countermarch,** koun'tėr-märch, *vi.* To march back.—*n.* A marching back; a returning; a change of measures.
**Countermark,** koun'tėr-märk, *n.* An additional mark made for greater security.—*vt.* To add a countermark to.
**Countermine,** koun'tėr-mīn, *n.* A mine formed to defeat the purpose of one made by an enemy; a counterplot,—*vt.* To defeat by a countermine; to frustrate by secret and opposite measures.
**Countermotion,** koun'tėr-mō-shon, *n.* An opposite motion.
**Counterpane,** koun'tėr-pān, *n.* A bed-cover.
**Counterpart,** koun'tėr-pärt, *n.* A corresponding part; a duplicate; a supplement.
**Counterplot,** koun'tėr-plot', *vi.* To oppose one plot by another.—*vt.* To plot against in order to defeat another plot; to baffle by an opposite plot.—*n.* A plot to frustrate another.
**Counterpoint,** koun'tėr-point, *n.* The art, in music, of adding to a given melody one or more melodies.
**Counterpoise,** koun'tėr-poiz, *vt.* To counterbalance.—*n.* A weight which balances another; equivalence of power or force; equilibrium.
**Counterscarp,** koun'tėr-skärp, *n.* The exterior slope of the ditch of a fortification.
**Counterseal,** koun-tėr-sēl', *vt.* To affix a seal beside another seal.
**Countersign,** koun-tėr-sīn', *vt.* To sign with an additional signature.—*n.* A military watchword.
**Counter-signature,** koun'tėr-sig-na-tūr, *n.* The name of a secretary countersigned to a writing.
**Counter-tenor,** koun'tėr-ten-ėr, *n.* In *music,* same as *Alto* or *Contralto.*
**Countervail,** koun-tėr-vāl', *vt.* To act against with equal power or effect.
**Counterwork,** koun-tėr-wėrk', *vt.* To work in opposition to; to counteract.
**Countess,** kount'es, *n.* The wife or widow of an earl or count.
**Countless,** kount'les, *a.* Innumerable.
**Country,** kun'tri, *n.* A large tract of land; a region; a kingdom or state; the inhabitants of a region; the public; rural parts.—*a.* Pertaining to the country; rural.
**Country-dance,** kun'tri-dans, *n.* A dance in which the partners are arranged opposite to each other in lines.
**Countryman,** kun'tri-man, *n.* One born in the same country with another; one who dwells in the country; a rustic.
**Country-side,** kun'tri-sīd, *n.* A tract of country, or the people inhabiting such.
**County,** koun'ti, *n.* A particular portion of a state or kingdom; a shire.—*a.* Pertaining to a county.
**Coupé,** kö-pā, *n.* A railway compartment seated on one side only; a closed motor car, usually a two-seater.
**Couple,** ku'pl, *n.* A band or leash; a pair; a brace; a man and his wife.—*vt.* and *i.* (coupling, coupled). To join together; to unite.
**Couplet,** kup'let, *n.* Two lines that rhyme.
**Coupling,** kup'ling, *n.* The act of one who couples; that which couples; a hook, chain, or other contrivance forming a connection.
**Coupon,** kö'pon, *n.* An interest certificate attached to a bond; one of a series of tickets which guarantee the holder to obtain a certain value or service for each at different periods.
**Courage,** ku'rij, *n.* Intrepidity; dauntlessness; hardihood.
**Courageous,** ku-rā'jē-us, *a.* Bold; brave; heroic, fearless.
**Courageously,** ku-rā'jē-us-li, *adv.* With courage; bravely; boldly; stoutly.
**Courier,** kö'rē-ėr, *n.* A messenger sent express with dispatches; a travelling attendant.
**Course,** kōrs, *n.* A running; passage; route; career; ground run over; line of conduct; order of succession; series of lectures, etc.; range of subjects taught; a layer of stones in masonry; part of a meal served at one time.—*vt.* (coursing, coursed). To hunt; to run through or over.—*vi.* To move with speed.
**Courser,** kōrs'ėr, *n.* A swift horse.
**Coursing,** kōrs'ing, *n.* The act or sport of chasing and hunting hares with greyhounds.
**Court,** kōrt, *n.* An inclosed area; residence of a sovereign; the family and retinue of a sovereign; judges assembled for deciding causes; the place where judges assemble; a judicial body; attention directed to gain favor; flattery.—*vt.* To endeavor to please by civilities; to woo; to seek.
**Court-day,** kōrt'dā, *n.* A day in which a court sits to administer justice.
**Courteous,** kōrt'ē-us, *a.* Polite; complaisant; affable; respectful.
**Courteously,** kōrt'ē-us-li, *adv.* In a courteous manner.
**Courter,** kōrt'ėr, *n.* One who courts; a wooer.
**Courtesan, Courtezan,** kōr'te-zan, *n.* A loose woman, a prostitute.
**Courtesy,** kōrt'e-si, *n.* Urbanity; complaisance; act of kindness or civility.

**Courthand,** kōrt'hand, *n*. The old manner of writing used in records, etc.
**Courthouse,** kōrt'hous, *n*. A house in which established courts are held.
**Courtier,** kōrt'i-ėr, *n*. A man who attends courts; a person of courtly manners; one who solicits favors.
**Courtliness,** kōrt'li-nes, *n*. Quality of being courtly; complaisance with dignity.
**Courtly,** kōrt'li, *a*. Relating to a court; elegant; polite with dignity; flattering.
**Court-martial,** kōrt'mär'shal, *n*.; pl. **Courts-martial.** A court consisting of military or naval officers for the trial of offenses of a military or naval character.
**Court-plaster,** kōrt'plas-tėr, *n*. Sticking plaster made of black silk.
**Courtship,** kōrt'ship, *n*. Act of courting a woman in view of marriage; wooing.
**Courtyard,** kōrt'yärd, *n*. A court or inclosure round or near a house.
**Cousin,** kuz'n, *n*. The son or daughter of an uncle or aunt; a kinsman.
**Cove,** kōv, *n*. A small inlet or bay; a sheltered recess in the sea-shore; a concave molding; a man, fellow.—*vt*. To arch over.
**Covenant,** kuv'en-ant, *n*. A contract; compact; a writing containing the terms of an agreement.—*vi*. To enter into a formal agreement; to stipulate.—*vt*. To grant by covenant.
**Covenanter,** kuv'en-ant-ėr, *n*. One who makes a covenant; a subscriber to the Solemn League and Covenant in Scotland in 1643.
**Cover,** kuv'ėr, *vt*. To overspread; to cloak; to secrete; to defend; to wrap up; to brood on; to be sufficient for; to include.—*n*. Anything spread over another thing; disguise; shelter; articles laid at table for one person.
**Covering,** kuv'ėr-ing, *n*. Envelope; cover.
**Coverlet,** kuv'ėr-let, *n*. The cover of a bed.
**Covert,** kuv'ėrt, *a*. Kept secret; private; insidious.—*n*. A shelter; a thicket.
**Covertly,** kuv'ėrt-li, *adv*. Secretly; insidiously.
**Coverture,** kuv'ėrt-ūr, *n*. Shelter; defense; the legal state of a married woman.
**Covet,** kuv'et, *vt*. To long for (in a good sense); to desire unlawfully; to hanker after.—*vi*. To have inordinate desire.
**Covetable,** kuv'et-a-bl, *a*. That may be coveted.
**Covetous,** kuv'et-us, *a*. Eager to obtain; inordinately desirous; avaricious.
**Covetously,** kuv'et-us-li, *adv*. In a covetous manner.
**Covetousness,** kuv'et-us-nes, *n*. Cupidity.
**Covey,** kuv'i, *n*. A hatch of birds; a small flock of birds (especially partridges) together; a company.
**Cow,** kou, *n*. The female of the bull, or of bovine animals generally.—*vt*. To sink the spirits or courage of; to dishearten.
**Coward,** kou'ėrd, *n*. A person who wants courage to meet danger; a craven; a dastard.—*a*. Destitute of courage; dastardly.
**Cowardice,** kou'ėrd-is, *n*. Want of courage to face danger.
**Cowardliness,** kou'ėrd-li-nes, *n*. Cowardice.
**Cowardly,** kou'ėrd-li, *a*. Wanting courage to face danger; faint-hearted; mean; base.—*adv*. In the manner of a coward.
**Cow-bane,** kou'bān, *n*. Water-hemlock.
**Cow-catcher,** kou'kach-ėr, *n*. A frame in front of locomotives to remove obstructions.
**Cower,** kou'ėr, *vi*. To crouch; to sink by bending the knees; to shrink through fear.
**Cowherd,** kou'hėrd, *n*. One who tends cows.
**Cowhide,** kou'hīd. *n*. The hide of a cow; a leather whip.—*vt*. To flog with a leather whip.
**Cowl,** koul, *n*. A monk's hood; a chimney cover which turns with the wind; a vessel carried on a pole by two persons.
**Cowled,** kould, *a*. Hooded; in shape of a cowl.
**Cow-pox,** kou'poks, *n*. The vaccine disease, which appears on the teats of the cow.
**Cowry,** kou'ri, *n*. A small shell used for coin in parts of Africa and S. Asia.
**Cowslip,** kou'slip, *n*. A species of primrose.
**Coxcomb,** koks'kōm, *n*. The comb worn by fools in their caps; the cap itself; a fop; a vain, showy fellow.
**Coxcombry,** koks'kōm-ri, *n*. Foppishness.
**Coxswain,** kok'sn, *n*. The man who steers a boat, or who has the care of a boat and its crew.
**Coy,** koi, *a*. Shy; reserved; bashful.
**Coyly,** koi'li, *adv*. With reserve; shyly.
**Coyness,** koi'nes, *n*. Shyness; bashfulness.
**Coz,** koz, *n*. A familiar contraction of *cousin*.
**Cozen,** kuz'n, *vt*. To cheat, to defraud; to beguile.—*vi*. To act deceitfully.
**Cozenage,** kuz'n-āj, *n*. Trickery; fraud.
**Cozener,** kuz'n-ėr, *n*. One who cheats.
**Crab,** krab, *n*. A crustaceous fish with strong claws; a portable windlass, etc.; Cancer, a sign of the zodiac; a wild sour apple; a morose person.
**Crabbed,** krab'ed, *a*. Perverse; peevish; perplexing.
**Crabbedly,** krab'ed-li, *adv*. Peevishly.
**Crack,** krak, *n*. A chink or fissure; a sudden or sharp sound; a sounding blow; a chat.—*vt*. and *i*. To break with a sharp, abrupt sound; to break partially; to snap; to boast of; to utter with smartness; to chat.
**Crack-brained,** krak'brānd, *a*. Crazy.
**Cracked,** krakt, *a*. Having fissures but not in pieces; impaired; crazy.
**Cracker,** krak'ėr, *n*. One who or that which cracks; a small firework; a hard biscuit.
**Crackle,** krak'l, *vi*. (crackling, crackled). To make small abrupt noises rapidly repeated.
**Crackling,** krak'ling, *n*. The act or noise of the verb to crackle; the brown skin of roasted pork.
**Cracknel,** krak'nel, *n*. A hard brittle cake or biscuit.
**Cradle,** krā'dl, *n*. A small bed in which infants are rocked; a frame to support or hold together.—*vt*. (cradling, cradled). To lay or rock in a cradle.
**Craft,** kraft, *n*. Ability; skill; artifice; guile; manual art; trade; a vessel or ship.
**Craftily,** kraf'ti-li, *adv*. Artfully; cunningly.
**Craftiness,** kraf'ti-nes, *n*. Artfulness.
**Craftsman,** krafts'man, *n*. An artificer.
**Crafty,** kraf'ti, *a*. Skillful; artful.
**Crag,** krag, *n*. A steep rugged rock; a cliff; gravel or sand mixed with shells.
**Cragged,** krag'ed, *a*. Full of crags; rugged.
**Craggy,** krag'i, *a*. Cragged.
**Crake,** krāk. *n*. The corn-crake or landrail.
**Cram,** kram, *vt*. (cramming, crammed). To thrust in by force; to stuff; to coach for an examination.—*vi*. To stuff; to eat beyond satiety; to prepare for an examination.
**Crambo,** kram'bō, *n*. A game of rhymes.
**Cramp,** kramp, *n*. A spasmodic contraction of a limb or muscle; restraint; piece of iron bent at the ends, to hold together pieces of timber, stones, etc.—*vt*. To affect with spasms; to restrain, hinder.
**Cramped,** krampt, *a*. Affected with spasm; restrained.
**Cranberry,** kran'be-ri, *n*. A wild sour berry.
**Crane,** krān, *n*. A migratory bird with long legs and neck; a machine for raising great weights; a crooked pipe for drawing liquor out of a cask.—*vi*. To stretch out one's neck.
**Crane's-bill,** krānz'bil, *n*. The geranium.
**Cranial,** krā'ni-al, *a*. Relating to the skull.
**Craniology,** krā-ni-ol'o-ji, *n*. The knowledge of the cranium or skull.
**Cranium,** krā'ni-um, *n*. The skull; the bones which inclose the brain.
**Crank,** krangk, *n*. A contrivance for producing a horizontal or perpendicular motion by means of a rotary motion, or the contrary; a bend or turn.—*a*. Liable to be overset; loose.
**Cranky,** krangk'i, *a*. Liable to overset; full of

whoms; crazy.
**Crannied,** kran'id, *a.* Having crannies.
**Cranny,** kran'ni, *n.* A narrow opening; chink.
**Crape,** krāp, *n.* A thin, transparent stuff of a crisp texture, much used in mourning.
**Crapulence,** krap'ū-lens, *n.* Drunkenness; sickness occasioned by intemperance.
**Crash,** krash, *vi.* To make the loud, clattering sound of many things falling and breaking at once.—*n.* The sound of things falling and breaking; a commercial collapse.
**Crasis,** krā'sis, *n.* The mixture of bodily constituents; temperament; constitution; the contraction of vowels into one long vowel.
**Crass,** kras, *a.* Gross; coarse; dense.
**Crate,** krāt, *n.* A basket of wicker-work, for crockery, etc.
**Crater,** krā'tėr, *n.* A bowl; the circular cavity or mouth of a volcano; hole in the ground caused by the explosion of a shell, bomb, or mine.
**Cravat,** kra-vat', *n.* A neck-cloth.
**Crave,** krāv, *vt.* (craving, craved). To ask earnestly or submissively; to desire strongly.—*n.* Strong desire.
**Craven,** krā'vn, *n.* A coward; a weak-hearted, spiritless fellow.—*a.* Cowardly.
**Craver,** krāv'ėr, *n.* One who craves or begs.
**Craving,** krāv'ing, *n.* Vehement desire; morbid demand of appetite.
**Craw,** kra, *n.* The crop or first stomach of fowls.
**Crawfish,** kra'fish, *n.* *See* CRAYFISH.
**Crawl,** kral, *vi.* To creep; to advance slowly, slyly, or weakly.
**Crawler,** kral'ėr, *n.* One who or that which crawls; a creeper; a reptile.
**Crayfish, Crawfish,** krā'fish, kra'fish, *n.* A crustacean found in streams; also the spiny lobster, a sea crustacean.
**Crayon,** krā'on, *n.* A pencil of colored clay, chalk, or charcoal, used in drawing; a drawing made with crayons.—*vt.* To sketch.
**Craze,** krāz, *vt.* (crazing, crazed). To shatter; to impair the intellect of.—*vi.* To become crazy.—*n.* An inordinate desire.
**Crazed,** krāzd, *a.* Decrepit; crazy.
**Crazy,** krāz'i, *a.* Decrepit; deranged; weakened or disordered in intellect.
**Creak,** krēk, *vi.* To make a grating sound.—*n.* A sharp, harsh, grating sound.
**Cream,** krēm, *n.* That part of a liquor which collects on the surface; the richer part of milk; best part of a thing.—*vt.* To take off cream from—*vi.* To gather cream; to mantle.
**Creamery,** krē'mėr-i, *n.* A place where milk is made into butter and cheese.
**Creamy,** krēm'i, *a.* Full of cream; like cream; luscious.
**Crease,** krēs, *n.* A mark made by folding; a hollow streak like a groove; lines near the wickets in cricket.—*vt.* (creasing, creased). To make a mark in by compressing or folding.
**Create,** krē-āt', *vt.* (creating, created). To bring into being from nothing; to cause to be; to shape; to beget; to bring about; to invest with a new character; to constitute or appoint.
**Creation,** krē-ā'shon, *n.* Act of creating; the aggregate of created things; the universe; conferring of a title or dignity.
**Creative,** krē-āt'iv, *a.* Having the power to create, or exerting the act of creation.
**Creator,** krē-āt'ėr, *n.* The being that creates; a producer; the Supreme Being.
**Creature,** krē'tūr, *n.* Something created; a human being; something imagined; a person who owes his rise to another; a mere tool.
**Crèche,** krāsh, *n.* A public nursery for children.
**Credence,** krē'dens, *n.* The act of believing; credit; trust.
**Credential,** krē-den'shi-al, *n.* That which gives a title to credit; (*pl.*) documents showing that one is entitled to credit, or is invested with authority.
**Credibility,** kred-i-bil'i-ti, *n.* State or quality of being credible.
**Credible,** kred'i-bl, *a.* Worthy of credit.
**Credit,** kred'it, *n.* Reliance on testimony; faith; reputed integrity; transfer of goods, etc., in confidence of future payment; reputation for pecuniary worth; time given for payment of goods sold on trust; side of an account in which payment is entered; money possessed or due.—*vt.* To trust; to believe; to sell or lend to, in confidence of future payment; to procure credit or honor to; to enter on the credit side of an account; to attribute.
**Creditable,** kred'it-a-bl, *a.* Estimable.
**Creditably,** kred'it-a-bli, *adv.* In a creditable manner; with credit.
**Creditor,** kred'it-ėr, *n.* One to whom a debt is due.
**Credulity,** kred-dū'li-ti, *n.* A disposition to believe on slight evidence.
**Credulous,** kred'ū-lus, *a.* Apt to believe without sufficient evidence; unsuspecting.
**Creed,** krēd, *n.* A system of principles believed or professed; a brief summary of the articles of Christian faith.
**Creek,** krēk, *n.* A small bay; a small harbor; a brook.
**Creel,** krēl, *n.* An osier basket or pannier.
**Creep,** krēp, *vi.* (creeping, crept). To move as a reptile; to crawl; to grow along the ground, or on another body; to move secretly, feebly, or timorously; to be servile; to shiver.
**Creeper,** krēp'ėr, *n.* A creeping plant; a small bird; a kind of grapnel for dragging.
**Creepy,** krēp-i, *a.* Producing horror or fear.
**Cremate,** krē-māt', *vt.* To burn; to dispose of (a human body) by burning.
**Cremation,** krē-mā'shon, *n.* The act or custom of cremating.
**Cremona,** krē-mō'na, *n.* A general name for violins made at Cremona in N. Italy.
**Crenate, Crenated,** krē'nāt, krē'nāt-ed, *a.* Notched; indented.
**Crenelle,** kre-nel', *n.* An embrasure in an embattled parapet to fire through.
**Creole,** krē'ōl, *n.* A native of the W. Indies or Spanish America, but not of indigenous blood.
**Creosote,** krē'ō-sōt, *n.* An antiseptic liquid obtained from wood-tar.
**Crepitate,** krep'i-tāt, *vi.* To crackle.
**Crepitation,** krep-it-ā'shon, *n.* A sharp crackling sound or rattle.
**Crepuscular,** krē-pus'kūl-ėr, *a.* Pertaining to twilight.
**Crescent,** kres'ent, *n.* The moon in her state of increase; anything resembling the shape of the new moon; the Turkish standard; buildings in the form of a crescent.
**Cress,** kres, *n.* The name of various plants, mostly cruciferous, used as a salad.
**Cresset,** kres'et, *n.* A fire-pan fixed on the top of a pole.
**Crest,** krest, *n.* A tuft on the head of certain birds; the plume of feathers or tuft on a helmet; the helmet itself; the top; a lofty mien; a sort of heraldic badge.—*vt.* To furnish with a crest.
**Crested,** krest'ed, *p.a.* Having a crest.
**Crestfallen,** krest'fal-en, *a.* Dejected.
**Cretaceous,** krē-tā'shus, *a.* Chalky.
**Cretin,** krē'tin, *n.* One afflicted with cretinism.
**Cretinism,** krē'tin-izm, *n.* A disease resembling rickets, but accompanied with idiocy.
**Cretonne,** kre-ton', *n.* A cotton cloth printed with colored patterns.
**Crevice,** kre'vis, *n.* A crack; cleft; cranny.
**Crew,** krö, *n.* A company; a gang; the company of sailors belonging to a vessel.
**Crewel,** krö'el, *n.* A kind of fine worsted.
**Crib,** krib, *n.* A child's bed; a small habitation; a rack; a stall for oxen; a framework; a literal translation.—*vt.* (cribbing, cribbed). To shut up in a narrow habitation; to pilfer.
**Cribbage,** krib'āj, *n.* A game at cards.
**Cribble,** krib'l, *n.* A coarse sieve; coarse flour or meal.

**Crick,** krik, *n.* A local spasm or cramp; a stiffness of the neck.
**Cricket,** krik'et, *n.* An insect which makes a creaking or chirping sound; an open-air game played with bats, ball, and wickets.
**Cricketer,** krik'et-ėr, *n.* One who plays cricket.
**Crier,** krī'ėr, *n.* One who cries; one who makes proclamation.
**Crime,** krīm, *n.* A breach of law, divine or human; any great wickedness.
**Criminal,** krim'in-al, *a.* Guilty; wicked; relating to crime.—*n.* A malefactor; a convict.
**Criminality,** krim-in-al'i-ti, *n.* The quality of being criminal; guiltiness.
**Criminally,** krim'in-al-li, *adv.* In a criminal manner; wickedly.
**Criminate,** krim'in-āt, *vt.* To charge with or involve in a crime.
**Crimination,** krim-in-ā'shon, *n.* Accusation.
**Criminative, Criminatory,** krim'in-āt-iv, krim'in-a-to-ri, *a.* Relating to or involving crimination or accusation.
**Criminous,** krim'in-us, *a.* Criminal.
**Crimp,** krimp, *a.* Easily crumbled; friable; brittle.—*vt.* To curl or crisp; to seize; to pinch; to decoy for the army or navy.
**Crimple,** krimp'l, *vt.* (crimpling, crimpled). To contract; to cause to shrink; to curl.
**Crimson,** krim'zn, *n.* A deep-red color; a red tinged with blue.—*a.* Of a beauitful deep-red.—*vt.* To dye of a deep-red color.—*vi.* To become of a deep-red color; to blush.
**Cringe,** krinj, *vi.* (cringing, cringed). To bend; to bend with servility; to fawn.—*n.* A bow; servile civility.
**Cringle,** kring'gl, *n.* A withe for fastening a gate; a ring or eye in a rope of a sail.
**Crinkle,** kring'kl, *vi.* (crinkling, crinkled). To bend in little turns; to wrinkle.—*vt.* To form with short turns or wrinkles.—*n.* A winding or turn; a wrinkle.
**Crinoline,** krin'o-līn, *n.* A fabric of horsehair and linen thread; a hooped petticoat.
**Cripple,** krip'l, *n.* A lame person.—*vt.* (crippling, crippled). To lame; to disable.
**Crisis,** krī'sis, *n.*; pl. **-ses.** Turning-point of a disease; a decisive stage; time when anything is at its height; conjuncture.
**Crisp,** krisp, *a.* Brittle; easily broken or crumbled; fresh; brisk.—*vt.* To curl; to make wavy.—*vi.* To form little curls.
**Crisper,** krisp-ėr, *n.* One who or that which crisps; an instrument for crisping cloth.
**Crisply,** krisp'li, *adv.* With crispness.
**Crispy,** krisp'i, *a.* Crisp; curled; brittle.
**Cristate,** kris'tāt, *a.* Crested; tufted.
**Criterion,** krī-tē'ri-un, *n.*; pl. **-ia.** Standard of judging; a measure; test.
**Critic,** kri'tik, *n.* One skilled in judging literary or artistic work; a reviewer; a severe judge.—*a.* Relating to criticism.
**Critical,** kri'tik-al, *a.* Relating to or containing criticism; nicely judicious; inclined to find fault; relating to a crisis; momentous.
**Critically,** kri'tik-al-li, *adv.* In a critical manner; at the crisis.
**Criticism,** kri'ti-sizm, *n.* Act or art of criticizing; exhibition of the merits of literary or artistic work; a critical essay; censure.
**Criticize,** kri'ti-sīz, *vi.* and *t.* (criticizing, criticized). To examine or judge critically; to pick out faults; to animadvert upon.
**Critique,** kri-tēk', *n.* A written estimate of the merits of a literary or artistic work.
**Croak,** krōk, *vi.* To make a low hoarse noise in the throat, as a frog or crow; to forebode evil without much cause; to murmur.—*n.* The low harsh sound of a frog, raven, etc.
**Croaker,** krōk'ėr, *n.* A grumbler.
**Croaking, Croaky,** krōk'ing, krōk'i, *a.* Uttering a croak; foreboding evil; grumbling.
**Crochet,** krō'shā, *n.* A species of knitting performed by means of a small hook.
**Crock,** krok, *n.* An earthen vessel; a pot; a person broken down in health.
**Crockery,** krok'ė-ri, *n.* Earthenware; vessels formed of clay, glazed and baked.
**Crocodile,** kro'kō-dīl, *n.* A large aquatic reptile of the lizard kind.—*a.* Pertaining to or like a crocodile; affected (tears).
**Crocus,** krō'kus, *n.* A bulbous plant of the iris family; saffron.
**Croft,** kroft, *n.* A little field adjoining a dwelling-house; a little farm.
**Crofter,** krof'tėr, *n.* One who occupies a croft; a tenant of a small holding in the Highlands of Scotland.
**Cromelch,** krom'lek, *n.* An ancient structure of large stones set on end, supporting a stone laid horizontally.
**Crone,** krōn, *n.* An old woman.
**Crony,** krō'ni, *n.* A familiar friend.
**Crook,** krök, *n.* A bend; a curving instrument; a shepherd's staff; a pastoral staff; a criminal, swindler.—*vt.* and *i.* To bend; to make a hook on.
**Crooked,** krök'ed, *a.* Bent; wry; deceitful.
**Crop,** krop, *n.* The first stomach of birds; the craw; harvest; corn, etc., while growing; act of cutting, as hair; a short whip without a lash.—*vt.* (cropping, cropped). To cut off the ends of; to cut close; to browse; to gather before it falls; to cultivate.
**Crop-eared,** krop'ērd, *a.* Having the ears cut short.
**Cropper,** krop'ėr, *n.* A breed of pigeons with a large crop; a fall as from horseback.
**Croquet,** krō'kā, *n.* An open-air game played with mallets, balls, hoops, and pegs.
**Crore,** krōr, *n.* In the E. Indies, ten millions.
**Crosier, Crozier,** krō'zhi-ėr, *n.* A bishop's crook or pastoral staff.
**Cross,** kros, *n.* An instrument of death, consisting of two pieces of timber placed transversely; the symbol of the Christian religion; the religion itself; a monument or sign in the form of a cross; anything that thwarts; a hybrid.—*a.* Athwart; adverse; fretful.—*vt.* To draw a line or lay a body across; to mark with a cross; to cancel; to pass from side to side of; to thwart; to perplex; to interbreed.—*vi.* To be athwart; to move across.
**Cross-bones,** kros'bōnz, *n.pl.* A symbol of death; two human thigh-bones places crosswise, generally in conjunction with a skull.
**Crossbow,** kros'bō, *n.* A weapon for shooting, formed by fixing a bow crosswise on a stock.
**Cross-breed,** kros'brēd, *n.* A breed from a male and female of different breeds.
**Cross-examination,** kros'egz-am-in-ā-shon, *n.* The examination of a witness called by one party by the opposite party.
**Cross-examine,** kros'egz-am-in, *vt.* To examine a witness of the opposite party.
**Cross-grained,** kros'grānd, *a.* Having the fiber across or irregular; perverse.
**Crossing,** kros'ing, *n.* Act of one who or that which crosses; a place where passengers cross.
**Crossly,** kros'li, *adv.* Peevishly; adversely.
**Cross-purpose,** kros'pėr-pus, *n.* A contrary purpose; a misunderstanding.
**Cross-question,** kros'kwes-chon, *vt.* To cross-examine.
**Cross-road,** kros'rōd, *n.* A road which crosses other roads.
**Cross-trees,** kros'trēz, *n.pl.* Horizontal pieces of timber on masts, to sustain the tops and extend the shrouds.
**Crosswise,** kros'wīz, *adv.* Transversely.
**Crossword puzzle,** kros'wėrd puz'l, *n.* A diagram of squares, each of which, except certain blanks, is to be filled with a letter so that the words formed, when read down and across, correspond to definitions given.
**Crotch,** kroch, *n.* A fork or forking.
**Crotchet,** kroch'et, *n.* A note in music, half the length of a minim; a whim; a perverse conceit; a

bracket in printing.
**Crotchety,** kroch'et-i, *a.* Whimsical.
**Croton,** krō'ton, *n.* An E. Indian shrub whose seeds yield a violently purgative oil.
**Crouch,** krouch, *vi.* To bend low; to lie close to the ground; to cringe.
**Croup,** kröp, *n.* A disease of the windpipe in children; the rump of certain animals; the place behind the saddle.
**Croupier,** krö'pē-ėr, *n.* One who at a public dinner sits at the lower end of the table; person in charge of the money at a gaming table.
**Crow,** krō, *n.* A black bird of the genus Corvus, including the raven, rook, jackdaw, etc.; a crowbar; the sound which a cock utters.—*vi.* (crowing, *pret.* crew, crowed, *pp.* crowed). To cry as a cock; to exult; to boast.
**Crowbar,** krō'bär, *n.* A bar of iron with a bent or forked end, used as a lever.
**Crowd,** kroud, *n.* A number of persons or things; a throng; the populace.—*vt.* To fill by pressing together; to fill to excess.—*vi.* To press in numbers; to throng.
**Crowded,** kroud'ed, *a.* Filled by a promiscuous multitude.
**Crow-flower,** krō'flou-ėr, *n.* A name of the buttercup and other plants.
**Crowfoot,** krō'fut, *n.* Cords used in ships to suspend the awnings. etc.; a buttercup.
**Crown,** kroun, *n.* An ornament for the head in the form of a wreath; a diadem; a badge of royalty; perfection; completion; the top of anything, especially the head; a coin.—*vt.* To invest with a crown; to cover; to adorn; to finish; to perfect.
**Crowned,** kround, *p.a.* Invested with a crown; surmounted.
**Crown-glass,** kroun'glas, *n.* The finest sort of window-glass.
**Crowning,** kroun'ing, *p.a.* Highest; perfecting; final.
**Crown-prince,** kroun'prins, *n.* The prince who is apparently successor to the crown.
**Crow-quill,** krō'kwil, *n.* The quill of the crow, formerly used in fine writing.
**Crow's-feet,** krōz'fēt, *n.pl.* The wrinkles at corners of the eyes, the effects of age.
**Crucial,** krö'shi-al, *a.* Relating to a cross; severe; searching; decisive.
**Crucible,** krö'si-bl, *n.* A melting pot, used by chemists and others.
**Cruciferous,** krö-sif'ėr-us, *a.* Having four petals in the form of a cross.
**Crucifix,** krö'si-fiks, *n.* A cross with the figure of Christ crucified on it.
**Crucifixion,** krö-si-fik'shon, *n.* The act of crucifying; the death of Christ.
**Cruciform,** krö'si-form, *a.* Cross-shaped.
**Crucify,** krö'si-fī, *vt.* (crucifying, crucified). To put to death by nailing the hands and feet of to a cross, to mortify; to torment.
**Crude,** kröd, *a.* Raw; unripe; in its natural state; not brought to perfection.
**Crudely,** kröd'li, *adv.* In a crude manner.
**Crudity,** kröd'i-ti, *n.* State of being crude; something in a crude state.
**Cruel,** krö'el, *a.* Unmerciful; hard-hearted; ferocious; brutal; severe.
**Cruelly,** krö'el-li, *adv.* In a cruel manner.
**Cruelty,** krö'el-ti, *n.* Quality of being cruel; inhumanity; barbarity; a cruel act.
**Cruet,** krö'et, *n.* A vial or small glass bottle for holding vinegar, oil, etc.
**Cruise,** kröz, *vi.* (cruising, cruised). To sail hither and thither.—*n.* A sailing to and fro in search of an enemy's ships, or for pleasure.
**Cruiser,** kröz'ėr, *n.* A person or a ship that cruises; a swift armed vessel to protect or destroy shipping.
**Crumb,** krum, *n.* A fragment; a small piece of bread broken off; the soft part of bread.—*vt.* To break into small pieces with the fingers; to cover with bread-crumbs.
**Crumble,** krum'bl, *vt.* (crumbling, crumbled). To break into small fragments; to pulverize.—*vi.* To part into small fragments; to decay.
**Crumby, Crummy,** krum'i, *a.* Full of crumbs; soft like the crumb of bread.
**Crump,** krump, *a.* Crooked; bent.
**Crumpet,** krum'pet, *n.* A sort of muffin.
**Crumple,** krum'pl, *vt.* (crumpling, crumpled). To press into wrinkles; to rumple.—*vi.* To shrink; to shrivel.
**Crumpled,** krum'pld, *p.a.* Wrinkled; curled.
**Crunch,** krunch, *vt.* To crush between the teeth.
**Crupper,** krup'ėr, *n.* A strap of leather to prevent a saddle from shifting forward; the buttocks.
**Crural,** krör'al, *a.* Belonging to the leg; shaped like a leg or root.
**Crusade,** krö-sād', *n.* A military expedition against the infidels of the Holy Land; a romantic or enthusiastic enterprise.
**Crusader,** krö-sād'ėr, *n.* A person engaged in a crusade.
**Cruse,** kröz, *n.* A small cup; cruet.
**Crush,** krush, *vt.* To squeeze; to bruise; to pound; to overpower; to oppress.—*vi.*. To be pressed; to force one's way amid a crowd.—*n.* A violent pressing or squeezing; a crowding.
**Crushing,** krush'ing, *p.a.* Overwhelming.
**Crust,** krust, *n.* The hard outer coat of anything; the outside of a loaf; a piece of hard bread; a deposit from wine.—*vt.* and *i.* To cover with a crust or hard coat.
**Crustacea,** krus-tā'shē-a, *n.pl.* A division of animals, comprising crabs, shrimps, etc., having an external skeleton or shell.
**Crustacean,** krus-tā'shė-an, *n.* and *a.* One of, or pertaining to, the crustaceans.
**Crustaceous,** krus-tā'shus, *a.* Having a shell; belonging to the Crustacea.
**Crustily,** krust'i-li, *adv.* Peevishly.
**Crusty,** krust'i, *a.* Pertaining to, having, or like a crust; snappish; surly.
**Crutch,** kruch, *n.* a staff with a cross-piece used by cripples; a support.
**Crutched,** krucht, *p.a.* Furnished with a crutch; badged with a cross.
**Cry,** krī, *vi.* (crying, cried). To utter the loud shrill sounds of weeping, joy, fear, surprise, etc.; to clamor; to weep.—*vt.* To shout; to proclaim.—*n.* The loud voice of man or beast; a shriek or scream; acclamation; weeping; importunate call; a political catchword.
**Crying,** krī'ing, *p.a.* Calling for vengenance or punishment; notorious; clamant.
**Crypt,** kript, *n.* A subterranean cell for burying purposes; a subterranean chapel.
**Cryptic, Cryptical,** krip'tik, krip'tik-al, *a.* Hidden; secret; occult.
**Cryptogam,** krip'tō-gam, *n.* One of those plants which do not bear true flowers, such as lichens, mosses, ferns, etc.
**Cryptogamy,** krip-tog'a-mi, *n.* Concealed fructification, as in cryptogams.
**Cryptogram, Cryptograph,** krip'tō-gram, krip'tō-graf, *n.* Something written in secret characters.
**Cryptography,** krip-tog'ra-fi, *n.* Art of writing in secret characters; cipher.
**Crystal,** kris'tal, *n.* Pure transparent quartz; a superior kind of glass; articles, collectively, made of this material; a regular solid mineral body with smooth surfaces.—*a.* Consisting of or like crystal; clear; pellucid.
**Crystalline,** kris'tal-īn, *a.* Pure; pellucid.
**Crystallization,** kris'tal-īz-ā''shon, *n.* Act or process of crystallizing.
**Crystallize,** kris'tal-īz, *vt.* and *i.* To form into crystals; to unite, and form a regular solid.
**Ctenoid,** ten'oid, *a.* Comb-shaped; having the posterior edge with teeth: said of the scales of fishes; having scales of this kind.
**Cub,** kub, *n.* The young of certain quadrupeds, as the bear and fox.—*vi.* (cubbing, cubbed). To bring forth cubs.
**Cube,** kūb, *n.* A regular solid body, with six equal

C

square sides, the third power, or the product from multiplying a number twice by itself.—*vt.* To raise to the third power.
**Cubic, Cubical,** kūb'ik, kūb'ik-al, *a.* Having the form or properties of a cube.
**Cubicle,** kū'bi-kl, *n.* A sleeping-place; a compartment for one bed in a dormitory.
**Cubit,** kū'bit, *n.* The forearm; the length from the elbow to the extremity of the middle finger, usually taken as 18 inches.
**Cuckold,** kuk'old, *n.* A man whose wife is false to his bed.—*vt.* To make a cuckold of.
**Cuckoo,** ku'kö, *n.* A migratory bird, so named from the sound of its note.
**Cucumber,** kū'kum-bėr, *n.* An annual plant of the gourd family.
**Cud,** kud, *n.* The food which ruminating animals bring up from the first stomach to chew.
**Cuddle,** kud'dl, *vi.* (cuddling, cuddled). To lie close and snug.—*vt.* To hug; to embrace; to fondle.
**Cuddy,** kud'i, *n.* A ship's cabin towards the stern; an ass; donkey.
**Cudgel,** kuj'el, *n.* A short thick stick; a club.—*vt.* (cudgelling, cudgelled). To beat with a cudgel; to beat in general.
**Cue,** kū, *n.* The last words of an actor's speech; catch-word; hint; the part which any man is to play in his turn; humor; the straight rod used in billiards.
**Cuff,** kuf, *n.* A blow; slap; part of a sleeve near the hand.—*vt.* To beat; to strike with talons or wings, or with fists.
**Cuirass,** kwi-ras', *n.* A breastplate.
**Cuirassier,** kwi-ras-sēr', *n.* A cavalryman who wears a cuirass or breastplate.
**Cuisine,** kwē-zēn', *n.* Style of cooking.
**Cul-de-sac,** köl'de-sak, *n.* A blind alley.
**Culinary,** kū'lin-a-ri, *a.* Relating to the kitchen, or cookery; used in kitchens.
**Cull,** kul, *vt.* To pick out, to gather.
**Cullender,** kul'en-dėr, *n.* A colander.
**Cullion,** kul'i-un, *n.* A mean wretch; a cully.
**Cully,** kul'li, *n.* A person easily deceived; a dupe.—*vt.* To deceive.
**Culm,** kulm, *n.* The straw of corn and grasses; anthracite shale.
**Culminate,** kul'min-āt, *vi.* To come or be in the meridian; to reach the highest point, as of rank, power, size, etc.
**Culmination,** kul-min-ā'shon, *n.* The transit of a heavenly body over the meridian; highest point; consummation.
**Culpability,** kulp-a-bil'i-ti, *n.* Blamableness; guiltiness.
**Culpable,** kulp'a-bl, *a.* Blameworthy; guilty; criminal; immoral; sinful.
**Culpably,** kulp'a-bli, *adv.* In a culpable manner; blamably.
**Culprit,** kul'prit, *n.* A person arraigned in court for a crime, or convicted of a crime; a criminal; an offender.
**Cult,** kult, *n.* A system of belief and worship; a subject of devoted study.
**Cultivable,** kul'ti-va-bl, *a.* Capable of being cultivated.
**Cultivate,** kul'ti-vāt, *vt.* To till; to refine; to foster; to improve.
**Cultivation,** kul-ti-vā'shon, *n.* Tillage; practice, care, or study directed to improvement; refinement; advancement.
**Cultivator,** kul'ti-vāt-ėr, *n.* One who cultivates; a kind of harrow.
**Culture,** kul'tūr, *n.* Cultivation; the rearing of certain animals, as oysters; the application of labor, or other means of improvement; the result of such efforts; refinement.—*vt.* To cultivate.
**Cultured,** kul'tūrd, *a.* Having education and taste; refined.
**Culverin,** kul'vėr-in, *n.* A long slender piece of ordnance formerly used.
**Culvert,** kul'vėrt, *n.* An arched drain under a road, railway, etc., for the passage of water.
**Cumber,** kum'bėr, *vt.* To embarrass; to entangle; to obstruct; to distract.
**Cumbersome,** kum'bėr-sum, *a.* Troublesome; unwieldy; unmanageable.
**Cumbrous,** kum'brus, *a.* Burdensome; troublesome; oppressive.
**Cumin, Cummin,** kum'in, *n.* An annual umbelliferous plant, whose seeds have stimulating and carminative properties.
**Cummer-bund,** kum'ėr-bund, *n.* A girdle or waistband.
**Cumulate,** kū-mū-lāt, *vt.* (cumulating, cumulated). To form a heap; to heap together.
**Cumulation,** kū-mū-lā'shon, *n.* A heaping up; a heap; accumulation.
**Cumulative,** kū-mū-lāt-iv, *a.* Forming a mass; that augments by addition.
**Cumulus,** kū'mū-lus, *n.*; pl. **-li.** A cloud in the form of dense convex or conical heaps.
**Cuneate, Cuneated, kū'nē-āt, kū'nē-āt-ed,** *a.* Wedge-shaped.
**Cuneiform,** kū-nē'i-form, *a.* Wedge-shaped; applied to the arrow-headed characters on old Babylonian and Persian inscriptions.
**Cunning,** kun'ing, *a.* Astute; artful.—*n.* Faculty or act of using stratagem; craftiness; artifice.
**Cunningly,** kun'ing-li, *adv.* In a cunning manner; craftily.
**Cup,** kup, *n.* A small vessel to drink out of; anything hollow, like a cup; a glass vessel for drawing blood; liquor in a cup.—*vt.* (cupping, cupped). To apply a cupping-glass.
**Cup-bearer,** kup'bār-ėr, *n.* An attendant at a feast, who serves the wine.
**Cupboard,** kup'bōrd, *n.* A case or inclosure for cups, plates, dishes, etc.
**Cupel,** kū'pel, *n.* A small cup or vessel used in refining precious metals.
**Cupellation,** kū-pel-lā'shon, *n.* The process of refining gold or silver in a cupel.
**Cupid,** kū'pid, *n.* The god of love.
**Cupidity,** kū-pid'i-ti, *n.* A longing to possess; inordinate or unlawful desire; covetousness.
**Cupola,** kū-pō-la, *n.* A spherical vault on the top of a building; a dome.
**Cupping,** kup'ing, *n.* A drawing of blood with a cupping-glass.
**Cupping-glass,** kup'ing-glas, *n.* A glass vessel like a cup, for drawing blood.
**Cupreous,** kū-prē-us, *a.* Coppery.
**Cur,** kėr, *n.* A mongrel dog; a contemptible man.
**Curable,** kūr'a-bl, *a.* That may be cured.
**Curaçoa, Curaçao,** kö-ra-sō'a, kö-ra-sä'o, *n.* A liqueur flavored with orange-peel, etc.
**Curacy, Curateship,** kū'ra-si, kū-rāt-ship, *n.* The office of a curate.
**Curate,** kū'rāt, *n.* One to whom the cure of souls is committed; a clergyman employed to assist in the duties of a rector or vicar.
**Curative,** kū'rāt-iv, *a.* Relating to the cure of diseases; tending to cure.
**Curator,** kū-rāt'ėr, *n.* A superintendent; custodian; guardian.
**Curb,** kėrb, *vt.* To control; to check; to restrain with a curb, as a horse; to strengthen by a curb-stone.—*n.* Check; restraint; part of a bridle; a curb-stone.
**Curb-stone,** kėrb'stōn, *n.* The outer edge of a foot-pavement.
**Curd,** kėrd, *n.* Coagulated milk.—*vt.* and *i.* To curdle; to congeal.
**Curdle,** kėrd'l, *vt.* and *i.* (curdling, curdled). To change into curds; to coagulate.
**Curdy,** kėrd'i, *a.* Like curd; coagulated.
**Cure,** kūr, *n.* Act of healing; a remedy; the care of souls; spiritual charge.—*vt.* (curing, cured). To heal; to remedy; to pickle.—*vi.* To effect a cure.
**Curé,** kū-rā, *n.* A curate; a parson.
**Cureless,** kūr'les, *a.* Incurable.
**Curer,** kūr'ėr, *n.* One who cures; a physician; one who preserves provisions.
**Curfew,** kėr'fū, *n.* An evening bell; an old utensil

for covering a fire.
**Curia,** kū'ri-a, *n.* The Roman see in its temporal aspect.
**Curio,** kū'ri-ō, *n.*; pl. **-os,** A curiosity; an interesting and curious article.
**Curiosity,** kū-ri-os'i-ti, *n.* Inquisitiveness; a thing unusual; a rarity.
**Curious,** kū'ri-us, *a.* Inquisitive; addicted to research or inquiry; strange; singular.
**Curiously,** kū'ri-us-li, *adv.* In a curious manner; inquisitively; unusually.
**Curl,** kėrl, *vt.* To form into ringlets,—*vi.* To take a twisted or coiled form; to play at the game of curling.—*n.* A ringlet of hair, or anything of a like form; a waving; flexure.
**Curler,** kėr'lėr, *n.* One who or that which curls; one who plays the game of curling.
**Curlew,** kėr'lū, *n.* A bird allied to the snipe and woodcock.
**Curling,** kėrl'ing, *n.* A winter game in which large smooth stones are propelled on the ice.
**Curly,** kėrl'i, *a.* Having curls; tending to curl.
**Curmudgeon,** kėr-muj'on, *n.* An avaricious churlish fellow; a miser; a churl.
**Currant,** ku'rant, *n.* A small dried grape; the name of several shrubs and of their fruit.
**Currency,** ku'ren-si, *n.* Circulation; circulating medium; the aggregate of coin, notes, etc., in circulation; general esteem; vogue.
**Current,** ku'rent, *a.* Running; circulating; general; present in its course.—*n.* A running; a stream; progressive motion of water; successive course; the passage of electricity from one pole of an apparatus to the other; often used for strength, amount, or intensity of current.
**Currently,** ku'rent-li, *adv.* In a current manner; generally.
**Curricle,** ku'ri-kl, *n.* A chaise with two wheels, drawn by two horses.
**Curriculum,** ku-rik'ū-lum, *n.* A course of study in a university, school, etc.
**Currier,** ku'ri-ėr, *n.* A man who dresses leather after it is tanned.
**Currish,** kėr'ish, *a.* Like a cur; snappish.
**Curry,** ku'ri, *n.* A highly spiced sauce or mixture; a dish cooked with curry.—*vt.* (currying, curried). To flavor with curry; to dress leather; to rub and clean (a horse) with a comb; to seek (favor).
**Curry-comb,** ku'ri-kōm, *n.* A comb for rubbing and cleaning horses.
**Curse,** kėrs, *vt.* (cursing, cursed). To utter a wish of evil against; a blight; to torment with calamities.—*vi.* To utter imprecations; to blaspheme.—*n.* Imprecation of evil; execration; torment.
**Cursed,** kėrs'ed, *a.* Deserving a curse; under a curse; execrable; detestable.
**Cursedly,** kėrs'ed-li, *adv.* In a cursed manner; confoundedly.
**Cursing,** kėrs'ing, *n.* The uttering of a curse; execration.
**Cursive,** kėr'siv, *a.* Running, flowing.
**Cursores,** kėr-sō'rēz, *n.pl.* The runners, an order of birds, such as the ostrich.
**Cursorily,** kėr'sō-ri-li, *adv.* In a hasty manner; slightly; hastily.
**Cursory,** kėr'so-ri, *a.* Hasty; superficial.
**Curt,** kėrt, *a.* Short; concise; somewhat rude.
**Curtail,** kėr-tāl', *vt.* To cut short; to abridge.
**Curtain,** kėr'tan, *n.* A hanging cloth for a window, bed, etc.; a screen in a theater—*vt.* To inclose or furnish with curtains.
**Curtain-lecture,** kėr'tan-lek-tūr, *n.* Lecture given in bed by a wife to her husband.
**Curtly,** kėrt'li, *adv.* Shortly; briefly.
**Curtsy, Curtsey,** kėrt'si, *n.* A gesture of respect by a female.—*vi.* (curtsying or curtseying, curtsied or curtseyed). To drop or make a crutsy.
**Curvature,** kėrv'a-tūr, *n.* A curving.
**Curve,** kėrv, *a.* Bending; inflected.—*n.* A bending without angles; a bent line.—*vt.* (curving, curved). To bend.
**Curvet,** kėr-vet', *n.* A leap of a horse, in which he raises his fore-legs together.—*vi.* (curvetting, curvetted). To leap and frisk.
**Curvilinear, Curvilineal,** kėrv-i-lin'ē-ėr, kėrv-i-lin'ē-al, *a.* Consisting of curved lines; bounded by curved lines.
**Curvirostral,** kėrv-i-ros'tral, *a.* Having a crooked beak.
**Cushat,** kush'at, *n.* The ring-dove.
**Cushion,** kush'on, *n.* A pillow for a seat; something resembling a pillow.—*vt.* To seat on a cushion; to furnish with cushions.
**Cusp,** kusp, *n.* The point of the moon, or other luminary; a point formed by the meeting of two curves.
**Custard,** kus'tėrd, *n.* A composition of milk and egg, sweetened, and baked or boiled.
**Custard-apple,** kus'tėrd-ap-pl, *n.* A West Indian tree or fruit.
**Custodial,** kus-tō'di-al, *a.* Relating to custody or guardianship.
**Custodian,** kus-tō'di-an, *n.* One who has care of a library, public building, etc.
**Custodier,** kus-tō'di-ėr, *n.* One who has something in custody; a keeper; a guardian.
**Custody,** kus'tō-di, *n.* A keeping; guardianship; imprisonment; security.
**Custom,** kus'tum, *n.* Habit; established practice; fashion; a buying of goods; business support; a tax on goods; *pl.* duties on merchandise imported or exported.
**Customable,** kus'tum-a-bl, *a.* Subject to the payment of customs.
**Customarily,** kus'tum-a-ri-li, *adv.* Habitually.
**Customary,** kus'tum-a-ri, *a.* According to custom; habitual; usual.
**Customer,** kus'tum-ėr, *n.* An accustomed buyer at a shop, etc., one who buys goods.
**Custom-house,** kus'tum-hous, *n.* The office where customs are paid.
**Cut,** kut, *vt.* (cutting, cut). To divide into pieces; to fell or mow; to clip; to carve; to affect deeply; to intersect; to castrate; to divide, as cards; to refuse to recognize.—*vi.* To make an incision; to be severed by a cutting instrument; to pass straight and rapidly.—*a.* Gashed; carved; intersected; deeply affected.—*n.* The action of an edged instrument; a wound; a stroke with a whip; a severe remark; a channel; any small piece; a lot; a near passage; a carving or engraving; act of dividing a pack of cards; form; fashion; refusal to recognize a person.
**Cutaneous,** kū-tā'nē-us, *a.* Pertaining to the skin.
**Cuticle,** kū'ti-kl, *n.* The thin exterior coat of the skin; a vesicular membrane in plants.
**Cutlass,** kut'las, *n.* A broad, curving sword.
**Cutler,** kut'lėr, *n.* One who makes or sharpens knives and other cutting instruments.
**Cutlery,** kut'lė-ri, *n.* Knives and edged instruments collectively.
**Cutlet,** kut'let, *n.* A small piece of meat for cooking, generally off the ribs.
**Cutpurse,** kut'pėrs, *n.* A thief; pickpocket.
**Cutter,** kut'ėr, *n.* One who or that which cuts; a vessel with one mast and a straight running bowsprit.
**Cut-throat,** kut'thrōt, *n.* A murderer.
**Cutting,** kut'ing, *p.a.* Serving to cut; wounding the feelings; severe.—*n.* A piece cut off; an incision; an excavation; a twig or scion.
**Cuttle, Cuttle-fish,** kut'tl, kut'tl-fish, *n.* A mollusc which ejects a black fluid to conceal itself..
**Cutwater,** kut'wa-tėr, *n.* The fore part of ship's prow, which cuts the water.
**Cyanean,** sī-ā'nē-an, *a.* Of a dark-blue color.
**Cyanide,** sī'an-id, *n.* A combination of cyanogen with a metallic base.
**Cyanogen,** sī-an'ō-jen, *n.* A poisonous gas of a strong and peculiar odor.
**Cycle,** sī'kl, *n.* An orbit in the heavens; a circle of years; a bicycle or tricycle.—*vi.* To recur in a cycle; to ride a bicycle.
**Cyclic, Cyclical,** sī'klik, sī'klik-al, *a.* Pertaining

C

to a cycle; connected with a series of legends.
**Cyclist,** sīk'list, *n.* One who uses a cycle.
**Cycloid,** sī'kloid, *n.* A geometrical curve.
**Cyclone,** sī'klōn, *n.* A circular storm; a rotatory system of winds revolving round a calm center, and advancing.
**Cyclopean,** sī-klō-pē'an, *a.* Pertaining to the Cyclops; gigantic; vast.
**Cyclops,** sī'klops, *n.sing.* and *pl.*; pl. also **Cyclopes,** sī-klō'pēz. A one-eyed race of giants in Greek fable.
**Cygnet,** sig'net, *n.* A young swan.
**Cylinder,** si'lin-dėr, *n.* An elongated round body of uniform diameter.
**Cylindric, Cylindrical,** si-lin'drik, si-lin'-drik-al, *a.* Having the form of a cylinder, or partaking of its properties.
**Cymbal,** sim'bal, *n.* A basin-shaped musical instrument of brass, used in pairs.
**Cymric,** kim'rik, *a.* Pertaining to the cymry (kim'ri) or Welsh.—*n.* The language of the Cymry or ancient Britons.
**Cynic,** sin'ik, *n.* One of a sect of Greek philosophers who professed contempt of riches, arts, etc.; a morose man.
**Cynic, Cynical,** sin'ik, sin'i-kal, *a.* Belonging to the Cynics; surly; sneering; captious.
**Cynicism,** sin'i-sizm, *n.* A morose contempt of the pleasures and arts of life.
**Cynosure,** sī'nō-zhör, *n.* The constellation of the Little Bear; a center of attraction.
**Cypher,** sī'fėr, *n.* Same as *Cipher.*
**Cypress,** sī'pres, *n.* An evergreen tree; the emblem of mourning.
**Cyst,** sist, *n.* A bag in animal bodies containing matter.
**Cytherean,** sith-e-rē'an, *a.* Pertaining to Venus.
**Czar,** tsär or zär, *n.* Formerly, the title of the Emperor of Russia.
**Czarevitch,** tsä're-vich, *n.* Formerly, the eldest son of the Czar: also *Cesarevitch* (tsā-zä-rä'vich).
**Czarina,** tsä-rē'na or zä-rē'na, *n.* Formerly, the title of the Empress of Russia.
**Czech,** chek, *n.* One of the Slavonic inhabitants of Bohemia; the language of the Czechs.

# D

**Dab,** dab, *vt.* (dabbing, dabbed). To hit lightly with something soft or moist.—*n.* A gentle blow; a small mass of anything soft or moist; a small flat fish; an adept or expert.
**Dabble,** dab'bl, *vt.* (dabbling, dabbled). To wet; to sprinkle.—*vi.* To play in water; to do anything in a superficial manner; to meddle.
**Dabbler,** dab'bl-ėr, *n.* One who dabbles; a superficial meddler.
**Dace,** dās, *n.* A small river fish.
**Dachshund,** däks'hunt, *n.* A long-bodied, short-legged dog, with short hair.
**Dacoit,** da-koit', *n.* An Indian name for a robber who is a member of a band of thieves.
**Dactyl,** dak'til, *n.* A poetical foot of one long or accented syllable followed by two short.
**Dactylic,** dak-til'ik, *a.* Pertaining to or consisting of dactyls.
**Dad, Daddy,** dad, dad'di, *n.* A childish or pet name for father.
**Dado,** dā'dō, *n.* That part of a pedestal between the base and the cornice; the finishing of the lower part of the walls in rooms.
**Daffodil,** daf'fō-dil, *n.* A plant of the amaryllis family with yellow flowers.
**Dagger,** dag'ėr, *n.* A short sharp-pointed sword.
**Daggle,** dag'gl, *vt.* (daggling, daggled). To trail in mud or wet grass; to dirty.
**Dago,** dā'gō, *n.* A contemptuous term for an Italian or Spaniard.
**Daguerreotype,** da-ger'ō-tīp, *n.* A photograph fixed on a metallic plate.
**Dahabieh,** da-ha-bē'ā, *n.* A Nile passenger boat.
**Dahlia,** da'li-a, *n.* A genus of composite plants, consisting of tuberous-rooted herbs.
**Daily,** dā'li, *a.* Happening or being every day; diurnal.—*adv.* Day by day.
**Daintily,** dān'ti-li, *adv.* Nicely; delicately.
**Dainty,** dān'ti, *a.* Toothsome; nice; delicate; elegant.—*n.* Something nice; a delicacy.
**Dairy,** dā'ri, *n.* The place where milk is converted into butter or cheese; a shop where milk, butter, etc., are sold.—*a.* Pertaining to the keeping of cows, managing of milk, etc.
**Dais,** dā'is, *n.* The high table at the upper end of the dining-hall; the raised floor on which the table stood; a canopy.
**Daisy,** dā'zi, *n.* The day's eye; a well-known plant, bearing a white flower with a tinge of red, and a yellow center.
**Dale,** dāl, *n.* A valley; a place between hills.
**Dalliance,** dal'yans, *n.* Acts of fondness; interchange of caresses; toying.
**Dally,** dal'li, *vi.* (dallying, dallied). To trifle; to wanton; to linger.
**Dalmatic,** dal-mat'ik, *n.* The ecclesiastical vestment used by deacons at mass, and worn also by bishops under the chasuble.
**Daltonism,** dal'ton-izm, *n.* Color-blindess.
**Dam,** dam, *n.* A female parent; a bank to confine or raise water.—*vt.* (damming, dammed). To obstruct or confine by a dam.
**Damage,** dam'āj, *n.* Hurt; injury; money compensation (generally in *pl.*).—*vt.* (damaging, damaged). To injure; to impair.
**Damageable,** dam'āj-a-bl, *a.* That may be damaged.
**Damask,** dam'ask, *n.* A fabric, of various materials, with figures of flowers, etc.; a pink color.—*a.* Pink or rosy.—*vt.* To form or imprint flowers or figures on.
**Damaskeen,** dam'as-kēn, *vt.* To inlay iron, steel, etc., with another metal, as gold or silver.
**Dame,** dām, *n.* A lady; the wife of a knight or baronet; title given to a woman who belongs to the first or second class of the Victorian Order or the Order of the British Empire.
**Damn,** dam, *vt.* To send to hell; to condemn.
**Damnable,** dam'na-bl, *a.* Deserving damnation; odious; pernicious.
**Damnably,** dam'na-bli, *adv.* In a damnable manner.
**Damnation,** dam-nā'shon, *n.* Condemnation; sentence to punishment in the future state.
**Damnatory,** dam'na-to-ri, *a.* Containing condemnation; condemnatory.
**Damned,** damd, *a.* Hateful; detestable.
**Damning,** dam'ing or dam'ning, *a.* That condemns or exposes to damnation.
**Damp,** damp, *a.* Moist; humid.—*n.* Moist air; fog; noxious exhalation from the earth; depression of spirits; discouragement.—*vt.* To moisten; to dispirit; to restrain.
**Dampen,** dam'pen, *vt.* and *i.* To make or become damp or moist.
**Damper,** dam'pėr, *n.* One who or that which damps; a plate across a flue or a furnace, etc., to regulate the draught of air.
**Dampish,** damp'ish, *a.* Moderately damp.
**Dampness,** damp'nes, *n.* Moisture; fogginess; moistness; moderate humidity.
**Damsel,** dam'zel, *n.* A young unmarried woman; a girl.
**Damson,** dam'zn, *n.* A small dark plum.
**Dance,** dans, *vi.* (dancing, danced). To move with measured steps, regulated by a tune; to leap and risk.—*vt.* To make to dance; to dandle.—*n.* A leaping or stepping to the measure of a tune; the tune itself.
**Dancer,** dans'ėr, *n.* One who dances.
**Dandelion,** dan'di-li-un, *n.* A composite plant bearing a bright yellow flower.
**Dandle,** dan'dl, *vt.* (dandling, dandled). To shake on the knee; as an infant; to fondle; to trifle with.

**Dandruff,** dan'druff, *n.* A scurf on the head.
**Dandy,** dan'di, *n.* A fop; a coxcomb.
**Dandyish,** dan'di-ish, *a.* Like a dandy.
**Dandyism,** dan'di-izm, *n.* The manners and dress of a dandy.
**Danger,** dān'jėr, *n.* Exposure to injury; jeopardy; risk.
**Dangerous,** dān'jėr-us, *a.* Perilous; causing risk of harm; unsafe; insecure.
**Dangerously,** dān'jėr-us-li, *adv.* With danger; perilously.
**Dangle,** dang'gl, *vi.* (dangling, dangled). To hang loose; to follow officiously.—*vt.* To carry suspended loosely; to swing.
**Dangler,** dang'gl-ėr, *n.* One who dangles; a man who hangs about women.
**Dank,** dangk, *a.* Damp; moist; humid.
**Danseuse,** däng-sėz, *n.* A female stage-dancer.
**Dapper,** dap'ėr, *a.* Little and active; neat.
**Dapple,** dap'l, *n.* A spot.—*a.* Marked with spots.—*vt.* (dappling, dappled). to variegate with spots.
**Dappled,** dap'pld, *a.* Spotted.
**Dare,** dãr, *vi.* (daring, *pret.* dared *pp.* dared). To have courage; to be bold enough; to venture.—*vt.* To challenge; to defy; to venture on.
**Dare-devil,** dãr'de-vil, *n.* A desperado; one who will fearlessly attempt anything.
**Daring,** dãr'ing, *a.* Bold; intrepid; fearless.—*n.* Courage; audacity.
**Daringly,** dãr'ing-li, *adv.* Boldly; fearlessly.
**Dark,** därk, *a.* Destitute of light; clouded; black or blackish; disheartening; involved in mystery; keeping designs in concealment.—*n.* Darkness; obscurity; secrecy; a state of ignorance.
**Darken,** därk'n, *vt.* To make dark.—*vi.* To grow dark or darker.
**Darkish,** därk'ish, *a.* Somewhat dark.
**Darkly,** därk'li, *adv.* Obscurely; dimly.
**Darkness,** därk'nes, *n.* Absence of light; blackness; gloom; ignorance; privacy.
**Darksome,** därk'sum, *a.* Dark; gloomy.
**Darling,** där'ling, *a.* Dearly beloved.—*n.* One much beloved; a favorite.
**Darn,** därn, *vt.* To mend by imitating the texture of the stuff with thread and needle; to sew together.—*n.* A place so mended.
**Darnel,** där'nel, *n.* A plant injurious to corn.
**Dart,** därt, *n.* A pointed missile thrown by the hand; a sudden rush or bound.—*vt.* To throw with a sudden thrust; to shoot.—*vi.* To fly or shoot, as a dart; to start and run.
**Darter,** därt'ėr, *n.* One who darts; a bird of the pelican tribe that darts after fish.
**Darwinism,** där'win-izm, *n.* The doctrine as to the origin and modifications of species taught by Darwin; evolution.
**Dash,** dash, *vt.* To cause to strike suddenly or violently; to throw or cast; to sprinkle; to mix slightly; to sketch out hastily; to obliterate; to frustrate; to abash.—*vi.* To rush with violence; to strike or be hurled.—*n.* A violent striking of two bodies; admixture; a rushing or onset; vigor in attack; bluster; a mark in writing or printing (—).
**Dash-board,** dash'bōrd, *n.* A board on a vehicle to keep off mud, etc., thrown by the horses' heels.
**Dashing,** dash'ing, *a.* Spirited; showy.
**Dastard,** das'tėrd, *n.* A coward.—*a.* cowardly.
**Dastardly,** das'tėrd-li, *a.* Cowardly; base.
**Data,** dā'ta, *n.pl. See* DATUM.
**Date,** dāt, *n.* The time when any event happened; era; age; a soft fleshy drupe, the fruit of the date-palm.—*vt.* (dating, dated). To note the time of.—*vi.* To reckon time; to have origin.
**Date-palm, Date-tree,** dāt'päm, dāt'trē, *n.* The kind of palms which bear dates.
**Dative,** dāt'iv, *a.* or *n.* A grammatical case, following verbs that express giving, etc.
**Datum,** dā'tum, *n.*; pl. **—ta.** A fact, proposition, etc., granted or known, from which other facts, etc., are to be deduced.
**Daub,** dab, *vt.* To smear; to cover with mud or other soft substance; to paint coarsely; to flatter grossly.—*n.* Coarse painting; a smear.
**Dauber,** dab'ėr, *n.* One who daubs; a coarse painter; a gross flatterer.
**Dauby,** dab'i, *a.* Viscous; glutinous.
**Daughter,** da'tėr, *n.* A female child or descendant.
**Daughter-in-law,** da'tėr-in-la, *n.* A son's wife.
**Daughterly,** da'tėr-li, *a.* Becoming a daughter.
**Daunt,** dant, *vt.* To subdue the courage of; to intimidate; to discourage.
**Dauntless,** dant'les, *a.* Fearless; intrepid.
**Dauphin,** da'fin, *n.* Formerly, the eldest son of the king of France.
**Davenport,** dav'en-port, *n.* A small ornamental writing-table fitted with drawers, etc.
**Davit,** dā'vit, *n.* One of a pair of projecting pieces over a ship's side, with tackle to hoist or lower a boat by.
**Daw,** da, *n.* A bird of the crow kind.
**Dawdle,** da'dl, *vi.* (dawdling, dawdled). To waste time; to trifle; to saunter.
**Dawn,** dan, *vi.* To begin to grow light in the morning; to glimmer obscurely; to begin to open or appear.—*n.* The break of day; beginning; first appearance.
**Dawning,** dan'ing, *n.* The first appearance of light in the morning; beginning.
**Day,** dā, *n.* The time between the rising and setting of the sun; the time of one revolution of the earth; or 24 hours; light; time specified; age; time; anniversary.
**Day-book,** dā'buk, *n.* A book in which are recorded the debts and credits of the day.
**Daybreak,** dā'brāk, *n.* The dawn; first appearance of light in the morning.
**Day-dream,** dā'drēm, *n.* A vision to the waking senses; a reverie.
**Daylight,** dā'līt, *n.* The light of the day.
**Dayspring,** dā'spring, *n.* The dawn.
**Day-star,** dā'stär, *n.* The star that ushers in the day; the morning-star, Lucifer.
**Daytime,** dā'tīm, *n.* The time of daylight.
**Daze,** dāz, *vt.* (dazing, dazed). To stupefy; to stun.
**Dazzle,** daz'zl, *vt.* (dazzling, dazzled). To overpower with light or splendor.—*vi.* To be intensely bright; to be overpowered by light.—*n.* A dazzling light; glitter.
**Deacon,** dē'kon, *n.* A person in the lowest degree of holy orders; a church officer; the president of an incorporated trade.
**Deaconess,** dē'kon-es, *n.* A female deacon.
**Deaconhood,** dē'kon-hud, *n.* The state of office of a deacon; deacons collectively.
**Deaconship, Deaconry,** dē'kon-ship, dē'kon-ri, *n.* The office of a deacon.
**Dead,** ded, *a.* Without life; deceased; perfectly still; dull; cold; tasteless; spiritless; utter; unerring.
**Deaden,** ded'n, *vt.* To abate in vigor, force, or sensation; to darken, dull, or dim.
**Dead-heat,** ded'hēt, *n.* A race in which the competitors finish at the same time.
**Dead-letter,** ded'let-tėr, *n.* A letter which cannot be delivered, and is returned to the sender; a law, treaty, etc., which has ceased to be acted on.
**Dead-light,** ded'līt, *n.* A kind of shutter in ships for a cabin-window.
**Dead-lock,** ded'lok, *n.* Complete stand-still.
**Deadly,** ded'li, *a.* That may cause death; mortal; implacable.—*adv.* In a deadly manner.
**Dead-march,** ded'märch, *n.* A piece of solemn music played at funerals.
**Dead-set,** ded'set, *n.* The fixed position of a dog in pointing game; a pointed attack.
**Dead-weight,** ded'wāt, *n.* A heavy or oppressive burden.
**Deaf,** def, *a.* Wanting the sense of hearing; not listening or regarding.
**Deafen,** def'n. *vt* To make deaf; to render impervi-

D

ous to sound.
**Deafening,** def'n-ing, *n.* Matter to prevent the passage of sound through floors, etc.
**Deaf-mute,** def'mūt, *n.* A deaf and dumb person.
**Deal,** dēl, *n.* A part; an indefinite quantity, degree, or extent; the distribution of playing cards; a board or plank; fir or pine timber.—*vt.* (dealing, dealt). to distribute.—*vi.* To traffic; to behave; to distribute cards.
**Dealer,** dēl'ėr, *n.* A trader; one who distributes cards.
**Dealing,** dēl'ing, *n.* Conduct; behavior; intercourse; traffic.
**Dean,** dēn, *n.* A dignitary in cathedral and collegiate churches who presides over the chapter; an officer in a university or college.
**Deanery,** dēn'ė-ri, *n.* The revenue, office, jurisdiction, or house of a dean.
**Deanship,** dēn'ship, *n.* The office of a dean.
**Dear,** dēr, *a.* Bearing a high price; valuable; expensive; a high estimation; beloved.—*n.* A darling.—*adv.* Dearly.
**Dearly,** dēr'li, *adv.* At a high price; With great fondness.
**Dearth,** dėrth, *n.* Scarcity; want; famine.
**Death,** deth, *n.* Extinction of life; decease; cause of decease; damnation.
**Death-bed,** deth'bed, *n.* The bed on which a person dies.
**Deathless,** deth'les, *a.* Not subject to death.
**Deathlike,** deth'līk, *a.* Resembling death; gloomy; quiet; motionless.
**Deathly,** deth'li, *a.* Deadly; fatal.
**Death-rate,** deth'rāt, *n.* The proportion of deaths in a town, country, etc.
**Death's-head,** deths'hed, *n.* A figure of a human skull; a kind of moth.
**Debacle,** de-bak'l, *n.* A sudden breaking up of ice; a confused rout; a crash in the social or political world.
**Debar,** dē-bär', *vt.* (debarring, debarred). To hinder from approach, entry, or enjoyment.
**Debark,** dē-bärk', *vt.* To disembark.
**Debase,** dē-bās', *vt.* (debasing, debased). To lower; to degrade; to vitiate.
**Debased,** dē-bāst', *p.a.* Adulterated; degraded; vile.
**Debasement,** dē-bās'ment, *n.* Act of debasing; state of being debased.
**Debatable,** dē-bāt'a-bl, *a.* Disputable.
**Debate,** dē-bāt', *n.* Contention in words or arguments; discussion; controversy.—*vt.* (debating, debated). To dispute; to argue; to discuss.—*vi.* To examine different arguments in the mind; to deliberate.
**Debater,** dē-bāt'ėr, *n.* One who debates.
**Debauch,** dē-bach', *vt.* To corrupt; to pervert.—*vi.* To riot; to revel.—*n.* Excess in eating or drinking; lewdness.
**Debauched,** dē-bacht', *p.a.* Vitiated in morals; profligate.
**Debauchee,** deb-o-shē', *n.* One addicted to debauchery; a libertine; a rake.
**Debaucher,** dē-bach'ėr, *n.* One who debauches or corrupts others.
**Debauchery,** dē-bach'ė-ri, *n.* Gluttony; intemperance; habitual lewdness.
**Debenture,** dē-ben'tūr, *n.* A deed charging property with the repayment of money lent, and with interest; a certificate of drawback.
**Debilitate,** dē-bil'i-tāt, *vt.* (debilitating, debilitated). To enfeeble; to enervate.
**Debility,** dē-bil'i-ti, *n.* Weakness; feebleness.
**Debit,** deb'it, *n.* A recorded item of debt; the left-hand page or debtor side of a ledger or account.—*vt.* To charge with debt.
**Debonair,** de-bō-nār', *a.* Gracious; courteous.
**Debouch,** dē-bösh', *vi.* To issue or march out of a narrow place.
**Debris,** dē-brē', *n.sing.* or *pl.* Fragments; rubbish.
**Debt,** det, *n.* That which is due from one person to another; obligation; guilt.
**Debtor,** det'ėr, *n.* One who owes money, goods, or services; one indebted.
**Début,** dā-bu', *n.* First appearance in public.
**Débutant,** dā-bu-tāng; *fem.* **Débutante,** dā-bu-tāngt, *n.* One who makes a début.
**Decade,** de'kād, *n.* The number of ten; a period of ten years.
**Decadence, Decadency,** dē-kā'dens, dē-kā'-den-si or dek'a-, *n.* A falling off; decay.
**Decadent,** dē-kā'dent or dek'a-, *a.* Decaying; deteriorating.
**Decagon,** de'ka-gon, *n.* A figure having ten sides.
**Decahedron,** de-ka-hē'dron, *n.* A solid figure or body having ten sides.
**Decalogue,** de'ka-log, *n.* The ten commandments given by God to Moses.
**Decamp,** dē-kamp', *vi.* To depart from a camp; to march off; to take oneself off.
**Decampment,** dē-kamp'ment, *n.* Departure from a camp; a marching off.
**Decant,** dē-kant', *vt.* To pour from one vessel into another.
**Decanter,** dē-kant'ėr, *n.* A glass bottle used for holding wine or other liquors.
**Decapitate,** dē-kap'it-āt, *vt.* (decapitating, decapitated). To behead.
**Decapitation,** dē-kap'it-ā''shon, *n.* Act of beheading.
**Decapod,** dek'a-pod, *n.* A crustacean having ten feet, as a crab; also a cuttle-fish with ten prehensile arms.
**Decarbonize, decarburize,** dē-kär'bon-īz, dē-kär'bū-rīz, *vt.* To deprive of carbon.
**Decay,** dē-kā', *vi.* To pass from a sound or prosperous state; to waste; to wither; to fail.—*n.* Gradual loss of strength, excellence, etc.; corruption; putrefaction.
**Decease,** dē-sēs', *n.* Departure from this life; death.—*vi.* (deceasing, deceased). To die.
**Deceased,** dē-sēst', *a.* Dead; often as a noun (with *the*).
**Deceit,** dē-sēt', *n.* Fraud; guile; cunning.
**Deceitful,** dē-sēt'ful, *a.* Fraudulent; delusive; false; hollow.
**Deceitfully, dē-sēt'fūl-li,** *adv.* In a deceitful manner.
**Deceivable,** dē-sēv'a-bl, *a.* Capable of being deceived; exposed to imposture.
**Deceive,** dē-sēv', *vt.* (deceiving, deceived). To mislead the mind of; to impose on; to delude; to frustrate (hopes, etc.).
**Deceiver,** dē-sēv'ėr, *n.* One who deceives.
**December,** dē-sem'bėr, *n.* The twelfth and last month of the year.
**Decemvir,** dē-sem'vėr, *n.*; pl. **-viri** or **-virs.** One of ten magistrates, who had absolute authority in Rome in B.C. 449 to 447.
**Decency,** dē'sen-si, *n.* The state or quality of being decent; decorum; modesty.
**Decennial,** dē-sen'ni-al, *a.* Consisting of ten years; happening every ten years.
**Decent,** dē'sent, *a.* Becoming; seemly; respectable; modest; moderate.
**Decently,** dē'sent-li, *adv.* In a decent manner.
**Decentralize,** dē-sen'tral-īz, *vt.* To remove from direct dependence on a central authority.
**Deception,** dē-sep'shon, *n.* Act of deceiving; state of being deceived; artifice practiced; fraud; double-dealing.
**Deceptive,** dē-sep'tiv, *a.* Tending to deceive; misleading; false; delusive.
**Decidable,** dē-sīd'a-bl, *a.* That may be decided.
**Decide,** dē-sīd', *vt.* (deciding, decided). To determine; to settle; to resolve.—*vi.* To determine; to pronounce a judgment.
**Decided,** dē-sīd'ed, *a.* Clear; resolute.
**Decidely,** dē-sīd'ed-li, *adv.* Clearly; indisputably.
**Deciduous,** dē-sid'ū-us, *a.* Not permanent; having leaves that fall in autumn.
**Decimal,** de'si-mal, *a.* Tenth; reckoned by ten.—*n.* A tenth.
**Decimate,** de'si-māt, *vt.* (decimating, decimated). To kill every tenth man of; to tithe; to destroy a large number of.

**Decimation**, de-si-mā'shon, *n*. Act of decimating; a tithing.
**Decipher**, dē-sī'fėr, *vt*. To explain what is written in ciphers; to read what is not clear; to interpret.
**Decipherable**, dē-sī'fėr-a-bl, *a*. That may be deciphered.
**Decipherer**, dē-sī'fėr-ėr, *n*. One who deciphers.
**Decision**, dē-si'zhon, *n*. Determination of a difference, doubt, or event; final judgment; firmness of purpose or character.
**Decisive**, dē-sī'siv, *a*. Conclusive; absolute; marked by prompt determination.
**Decisively**, dē-sī'siv-li, *adv*. Conclusively.
**Deck**, dek, *vt*. To clothe; to adorn; to furnish with a deck, as a vessel.—*n*. The platform or floor of a ship.
**Decker**, dek'ėr, *n*. One who decks; a ship having decks; as, a three-decker.
**Declaim**, dē-klām', *vi*. To make a formal speech; to harangue; to inveigh.
**Declaimer**, dē-klām'ėr, *n*. One who declaims.
**Declamation**, de-kla-mā'shon, *n*. The art or act of declaiming; a harangue.
**Declamatory**, dē-klam'a-to-ri, *a*. Relating to the practice of declaiming; rhetorical, without solid sense or argument.
**Declarable**, dē-klār'a-bl, *a*. That may be declared or proved.
**Declaration**, de-kla-rā'shon, *n*. Act of declaring; that which is declared; an explicit statement; a solemn affirmation.
**Declarative**, dē-klar'at-iv, *a*. Explanatory; making proclamation.
**Declaratory**, dē-kla'ra-to-ri, *a*. Making declaration or manifestation; expressive.
**Declare**, dē-klār', *vt*. (declaring, declared). To show clearly; to tell explicitly; to testify; to reveal.—*vi*. To make a declaration.
**Declared**, dē-klārd', *p.a*. Made known; avowed; openly professed.
**Declension**, dē-klen'shon, *n*. The act or state of declining; refusal; the change of the terminations of nouns, adjectives, and pronouns to form the oblique cases.
**Declinable**, dē-klīn'a-bl, *a*. That may be declined.
**Declination**, dē-klin-ā'shon, *n*. A bending downwards; decay; deviation from rectitude; angular distance of a heavenly body north or south from the equator; variation of the magnetic needle from the true meridian of a place.
**Decline**, dē-klīn', *vi*. (declining, declined). To bend downwards; to serve; to fail; not to comply.—*vt*. To bend downward; to refuse; to change the termination of a noun, etc.—*n*. A falling off; decay; deterioration; consumption.
**Declinometer**, dek-lī-nom'et-ėr, *n*. An instrument for measuring the declination of the magnetic needle.
**Declivity**, dē-kli'vi-ti, *n*. Inclining downward; a downward slope.
**Decoct**, dē-kokt', *vt*. To prepare by boiling; to digest by heat.
**Decoction**, dē-kok'shon, *n*. The act of boiling a substance in water to extract its virtues; the preparation thus obtained.
**Decollate**, dē-kol'āt, *vt*. To behead.
**Decolorate, Decolorize**, dē-kul'ėr-āt, dē-kul'ėr-īz, *vt*. To deprive of color.
**Decomposable**, dē-kom-pōz'a-bl, *a*. That may be decomposed.
**Decompose**, dē-kom-pōz, *vt*. To resolve into original elements.—*vi*. To become resolved into elementary particles; to decay.
**Decomposition**, dē-kom'pō-zi''shon, *n*. Act or process of decomposing; analysis; decay.
**Decompound**, dē-kom-pound', *a*. Compounded a second time.
**Decorate**, dek'ō-rāt, *vt*. (decorating, decorated). To adorn; to embellish.
**Decoration**, dek'ō-rā'shon, *n*. Act of decorating; that which adorns; a badge or medal.
**Decorative**, dek'ō-rāt-iv, *a*. Suited to adorn.
**Decorator**, dek'ō-rāt-ėr, *n*. One who decorates buildings by painting, etc.
**Decorous**, dē-kō'rus, *a*. Seemly; becoming; behaving with strict propriety.
**Decorum**, dē-kō'rum, *n*. Propriety of speech or behavior; seemliness.
**Decoy**, dē-koi', *n*. An enclosure for catching ducks or wild fowls; a lure.—*vt*. To lure into a snare; to entice.
**Decrease**, dē-krēs', *vi*. (decreasing, decreased). To grow less.—*vt*. To cause to become less.—*n*. Gradual diminution; decay; the wane of the moon.
**Decree**, dē-krē', *n*. An edict; an order or law; predetermined purpose; judicial decision.—*vt*. (decreeing, decreed). To enact; to award; to determine judicially.—*vi*. To make an edict; to appoint by edict.
**Decrement**, de'krē-ment, *n*. Decrease; quantity lost by diminution or waste.
**Decrepit**, dē-krep'it, *a*. Broken down with age; being in the last stage of decay.
**Decrepitate**, dē-krep'it-āt, *vt*. To calcine in a strong heat, with a continual crackling of the substance.—*vi*. To crackle when roasting.
**Decrepitation**, dē-krep'it-ā''shon, *n*. The separation of parts with a crackling noise.
**Decrepitude**, dē-krep'it-ūd, *n*. The crazy state of the body produced by decay or age.
**Decretal**, dē-krēt'al, *a*. Containing a decree.—*n*. A decree of the pope; a collection of papal decrees.
**Decretive**, dē-krēt'iv, *a*. Having the force of a decree; making a decree.
**Decretory**, de'krē-to-ri, *a*. Established by a decree; judicial; definitive.
**Decrial**, dē-krī-al, *n*. The act of decrying.
**Decry**, dē-krī', *vt*. To cry down; to rail against; to censure; to depreciate.
**Decumbent**, dē-kum'bent, *a*. Lying down; recumbent; prostrate.
**Decuple**, dē-kū-pl, *a*. Tenfold.—*n*. A number ten times repeated.
**Decussate**, dē-kus'āt, *vt*. and *i*. To intersect; to cross.—*a*. Crossing; intersected.
**Dedicate**, ded'i-kāt, *vt*. (dedicating, dedicated). To consecrate to a sacred purpose; to devote (often refl.); to inscribe to a friend.
**Dedication**, ded-i-kā'shon, *n*. Act of devoting to some person, use, or thing; inscription or address.
**Dedicator**, ded'i-kāt-ėr, *n*. One who dedicates.
**Dedicatory**, ded'i-kā-to-ri, *a*. Serving to dedicate, or as a dedication.
**Deduce**, dē-dūs', *vt*. (deducing, deduced). To draw or bring; to gather from premises; to infer; to derive.
**Deducible**, dē-dūs'i-bl, *a*. That may be deduced or inferred.
**Deduct**, dē-dukt', *vt*. To subtract.
**Deduction**, dē-duk'shon, *n*. Inference; abatement; discount.
**Deductive**, dē-duk'tiv, *a*. That is or may be deduced from premises.
**Deductively**, dē-duk'tiv-li, *adv*. In a deductive manner; by deduction.
**Deed**, dēd, *n*. That which is done; an act; feat; reality; a written agreement; an instrument conveying real estate.
**Deem**, dēm, *vt*. To judge; to think.—*vi*. To judge; to be of opinion; to estimate.
**Deemster**, dēm'stėr, *n*. One of the two chief-justices of the Isle of Man.
**Deep**, dēp, *a*. Being far below the surface; descending far downward; low in situation; not obvious; sagacious; designing; grave in sound; very still or solemn; thick; strongly colored; mysterious; heartfelt; absorbed.—*n*. The sea; the abyss of waters; any abyss.
**Deepen**, dēp'n, *vt*. To make deep or deeper.—*vi*. To become more deep.
**Deep-laid**, dēp'lād, *a*. Formed with great skill or artifice.

**Deeply,** dēp'li, *adv.* At or to a great depth; profoundly.
**Deer,** dēr, *n. sing.* and *pl.* A quadruped of several species, as the stag, the fallow-deer, the roebuck, the reindeer, etc.
**Deer-stalking,** dēr'stak-ing, *n.* The hunting of deer on foot, by stealing within shot of them unawares.
**Deface,** dē'fās', *vt.* To destroy or mar the surface of a thing; to disfigure; to erase.
**Defacement,** dē-fās'ment, *n.* Injury to the surface or beauty; obliteration; that which mars or disfigures.
**Defalcate,** dē-fal'kāt, *vt.* To take away or deduct.
**Defalcation,** dē-fal-kā'shon, *n.* A deficit; a fraudulent abstraction of money.
**Defalcator,** def'al-kāt-ėr, *n.* One guilty of defalcation or embezzlement.
**Defamation,** de-fa-mā'shon, *n.* Act of defaming; slander; calumny.
**Defamatory,** dē-fam'a-to-ri, *a.* Calumnious; slanderous.
**Defame,** dē-fām', *vt.* (defaming, defamed). To accuse falsely and maliciously; to slander.
**Defamer,** dē-fām'ėr, *n.* A slanderer.
**Default,** dē-falt', *n.* An omission; neglect to do what duty or law requires; failure to appear in court.—*vi.* To fail in fulfilling an engagement, contract, etc.
**Defaulter,** dē-falt'ėr, *n.* One who makes default; one who fails to account for money entrusted to his care; a delinquent.
**Defeat,** dē-fēt', *n.* Frustration; overthrow; loss of battle.—*vt.* To frustrate; to foil, to overthrow; to conquer.
**Defecate,** de'fē-kāt, *vt.* To clear from lees; to purify.—*vi.* To void excrement.
**Defecation,** de-fē-kā'shon, *n.* Act of separating from lees; purification.
**Defect,** dē-fekt', *n.* Want; a blemish; fault; flaw.
**Defection,** dē-fek'shon, *n.* Act of abandoning a person or cause; apostasy.
**Defective,** dē-fekt'iv, *a.* Having a defect; deficient; faulty.
**Defectively,** dē-fekt'iv-li, *adv.* In a defective manner.
**Defend,** dē-fend', *vt.* To guard; to support; to resist; to vindicate; to act as defendant.—*vi.* To make defense or opposition.
**Defendant,** dē-fen'dant, *n.* A defender; in *law,* the person that opposes a charge, etc.
**Defender,** dē-fend'ėr, *n.* One who defends; a protector, supporter, or vindicator.
**Defense,** dē-fens', *n.* A guarding against danger; protection; fortification; vindication; apology; plea; method adopted by one against whom legal proceedings are taken; skill in fencing.
**Defenseless,** dē-fens'les, *a.* Without defense; unprotected; weak.
**Defensible,** dē-fens'i-bl, *a.* That may be vindicated, maintained, or justified.
**Defensive,** dē-fens'iv, *a.* Proper for defense; carried on in resisting attack; in a state or posture to defend.—*n.* That which defends; state or posture of defense.
**Defensory,** dē-fens'o-ri, *a.* Tending to defend.
**Defer,** dē-fėr', *vt.* (deferring, deferred). To put off to a future time; to postpone.—*vi.* To yield to another's opinion; to submit courteously or from respect.
**Deference,** de'fėr-ens, *n.* A yielding in opinion; regard; respect; submission.
**Deferential,** de-fėr-en'shal, *a.* Expressing or implying deference; respectful.
**Deferentially,** de-fėr-en'shal-li, *adv.* With deference.
**Deferment,** dē-fėr-ment, *n.* Postponement.
**Defiance,** dē-fī'ans, *n.* Act of defying; a challenge to fight; contempt of opposition or danger.
**Defiant,** dē-fī'ant, *a.* Characterized by defiance, boldness, or insolence.
**Deficiency, Deficience,** de-fi'shen-si, de-fi'shens, *n.* Want; defect.
**Deficient,** de-fi'shent, *a.* Defective; imperfect; not adequate.
**Deficit,** de'fi-sit, *n.* Deficiency of revenue.
**Defile,** dē-fīl', *vt.* (defiling, defiled). To make foul; to pollute; to violate the chastity of; to march off in a line, or file by file.—*n.* A narrow way in which troops may march only in a line, or with a narrow front; a long narrow pass.
**Defilement,** dē-fīl'ment, *n.* Act of defiling, or state of being defiled.
**Defiler,** dē-fīl'ėr, *n.* One who defiles.
**Definable,** dē-fīn'a-bl, *a.* That may be defined.
**Define,** dē-fīn', *vt.* (defining, defined). To limit; to explain exactly.
**Definite,** de'fin-it, *a.* Having fixed limits; precise; exact; clear.
**Definitely,** de'fin-it-li, *adv.* Precisely.
**Definition,** de-fi-ni'shon, *n.* The act of defining; a brief description of a thing by its properties; an explanation in words.
**Definitive,** dē-fin'it-iv, *a.* Limiting; positive; determining; final.—*n.* A word used to limit the signification of a noun.
**Definitively,** dē-fin'it-iv-li, *adv.* In a definitive manner.
**Deflagrate,** de'flā-grāt, *vi.* To burn with a sudden and violent combustion.—*vt.* To set fire to.
**Deflagration,** de-flā-grā'shon, *n.* A sudden and violent combustion.
**Deflagrator,** de'flā-grāt-ėr, *n.* An instrument for producing rapid combustion.
**Deflect,** dē-flekt', *vi.* To deviate; to swerve.—*vt.* To cause to turn aside.
**Deflection, Deflexion, Deflexure,** dē-flek'shon, dē-flek'sūr, *n.* Deviation; a turning from a ture line or regular course.
**Defloration,** dē-flōr-ā'shon, *n.* Act of deflowering; rape.
**Deflower, Deflour,** dē-flou'ėr, dē-flour', *vt.* To strip of flowers, or of bloom and beauty; to deprive of virginity.
**Defluxion,** dē-fluk'shon, *n.* A discharge of fluid from a mucous membrane.
**Defoliation,** dē-fō'li-ā''shon, *n.* The fall of the leaf, or shedding of leaves.
**Deform,** dē-form', *vt.* To mar in form; to disfigure.
**Deformation,** dē-form-ā'shon, *n.* A disfiguring or defacing.
**Deformed,** dē-formd', *a.* Disfigured; distorted; misshapen.
**Deformity,** dē-form'i-ti, *n.* Want of proper form; distortion; gross deviation from propriety.
**Defraud,** dē-frad', *vt.* To deprive of or withhold from wrongfully.
**Defray,** dē-frā', *vt.* To discharge or pay, as the expenses of anything.
**Defrayal, Defrayment,** dē-frā'al, dē-frā'ment, *n.* The act of defraying.
**Deft,** deft, *a.* Apt; clever.
**Deftly,** deft'li, *adv.* Aptly; fitly; neatly.
**Defunct,** dē-fungkt', *a.* Dead; deceased.—*n.* A dead person; one deceased.
**Defy,** dē-fī', *vt.* (defying, defied). To provoke to combat; to dare; to challenge; to set at nought.
**De-gauss,** dē-gous, *vt.* To neutralize the magnetization of a ship so as to prevent it from exploding magnetic mines.
**Degeneracy,** dē-jen'ė-ra-si, *n.* a growing worse or inferior; decline in good qualities; departure from the virtue of ancestors.
**Degenerate,** dē-jen'ė-rat, *vi.* To become worse than one's kind; to decay in good qualities. —*a.* Fallen from primitive or natural excellence; mean; corrupt.
**Degeneration,** dē-jen'ė-rā''shon, *n.* A degenerate state; degeneracy; deterioration.
**Deglutition,** dē-glū-ti'shon, *n.* Act or power of swallowing.
**Degradation,** de-gra-dā'shon, *n.* Act of degrading; state of being degraded; debasement; disgrace; a gradual wasting away.
**Degrade,** dē-grād', *vt.* (degrading, degraded). To reduce to a lower rank; to strip of honors, to de-

base; to depose; to dishonor.
**Degraded,** dē-grād'ed, *p.a.* Sunk to an abject state; exhibiting degradation; debased.
**Degrading,** dē-grād'ing, *p.a.* Dishonoring.
**Degree,** dē-grē', *n.* A step; step in relationship, rank quality, etc.; measure; extent; the 360th part of the circumference of a circle; a mark of distinction conferred by universities; divisions marked on scientific instruments.
**Dehisce,** dē-his', *vi.* To open, as seed-vessels.
**Dehort,** dē-hort', *vt.* To dissuade.
**Dehydration,** dē-hī-drā'shon, *n.* Process of freeing a compound from water.
**Deiform,** dē'i-form, *a.* Of a god-like form.
**Deify,** dē'i-fī, *vt.* (deifying, deified). To exalt to the rank of a deity; to extol as an object of supreme regard.
**Deign,** dān, *vi.* To vouchsafe; to condescend.—*vt.* To condescend to give.
**Deism,** dē'izm, *n.* The doctrine of a deist.
**Deist,** dē'ist, *n.* One who acknowledges the existence of a God, but denies revealed religion; a freethinker.
**Deistic, Deistical,** dē-ist'ik, dē-ist'ik-al, *a.* Pertaining to deism or to deists.
**Deity,** dē'i-ti, *n.* Godhead; the Supreme Being; a fabulous god or goddess; a divinity.
**Deject,** dē-jekt', *vt.* To dispirit; to depress.
**Dejected,** dē-jekt'ed, *p.a.* Cast down; depressed; grieved; discouraged.
**Dejection,** dē-jek'shon, *n.* Depression; melancholy; lowness of spirits.
**Déjeuner,** dā-zhö-nā, *n.* Breakfast; luncheon.
**Delaine,** dē-lān', *n.* A figured muslin made of cotton and wool.
**Delay,** dē-lā', *vt.* To defer; to retard; to stop; to protract.—*vi.* To linger; to stop for a time.—*n.* A lingering; stay; hindrance.
**Delectable,** dē-lekt'a-bl, *a.* Delightful.
**Delectation,** dē-lek-tā'shon, *n.* A giving of pleasure or delight.
**Delegate,** de'lē-gāt, *vt.* (delegating, delegated). To send as a representative; to depute; to commit to another's care.—*n.* A representative; a deputy.
**Delegation,** de-lē-gā'shon, *n.* Act of delegating; persons delegated; a commission.
**Delete,** dē-lēt', *vt.* (deleting, deleted). To blot out; to erase; to efface.
**Deleterious,** de-lē-te'ri-us, *a.* Hurtful; poisonous; pernicious.
**Deletion,** dē-lē'shon, *n.* Act of deleting; an erasure; passage deleted.
**Delf,** delf, *n.* Earthenware, covered with enamel or white glazing in imitation of chinaware or porcelain.
**Deliberate,** dē-lib'ė-rāt, *vi.* To weigh well in one's mind; to consider; to consult; to debate.—*vt.* To balance well in the mind; to consider.—*a.* Cautious; discreet; well advised.
**Deliberately,** dē-lib'ė-rāt-li, *adv.* In a deliberate manner; slowly; cautiously.
**Deliberation,** dē-lib'ė-rā''shon, *n.* Thoughtful consideration; prudence; discussion of reasons for and against a measure.
**Deliberative,** dē-lib'ė-rāt-iv, *a.* Proceeding or acting by deliberation; having a right to deliberate.
**Delicacy,** de'li-ka-si, *n.* The quality of being delicate; fineness of texture; tenderness; minute accuracy; refined taste; a dainty.
**Delicate,** de'li-kāt, *a.* Pleasing to the taste or senses; choice; fine; soft; smooth; nice in forms; minute; easily hurt or affected; tender; not robust.
**Delicately,** de'li-kāt-li, *adv.* In a delicate manner; finely.
**Delicious,** dē-li'shus, *a.* Highly pleasing to the taste; delightful.
**Delight,** dē-līt', *n.* That which yields great pleasure; a high degree of pleasure; joy.—*vt.* To affect with great pleasure; to give high satisfaction to.—*vi.* To take great pleasure; to be rejoiced.
**Delighted,** dē-līt'ed, *a.* Experiencing delight; charmed.
**Delightful,** dē-līt'ful, *a.* Affording great pleasure and satisfaction; charming.
**Delimit,** dē-lim'it, *vt.* To mark or settle distinctly the limits of.
**Delimitation,** dē-lim'i-tā''shon, *n.* The act of delimiting; fixing of boundaries.
**Delineate,** dē-lin'ē-āt, *vt.* To draw the lines showing the form of; to sketch; to describe.
**Delineation,** dē-lin'ē-ā''shon, *n.* Act of delineating; outline; sketch; description.
**Delineator,** dē-lin'ē-āt-ėr, *n.* One who delineates.
**Delinquency,** dē-lin'kwen-si, *n.* An omission of duty; fault; offense; crime.
**Delinquent,** dē-lin'kwent, *a.* Neglecting duty.—*n.* One who fails to perform his duty; one who commits a fault or crime.
**Delirious,** dē-li'ri-us, *a.* Disordered in intellect; raving; frenzied; insane.
**Delirium,** dē-li'ri-um, *n.* Temporary disorder of the mind; violent excitement.
**Delitescence. Delitescency,** del-i-tes'ens, del-i-tes'en-si, *n.* The state of being concealed, or not active or manifest.
**Deliver,** dē-liv'ėr, *vt.* To free, as from danger or bondage; to disburden a woman of a child; to surrender; to commit; to give forth in words or in action.
**Deliverance,** dē-liv'ėr-ans, *n.* Release; rescue; an authoritative judgment.
**Deliverer,** dē-liv'ėr-ėr, *n.* One who delivers.
**Delivery,** dē-liv'ė-ri, *n.* Act of delivering; childbirth; rescue; surrender; distribution (of letters); manner of speaking.
**Dell,** del, *n.* A small valley; a glen.
**Delta,** del'ta, *n.* The space between diverging mouths of a river, as the Nile.
**Deltoid,** del'toid, *a.* Triangular.
**Delude,** dē-lūd', *vt.* (deluding, deluded). To impose on; to deceive; to circumvent.
**Deluge,** del'ūj, *n.* A flood; an inundation; the flood in the days of Noah; a sweeping or overwhelming calamity.—*vt.* (deluging, deluged). To inundate; to drown; to overwhelm.
**Delusion,** dē-lū'zhon, *n.* Act of deluding; a false belief; illusion; fallacy.
**Delusive,** dē-lū'siv, *a.* Apt to deceive.
**Delusory,** dē-lū'so-ri, *a.* Delusive.
**Delve,** delv, *vt.* and *i.* (delving, delved). To dig.
**Delver,** delv'ėr, *n.* One who delves.
**Demagnetize,** dē-mag'net-īz, *vt.* To deprive of magnetic polarity.
**Demagogue,** dem'a-gog, *n.* A leader of the people; a factious orator.
**Demand,** dē-mand', *vt.* To seek as due by right; to require; to interrogate.—*n.* A claim by virtue of a right; an asking with authority; debt; the calling for in order to purchase; desire to purchase or possess.
**Demandable,** dē-mand'a-bl, *a.* That may be demanded.
**Demandant,** dē-man'dant, *n.* One who demands; the plaintiff in a real action.
**Demarcation,** dē-mär-kā'shon, *n.* Act of setting a limit; a limit fixed.
**Demean,** dē-mēn', *vt.* To conduct; to behave; to debase (oneself).
**Demeanor,** dē-mēn'ėr, *n.* Manner of conducting oneself; behavior.
**Demented,** dē-ment'ed, *a.* Insane; infatuated.
**Demerit,** dē-me'rit, *n.* Fault; vice.
**Demesne,** de-mān', *n.* The land adjacent to a manor-house kept in the proprietor's own hands; a domain or region.
**Demi-god,** de'mi-god, *n.* Half a god; one partaking of the divine nature.
**Demi-monde,** demi'mongd, *n.* The class of fashionable courtesans.
**Demisable,** dē-mīz'a-bl, *a.* That may be demised.
**Demise,** dē-mīz', *n.* Death; conveyance of an estate by lease or will.—*vt.* (demising, demised).

To transfer; to lease; to bequeath.
**Demission,** dē-mi'shon, *n.* A laying down office; resignation; transference.
**Demit,** dē-mit', *vt.* (demitting, demitted). To lay down formally, as an office.
**Demiurge, Demiurgus,** dē'mi-ėrj, dē-mi-ėr-gus, *n.* A maker; the Creator.
**Demobilize,** dē-mō'bil-īz, *vt.* To disband.
**Democracy,** dē-mok'ra-si, *n.* A form of government in which the supreme power is vested in the people.
**Democrat,** dem'ō-krat, *n.* One who adheres to democracy.
**Democratic, Democratical,** dem-ō-krat'ik, dem-ō-krat'ik-al, *a.* Pertaining to democracy.
**Demogorgon,** dē-mō-gor'gon, *n.* A terrifying divinity in ancient mythology.
**Demoiselle,** dem-wä-zel', *n.* A damsel.
**Demolish,** dē-mol'ish, *vt.* To pull down; to destroy.
**Demolition,** dē-mō-li'shon, *n.* Act of demolishing; ruin; destruction.
**Demon,** dē'mon, *n.* A spirit, holding a place below the celestial deities of the pagans; an evil spirit; a devil; a fiend-like man.
**Demonetize,** dē-mon'e-tīz, *vt.* To deprive of standard value, as money; to withdraw from circulation.
**Demoniac,** dē-mō'ni-ak, *n.* A human being possessed by a demon.
**Demoniac, Demoniacal,** dē-mō'ni-ak, dē-mō-nī'ak-al, *a.* Pertaining to demons; influenced or produced by demons.
**Demonism,** dē'mon-izm, *n.* Belief in demons.
**Demonize,** dē'mon-īz, *vt.* To fill with the spirit of a demon.
**Demonology,** dē-mon-ol'o-ji, *n.* Knowledge of, or a treatise on, evil spirits.
**Demonstrable,** de-mon'stra-bl, *a.* That may be demonstrated or proved.
**Demonstrably,** de-mon'stra-bli, *adv.* In a manner to preclude doubt.
**Demonstrate,** de-mon'strāt, *vt.* (demonstrating, demonstrated). To prove beyond doubt; to make evident; to exhibit.
**Demonstration,** de-mon-strā'shon, *n.* Act or process of demonstrating; proof; massing of troops to deceive the enemy; a gathering to exhibit sympathy with a person or cause.
**Demonstrative,** de-mon'strāt-iv, *a.* Serving to demonstrate; outwardly expressive of feelings; indicating clearly.
**Demonstrator,** de'mon-strāt-ėr, *n.* One who demonstrates.
**Demoralization,** dē-mo'ral-īz-ā''shon, *n.* Act of demoralizing.
**Demoralize,** dē-mo'ral-īz, *vt.* To corrupt the morals of; to deprave.
**Demoralizing,** dē-mo'ral-īz-ing, *p.a.* Tending to destroy morals or moral principles.
**Demos,** dē'mos, *n.* The people at large.
**Demotic,** dē-mot'ik, *a.* Pertaining to the common people; applied to the popular alphabet of the ancient Egyptians, as distinguished from the *hieratic.*
**Demulcent,** dē-mul'sent, *a.* Softening; mollifying.—*n.* A medicine to soothe irritation.
**Demur,** dē-mėr, *vi.* (demurring, demurred). To hesitate; to object.—*n.* Pause; suspense of proceeding or decision; objection stated.
**Demure,** dē-mūr', *a.* Consciously grave; affectedly modest.
**Demurrage,** dē-mu'rāj, *n.* Delay of a vessel, railway wagon, etc., in loading or unloading; compensation for such delay; charge for the exchange of notes or coin into bullion.
**Demurrer,** dē-mėr'ėr, *n.* One who demurs; a stop at some point in law pleadings; an issue on matter of law.
**Demy,** dē-mī', *n.* A particular size of paper, generally 22 × 17 inches.
**Den,** den, *n.* A cave; a dell; a haunt.
**Denary,** dē-na-ri, *a.* Containing ten; proceeding by tens.—*n.* The number ten.
**Dendriform,** den'dri-form, *a.* Having the form or appearance of a tree.
**Dendritic, Dendritical,** den-drit'ik, den-drit'i-kal, *a.* Resembling a tree; marked by figures resembling shrubs, moss, etc.
**Denial,** dē-nī'al, *n.* Act of denying; contradiction; refusal to grant or acknowledge.
**Denigrate,** den'i-grāt, *vt.* To blacken; to sully.
**Denim,** den'im, *n.* A coarse cotton drill used for making aprons, overalls, etc.
**Denizen,** de'ni-zn, *n.* A stranger admitted to residence in a foreign country.
**Denominate,** dē-nom'in-āt, *vt.* (denominating, denominated). To name; to designate.
**Denomination,** dē-nom'in-ā''shon, *n.* Act of naming; title; class; religious sect.
**Denominational,** dē-nom'in-ā''shon-al, *a.* Pertaining to a denomination.
**Denominationalism,** dē-nom'in-ā''shon-al-izm, *n.* A class spirit; system of religious sects having each their own schools.
**Denominative,** dē-nom'in-āt-iv, *a.* That confers a distinct appellation.
**Denominator,** dē-nom'in-āt-ėr, *n.* One who or that which denominates; that number placed below the line in vulgar fractions.
**Denotable,** dē-nōt'a-bl, *a.* That may be denoted or marked.
**Denote,** dē-nōt', *vt.* To indicate; to imply.
**Dénouement,** dā-nö'mäng, *n.* The winding up of a plot in a novel or drama; solution of a mystery; issue; the event.
**Denounce,** dē-nouns', *vt.* (denouncing, denounced). To threaten; to accuse publicly; to stigmatize.
**Denouncement,** dē-nouns'ment, *n.* Act of denouncing; denunciation.
**Dense,** dens, *a.* Thick; close; compact.
**Density,** dens'i-ti, *n.* Closeness of constituent parts; compactness.
**Dent,** dent, *n.* A mark made by a blow on a solid body.—*vt.* To make a dent on.
**Dental,** den'tal, *a.* Pertaining to the teeth; pronounced by the teeth and the tip of the tongue.—*n.* A dental letter or sound, as *d, t, th.*
**Dentate, Dentated,** den'tāt, den'tāt-ed, *a.* Toothed; notched.
**Denticle,** den'ti-kl, *n.* A small tooth or projecting point.
**Denticulate, Denticulated,** den-tik'ū-lāt, den-tik'ū-lāt-ed, *a.* Having small teeth.
**Dentiform,** den'ti-form, *a.* Having the form of a tooth.
**Dentrifrice,** den'ti-fris, *n.* A powder or other substance for cleansing the teeth.
**Dentine,** den'tin, *n.* The ivory tissue forming the body of the tooth.
**Dentist,** den'tist, *n.* One whose occupation is to extract, repair, or replace teeth.
**Dentition,** den-ti'shon, *n.* The cutting of teeth in infancy; the system of teeth peculiar to an animal.
**Denture,** den'tūr, *n.* A set of false teeth.
**Denudation,** dē-nūd-ā'shon, *n.* Act of denuding; exposure of rocks by the action of water.
**Denude,** dē-nūd', *vt.* (denuding, denuded). To make bare; to divest; to uncover.
**Denunciation,** dē-nun'si-ā''shon, *n.* Act of denouncing; public menace; arraignment.
**Denunciator,** dē-nun'si-āt-ėr, *n.* One who denounces or threatens publicly.
**Denunciatory,** dē-nun'si-a-to-ri, *a.* Characterized by denunciation; ready to denounce.
**Deny,** dē-nī', *vt.* (denying, denied). To declare not to be true; to disavow; to refuse to grant or acknowledge; not to afford or yield.
**Deodorize,** dē-ō'dėr-īz, *vt.* (deodorizing, deodorized). To deprive of fetid odor.
**Deodorizer, Deodorant,** dē-ō'dėr-ī-zėr, dē-ō'dėr-ant, *n.* A substance which destroys fetid effluvia.
**Deoxidate, Deoxidize,** dē-ok'sīd-āt, dē-ok'sīd-īz,

*vt.* To reduce from the state of an oxide.
**Deoxidation,** dē-ok'sīd-ā''shon, *n.* The act or process of deoxidating.
**Depart,** dē-pärt', *vi.* To go away; to desist; to abandon; to deviate; to die.
**Department,** dē-pärt'ment, *n.* A separate part; a division of territory; a distinct branch, as of science, etc.
**Departmental,** dē-pärt'ment-al, *a.* Pertaining to a department.
**Departure,** dē-pärt'ūr, *n.* Act of going away; withdrawal; abandonment; death.
**Depend,** dē-pend', *vi.* To hang from; to be contingent or conditioned; to rest or rely solely; to trust.
**Dependant, Dependent,** dē-pend'ant, dē-pend'ent, *n.* One who depends on another; a retainer. (The spelling with *-ant* is more common in the noun, with *-ent* in the adj.).
**Dependence, Dependance,** dē-pend'ens, dē-pend'ans, *n.* State of being dependent; connection and support; reliance; trust.
**Dependency,** dē-pend'en-si, *n.* State of being dependent; that which is dependent; a subject territory.
**Dependent, Dependant,** dē-pend'ent, dē-pend'ant, *a.* Hanging down; subordinate; relying solely on another; contingent.
**Dependently, Dependantly,** dē-pend'ent-li, dē-pend'ant-li, *adv.* In a dependent manner.
**Depict,** dē-pikt', *vt.* To paint; to delineate; to represent in words.
**Depilate,** dep'i-lāt, *vt.* To strip of hair.
**Depilatory,** dē-pil'ā-to-ri, *n.* An application to remove hair from the skin.
**Deplete,** dē-plēt', *vt.* (depleting, depleted). To empty, reduce, or exhaust.
**Depletion,** dē-plē'shon, *n.* Act of depleting; act of diminishing the quantity of blood by blood-letting.
**Deplorable,** dē-plōr'a-bl, *a.* To be deplored; lamentable; grievous; pitiable.
**Deplorably,** dē-plōr'a-bli, *adv.* In a manner to be deplored.
**Deplore,** dē-plōr', *vt.* (deploring, deplored). To feel or express deep grief for; to bewail.
**Deploy,** dē-ploi', *vt.* To open out; to extend from column to line as a body of troops.—*vi.* To form a more extended front or line.
**Deployment,** dē-ploi'ment. The act of deploying.
**Deplume,** dē-plūm', *vt.* To strip of feathers.
**Depolarize,** dē-pō'lär-īz, *vt.* To deprive of polarity.
**Depone,** dē-pōn', *vi.* (deponing, deponed). To give testimony; to depose.
**Deponent,** dē-pōn'ent, *a.* Laying down; that has a passive form but an active signification.—*n.* One who gives testimony under oath; a deponent verb.
**Depopulate,** dē-po'pū-lāt, *vt.* To deprive of inhabitants; to dispeople.
**Depopulation,** dē-po'pū-lā''shon, *n.* Act or process of depopulating; decrease of population.
**Depopulator,** dē-po'pū-lāt-ėr, *n.* One who or that which depopulates.
**Deport,** dē-pōrt', *vt.* To transport; to demean; to conduct (oneself).
**Deportation,** dē-pōrt-ā'shon, *n.* Removal from one country to another; exile.
**Deportment,** dē-pōrt'ment, *n.* Carriage; demeanor; manner of acting.
**Deposable,** dē-pōz'a-bl, *a.* That may be deposed or deprived of office.
**Depose,** dē-pōz', *vt.* (deposing, deposed). To dethrone; to divest of office; to degrade.—*vi.* To bear witness; to give testimony in writing.
**Deposit,** dē-poz'it, *vt.* To lay down; to lodge in a place; to lay in a place for preservation; to intrust; to commit as a pledge.—*n.* Any matter laid down or lodged; anything intrusted to another; a thing given as security.
**Depositary,** dē-poz'it-a-ri, *n.* One to whom a thing is lodged in trust; a guardian.
**Deposition,** dē-pō-zi'shon, *n.* Act of depositing and of deposing; attested written testimony; declaration; act of dethroning a king, or degrading an official.
**Depositor,** dē-poz'it-ėr, *n.* One who makes a deposit; one who lodges money in a bank.
**Depository,** dē-poz'it-o-ri, *n.* A place where anything is lodged for safe-keeping.
**Depot,** dep'ō, *n.* A place of deposit; headquarters of a regiment; a railway-station.
**Depravation,** de-pra-vā'shon, *n.* Act of depraving; deterioration; degeneracy.
**Deprave,** dē-prāv', *vt.* (depraving, depraved). To make bad or worse; to impair the good qualities of; to corrupt; to vitiate.
**Depraved,** dē-prāvd', *a.* Given to evil courses; profligate; vitiated.
**Depravity,** dē-prav'i-ti, *n.* Corruption of moral principles; wickedness; profligacy.
**Deprecate,** de'prē-kāt, *vt.* (deprecating, deprecated). To pray for deliverance from; to plead against; to express regret or disapproval.
**Deprecation,** de-prē-kā'shon, *n.* Act of deprecating; protest; disapproval.
**Deprecatory, Deprecative,** de'prē-kā-to-ri, de'prē-kāt-iv, *a.* That serves to deprecate; containing protest or entreaty.
**Depreciate,** dēprē'shi-āt, *vt.* (depreciating, depreciated). To bring down the price or value of; to undervalue; to disparage; to traduce.—*vi.* To fall in value.
**Depreciation,** dē-prē'shi-ā''shon, *n.* Act of depreciating; the falling of value.
**Depreciative, Depreciatory,** dē-prē'shi-āt-iv, dē-prē'shi-ā-to-ri, *a.* Tending to depreciate or undervalue.
**Depredate,** de'prē-dāt, *vt.* To plunder; to waste.
**Depredation,** de-prē-dā'shon, *n.* Act of plundering; pillaging.
**Depredator,** de'prē-dāt-ėr, *n.* One who plunders or pillages; a spoiler.
**Depress,** dē-pres', *vt.* To press down; to lower; to humble; to deject.
**Depressed,** dē-prest', *a.* Dejected; dispirited; flattened in shape.
**Depression,** dē-pre'shon, *n.* Act of depressing; state of being depressed; a low state; a sinking of a surface; a hollow; abasement; dejection; a state of dulness.
**Depressive,** dē-pres'iv, *a.* Able or tending to depress or cast down.
**Deprivation,** de-pri-vā'shon, *n.* Act of depriving; state of being deprived; want; bereavement; deposition of a clergyman.
**Deprive,** dē-prīv', *vt.* (depriving, deprived). To take from; to dispossess; to hinder from possessing or enjoying.
**Depth,** depth, *n.* Deepness; a deep place; the darkest or stillest part, as of the night; the inner part; abstruseness; unsearchableness; intensity; extent of penetration.
**Deputy,** de'pū-ti, *n.* A person appointed to act for another; a substitute; a delegate; an agent.
**Deracinate,** dē-ras'in-āt, *vt.* To pluck up by the roots; to extirpate.
**Derange,** dē-rānj', *vt.* (deranging, deranged). To disturb the regular order of; to displace; to disconcert; to disorder the mind of.
**Deranged,** dē-rānjd', *p.a.* Disordered in mind; distracted.
**Derangement,** dē-rānj'ment, *n.* A putting out of order; disorder; insanity.
**Derelict,** de're-likt, *a.* Abandoned.—*n.* Anything forsaken or left, especially a ship.
**Dereliction,** de-re-lik'shon, *n.* Act of forsaking; state of being forsaken; neglect.
**Deride,** dē-rīd', *vt.* (deriding, derided). To laugh at in contempt; to ridicule; to jeer.
**Derider,** dē-rīd'ėr, *n.* A mocker; scoffer.
**Deridingly,** dē-rīd'ing-li, *adv.* By way of derision or mockery.
**Derision,** dē-ri'zhon, *n.* Act of deriding; scorn; ridicule; mockery.
**Derisive,** dē-rīs'iv, *a.* Mocking; ridiculing.

D

**Derivable,** dē-rīv'a-bl, *a*. That may be drawn or derived; deducible.
**Derivably,** dē-rīv'a-bli, *adv*. By derivation.
**Derivation,** de-ri-vā'shon, *a*. Act of deriving; the tracing of a word from its root; deduction.
**Derivative,** de-riv'āt-iv, *a*. Derived; secondary.—*n*. That which is derived; a word which takes its origin in another word.
**Derivatively,** de-riv'āt-iv-li, *adv*. In a derivative manner; by derivation.
**Derive,** de-rīv', *vt*. (deriving, derived). To draw or receive, as from a source or origin; to trace the etymology of.—*vi*. To come from.
**Derma, Dermis, Derm,** dėr'ma, dėr'mis, dėrm, *n*. The true skin, or under layer of the skin.
**Dermal,** dėr'mal, *a*. Pertaining to skin; consisting of skin.
**Dermatology,** dėr-ma-tol'o-ji, *n*. The science which treats of skin and its diseases.
**Dermo-skelton,** dėr'mo-skel''e-ton, *n*. The covering of scales, plates, shells, etc., of many animals, as crabs, crocodiles, etc.
**Derogate,** de'rō-gāt, *vt*. (derogating, derogated). To detract from; to disparage.—*vi*. To detract.
**Derogation,** de-rō-gā'shon, *n*. Act of derogating; detraction; disparagement.
**Derogatory,** dē-rog'ā-to-ri, *a*. Tending to lessen in repute, effect, etc.; disparaging.
**Derrick,** de'rik, *n*. A kind of crane for hoisting heavy weights.
**Dervish,** dėr'vish, *n*. A poor Mohammedan priest or monk.
**Descant,** des'kant, *n*. A discourse; discussion; a song or tune with various modulations.—*vi*. des-kant'. To discourse or animadvert freely; to add a part to a melody.
**Descend,** dē-send', *vi*. To pass or move down; to invade; to be derived; to pass to an heir.—*vt*. To pass or move down, on, or along.
**Descendant,** dē-send'ant, *n*. Offspring from an ancestor; issue.
**Descendent,** dē-send'ent, *a*. Descending; proceeding from an original or ancestor.
**Descendible,** dē-send'i-bl, *a*. That may be descended or passed down; that may descend from an ancestor to an heir.
**Descending,** dē-send'ing, *p.a*. Moving or bent downward; gradually decreasing.
**Descent,** dē-sent', *n*. Act of descending; declivity; invasion; a passing from an ancestor to an heir; lineage; distance drom the common ancestor; descendants; a rank in the scale of subordination.
**Describable,** dē-skrīb'a-bl, *a*. That may be described.
**Describe,** dē-skrīb', *vt*. (describing, described). To mark or trace out; to represent on paper, etc.; to portray; to relate.
**Description,** dē-skrip'shon, *n*. Act of describing; account; relation; class, species, kind.
**Descriptive,** dē-skrip'tiv, *a*. Containing description; having the quality of representing.
**Descry,** dē-skrī', *vt*. (descrying, descried). To espy; to discover from a distance.
**Desecrate,** de'sē-krāt, *vt*. (desecrating, desecrated). To divert from a sacred purpose; to profane.
**Desecration,** de-sē-krā'shon, *n*. Act of desecrating; profanation.
**Desert,** de'zėrt, *a*. Waste; uncultivated.—*n*. An uninhabited tract; a vast sandy plain.
**Desert,** dē-zėrt', *vt*. To leave, as service; to abandon; to quit.—*vi*. To run away; to quit a service without permission.—*n*. That which is deserved; merit or demerit; reward.
**Deserter,** dē-zėrt'ėr, *n*. One who deserts; a soldier or seaman who quits the service without permission.
**Desertion,** dē-zėr'shon, *n*. Act of deserting; state of being deserted.
**Deserve,** dē-zėrv', *vt*. (deserving, deserved). To merit by qualities or services; to be worthy of.—*vi*. To merit; to be worthy of.
**Deservedly,** dē-zėrv'ed-li, *adv*. Justly; according to desert.
**Deserving,** dē-zėrv'ing, *a*. Worthy of reward or praise; meritorious.
**Deshabille,** dez-a-bēl', *n*. The state of being in undress, or not fully dressed.
**Desiccant, Desiccative,** des'i-kant, or dē-sik'ant, dē-ski'a-tiv, *a*. Drying.—*n*. An application that dries a sore.
**Desiccate,** dē-sik'āt, *vt*. To exhaust of moisture; to dry.
**Desiderate,** dē-sid'ėr-āt, *vt*. To desire; to want; to miss.
**Desiderative,** dē-sid'ėr-āt-iv, *a*. Having, implying, or denoting desire.
**Desideratum,** dē-sid'ėr-ā''tum, *n*.; pl. **-ata** That which is not possessed, but is desirable; something much wanted.
**Design,** dē-sīn', *vt*. To delineate by drawing the outline of; to form in idea; to plan; to propose; to mean.—*vi*. To intend.—*n*. A representation of a thing by an outline; first idea represented by lines; a plan drawn out in the mind; purpose; aim; project.
**Designate,** de'sig-nāt, *vt*. (designating, designated). To point out; to name; to characterize; to appoint; to allot.
**Designation,** de-sig-nā'shon, *n*. Act of designating; appointment; assignment; appellation.
**Designedly,** dē-sīn'ed-li, *adv*. By design; purposely; intentionally.
**Designer,** dē-sīn'ėr, *n*. One who designs; a contriver; a plotter.
**Designing,** dē-sīn'ing, *a*. Artful; intriguing; deceitful; treacherous.
**Desirability,** dē-zīr'a-bil''i-ti, *n*. The state or quality of being desirable.
**Desirable,** dē-zīr'a-bl, *a*. Worthy of desire; pleasing; agreeable.
**Desirably,** dē-zīr'a-bli, *adv*. In a desirable manner.
**Desire,** dē-zīr', *n*. Eagerness to obtain or enjoy; aspiration; longing; a request to obtain; the object of desire; love; lust.—*vt*. (desiring, desired). To wish for the possession or enjoyment of; to covet; to ask; to petition.
**Desirous,** dē-zīr'us, *a*. Full of desire; solicitous to possess and enjoy; eager.
**Desist,** dē-sist', *vi*. To cease to act or proceed; to forbear; to leave off. (With *from*.)
**Desk,** desk, *n*. An inclining table to write or read upon; a portable case for the same purpose; a lectern; a pulpit.
**Desolate,** de'sō-lāt, *a*. Destitute of inhabitants; waste; laid waste; afflicted; forlorn.—*vt*. (desolating, desolated). To deprive of inhabitants; to make desert; to ravage.
**Desolately,** de'sō-lāt-li, *adv*. In a desolate manner.
**Desolation,** de-sō-lā'shon, *n*. Act of desolating; a desolate state or place; melancholy.
**Despair,** dē-spār', *n*. A hopeless state; despondency; that which causes despair; loss of hope.—*vi*. To give up all hope; to despond.
**Desperado,** des-pė-rā'dō, *n*. A desperate fellow; a reckless ruffian.
**Desperate,** des'pė-rāt, *a*. Without care of safety; reckless; frantic; beyond hope; past cure.
**Desperately,** des'pē-rāt-li, *adv*. In a desperate manner.
**Desperation,** des-pė-rā'shon, *n*. A giving up of hope; fury; disregard of danger; despair.
**Despicable,** des'pik-a-bl, *a*. Contemptible; vile; base; mean.
**Despicably,** des'pik-a-bli, *adv*. Meanly.
**Despisable,** dē-spīz'a-bl, *a*. That may be despised; despicable; contemptible.
**Despise,** dē-spīz', *vt*. (despising, despised). To hold in contempt; to scorn; to disdain.
**Despiser,** dē-spīz'ėr, *n*. A contemner; scorner.
**Despite,** dē-spīt', *n*. Extreme malice; defiance with contempt; an act of malice.—*vt*. To despise; to spite.—*prep*. In spite of; notwithstanding.

**Despiteful,** dē-spīt'ful, *a*. Full of spite; malignant.
**Despoil,** dē-spoil', *vt*. To take from by force; to rob; to bereave; to rifle.
**Despond,** dē-spond', *vi*. To be cast down or dejected; to lose heart, hope, or resolution.
**Despondence, Despondency,** dē-spond'ens, dē-spond'en-si, *n*. Hopelessness; dejection.
**Despondent,** dē-spond'ent, *a*. Depressed and inactive in despair; desponding.
**Despondently, Despondingly,** dē-spond'ent-li, dē-spond'ing-li, *adv*. In a despondent manner; without hope.
**Despot,** des'pot, *n*. An absolute ruler (generally in a bad sense); a tyrant.
**Despotic, Despotical,** des-pot'ik, des-pot'ik-al, *a*. Belonging to a despot; absolute in powr; arbitrary; tyrannical.
**Desquamate,** dē-skwā'māt, *vt*. or *i*. to come off in scales; to peel off.
**Dessert,** dē-zėrt', *n*. That which is served at the close of a dinner, as fruits, etc.
**Destination,** des-tin-ā'shon, *n*. Act of destining; ultimate design; predetermined end.
**Destine,** des'tin, *vt*. (destining, destined). To set or appoint to a purpose; to design; to doom; to ordain.
**Destiny,** des'ti-ni, *n*. State appointed or predetermined; fate; invincible necessity.
**Destitute,** des'ti-tūt, *a*. Wanting; needy; comfortless; forlorn.
**Destitution,** des-ti-tū'shon, *n*. Want; poverty; indigence.
**Destroy,** dē-stroi', *vt*. To pull down; to overthrow; to devastate; to annihilate.
**Destroyer,** dē-stroi'ėr, *n*. One who or that which destroys; a swift class of vessel intended for the destruction of torpedo-craft, and itself armed with guns and torpedoes.
**Destructible,** dē-strukt'i-bl, *a*. Liable to destruction.
**Destruction,** dē-struk'shon, *n*. A pulling down; demolition; overthrow; death; slaughter; cause of destruction.
**Destructive,** dē-strukt'iv, *a*. Causing destruction; pernicious; mischievous.
**Destructively,** dē-strukt'iv-li, *adv*. With destruction; ruinously.
**Desuetude,** des'wē-tūd, *n*. Disuse.
**Desultorily,** de'sul-to-ri-li, *adv*. In a desultory manner; without method.
**Desultory,** de'sul-to-ri, *a*. Passing from one subject to another, without order; unconnected; rambling.
**Detach,** dē-tach', *vt*. To separate; to disengage.
**Detached,** dē-tacht', *p.a*. Separate.
**Detachment,** dē-tach'ment, *n*. Act of detaching; a body of troops, or number of ships, sent from the main army or fleet.
**Detail,** dē-tāl, *vt*. To relate in particulars; to specify; in military affairs, to appoint to a particular service.—*n*. dē-tāl' or dē'tāl. An individual fact, circumstance, or portion; an item; a report of particulars.
**Detailed,** dē-tāld', *p.a*. Related in particulars; exact.
**Detain,** dē-tān', *vt*. To keep back or from; to withhold; to arrest; to check; to retard.
**Detainer,** dē-tān'ėr, *n*. One who detains; a holding of what belongs to another.
**Detainment,** dē-tān'ment, *n*. Detention.
**Detect,** dē-tekt', *vt*. To discover; to bring to light.
**Detection,** dē-tek'shon, *n*. Act of detecting; discovery of a person or thing.
**Detective,** dē-tek'tiv, *a*. Skilled or employed in detecting.—*n*. A police officer whose duty is to detect criminals; one who investigates cases for hire.
**Detent,** dē-tent', *n*. A pin, stud, or lever forming a check in a clock, watch, etc.
**Detention,** dē-ten'shon, *n*. Act of detaining; confinement; delay.
**Deter,** dē-tėr', *vt*. (deterring, deterred). To prevent by prohibition or danger; to discourage.
**Deterge,** dē-tėrj', *vt*. To cleanse, purge.
**Detergent,** dē-tėrj'ent, *a*. Cleansing; purging.—*n*. That which cleanses.
**Deteriorate,** dē-tē'ri-ō-rāt, *vi*. (deteriorating, deteriorated). To grow worse; to degenerate.—*vt*. To reduce in quality.
**Deterioration,** dē-tē'ri-o-rā''shon, *n*. The state or process of deteriorating.
**Determent,** dē-tėr'ment, *n*. Act of deterring; that which deters.
**Determinable,** dē-tėr'min-a-bl, *a*. That may be decided or determined.
**Determination,** dē-tėr'min-ā''shon, *n*. Act of determining; firm resolution; judgment; strong direction to a given point; end.
**Determine,** dē-tėr'min, *vt*. (determining, determined). To bound; to fix permanently; to decide; to establish; to give a direction to; to resolve on; to bring to an end.—*vi*. To resolve; to conclude.
**Determined,** dē-tėr'mind, *a*. Resolute.
**Deterrent,** dē-tėr'ent, *a*. Tending or able to deter.—*n*. That which deters.
**Detest,** dē-test', *vt*. To abhor; to loathe.
**Detestable,** dē-test'a-bl, *a*. Extremely hateful; abominable; odious.
**Detestably,** dē-test'a-bli, *adv*. Abominably.
**Detestation,** dē-test-ā'shon, *n*. Extreme hatred; abhorrence; loathing.
**Dethrone,** dē-thrōn', *vt*. (dethroning, dethroned). To divest of royal authority and dignity; to depose.
**Dethronement,** dē-thrōn'ment, *n*. Removal from a throne; deposition.
**Detonate,** de'tō-nāt, *vt*. (detonating, detonated). To cause to explode; to cause to burn with a sudden repot.—*vi*. To explode.
**Detonation,** de-tō-nā'shon, *n*. An explosion made by the inflammation of certain combustible bodies.
**Detonator,** det'ō-nā-tėr, *n*. The device by which fulminate of mercury is made to explode the charge in a torpedo, submarine mine, etc.
**Detract,** dē-trakt', *vt*. To draw away; to disparage.—*vi*. To take away from (especially reputation).
**Detraction,** dē-trak'shon, *n*. Act of detracting; depreciation; slander.
**Detractor,** dē-trakt'ėr, *n*. One who detracts; a slanderer; a muscle which detracts.
**Detriment,** de'tri-ment, *n*. Loss; damage; injury; prejudice; mischief; harm.
**Detrimental,** de-tri-ment'al, *a*. Causing detriment; injurious; hurtful.
**Detritus,** dē-trīt'us, *n*. A mass of matter worn off from solid bodies by attrition; disintegrated materials of rocks.
**Detruncate,** dē-trung'kāt, *vt*. To cut off; to lop; to shorten by cutting.
**Detruncation,** dē-trung-kā'shon, *n*. Act of cutting off.
**Deuce,** dūs, *n*. A card or die with two spots; the devil; perdition.
**Deuterogamist,** dū-tėr-og'a-mist, *n*. One who marries the second time.
**Deuterogamy,** dū-tėr-og'a-mi, *n*. A second marriage.
**Deuteronomy,** dū-tėr-on'o-mi, *n*. The second law, or second giving of the law by Moses; the fifth book of the Pentateuch.
**Devastate,** de'vas-tāt, *vt*. (devastating, devastated). To lay waste; to ravage.
**Devastation,** de-vas-tā'shon, *n*. Act of devastating; state of being devastated; havoc.
**Develop,** dē-vel'up, *vt*. To unfold; to lay open to view; to make to grow.—*vi*. To be unfolded; to become manifest; to grow or expand; to be evolved.
**Development,** dē-vel'up-ment, *n*. Act or process of developing; expansion; growth.
**Deviate,** dē'vi-āt, *vi*. (deviating, deviated). To stray; to wander; to swerve; to err.
**Deviation,** dē-vi-ā'shon, *n*. A turning aside from the right way, course, or line.

**Device,** dē-vīs', *n.* That which is devised; contrivance; scheme; an emblem.
**Devil,** de'vil, *n.* An evil spirit; Satan; a very wicked person; a machine for cutting, tearing, etc.—*vt.* (devilling, devilled). To pepper excessively and broil; to tease or cut up.
**Devilish,** de'vil-ish, *a.* Partaking of the qualities of the devil; diabolical; infernal.
**Devil-may-care,** de'vil-mā-kār, *a.* Rollicking; reckless.
**Devilment,** de'vil-ment, *n.* Roguery.
**Devilry,** de'vil-ri, *n.* Extreme wickedness; wicked mischief.
**Devious,** dē'vi-us, *a.* Out of the common way or track; erring; rambling.
**Devisable,** dē-vīz'a-bl, *a.* That may be devised; that may be bequeathed.
**Devise,** dē-vīz', *vt.* (devising, devised). To form in the mind; to contrive; to invent; to give or bequeath by will.—*n.* Act of bequeathing by will; a will; a share of estate bequeathed.
**Deviser,** de-vīz'ėr, *n.* A contriver; inventor.
**Devisor,** de-vīz'ėr, *n.* One who bequeaths.
**Devoid,** dē-void', *a.* Destitute; not possessing; free from.
**Devoir,** de-vwär', *n.* Service or duty; act of civility or respect.
**Devote,** dē-vōt', *vt.* (devoting, devoted). To set apart by vow; to consecrate; to addict (oneself); to apply closely to; to consign.
**Devoted,** dē-vōt'ed, *a.* Ardent; zealous; strongly attached.
**Devotee,** dev-o-tē', *n.* One wholly devoted, particularly to religion; a votary.
**Devotion,** dē-vō'shon, *n.* Act of devoting or state of being devoted; prayer; devoutness; ardent love or affection; attachment; earnestness.
**Devotional,** dē-vō'shon-al, *a.* Pertaining to devotion; used in devotion.
**Devour,** dē-vour', *vt.* To eat ravenously; to swallow up; to waste; to look on with keen delight.
**Devout,** dē-vout', *a.* Pious; expressing devotion; earnest; solemn.
**Devoutly,** dē-vout'li, *adv.* Piously.
**Dew,** dū, *n.* Moisture from the atmosphere condensed into drops on the surface of cold bodies, as grass, etc.; damp.—*vt.* To wet with dew; to moisten; to damp.
**Dewiness,** dū'i-nes, *n.* State of being dewy.
**Dew-lap,** dū'lap, *n.* The fold of skin that hangs from the throat of oxen, etc.
**Dew-point,** dū'point, *n.* The temperature at which dew begins to form.
**Dewy,** dū'i, *a.* Pertaining to dew; like dew; moist with dew.
**Dexter,** deks'tėr, *a.* Right, as opposed to left.
**Dexterity,** deks-te'ri-ti, *n.* Right-handedness; adroitness; expertness; skill.
**Dexterous,** deks'tėr-us, *a.* Expert in manual acts; adroit; done with dexterity.
**Dexterously,** deks'tėr-us-li, *adv.* With dexterity; expertly; skilfully; artfully.
**Dextrine,** deks'trin, *n.* A gummy matter prepared from starch.
**Dextrose,** deks'tros, *n.* Grape-sugar.
**Dhow,** dou, *n.* An Arab trading vessel.
**Dhurra,** dur'ra, *n.* A kind of millet cultivated in Africa and elsewhere.
**Diabetes,** dī-a-bē'tēz, *n.* Disease characterized by a morbid discharge of urine.
**Diabolic, Diabolical,** dī-a-bol'ik, dī-a-bol'ik-al, *a.* Devilish; atrocious.
**Diabolically,** dī-a-bol'ik-al-li, *adv.* In a diabolical manner; very wickedly.
**Diaconal,** dī-ak'on-al, *a.* Pertaining to a deacon.
**Diaconate,** dī-ak'on-āt, *n.* Office of a deacon; body of deacons.
**Diacoustics,** dī-a-kous'tiks, *n.* The science of refracted sound.
**Diacritical,** dī-a-krit'ik-al, *a.* Separating; distinctive; applied to a mark used to distinguish letters similar in form.
**Diadem,** dī'a-dem, *n.* A badge of royalty worn on the head; a crown; a coronet.
**Diaeresis,** dī-ē're-sis, *n.* Separation of one syllable into two; a mark signifying such a division, as in *aërial.*
**Diagnose,** dī-ag-nōs', *vt.* To ascertain from symptoms the true nature of.
**Diagnosis,** dī-ag-nō'sis, *n.* The ascertaining from symptoms the true nature of diseases.
**Diagnostic,** dī-ag-nōs'tik, *a.* Pertaining to diagnosis.—*n.* A symptom.
**Diagonal,** dī-ag'on-al, *a.* Extending from one angle to another of a quadrilateral figure; lying in an oblique direction.—*n.* A straight line drawn between opposite angles of a quadrilateral figure.
**Diagonally,** dī-ag'on-al-li, *adv.* In a diagonal direction.
**Diagram,** dī'a-gram, *n.* A drawing to demonstrate the properties of any figure; an illustrative figure in outline.
**Dial,** dī'al, *n.* An instrument for showing the hour by the sun's shadow; face of a clock, etc.
**Dialect,** dī'a-lekt, *n.* The idiom of a language peculiar to a province; language; manner of speaking.
**Dialectal,** dī-a-lek'tal, *a.* Pertaining to a dialect.
**Dialectic, Dialectical,** dī-a-lek'tik, dī-a-lek'tik-al, *a.* Relating to dialectics; pertaining to a dialect or dialects.
**Dialectician,** dī'a-lek-ti''shan, *n.* One skilled in dialectics; a logician; a reasoner.
**Dialectics,** dī-a-lek'tiks, *n.sing.* The art of reasoning; that branch of logic which teaches the rules and modes of reasoning; word-fence. Also **Dialectic** in same sense.
**Dialling,** dī'al-ing, *n.* The science which explains the principles of measuring time by dials; the art of constructing dials.
**Dialogue,** dī'a-log, *n.* A conversation between two or more persons.
**Dial-plate,** dī'al-plāt, *n.* The plate or face of a dial, clock, or watch.
**Diamagnetic,** dī-a-mag-net''ik, *a.* Applied to substances which, when under the influence of magnetism, point east and west.
**Diameter,** dī-am'et-ėr, *n.* A straight line passing through the center of a circle, and terminated by the circumference; the distance through the center of any object.
**Diametric, Diametrical,** dī-a-met'rik, dī-a-met'rik-al, *a.* Of or pertaining to a diameter.
**Diametrically,** dī-a-met'rik-al-li, *adv.* In a diametrical direction; directly.
**Diamond,** dī'a-mond, *n.* A valuable gem, remarkable for its hardness and transparency; a rhombus; a card of the suit marked with such figures in red; a very small printing type.—*a.* Resembling a diamond; set with diamonds.
**Diapason,** dī-a-pā'zon, *n.* The entire compass of a voice or instrument; an organ stop.
**Diaper,** dī'a-pėr, *n.* A figured linen or cotton cloth.—*vt.* To variegate or diversify with figures.—*vi.* To draw flowers or figures on.
**Diaphanous,** dī-af'an-us, *a.* Having power to transmit rays of light; transparent.
**Diaphragm,** dī'a-fram, *n.* The midriff, a muscular partition separating the thorax from the abdomen.
**Diarrhea,** dī-a-rē'a, *n.* A morbidly frequent evacuation of the intestines.
**Diary,** dī'a-ri, *n.* A register of daily events or transactions; a journal.
**Diastole,** dī-as'to-lē, *n.* Dilatation of the heart in beating.
**Diathermal, Diathermous,** dī-a-thėr'mal, dī-a-thėr'mus, *a.* Freely permeable by heat.
**Diathesis,** dī-ath'e-sis, *n.* Predisposition.
**Diatomic,** dī-a-tom'ik, *a.* Consisting of two atoms.
**Diatonic,** dī-a-ton'ik, *a.* In *music,* applied to the major or minor scales.
**Diatribe,** dī'a-trīb, *n.* A continued disputation; a lengthy invective.
**Dibble,** dib'bl, *n.* A pointed instrument to make

holes for planting seeds, etc.—*vt.* (dibbling, dibbled). To make holes for planting seeds, etc.
**Dice,** dīs, *n.*; pl. of **Die,** for gaming.—*vi.* (dicing, diced). To play with dice.
**Dichotomous,** dī-kot'o-mus, *a.* In *botany,* regularly divided by pairs from top to bottom.
**Dickey, Dicky,** dik'i, *n.* A false shirt-front; the driver's seat in a carriage.
**Dicotyledon,** dī'kot-i-lē''don, *n.* A plant whose seeds contain a pair of cotyledons.
**Dictaphone,** dik'ta-fōn, *n.* Trade name for an instrument into which correspondence is dictated, to be transcribed afterwards.
**Dictate,** dik'tāt, *vt.* (dictating, dictated). To deliver, as an order or direction; to prescribe; to tell what to say or write; to instigate.—*n.* An order delivered; an authoritative precept or maxim; an impulse.
**Dictation,** dik-tā'shon, *n.* Act of dictating; the art or practice of speaking that another may write down what is spoken.
**Dictator,** dik-tāt'ėr, *n.* One invested with absolute authority.
**Dictatorial,** dik-ta-tō'ri-al, *a.* Pertaining to a dictator; absolute; overbearing.
**Dictatorship,** dik-tāt'ėr-ship, *n.* The office of a dictator.
**Diction,** dik'shon, *n.* Choice of words; mode of expression; style.
**Dictionary,** dik'shon-a-ri, *n.* A book containing the words of a language arranged alphabetically, with their meanings, etc.; a work explaining the terms, etc., of any subject under heads alphabetically arranged.
**Dictum,** dik'tum, *n.*; pl. **Dicta.** An authoritative saying or assertion.
**Did,** did, *pret* of *do.*
**Didactic, Didactical,** di-dak'tik, di-dak'tik-al, *a.* Adapted to teach; instructive.
**Didactics,** di-dak'tiks, *n.* The art or science of teaching.
**Diddle,** did'l, *vt.* To cheat or trick.
**Die,** dī, *vi.* (dying, died). To cease to live; to expire; to sink gradually; to vanish.
**Die,** dī, *n.*; pl. **Dice,** dīs, in first sense, in the others **Dies,** dīz. A small cube with numbered faces; any cubic body; the dado of a pedestal; a stamp used in coining money; an implement for turning out things of a regular shape.
**Dielectric,** dī-ē-lek'trik, *n.* Any medium through or across which electric induction takes place between two conductors.
**Diesel,** dēs'el, *n.* An oil-burning internal-combustion engine.
**Diet,** dī'et, *n.* A person's regular food; food prescribed medically; a meeting of dignitaries or delegates for legislative or other purposes.—*vt.* To furnish provisions for.—*vi.* To eat according to rules prescribed.
**Dietary,** dī'et-a-ri, *a.* Pertaining to diet.—*n.* A system of diet; allowance of food.
**Dietetic, Dietetical,** dī-et-et'ik, dī-et-et'ikal, *a.* Pertaining to diet.
**Dietetics,** dī-et-et'iks, *n.* Principles for regulating the diet.
**Differ,** dif'ėr, *vi.* To be unlike or distinct; to disagree; to be at variance.
**Difference,** dif'ėr-ens, *n.* State of being different; dissimilarity; that which distinguishes; dispute; point in dispute; remainder after a sum is subtracted.
**Different,** dif'ėr-ent, *a.* Distinct; dissimilar. (With *from.*)
**Differential,** dif-ėr-en'shi-al, *a.* Creating a difference; discriminating.—*n.* An infinitesimal difference between two states of a variable quantity; a differential gear.
**Differentiate,** dif-ėr-en'shi-āt, *vt.* To mark or distinguish by a difference.—*vi.* To acquire a distinct character.
**Differently,** dif-ėr-ent-li, *adv.* In a different manner; variously.
**Difficult,** dif'fi-kult, *a.* Not easy to be done, etc.; perplexed; hard to please; unyielding.
**Difficulty,** dif'fi-kul-ti, *n.* Hardness to be done; obstacle; perplexity; objection.
**Diffidence,** dif'fi-dens, *n.* Want of confidence; modest reserve; bashfulness.
**Diffident,** dif'fi-dent, *a.* Wanting confidence; bashful.
**Diffidently,** dif'fi-dent-li, *adv.* In a diffident manner; modestly.
**Diffract,** dif-frakt', *vt.* To bend from a straight line; to deflect.
**Diffraction,** dif-frak'shon, *n.* The modifications which light undergoes when it passes by the edge of an opaque body; deflection.
**Diffuse,** dif-fūz', *vt.* (diffusing, diffused). To pour out and spread; to circulate; to proclaim.—*a.* dif-fūs'. Widely spread; prolix; verbose.
**Diffusely,** dif-fūs'li, *adv.* In a diffuse manner; copiously; with too many words.
**Diffusible,** dif-fūz'i-bl, *a.* That may be diffused or dispersed.
**Diffusion,** dif-fū'zhon, *n.* A spreading or scattering; dispersion; circulation.
**Diffusive,** dif-fūs'iv, *a.* Having the quality of diffusing; spread widely; verbose.
**Diffusively,** dif-fūs'iv-li, *adv.* Widely.
**Dig,** dig, *vt.* (digging, digged or dug). To open and turn up with a spade; to excavate.—*vi.* To work with a spade.
**Digest,** di-jest', *vt.* To arrange under proper heads; to think out; to dissolve in the stomach; to soften by a heated liquid; to bear with patience.—*vi.* To undergo digestion, as food.—*n.* dī'jest. A collection of laws; systematic summary.
**Digester,** di-jest'ėr, *n.* That which assists the digestion of food.
**Digestible,** di-jest'i-bl, *a.* Capable of being digested.
**Digestion,** di-jest'yon, *n.* Act of digesting; process of dissolving aliment in the stomach; operation of heating with some solvent.
**Digestive,** di-jest'iv, *a.* Having the power to cause digestion in the stomach.—*n.* A medicine which aids digestion.
**Digging,** dig'ing, *n.* The act of one who digs; *pl.* localities where gold is mined.
**Dight,** dīt, *vt.* To put in order; to array.
**Digit,** di'jit, *n.* A finger; three-fourths of an inch; the twelfth part of the diameter of the sun or moon; any integer under 10.
**Digital,** di'jit-al, *a.* Pertaining to the fingers or to digits.
**Digitate, Digitated,** di'jit-āt, di'jit-āt-ed, *a.* Branching into divisions like fingers.
**Dignified,** dig'ni-fīd, *a.* Marked with dignity; stately; grave.
**Dignify,** dig'ni-fī, *vt.* (dignifying, dignified). To invest with dignity; to exalt in rank or office; to make illustrious.
**Dignitary,** dig'ni-ta-ri, *n.* One of exalted rank or office; an ecclesiastic who has preeminence over priests and canons.
**Dignity,** dig'ni-ti, *n.* Nobleness or elevation of mind; honorable place; degree of excellence; grandeur of mien; an elevated office; one who holds high rank.
**Digress,** di-gres' or dī'gres, *vi.* To depart from the main subject; to deviate.
**Digression,** di-gre'shon or dī-, *n.* Act of digressing; departure from the main subject; the part of a discourse which digresses.
**Digressional, Digressive,** di-gre'shon-al, di-gres'iv, *a.* Pertaining to or consisting in digression.
**Dike, Dyke,** dīk, *n.* A ditch; an embankment; a wall; a vein of igneous rock.—*vt.* (diking, diked). To surround with a dike; to secure by a bank; to drain by ditches.
**Dilacerate,** dī-la'sė-rāt, *vt.* To rend asunder; to separate by force.
**Dilapidate,** di-la'pi-dāt, *vt.* To make ruinous; to squander.—*vi.* To go to ruin; to fall by decay.

**Dilapidated,** di-la'pi-dāt-ed, *p.a.* In a ruinous condition.
**Dilapidation,** di-la'pi-dā''shon, *n.* Decay; ruin; destruction; ruining or suffering to decay of a church building.
**Dilatability,** dī-lāt'a-bil''i-ti, *n.* Quality of being dilatable.
**Dilatable,** dī-lāt'a-bl, *a.* Capable of expansion; possessing elasticity; elastic.
**Dilatation, Dilation,** dil-at-ā'shon, dī-lā'shon, *n.* Act of dilating; expansion; state of being expanded or distended.
**Dilate,** dī-lāt', *vt.* (dilating, dilated). To expand; to distend.—*vi.* To swell or extend in all directions; to speak copiously; to dwell on in narration (with *on* or *upon*).
**Dilatorily,** di'la-to-ri-li, *adv.* With delay.
**Dilatory,** di'la-tō-ri, *a.* Tardy; given to procrastination; making delay; sluggish.
**Dilemma,** di-lem'ma, *n.* An argument with two alternatives, each conclusive against an opponent; a difficult or doubtful choice.
**Dilettante,** dil-e-tan'tā, *n.*; pl. **Dilettanti,** dil-e-tan'tē. An amateur or trifler in art.
**Diligence,** di'li-jens, *n.* Steady application; assiduity; a four-wheeled stage-coach.
**Diligent,** di'li-jent, *a.* Steady in application; industrious; persevering; prosecuted with care and constant effort.
**Dilly-Dally,** dil'i-dal-i, *vi.* To loiter, trifle.
**Diluent,** dil'ū-ent, *a.* Diluting.—*n.* That which dilutes; a substance which increases the proportion of fluid in the blood.
**Dilute,** di-lūt', *vt.* (diluting, diluted). To render liquid or more liquid; to weaken by admixture of water.—*vi.* To become attenuated or diluted.—*a.* Thin; reduced in strength.
**Dilution,** di-lū'shon, *n.* Act of diluting.
**Diluvial, Diluvian,** di-lū'vi-al, di-lū'vi-an, *a.* Pertaining to a flood or deluge; effected or produced by a deluge.
**Diluvium,** di-lū'vi-um, *n.* A deluge or inundation; a deposit of sand, gravel, etc., caused by a flood.
**Dim,** dim, *a.* Not seeing clearly; not clearly seen; mysterious; tarnished.—*vt.* (dimming, dimmed). To dull; to obscure; to sully.
**Dime,** dīm, *n.* A silver coin the tenth of a dollar.
**Dimension,** di-men'shon, *n.* Extension in a single direction; measure of a thing, its size, extent, capacity, (usually in *pl.*).
**Diminish,** di-min'ish, *vt.* To reduce; to abate; to degrade.—*vi.* To become less.
**Diminution,** di-min-ū'shon, *n.* Act of diminishing; state of becoming less.
**Diminutive,** di-min'ūt-iv, *a.* Small; little.—*n.* A word formed from another word to express a little thing of the kind.
**Dimissory,** di-mis'so-ri, *a.* Dismissing to another jurisdiction; granting leave to depart.
**Dimity,** di'mi-ti, *n.* A stout cotton fabric woven with raised stripes or figures.
**Dimly,** dim'li, *adv.* Obscurely.
**Dimmish,** dim'ish, *a.* Somewhat dim.
**Dimple,** dim'pl, *n.* A small natural depression in the cheek or chin.—*vi.* (dimpling, dimpled). To form dimples.
**Dimpled,** dim'pld, *a.* Set with dimples.
**Din,** din, *n.* A loud sound long continued.—*vt.* (dinning, dinned). To stun with noise; to harass with clamor.
**Dine,** dīn, *vi.* (dining, dined). To eat a dinner.—*vt.* To give a dinner to.
**Dinghy,** ding'gi, *n.* A small boat used by a ship.
**Dingle,** ding'gl, *n.* A small secluded valley.
**Dingy,** din'ji, *a.* Of a dusky color; soiled.
**Dinner,** din'ėr, *n.* The principal meal of the day.
**Diocesan,** dī-os'es-an, *a.* Pertaining to a diocese.—*n.* A bishop; one in possession of a diocese.
**Diocese,** dī'ō-sēs, *n.* An ecclesiastical division of a state, subject to a bishop.
**Dioptric, Dioptrical,** dī-op'trik, dī-op'trik-al, *a.* Pertaining to refracted light.
**Dioptrics,** dī-op-triks, *n.* The science of the refractions of light passing through mediums, as air, water, or lenses.
**Diorama,** dī-ō-rä'ma, *n.* A contrivance for giving a high degree of optical illusion to painted scenes.
**Dioramic,** dī-ō-ram'ik, *a.* Pertaining to a diorama.
**Dip,** dip, *vt.* (dipping, dipped). To plunge in a liquid; to baptize by immersion.—*vi.* To dive into a liquid and emerge; to engage in a desultory way; to look cursorily; to choose by chance; to incline.—*n.* Act of dipping; a bath; candle; downward slope.
**Diphtheria,** dif-thē'ri-a, *n.* An epidemic inflammatory disease of the throat.
**Diphthong,** dif'thong, *n.* A union of two vowels pronounced in one syllable.
**Diploma,** di-plō-ma, *n.* A document conferring some power, privilege, or honor.
**Diplomacy,** di-plō'ma-si, *n.* The art or practice of conducting international negotiations; skill in securing advantages.
**Diplomat,** dip'lō-mat, *n.* A diplomatist.
**Diplomatic, Diplomatical,** dip-lō-mat'ik, dip-lō-mat'ik-al, *a.* Pertaining to diplomacy; skilful in gaining one's ends by tact; relating to diplomatics.
**Diplomatics,** dip-lō-mat'iks, *n.* The science of deciphering ancient writings, and of ascertaining their authenticity, date, etc.
**Diplomatist,** di-plō'mat-ist, *n.* One skilled or engaged in diplomacy.
**Dipper,** dip'ėr, *n.* He or that which dips; a ladle; a bird, the water-ousel.
**Dipsomania,** dip-sō-mā'ni-a, *n.* An uncontrollable craving for stimulants.
**Dire,** dīr, *a.* Dreadful; dismal; terrible.
**Direct,** di-rekt', *a.* Straight; right; in the line of father and son; not ambiguous; express.—*vt.* To point or aim at; to show the right course to; to conduct; to order; to instruct.
**Direction,** di-rek'shon, *n.* Act of directing; a pointing toward; course; guidance; command; address on a letter; a body of directors.
**Directive,** di-rekt'iv, *a.* Giving direction.
**Directly,** di-rekt'li, *adv.* In a direct manner; without delay; expressly.
**Director,** di-rekt'ėr, *n.* One who or that which directs; a superintendent; an instructor; a counsellor; one appointed to transact the affairs of a company.
**Directorate,** di-rek'tėr-āt, *n.* Office of a director; body of directors.
**Directorship,** di-rek'tėr-ship, *n.* The condition or office of a director.
**Directory,** di-rek'to-ri, *n.* A rule to direct; a book containing directions for public worship; a book containing a list of the inhabitants of a place, with their addresses; a board of directors.
**Directress, Directrix,** di-rekt'res, di-rekt'riks, *n.* A female who directs.
**Direful,** dīr'ful, *a.* Dire; dreadful; calamitous.
**Direfully,** dīr'ful-li, *adv.* Dreadfully.
**Dirge,** dėrj, *n.* A song or tune intended to express grief, sorrow, and mourning.
**Dirk,** dėrk, *n.* A kind of dagger or poniard.
**Dirt,** dėrt, *n.* Any foul or filthy substance.—*vt.* To make foul; to defile.
**Dirtily,** dėrt'i-li, *adv.* In a dirty manner; foully; meanly.
**Dirty,** dėrt'i, *a.* Soiled with dirt; mean; despicable; rainy; squally, etc.—*vt.* (dirtying, dirtied). To soil; to sully.
**Disability,** dis-a-bil'i-ti, *n.* Want of ability; incompetence; want of legal qualification.
**Disable,** dis-ā'bl, *vt.* (disabling, disabled). To deprive of power; to disqualify; to incapacitate.
**Disabuse,** dis-a-būz', *vt.* To undeceive.
**Disadvantage,** dis-ad-van'tāj, *n.* Want of advantage; unfavorable state; detriment.

**Disadvantageous,** dis-ad'van-tāj''us, *p.a.* Unfavorable to success or prosperity.
**Disaffect,** dis-af-fekt', *vt.* To make less faithful or friendly; to make discontented.
**Disaffected,** dis-af-fek'ted, *a.* Indisposed to favor or support; unfriendly.
**Disaffection,** dis-af-fek'shon, *n.* Alienation of affection; disloyalty, hostility.
**Disaffirm,** dis-af-fėrm', *vt.* To deny; to annul.
**Disagree,** dis-a-grē', *vi.* To be of a different opinion; to dissent; to be unfriendly; to be unsuitable.
**Disagreeable,** dis-a-grē'a-bl, *a.* Not agreeable; offensive; displeasing.
**Disagreeably,** dis-a-grē'a-bli, *adv.* Unpleasantly.
**Disagreement,** dis-a-grē'ment, *n.* Difference; unsuitableness; discrepancy; discord.
**Disallow,** dis-al-lou', *vt.* To refuse to allow; to disapprove of; to reject.
**Disallowable,** dis-al-lou'a-bl, *a.* Not allowable.
**Disallowance,** dis-al-lou'ans, *n.* Refusal to allow; disapprobation; rejection.
**Disannul,** dis-an-nul', *vt.* To annul.
**Disappear,** dis-ap-pēr', *vi.* To vanish from sight; to cease, or seem to cease, to be.
**Disappearance,** dis-ap-pēr'ans, *n.* Act of disappearing; removal from sight.
**Disappoint,** dis-ap-point', *vt.* To defeat of expectation or intention; to frustrate.
**Disappointed,** dis-ap-point'ed, *a.* Balked; soured in life.
**Disappointment,** dis-ap-point'ment, *n.* Failure of expectation or intention.
**Disapprobation,** dis-ap'prō-bā''shon, *n.* Disapproval; censure, expressed or unexpressed.
**Disapproval,** dis-ap-prōv'al, *n.* The act of disapproving; dislike.
**Disapprove,** dis-ap-prōv', *vt.* To censure as wrong; to regard with dislike; to reject.
**Disapprovingly,** dis-ap-prōv'ing-li, *adv.* By disapprobation.
**Disarm,** dis-ärm', *vt.* To take the arms or weapons from; to render harmless.—*vi.* To lay down arms; to disband.
**Disarmament,** dis-ärm'a-ment, *n.* Act of disarming.
**Disarrange,** dis-a-rānj', *vt.* To put out of arrangement or order; to derange.
**Disarrangement,** dis-a-rānj'ment, *n.* Act of disturbing order; disorder.
**Disarray,** dis-a-rā', *vt.* To undress; to throw into disorder.—*n.* Disorder; undress.
**Disaster,** diz-as'tėr, *n.* An unfortunate event; mishap; catastrophe; reverse.
**Disastrous,** diz-as'trus, *a.* Occasioning, accompanied by, or threatening disaster; calamitous; dismal.
**Disavouch,** dis-a-vouch', *vt.* To disavow.
**Disavow,** dis-a-vou', *vt.* To deny to be true; to reject; to dissent from.
**Disavowal,** dis-a-vou'al, *n.* Denial; repudiation.
**Disband,** dis-band', *vt.* To dismiss from military service; to disperse.—*vi.* To retire from military service; to dissolve connection.
**Disbar,** dis-bär', *vt.* To expel from being a member of the bar.
**Disbelief,** dis-bē-lēf', *n.* Refusal of credit or faith; distrust.
**Disbelieve,** dis-bē-lēv', *vt.* To refuse to credit.
**Disburden,** dis-bėr'dn, *vt.* To remove a burden from; to relieve.
**Disburse,** dis-bėrs', *vt.* (disbursing, disbursed). To pay out, as money; to expend.
**Disbursement,** dis-bėrs'ment, *n.* Act of disbursing; the sum paid out.
**Disburthen,** dis-bėr'THen, *vt.* and *i.* A different orthography of *disburden.*
**Disc, Disk,** disk, *n.* A flat circular plate; the face of the sun, or a planet; the central part of a composite flower.
**Discard,** dis-kärd', *vt.* To throw away; to cast off; to dismiss; to discharge.
**Discern,** dis-sėrn' or di-zėrn', *vt.* To distinguish; to discriminate; to descry.—*vi.* To see or understand difference; to have clearness of mental sight.
**Discerner,** dis-sėrn'ėr, *n.* One who discerns; a clear-sighted observer.
**Discernible,** dis-sėrn'i-bl, *a.* That may be discerned; perceptible.
**Discerning,** dis-sėrn'ing, *p.a.* Having power to discern; sharp-sighted; acute.
**Discerningly,** dis-sėrn'ing-li, *adv.* With discernment; acutely; with judgment.
**Discernment,** dis-sėrn'ment, *n.* Act or power of discerning; judgment; sagacity.
**Discharge,** dis-chärj', *vt.* To unload; to let fly or go, as a missile; to fire off; to give vent to; to clear off by payment; to perform; to acquit; to dismiss; to release.—*vi.* To get rid of or let out a charge or contents.—*n.* Act of discharging; unloading; a firing off; emission; dismissal; release from obligation, debt, or penalty; absolution from a crime; ransom; performance; release; payment, as of a debt.
**Disciple,** dis-sī'pl, *n.* A learner; a pupil; an adherent to the doctrines of another.
**Discipleship,** dis-sī'pl-ship, *n.* The state or position of a disciple.
**Disciplinable,** dis'si-plin-a-bl, *a.* Capable of discipline, or of instruction.
**Disciplinarian,** dis'si-plin-ā''ri-an, *a.* Pertaining to discipline.—*n.* One who enforces discipline; a martinet.
**Disciplinary,** dis'si-plin-a-ri, *a.* Pertaining to discipline; intended for discipline.
**Discipline,** dis'si-plin, *n.* Training; method of government; order; subjection to laws; punishment; correction; execution of ecclesiastical laws.—*vt.* (disciplining, disciplined). To subject to discipline; to train up well; to chastise.
**Disclaim,** dis-klām', *vt.* To deny all claim to; to reject; to disown.
**Disclaimer,** dis-klām'ėr, *n.* One who disclaims; formal disavowal; renunciation.
**Disclose,** dis-klōz', *vt.* To open; to uncover; to reveal; to divulge.
**Disclosure,** dis-klō'zhūr, *n.* Act of disclosing; utterance of what was secret; that which is disclosed.
**Discoloration,** dis-kul'ėr-ā''shon, *n.* Act of discoloring; alteration of color; stain.
**Discolor,** dis-kul'ėr, *vt.* To alter the color of; to stain; to tinge.
**Discomfit,** dis-kom'fit, *vt.* To rout; to defeat.—*n.* Rout; overthrow.
**Discomfiture,** dis-kom'fit-ūr, *n.* Rout; overthrow, frustration; disappointment.
**Discomfort,** dis-kum'fėrt, *n.* Want of comfort; uneasiness; inquietude.—*vt.* To deprive of comfort; to grieve.
**Discommend,** dis-kom-mend', *vt.* To blame; to censure; to mention with disapprobation.
**Discompose,** dis-kom-pōz', *vt.* To disturb.
**Discomposure,** dis-kom-pō'zhūr, *n.* Disorder; agitation; disturbance; perturbation.
**Disconcert,** dis-kon-sėrt', *vt.* To disturb; to unsettle; to confuse; to ruffle.
**Disconnect,** dis-kon-nekt', *vt.* To separate; to disunite.
**Disconnection,** dis-kon-nek'shon, *n.* Separation; want of union.
**Disconsolate,** dis-kon'sō-lāt, *a.* Comfortless; hopeless; gloomy; cheerless.
**Discontent,** dis-kon-tent', *n.* Want of content; uneasiness of mind; dissatisfaction.
**Discontented,** dis-kon-tent'ed, *a.* Dissatisfied; given to grumble.
**Discontentment,** dis-kon-tent'ment, *n.* Discontent; uneasiness; inquietude.
**Discontinuance,** dis-kon-tin'ū-ans, *n.* A breaking off; cessation.
**Discontinuation,** dis-kon-tin'ū-ā''shon, *n.* Act of discontinuing; discontinuance.
**Discontinue,** dis-kon-tin'ū, *vt.* To leave off; to cause to cease; to cease to take or receive.—*vi.*

D

To cease.
**Discontinuous,** dis-kon'tin'ū-us, *a.* Not continuous; broken off; interrupted.
**Discord,** dis'kord, *n.* Want of concord; disagreement; disagreement of sounds.
**Discordance, Discordancy,** dis-kord'ans, dis-kord'an-si, *n.* Want of concord; disagreement; inconsistency; discord.
**Discordant,** dis-kord'ant, *a.* Wanting agreement; incongruous; dissonant; jarring.
**Discount,** dis'kount, *n.* A sum deducted for prompt or advanced payment.—*vt.* dis-kount'. To advance the amount of, as of a bill, deducting a certain rate per cent; to make an allowance for supposed exaggeration; to disregard.
**Discountable,** dis-kount'a-bl, *a.* That may be discounted.
**Discountenance,** dis-koun'ten-ans, *vt.* To restrain by censure, cold treatment, etc.
**Discounter,** dis'kount-ėr, *n.* One who discounts bills and financial documents.
**Discourage,** dis-ku'rāj, *vt.* (discouraging, discouraged). To dishearten; to dissuade.
**Discouragement,** dis-ku'rāj-ment, *n.* Act of discouraging; that which discourages.
**Discouraging,** dis-ku'rāj-ing, *a.* Tending to discourage.
**Discourse,** dis-kōrs', *n.* A speech; treatise; sermon; conversation.—*vi.* (discoursing, discoursed). To talk; to converse; to treat of formally; to expatiate.—*vt.* To utter.
**Discourteous,** dis-kōr'tē-us, *a.* Void of courtesy; rude.
**Discourtesy,** dis-kōr'te-si, *n.* Incivility; rudeness; act of disrespect.
**Discover,** dis-kuv'ėr, *vt.* To lay open to view; to reveal; to have the first sight of; to find out; to detect.
**Discoverable,** dis-kuv'ėr-a-bl, *a.* That may be discovered.
**Discoverer,** dis-kuv'ėr-ėr, *n.* One who discovers; an explorer.
**Discovery,** dis-kuv'ė-ri, *n.* Act of discovering; disclosure; that which is discovered.
**Discredit,** dis-kred'it, *n.* Want of credit; disrepute; disbelief; distrust.—*vt.* To give no credit to; to deprive of credit; to make less reputable; to bring into disesteem.
**Discreditable,** dis-kred'it-a-bl, *a.* Tending to discredit; injurious to reputation.
**Discreet,** dis-krēt, *a.* Prudent; wary; judicious.
**Discrepance, Discrepancy,** dis-krep'ans, dis-krep'an-si, *n.* Discordance; disagreement.
**Discrete,** dis'krēt, *a.* Separate; distinct.
**Discretionary,** dis-kre'shon-a-ri, *a.* Unrestrained except by discretion.
**Discretive,** dis-krēt'iv, *a.* Disjunctive; implying opposition or distinction.
**Discriminate,** dis-krim'in-āt, *vt.* (discriminating, discriminated). To distinguish; to select from.—*vt.* To make a distinction.—*a.* Having the difference marked; distinct.
**Discriminately,** dis-krim'in-āt-li, *adv.* In a discriminate manner.
**Discriminating,** dis-krim'in-āt-ing, *p.a.* Distinguishing; able to make nice distinctions.
**Discrimination,** dis-krim'in-ā''shon, *n.* Discernment; judgment; distinction.
**Discriminative,** dis-krim'in-āt-iv, *a.* That discriminates or distinguishes.
**Discriminator,** dis-krim'in-āt-ėr, *n.* One who discriminates.
**Discursive,** dis-kėrs'iv, *a.* Passing from one subject to another, desultory; rambling.
**Discus,** dis'kus, *n.* A round, flat piece of iron, etc., thrown in play; a quoit.
**Discuss,** dis-kus', *vt.* To drive away or dissolve (a tumor, etc.); to debate; to examine by disputation; to make a trial of, as food; to consume.
**Discussion,** dis-ku'shon, *n.* Dispersion; debate; examination.
**Disdain,** dis-dān', *vt.* To think unworthy; to deem worthless; to scorn; to contemn.—*n.* Contempt; scorn; haughtiness; pride.
**Disdainful,** dis-dān'ful, *a.* Contemptuous; scornful; haughty; indignant.
**Disdainfully,** dis-dān'ful-li, *adv.* With scorn.
**Disease,** diz-ēz', *n.* Any state of a living body in which the natural functions are disturbed; illness; disorder.—*vt.* (diseasing, diseased). To afflict with disease; to infect; to derange.
**Disembark,** dis-em-bärk', *vt.* To remove from a vessel to the land.—*vi.* To go ashore.
**Disembarkation,** dis-em'bärk-ā''shon, *n.* Act of disembarking.
**Disembarrass,** dis-em-ba'ras, *vt.* To free from perplexity; to clear; to extricate.
**Disembody,** dis-em-bo'di, *vt.* To divest of body; to free from connection with the human body; to disband (troops).
**Disembowel,** dis-em-bou'el, *vt.* (disembowelling, disembowelled). To take out the bowels of.
**Disembroil,** dis-em-broil', *vt.* To disentangle; to free from perplexity.
**Disenchant,** dis-en-chant', *vt.* To free from enchantment.
**Disencumber,** dis-en-kum'bėr, *vt.* To free from encumbrance or obst uction.
**Disencumbrance,** dis-en-kum'brans, *n.* The act of disencumbering.
**Disendow,** dis-en-dou', *vt.* To deprive of endowment, as a church.
**Disendowment,** dis-en-dou'ment, *n.* The act of disendowing.
**Disengage,** dis-en-gāj', *vt.* To free from engagement; to detach; to release; to extricate.
**Disengaged,** dis-en-gājd', *p.a.* At leisure; not particularly occupied.
**Disengagement,** dis-en-gāj'ment, *n.* Release from engagement; separation; extrication; leisure.
**Disennoble,** dis-en-nō'bl, *vt.* To deprive of that which ennobles; to deprive of title.
**Disentail,** dis-en-tāl', *vt.* To free from being entailed.—*n.* The act of breaking the entail of an estate.
**Disentangle,** dis-en-tang'gl, *vt.* To free from entanglement; to clear.
**Disenthrall,** dis-en-thral', *vt.* To give freedom to.
**Disentitle,** dis-en-tī'tl, *vt.* To deprive of title.
**Disestablish,** dis-es-tab'lish, *vt.* To cause to cease to be established; to withdraw (a church) from connection with the state.
**Disestablishment,** dis-es-tab'lish-ment, *n.* The act of disestablishing.
**Disesteem,** dis-es-tēm', *n.* Want of esteem.—*vt.* To dislike moderately; to slight.
**Disfavor,** dis-fā'vėr, *n.* Want of favor; unfavorable regard.—*vt.* To withhold favor from; to discountenance.
**Disfiguration,** dis-fi'gūr-ā''shon, *n.* Act of disfiguring; some degree of deformity.
**Disfigure,** dis-fi'gūr, *vt.* (disfiguring, disfigured). To mar the figure of; to impair the beauty, symmetry, or excellence of.
**Disfigurement,** dis-fi'gūr-ment, *n.* Act of disfiguring, that which disfigures.
**Disfranchise,** dis-fran'chīz, *vt.* To deprive of the rights of a free citizen.
**Disfranchisement,** dis-fran'chiz-ment, *n.* Act of disfranchising.
**Disgorge,** dis-gorj', *vt.* To vomit; to discharge violently; to surrender.
**Disgrace,** dis-grās', *n.* State of being deprived of grace or favor; cause of shame; dishonor.—*vt.* (disgracing, disgraced). To bring to shame; to degrade; to dishonor.
**Disgraceful,** dis-grās'ful, *a.* Shameful; causing shame; sinking reputation.
**Disguise,** dis-gīz', *vt.* (disguising, disguised). To conceal by an unusual habit or mask; to dissemble; to give an unusual appearance to.—*n.* A dress intended to conceal; an assumed appearance, intended to deceive.
**Disgust,** dis-gust', *n.* Distaste; loathing; repugnance.—*vt.* To cause distaste in; to offend

the mind or moral taste of.
**Disgustful,** dis-gust'ful, *a.* Exciting aversion in the natural or moral taste.
**Disgusting,** dis-gust'ing, *a.* Provoking disgust; loathsome; nasty.
**Dish,** dish, *n.* A broad open vessel for serving up meat at table; the meat served; any particular kind of food.—*vt.* To put in a dish; to make (a wheel) hollow or concave.
**Dishearten,** dis-härt'n, *vt.* To discourage; to depress.
**Dishevel,** di-she'vel, *vt.* (dishevelling, dishevelled). To put out of order, or spread loosely, as the hair.
**Dishonest,** dis-on'est, *a.* Void of honesty; fraudulent; knavish; perfidious.
**Dishonesty,** dis-on'est-i, *n.* Want of honesty or integrity.
**Dishonor,** dis-on'ėr, *n.* Want of honor; disgrace; ignominy.—*vt.* To deprive of honor; to treat with indignity; to violate the chastity of; to decline to accept or pay, as a draft.
**Dishonorable,** dis-on'ėr-a-bl, *a.* Destitute of honor; base; vile.
**Disillusionize,** dis-il-lū'zhon-īz, *vt.* To free from illusion.
**Disinclination,** dis-in'klin-ā''shon, *n.* Want of propensity, desire, or affection.
**Disincline,** dis-in-klīn', *vt.* To take away inclination from; to make disaffected.
**Disinfect,** dis-in-fekt', *vt.* To cleanse from infection.
**Disinfectant,** dis-in-fek'tant, *n.* An agent for removing the causes of infection.
**Disinfection,** dis-in-fek'shon, *n.* Purification from infecting matter.
**Disingenuous,** dis-in-jen'ū-us, *a.* Not open, frank, and candid; crafty; cunning.
**Disinherit,** dis-in-he'rit, *vt.* To cut off from hereditary right.
**Disinheritance,** dis-in-he'rit-ans, *n.* Act of disinheriting.
**Disintegrable,** dis-in'tē-gra-bl, *a.* That may be disintegrated.
**Disintegrate,** dis-in'tē-grāt, *vt.* To separate, as the integral parts of a body.
**Disintegration,** dis-in'tē-grā''shon, *n.* Act of separating integral parts of a substance.
**Disinter,** dis-in-tėr', *vt.* To take out of a grave; to bring into view.
**Disinterested,** dis-in'tėr-est-ed, *a.* Not interested; free from self-interest; not dictated by private advantage; impartial.
**Disinterment,** dis-in-tėr'ment, *n.* Act of disinterring or taking out of the earth.
**Disinthrall,** dis-in-thral', *vt.* *See* DISENTHRALL.
**Disjoin,** dis-join', *vt.* To part asunder; to sever.—*vi.* To part.
**Disjoint,** dis-joint', *vt.* To separate, as parts united by joints; to put out of joint; to make incoherent.
**Disjointed,** dis-joint'ed, *p.a.* Unconnected; incoherent; out of joint.
**Disjunct,** dis-jungkt', *a.* Disjoined.
**Disjunction,** dis-jungk'shon, *n.* Act of disjoining; disunion.
**Disjunctive,** dis-jungk'tiv, *a.* Separating; uniting words or sentences in construction, but disjoining the sense.—*n.* A word that disjoins, as *or, nor.*
**Disk,** disk, *n.* *See* DISC.
**Dislike,** dis-līk', *n.* A feeling the opposite of liking; a moderate degree of hatred; aversion; antipathy.—*vt.* To regard with some aversion or displeasure.
**Dislocate,** dis'lō-kāt, *vt.* To displace; to put out of joint.
**Dislocation,** dis-lō-kā'shon, *n.* Act of dislocating; displacement.
**Dislodge,** dis-loj', *vt.* To remove or drive from a place of rest or a station.—*vi.* To go from a place of rest.
**Dislodgment,** dis-loj'ment, *n.* Act of dislodging; displacement.
**Disloyal,** dis-loi'al, *a.* Void of loyalty; false to a sovereign; faithless.
**Disloyally,** dis-loi'al-li, *adv.* In a disloyal manner; perfidiously.
**Disloyalty,** dis-loi'al-ti, *n.* Want of loyalty or fidelity; violation of allegiance.
**Dismal,** diz'mal, *a.* Dark; gloomy; doleful; calamitous; sorrowful.
**Dismally,** diz'mal-li, *adv.* Gloomily.
**Dismantle,** dis-man'tl, *vt.* To strip; to divest; to unrig; to deprive or strip, as of military equipment or defenses; to break down.
**Dismask,** dis-mask', *vt.* To strip off a mask from; to uncover.
**Dismast,** dis-mast', *vt.* To break and carry away the masts from.
**Dismay,** dis-mā', *vt.* To produce terror in; to appal; to dishearten.—*n.* Loss of courage; consternation; fright.
**Dismember,** dis-mem'bėr, *vt.* To sever limb from limb; to separate; to mutilate.
**Dismemberment,** dis-mem'bėr-ment, *n.* The act of dismembering.
**Dismiss,** dis-mis', *vt.* To send away; to permit to depart; to discharge.
**Dismissal,** dis-mis'al, *n.* Dismission.
**Dismission,** dis-mi'shon, *n.* Act of sending away; leave to depart; discharge.
**Dismount,** dis-mount', *vi.* To descend from a horse, etc.—*vt.* To unhorse; to throw cannon from their carriages or fixed positions.
**Disobedience,** dis-ō-bē'di-ens, *n.* Neglect or refusal to obey.
**Disobedient,** dis-ō-bē'di-ent, *a.* Neglecting or refusing to obey; refractory.
**Disobey,** dis-ō-bā', *vt.* To neglect or refuse to obey; to violate an order.
**Disoblige,** dis-ō-blīj', *vt.* To fail to oblige; to be unaccommodating to.
**Disobligement,** dis-ō-blīj'ment, *n.* Act of disobliging.
**Disobliging,** dis-ō-blīj'ing, *p.a.* Not disposed to gratify the wishes of another; unaccommodating.
**Disorder,** dis-or'dėr, *n.* Want of order; confusion; disease.—*vt.* To put out of order; to disturb; to produce indisposition; to craze.
**Disordered,** dis-or'dėrd, *p.a.* Deranged.
**Disorderly,** dis-or'dėr'li, *a.* Being without proper order; confusedly; unruly.
**Disorganization,** dis-or'gan-īz-ā''shon, *n.* Act of disorganizing; state of being disorganized.
**Disorganize,** dis-or'gan-īz, *vt.* To destroy organic structure or connected system in; to throw into confusion.
**Disown,** dis-ōn', *vt.* To refuse to acknowledge; to renounce; to repudiate.
**Disparage,** dis-pa'rāj, *vt.* (disparaging, disparaged). To dishonor by comparison with something inferior; to derogate from; to decry.
**Disparagement,** dis-pa'rāj-ment, *n.* Injury by union or comparison with something inferior; indignity; detraction.
**Disparagingly,** dis-pa'rāj-ing-li, *adv.* In a manner to disparage.
**Disparate,** dis'pa-rāt, *a.* Unequal; unlike.
**Disparity,** dis-pa'ri-ti, *n.* Inequality; difference in degree, age, rank, etc.
**Dispark,** dis-pärk', *vt.* To cause to be no longer a park; to throw open.
**Dispart,** dis-pärt', *vt.* and *i.* To separate.
**Dispassionate,** dis-pa'shon-āt, *a.* Free from passion; cool; impartial.
**Dispassionately,** dis-pa'shon-āt-li, *adv.* Without passion; calmly; coolly.
**Dispatch,** dis-pach', *vt.* To send away in haste; to put to death; to perform quickly; to conclude.—*n.* Act of dispatching; communication on public business; speedy performance; due diligence.
**Dispeace,** dis-pēs', *n.* Want of peace or quiet; dissension; quarrelling.
**Dispel,** dis-pel', *vt.* (dispelling, dispelled). To scat-

D

ter; to banish.—*vi.* To fly different ways; to disappear.
**Dispensable,** dis-pens'a-bl, *a.* That may be dispensed with.
**Dispensary,** dis-pens'a-ri, *n.* A place where medicines are dispensed to the poor, and medical advice is given gratis; a place where medicines are compounded.
**Dispensation,** dis-pens-ā'shon, *n.* Act of dispensing; distribution; good or evil dealt out by providence; exemption.
**Dispensatory,** dis-pens'a-to-ri, *a.* Having power to grant dispensations.—*n.* A book containing the method of preparing the various kinds of medicines.
**Dispense,** dis-pens', *vt.* (dispensing, dispensed). To deal out in portions; to administer; to apply; to exempt; to grant dispensation for.—*vi.* To do without (with *with*).
**Dispenser,** dis-pens'ėr, *n.* One who dispenses, distributes, or administers.
**Dispensing,** dis-pens'ing, *p.a.* Granting dispensation or exemption.
**Dispeople,** dis-pē'pl, *vt.* To depopulate.
**Disperse,** dis-pėrs', *vt.* To scatter; to dispel; to diffuse; to distribute.—*vi.* To be scattered; to vanish.
**Dispersion,** dis-pėr'shon, *n.* Act of dispersing; diffusion; dissipation.
**Dispirit,** dis-pi'rit, *vt.* To deprive of spirit; to discourage; to daunt.
**Dispirited,** dis-pi'rit-ed, *p.a.* Dejected; tame.
**Dispiriting,** dis-pi'rit-ing, *p.a.* Discouraging.
**Displace,** dis-plās', *vt.* To remove from its place; to derange; to dismiss.
**Displacement,** dis-plās'ment, *n.* Act of displacing; quantity of water displaced by a floating body.
**Displant,** dis-plant', *vt.* To pluck up from the spot where planted; to remove from the usual place of residence; to depopulate.
**Display,** dis-plā', *vt.* To unfold; to spread before the eyes or mind; to show; to parade.—*vi.* To make a show; to talk without restraint.—*n.* An opening or unfolding; exhibition; parade.
**Displease,** dis-plēz, *vt.* To offend; to dissatisfy; to provoke.—*vi.* To disgust.
**Displeased,** dis-plēzd', *p.a.* Annoyed.
**Displeasing,** dis-plēz'ing, *p.a.* Disgusting; disagreeable.
**Displeasure,** dis-ple'zhūr, *n.* Dissatisfaction; resentment.
**Disposable,** dis-pōz'a-bl, *a.* Subject to disposal; free to be used or employed.
**Disposal,** dis-pōz'al, *n.* Act or power of disposing; disposition; control.
**Dispose,** dis-pōz', *vt.* (disposing, disposed). To arrange; to apply to a particular purpose; to incline.—*vi.* To regulate; (with *of*) to part with, to employ.
**Disposed,** dis-pōzd', *p.a.* Inclined.
**Disposer,** dis-pōz'ėr, *n.* One who disposes.
**Disposition,** dis-pō-zi'shon, *n.* Act of disposing; state of being disposed; arrangement; natural fitness; frame of mind; inclination.
**Dispossess,** dis-poz-zes', *vt.* To deprive of possession.
**Dispossession,** dis-poz-ze'shon, *n.* Act of putting out of possession.
**Dispraise,** dis-prāz, *n.* The opposite of praise; blame; censure.—*vt.* To blame; to mention with disapprobation.
**Disproof,** dis-prōf', *n.* Refutation.
**Disproportion,** dis-prō-pōr'shon, *n.* Want of proportion or symmetry.—*vt.* To violate proportion; to join unfitly.
**Disproportional,** dis-prō-pōr'shon-al, *a.* Showing disproportion; inadequate.
**Disproportionate,** dis-prō-pōr'shon-āt, *a.* Not proportioned; unsymmetrical; inadequate.
**Disproval,** dis-prōv'al, *n.* Act of disproving; disproof.
**Disprove,** dis-prōv', *vt.* To prove to be false; to confute.
**Disputable,** dis-pūt'a-bl or dis'pūt-a-bl, *a.* That may be disputed; controvertible.
**Disputant,** dis-pūt-ant, *n.* One who argues in opposition to another.
**Disputation,** dis-pūt-ā'shon, *n.* Act of disputing; controversy in words; debate.
**Disputatious,** dis-pūt-ā'shus, *a.* Inclined to dispute; apt to controvert.
**Disputative,** dis-pūt'at-iv, *a.* Disputatious.
**Dispute,** dis-pūt', *vi.* (disputing, disputed). To contend in argument; to debate; to strive with.—*vt.* To attempt to prove to be false; to impugn; to contest; to strive to maintain.—*n.* Controversy in words; strife.
**Disputer,** dis-pūt'ėr, *n.* One who disputes or who is given to disputes.
**Disqualification,** dis-kwo'li-fi-kā''shon, *n.* Act of disqualifying; that which disqualifies.
**Disqualify,** dis-kwo'li-fī, *vt.* To divest of qualifications; to incapacitate.
**Disquiet,** dis-kwī'et, *n.* Uneasiness; anxiety.—*vt.* To make uneasy or restless.
**Disquieting,** dis-kwī'et-ing, *p.a.* Tending to disturb the mind.
**Disquietude,** dis-kwī'et-ūd, *n.* Uneasiness; anxiety.
**Disquisition,** dis-kwi-zi'shon, *n.* A systematic inquiry into any subject, by arguments; a treatise or dissertation.
**Disregard,** dis-rē-gärd', *n.* Neglect; slight.—*vt.* To omit to take notice of; to slight.
**Disregardful,** dis-rē-gärd'ful, *a.* Neglectful; negligent; heedless.
**Disrelish,** dis-rel'ish, *n.* Distaste; dislike.—*vt.* To dislike the taste of; to feel some disgust at.
**Disrepair,** dis-rē-pār', *n.* A state of being not in repair.
**Disreputable,** dis-re'pūt-a-bl, *a.* Discreditable; low; mean.
**Disrepute,** dis-rē-pūt', *n.* Loss or want of reputation; disesteem; disgrace.
**Disrespect,** dis-rē-spekt', *n.* Want of respect; incivility.—*vt.* To show disrespect to.
**Disrespectful,** dis-rē-spekt'ful, *a.* Irreverent; discourteous; rude.
**Disrobe,** dis-rōb, *vt.* To undress; to uncover; to divest of any surrounding appendage.
**Disroot,** dis-röt', *vt.* To tear up the roots.
**Disruption,** dis-rup'shon, *n.* Act of rending asunder; breach; rent; rupture.
**Disruptive,** dis-rupt'iv, *a.* Causing, or produced by, disruption.
**Dissatisfaction,** dis-sa'tis-fak''shon, *n.* Want of satisfaction; discontent.
**Dissatisfied,** dis-sa'tis-fīd, *p.a.* Discontented; offended.
**Dissatisfy,** dis-sa'tis-fī, *vt.* To fail to satisfy; to render discontented.
**Dissect,** dis-sekt', *vt.* To cut up; to anatomize; to divide and examine minutely.
**Dissecting,** dis-sekt'ing, *p.a.* Used in dissection.
**Dissection,** dis-sek'shon, *n.* Act of cutting up anatomically; act of separating into parts for the purpose of critical examination.
**Dissector,** dis-sekt'ėr, *n.* An anatomist.
**Dissemble,** dis-sem'bl, *vt.* and *i.* (dissembling, dissembled). To hide under a false appearance; to conceal under some pretense.
**Dissembler,** dis-sem'bl-ėr, *n.* One who dissembles.
**Disseminate,** dis-se'min-āt, *vt.* (disseminating, disseminated). To scatter; to spread.
**Dissemination,** dis-se'min-ā''shon, *n.* Act of disseminating; propagation.
**Disseminator,** dis-se'min-āt-ėr, *n.* One who disseminates.
**Dissension,** dis-sen'shon, *n.* Disagreement in opinion; discord; strife.
**Dissent,** dis-sent', *vi.* To disagree in opinion; to separate from an established church, in doctrines, rites, or government.—*n.* Disagreement; separation from an established church.

**Dissenter,** dis-sent'ėr, *n.* One who withdraws from an established church; a nonconformist.
**Dissentient,** dis-sen'shi-ent, *a.* Declaring dissent; disagreeing.—*a.* One who declares his dissent.
**Dissenting,** dis-sent'ing, *p.a.* Disagreeing; connected with a body of dissenters.
**Dissertation,** dis-sėr-tā'shon, *n.* A formal discourse; treatise; disquisition.
**Disserve,** dis-sėrv', *vt.* To do an ill service to; to harm.
**Disservice,** dis-sėr'vis, *n.* An ill-service; injury; harm; mischief.
**Dissever,** dis-sev'ėr, *vt.* To part in two; to disunite.
**Dissident,** dis'si-dent, *a.* Dissenting.—*n.* A dissenter.
**Dissilient,** dis-si'li-ent, *a.* Starting asunder; opening with an elastic force.
**Dissimilar,** dis-si'mi-lėr, *a.* Unlike.
**Dissimilarity,** dis-si'mi-la''ri-ti, *n.* Unlikeness; want of resemblance.
**Dissimilitude,** dis-si-mil'i-tūd, *n.* Unlikeness; want of resemblance.
**Dissimulate,** dis-sim'ū-lāt, *vt.* and *i.* To dissemble.
**Dissimulation,** dis-si'mū-lā''shon, *n.* Act of dissembling; false pretension; hypocrisy.
**Dissipate,** dis'si-pāt, *vt.* (dissipating, dissipated). To scatter; to spend; to squander.—*vi.* To scatter; to disperse; to vanish.
**Dissipated,** dis'si-pāt'ed, *p.a.* Dissolute; devoted to pleasure and vice.
**Dissipation,** dis-si-pā'shon, *n.* Dispersion; waste; dissolute conduct; diversion.
**Dissociate,** dis-sō'shi-āt, *vt.* (dissociating, dissociated). To separate, as from society; to disunite; to part.
**Dissociation,** dis-sō'shi-ā''shon, *n.* Act of dissociating; state of separation; disunion.
**Dissolubility,** dis-so'lū-bil''i-ti, *n.* State of being dissoluble.
**Dissoluble,** dis'so-lū-bl, *a.* Capable of being dissolved.
**Dissolute,** dis'sō-lūt, *a.* Loose in behavior and morals; licentious; debauched.
**Dissolution,** dis-sō-lū'shon, *n.* Act of dissolving; a melting or liquefaction; separation of parts; decomposition; death; destruction; the breaking up of an assembly.
**Dissolvable,** diz-zolv'a-bl, *a.* That may be dissolved, melted, or converted into fluid.
**Dissolve,** diz-zolv', *vt.* To melt; to break up; to put an end to; to cause to vanish.—*vi.* To be melted; to become soft or languid; to waste away; to perish; to break up.
**Dissolvent,** diz-zolv'ent, *a.* Having power to dissolve.—*n.* That which has the power of melting; a solvent.
**Dissolver,** diz-zolv'ėr, *n.* One who or that which dissolves.
**Dissonance,** dis'sō-nans, *n.* Disagreement in sound; discord.
**Dissonant,** dis'sō-nant, *a.* Discordant in sound; harsh; jarring; incongruous.
**Dissuade,** dis-swād', *vt.* (dissuading, dissuaded). To exhort against; to turn from a purpose by argument.
**Dissuasion,** dis-swā'zhon, *n.* Act of dissuading; advice in opposition to something.
**Dissuasive,** dis-swā'siv, *a.* Tending to dissuade.—*n.* Argument or motive that deters.
**Dissuasively,** dis-swā'siv-li, *adv.* In a way to dissuade.
**Dissyllabic,** dis-sil-lab'ik, *a.* Consisting of two syllables only.
**Dissyllable,** dis'sil-la-bl, *n.* A word of two syllables only.
**Distaff,** dis'taf, *n.* The staff to which a bunch of flax or tow is tied, and from which the thread is drawn in spinning.
**Distain,** dis-tān', *vt.* To discolor; to stain.
**Distance,** dis'tans, *n.* Remoteness in place or time; extent of interval between two things; the remoteness which respect requires; reserve; coldness.—*vt.* (distancing, distanced). To leave behind in a race; to outdo or excel.
**Distant,** dis'tant, *a.* Remote in place, time, relationship, etc.; implying haughtiness, indifference, etc.; cool; shy.
**Distantly,** dis'tant-li, *adv.* Remotely; at a distance; with reserve.
**Distaste,** dis-tāst', *n.* Aversion of the taste or mind; dislike.—*vt.* To dislike.
**Distasteful,** dis-tāst'ful, *a.* Unpleasant to the taste; nauseous; displeasing.
**Distemper,** dis-tem'pėr, *n.* Any morbid state of the body; disorder; a disease of young dogs; bad constitution of the mind; a kind of painting in which the pigments are mixed with size; a pigment so mixed.—*vt.* To disease; to derange; to ruffle.
**Distemperature,** dis-tem'pėr-ā-tūr, *n.* Tumult; perturbation of mind.
**Distempered,** dis-tem'pėrd, *p.a.* Diseased in body, or disordered in mind; biassed.
**Distend,** dis-tend', *vt.* To stretch by force from within; to swell.—*vi.* To swell; to dilate.
**Distensible,** dis-tens'i-bl, *a.* Capable of being distended or dilated.
**Distention,** dis-ten'shon, *n.* Act of distending; state of being distended.
**Distich,** dis'tik, *n.* A couple of poetic lines.
**Distil,** dis'til', *vi.* (distilling, distilled). To fall in drops; to practice distillation.—*vt.* To let fall in drops; to extract spirit from, by evaporation and condensation.
**Distillation,** dis-til-ā'shon, *n.* Act or process of distilling.
**Distillatory,** dis-til'ā-to-ri, *a.* Belonging to distillation.—*n.* A still.
**Distiller,** dis-til'ėr, *n.* One who distils.
**Distillery,** dis-til'ė-ri, *n.* The building where distilling is carried on.
**Distinct,** dis-tingkt', *a.* Separated by some mark; not the same in number or kind; separate in place; clear; definite.
**Distinction,** dis-tingk'shon, *n.* Act of distinguishing; that which distinguishes; difference; elevation of rank in society; eminence; a title or honor.
**Distinctive,** dis-tingkt'iv, *a.* Marking distinction; having power to distinguish.
**Distinctively,** dis-tingkt'iv-li, *adv.* In a distinctive manner; with distinction; plainly.
**Distinctly,** dis-tingkt'li, *adv.* In a distinct manner; clearly; plainly; obviously.
**Distinctness,** dis-tingkt'nes, *n.* Quality or state of being distinct; clearness; precision.
**Distinguish,** dis-ting'gwish, *vt.* To mark out by some peculiarity; to perceive; to make eminent; to signalize.—*vi.* To make a distinction; to find or show the difference.
**Distinguishable,** dis-ting'gwish-a-bl, *a.* Capable of being distinguished; worthy of note.
**Distinguished,** dist-ing'gwisht, *p.a.* Eminent.
**Distinguishing,** dis-ting'gwish-ing, *p.a.* Constituting distinction; characteristic.
**Distort,** dis-tort', *vt.* To twist; to pervert.
**Distortion,** dis-tor'shon, *n.* Act of distorting; a writhing motion; deformity; perversion of the true meaning of words.
**Distract,** dis-trakt', *vt.* To draw towards different objects; to perplex; to disorder the reason of; to render furious.
**Distracted,** dis-trakt'ed, *p.a.* Disordered in intellect; crazy; frantic; insane.
**Distractedly,** dis-trakt'ed-li, *adv.* Madly; furiously; wildly.
**Distracting,** dis-trakt'ing, *p.a.* Perplexing.
**Distraction,** dis-trak'shon, *n.* Derangement; frenzy; diversion.
**Distrain,** dis-trān', *vt.* To seize, as goods, for debt.—*vi.* To make seizure of goods.
**Distrainable,** dis-trān'a-bl, *a.* Liable to be distrained.
**Distrainer, Distrainor,** dis-trān'ėr, *n.* One who seizes goods for debt.

D

**Distraint,** dis-trānt, *n.* A distraining of goods.
**Distraught,** dis-trat', *a.* Distracted.
**Distress,** dis-tres', *n.* Anguish of body or mind; affliction; state of danger or destitution; act of distraining.—*vt.* To afflict with pain or anguish; to perplex.
**Distressed,** dis-trest', *p.a.* Afflicted; oppressed with calamity or misfortune.
**Distressful,** dis-tres'ful, *a.* Full of distress; proceeding from pain or anguish; calamitous; indicating distress.
**Distressfully,** dis-tres'ful-li, *adv.* In a distressful or painful manner.
**Distressing,** dis-tres'ing, *p.a.* Afflicting; grievous.
**Distributable,** dis-tri'būt-a-bl, *a.* That may be distributed.
**Distribute,** dis-tri'būt, *vt.* (distributing, distributed). To divide among two or more; to apportion: to administer, as justice; to classify.
**Distributor,** dis-tri'būt'ėr, *n.* One who distributes.
**Distribution,** dis-tri-bū'shon, *n.* Act of distributing; apportionment.
**Distributive,** dis-tri'būt-iv, *a.* That distributes; expressing separation or division.—*n.* A word that divides or distributes, as *each, every, either.*
**Distributively,** dis-tri'būt-iv-li, *adv.* Singly; not collectively.
**District,** dis'trikt, *n.* A limited extent of country; a circuit; a region.
**Distrust,** dis-trust', *vt.* To have no trust in; to doubt; to suspect.—*n.* Want of trust; doubt; suspicion; discredit.
**Distrustful,** dis-trust'ful, *a.* Apt to distrust; suspicious; not confident.
**Disturb,** dis-tėrb', *vt.* To throw into disorder; to agitate; to hinder; to move.
**Disturbance,** dis-tėrb'ans, *n.* State of being disturbed; commotion; excitement; interruption of a right.
**Disturber,** dis-tėrb'ėr, *n.* One who or that which disturbs.
**Ditch,** dich, *n.* A trench in the earth for drainage or defense.—*vi.* To dig a ditch.—*vt.* To dig a ditch in; to drain by a ditch; to surround with a ditch.
**Ditcher,** dich'ėr, *n.* One who digs ditches.
**Dithyramb,** di'thi-ramb, *n.* An ancient hymn in honor of Bacchus; a poem of impetuous and irregular character.
**Ditto,** dit'tō, *n.* A word used in lists, etc., meaning same as above; often written *Do.*
**Ditty,** dit'ti, *n.* A song; a poem to be sung.
**Diuretic,** dī-ū-rēt'ik, *a.* Tending to produce discharges of urine.—*n.* A medicine that has this effect.
**Diurnal,** dī-ėrn'al, *a.* Relating to day; daily.—*n.* In the Roman Catholic Church, a book containing the office of each day.
**Diurnally,** dī-ėrn'al-li, *adv.* Daily.
**Divagation,** dī-va-gā'shon, *n.* Deviation.
**Divan,** di-van', *n.* Among the Turks, a court of justice; a council or council-chamber; a cushioned seat standing against the wall of a room.
**Divaricate,** dī-va'ri-kāt, *vi.* To branch off; to fork.
**Divarication,** dī-va'ri-kā''shon, *n.* A parting into two branches; a crossing of fibers at different angles.
**Dive,** dīv, *vi.* (diving, dived). To plunge into water head-foremost; to go under water to execute some work; to go deep.
**Dive-bomber,** dīv-bom'ėr, *n.* An airplane specially designed for diving low in order to drop its bombs.
**Diver,** dīv'ėr, *n.* One who dives; one who works under water; a bird which dives.
**Diverge,** di-vėrj', *vi.* (diverging, diverged). To proceed from a point in different directions; to deviate; to vary.
**Divergence, Divergency,** di-vėrj'ens, di-vėr'jen-si, *n.* Act of diverging; a receding from each other.
**Divergent,** di-vėrj'ent, *a.* Diverging; receding from each other.
**Divers,** dī'vėrz, *a.* Different; various; sundry; more than one, but not many.
**Diverse,** di-vėrs', *a.* Different; unlike; various.
**Diversely,** di-vėrs'li, *adv.* In a diverse manner; variously.
**Diversifiable,** di-vėrs'i-fī-a-bl, *a.* Capable of being diversified.
**Diversification,** di-vėrs'i-fi-kā''shon, *n.* Act of diversifying; variation; variegation.
**Diversified,** di-vėrs'i-fīd, *p.a.* Distinguished by various forms; variegated.
**Diversify,** di-vėrs'i-fī, *vt.* (diversifying, diversified). To make diverse in form or qualities; to variegate; to give diversity to.
**Diversion,** di-vėr'shon, *n.* Act of diverting; that which diverts; amusement; a feigned attack.
**Diversity,** di-vėrs'i-ti, *n.* State of being diverse; contrariety; variety.
**Divert,** di-vėrt', *vt.* To turn aside; to amuse.
**Diverting,** di-vėrt'ing, *p.a.* Amusing.
**Divest,** di-vest', *vt.* To strip of clothes; to deprive.
**Dividable,** di-vīd'a-bl, *a.* Divisible.
**Divide,** di-vīd', *vt.* (dividing, divided). To part asunder; to separate; to keep apart; to distribute, allot; to set at variance.—*vi.* To part; to be of different opinions; to vote by the division of a legislative house into parties.
**Dividend,** di'vi-dend, *n.* A number which is to be divided; share of profit; share divided to creditors.
**Divider,** di-vīd'ėr, *n.* One who or that which divides; a distributor; *pl.* compasses.
**Divination,** di-vin-ā'shon, *n.* Act of divining; a foretelling future events, or discovering things secret, by magical means.
**Divine,** di-vīn', *a.* Of or belonging to God; excellent in the highest degree.—*n.* One versed in divinity; a clergyman.—*vt.* (divining, divined). To foretell; to presage; to guess.—*vi.* To practice divination; to have or utter presages; to guess.
**Diviner,** di-vīn'ėr, *n.* One who divines; one who professes divination, a soothsayer.
**Diving-bell,** dīv'ing-bel, *n.* An apparatus by means of which persons may descend below water to execute various operations.
**Divining-rod,** di-vīn'ing-rod, *n.* A hazel rod, which is said to point downwards over a spot where water or treasure is to be found.
**Divinity,** di-vin'i-ti, *n.* The state of being divine; God; a deity; the science of divine things; theology.
**Divisibility,** di-viz'i-bil''i-ti, *n.* Quality of being divisible.
**Divisible,** di-viz'i-bl, *a.* Capable of division; separable.
**Division,** di-vi'zhon, *n.* Act of dividing; state of being divided; separation; partition; portion; a separate body of men; a process or rule in arithmetic; part of an army, comprising all arms and services in due proportion.
**Divisional,** di-vizh'on-al, *a.* Pertaining to division; belonging to a division or district.
**Divisive,** di-vīz'iv, *a.* Creating division or discord.
**Divisor,** di-vīz'or, *n.* In *arithmetic,* the number by which the dividend is divided.
**Divorce,** di-vōrs', *n.* A legal dissolution of marriage; disunion of things closely united.—*vt.* (divorcing, divorced). To dissolve the marriage contract between; to separate.
**Divorcement,** di-vōrs'ment, *n.* The act of divorcing.
**Divot,** div'ot, *n.* A piece of turf cut out by a golfer when striking the ball.
**Divulge,** di-vulj', *vt.* (divulging, divulged). To make public; to disclose.
**Divulsion,** di-vul'shon, *n.* A pulling, tearing, or rending asunder, or separating.
**Dizen,** diz'n, *vt.* To dress; to bedizen.
**Dizziness,** diz'zi-nes, *n.* Giddiness; vertigo.
**Dizzy,** diz'zi, *a.* Having a sensation of whirling in the head; giddy; causing giddiness.—*vt.* (dizzying, dizzied). To make giddy.

**Djereed, Djerid,** je-rēd', *n.* A blunt javelin used in oriental military sports.
**Do,** dö, *vt.* or *auxiliary* (doing, pret. did, pp. done). To perform; to bring about; to pay (as honor, etc.); to transact; to finish; to prepare; to cook.—*vi.* To act or behave; to fare in health; to succeed; to suffice; to avail.
**Docile,** dō'sīl, *a.* Easily taught; ready to learn; tractable; pliant.
**Docility,** dō-si'li-ti, *n.* Quality of being docile.
**Dock,** dok, *n.* A troublesome weed; the tail of a beast cut short; the stump of a tail; an inclosed area on the side of a harbor or bank of a river for ships; the place where the accused stands in court.—*vt.* To cut off; to curtail; to deduct from; to put a ship in dock.
**Dockage,** dok'āj, *n.* Pay for using a dock.
**Docket,** dok'et, *n.* A summary; a bill tied to goods; a list of cases in a court.—*vt.* To make an abstract of; to mark the contents of papers on the back; to attach a docket to.
**Dockyard,** dok'yärd, *n.* A yard near a dock for naval stores.
**Doctor,** dok'tėr, *n.* A person who has received the highest degree in a university faculty; one licensed to practice medicine; a physician.—*vt.* To treat medically; to adulterate.
**Doctorate,** dok'tėr-āt, *n.* The degree of a doctor.
**Doctrinaire,** dok-tri-nār', *n.* A political theorist.
**Doctrinal,** dok'trin-al, *a.* Pertaining to doctrine; containing a doctrine.
**Doctrine,** dok'trin, *n.* Instruction; whatever is taught; a principle in any science; dogma; a truth of the gospel.
**Document,** do'kū-ment, *n.* Written evidence or proof; any authoritative paper containing instructions or proof.—*vt.* To furnish with documents.
**Documentary,** do-kū-ment'a-ri, *a.* Pertaining to or consisting in documents.
**Dodecagon,** dō-de'ka-gon, *n.* A figure with twelve sides.
**Dodge,** doj, *vt.* (dodging, dodged). To start aside; to quibble.—*vt.* To evade by a sudden shift of place.—*n.* An artifice; an evasion.
**Dodo,** dō'dō, *n.* An extinct bird of Mauritius, having a massive, clumsy body, short strong legs, and wings useless for flight.
**Doe,** dō, *n.* A female deer.
**Doer,** dö'ėr, *n.* One who does; actor; agent.
**Does,** duz. The third sing. present of *do.*
**Doeskin,** dō'skin, *n.* The skin of a doe; a compact twilled woollen cloth.
**Doff,** dof, *vt.* To put off.
**Dog,** dog, *n.* A domestic quadruped of many varieties; a mean fellow; a gay young man.—*vt.* (dogging, dogged). To follow insidiously; to worry with importunity.
**Dog-cart,** dog'kärt, *n.* A carriage with a box for holding sportsmen's dogs; a sort of double-seated gig.
**Dog-day,** dog'dā, *n.* One of the days when Sirius, the Dog-star, rises and sets with the sun.
**Doge,** dōj, *n.* The chief magistrate in republican Venice.
**Dog-eared,** dog'ērd, *a.* Having the corners of the leaves turned down (said of a book).
**Dog-fish,** dog'fish, *n.* A species of shark.
**Dogged,** dog'ed, *a.* Determined; pertinacious.
**Doggedly,** dog'ed-li, *adv.* With obstinate resolution.
**Dogger,** dog'ėr, *n.* A two-masted Dutch fishing-boat.
**Doggerel,** dog'ė-rel, *n.* A loose irregular kind of versification; wretched verse.
**Doggish,** dog'ish, *a.* Churlish; snappish.
**Dogma,** dog'ma, *n.* A settled opinion or belief; tenet; a doctrinal point.
**Dogmatic, Dogmatical,** dog-mat'ik, dog-mat'ik-al, *a.* Pertaining to a dogma; asserting, or asserted, with authority or arrogance; positive.
**Dogmatics,** dog-mat'iks, *n.* Doctrinal theology; essential doctrines of Christianity.
**Dogmatism,** dog'mat-izm, *n.* Positiveness in assertion; arrogance in opinion.
**Dogmatist,** dog'mat-ist, *n.* A dogmatic asserter; an arrogant advancer of principles.
**Dogmatize,** dog'mat-īz, *vi.* (dogmatizing, dogmatized). To assert with undue confidence; to advance principles with arrogance.
**Dog-star,** dog'stär, *n.* Sirius, a star of the first magnitude.
**Dog-tooth,** dog'töth, *n.* An eye-tooth.
**Doily,** doi'li, *n.* A small ornamental mat for glasses, etc.
**Doings,** dö'ingz, *n.pl.* Things done; transactions; conduct; bustle.
**Doit,** doit, *n.* A small Dutch copper coin; any small piece of money; a trifle.
**Doldrums,** dol'drumz, *n.pl.* The dumps.
**Dole,** dōl, *n.* That which is dealt out; share; gratuity; grief; sorrow.—*vt.* (doling, doled). To deal out; to distribute.
**Doleful,** dōl'ful, *a.* Full of pain, grief, etc.; expressing or causing grief; gloomy.
**Dolefully,** dōl'ful-li, *adv.* In a doleful manner; sorrowfully; dismally; sadly.
**Dolichocephalic, Dolichocephalous,** dol'i-kō-se-fal''ik, dol'i-kō-sef''a-lus, *a.* Long-skulled; used to denote skulls in which the diameter from side to side is small in proportion to the diameter from front to back.
**Doll,** dol, *n.* A child's puppet in human form.
**Dollar,** dol'lėr, *n.* A coin of the United States and Canada (= 100 cents).
**Dolman,** dol'man, *n.* A lady's mantle.
**Dolmen,** dol'men, *n.* An ancient structure consisting of one large unhewn stone resting on others; a cromlech.
**Dolomite,** dol'o-mīt, *n.* A granular crystalline or schistose rock compounded of carbonate of magnesia and carbonate of lime.
**Dolorous,** dō'lėr-us, *a.* Sorrowful; doleful.
**Dolorously,** dō'lėr-us-li, *adv.* Sorrowfully.
**Dolor,** dō'lėr, *n.* Sorrow; lamentation.
**Dolphin,** dol'fin, *n.* A small species of whale remarkable for gambolling in the water; a fish celebrated for its changes of color when dying.
**Dolt,** dōlt, *n.* A blockhead.
**Doltish,** dōlt'ish, *a.* Dull in intellect.
**Domain,** dō-mān', *n.* Territory governed; estate; a demesne.
**Dome,** dōm, *n.* A hemispherical roof of a building; a large cupola.
**Domestic,** dō-mes'tik, *a.* Belonging to the house or home; tame; not foreign.—*n.* A household servant.
**Domesticate,** dō-mes'tik-āt, *vt.* To accustom to remain much at home; to tame.
**Domestication,** dō-mes'tik-ā''shon, *n.* Act of domesticating; state of being domesticated.
**Domicile,** do'mi-sīl, *n.* A habitation; family residence.—*vt.* (domiciling, domiciled). To establish in a residence.
**Domiciliary,** do-mi-si'li-a-ri, *a.* Pertaining to a domicile.
**Dominant,** dom'in-ant, *a.* Governing; predominant; ascendant.
**Dominate,** dom'in-āt, *vt.* (dominating, dominated). To rule; to predominate over.
**Domination,** dom-in-ā'shon, *n.* Rule; tyranny.
**Domineer,** dom-in-ēr', *vi.* To rule tyrannically or with insolence (with *over*).
**Domineering,** dom-in-ēr'ing, *p.a.* Overbearing; insolent.
**Dominical,** dō-min'ik-al, *a.* Noting Sunday; relating to God.
**Dominican,** dō-min'ik-an, *n.* A Black-friar.
**Dominie,** dom'i-ni, *n.* A pedagogue.
**Dominion,** dō-min'i-on, *n.* Sovereign authority; district governed; region.
**Domino,** do'mi-nō, *n.* A masquerade dress; a half-mask; a person wearing a domino; *pl.* **(Dominoes),** a game played with pieces of ivory or bone dotted like dice.
**Don,** don, *n.* A Spanish title, corresponding to

D

Eng. Mr.; an important personage; a resident Fellow of a college at Oxford or Cambridge.—*vt.* (donning, donned). To put on; to invest with.
**Donate,** dō'nāt, *vt.* To bestow.
**Donation,** dō-nā'shon, *n.* Act of giving; that which is given; a gift; a present.
**Donative,** don'at-iv, *n.* A gift; a largess; a benefice given by the patron, without presentation, institution, or introduction by the ordinary.—*a.* Vested or vesting by donation.
**Donee,** dō-nē', *n.* One to whom a gift is made.
**Donjon,** don'jon, *n.* The principal tower of a castle; the keep.
**Donkey,** dong'ki, *n.* An ass.
**Donna,** don'na, *n.* A lady; as, *prima donna,* the first female singer in an opera, etc.
**Donor,** dō'nėr, *n.* One who gives.
**Dooly,** dö'li, *n.* A light palanquin or litter.
**Doom,** döm, *n.* Judicial sentence; fate; ruin.—*vt.* To condemn to punishment; to destine.
**Doomed,** dömd, *p.a.* Having the doom or fate settled; destined to speedy destruction.
**Doomsday,** dömz'dā, *n.* The day of judgment.
**Door,** dōr, *n.* The entrance of a house or room; the frame of boards that shuts such an entrance; avenue; means of approach.
**Dor, Dorr,** dor, *n.* A common British beetle.
**Dorian,** dō'ri-an, *n.* Pertaining to Doris in Greece.—*n.* A Greek of Doris.
**Doric,** dor'ik, *a.* Pertaining to Doris in Greece; denoting the earliest and plainest of the Grecian orders of architecture.
**Dormancy,** dor'man-si, *n.* State of being dormant; quiescence; sleep; abeyance.
**Dormant,** dor'mant, *a.* Sleeping; not used; inactive.
**Dormer, Dormer-window,** dor'mėr, dor'mėr-win-dō, *n.* A window in a sloping roof, the frame being placed vertically.
**Dormitory,** dor'mi-to-ri, *n.* A place to sleep in; a room in which a number sleep.
**Dormouse,** dor'mous, *n.*; pl. **Dormice,** dor'mīs. A small rodent which passes the winter in a lethargic or torpid state.
**Dormy,** dor'mi, *a.* In golf, applied to a player leading by as many holes as still remain to be played.
**Dorsal,** dor'sal, *a.* Pertaining to the back.
**Dory,** dō'ri, *n.* A European yellow fish, with a protrusible mouth; a small boat.
**Dose,** dōs, *n.* The quantity of medicine given at one time; something given to be swallowed.—*vt.* (dosing, dosed). To give in doses; to give medicine to.
**Dossier,** dos'ē-ā, *n.* A collection of documents of information about a person or incident.
**Dot,** dot, *n.* A small point, as made with a pen, etc.; a speck.—*vt.* (dotting, dotted). To mark with a dot; to diversify with small objects.—*vi.* To make dots.
**Dotage,** dōt'āj, *n.* Feebleness of mind, particularly in old age; excessive fondness.
**Dotal,** dōt'al, *a.* Pertaining to dower.
**Dotard,** dōt'ėrd, *n.* One whose mind is impaired by age; one foolishly fond.
**Dotation,** dō-tā'shon, *n.* Act of bestowing a marriage portion on a woman; endowment.
**Dote,** dōt, *vi.* (doting, doted). To have the intellect impaired by age; to be foolishly fond.
**Doting,** dōt'ing, *p.a.* Having the mind impaired by age; foolishly fond.
**Dotterel, Dottrel,** dot'tėr-el, dot'trel, *n.* A species of plover; a booby; a dupe.
**Double,** du'bl, *a.* Twofold; forming a pair; of extra size, quality, etc.; deceitful.—*vt.* (doubling, doubled). To make twofold; to fold; to increase by adding an equal amount to; to sail round (a cape, etc.).—*vi.* To increase twofold; to turn or wind in running; to use sleights.—*n.* Twice as much; a turn in running; a shift; a duplicate; a wraith.
**Double-bass,** du'bl-bās, *n.* The lowest-toned instrument of the violin class.
**Double-dealing,** du'bl-dēl-ing, *n.* Deceitful practice; duplicity.
**Double-entry,** du'bl-en-tri, *n.* A mode of book-keeping in which every transaction is entered on the debit side of one account and the credit side of another.
**Double-star,** du'bl-stär, *n.* A star which in the telescope is resolved into two stars.
**Doublet,** du'blet, *n.* A close-fitting body garment; one of a pair; one of two words really the same but different in form.
**Doubling,** du'bl-ing, *n.* Act of making double; a fold; a lining.
**Doubloon,** dub-lön', *n.* A Spanish gold coin.
**Doubly,** du'bli, *adv.* In twice the quantity; to twice the degree.
**Doubt,** dout, *vi.* To waver in opinion or judgment; to question; to suspect.—*vt.* To deem uncertain; to distrust.—*n.* A wavering in opinion; uncertainty; suspicion.
**Doubter,** dout'ėr, *n.* One who doubts.
**Doubtful,** dout'ful, *a.* Full of doubt or doubts; hesitating; ambiguous; precarious; suspicious.
**Doubtfully,** dout'ful-li, *adv.* In a doubtful manner; dubiously.
**Doubtless,** dout'les, *adv.* Without doubt; unquestionably.
**Doubtlessly,** dout'les-li, *adv.* Doubtless.
**Douceur,** dö-sėr', *n.* A gift; bribe; gratuity.
**Douche,** dösh, *n.* A jet of water directed upon some part of the body.
**Dough,** dō, *n.* Flour or meal moistened and kneaded, but not baked; paste of bread.
**Doughtily,** dou'ti-li, *adv.* In a doughty manner.
**Doughty,** dou'ti, *a.* Noble; brave; valiant.
**Doughy,** dō'i, *a.* Like dough; soft; pale.
**Douse, Dowse,** dous, *vt.* and *i.* To plunge into water; to drench.
**Dove,** duv, *n.* A pigeon; a word of endearment.
**Dove-cot, Dove-cote,** duv'kot, duv'kōt, *n.* A place for pigeons.
**Dovetail,** duv'tāl, *n.* A mode of joining boards by letting one piece into another in the form of a dove's tail spread, or wedge reversed.—*vt.* and *i.* To unite by the above method; to fit exactly.
**Dowager,** dou'ā-jėr, *n.* A title given to the widow of a person of title, provided that she is mother, grandmother, or stepmother of the successor.
**Dowdy,** dou'di, *n.* An awkward, ill-dressed woman.—*a.* Ill-dressed; vulgar-looking.
**Dowel,** dou'el, *n.* A pin of wood or iron to join boards, etc.—*vt.* (dowelling, dowelled). To fasten by dowels.
**Dower,** dou'ėr, *n.* That portion of the property of a man which his widow enjoys during her life; the property which a woman brings to her husband in marriage; dowry.
**Dowlas,** dou'las, *n.* A coarse linen cloth.
**Down,** doun, *n.* The fine soft feathers of birds; fine hair; the pubescence of plants; a hill; a dune; a tract of naked, hilly land.—*adv.* In a descending direction; on the ground; into less bulk; paid in ready money.—*prep.* Along in descent; toward the mouth of.—*a.* Downcast; dejected.
**Downcast,** doun'kast, *a.* Cast downward; dejected.
**Down-come,** doun'kum, *n.* A sudden or heavy fall; ruin; destruction.
**Downfall,** foun'fal, *n.* A falling down; loss of wealth or high position; ruin.
**Downhill,** doun'hil, *a.* Descending; easy.—*adv.* Down a hill or slope.
**Downpour,** doun'pōr, *n.* A pouring down; especially, a heavy or continuous shower.
**Downright,** doun'rīt, *adv.* Right down; in plain terms; utterly.—*a.* Directly to the point; plain; blunt; utter.
**Downstairs,** doun'stārz, *a.* or *adv.* Descending the stairs; on a lower flat.
**Downthrow,** doun'thrō, *n.* A throwing down; a falling or sinking of strata.
**Downtrodden,** doun'trod-n, *a.* Trodden down; oppressed.

**Downward, Downwards,** doun'wėrd, doun'wėrdz, *adv.* From a higher place or state to a lower; in direction from a head or source.
**Downward,** *a.* Sloping down; descending.
**Downy,** doun'i, *a.* Covered with, or pertaining to, down, soft; soothing.
**Dowry,** dou'ri, *n.* The property which a woman brings to her husband in marriage; a dower; gift.
**Doxology,** doks-ol'o-ji, *n.* A hymn or form of giving glory to God.
**Doze,** dōz, *vi.* (dozing, dozed). To sleep lightly; to be half asleep.—*vt.* To pass or spend in drowsiness.—*n.* A slight sleep; a slumber.
**Dozen,** du'zn, *n.* Twelve things regarded collectively.
**Dozy,** dōz'i, *a.* Drowsy; sleepy; sluggish.
**Drab,** drab, *n.* A sluttish woman; a strumpet; a thick woollen cloth of a dun color; a dull brownish color.—*a.* Of a dull brown color.
**Drachm,** dram, *n.* Same as *Drachma, Dram.*
**Drachma,** drak'ma, *n.* A Greek silver coin value one franc; a Greek weight of about 2 dwts. 7 grains troy.
**Draconic, Draconian,** drā-kon'ik, drā-kō'ni-an, *a.* Relating to Draco, the Athenian lawgiver; extremely severe.
**Draff,** draf, *n.* Refuse; dregs; waste matter.
**Draft,** dräft, *n.* A detachment of men or things; an order for money; the first sketch of any writing; a sketch.—*vt.* To make a draft of; to sketch; to select.
**Draftsman,** dräfts'man, *n. See* DRAUGHTSMAN.
**Drag,** drag, *vt.* (dragging, dragged). To draw along the ground by main force; to haul; to explore with a drag.—*vi.* To hang so as to trail on the ground; to move slowly.—*n.* A net drawn along the bottom of the water; an instrument to catch hold of things under water; a machine for dredging; a low cart; a long coach; a contrivance to stop a wheel of a carriage; whatever serves to retard.
**Draggle,** drag'gl, *vt.* (draggling, draggled). To dirty by drawing on the ground.—*vi.* To become dirty by being drawn on the ground.
**Drag-net,** drag'net, *n.* A net to be drawn along the bottom of a river or pond.
**Dragoman,** drag'ō-man, *n.*; pl. **Dragomans.** An interpreter and traveller's guide or agent in eastern countries.
**Dragon,** dra'gon, *n.* A fabulous winged monster; a fierce person; a kind of small lizard.
**Dragonet,** dra'gon-et, *n.* A little dragon; a small fish of the goby family.
**Dragon-fly,** dra'gon-flī, *n.* A fly that preys upon other insects.
**Dragonish,** dra'gon-ish, *a.* In the form of a dragon; dragon-like.
**Dragon's-blood,** dra'gonz-blud, *n.* The red juice of certain tropical plants, used for coloring varnishes, staining marble, etc.
**Dragoon,** dra-gön', *n.* A heavy cavalry soldier.—*vt.* To harass; to compel by force.
**Drain,** drān, *vt.* To draw off; to filter; to make dry; to exhaust.—*vi.* To flow off gradually.—*n.* A channel for liquid; a sewer; gradual or continuous withdrawal.
**Drainage,** drān'āj, *n.* The act or art of draining; the system of drains; that which flows out of drains.
**Drainer,** drān'ėr, *n.* A utensil on which articles are placed to drain; one who or that which drains.
**Drake,** drāk, *n.* The male of ducks.
**Dram,** dram, *n.* The eighth part of an ounce, or sixty grains apothecaries' measure; the sixteenth part of an ounce avoirdupois; as much spirituous liquor as is drunk at once.
**Drama,** drä'ma, *n.* A representation on a stage; a play; dramatic literature.
**Dramatic, Dramatical,** dra-mat'ik, dra-mat'ik-al, *a.* Pertaining to the drama; represented by action; theatrical.
**Dramatist,** drä'mat-ist, *n.* The author of a dramatic composition.
**Dramatize,** drä'mat-īz, *vt.* To compose in the form of the drama.
**Dramaturgy,** dräm'a-tėr-ji, *n.* The science of dramatic composition and representation.
**Drape,** drāp, *vt.* (draping, draped). To cover with cloth or drapery.
**Draper,** drāp'ėr, *n.* One who sells cloths.
**Drapery,** drāp'ė-ri, *n.* The occupation of a draper; fabrics of wool or linen; clothes or hangings.
**Drastic,** dras'tik, *a.* Acting with strength or violence.—*n.* A strong purgative.
**Draught,** dräft, *n.* The act of drawing; quantity drunk at once; a sketch or outline; the depth a ship sinks in water; a current of air; *pl.* a game played on a checkered board.—*vt.* To draw out; to draft.—*a.* Used for drawing; drawn from the barrel, etc.
**Draughtsman,** dräfts'man, *n.* One who draws plans or designs; one of the pieces in the game of draughts.
**Draughty,** dräf'ti, *a.* Of or pertaining to draughts of air; exposed to draughts.
**Dravidian,** dra-vid'yan, *a.* Pertaining to Dravida, an old province of S. India: applied to a distinct family of tongues spoken in S. India, Ceylon, etc.
**Draw,** dra, *vt.* (drawing, pret. drew, pp. drawn). To pull along or towards; to cause to come; to unsheathe; to suck; to attract; to inhale; to stretch; to lead, as a motive; to represent by lines drawn on a surface; to describe; to infer; to derive; to draft; to require a certain depth of water; to bend (a bow); to end indecisively.—*vi.* To pull; to shrink; to advance; to practice drawing; to make a written demand for money.—*n.* Act of drawing; the lot or chance drawn; a drawn game.
**Drawback,** dra'bak, *n.* What detracts from profit or pleasure; duties on goods paid back when exported.
**Drawbridge,** dra'brij, *n.* A bridge which may be raised or drawn aside.
**Drawer,** dra'ėr, *n.* One who or that which draws; he who draws a bill; a sliding box in a case, etc.; *pl.* an under-garment for the lower limbs.
**Drawing,** dra'ing, *n.* Act of one who draws; representation of objects by lines and shades; delineation.
**Drawing-room,** dra'ing-röm, *n.* A room for receiving company in; formal reception of company at a court.
**Drawl,** dral, *vi.* To speak with slow, prolonged utterance.—*vt.* To utter in a slow tone.—*n.* A lengthened utterance.
**Draw-well,** dra'wel, *n.* A deep well from which water is drawn by a long cord or pole.
**Dray,** drā, *n.* A low cart or carriage on wheels, drawn by a horse.
**Dread,** dred, *n.* Fear, united with respect; terror; the person or the thing dreaded.—*a.* Exciting great fear; terrible; venerable.—*vt.* and *i.* To fear in a great degree.
**Dreadful,** dred'ful, *a.* Awful; terrible.
**Dreadfully,** dred'ful-li, *adv.* Terribly.
**Dreadless,** dred'les, *a.* Fearless; intrepid.
**Dreadnought,** dred'nat, *n.* A person that fears nothing; a thick cloth with a long pile; a garment made of such cloth; a general term for a battleship.
**Dream,** drēm, *n.* The thought of a person in sleep; a vain fancy.—*vi.* To have images in the mind, in sleep; to imagine; to think idly.—*vt.* To see in a dream; to spend idly.
**Dreamer,** drēm'ėr, *n.* One who dreams; a fanciful man; a visionary.
**Dreamless,** drēm'les, *a.* Free from dreams.
**Dreamy,** drēm'i, *a.* Full of dreams; visionary.
**Drear,** drēr, *a.* Dismal; gloomy.
**Drearily,** drē'ri-li, *adv.* Gloomily.
**Dreary,** drē'ri, *a.* Dismal; gloomy; oppressively

D

monotonous.

**Dredge,** drej, *n.* An oyster net; a dredging-machine.—*vt.* (dredging, dredged). To take with a dredge; to deepen with a dredging-machine; to powder; to sprinkle flour on meat while roasting.

**Dredger,** drej'ėr, *n.* One who uses a dredge; a utensil for scattering flour on meat while roasting; a dredging-machine.

**Dredging-machine,** drej'ing-ma-shēn, *n.* A machine to take up mud, etc., from the bottom of rivers or docks.

**Dreggy,** dreg'i, *a.* Containing dregs; foul.

**Dregs,** dregz, *n.pl.* Lees; grounds; the most vile and despicable part.

**Drench,** drensh, *vt.* To wet thoroughly; to soak; to purge violently.—*n.* A draught; a large dose of liquid medicine for an animal.

**Dress,** dres, *vt.* To make straight; to put in good order; to cleanse and cover a wound; to prepare; to curry, rub, and comb; to clothe; to array; to trim.—*vi.* To arrange in a line; to put on clothes; to pay regard to dress.—*n.* Apparel; attire; a lady's gown.

**Dresser,** dres'ėr, *n.* One who dresses; a table on which food is dressed; a low cupboard for dishes.

**Dressing,** dres'ing, *n.* Act of one who dresses; manure; application to a sore; stuffing of fowls, pigs, etc.; starch, etc., used in finishing silk, linen, etc.; moulding round doors, windows, etc.

**Dressing-case,** dres'ing-kās, *n.* A box containing toilet requisites.

**Dressing-room,** dres'ing-röm, *n.* A room for dressing in.

**Dressy,** dres'i, *a.* Showy in dress.

**Dribble,** drib'l, *vi.* (dribbling, dribbled). To fall in a quick succession of drops; to trickle; to take a football up the field by means of a series of short kicks, keeping the ball near to the foot and under control.—*vt.* To throw down in drops.

**Driblet,** drib'let, *n.* A small drop; a small sum, as one of a series.

**Drift,** drift, *n.* That which is driven by wind or water; impulse; tendency; aim; velocity of a current; the distance a vessel is driven by a current; rocks conveyed by glaciers and deposited over a country while submerged; in S. Africa, a ford.—*vi.* To move along like anything driven; to accumulate in heaps; to float or be driven by a current.—*vt.* To drive into heaps.—*a.* Drifted by wind or currents.

**Driftless,** drift'les, *a.* Aimless.

**Drill,** dril, *vt.* To pierce with a drill; to teach soldiers their proper movements, etc.; to teach by repeated exercise; to sow in rows; to furrow.—*vi.* To sow in drills; to muster for exercise.—*n.* A pointed instrument for boring holes; act of training soldiers; a row of seeds; a furrow.

**Drill,** dril, *n.* A kind of coarse linen or cotton cloth.

**Drink,** dringk, *vi.* (drinking, pret. drank, pp. drunk or drunken). To swallow liquor; to take spirituous liquors to excess.—*vt.* To swallow, as liquids; to absorb.—*n.* Liquor to be swallowed; any beverage; potion.

**Drinkable,** dringk'a-bl, *a.* That may be drunk; fit or suitable for drink.

**Drinker,** dringk'ėr, *n.* One who drinks; a tippler.

**Drip,** drip, *vi.* (dripping, dripped). To fall in drops.—*vt.* To let fall in drops.—*n.* A falling in drops; the eaves; a projecting moulding.

**Dripping,** drip'ing, *n.* A falling in drops; the fat which falls from meat in roasting.

**Drive,** drīv, *vt.* (driving, pret. drove, pp. driven). To impel; to hurry on; to impel and guide; to convey in a carriage; to carry on.—*vi.* To be impelled along; to aim at; to strike with force.—*n.* A journey in a vehicle; a road for driving on; a sweeping blow.

**Drivel,** dri'vel, *vi.* (drivelling, drivelled). To slaver; to dote; to talk rubbish.—*n.* Slaver; senseless twaddle.

**Driveller,** dri'vel-ėr, *n.* An idiot, twaddler.

**Driver,** drīv'ėr, *n.* One who or that which drives; a large quadrilateral sail; a main wheel; a golf club for long strokes.

**Drizzle,** driz'l, *vi.* (drizzling, drizzled). To rain in small drops.—*vt.* To shed in small drops or particles.—*n.* A small or fine rain.

**Drizzly,** driz'li, *a.* Shedding small rain.

**Droll,** drōl, *a.* Comic; queer; facetious.—*n.* A jester; a farce.

**Drollery,** drōl'ė-ri, *n.* Buffoonery; comical stories.

**Dromedary,** drom'ē-da-ri, *n.* A swift camel, usually the Arabian, with one hump, in distinction from the Bactrian, which has two.

**Drone,** drōn, *n.* The male or non-working bee; an idler; a low humming sound; a large tube of the bagpipe.—*vi.* (droning, droned). To give a low dull sound; to hum.

**Dronish,** drōn'ish, *a.* Idle; sluggish.

**Droop,** dröp, *vi.* To hang down; to languish; to fail; to be dispirited.—*vt.* To let sink or hang down.—*n.* A drooping position or state.

**Drop,** drop, *n.* A globule of any liquid; an earring; a small quantity; part of a gallows; a distance to fall.—*vt.* (dropping, dropped). To pour or let fall in drops; to let fall; to let down; to quit; to utter casually.—*vi.* To fall in drops; to fall; to cease; to come unexpectedly.

**Dropping,** drop'ing, *n.* A falling in drops; that which drops; *pl.* the dung of animals.

**Drop-scene,** drop'sēn, *n.* A scenic picture, which descends in front of the stage.

**Dropsical,** drop'sik-al, *a.* Diseased with, or inclined to, dropsy; of the nature of dropsy.

**Dropsy,** drop'si, *n.* An unnatural collection of water in any part of the body.

**Drosky,** dros'ki, *n.* A light four-wheeled open carriage.

**Dross,** dros, *n.* The scum of metals; waste matter; refuse.

**Drossy,** dros'i, *a.* Like or pertaining to dross; full of dross; foul.

**Drought,** drout, *n.* Dry weather; want of rain; aridness; thirst; lack.

**Droughty,** drout'i, *a.* Dry; wanting rain.

**Drove,** drōv, *n.* A collection of cattle driven; a crowd of people in motion.

**Drover,** drōv'ėr, *n.* One who drives cattle or sheep to market.

**Drown,** droun, *vt.* To deprive of life by immersion in water, etc.; to inundate; to overwhelm.—*vi.* To be suffocated in water, etc.

**Drowse,** drouz, *vi.* (drowsing, drowsed). To nod in slumber; to doze; to look heavy.—*vt.* To make heavy with sleep, or stupid.

**Drowsily,** drou'zi-li, *adv.* Sleepily.

**Drowsy,** drou'zi, *a.* Inclined to sleep; dull; sluggish; lulling.

**Drub,** drub, *vt.* (drubbing, drubbed). To cudgel; to thrash.—*n.* A blow; a thump.

**Drubbing,** drub'ing, *n.* A sound beating.

**Drudge,** druj, *vi.* (drudging, drudged). To labor at mean work.—*n.* One who labors hard in servile employments; a slave.

**Drudgery,** druj'ė-ri, *n.* Hard labor; toilsome work; ignoble toil.

**Drug,** drug, *n.* Any substance used in medicine; an article of slow sale.—*vt.* (drugging, drugged). To mix with drugs; to introduce a narcotic into; to dose to excess with drugs.

**Drugget,** drug'et, *n.* A coarse woollen cloth or felted stuff.

**Druggist,** drug'ist, *n.* One who deals in drugs.

**Druid,** drū'id, *n.* A priest and judge among the ancient Celtic nations.

**Druidic, Druidical,** drū-id'ik, drū-id'ik-al, *a.* Pertaining to the Druids.

**Druidism,** drū'id-izm, *n.* The doctrines, rites, and ceremonies of the Druids.

**Drum,** drum, *n.* A hollow cylindrical instrument of music beaten with sticks; something in the form of a drum; the tympanum of the ear.—*vi.* (drumming, drummed). To beat a drum; to beat with the fingers, as with drumsticks; to beat rapidly.—*vt.* To expel or summon by beat of drum.

**Drumhead,** drum'hed, *n.* The head of a drum; the top part of a capstan.

**Drum-major,** drum'mā-jėr, *n.* The chief drummer of a regiment.

**Drummer,** drum'ėr, *n.* One whose office is to beat the drum in military exercises.

**Drunk,** drungk, *a.* Overcome with alcoholic liquor; intoxicated.

**Drunkard,** drungk'ėrd, *n.* A person who is habitually or frequently drunk.

**Drunken,** drungk'en, *p.a.* Inebriated; given to drunkenness; proceeding from intoxication.

**Drunkenness,** drungk'en-nes, *n.* Intoxication; inebriety.

**Drupe,** dröp, *n.* A stone fruit, as the plum.

**Dry,** drī, *a.* Destitute of moisture; arid; free from juice; thirsty; uninteresting; sarcastic; harsh; cold.—*vt.* (drying, dried). To free from moisture; to deprive of natural juice; to drain.—*vi.* To lose moisture; to evaporate wholly.

**Dryad,** drī'ad, *n.* A nymph of the woods.

**Dryer, Drier,** drī'ėr, *n.* One who or that which dries; that which exhausts moisture.

**Dryly, Drily,** drī'li, *adv.* In a dry manner; coldly; sarcastically.

**Dryness,** drī'nes, *n.* State or quality of being dry; jejuneness; causticity.

**Dry-nurse,** drī'nėrs, *n.* A nurse who attends but does not suckle a child.

**Dry-rot,** drī'rot, *n.* A decay of timber, occasioned by various species of fungi.

**Dual,** dū'al, *a.* Expressing the number two; existing as two; twofold.

**Dualism,** dū'al-izm, *n.* A twofold division; the belief in two gods, the one good, the other evil; the doctrine of the existence of spirit and matter as distinct entities.

**Dualist,** dū'al-ist, *n.* One who holds the doctrine of dualism.

**Duality,** dū-al'i-ti, *n.* The state of being dual or twofold.

**Dub,** dub, *vt.* (dubbing, dubbed). To tap with a sword and make a knight; to speak of as; to smooth; to trim.

**Dubiety,** dū-bī'e-ti, *n.* Doubtfulness.

**Dubious,** dū'bi-us, *a.* Wavering in opinion; doubtful; uncertain.

**Dubiously,** dū'bi-us-li, *adv.* Doubtfully.

**Ducal,** dūk'al, *a.* Pertaining to a duke.

**Ducally,** dūk'al-li, *adv.* In a ducal manner.

**Ducat,** duk'at, *n.* A coin formerly common in Europe, either of silver or gold.

**Duchess,** duch'es, *n.* The wife of a duke; a lady who has the sovereignty of a duchy.

**Duchy,** duch'i, *n.* The dominion of a duke.

**Duck,** duk, *vt.* and *i.* To plunge in water; to bow, stoop, or nod.—*n.* A water-fowl; a term of endearment; an inclination of the head; a canvas or coarse cloth.

**Duckling,** duk'ling, *n.* A young duck.

**Duct,** dukt, *n.* A canal or tube, especially in animal bodies and plants.

**Ductile,** duk'tīl, *a.* That may be drawn out; docile; tractable; flexible.

**Ductility,** duk-til'i-ti, *n.* The property of metals which renders them capable of being drawn out without breaking; obsequiousness; ready compliance.

**Dud,** dud, *n.* A shell which fails to explode; hence an incompetent person or a defective thing.

**Dude,** dūd, *n.* A dandy of the first water; a brainless exquisite.

**Dudgeon,** du'jon, *n.* A small dagger, or the handle of a dagger; ill-will; sullenness.

**Due,** dū, *a.* Owed; owing; suitable; proper; attributable; that ought to have arrived by the time specified.—*adv.* Directly.—*n.* That which law, office, rank, etc., require to be paid or done; fee; right; just title.

**Duel,** dū'el, *n.* A premeditated combat between two persons; single combat; contest.

**Duellist,** dū'el-ist, *n.* One who fights duels.

**Duello,** dū-el'lō, *n.* The art of duelling; the code of laws which regulate it.

**Duenna,** dö-en'na, *n.* Formerly, the chief lady in waiting on the Queen of Spain; an elderly woman in charge of a younger; a governess.

**Duet,** dū'et, *n.* A piece of music for two performers, vocal or instrumental.

**Dug,** dug, *n.* The pap or nipple: now applied only to beasts, unless in contempt.

**Dug-out,** dug out, *n.* A rudely hollowed-out canoe from trunk of tree; an underground shelter from shells; an elderly officer recalled to duty from retirement.

**Duke,** dūk, *n.* One of the highest order of nobility; a sovereign prince.

**Dukedom,** dūk'dum, *n.* The jurisdiction, possessions, title, or quality of a duke.

**Dulcet,** dul'set, *a.* Sweet; harmonious.

**Dulcimer,** dul'si-mėr, *n.* A stringed instrument of music, played on by two sticks.

**Dull,** dul, *a.* Stupid; slow; blunt; drowsy; cheerless; not bright or clear; tarnished; uninteresting.—*vt.* To make dull; to stupefy; to blunt; to make sad; to sully.—*vi.* To become dull, blunt, or stupid.

**Dullard,** dul'ėrd, *n.* A stupid person; dolt.

**Dully,** dul'li, *adv.* Stupidly; sluggishly.

**Dulness, Dullness,** dul'nes, *n.* Stupidity; heaviness; slowness; dimness.

**Dulse,** duls, *n.* An edible sea-weed.

**Duly,** dū'li, *adv.* Properly; fitly.

**Dumb,** dum, *a.* Incapable of speech; mute; silent; not accompanied with speech.

**Dumb-bell,** dum'bel, *n.* One of a pair of weights used for exercise.

**Dumbly,** dum'li, *adv.* Mutely.

**Dumdum,** dum-dum, *n.* A soft-nosed bullet which expands and lacerates on striking.

**Dumfound, Dumbfound,** dum-found', *vt.* To strike dumb; to confuse. Also *Dumfounder.*

**Dummy,** dum'i, *n.* One who is dumb; the exposed hand when three persons play at whist; a sham article.

**Dump,** dump, *n.* A dull state of the mind; sadness; a thud; a clumsy piece; *pl.* low spirits; gloom.

**Dump,** dump, *n.* A heap of refuse; a place where refuse is deposited; a large concentration of military stores, especially of ammunition.

**Dumpish,** dump'ish, *a.* Melancholy; depressed in spirits.

**Dumpling,** dump'ling, *n.* A pudding of boiled suet paste, with or without fruit.

**Dumpy,** dump'i, *a.* Short and thick.

**Dun,** dun, *a.* Of a dark dull color; swarthy.—*vt.* (dunning, dunned). To demand a debt from; to urge importunately.—*n.* An importunate creditor; urgent demand for payment.

**Dunce,** duns, *n.* One slow at learning; a dullard; a dolt.

**Dunderhead,** dun'dėr-hed, *n.* A dolt.

**Dune,** dūn, *n.* A sand-hill on the sea-coast.

**Dung,** dung, *n.* The excrement of animals.—*vt.* To manure; to immerse (calico) in cow-dung and water.—*vi.* To void excrement.

**Dungeon,** dun'jon, *n.* A strong tower in the middle of a castle; a deep, dark place of confinement.

**Dunghill,** dung'hil, *n.* A heap of dung.—*a.* Sprung from the dunghill; mean; low.

**Dunlin,** dun'lin, *n.* A species of sandpiper.

**Dunnage,** dun'āj, *n.* Branches of brushwood, etc., used as a support for cargo.

**Dunnish,** dun'ish, *a.* Inclined to a dun color; somewhat dun.

**Duodecimal,** dū-ō-de'si-mal, *a.* Proceeding in computation by twelves; twelfth.

**Duodecimo,** dū-ō-de'si-mō, *a.* Consisting of twelve leaves to a sheet.—*n.* A book in which a sheet is folded into twelve leaves.

**Duodenum,** dū-ō-dē'num, *n.* The first portion of

D

the small intestines.
**Dupe,** dūp, *n.* One who is cheated; one easily deceived.—*vt.* (duping, duped). To impose on.
**Duplex,** dū'pleks, *a.* Double; twofold.
**Duplicate,** dū'pli-kāt, *a.* Double; twofold.—*n.* A copy; a transcript.—*vt.* To double.
**Duplication,** dū-pli-kā'shon, *n.* Act of doubling; a fold; multiplication by 2.
**Duplicity,** dū-pli'si-ti, *n.* Doubleness of heart or speech; guile; deception.
**Durability,** dūr-a-bil'i-ti, *n.* Quality of being durable.
**Durable,** dūr'a-bl, *a.* Having the quality of lasting long; permanent; firm.
**Durably,** dūr'a-bli, *adv.* In a durable manner.
**Dura-mater,** dū'ra-mā-tėr, *n.* The outer membrane of the brain.
**Duramen,** dū-rā'men, *n.* The heart-wood of an exogenous tree.
**Durance,** dūr'ans, *n.* Imprisonment; custody.
**Duration,** dūr-ā'shon, *n.* Continuance in time; power of continuance; permanency.
**Durbar,** dėr'bär, *n.* An Indian state levee or audience.
**Duress,** dūr'es, *n.* Constraint; imprisonment.
**During,** dūr'ing, *prep.* For the time of the continuance of.
**Dusk,** dusk, *a.* Tending to darkness; moderately black.—*n.* A middle degree between light and darkness; twilight.
**Duskish,** dusk'ish, *a.* Moderately dusky.
**Dusky,** dusk'i, *a.* Partially dark; dark colored; not bright.
**Dust,** dust, *n.* Fine dry particles of earth, etc.; powder; earth as symbolic of mortality; a low condition.—*vt.* To free from dust; to sprinkle, as with dust.
**Duster,** dust'ėr, *n.* A cloth, etc., for removing dust; a sieve.
**Dusty,** dust'i, *a.* Covered with dust; like dust.
**Dutch,** duch, *a.* Pertaining to Holland, or to its inhabitants.—*n.pl.* The people of Holland; *sing.* their language.
**Duteous,** dū'tē-us, *a.* Pertaining to duty; dutiful.
**Dutiful,** dū'ti-ful, *a.* Regularly performing duties required toward superiors; respectful.
**Duty,** dū'ti, *n.* That which a person is bound to perform; obligation; act of reverence or respect; business, service, or office; tax, impost or customs.
**Dwarf,** dwarf, *n.* A person or plant much below the ordinary size.—*vt.* To stunt; to make or keep small; to cause to appear small by comparison.—*a.* Below the common size; stunted.
**Dwarfish,** dwarf'ish, *a.* Like a dwarf; very small; petty.
**Dwell,** dwel, *vi.* (pret. and pp. dwelled). To live in a place; to reside; to hang on with fondness; to continue.
**Dweller,** dwel'ėr, *n.* An inhabitant.
**Dwelling,** dwel'ing, *n.* Habitation; abode.
**Dwindle,** dwin'dl, *vi.* (dwindling, dwindled). To diminish gradually; to shrink; to sink.
**Dye,** dī, *vt.* (dyeing, dyed). To stain; to give a new and permanent color to.—*n.* A coloring liquid or matter; tinge.
**Dyer,** dī'ėr, *n.* One whose occupation is to dye cloth and the like.
**Dying,** dī'ing, *a.* Mortal; destined to death; uttered, given, etc., just before death; pertaining to death; fading away.
**Dyke,** dīk. *See* DIKE.
**Dynamic, Dynamical,** dī-nam'ik, dī-nam'ik-al, *a.* Pertaining to strength, or to dynamics.
**Dynamics,** dī-nam'iks, *n.* The science which investigates the action of force.
**Dynamite,** din'a-mīt, *n.* An explosive substance consisting of some powdery matter impregnated with nitro-glycerine.
**Dynamo,** dī'na-mō, *n.* A machine for producing an electric current by mechanical power.
**Dynasty,** di'nas-ti, *n.* A race of kings of the same family.
**Dyne,** dīn, *n.* A unit of force, being that force which, acting on a gram for one second, generates a velocity of a centimeter per second.
**Dysentery,** dis'en-te-ri, *n.* A disorder of the intestines; a flux in which the stools consist chiefly of blood and mucus.
**Dyspepsia, Dyspepsy,** dis-pep'si-a, dis-pep'si, *n.* Indigestion; difficulty of digestion.
**Dyspeptic,** dis-pep'tik, *a.* Afflicted with dyspepsia; pertaining to dyspepsia.—*n.* A person afflicted with bad digestion.

# E

**Each,** ēch, *a.* and *pron.* Every one of any number considered individually.
**Eager,** ē'gėr, *a.* Sharp; ardent; keenly desirous; impetuous; earnest; intense.
**Eagerly,** ē-gėr-li, *adv.* With great ardor of desire; ardently; earnestly.
**Eagerness,** ē'gėr-nes, *n.* Ardent desire; vehemence; fervor; avidity.
**Eagle,** ē'gl, *n.* A large bird of prey, of great powers of flight and vision; a military standard.
**Eaglet,** ē'gl-et, *n.* A young eagle.
**Eagle-wood,** ē'gl-wud, *n.* A fragrant wood, burned by Asiatics as incense.
**Ear,** ēr, *n.* The organ of hearing; power of distinguishing musical sounds; heed; regard; anything resembling an ear or ears; a spike, as of corn.—*vi.* To form ears, as corn.—*vt.* To plow or till.
**Ear-ache,** ēr'āk, *n.* Pain in the ear.
**Ear-drum,** ēr'drum, *n.* The tympanum or middle ear.
**Earl,** ėrl, *n.* A British title of nobility, below a marquis and above a viscount.
**Earldom,** ėrl'dum, *n.* The domain, title, or dignity of an earl.
**Earless,** ēr'les, *a.* Without ears.
**Earn,** ėrn, *vt.* To gain by labor; to deserve.
**Earnest,** ėrn'est, *a.* Ardent in the pursuit of an object; eager; zealous; serious.—*n.* Seriousness; a reality; first-fruits; a part given beforehand as a pledge for the whole; indication; token.
**Earnestly,** ėrn'est-li, *adv.* Warmly; zealously; importunately; eagerly.
**Earnest-money,** ėrn'est-mun-i, *n.* Money paid as earnest, to bind a bargain, etc.
**Earnings,** ėrn'ingz, *n.pl.* That which is gained or merited by labor or performance; wages; reward.
**Ear-ring,** ēr'ring, *n.* A jewel or ornament worn in the ear; a pendant.
**Ear-shot,** ēr'shot, *n.* The distance at which words may be heard.
**Earth,** ėrth, *n.* The globe we inhabit; the world; the fine mold on the surface of the globe; dry land; the ground; the hiding hole of a fox, etc.—*vt.* To cover with earth.—*vi.* To retire underground; to burrow.
**Earthen,** ėrth'en, *a.* Made of earth.
**Earthenware,** ėrth'en-wār, *n.* Ware made of clay; crockery; pottery.
**Earthling,** ėrth'ling, *n.* An inhabitant of the earth; a mortal; a frail creature.
**Earthly,** ėrth'li, *a.* Pertaining to the earth; sordid; worldly; sensual; conceivable.
**Earthquake,** ėrth'kwāk, *n.* A shaking, trembling, or concussion of the earth.
**Earthward,** ėrth'wėrd, *adv.* Toward the earth.
**Earth-work,** ėrth'wėrk, *n.* A rampart or fortification of earth.
**Earth-worm,** ėrth'wėrm, *n.* The common worm; a mean, sordid wretch.
**Earthy,** ėrth'i, *a.* Consisting of or resembling earth; gross; not refined.
**Ear-trumpet,** ēr'trum-pet, *n.* An instrument in form of a tube, to aid in hearing.
**Earwig,** ēr'wig, *n.* A well-known insect, errone-

ously supposed to creep into the human brain through the ear.

**Ear-witness,** ēr'wit-nes, *n.* One who can testify to a fact from his own hearing.

**Ease,** ēz, *n.* Freedom from toil, pain, anxiety, etc.; freedom from difficulty; freedom from stiffness or formality; unaffectedness.—*vt.* (easing, eased). To give ease to; to relieve; to calm; to alleviate; to shift a little.

**Easel,** ēz'el, *n.* The frame on which pictures are placed while being painted.

**Easement,** ēz'ment, *n.* That which gives ease; accommodation; privilege.

**Easily,** ēz'i-li, *adv.* In an easy manner.

**East,** ēst, *n.* That part of the heavens where the sun rises; the countries east of Europe.—*a.* In or toward the east; easterly.—*adv.* Eastwards.

**Easter,** ēs'tėr, *n.* A festival of the Christian church in March or April, in commemoration of Christ's resurrection.

**Easterling,** ēst'ėr-ling, *n.* A native of some country east of Britain; a Baltic trader.

**Easterly,** ēst'ėr-li, *a.* Coming from the east, as wind; situated or moving toward the east.—*adv.* On the east; in the direction of east.

**Eastern,** ēst'ėrn, *a.* Belonging to the east; toward the east; oriental.

**Eastertide,** ēst'ėr-tīd, *n.* The time at which Easter is celebrated.

**Eastward,** ēst'wėrd, *adv.* and *a.* Toward the east.

**Easy,** ēz'i, *a.* Being at ease; free from pain or anxiety; not difficult; gentle; complying; affluent; not stiff or formal.

**Easy-chair,** ēz'i-chār, *n.* A large, padded armchair.

**Eat,** ēt, *vt.* (pret. ate, pp. eaten or eat). to chew and swallow, as food; to wear away; to gnaw; to consume.—*vi.* To take food; to taste or relish; to corrode.

**Eatable,** ēt'a-bl, *a.* That may be eaten; proper for food.—*n.* That which is fit for, or used as food.

**Eating,** ēt'ing, *n.* The act of chewing and swallowing food; what is eaten.

**Eau de Cologne,** ō dė ko-lōn, *n.* A perfumed spirit.—**Eau de vie,** ō dė vē, *n.* Brandy.

**Eaves,** ēvz, *n.pl.* That part of the roof of a building which overhangs the walls.

**Eavesdrop,** ēvz'drop, *n.* The water which drops from the eaves.—*vi.* To listen to what is said within doors; to watch for opportunities of hearing private conversation.

**Eavesdropper,** ēvz'drop-ėr, *n.* One who tries to hear private conversation.

**Ebb,** eb, *n.* The flowing back of the tide; decline; decay.—*vi.* To flow back; to decay; to decline.

**E-boat,** ē-bōt, *n.* A German motor torpedo-boat.

**Ebon,** eb'on, *a.* Consisting of ebony; like ebony; black.

**Ebonite,** eb'o-nīt, *n.* Vulcanite.

**Ebonize,** eb'o-nīz, *vt.* To make black or like ebony.

**Ebony,** eb'on-i, *n.* A hard, heavy, dark wood admitting of a fine polish.

**Ebriety,** ē-brī'e-ti, *n.* Drunkenness.

**Ebullient,** ē-bul'yent, *a.* Boiling over, as a liquor; over enthusiastic.

**Ebullition,** ē-bul-li'shon, *n.* The operation of boiling; a sudden burst, as of passion; an overflowing; outbreak.

**Eburnean, Eburnine,** ē-bėr'nē-an, ē-bėr'nīn, *a.* Relating to or made of ivory.

**Ecarté,** ā-kär-tā, *n.* A game of cards for two persons with thirty-two cards.

**Eccentric,** ek-sen'trik, *a.* Not having its axis in the center; not having the same center; deviating from usual practice, etc.; anomalous; whimsical.—*n.* An eccentric person; mechanical contrivance for converting circular into reciprocating rectilinear motion.

**Eccentrically,** ek-sen'trik-al-li, *adv.* In an eccentric manner.

**Eccentricity,** ek-sen-tris'i-ti, *n.* State or quality of being eccentric; distance of the center of a planet's orbit from the center of the sun; singularity; oddness.

**Ecclesiastes,** ek-klē'zi-as''tēz, *n.* A canonical book of the Old Testament.

**Ecclesiastic,** ek-klē'zi-as-tik, *a.* Ecclesiastical.—*n.* A priest; a clergyman.

**Ecclesiastical,** ek-klē'zi-as''tik-al, *a.* Pertaining to the church; not civil or secular.

**Echelon,** esh'e-lon, *n.* The position of troops or ships in parallel lines, each line being a little to the right or left of the preceding one.

**Echinus,** ē-kī'nus, *n.* The sea-urchin; a form of molding.

**Echo,** e'kō, *n.* A sound repeated or reverberated.—*vi.* To give out an echo.—*vt.* To reverberate or send back, as sound; to repeat with assent.



**Eclat,** e-klä', *n.* A burst of applause; renown; splendor.

**Eclectic,** ek-lek'tik, *a.* Proceeding by the method of selection; applied to certain philosophers who selected from the principles of various schools what they thought sound.—*n.* One who follows an eclectic method in philosophy, etc.

**Eclecticism,** ek-lek'ti-sizm, *n.* The doctrine or practice of an eclectic.

**Eclipse,** ē-klips', *n.* An interception of the light of the sun, moon, etc., by some other body; darkness; obscuration.—*vt.* (eclipsing, eclipsed). To cause an eclipse of; to excel.

**Ecliptic,** ē-klip'tik, *n.* The apparent path of the sun round the earth.—*a.* Pertaining to the ecliptic or an eclipse; suffering an eclipse.

**Eclogue,** ek'log, *n.* A pastoral poem.

**Economic, Economical,** ē-kon-om'ik, ē-kon-om'ik-al, *a.* Pertaining to economy or economics; frugal; careful.

**Economically,** ē-kon-om'ik-al-li, *adv.* With economy.

**Economics,** ē-kon-om'iks, *n.* The science of the application of wealth; political economy.

**Economist,** ē-kon'om-ist, *n.* One who practices economy; one versed in economics.

**Economize,** ē-kon'om-īz, *vt.* and *i.* (economizing, economized). To manage with prudence or frugality.

**Economy,** ē-kon'o-mi, *n.* Frugal use of money; the regular operations of nature; due order of things; judicious management.

**Ecstasy,** ek'sta-si, *n.* A trance; excessive joy; rapture; enthusiasm.

**Ecstatic, Ecstatical,** ek-stat'ik, ek-stat'ik-al, *a.* Causing or pertaining to ecstasy; entrancing; delightful beyond measure.

**Ecumenic, Ecumenical,** ek-ū-men'ik, ek-ū-men'i-kal, *a.* General; universal: applied to church councils.

**Eczema,** ek'ze-ma, *n.* A skin disease.

**Edacious,** ē-dā'shus, *a.* Voracious.

**Eddy,** ed'i, *n.* A circular current of water or air.—*a.* Whirling.—*vi.* (eddying, eddied). To move circularly, or as an eddy.

**Edelweiss,** ā'dl-vīs, *n.* An Alpine plant.

**Eden,** ē'den, *n.* The garden of Adam and Eve; a delightful region or residence.

**Edentata,** ē-den-tā'ta, *n.pl.* An order of mammals with no, or rudimentary, teeth.

**Edge,** ej, *n.* The cutting side of an instrument; an abrupt border or margin; sharpness; keenness.—*vt.* (edging, edged). To bring to an edge; to sharpen; to fringe; to exasperate; to move by little and little.—*vi.* To move sideways or gradually.

**Edged,** ejd, *a.* Sharp; keen.

**Edge-tool,** ej'töl, *n.* An instrument with a sharp edge.

**Edgeways, Edgewise,** ej'wāz, ej'wīz, *adv.* With the edge forward or towards; sideways.

**Edging,** ej'ing, *n.* A border; fringe.

**Edible,** ed'i-bl, *a.* Eatable.

**Edict,** ē'dikt, *n.* An order issued by a prince; a decree; manifesto.

**Edification,** ed'i-fi-kā''shon, *n.* A building up; im-

provement in knowledge, morals, etc.; instruction.
**Edifice,** ed'i-fis, *n*. A structure; a fabric; a large or splendid building.
**Edify,** ed'i-fi, *vt.* (edifying, edified). To build up, in a moral sense; to instruct or improve generally.
**Edifying,** ed'i-fi-ing, *p.a.* Improving; adapted to instruct.
**Edit,** ed'it, *vt.* To prepare for publication; to conduct, as regards literary contents.
**Edition,** ē-di'shon, *n*. A published book as characterized by form or editorial labors; the whole number of copies of a work published at once.
**Editor,** ed'it-ėr, *n*. One who prepares or superintends for publication.
**Editorial,** ed-i-tō'ri-al, *a*. Pertaining to or written by an editor.—*n*. A leading article in a newspaper.
**Editorship,** ed'it-ėr-ship, *n*. The office or business of an editor.
**Educate,** ed'ū-kāt, *vt.* (educating, educated). To teach; to cultivate and train; to enlighten.
**Education,** ed-ū-kā'shon, *n*. Act of educating; instruction and discipline; schooling.
**Educational,** ed'ū-kā'shon-al, *a*. Pertaining to education.
**Educationist,** ed-ū-kā'shon-ist, *n*. One who is versed in or promotes education.
**Educative,** ed'ū-kāt-iv, *a*. Tending or able to educate; imparting education.
**Educator,** ed'ū-kāt-ėr, *n*. One who educates.
**Educe,** ē-dūs', *vt.* (educing, educed). To draw out; to elicit; to extract.
**Educible,** ē-dūs'i-bl, *a*. That may be educed.
**Eduction,** ē-duk'shon, *n*. Act of drawing out or bringing into view.
**Eel,** ēl, *n*. A slimy serpent-like fish.
**Eerie,** ē'ri, *a*. Inspiring superstitious fear; weird.
**Efface,** ef-fās', *vt.* To remove from the face or surface of anything; to render illegible; to blot out; to wear away.
**Effacement,** ef-fās'ment, *n*. Act of effacing.
**Effect,** ef-fekt', *n*. That which is produced; result; purpose; validity; striking appearance; impression produced by a work of art, etc.; *pl.* goods; movables; personal estate.—*vt.* To produce; to cause; to fulfil; to execute.
**Effective,** ef-fekt'iv, *a*. Having the power to produce; efficacious; efficient; effectual; fit for duty or service.
**Effectively,** ef-fekt'iv-li, *adv.* With effect.
**Effectual,** ef-fek'tū-al, *a*. Producing the effect desired or intended; valid.
**Effectuate,** ef-fek'tū-āt, *vt.* To carry into effect; to bring to pass; to fulfil.
**Effeminacy,** ef-fem'in-a-si, *n*. State or character of being effeminate.
**Effeminate,** ef-fem'in-āt, *a*. Womanish; unmanly; weak; voluptuous.—*vt.* To unman; to weaken.—*vi.* To grow womanish or weak.
**Effeminately,** ef-fem'in-āt-li, *adv.* In an effeminate manner; womanishly; weakly.
**Effendi,** ef-fen'di, *n*. A Turkish title of respect.
**Effervesce,** ef-fėr-ves', *vi.* To bubble or sparkle, as any fluid when part escapes in gas; to exhibit signs of excitement.
**Effervescence,** ef-fėr-ves'ens, *n*. Act of effervescing; strong excitement.
**Effervescent,** ef-fėr-ves'ent, *a*. Boiling or bubbling, by means of the disengagement of gas.
**Effete,** ef-fēt', *a*. Worn out; exhausted; barren.
**Efficacious,** ef-fi-kā'shus, *a*. Producing the effect intended; having adequate power.
**Efficacy,** ef'fi-ka-si, *n*. Power to produce effects; production of the effect intended; virtue; force; energy.
**Efficiency,** ef-fi'shen-si, *n*. The state or character of being efficient; effectual agency.
**Efficient,** ef-fi'shent, *a*. Effecting; capable; qualified for duty.
**Effigy,** ef'fi-ji, *n*. The image or likeness of a person; portrait; figure.
**Effloresce,** ef-flo-res', *vi.* To bloom; to show a powdery substance on the surface.
**Efflorescence,** ef-flo-res'ens, *n*. The time, act, or process of flowering; a redness of the skin; mealy powder or minute crystals forming on a surface.
**Efflorescent,** ef-flo-res'ent, *a*. Showing efflorescence; liable to effloresce.
**Effluence,** ef'flu-ens, *n*. A flowing out; that which issues from any body or substance.
**Effluent,** ef'flu-ent, *a*. Flowing out.—*n*. A stream that flows out of another, or out of a lake.
**Effluvial,** ef-flū'vi-al, *a*. Pertaining to effluvia; containing effluvia.
**Effluvium,** ef-flū'vi-um, *n.*; pl. **-via.** Something flowing out invisibly; a disagreeable odor; a noxious exhalation.
**Efflux,** ef'fluks, *n*. Act or state of flowing out in a stream; flow; emanation.
**Effluxion,** ef-fluk'shon, *n*. Act of flowing out; that which flows out; emanation.
**Effort,** ef'fōrt, *n*. An exertion of strength; strenuous endeavor; struggle.
**Effrontery,** ef-frun'te-ri, *n*. Audacious impudence; shameless boldness.
**Effulgence,** ef-fulj'ens, *n*. A flood of light; great luster; splendor.
**Effulgent,** ef-fulj'ent, *a*. Sending out a flood of light; gleaming; splendid.
**Effuse,** ef-fūz', *vt.* (effusing, effused). To pour out; to shed.—*vi.* To emanate.
**Effusion,** ef-fū'zhon, *n*. Act of pouring out; that which is poured out; in *pathology,* the escape of fluid out of its proper vessel into another part; cordiality of manner; a literary production.
**Effusive,** ef-fūs'iv, *a*. Pouring out; showing overflowing kindness.
**Eft,** eft, *n*. A newt.
**Egg,** eg, *n*. A roundish body produced by many female animals besides birds, from which their young is produced; something resembling an egg.—*vt.* To urge on; to instigate.
**Eglantine,** eg'lan-tīn, *n*. The sweet-brier.
**Egoism,** eg'ō-izm or ē', *n*. The doctrine which refers all knowledge to the phenomena of personal existence; egotism.
**Egoist,** eg'ō-ist or ē', *n*. An egotist; one holding the doctrine of egoism.
**Egotism,** eg'ot-izm or ē', *n*. The practice of too frequently using the word *I*; an exaggerated love of self; self-exaltation.
**Egotist,** eg'ot-ist or ē', *n*. One always talking of himself; one who magnifies his own achievements.
**Egotistic, Egotistical,** eg-ot-is'tik, eg-ot-is'tik-al, or ē-, *a*. Addicted to egotism; vain.
**Egotize,** eg'ot-īz or ē', *vi.* (egotizing, egotized). To talk or write much of oneself.
**Egregious,** e-grē'jus, *a*. Remarkable; extraordinary; enormous.
**Egress,** ē'gres, *n*. Act of going out; power of departing from any confined place; exit.—*vi.* To go out.
**Egret,** eg'ret or ē'gret, *n*. A species of heron; an aigret.
**Egyptian,** ē-jip'shun, *a*. Pertaining to Egypt.—*n*. A native of Egypt; a gipsy.
**Egyptology,** ē-jip-tol'o-ji, *n*. The science of Egyptian antiquities.
**Eh,** eh, *exclam.* Denoting inquiry or slight surprise.
**Eider, Eider-duck,** ī'dėr, ī'dėr-duk, *n*. A species of sea-duck, producing down of the finest and softest kind.
**Eider-down,** ī'dėr-doun, *n*. Down or soft feathers of the eider-duck.
**Eight,** āt, *a*. One more than seven and less than nine.—*n*. This number; the symbol representing this number; an eight-oared racing boat or its crew.
**Eighteen,** āt'ēn, *a*. and *n*. Eight and ten united.
**Eighteenth,** āt'ēnth, *a*. and *n*. Next in order after the seventeenth; one of eighteen parts.
**Eighth,** ātth, *a*. and *n*. Next after the seventh; one

of eight parts; an octave.
**Eighthly,** āth'li, *adv.* In the eighth place.
**Eightieth,** āt'i-eth, *a.* and *n.* The ordinal of eighty.
**Eighty,** āt'i, *a.* Eight times ten.
**Eisteddfod,** īs-teTH-vōd', *n.* A meeting of Welsh bards and minstrels; a periodical Welsh festival for the recitation of poems, etc.
**Either,** ē'THėr or ī'THėr, *a.* or *pron.* One or the other; one of two; each;—*conj.* or *adv.* Used disjunctively as correlative to *or.*
**Ejaculate,** ē-jak'ū-lāt, *vt.* To exclaim; to utter suddenly and briefly.
**Ejaculation,** ē-jak'ū-lā''shon, *n.* Exclamation; a short prayer.
**Ejaculatory,** ē-jak'ū-la-to-ri, *a.* Of the nature of an ejaculation.
**Eject,** ē'jekt, *vt.* To throw out; to dismiss; to dispossess of land or estate; to expel.
**Ejection,** ē-jek'shon, *n.* Act of casting out; expulsion; dismission.
**Ejectment,** ē-jekt'ment, *n.* Act or process of ejecting; removal of a person from the wrongful possession of land or tenements.
**Ejector,** ē-jekt'or, *n.* One who or that which ejects.
**Eke,** ēk, *vt.* (eking, eked). To add to; to lengthen; to prolong.—*n.* An addition.—*adv.* Also; in addition.
**Elaborate,** ē-lab'o-rāt, *vt.* (elaborating, elaborated). To produce with labor; to refine by successive operations.—*a.* Wrought with labor; studied; high-wrought.
**Elaborately,** ē-lab'o-rāt-li, *adv.* In an elaborate manner.
**Elaboration,** ē-lab'o-rā''shon, *n.* Refinement by successive operations; the process in animal and vegetable organs by which something is produced.
**Eland,** ē'land, *n.* An African species of antelope.
**Elapse,** ē-laps', *vi.* (elapsing, elapsed). To slip or glide away.
**Elastic,** ē-las'tik, *a.* Having the power of returning to the form from which it is bent or distorted; rebounding.—*n.* Cord or ribbon made of cotton or silk, etc., with strands of rubber.
**Elastically,** ē-las'tik-al-li, *adv.* In an elastic manner; with a spring.
**Elasticity,** ē-las-tis'i-ti, *n.* State or property of being elastic.
**Elate,** ē-lāt', *a.* Elevated in mind; flushed, as with success.—*vt.* (elating, elated). To exalt; to puff up; to make proud.
**Elated,** ē-lāt'ed, *p.a.* Elate.
**Elation,** ē-lā'shon, *n.* Elevation of mind or spirits; buoyancy.
**Elbow,** el'bō, *n.* The bend or joint of the arm; an angle.—*vt.* To push with the elbow; to push, as through a crowd.—*vi.* To project; to push one's way.
**Eld,** eld, *n.* Old age; old time.
**Elder,** eld'ėr, *a.* Older; having lived a longer time; senior.—*n.* One who is older; an office-bearer in the Presbyterian Church; a small tree with a spongy pitch and dark purple or red berries.
**Elderly,** eld'ėr-li, *a.* Somewhat old; beyond middle age.
**Eldership,** eld'ėr-ship, *n.* Seniority; office of an elder; order of elders.
**Eldest,** eld'est, *a.* Oldest; most aged.
**Elect,** ē-lekt', *vt.* To pick or choose; to select for an office.—*a.* Chosen; chosen to an office, but not yet in office.—*n. sing.* or *pl.* One or several chosen; those favored by God.
**Election,** ē-lek'shon, *n.* Act of choosing; choice; voluntary preference; divine choice; predestination.
**Electioneer,** ē-lek'shon-ēr'', *vi.* To work for a candidate at an election.
**Electioneering,** ē-lek'shon-ēr''ing, *n.* The arts used to secure the election of a candidate.
**Elective,** ē-lekt'iv, *a.* Pertaining to or consisting in choice; exerting the power of choice.
**Elector,** ē-lekt'ėr, *n.* One who elects or has the right of voting.
**Electoral,** ē-lekt'ėr-al, *a.* Pertaining to election or electors.
**Electorate,** ē-lekt'ėr-āt, *n.* A body of electors.
**Electric, Electrical,** ē-lek'trik, ē-lek'tri-kal, *a.* Containing, conveying, or produced by electricity; full of fire or spirit, and capable of communicating it.
**Electrically,** ē-lek'tri-kal-li, *adv.* In the manner of electricity; by electricity.
**Electrician,** ē-lek-trish'an, *n.* One versed in the science of electricity.
**Electricity,** ē-lek-tris'i-ti, *n.* The force that manifests itself in lightning and in many other phenomena; the science which deals with these phenomena.
**Electrifiable,** ē-lek'tri-fī-a-bl, *a.* Capable of being electrified.
**Electrify,** ē-lek'tri-fī, *vt.* (electrifying, electrified). To communicate electricity to; to thrill.—*vi.* To become electric.
**Electro,** ē-lek'trō, *n.* An electrotype.
**Electro-biology,** ē-lec'trō-bī-ol''o-ji, *n.* The science of electric currents in living organisms; mesmerism or animal magnetism.
**Electrocute,** ē-lek'trō-kūt, *vt.* To execute a criminal by means of electricity.
**Electrode,** ē-lek'trōd, *n.* One of the terminals or poles of the voltaic circle.
**Electro-dynamics,** ē-lek'trō-di-nam''iks, *n.* The science of mechanical actions exerted on one another by electric currents.
**Electrolysis,** ē-lek-trol'i-sis, *n.* Decomposition by means of electricity.
**Electrolyte,** ē-lek'trō-līt, *n.* A compound decomposable by electricity.
**Electrometer,** ē-lek-trom'e-tėr, *n.* An instrument for measuring electricity.
**Electron,** ē-lek'tron, *n.* One of the extremely small particles of negative electricity, which form essential constituents of atoms, and by which, according to the electron theory, heat and electricity are conducted.
**Electroplate,** ē-lek'trō-plāt, *vt.* To give a coating of silver or other metal by means of electricity.—*n.* Articles so coated.
**Electrotype,** ē-lek'trō-tīp, *n.* The art of producing copies of types, wood-cuts, etc., by the electric deposition of copper on a cast from the original; a copy thus produced.
**Electuary,** ē-lek'tū-a-ri, *n.* A medicine incoporated with some conserve or syrup.
**Eleemosynary,** el-ē-mos'i-na-ri, *a.* Given in or relating to charity; founded to dispense some gratuity.—*n.* One who subsists on charity.
**Elegance, Elegancy,** el'ē-gans, el'ē-gan-si, *n.* Quality of being elegant; beauty resulting from propriety; refinement.
**Elegant,** el'ē-gant, *a.* Pleasing to good taste; graceful; polished; refined; symmetrical.
**Elegiac,** el'ē-jī'ak, *a.* Belonging to elegy; plaintive.—*n.* Elegiac verse.
**Elegiast, Elegist,** e-lē'jī-ast, el'ē-jist, *n.* A writer of elegies.
**Elegy,** el'ē-ji, *n.* A poem or a song expressive of sorrow and lamentation.
**Element,** el'ē-ment, *n.* A fundamental part or principle; an ingredient; proper sphere; suitable state of things; *pl.* first principles of an art or science; data employed in a calculation; the bread and wine used in the Lord's supper.
**Elemental,** el-ē-ment'al, *a.* Pertaining to or produced by elements.
**Elementary,** el-ē-ment'ar-i, *a.* Primary; uncompounded; teaching first principles or rudiments.
**Elephant,** el'ē-fant, *n.* A huge quadruped, having a long trunk and tusks.
**Elephantine,** el'ē-fant'īn, *a.* Pertaining to the elephant; huge; clumsy.
**Elevate,** el'ē-vāt, *vt.* (elevating, elevated). To raise; to refine or dignify; to elate; to cheer.
**Elevation,** el-ē-vā'shon, *n.* Act of elevating; state of being elevated; an elevated station; a hill;

representation of a building in vertical section.

**Elevator,** el'ē-vāt-ėr, *n*. One who or that which elevates; a hoist.

**Eleven,** ē-lev'n, *a*. Ten and one added.—*n*. The sum of ten and one; the symbol representing this number; a side of players in association football, cricket, etc.

**Eleventh,** ē-lev'nth, *a*. and *n*. Next after the tenth; one of eleven parts.

**Elf,** elf, *n*.; pl. **Elves,** elvz. A fairy; a goblin; a mischievous person.

**Elfin,** elf'in, *a*. Relating to elves.—*n*. An elf; a little urchin.

**Elfish,** elf'ish, *a*. Resembling or pertaining to elves.

**Elicit,** ē-lis'it, *vt*. To draw out by reasoning, discussion, etc.; to educe.

**Elide,** ē-līd', *vt*. (eliding, elided). To strike out; to cut off or suppress (a syllable).

**Eligibility,** el'i-ji-bil''i-ti, *n*. Worthiness or fitness to be chosen.

**Eligible,** el'i-ji-bl, *a*. Fit to be chosen; suitable; legally qualified.

**Eligibly,** el'i-ji-bli, *adv*. In a manner to be worthy of choice; suitably.

**Eliminate,** ē-lim'in-āt, *vt*. (eliminating, eliminated). To throw off; to cancel; to leave out of consideration.

**Elimination,** ē-lim'in-ā''shon, *n*. Act of eliminating.

**Elision,** ē-li'zhon, *n*. Act of eliding; suppression of a vowel or syllable.

**Elite,** ā-lēt', *n.pl*. A select body; the best.

**Elixir,** ē-lik'sėr, *n*. A liquor sought by the alchemists to transmute metals into gold or to prolong life; quintessence; a cordial.

**Elizabethan,** ē-liz'a-bēth''an, *a*. Pertaining to Queen Elizabeth or her times.

**Elk,** elk, *n*. The largest species of deer.

**Ellipse,** el-lips', *n*. An oval figure.

**Ellipsis,** el-lips'is, *n*.; pl. **-ses.** A figure of syntax by which words are omitted; suppression of letters or words in printing.

**Elliptic, Elliptical,** el-lip'tik, el-lip'tik-al, *a*. Pertaining to an ellipse or ellipsis; having a part omitted.

**Ellipticity,** el-lip-tis'i-ti, *n*. Amount of divergence from a circle.

**Elm,** elm, *n*. A tree valuable for its timber.

**Elocution,** e-lō-kū'shon, *n*. Management of the voice and gesture in speaking; pronunciation; delivery.

**Elocutionary,** e-lō-kū'shon-a-ri, *a*. Pertaining to elocution.

**Elocutionist,** e-lō-kū'shon-ist, *n*. One who is versed in, or teaches, elocution.

**Elogium,** ē-lō'ji-um, *n*. A panegyric.

**Elongate,** ē-long'gāt, *vt*. (elongating, elongated). To lengthen.—*vi*. To recede apparently from the sun.—*a*. Long and slender.

**Elongation,** ē-long-gā'shon, *n*. Act of lengthening; state of being extended; continuation; apparent distance of a planet from the sun.

**Elope,** ē-lōp', *vi*. (eloping, eloped). To escape privately; to run away with a lover.

**Elopement,** ē-lōp'ment, *n*. Act of eloping; running away of a woman with a lover.

**Eloquence,** e'lō-kwens, *n*. The quality or faculty of being eloquent; oratory.

**Eloquent,** e'lō-kwent, *a*. Having the power of fluent, elegant, or forcible speech; characterized by eloquence.

**Eloquently,** e'lō-kwent-li, *adv*. With eloquence; in an eloquent manner.

**Else,** els, *a*. or *adv*. Other; besides; in addition.—*conj*. Otherwise; in the other case.

**Elsewhere,** els'whār, *adv*. In any other place; in some other place.

**Elucidate,** ē-lū'sid-āt, *vt*. To make clear; to free from obscurity; to explain.

**Elude,** ē-lūd', *vt*. (eluding, eluded). To avoid by artifice or dexterity; to baffle; to evade.

**Elusion,** ē-lū'zhon, *n*. Act of eluding; evasion.

**Elusive,** ē-lū'siv, *a*. Practicing elusion; evasive.

**Elusory,** ē-lū'so-ri, *a*. Tending to elude; evasive; fallacious.

**Elvan,** el'van, *n*. A granitic and felspar porphyritic rock.

**Elvish,** elv'ish, *a*. Elfish.

**Elysian,** ē-li'zhi-an, *a*. Pertaining to Elysium; exceedingly delightful.

**Elysium,** ē-li'zhi-um, *n*. The place of future happiness; any delightful place.

**Elytron, Elytrum,** el'i-tron, el'i-trum, *n*.; pl. **Elytra,** el'i-tra. The wing-sheath which covers the true wing in beetles.

**Emaciate,** ē-mā'shi-āt, *vi*. and *t*. (emaciating, emaciated). To become or make lean.

**Emaciation,** ē-mā'shi-ā''shon, *n*. Act of emaciating; leanness.

**Emanant,** em'a-nant, *a*. Emanating.

**Emanate,** em'a-nāt, *vi*. (emanating, emanated). To flow out; to issue; to spring.

**Emanation,** em-a-nā-shon, *n*. Act of emanating; that which issues from any source or substance; effluvium.

**Emancipate,** ē-man'si-pāt, *vt*. (emancipating, emancipated). To set free from slavery; to liberate.

**Emancipation,** ē-man'si-pā''shon, *n*. Liberation; freedom; enfranchisement.

**Emancipator,** ē-man'si-pāt-ėr, *n*. One who emancipates from bondage or restraint.

**Emasculate,** ē-mas'kū-lāt, *vt*. To castrate; to render effeminate; to expurgate.

**Emasculation,** ē-mas'kū-lā''shon, *n*. Castration; effeminacy.

**Embalm,** em-bām', *vt*. To preserve a dead body by aromatics; to cherish the memory of.

**Embank,** em-bangk', *vt*. To inclose or defend with a bank, mounds, or dikes.

**Embankment,** em-bangk'ment, *n*. Act of embanking; a bank raised for protecting against inundation, or for a railway, etc.

**Embargo,** em-bär'gō, *n*. Prohibition on ships from sailing; restraint or hindrance.—*vt*. To put an embargo on.

**Embark,** em-bärk', *vt*. To put on board a ship; to engage in.—*vi*. To go on board of a ship; to engage in; to take a share.

**Embarkation,** em-bärk-ā'shon, *n*. Act of embarking; that which is embarked.

**Embarrass,** em-ba'ras, *vt*. To involve in difficulties; to entangle; to disconcert.

**Embarrassed,** em-ba'rast, *p.a*. Entangled; confused; disconcerted; unable to pay.

**Embarrassment,** em-ba'ras-ment, *n*. Entanglement; trouble; abashment.

**Embassy,** em'bas-si, *n*. The mission, charge or residence of an ambassador; an important message.

**Embattle,** em-bat'l, *vt*. To arrange in order of battle; to furnish with battlements.—*vi*. To be ranged in order of battle.

**Embay,** em-bā', *vt*. To inclose in a bay; to landlock.

**Embellish,** em-bel'lish, *vt*. To make beautiful; to adorn.

**Embellishment,** em-bel'lish-ment, *n*. Act of embellishing; that which embellishes.

**Ember,** em'bėr, *n*. A glowing cinder; chiefly in *pl*.

**Ember-days,** em'bėr-dāz, *n.pl*. Days appointed for fasting, being a Wednesday, Friday, and Saturday in each of the four seasons.

**Ember-week,** em'bėr-wēk, *n*. A week in which ember-days fall.

**Embezzle,** em-bez'l, *vt*. (embezzling, embezzled). To appropriate by breach of trust.

**Embezzlement,** em-bez'l-ment, *n*. Act of fraudently appropriating money, etc., intrusted to one's care.

**Embezzler,** em-bez'l-ėr, *n*. One who embezzles.

**Embitter,** em-bit'ėr, *vt*. To make bitter or more bitter; to exasperate.

**Emblaze,** em-blāz', *vt*. To kindle; to blazon.

**Emblazon,** em-blā'zon, *vt*. To adorn with figures

of heraldry; to sing the praises of.
**Emblazoner,** em-blā'zon-ėr, *n.* A blazoner.
**Emblazonment,** em-blā'zn-ment, *n.* Act of emblazoning; that which is emblazoned.
**Emblazonry,** em-blā'zn-ri, *n.* Blazonry; heraldic decoration.
**Emblem,** em'blem, *n.* A picture representing one thing and suggesting another; a symbol; type; device.
**Emblematic, Emblematical,** em-ble-mat'ik, em-ble-mat'ik-al, *a.* Pertaining to or comprising an emblem; symbolic.
**Embodiment,** em-bo'di-ment, *n.* Act of embodying; state of being embodied; that in which something is embodied; incarnation.
**Embody,** em-bo'di, *vt.* (embodying, embodied). To invest with a body; to form into a body (as troops), or into a system; to collect.
**Embogue,** em-bōg', *vi.* To discharge itself, as a river.
**Embolden,** em-bōld'en, *vt.* To give boldness to; to encourage.
**Embolism,** em'bol-izm, *n.* Obstruction of a blood-vessel by a clot of blood.
**Emboss,** em-bos', *vt.* To form bosses on; to fashion in relievo or raised work.
**Embossment,** em-bos'ment, *n.* Act of embossing; figures in relievo; raised work.
**Embouchure,** em'bö-shör, *n.* A mouth or aperture, as of a river, cannon, etc.
**Embowel,** em-bou'el, *vt.* To take out the bowels of; to eviscerate; to imbed.
**Embower,** em-bou'ėr, *vt.* To inclose in or cover with a bower; to shade.
**Embrace,** em-brās', *vt.* (embracing, embraced). To take within the arms; to press to the bosom; to seize ardently; to include; to accept.—*vi.* To join in an embrace.—*n.* Clasp with the arms; a hug; conjugal endearment.
**Embraceor, Embrasor,** em-brā'sėr, *n.* One who attempts to influence a jury illegally.
**Embrasure,** em-brā'zhūr, *n.* An opening in a wall or parapet through which cannon are fired.
**Embrocate,** em'brō-kāt, *vt.* To moisten and rub, as a diseased part of the body.
**Embrocation,** em-brō-kā'shon, *n.* Act of embrocating; the liquid used in embrocating.
**Embroider,** em-broi'dėr, *vt.* To adorn with ornamental needlework or figures.
**Embroidery,** em-broi'de-ri, *n.* Embroidered work; variegated needlework.
**Embroil,** em-broil', *vt.* To confuse; to disorder; to involve in troubles; to disturb.
**Embroilment,** em-broil'ment, *n.* The act of embroiling; state of contention, perplexity, or confusion; disturbance.
**Embryo,** em'bri-ō, *n.* The first rudiments of an animal in the womb or of a plant in the seed; the first state of anything.—*a.* Pertaining to anything in its first rudiments.
**Embryology,** em-bri-ol'o-ji, *n.* The doctrine of the development of embryos.
**Embryonic,** em-bri-on'ik, *a.* Pertaining to an embryo, or the embryo state.
**Emend,** ē-mend', *vt.* To remove faults from; to improve the text or reading of.
**Emendation,** ē-mend-ā'shon, *n.* Correction in a text, writing, etc.; alteration for the better.
**Emendator,** ē-mend'āt-ėr, *n.* One who emends.
**Emendatory,** ē-mend'a-to-ri, *a.* Contributing to emendation.
**Emerald,** e'me-rald, *n.* A precious stone, akin to the beryl, usually green; a small printing type.—*a.* Of a bright-green color.
**Emerge,** ē-mėrj', *vi.* (emerging, emerged). To rise out of a fluid or other substance; to issue; to rise into view; to reappear.
**Emergence,** ė-mėrj'ens, *n.* Act of emerging.
**Emergency,** ē-mėrj'en-si, *n.* Act of emerging; unforeseen occurrence; pressing necessity.
**Emergent,** ē-mėrj'ent, *a.* Rising out of; issuing from; sudden; casual; pressing.
**Emeritus,** ė-mer'i-tus, *a.* Discharged from duty with honor on account of infirmity, age, or long service.
**Emersion,** ē-mėr'shon, *n.* Act of rising out of a fluid or other substance; reappearance of a heavenly body after eclipse, etc.
**Emery,** e'me-ri, *n.* A hard mineral used in cutting gems and for polishing.
**Emetic,** ē-met'ik, *a.* Causing vomiting.—*n.* A medicine that provokes vomiting.
**Emeute,** ā-möt', *n.* A seditious commotion; a riot; a tumult.
**Emigrant,** em'i-grant, *a.* Emigrating; pertaining to emigration or emigrants.—*n.* One who emigrates.
**Emigrate,** em'i-grāt, *vi.* (emigrating, emigrated). To remove from one country or state to another for the purpose of residence.
**Emigration,** em-i-grā'shon, *n.* Act of emigrating; a body of emigrants.
**Eminence,** em'in-ens, *n.* A rising ground; elevation; top; distinction; fame; a title of honor given to cardinals, etc.
**Eminent,** em'in-ent, *a.* Exalted; high in office; distinguished; illustrious.
**Eminently,** em'in-ent-li, *adv.* In an eminent manner or position.
**Emir,** em'ēr, *n.* An independent Mohammedan chief; a descendant of Mohammed; the head of certain departments in Mohammedan countries.
**Emissary,** em'is-sa-ri, *n.* One sent on private business; a secret agent; a spy.
**Emission,** ē-mi'shon, *n.* Act of emitting; that which is emitted.
**Emissive,** ē-mis'iv, *a.* Sending out; emitting.
**Emissory,** ē-mis'o-ri, *a.* Sending out; excretory.
**Emit,** ē-mit', *vt.* (emitting, emitted). To send out; to discharge; to vent.
**Emmet,** em'met, *n.* An ant.
**Emollient,** ē-mol'li-ent, *a.* Softening; making supple.—*n.* A substance which softens or allays irritation.
**Emolument,** ē-mol'ū-ment, *n.* Profit arising from office or employment; salary; gain.
**Emotion,** ē-mō'shon, *n.* Any agitation of mind; feeling.
**Emotional,** ē-mō'shon-al, *a.* Pertaining to or characterized by emotion.
**Empale,** em-pāl', *vt.* (empaling, empaled). To put to death by fixing on a stake.
**Emperor,** em'pėr-ėr, *n.* The sovereign of an empire.
**Emphasis,** em'fa-sis, *n.* A stress laid on a word or clause to enforce a meaning; impressiveness; weight.
**Emphasize,** em'fa-sīz, *vt.* (emphasizing, emphasized). To place emphasis on.
**Emphatic, Emphatical,** em-fat'ik, em-fat'ik-al, *a.* Characterized by emphasis; expressive; strong; energetic.
**Emphatically,** em-fat'ik-al-li, *adv.* With emphasis; strongly; forcibly.
**Empire,** em'pīr, *n.* Supreme power in governing; sway; dominion of an emperor; region over which dominion is extended.
**Empiric,** em-pi'rik, *n.* One whose knowledge is founded exclusively on experience; a quack; a charlatan.
**Empirical,** em-pi'rik-al, *a.* Pertaining to or derived from experience; relying on experience without due regard to theory.
**Empiricism,** em-pi'ri-sizm, *n.* The methods or practice of an empiric; quackery; the doctrine that knowledge comes solely from experience.
**Employ,** em-ploi', *vt.* To occupy; to engage in one's service; to keep at work; to make use of.—*n.* Business; occupation; engagement.
**Employee,** em-ploi'ē, *n.* One who works for an employer.
**Employer,** em-ploi'ėr, *n.* One who employs; one who keeps men in service.
**Employment,** em-ploi'ment, *n.* Act of employing; office; trade; profession; function.

E

**Emporium,** em-pō'ri-um, *n.*; pl. **-ia** or **-iums.** A commercial center; a warehouse or shop.
**Empower,** em-pou'ėr, *vt.* To give legal or moral power to; to authorize.
**Empress,** em'pres, *n.* The consort of an emperor; a female invested with imperial power.
**Empty,** em'ti, *a.* Containing nothing, or nothing but air; void; unsatisfactory; unburdened; hungry; vacant of head.—*vt.* (emptying, emptied). To make empty.—*vi.* To become empty.—*n.* An empty packingcase, etc.
**Empyreal,** em-pi-rē'al or em-pi'rē-al, *a.* Formed of pure fire or light; pertaining to the highest region of heaven.
**Empyrean,** em-pi-rē'an, em-pi'rē-an, *a.* The highest heaven.
**Emu, Emeu,** ē-mū', *n.* A large Australian bird, allied to the ostrich and cassowary.
**Emulate,** em'ū-lāt, *vt.* (emulating, emulated). To strive to equal or excel; to vie with.
**Emulation,** em-ū-lā'shon, *n.* Act of emulating; rivalry; envy.
**Emulative,** em'ū-lāt-iv, *a.* Inclined to emulation; rivalling.
**Emulator,** em'ū-lāt-ėr, *n.* A rival; competitor.
**Emulous,** em'ū-lus, *a.* Eager to emulate; rivalling; engaged in competition.
**Emulsion,** ē-mul'shon, *n.* A soft liquid remedy resembling milk; any milk-like mixture.
**Emulsive,** ē-muls'iv, *a.* Milk-like; softening; yielding a milk-like substance.
**Enable,** en-ā'bl, *vt.* (enabling, enabled). To make able; to empower; to authorize.
**Enact,** en-akt', *vt.* To establish by law; to decree; to perform; to act.
**Enactive,** en-akt'iv, *a.* Having power to enact or establish as a law.
**Enactment,** en-akt'ment, *n.* The passing of a bill into a law; a decree; an act.
**Enactor,** en-akt'ėr, *n.* One who enacts.
**Enamel,** en-am'el, *n.* A substance of the nature of glass, used as a coating; that which is enamelled; a smooth glossy surface of various colors; the smooth substance on a tooth.—*vt.* (enamelling, enamelled). To lay enamel on; to paint in enamel; to form a surface like enamel; to adorn with different colors.—*vi.* To practice the art of enamelling.
**Enamor,** en-am'ėr, *vt.* To inspire with love; to charm; to fill with delight.
**Encage,** en-kāj', *vt.* To put into or confine in a cage.
**Encamp,** en-kamp', *vi.* To take up position in a camp; to make a camp.—*vt.* To form into or place in a camp.
**Encampment,** en-kamp'ment, *n.* Act of encamping; a camp.
**Encaustic,** en-kas'tik, *a.* Pertaining to the art of enamelling and to painting in colors that are fixed by burning.
**Encave,** en-kāv', *vt.* To put into a cave; to hide in a cave or recess.
**Enceinte,** ang-sangt, *n.* The rampart which surrounds a fortress; the area thus surrounded.—*a.* Pregnant; with child.
**Encenia,** en-sē'ni-a, *n.pl.* A commemorative ceremonial.
**Encephalic,** en-sē-fal'ik, *a.* Belonging to the encephalon or brain.
**Encephalon,** en-sef'a-lon, *n.* The contents of the skull; the brain.
**Enchain,** en-chān', *vt.* To fasten with a chain; to hold in bondage; to confine.
**Enchant,** en-chant', *vt.* To practice sorcery on; to charm; to enrapture; to fascinate.
**Enchanted,** en-chant'ed, *p.a.* Affected by sorcery; delighted beyond measure.
**Enchanter,** en-chant'ėr, *n.* A sorcerer; one who charms or delights.
**Enchanting,** en-chant'ing, *p.a.* Charming; delighting; ravishing.
**Enchantment,** en-chant'ment, *n.* Act of enchanting; incantation; magic; overpowering influence of delight; fascination.
**Enchantress,** en-chant'res, *n.* A female enchanter; a sorceress.
**Enchase,** en-chās', *vt.* To inclose in a border; to surround with an ornamental setting; to adorn by embossed work.
**Enchorial,** en-kō'ri-al, *a.* Belonging to or used in a country; native; demotic.
**Encircle,** en-sėr'kl, *vt.* To inclose with a circle; to encompass; to embrace.
**Enclasp,** en-klasp', *vt.* To clasp; to fasten with a clasp.
**Enclave,** en-klāv or ang-klav, *n.* A place surrounded entirely by the territories of another power.
**Enclitic, Enclitical,** en-klit'ik, en-klit'ik-al, *a.* Said of a particle or word so united to the preceding word as to seem a part of it; throwing back the accent on the foregoing syllable.—*n.* An enclitic word.
**Enclose,** en-klōz', *vt.* To inclose.
**Enclosure,** en-klō'zhūr, *n.* Inclosure.
**Encomiast,** en-kō'mi-ast, *n.* One who praises another; a panegyrist.
**Encomiastic, Encomiastical,** en-kō'mi-as''tik, en-kō'mi-ast''ik-al, *a.* Containing encomium; bestowing praise; laudatory.
**Encomium,** en-kō'mi-um, *n.*; pl. **-iums.** Panegyric; eulogy; praise.
**Encompass,** en-kum'pas, *vt.* To encircle; to hem in; to go or sail round.
**Encore,** ang-kōr'. Again; once more; a call for a repetition of a performance.—*vt.* (encoring, encored). To call for a repetition of.
**Encounter,** en-koun'tėr, *n.* A meeting in contest; a conflict; a meeting; controversy; debate.—*vt.* To meet face to face; to meet suddenly; to strive against.—*vi.* To meet unexpectedly; to conflict.
**Encourage,** en-ku'rāj, *vt.* (encouraging, encouraged). To give courage to; to stimulate; to embolden; to countenance.
**Encouragement,** en-ku'rāj-ment, *n.* Act of encouraging; incentive; favor.
**Encourager,** en-ku'rāj-ėr, *n.* One who encourages.
**Encouraging,** en-ku'rāj-ing, *p.a.* Furnishing ground to hope for success.
**Encrimson,** en-krim'zn, *vt.* To cover with a crimson color.
**Encroach,** en-krōch', *vi.* To trespass on the rights and possessions of another; to intrude; to infringe; with *on* or *upon.*
**Encroacher,** en-krōch'ėr, *n.* One who encroaches.
**Encroachment,** en-krōch-ment, *n.* Act of encroaching; invasion; inroad; that which is taken by encroaching.
**Encrust,** en-krust', *vt.* To cover with a crust.
**Encumber,** en-kum'bėr, *vt.* To impede the motion of with a load; to embarrass; to load with debts or legal claims.
**Encumbrance,** en-kum'brans, *n.* That which encumbers; burden; hindrance; legal claims or liabilities; mortgage.
**Encyclic, Encyclical,** en-sī'klik, en-sī'kli-kal, *a.* Sent to many persons or places; circular.—*n.* A letter on some important occasion sent by the pope to the bishops.
**Encyclopedia, Encyclopaedia,** en-sī'klō-pē''di-a, *n.* A collection, usually alphabetical, of articles on one or more branches of knowledge.
**Encyclopedic, Encyclopaedic,** en-sī'klō-pē''dik, *a.* Pertaining to an encyclopedia; universal as regards information.
**Encyclopedist, Encyclopaedist,** en-sī'klō-pēd''ist, *n.* The compiler of an encyclopedia; one whose knowledge is very wide.
**End,** end, *n.* The extreme point; the last part; final state; completion; close of life; death; issue; result; aim; drift.—*vt.* To bring to an end; to conclude; to destroy.—*vi.* To come to an end; to close; to cease.
**Endanger,** en-dān'jėr, *vt.* To bring into danger; to expose to loss or injury.

**Endear,** en-dēr', *vt.* To make dear; to make more beloved.

**Endearing,** en-dēr'ing, *p.a.* Making dear or more beloved; exciting affection.

**Endearment,** en-dēr'ment, *n.* The act of endearing; tender affection; a caress.

**Endeavor,** en-dev'ėr, *n.* Effort; attempt; exertion; essay; aim.—*vi.* To try; to strive; to aim.—*vt.* To try to effect; to strive after.

**Endemic, Endemical,** en-dem'ik, en-dem'ik-al, *a.* Peculiar to a people or region, as a disease,—*n.* A disease of endemic nature.

**Ending,** end'ing, *n.* Termination.

**Endive,** en'div, *n.* A plant allied to chicory; garden succory.

**Endless,** end'les, *a.* Without end; everlasting; infinite; incessant.

**Endlessly,** end'les-li, *adv.* Incessantly.

**Endlong,** end'long, *adv.* With the end forward; lengthwise.

**Endogen,** en'dō-jen, *n.* A plant whose stem grows by additions developed from the inside, as palms and grasses.

**Endogenous,** en-doj'e-nus, *a.* Pertaining to endogens; developing from within.

**Endorse,** en-dors', *vt.* (endorsing, endorsed). To write on the back of, as one's name on a bill; to assign by endorsement; to ratify.

**Endorsement,** en-dors'ment, *n.* The act of endorsing; a docket; signature of one who endorses; sanction or approval.

**Endoskeleton,** en'dō-skel-e-ton, *n.* The internal bony structure of animals.

**Endosmose,** en'dos-mōs, *n.* The transmission of fluids or gases through porous partitions from the exterior to the interior.

**Endow,** en-dou', *vt.* To settle a dower on; to enrich or furnish, as with any gift, quality, or faculty; to indue; to invest.

**Endowment,** en-dou'ment, *n.* Act of endowing; revenue permanently appropriated to any object; natural capacity.

**Endurable,** en-dūr'a-bl, *a.* That can be endured.

**Endurance,** en-dūr'ans, *n.* State of enduring; continuance; patience; fortitude.

**Endure,** en-dūr', *vi.* (enduring, endured). To continue in the same state; to last; to abide; to submit.—*vt.* To sustain; to bear; to undergo; to tolerate.

**Enduring,** en-dūr'ing, *p.a.* Lasting long; permanent.

**Endwise,** end'wīz, *adv.* In an upright position; with the end forward.

**Enema,** en'e-ma, *n.* A liquid or gaseous medicine injected into the rectum; a clyster.

**Enemy,** en'e-mi, *n.* One who is unfriendly; an antagonist; a hostile army.

**Energetic, Energetical,** en-ėr-jet'ik, en-ėr-jet'ik-al, *a.* Acting with energy; forcible; potent; active; vigorous.

**Energetically,** en-ėr-jet'ik-al-li, *adv.* With energy and effect.

**Energize,** en'ėr-jīz, *vi.* (energizing, energized). To act with energy.—*vt.* To give energy to.

**Energy,** en'ėr-ji, *n.* Inherent power to operate or act; power exerted; force; vigor; strength of expression; emphasis; in physics, power to do work; it may be mechanical, electrical, thermal, chemical, etc.

**Enervate,** en'ėr-vāt or ē-nėrv'āt, *vt.* (enervating, enervated). To deprive of strength or force; to unnerve; to debilitate.

**Enervation,** en-ėr-vā'shon, *n.* Act of enervating; state of being enervated; effeminacy.

**Enfeeble,** en-fē'bl, *vt.* (enfeebling, enfeebled). To make feeble; to weaken.

**Enfeeblement,** en-fē'bl-ment, *n.* The act of weakening; enervation.

**Enfeoff,** en-fef', *vt.* To invest with the fee of an estate.

**Enfilade,** en-fi-lād, *vt.* (enfilading, enfiladed). To rake with shot through the whole length of a line or work; to fire in the flank of.—*n.* A firing in such a manner; the line of fire.

**Enforce,** en-fōrs', *vt.* To urge with energy; to impress on the mind; to compel; to put in execution.

**Enforceable, Enforcible,** en-fōrs'a-bl, en-fōrs'i-bl, *a.* Capable of being enforced.

**Enforcement,** en-fōrs'ment, *n.* Act of enforcing; compulsion; a giving of force or effect to; a putting in execution, as law.

**Enfranchise,** en-fran'chīz, *vt.* (enfranchising, enfranchised). To set free; to admit to the privileges of a citizen; to endow with the franchise.

**Enfranchisement,** en-fran'chīz-ment, *n.* Act of enfranchising; state of being enfranchised.

**Engage,** en-gāj', *vt.* (engaging, engaged). To bind by pledge or contract; to attach; to attract; to attack.—*vi.* To bind oneself; to embark on any business; to begin to fight.

**Engaged,** en-gājd', *p.a.* Pledged; affianced; attached to a wall (said of a column).

**Engagement,** en-gāj'ment, *n.* Act of engaging; obligation; betrothal; avocation; business; conflict; battle.

**Engaging,** en-gāj'ing, *p.a.* Winning; attractive; pleasing.

**Engender,** en-jen'dėr, *vt.* To breed; to beget; to occasion.—*vi.* To be caused or produced.

**Engine,** en'jin, *n.* Any instrument in some degree complicated; a machine to drive machinery, to propel vessels, railway trains, etc.—*vt.* (engining, engined). To furnish with an engine or engines.

**Engineer,** en-ji-nēr', *n.* One who constructs or manages engines; one who plans works for offense or defense; one who constructs roads, railways, etc.—*vt.* To direct the making of in the capacity of engineer.

**Engineering,** en-ji-nēr'ing, *n.* The art or business of an engineer.

**Engird,** en-gėrd', *vt.* To gird round; to encircle.

**English,** ing'glish, *a.* Belonging to England, or to its inhabitants.—*n.* The people or language of England.—*vt.* To translate into English.

**Englishry,** ing'glish-ri, *n.* A population of English descent; the persons of English descent in Ireland.

**Engraft,** en-grăft', *vt.* To ingraft.

**Engrail,** en-grāl', *vt.* To notch; to indent; to jag at the edges.

**Engrain,** en-grān', *vt.* To dye with grain; to dye deep; to paint in imitation of wood.

**Engrave,** en-grāv', *vt.* (engraving, engraved). To cut figures on with a burin; to represent by incisions; to imprint; to impress deeply.

**Engraver,** en-grāv'ėr, *n.* One who engraves; a cutter of figures on metal, wood, etc.

**Engraving,** en-grāv'ing, *n.* Act or art of engraving; an engraved plate; an impression from an engraved plate.

**Engross,** en-grōs', *vt.* To take up the whole of; to occupy, engage; to write a correct copy in legible characters; to take in undue quantities or degrees.—*vi.* To be employed in making fair copies of writings.

**Engrosser,** en-grōs'ėr, *n.* One who engrosses.

**Engrossment,** en-grōs'ment, *n.* Act of engrossing; state of being engrossed; exorbitant acquisition; copy of a deed in clear writing.

**Engulf,** en-gulf', *vt.* To ingulf; to swallow up.

**Enhance,** en-hans', *vt.* (enhancing, enhanced). To raise to a higher point; to increase; to aggravate.—*vi.* To grow larger.

**Enhancement,** en-hans'ment, *n.* Act of enhancing; rise; augmentation.

**Enigma,** ē-nig'ma, *n.* An obscure statement or question; riddle; anything inexplicable.

**Enigmatic, Enigmatical,** ē-nig-mat'ik, ē-nig-mat'ik-al, *a.* Relating to or containing an enigma; obscure; ambiguous.

**Enigmatist,** ē-nig'mat-ist, *n.* A maker of or dealer in enigmas.

**Enjoin,** en-join', *vt.* To order with urgency; to admonish; to prescribe.

E

**Enjoy**, en-joi', *vt*. To feel gladness in; to have, use, or perceive with pleasure.
**Enjoyable**, en-joi'a-bl, *a*. Capable of being enjoyed.
**Enjoyment**, en-joi'ment, *n*. State of enjoying; pleasure; satisfaction; fruition.
**Enkindle**, en-kin'dl, *vt*. To kindle.
**Enlarge**, en-lärj', *vt*. (enlarging, enlarged). To make large or larger; to set free.—*vi*. To grow large or larger; to expatiate.
**Enlarged**, en-lärjd', *p.a*. Not narrow nor confined; broad; comprehensive; liberal.
**Enlargement**, en-lärj'ment, *n*. Act of enlarging; state of being enlarged; expansion; release; addition.
**Enlighten**, en-līt'en, *vt*. To make clear; to enable to see more clearly; to instruct.
**Enlightened**, en-līt'end, *p.a*. Instructed; informed; unprejudiced.
**Enlist**, en-list', *vt*. To enter on a list; to engage in public service, especially military; to engage the services of.—*vi*. To engage voluntarily in public service; to enter heartily into a cause.
**Enlistment**, en-list'ment, *n*. Act of enlisting; voluntary engagement to serve as a soldier, sailor or airman.
**Enliven**, en-līv'en, *vt*. To give life or vivacity to; to gladden; to invigorate.
**Enlivener**, en-līv'en-ėr, *n*. One who or that which enlivens or animates.
**Enmity**, en'mi-ti, *n*. Quality of being an enemy; hostility; ill-will; opposition.
**Ennoble**, en-nō'bl, *vt*. (ennobling, ennobled). To make noble; to exalt; to dignify.
**Ennui**, än-nwē, *n*. Dullness of spirit; weariness; listlessness; tedium.
**Enormity**, ē-nor'mi-ti, *n*. State or quality of being enormous; depravity; atrocity.
**Enormous**, ē-nor'mus, *a*. Great beyond the common measure; huge; outrageous.
**Enormously**, ē-nor'mus-li, *adv*. Excessively.
**Enough**, ē-nuf', *a*. That satisfies desire; that may answer the purpose.—*n*. A sufficiency; that which is equal to the powers or abilities.—*adv*. Sufficiently; tolerably.
**Enrage**, en-rāj', *vt*. To excite rage in; to incense.
**Enrapture**, en-rap'tūr, *vt*. To transport with rapture; to delight beyond measure.
**Enrich**, en-rich', *vt*. To make rich; to fertilize; to supply with an abundance of anything desirable; to adorn.
**Enrichment**, en-rich'ment, *n*. Act of enriching; something that enriches.
**Enrobe**, en-rōb', *vt*. To attire.
**Enroll, Enrol**, en-rōl', *vt*. To write in a roll or register; to record.
**Enrolment**, en-rōl'ment, *n*. Act of enrolling; a register; a record.
**Ensanguine**, en-sang'gwin, *vt*. To stain or cover with blood; to smear with gore.
**Ensconce**, en-skons', *vt*. To cover, as with a sconce; to protect; to hide.
**Ensemble**, ong-säm-bl, *n*. All parts of a thing considered together; general effect.
**Enshrine**, en-shrīn', *vt*. To inclose in a shrine or chest; to cherish.
**Enshroud**, en-shroud', *vt*. To cover with a shroud; to envelop.
**Ensiform**, en'si-form, *a*. Sword-shaped.
**Ensign**, en'sīn, *n*. A mark of distinction; the flag of a company of soldiers or a vessel; formerly the lowest rank of commissioned officer in the infantry.
**Ensigncy, ensignship**, en'sīn-sī, en'sīn-ship, *n*. Rank or commission of an ensign.
**Ensilage**, en'sil-āj, *n*. A mode of storing green fodder, vegetables, etc., by burying in pits or silos.
**Enslave**, en-slāv', *vt*. (enslaving, enslaved). To reduce to slavery; to overpower.
**Enslavement**, en-slāv'ment, *n*. Act of enslaving; slavery; servitude.
**Enslaver**, en-slāv'ėr, *n*. One who enslaves.
**Ensnare**, en-snār, *vt*. To entrap; to insnare.
**Ensue**, en-sū', *vi*. (ensuing, ensued). To follow as a consequence; to succeed.
**Ensure**, en-shör', *vt*. To make sure.
**Entablature**, en-tab'la-tūr, *n*. That part of a structure which lies upon the capitals of columns.
**Entail**, en-tāl', *vt*. To cut off an estate from the heirs general; to settle, as the descent of lands by gift to a man and to certain heirs; to devolve as a consequence or of necessity.—*n*. The act of entailing; an estate entailed; rule of descent settled for an estate.
**Entailment**, en-tāl'ment, *n*. Act of entailing; state of being entailed.
**Entangle**, en-tang'gl, *vt*. To knit or interweave confusedly; to involve; to hamper.
**Entanglement**, en-tang'gl-ment, *n*. Act of entangling; state of being entangled.
**Enter**, en'tėr, *vt*. To go or come into; to begin; to set down in writing; to register; to take possession of.—*vi*. To go or come in; begin; engage in; be an ingredient in.
**Enteric**, en-ter'ik, *a*. Belonging to the intestines.—*Enteric fever*, same as *Typhoid fever*.
**Enterprise**, en'tėr-prīz, *n*. That which is undertaken; a bold or hazardous attempt; adventurous spirit; hardihood.—*vt*. To undertake.
**Enterprising**, en'tėr-prīz-ing, *a*. Bold or prompt to attempt; venturesome.
**Entertain**, en-tėr-tān', *vt*. To receive as a guest; to cherish; to treat with conversation; to please; to admit, with a view to consider.—*vi*. To give entertainments.
**Entertaining**, en-tėr-tān'ing, *p.a*. Pleasing; amusing; diverting.
**Entertainment**, en-tėr-tān'ment, *n*. Act of entertaining; hospitable treatment; a festival; amusement.
**Enthrall, Enthral**, en-thral', *vt*. To reduce to the condition of a thrall; to enslave.
**Enthrone**, en-thrōn, *vt*. (enthroning, enthroned). To place on a throne.
**Enthusiasm**, en-thū'zi-azm, *n*. An ecstasy of mind, as if from divine or spiritual influence; ardent zeal; elevation of fancy.
**Enthusiast**, en-thū'zi-ast, *n*. One possessed of enthusiasm; a person of ardent zeal; one of elevated fancy.
**Enthusiastic**, en-thū'zi-as''tik, *a*. Filled with enthusiasm; ardent; devoted; visionary.
**Entice**, en-tīs', *vt*. (enticing, enticed). To draw on, by exciting hope or desire; to allure.
**Enticement**, en-tīs'ment, *n*. Act or means of enticing; blandishment; wile.
**Enticing**, en-tīs'ing, *p.a*. Having the qualities that entice; fascinating.
**Entire**, en-tīr', *a*. Whole; unshared; complete; sincere; hearty; in full strength.
**Entirely**, entīr'li, *adv*. Wholly; fully.
**Entitle**, en-tī'tl, *vt*. (entitling, entitled). To give a title to; to style; to characterize; to give a claim to; to qualify.
**Entity**, en'ti-ti, *n*. Being; essence; existence.
**Entomb**, en-töm', *vt*. To deposit in a tomb; to bury; to inter.
**Entombment**, en-töm'ment, *n*. Burial.
**Entomologist**, en-to-mol'o-jist, *n*. One versed in the science of insects.
**Entomology**, en-to-mol'o-ji, *n*. That branch of zoology which treats of the structure, habits, and classification of insects.
**Entozoon**, en-to-zō'on, *n*.; pl. **-zoa.** An intestinal worm; an animal living in some part of another animal.
**Entrail**, en'trāl, *n*. One of the intestines; generally in *pl*.; the bowels.
**Entrain**, en-trān', *vt*. To put on board a railway train.—*vi*. To take places in a train.
**Entrance**, en'trans, *n*. Act or power of entering into a place; the door or avenue by which a place may be entered; beginning; act of taking possession.
**Entrance**, en-trans', *vt*. To put in a trance or ec-

stasy; to enrapture; to transport.
**Entrant,** en'trant, *n.* One who enters.
**Entrap,** en-trap', *vt.* To catch in a trap; to inveigle; to decoy.
**Entreat,** en-trēt', *vt.* To beg earnestly; to beseech; to supplicate.—*vi.* To make an earnest request; to pray.
**Entreaty,** en-trēt'i, *n.* Urgent prayer; earnest petition; solicitation.
**Entrée,** äng-trā, *n.* Freedom of access; a dish served at table.
**Entremets,** äng-tr-mā, *n.* A side-dish or minor dish at table, as an omelet, a jelly, etc.
**Entrench,** en-trensh', *vt.* Same as *Intrench.*
**Entresol,** en'tėr-sol or äng-tr-sol, *n.* A low story between the ground story and one of greater height above.
**Entry,** en'tri, *n.* Act of entering; entrance; the passage by which persons enter a house; act of taking possession of lands, etc.; act of committing to writing.
**Entwine,** en-twīn', *vt.* To twine; to twist round; to intwine.
**Entwist,** en-twist', *vt.* To twist round.
**Enumerate,** ē-nū'me-rāt, *vt.* (enumerating, enumerated). To count number by number; to reckon or mention a number of things, each separately.
**Enumeration,** ē-nū'me-rā''shon, *n.* Act of enumerating; detailed account; a summing up.
**Enunciate,** ē-nun'si-āt, *vt.* (enunciating, enunciated). To utter; to pronounce; to proclaim.
**Enunciation,** ē-nun'si-ā''shon, *n.* Act or manner of enunciating; expression; declaration; public attestation.
**Enunciatory,** ē-nun'si-a-to-ri, *a.* Containing enunciation; declarative.
**Envelop,** en-vel'op, *vt.* To cover by wrapping or folding; to lie around and conceal.
**Envelope,** en'vel-ōp, *n.* That which infolds; a wrapper; a covering for a letter, etc.; an investing integument.
**Envelopment,** en-vel'op-ment, *n.* The act of enveloping; that which envelops.
**Envenom,** en-ven'om, *vt.* To poison; to taint with malice; to exasperate.
**Enviable,** en'vi-a-bl, *a.* Exciting or capable of exciting envy.
**Envious,** en'vi-us, *a.* Feeling or harboring envy; tinctured with or excited by envy.
**Environ,** en-vī'ron, *vt.* To encompass; to encircle; to besiege; to invest.
**Environment,** en-vī'ron-ment, *n.* Act of environing; state of being environed; that which environs; conditions under which one lives.
**Environs,** en-vī'rons, *n.pl.* Neighborhood; vicinity.
**Envisage,** en-viz'āj, *vt.* To look in the face of; to apprehend directly or by intuition.
**Envoy,** en'voi, *n.* One sent on a mission; a person next in rank to an ambassador, deputed to transact business with a foreign power.
**Envy,** en'vi, *n.* Pain or discontent excited by another's superiority or success; malice; object of envy.—*vt.* (envying, envied). To feel envy towards or on account of; to begrudge.—*vi.* To be affected with envy.
**Enwrap,** en-rap', *vt.* To envelop; to inwrap.
**Eocene,** ē'ō-sēn, *a.* and *n.* A term applied to the series of strata at the base of the tertiary formations.
**Eolithic,** ē-ō-lith'ik, *a.* Pertaining to the early part of the palaeolithic period.
**Eozoic,** ē-ō-zō'ik, *a.* Pertaining to the oldest fossiliferous rocks.
**Epact,** ē'pakt, *n.* Days forming the excess of the solar over the lunar year; the moon's age at the end of the year.
**Epaulet, Epaulette,** e'pal-et, *n.* A shoulder knot; a badge worn on the shoulder by military men or naval officers.
**Epergne,** e-pärn', *n.* An ornamental stand for the center of a table.
**Ephemera,** e-fem'e-ra, *n.*; pl. **-rae.** A fly that lives one day only; a short-lived insect.
**Ephemeral,** e-fē'me-ral, *a.* Continuing one day only; short-lived; fleeting.
**Ephemeris,** e-fem'e-ris, *n.*; pl. **Ephemerides,** e-fe-me'ri-dēz. A diary; an astronomical almanac; periodical literature.
**Ephod,** e'fod, *n.* A vestment worn by the Jewish high-priest.
**Epic,** ep'ik, *a.* Composed in a lofty narrative style; heroic.—*n.* A poem of elevated character, describing the exploits of heroes.
**Epicarp,** ep'i-kärp, *n.* The outer skin of fruits.
**Epicure,** ep'i-kūr, *n.* One devoted to sensual enjoyments; a voluptuary.
**Epicurean,** ep'i-kū-rē''an, *a.* Luxurious; given to luxury.—*n.* A follower of Epicurus; a luxurious eater; an epicure.
**Epicurism,** ep'i-kūr-izm, *n.* The doctrines or practices of an epicure.
**Epicycle,** ep'i-sī-kl, *n.* A little circle whose center moves round in the circumference of a greater circle.
**Epideictic, Epideictical,** ep-i-dīk'tik, ep-i-dīk'ti-kal, *a.* Serving to display; having a rhetorical character; demonstrative.
**Epidemic, Epidemical,** ep-i-dem'ik, ep-i-dem'ik-al, *a.* Affecting a whole community, as a disease; prevalent.—**Epidemic,** ep-i-dem'ik, *n.* A disease which attacks many people at the same period.
**Epidermis,** ep-i-dėr'mis, *n.* The cuticle or scarf-skin of the body; the exterior coating of the leaf or stem of a plant.
**Epiglottis,** ep-i-glot'is, *n.* The cartilage at the root of the tongue that covers the glottis during the act of swallowing.
**Epigram,** ep'i-gram, *n.* A short poem, usually keenly satirical; a pointed or antithetical saying.
**Epigrammatic, Epigrammatical,** ep'i-gram-mat''ik, ep'i-gram-mat''ik-al, *a.* Pertaining to epigrams; like an epigram; pointed.
**Epigrammatist,** ep-i-gram'mat-ist, *n.* One who composes or deals in epigrams.
**Epigraph,** ep'i-graf, *n.* An inscription; quotation; motto.
**Epilepsy,** ep'i-lep-si, *n.* The falling-sickness; a disease characterized by spasms and loss of sense.
**Epileptic,** ep-i-lep'tik, *a.* Pertaining to epilepsy.—*n.* One affected with epilepsy.
**Epilogue,** ep'i-log, *n.* A speech or short poem spoken by an actor at the end of a play.
**Epiphany,** ē-pif'a-ni, *n.* A church festival on January 6th, celebrating the manifestation of Christ to the wise men of the East.
**Epiphyte,** ep'i-fīt, *n.* A plant growing upon another plant, but not nourished by it.
**Episcopacy,** ē-pis'kō-pa-si, *n.* Ecclesiastical government by bishops; the collective body of bishops.
**Episcopal,** ē-pis'kō-pal, *a.* Belonging to or vested in bishops.
**Episcopalian,** ē-pis'kō-pā''li-an, *a.* Pertaining to bishops, or government by bishops.—*n.* One who belongs to an episcopal church.
**Episcopalianism,** ē-pis'kō-pā''li-an-izm, *n.* The system of episcopal government.
**Episcopate,** ē-pis'kō-pāt, *n.* A bishopric; the collective body of bishops.
**Episode,** ep'i-sōd, *n.* A separate story introduced to give greater variety to the events related in a poem, etc.; an incident.
**Episodic, Episodical,** ep-i-sod'ik, ep-i-sod'ik-al, *a.* Pertaining to an episode; contained in an episode.
**Epistle,** ē-pis'l, *n.* A writing communicating intelligence to a distant person; a letter.
**Epistolary,** ē-pis'tō-la-ri, *a.* Pertaining to epistles; suitable to correspondence.
**Epitaph,** ep'i-taf, *n.* That which is written on a tomb; an inscription, or a composition, in honor

of the dead.
**Epithalamium,** ep'i-tha-lā'mi-um, *n.*; pl. **-iums** or **-ia.** A nuptial song or peom.
**Epithet,** ep'i-thet, *n.* Any word implying a quality attached to a person or thing.
**Epitome,** e-pit'o-mi, *n.* A brief summary; abridgment; compendium.
**Epitomist, Epitomizer,** e-pit'o-mist, e-pit'o-mī-zėr, *n.* The writer of an epitome.
**Epitomize,** e-pit'om-īz, *vt.* To make an epitome of; to abstract; to condense.
**Epoch,** ē'pok, *n.* A fixed point of time from, which years are numbered; period; era; date.
**Epode,** ep'ōd, *n.* The third and last part of an ode, succeeding the antistrophe; a lyric in which a verse is followed by a shorter verse.
**Eponym,** ep'o-nim, *n.* A name of a place or people derived from that of a person.
**Epopee,** e-po-pē', *n.* An epic poem; the subject of an epic poem.
**Epsom-salt,** ep'sum-salt, *n.* The sulphate of magnesia, a cathartic.
**Equability,** ē-kwa-bil'i-ti, *n.* State or quality of being equable.
**Equable,** ē-kwa-bl, *a.* Uniform; even; steady.
**Equably,** ē'kwa-bli, *adv.* In an equable or uniform manner.
**Equal,** ē'kwal, *a.* The same in extent, number, degree, rank, etc.; same in qualities; uniform; proportionate; adequate; just.—*n.* One not inferior or superior to another.—*vt.* (equalling, equalled). To make equal to; to become or be equal to.
**Equality,** ē-kwal'i-ti, *n.* State or quality of being equal; likeness; evenness; plainness.
**Equalization,** ē'kwal-īz-ā''shon, *n.* Act of equalizing; state of being equalized.
**Equalize,** ē-kwal-īz, *vt.* (equalizing, equalized). To make equal, even, or uniform.
**Equally,** ē'kwal-li, *adv.* In an equal manner; alike; impartially.
**Equanimity,** ē-kwa-nim'i-ti or ek-, *n.* Evenness of mind; steadiness of temper.
**Equate,** ē-kwāt, *vt.* (equating, equated). To make equal; to reduce to an equation; to reduce to mean time or motion.
**Equation,** ē-kwā'shon, *n.* The act of equating; an expression asserting the equality of two quantities; a quantity to be taken into account in order to give a true result.
**Equator,** ē-kwā'tėr, *n.* The great circle of our globe which divides it into the northern and southern hemispheres; a circle in the heavens coinciding with the plane of the earth's equator.
**Equatorial,** ē-kwa-tō'ri-al, *a.* Pertaining to the equator.—*n.* An astronomical instrument.
**Equerry,** e'kwe-ri or ē-kwe'ri, *n.* An officer of princes or nobles who has the care of their horses.
**Equestrian,** ē-kwes'tri-an, *a.* Pertaining to horses or horsemanship; on horseback; skilled in horsemanship.—*n.* A horseman.
**Equiangular,** ē-kwi-ang'gū-lėr, or ek-, *a.* Consisting of or having equal angles.
**Equidistant,** ē-kwi-dis'tant or ek-, *a.* Being at an equal distance from.
**Equilateral,** ē-kwi-lat'ėr-al or ek-, *a.* Having all the sides equal.
**Equilibrist,** ē-kwil'i-brist or ek-, *n.* One who keeps his balance in unnatural positions.
**Equilibrium,** ē-kwi-li'bri-um or ek-, *n.* State of rest produced by the counteraction of forces; balance.
**Equimultiple,** ē-kwi-mul'ti-pl or ek-, *a.* Multiplied by the same number or quantity.—*n.* Any number or quantity multiplied by the same number or quantity as another.
**Equine,** ē-kwīn,', *a.* Pertaining to a horse; denoting the horse kind.
**Equinoctial,** ē-kwi-nok'shal, or ek-, *a.* Pertaining to the equinoxes.—*n.* The celestial equator: when the sun is on it, the days and nights are of equal length.
**Equinox,** ē'kwi-noks or ek', *n.* The time when the day and night are of equal length, about March 21st and September 23rd.
**Equip,** ē-kwip', *vt.* (equipping, equipped). To fit out or furnish, as for war; to dress; to array.
**Equipage,** ek'wi-pāj, *n.* An equipment; retinue; carriage of state and attendants; accoutrements.
**Equipment,** ē-kwip'ment, *n.* Act of equipping; habiliments; warlike apparatus; necessary adjuncts.
**Equipose,** ē'kwi-poiz or ek', *n.* Equality of weight or force; equilibrium.
**Equipollence, Equipollency,** ē-kwi-pol'lens, ē-kwi-pol'len-si or ek-, *n.* Equality of power or force.
**Equipollent,** ē-kwi-pol'lent or ek-, *a.* Having equal power; equivalent.
**Equiponderance,** ē-kwi-pon'dėr-ans or ek-, *n.* Equality of weight; equipoise.
**Equiponderant,** ē-kwi-pon'dėr-ant or ek-, *a.* Being of the same weight.
**Equitable,** ek'wit-a-bl, *a.* Distributing equal justice; just; upright; impartial.
**Equitably,** ek'wit-a-bl, *adv.* In an equitable manner; justly; impartially.
**Equity,** ek'wi-ti, *n.* The giving to each man his due; impartiality; uprightness; a system of supplementary law founded upon precedents and established principles.
**Equivalence,** ē-kwiv'a-lens or ek-, *n.* State of being equivalent; equality of value.
**Equivalent,** ē-kwiv'a-lent or ek-, *a.* Equal in excellence, worth, or weight; of the same import or meaning.—*n.* That which is equal in value, etc.; compensation.
**Equivocal,** ē-kwiv'ō-kal, *a.* Capable of a double interpretation; doubtful.
**Equivocate,** ē-kwiv'ō-kāt, *vi.* To use ambiguous expressions to mislead; to quibble.
**Equivocation,** ē-kwiv'ō-kā''shon, *n.* Act of equivocating; ambiguity.
**Equivocator,** ē-kwiv'ō-kāt-ėr, *n.* One who equivocates.
**Equivoke, Equivoque,** ē'kwi-vōk, *n.* An ambiguous term; equivocation.
**Era,** ē'ra, *n.* A fixed point of time, from which years are counted; epoch; age.
**Eradicate,** ē-rad'i-kāt, *vt.* To root out; to destroy; to exterminate.
**Eradication,** ē-rad'i-kā''shon, *n.* Act of eradicating; total destruction.
**Erase,** ē-rās', *vt.* (erasing, erased). To scrape out; to efface; to expunge.
**Erasement,** ē-rās'ment, *n.* A rubbing out; obliteration.
**Eraser,** ē-rās'ėr, *n.* One who erases; an appliance to erase writing, etc.
**Erastian,** ē-ras'ti-an, *n.* A follower of Thomas Erastus, a 16th-century German, who maintained that the church is dependent on the state for its government and discipline.—*a.* Relating to the Erastians or their principles.
**Erastianism,** ē-ras'ti-an-izm, *n.* the principles of the Erastians.
**Erasure,** ē-rā'zhūr, *n.* Act of erasing; obliteration.
**Ere,** ār, *adv. conj.*, and *prep.* Before; sooner than.
**Erect,** ē-rekt', *a.* Upright; bold; undismayed.—*vt.* To raise and set upright; to build; to found; to cheer.
**Erecter, Erector,** ē-rekt'ėr, *n.* One who erects.
**Erectile,** ē-rekt'īl, *a.* That may be erected.
**Erection,** ē-rek'shon, *a.* Act of erecting; formation; anything erected; structure.
**Eremite,** e'rē-mīt, *n.* One who lives in a desert or wilderness; a hermit.
**Ergo,** ėr'gō, *adv.* Therefore.
**Ergot,** ėr'got, *n.* A disease of rye and other grasses; this diseases growth, used in medicine.
**Ermine,** ėr'mīn, *n.* An animal of the weasel kind, a native of N. Europe and America, valued for its white fur; the fur of the ermine.

**Erode,** ē-rōd', *vt.* (eroding, eroded). To gnaw off or away; to corrode.
**Erosion,** ē-rō'zhon, *n.* Act of eroding; state of being eaten away; corrosion.
**Erotic,** ē-rot'ik, *a.* Pertaining to or prompted by love; treating of love.
**Err,** er, *vi.* To wander; to stray; to depart from rectitude; to blunder.
**Errand,** e'rand, *n.* A message; mandate; business to be transacted by a messenger.
**Errant,** e'rant, *a.* Roving; wandering about in search of adventures.
**Errantry,** e'rant-ri, *n.* A wandering state; a roving or rambling; the employment of a knight-errant.
**Erratic,** e-rat'ik, *a.* Wandering; irregular; eccentric.
**Erratum,** e-rā'tum, *n.*; pl. **-ata.** An error or mistake in writing or printing.
**Erroneous,** e-rō'nē-us, *a.* Characterized by or containing error; wrong; mistaken.
**Error,** e'rėr, *n.* A deviation from truth or what is right; a mistake; a blunder; fault; offense.
**Erse,** ėrs, *n.* The Celtic language of the Highlands of Scotland; Gaelic; also the language spoken in parts of Ireland.
**Erst,** ėrst, *adv.* At first; long ago; hitherto.
**Erubescence,** e-rū-bes'ens, *n.* A becoming red; redness; a blushing.
**Erubescent,** e-rū-bes'ent, *a.* Red; blushing.
**Eructate,** ē-rukt'āt, *vt.* To belch up; to eject from the stomach, as wind. Also **Eruct.**
**Eructation,** ē-ruk-tā'shon, *n.* Act of belching; a belch; a violent bursting forth or ejection of matter from the earth.
**Erudite,** e'rū-dīt, *a.* Fully instructed; deeply read; learned.
**Erudition,** e-rū-di'shon, *n.* Learning; knowledge gained by study; scholarship.
**Erupt,** ē-rupt', *vt.* To throw out by volcanic action.
**Eruption,** ē-rup'shon, *n.* A breaking forth; a violent emission; a sudden hostile excursion; a breaking out of pimples, pustules, etc.
**Eruptive,** ē-rup'tiv, *a.* Bursting out or forth; produced by eruption.
**Erysipelas,** e-ri-si'pe-las, *n.* A disease accompanied by fever and an eruption of a fiery acrid humor, chiefly on the face.
**Escalade,** es-ka-lād', *n.* The assault of a fortress by scaling the walls.—*vt.* To scale; to mount and pass or enter by means of ladders.
**Escalator,** es'ka-lā-tėr, *n.* A mechanism consisting of a series of steps which are carried up and down by means of a continuous chain; a moving stairway.
**Escallop,** es-kol'op, *n.* A bivalve shell; a scallop.
**Escapade,** es-ka-pād', *n.* A runaway adventure; a freak; a mad prank.
**Escape,** es-kāp', *vt.* (escaping, escaped). To get out of the way of; to pass without harm; to pass unobserved; to avoid.—*vi.* To be free; to avoid; to regain one's liberty.—*n.* Flight; to shun danger; an evasion of legal retraint or custody.
**Escapement,** es-kāp'ment, *n.* Means of escaping; that part of a time-piece by which the circular motion of the wheels is converted into a vibrating one.
**Escarp,** es-kärp', *vt.* To form into a scarp; to make to slope suddenly.—*n.* A sudden slope.
**Escarpment,** es-kärp'ment, *n.* A steep declivity; ground cut away nearly vertically.
**Eschatology,** es-ka-tol'o-ji, *n.* The doctrine of the last or final things, as death.
**Escheat,** es-chēt', *n.* The reversion of property to the original proprietor, or to the state, through failure of heirs or by forfeiture; the property itself.—*vi.* To revert, as land.—*vt.* To cause to be an escheat; to forfeit.
**Eschew,** es-chö', *vt.* To shun; to avoid.
**Escort,** es'kort, *n.* A guard attending an officer or baggage, etc.; persons attending as a mark of honor.—*vt.* es-kort'. To attend and guard.
**Escritoire,** es-kri-twär', *n.* A chest of drawers with appliances for writing; a writing-desk.
**Esculent,** es'kū-lent, *a.* Eatable; that may be used by man for food.—*n.* An edible.
**Escutcheon,** es-kuch'on, *n.* A shield; the shield on which a coat of arms is represented.
**Esophagus,** ē-sof'a-gus, *n.* The gullet; the canal through which food and drink pass to the stomach.
**Esoteric,** es-ō-te'rik, *a.* Taught to a select few; private; select.
**Espalier,** es-pa'li-ėr, *n.* A trellis-work or lattice-work on which to train fruit-trees and shrubs; a tree or row of trees so trained.
**Esparto,** es-pär'tō, *n.* A grass found in S. Spain and N. Africa, extensively exported for the manufacture of paper, matting, etc.
**Especial,** es-pe'shal, *a.* Distinct; chief; special.
**Especially,** es-pe'shal-li, *adv.* In an uncommon degree; specially.
**Esperanto,** es-pėr-ant'ō, *n.* A language invented by Dr. Zamenhof (about 1887) for the purpose of enabling the inhabitants of all countries to converse with each other.
**Espial,** es-pī'al, *n.* Act of espying.
**Espionage,** es'pi-on-āj, *n.* Practice or employment of spies; practice of watching others without being suspected.
**Esplanade,** es-pla-nād', *n.* An open space between the glacis of a citadel and the houses of the town; any level space near a town for walks or drives; a terrace by the sea-side.
**Espousal,** es-pouz'al, *n.* Betrothal; nuptials: in this sense generally in *pl*; the adopting of a cause.
**Espouse,** es-pouz', *vt.* (espousing, espoused). To give or take in marriage; to betroth; to wed; to embrace or adopt; to uphold.
**Espouser,** es-pouz'ėr, *n.* One who espouses.
**Esprit,** es-prē, *n.* Soul; spirit; mind; wit.
**Espy,** es-pī', *vt.* (espying, espied). To see at a distance; to descry; to discover.
**Esquire,** es-kwīr', *n.* A shield-bearer; a title of dignity next to a knight; a title of courtesy.
**Essay,** es-sā', *vt.* To try; to make experiment of.—*n.* es'sā. An endeavor or experiment; a literary composition to prove or illustrate a particular subject; a short treatise.
**Essayist,** es'sā-ist, *n.* A writer of an essay or essays.
**Essence,** es'sens, *n.* The nature, substance, or being of anything; predominant qualities of a plant or drug; an extract; perfume; fundamental doctrines, facts, etc., of a statement, etc.—*vt.* To perfume; to scent.
**Essential,** es-sen'shal, *a.* Relating to or containing the essence; necessary to the existence of; indispensable; highly rectified; volatile; diffusible (oils).—*n.* Something necessary; the chief point; constituent principle.
**Essentiality,** es-sen'shi-al''i-ti, *n.* The quality of being essential.
**Establish,** es-tab'lish, *vt.* To make stable; to found permanently; to institute; to enact; to sanction; to confirm; to make good.
**Established,** es-tab'lisht, *p.a.* Ratified; confirmed; set up and supported by the state.
**Establishment,** es-tab'lish-ment, *n.* Act of establishing; state of being established; confirmation; sanction; that which is established; a civil or military force or organization; form of doctrine and church government established under state control; place of residence or business; the number of men in a regiment, etc.
**Estate,** es-tāt', *n.* State; condition; rank; landed property; possessions; an order or class of men in the body politic.
**Esteem,** es-tēm', *vt.* To set a value on; to regard with respect; to prize.—*n.* Judgment of merit or demerit; estimation; great regard.
**Estimable,** es'tim-a-bl, *a.* Capable of being estimated; worthy of esteem or respect.
**Estimate,** es'tim-āt, *vt.* (estimating, estimated).

To form an opinion regarding; to calculate; to appraise; to esteem,—*n*. Valuation; calculation of probable cost.

**Estimation,** es-tim-ā'shon, *n*. Act of estimating; valuation; opinion; esteem.

**Estrange,** es-trānj', *vt*. (estranging, estranged). To alienate, as the affections.

**Estrangement,** es-trānj'ment, *n*. Alienation of affection or friendship.

**Estray,** es-trā', *n*. A domestic animal found straying.

**Estreat,** es-trēt', *n*. In *law*, a true copy of a writing under which fines are to be levied.—*vt*. To levy (fines) under an estreat.

**Estuary,** es'tū-a-ri, *n*. The mouth of a river where the tide meets the current; a firth.

**Etch,** ech, *vt*. To produce designs on a copper or other plate by lines drawn through a thin coating, and then eaten into the plate by a strong acid; to draw finely in ink.—*vi*. To practice etching.

**Etcher,** ech'ėr, *n*. One who etches.

**Etching,** ech'ing, *n*. The act or art of the etcher; a mode of engraving; the impression taken from an etched plate.

**Eternal,** ē-tėrn'al, *a*. Everlasting; without beginning or end of existence; unchangeable.—*n*. An appellation of God.

**Eternally,** ē-tėrn'al-li, *adv*. Forever; unchangeably; without intermission.

**Eternity,** ē-tėrn'i-ti, *n*. Continuance without beginning or end; duration without end; the state or time after death.

**Eternize,** ē-tėrn'īz, *vt*. To make eternal or endless; to immortalize.

**Etesian,** e-tē'zi-an, *a*. Yearly; periodical.

**Ether,** ē'thėr, *n*. The clear upper air; refined air; a hypothetical medium of extreme tenuity universally diffused, and the medium of the transmission of light, heat, etc.; a very light, volatile, and inflammable fluid obtained from alcohol, used as a stimulant and anesthetic.

**Ethereal,** ē-thē'rē-al, *a*. Formed of ether; heavenly; aerial; intangible.

**Etherealize,** ē-thē'rē-al-īz, *vt*. To convert into ether; to render ethereal.

**Etherize,** ē'thėr-īz, *vt*. To convert into ether; to treat with ether; to stupefy with ether.

**Ethic, Ethical,** eth'ik, eth'ik-al, *a*. Relating to morals; treating of morality; delivering precepts of morality.

**Ethically,** eth'ik-al-li, *adv*. In an ethical manner; according to morality.

**Ethics,** eth'iks, *n*. The doctrine of morals; moral philosophy; a system of moral principles.

**Ethiop, Ethiopian,** ē'thi-ōp, ē-thi-ō'pi-an, *n*. A native of Ethiopia.

**Ethiopic,** e-thi-op'ik, *n*. The language of Ethiopia.—*a*. Relating to Ethiopia.

**Ethnic, Ethnical,** eth'nik, eth'nik-al, *a*. Pertaining to the gentiles; pagan; ethnological.

**Ethnography,** eth-nog'ra-fi, *n*. That branch of science which treats of the manners, customs, etc., peculiar to different nations.

**Ethnologic, Ethnological,** eth-no-loj'ik, eth-no-loj'ik-al, *a*. Relating to technology.

**Ethnologist,** eth-nol'o-jist, *n*. One skilled in ethnology; a student of ethnology.

**Ethnology,** eth-nol'o-ji, *n*. That branch of science which treats of the different races of men.

**Ethology,** eth-ol'o-ji, *n*. The science of ethics; the doctrine of the formation of character.

**Etiolate,** ē'ti-ō-lāt, *vi*. To be whitened by exclusion of sunlight.—*vt*. To whiten.

**Etiquet,** et-i-ket', *n*. Forms of ceremony or decorum; social observances.

**Etruscan,** ē-trus'kan, *a*. Relating to Etruria, an ancient country in Italy.—*n*. A native of ancient Etruria.

**Etui,** et-wē', *n*. A pocket-case for small articles.

**Etymologic, Etymological,** et'i-mo-loj''ik, et'i-mo-loj''ik-al, *a*. Pertaining to etymology.

**Etymologist,** et-i-mol'o-jist, *n*. One versed in etymology.

**Etymology,** et-i-mol'o-ji, *n*. that part of philology which traces the origin of words; the derivation or history of any word.

**Etymon,** e'ti-mon, *n*. An original root or primitive word.

**Eucalyptus,** ū-ka-lip'tus, *n*.; pl. **-tuses** or **-ti.** The generic name of some Australian trees of the myrtle order, usually called gum-trees.

**Eucharist,** ū'ka-rist, *n*. The sacrament of the Lord's Supper.

**Eucharistic, Eucharistical,** ū-ka-rist'ik, ū-ka-rist'ik-al, *a*. Pertaining to the Lord's Supper.

**Euchre,** ū'kėr, *n*. A game of cards played by two, three, or four players.

**Eugenics,** ū-jen'iks, *n*. The theory dealing with the production or treatment of a fine, healthy race.

**Eulogist,** ū'lo-jist, *n*. One who eulogizes.

**Eulogistic,** ū-lo-jis'tik, *a*. Commendatory; full of praise.

**Eulogium,** ū-lō'ji-um, *n*. Eulogy; encomium.

**Eulogize,** ū'lo-jiz, *vt*. (eulogizing, eulogized). To praise; to extol.

**Eulogy,** ū'lo-ji, *n*. A speech or writing in commendation; praise; panegyric.

**Eunuch,** ū'nuk, *n*. A castrated man.

**Eupepsia, Eupepsy,** ū-pep'si-a, ū-pep'si, *n*. Good digestion.

**Eupeptic,** ū-pep'tik, *a*. Having good digestion; easy of digestion.

**Euphemism,** ū'fem-izm, *n*. A mode of speaking by which a delicate word or expression is substituted for one which is offensive; a word or expression so substituted.

**Euphemistic,** ū-fem-is'tik, *a*. Rendering more decent or delicate in expression.

**Euphonic, Euphonious,** ū-fōn'ik, ū-fō'ni-us, *a*. Having euphony; agreeable in sound.

**Euphony,** ū'fo-ni, *n*. An easy, smooth enunciation of sounds; harmony of sound.

**Euphuism** ū'fū-izm, *n*. Excessive elegance and refinement of language.

**Eurasian,** ū-rā'shi-an, *n*. One born in India of a native mother and European father.

**European,** ū-rō-pē'an, *a*. Pertaining to Europe.—*n*. A native of Europe.

**Euthanasia,** ū-tha-nā'zi-a, *n*. An easy death; a putting to death by painless means.

**Evacuate,** ē-vak'ū-āt, *vt*. (evacuating, evacuated). To make empty; to quit; to withdraw from; to discharge.

**Evacuation,** ē-vak'ū-ā''shon, *n*. Act of evacuating; that which is discharged.

**Evacuee,** ē-vak'ū-ē, *n*. A person transferred from a vulnerable to a safe area on account of air-raids, etc.

**Evade,** ē-vād', *vt*. (evading, evaded). To avoid by dexterity; to slip away from; to elude; to baffle.—*vi*. To practice evasion.

**Evaluate,** ē-val'ū-āt, *vt*. To value carefully; to ascertain the amount of.

**Evanesce,** ev-a-nes', *vi*. To vanish.

**Evanescence,** ev-an-es'ens, *n*. A vanishing away; state of being liable to vanish.

**Evanescent,** ev-an-es'ent, *a*. Vanishing; fleeting; passing away.

**Evangel,** ē-van'jel, *n*. The gospel.

**Evangelic, Evangelical,** ē-van-jel'ik, ē-van-jel'ik-al, *a*. Pertaining to or according to the gospel; sound in the doctrines of the gospel; fervent and devout.

**Evangelicism,** ē-van-jel'i-sizm, *n*. Evangelical principles.

**Evangelist,** ē-van'jel-ist, *n*. One of the four writers of the history of Jesus Christ; a preacher of the gospel; a missionary.

**Evangelize,** ē-van'jel-īz, *vt*. and *i*. (evangelizing, evangelized). To preach the gospel to and convert.

**Evanish,** ē-van'ish, *vi*. To vanish away.

**Evaporable,** ē-va'pėr-a-bl, *a*. That may evaporate or be evaporated.

**Evaporate,** ē-va'pėr-āt, *vi.* (evaporating, evaporated). To pass off in vapor; to exhale; to be wasted.—*vt.* To convert into vapor; to disperse in vapors.
**Evaporation,** ē-va'pėr-ā''shon, *n.* Act of evaporating; conversion of a fluid or solid into vapor.
**Evasion,** ē-vā'zhon, *n.* Act of evading; artifice to elude; shift; equivocation.
**Evasive,** ē-vā'siv, *a.* That evades; shuffling; equivocating.
**Eve,** ēv, *n.* Evening; the evening before a church festival; the period just preceding some event.
**Even,** ē'vn, *a.* Level; smooth; equable; on an equality; just; settled; balanced; capable of being divided by 2 without a remainder.—*vt.* To make even or level; to equalize; to balance.—*adv.* Just; exactly; likewise; moreover.—*n.* The evening.
**Even-handed,** ē-vn-hand-ed, *a.* Impartial.
**Evening,** ē'vn-ing, *n.* The close of the day; the decline of anything.—*a.* Being at the close of day.
**Event,** ē'vent', *n.* That which happens; an incident; the consequence of anything; issue; result; conclusion.
**Eventful,** ē-vent'ful, *a.* Full of incidents; producing numerous or great changes.
**Eventide,** ē-vn-tīd, *n.* The time of evening.
**Eventual,** ē-vent'ū-al, *a.* Pertaining to a final issue; happening as a consequence; final; ultimate.
**Eventuality,** ē-vent'ū-al''i-ti, *n.* That which happens; a contingent result.
**Eventuate,** ē-vent'ū-āt, *vi.* To come to pass.
**Ever,** ev'ėr, *adv.* At all times; at any time; continually; in any degree.
**Evergreen,** ev'ėr-grēn, *n.* A plant that always retains its greenness.—*a.* Always green.
**Everlasting,** ev-ėr-last'ing, *a.* Enduring forever; eternal.—*n.* Eternity; the Eternal Being; a plant whose flowers endure for many months after being plucked.
**Everlastingly,** ev-ėr-last'ing-li, *adv.* Eternally; perpetually; continually.
**Evermore,** ev'ėr-mōr, *adv.* At all times; eternally.
**Eversion,** ē-vėr'shon, *n.* An overthrowing; destruction; subversion.
**Every,** ev'ri, *a.* Each one; all taken separately.
**Everybody,** ev'ri-bod-i, *n.* Every person.
**Everyday,** ev'ri-dā, *a.* Common;; usual.
**Everyone,** ev'ri-wun, *n.* Every person.
**Everywhere,** ev'ri-whār, *adv.* In every place; in all places.
**Evict,** ē-vikt', *vt.* To dispossess by judicial process; to expel from lands, etc., by law.
**Eviction,** ē-vik'shon, *n.* Act of evicting; expulsion of a tenant.
**Evidence,** ev'i-dens, *n.* That which demonstrates that a fact is so; testimony; proof; witness.—*vt.* To make evident; to prove.
**Evident,** ev'i-dent, *a.* Clear; obvious; plain.
**Evidential,** ev-i-den'shal, *a.* Pertaining to evidence; affording evidence.
**Evil,** ē'vil, *a.* Not good; bad; wrong; unhappy; calamitious.—*n.* That which is not good; anything which produces pain, calamity, etc.; wrong; malady.—*adv.* Not well; ill.
**Evince,** ē-vins', *vt.* (evincing, evinced). To show in a clear manner; to manifest.
**Eviscerate,** ē-vis'sė-rāt, *vt.* To take out the entrails of; to disembowel.
**Evisceration,** ē-vis'sė-rā''shon, *n.* Act of eviscerating.
**Evocation,** ev-ō-kā'shon, *n.* A calling forth.
**Evoke,** ē-vōk', *vt.* (evoking, evoked). To call forth or out; to summon forth.
**Evolution,** ev-o-lū'shon, *n.* An unfolding; development; extraction of roots in arithmetic and algebra; systematic movement of troops or ships in changing their position; that theory which sees in the history of all things a gradual advance from a rudimentary condition to one more complex and of higher character.
**Evolutional, Evolutionary,** ev-o-lū'shon-al, ev-ō-lū'shon-a-ri, *a.* Pertaining to evolution; produced by or due to evolution.
**Evolutionist,** ev-o-lū'shon-ist, *n.* and *a.* A believer in the doctrine of evolution.
**Evolve,** ē-volv', *vt.* (evolving, evolved). To unfold; to develop; to open and expand.—*vi.* To open or disclose itself.
**Evulsion,** ē-vul'shon, *n.* Act of plucking out.
**Ewe,** ū, *n.* A female sheep.
**Ewer,** ū'ėr, *n.* A kind of pitcher or vessel for holding water.
**Exacerbate,** eks-as'ėr-bāt, *vt.* To exasperate; to increase the violence of.
**Exacerbation,** eks-as'ėr-bā''shon, *n.* Increase of malignity; periodical increase of violence in a disease.
**Exact,** egz-akt', *a.* Strictly accurate; methodical; precise; true.—*vt.* To extort by means of authority; to demand of right; to compel.—*vi.* To practice extortion.
**Exacting,** egz-akt'ing, *p.a.* Disposed to exact or claim too much.
**Exaction,** egz-ak'shon, *n.* Act of exacting; extortion; that which is exacted.
**Exactitude,** egz-ak'ti-tūd, *n.* Accuracy.
**Exactly,** egs-akt'li, *adv.* In an exact manner; precisely; nicely; accurately.
**Exactor,** egz-akt'ėr, *n.* One who exacts; one unreasonably severe in his demands.
**Exaggerate,** egz-aj'ė-rāt, *vt.* (exaggerating, exaggerated). To increase beyond due limits; to depict extravagantly.
**Exaggeration,** egz-aj'ė-rā''shon, *n.* Representation of things beyond the truth.
**Exalt,** egz-alt', *vt.* To raise high; to raise to power or dignity; to extol.
**Exaltation,** egz-alt-ā'shon, *n.* Elevation to power, office, etc.; elevated estate.
**Examination,** egz-am'in-ā''shon, *n.* Act of examining; inquiry into facts, etc., by interrogation; scrutiny by study.
**Examine,** egz-am'in, *vt.* (examining, examined). To inspect carefully; to inquire into; to interrogate, as a witness, a student, etc.; to discuss.
**Examiner,** egz-am'in-ėr, *n.* One who examines.
**Examining,** egz-am'in-ing, *p.a.* Having power to examine; appointed to examine.
**Example,** egz-am'pl, *n.* A sample; pattern; model; precedent; instance.
**Exasperate,** egz-as'pė-rāt, *vt.* (exasperating, exasperated). To irritate; to enrage; to make worse; to aggravate.
**Exasperation,** egz-as'pė-rā''shon, *n.* Irritation; rage; fury.
**Excavate,** eks'ka-vāt, *vt.* (excavating, excavated). To hollow out.
**Excavation,** eks-ka-vā'shon, *n.* Act of hollowing out; a cavity.
**Excavator,** eks'ka-vāt-ėr, *n.* One who excavates; a machine for excavating.
**Exceed,** ek-sēd', *vt.* To go beyond, as any limit; to surpass; to outdo.—*vi.* To go too far; to bear the greater proportion.
**Exceeding,** ek-sēd'ing, *a.* Great in extent, quantity, or duration.—*adv.* In a very great degree.
**Exceedingly,** ek-sēd'ing-li, *adv.* Greatly; very much.
**Excel,** ek-sel', *vt.* (excelling, excelled). To surpass; to transcend; to outdo.—*vi.* To be eminent or distinguished.
**Excellence, Excellency,** ek'sel-lens, ek'sel-len-si, *n.* Superiority; pre-eminence; any valuable quality; an official title of honor.
**Excellent,** ek'sel-lent, *a.* Of great value; distinguished in attainments; exquisite.
**Except,** ek-sept', *vt.* To take or leave out of any number specified; to exclude.—*vi.* to object; to make objection.—*prep.* Exclusively of; without.—*conj.* Unless.
**Excepting,** ek-sept'ing, *prep.* and *conj.* With exception of; excluding; except.
**Exception,** ek-sep'shon, *n.* Act of excepting; state of being excepted; that which is excepted; an

E

objection; offense.
**Exceptionable,** ek-sep'shon-a-bl, *a.* Liable to objection; objectionable.
**Exceptional,** ek-sep'shon-al, *a.* Forming or making an exception.
**Exceptious,** ek-sep'shus, *a.* Disposed to make objections; captious.
**Excerpt,** ek-sėrpt', *n.* An extract; a passage selected from an author.—*vt.* To pick out from a book, etc.; to cite.
**Excess,** ek-ses', *n.* That which exceeds; superabundance; intemperate conduct; that by which one thing exceeds another.
**Excessive,** ek-ses'iv, *a.* Beyond any given degree or limit; intemperate; extreme.
**Excessively,** ek-ses'iv-li, *adv.* Exceedingly.
**Exchange,** eks-chānj', *vt.* To change one thing for another; to commute; to bargain.—*n.* Act of exchanging; interchange; barter; the thing interchanged; place where merchants, etc., of a city meet to transact business; a method of finding the equivalent to a given sum in the money of another country.
**Exchangeability,** eks-chānj'a-bil''i-ti, *n.* Quality of being exchangeable.
**Exchangeable,** eks-chānj'a-bl, *a.* Capable, fit, or proper to be exchanged.
**Exchanger,** eks-chānj-ėr, *n.* One who exchanges; one who practices exchange.
**Exchequer,** eks-chek'ėr, *n.* An ancient English court for the care of the royal revenues, now a division of the High Court of Justice; a state treasury; pecuniary property.
**Excisable,** ek-sīz'a-bl, *a.* Liable or subject to excise.
**Excise,** ek-sīz', *n.* A tax on certain commodities of home production and consumption, as beer, etc.; also for licenses to deal in certain commodities.—*vt.* (excising, excised). To impose a duty on articles produced and consumed at home; to cut out.
**Exciseman,** ek-sīz'man, *n.* One who collects excise duties, or prevents the evasion of them.
**Excision,** ek-si'zhon, *n.* A cutting out or off; amputation; extirpation.
**Excitability,** ek-sīt'a-bil''i-ti, *n.* The state or quality of being excitable.
**Excitable,** ek-sīt'a-bl, *a.* Capable of being excited; prone to excitement.
**Excite,** ek-sīt', *vt.* (exciting, excited). To call into action; to rouse; to stimulate.
**Excitement,** ek-sīt'ment, *n.* Act of exciting; stimulation; agitation.
**Exciting,** ek-sīt'ing, *p.a.* Producing excitement; deeply interesting; thrilling.
**Exclaim,** eks-klām', *vi.* To call out; to shout.—*vt.* To declare with loud vociferation.
**Exclamation,** eks-klam-ā'shon, *n.* A loud outcry; a passionate sentence; a note by which emphatical utterance is marked, thus, !; an interjection.
**Exclamatory,** eks-klam'a-to-ri, *a.* Containing or expressing exclamation.
**Exclude,** eks-klūd', *vt.* (excluding, excluded). To shut out; to thrust out; to debar; to prohibit; to except.
**Exclusion,** eks-klū'zhon, *n.* Act of excluding; state of being excluded; prohibition; ejection.
**Exclusionist,** eks-klū'zhon-ist, *n.* One who would preclude another from a privilege.
**Exclusive,** eks-klū'siv, *a.* Excluding; not including; debarring from fellowship; illiberal.
**Excogitate,** eks-ko'jit-āt, *vt.* To invent or devise by thinking; to think out.
**Excommunicate,** eks-kom-mū'ni-kāt, *vt.* To eject from the communion of the church; to expel from fellowship.
**Excommunication,** eks-kom-mū'ni-kā''shon, *n.* Expulsion from the communion of a church.
**Excoriate,** eks-kō'ri-āt, *vt.* To break or wear off the cuticle of.
**Excorticate,** eks-kor'ti-kāt, *vt.* To strip of the bark or rind.
**Excrement,** eks'krē-ment, *n.* That which is separated from the nutriment by digestion, and discharged from the body; ordure; dung.
**Excremental, Excrementitial, Excrementitious,** eks-krē-men'tal, eks'krē-men-tish''al, eks'krē-men-tish''us, *a.* Pertaining to or consisting of excrement.
**Excrescence,** eks-kres'ens, *n.* Anything which grows out of something else and is useless or disfiguring; a troublesome superfluity.
**Excrescent,** eks-kres'ent, *a.* Growing out of something else abnormally; superfluous.
**Excrete,** eks-krēt', *vt.* (excreting, excreted). To separate and discharge from the body by vital action.
**Excretion,** eks-krē'shon, *n.* Act or process of excreting; that which is excreted.
**Excruciate,** eks-krö'shi-āt, *vt.* To torture; to rack.
**Excruciating,** eks-krö'shi-āt-ing, *p.a.* Extremely painful; agonizing; distressing.
**Excruciation,** eks-krö'shi-ā''shon, *n.* Act of excruciating; agony; torture.
**Exculpate,** eks-kul'pāt, *vt.* To clear from a charge of fault or guilt; to absolve.
**Exculpation,** eks-kul-pā'shon, *n.* Act of exculpating; excuse.
**Exculpatory,** eks-kul'pa-to-ri, *a.* Serving to exculpate; clearing from blame.
**Excursion,** eks-kėr'shon, *n.* A journey for pleasure or health; a ramble; a trip.
**Excursionist,** eks-kėr'shon-ist, *n.* One who joins in an excursion for pleasure.
**Excursive,** eks-kėr'siv, *a.* Rambling; wandering; deviating.
**Excursus,** eks-kėr'sus, *n.*; pl. **-suses.** A dissertation appended to a book; digression.
**Excusable,** eks-kūz'a-bl, *a.* Admitting of excuse or justification; pardonable.
**Excuse,** eks-kūz', *vt.* (excusing, excused). To acquit of guilt; to pardon; to free from a duty.—*n.* eks-kūs'. A plea in extenuation of a fault; apology; that which excuses.
**Excuser,** eks-kūz'ėr, *n.* One who offers excuses, or pleads for another.
**Execrable,** ek'sē-kra-bl, *a.* Deserving to be execrated or cursed; hateful; detestable.
**Execrate,** ek'sē-krāt, *vt.* (execrating, execrated). To curse; to abominate.
**Execration,** ek-sē-krā'shon, *n.* Act of execrating; a curse; imprecation.
**Executant,** eks-ek'ū-tant, *n.* A performer.
**Execute,** ek'sē-kūt, *vt.* (executing, executed). To effect; to achieve; to inflict capital punishment on; to make valid, as by signing and sealing; to perform.—*vi.* To perform.
**Execution,** ek-sē-kū'shon, *n.* Act of executing; act of signing and sealing a legal instrument; capital punishment; mode of performing a work of art; facility of voice or finger in music.
**Executioner,** ek-sē-kū'shon-ėr, *n.* One who puts to death by law.
**Executive,** egz-ek'ūt-iv, *a.* That executes; carrying laws into effect, or superintending their enforcement.—*n.* The person or persons who administer the government.
**Executor,** egz-ek'ūt-ėr, *n.* One who executes or performs; the person appointed by a testator to execute his will.
**Executorship,** egz-ek'ūt-ėr-ship, *n.* The office of an executor.
**Executory,** egz-ek'ū-to-ri, *a.* That executes; performing official duties.
**Executrix,** egz-ek'ū-triks, *n.* A female executor.
**Exegesis,** eks-ē-jē'sis, *n.* An exposition; the science or art of literary interpretation, particularly of the Bible.
**Exegetic, Exegetical,** eks-ē-jet'ik, eks-ē-jet'ik-al, *a.* Explanatory; expository.
**Exegetics,** eks-ē-jet'iks, *n.pl.* A branch of theology dealing with scriptural interpretation.
**Exemplar,** egz-em'plėr, *n.* A pattern; copy.
**Exemplarily,** egz'em-pla-ri-li, *adv.* In an exemplary manner.

**Exemplary,** egz'em-pla-ri, *a*. Serving as a pattern; worthy of imitation; explanatory.
**Exemplification,** egz-em'pli-fi-kā''shon, *n*. A showing by example; instance.
**Exemplify,** egz-em'pli-fī, *vt*. (exemplifying, exemplified). To show by example; to serve as an instance of.
**Exempt,** egz-emt', *vt*. To free from; to privilege; to grant immunity from.—*a*. Free by privilege; not liable.
**Exemption,** egz-em'shon, *n*. Act of exempting; state of being exempt; immunity.
**Exequatur,** ek-sē-kwā'tėr, *n*. A warrant.
**Exequies,** eks'ē-kwiz, *n.pl*. Funeral rites.
**Exercise,** eks'ėr-sīz, *n*. Practice; use; drill; act of divine worship; application; a lesson or example for practice.—*vt*. (exercising, exercise). To employ; to practice; to train; to give anxiety to; to afflict.—*vi*. To take exercise.
**Exert,** egz-ėrt, *vt*. To put forth, as strength; to put in action. (*refl.*) to use efforts; to strive.
**Exertion,** egz-ėr'shon, *n*. Act of exerting.
**Exfoliate,** eks-fō'li-āt, *vt*. and *i*. To scale off.
**Exhalation,** egz-hāl-ā'shon, *n*. Act of exhaling; that which is exhaled; vapor; effluvia.
**Exhale,** egz-hāl', *vt*. (exhaling, exhaled). To breathe out; to cause to be emitted in vapor or minute particles; to evaporate.—*vi*. To fly off as vapor.
**Exhaust,** egz-ast', *vt*. To drain off contents; to expend entirely; to treat thoroughly; to tire.
**Exhausted,** egz-ast'ed, *p.a*. Wholly expended; fatigued.
**Exhibit,** egz-ib'it, *vt*. To show; to display; to administer by way of remedy.—*n*. Anything exhibited.
**Exhibiter, Exhibitor,** egz-ib'it-ėr, *n*. One who exhibits.
**Exhibition,** eks-i-bi'shon, *n*. Act of exhibiting; display; any public show; a benefaction for students in English universities.
**Exhibitioner,** eks-i-bi'shon-ėr, *n*. One maintained at an English university by an exhibition.
**Exhibitory,** egz-ib'i-to-ri, *a*. Exhibiting; showing; displaying.
**Exhilarate,** egz-il'a-rāt, *vt*. (exhilarating, exhilarated). To make cheerful; to inspirit.
**Exhilaration,** egz-il'a-rā''shon, *n*. Act of exhilarating; cheerfulness; gaiety.
**Exhort,** egz-hort', *vt*. To urge to a good deed; to encourage; to warn.
**Exhortation,** egz-hor-tā'shon, *n*. Act of exhorting; a persuasive discourse.
**Exhortatory,** egz-hor'ta-to-ri, *a*. Tending to exhort; serving for exhortation.
**Exhorter,** egz-hort'ėr, *n*. One who exhorts.
**Exhumation,** eks-hūm-ā'shon, *n*. Act of exhuming; disinterring of a corpse.
**Exhume,** eks'hūm, *vt*. (exhuming, exhumed). To unbury; to disinter.
**Exigence, Exigency,** eks'i-jens, eks'i-jen-si, *n*. Pressing necessity; urgency.
**Exigent,** eks'i-jent, *a*. Urgent; pressing.
**Exigible,** eks'i-ji-bl, *a*. That may be exacted.
**Exiguous,** ek-sig'ū-us, *a*. Slender.
**Exile,** eks'īl or egz'īl, *n*. State of being expelled from one's native country; banishment; the person banished.—*vt*. (exiling, exiled). To banish from one's country.
**Exist,** egz-ist', *vi*. To be; to live; to endure.
**Existence,** egz-ist'ens, *n*. State of being; life; continuation; anything that exists.
**Existent,** egz-ist'ent, *a*. Being; existing.
**Exit,** eks'it, *n*. A going out; the departure of a player from the stage; death; a way out.
**Exodus,** eks'ō-dus, *n*. Way out; departure; the second book of the Old Testament.
**Exogen,** eks'o-jen, *n*. A plant whose stem grows by additions to the outside of the wood.
**Exogenous,** eks-oj'en-us, *a*. Pertaining to the exogens or their mode of growth.
**Exonerate,** egz-on'ē-rāt, *vt*. To exculpate; to acquit; to justify.
**Exonerative,** egz-on'ė-rāt-iv, *a*. That exonerates; freeing from an obligation.
**Exorable,** eks'ōr-a-bl, *a*. That can be persuaded; placable.
**Exorbitance, Exorbitancy,** egz-or'bit-ans, egz-or'bit-an-si, *n*. A going beyond fair or usual limits; enormity; extravagance.
**Exorbitant,** egz-or'bit-ant, *a*. Excessive; extravagant.
**Exorbitantly,** egz-or'bit-ant-li, *adv*. Enormously; excessively.
**Exorcise,** eks'or-sīz, *vi*. (exorcising, exorcised). To purify from evil spirits by adjurations.
**Exorcism,** eks'or-sism, *n*. The act or ceremony of exorcising.
**Exorcist,** eks'or-sist, *n*. One who exorcises.
**Exordium,** egz-or'di-um, *n*. The introductory part of a discourse.
**Exoskeleton,** ek'sō-skel-e-ton, *n*. The external skeleton, as the shell of a crustacean; the dermoskeleton.
**Exosmose,** ek'sos-mōs, *n*. The passage of gases or liquids through membrane or porous media, from within outward.
**Exoteric, Exoterical,** eks-ō-te'rik, eks-ō-te'rik-al, *a*. Suitable to be imparted to the public; public; opposed to *esoteric* or secret.
**Exotic,** egz-ot'ik, *a*. Introduced from a foreign country; not native.—*n*. *a*. Anything introduced from a foreign country.
**Expand,** ek-spand', *vt*. and *i*. To spread out; to enlarge; to distend; to dilate.
**Expanse,** ek-spans', *n*. A surface widely extended; a wide extent of space or body.
**Expansibility,** ek-spans'i-bil''i-ti, *n*. The capacity of being expanded.
**Expansible,** ek-spans'i-bl, *a*. Capable of being expanded.
**Expansile,** ek-spans'īl, *a*. Expansible; producing expansion.
**Expansion,** ek-span'shon, *n*. Act of expanding; state of being expanded; dilatation; distension; enlargement.
**Expansive,** ek-spans'iv, *a*. Having the power to expand; widely extended or extending.
**Ex-parte,** eks-pär'te, *a*. One-sided; partial.
**Expatiate,** ek-spā'shi-āt, *vi*. (expatiating, expatiated). To move at large; to enlarge in discourse or writing.
**Expatriate,** eks-pā'tri-āt, *vt*. (expatriating, expatriated). To exile.
**Expatriation,** eks-pā'tri-ā''shon, *n*. Exile; the forsaking of one's own country.
**Expect,** ek-spekt', *vt*. To wait for; to look for to happen; to anticipate.
**Expectance, Expectancy,** ek-spek'tans, ek-spek'tan-si, *n*. Act or state of expecting; expectation; hope.
**Expectant,** ek-spek'tant, *a*. Expecting; awaiting.—*n*. One who expects; one who waits in expectation.
**Expectation,** ek-spek-tā'shon, *n*. Act or state of expecting; prospect of good to come; prospect of reaching a certain age.
**Expectorant,** eks-pek'tō-rant, *a*. Having the quality of promoting discharges from the lungs.—*n*. A medicine which promotes expectoration.
**Expectorate,** eks-pek'tō-rāt, *vt*. (expectorating, expectorated). To expel, as phlegm, by coughing; to spit out.
**Expectoration,** eks-pek'tō-rā''shon, *n*. Act of expectorating; matter expectorated.
**Expedience, Expediency,** eks-pē'di-ens, eks-pē'di-en-si, *n*. Quality of being expedient; propriety; advisability.
**Expedient,** eks-pē'di-ent, *a*. Tending to promote the object proposed; proper under the circumstances; advantageous.—*n*. Means to an end; shift; plan.
**Expediently,** eks-pē'di-ent-li, *adv*. Fitly; suitably.
**Expedite,** eks'pē-dīt, *vt*. (expediting, expedited). To free from hindrance; to accelerate; to hasten by making easier.

**Expedition,** eks-pē-di'shon, *n.* State of being unimpeded; dispatch; a march or voyage for hostile purposes; journey by a body of men for some valuable end; such body of men.
**Expeditionary,** eks-pē-di'shon-a-ri, *n.* Consisting in or forming an expedition.
**Expeditious,** eks-pē-di'shus, *a.* Speedy; prompt; nimble; active.
**Expel,** eks-pel', *vt.* (expelling, expelled). To drive out; to eject; to banish.
**Expend,** ek-spend', *vt.* To spend; to use or consume; to waste.
**Expenditure,** ek-spend'i-tūr, *n.* Act of expending; a laying out, as of money; money expended; expense.
**Expense,** ek-spens', *n.* That which is expended; cost; charge; price.
**Expensive,** ek-spens'iv, *a.* Requiring much expense; dear; lavish.
**Expensively,** ek-spens'iv-li, *adv.* In an expensive manner; at great cost or charge.
**Experience,** eks-pē'ri-ens, *n.* Personal trial; continued observation; knowledge gained by trial or observation; trial and knowledge from suffering or enjoyment; suffering itself.—*vt.* (experiencing, experienced). To try; to know by trial; to have happen; to undergo.
**Experienced,** eks-pē'ri-enst, *p.a.* Taught by experience; skillful by use or observation.
**Experiment,** eks-pe'ri-ment, *n.* A trial; an operation designed to discover something unknown, or to establish it when discovered.—*vi.* To make trial or experiment.
**Experimental,** eks-pe'ri-men''tal, *a.* Pertaining to, known by, or derived from experiment; having personal experience.
**Experimentalist,** eks-pe'ri-men''tal-ist, *n.* One who makes experiments.
**Experimentally,** eks-pe'ri-men''tal-li, *adv.* In an experimental way; by trial.
**Experimenter,** eks-pe'ri-men-tėr, *n.* One who makes experiments.
**Expert,** eks-pėrt', *a.* Skillful; dexterous; adroit.—*n.* eks'pėrt. An expert person; a scientific witness.
**Expertly,** eks-pėrt'li, *adv.* In a skillful or dexterous manner; adroitly.
**Expiable,** eks'pi-a-bl, *a.* That may be expiated or atoned for.
**Expiate,** eks'pi-āt, *vt.* (expiating, expiated). To atone for; to make reparation for.
**Expiation,** eks-pi-ā'shon, *n.* Act of expiating; atonement; reparation.
**Expiator,** eks'pi-āt-ėr, *n.* One who expiates.
**Expiatory,** eks'pi-a-to-ri, *a.* Able to make atonement.
**Expiration,** eks-pīr-ā'shon, *n.* Act of breathing out; death; end; expiry.
**Expiratory,** eks-pīr'-to-ri, *a.* Pertaining to the expiration of breath.
**Expire,** eks-pīr', *vt.* (expiring, expired). To breathe out; to exhale.—*vi.* To emit the last breath; to die; to terminate.
**Expiry,** eks'pi-ri, *n.* Termination.
**Explain,** eks-plān', *vt.* To make plain or intelligible; to expound; to elucidate.—*vi.* To give explanations.
**Explanation,** eks-pla-nā'shon, *n.* Act of explaining; interpretation; clearing up of matters between parties at variance.
**Explanatory,** eks-plan'a-to-ri, *a.* Serving to explain.
**Expletive,** eks'plēt-iv, *a.* Serving to fill out; superfluous.—*n.* A word or syllable inserted to fill a vacancy or for ornament; an oath or interjection.
**Expletory,** eks'ple-to-ri, *a.* Expletive.
**Explicable,** eks'pli-ka-bl, *a.* Capable of being explained.
**Explicate,** eks'pli-kāt, *vt.* To unfold the meaning of; to explain.
**Explication,** eks-pli-kā'shon, *n.* Explanation.
**Explicit,** eks-plis'it, *a.* Plain in language; express, not merely implied; open.
**Explicitly,** eks-plis'it-li, *adv.* In an explicit manner; plainly; expressly.
**Explode,** eks-plōd', *vt.* (exploding, exploded). To drive out of use or belief; to cause to burst with violence and noise.—*vi.* To burst with noise; to burst into activity or passion.
**Exploit,** eks-ploit', *n.* A deed; a heroic act; a deed of renown.—*vt.* To make use of; to work.
**Exploitation,** eks-ploi-tā'shon, *n.* Successful application of industry on any object, as land, mines, etc.
**Exploration,** eks-plō-rā'shon, *n.* Act of exploring; strict or careful examination.
**Explore,** eks-plōr', *vt.* (exploring, explored). To travel with the view of making discovery; to search; to examine closely.
**Explorer,** eks-plōr'ėr, *n.* One who explores; a traveler in unknown regions.
**Explosion,** eks-plō'zhon, *n.* Act of exploding; a bursting with noise; a violent outburst of feeling.
**Explosive,** eks-plō'siv, *a.* Causing explosion; readily exploding.—*n.* Anything liable to explode, as gunpowder; a mute or non-continuous consonant, as *k, t, b*.
**Exponent,** eks-pō'nent, *n.* One who explains or illustrates; that which indicates; the index of a power in algebra.
**Export,** eks-pōrt', *vt.* To convey, in traffic, to another country.—*n.* eks'pōrt. Act of exporting; quantity of goods exported; a commodity exported.
**Exportable,** eks-pōrt'a-bli, *a.* That may be exported.
**Exportation,** eks-pōr-tā'shon, *n.* Act of conveying goods to another country.
**Exporter,** eks-pōrt'ėr, *n.* One who exports.
**Expose,** eks-pōz', *vt.* (exposing, exposed). To put or set out; to disclose; to lay open to attack, censure, &c; to make liable; to exhibit.
**Exposé,** eks-po-zā, *n.* Exposure; statement.
**Exposed,** eks-pōzd', *p.a.* In danger; liable; unsheltered.
**Exposition,** eks-pō-zi'shon, *n.* Act of exposing; explanation; exhibition.
**Expositor,** eks-poz'it-ėr, *n.* One who expounds; an interpreter.
**Expository,** eks-poz'i-to-ri, *a.* Containing exposition; explanatory.
**Ex-post-facto,** eks-pōst-fak'tō, *a.* After the deed is done; retrospective.
**Expostulate,** eks-pos'tū-lāt, *vi.* To remonstrate; to reason earnestly with a person on some impropriety.
**Expostulation,** eks-pos'tū-lā''shon, *n.* Act of expostulating; remonstrance.
**Expostulatory,** eks-pos'tu-la-to-ri, *a.* Containing expostulation.
**Exposure,** eks-pō-zhūr, *n.* Act of exposing; state of being exposed; situation.
**Expound,** eks-pound', *vt.* To explain; to interpret; to unfold.
**Expounder,** eks-pound'ėr, *n.* One who expounds; an explainer; an interpreter.
**Express,** eks-pres', *vt.* To press out; to set forth in words; to declare; to make known by any means; *(refl.)* to say what one has got to say.—*a.* Clearly exhibited; given in direct terms; intended or sent for a particular purpose; traveling with special speed.—*n.* A messenger or vehicle sent on a particular occasion; a message specially sent; a specially fast railway train.—*adv.* For a particular purpose; with special haste.
**Expressible,** eks-pres'i-bl, *a.* That may be expressed.
**Expression,** eks-pre'shon, *n.* Act of expressing; a phrase or mode of speech; manner of utterance; a natural and lively representation in painting and sculpture; musical tone, grace, or modulation; play of features; representation of a quantity in algebra.

**Expressionless,** eks-pre'shon-les, *a.* Destitute of expression.
**Expressive,** eks-pres'iv, *a.* Serving to express; representing with force; emphatical.
**Expressively,** eks-pres'iv-li, *adv.* In an expressive manner; with expression.
**Expressly,** eks-pres'li, *adv.* In direct terms; of set purpose.
**Expropriate,** eks-prō'pri-āt, *vt.* To take for public use; to dispossess.
**Expropriation,** eks-prō-pri-ā''shon, *n.* Act of dispossessing of proprietary rights.
**Expulsion,** eks-pul'shon, *n.* A driving away by violence; state of being driven away.
**Expulsive,** eks-puls'iv, *q.* Having the power of expelling; serving to expel.
**Expunge,** ek spunj', *vt.* (expunging, expunged). To blot out, as with a pen; to erase; to obliterate.
**Expurgate,** eks-pėr'gāt or eks'pėr-gāt, *vt.* (expurgating, expurgated). To render pure; to strike offensive passages out of (a book).
**Expurgation,** eks-pėr-gā'shon, *n.* Act of purging or cleansing; purification.
**Expurgatory,** eks-pėr'ga-to-ri, *a.* Serving to expurgate.
**Exquisite,** eks'kwi-zit, *a.* Select; highly finished; excellent; extreme; matchless, as pain or pleasure keenly felt.—*n.* A fop; a dandy.
**Exscind,** ek-sind', *vt.* To cut out or off.
**Exsiccate,** ek-sikakrt, *vt,* To dry up completely.
**Extant,** eks'tant, *a.* Still existing; in being.
**Extemporaneous,** eks-tem'pō-rā''nē-us, *a.* Arising out of the time or occasion; on the spur of the moment; unpremeditated.
**Extemporary,** eks-tem'pō-ra-ri, *a.* Arising out of the time or occasion; extemporaneous.
**Extempore,** eks-tem'po-rē, *adv.* and *a.* Without study or preparation; extemporary.
**Extemporize,** eks-tem'pō-rīz, *vi.* To speak without preparation.—*vt.* To make without forethought; to prepare in haste.
**Extend,** eks-tend', *vt.* To stretch out; to spread; to prolong; to bestow on.—*vi.* To stretch; to reach; to become larger.
**Extensibility,** eks-ten'si-bil''i-ti, *n.* The capacity of suffering extension.
**Extensible,** eks-ten'si-bl, *a.* That may be extended; susceptible of enlargement.
**Extensile,** eks-ten'sīl, *a.* Extensible.
**Extension,** eks-ten'shon, *n.* Act of extending; state of being extended; that property of a body by which it occupies a portion of space; enlargement; in *logic,* the objects to which a term may be applied.
**Extensive,** eks-ten'siv, *a.* Having great extent; large; comprehensive.
**Extensor,** eks-ten'sėr, *n.* A muscle which serves to extend or straighten.
**Extent,** eks-tent', *n.* Space or degree to which a thing is extended; compass; size.
**Extenuate,** eks-ten'ū-āt, *vt.* To lessen; to weaken the force of; to palliate.
**Extenuation,** eks-ten'ū-ā''shon, *n.* Act of extenuating; palliation; mitigation.
**Exterior,** eks-tē'ri-ėr, *a.* External; on the outside; foreign.—*n.* The outward surface; that which is external.
**Exterminate,** eks-tėr'min-āt, *vt.* To destroy utterly; to extirpate; to root out.
**Extermination,** eks-tėr'min-ā''shon, *n.* Act of exterminating; eradication; extirpation.
**Exterminative,** eks-tėr'min-āt-iv, *a.* That exterminates or destroys.
**Extern,** eks-tėrn', *a.* External. [Poetic.].
**External,** eks-tėr'nal, *a.* On the outside; exterior; not being within, as causes or effects visible; foreign.
**Externals,** eks-tėr'nalz, *n.pl.* Outward parts; exterior form; outward ceremonies.
**Exterritorial,** eks-ter'i-tō''ri-al, *a.* Beyond the jurisdiction of the country in which one resides.
**Extinct,** ek-stingkt', *a.* Extinguished; abolished; having died out.
**Extinction,** ek-stingk'shon, *n.* Act of extinguishing; state of being extinguished; destruction; extermination.
**Extinguish,** ek-sting'gwish, *vt.* To put out; to quench; to destroy; to eclipse.
**Extinguishable,** ek-sting'gwish-a-bl, *a.* That may be quenched or destroyed.
**Extinguisher,** ek-sting'gwish-ėr, *n.* One who or that which extinguishes; a hollow, conical utensil to extinguish a candle.
**Extinguishment,** ek-sting'gwish-ment, *n.* Act of extinguishing; extinction.
**Extirpate,** eks-tėrp'āt or eks'terp-āt, *vt.* To root out; to eradicate; to destroy totally.
**Extirpation,** eks-tėrp-ā'shon, *n.* Act of rooting out; eradication; total destruction.
**Extirpator,** eks-tėrp'āt-ėr or eks'terp-āt-ėr, *n.* One who extirpates.
**Extol,** eks-tol', *vt.* (extolling; extolled). To exalt in eulogy; to magnify; to glorify.
**Extort,** eks-tort', *vt.* To exact by force; to wrest or wring.
**Extortion,** eks-tor'shon, *n.* Act of extorting; illegal or oppressive exaction.
**Extortionate,** eks-tor'shon-āt, *a.* Excessive in amount; oppressive in exacting money.
**Extortioner, Extortionist,** eks-tor'shon-ėr, eks-tor'shon-ist, *n.* One who practices extortion.
**Extra,** eks'tra, *a.* and *adv.* Additional; beyond what is usual, due, etc.—*n.* Something in addition.
**Extract,** eks-trakt', *vt.* To draw out or forth; to select; to draw or copy out; to find the root of a number.—*n.* eks'trakt. That which is extracted; a quotation; an essence, tincture, etc.
**Extraction,** eks-trak'shon, *n.* Act of extracting; lineage; operation of drawing essences; tinctures; etc.; operation of finding the roots of numbers.
**Extractive,** eks-trakt'iv, *a.* Capable of being extracted; serving to extract.—*n.* A base supposed to exist in all vegetable extracts.
**Extractor,** eks-trakt'ėr, *n.* One who extracts; an instrument for extracting teeth, etc.
**Extradite,** eks'tra-dīt, *vt.* To deliver up (a criminal) to the authorities of the country from which he has come.
**Extradition,** eks-traa-di'shon, *n.* The delivery, under a treaty, of a fugitive from justice by one government to another.
**Extrados,** eks-trā'dos, *n.* The exterior curve of an arch.
**Extrajudicial,** eks'tra-jū-di''shal, *a.* Out of the ordinary course of legal procedure; out of the proper court.
**Extramundane,** eks-tra-mun'dān, *a.* Beyond the limit of the material world.
**Extramural,** eks-tra-mūr'al, *a.* Outside the walls, as of a fortified city or university.
**Extraneous,** eks-trā'nē-us, *a.* That is without; foreign; not intrinsic; irrelevant.
**Extraordinarily,** eks-tra-or'din-a-ri-li, *adv.* In an extraordinary manner; unusually.
**Extraordinary,** eks-tra-or'din-a-ri, *a.* Beyond that which is ordinary; unusual; remarkable; special.
**Extravagance, Extravagancy,** eks-trav'-a-gans, eks-trav'a-gan-si, *n.* A going beyond due bounds; excess; wastefulness.
**Extravagant,** eks-trav'-a-gant, *a.* Exceeding due bounds; fantastic; wasteful; lavish.
**Extravagantly,** eks-trav'a-gant-li, *adv.* Unreasonably; excessively; wastefully.
**Extravaganza,** eks-trav'a-gan''za, *n.* A wild literary or musical composition.
**Extravasate,** eks-trav'a-sāt, *vt.* To force or let out of the proper vessels, as the blood.
**Extreme,** eks-trēm', *a.* Outermost; furthest; most violent; last; worst or best; most pressing.—*n.* The utmost point or verge of a thing; end; furthest or highest degree; *(pl.)* points at the greatest distance from each other.
**Extremely,** eks-trēm'li, *adv.* In the utmost de-

E

gree; to the utmost point.
**Extremist,** eks-trēm'ist, *n.* A supporter of extreme doctrines or practice.
**Extremity,** eks-trem'i-ti, *n.* That which is extreme; utmost point, part, or degree; utmost distress or violence.
**Extricable,** eks'tri-ka-bl, *a.* That can be extricated.
**Extricate,** eks'tri-kāt, *vt.* (extricating, extricated). To disentangle; to set free.
**Extrication,** eks-tri-kā'shon, *n.* Act of extricating.
**Extrinsic, Extrinsical,** eks-trin'sik, eks-trin'-sik-al, *a.* Being on the outside; extraneous; accessory.
**Extrude,** eks-tröd', *vt.* (extruding, extruded). To thrust out; to expel.
**Extrusion,** eks-trö'zhon, *n.* Act of extruding; a driving out; expulsion.
**Exuberance, Exuberancy,** eks-ū'bė-rans, eks-ū'bė-ran-si, *n.* Superabundance; overflowing fullness; rankness; luxuriance.
**Exuberant,** eks-ū-bė-rant, *a.* Superabundant; ovrflowing; luxuriant.
**Exudation,** eks-ūd-ā'shon, *n.* Act or process of exuding; something exuded.
**Exude,** eks-ūd, *vt.* (exuding, exuded). To discharge through the pores; to let ooze out.—*vi.* To flow through pores; to ooze out like sweat.
**Exulcerate,** eg-zul'sėr-āt, *vt.* To produce an ulcer on; to exasperate.
**Exult,** egz-ult', *vi.* To rejoice exceedingly; to triumph.
**Exultant,** egz-ult'ant, *a.* Rejoicing triumphantly.
**Exultation,** egz-ult-ā'shon, *n.* Lively joy; triumph; rapture; ecstasy.
**Exuviae,** egz-ū'vi-ē, *n.pl.* Any parts of animals which are shed or cast off, as the skins of serpents, etc.
**Exuviate,** egz-ū'vi-āt, *vi.* To cast or throw off exuviae.
**Eyalet,** ī'a-let, *n.* A Turkish province administered by a vizier or pacha.
**Eyas,** ī'as, *n.* A nestling; a young hawk still unable to prey for itself.
**Eye,** ī, *n.* The organ of vision; sight or view; power of perception; something resembling an eye in form; a small hole; a loop or ring for fastening.—*vt.* (eyeing, eyed). To fix the eye on; to observe or watch narrowly.
**Eyeball,** ī'bal, *n.* The ball of the eye.
**Eyebrow,** ī'brou, *n.* The brow or hairy arch about the eye.
**Eyed,** īd, *a.* Having eyes.
**Eye-glass,** ī'glas, *n.* A glass to assist the sight.
**Eyelash,** ī'lash, *n.* The line of hair that edges the eyelid.
**Eyeless,** ī'les, *a.* Wanting eyes; blind.
**Eyelet, Eyelet-hole,** ī'let, ī'let-hōl, *n.* A small eye or hole to receive a lace.
**Eyelid,** ī'lid, *n.* The cover of the eye; the movable skin with which an animal covers or uncovers the eyeball.
**Eye-service,** ī'sėr-vis, *n.* Service performed only under the eye of an employer.
**Eyeshot,** ī'shot, *n.* Range of vision; view.
**Eyesight,** ī'sīt, *n.* The sight of the eye; view; observation; the sense of seeing.
**Eyesore,** ī'sōr, *n.* Something ugly to look at.
**Eye-tooth,** ī'töth, *n.* A tooth under the eye; a canine tooth; a fang.
**Eye-witness,** ī'wit-nes, *n.* One who sees a thing done.
**Eyot,** īot, *n.* A small river islet.
**Eyre,** ār, *n.* A circuit of a court of justice; a court of itinerant justices.
**Eyrie, Eyry,** ī'ri, *n.* An aerie; nest of a bird of prey.

# F

**Fabaceous,** fā-ba'shus, *a.* Having the nature of the bean.
**Fabian,** fā'bi-an, *a.* Delaying; lingering.
**Fable,** fā'bl, *n.* A fictitious narrative to instruct or amuse, often to enforce a precept; falsehood; an idle story; the plot in a poem or drama.—*vi.* (fabling, fabled). To tell fables or falsehoods.—*vt.* To feign; to invent.
**Fabled,** fā'bld, *p.a.* Told in fables.
**Fabliau,** fab-lē-ō, *n.*; pl. **-iaux.** A kind of metrical tale common in early French literature.
**Fabric,** fab'rik, *n.* Frame or structure of anything; a building; texture; cloth.
**Fabricate,** fab'rik-āt, *vt.* (fabricating, fabricated). To make or fashion; to form by art or labor; to devise falsely.
**Fabrication,** fab-rik-ā'shon, *n.* Act of fabricating; that which is fabricated; fiction.
**Fabricator,** fab'rik-āt-ėr, *n.* One who fabricates.
**Fabulist,** fa'bū-list, *n.* An inventor or writer of fables.
**Fabulous,** fa'bū-lus, *a.* Containing or abounding in fable; feigned; mythical; incredible.
**Façade, Facade,** fa-säd', fa-säd', *n.* Front view or elevation of an edifice.
**Face,** fās, *n.* The front part of an animal's head, particularly of the human head; the visage; front; effrontery; assurance; dial of a watch, etc.—*vt.* (facing; faced). To meet in front; to stand opposite to; to oppose with firmness; to finish or protect with a thin external covering; to dress the face of (a stone, etc.).—*vi.* To turn the face; to look.
**Facet, Facette,** fas'et, fa-set', *n.* A small flat portion of a surface.
**Facetiae,** fa-sē'shi-ē, *n.pl.* Jests; witticisms.
**Facetious,** fa-sē'shus, *a.* Witty; humorous; jocose; sprightly.
**Facial,** fā'shi-al, *a.* Pertaining to the face.
**Facile,** fa'sil, *a.* Easy; easily persuaded; yielding; dexterous.
**Facilitate,** fa-sil'it-āt, *vt.* To make easy; to lessen the labor of.
**Facility,** fa-sil'i-ti, *n.* Easiness to be performed; dexterity; readiness of compliance; *pl.* means to render easy; convenient advantages.
**Facing,** fās'ing, *n.* A covering in front for ornament or defense; a mode of adulterating tea; the movement of soldiers in turning round to the left, right, etc.; *pl.* trimmings on regimental garments.
**Facsimile,** fak-sim'i-lē, *n.* An exact copy or likeness.
**Fact,** fakt, *n.* Anything done; a deed; event; circumstance; reality; truth.
**Faction,** fak'shon, *n.* A party in political society in opposition to the ruling power; a party unscrupulously promoting its private ends; discord; dissension.
**Factionary,** fak'shon-a-ri, *n.* A party man; one of a faction.
**Factionist,** fak'shon-ist, *n.* One who takes part in or promotes faction.
**Factious,** fak'shus, *a.* Given to faction; prone to clamor against public measures or men; pertaining to faction.
**Factitious,** fak-ti'shus, *a.* Made by art; artificial.
**Factitive,** fak'ti-tiv, *a.* Causative: applied to verbs expressing an action that produces a new condition in the object.
**Factor,** fak'tėr, *n.* An agent, particularly a mercantile agent; in Scotland, one appointed to manage an estate; one of two or more numbers or quantities, which, when multiplied together, form a product; one of several elements which contribute to a result.
**Factorage,** fak'tėr-āj, *n.* Agency of a factor; commission paid to a factor.
**Factorship,** fak'tėr-ship, *n.* The business of a factor.
**Factory,** fak'to-ri, *n.* An establishment where factors in foreign countries reside to transact business for their employers; buildings appropriated to the manufacture of goods; a manufactory.

**Factotum,** fak-tō'tum, *n.* A person employed to do all kinds of work; confidential agent.
**Facula,** fak'ū-lē, *n.pl.* Spots sometimes seen on the sun's disc, which appear brighter than the rest of the surface.
**Facultative,** fak'ul-tāt-iv, *a.* Optional.
**Faculty,** fak'ul-ti, *n.* Any mental or bodily power; capacity; special power or authority; the body of individuals constituing one of the learned professions; a department of a university, or its professors.
**Fad,** fad, *n.* A favorite theory; crotchet; hobby.
**Faddist,** fad'ist, *n.* One who deals in fads.
**Fade,** fād, *vi.* (fading, faded). To lose color, strength, or freshness; to wither; to perish; to become indistinct.—*vt.* To cause to wither.
**Fading,** fād'ing, *p.a.* Liable to fade; transient.
**Fag,** fag, *vi.* (fagging, fagged). To become weary; to drudge.—*vt.* To use as a drudge; to tire by labor.—*n.* A laborious drudge; a public schoolboy in England who performs certain tasks for a senior.
**Fag-end,** fag'end, *n.* The end of a web of cloth; the untwisted end of a rope; the refuse or meaner part of anything.
**Faggot, Fagot,** fag'ot, *n.* A bundle of sticks or twigs; a bundle of pieces of iron or steel for remanufacture; one hired to take the place of another at the muster of a military company; a shriveled old woman.—*vt.* To tie up; to collect promiscuously.
**Faggot-vote,** fag'ot-vōt, *n.* A vote procured by the purchase or property, which is divided among a number so as to constitute a nominal voting qualification for each.
**Fahrenheit,** fä'ren-hīt, *a.* The name of the thermometer in which the freezing point is 32° and the boiling 212°.
**Faience,** fä-yängs, *n.* A sort of fine glazed pottery painted in various designs.
**Fail,** fāl, *vi.* To become deficient; to decline; to become extinct; not to produce the effect; to be unsuccessful; to be guilty of omission or neglect; to become bankrupt.—*vt.* To cease or omit to afford aid, supply, or strength to; to forsake.—*n.* Omission; failure; want.
**Failing,** fāl'ing, *n.* A natural weakness; foible; fault in character or disposition.
**Failure,** fāl'ūr, *n.* A failing; cessation of supply or total defect; non-performance; want of success; a becoming bankrupt.
**Fain,** fān, *a.* Glad; pleased; inclined; content to accept.—*adv.* Gladly.
**Faint,** fānt, *vi.* To become feeble; to become senseless and motionless; to swoon; to lose spirit; to vanish.—*a.* Enfeebled so as to be inclined to swoon; weak; indistinct; depressed.—*n.* A fainting fit; a swoon.
**Faint-hearted,** fānt'härt-ed, *a.* Cowardly; timorous; dejected.
**Faintly,** fānt'li, *adv.* Feebly; languidly; without vigor, vividness, or distinctness.
**Fair,** fār, *a.* Pleasing to the eye; beautiful; white or light in respect of complexion; not stormy or wet; favorable; reasonable; impartial; honorable; plain; unspotted; moderately good; middling.—*adv.* Openly; frankly; honestly; on good terms.—*n.* A fair woman; *the fair,* the female sex; a stated market.
**Fairing,** fār'ing, *n.* A present given at a fair.
**Fairish,** fār'ish, *a.* Moderately fair.
**Fairly,** fār'li, *adv.* Honestly, justly, equitably, reasonably, tolerably, etc.
**Fair-spoken,** fār'spōk-en, *a.* Using fair speech; courteous; plausible; bland.
**Fairy,** fā'ri, *n.* An imaginary being of human form, supposed to play a variety of pranks.—*a.* Belonging to fairies; given by fairies.
**Faith,** fāth, *n.* Belief; trust; confidence; conviction in regard to religion; system of religious beliefs; strict adherence to duty and promises; word or honor pledged.
**Faithful,** fāth'ful, *a.* Full of faith; form in adherence to duty; loyal; trusty; observant of compacts, vows, etc.
**Faithfully,** fāth'ful-li, *adv.* In a faithful manner; loyally; sincerely.
**Faithless,** fāth'les, *a.* Destitute of faith; false; not observant of promises; deceptive.
**Fake,** fāk, *vt.* To lay (a rope) in coils.—*n.* Single coil of a rope.
**Fakir, Fakeer,** fā-kēr', *n.* An oriental ascetic or begging monk.
**Falange,** fal-an'gi, *n.* The spanish fascist party.
**Falcate, Falcated,** fal'kāt, fal'kāt-ed, *a.* Bent like a sickle or scythe; hooked; curved.
**Falchion,** fal'shon, *n.* A short, broad, curved sword; a scimitar.
**Falcon,** fa'kn, or fal'kon, *n.* The name of various small or medium-sized raptorial birds; a hawk of any kind trained to sport.
**Falconer,** fa'kn-ėr, *n.* A person who breeds and trains hawks, or sports with hawks.
**Falconry,** fa'kn-ri, *n.* The art of training hawks; hawking.
**Faldstool,** fald'stöl, *n.* A folding stool; desk at which litany is said.
**Fall,** fal, *vi.* (pret. fell, pp. fallen). To sink to a lower position; to drop down; to empty or disembogue; to sink into sin, weakness, or disgrace; to come to an end suddenly; to decrease; to assume an expression of dejection, etc.; to happen; to pass or be transferred; to belong or appertain; to be uttered carelessly.—*n.* Descent; tumble; death; ruin; cadence; a cascade or cataract; extent of descent; declivity; autumn; that which falls; a kind of ladies' veil; lapse or declension from innocence or goodness; *naut.* the part of a tackle to which the power is applied in hoisting.
**Fallacious,** fal-lā'shus, *a.* Deceitful; misleading; sophistical; delusive.
**Fallacy,** fal'la-si, *n.* Deception; deceitfulness; a misleading or mistaken argument.
**Fallibility,** fal-i-bil'i-ti, *n.* Quality or state of being fallible.
**Fallible,** fal'i-bl, *a.* Liable to mistake or be deceived.
**Falling-sickness,** fal'ing-sik-nes, *n.* Epilepsy.
**Fallow,** fal'ō, *a.* Pale red or pale yellow; ploughed, but not sowed; uncultivated.—*n.* Land left unsown after being ploughed.—*vt.* To plough and harrow land without seeding it.
**Fallow-deer,** fal'ō-dēr, *n.* A kind of deer smaller than the stag, and common in England in parks.
**False,** fals, *a.* Not true; forged; feigned; fraudulent; treacherous; inconstant; constructed for show or a subsidiary purpose.
**False-hearted,** fals'härt-ed, *a.* Deceitful; treacherous; perfidious.
**Falsehood,** fals'höd, *n.* Quality of being false; untruth; fiction; a lie.
**Falsely,** fals'li, *adv.* In a false manner.
**Falsetto,** fal-set'tō, *n.* A false or artifical voice; the tones above the natural compass of the voice.
**Falsification,** fals'i-fi-kā''shon, *n.* Act of falsifying; willful misrepresentation.
**Falsifier,** fals'i-fī-ėr, *n.* One who falsifies.
**Falsify,** fals'i-fī, *vt.* (falsifying, falsified). To make false; to garble; to prove to be false; to break by falsehood.—*vi.* To violate the truth.
**Falsity,** fals'i-ti, *n.* The quality of being false; that which is false; a falsehood.
**Falter,** fal'tėr, *vi.* To hestiate in speech; to fail in exertion; to fail in the regular exercise of the understanding.
**Faltering,** fal'tėr-ing, *p.a.* Hesitating.
**Fama,** fā'ma, *n.* A widely prevailing rumor affecting the moral character of any one.
**Fame,** fām, *n.* A public report or rumor; favorable report; celebrity; reputation.
**Famed,** fāmd, *a.* Renowned; celebrated.
**Fameless,** fām'les, *a.* Without renown.
**Familiar,** fa-mil'i-ėr, *a.* Well acquainted; inti-

mate; affable; well known; free; unconstrained.—*n*. An intimate; one long acquainted; a demon supposed to attend at call.

**Familiarity,** fa-mil'i-a''ri-ti, *n*. State of being familiar; affability; freedom from ceremony; intimacy.

**Familiarize,** fa-mil'i-ėr-īz, *vt*. To make familiar; to accustom.

**Family,** fam'i-li, *n*. Household; the parents and children alone; the children as distinguished from the parents; kindred; line of ancestors; honorable descent; a group or class of animals or plants.

**Famine,** fam'in, *n*. Scarcity of food; dearth.

**Famish,** fam'ish, *vt*. To kill or exhaust with hunger; to starve; to kill by denial of anything necessary.—*vi*. To die of hunger; to suffer extreme hunger or thirst.

**Famous,** fām'us, *a*. Much talked of and praised; renowned; distinguished; admirable.

**Famously,** fām'us-li, *adv*. In a famous manner; capitally.

**Fan,** fan, *n*. An instrument for winnowing grain; an instrument to agitate the air and cool the face; something by which the air is moved; a wing.—*vt*. (fanning, fanned). To cool and refresh by moving the air with a fan; to winnow, to stimulate.

**Fanatic, Fanatical,** fa-nat'ik, fa-nat'ik-al, *a*. Wild in opinions, particularly in religious opinions; excessively enthusiastic.—**Fanatic,** fa-nat'ik, *n*. A person affected by excessive enthusiasm, particularly on religious subjects; an enthusiast; a visionary.

**Fanatically,** fa-nat'ik-al-li, *adv*. With wild enthusiasm.

**Fanaticism,** fa-nat'i-sizm, *n*. Excessive enthusiasm; religious frenzy.

**Fancied,** fan'sid, *p.a*. Imagined; fanciful.

**Fancier,** fan'si-ėr, *n*. One who fancies; one who has a hobby for certain things.

**Fanciful,** fan'si-ful, *a*. Full of fancy; dictated by fancy; visionary; whimsical.

**Fancy,** fan'si, *n*. A phase of the intellect of a lighter cast than the imagination; thought due to this faculty; embodiment of such in words; opinion or notion; liking; caprice; false notion.—*vi*. (fancying, fancied). To imagine; to suppose without proof.—*vt*. To imagine; to like; to be pleased with.—*a*. Fine; ornamental; adapted to please the fancy; beyond intrinsic value.

**Fancy-free,** fan'si-frē, *a*. Free from the power of love.

**Fandango,** fan-dang'gō, *n*. A lively Spanish dance by two persons, male and female.

**Fane,** fān, *n*. A temple; a church.

**Fanfare,** fan'fār, *n*. A flourish of trumpets; an ostentatious boast; a bravado.

**Fanfaron,** fan'fa-ron, *n*. A braggart, ostentation.

**Fanfaronade,** fan'fa-ron-ād, *n*. A swaggering; vain boasting; bluster.

**Fang,** fang, *n*. A long, pointed tooth; the tusk of an animal; the hollow poison tooth of a serpent; a prong; a claw or talon.

**Fanged,** fangd, *p.a*. Furnished with fangs.

**Fan-light,** fan'līt, *n*. A window over a door and forming part of the door-opening.

**Fanner,** fan'ėr, *n*. One who fans; a ventilator; *pl*. a machine for winnowing grain.

**Fan-palm,** fan'päm, *n*. A palm of the E. Indies with enormous leaves, the taliput-palm.

**Fantail,** fan'tāl, *n*. A variety of the domestic pigeon.

**Fantasia,** fan-tä'zē-a, *n*. A species of music ranging amidst various airs and movements.

**Fantastic, Fantastical,** fan-tas'tik, fan-tas'tik-al, *a*. Pertaining to fantasy or fancy; whimsical; fanciful; odd; grotesque.

**Fantasy,** fan'ta-si, *n*. Fancy; a vagary of the imagination; a fanciful artistic production.—*vt*. To picture in fancy.

**Far,** fär, *a*. Remote; distant, *adv*. To a great extent or distance in space or in time; in great part; very much; to a certain point.

**Farad,** far'ad, *n*. The unit of quantity in the measurement of electricity.

**Farce,** färs, *n*. A play full of extravagant drollery; absurdity; mere show.—*vt*. To stuff with forcemeat or mingled ingredients.

**Farcical,** färs'ik-al, *a*. Belonging to a farce; droll; ludicrous; ridiculous.

**Fardel,** fär'del, *n*. A bundle or little pack; a burden.

**Fare,** fār, *vi*. (faring, fared). To go; to travel; to be in any state, good or bad; to be entertained with food; to happen well or ill.—*n*. Sum charged for conveying a person; person conveyed; food; provisions of the table.

**Farewell,** fär'wel, *interj*. May you fare or prosper well.—*n*. Good-bye; departure; final attention.—*a*. Leave-taking; valedictory.

**Far-fetched,** fėr'fect, *a*. Brought from afar; not naturally introduced; forced.

**Farina,** fa-rī'na, *n*. Meal; flour.

**Farinaceous,** fa-rin-ā'shus, *a*. Made of farina; yielding farina; mealy.

**Farm,** färm, *n*. A portion of land under cultivation; ground let to a tenant for tillage, pasture, etc.—*vt*. To let out or take on lease, as lands; to cultivate; to lease, as taxes, imposts, etc.—*vi*. To cultivate the soil.

**Farmer,** färm'ėr, *n*. One who cultivates a farm; one who collects taxes, etc., for a certain rate per cent.

**Farming,** färm'ing, *a*. Pertaining to agriculture.—*n*. The business of a farmer; agriculture; husbandry; tillage of land.

**Farmost,** fär'most, *a*. Most distant or remote.

**Farrago,** fa-rā'gō, *n*. A mass composed of various materials; a medley.

**Farrier,** fa'ri-ėr, *n*. A smith who shoes horses; one who combines horse-shoeing with veterinary surgery.

**Farriery,** fa'ri-ė-ri, *n*. The art of the farrier; the veterinary art.

**Farrow,** fa'rō. *n*. A pig; a litter of pigs,—*vt*. or *i*. To bring forth pigs.

**Farther,** fär'ᴛʜėr-mėr, *a*. *comp*. More remote.—*adv*. At or to a greater distance; beyond; moreover; in addition.

**Farthermore,** fär'ᴛʜėr-mōr, *adv*. Futhermore; moreover; besides.

**Farthermost,** fär'ᴛʜėr-mōst, *a*. *superl*. Being at the greatest distance.

**Farthest,** färᴛʜest, *a*. *superl*. Most distant.—*adv*. At or to the greatest distance.

**Farthing,** fär'ᴛʜing, *n*. The fourth of a penny.

**Farthingale,** fär'ᴛʜing-gāl, *n*. A hoop-petticoat; circles of hoops used to extend the petticoat.

**Fascia,** fash'i-a, *n*.; pl. **-iae.** A band or fillet, or something resembling this in shape.

**Fascicle,** fas'si-kl, *n*. A small bundle; a collection.

**Fascicule, Fasciculus,** fas'si-kūl, fas-sik'ū-lus, *n*. A fascicle; one of the separate divisions in which a book is published.

**Fascinate,** fas'si-nāt, *vt*. (fascinating, fascinated). To bewitch; to charm; to captivate.

**Fascinating,** fas'si-nāt-ing, *p.a*. Bewitching; enchanting; charming.

**Fascination,** fas-si-nā'shon, *n*. Act of bewitching; enchantment; charm; spell.

**Fascine,** fas-sēn', *n*. A faggot or bundle or sticks used in military defense.

**Fascist,** fash'ist, *n*. A member of an Italian organization formed to oppose Bolshevism, Communism, and Socialism in all their forms.

**Fashion,** fa'shon, *n*. The make or form of anything; external appearance; form of a garment; prevailing mode; custom; genteel life—*vt*. To give shape to; to mold; to adapt.

**Fashionable,** fa'shon-a-bl, *a*. According to the prevailing mode; established by custom; prevailing at a particular time; observant of the fashion; stylish.

**Fast,** fäst, *a*. Firmly fixed; closely adhering; steadfast; durable; swift; dissipated.—*adv*.

Firmly; rapidly; durably; near; with dissipation.—*vi.* To abstain from eating and drinking, or from particular kinds of food.—*n.* Abstinence from food; a religious mortification by abstinence; the time of fasting.

**Fasten,** fäs'n, *vt.* To fix firmly, closely, or tightly; to hold together; to affix.—*vi.* To become fixed; to seize and hold on.

**Fastener,** fäs'n-ėr, *n.* One who or that which fastens.

**Fastening,** fäs'n-ing, *n.* Anything that binds and makes fast.

**Fastidious,** fas-tid'i-us, *a.* Squeamish; delicate to a fault; difficult to please.

**Fastness,** fäst'nes, *n.* State of being fast; a stronghold; a fortress or fort.

**Fat,** fat, *a.* Fleshy; plump; unctuous; heavy; stupid; rich; fertile.—*n.* A solid oily substance found in parts of animal bodies; the best or richest part of a thing.—*vt.* (fatting, fatted). To make fat.

**Fatal,** fāt'al, *a.* Proceeding from fate; causing death; deadly; calamitous.

**Fatalism,** fāt'al-izm, *n.* The doctrine that all things take place by inevitable necessity.

**Fatalist,** fāt'al-ist, *n.* One who maintains that all things happen by inevitable necessity.

**Fatality,** fa-tal'i-ti, *n.* State of being fatal; invincible necessity; fatalism; fatal occurence; calamitous accident.

**Fatally,** fāt'al-li, *adv.* In a fatal manner; by decree of destiny; mortally.

**Fate,** fāt, *n.* Destiny; inevitable necessity; death; doom; lot; *pl.* the three goddesses supposed to preside over the birth and life of men.

**Fated,** fāt'ed, *a.* Decreed by fate; destined.

**Fateful,** fāt'ful, *a.* Producing fatal events.

**Father,** fä'THėr, *n.* A male parent; the first ancestor; the oldest member of a society or profession; the first to practice any art; a creator; a name given to God; a dignitary of the church; one of the early expounders of Christianity.—*vt.* To become a father to; to adopt; to profess to be the author of; to ascribe to one as his offspring or production.

**Fatherhood,** fä'THėr-hud, *n.* State of being a father; character or aüthority of a father.

**Father-in-law,** fä'THėr-in-la, *n.* The father of one's husband or wife.

**Fatherland,** fä'THėr-land, *n.* One's native country.

**Fatherless,** fä'THėr-les, *a.* Destitute of a living father; without a known author.

**Fatherly,** fä'THėr-li, *a.* Like a father, in affection and care; tender; paternal.

**Fathom,** faTH'um, *n.* A measure of length containing six feet.—*vt.* To try the depth of; to sound; to master; to comprehend.

**Fathomable,** faTH'um-a-bl, *a.* Capable of being fathomed.

**Fathomless,** faTH'um-les, *a.* That cannot be fathomed; bottomless; incomprehensible.

**Fatigue,** fa-tēg', *vt.* (fatiguing, fatigued). To employ to weariness; to tire; to harass with toil or labor.—*n.* Weariness from bodily or mental exertion; exhaustion; toil; labors of soldiers distinct from the use of arms.

**Fatling,** fat'ling, *n.* A young animal fattened for slaughter; a fat animal.

**Fatness,** fat'nes, *n.* Quality or state of being fat; greasy matter; richness; fertility.

**Fatten,** fat'n, *vt.* To make fat; to feed for slaughter; to make fertile.—*vi.* To grow fat.

**Fatty,** fat'i, *a.* Having the qualities of fat; greasy.

**Fatuity,** fa-tū'i-ti, *n.* State or quality of being fatuous; foolishness; imbecility.

**Fatuous,** fa'tū-us, *a.* Foolish; silly; feeble in mind; imbecile.

**Fauces,** fa'sēz, *n.pl.* The back part of the mouth.

**Faucet,** fa'set, *n.* A pipe to be inserted in a cask, for drawing liquor.

**Faugh,** fa, *interj.* An exclamation of contempt or abhorrence.

**Fault,** falt, *n.* A slight offence; a defect; a flaw; a break or dislocation of strata.

**Faultily,** falt'i-li, *adv.* In a faulty manner; defectively.

**Faultless,** falt'les, *a.* Without fault; free from blemish; perfect.

**Faulty,** falt'i, *a.* Marked by faults; defective; imperfect; blamable; bad.

**Faun,** fan, *n.* Among the Romans, a rural deity, the protector of agriculture and of shepherds; a sylvan deity.

**Fauna,** fa'na, *n.* A collective term for the animals peculiar to a region or epoch.

**Fauteuil,** fō-tė-yė, *n.* An arm-chair.

**Faux-pas,** fō-pä, *n.* A false step; a breach of manners or moral conduct.

**Faveolate,** fa-vē'o-lāt, *a.* Formed like a honeycomb; alveolate.

**Favor,** fā'vėr, *n.* Good-will; kindness; a kind act; leave; a yielding to another; a token of goodwill; a knot of ribbons; advantage; prejudice.—*vt.* To regard with good-will or kindness; to befriend; to show partiality to; to facilitate; to resemble in features.



**Favorable,** fā'vėr-a-bl, *a.* Kindly disposed; propitious; conducive, advantageous.

**Favored,** fā'vėrd, *p.a.* Regarded with favor; having special facilities; featured.

**Favorer,** fā'vėr-ėr, *n.* One who favors.

**Favorite,** fā'vėr-it, *n.* A person or thing regarded with peculiar favor; a darling; a minion; one unduly favored.—*a.* Regarded with particular favor.

**Favoritism,** fā'vėr-it-izm, *n.* Disposition to favor one or more persons or classes, to the neglect of others having equal claims; exercise of power by favorites.

**Favose,** fa-vōs', *a.* Resembling a honey-comb.

**Fawn,** fan, *n.* A young deer; a buck or doe of the first year; a light-brown color; a servile cringe or bow; mean flattery.—*vi.* To bring forth a fawn; to show a servile attachment; to cringe to gain favor.—*a.* Light brown.

**Fawningly,** fan'ing-li, *adv.* In a cringing servile way; with mean flattery.

**Fay,** fā, *n.* A fairy; an elf.—*vt.* To fit pieces of timber together.

**Fealty,** fē'al-ti, *n.* Fidelity to a superior; loyalty.

**Fear,** fār, *n.* Painful emotion excited by apprehension of impending danger; dread; the object of fear; filial regard mingled with awe; reverence.—*vt.* To feel fear; to apprehend; to dread; to reverence.—*vi.* To be in apprehension of evil; to be afraid.

**Fearful,** fēr'ful, *a.* Filled with fear; apprehensive; timid; impressing fear; dreadful.

**Fearless,** fēr'les, *a.* Free from fear; undaunted; courageous; bold; intrepid.

**Feasibility,** fēz-i-bil'i-ti, *n.* Quality of being feasible; practicability.

**Feasible,** fēz-i-bl, *a.* That may be done; practicable.

**Feasibly,** fēz'bli, *adv.* Practicably.

**Feast,** fēst, *n.* A festal day; a sumptuous enterainment; a banquet; a festival; that which delights and entertains.—*vi.* To partake of a feast; to eat sumptuously; to be highly gratified.—*vt.* To entertain sumptuously.

**Feat,** fēt, *n.* An exploit, an extraordinary act of strength, skill, or cunning.

**Feather,** feTH'ėr, *n.* One of the growths which form the covering of birds; a plume; projection on a board to fit into another board; kind of nature; birds collectively; a trifle.—*vt.* To cover or fit with feathers; to turn (an oar) horizonatally over the water.

**Feathery,** feTH'ėr-i, *a.* Clothed or covered with feathers; resembling feathers.

**Feature,** fē'tūr, *n.* The make or cast of any part of the face; any single lineament; a prominent part or characteristic.

**Featured,** fē'tūrd, *a.* Having features of a certain cast.

**Featureless,** fē'tūr-les, *a.* Having no distinct features.

**Feaze,** fēz, *vt.* To untwist the end of anything made of threads of fibers.

**Febrifuge,** fe'bri-fūj, *n.* Any medicine that drives away or mitigates fever.—*a.* Dispelling or mitigating fever.

**Febrile,** fē'bril, *a.* Pertaining to fever; indicating fever, or derived from it.

**February,** feb'rū-a-ri, *n.* The second month in the year.

**Feces,** fē'sēz, *n.pl.* Grounds; dregs; excrement.

**Feculence,** fe'kū-lens, *n.* State or quality of being feculent; foulness; dregs.

**Feculent,** fe'kū-lent, *a.* Abounding with sediment; foul or filthy; impure.

**Fecund,** fē'kund, *a.* Fruitful in progeny; prolific; fertile; productive.

**Fecundate,** fē'kund-āt, *vt.* To make fruitful or prolific; to impregnate.

**Fecundation,** fē-kund-ā'shon, *n.* Act of fecundating; impregnation.

**Fecundity,** fē-kund'i-ti, *n.* State or quality of being fecund; fertility; richness of invention.

**Federal,** fed'ėr-al, *a.* Pertaining to a league or contract; confederated; founded on alliance between states which unite for national purposes.—*n.* One who upholds federal government.

**Federalism,** fed'ėr-al-izm, *n.* The principles of federal government.

**Federalist,** fed'ėr-al-ist, *n.* A federal.

**Federalize,** fed'ėr-al-īz, *vt.* or *i.* To unite in a federal compact.

**Federate,** fed'ėr-āt, *a.* Joined in confederacy.

**Federation,** fed-ėr-ā'shon, *n.* Act of uniting in a league; confederacy.

**Federative,** fed'ėr-āt-iv, *a.* Uniting in a confederacy.

**Fee,** fē, *n.* A reward for services; recompense for professional services; a fief; a freehold estate held by one who is absolute owner.—*vt.* (feeing, feed). To pay a fee to; to engage in one's service by advancing a fee to.

**Feeble,** fē'bl, *a.* Weak; impotent; deficient in vigor, as mental powers, sound, light, etc.

**Feebly,** fē'bli, *adv.* Weakly; without strength.

**Feed,** fēd, *vt.* (feeding, fed). To give food to; to furnish with anything of which there is constant consumption; to fatten.—*vi.* To take food; to eat; to prey; to graze; to grow fat.—*n.* That which is eaten; fodder; portion of provender given to a horse, cow, etc.

**Feeder,** fēd'ėr, *n.* One who or that which feeds; an encourager; an affluent; a branch railway; napkin tied round a child's neck at meal-times.

**Feeding,** fēd'ing, *n.* Act of giving food; act of eating; that which is eaten; provender.

**Feel,** fēl, *vt.* (feeling, felt). To perceive by the touch; to have the sense of; to be affected by; to examine by touching.—*vi.* To have perception by the touch; to have the sensibility moved; to have perception mentally.—*n.* Act of feeling; perception caused by the touch.

**Feeler,** fēl'ėr, *n.* One who feels; an observation, etc., put forth to ascertain the views of others; an organ of touch in the lower animals.

**Feeling,** fēl'ing, *a.* Possessing great sensibility; sensitive; sympathetic.—*n.* The sense of touch; sensation; sensibility; emotion; sympathy.

**Feelingly,** fēl'ing-li, *adv.* In a feeling manner; tenderly.

**Feet,** fēt, *n.pl.* of *foot.*

**Feign,** fān, *vt.* To pretend; to counterfeit; to simulate.—*vi.* To represent falsely; to pretend.

**Feigned,** fānd, *p.a.* Simulated; assumed.

**Feignedly,** fēn'ed-li, *adv.* In pretense.

**Feint,** fānt, *n.* A pretense; an appearance of aiming at one part when another is intended to be struck.—*vi.* To make a feigned blow or thrust.

**Feldspar.,** *See* FELSPAR.

**Felicitate,** fē-lis'it-āt, *vt.* To congratulate.

**Felicitation,** fē-lis'it-ā''shon, *n.* Congratulation.

**Felicitous,** fē-lis'it-us, *a.* Happy; extremely appropriate; managed with skill.

**Felicity,** fē-lis'i-ti, *n.* State of being in extreme enjoyment; bliss; the joys of heaven; skillfulness; appropriateness.

**Feline,** fē'līn, *a.* Pertaining to cats; like a cat.

**Fell,** fel, *a.* Cruel; fierce; savage.—*n.* A skin or hide of an animal; a seam sewed down level with the cloth; a stony or barren hill.—*vt.* To cause to fall; to hew down; to sew down a seam level with the cloth.

**Fellah,** fel'lä, *n.* An Egyptian peasant.

**Felloe,** fel'ō. Same as *Felly.*

**Fellow,** fel'ō, *n.* A partner; a companion; one of the same kind; an appellation of contempt; a member of a college or incorporated society.

**Fellowship,** fel'ō-ship, *n.* Companionship; joint interest; an association; an establishment in colleges for maintaining a fellow.

**Felly,** fel'i, *n.* One of the curved pieces which form the circular rim of a wheel.

**Felon,** fe'lon, *n.* One who has committed felony; a culprit; a whitlow.—*a.* Fierce; malignant; malicious.

**Felonious,** fe-lō'ni-us, *a.* Villainous; done with purpose to commit a crime.

**Felony,** fe'lon-i, *n.* Any crime which incurs the forfeiture of lands or goods; a heinous crime.

**Felspar,** fel'spär, *n.* A mineral consisting of silica and alumina, with potash, soda, or lime, a principal constitutent in granite, porphyry, etc. Called also *Feldspar, Felspath.*

**Felt,** felt, *n.* A fabric made of wool, or wool and fur, wrought into a compact substance by rolling, beating, etc.; an article made of felt.—*vt.* To make into felt; to cover with felt.

**Felting,** felt'ing, *n.* Process of making felt; materials of which felt is made; felt.

**Felucca,** fe-luk'ka, *n.* A narrow Mediterranean vessel with lateen sails.

**Female,** fē'māl, *n.* One of that sex which conceives and brings forth young.—*a.* Belonging to the sex which produces young; feminine; weak.

**Feminine,** fem'in-in, *a.* Pertaining to females; womanly; effeminate; denoting the gender of words which signify females.

**Femme-de-chambre,** fam-dė-shäm-br, *n.* A lady's-maid; a chamber-maid.

**Femoral,** fem'ō-ral, *a.* Belonging to the thigh.

**Femur,** fē'mėr, *n.* The thigh-bone.

**Fen,** fen, *n.* A marsh; bog; swamp where water stagnates.

**Fence,** fens, *n.* That which defends or guards; a wall, railing, etc., forming a boundary, etc.; defense; fencing; skill in fencing or argument; a purchaser or receiver of stolen goods.—*vt.* (fencing, fenced). To defend; to secure by an enclosure; to ward off by argument or reasoning.—*vi.* To practice the swordsman's art; to parry arguments; to prevaricate.

**Fencer,** fens'ėr, *n.* One who fences; one who teaches or practices the art of fencing.

**Fencible,** fen'si-bl, *n.* A soldier for defense of the country, not liable to serve abroad.

**Fencing,** fens'ing, *n.* The art of using a sword or foil in attack or defense; material used in making fences; that which fences.

**Fend,** fend, *vt.* To keep or ward off.—*vi.* To act on the defensive; to provide a livelihood.

**Fender,** fend'ėr, *n.* That which defends; a utensil to confine coals to the fireplace; something to protect the side of a vessel from injury.

**Fenestration,** fen-es-trā'shon, *n.* The arrangement of windows in a building.

**Fenian,** fē'ni-an, *n.* A member of a secret society, the object of which was the erection of an independent Irish republic.

**Fennel,** fen'el, *n.* A plant cutivated for the aromatic flavor of its seeds and for its leaves.

**Fenny,** fen'i, *a.* Growing in fens; marshy.

**Fent,** fent, *n.* A placket of a dress.

**Feoff,** fef, *n.* A fief or fee.

**Feoffment,** fef'ment, *n.* The gift or grant of a fee;

the instrument or deed conveying it.
**Feracious,** fē-rā'shus, *a*. Fruitful.
**Feral,** fē'ral, *a*. Having become wild after a state of domestication or cultivation.
**Feretory,** fe'rē-to-ri, *n*. A movable shrine containing the relics of saints.
**Ferial,** fē'ri-al, *a*. Pertaining to holidays.
**Ferine,** fē'rin, *a*. Pertaining to wild beasts.
**Ferment,** fėr'ment, *n*. That which causes fermentation, as yeast, etc.; intestine motion; agitation.—*vt*. fėr-ment'. To produce fermentation in; to set in agitation.—*vi*. To undergo fermentation; to be in agitation.
**Fermentation,** fėr-ment-ā'shon, *n*. Decomposition or conversion of an organic substance into new compounds by a ferment, indicated by the development of heat, bubbles, etc.; process by which grape juice is converted into wine; agitaion; excitement.
**Fermentative,** fėr-ment'a-tiv, *a*. Causing fermentation; consisting in fermentation.
**Fern,** fėrn, *n*. The name of many cryptogams producing leaves called fronds.
**Fernery,** fėr'nėr-i, *n*. A place where ferns are artifically grown.
**Ferny,** fėrn'i, *a*. Abounding with fern.
**Ferocious,** fē-rō'shus, *a*. Fierce; savage; cruel.
**Ferocity,** fē-ros'i-ti, *n*. Savage wildness; fury; fierceness.
**Ferreous,** fe'rē-us, *a*. Partaking of or pertaining to iron.
**Ferret,** fe'ret, *n*. An animal allied to the weasel, employed in unearthing rabbits; a narrow tape made of woolen thread, cotton, or silk.—*vt*. To hunt with ferrets; to search out cunningly.
**Ferriferous,** fe-rif'ėr-us, *a*. Producing or yielding iron.
**Ferruginous,** fe-rū'jin-us, *a*. Of the color of the rust or oxide of iron; partaking of or containing iron.
**Ferrule,** fe'rūl, *n*. A ring of metal round the end of a stick to strengthen it.
**Ferry,** fe'ri, *vt*. (ferrying, ferried). To carry over a river or other water in a boat.—*n*. Place where boats pass over to convey passengers; regular conveyance provided at such a place; a boat that plies at a ferry.
**Ferryman,** fe'ri-man, *n*. One who keeps a ferry.
**Fertile,** fėr'tīl, *a*. Fruitful; prolific; inventive; able to produce abundantly.
**Fertility,** fėr-til'i-ti, *n*. Fruitfulness; rickness; fertile invention.
**Fertilize,** fėr'til-iz, *vt*. To make fertile or fruitful; to enrich; to impregnate.
**Ferule,** fe'rūl, *n*. A flat piece of wood, or rod, used to punish children.—*vt*. To punish with a ferule.
**Fervency,** fėr'ven-si, *n*. Eagerness; ardor; warmth of devotion.
**Fervent,** fėr'vent, *a*. Burning; vehement; ardent; earnest.
**Fervid,** fėr'vid, *a*. Burning Zealous; eager; earnest.
**Fervor,** fėr'vėr, *n*. Heat or warmth; ardor; intensity of feeling; zeal.
**Festal,** fest'al, *a*. Pertaining to a feast; joyous; gay; mirthful.
**Fester,** fes'tėr, *vi*. To suppurate; to rankle; to putrefy; to grow virulent.—*n*. A small inflammatory tumor.
**Festival,** fes'tiv-al, *a*. Festive; joyous.—*n*. The time of feasting; a feast; an anniversary day of joy, civil or religious.
**Festivity,** fes-tiv'i-ti, *n*. Festive gaiety; social joy or mirth at an entertainment.
**Festoon,** fes-tön', *n*. A string of flowers, foliage, etc., suspended in a curve or curves; carved work in the form of a wreath of flowers, etc.—*vt*. To form in festoons; to adorn with festoons.
**Fetch,** fech, *vt*. To bring or draw; to make; to heave, as a sigh; to obtain as its price.—*vi*. To move or turn; to bring things.—*n*. A stratagem or trick; a wraith.
**Fête,** fāt, *n*. A feast or festival; a holiday.—*vt*. To honor with a feast.
**Fetlock,** fet'lok, *n*. The tuft of hair that grows behind on a horse's feet; the joint on which this hair grows; an instrument fixed to a horse's leg to prevent him from running off.
**Fetter,** fet'ėr, *n*. A chain for the feet; anything that confines or restrains from motion; generally in *pl*.—*vt*. To put fetters upon; to restrain.
**Fetus,** fē'tus, *n*.; **pl. -uses.** The young or an animal in the womb, or in the egg, after being perfectly formed.
**Feud,** fūd, *n*. Hostility; a hereditary quarrel; a fief.
**Feudal,** Fūd'al, *a*. Pertaining to feuds or fiefs; pertaining to the system of holding hands by military services.
**Feudalism,** fūd'al-izm, *n*. The system by which land was held in return for military service; the feudal system.
**Feu-de-jole,** Fu-dė-zhwä. A bonfire, or a firing of guns in token of joy.
**Fever,** Fē'vėr, *n*. A disease characterized by an accelerated pulse, heat, thirst, and diminished strength; agitation; excitement.—*vt*. To put in a fever.—*vt*. To be seized with fever.
**Feverish,** Fē'ver-ish, *a*. Having a slight fever; pertaining to fever; agitated; inconstant.
**Few,** fū, *a*. Not many; small in number.
**Fey,** fā, *a*. On the verge of a sudden or violent death; fated soon to die and often showing this by unnatural gaiety.
**Fez,** fez, *n*. A close-fitting red cap with a tassel, worn in Turkey, Egypt, etc.
**Fiancé, Fiancée,** fē-äng-sā, *n*., *masc.* and *fem*. An affianced or betrothed person.
**Fiasco,** fē-as'kō, *n*. An ignominious failure.
**Fiat,** fī'at, *n*. A decree; a command.
**Fib,** fib, *n*. A falsehood (a softer expression than *lie*).—*vi*. (fibbing, fibbed). To tell fibs.
**Fiber,** fībėr, *n*. A thread; a fine, slender body which constitutes a part of animals, plants, or minderals.
**Fibril,** fī'ril, *n*. A small fiber.
**Fibrositis,** fī-brō-sī'tis, *n*. Non-articular rheumatism; rheumatic inflammation of fibrous tissue.
**Fibrous,** fī'brus, *a*. Composed or consisting of fibers; containing fibers.
**Fickle,** fik'l, *a*. Of a changeable mind; vacillating; capricious.
**Fickleness,** fik'l-nes, *n*. Inconstancy.
**Fictile,** fik'tīl, *a*. Molded by art; made of clay; manufactured by the potter.
**Fiction,** fik'shon, *n*. A feigned story; literature in the form of novels, tales, etc., a falsehood; fabrication.
**Fictitious,** fik-ti'shus, *a*. Containing fiction; imaginary; counterfeit.
**Fid,** fid, *n*. A bar of wood or metal; a pin for various purposes on board ship.
**Fiddle,** fid'l, *n*. A stringed instrument of music; a violin; the wooden framework fixed on tables on board ship in rough weather, to keep the crockery from sliding off.—*vt*. (fiddling, fiddled). To play on a fiddle; to trifle; to trifle with the hands.—*vt*. To play on a fiddle.
**Fiddler,** fid'l-ėr, *n*. One who plays a fiddle.
**Fidelity,** fi-del'i-ti, *n*. Faithfulness; trustiness; loyalty; integrity.
**Fidget,** fij'et, *vi*. To move uneasily or in fits and starts.—*n*. An uneasy restless motion.
**Fiduciary,** fi-dū'shi-a-ri, *a*. Held in trust; having the nature of a trust.—*n*. One who holds a thing in trust; a trustee.
**Fief,** fēf, *n*. An estate held of a superior on condition of military service.
**Field,** fēld, *n*. A piece of land suitable for tillage or pasture; piece of enclosed land; place of battle; battle; open space for action; sphere; blank space on which figures are drawn; those taking part in a hunt or race.—*vi*. and *t*. To watch and catch the ball, as in cricket.
**Field-book,** fēld'bụk, *n*. A book used in surveying
**Field-day,** fēld'dā, *n*. A day when troops are

drawn out for instruction in field exercises and evolutions.
**Fieldfare,** fēld-fär, *n.* A species of thrush found in Great Britain during the winter.
**Field-glass,** fēld'gläs, *n.* A kind of binocular telescope.
**Field-marshal,** fēld-mär'shal, *n.* A military officer of the highest rank.
**Field-officer,** fēld'of-fis-ėr, *n.* A major, lieutenant-colonel, or colonel.
**Field-train,** fēld-trān, *n.* A department of artillery that supplies ammunition on the field.
**Fiend,** fēnd, *n.* A demon; the devil; a wicked or cruel person.
**Fiendish,** fēnd'ish, *a.* Like a fiend; diabolic.
**Fierce,** fērs, *a.* Wild; savage; outrageous; violent.
**Fiercely,** fērs'li, *adv.* Violently; with rage.
**Fierily,** fī'ė-ri-li, *adv.* In a fiery manner.
**Fiery,** fī'ė-ri, *a.* Consisting of fire; like fire; impetuous; irritable; fierce.
**Fife,** fif, *n.* A small wind-instrument used chiefly in martial music.—*vi.* (fifing, fifed). To play on a fife.
**Fifer,** fif'ėr, *n.* One who plays on a fife.
**Fifteen,** fif'tēn, *a.* and *n.* Five and ten; a Rugby football team.
**Fifteenth,** fif'tēnth, *a.* The ordinal of fifteen.—*n.* A fifteenth part.
**Fifth,** fifth, *a.* The ordinal of five.—*n.* A fifth part.
**Fifth column,** fifth ko'lum, *n.* The individuals and organizations in a country which are prepared to give help to an enemy.
**Fifthly,** fifth'li, *adv.* In the fifth place.
**Fiftieth,** fif'ti-eth, *a.* The ordinal of fifty.—*n.* A fiftieth part.
**Fifty,** fif'ti, *a.* and *n.* Five tens; five times ten.
**Fig,** fig, *n.* The fruit of a tree of the mulberry family; the tree itself; a mere trifle; dress.
**Fight,** fit, *vi.* (fighting, fought). To strive for victory; to contend in arms.—*vt.* To war against; to contend with in battle; to win by struggle.—*n.* A struggle for victory; a battle; an encounter.
**Fighter,** fit'ėr, *n.* One who fights; a combatant; a warrior; an aeroplane designed for aerial combat.
**Fighting,** fit'ing, *a.* Qualified for war; fit for battle; occupied in war.
**Figment,** fig'ment, *n.* A fiction; fabrication.
**Figurant,** fig'ūr-ant, *n.* A character on the stage who has nothing to say.
**Figurate,** fig'ūr-āt, *a.* Of a certain determinate form.
**Figuration,** fig-ūr-ā'shon, *n.* Act of giving figure; configuration; form.
**Figurative,** fig'ūr-āt-iv, *a.* Containing a figure or figures; representing by resemblance; typical metaphoric; abounding in figures of speech.
**Figure,** fig'ūr, *n.* The form of anything as expressed by the outline; appearance; representation; a statue; a character denoting a number; a diagram; type; mode of expression in which words are turned from their ordinary signification; price.—*vt.* (figuring, figured). To make a likeness of; to represent by drawing, etc.; to cover or mark with figures; to image in the mind.—*vi.* To make a figure; to be distinguished.
**Figured,** fig'ūrd, *a.* Adorned with figures; free and florid.
**Figure-head,** fig'ūr-hed, *n.* The ornamental figure on a ship under the bowsprit.
**Figuring,** fig'ūr-ing, *n.* Act of making figures; figures collectively.
**Filaceous,** fil-ā'shus, *a.* Composed of threads.
**Filament,** fil'a-ment, *n.* A slender thread; a fine fiber.
**Filamentary, Filamentose, Filamentous,** fil-a-men'ta-ri, fil-a-men'tōs, fil-a-men'tus, *a.* Consisting of filaments.
**Filatory,** fil'a-to-ri, *n.* A machine which spins threads.
**Filature,** fil'a-tūr, *n.* The reeling off silk from cocoons; an establishment for reeling silk; a filatory.
**Filbert,** fil'bėrt, *n* The fruit of the cultivated hazel.
**Filch,** filsh or filch, *vt.* To pilfer; to steal.
**Filcher,** filsh'ėr, *n.* A petty thief.
**File,** fīl, *n.* A line or wire on which papers are strung; the papers so strung; a row of soldiers one behind another; a steel instrument for cutting and smoothing iron, wood, etc.—*vt.* (filing, filed). To arrange or place on or in a file; to bring before a court by presenting the proper papers; to rub or cut with a file; to polish.—*vi.* To march in a line one after the other.
**Filial,** fil'i-al, *a.* Pertaining to or becoming a son or daughter.
**Filiate,** fil'i-āt, *vt.* To affiliate.
**Filiation,** fil-i-ā'shon, *n.* Affiliation.
**Filibuster,** fil'i-bus-tėr, *n.* A buccaneer; one of those lawless adventurers who in the present century have invaded a foreign country.—*vi.* To act as a filibuster.
**Filiform,** fil'i-form, *a.* Having the form of a thread or filament; slender.
**Filigree,** fil'i-grē, *n.* Ornamental open work in fine gold or silver wire.
**Filings,** fil'ingz, *n.pl.* Fragments or particles rubbed off by the act of filing.
**Fill,** fil, *vt.* To make full; to occupy; to pervade; to satisfy; to surfeit; to supply with an occupant; to hold; to possess and perform the duties of.—*vi.* To grow or become full.—*n.* As much as fills or supplies want.
**Filler,** fil'ėr, *n.* One who fills; a tube for filling bottles, etc.
**Fillet,** fil'et, *n.* A little band to tie about the hair; the fleshy part of the thigh in veal; meat rolled together and tied round; something resembling a fillet or band.—*vt.* (filleting, filleted). To bind with a little band.
**Fillibeg,** fil'i-beg, *n.* The kilt worn by the Highlanders of Scotland.
**Filling,** fil'ing, *n.* A making full; materials for making full; woof of a fabric.
**Fillip,** fil'ip, *vt.* To strike with the nail of the finger, forced from the thumb with a sudden spring.—*n.* A jerk of the finger; something which tends to stimulate at once.
**Filly,** fil'i, *n.* A female colt; a wanton girl.
**Film,** film, *n.* A thin skin; a pellicle; *(pl.)* a cinema-show; the pictures.—*vt.* To cover with a thin skin.
**Filmy,** film'i, *a.* Like a film; composed of thin membranes or pellicles.
**Filter,** fil'tėr, *n.* A strainer; any substance through which liquors are passed.—*vt.* To purify by passing through a filter.—*vi.* To percolate; to pass through a filter.
**Filth,** filth, *n.* That which defiles; dirt; pollution.
**Filthily,** filth'i-li, *adv.* In a filthy manner.
**Filthy,** filth'i, *a.* Abounding in filth; dirty; foul; nasty; obscene.
**Filtrate,** fil'trāt, *vt.* To filter.
**Filtration,** fil-trā'shon, *n.* Act or process of filtering.
**Fimbriate,** fim'bri-āt, *a.* Fringed. Also *Fimbriated.*
**Fin,** fin, *n.* One of the organs which enable fishes to balance themselves and regulate their movements; anything resembling a fin.
**Finable,** fīn'a-bl, *a.* Liable to a fine.
**Final,** fīn'al, *a.* Pertaining to the end; last; ultimate; conclusive; decisive.
**Finale,** fē-nä'lā, *n.* The last part of a piece of music; the last piece or scene in a performance.
**Finality,** fī-nal'i-ti, *n.* Final state; state of being final; the doctrine that nothing exists except for a determinate end.
**Finally,** fīn'al-li, *adv.* Ultimately; lastly; completely; beyond recovery.
**Finance,** fi-nans', *n.* The science of public revenue and expenditure; management of money matters; *pl.* public funds or resources of money; private income.—*vi.* (financing, financed). To

conduct financial operations.—*vt.* To manage the financial affairs of.

**Financial,** fi-nan'shal, *a.* Pertaining to finance.

**Financier,** fi-nan'sėr, *n.* One skilled in matters of finance.

**Finch,** finsh, *n.* A small singing bird.

**Find,** fīnd, *vt.* (finding, found). To come upon; to discover; to recover; to get; to perceive; to supply; to declare by verdict.—*n.* A discovery; the thing found.

**Finding,** fīnd'ing, *n.* Discovery; act of discovering; that which is found; a verdict.

**Fine,** fīn, *a.* Slender; minute; keen; delicate; refined; elegant; amiable; noble; splendid.—*n.* Payment of money imposed as a punishment; conclusion *(in fine).*—*vt.* (fining, fined). To make fine; to purify; to impose a pecuniary penalty on.

**Finedraw,** fīn'dra, *vt.* To sew up (a rent) neatly.

**Finedrawn,** fīn'dran, *p.a.* Drawn out to too great fineness, or with too much subtlety.

**Finely,** fīn'li, *adv.* In a fine manner; gaily; handsomely; delicately.

**Finer,** fīn'ėr, *n.* One who refines or purifies.

**Finery,** fīn'ė-ri, *n.* Fine things; showy articles of dress; a furnace where cast-iron is converted into malleable iron.

**Finespun,** fīn'spun, *a.* Drawn to a fine thread; minute; over-elaborated.

**Finesse,** fi-nes', *n.* Artifice; stratagem.—*vi.* To use finesse or artifice.

**Fin-footed,** fin'fut-ed, *a.* Having feet with toes connected by a membrane.

**Finger,** fing'gėr, *n.* One of the five members of the hand; something resembling a finger; skill in playing on a keyed instrument.—*vt.* To handle with the fingers; to touch lightly; to pilfer.—*vi.* To dispose the fingers aptly in playing on an instrument.

**Fingered,** fing'gėrd, *a.* Having fingers, or parts like fingers.

**Fingering,** fing'gėr-ing, *n.* Act of touching lightly; manner of touching an instrument of music; a loose worsted for stockings, etc.

**Finger-post,** fing'gėr-pōst, *n.* A post for the direction of travelers.

**Finger-stall,** fing'gėr-stal, *n.* A cover for protection of a finger when injured.

**Finical,** fin'i-kal, *a.* Unduly particular about trifles; idly busy. Also *finicking* and *finikin.*

**Fining,** fīn'ing, *n.* The process of refining; that which is used to fine liquors.

**Finis,** fī'nis, *n.* An end; conclusion.

**Finish,** fin'ish, *vt.* To bring to an end; to perfect; to polish to a high degree.—*vi.* To come to an end; to expire.—*n.* Completion; the last touch to a work; polish.

**Finite,** fī'nīt, *a.* Limited; bounded; circumscribed; not infinite.

**Finitely,** fī'nīt-li, *adv.* In a finite manner or degree.

**Finless,** fin'les, *a.* Destitute of fins.

**Finn,** fin, *n.* A native of Finland.

**Finnish,** fin'ish, *a.* Relating to the Finns.—*n.* Their language.

**Finny,** fin'i, *a.* Furnished with fins.

**Fiord, Fjord,** fyord, *n.* An inlet of the sea, such as are common in Norway.

**Fir,** fėr, *n.* A resinous coniferous tree.

**Fire,** fīr, *n.* Heat and light emanating from a body; fuel burning; a conflagration; discharge of firearms; splendor; violence of passion; vigor of fancy; animation; ardent affection; affliction.—*vt.* (firing, fired). To set on fire; to irritate; to animate; to bake; to cause to explode; to discharge (firearms).—*vi.* To take fire; to be inflamed with passion; to discharge firearms.

**Firearm,** fīr'ärm, *n.* A weapon which expels its projectile by the combustion of powder.

**Fire-brand,** fīr'brand, *n.* A piece of wood kindled; an incendiary; one who inflames factions.

**Fire-brigade,** fīr'bri-gād, *n.* A body of men organized to extinguish fires.

**Fire-damp,** fīr'damp, *n.* The explosive carbureted hydrogen of coal-mines.

**Fire-engine,** fīr'en-jin, *n.* An engine for throwing water to extinguish fire.

**Fire-escape,** fīr'es-kāp, *n.* A machine to facilitate escape from a building on fire.

**Fire-fly,** fīr'flī, *n.* A winged insect which emits a brilliant light at night.

**Fire-irons,** fīr'ī-ėrnz, *n.pl.* A shovel, tongs, poker, etc.

**Fireman,** fīr'man, *n.* A man who extinguishes fires, or tends the fires of an engine.

**Fire-new,** fīr'nū, *a.* Brand-new.

**Fire-proof,** fīr'pröf, *a.* Incombustible.

**Fire-ship,** fīr'ship, *n.* A vessel filled with combustibles and furnished with grappling irons, to hook and set fire to an enemy's ships.

**Fire-side,** fīr'sīd, *n.* A place near the fire or hearth; home; domestic life.

**Fire-watcher,** fīr-woch'ėr, *n.* Person detailed to keep watch in a building or street in case of an outbreak of fire caused by incendiary bombs.

**Firework,** fīr'wėrk, *n.* Preparation of gunpowder, sulphur, etc., used for making a show, a signal, etc.

**Firing,** fīr'ing, *n.* Act of one who fires; act of discharging firearms; application of fire; fuel; process of treating articles with fire.

**Firkin,** fėr'kin, *n.* An old measure equal to 7½ gallons; a small cask for butter.

**Firm,** fėrm, *a.* Steady; stable; strong; dense; hard; not fluid; fixed; resolute.—*n.* A partnership or commercial house.—*vt.* To make firm or solid.—*vi.* To become firm.

**Firmament,** fėrm'a-ment, *n.* The sky or heavens; region of the air; an expanse.

**Firmly,** fėrm'li, *adv.* In a firm manner; steadfastly; resolutely.

**First,** fėrst, *a.* Foremost in time, place, rank, value, etc.; chief; highest; the ordinal of *one.*—*adv.* Before all others in time, place, etc.

**First-born,** fėrst'born, *a.* Eldest.

**First-class,** fėrst'klas, *a.* First-rate.

**First-fruit,** fėrst'fröt, *n.* The fruit or produce first collected; first profits; first or earliest effect, in good or bad sense.

**First-hand,** fėrst'hand, *a.* Obtained direct from the first source, producer, maker, etc.

**Firstling,** fėrst'ling, *n.* The first produce or offspring, as of sheep or cattle.

**Firstly,** fėrst'li, *adv.* In the first place; first.

**First-rate,** fėrst'rāt, *a.* Of highest excellence; pre-eminent; of largest size.

**Firth,** fėrth, *n.* An arm of the sea into which a river discharges; a channel. Also *Frith.*

**Fiscal,** fis'kal, *a.* Pertaining to the public treasury.—*n.* A treasurer; a public prosecutor, as in Scotland.

**Fish,** fish, *n.* An animal that lives in water; the flesh of such animals used as food.—*vi.* To attempt to catch fish; to attempt to obtain by artifice.—*vt.* To catch or try to catch fish in; to draw out or up when in water.

**Fisher,** fish'ėr, *n.* One employed in fishing.

**Fisherman,** fish'ėr-man, *n.* One whose occupation is to catch fish.

**Fishery,** fish'ė-ri, *n.* The business of catching fish; a place for catching fish.

**Fishing,** fish'ing, *a.* Used in catching fish.—*n.* Art or practice of catching fish; place to fish in.

**Fishmonger,** fish'mung-gėr, *n.* A dealer in fish.

**Fishwife, Fishwoman,** fish'wīf, fish-wụ'man, *n.* A woman who sells fish.

**Fishy,** fish'i, *a.* Consisting of fish; like fish; worn out; dubious; unsafe.

**Fissile,** fis'sīl, *a.* That may be split in the direction of the grain, or of natural joints.

**Fission,** fi'shon, *n.* The act of splitting into parts; reproduction in animals of a low type through the body dividing into parts.

**Fissure,** fi'shūr, *n.* A cleft; a longitudinal opening.—*vt.* To cleave; to crack.

**Fist,** fist, *n.* The hand clenched; the hand with the

F

fingers doubled into the palm.—*vt*. To strike with the fist.
**Fistic,** fis'tik, *a*. Pertaining to boxing.
**Fisticuffs,** fis'ti-kufs, *n*. A blow with the fist; commonly in *pl*. boxing.
**Fistula,** fis'tū-la, *n*. A shepherd's pipe; a deep, narrow, sinuous ulcer.
**Fistular,** fis'tū-lėr, *a*. Hollow like a pipe.
**Fit,** fit, *n*. A sudden activity followed by a relaxation; paroxysm; convulsion; due adjustment of dress to the body.—*a*. Conformable to a standard of right, duty, taste, etc.; suitable; proper; congruous; qualified; adequate.—*vt*. (fitting, fitted). To make fit or suitable; to furnish with anything; to adapt; to qualify for.—*vi*. To be proper or becoming; to suit; to be adapted.
**Fitful,** fit'ful, *a*. Full of fits; varied by sudden impulses; spasmodic; chequered.
**Fitly,** fit'li, *adv*. Suitably; properly.
**Fitter,** fit'ėr, *n*. One who fits; one who puts the parts of machinery together.
**Fitting,** fit'ing, *a*. Fit; appropriate.—*n.pl*. Things fixed on; permanent appendages.
**Fittingly,** fit'ing-li, *adv*. Suitably.
**Five,** fiv, *a*. and *n*. Four and one added; the half of ten.
**Fix,** fiks, *vt*. To make fast or firm; to settle; to define; to appoint; to deprive of volatility.—*vi*. To settle or remain permanently; to cease to be fluid; to congeal.—*n*. A condition of difficulty; dilemma.
**Fixation,** fiks-ā'shon, *n*. Act of fixing; state in which a body resists evaporation.
**Fixative,** fiks'a-tiv, *a*. Tending or causing to fix.—*n*. A substance that causes something to be stable or not fleeting.
**Fixed,** fikst, *p.a*. Firm; fast; settled; deprived of volatility.
**Fixture,** fiks'tūr, *n*. That which is fixed; that which is permanently attached; an appendage.
**Fizz, Fizzle,** fiz, fiz'l, *vi*. To make a hissing sound. Also used as a noun.
**Flabbergast,** flab'ėr-gast, *vt*. To strike with astonishment or dismay.
**Flabby,** flab'i, *a*. Soft; yielding to the touch; languid; feeble.
**Flaccid,** flak'sid, *a*. Flabby; soft and weak; drooping; limber.
**Flaccidity,** flak-sid'i-ti, *n*. State or quality of being flaccid; want of firmness.
**Flag,** flag, *n*. A cloth, usually attached to a pole, and bearing devices expressive of nationality, etc.; a banner; a flat stone for paving; an aquatic plant with sword-shaped leaves.—*vi*. (flagging, flagged). To hang loose; to droop; to languish; to slacken.—*vt*. To lay with broad flat stones.
**Flagellant,** fla'jel-lant, *n*. One who whips himself in religious discipline.
**Flagellate,** fla'jel-lāt, *vt*. To whip.
**Flagellation,** fla-jel-lā'shon, *n*. A flogging; the discipline of the scourge.
**Flageolet,** fla'jel-et, *n*. A small wind-instrument like a flute with a mouth-piece.
**Flagging,** flag'ing, *n*. Flag-stones; a pavement or side-walk of flag-stones.
**Flaggy,** flag'i, *a*. Flexible; abounding with the plant flag; resembling flag-stone.
**Flagitious,** fla-ji'shus, *a*. Deeply criminal; corrupt; profligate; heinous.
**Flag-officer,** flag of'is-ėr, *n*. An admiral, vice-admiral or rear-admiral. **Flag-ship,** *n*. Ship flying the flag of the admiral commanding the fleet.
**Flagon,** fla'gon, *n*. A vessel with a narrow mouth, used for liquors.
**Flagrancy,** flā'gran-si, *n*. Quality of being flagrant; enormity.
**Flagrant,** flā'grant, *a*. Flaming in notice; glaring; notorious; enormous.
**Flagrantly,** flā'grant-li, *adv*. Glaringly; notoriously.
**Flail,** flāl, *n*. A wooden instrument for thrashing or beating grain, etc.
**Flake,** flāk, *n*. A loose, filmy mass of anything; a scale; a fleecy or feathery particle, as of snow; a flock, as of wool.—*vt*. (flaking, flaked). To form into flakes.—*vi*. To break in layers; to peel off.
**Flaky,** flāk'i, *a*. Consisting of flakes; lying in flakes; like flakes or scales.
**Flambeau,** flam'bō, *n*. A light made of thick wicks covered with wax; a torch.
**Flamboyant,** flam-boi'ant, *a*. Noting that style of gothic architecture characterized by wavy tracery in the windows; florid.
**Flame,** flām, *n*. Light emitted from fire; a blaze; fire; heat of passion; ardor of temper or imagination; ardent love; rage; one beloved.—*vi*. (flaming, flamed). To blaze; to glow; to rage.
**Flaming,** flām'ing, *p.a*. Emitting a flame, violent; vehement.
**Flamingly,** flām'ing-li, *adv*. Most brightly; with great show or vehemence.
**Flamingo,** fla-ming'gō, *n*. A web-footed, long-necked bird about 5 to 6 feet high.
**Flamy,** flām'i, *a*. Having the nature or color of flame.
**Flange,** flanj, *n*. A projecting rim or edge on any substance; a raised edge on a wheel, etc.—*vt*. (flanging, flanged). To furnish with a flange.
**Flank,** flangk, *n*. The part of the side of an animal, between the ribs and the hip; the side of an army; the extreme right or left; the side of any building.—*vt*. To be situated at the side of; to place troops so as to command or attack the flank; to pass round the side of.
**Flannel,** flan'el, *n*. A soft, nappy, woollen cloth of loose texture; garment made of flannel.
**Flap,** flap, *n*. Something broad and flexible that hangs loose; the motion or sound of anything broad and loose, or a stroke with it; tail of a coat, etc.—*vt*. (flapping, flapped). To beat with a flap; to move; as something broad.—*vi*. To move, as wings; to wave loosely.
**Flap-dragon,** flap'dra-gon, *n*. A game of snatching raisins out of burning brandy.
**Flap-eared,** flap'ērd, *a*. Having broad loose ears.
**Flap-jack,** flap'jak, *n*. A sort of broad pancake; an apple-puff; a flat powder-compact.
**Flapper,** flap'ėr, *n*. One who or that which flaps; a young wild duck; a young girl *(colloq.)*.
**Flare,** flār, *vi*. (flaring, flared). To burn with an unsteady light; to glitter with transient luster; to give out a dazzling light.—*n*. An unsteady strong light.
**Flaring,** flār'ing, *p.a*. Glittering; showy.
**Flash,** flash, *n*. A sudden burst of flame and light; a gleam.—*a*. Vulgarly showy; counterfeit,—*vi*. To burst or break forth with a flash; to dart.—*vt*. To throw out like a burst of light.
**Flashily,** flash'i-li, *adv*. Gaudily; showily.
**Flash-point, Flashing-point,** flash'point, flash'ing-point, *n*. The temperature at which the vapor of oils will ignite and flash.
**Flashy,** flash'i, *a*. Charactertized by empty show; gaudy; impulsive.
**Flask,** flask, *n*. A kind of bottle; a bottle for the pocket; a vessel for powder.
**Flat,** flat, *a*. Having an even surface; level; fallen; tasteless; vapid; depressed; dull; absolute; below the true pitch, as a sound.—*n*. A level; a shallow; the broad side of something; a mark in music ♭ indicating lowering of pitch; a story or floor of a house; a simpleton.
**Flatly,** flat'li, *adv*. In a flat manner; horizontally; evenly; without spirit; positively.
**Flatten,** flat'n, *vt*. To make flat; to level; to render less acute or sharp, as a sound.—*vi*. To grow or become flat.
**Flatter,** flat'ėr, *vt*. To gratify by praise; to compliment; to praise falsely.
**Flatterer,** flat'ėr-ėr, *n*. One who flatters; a fawner; a wheedler.
**Flattering,** flat'ėr-ing, *a*. Bestowing flattery; agreeable to one's self-love; gratifying.
**Flattery,** flat'ė-ri, *n*. False praise; sycophancy; ca-

jolery.

**Flatulence, Flatulency,** flat'ū-lens, flat'ū-len-si, *n.* State of being flatulent.

**Flatulent,** flat'ū-lent, *a.* Affected with gases in the stomach and intestines; generating wind in the stomach; empty; puffy.

**Flatwise,** flat'wīz, *a.* or *adv.* With the flat side downward or next to another object.

**Flaunt,** flant, *vi.* and *t.* To display ostentatiously.—*n.* Bold or impudent parade.

**Flaunty, Flaunting,** flant'i, flant'ing, *a.* Apt to flaunt; ostentatious; gaudy.

**Flavor,** flā'vėr, *n.* The quality of a substance which affects the smell or taste; relish; zest.—*vt.* To give a flavor to.

**Flaw,** fla, *n.* A crack; a defect; a speck; a gust of wind.—*vt.* To make a flaw in.

**Flawless,** fla'les, *a.* Without defect; perfect.

**Flawy,** fla'i, *a.* Full of flaws or cracks.

**Flax,** flaks, *n.* A plant, the fibers of which are formed into linen threads; the fibers prepared for manufacture.

**Flax-dresser,** flaks'dres-ėr, *n.* One who combs and prepares flax for the spinner.

**Flaxen,** flaks'n, *a.* Made of or like flax; of the color of flax; fair.

**Flaxy,** flaks'i, *a.* Like flax; flaxen.

**Flay,** flā, *vt.* To strip the skin off an animal.

**Flea,** flē, *n.* An insect that leaps with great agility, and whose bite causes itch.

**Flea-bite,** flē'bīt, *n.* The bite of a flea; a thing of no moment.

**Fleam,** flēm, *n.* An instrument for opening the veins of animals to let blood.

**Fleck,** flek, *n.* A spot; streak; dapple.—*vt.* To spot; to streak or stripe; to dapple.

**Flection,** flek'shon, *n.* Act of bending; state of being bent.

**Fledge,** flej, *vt.* (fledging, fledged). To supply with the feathers necessary for flight.

**Fledgling,** flej'ling, *n.* A bird just fledged.

**Flee,** flē, *vi.* (fleeing, fled). To run away; to hasten from.—*vt.* To shun.

**Fleece,** flēs, *n.* The coat of wool that covers a sheep, or is shorn at one time.—*vt.* (fleecing, fleeced). To strip of the fleece; to rob or cheat heartlessly; to cover as with a fleece.

**Fleecy,** flēs'i, *a.* Resembling wool or a fleece; covered with wool; woolly.

**Fleer,** flēr, *vi.* To grin with an air of civility; to mock; to leer.—*n.* A leer; derision or mockery expressed by words or looks.

**Fleet,** flēt, *n.* A squadron or body of ships; navy.—*a.* Swift of pace; nimble.—*vi.* To fly swiftly; to be in a transient state.

**Fleeting,** flēt'ing, *a.* Not durable; transient; momentary.

**Fleetly,** flēt'li, *adv.* Rapidly; swiftly.

**Fleming,** flem'ing, *n.* A native of Flanders.

**Flemish,** flem'ish, *a.* Pertaining to Flanders.—*n.* The language of the Flemings.

**Flesh,** flesh, *n.* The muscular part of an animal; animal food; beasts and birds used as food; the body, as distinguished from the soul; mankind; corporeal appetities; kindred; family.—*vt.* To feed with flesh; to initiate to the taste of flesh.

**Flesh-brush,** flesh'brush, *n.* A brush for exciting action in the skin by friction.

**Fleshed,** flesht, *a.* Fat; fleshy; having flesh of a particular kind.

**Flesher,** flesh'ėr, *n.* A butcher.

**Flesh-fly,** flesh'flī, *n.* A fly that feeds on flesh, and deposits her eggs in it.

**Fleshings,** flesh'ingz, *n.pl.* Tight-fitting flesh-colored garments.

**Fleshly,** flesh'li, *a.* Carnal; worldly; lascivious; human; not spiritual.

**Flesh-wound,** flesh'wönd, *n.* A wound which affects the flesh only.

**Fleshy,** flesh'i, *a.* Muscular; fat; corpulent; plump; pulpy.

**Flex,** fleks, *vt.* To bend.

**Flexibility,** fleks-i-bil'i-ti, *n.* Quality of being flexible; pliancy; readiness to comply.

**Flexible,** fleks'i-bl, *a.* That may be bent; pliant; supple; tractable; plastic.

**Flexile,** fleks'īl, *a.* Pliant.

**Flexion,** flek'shon, *n.* Act of bending; a bend; part bent.

**Flexor,** fleks'ėr, *n.* A muscle which produces flexion.

**Flexuous, Flexuose,** fleks'ū-us, fleks'ū-ōs, *a.* Winding; bending.

**Flexure,** fleks'ūr, *n.* A bending; form of bending; part bent.

**Flick,** flik, *n.* A sharp sudden stroke, as with a whip; a flip.—*vt.* To strike with a flick; to flip.

**Flicker,** flik'ėr, *vi.* To flutter; to waver, as an unsteady flame.—*n.* A wavering gleam.

**Flier, Flyer,** flī'ėr, *n.* One who flies or flees; a part of a machine which moves rapidly.

**Flight,** flīt, *n.* Act of fleeing or flying; power or manner of flying; a flock of birds; a volley, as of arrows; pace passed by flying; a soaring; lofty elevation, as of fancy; extravagant sally; a series of steps or stairs.

F

**Flighty,** flīt'i, *a.* Full of flights or sallies of imagination, caprice, etc.; volatile; giddy.

**Flimsy,** flim'zi, *a.* Thin; slight; weak; without force; shallow.

**Flinch,** flinsh, *vi* to shrink; to withdraw; to wince; to fail.

**Fling,** fling, *vt.* (flinging, flung). To cause to fly from the hand; to hurl; to scatter; to throw to the ground.—*vi.* To fly into violent and irregular motions; to flounce; to rush away angrily.—*n.* A throw; a gibe; a lively Scottish dance.

**Flint,** flint, *n.* A very hard siliceous stone, which strikes fire with steel; anything proverbially hard.

**Flint-lock,** flint'lok, *n.* A musket-lock in which fire is produced by a flint.

**Flinty,** flint'i, *a.* Consisting of or like flint; very hard; cruel; inexorable.

**Flip,** flip, *n.* A flick; a drink consisting of beer and spirit sweetened, and heated by a hot iron.—*vt.* To flick.

**Flippancy,** flip'an-si, *n.* Quality of being flippant; heedless pertness; undue levity.

**Flippant,** flip'ant, *a.* Speaking confidently, without knowledge; heedlessly pert; shallow.

**Flipper,** flip'ėr, *n.* The paddle of a sea-turtle; the broad fin of a fish; the arm of a seal.

**Flirt,** flėrt, *vt.* To throw with a jerk; to make coquettish motions with (a fan).—*vi.* To run and dart about; to coquette; to play at courtship.—*n.* A sudden jerk; one who plays at courtship; a coquette.

**Flirtation,** flėrt-ā'shon, *n.* Playing at courtship; coquetry.

**Flit,** flit, *vi.* (flitting, flitted). To fly or dart along; to flutter; to change habitation (Scottish in this sense).

**Float,** flōt, *n.* That which is borne on water or any fluid; a raft.—*vi.* To be borne on the surface of a fluid; to be buoyed up; to move with a light, irregular course.—*vt.* To cause to be conveyed on water; to flood; to get (a company, scheme, etc.) started.

**Floatage,** flōt'āj, *n.* Anything that floats on the water; floating capacity or buoyancy.

**Float-board,** flōt'bōrd, *n.* A board of an undershot water-wheel, on which the water strikes; board of a paddle-wheel.

**Floating,** flōt'ing, *p.a.* Circulating; fluctuating; not fixed or invested; unattached.

**Flocculent,** flok'ū-lent, *a.* Adhering in locks or flakes; fleecy.

**Flock,** flok, *n.* A lock of wool or hair; stuffing for mattresses, etc.; a company, as of sheep, birds, etc.; a Christian congregation in relation to their pastor.—*vi.* To gather in companies; to crowd; to move in crowds.

**Flock-bed,** flok'bed, *n.* A bed stuffed with flocks of wool, or cloth cut up fine.

**Flock-paper,** flok'pā-per, *n.* A wall-paper having

raised figures made of powdered wool attached by size and varnish.

**Floe,** flō, *n.* A mass of ice floating in the ocean.

**Flog,** flog, *vt.* (flogging, flogged). To whip; to chastise with repeated blows.

**Flogging,** flog'ing, *n.* A whipping for punishment.

**Flood,** flud, *n.* A great flow of water; a deluge; a river; the flowing of the tide; a great quantity; abundance.—*vt.* To overflow; to deluge; to overwhelm.

**Flood-gate,** flud'gāt, *n.* A gate to stop or let out water.

**Flood-mark,** flud'märk, *n.* The line to which the tide rises; high-water mark.

**Flood-tide,** flud'tīd, *n.* The rising tide.

**Floor,** flōr, *n.* That part of a building on which we walk; bottom of a room; story in a building; a flat, hard surface of loam, lime, etc., used in some kinds of business, as in malting.—*vt.* To lay a floor upon; to strike down.

**Flooring,** flōr'ing, *n.* A floor; materials for floors.

**Flop,** flop, *vt.* and *i* (flopping, flopped). To clap or flap; to let down suddenly; to plump down.—*n.* A sudden sinking to the ground.

**Flora,** flō'ra, *n.* The plants of a particular district or period; a work describing them.

**Floral,** flō'ral, *a.* Pertaining to or made of flowers.

**Florescence,** flō-res'ens, *n.* A flowering; season when plants expand their flowers.

**Floret,** flō'ret, *n.* A floweret; the separate little flower of an aggregate flower; a fencing foil; silk yarn or floss.

**Floriculture,** flō'ri-kul-tūr, *n.* The culture of flowers or flowering plants.

**Floriculturist,** flō'ri-kul-tūr-ist, *n.* One skilled in the cultivation of flowers.

**Florid,** flo'rid, *a.* Flowery; bright in color; flushed with red; embellished with flowers of rhetoric; highly decorated.

**Florin,** flo'rin, *n.* A coin of different countries; a British coin.

**Florist,** flo'rist, *n.* A cultivator of flowers; one who writes a flora.

**Floscule,** flos'kūl, *n.* A little flower; a floret.

**Floss,** flos, *n.* A downy or silky substance in plants; fine untwisted silk used in embroidery.

**Flossy,** flos'i, *a.* Composed of or like floss.

**Flotation,** flōt-ā'shon, *n.* Act of floating; the doctrine of floating bodies.

**Flotilla,** flō-til'la, *n.* A little fleet, or fleet of small vessels.

**Flotsam,** flot'sam, *n.* Portion of a wreck that continues floating.

**Flounce,** flouns, *vi.* (flouncing, flounced). To spring or turn with sudden effort; to start away in anger.—*vt.* To deck with a flounce or flounces.—*n.* A strip of cloth sewed around a gown with the lower border loose and spreading.

**Flounder,** floun'dėr, *n.* A flat fish found in the sea near the mouths of rivers.—*vi.* To struggle, as in mire; to roll, toss, and tumble.

**Flour,** flour, *n.* Finely ground meal of wheat or other grain; fine powder of any substance.—*vt.* To convert into flour; to sprinkle with flour.

**Flourish,** flu'rish, *vi.* To grow luxuriantly; to thrive; to live; to use florid language; to make ornamental strokes in writing, etc.; to move in bold and irregular figures.—*vt.* To adorn with flowers or figures; to ornament with anything showy; to brandish.—*n.* Showy splendor; parade of words and figures; fanciful stroke of the pen; decorative notes in music; brandishing.

**Flourishing,** flu'rish-ing, *p.a.* Prosperous; growing luxuriantly.

**Floury,** flour'i, *a.* Resembling flour.

**Flout,** flout, *vt.* To mock or insult; to jeer at.—*n.* A mock; an insult.

**Flow,** flō, *vi.* To move, as water; to issue; to abound; to glide smoothly; to hang loose and waving; to rise, as the tide; to circulate, as blood.—*vt.* To flow over; to flood.—*n.* A moving along, as of water; stream; current; rise of water; fullness; free expression; feeling.

**Flower,** flou'ėr, *n.* The delicate and gaily-colored leaves or petals on a plant; a bloom or blossom; youth; the prime; the best part; one most distinguished; an ornamental expression; *pl.* a powdery substance.—*vi.* To blossom; to bloom.—*vt.* To embellish with figures of flowers.

**Floweret,** flou'ėr-et, *n.* A small flower.

**Flowering,** flou'ėr-ing, *p.a.* Having flowers; blossoming.

**Flowery,** flou'ėr-i, *a.* Full of flowers; embellished with figurative language; florid.

**Flowing,** flō'ing, *p.a.* Moving as a steam; abounding; fluent; undulating.

**Flown,** flōn, pp. of *fly*.

**Fluctuate,** fluk'tū-āt, *vi.* To move as a wave; to waver; to hesitate; to experience vicissitudes.

**Fluctuating,** fluk'tū-āt-ing, *p.a.* Unsteady; wavering.

**Fluctuation,** fluk-tū-ā'shon, *n.* A rising and falling; change; vicissitude.

**Flue,** flö, *n.* A passage for smoke or heated air; a pipe for conveying heat; light downy matter; fluff.

**Fluency,** flu'en-si, *n.* Quality of being fluent; facility of words; volubility.

**Fluent,** flu'ent, *a.* Flowing; ready in the use of words; voluble; smooth.

**Fluently,** flu'ent-li, *adv.* In a fluent manner; with ready flow of words.

**Fluff,** fluf, *n.* Light down or nap such as rises from beds, cotton, etc.

**Fluid,** flu'id, *a.* Capable of flowing; liquid or gaseous.—*n.* Any substance whose parts easily move and change their relative position without separation; a liquid.

**Fluidity,** flu-id'i-ti, *n.* Quality or state of being fluid.

**Fluke,** flök, *n.* That part of an anchor which fastens in the ground; an accidental success; a flat-fish; a parasitic worm.

**Flume,** flöm, *n.* A channel for the water that drives a mill-wheel; an artifical channel for gold-washing.

**Flummery,** flum'mė-ri, *n.* A sort of jelly made of flour or meal; flattery; nonsense.

**Flunkey,** flung'ki, *n.* A male servant in livery; a cringing flatterer; a toady.

**Fluor-spar,** flö'or-spär, *n.* A mineral exhibiting yellow, green, blue, and red tints.

**Flurry,** flu'ri, *n.* Bustle; hurry; a gust of wind; light things carried by the wind.—*vt.* (flurrying, flurried). To agitate or alarm.

**Flush,** flush, *vi.* To become suddenly red, to blush.—*vt.* To cause to redden suddenly; to elate; to excite; to wash out by copious supplies of water; to cause to start up.—*n.* A sudden flow of blood to the face; sudden thrill; vigor; flow of water; run of cards of the same suit.—*a.* Fresh; full of vigor; affluent; even with the adjacent surface.

**Fluster,** flus'tėr, *vt.* To agitate; to make hot with drink.—*n.* Agitation; confusion; heat.

**Flute,** flöt, *n.* A small wind-instrument with holes and keys; a channel cut along the shaft of a column; a similar channel.—*vi.* (fluting, fluted). To play on a flute.—*vt.* To play or sing in notes like those of a flute; to form flutes or channels in.

**Fluted,** flöt'ed, *p.a.* Channeled; furrowed.

**Fluting,** flöt'ing, *n.* A channel or furrow; fluted work; sound like that of a flute.

**Flutist,** flöt'ist, *n.* A performer on the flute.

**Flutter,** flut'ėr, *vi.* To move or flap the wings rapidly; to be in agitation; to fluctuate.—*vt.* To agitate; to throw into confusion.—*n.* Quick, confused motion; agitation; disorder.

**Fluty,** flöt'i, *a.* Having the sound of a flute.

**Fluvial,** flö'vi-al, *a.* Belonging to rivers.

**Fluviatile,** flö'vi-a-tīl, *a.* Belonging to rivers; produced by river action.

**Flux,** fluks, *n.* Act of flowing, any flow of matter;

dysentery; flow of the tide; anything used to promote fusion; fusion; liquid state from the operation of heat.—*vt*. To melt; to fuse.

**Fluxion,** fluk'shon, *n*. Act of flowing; flux; a flow of blood or other fluid; an infintely small quantity; *pl*. the analysis of infintely small variable quantities.

**Fluxional, Fluxionary,** fluk'shon-al, fluk'-shon-a-ri, *a*. Pertaining to mathematical fluxions.

**Fly,** flī, *vi*. (flying, pret. flew, pp. flown). To move through air by wings; to move in air by the force of wind, etc.; to rise in air; to move rapidly; to pass away; to depart suddenly; to spring; to flutter.—*vt*. To flee from; to cause to float in the air.—*n*. A winged insect; a revolving mechanism to regulate the motion of machinery; a light carriage; a cab.

**Fly-blow,** flī'blō, *vt*. To taint with eggs which produce maggots.—*n*. The egg of a fly.

**Fly-fishing,** flī'fish-ing, *n*. Angling for fish with flies, natural or artifical.

**Flying-bomb,** flī'ing-bom, *n*. A large self-propelled projectile, first used by the Germans in 1944.

**Flying-fish,** flī'ing-fish, *n*. A fish which can sustain itself in the air for a time by means of its long pectoral fins.

**Fly-leaf,** flī'lēf, *n*. A leaf of blank paper at the beginning and end of a book.

**Fly-paper,** flī'pā-pėr, *n*. A paper for destroying flies.

**Fly-wheel,** flī'whēl, *n*. A wheel to equalize the motive power of a machine.

**Foal,** fōl, *n*. The young of a mare, she-ass, etc.; a colt or filly.—*vt*. To bring forth, as a colt or filly.—*vi*. To bring forth a foal.

**Foam,** fōm, *n*. Froth; spume.—*vi*. To froth; to show froth at the mouth; to rage.—*vt*. To cause to give out foam; to throw out with rage or violence.

**Foamy,** fōm'i, *a*. Covered with foam; frothy.

**Fob,** fob, *n*. A little pocket for a watch in the waistband of the breeches.

**Focal,** fō'kal, *a*. Belonging to a focus.

**Focus,** fō'kus, *n*.; pl. **-cuses** or **-ci.** A point in which rays of light meet after being reflected or refracted; point of concentration.—*vt*. To bring to a focus.

**Fodder,** fod'ėr, *n*. Food for cattle, etc.—*vt*. To furnish with fodder.

**Foe,** fō, *n*. An enemy; an opposing army; one who opposes anything.

**Foeman,** fō'man, *n*. A personal antagonist.

**Fog,** fog, *n*. A dense vapor near the surface of the land or water; mental confusion; dimness; second growth of grass; long grass that remains in pastures till winter.

**Fogey, Fogy,** fō'gi, *n*.; pl. **-eys, -ies.** A stupid fellow; an old-fashioned person.

**Foggage,** fog'āj, *n*. Rank or coarse grass not eaten down.

**Foggy,** fog'i, *a*. Filled with fog; cloudy; misty; producing fogs; stupid.

**Foible,** foi'bl, *n*. A weak point in character; a failing; the weak part of a sword.

**Foil,** foil, *vt*. To frustrate; to baffle; to balk.—*n*. Defeat; frustration; a sword used in fencing; a thin leaf of metal; anything which serves to set off a thing to advantage; something resembling a leaf; a curve in the tracery of Gothic windows, etc.

**Foist,** foist, *vt*. To introduce or insert surreptitiously or without warrant; to palm off.

**Fold,** fōld, *n*. The doubling or doubled part of any flexible substance; a plait; an enclosure for sheep; a flock of sheep; the Church.—*vt*. To double; to lay in plaits; to embrace; to confine, as sheep in a fold.—*vi*. To close together; to become folded.

**Folder,** fōld'ėr, *n*. One who folds; an instrument used in folding paper.

**Foliaceous,** fō-li-ā'shus, *a*. Leafy; of the nature or form of a leaf.

**Foliage,** fō'li-āj, *n*. Leaves collectively; ornamental representation of leaves.

**Foliate,** fō'li-āt, *vt*. To beat into a leaf or thin plate of lamina.

**Foliated,** fō'li-āt-ed, *p.a*. Covered with a thin plate; being in laminae; having leaf-shaped ornaments.

**Foliation,** fō-li'ā'shon, *n*. The leafing of plants; operation of spreading foil over a surface; property in certain rocks of dividing into laminae; tracery of Gothic windows.

**Folio,** fō'li-ō, *n*. A book of the largest size, formed by sheets of paper once doubled; a page; number appended to each page; a written page of a certain number of words.

**Folk,** fōk, *n*. People in general; certain people discriminated from others, as old *folks*.

**Folk-lore,** fōk'lōr, *n*. Rural superstitions, tales, traditions, or legends.

**Follicle,** fol'li-kl, *n*. A little bag or vesicle in animals or plants.

F

**Follow,** fol'ō, *vt*. To go or come after; to chase; to accompany; to succeed; to result from; to understand; to copy; to practice; to be occupied with; to be guided by.—*vi*. To come after another, to ensure, to result.

**Follower,** fol'ō-ėr, *n*. An adherent; disciple; imitator; attendant; dependent.

**Following,** fol'ō-ing, *n*. A body of followers.—*p.a*. Being next after; succeeding.

**Folly,** fol'i, *n*. Foolishness; imbecility; a weak or foolish act; criminal weakness.

**Foment,** fō-ment', *vt*. To apply warm lotions to; to abet; to stir up (in a bad sense).

**Fomentation,** fō-ment-ā'shon, *n*. Act of fomenting; lotion applied; instigation; encouragement.

**Fomenter,** fō-ment'ėr, *n*. One who foments; one who encourages or instigates.

**Fond,** fond, *a*. Foolish; foolishly tender and loving; doting; loving; relishing.

**Fondle,** fon'dl, *vt*. (fondling, fondled). To treat with fondness; to caress.

**Fondly,** fond'li, *adv*. Foolishly; lovingly.

**Fondness,** fond'nes, *n*. Affection; great liking.

**Font,** font, *n*. A large basin in which water is contained for baptizing; a complete assortment of printing types of one size.

**Food,** föd, *n*. Whatever supplies nourishment to animals or plants; nutriment; provisions; whatever feeds or augments.

**Fool,** föl, *n*. One destitute of reason; a simpleton; a silly person; a buffoon.—*vi*. To play the fool; to trifle.—*vt*. To make a fool of; to deceive.

**Foolery,** föl'ė-ri, *n*. Habitual folly; act of folly; absurdity.

**Foolhardy,** föl'här-di, *a*. Daring without judgment; foolishly bold; venturesome.

**Foolish,** föl'ish, *a*. Void of understanding; acting without judgment or discretion; silly; ridiculous; unwise.

**Foolishly,** föl'ish-li, *adv*. Unwisely; absurdly.

**Foolscap,** fölz'kap, *n*. Paper of the smallest regular size but one, about 17 inches by 14.

**Foot,** fut, *n*.; pl. **feet,** fēt. The lower extremity of the leg; that on which a thing stands; the base; infantry; a measure of twelve inches; a measure of syllables in a verse.—*vi*. to dance; to tread to measure or music; to skip; to walk.—*vt*. To tread; to dance; to trip; to add a foot to, as to a stocking.

**Football,** fut'bal, *n*. An inflated leather ball to be driven by the foot; a game played with such a ball.

**Foot-boy,** fut'boi, *n*. An attendant in livery.

**Foot-cloth,** fut'kloth, *n*. The covering of a horse, reaching down to his heels.

**Footfall,** fut'fal, *n*. A footstep; a stumble.

**Foothold,** fut'hōld, *n*. That on which one may tread or rest securely; firm standing.

**Footing,** fut'ing, *n*. Ground for the foot; established place; basis; tread.

**Foot-lights,** fut'līts, *n.pl*. A row of lights in a theater on the front of the stage.

**Footman,** fut'man, *n*. A menial servant; a runner;

a servant in livery.
**Footmark,** fut'märk, *n.* Mark of a foot.
**Footpad,** fut'pad, *n.* A highwayman or robber on foot.
**Footpath,** fut'path, *n.* A narrow path for foot passengers only.
**Foot-pound,** fut'pound, *n.* The unit of work done by a mechanical force, representing one pound weight raised through a height of one foot.
**Footprint,** fut'print, *n.* The impression of the foot.
**Foot-sore,** fut'sōr, *a.* Having the feet sore or tender, as by much walking.
**Foot-stalk,** fut'stak, *n.* The stalk of a leaf.
**Footstep,** fut'step, *n.* A track; the mark of the foot; vestige; *pl.* example; course.
**Footstool,** fut'stöl, *n.* A stool for the feet.
**Fop,** fop, *n.* A coxcomb; a dandy.
**For,** for, *prep.* In the place of; because of; in favor of; toward; during; in quest of; according to; as far as; notwithstanding; in proportion to.—*conj.* Because.
**Forage,** fo'rāj, *n.* Food for horses and cattle; act of providing forage.—*vi.* (foraging, foraged). To collect forage; to rove in search of food.—*vt.* To strip of provisions for horses, etc.; to supply with forage. **Forage cap,** *n.* Undress cap worn by soldiers of all branches of the army.
**Forager,** fo'rāj-ėr, *n.* One who forages.
**Forament,** fō-rā'men, *n.*; pl. **Foramina,** fō-ram'in-a. A small natural opening in animals or plants.
**Foraminifera,** fō-ram'i-nif''ėr-a, *n.pl.* An order of minute animals furnished with a shell perforated by pores.
**Foraminous,** fō-ram'in-us, *a.* Full of minute holes; porous.
**Forasmuch,** for-az-much', *conj.* In consideration of; because that.
**Foray,** fo'rā, *vt.* To ravage; to pillage.—*n.* A predatory excursion; a raid.
**Forbear,** for-bār', *vi.* To keep away; to cease; to delay; to refrain.—*vt.* To abstain from; to avoid doing.
**Forbearance,** for-bār'ans, *n.* Act of forbearing; restraint of passion; long-suffering; mildness.
**Forbearing,** for-bār'ing, *p.a.* Patient; long-suffering.
**Forbid,** for-bid', *vt.* To prohibit; to oppose; to obstruct.—*vi.* To utter a prohibition.
**Forbidden,** for-bid'n, *p.a.* Prohibited.
**Forbidding,** for-bid'ing, *p.a.* Repelling approach; disagreeable; repulsive.
**Force,** fōrs, *n.* Strength; active power; might; violence; coercion; cogency; efficacy; power for war; troops; a waterfall.—*vt.* (forcing, forced). To compel; to impel; to take by violence; to ravish; to twist or overstrain; to ripen by artificial means; to stuff; to farce.—*vi.* To use force or violence.
**Forced,** fōrst, *p.a.* Affected; overstrained; unnatural.
**Forceful,** fōrs'ful, *a.* Possessing force; acting with power; impetuous.
**Forceless,** fōrs'les, *a.* Feeble; impotent.
**Forcemeat,** fōrs'mēt, *n.* Meat chopped and seasoned, served up alone or as stuffing.
**Forceps,** for'seps, *n.* A surgical instrument on the principle of pincers for holding anything difficult to be held by the hand.
**Forcible,** fōrs'i-bl, *a.* Efficacious; potent; cogent; done by force; suffered by force.
**Forcing,** fōrs'ing, *n.* Art of raising plants or fruits, at an earlier season than the natural one, by artifical heat.
**Forclosure,** *See* FORECLOSE.
**Ford,** fōrd, *n.* A shallow place in a river or other water, where it may be passed on foot.—*vt.* To cross by walking; to wade through.
**Fordable,** fōrd'a-bl, *a.* That may be forded.
**Fore,** fōr, *a.* In front of; anterior; coming first in time; prior.—*adv.* In the part that precedes or goes first.
**Fore-and-aft,** fōr'and-äft, *a.* In a direction from stem to stern.
**Fore-arm,** fōr'ärm, *n. vt.* The part of the arm between the elbow and the wrist.
**Forearm,** fōr'ärm', *vt.* To arm for attack or resistance before the time of need.
**Forebode,** fōr-bōd', *vt.* To foretell; to prognosticate; to be prescient of.
**Forecast,** fōr-käst', *vt.* To foresee; to scheme beforehand.—*vi.* To foresee.—*n.* fōr'käst. Contrivance beforehand; foresight; estimate of what will happen.
**Forecastle,** fōr'kas-l, *n.* That part of the upper deck of a vessel forward of the foremast; the forward part of a merchant vessel.
**Foreclose,** fōr-klōz', *vt.* To preclude; to stop.
**Foreclosure,** fōr-klōz'ūr, *n.* Prevention.
**Foredoom,** fōr-döm', *vt.* To doom beforehand.
**Forefather,** fōr'fä-THėr, *n.* A progenitor; an ancestor.
**Forefinger,** fōr'fing-gėr, *n.* The finger next to the thumb.
**Fore-foot,** fōr'fut, *n.* One of the anterior feet of a quadruped.
**Forefront,** fōr'frunt, *n.* The foremost part.
**Forego,** fōr-gō', *vt.* To go before; to precede. *See* FORGO.
**Foregone,** fōr-gon', or fōr'gon, *p.a.* Past; preceding; predetermined.
**Foreground,** fōr'ground, *n.* The part of a scene or picture represented as nearest the observer.
**Forehand,** fōr'hand, *a.* Done sooner than is regular or necessary; anticipative.
**Forehanded,** fōr'hand-ed, *a.* Early; timely; seasonable; prosperous.
**Forehead,** fōr'hed or fo'red, *n.* The part of the face above the eyes; the brow.
**Foreign,** fo'rin, *a.* Belonging to another nation or country; alien; not to the purpose; irrelevant.
**Foreigner,** fo'rin-ėr, *n.* A person born in a foreign country; an alien.
**Forejudge,** fōr-juj', *vt.* To judge beforehand, or before hearing the facts and proof.
**Forejudgment,** fōr-juj'ment, *n.* Judgment previously formed.
**Foreknow,** fōr-nō', *vt.* To know beforehand; to foresee.
**Foreknowledge,** fōr-nol'ej, *n.* Knowledge of a thing before it happens.
**Foreland,** fōr'land, *n.* Headland; cape.
**Foreleg,** fōr'leg, *n.* One of the anterior legs of an animal, chair, etc.
**Forelock,** fōr'lok, *n.* The lock of hair that grows from the fore part of the head.
**Foreman,** fōr'man, *n.* The first or chief man; chief man of a jury; chief workman.
**Foremast,** fōr'mast, *n.* The forward mast in any vessel.
**Foremost,** fōr'mōst, *a.* First in place, time, rank, or dignity; most advanced.
**Forenoon,** fōr'nön, *n.* The part of the day before noon, or from morning to noon.
**Forensic,** fō-ren'sik, *a.* Belonging to courts of justice, or to public debate; used in courts or legal proceedings.
**Forepart,** fōr'pärt, *n.* The anterior part; part first in time; part most advanced in place; beginning.
**Forerun,** fōr-run', *vt.* To run before; to usher in; to prognosticate.
**Forerunner,** fōr'run-ėr, *n.* One who runs before; harbinger; precursor; prognostic.
**Foresaid,** fōr'sed, *p.a.* Aforesaid.
**Foresail,** fōr'sāl, *n.* The lowermost square sail set on the foremast; a large fore-and-aft sail on a schooner's foremast.
**Foresee,** fōr-sē', *vt.* To see beforehand; to foreknow.
**Foreshadow,** fōr-sha'dō, *vt.* To shadow or typify beforehand.
**Foreshore,** fōr'shōr, *n.* The sloping part of a shore between high and low water-mark.
**Foreshorten,** fōr-short'n, *vt.* To shorten, in drawing and painting, the parts of figures that stand

forward.
**Foresight,** fōr'sit, *n.* Foreknowledge; provident care; forethought; sight on muzzle of gun or rifle.
**Forest,** fo'rest, *n.* An extensive wood; a district devoted to the purposes of the chase; a tract once a royal forest.—*a.* Relating to a forest; sylvan; rustic.—*vt.* To convert into a forest.
**Forestall,** fōr-stąl', *vt.* To anticipate; to hinder by preoccupation.
**Forester,** fo'rest-ėr, *n.* One who watches a forest and preserves the game; one who manages the timber on an estate; an inhabitant of a forest.
**Forestry,** fo'rest-ri, *n.* Art of cultivating forests, or of managing growing timber.
**Foretaste,** fōr'tāst, *n.* A taste beforehand; anticipation.—*vt.* to taste before possession; to anticipate.
**Foretell,** fōr-tel', *vt.* To tell beforehand; to predict.—*vi.* To utter prophecy.
**Forethought,** fōr'that, *n.* A thinking beforehand; foresight; provident care.
**Foretoken,** fōr-tō'kn, *vt.* To betoken beforehand.—*n.* A previous sign; prognostic.
**Foretop,** fōr'top, *n.* Hair on the forepart of the head; platform at the head of a foremast.
**Forever,** for-ev'ėr, *adv.* At all times; through endless ages; eternally.
**Fore-vouched,** fōr-voucht', *a.* Affirmed before.
**Forewarn,** fōr-warn', *vt.* To warn beforehand, to give previous notice to.
**Foreword,** fōr'wėrd, *n.* A preface.
**Forfeit,** for'fit, *vt.* To lose by a misdeed.—*n.* That which is forfeited; fine; penalty.
**Forfeitable,** for'fit-a-bl, *a.* Liable to be forfeited.
**Forfeiture,** for'fit-ūr, *n.* Act of forfeiting; loss of some right, estate, honor, etc., by a crime or fault; fine; penalty.
**Forfend,** for-fend', *vt.* To ward off; to avert.
**Forgather,** for-gaᴛʜ'ėr, *vi.* To meet.
**Forge,** fōrj, *n.* A furnace in which iron is heated and wrought; a smithy.—*vt.* (forging, forged). To frame or fabricate; to form by heating and hammering; to counterfeit.—*vi.* To commit forgery; to move on slowly and laboriously; to work one's way.
**Forger,** fōrj'ėr, *n.* One who forges; one who counterfeits.
**Forgery,** fōrj'ė-ri, *n.* The crime of counterfeiting; that which is forged or counterfeited.
**Forget,** for-get', *vt.* (forgetting, pret, forgot, pp. forgot, forgotten). To lose the remembrance of; to slight; to neglect.
**Forgetful,** for-get'ful, *a.* Apt to forget; neglectful; oblivious.
**Forgetfulness,** for-get'ful-nes, *n.* Oblivion; obliviousness; inattention.
**Forget-me-not,** for-get'mē-not, *n.* A small, bright blue flower.
**Forging,** fōrj'ing, *n.* The act of one who forges; an article of metal forged.
**Forgive,** for-giv', *vt.* (forgiving, pret. forgave, pp. forgiven). To pardon; to remit; to overlook.
**Forgiveness,** for-giv'nes, *n.* Act of forgiving; pardon; disposition to pardon; remission.
**Forgiving,** for-giv'ing, *p.a.* Disposed to forgive; merciful; compassionate.
**Forgo,** for-gō', *vt.* To forbear to enjoy or possess; to renounce; to resign.
**Forisfamiliate,** fō'ris-fa-mil''i-āt, *vt.* To free from parental authority; to put in possession of property in his father's lifetime.
**Fork,** fork, *n.* An instrument with two or more prongs, used for lifting or pitching anything; a branch or division; a prong.—*vi.* To shoot into branches; to divide into two.—*vt.* To raise or pitch with a fork, as hay, etc.
**Forked,** forkt, *a.* Opening into two or more prongs or shoots.
**Forky,** fork'i, *a.* Forked.
**Forlorn,** for-lorn', *a.* Deserted; abandoned; miserable.—**Forlorn hope,** a body of men appointed to perform some specially perilous service.
**Form,** form, *n.* Shape; manner; pattern; order; empty show; prescribed mode; ceremony; schedule; a long seat; a bench; a class; the seat or bed of a hare.—*vt.* To shape or mold; to arrange; to invent; to make up.—*vi.* To take a form.
**Formal,** form'al, *a.* Relating to outward form; according to form; precise; ceremonious; having mere appearance.
**Formalism,** form'al-izm, *n.* Quality of being addicted to mere forms; ceremonial religion.
**Formalist,** form'al-ist, *n.* One who observes forms.
**Formality,** form-al'i-ti, *n.* Quality of being formal; ceremony; a mere form.
**Formally,** form'al-li, *adv.* In a formal manner; precisely.
**Format,** for'mä, *n.* Size of a book as regards length and breadth; get-up.
**Formation,** form-ā'shon, *n.* Act of forming; production; manner in which a thing is formed; any assemblage of rocks or strata, referred to a common origin; arrangement.
**Formative,** form'at-iv, *a.* Giving form; plastic; derivative.—*n.* That which serves to give form to a word, and is no part of the root.
**Former,** form'ėr, *n.* He who forms.—*a. comp. deg.* Before in time; long past; mentioned before another.
**Formerly,** form'ėr-li, *adv.* In time past; of old; in days of yore.
**Formic,** for'mik, *a.* Pertaining to ants.
**Formicary,** for'mi-ka-ri, *n.* A colony of ants; an ant-hill.
**Formidable,** for'mid-a-bl, *a.* Exciting fear or apprehension; difficult to deal with or undertake.
**Formless,** form'les, *a.* Without a determinate form; shapeless.
**Formula,** for'mū-la, *n.*; pl. **-lae.** A prescribed form; a confession of faith; expression for resolving certain problems in mathematics; expression of chemical composition.
**Formulary,** for'mū-la-ri, *n.* A book containing prescribed forms, as of oaths, declarations, prayers; a book of precedents.—*a.* Prescribed; ritual.
**Formulate,** for'mū-lāt, *vt.* To express in a formula; to put into a precise and comprehensive statement.
**Fornicate,** for'ni-kāt, *vi.* To have unlawful sexual intercourse.
**Fornication,** for-ni-kā'shon, *n.* Incontinence of unmarried persons.
**Fornicator,** for'ni-kāt-ėr, *n.* One guilty of fornication.
**Forsake,** for-sāk', *vt.* (forsaking, pret, forsook, pp. forsaken). To abandon; to renounce; to withdraw from.
**Forswear,** for-swār', *vt.* To renounce upon oath; to abjure; to swear falsely; to perjure oneself.—*vi.* To swear falsely.
**Fort,** fōrt, *n.* A fortified place; a fortress.
**Fortalice,** fōr'ta-lis, *n.* A small fort; outwork of a fortification.
**Forte,** fōr'tā, *adv.* A direction to sing or play with force.
**Forte,** fōrt, *n.* The strong portion of a swordblade; peculiar talent; strong point; chief excellence.
**Forth,** fōrth, *adv.* Forward in place or order; out into public view; abroad; onward in time.
**Forthcoming,** fōrth-kum'ing, *a.* Coming forth; making appearance; ready to appear.
**Forthright,** fōrth'rīt, *adv.* Straight forward; straightway.—*a.* Straightforward; direct.
**Forthwith,** fōrth-with', *adv.* Without delay.
**Fortification,** for'ti-fi-kā''shon, *n.* The art or science of fortifying places; the works erected in defense; a fortified place; additional strength.
**Fortify,** for'ti-fī, *vt.* (fortifying, fortified). To make strong; to strengthen by forts, batteries, etc.; to invigorate; to increase the strength of.
**Fortissimo,** for-tis'sē-mō, *adv.* Direction to sing

or play with the utmost loudness.

**Fortitude,** for'ti-tūd, *n*. Firmness of mind to encounter danger or to bear pain or adversity; resolute endurance.

**Fortnight,** fort'nīt, *n*. The space of fourteen days; two weeks.

**Fortress,** fort'res, *n*. A fortified place; stronghold; place of security.

**Fortuitous,** for-tū'it-us, *a*. Happening by chance; accidental; incidental.

**Fortunate,** for'tū-nāt, *a*. Having good fortune; successful; coming by good luck.

**Fortunately,** for'tū-nāt-li, *adv*. By good fortune; happily.

**Fortune,** for'tūn, *n*. Chance; luck; the good or ill that befalls man; means of living; estate; great wealth; destiny; the power regarded as determining the lots of life.

**Fortune-hunter,** for'tūn-hunt-ėr, *n*. A man who seeks to marry a rich woman.

**Fortune-teller,** for'tūn-tel-ėr, *n*. One who pretends to foretell the events of one's life.

**Forty,** for'ti, *a*. and *n*. Four times ten.

**Forum,** fō'rum, *n*. A public place in ancient Rome, where causes were tried; a tribunal; jurisdiction.

**Forward,** for'wėrd, *adv*. Toward a place in front; onward.—*a*. Near or towards the forepart; in advance of something; ready; bold; pert; advanced beyond the usual degree; too ready.—*vt*. To help onward; to hasten; to send forward; to transmit.—*n*. In football, hockey, etc., one of the players in the front line.

**Forwardly,** for'wėrd-li, *adv*. Eagerly; hastily; pertly; saucily.

**Forwardness,** for'wėrd-nes, *n*. Promptness; eagerness; want of due reserve or modesty; pertness; earliness.

**Forwards,** for'wėrdz, *adv*. Same as *Forward*.

**Fosse,** fos, *n*. A ditch or moat; a trench; a kind of cavity in a bone.

**Fossick,** fos'ik, *vi*. To search for waste gold in relinquished workings, etc.

**Fossil,** fos'sil, *a*. Dug out of the earth; petrified and preserved in rocks.—*n*. Petrified remains of plants and animals found in the strata composing the surface of our globe.

**Fossiliferous,** fos-sil-if'ėr-us, *a*. Containing fossils.

**Fossilize,** fos'sil-īz, *vt*. To convert into a fossil state.—*vi*. To be changed into a fossil state; to become antiquated.

**Fossorial,** fos-sō'ri-al, *a*. Digging; burrowing.

**Foster,** fos'tėr, *vt*. To nourish; to bring up; to encourage; to promote.

**Foster-child,** fos'tėr-chīld, *n*. A child nursed by a woman not the mother; or bred by a man not the father. (Also *foster-brother, -mother, -parent,* etc.).

**Fother,** foᴛʜ'ėr, *n*. A weight for lead = 19½ cwts.—*vt*. To stop a leak by letting down a sail over it.

**Foul,** foul, *a*. Covered with or containing extraneous matter which is offensive; turbid; obscene; rainy or tempestuous; unfair; loathsome; entangled or in collision.—*vt*. To defile; to dirty.—*vi*. To become dirty; to come into collision; to become clogged.—*n*. A colliding, or impeding due motion; an unfair piece of play.

**Foulard,** fö-lärd', *n*. A thin silk fabric, without twill; a silk handkerchief.

**Foully,** foul'li, *adv*. Fithily; unfairly.

**Foul-mouthed,** foul'mouᴛʜd, *a*. Using scurrilous or abusive language.

**Found,** found, *vt*. To lay the base of; to establish; to institute; to form by melting metal and pouring it into a mold; to cast.—*vi*. To rest or rely (with *on* or *upon*). Pret. and pp. of *find*.

**Foundation,** found-ā'shon, *n*. Act of founding; base of an edifice; base; endowment; endowed institution.

**Foundationer,** found-ā'shon-ėr, *n*. One who derives support from the funds or foundation of a college or endowed school.

**Founder,** found'ėr, *n*. One who lays a foundation; an originator; an endower; one who casts metal.—*vi*. To fill with water and sink; to miscarry; to go lame, as a horse.

**Foundery,** found'ė-ri, *n*. The art of founding or casting; a foundry.

**Foundling,** found'ling, *n*. A child found without anyone to care for it.

**Foundry,** found'ri, *n*. An establishment for casting metals.

**Fount,** fount, *n*. A fountain *(poetical)*; a complete stock of printing type; a font.

**Fountain,** fount'ān, *n*. A spring or source of water; an artificial jet or shower; head of a river; original; source.

**Fountainhead,** fount'ān-hed, *n*. The head of a stream; primary source; origin.

**Fountain-pen,** fount'ān-pēn, *n*. A pen with a reservoir for ink.

**Four,** fōr, *a*. and *n*. Twice two; three and one.

**Fourfold,** fōr'fōld, *a*. and *adv*. Quadruple; four times told.—*n*. Four times as much.

**Four-in-hand,** fōr'in-hand, *n*. A vehicle drawn by four horses guided by one driver.

**Fourscore,** fōr'skōr, *a*. and *n*. Eighty.

**Foursquare,** fōr-skwār, *a*. Having four sides and four angles equal; quadrangular.

**Fourteen,** fōr'tēn, *a*. and *n*. Four and ten.

**Fourteenth,** fōr'tēnth, *a*. The ordinal or fourteen.—*n*. One of fourteen equal parts.

**Fourth,** fōrth, *a*. The ordinal of four.—*n*. One of four equal parts.

**Fourthly,** fōrth'li, *adv*. In the fourth place.

**Foveate, Foveolate,** fō'vē-āt, fō'vē-ō-lāt, *a*. Marked by little depressions or pits.

**Fowl,** foul, *n*. A bird; a domestic or barndoor bird.—*vt*. To catch wild fowls for game or food.

**Fowler,** foul'ėr, *n*. A sportsman who pursues wild fowls.

**Fowling-piece,** foul'ing-pēs, *n*. A light gun for shooting wild fowl.

**Fox,** foks, *n*. A carnivorous animal, remarkable for cunning; a sly cunning fellow.—*vt*. and *i*. To turn sour; to become marked with brown spots, as paper.

**Foxglove,** foks'gluv, *n*. A British plant yielding a powerful medicine, both sedative and diuretic; digitalis.

**Fox-hound,** foks'hound, *n*. A hound for chasing foxes.

**Fox-trot,** foks-trot, *n*. A dance of American origin.

**Foxy,** foks'i, *a*. Pertaining to foxes; wily; cunning; stained with reddish marks; sour.

**Fracas,** fra-käs', *n*. An uproar; a brawl.

**Fraction,** frak'shon, *n*. A fragment; a very small part; one or more of the equal parts into which a unit or number is divided.

**Fractional,** frak'shon-al, *a*. Belonging to a fraction; pertaining to a method of distillation by which products of different kinds are successively got from the substance treated.

**Fractionize, Fractionate,** frak'shon-īz, frak'-shon-āt, *vt*. To subject to the process of fractional distillation.

**Fractious,** frak'shus, *a*. Snappish; peevish; cross.

**Fracture,** frak'tūr, *n*. A breach or break; breaking of a bone; manner in which a mineral breaks.—*vt*. (fracturing, fractured). To break.

**Fragile,** fra'jīl, *a*. Easily broken; frail; weak.

**Fragility,** fra-jil'i-ti, *n*. Quality of being fragile; delicacy of substance.

**Fragment,** frag'ment, *n*. A part broken off; an imperfect thing.

**Fragmentary,** frag'ment-a-ri, *a*. Composed of fragments; not complete; disconnected.

**Fragrance, Fragrancy,** frā'grans, frā'gran-si, *n*. Quality of being fragrant; sweetness of smell; perfume.

**Fragrant,** frā'grant, *a*. Sweet-smelling; spicy; balmy; aromatic.

**Frail,** frāl, *a*. Easily broken; weak; liable to fail and decay.—*n*. A kind of basket.

**Frailty,** frāl'ti, *n.* State or quality of being frail; infirmity; liableness to be deceived or seduced; failing; foible.
**Frame,** frām, *vt.* (framing, framed). To make; to construct; to devise; to adjust; to shape; to place in a frame.—*n.* Anything composed of parts fitted together; structure; bodily structure; framework; particular state, as of the mind; mood or disposition.
**Framework,** frām'wėrk, *n.* A structure or fabric for supporting anything; a frame.
**Framing,** frām'ing, *n.* Act of constructing a frame; frame thus constructed; rough timber-work of a house.
**Franc,** frangk, *n.* A coin of France.
**Franchise,** fran'chīz, *n.* Right granted by a sovereign or government; right of voting for a member of parliament.
**Franciscan,** fran-sis'kan, *n.* A mendicant friar of the order of St. Francis; a Gray Friar.
**Francolin,** frang'ko-lin, *n.* A bird allied to the partridge.
**Frangibility,** fran-ji-bil'i-ti, *n.* The state or quality of being frangible.
**Frangible,** fran'ji-bl, *a.* That may be broken; brittle; fragile.
**Frank,** frangk', *n.* One of the ancient German race of the Franks; a name given by Orientals to inhabitants of W. Europe.
**Frank,** frangk, *a.* Free in uttering real sentiments; candid; outspoken.—*n.* Signature of a privileged person formerly securing free transmission of a letter.—*vt.* To exempt from postage.
**Frankincense,** frangk'in-sens, *n.* An odoriferous gum-resin used as a perfume.
**Franklin,** frangk'lin, *n.* Formerly an English freeholder; a yeoman.
**Frankly,** frangk'li, *adv.* In a frank manner; openly; freely; unreservedly.
**Frantic,** fran'tik, *a.* Mad; raving; furious; outrageous; distracted.
**Franticly, Frantically,** fran'tik-li, fran'tik-al-li, *adv.* Madly; outrageously.
**Fraternal,** fra-tėr'nal, *a.* Brotherly; pertaining to brethren; becoming brothers.
**Fraternity,** fra-tėr'ni-ti, *n.* State or relationship of a brother; brotherhood; society, class, or profession.
**Fraternize,** frat'ėr-nīz, *vi.* (fraternizing, fraternized). To associate as brothers, or as men of like occupation or disposition.
**Fratricidal,** fra-tri-sīd'al, *a.* Pertaining to fratricide.
**Fratricide,** fra'tri-sīd, *n.* Murder of a brother; one who murders a brother.
**Frau,** frou, *n.* German married woman or widow; title equivalent to *Mrs.*
**Fraud,** frad, *n.* Artifice by which the right or interest of another is injured; deception.
**Fraudful,** frad'ful, *a.* Full of fraud; deceitful.
**Fraudfully,** frad'ful-li, *adv.* In a fraudful or fraudulent manner.
**Fraudulence, Fraudulency,** frad'ū-lens, frad'ū-len-si, *n.* Quality of being fradulent.
**Fraudulent,** frad'ū-lent, *a.* Using fraud in bargains, etc.; founded on fraud; dishonest.
**Fraudulently,** frad'ū-lent-li, *adv.* By fraud, artifice, or imposition.
**Fraught,** frat, *a.* Freighted; stored; abounding; pregnant.
**Fräulein,** froi'līn, *n.* German unmarried woman; title equivalent to *Miss.*
**Fray,** frā, *n.* An affray; a broil; a night; a frayed place in cloth.—*vt.* To rub; to fret, as cloth, by wearing.—*vi.* Top become worn by rubbing.
**Freak,** frēk, *n.* A sudden causeless turn of the mind; a caprice; a sport.—*vt.* To variegate.
**Freakish,** frēk'ish, *a.* Capricious; grotesque.
**Freckle,** frek'l, *n.* A yellowish spot in the skin; any small spot or discoloration.—*vt.* or *i.* (freckling, freckled). To give or acquire freckles.
**Freckly,** frek'li, *a.* Sprinkled with freckles.
**Free,** frē, *a.* Being at liberty; instituted by a free people; not arbitrary or despotic; open; clear; disjoined; licentious; candid; generous; gratuitous; guiltless.—*vt.* (freeing, freed). To set free; to liberate; to disentangle; to exempt; to absolve from some charge.
**Freebooter,** frē'böt-ėr, *n.* A robber; a pillager; a plunderer.
**Freebooting,** frē'böt-ing, *a.* Pertaining to or like freebooters.
**Freeborn,** frē'born, *a.* Born free; inheriting liberty.
**Freedman,** frēd'man, *n.* A man who has been a slave and is set free.
**Freedom,** frē'dum, *n.* State of being free; liberty; particular privilege; facility of doing anything; frankness; undue familiarity.
**Freehand,** frē'hand, *a.* Applied to drawing in which the hand is not assisted by any guiding or measuring instruments.
**Freehanded,** frē'hand-ed, *a.* Open-handed; liberal.
**Freehold,** frē'hōld, *n.* An estate for which the owner owes no service except to the crown; tenure by which such an estate is held.
**Freeholder,** frē'hōld-ėr, *n.* The possessor of a freehold.
**Free-lance,** frē'lans, *n.* A mercenary soldier of the middle ages; one unattached to any party.
**Freely,** frē'li, *adv.* In a free manner; readily; liberally.
**Freeman,** frē'man, *n.* One who is free; one who enjoys or is entitled to a franchise.
**Freemason,** frē'mā-sn, *n.* A member of a secret friendly society or organization.
**Freemasonry,** frē'mā-sn-ri, *n.* The mysteries in which freemasons are initiated.
**Freeness,** frē'nes, *n.* State or quality of being free; openness; frankness; liberality.
**Free-spoken,** frē'spōk-n, *a.* Accustomed to speak without reserve.
**Freestone,** frē'stōn, *n.* Any stone composed of sand or grit, easily cut.
**Free-thinker,** frē'thingk-ėr, *n.* One who is free from the common modes of thinking in religious matters; a deist; a sceptic.
**Free-trade,** frē'trād, *n.* Commerce free from customs on foreign commodities.
**Free-will,** frē'wil, *n.* The power of directing our own actions, without restraint by necessity or fate.—*a.* Spontaneous.
**Freeze,** frēz, *vi.* (freezing, pret. froze, pp. frozen or froze). To be congealed by cold; to be hardened into ice; to be of that degree of cold at which water congeals; to stagnate; to shiver or stiffen with cold.—*vt.* To congeal; to chill; to make credits, etc., temporarily unrealizable.
**Freezing,** frēz'ing, *a.* Such as to freeze; chilling.
**Freight,** frāt, *n.* The cargo of a ship; lading; hire of a ship; charge for the transportation of goods.—*vt.* To load with goods; to hire for carrying goods.
**Freightage,** frāt'āj, *n.* Act of freighting; money paid for freight.
**Freighter,** frāt'ėr, *n.* One who charters and loads a ship.
**French,** frensh, *a.* Pertaining to France or its inhabitants.—*n.* The language spoken by the people of France; the people of France.
**Frenetic, Frenetical,** fre-net'ik, fre-net'ik-al, *a.* Frenzied; frantic.
**Frenzied,** fren'zid, *a.* Affected with frenzy; proceeding from frenzy.
**Frenzy,** fren'zi, *n.* Madness; distraction; violent agitation of the mind.
**Frequency,** frē'kwen-si, *n.* State or character of being frequent; repetition.
**Frequent,** frē'kwent, *a.* That takes place repeatedly; often seen or done; doing a thing often.—*vt.* frē-kwent'. To visit often; to resort to habitually.
**Frequentative,** frē-kwent'at-iv, *a.* Denoting frequent repetition of an action.—*n.* A verb denoting frequent repetition.

F

**Frequently,** frē'kwent-li, *adv.* Often; many times at short intervals; commonly.
**Fresco,** fres'kō, *n.* A method of painting with mineral and earthy pigments on walls of which the plaster is not quite dry.
**Fresh,** fresh, *a.* Full of health and strength; vigorous; brisk; bright; not faded; in good condition; not stale; cool and agreeable; clearly remembered; new; not salt; unpracticed; unused.
**Freshen,** fresh'n, *vt.* To make fresh; to revive.—*vi.* To grow fresh.
**Freshet,** fresh'et, *n.* A small stream of fresh water; flood of a river.
**Freshly,** fresh'li, *adv.* In a fresh manner; with freshness; newly; recently; anew.
**Freshman,** fresh'man, *n.* A novice; a first year student at an English university.
**Freshness,** fresh'nes *n.* State or quality of being fresh, in all senses.
**Fret,** fret, *vt.* (fretting, fretted). To eat into; to corrode; to wear away; to chafe; to vex; to ornament or furnish with frets; to variegate.—*vi.* To be vexed; to utter peevish expressions; to rankle.—*n.* Irritation; peevishness; an ornament of bands or fillets; a piece of perforated work; one of the crossbars on the finger-board of some stringed instruments.
**Fretful,** fret'ful, *a.* Disposed to fret; peevish; irritable; petulant; angry.
**Fretwork,** fret'wėrk, *n.* Ornamental work consisting of a series or combination of frets.
**Friability, Friableness,** frī-a-bil'i-ti, frī'a-bl-nes, *n.* Quality of being friable.
**Friable,** frī'a-bl, *a.* Easily rubbed down, crumbled, or pulverized.
**Friar,** frī'ėr, *n.* A monk; a male member of a monastery.
**Fricassee,** fri-kas-sē', *n.* A dish made by cutting chickens or rabbits, etc., into pieces, and dressing them in a frying-pan, etc., with strong sauces.
**Fricasseed,** fri-kas-sēd', *a.* Dressed in fricassee.
**Friction,** frik'shon, *n.* A rubbing; effect of rubbing; resistance which a moving body meets with from the surface on which it moves.
**Friday,** frī'dā, *n.* The sixth day of the week.—**Good Friday,** the Friday preceding Easter, sacred as the day of Christ's crucifixion.
**Friend,** frend, *n.* One attached to another by affection; a favorer; one who is propitious; a favorite; a Quaker.
**Friendless,** frend'les, *a.* Destitute of friends; wanting support; forlorn.
**Friendliness,** frend'li-nes, *n.* Friendly disposition.
**Friendly,** frend'li, *a.* Like or becoming a friend; kind; favorable; disposed to peace.
**Friendship,** frend'ship, *n.* Intimacy resting on mutual esteem; kindness; aid.
**Frieze,** frēz, *n.* A coarse woolen cloth with a nap on one side; that part of the entablature of a column between the architrave and the cornice; upper part of the wall of a room and its decoration.—*vt.* (friezing, friezed). To form a nap on cloth; to frizzle; to curl.
**Friezed,** frēzd, *p.a.* Shaggy with nap or frieze.
**Frigate,** fri'gāt, *n.* A large fast sailing-ship which performed the functions of the modern cruiser.
**Fright,** frīt, *n.* Sudden and violent fear; terror; consternation; an ugly or ill-dressed person.—*vt.* To frighten.
**Frighten,** frīt'n, *vt.* To strike with fright or fear; to terrify; to scare; to alarm.
**Frightful,** frīt'ful, *a.* Causing fright; terrible; dreadful; fearfül.
**Frightfully,** frīt'ful-li, *adv.* In a frightful manner; dreadfully; terrībly.
**Frigid,** fri'jid, *a.* Cold; wanting spirit or zeal; stiff; formal; lifeless.
**Frigidity,** fri-jid'i-ti, *n.* Coldness; coldness of affection; dullness.
**Frigidly,** frij'id-li, *adv.* Coldly; dully.
**Frigorific,** fri-go-rif'ik, *a.* Causing cold; cooling.
**Frill,** fril, *n.* A crisp or plaited edging on an article of dress; a ruffle.—*vt.* To decorate with frills.
**Frilling,** fril'ing, *n.* Frills collectively; ruffles; gathers, etc.
**Fringe,** frinj, *n.* An ornamental appendage to furniture or dress, consisting of loose threads; margin; extremity.—*vt.* (fringing, fringed). To border with fringe or a loose edging.
**Fringed,** frinjd, *p.a.* Bordered with fringe; having a certain kind of border or margin.
**Frippery,** frip'ė-ri, *n.* Old worn-out clothes; waste matter; trifles; trumpery.—*a.* Trifling; contemptible.
**Frisian,** friz'i-an, *a.* Belonging to Friesland.—*n.* A native or the language of Friesland.
**Frisk,** frisk, *vi.* To dance, skip, and gambol in frolic and gaiety.—*n.* A frolic; a fit of wanton gaiety.
**Frisket,** fris'ket, *n.* A frame to keep paper in position when printing.
**Frisky,** fris'ki, *a.* Jumping with gaiety; gay; frolicsome; lively.
**Frit,** frit, *n.* The matter of which glass is made after it has been calcined.
**Frith,** frith, *n.* Same as *Firth.*
**Fritillary,** frit'il-la-ri, *n.* A genus of herbaceous bulbous plants, natives of north temperate regions; also a British butterfly.
**Fritter,** frit'ėr, *n.* A kind of small cake fried; a small piece of meat fried; a small piece.—*vt.* To cut into small pieces to be fried; to break into small pieces; to waste by degrees (with *away*).
**Frivolity,** fri-vol'i-ti, *n.* Acts or habit of trifling; unbecoming levity.
**Frivolous,** fri'vol-us, *a.* Trivial; trifling; petty.
**Frizz,** friz, *vt.* To curl; to crisp; to form the nap of cloth into little burs.
**Frizzle,** friz'l, *vi.* (frizzling, frizzled). To curl; to crisp; as hair; to make crisp by cooking.—*n.* A curl; a lock of hair crisped.
**Fro,** frō, *adv.* From; away; back or backward.
**Frock,** frok, *n.* An ecclesiastical garment; a lady's gown; a child's dress; a blouse for men.
**Frock-coat,** frok'kōt, *n.* A coat with full skirts of the same length before and behind.
**Frog,** frog, *n.* An amphibious animal, remarkable for its activity in swimming and leaping; a kind of button or tassel on a coat or vestment; a loop used to support a sword or bayonet; horny growth on sole of horse's hoof.
**Frolic,** fro'lik, *a.* Joyous; merry; frisky; *poetic.*—*n.* A merry prank; merry-making.—*vi.* To play merry pranks; to gambol.
**Frolicsome,** fro'lik-sum, *a.* Full of frolics; given to pranks.
**From,** from, *prep.* Out of the neighborhood or presence of; by reason of; denoting source, distance, absence, departure, etc.
**Frond,** frond, *n.* The leaf of a fern or other cryptogamic plant.
**Frondescence,** frond-es'ens, *n.* The time, act, or state of unfolding leaves.
**Front,** frunt, *n.* The forehead; the whole face; the fore part; boldness; impudence; the area of military operations.—*a.* Relating to the front or face.—*vt.* To stand with the front opposed to; to oppose; to face; to supply with a front.—*vi.* To face; to look.
**Frontage,** frunt'āj, *n.* The front part of an edifice, quay, etc.
**Frontal,** frunt'al, *a.* Belonging to the forehead.—*n.* An ornament for the forehead; a frontlet; a small pediment.
**Fronted,** frunt'ed, *p.a.* Formed with a front.
**Frontier,** fron'tēr, *n.* That part of a country which fronts another country; extreme part of a country.—*a.* Bordering; conterminous.
**Frontispiece,** fron'tis-pēs, *n.* The principal face of a building; an illustration facing the title- page of a book.
**Frontless,** frunt'les, *a.* Wanting shame or modesty; not diffident.
**Frontlet,** frunt'let, *n.* A fillet or band worn on the forehead.

**Frore,** frōr, *a.* Frozen; frosty: *poetical.*
**Frost,** frost, *n.* That temperature of the air which causes freezing; frozen dew; rime; coldness or severity of manner.—*vt.* To injure by frost; to ornament with anything resembling hoar-frost; to frunish with frost-nails.
**Frost-bite,** frost'bīt, *n.* Insensibility or deadness in any part of the body caused by exposure to frost.—*vt.* To affect with frost-bite.
**Frostily,** frost'i-li, *adv.* With frost or excessive cold; coldly.
**Frosting,** frost'ing, *n.* The composition, resembling hoar-frost, used to cover cake, etc.
**Frost-nail,** frost'nāl, *n.* A nail driven into a horse-shoe to prevent slipping on ice.
**Frosty,** frost'i, *a.* Producing or characterized by frost; chill in affection; resembling hoarfrost; gray-haired.
**Froth,** froth, *n.* Bubbles caused by fermentation or agitation; spume; empty talk; light unsubstantial matter.—*vt.* To cause to foam.—*vi.* To foam; to throw up spume.
**Frothy,** froth'i, *a.* Full or consisting of froth; not firm or solid.
**Frounce,** frouns, *n.* Old form of *flounce.*
**Frouzy, Frowzy,** frou'zi, *a.* Fetid; musty; dingy; in disorder; slatternly.
**Froward,** frō'wėrd, *a.* Perverse; ungovernable; disobedient; peevish.
**Frown,** froun, *vi.* To express displeasure by contracting the brow; to look stern; to scowl.—*n.* A wrinkling of the brow; a sour or stern look; any expression of displeasure.
**Frozen,** frōz'en, *p.a.* Congealed by cold; frosty; chill.
**Fructescence,** fruk-tes'ens, *n.* The fruiting season.
**Fructiferous,** fruk-tif'ėr-us, *a.* Bearing fruit.
**Fructification,** fruk'ti-fi-kā''shon, *n.* Act of fructifying; the bearing of fruit; arrangement of the organs of reproduction in plants.
**Fructify,** fruk'ti-fī, *vt.* (fructifying, fructified). To make fruitful; to fertilize.—*vi.* To bear fruit.
**Frugal,** frö'gal, *a.* Economical; careful; thrifty.
**Frugality,** frö-gal'i-ti, *n.* Prudent economy; thrift.
**Frugally,** frö'gal-li, *adv.* In a frugal manner; with economy.
**Frugiferous,** frö-jif'ėr-us, *a.* Producing fruit or crops; fruitful.
**Frugivorous,** frö-jiv-ėr-us, *a.* Feeding on fruits, seeds, or corn, as birds.
**Fruit,** fröt, *n.* Whatever of a vegetable nature is of use to man or animals; the reproductive produce of a plant; such products collectively; the seed or matured ovary; that which is produced; offspring; effect; outcome.—*vi.* To produce fruit.
**Fruitage,** fröt'āj, *n.* Fruit collectively.
**Fruiterer,** fröt'ėr-ėr, *n.* One who deals in fruit.
**Fruitery,** fröt'ė-ri, *n.* A repository for fruit.
**Fruitful,** fröt'ful, *a.* Very productive; fertile; plenteous; prolific.
**Fruitfully,** fröt'ful-li, *adv.* In a fruitful manner; plenteously; abundantly.
**Fruition,** frö-i'shon, *n.* A using or enjoying; enjoyment; gratification; pleasure derived from use or possession.
**Fruitless,** fröt'les, *a.* Destitute of fruit; unprofitable; abortive; ineffectual.
**Fruity,** frö'ti, *a.* Resembling fruit; having the taste or flavor of fruit.
**Frumentaceous,** frö-men-tā'shus, *a.* Having the character of or resembling wheat or other cereal.
**Frumpt,** frump, *n.* A cross-tempered, old-fashioned female.
**Frustrate,** frus'trāt, *vt.* (frustrating, frustrated). To balk; to foil; to bring to nothing; to render of no effect.
**Frustration,** frus-trā'shon, *n.* Disappointment; defeat.
**Frustum,** frus'tum, *n.*; pl. **-tums** or **-ta.** A piece; the part which remains of a cone, pyramid, etc., when the top is cut off by a plane parallel to the base.
**Frutescent, Fruiticose, Fruticous,** frö-tes'ent, frö'tik-ōs, frö'tik-us, *a.* Shrub-like; shrubby.
**Fry,** frī, *vt.* (frying, fried). To cook by roasting over a fire.—*vi.* To be cooked as above; to simmer; to be in agitation.—*n.* A dish of anything fried; state of mental ferment; young fishes at an early stage; swarm of small fishes, etc.; insignificant objects.
**Fuchsia,** fū'shi-a, *n.* A beautiful flowering shrub.
**Fuddle,** fud'l, *vt.* (fuddling, fuddled). To make stupid by drink; to spend in drinking.—*vi.* To drink to excess.
**Fudge,** fuj, *n.* or *interj.* Stuff; nonsense.
**Fuel,** fū'el, *n.* That which serves to feed fire, or to increase excitement. etc.—*vt.* To feed or furnish with fuel.
**Fugacious,** fū-gā'shus, *a.* Flying or fleeing away; volatile; soon shed or dropped.
**Fugacity,** fū-gas'i-ti, *n.* Quality of flying away; volatility; instability.
**Fugitive,** fū-jit-iv, *a.* Apt to flee away; volatile; fleeting; vagabond; temporary.—*n.* One who flees from duty or danger; refugee.
**Fugleman,** fū'gl-man, *n.* One who stands in front of soldiers at drill, and whose movements they copy; an example.
**Fugue,** fūg, *n.* A musical composition in which the parts seem to chase each other.
**Fulcrum,** ful'krum, *n.*; pl. **-ra** or **-rums.** A support; that by which a lever is sustained, or the point about which it moves.
**Fulfill,** ful-fil', *vt.* To carry into effect, as a prophecy, promise, etc.; to answer in execution or event; to perform; to complete.
**Fulfillment,** ful-fil'ment, *n.* Accomplishment; execution; performance.
**Fulgency,** ful'jen-si, *n.* Splendor; glitter.
**Fulgent,** ful'jent, *a.* Glittering; shining.
**Fuliginous,** fū-lij'in-us, *a.* Sooty.
**Full,** ful, *a.* Having all it can contain; abounding; crowded; entire; strong; loud; clear; mature; perfect; ample.—*n.* Complete measure; the highest state or degree (usually with *the*).—*adv.* Quite; altogether; exactly; directly.—*vt.* To scour and thicken, as woolen cloth, in a mill.
**Full-blown,** ful'blōn, *a.* Fully expanded, as a blossom.
**Fuller,** ful'ėr, *n.* One who fulls cloth.
**Fuller's-earth,** ful'ėrz-ėrth, *n.* A soft friable clay, wihch absorbs grease, and is much used in fulling cloth.
**Fulling,** ful'ing, *n.* The art or practice of fulling cloth, and making it compact and firm.
**Fully,** ful'li, *adv.* With fullness; amply; perfectly.
**Fulmar,** ful'mär, *n.* A kind of petrel of the northern seas.
**Fulminate,** ful'min-āt, *vi.* (fulminating, fulminated). To lighten and thunder; to detonate; to issue threats, denunciations, etc.—*vt.* To utter or send out, as a denunciation or censure; to cause to explode.—*n.* A compound substance which explodes by percussion, friction, or heat.
**Fulmination,** ful-min-ā'shon, *n.* Act of fulminating; that which is fulminated; censure, anathema; chemical explosion.
**Fulness, Fullness,** ful'nes, *n.* State of being full; abundance; extent; loudness.
**Fulsome,** ful'sum, *a.* Offensive from excess of praise; gross; nauseous.
**Fulvous,** ful'vus, *a.* Tawny; dull yellow.
**Fumble,** fum'bli, *vi.* (fumbling, fumbled). To grope about awkwardly; to attempt or handle something bunglingly.
**Fume,** fūm, *n.* Smoke; vapor; exhalation from the stomach, as of liquor; heat of passion.—*vi.* (fuming, fumed). To yield vapor or visible exhalations; to be hot with anger.—*vt.* To smoke; to perfume; to disperse in vapors.
**Fumigate,** fūm'i-gāt, *vt.* (fumigating, fumigated). To smoke; to purify from infection, etc.
**Fumigation,** fūm-i-gā'shon, *n.* Act of fumigating, to purify from infection.

F

**Fumy,** fūm-'i, *a.* Producing fume or smoke; full of vapor.
**Fun,** fun, *n.* Sportive acts or words; merriment.
**Funambulist,** fū-nam'bū-list, *n.* A rope walker or dancer.
**Function,** fungk'shon, *n.* Performance; office; duty; proper office of any organ in animals or vegetables; a ceremonial; a mathematical quantity connected with and varying with another.
**Functional,** fungk'shon-al, *a.* Pertaining to functions, or to some office or function.
**Functionary,** fungk'shon-a-ri, *n.* One who holds an office or trust.
**Fund,** fund, *n.* A stock or capital; money set apart for any object more or less permanent; store; supply.—*vt.* To provide and appropriate a fund for paying the interest of, as a debt; to place in a fund, as money.
**Fundament,** fun'da-ment, *n.* The part of the body on which one sits; the anus.
**Fundamental,** fun-da-ment'al, *a.* Pertaining to the foundation; essential; primary.—*n.* A leading principle which serves as the groundwork of a system; an essential.
**Fundamentalist,** fun-da-ment'al-ist, *n.* One who believes in the literal interpretation and the infallibility of the Bible.
**Funeral,** fū'nė-ral, *n.* Burial; ceremony of burying a dead body.—*a.* Used at the interment of the dead.
**Funereal,** fū-nē'rė-al, *a.* Suiting a funeral; dark; dismal; mournful.
**Fungous,** fung'gus, *a.* Like a mushroom or fungus; excrescent; growing suddenly, but not substantial or durable.
**Fungus,** fung'gus, *n.*; pl. **Fungi** or **Funguses,** fun'jī, fung'gus-es. A mushroom; a toadstool; spongy excrescence in animal bodies; as proud flesh formed in wounds.
**Funicle,** fū'ni-kl, *n.* A small cord or ligament.
**Funicular,** fū-nik'ū-lėr, *a.* Consisting of a small cord; dependent on the tension of a cord.
**Funnel,** fun'el, *n.* A utensil for conveying liquids into close vessels; the shaft of a chimney through which smoke ascends.
**Funnily,** fun'i-li, *adv.* In a droll manner.
**Funny,** fun'i, *a.* Making fun; droll; comical.
**Fur,** fėr, *n.* The short, fine, soft hair of certain animals, growing thick on the skin; furred animals collectively; something resembling fur.—*a.* Pertaining to or made of fur.—*vt.* (furring, furred). To line or cover with fur.
**Furbelow,** fėr'bē-lō, *n.* A kind of flounce; plaited border of a petticoat or gown.
**Furbish,** fėr'bish, *vt.* To rub or scour to brightness; to burnish.
**Furbisher,** fėr'bish-ėr, *n.* One who or that which furbishes.
**Furcate, Furcated,** fėr'kāt, fėr'kāt-ed, *a.* Forked; branching like the prongs of a fork.
**Furfur,** fėr'fėr, *n.* Dandruff; scales like bran.
**Furious,** fū'ri-us, *a.* Full of rage; violent; impetuous; frantic.
**Furiously,** fū'ri-us-li, *adv.* With fury; vehemently; violently.
**Furl,** fėrl, *vt.* To wrap a sail close to a yard, etc., and fasten by a cord.
**Furlong,** fėr'long, *n.* The eighth of a mile.
**Furlough,** fėr'lō, *n.* Leave of absence to a soldier for a limited time.—*vt.* To grant leave of absence from military service.
**Furnace,** fėr'nās, *n.* A structure in which a vehement fire may be maintained for melting ores, heating water, etc.; place or occasion of torture or trial.
**Furnish,** fėr'nish, *vt.* To supply; to equip; to yield; to provide.
**Furniture,** fėr'ni-tūr, *n.* That with which anything is furnished; equipment; outfit; movable wooden articles in a house.
**Furor,** fū'ror, *n.* Fury; rage.
**Furore,** fū-rō'rā, *n.* Great enthusiasm or excitement; commotion; mania; rage.
**Furrier,** fu'ri-ėr, *n.* A dealer in furs; one who dresses furs.
**Furriery,** fu'ri-ė-ri, *n.* Furs in general; the trade in furs; dressing of furs.
**Furrow,** fu'rō, *n.* A trench made by a plough; a groove; a wrinkle.—*vt.* To make furrows in; to groove; to wrinkle.
**Furrowy,** fu'rō-i, *a.* Full of furrows.
**Furry,** fėr'i, *a.* Covered or coated with fur; resembling fur.
**Further,** fėr'THėr, *adv.* More in advance; besides; farther.—*a.* More distant; farther.—*vt.* To help forward; to advance.
**Furtherance,** fėr'THėr-ans, *n.* A helping forward; promotion; advancement.
**Furtherer,** fėr'THėr-ėr, *n.* A promoter.
**Furthermore,** fėr'THėr-mōr, *adv.* More in addition; moreover; besides.
**Furthermost,** fėr'THėr-mōst, *a.* Most remote.
**Furthest,** fėr'THest, *a.* and *adv.* Most advanced; farthest.
**Furtive,** fėr'tiv, *a.* Stolen; sly; stealthy.
**Furtively,** fėr'tiv-li, *adv.* By stealth.
**Fury,** fū'ri, *n.* Rage; a violent rushing; frenzy; a goddess of vengeance, in mythology; a violent woman.
**Furze,** fėrz, *n.* A prickly evergreen shrub; whin; gorse.
**Fuscous,** fus'kus, *a.* Dark; swarthy; dusky.
**Fuse,** fūz, *n.* A length of easily melted metal inserted in an electrical circuit as a safety device.—*vt.* (fusing, fused). To liquefy by heat; to dissolve; to blend or unite.—*vi.* To be melted; to become blended.
**Fuse, Fuze,** fūz, *n.* A tube or case filled with combustible matter, used in blasting or in discharging a shell, etc.
**Fusee,** fū-zē', *n.* The conical part of a watch or clock, round which is wound the chain or cord; a fusil; match used by smokers.
**Fuselage,** fū'sel-āj, *n.* The long, narrow, somewhat spindle-shaped body of an airplane.
**Fusel-oil,** fū'zel-oil, *n.* A colorless oily spirit separated in the rectification of ordinary distilled spirits.
**Fusible,** fūz'i-bl, *a.* That may be fused.
**Fusil,** fū'sil, *a.* A light musket or firelock.
**Fusilier,** fū-sil-ēr', *n.* An infantry soldier of a regiment formerly armed with fusils.
**Fusillade,** fū'zi-lād, *n.* A simultaneous discharge of musketry.
**Fusion,** fū'zhon, *n.* Act or operation of fusing; state of being melted or blended; complete union.
**Fuss,** fus, *n.* Bustle; much ado about trifles.—*vi.* To make a fuss or bustle.
**Fussily,** fus'i-li, *adv.* In a bustling manner.
**Fussy,** fus'i, *a.* Making a fuss; bustling.
**Fusted,** fus'ted, *a.* Moldy; ill-smelling.
**Fustian,** fus'tyan, *n.* A coarse cotton stuff with a pile like velvet; mere stuff; bombast; an inflated style.—*a.* Made of fustian; bombastic.
**Fustic,** fus'tik, *n.* The wood of a West Indian tree, used in dyeing yellow.
**Fustigate,** fus'ti-gāt, *vt.* To cudgel.
**Fusty,** fus'ti, *n.* Tasting or smelling of a foul or moldy cask; moldy; ill-smelling.
**Futile,** fū'til *a.* Serving no useful end; trivial; worthless.
**Futility,** fū-til'i-ti, *n.* Quality of being futile; worthlessness; unimportance.
**Future,** fū'tūr, *a.* That is to be; pertaining to time to come.—*n.* The time to come; all that is to happen; the future tense.
**Futurity,** fū-tūr'i-ti, *n.* State of being future; time to come; after-ages.
**Fuzz,** fuz, *vi.* To fly off in minute particles.—*n.* Fine particles; loose, volatile matter.
**Fuzzy,** fuz'i, *a.* Like, or covered with, fuzz.

# G

**Gab**, gab, *vi*. (gabbling, gabbed). To talk much; to chatter.—*n*. Idle talk.
**Gabardine, Gaberdine**, gab'ar-dēn, gab'ėr-dēn, *n*. A coarse upper garment.
**Gabble**, gab'l, *vi*. (gabbling, gabbled). To talk fast, or without meaning.—*n*. Rapid talk without meaning; inarticulate sounds rapidly uttered.
**Gabel, Gabelle**, ga-bel', *n*. A tax or impost in some continental countries.
**Gabion**, gā'bi-on, *n*. A cylindrical wickerbasket filled with earth, used in fortifications.
**Gable**, gā'bl, *n*. The pointed end of a house; the triangular part of the end of a house.
**Gaby**, gā'bi, *n*. A silly person; a simpleton.
**Gad**, gad, *n*. A spike; a wedge or ingot of steel or iron.—*vi*. (gadding, gadded). To rove or ramble idly.
**Gadabout**, gad'a-bout, *n*. One who roves about idly.
**Gadder**, gad'ėr, *n*. A gadabout.
**Gadfly**, gad'flī, *n*. A fly which bites cattle.
**Gadget**, gad'jet, *n*. A tool, appliance, or contrivance.
**Gadhelic**, gad'e-lik, *a*. Pertaning to the branch of the Celtic race comprising the Erse of Ireland, the Gaels of Scotland, and the Manx.—*n*. Their language.
**Gadwall**, gad'wal, *n*. A species of duck.
**Gael**, gāl, *n*. A Scottish Highlander.
**Gaelic**, gāl'ik, *a*. Pertaining to the Celtic inhabitants of Scotland.—*n*. Their language.
**Gaff**, gaf, *n*. A hook used by anglers in landing large fish; a spar to entend the upper edge of some fore-and-aft sails.—*vt*. To strike or secure (a salmon) by means of a gaff.
**Gaffer**, gaf'ėr, *n*. An old rustic; a foreman.
**Gag**, gag, *vt*. (gagging, gagged). To prevent from speaking by fixing something in the mouth; to silence by authority or force.—*n*. Something thrust into the mouth to hinder speaking; interpolations in an actor's part.
**Gage**, gāj, *n*. A pledge; a security; a kind of plum.—*vt*. (gaging, gaged). To pledge; to bind by pledge or security; to engage. *See* GAUGE.
**Gaiety**, gā'e-ti, *n*. State or quality of being gay; mirth; entertainment; showiness.
**Gaily**, gā'li, *adv*. In a gay manner; joyful; merrily; with finery or showiness.
**Gain**, gān, *vt*. To obtain; to get, as profit or advantage; to receive, as honor; to win to one's side; to conciliate; to reach, arrive at.—*vi*. To reap advantage or profit; to make progress.—*n*. Something obtained as an advantage; profit; benefit.
**Gainful**, gān'ful, *a*. Full of gain; profitable; advantageous; lucrative.
**Gaining**, gān'ing, *n*. That which one gains; usually in the *pl*. earnings.
**Gainless**, gān'les, *a*. Not producing gain; unprofitable.
**Gainsay**, gān'sā, *vt*. To contradict; to oppose in words; to dispute.
**Gainsayer**, gān'sā-ėr, *n*. One who gainsays.
**'Gainst**, genst, *See* AGAINST.
**Gait**, gāt, *n*. Walk; manner of walking or stepping; carriage.
**Gaiter**, gā'tėr, *n*. A covering for the leg fitting over the shoe.—*vt*. To dress with gaiters.
**Gala**, gal'a, *n*. An occasion of public festivity.
**Galantine**, gal-an-tēn', *n*. A dish of veal or chicken, without bones, served cold.
**Galaxy**, ga'lak-si, *n*. The Milky Way; that long, luminous track in the heavens, formed by a multitude of stars; an assemblage of splendid persons or things.
**Gale**, gāl, *n*. A strong wind; a storm; a small shrub found in bogs.
**Galena**, ga-lē'na, *n*. The principal ore of lead.
**Galiot, Galliot**, gal'i-ot, *n*. A two-masted Duch cargo vessel, with rounded ribs and flattish bottom.
**Gall**, gal, *n*. A bitter fluid secreted in the liver; bile; rancor; malignity; an excrescence produced by the egg of an insect on a plant, especially the oak; a sore place in the skin from rubbing.—*vt*. To make a sore in the skin of by rubbing; to fret; to vex; to harass.
**Gallant**, gal'ant, *a*. Gay in attire; handsome; brave; showing politeness and attention to ladies (in this sense also pron. ga-lant').—*n*. A gay sprightly man; a daring spirit; (pron. also ga-lant') a man attentive to ladies; suitor; paramour.—*vt*. ga-lant'. To act the gallant towards; to be very attentive to (a lady).
**Gallantly**, gal'ant-li, *adv*. Gaily; bravely; nobly; in the manner of a wooer.
**Gallantry**, gal'ant-ri, *n*. Show; bravery; intrepidity; polite attentions to ladies; vicious love or pretentions to love.
**Galleon**, gal'ē-un, *n*. A large ship formerly used by the Spaniards.
**Gallery**, gal'ė-ri, *n*. A long apartment serving as a passage of communication, or for the receptio of pictures, etc.; upper floor of a church, theatre, etc.; a covered passage; frame like a balcony projected from a ship.
**Galley**, gal'i, *n*. A low, flat-built vessel navigated with sails and oars; the cook-room of a large ship; a frame used in printing.
**Galley-slave**, gal'i-slāv, *n*. A person condemned to work on board a galley.
**Gallic**, gal'ik, *a*. Pertaining to Gaul, or France.
**Gallic**, gal'ik, *a*. Belonging to or derived from galls, or oak-apples.
**Gallicism**, gal'i-sizm, *n*. A French idiom.
**Galligaskins**, gal-li-gas'kinz, *n.pl*. Large open hose; leather guards for the legs.
**Gallimaufry**, gal-i-ma'fri, *n*. A hash; medley.
**Gallinaceous**, gal-li-nā'shus, *a*. Pertaining to that order of birds which includes the domestic fowl, pheasant, turkey, etc.
**Galling**, gal'ing, *p.a*. Adapted to gall or chagrin; keenly annoying.
**Gallipot**, gal'li-pot, *n*. A small pot painted and glazed, used for holding medicines.
**Gallon**, gal'lun, *n*. A liquid measure of four quarts or eight pints.
**Galloon**, gal-lōn', *n*. A narrow close lace.
**Gallop**, gal'up, *vi*. To move or run with leaps; to ride at this pace; to move very fast.—*n*. The pace of a horse, by springs or leaps.
**Gallopade**, gal-up-ād', *n*. A sidelong or curveting kind of gallop; a kind of dance.—*vi*. To gallop; to dance a gallopade.
**Galloper**, gal'up-ėr, *n*. A horse or man that gallops.
**Gallows**, gal'ōz, *n. sing*. or *pl*.; also **Gallowses**, gal'ōz-ez, in *pl*. A structure for the hanging of criminals; one of a pair of braces for the trousers.
**Galoche, Galosh**, ga-losh', *n*. A shoe worn over another shoe to keep the foot dry.
**Galop**, ga-lop', *n*. A quick lively dance somewhat resembling a waltz.
**Galore**, ga-lōr,', *n*. Abundance; plenty.
**Galvanic**, gal-van'ik, *a*. Pertaining to galvanism; containing or exhibiting it.
**Galvanism**, gal'van-izm, *n*. A species of electricity developed by the action of various metals and chemicals upon each other.
**Galvanist**, gal'van-ist, *n*. One versed in galvanism.
**Galvanize**, gal'van-īz, *vt*. (galvanizing, galvanized). To affect with falvanism; to electroplate; to coat with tin or zinc; to restore to consciousness; to give spurious life to.
**Galvanometer**, gal-van-om'et-ėr, *n*. An instrument for detecting the existence and determining the strength and direction of an electric current.
**Gambadoes**, gam-bā'dōz, *n.pl*. Leather cover-

ings for the legs in riding.
**Gambit,** gam'bit, *n.* An opening in chess incurring the sacrifice of a pawn.
**Gamble,** gam'bl, *vi.* (gambling, gambled). To play for money.
**Gambler,** gam'bl-ėr, *n.* One who plays for money or other stake.
**Gambling,** gam'bl-ing, *n.* The act or practice of gaming for money or anything valuable.
**Gamboge,** gam-bōj', *n.* A concrete vegetable juice, used as a pigment and cathartic.
**Gambol,** gam'bol, *vi.* (gamboling, gamboled). To skip about in sport; to frisk; to frolic.—*n.* A skipping about in frolic; a prank.
**Gambrel,** gam'brel, *n.* The prominent bend of a horse's hind leg.
**Game,** gām, *n.* Sport of any kind; exercise for amusement, testing skill, etc.; scheme pursued; field-sports; animals hunted.—*vi.* (gaming, gamed). To play at any sport; to play for a stake or prize; to practice gaming. **To die game,** to maintain a bold spirit to the last.
**Game-cock,** gām'kok, *n.* A cock bred or used to fight.
**Gamekeeper,** gām'kēp-ėr, *n.* One who has the care of game on an estate.
**Gamesome,** gām'sum, *a.* Sportive; playful.
**Gamester,** gām'stėr, *n.* A person addicted to gaming; a gambler.
**Gamin,** gam'in, *n.* A street arab; a neglected street-boy.
**Gaming,** gām'ing, *n.* The act or practice of gambling.
**Gammer,** gam'ėr, *n.* An old woman in humble life.
**Gammon,** gam'un, *n.* The thigh of a hog, pickled and smoked or dried; a smoked ham; an imposition or hoax.—*vt.* To pickle and dry in smoke; to hoax or humbug.
**Gamut,** gam'ut, *n.* A scale on which notes in music are written, consisting of lines and spaces; range or compass.
**Gamy, Gamey,** gām'i, *a.* Having the flavor of game; courageous.
**Gander,** gan'dėr, *n.* The male of the goose.
**Gang,** gang, *n.* A crew or band; a squad; a vein in mining; a gangue.
**Gangliated,** gang'gli-āt-ed, *a.* Having ganglions; forming a ganglion.
**Ganglion,** gang'gli-on, *n.*; pl. **-ia** or **-ions.** An enlargement in the course of a nerve; a mass of nervous matter giving origin to nervefibers; a tumor on a tendon.
**Ganglionic,** gang-gli-on'ik, *a.* Pertaining to a ganglion.
**Gangrene,** gang'grēn, *n.* An eating away of the flesh; first stage of mortification.—*vt.* (gangrening, gangrened). To mortify.—*vi.* To become mortified.
**Gangrenous,** gang'grēn-us, *a.* Mortified; attacked by gangrene.
**Gangster,** gang'stėr, *n.* A member of a criminal organization.
**Gangue,** gang, *n.* The mineral substance which encloses any metallic ore in the vein.
**Gangway,** gang'wā, *n.* A means of access formed of planks or boards; a passage across the House of Commons.
**Gannet,** gan'et, *n.* The solan-goose, an aquatic bird of the pelican tribe.
**Ganoid,** gan'oid, *a.* Applied to an order to fishes with scales of horny or bony plates covered with glossy enamel.
**Gantlet,** gänt'let, *n.* *See* GAUNTLET.
**Gantlet, Gantlope,** gant'let, gant'lōp, *n.* A punishment, in which the culprit was compelled to run between two ranks of men and receive a blow from each man.
**Gaol,** jāl, *n.* *See* JAIL.
**Gap,** gap, *n.* An opening; breach; hiatus; chasm.
**Gape,** gāp, *vi.* (gaping, gaped). To open the mouth wide; to yawn; to open in fissures; to stand open.—*n.* A gaping; the width of the mouth when opened, as of a bird, fish, etc.
**Garage,** gar'aj, *n.* A place for housing or repairing motor-cars.
**Garb,** gärb, *n.* Dress; clothes; mode of dress.—*vt.* To dress.
**Garbage,** gärb'āj, *n.* Waste matter; offal; vegetable refuse.
**Garble,** gär'bl, *vt.* (garbling, garbled). To pick out such parts as may serve a purpose; to falsify by leaving out parts; to corrupt.
**Garden,** gär'dn, *n.* A piece of ground appropriated to the cultivation of plants; a rich, well-cultivated tract; a delightful spot.—*a.* Pertaining to or produced in a garden.—*vi.* To lay out and to cultivate a garden.
**Gardener,** gär'dn-ėr, *n.* One whose occupation is to tend or keep a garden.
**Gardening,** gär'dn-ing, *n.* The act or art of cultivating gardens; horticulture.
**Gargle,** gär'gl, *vt.* (gargling, gargled). To wash, as the throat.—*n.* Any liquid preparation for washing the throat.
**Gargoyle,** gär'goil, *n.* A projecting waterspout on a building, often grotesque.
**Garish,** gär'ish, *a.* Gaudy; showy; dazzling.
**Garland,** gär'land, *n.* A wreath or chaplet of flowers, leaves, etc.; a collection of pieces of prose or verse.—*vt.* To deck with a garland.
**Garlic,** gär'lik, *n.* A plant allied to the onion, with a pungent taste and strong odor.
**Garment,** gär'ment, *n.* An article of clothing, as a coat, a gown, etc.
**Garner,** gär'nėr, *n.* A granary; a store.—*vt.* To store in a granary; to store up.
**Garnet,** gär'net, *n.* A precious stone, generally of a red color.
**Garnish,** gär'nish, *vt.* To adorn; to embellish (a dish) with something laid round.—*n.* Ornament; an embellishment round a dish.
**Garnishing, Garnishment,** gär'nish-ing, gär'nish-ment, *n.* That which garnishes.
**Garniture,** gär'ni-tūr, *n.* Ornamental appendages; furniture; dress.
**Garret,** ga'ret, *n.* A room in a house on the uppermost floor, immediately under the roof.
**Garrison,** ga'ri-sn, *n.* A body of troops stationed in a fort or town.—*vt.* To place a garrison in.
**Garrotte,** ga-rot', *vt.* To rob by seizing a person and compressing his windpipe till he become helpless.
**Garrotter,** ga-rot'ėr, *n.* One who commits the act of garrotting.
**Garrulity,** ga-rū'li-ti, *n.* Loquacity; practice or habit to talking much.
**Garrulous,** ga'rū-lus, *a.* Talkative; loquacious; characterized by long prosy talk.
**Garter,** gär'tėr, *n.* A band to hold up a stocking; the badge of the highest order or knighthood in Great Britain; the order itself.—*vt.* To bind with a garter.
**Gas,** gas, *n.* An elastic aeriform fluid; coalgas, used for giving light; any similar substance.
**Gasalier, Gaselier,** gas-a-lēr', gas'e-lēr, *n.* A hanging appartus with branches for burning gas.
**Gascon,** gas'kon, *n.* A native of Gascony in France.
**Gasconade,** gas-kon-ād', *n.* A boast or boasting; a bravado.—*vi.* To boast; to brag.
**Gaseous,** gā'sē-us, *a.* In the form of gas.
**Gas-fitter,** gas'fit-ėr, *n.* One who fits up the pipes, brackets, etc., for gas-lighting.
**Gash,** gash, *vt.* To make a long deep incision in; to cut; to slash.—*n.* A deep and long cut, particularly in flesh.
**Gasholder,** gas'hōld-ėr, *n.* A large vessel for storing, ordinary coal-gas.
**Gasification,** gas'i-fi-kā''shon, *n.* Act or process of converting into gas.
**Gasify,** gas'i-fi, *vt.* To convert into gas by heat.
**Gasket,** gas'ket, *n.* A cord on the yard of a ship to tie the sail to it; material used for packing joints, etc.
**Gas-mask,** gas-mask, *n.* A covering for the face

used to give protection against poisonous gases in warfare.
**Gasogene,** gas'o-jēn, *n.* An apparatus for manufacturing aerated waters for domestic use.
**Gasometer,** gaz-om'et-ėr, *n.* An instrument to measure, mix, or store gases.
**Gasp,** gasp, *vi.* To open the mouth wide to catch breath; to labor for breath; to pant.—*vt.* To emit with a gasp.—*n.* Short painful catching of the breath.
**Gasteropod, Gastropod,** gas'tėr-o-pod, gas'trō-pod, *n.* A mollusc such as snails, having a broad muscular foot attached to the ventral surface.
**Gastric,** gas'trik, *a.* Belonging to the stomach.
**Gastronomy,** gas-tron'o-mi, *n.* The art or science of good eating; epicurism.
**Gate,** gāt, *n.* A large door or entrance; a frame of timber, iron, etc., closing an entrance, etc.; a way or passage; the frame which stops the passage of water through a dam, lock, etc.
**Gate-crasher,** gāt-krash'ėr, *n.* An uninvited guest; one who obtains admission to a public entertainment without a ticket.
**Gateway,** gāt'wā, *n.* A way through the gate of some enclosure; the gate itself.
**Gather,** gaᴛʜ'ėr, *vt.* To bring together; to collect; to acquire; to pucker; to deduce by inference.—*vi.* To assemble; to increase.—*n.* A fold in cloth, made by drawing; a pucker.
**Gatherer,** gaᴛʜ'ėr-ėr. One who gathers.
**Gathering,** gaᴛʜ'ėr-ing, *n.* The act of collecting or assembling; an assembly; a collection of pus; an abscess.
**Gatling-gun,** gat'ling-gun, *n.* A type of machine-gun.
**Gaucherie,** gōsh-rē, *n.* Awkwardness.
**Gaucho,** gou'chō, *n.* A native of the S. American Pampas, of Spanish descent.
**Gaud,** gad, *n.* A piece of showy finery.
**Gaudily,** gad'i-li, *adv.* Showily; with ostentation of fine dress.
**Gaudy,** gad'i, *a.* Showy; ostentatiously fine; tastelessly or glaringly adorned.
**Gauge,** gāj, *vt.* (gauging, gauged). To ascertain the contents of; to measure.—*n.* A measuring-rod; a measure; distance between the rails of a railway, caliber; size or dimensions.
**Gaul,** gal, *n.* An inhabitant of Gaul, or ancient France.
**Gaunt,** gant, *a.* Emaciated; lean; thin; famished.
**Gauntlet,** gant'let, *n.* A large iron glove formerly worn as armor; a long glove covering the hand and wrist.
**Gauze,** gaz, *n.* A very thin, slight, transparent stuff.
**Gauzy,** gaz'i, *a.* Like gauze; thin as gauze.
**Gavotte,** ga-vot', *n.* A sprightly dance; music for the dance.
**Gawky,** gak'i, *a.* Awkward; clumsy; foolish.—*n.* A stupid clumsy fellow.
**Gay,** gā, *a.* Merry; frolicsome; showy; dressed out; dissipated.
**Gaze,** gāz, *vi.* (gazing, gazed). To fix the eyes and look earnestly; to stare.—*n.* A fixed look; a look of eagerness, wonder or admiration.
**Gazelle,** ga-zel', *n.* A small elegant species of antelope, with soft, lustrous eyes.
**Gazette,** ga-zet', *n.* A newspaper, especially an official newspaper.—*vt.* (gazetting, gazetted). To insert in a gazette; to announce or public officially.
**Gazetteer,** ga-zet-tēr', *n.* A writer or publisher of news; a dictionary of geographical information.
**Gazing-stock,** gēz'ing-stok, *n.* A person gazed at; an object of curiosity or contempt.
**Gear,** gēr, *n.* Dress; ornaments; apparatus; harness; tackle; a train of toothed wheels.—*vt.* To put gear on; to harness.
**Gearing,** gēr'ing, *n.* Harness; a train of toothed wheels working into each other.
**Geese,** gēs, *n.pl.* of *goose.*
**Gelatine,** jel'a-tin, *n.* A concrete transparent substance obtained by boiling from certain parts of animals; the principle of jelly; glue.
**Gelatinous,** je-lat'in-us, *a.* Of the nature of gelatine; containing jelly.
**Geld,** geld, *vt.* To castrate; to emasculate.
**Gelding,** geld'ing, *n.* Act of castrating; a castrated animal, but chiefly a horse.
**Gelid,** je'lid, *a.* Icy cold; frosty or icy.
**Gem,** jem, *n.* A precious stone of any kind; a jewel; anything remarkable for beauty or rarity.—*vt.* (gemming, gemmed). To adorn, as with gems; to bespangle; to embellish.
**Geminate,** jem'i-nāt, *vt.* To double.—*a.* Twin; combined in pairs.
**Gemini,** jem'i-nī, *n.pl.* The Twins, a sign of the zodiac, containing the two stars Castor and Pollux.
**Gemma,** jem'a, *n.*; pl. **-ae.** A bud; a leafbud.
**Gemmation,** jem'ē'shon, *n.* A budding; arrangement of parts in the bud.
**Gemmeous,** jem'ē-us, *a.* Pertaining to or resembling gems.
**Gemmy,** jem'i, *a.* Full of gems; glittering.
**Gendarme,** zhäng-därm, *n.* A private in the armed police of France.
**Gender,** jen'dėr, *n.* Sex, male or female; difference in words to express distinction of sex.—*vt.* To beget.—*vi.* To beget.—*vi.* To copulate; to breed.
**Genealogical,** jen'ē-a-loj''ik-al, *a.* Pertaining to genealogy.
**Genalogist,** jen-ē-al'o-jist, *n.* One who traces genealogies or writes on genealogy.
**Genealogy,** jen-ē-al'o-ji, *n.* An account of the descent of a person or family from an ancestor; pedigree; lineage.
**Genera,** jen'ė-ra, *n.pl.* *See* Genus.
**Generable,** jen'ė-ra-bl, *a.* That may be generated.
**General,** jen'ė-ral, *a.* Of or belonging to a genus;, not special; public; common; extensive, though not universal; usual; taken as a whole.—*n.* The whole; a comprehensive notion; a military officer of the highest rank.
**Generalissimo,** jen'ė-ral-is''si-mō, *n.* The supreme commander of an army.
**Generality,** jen-ė-ral'i-ti, *n.* State of being general; the bulk; the greatest part.
**Generalization,** jen'ė-ral-īz-ā''shon, *n.* Act of generalizing; general inference.
**Generalize,** jen'ė-ral-īz, *vt.* To make general; to bring under a general law or statement.—*vi.* To classify under general heads; to reason by induction.
**Generally,** jen'ė-ral-li, *adv.* In general; commonly; without detail.
**Generalship,** jen'ė-ral-ship, *n.* The office, skill, or conduct of a general officer.
**Generate,** jen'ė-rāt, *vt.* (generating, generated). To beget; to produce; to cause to be.
**Generation,** jen-ė-rā'shon, *n.* Act of generating; single succession in natural descent; people living at the same time; race.
**Generative,** jen'ė-rāt-iv, *a.* Having the power of generating; belonging to generation.
**Generator,** jen'ė-rāt-ėr, *n.* One who or that which generates.
**Generic, Generical,** jē-ne'rik, jē-ne'rik-al, *a.* Pertaining to a genus.
**Generically,** jē-ne'rik-al-li, *adv.* With regard to a genus.
**Generosity,** jen-ė-ros'i-ti, *n.* Nobleness of soul; liberality; munificence.
**Generous,** jen'ė-rus, *a.* Noble; bountiful; liberal; full of spirit, as wine; courageous, as a steed.
**Generously,** jen'ė-rus-li, *adv.* Nobly; magnanimously; liberally.
**Genesis,** jen'e-sis, *n.* Act of producing; origin; first book of the Old Testament.
**Genetic, Genetical,** jen-net'ik, je-net'ik-al, *a.* Relating to origin or production.
**Geneva,** je-nē'va, *n.* A spirit distilled from grain or malt, with the addition of juniper berries; gin.
**Genial,** jē'ni-al, *a.* Cordial kindly; contributing to

G

life and cheerfulness.
**Geniality,** jē-ni-al'i-ti, *n.* Sympathetic cheerfulness or cordiality.
**Genially,** jē'ni-al-li, *adv.* Cordially; cheerfully.
**Geniculated, Geniculate,** je-nik'ū-lāt-ed, je-nik'ū-lāt, *a.* Kneed; knotted; having joints like the knee, a little bent.
**Genital,** jen'it-al, *a.* Pertaining to generation or birth.
**Genitals,** jen'it-alz, *n.pl.* the parts of generation; sexual organs.
**Genitive,** jen'it-iv, *a.* and *n.* Applied to a case of nouns, pronouns, etc., in English called the possessive.
**Genius,** je'ni-us, *n.*; pl. **Geniuses,** jē'ni-us-ez; in first sense **Genii,** jē'ni-ī. A tutelary deity; aptitude of mind for a particular study or course of life; uncommon powers of intellect; a man with uncommon intellectual faculties; nature; peculiar character.
**Genre,** zhäng-r, *n.* A term applied to the department of painting which depicts scenes of ordinary life.
**Genteel,** jen-tēl, *a.* Having the manners of well-bred people; refined; elegant.
**Genteelly,** jen-tēl'li, *adv.* In a genteel manner; politely; fashionably.
**Gentian,** jen'shan, *n.* A bitter herbaceous plant, valued medicinally as a tonic.
**Gentile,** jen'tīl, *a.* Pertaining to a family, race, or nation; pertaining to pagans.—*n.* Any person not a Jew or a Christian; a heathen.
**Gentility,** jen-til'i-ti, *n.* Politeness of manners; fashionable style or circumstances.
**Gentle,** jen'tl, *a.* Well-born; refined in manners; mild; placid; not rough, violent, or wild; soothing.—*n.* A person of good birth.
**Gentlefolk,** jen'tl-fōk, *n.* Persons of good breeding and family: more generally in *pl. gentlefolks*.
**Gentleman,** jen'tl-man, *n.* A man of good social position; technically any man above the rank of yeoman, comprehending noblemen; a man of good breeding or of high honor; a polite equivalent for 'man.'
**Gentleness,** jen'tl-nes, *n.* Quality of being gentle; tenderness; mild treatment.
**Gentlewoman,** jen'tl-wu-man, *n.* A woman of good family or of good breeding.
**Gently,** jen'tli, *adv.* Softly; meekly; mildly; with tenderness.
**Gentry,** jen'tri, *n.* Wealthy or well-born people; people of a rank below the nobility.
**Genuflection,** jen-ū-flek'shon, *n.* The act of bending the knee, particularly in worship.
**Genuine,** jen'ū-in, *a.* Belonging to the original stock; real; pure; true.
**Genus,** jē'nus, *n.*; pl. **Genera** jen'ė-ra. A kind, class, or sort; an assemblage of species having distinctive characteristics in common.
**Geocentric, Geocentrical,** jē-o-sen'trik, jē-o-sen'trik-al, *a.* Having reference to the earth as a center, applied to the position of a celestial object.
**Geodesic, Geodetic,** jē-o-des'ik, jē-o-det'ik, *a.* Pertaining to geodesy.
**Geodesy,** jē-od'e-si, *n.* The geometry of the earth.
**Geognosy,** jē-of'no-si, *n.* The science of the structure of the earth.
**Geographer,** jē-og'ra-fėr, *n.* One versed in geography or who writes on it.
**Geographic, Geographical,** jē-o-graf'ik, jē-o-graf'ik-al, *a.* Pertaining to geography; containing information regarding geography.
**Geography,** jē-og'ra-fi, *n.* The science of the external features of the world; a book describing the earth or part of it.
**Geological,** jē-o-loj'ik-al, *a.* Pertaining to geology.
**Geologist,** jē-ol'o-jist, *n.* One versed in the science of geology.
**Geology,** jē-ol'o-ji, *n.* The science of the structure of the earth as to its rocks, strata, soil, minerals, organic remains, and changes.
**Geomancy,** jē'o-man-si, *n.* A kind of divination by figures made on the ground or paper.
**Geometer,** jē-om'et-ėr, *n.* One skilled in geometry; a geometrician.
**Geometric, Geometrical,** jē-o-met'rik, jē-o-met'rik-al, *a.* Pertaining to geometry; according to the principles of geometry.
**Geometrician,** jē-om'e-tri''shan, *n.* One skilled in geometry.
**Geometry,** jē-om'e-tri, *n.* The science of magnitude; that branch of mathematics which treats of the properties and relations of lines, angles, surfaces, and solids.
**George,** jorj, *n.* A figure of St. George on horseback, worn by knights of the Garter.
**Georgian,** jorj'i-an, *a.* Relating to the reigns of the four Georges, kings of Great Britain.
**Georgic,** jorj'ik, *n.* A rural poem; a poetical composition on husbandry, etc.
**Geothermic,** jē-o-thėr'mik, *a.* Pertaining to the internal heat of the earth.
**Geranium,** jė-rā'ni-um, *n.* A plant cultivated for its beautiful flowers; the crane's-bill genus of plants.
**Germ,** jėrm, *n.* The earliest form of any animal or plant; origin; microbe; bacillus.
**German,** jėr'man, *a.* Come of the same parents. Cousins *german* are the sons or daughters of brothers or sisters, first cousins.
**German,** jėr'man, *a.* Belonging to Germany.—*n.* A native of Germany; the German language.
**Germane,** jėr'mān, *a.* Closely allied; relevant; pertinent.
**Germanic,** jėr-man'ik, *a.* Pertaining to Germany; Teutonic.
**Germinal,** jėrm'in-al, *a.* Pertaining to a germ.
**Germinate,** jėrm'in-āt, *vi.* (germinating, germinated). To sprout; to bud; to begin to vegetate or grow, as seeds.
**Gerrymander,** ge'ri-man-dėr, *vt.* To arrange so as to get an unfair result from the distribution of voters in political elections.
**Gerund,** je'rund, *n.* A kind of verbal noun in Latin; a verbal noun, such as 'teaching' in 'fit for teaching boys.'
**Gerundial,** je-run'di-al, *a.* Pertaining to or like a gerund.
**Gestapo,** ges-ta'pō, *n.* The German secret police, a terrorist organization.
**Gestation,** jest-ā'shon, *n.* The carrying of young in the womb from conception to delivery; pregnancy.
**Gesticulate,** jes-tik'ū-lāt, *vi.* To make gestures or motions, as in speaking.—*vt.* To represent by gesture; to act.
**Gesture,** jes'tūr, *n.* A posture or motion of the body of limbs; action intended to express an idea or feeling; or to enforce an argument.
**Get,** get, *vt.* (getting, pret. got, pp. got, gotten). To obtain; to gain; to reach; to beget; to learn; to induce.—*vi.* To arrive at any place or state by degrees; to become; to make gain.
**Get-up,** get'up, *n.* Equipment; dress.
**Gewgaw,** gū'ga, *n.* A showy trifle; a toy; a splendid plaything.
**Geyser,** gī'zėr, *n.* A hot-water spring, the water rising in a column.
**Ghastly,** gast'li, *a.* Deathlike in looks; hideous; frightful, as wounds.
**Ghat, Ghaut,** gät, gat, *n.* In India, a mountain pass; a chain of hills; a river landing-place.
**Ghee,** gē, *n.* In India, the butter made from buffalo milk converted into a kind of oil.
**Gherkin,** gėr'kin, *n.* A small-fruited variety of cucumber used for pickling.
**Ghetto,** get'to, *n.* A small portion or section of a city, generally limited to where large numbers of minority people live.
**Ghost,** gōst, *n.* The soul of man; a disembodied spirit; apparition; shadow.
**Ghostly,** gōst'li, *a.* Relating to the soul; spiritual; not carnal or secular; pertaining to apparitions.

**Ghoul,** gōl, *n.* An imaginary evil being which preys upon human bodies.

**Giant,** jī'ant, *n.* A man of extraordinary stature; a person of extraordinary powers, bodily or intellectual.—*a.* Like a giant; extraordinary in size.

**Giaour,** jour, *n.* A Turkish name for a non-Mohammedan; a Christian.

**Gibberish,** gib'bėr-ish, *n.* Rapid and inarticulate talk; unmeaning words.

**Gibbet,** jib'bet, *n.* A gallows; the projecting beam of a crane, on which the pulley is fixed.—*vt.* To hang on a gibbet; to expose to scorn, infamy, etc.

**Gibbon,** gib'on, *n.* A long-armed ape of the Indian Archipelago.

**Gibbosity,** gib-os'i-ti, *n.* A round or swelling prominence; convexity.

**Gibbous,** gib'us, *a.* Protuberant; convex.

**Gibe,** jīb, *vi.* (gibing, gibed). To utter taunting, sarcastic words; to flout; to sneer.—*vt.* To scoff at; to mock.—*n.* A scoff; taunt; reproach.

**Giber,** jīb'ėr, *n.* One who gibes.

**Gibingly,** jīb'ing-li, *adv.* With gibes; scornfully.

**Giblet,** jib'let, *n.* One of those parts of poultry usually excluded in roasting, as the head, gizzard, liver, etc.: usually in *pl.*

**Giddy,** gid'i, *a.* Having in the head a sensation of whirling or swimming; dizzy; fickle; heedless; rendered wild by excitement.

**Gier-eagle,** jēr'ē-gl, *n.* A kind of eagle.

**Gift,** gift, *n.* Anything given; act of giving; power of giving; talent or faculty.—*vt.* To endow with any power or faculty.

**Gifted,** gift'ed, *p.a.* Furnished with any particular talent; talented.

**Gig,** gig, *n.* A light one-horse carriage with one pair of wheels; a ship's light boat; a long narrow rowing-boat, adapted for racing.

**Gigantic,** jī-gan'tik, *a.* Like a giant; huge; colossal; immense.

**Giggle,** gig'l, *n.* A kind of laugh, with short catches of the voice or breath.—*vi.*(giggling, giggled). To laugh with short catches of the breath; to titter.

**Giglet, Giglot,** gig'let, gig'lot, *n.* A giggler; a giddy girls.—*a.* Giddy; wanton.

**Gigot,** jig'ot, *n.* A leg of mutton.

**Gilbertian,** gil-bėr'shan, *a.* Whimsically topsy-turvy; resembling the humor of Sir W. S. Gilbert (1836-1911), author of the Savoy Operas and the *Bab Ballads.*

**Gild,** gild, *vt.* (pret. and pp. gilded or gilt). To overlay with gold in leaf or powder; to illuminate; to give a fair and agreeable appearance to.

**Gild,** gild, *n.* Same as *Guild.*

**Gilder,** gild'ėr, *n.* One who gilds; one whose occupation is to overlay things with gold.

**Gilding,** gild'ing, *n.* The art or practice of overlaying things with gold; a thin coating of gold; fair superficial show.

**Gill,** gil, *n.* The organ of respiration in fishes; the flap below the beak of a fowl; the flesh on the lower part of the cheeks.

**Gill,** jil, *n.* The fourth part of a pint; a sweetheart; a wanton girl.

**Gillie,** gil'i, *n.* A Highland male servant who attends on sportsmen.

**Gillyflower,** jil'li-flou-ėr, *n.* A name for the pink or carnation, the wallflower, etc.

**Gilt,** gilt, pp. of *gild.* Overlaid with gold; brightly adorned.—*n.* Gold laid on the surface of a thing; gilding.

**Gimbals,** jim'balz, *n.pl.* A contrivance of two movable hoops, used to keep the mariner's compass, etc., always horizontal.

**Gimlet,** gim'let, *n.* A small borer with a pointed screw at the end.

**Gimp,** gimp, *n.* A kind of silk twist or edging.

**Gin,** jin, *n.* A distilled spirit flavored with juniper berries; a machine for driving piles, raising great weights, etc.; a machine for separating the seeds from cotton; a trap, snare.—*vt.* (ginning, ginned). To clear of seeds by a cotton-gin; to catch in a trap.

**Ginger,** jin'jėr, *n.* A tropical plant, the root of which has a hot, spicy quality.

**Gingerly,** jin'jėr-li, *adv.* Cautiously; timidly; delicately; gently.

**Gingham,** ging'am, *n.* A kind of striped cotton cloth.

**Ginseng,** jin'seng, *n.* The name of two plants, the roots of which are a favorite Chinese medicine.

**Gipsy,** jip'si, *n.* One of an oriental vagabond race scattered over Europe, etc., believed to have come originally from India; the language of the Gipsies; a name of slight reproach to a woman, implying roguishness.—*a.* Pertaining to or resembling the Gipsies.

**Giraffe,** ji-raf', *n.* The camelopard, the tallest of animals.

**Gird,** gėrd, *vt.* (pp. girded or girt). To bind; to make fast by binding; to invest; to encompass.—*vi.* To gibe; to sneer.—*n.* A stroke with a whip; a twitch; a sneer.

**Girder,** gėrd'ėr, *n.* One who girds; a main beam supporting a superstructure.

**Girdle,** gėr'dl, *n.* That which girds; a band or belt; something drawn round the waist and tied or buckled.—*vt.* (girdling, girdled). To bind with a girdle; belt, or sash; to gird.

**Girl,** gėrl, *n.* A female child; young woman.

**Girl Guide,** gėrl gīd, *n.* Member of an organization for young girls analogous to the Boy Scout organization, and also founded by Lord Baden-Powell.

**Girlhood,** gėrl'hud, *n.* The state of a girl.

**Girlish,** gėrl'ish, *a.* Like a girl; befitting a girl.

**Girt,** gėrt, pret. and pp. of *gird.*

**Girt,** gėrt, *vt.* To gird; to surround.

**Girth,** gėrth, *n.* That which girds; band fastening a saddle on a horse's back; measure round a person's body or anything cylindrical.

**Gist,** jist, *n.* The main point of a question; substance or pith of a matter.

**Give,** giv, *vt.* (giving, pret. gave, pp. given). To bestow; to deliver; to impart; to yield; to afford; to utter; to show; to send forth; to devote (oneself); to pledge; to allow; to ascribe.—*vi.* To make gifts; to yield to pressure; to recede.

**Giver,** giv'ėr, *n.* One who gives; a donor.

**Gizzard,** giz'ėrd, *n.* The muscular stomach of a bird.

**Glacial,** glā'shi-al, *a.* Icy; frozen; relating to glaciers.

**Glacier,** glā'shi-ėr, *n.* An immense mass of ice formed in valleys above the snow-line, and having a slow movement downwards.

**Glacis,** glā'sis, *n.* The outer slope of a fortification.

**Glad,** glad, *a.* Affected with pleasure; pleased; cheerful; imparting pleasure.—*vt.* (gladding, gladded). To make glad; to gladden.

**Gladden,** glad'n, *vt.* To make glad.—*vi.* To become glad; to rejoice.

**Glade,** glād, *n.* A green clear space or opening in a wood.

**Gladiator,** glad'i-ā-tėr, *n.* Among the Romans, one who fought with swords, etc., for the entertainment of the people; a prize-fighter.

**Gladiatorial,** glad'i-a-tō''ri-al, *a.* Pertaining to gladiators.

**Gladiolus,** gla-dī-ō'lus, *n.*; pl. **-li.** A beautiful genus of bulbous-rooted plants, abundant in S. Africa; sword-lily.

**Gladly,** glad'li, *adv.* With pleasure; joyfully.

**Gladsome,** glad'sum, *a.* Joyful; cheerful; pleasing.

**Glair,** glār, *n.* The white of an egg, used as a varnish for paintings; any substance resembling the white of an egg.

**Glamor,** glam'ėr, *n.* Magic influence causing a person to see objects differently from what they really are; witchery.

**Glance,** glāns, *n.* A sudden shoot of light or splendor; a glimpse or sudden look.—*vi.* (glancing,

G

glanced). To shine; to gleam; to dart aside; to look with a sudden rapid cast of the eye; to move quickly; to hint.—*vt.* To shoot or dart suddenly or obliquely; to cast for a moment.

**Glancingly,** glans'ing-li, *adv.* By glancing; in a glancing manner; transiently.

**Gland,** gland, *n.* An acorn; any acorn-shaped fruit; a roundish organ in many parts of the body secreting some fluid; a secreting organ in plants.

**Glanders,** glan'dėrz, *n.* A disease of the mucous membrane about the mouth in horses.

**Glandular,** gland'ū-lėr, *a.* Having the character of a gland; consisting of glands.

**Glandule,** gland'ūl, *n.* A small gland.

**Glare,** glār, *n.* A bright dazzling light; a fierce piercing look.—*vi.* (glaring, glared). To shine with excessive luster; to look with fierce piercing eyes.

**Glaring,** glār'ing, *p.a.* Excessively bright; vulgarly splendid; notorious; barefaced.

**Glaringly,** glār'ing-li, *adv.* Oenly; notoriously.

**Glass,** gläs, *n.* A hard transparent substance; a small drinking vessel of glass; a mirror; quantity of liquor that a glass vessel contains; a lens; a telescope; a barometer; *pl.* spectacles.—*a.* Made of glass; vitreous.

**Glass-blower,** gläs'blō-ėr, *n.* One who blows and fashions glass vessels.

**Glass-house,** gläs'hous, *n.* A house where glass is made; a house made of glass.

**Glass-paper,** gläs'pā-pėr, *n.* A polishing paper covered with finely-pounded glass.

**Glass-work,** gläs'wėrk, *n.* The manufacture of glass; a place where glass is made.

**Glass,** gläs'i, *a.* Made of glass; vitreous; resembling glass in its properties.

**Glaucoma, Glaucosis,** gla-kō'ma, gla-kō'sis, *n.* An opacity of the vitreous humor of the eye, giving it a bluish-green tint.

**Glaucous,** gla'kus, *a.* Of a sea-green color; covered with a fine bluish or greenish bloom or powder.

**Glaze,** glāz, *vt.* (glazing, glazed). To furnish with glass; to incrust with a vitreous substance; to make smooth and glossy.—*n.* A vitreous or transparent coating.

**Glazer,** glā'zėr, *n.* One who or that which glazes.

**Glazier,** glā'zhėr, *n.* One whose business is to set window-glass.

**Glazing,** glāz'ing, *n.* Act or art of one who glazes; enamel; glaze.

**Gleam,** glēm, *n.* A small stream of light; brightness.—*vi.* To shoot or dart, as rays of light; to shine; to flash.

**Gleamy,** glēm'i, *a.* Darting beams of light; casting light in rays.

**Glean,** glēn, *vt.* and *i.* To gather stalks and ears of grain left behind by reapers; to pick up here and there; to gather slowly and assiduously.

**Gleaner,** glēn'ėr, *n.* One who gleans.

**Glebe,** glēb, *n.* Soil; ground; land belonging to a parish church or ecclesiastical benefice.

**Glede,** glēd, *n.* A bird of prey, the common kite of Europe.

**Glee,** glē, *n.* Joy; mirth; a composition for voices in three or more parts.

**Gleeful, Gleesome,** glē'ful, glē'sum, *a.* Full of glee; merry; gay; joyous.

**Gleet,** glēt, *n.* A transparent mucous discharge from the urethra; a thin ichor.

**Glen,** glen, *n.* A narrow valley; a dale; a depression or space between hills.

**Glib,** glib, *a.* Smooth; slippery; having plausible words always ready.

**Glide,** glīd, *vi.* (gliding, glided). To flow gently; to move or slip along with ease.—*n.* Act of moving smoothly.

**Glider,** glīd'ėr, *n.* A modification of the airplane, which can travel through the air for a certain time without engine power.

**Glimmer,** glim'ėr, *vi.* To shine faintly, and with frequent intermissions; to flicker.—*n.* A faint light; a twinkle.

**Glimmering,** glim'ėr-ing, *p.a.* Shining faintly.—*n.* A glimmer; faint view; glimpse.

**Glimpse,** glimps, *n.* A gleam or flash of light; short transitory view; faint resemblance; slight tinge.—*vi.* To appear by glimpses.

**Glint,** glint, *vi.* To glance; to give a flash of light.—*n.* A glance, flash, gleam.

**Glisten,** glis'n, *vi.* To glitter; to sparkle.

**Glister,** glis'tėr, *vi.* To glisten; to be bright; to sparkle.—*n.* Glitter; luster.

**Glitter,** glit'ėr, *vi.* To sparkle with light; to be showy, specious, or striking.—*n.* Brightness; luster.

**Gloaming,** glōm'ing, *n.* Fall of the evening; the twilight; decline.

**Gloat,** glōt, *vi.* To gave earnestly; to feast the eyes; to contemplate with evil satisfaction.

**Globate, Globated,** glōb'āt, glōb'āt-ed, *a.* Having the form of a globe; spherical.

**Globe,** glōb, *n.* A round solid body; a sphere; the earth; an artificial sphere on whose surface is drawn a map of the earth or heavens.—*vt.* To gather into a round mass.

**Globular,** glob'ū-lėr, *a.* Having the form of a ball or sphere; spherical.

**Globule,** glob'ūl, *n.* A little globe; a small spherical particle; one of the red particles of the blood.

**Globulin,** glob'ū-lin, *n.* The main ingredient of blood globules and resembling albumen.

**Glomerate,** glom'ė-rāt, *vt.* To gather or wind into a ball.

**Glomeration,** glom-ė-rā'shon, *n.* Act of glomerating; body formed into a ball.

**Gloom,** glöm, *n.* Obscurity; thick shade; sadness; aspect of sorrow; darkness of prospect or aspect.—*vi.* To shine obscurely; to be cloudy or dark; to be sullen or sad.

**Gloomily,** glöm-i-li, *adv.* Darkly; dismally; sullenly.

**Gloomy,** glöm'i, *a.* Dark; dismal; downcast; sad.

**Glorification,** glō'ri-fi-kā''shon, *n.* Act of glorifying; laudation.

**Glorify,** glō'ri-fī, *vt.* (glorifying, glorified). to make glorious; to ascribe glory or honor to; to extol.

**Gloriole,** glō'ri-ōl, *n.* A circle, as of rays, in paintings surrounding the heads of saints.

**Glorious,** glō'ri-us, *a.* Full of glory; renowned; celebrated; grand; brilliant.

**Gloriously,** glō'ri-us-li, *adv.* In a glorious manner; splendidly; illustriously.

**Glory,** glō'ri, *n.* Praise, honor, admiration, or distinction; renown; magnificence; celestial bliss; the divine presence; the divine perfections; that of which one may be proud.—*vi.* (glorying, gloried). To boast; to rejoice; to be proud with regard to something.

**Gloss,** glos, *n.* Brightness from a smooth surface; sheen; specious appearance; an interpretation; comment.—*vt.* To give superficial luster to; to give a specious appearance to; to render plausible; to comment; to annotate.

**Glossarial,** glos-sā'ri-al, *a.* Containing explanation.

**Glossary,** glos'a-ri, *n.* A vocabulary explaining antiquated or difficult words or phrases.

**Glosser,** glos'ėr, *n.* A writer of glosses.

**Glossographer,** glos-og'ra-fėr, *n.* A writer of glosses; a scholiast.

**Glossology, Glottology,** glos-ol'o-ji, glot-ol'o-ji, *n.* The science of language; comparative philology.

**Glossy,** glos'i, *a.* Smooth and shining; highly polished.

**Glottal,** glot'al, *a.* Pertaining to the glottis.

**Glottis,** glot'is, *n.* The narrow opening at the upper part of the windpipe.

**Glove,** gluv, *n.* A cover for the hand.—*vt.* (gloving, gloved). To cover with a glove.

**Glover,** gluv'ėr, *n.* One who makes or sells gloves.

**Glow,** glō, *vi.* To burn with intense heat, especialy without flame; to feel great heat of body; to be flushed; to be ardent; to rage.—*n*. White heat; brightness of color; animation.

**Glowing,** glō'ing, *p.a.* Exhibiting a bright color; vehement; inflamed, fervent.

**Glowworm,** glō'wėrm, *n*. A wingless female beetle which emits a greenish light.

**Glucose,** glö'kōs, *n*. Grape-sugar, a sugar produced from grapes, starch, etc.

**Glue,** glö, *n*. A tenacious, viscid matter which serves as a cement.—*vt*. (gluing, glued). To join with glue; to unite.

**Gluey,** glö'i, *a*. Viscous; glutinous.

**Glum,** glum, *a*. Sullen; moody; dejected.

**Glume,** glöm, *n*. The husk or chaff of grain; a bract of plants.

**Glut,** glut, *vt*. (glutting, glutted). To swallow greedily; to cloy; to satiate; to furnish beyond sufficiency.—*n*. Plenty, even to loathing; supply of an article beyond the demand.

**Gluten,** glö'ten, *n*. A tough, elastic, nitrogenous substance in the flour of wheat, etc.

**Glutinate,** glö'tin-āt, *vt*. To unite with glue.

**Glutinous,** glö'tin-us, *a*. Gluey; viscous; viscid; tenacious; resembling glue.

**Glutton,** glut'n, *n*. One who eats to excess; one eager of anything to excess; a carnivorous quadruped.

**Gluttonize,** glut'n-īz, *vi*. To indulge in guttony.

**Gluttonous,** glut'n-us, *a*. Given to excessive eating; insatiable.

**Gluttony,** glut'n-i, *n*. Excess in eating; voracity of appetite.

**Glycerine,** glis'ėr-in, *n*. A transparent, colorless, sweet liquid obtained from fats.

**Glyphic,** glif'ik, *a*. Of or pertaining to carving or sculpture.

**Glyptic,** glip'tik, *a*. Pertaining to the art of engraving on precious stones.

**Glyptography,** glip-tog'ra-fi, *n*. The art of engraving on gems.

**Gnarl,** närl, *n*. A protuberance on the outside of a tree; a knot.

**Gnarled,** närld, *a*. Knotty; perverse.

**Gnarr, Gnarl,** när, närl, *vi*. To growl to murmur; to snarl.

**Gnash,** nash, *vt*. To strike together, as the teeth.—*vi*. To strike or dash the teeth together, as in rage or pain.

**Gnat,** nat, *n*. A small two-winged fly, the female of which bites.

**Gnaw,** nä, *vt*. To bite by little and little; to bite in agony or rage; to fret; to corrode.—*vi*. To use the teeth in biting; to cause steady annoying pain.

**Gneiss,** nīs, *n*. A species of rock composed of quartz, feldspar, and mica, and having a slaty structure.

**Gnome,** nōm, *n*. A sprite supposed to inhabit the inner parts of the earth; a dwarf; a maxim, aphorism.

**Gnomic, Gnomical,** nō'mik, nō'mik-al, *a*. Containing or dealing in maxims.

**Gnomon,** nō'mon, *n*. The style or pin of a dial; a geometrical figure.

**Gnostic,** nos'tik, *n*. One of an early religious sect whose doctrines were based partly on Christianity and partly on Greek and Oriental philosophy.

**Gnosticism,** nos'ti-sizm, *n*. The doctrines of the Gnostics.

**Gnu,** nū, *n*. A large south African antelope.

**Go,** gō, *vi*. (going, pret, went, pp. gone). To move; to proceed; to depart; to be about to do; to circulate; to tend; to be guided; to be alienated or sold; to reach; to avail; to conduce; to die; to fare; to become.

**Goad,** gōd, *n*. A pointed instrument to make a beast move faster; anything that stirs into action. *vt*. To drive with a goad; to instigate.

**Goal,** gōl, *n*. The point set to bound a race; a mark that players in some outdoor sport must attain; a success scored by reaching this; final purpose; end.

**Goat,** gōt, *n*. A ruminant quadruped with long hair and horns.

**Goatherd,** gōt'hėrd, *n*. One whose occupation is to tend goats.

**Goatish,** gōt'ish, *a*. Resembling a goat; of a rank smell.

**Goat-skin,** gōt'skin, *n*. Leather made from the skin of goats.

**Goat-sucker,** gōt'suk-ėr, *n*. A bird that preys on nocturnal insects: the night-jar.

**Gobbet,** gob'et, *n*. A mouthful; a lump.

**Gobble,** gob'l, *vt*. (gobbling, gobbled). To swallow in large pieces or hastily.—*vi*. To make a noise in the throat, as a turkey.

**Gobbler,** gob'lėr, *n*. One who gobbles; a greedy eater; a gormandizer; a turkey-cock.

**Go-between,** gō'bē-twēn, *n*. Intermediary.

**Goblet,** gob'let, *n*. A kind of cup or drinking vessel without a handle.

**Goblin,** gob'lin, *n*. A mischievous sprite; an elf.

**Goby,** gō'bi, *n*. A name of various small fishes.

**Go-by,** gō-bī', *n*. A passing without notice; intentional disregard or avoidance.

**God,** god, *n*. The Supreme Being; a divinity; a deity.

**Goddess,** god'es, *n*. A female deity; a woman of superior charms.

**Godfather,** god'fä-ᴛʜėr, *n*. A man who becomes sponsor for a child at baptism. (Also *godmother, -son, -daughter,* and *-child.*).

**Godhead,** god'hed, *n*. Godship; divinity; divine nature or essence.

**Godless,** god'les, *a*. Having or acknowledging no God; ungodly; atheistical.

**Godlike,** god'līk, *a*. Resembling God; divine; resembling a deity; of superior excellence.

**Godliness,** god'li-nes, *n*. Quality of being godly; piety; reverence for God.

**Godly,** god'li, *a*. Reverencing God; pious; devout; holy; religious; righteous.

**Godsend,** god'send, *n*. An unexpected acquisition or good fortune.

**Godship,** god'ship, *n*. Deity; rank of a god.

**God-speed,** god'spēd, *n*. Success; prosperity.

**Godwit,** god'wit, *n*. A bird resembling a curlew.

**Goer,** gō'ėr, *n*. One who or that which goes; a runner or walker.

**Goffer,** gof'ėr, *vt*. To plait or flute.

**Goggle,** gog'l, *vi*. (goggling, goggled). To roll or strain the eyes.—*a*. Prominent, rolling, or staring (eyes).—*n*. A strained or affected rolling of the eye; *pl*. a kind of spectacles to protect the eyes or cure squinting.

**Goggle-eyed,** gog'l-īd, *a*. Having prominent, distorted, or rolling eyes.

**Going,** gō'ing, *n*. Act of one who goes; departure; way; state of roads.—**Goings-on,** actions; behavior.

**Goiter,** goi'tėr, *n*. A morbid enlargment of the thyroid gland, forming a masss on the front of the neck.

**Gold,** gōld, *n*. A precious metal of a bright yellow color; money; something pleasing or valuable; a bright yellow color.—*a*. Made or consisting of gold.

**Gold-beater,** gōld'bēt-ėr, *n*. One who beats gold into thin leaves for gilding.

**Gold-crest,** gōld-krest, *n*. The smallest British bird; the golden-crested wren.

**Golden,** gōld'n, *a*. Made of gold; like gold; splendid; most valuable; auspicious.

**Gold-field,** gōld'fēld, *n*. District or region where gold is found.

**Goldfinch,** gōld'finsh, *n*. A beautiful singing bird.

**Gold-fish,** gōld'fish, *n*. A fresh-water fish of the carp family, of a bright orange color.

**Gold-leaf,** gōld'lēf, *n*. Gold beaten into a thin leaf.

**Goldsmith,** gōld'smith, *n*. One who manufacturers articles of gold and silver.

**Goldylocks,** gōld'i-loks, *n*. A plant with yellow flowers; a ranunculus.

**Golf,** golf, *n*. A game played over links with a small ball driven by clubs.—*vi*. To play golf.

**Golfer,** gol'fėr, *n.* One who plays golf.
**Golfing,** golf'ing, *n.* Act of playing golf.
**Gondola,** gon'dō-la, *n.* A long narrow pleasure-boat, used in Venice.
**Gondolier,** gon-dō-lēr', *n.* A man who rows a gondola.
**Gong,** gong, *n.* A kind of metallic drum; a similar article used instead of a bell.
**Gonidium,** gon-nid'i-um, *n.*; pl. **-dia.** A secondary reproductive cell in the thallus of lichens.
**Goniometer,** gō-ni-om'et-ėr, *n.* An instrument for measuring solid angles.
**Good,** gud, *a.* The opposite of bad; wholesome; useful; fit; virtuous; valuable; benevolent; clever; adequate; valid; able to fulfil engagements; considerable; full or complete; immaculate.—*n.* What is good or desirable; advantage; welfare; virtue; *pl.* commodities, chattels, movables.—**For good,** to close the whole business; finally.—*interj.* Well; right.
**Good-bye,** gud-bī, *n.* or *interj.* A salutation at parting; farewell.
**Good-day,** gud-dā', *n.* or *interj.* A salutation at meeting or parting; farewell.
**Good-for-nothing,** gud'for-nu-thing, *n.* An idle; worthless person.—*a.* Worthless.
**Good-humor,** gud-hū'mėr, *n.* A cheerful temper or state of mind.
**Good-humored,** gud-hū'mėrd, *a.* Being of a cheerful temper.
**Goodly,** gud'li, *a.* Good-looking; handsome; graceful; desirable.
**Good-morning,** gud-morn'ing, *n.* or *interj.* A form of morning salutation .
**Good-nature,** gud-nā'tūr, *n.* Natural mildness and kindness of disposition.
**Good-natured,** gud-nā'tūrd, *a.* Naturally mild in temper; not easily provoked.
**Goodness,** gud'nes, *n.* State or quality of being good; excellence, virtue, etc.; a euphemism for God.
**Good-night,** gud-nīt', *n.* or *interj.* A form of salutation in parting for the night.
**Good-sense,** gud-sens', *n.* Sound judgment.
**Good-will,** gud-wil', *n.* Benevolence; business connecton of some established business.
**Goody, Goody-good, Goody-goody,** gud'i, gud'i-gud, gud'i-gud-i, *a.* Affected wth mawkish morality; squeamish in morals.
**Googly,** gō-gli, *n.* At cricket, a ball which breaks in from the off while delivered with a leg-break action.
**Goosander,** gös'an-dėr, *n.* A swimming bird allied to the ducks and divers.
**Goose,** gös, *n.*; pl. **Geese,** gēs. A swimming bird larger than the duck; a tailor's smoothing-iron; a silly person.
**Gooseberry,** gös'be-ri, *n.* The fruit of a prickly shrub, and the shrub itself.
**Goose-quill,** gös'kwil, *n.* The large feather or quill of a goose, or a pen made with it.
**Goosery,** gös'ė-ri, *n.* A place for geese; qualities of a goose; folly.
**Goose-step,** gös-step, *n.* Act of marking time by raising the feet alternately without advancing.
**Gopher,** gō'fėr, *n.* The name given in America to several burrowing animals.
**Gor-cock,** gor'kok, *n.* The moor-cock or red grouse.
**Gordian knot,** gor'di-an not. An inextricable difficulty; *to cut the Gordian knot,* to remove a diffculity by bold measures.
**Gore,** gōr, *n.* Blood that is shed; thick or clotted blood; a wedge-shaped piece of land or cloth; a gusset.—*vt.* (goring, gored). To cut in a triangular form; to pierce with a pointed instrument, or an animal's horns.
**Gorge,** gorj, *n.* The throat; the gullet; a narrow passage between hills or mountains; entrance into a bastion.—*vt.* and *i.* (gorging, gorged). To swallow with greediness; to glut; to satiate.
**Gorgeous,** gor'jus, *a.* Showy; splendid; magnificent.
**Gorget,** gor'jet, *n.* A piece of armor for defending the neck; a pendent ornament formerly worn by officers when on duty.
**Gorgon,** gor'gon, *n.* A monster of Greek mythology, one of three sisters.—*a.* Like a gorgon; very ugly or terrific.
**Gorgonzola,** gor-gon-zō'la, *n.* A kind of Italian ewe-milk cheese.
**Gorilla,** gor-il'la, *n.* The largest animal of the ape kind.
**Gormand,** gor'mand, *n.* A glutton.
**Gormandize,** gor'mand-īz, *vi.* To eat greedily or to excess.
**Gormandizer,** gor'mand-īz-ėr, *n.* A glutton.
**Gorse,** gors, *n.* A shrubby plant; furze; whin.
**Gorsy,** gors'i, *a.* Abounding in gorse.
**Gory,** gō'ri, *a.* Covered with gore; bloody; murderous.
**Goshawk,** gos'hak, *n.* A large bird of the hawk family.
**Gosling,** goz'ling, *n.* A young goose.
**Gospel,** gos'pel, *n.* The history of Jesus Christ; any of the four records of Christ's life by his apostles; scheme of salvation as taught by Christ; any general doctrine.—*a.* Relating to the gospel; accordant with the gospel.
**Gospeller,** gos'pel-ėr, *n.* An evangelist; he who reads the gospel in the church service.
**Gossamer,** gos'a-mėr, *n.* A fine, filmy substance, like cobwebs, floating in the air in calm, sunny weather; a thin fabric.
**Gossip,** gos'ip, *n.* An idle tattler; idle talk. *vi.* To prate; to run about and tattle.
**Gossipry,** gos'ip-ri, *n.* Relationship by baptismal rites; idle talk or gossip.
**Gossipy,** gos'ip-i, *a.* Full of gossip.
**Goth,** goth, *n.* One of an ancient Teutonic race; a barbarian; one defective in taste.
**Gothic,** goth'ik, *a.* Pertaining to the Goths; rude; barbarous; denoting the style of architecture characterized by the pointed arch.—*n.* The language of the Goths: the Gothic order of architecture.
**Gothicism,** goth'i-sizm, *n.* Rudeness of manners; conformity to the Gothic style of architecture.
**Gouda,** gou'da, *n.* A kind of cheese from *Gouda,* A town in Holland.
**Gouge,** gouj, göj, *n.* A chisel with a hollow or grooved blade.—*vt.* (gouging, gouged). To scoop out with, or as with, a gouge.
**Gourd,** gōrd, *n.* The popular name of the family of plants represented by the melon, cucumber, etc.; a cup made from the rind of a gourd.
**Gourmand,** gör'mänd, *n.* A glutton; a gourmet.
**Gourmandize,** gör'mand-īz, *vi.* To gormandize.
**Gourmet,** gör-mā or gör'met, *n.* A connoisseur in wines and meats; a nice feeder.
**Gout,** gout, *n.* A painful disease, affecting generally the small joints; a drop; a clot or coagulation.
**Gout,** gö, *n.* Taste; relish.
**Gouty,** gout'i, *a.* Diseased with or subject to gout; pertaining to gout.
**Govern,** gu'vėrn, *vt.* To direct and control; to regulate; to steer; to affect so as to determine the case, etc., in grammar.—*vi.* To exercise authority; to administer the laws.
**Governable,** gu'vėrn-a-bl, *a.* That may be governed.
**Governance,** gu'vėrn-ans, *n.* Exercise of authority; control.
**Governess,** gu'vėrn-es, *n.* A female who governs or instructs.
**Government,** gu'vėrn-ment, *n.* Rule; control; administration of public affairs; system of polity in a state; territory ruled by a governor; executive power; the influence of a word in grammar in regard to construction.
**Governmental,** gu-vėrn-ment'al, *a.* Pertaining to or sanctioned by government.
**Governor,** gu'vėrn-ėr, *n.* One who governs; one invested with supreme authority; a tutor; a contrivance in machinery for maintaining a

uniform velocity.

**Governorship,** gu'vėrn-ėr-ship, *n.* The office of a governor.

**Gowan,** gou'an, *n.* The common daisy.

**Gown,** goun, *n.* A woman's outer garment; a long, loose garment worn by professional men, as divines.—*vt.* To put on a gown.

**Gownsman,** gounz'man, *n.* One whose professional habit is a gown, particularly a member of an English university.

**Grab,** grab, *vt.* (grabbing, grabbed). To seize; to snatch.—*n.* A sudden grasp; implement for clutching objects.

**Grace,** grās, *n.* Favor; kindness; love and favor of God; state of reconciliation to God; pardon; license or privilege; expression of thanks before or after meals; title of a duke or archbishop; elegance with appropriate dignity; an embellishment; one of three ancient goddesses in whose gift were grace and beauty; in *music,* a trill, shake, etc.—*vt.* (gracing, graced). To lend grace to; to adorn; to favor.

**Graceful,** grās'ful, *a.* Full of grace; beautiful with dignity; elegant.

**Gracefully,** grās'ful-li, *adv.* In a graceful manner; elegantly.

**Graceless,** grās'les, *a.* Void of grace; unregenerate; unsanctified; profligate.

**Gracile,** gras'īl, *a.* Slight and elegant.

**Gracious,** grā'shus, *a.* Full of grace; favorable; disposed to forgive offenses and impart blessings; benignant; condescending.

**Graciously,** grā'shus-li, *adv.* Kindly; favorably, with kind condescension.

**Gradation,** gra-dā'shon, *n.* Arrangement by grades; regular advance step by step; rank; series; regular process by degrees.

**Gradatory,** grā'da-to-ri, *a.* Proceeding step by step; marking gradation.—*n.* Steps from the cloisters into the church.

**Grade,** grād, *n.* A step; degree; rank; gradient.—*vt.* (grading, graded). To arrange in order of rank, etc.; to reduce to a suitable slope.

**Gradient,** grā'di-ent, *a.* Moving by steps; rising or descending by regular degrees.—*n.* The degree of ascent or descent in a road, etc.; part of a road which slopes.

**Gradual,** grad'ū-al, *a.* Advancing step by step; regular and slow.—*n.* An order of steps.

**Gradually,** grad'ū-al-li, *adv.* By degrees; step by step; regularly; slowly.

**Graduate,** grad'ū-āt, *vt.* (graduating, graduated). To divide into regular intervals or degrees; to mark with such; to arrange by grades; to confer a university degree on; to reduce to a certain consistency by evaporation.—*vi.* To receive a university degree; to change gradually.—*n.* One who has received a degree of a university, etc.

**Graduation,** grad-ū-ā'shon, *n.* Marks to indicate degrees, etc.; regular progression; act of conferring or receiving academical degrees.

**Graft,** graft, *n.* A small scion of a tree inserted in another tree which is to support and nourish the scion; corrupt gains or practices in politics.—*vt.* To insert a graft on; to propagate by a graft; to join on as if organically; a part.

**Grail, Graal,** grāl, *n.* The holy vessel containing the last drops of Christ's blood, brought to England by Joseph of Arimathea, and, being afterwards lost, eagerly sought for by King Arthur's knights.

**Grain,** grān, *n.* A single seed of a plant; corn in general; a minute particle; a small weight; fibers of wood with regard to their arrangement; substance of a thing with respect to the size, form, or direction of the constituent particles; texture; dye.—*vt.* To paint in imitation of fibers; to granulate.

**Grained,** grānd, *p.a.* Having a certain grain or texture; having a granular surface.

**Graining,** grān'ing, *n.* A kind of painting in imitation of the grain of wood.

**Grallatorial,** gral-a-tō'ri-al, *a.* Pertaining to the Grallatores, an order of birds including cranes, snipes, etc., called also the *waders.*

**Gram,** gram, *n.* The French unit of weight, equal to 15.43 grains troy.

**Gramineal, Gramineous,** gra-min'ē-al, gra-min'ē-us, *a.* Grassy; pertaining to grass.

**Graminivorous,** gra-min-iv'ō-rus, *a.* Feeding on grass.

**Grammar,** gram'ėr, *n.* A system of principles and rules for speaking or writing a language; propriety of speech; an outline of any subject.

**Grammarian,** gram-mā'ri-an, *n.* One who is versed in or who teaches grammar.

**Grammatical, Grammatic,** gram-mat'ik-al, gram-mat'ik, *a.* Belonging to grammar; according to the rules of grammar.

**Grammatically,** gram-mat'ik-al-li, *adv.* According to grammar.

**Grammaticize,** gram-mat'i-sīz, *vt.* To render grammatical.

**Gramophone,** gram'o-fōn, *n.* An instrument for recording and reproducing speech and music by purely mechanical means.

**Grampus,** gram'pus, *n.* A large marine mammal.

**Granary,** gra'na-ri, *n.* A storehouse for grain after it is thrashed.

**Grand,** grand, *a.* Great, figuratively; majestic; magnificent; noble.

**Grandam,** gran'dam, *n.* An old woman; a grandmother.

**Grandchild,** grand'chīld, *n.* A son's or daughter's child.

**Granddaughter,** grand'da-tėr, *n.* The daughter of a son or daughter.

**Grandee,** gran-dē', *n.* A man of elevated rank; a nobleman.

**Grandeur,** grand'yūr, *n.* Greatness; sublimity; splendor; magnificence.

**Grandfather,** grand'fä-THėr, *n.* A father's or mother's father.

**Grandiloquence,** grand-il'ō-kwens, *n.* Lofty speaking; pompous language.

**Grandiose,** gran'di-ōs, *a.* Impressive from grandeur; bombastic; turgid.

**Grandly,** grand'li, *adv.* In a grand or lofty manner; splendidly; sublimely.

**Grandmother,** grand'muTH-ėr, *n.* The mother of one's father or mother.

**Grandsire,** grand'sīr, *n.* A grandfather; any ancestor.

**Grandson,** grand'sun, *n.* The son of a son or daughter.

**Grandstand,** grand'stand, *n.* An erection of a race-course, etc., affording a good view.

**Grange,** grānj, *n.* A farm, with the buildings, stables, etc.

**Granite,** gran'it, *n.* A rock composed of quartz, feldspar, and mica, or at least of two of them, confusedly crystallized.

**Granitic,** gran-it'ik, *a.* Like granite; pertaining to or consisting of granite.

**Granivorous,** grān-iv'ō-rus, *a.* Feeding on grain or seeds.

**Grant,** grant, *vt.* To bestow; to confer on; to admit as true; to convey by deed or writing; to cede.—*n.* A bestowing; a gift; a conveyance in writing; the thing conveyed.

**Grantor,** grant'or, *n.* The person who grants or conveys lands, etc.

**Granular,** gran'ū-lėr, *a.* Consisting of or resembling grains.

**Granulate,** gran'ū-lāt, *vt.* and *i* (granulating, granulated). To form into grains; to make or become rough on the surface.

**Granulation,** gran-ū-lā'shon, *n.* Act of forming into grains; a process by which minute fleshy bodies are formed on wounds during healing; the fleshy grains themselves.

**Granule,** gran'ūl, *n.* A little grain.

**Granulous, Granulose,** gran-ūl-us, gran'ūl-ōs, *a.* Full of granules.

G

**Grape,** grāp, *n.* A single berry of the vine; grape-shot.
**Grapefruit,** grāp'fröt, *n.* A pale-yellow fruit akin to the orange, but larger and sourer.
**Grape-shot,** grāp'shot, *n.* A cluster of small balls, confined in a cavas bag, to be fired from ordnance.
**Graph,** graf, *n.* A diagram representing the relation between two varying magnitudes by means of a curve or series of lines.
**Graphic, Graphical,** graf'ik, graf'ik-al, *a.* Pertaining to the art of writing or delineating; pictorial; vivid.
**Graphically,** graf'ik-al-li, *adv.* In a vivid and forcible way.
**Graphite,** graf'īt, *n.* A form of carbon, made into pencils; plumbago; black-lead.
**Grapnel,** grap'nel, *n.* A small anchor with four or five claws.
**Grapple,** grap'l, *vt.* (grappling, grappled). To lay fast hold on, with hands or hooks.—*vi.* To contend in close fight, as wrestlers.—*n.* A seizing; close hug in contest; grappling-iron.
**Grappling-iron,** grap'ling-ī-ėrn, *n.* An instrument of four or more iron claws for grappling and holding fast; a grapnel.
**Graphy,** grāp'i, *a.* Like grapes; full of grapes; made of grapes.
**Grasp,** gräsp, *vt.* To seize and hold by the fingers or arms; to take possession of; to comprehend.—*vi.* To make a clutch or catch.—*n.* Gripe of the hand; reach of the arms; power of seizing or comprehending.
**Grasping,** gräsp'ing, *p.a.* Avaricious; greedy.
**Grass,** gräs, *n.* Herbage; any plant of the family to which belong the grain-yielding and pasture plants.—*vt.* To cover with grass; to bleach on the grass.
**Grasshopper,** gräs'hop-ėr, *n.* An insect that hops among grass, allied to the locusts.
**Grate,** grāt, *n.* A frame composed of parallel or cross-bars; grating; iron frame for holding coals used as fuel.—*vt.* (grating, grated). To furnish or make fast with cross-bars; to wear away in small particles by rubbing; to offend, as by a discordant sound.—*vi.* To rub roughly on; to have an annoying effect; to sound harshly.
**Grateful,** grāt'ful, *a.* Pleasing; gratifying; feeling or expressing gratitude.
**Grater,** grāt'er, *n.* An instrument for rubbing off small particles of a body.
**Gratification,** grat'i-fi-kā''shon, *n.* Act of gratifying; that which affords pleasure; satisfaction; recompense.
**Gratify,** grat'i-fī, *vt.* (gratifying, gratified). To please; to indulge, delight, humor.
**Gratifying,** grat'i-fī-ing, *p.a.* Giving pleasure; affording satisfaction.
**Grating,** grāt'ing, *n.* A frame or partition of bars or lattice-work.
**Gratis,** grā'tis, *adv.* Without recompense; freely.—*a.* Given or done for nothing.
**Gratitude,** grat'i-tūd, *n.* Quality of being grateful; an emotion of the heart, excited by a favor received; thankfulness.
**Gratuitous,** gra-tū'it-us, *a.* That is done out of favor; free; voluntary; asserted or taken without proof.
**Gratuitously,** gra-tū'it-us-li, *adv.* Freely; voluntarily.
**Gratuity,** gra-tū'i-ti, *n.* A free gift; donation; something given in return for a favor.
**Gratulate,** grat'ū-lāt, *vt.* To congratulate.
**Gratulation,** grat-ū-lā'shon, *n.* Congratulation.
**Gratulatory,** grat'ū-la-to-ri, *a.* Congratulatory.
**Gravamen,** gra-vā'men, *n.* Ground or burden of complaint.
**Grave,** grāv, *vt.* (graving, pret. graved, pp. graven, graved). To make incisions on; to engrave; to impress deeply; as on the mind; to clean, as a ship's bottom, and cover with pitch.—*n.* A pit for the dead; a tomb.—*a.* Weighty; serious; staid; thoughtful; not gay; not tawdry; in *music*, low.
**Grave-digger,** grāv'dig-ėr, *n.* One whose occupation is to dig graves.
**Gravel,** gra'vel, *n.* Small pebbles; a disease produced by small concretions in the kidneys and bladder.—*vt.* (gravelling, gravelled). To cover with gravel; to cause to stick in the sand or gravel; to puzzle.
**Gravelly,** gra'vel-i, *a.* Abounding with gravel; consisting of gravel.
**Gravely,** grāv'li, *adv.* In a grave, solemn manner; soberly; seriously.
**Graver,** grāv'ėr, *n.* One who engraves; an engraving tool; a burin.
**Gravid,** grav'id, *a.* Being with young; pregnant.
**Graving-dock,** grāv'ing-dok, *n.* A dock in which a ship's bottom may be graved or cleaned; a dry-dock.
**Gravitate,** grav'i-tāt, *vt.* To be affected by gravitation; to tend towards the center.
**Gravitation,** grav-i-tā'shon, *n.* The force by which bodies are drawn towards the center of the earth; tendency of all matter toward all other matter.
**Gravity,** grav'i-ti, *n.* The tendency of matter toward some attracting body, particularly toward the center of the earth; state or character of being grave; weight; enormity.
**Gravy,** grā'vi, *n.* The juice that comes from flesh in cooking.
**Gray,** grā, *a.* Of the color of hair whitened by age; white with a mixture of black; having gray hairs.—*n.* A gray color; a gray animal, as a horse; early morning twilight.
**Gray-beard,** grā'bērd, *n.* An old man; an earthen jar for holding liquor.
**Grayish,** grā'ish, *a.* Somewhat gray.
**Grayling,** grā'ling, *n.* A fish of the salmon tribe.
**Graywacke, Grauwacke,** grā-wak'e, grou-wak'e, *n.* A sandstone in which fragments of minerals or rocks are embedded.
**Gray-wether,** grā'weтн-ėr, *n.* A large boulder of siliceous sandstone.
**Graze,** grāz, *vt.* (grazing, grazed). To rub or touch lightly in passing; to feed with growing grass, as cattle; to feed on.—*vi.* to pass so as to rub lightly; to eat grass; to supply grass.—*n.* A slight rub or brush.
**Grazier,** grā'zhėr, *n.* One who pastures cattle, and who rears them for market.
**Grazing,** grāz'ing, *n.* The act of feeding on grass; pasture.
**Grease,** grēs, *n.* Animal fat in a soft state; oily matter.—*vt.* (greasing, greased). To smear with grease.
**Greasy,** grēz'i, *a.* Smeared with grease; fatty; unctuous; like grease.
**Great,** grāt, *a.* Large in bulk or number; long-continued; of vast power and excellence; eminent; majestic; pregnant; distant by one more generation, as *great*-grandfather, etc.
**Greatcoat,** grāt'kōt, *n.* An overcoat.
**Great-hearted,** grāt'härt-ed, *a.* High-spirited; magnanimous; noble.
**Greatly,** grāt'li, *adv.* In a great degree; much; nobly; illustriously; bravely.
**Greatness,** grāt'nes, *n.* Quality of being great; magnitude; nobleness; grandeur.
**Greave,** grēv, *n.* Armor worn on the front of the lower part of the leg: generally in *pl.*.
**Grecian,** grē'shan, *a.* Pertaining to Greece.—*n.* A Greek; one well versed in the Greek language.
**Greed,** grēd, *n.* Eager desire; avarice.
**Greedily,** grēd'i-li, *adv.* Ravenously; eagerly.
**Greedy,** grēd'i, *a.* Having a keen appetite for food or drink; covetous; avaricious.
**Greek,** grēk, *a.* Pertaining to Greece.—*n.* A native of Greece; the language of Greece.
**Green,** grēn, *a.* Having the color of growing plants; verdant; fresh; containing its natural juices; unripe; young; easily imposed upon.—*n.* A green color; a grassy plain or plot; *pl.* leaves and stems of young plants used in cookery.—*vt.*

and *i*. To make or grow green.
**Green-gage**, grēn'gāj, *n*. A species of plum.
**Greenhorn**, grēn'horn, *n*. One easily imposed upon; a raw inexperienced person.
**Greenhouse**, grēn'hous, *n*. A building in which tender plants are cultivated.
**Greenish**, grēn'ish, *a*. Somewhat green.
**Greenness**, grēn'nes, *n*. Viridity; unripeness; freshness; vigor.
**Green-room**, grēn'röm, *n*. A retiring-room for actors in a theater.
**Greet**, grēt, *vt*. To salute; to meet and address with kindness.—*vi*. To meet and salute.
**Greeting**, grēt'ing, *n*. Salutation at meeting; compliment from one absent.
**Gregarious**, grē-gā'ri-us, *a*. Assembling or living in a flock; not habitually solitary.
**Gregorian**, gre-gō'ri-an, *a*. Pertaining to persons named Gregory.
**Grenade**, gre-nād', *n*. A small bomb, thrown by hand or fired from a rifle.
**Grenadier**, gren-a-dēr', *n*. A tall foot-soldier, one of a regiment of British guards.
**Grey**, grā, *See* GRAY.
**Greyhound**, grā'hound, *n*. A tall, slender, fleet dog kept for the chase.
**Grice**, grīs, *n*. A little pig.
**Grid**, grid, *n*. A grating; a gridiron.
**Grid**, grid, *n*. A grating; a gridiron.
**Griddle**, grid'l, *n*. A circular plate of iron, or a shallow pan, for baking cakes.
**Gride**, grīd, *vt*. and *i* (griding, grided). To pierce; to wound; to cause to grate; to scrape or graze along.
**Gridiron**, grid'ī-ėrn, *n*. A grated utensil for broiling flesh and fish; a frame upon which a ship rests, for inspection or repair.
**Grief**, grēf, *n*. Pain of mind produced by loss, misfortune, etc.; sorrow; cause of sorrow; trouble.
**Grievance**, grēv'ans, *n*. A wrong suffered; cause of complaint; trouble.
**Grieve**, grēv, *vt*. (grieving, grieved). To cause grief to; to deplore.—*vi*. To feel grief; to sorrow; to lament.
**Grievous**, grēv'us, *a*. Causing grief; hard to be borne; atrocious.
**Griffin, Griffon**, grif'in, grif'on, *n*. A fabled monster, in the fore part an eagle, in the hinder a lion.
**Grill**, gril, *vt*. To broil on a gridiron; to torment, as if by broiling.—*vi*. To suffer, as if from grilling.—*n*. A grated utensil for broiling meat, etc.
**Grilse**, grils, *n*. A young salmon on its first return to fresh water.
**Grim**, grim, *a*. of a forbidding or fear-inspiring aspect; stern; sullen; surly; ugly.
**Grimace**, gri-mās', *n*. A distortion of the countenance; air of affectation.—*vi*. To make grimaces.
**Grimalkin**, gri-mal'kin, *n*. An old cat.
**Grime**, grīm, *n*. Foul matter.—*vt*. (griming, grimed). To sully or soil deeply.
**Grimly**, grim'li, *adv*. Fiercely; sullenly.
**Grimy**, grīm'i, *a*. Full of grime; foul.
**Grin**, grin, *vi*. (grinning, grinned). To show the teeth, as in laughter, scorn, or anguish—*n*. Act of showing the teeth; a forced smile or restrained laugh.
**Grind**, grīnd, *vt*. (grinding, ground). To reduce to fine particles; to sharpen or polish by friction; to rub together; to oppress; to crush in pieces.—*vi*. To turn a mill; to be moved or rubbed together; to be puverized by friction; to study hard.—*n*. Act of one who grinds; a laborious spell of work.
**Grinder**, grīnd'ėr, *n*. One who or that which grinds; a molar tooth.
**Grindstone**, grīnd'stōn, *n*. A circular stone, made to revolve, to sharpen tools.
**Grip**, grip, *n*. The act of grasping; grasp; a fast hold; a hilt or handle.—*vt*. and *i* (gripping, gripped). To grasp by the hand; to clutch; to hold fast.
**Gripe**, grīp, *vt*. and *i* (griping, griped). To grasp by the hand; to hold fast; to pinch; to give pain to the bowels.—*n*. Grasp; grip; something which grasps; *pl*. pinching pain in the bowels.
**Griping**, grīp'ing, *p.a*. Grasping; extortionate; oppressing; distressing the bowels.
**Grisette**, gri-zet', *n*. A young French woman of the working-class, especially a dress-maker.
**Grisly**, griz'li, *a*. Dreadful; fearful; ghastly.
**Grist**, grist, *n*. Corn ground, or for grinding.
**Gristle**, gris'l, *n*. Cartilage.
**Gristly**, gris'li, *a*. Consisting of gristle; cartilaginous.
**Grit**, grit, *n*. Sand or gravel; hard sandstone; texture of a stone; firmness of mind; coarse part of meal.
**Gritty**, grit'i, *a*. Containing sand or grit; consisting of grit; sandy.
**Grizzle**, griz'l, *n*. Gray; a gray color.
**Grizzled**, griz'ld, *a*. Gray; of a mixed color.
**Grizzly**, griz'li, *a*. Somewhat gray; gray with age.
**Groan**, grōn, *vi*. To utter a mournful voice, as in pain or sorrow; to moan.—*n*. A deep, mournful sound, uttered in pain, sorrow, or disapprobation; any low rumbling sound.
**Groat**, grōt, *n*. A former English coin and money of account, equal to fourpence; a small sum.
**Groats**, grōts, *n.pl*. Oats or wheat with the husks taken off.
**Grocer**, grō'sėr, *n*. A merchant who deals in tea, sugar, spices, etc.
**Grocery**, grō'sė-ri, *n*. A grocer's shop; the commodities sold by grocers.
**Grog**, grog, *n*. A mixture of spirit and water not sweetened.
**Groggy**, grog'i, *a*. Overcome with grog; tipsy; moving in an uneasy, hobbling manner.
**Grogram, Grogran**, grog'ram, grog'ran, *n*. A kind of coarse stuff made of silk and mohair, or silk and wool.
**Groin**, groin, *n*. The part of the human body between the belly and thigh in front; the angular projecting curve made by the intersection of simple vaults at any angle.
**Groined**, groind, *a*. Having a groin or groins; formed of groins meeting in a point.
**Groom**, gröm, *n*. A man or boy who has the charge of horses; a bridegroom.—*vt*. To feed and take care of, as a groom does horses.
**Groomsman**, grömz'man, *n*. One who acts as attendant on a bridegroom at his marriage.
**Groove**, gröv, *n*. A channel or long hollow cut by a tool; fixed routine of life.—*vt*. (grooving, grooved). To cut a groove in; to furrow.
**Grope**, grōp, *vi*. (groping, groped). To search in the dark by feeling; to feel one's way.—*vt*. To search out by feeling in the dark.
**Gropingly**, grōp'ing-li, *adv*. In a groping manner.
**Gross**, grōs, *a*. Thick; coarse; obscene; palpable; dense; shameful; dull; whole.—*n*. Main body; bulk; the number of twelve dozen.
**Grossbeak, Grosbeak**, grōs'bēk, *n*. A finch with a thick and strong bill.
**Grossly**, grōs'li, *adv*. Greatly; shamefully.
**Grot**, grot, *n*. A grotto; *poetical*.
**Grotesque**, grō-tesk', *a*. Wildly formed; extravagant; fantastic.—*n*. Whimsical figures or scenery.
**Grotto**, grot'tō, *n*. A natural cave; an artificial ornamented cave.
**Ground**, ground, *n*. Surface of the earth; soil; land; basis; reason; foil or background; predominating color; *pl*. dregs, sediment; ornamental land about a mansion—*vt*. To set on the ground; to found; to fix firmly; to instruct in first principles.—*vi*. To strike the bottom and remain fixed, as a ship.
**Ground-floor**, ground'flōr, *n*. Floor of a house o a level with the exterior ground.
**Groundless**, ground'les, *a*. Wanting foundation or reason; baseless; false.
**Groundling**, ground'ling, *n*. A fish that keeps at the bottom of the water.

**Ground-rent**, ground'rent, *n*. Rent for the privilege of building.
**Groundsel, Groundsill**, ground'sel, ground'sil, *n*. The timber of a building which lies on the ground; a sill.
**Groundsel**, ground'sel, *n*. A common annual weed, used as food for caged birds.
**Ground-swell**, ground'swel, *n*. Heaving of the sea caused by a distant storm.
**Groundwork**, ground'wėrk, *n*. Basis; fundamentals.
**Group**, gröp, *n*. A cluster; an assemblage; an artistic combination of figures; a class.—*vt*. To form into a group or groups.
**Grouping**, gröp'ing, *n*. The art of arranging or mode of arrangement in a picture or work of art.
**Grouse**, grous, *n*. The name of several wild rasorial birds, more particularly the moorfowl or red grouse of Britain.
**Grout**, grout, *n*. Coarse meal; a thin mortar; dregs.—*vt*. To fill up with grout or mortar.
**Grove**, grōv, *n*. A shady cluster of trees; a small wood.
**Grovel**, gro'vel, *vi*. (grovelling, grovelled). To lie prone, or creep on the earth; to be low or mean.
**Groveller**, gro'vel-ėr, *n*. One who grovels; an abject wretch.
**Grovelling**, gro'vel-ing, *p.a*. Apt to grovel; abject; base.
**Grow**, grō, *vi*. (pret. grew, pp. grown). To be augmented by natural process; to increase; to make progress; to become; to accrue; to swell.—*vt*. To raise from the soil; to produce.
**Grower**, grō'ėr, *n*. One who grows.
**Growl**, groul, *vi*. To murmur or snarl, as a dog; to utter an angry, grumbling sound.—*vt*. to express by growling.—*n*. Angry sound of a dog; grumbling murmur.
**Growler**, groul'ėr, *n*. One that growls; a grumbler.
**Grown**, grōn, *p.a*. Increased in growth; having arrived at full size or stature.
**Grown-up**, grōn'up, *a*. Adult.
**Growth**, grōth, *n*. Act or process of growing; product; increase; advancement.
**Groyne**, groin, *n*. A kind of small breakwater.
**Grub**, grub, *vi*.(grubbing, grubbed). To dig; to be employed meanly.—*vt*. To dig; to root out by digging.—*n*. The larva of an insect; caterpillar; maggot.
**Grubber**, grub'ėr, *n*. One who grubs; an instrument for digging up roots, weeds, etc.
**Grudge**, gruj, *vi*. (grudging, grudged). To cherish ill-will; to be envious.—*vt*. To permit or grant with reluctance; to envy.—*n*. Reluctance in giving; secret enmity.
**Grudgingly**, gruj'ing-li, *adv*. In a grudging unwilling, or envious manner.
**Gruel**, grū'el, *n*. A light food made by boiling meal in water.
**Gruesome**, grö'sum, *a*. Causing one to shudder; frightful; horrible; repulsive.
**Gruff**, gruf, *a*. Of a rough or stern manner or voice; surly; harsh.
**Gruffly**, gruf'li, *adv*. Roughly; harshly.
**Grum**, grum, *a*. Morose; surly; glum.
**Grumble**, grum'bl, *vi*. (grumbling, grumbled). To murmur with discontent.
**Grumbler**, grum'bl-ėr, *n*. One who grumbles; a discontented man.
**Grume**, gröm, *n*. A fluid of a thick, viscid consistence; a clot, as of blood.
**Grumpy, Grumpish**, grum'pi, grum'pish, *a*. Surly; angry; gruff; *colloq*.
**Grunt**, grunt, *vi*. To make a noise like a hog; to utter a deep guttural sound.—*n*. A deep guttural sound, as of a hog.
**Grunter**, grunt'ėr, *n*. One who grunts; a pig.
**Gruyère**, grü-yār, *n*. Cheese made from a mixture of goats' and ewes' milk.
**Guano**, gwä'nō, *n*. A rich manure composed chiefly of the excrements of sea-fowls, and brought from S. America and the Pacific.
**Guarantee**, ga-ran-tē', *n*. An undertaking by a third person that a covenant shall be observed by the contracting parties or by one of them; one who binds himself to see the stipulations of another performed.—*vt*. (guaranteeing, guaranteed). To warrant; to pledge oneself for.
**Guarantor**, gar-an-tor', *n*. One who gives a guarantee.
**Guard**, gärd, *vt*. To keep watch over; to secure against injury, loss, or attack.—*vi*. To watch, by way of caution or defense; to be in a state of caution or defense.—*n*. Defense; protector; sentinel; escort; attention; caution; posture of defense.
**Guarded**, gärd'ed, *p.a*. Circumspect; framed or uttered with caution.
**Guardedly**, gärd'ed-li, *adv*. With circumspection.
**Guard-house, Guard-room**, gärd'hous, gärd'röm, *n*. A house or room for the accommodation of a guard of soldiers, and where military defaulters are confined.
**Guardian**, gärd'i-an, *n*. One who guards; one appointed to take charge of an orphan or ward.—*a*. Protecting.
**Guardianship**, gärd'i-an-ship, *n*. The office of a guardian; protection; care.
**Guardsman**, gärdz'man, *n*. An officer or a private in a body of guards.
**Guava**, gwä'va, *n*. A small tropical tree of the myrtle family.
**Gudgeon**, gu'jon, *n*. A metallic piece let into the end of a wooden shaft; a small fresh-water fish; a person easily cheated.
**Guerdon** gėrdon', *n*. A reward; requital; recompense.—*vt*. To reward.
**Guerrilla, Guerilla**, ge-ril'la, *n*. An irregular petty war; one engaged in such.
**Guess**, ges, *vt*. To conjecture; to form an opinion without certain means of knowledge; to surmise.—*vi*. To conjecture; to judge at random.—*n*. Conjecture; surmise.
**Guess-work**, ges'wėrk, *n*. Work performed at hazard or by mere conjecture.
**Guest**, gest, *n*. A visitor or friend entertained in the house or at the table of another.
**Guffaw**, guf-fa', *n*. A loud burst of laughter.—*vi*. To burst into a loud laugh.
**Guggle**, gug'l, *vi*. To gurgle.
**Guidance**, gīd'ans, *n*. The act of guiding; direction; government; a leading.
**Guide**, gīd, *vt*. (guiding, guided). To lead; to direct; to influence; to regulate.—*n*. A person who guides; a director; a regulator; a guide-book.
**Guide-book**, gīd'buk, *n*. A book for the guidance of travellers.
**Guide-post**, gīd'pōst, *n*. A post for directing travellers the way; a finger-post.
**Guild, Gild**, gild, *n*. A corporation of craftsmen, etc., for mutual aid and protection.
**Guilder**, gil'der, *n*. A Dutch coin.
**Guildhall**, gild-hal', *n*. Hall where a guild assembles; a town or corporation hall.
**Guile**, gīl, *n*. Wile; fraud; duplicity.
**Guileful**, gīl'ful, *a*. Cunning; fraudulent.
**Guileless**, gīl'les, *a*. Artless; sincere; honest.
**Guillemot**, gil'e-mot, *n*. A marine swimming bird allied to the auks and divers.
**Guillotine**, gil-ō-tēn', *n*. A machine for beheading persons; a machine for cutting paper.—*vt*. To behead by the guillotine.
**Guilt**, gilt, *n*. Criminality; sin; wickedness.
**Guiltily**, gilt'i-li, *adv*. In a guilty manner.
**Guiltless**, gilt'les, *a*. Free from guilt.
**Guilty**, gilt'i, *a*. Justly chargeable with guilt; criminal; pertaining to or indicating guilt.
**Guinea**, gin'ē, *n*. A former British gold coin, or a sum of money.
**Guinea-fowl**, gin'ē-foul, *n*. A fowl allied to the peacocks and pheasants.
**Guinea-pig**, gin'ē-pig, *n*. A tailless rodent about 7 inches in length.
**Guipure**, gē-pūr', *n*. An imitation of antique lace.
**Guise**, gīz, *n*. External appearance; dress; mien;

cast of behavior.
**Guiser,** gīz'ėr, *n.* A person in disguise; a Christmas masker or mummer.
**Guitar,** gi-tär', *n.* A musical instrument having six strings.
**Gulch,** gulch, *n.* A gully; dry bed of a torrent.
**Gules,** gūlz, *n.* Red (in *heraldry*).
**Gulf,** gulf, *n.* An arm of the sea extending into the land; bay; chasm; whirlpool; anything insatiable; a wide interval.
**Gull,** gul, *vt.* To cheat.—*n.* One easily cheated; a simpleton; a marine swimming bird.
**Gullet,** gul'et, *n.* The passage in the neck of an animal by which food and liquor are taken into the stomach.
**Gullible,** gul'i-bl, *a.* Easily gulled or cheated.
**Gully,** gul'i, *n.* A channel worn by water; a ravine.—*vt.* To wear into a gully.
**Gulp,** gulp, *vt.* To swallow eagerly.—*n.* Act of taking a large swallow.
**Gum,** gum, *n.* The fleshy substance of the jaws round the teeth; a juice which exudes from trees, etc., and thickens; a viscous substance. *vt.* (gumming, gummed). To smear with or unite by a viscous substance.
**Gum-boil,** gum'boil, *n.* A boil on the gum.
**Gummy,** gum'i, *a.* Of the nature of gum; productive of gum; covered with gum.
**Gumption,** gum'shon, *n.* Understanding; capacity; shrewdness: *colloq.*
**Gun,** gun, *n.* Any species of firearm.
**Gun-boat,** gun'bōt, *n.* A small vessel of light draught, fitted for carrying one or more guns.
**Gun-cotton,** gun'kot-n, *n.* An explosive produced by soaking cotton, etc., in nitric and sulphuric acids, and leaving it to dry.
**Gunman,** gun'man, *n.* An armed bandit.
**Gun-metal,** gun'met-l, *n.* An alloy of copper and tin used for cannon, etc.
**Gunner,** gun'ėr, *n.* One who has the charge of ordnance.
**Gunnery,** gun'ė-ri, *n.* The art of firing cannon; the science of artillery.
**Gunpowder,** gun'pou-dėr, *n.* An explosive mixture of saltpeter, sulphur, and charcoal.
**Gunshot,** gun'shot, *n.* Range of a cannon-shot; firing of a gun.—*a.* Made by the shot of a gun.
**Gunwale, Gunnel,** gun'wāl, gun'el, *n.* The upper edge of a ship's side.
**Gurgle,** gėr'gl, *vi.* (gurgling, gurgled). To run or flow in a broken noisy current.—*n.* Sound produced by a liquid flowing from or through a narrow opening.
**Gurnard, Gurnet,** gėr'närd, gėr'net, *n.* A marine fish with an angular bony head.
**Gush,** gush, *vi.* To issue with violence and rapidity, as a fluid; to be effusively sentimental.—*n.* A sudden and violent issue of a fluid; the fluid thus emitted; effusive display of sentiment.
**Gushing,** gush'ing, *p.a.* Rushing forth with a gush; demonstratively affectionate.
**Gusset,** gus'et, *n.* A piece of cloth inserted in a garment.
**Gust,** gust, *n.* Taste; relish; a sudden blast of wind; a violent burst of passion.
**Gustatory,** gust'a-to-ri, *a.* Pertaining to taste.
**Gusto,** gust'ō, *n.* Relish; zest; taste.
**Gusty,** gust'i, *a.* Subject to sudden blasts of wind; stormy.
**Gut,** gut, *n.* The intestinal canal of an animal; *pl.* the entrails; a preparation of the intestines for various purposes; a channel.-*vt.* (gutting, gutted). To take out the entrails of; to plunder of contents; to destroy the interior of.
**Gutta-percha,** gut'ta-pėr'cha, *n.* The hardened milky juice of a tree of E. Asia.
**Gutter,** gut'ėr, *n.* A channel at the side of a road, etc., for water.—*vt.* To cut or form gutters in.—*vi.* To become channelled.
**Guttle,** gut'l, *vt.* and *t.* To guzzle.
**Guttural,** gut'tėr-al, *a.* Pertaining to the throat; formed in the throat.—*n.* A letter pronounced in the throat; any guttural sound.
**Guy,** gī, *n.* A rope to steady anything; a person of queer looks or dress.—*vt.* To steady or direct by means of a guy.
**Guzzle,** guz'l, *v.* and *t.* (guzzling, guzzled). To swallow greedily or frequently.—*n.* A debauch.
**Gymnasium** jim-nā'zi-um, *n.*; pl. **ia** or **-iums.** A place for athletic exercises; a school for the higher branches of education.
**Gymnast,** jim'nast, *n.* One who teaches or practices gymnastic exercises.
**Gymnastic,** jim-nast'ik, *a.* Pertaining to athletic exercises.
**Gymnastics,** jim-nast'iks, *n.pl.* The art of performing athletic exercises.
**Gynecocracy,** jīn- or jin-ē-kok'ra-si, *n.* Female rule.
**Gynecology,** jīn- or jin-ē-kol'o-ji, *n.* The medical science of the functions and diseases peculiar to women.
**Gyneolatry,** jīn- or jin-ē-ol'a-tri, *n.* The extravagant admiration of woman.
**Gypseous,** jip'sē-us, *a.* Like gypsum.
**Gypsum** jip'sum, *n.* A mineral found as alabaster or as plaster of Paris.
**Gypsy,** jip'si, *n.* *See* GIPSY.
**Gyrate,** jī'rāt, *vi.* (gyrating, gyrated). To move in a circle or spirally.—*a.* Moving in a circle.
**Gyration,** jī-rā'shon, *n.* A turning or whirling round.
**Gyratory,** jī'ra-to-ri, *a.* Moving in a circle.
**Gyre,** jīr, *n.* A circular motion, or a circle described by a moving body; a turn.
**Gyrfalcon,** jėr'fa-kn, *n.* A species of falcon.
**Gyroscope, Gyrostat,** jī'rō-skōp, jī'rō-stat, *n.* An apparatus for illustrating peculiarities of rotation.
**Gyve,** jīv, *n.* A fetter or shackle.—*vt.* (gyving, gyved). To fetter; to shackle.

# H

**Ha,** hä. An exclamation denoting surprise, joy, grief, etc.
**Haberdasher,** ha'bėr-dash-ėr, *n.* A dealer in drapery goods, as woollens, silks, ribbons, etc.
**Haberdashery,** ha'bėr-dash-ė-ri, *n.* The wares sold by a haberdasher.
**Habergeon,** ha'bėr-jon or ha-bėr'jon, *n.* A coat of mail consisting of a jacket without sleeves.
**Habiliment,** ha-bil'i-ment, *n.* A garment: usually in *pl.*
**Habilitate,** ha-bil'i-tāt, *vi.* To qualify.
**Habit,** ha'bit, *n.* State of body, natural or acquired; mode of growth of a plant; aptitude acquired by practice; custom; manner; dress; outer dress worn by ladies on horseback.—*vt.* To dress; to clothe; to array.
**Habitable,** ha'bit-a-bl, *a.* That may be inhabited.
**Habitat,** ha'bit-at, *n.* The natural abode or locality of a plant or animal.
**Habitation,** ha-bit-ā'shon, *n.* Occupancy; abode; residence.
**Habited,** ha'bit-ed, *p.a.* Clothed; dressed.
**Habitual,** ha-bit'ū-al, *a.* Formed or acquired by habit; customary; usual.
**Habitually,** ha-bit'ū-al-li, *adv.* By habit; constantly.
**Habituate,** ha-bit'ū-āt, *vt.* (habituating, habituated). To train to a habit; to make familiar by frequent use; to inure.
**Habitude,** ha'bit-ūd, *n.* Customary manner of life; long custom; habit.
**Habitué,** a-bē-tu-ā, *n.* A habitual frequenter of any place.
**Hachure,** hach'ūr or ā-shur, *n.* Short lines marking half-tints and shadows in engraving, etc.
**Hack,** hak, *n.* A notch; cut; kick at football; a horse kept for hire; a worn-out horse; a literary drudge; frame for drying fish, etc.; rack for cattle.—*vt.* To cut irregularly; to notch; to mangle; to let out for hire.—*a.* Hired; much used or

worn.

**Hackery,** hak'ėr-i, *n.* A rude two-wheeled cart of India drawn by oxen.

**Hacking,** hak'ing, *p.a.* Short and interrupted; as, a *hacking* cough.

**Hackle,** hak'l, *n.* A comb for dressing flax; raw silk; any flimsy substance unspun; a long pointed feather; a fly for angling.—*vt.* (hackling, hackled). To comb (flax or hemp).

**Hackney,** hak'ni, *n.* A horse kept for hire; a coach kept for hire; nag; drudge.—*a.* Let out for hire; much used; trite.—*vt.* To use much; to make trite.

**Hackneyed,** hak'nid, *p.a.* Much used; trite.

**Haddock,** had'ok, *n.* A sea-fish allied to the cod.

**Hades,** hā'dēz, *n.* The abode of the dead; state of departed souls.

**Hadji, Hadjee,** haj'ē, *n.* A Mohammedan who has performed the pilgrimage to Mecca.

**Haft,** haft, *n.* A handle; that part of an instrument which is taken into the hand.—*vt.* To set in a haft.

**Hag,** hag, *n.* An ugly old woman; a witch; an eel-shaped fish that eats into other fishes.

**Haggard,** hag'ärd, *a.* Wild; intractable; having the face worn and pale; gaunt.—*n.* An untrained or refractory hawk.

**Haggis,** hag'is, *n.* A Scottish dish, commonly made of a sheep's stomach, with the heart, lungs, and liver minced, and mixed with suet, onions, oatmeal, salt, etc., inside.

**Haggish,** hag'ish, *a.* Of the nature of a hag; deformed; ugly.

**Haggle,** hag'l, *vt.* (haggling, haggled). To cut into small pieces; to mangle.—*vi.* To be difficult in bargaining; to stick at small matters; to chaffer.

**Hagiology,** hā-ji-ol'o-ji, *n.* That branch of literature which has to do with the lives and legends of the saints.

**Hah,** häh. Same as *Ha.*

**Ha-ha,** hä'hä, *n.* A sunk fence or ditch.

**Hail,** hāl, *n.* Frozen drops of rain; a wish of health; a call.—*vi.* To pour down hail; to have as one's residence, or belong to (with *from*).—*vt.* To pour down in the manner of hail; to salute; to call to; to designate as.—*interj.* A salutation expressive of well-wishing.

**Hailstone,** hāl'stōn, *n.* A single pellet of hail falling from a cloud.

**Hair,** hār, *n.* A small filament issuing from the skin of an animal; the mass of filaments growing from the skin of an animal; anything similar; a very small distance.

**Hair-breadth, Hair's-breadth,** hār'bredth, hārz'bredth, *n.* The diameter of a hair; a very small distance.—*a.* Of the breadth of a hair; very narrow.

**Hair-cloth,** hār'kloth, *n.* A cloth made of hair or in part of hair.

**Hair-dresser,** hār'dres-ėr, *n.* A barber.

**Hairless,** hār'les, *a.* Destitute of hair; bald.

**Hair-splitting,** hār'split-ing, *n.* The making minute distinctions in reasoning.

**Hairy,** hār'i, *a.* Overgrown with hair; consisting of hair; resembling hair.

**Hake,** hāk, *n.* A fish of the cod family.

**Halberd,** hal'bėrd, *n.* An ancient weapon consisting of a long pole ending with an axe and sharp head.

**Halberdier,** hal-bėrd-ēr', *n.* One who is armed with a halberd.

**Halcyon,** hal'si-on, *n.* The kingfisher, fabled to have the power of producing calm weather during the period of incubation.—*a.* Calm; peaceful.

**Hale,** hāl, *a.* Sound; healthy; robust.—*n.* A violent pull.—*vt.* (haling, haled). To take, pull, or drag by force.

**Half,** häf, *n.*; pl. **Halves,** hävz. One part of a thing divided into two equal parts.—*a.* Consisting of a half.—*adv.* In part, or in a equal part or degree.

**Half-back,** häf-bak, *n.* Player in football or hockey who plays between the forwards and the backs.

**Half-brother,** häf'bruᴛʜ-ėr, *n.* A brother by one parent, but not by both.

**Half-caste,** häf'kast, *n.* One born of a Hindu and a European.

**Half-crown,** haf'kroun, *n.* An old British silver coin.

**Half-dead,** häf-ded', *a.* Almost dead.

**Half-hearted,** häf-härt'ed, *a.* Far from enthusiastic; lukewarm.

**Half-length,** häf'length, *a.* Containing one-half of the length.—*n.* Portrait showing only the upper half of the body.

**Half-pay,** häf'pā, *n.* Reduced allowance to an officer on retirement or when not in actual service.—*a.* Receiving half-pay.

**Halfpenny,** hā'pen-i, *n.*; pl. **Halfpence,** häf'pens or hā'pens. A copper coin, value half a penny.

**Half-sister,** häf'sis-tėr, *n.* A sister by one partent, but not by both.

**Half-sovereign,** häf'sov-ėr-in, *n.* A British gold coin.

**Half-witted,** häf-wit'ed, *a.* Weak in intellect.

**Halibut,** ha'li-but, *n.* A large flat-fish allied to the turbot.

**Halidom,** hal'i-dom, *n.* Holiness; sacred word of honor.

**Hall,** hal, *n.* A large room, especially a large public room; a large room at the entrance of a house; a manor-house; the name of certain colleges at Oxford and Cambridge.

**Halleluiah, Hallelujah,** hal-lē-lu'ya, *n.* and *interj.* A word used in sacred songs of praise, signifying *praise ye Jehovah.*

**Halliard.** *See* HALYARD.

**Hall-mark,** hal'märk, *n.* The official stamp affixed to articles of gold and silver, as a mark of their legal quality.

**Hallo,** ha-lō', *interj.* Nearly equal to *halloo.*

**Halloo,** ha-lō', *interj.* and *n.* An exclamation to invite attention; hunting cry to a dog.—*vi.* (hallooing, hallooed). To cry out.—*vt.* To encourage with shouts; to call or shout to.

**Hallow,** hal'ō, *vt.* To make holy; to set apart for religious use; to treat as sacred.

**Hallow-e'en, Hallow-even,** hal'ō-ēn, hal'ō-ē-vn, *n.* The eve or vigil of All-Hallows' or All-Saints' Day.

**Hallowmas,** hal'ō-mas, *n.* The feast of All-Saints or the time at which it is held.

**Hallucination,** hal-lū'si-nā''shon, *n.* A mistaken notion; mere dream or fancy; morbid condition in which objects are believed to be seen and sensations experienced; object or sensation thus erroneously perceived.

**Halo,** hā'lō, *n.* A luminous ring round the sun or moon; any circle of light, as the glory round the head of saints; an ideal glory investing an object.—*vi.* To form itself into a halo.—*vt.* To surround with a halo.

**Halt,** halt, *vi.* To limp; to be lame; to hesitate; to cease marching.—*vt.* To stop; to cause to cease marching.—*a.* Lame; limping.—*n.* A limp; a stopping; stoppage on march.

**Halter,** hal'tėr, *n.* A rope or strap and headstall for leading or confining a horse; a rope for hanging.—*vt.* To put a halter on.

**Halve,** häv, *vt.* (halving, halved). To divide into two equal parts.

**Halyard,** hal'yärd, *n.* Rope or tackle for raising and lowering the yards.

**Ham,** ham, *n.* The hind part of the knee; the back of the thigh; the thigh of an animal, particularly of a hog, salted and dried in smoke.

**Hamadryad,** ham'a-drī-ad, *n.* A wood-nymph, believed to die with the tree to which she was attached; the king cobra of India; the sacred baboon of ancient Egypt.

**Hamlet,** ham'let, *n.* A small village.

**Hammer,** ham'ėr, *n.* An instrument for driving nails, beating metals, and the like.—*vt.* To beat or forge with a hammer; to contrive by intellec-

tual labor.—*vi.* To work with a hammer; to labor in contrivance.
**Hammock,** ham'ok, *n.* A kind of hanging bed.
**Hamper,** ham'pėr, *n.* A large basket for conveying things to market, etc.; something that encumbers; a clog.—*vt.* To put into a hamper; to hinder or impede; to embarrass.
**Hamstring,** ham'string, *n.* One of the tendons of the ham.—*vt.* (pp. hamstrung or hamstringed). To cut the tendons of the ham, and thus to lame or disable.
**Hand,** hand, *n.* The extremity of the arm, consisting of the palm and fingers; a measure of four inches; side or direction; skill; manner of acting; power; cards held at a game; a game; an index; a male or female in relation to an employer; a person with some special faculty; style of penmanship.—*vt.* To give with the hand; to lead with the hand; to conduct; to handle.—*a.* Belonging to, or used by the hand.
**Handbill,** hand'bil, *n.* A loose printed sheet, etc., to be circulated.
**Handbook,** hand'buk, *n.* A book for the hand; a manual; a guide-book.
**Handbreadth,** hand'bredth, *n.* A space equal to the breadth of the hand.
**Handcuff,** hand'kuf, *n.* A fetter for the hands or wrists.—*vt.* To manacle with handcuffs.
**Handed,** hand'ed, *a.* Having hands of this or that character: especially in compounds.
**Handful,** hand'ful, *n.* As much as the hand will grasp or hold; a small quantity or number.
**Hand-gallop,** hand-gal'up, *n.* A slow and easy gallop.
**Handicap,** hand'i-kap, *n.* In racing, games, etc., an allowance to bring superior competitors to an equality with the others; a race or contest so arranged.—*vt.* To put a handicap on; to equalize by a handicap.
**Handicraft,** hand'i-kraft, *n.* Work performed by the hand; manual occupation.
**Handicraftsman,** hand'i-krafts-man, *n.* A man skilled in a handicraft; an artisan.
**Handily,** hand'i-li, *adv.* In a handy manner.
**Handiwork,** hand'i-wėrk, *n.* Product of manual labor; work or deed of any person.
**Handkerchief,** hand'kėr-chif, *n.* A cloth carried about the person for wiping the mouth, nose, etc.; a cloth worn about the neck.
**Handle,** hand'dl, *vt.* (handling, handled). To feel, use, or hold with the hand; to discuss; to deal with; to treat or use well or ill.—*n.* That part of an instrument, etc., held in the hand; instrument for effecting a purpose.
**Handline,** hand'līn, *n.* A small line used in fishing from boats at sea.
**Handmaid, Handmaiden,** hand'mād, hand'mād-n, *n.* Female servant or attendant.
**Hand-mill,** hand'mil, *n.* A mill worked by the hand.
**Handrail,** hand'rāl, *n.* A rail for the hand, supported by balusters, etc., as in staircases.
**Handsel,** hand'sel, *n.* An earnest; a new-year's gift; the first act of using anything.—*vt.* (handseling, handseled). To give a handsel to; to use or do for the first time.
**Handsome,** hand'sum, *a.* Well formed; having a certain share of beauty along with dignity; ample; generous.
**Handsomely,** hand'sum-li, *adv.* In a handsome manner; amply; generously.
**Handwriting,** hand-rīt'ing, *n.* The writing peculiar to each person; any writing.
**Handy,** hand'i, *a.* Skilled in using the hands; dexterous; ready; convenient for use.
**Hang,** hang, *vt.* (pret. and pp. hung and hanged). To suspend; to furnish with anything suspended; to cause to droop; to fit so as to allow of free motion; to put to death by suspending by the neck.—*vi.* To be suspended; to dangle; to adhere; to linger; to lean; to have a steep declivity; to be executed.
**Hangar,** hang'ar, *n.* A shed for housing airplanes.
**Hang-dog,** hang'dog, *n.* A degraded character.—*a.* Having a low or blackguard-like appearance.
**Hanger,** hang'ėr, *n.* One who or that which hangs; a short broad sword; that from which something is hung.
**Hanger-on,** hang'ėr-on', *n.*; pl. **Hangers-on.** A servile dependant; a parasite.
**Hanging,** hang'ing, *n.* Act of suspending; death by the halter; *pl.* linings for rooms, of tapestry, paper, etc.
**Hangman,** hang'man, *n.* A public executioner.
**Hank,** hangk, *n.* A skein of silk, yarn, etc.; a coil.—*vt.* To form into hanks.
**Hanker,** hang'kėr, *vi.* To desire eagerly; to think of something longingly (with *after*).
**Hansom, Hansom-cab,** han'sum, han'sum-kab, *n.* A two-wheeled cab.
**Hap,** hap, *n.* Chance; luck; fortune.—*vi.* To happen; to befall.
**Haphazard,** hap-ha'zėrd, *n.* Chance; accident.
**Hapless,** hap'les, *a.* Unlucky; unhappy.
**Haply,** hap'li, *adv.* By hap or chance; perhaps
**Happen,** hap'n, *vi.* To come by chance; to occur.
**Happily,** hap'i-li, *adv.* In a happy manner; fortunately; gracefully.
**Happiness,** hap'i-nes, *n.* State of being happy; enjoyment of pleasure; good luck.
**Happy,** hap'i, *a.* Being in the enjoyment of agreeable sensations from the possession of good; fortunate; propitious; well suited; apt.
**Harangue,** ha-rang', *n.* A noisy or pompous address; a declamatory public address; a tirade.—*vi.* (haranguing, harangued). To make a harangue.—*vt.* To address by a harangue.
**Harass,** ha'ras, *vt.* To vex; to tire with labor; to fatigue with importunity.
**Harassing,** ha'ras-ing, *p.a.* Fatiguing; tending to wear with care or anxiety.
**Harbinger,** här'bin-jėr, *n.* A forerunner; that which precedes and gives notice of something else.—*vt.* To precede as harbinger.
**Harbor,** här'bėr, *n.* A shelter; a haven for ships; an asylum.—*vt.* To shelter; to entertain in the mind.—*vi.* To take shelter; to lodge or abide for a time.
**Hard,** härd, *a.* Not easily penetrated or separated; firm; difficult to understand; arduous; unfeeling; severe; unjust; harsh; stiff; grasping: applied to certain sounds, as sibilants contrasted with gutturals: applied to water not suitable for washing, from holding minerals.—*adv.* Close; diligently; with difficulty; fast; copiously; with force.
**Harden,** härd'n, *vt.* To make hard or more hard; to confirm in effrontery, obstinacy, wickedness, etc.; to make unfeeling; to inure; to render less liable to injury by exposure or use.—*vi.* To become hard or more hard; to become unfeeling; to become inured.
**Hardened,** härd'nd, *p.a.* Made hard or more hard; obstinate; confirmed; callous.
**Hard-fisted,** härd'fist-ed, *a.* Having hard or strong hands; covetous.
**Hard-headed,** härd'hed-ed, *a.* Shrewd; intelligent.
**Hard-hearted,** härd'härt-ed, *a.* Having an unfeeling heart; pitiless.
**Hardihood,** härd'i-hud, *n.* Quality of being hardy; boldness; intrepidity; audacity; effrontery.
**Hardily,** härd'i-li, *adv.* In a hardy manner; boldly; stoutly; with endurance.
**Hardish,** härd'ish, *a.* Somewhat hard.
**Hardly,** härd'li, *adv.* With difficulty; scarcely; harshly.
**Hardness,** härd'nes, *n.* State or quality of being hard in all its senses; firmness; difficulty; obduracy; rigor; niggardliness, etc.
**Hards,** härdz, *n. pl.* The refuse or coarse part of flax or wool.
**Hardship,** härd'ship, *n.* Privation; affliction; op-

pression; injustice; grievance.
**Hardware,** härd'wãr, *n.* Wares made of iron or other metal, as pots, knives, etc.
**Hardy,** härd'i, *a.* Bold; intrepid; full of assurance; inured to fatigue; capable of bearing exposure.
**Hare,** hãr, *n.* A rodent animal allied to the rabbit, but not making burrows.
**Harebell,** hãr'bel, *n.* A plant with a slender stem and pale-blue bell-shaped flowers.
**Hare-brained,** hãr'brãnd, *a.* Wild as a hare; giddy; volatile; heedless.
**Harelip,** hãr'lip, *n.* A perpendicular division of one or both lips, but commonly the upper one, like that of a hare.
**Harem,** hā'rem, *n.* The apartments of the female members of a Mohammedan family; the occupants.
**Haricot,** ha'ri-kō, *n.* A ragout of meat and roots; the kidney-bean or French bean.
**Hark,** härk, *vi.* To listen; to lend the ear.
**Harlequin,** här'le-kwin, *n.* A performer in a pantomime, masked, dressed in tight spangled clothes, and armed with a magic wand; a buffoon in general.
**Harlequinade,** här'le-kwin-ād'', *n.* Portion of a pantomime in which the harlequin appears; buffoonery.
**Harlot,** här'lot, *n.* A prostitute.
**Harlotry,** här'lot-ri, *n.* The trade or practice of prostitution.
**Harm,** härm, *n.* Injury; hurt; evil.—*vt.* To hurt; to damage; to impair.
**Harmful,** härm'ful, *a.* Hurtful; injurious; noxious; mischievous.
**Harmless,** härm'les, *a.* Free from harm; not causing harm; inoffensive; uninjured.
**Harmlessly,** härm'les-li, *adv.* Without causing or receiving harm.
**Harmonic, Harmonical,** här-mon'ik, här-mon'ik-al, *a.* Pertaining to harmony; concordant; musical.—**Harmonic,** här-mon'ik, *n.* A less distinct tone accompanying a principal tone.
**Harmonica,** här-mon'i-ka, *n.* A musical toy played by striking rods or plates of glass or metal with small hammers.
**Harmonicon,** här-mon'i-kon, *n.* A kind of large and complicated barrel-organ.
**Harmonics,** här-mon'iks, *n.* The doctrine of harmony or of musical sounds.
**Harmonious,** här-mō'ni-us, *a.* Having harmony; having the parts adapted to each other; concordant; friendly.
**Harmonist,** här'mon-ist, *n.* One skilled in harmony; a musician; one who harmonizes.
**Harmonium,** här-mō'ni-um, *n.* A musical wind-instrument resembling a small organ.
**Harmonize,** här'mon-iz, *vi.* To be in harmony; to agree in sound or sense; to be in friendship.—*vt.* To bring into harmony; to set accompanying parts to.
**Harmony,** här'mo-ni, *n.* The just adaptation of parts to each other; musical concord; agreement; peace and friendship.
**Harness,** här'nes, *n.* Armor; furniture of a carriage or draft horse.—*vt.* To dress in armor; to put harness on.
**Harp,** härp, *n.* A stringed musical instrument of triangular form played with the fingers.—*vi.* To play on the harp; to dwell on tediously.
**Harper, Harpist,** härp'ėr, härp'ist, *n.* A player on the harp.
**Harpoon,** här-pön', *n.* A spear or javelin, used to strike whales, etc.—*vt.* To strike, catch, or kill with a harpoon.
**Harpooner,** här-pön'ėr, *n.* One who uses a harpoon.
**Harpischord,** härp'si-kord, *n.* An obsolete stringed musical instrument something like a horizontal grand pianoforte.
**Harpy,** här'pi, *n.* A fabulous winged monster with the face of a woman; any rapacious animal; an extortioner.
**Harridan,** ha'ri-dan, *n.* A hag; an odious old woman; a vixenish woman; a trollop.
**Harrier,** ha'ri-ėr, *n.* A small kind of hound for hunting hares; a kind of hawk.
**Harrow,** ha'rō, *n.* A frame set with spikes, to prepare plowed land for seed or to cover the seed.—*vt.* To draw a harrow over; to lacerate; to torment.
**Harrowing,** ha'rō-ing, *p.a.* Causing acute distress to the mind.
**Harry,** ha'ri, *vt.* (harrying, harried). To pillage; to plunder; to ravage.
**Harsh,** härsh, *a.* Grating to the touch, taste, or ear; jarring; rough; severe.
**Harshly,** härsh'li, *adv.* In a harsh manner; severely; rudely.
**Hart,** härt, *n.* A stag or male of the red-deer.
**Hart's-horn,** härts'horn, *n.* Horn of the hart; ammoniacal preparation obtained from the horn; solution of ammonia.
**Hart's-tongue,** härts'tung, *n.* A common British fern.
**Harum-scarum,** hā'rum-skā'rum, *a.* Hare-brained; unsettled; giddy; rash.
**Harvest,** här'vest, *n.* The season of gathering a crop, especially corn; the crop gathered; the product of labor; fruit or fruits; effects; consequences.—*vt.* To reap or gather.
**Harvester,** här'vest-ėr, *n.* A reaper; alborer in gathering grain; reaping-machine.
**Harvest-home,** här'vest-hōm, *n.* The bringing home of the harvest; the feast celebrating it.
**Hash,** hash, *vt.* To hack; to chop; to mince and mix.—*n.* That which is chopped; cooked meat chopped up and served again; a repetition; bungle.
**Hashish,** hash'ēsh, *n.* Bhang.
**Hasp,** hasp, *n.* A clasp that passes over a staple to be fastened by a padlock.—*vt.* To fasten with a hasp.
**Hassock,** has'ok, *n.* A thick mat or cushion used for kneeling on, etc.
**Haste,** hāst, *n.* Speed; hurry; sudden excitement of passion; precipitance.—*vt.* (hasting, hasted). To drive or urge forward; to hurry.—*vi.* To move with celerity; to be speedy.
**Hasten,** hās'n, *vt.* and *i.* To haste.
**Hastily,** hāst'i-li, *adv.* In a hasty manner; speedily; rashly; precipitately; passionately.
**Hasty,** hāst'i, *a.* Speedy; precipitate; rash; irritable; irascible; early ripe.
**Hat,** hat, *n.* A covering for the head.
**Hatch,** hach, *vt.* To produce from eggs; to contrive; to shade by crossing lines in drawing, etc.—*vi.* To produce young; to bring the young to maturity.—*n.* A brood; act of exclusion from the egg; frame of cross-bars over the opening in a ship's deck; the opening itself; hatchway; trap-door.
**Hatchel,** hach'el, *n.* A hackle or heckle.—*vt.* To hackle or heckle.
**Hatchet,** hach'et, *n.* A small axe with a short handle, used with one hand.
**Hatchment,** hach'ment, *n.* The coat of arms of a deceased person, set in a prominent position.
**Hatchway,** hach'wā, *n.* An opening in a ship's deck for communication with the interior.
**Hate,** hāt, *vt.* (hating, hated). To detest; to loathe; to abhor.—*n.* Great dislike; hatred.
**Hateful,** hāt'ful, *a.* Exciting hate; odious; loathsome; malignant.
**Hatefully,** hāt'ful-li, *adv.* Odiously; malignantly; maliciously.
**Hatred,** hāt'red, *n.* Great dislike or aversion; ill-will; rancor; abhorrence.
**Hatter,** hat'ėr, *n.* A maker or seller of hats.
**Hauberk,** ha'bėrk, *n.* A coat of mail.
**Haugh,** hah, *n.* In Scotland, a low-lying meadow beside a stream; a holm.
**Haughty,** hat'i, *a.* Proud and disdainful; lofty and arrogant.
**Haul,** hal, *vt.* To pull or draw with force; to drag; to compel to go.—*n.* A violent pull; draught of fish in a net; that which is taken or gained at

once.

**Haulage,** hal'āj, *n.* A hauling; length hauled; charge for hauling.

**Haulum, Haum,** halm, ham, *n.* The stem or stalk of a plant, especially when dry.

**Haunch,** hansh, *n.* The hip; the thigh; part of an arch between the springing and the crown; the flank.

**Haunt,** hant, *vt.* To frequent; to resort to often; to appear in or about, as a specter.—*vi.* To be much about; to visit often.—*n.* A place much frequented; a favorite resort.

**Haunted,** hant'ed, *p.a.* Frequently visited by apparitions; troubled by spectral visitants.

**Hautboy, Hautbois,** hō'boi, *n.*; pl. *Hautboys, Hautbois,* hōboiz. An oboe; a wind-instrument of wood, sounded through a double-reed.

**Hauteur,** ō-tėr', *n.* Haughty manner or spirit; pride.

**Have,** hav, *vt.* (having, had). To possess; to accept; to enjoy; to hold in opinion; to be under necessity, or impelled by duty; to procure; to bring forth.

**Haven,** hā'vn, *n.* A harbor; port; shelter.

**Haversack,** hav'ėr-sak, *n.* A soldier's bag for provisions on the march.

**Having,** hav'ing, *n.* What one has; possession; goods.

**Havoc,** hav'ok, *n.* Devastation; wide and general destruction; slaughter.

**Haw,** ha, *n.* A hedge or fence; the berry and seed of the hawthorn; hesitation of speech.—*vi.* To speak with hesitation.

**Hawhaw,** ha'ha, *n.* Same as *Ha-ha.*

**Hawk,** hak, *n.* A rapacious bird of the falcon family.—*vi.* To catch birds by means of hawks; to practice falconry; to take prey on the wing; to force up phlegm with noise.—*vt.* To carry about for sale from place to place.

**Hawker,** hak'ėr, *n.* One who goes about selling wares; a peddler.

**Hawking,** hak'ing, *n.* Sport of taking wild fowls by means of hawks; falconry.

**Hawse,** has, *n.* That part of a vessel's bow where the holes for the cables are cut; the hole in the vessel's bow.

**Hawser,** ha'sėr, *n.* A small cable.

**Hawthorn,** ha'thorn, *n.* The hedge-thorn; the white-thorn, much used for hedges.

**Hay,** hā, *n.* Grass cut and dried for fodder.—*vt.* To make into hay.

**Haymaker,** hā'māk-ėr, *n.* One who cuts and dries grass for fodder.

**Haymaking,** hā'māk-ing, *n.* The business of cutting grass and preparing it for hay.

**Hazard,** ha'zėrd, *n.* A game at dice, etc.; risk; venture; chance; fortuitous event.—*vt.* To risk; to put in danger of loss or injury.

**Hazardous,** ha'zėrd-us, *a.* Perilous; risky.

**Haze,** hāz, *n.* Vapor which renders the air thick, though not so damp as in foggy weather; dimness; mental fog.

**Hazel,** hā'zl, *n.* A small tree of the oak family that bears edible nuts.—*a.* Pertaining to the hazel; of a light-brown color.

**Hazy,** hāz'i, *a.* Thick with haze; mentally obscure or confused.

**He,** hē, *pron.* of the third person, nominative. A substitute for the third person masculine, representing the man or male named before; prefixed to names of animals to specify the male.

**Head,** hed, *n.* The anterior part of animals; uppermost part of the human body; seat of the brain; etc.; intellect; an individual; a chief; first place; top; chief part; principal source; crisis; height; promontory; division of discourse; headway.—*vt.* To form a head to; to behead; to lead; to go in front of in order to stop; to oppose.—*vi.* To form a head; to be directed, as a ship.

**Headache,** hed'āk, *n.* Pain in the head.

**Head-dress,** hed'dres, *n.* The covering or ornaments of a woman's head.

**Head-gear,** hed'gēr, *n.* Covering or ornaments of the head.

**Headily,** hed'i-li, *adv.* Hastily; rashly.

**Heading,** hed'ing, *n.* That which stands at the head; title of a section; passage excavated in the line of an intended tunnel.

**Headland,** hed'land, *n.* A cape; a promontory; a ridge or strip of unplowed land at the end of furrows.

**Headless,** hed'les, *a.* Having no head.

**Headlong,** hed'long, *adv.* With the head foremost; precipitately.—*a.* Steep; precipitous; precipitate.

**Head-mark,** hed'märk, *n.* Distinctive mark or characteristic.

**Head-money,** hed'mu-ni, *n.* A tax levied on each individual; money paid for the heads of enemies or for prisoners caught.

**Headmost,** hed'mōst, *a.* Most advanced.

**Head-piece,** hed'pēs, *n.* Armor for the head; a helmet.

**Headquarters,** hed-kwar'tėrz, *n.pl.* The quarters of a commander; place where one chiefly resides or carries on business.

**Headship,** hed'ship, *n.* Office of a head or principal; authority; chief place.

**Headsman,** hedz'man, *n.* An executioner.

**Head-stone,** hed'stōn, *n.* The chief or corner stone; stone at the head of a grave.

**Headstrong,** hed'strong, *a.* Resolute; obstinate; violent.

**Headway,** hed'wā, *n.* Progress made by a ship in motion; progress or success.

**Head-wind,** hed'wind, *n.* A wind that blows right against a ship, etc.

**Head-work,** hed'wėrk, *n.* Mental or intellectual labor.

**Heady,** hed'i, *a.* Rash; hasty; headstrong; intoxicating.

**Heal,** hēl, *vi.* To make hale or sound; to cure; to reconcile.—*vt.* To grow whole or sound; to recover.

**Healing,** hēl'ing, *p.a.* Tending to cure; mild; mollifying.—*n.* Act or process by which a cure is effected.

**Health,** helth, *n.* A sound state of body or mind; freedom from disease; bodily conditions; wish of health and happiness (used in drinking).

**Healthful,** helth'ful, *a.* Full of health; healthy; wholesome; salubrious.

**Healthily,** helth'i-li, *adv.* Without disease; soundly.

**Healthy,** helth'i, *a.* Being in health; sound; hale; salubrious; wholesome.

**Heap,** hēp, *n.* A mass; large quantity; pile.—*vt.* To raise in a heap; to amass; to pile.

**Hear,** hēr, *vt.* (hearing, heard). To perceive by the ear; to give audience to; to listen; to obey; to regard; to attend favorably; to try in a court of law; to learn; to approve.—*vi.* To enjoy the faculty of perceiving sound; to listen; to be told; to receive by report.

**Hearer,** hēr'ėr, *n.* One who hears; an auditor.

**Hearing,** hėr'ing, *n.* The faculty or sense by which sound is perceived; audience; opportunity to be heard; judicial trial; reach of the ear.

**Hearken,** härk'n, *vi.* To lend the ear; to listen; to give heed.

**Hearsay,** hēr'sā, *n.* Report; rumor.—*a.* Given at second hand.

**Hearse,** hėrs, *n.* A carriage for conveying the dead to the grave; bier.

**Heart,** härt, *n.* The primary organ of the blood's motion; the inner, vital, or most essential part; seat of the affections, will, etc.; disposition of mind; conscience; courage; spirit; what represents a heart; one of a suit of playing cards marked with such a figure.

**Heartache,** härt'āk, *n.* Sorrow; anguish.

**Heart-breaking,** härt'brāk-ing, *a.* Overpowering with grief or sorrow.

**Heart-broken,** härt'brōk-n, *a.* Deeply afflicted or grieved.

H

**Heartburn,** härt'bėrn, *n.* A burning sensation in the stomach from indigestion.
**Heart-burning,** härt'bėrn-ing, *n.* Discontent; secret enmity.
**Hearten,** härt'n, *vt.* To give heart or courage to; to encourage; to animate.
**Heartfelt,** härt'felt, *a.* Deeply felt; deeply affecting, either as joy or sorrow.
**Hearth,** härth, *n.* The part of a floor on which a fire is made; the house and its inmates; the fireside.
**Hearthstone,** härth'stōn, *n.* Stone forming the hearth; fireside.
**Heartily,** härt'i-li, *adv.* From the heart; sincerely; warmly; with keen relish.
**Heartless,** härt'les, *a.* Without heart; spiritless; without feeling or affection.
**Heart-rending,** härt'rend-ing, *a.* Overpowering with anguish; deeply afflictive.
**Heart's-ease,** härts'ēz, *n.* A plant, a species of violet; the pansy.
**Heart-sick,** härt'sik, *a.* Sick at heart; pained in mind; deeply depressed.
**Heart-whole,** härt'hōl, *a.* Whole at heart; not affected with love; of good courage.
**Hearty,** härt'i, *a.* Warm; cordial; healthy; having a keen appetite; large to satisfaction.
**Heat,** hēt, *n.* The sensation produced by bodies that are hot; hot air; hot weather; high temperature; degree of temperature; a single effort; a course at a race; animal excitement; rage; ardor; animation in thought or discourse; fermentation.—*vt.* To make hot; to warm with passion or desire; to rouse into action.—*vi.* To grow warm or hot.
**Heater,** hēt'ėr, *n.* One who or that which heats; metal for heating a smoothing-iron.
**Heath,** hēth, *n.* A small flowering shrub growing on waste or wild places; a place overgrown with heath; waste tract.
**Heath-bell,** hēth'bel, *n.* The flower of a species of heath.
**Heath-cock,** hēth'kok, *n.* The black-cock, a species of grouse.
**Heathen,** hē'ᴛʜen, *n.* A pagan; one who worships idols; a barbarous person.—*a.* Gentile; pagan.
**Heathendom,** hē'ᴛʜen-dum, *n.* That part of the world where heathenism prevails.
**Heathenish,** hē'ᴛʜen-ish, *a.* Belonging to pagans; idolatrous; barbarous.
**Heathenism,** hē'ᴛʜen-izm, *n.* Paganism; idolatry.
**Heather,** heᴛʜ'ėr, *n.* Common heath, a low shrub with clusters of rose-colored flowers.
**Heating,** hēt'ing, *p.a.* Exciting action; stimulating.
**Heave,** hēv, *vt.* (heaving, pret. and pp. heaved, hove). To lift; to move upward; to cause to swell; to raise or force from the breast, as a groan; to throw; to turn in some direction.—*vi.* To rise; to swell, as the sea; to pant; to retch; *to heave in sight,* to appear, as a ship.—*n.* A rising or swell; an effort upward; a throw; a swelling, as of the breast.
**Heaven,** hev'n, *n.* The blue expanse surrounding the earth; the sky; the abode of God and of his angels; God or Providence; supreme felicity; bliss.
**Heavenly,** hev'n-li, *a.* Pertaining to heaven; divine; inhabiting heaven; enchanting.—*adv.* In a heavenly manner.
**Heavenward, Heavenwards,** hev'n-wėrd, hev'n-wėrdz, *adv.* Toward heaven.
**Heave-offering,** hēv'of-fėr-ing, *n.* Among the Jews, an offering to God.
**Heaver,** hēv'ėr, *n.* One who heaves; one who unloads coals from vessels.
**Heavily,** he'vi-li, *adv.* In a heavy manner; dully; gloomily; laboriously; densely.
**Heaviness,** he'vi-nes, *n.* Weight; gloom; dullness; oppressiveness.
**Heavy,** he'vi, *a.* That is heaved or lifted with difficulty; weighty; sad; grievous; burdensome; drowsy; wearisome; not easily digested; soft and miry; difficult; large in amount; dense; abundant; forcible.
**Hebdomadal,** heb-dom'ad-al, *a.* Consisting of seven days, or occurring every seven days; weekly.
**Hebetate,** heb'ē-tāt, *vt.* To dull; to blunt; to stupefy.
**Hebetude,** heb'ē-tūd, *n.* Dullness; stupidity.
**Hebraic, Hebraical,** hē-brā'ik, hē-brā'ik-al, *a.* Pertaining to the Hebrews or their language; Jewish.
**Hebraist,** hē'brā-ist, *n.* One versed in the Hebrew language.
**Hebrew,** hē'brö, *n.* An Israelite; a Jew; the Hebrew language.—*a.* Pertaining to the Hebrews.
**Hebridean, Hebridian,** heb-ri-dē'an, hē-brid'i-an, *a.* Pertaining to the Hebrides of Scotland.—*n.* A native of the Hebrides.
**Heckle,** hek'l, *n.* A sort of comb for flax or hemp; a hackle or hatchel.—*vt.* (heckling, heckled). To dress with a heckle; to question or catechize severely.
**Hectare,** hek'tār, *n.* A French measure equal to 2.47 acres.
**Hectic,** hek'tik, *a.* A term applied to the fever which accompanies consumption; consumptive; feverish.—*n.* A hectic fever; a flush.
**Hector,** hek'tėr, *n.* A bully.—*vt.* To bully; to treat with insolence.—*vi.* To play the bully.
**Hedge,** hej, *n.* A fence consisting of thorns or shrubs.—*vt.* (hedging, hedged). To enclose with a hedge; to surround or restrain.—*vi.* To hide oneself; to bet on both sides; to skulk; to dodge or trim.—*a.* Pertaining to a hedge; mean; rustic.
**Hedgehog,** hej'hog, *n.* A small insectivorous quadruped covered with prickly spines.
**Hedger,** hej'ėr, *n.* One who makes or trims hedges.
**Hedgerow,** hej'rō, *n.* A row of shrubs forming a hedge.
**Hedonic,** hē-don'ik, *a.* Pertaining to pleasure.
**Hedonism,** hē'don-izm, *n.* The doctrine that the chief good of man lies in pursuit of pleasure.
**Hedonist,** hē'don-ist, *n.* One who professes hedonism.
**Heed,** hēd, *vt.* To look to or after; to regard with care; to notice.—*vi.* To mind; to consider.—*n.* Care; attention; regard.
**Heedful,** hēd'ful, *a.* Giving heed; attentive; watchful; cautious; wary.
**Heedless,** hēd'les, *a.* Inattentive; careless; remiss; negligent.
**Heel,** hēl, *n.* The hind part of the foot; a cant.—*vt.* To add a heel to; to furnish with heels, as shoes.—*vi.* To cant over from a vertical position.
**Heelball,** hēl'bal, *n.* A composition for blackening the heels of shoes, etc.
**Heel-tap,** hēl'tap, *n.* A piece of leather for the heel of a shoe; a small portion of liquor left in a glass.
**Heft,** heft, *n.* The act of heaving; effort; weight; gist.
**Hegelian,** he-gē'li-an, *a.* Pertaining to Hegel (hā'gl) or his system of philosophy.—*n.* A follower of Hegel.
**Hegelianism,** he-gē'li-an-izm, *n.* The system of philosophy of Hegel.
**Hegemony,** hē-jem'o-ni (or with g hard), *n.* Leadership; preponderance of one state among others.
**Hegira,** hej'i-ra, *n.* The flight of Mohammed from Mecca (July 16th, 622); the beginning of the Mohammedan era.
**Heifer,** hef'ėr, *n.* A young cow.
**Height,** hīt, *n.* The condition of being high; distance of anything above its base or above the earth; eminence; any elevated ground; extent; degree; utmost degree.
**Heighten,** hīt'n, *vt.* To raise higher; to improve; to increase.
**Heinous,** hān'us, *a.* Hateful; characterized by great wickedness; flagrant.
**Heir,** ār, *n.* One who succeeds or is to succeed an-

other in the possession of property.

**Heiress,** ār'es, *n.* A female heir.

**Heirloom,** ār'lōm, *n.* Any personal chattel which, by law, descends to the heir or has belonged to a family for a long time.

**Heirship,** ār'ship, *n.* The state, character, or privileges of an heir; right of inheriting.

**Heliacal,** hē-lī'ak-al, *a.* Coincident with the rising or setting of the sun.

**Helicopter,** hel-i-kop'tėr, hel'i-kop-tėr, *n.* A type of aircraft supported in flight by a propeller rotating about a vertical axis. It can rise and descend vertically.

**Heliocentric,** hē'li-o-sen''trik, *a.* Relating to the sun as a center; appearing as if seen from the sun's center.

**Heliograph, Heliostat,** hē'li-o-graf, hē'li-o-stat, *n.* A sun telegraph; apparatus for reflecting the sun's light to a distance.

**Heliotrope,** hē'li-o-trōp, *n.* Blood-stone; a heliostat; a fragrant garden plant.

**Heliotype,** hē'li-o-tīp, *n.* A surface-printed picture direct from a photograph.

**Helium,** hē'li-um, *n.* An inert gas present in the air in small quantities, the lightest element next to hydrogen.

**Helix,** hē'liks, *n.*; pl. **Helices,** hel'i-sēz. A spiral line, as of wire in a coil; something that is spiral.

**Hell,** hel, *n.* The place or state of punishment for the wicked after death; the abode of the devil and his angels; the infernal powers; a gambling-house.

**Hellebore,** hel'e-bōr, *n.* A plant used by the ancients as a remedy for mental diseases, epilepsy, etc.

**Hellenic,** hel-len'ik or hel-lēn'ik, *a.* Pertaining to the inhabitants of Greece; Greek.

**Hellenism,** hel'len-izm, *n.* A Greek idiom; type of character peculiar to the Greeks.

**Hellenist,** hel'len-ist, *n.* A Grecian Jew; one skilled in the Greek language.

**Hellish,** hel'ish, *a.* Pertaining to hell; infernal; malignant; detestable.

**Helm,** helm, *n.* A helmet; instrument by which a ship is steered; the rudder, tiller, etc.; place or post of management.—*vt.* To cover or furnish with a helmet..

**Helmet,** hel'met, *n.* A covering for the head in war; head armor; a head-piece.

**Helmsman,** helmz'man, *n.* The man at the helm of a ship.

**Helot,** he'lot or hē'lot, *n.* A slave, originally a serf in ancient Sparta.

**Help,** help, *vt.* To lend strength or means towards effecting a purpose; to aid; to relieve; to remedy; to prevent; to avoid.—*vi.* To lend aid.—*n.* Aid; remedy; an assistant.

**Helper,** help'ėr, *n.* One who helps; an assistant; an auxiliary.

**Helpful,** help'ful, *a.* That gives help, aid, or assistance; useful.

**Helpless,** help'les, *a.* Without help in oneself; needing help; affording no help; beyond help.

**Helpmate,** help'māt, *n.* A companion who helps; an assistant; a wife.

**Helter-skelter,** hel'tėr-skel'tėr, *adv.* A word suggestive of hurry and confusion.

**Helve,** helv, *n.* The handle of an axe or hatchet.—*vt.* (helving, helved). To furnish with a helve, as an axe.

**Helvetian, Helvetic,** hel-vē'shan, hel-vet'ik, *a.* Of or pertaining to Switzerland.

**Hem,** hem, *n.* The border of a garment, doubled and sewed to strengthen it; edge; border.—*interj.* and *n.* A sort of half cough, suggested by some feeling.—*vt.* (hemming, hemmed). To form a hem or border on; to enclose and confine; to make the sound expressed by the word *hem*.

**Hematite,** he'ma-tit, *n.* A name of two ores of iron, red hematite and brown hematite.

**Hemisphere,** he'mi-sfēr, *n.* One half of a sphere; half the celestial or terrestrial sphere.

**Hemispheric, Hemispherical,** he-mi-sfe'rik, he-mi-sfe'rik-al, *a.* Pertaining to or forming a hemisphere.

**Hemistich,** he'mi-stik, *n.* Half a poetic line or verse, or a verse not completed.

**Hemlock,** hem'lok, *n.* An umbelliferous plant whose leaves and root are poisonous.

**Hemorrhage,** he'mor-āj, *n.* A bursting forth of blood; any discharge of blood from the blood-vessels.

**Hemorrhoids,** he'mor-oidz, *n.pl.* Piles.

**Hemp,** hemp, *n.* An annual herbaceous plant of the nettle family, the fiber of which, also called hemp, is made into sail-cloth, ropes, etc.

**Hempen,** hemp'n, *a.* Made of hemp.

**Hemp-seed,** hemp'sēd, *n.* The seed of hemp, used as food for fowls, and yielding an oil.

**Hen,** hen, *n.* The female of the domestic fowl; any female bird.

**Henbane,** hen'bān, *n.* A poisonous herb of the potato family used in medicine.

**Hence,** hens, *adv.* From this place, time, source, reason, etc.

**Henceforth,** hens-forth', *adv.* From this time forward.

**Henceforward,** hens-for'wėrd, *adv.* From this time forward; henceforth.

**Henchman,** hensh'man, *n.* A servant; a male attendant.

**Hennery,** hen'ėr-i, *n.* An enclosed place for hens.

**Henpeck,** hen'pek, *vt.* To rule: said of a wife who has the upper hand of her husband.

**Hepatic,** hē-pat'ik, *a.* Pertaining to the liver.

**Heptagon,** hep'ta-gon, *n.* A plane figure having seven angles and seven sides.

**Heptamerous,** hep-tam'ėr-us, *a.* Consisting of seven parts.

**Heptangular,** hep-tang'gū-lėr, *a.* Having seven angles.

**Heptarchy,** hep'tär-ki, *n.* A government by seven persons, or the country governed by seven persons.

**Heptateuch,** hep'ta-tūk, *n.* The first seven books of the Old Testament.

**Her,** hėr, *pron.* The possessive and objective case of *she*: when the possessive is used without a noun it becomes *hers*.

**Herald,** he'rald, *n.* An officer whose business was to proclaim war or peace, bear messages, etc.; a forerunner; an officer who regulates matters relating to public ceremonies; one who records and blazons arms, etc.—*vt.* To introduce, as by a herald; to proclaim.

**Heraldic,** he-rald'ik, *a.* Pertaining to heralds or heraldry.

**Heraldry,** he'rald-ri, *n.* Art or office of a herald; art of recording genealogies and blazoning arms; heraldic figures or symbols.

**Herb,** hėrb, *n.* Any plant with a succulent stem which dies to the root every year.

**Herbaceous,** hėrb-ā'shus, *a.* Pertaining to herbs; having the nature of a herb.

**Herbage,** hėrb'āj, *n.* Herbs collectively; grass; pasture.

**Herbal,** hėrb'al, *n.* A book that contains descriptions of herbs or plants.

**Herbalist,** hėrb'al-ist, *n.* One skilled in herbs, or who makes collections of them.

**Herbarium,** hėr-bā'ri-um, *n.*; pl. **-iums and -ia.** A collection of herbs or plants dried and preserved.

**Herbivorous,** hėrb-iv'or-us, *a.* Eating herbs; subsisting on herbaceous plants.

**Herb-Robert,** hėrb'ro-bert, *n.* A very common British species of wild geranium.

**Herculean,** hėr-kū'lē-an, *a.* Belonging to or resembling Hercules; of extraordinary strength; very great or difficult.

**Herd,** hėrd, *n.* A number of animals feeding or driven together; flock; crowd; rabble; a keeper of cattle or sheep.—*vi.* and *t.* To unite into a herd, as beasts; to congregate.

**Herdsman,** hėrdz'man, *n.* One employed in tend-

ing herds of cattle.
**Here,** hēr, *adv.* In this place; at this point; hither.
**Hereabout, Hereabouts,** hēr'a-bout, hēr'a-bouts, *adv.* About this place.
**Hereafter,** hēr-af'tėr, *adv.* After this time; in a future state.—*n.* The time after this; a future state.
**Hereby,** hēr-bī', *adv.* By this; close by; near.
**Hereditable,** he-red'i-ta-bl, *a.* Heritable.
**Hereditament,** he-re-dit'a-ment, *n.* Any species of property that may be inherited.
**Hereditarily,** he-red'it-a-ri-li, *adv.* By inheritance.
**Hereditary,** he-red'it-a-ri, *a.* Relating to an inheritance; descending to an heir; that is or may be transmitted from a parent to a child.
**Heredity,** he-red'i-ti, *n.* Hereditary transmission of qualities; the doctrine that the offspring inherits parental characteristics.
**Herein,** hēr-in', *adv.* In this.
**Hereinafter,** hēr-in-äf'tėr, *adv.* In this writing or document afterwards.
**Hereof,** hēr-of', *adv.* Of this; from this.
**Hereon,** hēr-on', *adv.* On this.
**Heresy,** he're-si, *n.* A fundamental error in religion; error in doctrine; heterodoxy.
**Heretic,** he're-tik, *n.* One guilty of heresy.
**Heretical,** he-ret'ik-al, *a.* Containing heresy; contrary to the established faith.
**Hereto,** hēr-tö', *adv.* To this.
**Heretofore,** hēr-tö-fōr', *adv.* Before or up to the present; formerly.
**Hereupon,** hēr-up-on', *adv.* On this; hereon.
**Herewith,** hēr-with', *adv.* With this.
**Heritable,** he'rit-a-bl, *a.* Capable of being inherited; that may inherit.
**Heritage,** he'rit-āj, *n.* Inheritance; lot or portion by birth.
**Heritor,** he'rit-or, *n.* One who inherits; an heir; *Scots law,* a proprietor liable to pay public burdens.
**Hermaphrodite,** hėr-maf'rod-īt, *n.* An animal in which the characteristics of both sexes are really or apparently combined; a flower that contains both the stamen and the pistil.—*a.* Including or being of both sexes.
**Hermeneutic, Hermeneutical,** hėr-mē-nū'tik, hėr-mē-nū'tik-al, *a.* Interpreting; explaining.
**Hermeneutics,** hėr-mē-nū'tiks, *n.* The science of interpretation, particularly of interpreting the Scriptures.
**Hermetic, Hermetical,** hėr-met'ik, hėr-met'ik-al, *a.* Pertaining to alchemy or to occult science; effected by fusing together the edges of the aperture, as of a bottle; perfectly close and airtight.
**Hermetically,** hėr-met'ik-al-li, *adv.* Chemically; by fusing the edges together.
**Hermit,** hėr'mit, *n.* One who lives in solitude; a recluse.
**Hermitage,** hėr'mit-āj, *n.* The habitation of a hermit.
**Hernia,** hėr'ni-a, *n.* A protrusion of some organ of the abdomen through an interstice; a rupture.
**Hero,** hē'rō, *n.*; pl. **Heroes,** hē'rōz. A man of distinguished valor; the person who has the principal share in some exploit, or in a play, novel, etc.
**Heroic,** he-rō'ik, *a.* Pertaining to a hero or heroes; intrepid and noble; reciting achievements of heroes; epic.
**Heroically,** he-rō'ik-al-li, *adv.* In a heroic manner; like a hero.
**Heroin,** her'o-in, *n.* A narcotic drug derived from morphia.
**Heroine,** he'rō-in, *n.* A female hero.
**Heroism,** he'rō-izm, *n.* The qualities of a hero; intrepidity; magnanimity.
**Heron,** her'un, *n.* A wading bird with a long bill, long slender legs and neck.
**Heronry,** he'run-ri, *n.* A place where herons breed.
**Heronshaw,** her'un-sha, *n.* A young heron.
**Hero-worship,** hē'rō-wėr-ship, *n.* Extravagant admiration of great men.
**Herpes,** hėr'pez, *n.* A skin disease characterized by eruption or inflamed vesicles.
**Herpetology,** hėr-pe-tol'o-ji, *n.* The natural history of reptiles.
**Herr,** här, *n.* The German equivalent of the English Mr.
**Herring,** he'ring, *n.* One of those small food fishes which go in shoals in northern seas.
**Herring-bone,** he'ring-bōn, *a.* Applied to masonry, sewing, etc., which bears resemblance to the backbone of a herring.
**Hers,** hėrz, *pron. possessive. See* Her.
**Herse,** hėrs, *n.* A frame in form of a harrow; frame carrying candles in funerals, etc.
**Herself,** hėr-self', *pron.* The emphatic and reflexive form of *she* and *her.*
**Hesitancy,** he'zi-tan-si, *n.* A hesitating; vacillation.
**Hesitate,** he'zi-tāt, *vi.* (hesitating, hesitated). To pause respecting decision or action; to stop in speaking; to stammer.
**Hesitation,** he-zi-tā'shon, *n.* Act of hesitating; doubt; a stopping in speech.
**Hesperian,** hes-pē'ri-an, *a.* Western; situated at the west.
**Hest,** hest, *n.* Command.
**Hetarism, Hetairism,** het'a-rizm, he-tī'rizm, *n.* That primitive state of society in which the women are held in common.
**Heteroclite,** he'te-rō-klīt, *n.* A word irregular in declension or conjugation; something abnormal or anomalous.
**Heterodox,** he'te-rō-doks, *a.* Holding opinions different from those established or prevalent; not orthodox; heretical.
**Heterodoxy,** he'te-rō-dok-si, *n.* The holding of heterodox opinions; heresy.
**Heterogeneous,** he'te-rō-jē''nē-us, *a.* Of a different kind or nature; composed of dissimilar parts.
**Hew,** hū, *vt.* (pret. hewed, pp. hewed or hewn). To cut with an axe, etc.; to cut; to hack; to make smooth, as stone; to shape.
**Hewer,** hū-ėr, *n.* One who hews wood or stone.
**Hexagon,** heks'a-gon, *n.* A plane figure of six angles and six sides.
**Hexagonal,** heks-ag'on-al, *a.* Having six angles and six sides.
**Hexahedron,** heks-a-hē'dron, *n.* A regular solid body of six sides; a cube.
**Hexameter,** heks-am'et-ėr, *n.* A verse of six metrical feet.—*a.* Having six metrical feet.
**Hexangular,** heks-ang'gū-lėr, *a.* Having six angles or corners.
**Hey,** hā, *interj.* An exclamation of joy or to call attention.
**Heyday,** hā'dā, *interj.* An exclamation of cheerfulness.—*n.* The bloom or height; the wildness or frolicsome period of youth.
**Hiatus,** hī-ā'tus, *n.*; pl. **Hiatuses.** A gap; break; lacuna; meeting of vowel sounds.
**Hibernal,** hī-bėr'nal, *a.* Belonging to winter; wintry.
**Hibernate,** hī-bėr'nāt, *vt.* To pass the winter in sleep or seculsion; to winter.
**Hibernation,** hī-bėr-nā'shon, *n.* Act of hibernating.
**Hibernian,** hī-bėr'ni-an, *a.* Pertaining to Ireland; Irish.—*n.* A native of Ireland.
**Hiccup, Hiccough,** hik'up, *n.* A spasmodic affection of the diaphragm and glottis; a convulsive catch of the respiratory muscles.—*vt.* and *i.* To have a hiccup; to utter with hiccups.
**Hickory,** hik'ō-ri, *n.* An American tree of the walnut family, valuable for timber.
**Hid, Hidden,** hid, hid'n, *p.a.* Unseen; unknown; abstruse; profound.
**Hide,** hīd, *vt.* (hiding, pret. hid, pp. hid, hidden). To withhold or withdraw from sight or knowledge; to screen; to secrete.—*vi.* To be or to lie concealed; to keep oneself out of view.—*n.* The skin

of an animal, either raw or dressed; the human skin; an old measure of land of about 80 acres.
**Hide-bound,** hīd'bound, *a.* Having the hide abnormally tight; having the bark so close or firm as to hinder growth.
**Hideous,** hid'ē-us, *a.* Frightful; shocking to the eye or ear.
**Hideously,** hid'ē-us-li, *adv.* Dreadfully; shockingly.
**Hiding,** hīd'ing, *n.* Concealment; state of being hidden.
**Hie,** hī, *vi.* (hying, hied). To hasten; to speed.
**Hiemal,** hī-em'al, *a.* Wintry; pertaining to winter.
**Hiemation,** hī-e-mā''shon, *n.* The spending or passing of winter.
**Hierarch,** hī-ėr-ärk, *n.* One who has authority in sacred things.
**Hierarchical, Hierarchal,** hī-ėr-ärk'ik-al, hī-ėr-är'kal, *a.* Pertaining to a hierarchy.
**Hierarchy,** hī'ėr-är-ki, *n.* Authority in sacred things; clergy in whom is confided the direction of sacred things; ecclesiastical or clerical rule.
**Hieratic,** hī-ėr-at'ik, *a.* Sacred; pertaining to priests; applied to a kind of developed hieroglyphics used by the ancient Egyptian priests.
**Hieroglyph, Hieroglyphic,** hī'ėr-o-glif, hī'ėr-o-glif''ik, *n.* A figure of an animal, plant, etc., implying a word, idea, or sound, such as those in use among the ancient Egyptians; a character difficult to decipher.
**Hieroglyphic, Hieroglyphical,** hī'ėr-o-glif''ik, hī'ėr-o-glif''ik-al, *a.* Forming a hieroglyph; relating to hieroglyphics; emblematic.
**Hierology,** hī'ėr-ol'o-ji, *n.* Sacred lore; knowledge of hieroglyphics or sacred writing.
**Hierophant,** hī'ėr-o-fant, *n.* A priest; one who teaches the mysteries of religion.
**High,** hī, *a.* Having a great extent from base to summit; elevated; lofty; far above the earth; elevated in rank or office; dignified; proud; violent; solemn; strong; vivid; dear; remote; sharp; far advanced; committed against the sovereign or state; tending towards putrefaction; strong-scented.—*adv.* In a high manner; to a great altitude or degree; eminently; greatly.
**High-born,** hī'born, *a.* Being of noble birth or extraction.
**High-bred,** hī'bred, *a.* Bred in high life.
**Highbrow,** hī'brou, *n.* A person who pretends to be of a superior culture to the majority.
**High-flown,** hī'flōn, *a.* Elevated; turgid; extravagant.
**High-flying,** hī'flī-ing, *a.* Extravagant in claims or opinions.
**High-handed,** hī'hand-ed, *a.* Violent; overbearing; oppressive.
**Highland,** hī'land, *n.* A mountainous region: often in pl.—*a.* Pertaining to mountainous regions, or to the Highlands of Scotland.
**Highlander,** hī'land-ėr, *n.* An inhabitant of the mountains; a native of the Highlands of Scotland.
**Highly,** hī'li, *adv.* In a high manner; in a great degree; decidedly; markedly.
**High-minded,** hī'mind-ed, *a.* Proud; arrogant; having honorable pride.
**Highness,** hī'nes, *n.* State or quality of being high; height; title of honor given to princes, etc.; used with poss. prons. *his, her,* etc.
**High-pressure,** hī'prē-shūr, *a.* Having or involving a pressure exceeding that of the atmosphere, or having a pressure greater than 50 lbs. to the square inch.
**High-priest,** hī'prēst, *n.* A chief priest.
**Highroad,** hī'rōd, *n.* A highway or much-frequented road.
**High-souled,** hī'sōld, *a.* Having a high or lofty spirit; highly honorable.
**High-sounding,** hī'sound-ing, *a.* Making a loud sound; bombastic; ostentatious.
**High-spirited,** hī'spi-rit-ed, *a.* Full of spirit; bold; daring.
**High-strung,** hī'strung, *a.* Strung to a high pitch; high-spirited; sensitive.
**High-toned,** hī'tōnd, *a.* High in tone or pitch; noble; elevated.
**Highway,** hī'wā, *n.* A public road; direct course; train of action.
**Highwayman,** hī'wā-man, *n.* One who robs on the public road or highway.
**High-wrought,** hī'rat, *a.* Wrought with exquisite art or skill; inflamed to a high degree; keenly felt; intense.
**Hike,** hīk, *vi.* To tramp; to go on a long or fairly long walking expedition.
**Hilarious,** hi-lā'ri-us, *a.* Full of hilarity; gay; mirthful; merry.
**Hilarity,** hi-la'ri-ti, *n.* Cheerfulness; merriment; good humor; jollity.
**Hill,** hil, *n.* A natural elevation of less size than a mountain; an eminence.
**Hillock,** hil'ok, *n.* A small hill.
**Hilly,** hil'i, *a.* Abounding with hills.
**Hilt,** hilt, *n.* A handle, particularly of a sword.
**Him,** him, *pron.* The objective case of *he.*
**Himself,** him-self', *pron.* The emphatic and reflexive form of *he* and *him.*
**Hind,** hīnd, *n.* The female of the red-deer or stag; a farm servant; a rustic.—*a.* Backward; back; pertaining to the backward part.
**Hinder,** hīnd'ėr, *a.* Posterior; in the rear; latter; after.
**Hinder,** hin'dėr, *vt.* To prevent from moving or acting; to obstruct; to thwart; to check.—*vi.* To interpose obstacles or impediments.
**Hindmost, Hindermost,** hīnd'mōst, hīnd'ėr-mōst, *a.* Farthest behind; last.
**Hindrance,** hin'drans, *n.* Act of hindering; impediment; obstruction.
**Hindu, Hindoo,** hin-dö' or hin'dö, *n.* and *a.* A person of Aryan race native to Hindustan; pertaining to such.
**Hinge,** hinj, *n.* The hook or joint on which a door, etc., hangs and turns; that on which anything depends or turns.—*vt.* (hinging, hinged). To furnish with hinges.—*vi.* To stand or turn, as on a hinge.
**Hinny,** hin'i, *n.* A mule; the produce of a stallion and a she-ass.
**Hint,** hint, *vt.* To suggest indirectly; to insinuate.—*vi.* To make an indirect allusion.—*n.* A distant allusion; a suggestion.
**Hip,** hip, *n.* The fleshy projecting part of the thigh; the haunch; the joint of the thigh; the fruit of the dog-rose or wild brier.—*interj.* Exclamation expressive of a call to anyone. *Hip, hip, hurrah!* the signal to cheer.
**Hippocras,** hip'ō-kras, *n.* A medicinal drink of wine and spices, etc.
**Hippodrome,** hip'ō-drōm, *n.* A racecourse for horses and chariots; a circus.
**Hippophagy,** hip-pof'a-ji, *n.* The act or practice of feeding on horse-flesh.
**Hippopotamus,** hip-ō-pot'a-mus, *n.*; pl. **-amuses** or **-ami.** A large, hoofed pachydermatous animal, inhabiting the Nile and other rivers in Africa.
**Hip-shot,** hip'shot, *a.* Having the hip dislocated.
**Hircine,** hėr'sīn, *a.* Pertaining to or resembling a goat.
**Hire,** hīr, *vt.* (hiring, hired). To procure for temporary use, at a certain price; to engage in service for a stipulated reward; to let; to lease (with *out*).—*n.* Price paid for temporary use of anything; recompense for personal service; wages; pay.
**Hirsute,** hėr-sūt', *a.* Hairy; shaggy.
**His,** hiz, *pron.* The possessive case of *he.*
**Hispid,** his'pid, *a.* Rough with bristles; bristry.
**Hiss,** his, *vi.* To make a sound like that of the letter *s,* in contempt or disapprobation; to emit a similar sound; to whizz.—*vt.* To condemn by hissing.—*n.* The sound expressed by the verb.
**Hist,** hist, *interj.* A word commanding silence, equivalent to hush, whist, be silent.
**Histology,** his-tol'o-ji, *n.* The doctrine of animal

or vegetable tissues.
**Historian,** his-tō'ri-an, *n.* A writer or compiler of history.
**Historic, Historical,** his-to'rik, his-to'rik-al, *a.* Pertaining to, connected with, contained in, or deduced from history.
**Historically,** his-to'rik-al-li, *adv.* In a historical manner; according to history.
**Historiette,** his-tō'ri-et'', *n.* A short history or story; a tale; a novel.
**Historiographer,** his'tō-ri-og''ra-fėr, *n.* A writer of history; an official historian.
**History,** his'to-ri, *n.* An account of facts, particularly respecting nations or states; that branch of knowledge which deals with past events; narration; a story; an account of existing things, as animals or plants.
**Histrionic, Histrionical,** his-tri-on'ik, his-tri-on'ik-al, *a.* Pertaining to an actor or stage-playing; theatrical.
**Histrionics,** his-tri-on'iks, *n.* The art of theatrical representation.
**Hit,** hit, *vt.* (hitting, hit). To strike or touch with some force; to give a blow to; not to miss; to reach; to light upon; to suit.—*vi.* To strike; to come in contact; to reach the intended point; to succeed.—*n.* A stroke; a blow; a lucky chance; happy thought or expression.
**Hitch,** hich, *vi.* To move by jerks; to be entangled, hooked, or yoked.—*vt.* To fasten; to hook; to raise by jerks.—*n.* A catch; act of catching, as on a hook, etc.; knot or noose in a rope; a jerk; a temporary obstruction.
**Hither,** hiTH'ėr, *adv.* To this place.—*a.* Nearer; toward the person speaking.
**Hithermost,** hiTH'ėr-mōst, *a.* Nearest on this side.
**Hitherto,** hiTH'ėr-tö, *adv.* To this time; till now; to this place or limit.
**Hitherward,** hiTH'ėr-wėrd, *adv.* This way; toward this place.
**Hitter,** hit'ėr, *n.* One that hits.
**Hive,** hīv, *n.* A box or receptacle for honey-bees; the bees inhabiting a hive; a place swarming with busy occupants.—*vt.* (hiving, hived). To collect into a hive; to lay up in store.—*vi.* To take shelter together; to reside in a collective body.
**Ho,** hō, *interj.* A cry to excite attention, give notice, etc.
**Hoar,** hōr, *a.* White or whitish; hoary.—*vi.* To become moldy or musty.
**Hoard,** hōrd, *n.* A store, stock, or large quantity of anything; a hidden stock.—*vt.* To collect; to store secretly.—*vi.* To form a hoard; to lay up in store.
**Hoarding,** hōrd'ing, *n.* A timber enclosure round a building, etc.
**Hoar-frost,** hōr'frost, *n.* The white particles of frozen dew; rime.
**Hoarhound,** hōr'hound, *n.* A labiate plant with hoary foliage; a popular remedy for colds.
**Hoarse,** hōrs, *a.* Having a grating voice, as when affected with a cold; discordant; rough; grating.
**Hoarsely,** hōrs'li, *adv.* With a rough, harsh, grating voice or sound.
**Hoary,** hōr'i, *a.* White or whitish; white or gray with age.
**Hoax,** hōks, *n.* Something done for deception or mockery; a practical joke.—*vt.* To deceive; to play a trick upon without malice.
**Hob,** hob, *n.* The part of a grate on which things are placed to be kept warm.
**Hobble,** hob'l, *vi.* (hobbling, hobbled). To walk lamely or awkwardly; to limp; to halt.—*vt.* To hopple.—*n.* An unequal, halting gait; perplexity.
**Hobbledehoy,** hob'l-dē-hoi, *n.* A raw gawky youth approaching manhood.
**Hobby,** hob'i, *n.* A small but strong British falcon; an active, ambling nag; a hobby-horse; any favorite object or pursuit.
**Hobby-horse,** hob'i-hors, *n.* A wooden horse for children; a favorite object of pursuit.
**Hobgoblin,** hob-gob'lin, *n.* A goblin; an imp; something that causes terror.
**Hobnail,** hob'nāl, *n.* A nail with a thick, strong head.
**Hobnob,** hob'nob, *vi.* (hobnobbing, hobnobbed). To drink familiarly; to be boon companions.
**Hock, Hough,** hok, *n.* The joint between the knee and fetlock; in man, the posterior part of the knee-joint.—*vt.* To hamstring.
**Hock,** hok, *n.* A light Rhenish wine.
**Hockey,** hok'i, *n.* A game at ball played with a club curved at the lower end.
**Hocus,** hō'kus, *vt.* (hocussing, hocussed). To impose upon; to cheat; to drug.
**Hocus-pocus,** hō'kus-pō'kus, *n.* A juggler's trick; trickery used by conjurers.
**Hod,** hod, *n.* A kind of trough for carrying mortar and brick on the shoulder.
**Hodge,** hoj, *n.* A rustic or clown.
**Hodge-podge,** hoj'poj, *n.* A mixed mass; a medley of ingredients; a hotch-potch.
**Hodiernal,** ho-di-ėrn'al, *a.* Modern.
**Hodometer,** ho-dom'et-ėr, *n.* An instrument for measuring the distance travelled by any vehicle.
**Hoe,** hō, *n.* An instrument to cut up weeds and loosen the earth.—*vt.* (hoeing, hoed). To dig or clean with a hoe.—*vi.* To use a hoe.
**Hog,** hog, *n.* A swine; a castrated boar; a sheep of a year old; a brutal or mean fellow.—*vi.* To bend, as a ship's bottom.
**Hoggish,** hog'ish, *a.* Brutish; filthy.
**Hogshead,** hogz'hed, *n.* A large cask; an old measure of capacity, containing about 52$^1/_2$ imperial gallons.
**Hog-skin,** hog'skin, *n.* Leather made of the skin of swine.
**Hog-wash,** hog'wosh, *n.* Refuse of a kitchen, brewery, etc., given to swine; swill.
**Hoiden,** hoi'den, *n.* A rude, bold girl; a romp.—*a.* Rude; bold; inelegant; rustic.—*vi.* To romp rudely or wildly.
**Hoist,** hoist, *vt.* To heave up; to lift upward by means of tackle.—*n.* Act of raising; apparatus for raising goods, etc.; an elevator.
**Hoity-toity,** hoi ti-toi'ti, *a.* Frolicsome; haughty.—*interj.* An exclamation denoting surprise, with some degree of contempt.
**Hold,** hōld, *vt.* (pret. held, pp. held,). To have in the grasp; to keep fast; to confine; to maintain; to consider; to contain; to possess; to withhold; to continue; to celebrate.—*vi.* To take or keep a thing in one's grasp; to stand as a fact or truth; not to give way or part; to refrain; to adhere; to derive title (with *of*).—*n.* A grasp; something which may be seized for support; power of keeping, seizing, or directing; influence; place of confinement; stronghold; interior cavity of a ship.
**Holder,** hōld'ėr, *n.* One who or that which holds; something by which a thing is held; one who possesses.
**Holdfast,** hōld'fast, *n.* That which holds fast; a catch, hook, etc.
**Hole,** hōl, *n.* A hollow place in any solid body; a perforation, crevice, etc.; a den; a subterfuge.—*vt.* (holing, holed). To make a hole or holes in; to drive into a hole.
**Hole-and-corner,** hōl'and-kor-nėr, *a.* Clandestine; underhand.
**Holiday,** ho'li-dā, *n.* A holy or sacred day; a festival; day of exemption from labor.—*a.* Pertaining to a festival.
**Holiness,** hō'li-nes, *n.* State or quality of being holy; moral goodness; sanctity.—**His Holiness,** a title of the pope.
**Holism,** hol'izm, *n.* A philosophical theory according to which a fundamental feature of nature is the existence of 'wholes,' which are more than assemblages of parts, and which are always tending to become more highly developed and comprehensive.
**Holland,** hol'land, *n.* Fine linen.
**Hollands,** hol'landz, *n.* Gin manufactured in Hol-

land.
**Hollow,** hol'lō, *a.* Containing an empty space; not solid; deep; false; deceitful.—*n.* A depression or excavation; a cavity.—*vt.* To make a hole in; to excavate.
**Hollow-ware,** hol'ō-wār, *n.* A trade name for such iron articles as cauldrons, kettles, etc.
**Holly,** hol'i, *n.* An evergreen tree or shrub, with thorny leaves and scarlet berries.
**Hollyhock,** hol'i-hok, *n.* a tall biennial plant of the mallow family.
**Holm,** hōm or hōlm, *n.* A river isle; tract of rich land on the banks of a river.
**Holm-oak,** hōm'ōk or hōlm'ōk, *n.* The evergreen oak.
**Holocaust,** hol'o-kast, *n.* A burnt-sacrifice, of which the whole was consumed by fire; a great slaughter.
**Holograph,** hol'o-graf, *n.* A deed or document written wholly by the person from whom it proceeds.
**Holometabolic,** hol'o-met-a-bol''ik, *a.* Applied to insects which undergo a complete metamorphosis.
**Holster,** hōl'stėr, *n.* A leathern case for a pistol.
**Holt,** hōlt, *n.* A wood or woodland; a grove.
**Holy,** hō'li, *a.* Free from sin; immaculate; consecrated; sacred.
**Holy-day,** hō'li-dā. *See* HOLIDAY.
**Holy-stone,** hō'li-stōn, *n.* A soft sandstone used for cleaning the decks of ships.—*vt.* To scrub with holy-stone.
**Homage,** hom'āj, *n.* An act of fealty on the part of a vassal to his lord; obeisance; reverential worship.
**Home,** hōm, *n.* One's own abode; the abode of one's family; residence; one' own country; an establishment affording the comforts of a home.—*a.* Domestic; close; severe; poignant.—*adv.* To one's own habitation or country; to the point; effectively.
**Home-bred,** hōm'bred, *a.* Native; domestic; not polished by travel.
**Homefelt,** hōm'felt, *a.* Felt in one's own breast; inward; private.
**Home Guard,** hōm gärd, *n.* A voluntary unpaid force raised in 1940 for local defense.
**Homeless,** hōm'les, *a.* Destitute of a home.
**Homely,** hōm'li, *a.* Belonging to home; of plain features; plain; coarse.
**Homeopathic,** hō'mē-o-path''ik, *a.* Pertaining to homeopathy.
**Homeopathy,** hō-mē-op'a-thi, *n.* A system of curing diseases by drugs (usually in very small doses) which produce in healthy persons symptoms like those of the disease.
**Homer,** hō'mėr, *n.* A Hebrew measure of about 75 gallons or 11 bushels.
**Homeric,** hō-me'rik, *a.* Pertaining to or like Homer or his poetry.
**Home-rule,** hom'rōl, *n.* Self-government for a detached part of a country.
**Home-sick,** hōm'sik, *a.* Affected with homesickness.
**Home-sickness,** hōm'sik-nes, *n.* Depression of spirits occasioned by absence from one's home or country; nostalgia.
**Homespun,** hōm'spun, *a.* Spun or wrought at home; plain; coarse; homely.
**Homestead,** hōm'sted, *n.* A house with the grounds and buildings contiguous; a home; native seat.
**Homeward,** hōm'wėrd, *adv.* Toward one's habitation or country.—*a* Being in the direction of home.
**Homewards,** hōm'wėrdz, *adv.* Homeward.
**Homicidal,** ho-mi-sīd'al, *a.* Pertaining to homicide; murderous.
**Homicide,** ho'mi-sīd, *n.* Manslaughter; a person who kills another.
**Homiletic,** ho-mi-let'ik, *a.* Pertaining to homilies or homiletics.
**Homiletics,** ho-mi-let'iks, *n.* The art of preaching.
**Homilist,** ho'mi-list, *n.* One who writes or preaches homilies.
**Homily,** ho'mi-li, *n.* A sermon; a familiar religious discourse; a serious discourse or admonition.
**Homing,** hōm'ing, *a.* Coming home: applied to birds such as the carrier-pigeons.
**Hominy,** hom'i-ni, *n.* Maize hulled or coarsely ground, prepared for food by being boiled.
**Homogeneous,** ho-mō-jē'nē-us, *a.* Of the same kind or nature; consisting of similar parts or elements.
**Homogenesis,** ho-mō-jen'e-sis, *n.* Sameness of origin; reproduction of offspring similar to their parents.
**Homologate,** hō-mol'o-gāt, *vt.* To approve; to ratify.
**Homologous,** hō-mol'o-gus, *a.* Having the same relative position, proportion, or structure; corresponding.
**Homonym,** ho'mō-nim, *n.* A word which agrees with another in sound, and perhaps in spelling, but differs in signification.
**Homuncule, Homunculus,** hō-mung'kūl, hō-mung'kūl-us, *n.* A manikin; dwarf.
**Hone,** hōn, *n.* A stone of a fine grit, used for sharpening instruments.—*vt.* (honing, honed). To sharpen on a hone.
**Honest,** on'est, *a.* Free from fraud; upright; just; sincere; candid; virtuous.
**Honestly,** on'est-li, *adv.* In an honest manner; with integrity; frankly.
**Honesty,** on'est-i, *n.* State or quality of being honest; integrity; candor; truth.
**Honey,** hun'i, *n.* A sweet viscous juice collected by bees from flowers; sweetness; a word of tenderness.—*vt.* To sweeten.
**Honey-comb,** hun'i-kōm, *n.* The waxy structure formed by bees for honey; anything having cells like a honey-comb.
**Honey-combed,** hun'i-kōmd, *p.a.* Having little cells resembling honey-combs.
**Honey-dew,** hun'i-dū, *n.* A sweet substance found on certain plants in small drops.
**Honeyed,** hun'id, *a.* Covered with honey; sweet.
**Honeymoon,** hun'i-mōn, *n.* The first month after marriage; interval spent by a newly-married pair before settling down at home.
**Honeysuckle,** hun'i-suk-l, *n.* A beautiful flowering and climbing shrub; woodbine.
**Honorarium,** on-ėr-ā'ri-um, *n.* A fee for professional services.
**Honorary,** on'ėr-a-ri, *a.* Relating to honor; conferring honor; possessing a title or place without performing services or without receiving a reward.
**Honor,** on'ėr, *n.* Respect; esteem; testimony of esteem; dignity; good name; a nice sense of what is right; scorn of meanness; a title of respect or distinction; one of the highest trump cards; *pl.* civilities paid; public marks of respect; academic and university distinction.—*vt.* To regard or treat with honor; to bestow honor upon; to exalt; to accept and pay when due, as a bill.
**Honorable,** on'ėr-a-bl, *a.* Worthy of honor; actuated by principles of honor; conferring honor; consistent with honor; performed with marks of honor; not base; honest; fair; a title of distinction.
**Honorably,** on'ėr-a-bli, *adv.* In an honorable manner.
**Hood,** hud, *n.* A soft covering for the head; a cowl; a garment worn as part of academic dress, which indicates by its colors, material and shape the degree and University of its wearer; anything resembling a hood.—*vt.* To dress in a hood; to cover; to blind.
**Hooded,** hud'ed, *a.* Covered with a hood.
**Hooded crow,** a grayish crow with a black head.
**Hoodwink,** hud'wingk, *vt.* To blind by covering the eyes of; to impose on.
**Hoof,** höf, *n.*; pl. **Hoofs,** rarely **Hooves.** The horny substance that covers the feet of certain ani-

H

mals, as the horse.
**Hoof-mark,** höf'märk, *n*. The mark of an animal's hoof on the ground.
**Hook,** hök, *n*. A bent piece of iron or other metal for catching; that which catches; a sickle.—*vt*. To catch with a hook; to ensnare.—*vi*. To bend; to be curving.
**Hookah,** hö'kä, *n*. A tobacco-pipe with a large bowl and long pliable tube, so constructed that the smoke passes through water.
**Hooked,** hökt, *a*. Curved; bent; aquiline.
**Hooligan,** hō'li-gan, *n*. One of a gang of street roughs.
**Hoop,** hōp, *n*. A band of wood or metal confining the staves of casks, tubs, etc.; a crinoline; a ring; a loud shout.—*vt*. To bind with hoops; to encircle.—*vi*. To shout; to whoop.
**Hooping-cough,** höp'ing-kof, *n*. A contagious ailment common in childhood, characterized by a convulsive cough.
**Hoot,** höt, *vi*. To shout in contempt; to cry as an owl.—*vt*. To utter contemptuous cries at.—*n*. A cry or shout in contempt.
**Hop,** hop, *n*. A leap on one leg; a spring; a bitter plant of the hemp familyused to flavor malt liquors.—*vi*. To leap or spring on one leg; to skip; to limp; to pick hops.—*vt*. To impregnante with hops.
**Hope,** hōp, *n*. A desire of some good, accompanied with a belief that it is attainable; trust; one in whom trust or confidence is placed; the object of hope.—*vi*. (hoping, hoped). To entertain hope; to trust.—*vt*. To desire with some expectation of attainment.
**Hopeful,** hōp'ful, *a*. Full of hope; having qualities which excite hope; promising.
**Hopeless,** hōp'les, *a*. Destitute of hope; desponding; promising nothing desirable.
**Hopper,** hop'ėr, *n*. One who hops; a wooden trough through which grain passes into a mill; a boat to convey dredged matter.
**Hop-yard, Hop-garden,** hop'yärd, hop'gär-dn, *n*. A field where hops are raised.
**Horal,** hör'al, *a*. Relating to an hour.
**Horary,** hōr'a-ri, *a*. Hourly; noting the hours; continuing an hour.
**Horatian,** ho-rā'shan, *a*. Relating to or resembling Horace or his poetry.
**Horde,** hōrd, *n*. A tribe or race of nomads; a gang; migratory crew; rabble.—*vi*. (hording, horded). To live together like migratory tribes.
**Horehound,** hōr'hound, *n*. *See* HOARHOUND.
**Horizon,** ho-rī'zon, *n*. The circle which bounds tht part of the earth's surface visible from given point; the apparent junction of the earth and sky.
**Horizontal,** ho-ri-zon'tal, *a*. Parallel to the horizon; level; near the horizon.
**Hormones,** hor'mōnz, *n.pl*. Products of the ductless glands, affecting other organs by way of the blood stream.
**Horn,** horn, *n*. A hard projection on the heads of certain animals; the material of such horns; wind-instrument of music; extremity of the moon; drinking-cup; powder-horn; something resembling a horn; the feeler of a snail, etc.
**Hornblende,** horn'blend, *n*. A dark green or black lustrous mineral, an important constituent of several rocks.
**Horned,** hornd, *a*. Furnished with horns, or projections resembling horns; having two tufts of feathers on the head, as owls.
**Hornet,** horn'et, *n*. A large stinging species of wasp.
**Hornpipe,** horn'pip, *n*. An old Welsh instrument of music; a lively air or tune, of triple time; a dance to the tune.
**Hornwork,** horn'wėrk, *n*. An outwork in fortification, having angular points or horns.
**Horny,** horn'i, *a*. Consisting of horn; resembling horns; hardened by labor; callous.
**Horologe,** ho'ro-lōj, *n*. A time-piece of any kind.
**Horological,** ho-ro-loj'ik-al, *a*. Pertaining to horology.
**Horology,** ho-rol'o-ji, *n*. The science of measuring time; art of constructing machines for measuring time, as clocks, dials.
**Horoscope,** hor'os-kōp, *n*. In *astrology*, a figure or scheme of the heavens from which to cast nativities and foretell events.
**Horrible,** hor'ri-bl, *a*. Exciting horror; dreadful; frightful; awful; hideous.
**Horribly,** hor'ri-bli, *adv*. In a manner to excite horror; dreadfully; terribly.
**Horrid,** hor'rid, *a*. That does or may excite horror; horrible; shocking.
**Horridly,** hor'rid-li, *adv*. In a horrid manner; dreadfully; shockingly.
**Horrific,** hor'rif-ik, *a*. Causing horror.
**Horrify,** hor'ri-fi, *vt*. (horrifying, horrified). To strike or impress with horror.
**Horror,** hor'rėr, *n*. A powerful feeling of fear and abhorrence; that which may excite terror; something frightful or shocking.
**Horse,** hors, *n*. A well-known quadruped, used for draft and carriage in war; the male animal; cavalry; a name of various things resembling or analogous to a horse.—*vt*. (horsing, horsed). To supply with a horse; to carry on the back; to bestride.
**Horseback,** hors'bak, *n*. The back of a horse.
**Horse-chestnut,** hors'ches-nut, *n*. A flowering tree, the nuts of which have been used as food for animals.
**Horse-cloth,** hors'kloth, *n*. A cloth to cover a horse.
**Horse Guards,** hors'gärdz, *n.pl*. A body of cavalry for guards.
**Horse-leech,** hors'lēch, *n*. A large leech; one who cures horses.
**Horseman,** hors'man, *n*. A rider on horseback; a man skilled in riding; a soldier who serves on horseback.
**Horsemanship,** hors'man-ship, *n*. Act of riding, and of training and managing horses.
**Horse-play,** hors'plā, *n*. Rough or rude practical jokes or the like; rude pranks.
**Horse-power,** hors'pou-ėr, *n*. The power of a horse, or its equivalent, estimated as a power which will raise 32,000 lbs. avoirdupois one foot per minute: the standard for estimating the power of a steam-engine or motor, etc.
**Horseradish,** hors'rad-ish, *n*. A perennial plant, having a root of a pungent taste.
**Horseshoe,** hors'shö, *n*. A shoe for horses, commonly of iron shaped like the letter U; anything shaped like a horse-shoe.—*a*. Having the form of a horse-shoe.
**Horsewhip,** hors'whip, *n*. A whip for driving horses.—*vt*. To lash.
**Horsy, Horsey,** hor'si, *a*. Connected with, fond of, or much taken up with horses.
**Hortation,** hor-tā'shon, *n*. Exhortation.
**Hortative,** hort'at-iv, *a*. Giving exhortation.
**Hortatory,** hort'a-to-ri, *a*. Giving exhortation or advice; encouraging.
**Horticulture,** hor'ti-kul-tūr, *n*. The art of cultivating gardens.
**Horticulturist,** hor-tik-ul'tūr-ist, *n*. One skilled in horticulture.
**Hosanna,** hō-zan'na, *n*. An exclamation of praise to God, or an invocation of blessings.
**Hose,** hōz, *n*. *sing*. or *pl*. A covering for the thighs, legs, or feet; close-fitting breeches· stockings; in these senses plural; a flexible pipe used for conveying water.
**Hosier,** hō'zhi-ėr, *n*. One who deals in stockings, etc., or underclothing generally.
**Hosiery,** hō'zhi-ė-ri, *n*. The goods of a hosier; underclothing in general.
**Hospice,** hos'pis, *n*. A place of refuge and entertainment for travellers, as among the Alps.
**Hospitable,** hos'pit-a-bl, *a*. Kind to strangers and guests.
**Hospitably,** hos'pit-a-bli, *adv*. In a hospitable manner.

**Hospital,** hos'pit-al, *n.* A building for the sick, wounded, etc., or for any class of persons requiring public help.
**Hospitality,** hos-pit-al'i-ti, *n.* Quality of being hospitable.
**Hospitaller,** hos'pit-al-ėr, *n.* One of a religious community, whose office it was to relieve the poor, the stranger, and the sick; one of the Knights of Malta.
**Host,** hōst, *n.* One who entertains a stranger or guest; an innkeeper; an army; any great number or multitude; the consecrated bread in the R. Catholic sacrament of the mass.
**Hostage,** host'āj, *n.* A person delivered to an enemy, as a pledge to secure the performance of conditions.
**Hostel, Hostelry,** hos'tel, hos'tel-ri, *n.* An inn; a lodging-house.
**Hostess,** hōst'es, *n.* A female host; a woman who keeps an inn.
**Hostile,** hos'tīl, *a.* Belonging to an enemy; unfriendly; antagonistic; adverse.
**Hostility,** hos-til'i-ti, *n.* State or quality of being hostile; state of war between nations or states; the actions of an open enemy (in *pl.*); animosity; enmity; opposition.
**Hostler,** os'lėr, *n.* The person who has the care of horses at an inn.
**Hot,** hot, *a.* Having sensible heat; burning; glowing; easily exasperated; vehement; eager; lustful; biting; pungent in taste.
**Hot-bed,** hot'bed, *n.* A bed of earth heated by fermenting substances, and covered with glass, used for early or exotic plants; a place which favors rapid growth.
**Hot-blast,** hot'blast, *n.* A current of heated air injected into a smelting furnace by means of a blowing-engine.
**Hot-blooded,** hot'blud-ed, *a.* High-spirited; irritable.
**Hotchpot,** hoch'pot, *n.* A hodge-podge or mixture; a commixture of property for equality of division.
**Hotch-potch,** hoch'poch, *n.* A mixture of miscellaneous things; jumble; in Scotland, a thick soup of vegetables boiled with meat.
**Hotel,** hō-tel', *n.* A superior house for strangers or travellers; an inn; in France, a large mansion in a town.
**Hot-headed,** hot'hed-ed, *a.* Of ardent passions; vehement; violent; rash.
**Hot-house,** hot'hous, *n.* A house kept warm to shelter tender plants; a conservatory.
**Hotly,** hot'li, *adv.* With heat; ardently.
**Hot-press,** hot'pres, *vt.* To press paper, etc., between hot plates to produce a glossy surface.
**Hotspur,** hot'spėr, *n.* A fiery, violent, or rash man.
**Hot-tempered,** hot'tem-pėrd, *a.* Of a fiery wrathful temper.
**Hottentot,** hot'n-tot, *n.* A member of a native race of S. Africa; their language.
**Houdah,** hou'da, *n. See* HOWDAH.
**Hough,** hok, *n.* The hock of an animal.—*vt.* To hamstring.
**Hound,** hound, *n.* A dog; a dog used in the chase; a dog-fish.—*vt.* To set on in chase; to hunt; to urge on.
**Hour,** our, *n.* The twenty-fourth part of a day, consisting of sixty minutes; the particular time of the day; an appointed time; *pl.* certain prayers in the R. Catholic Church.
**Hour-glass,** our'glas, *n.* A glass for measuring time by the running of sand from one compartment to the other.
**Houri,** hou'ri or hö'ri, *n.* Among Mohammedans, a nymph of Paradise.
**Hourly,** our'li, *a.* Happening or done every hour; often repeated; continual.—*adv.* Every hour; frequently.
**House,** hous, *n.*; pl. **Houses,** hou'zez. A building or erection for the habitation or use of man; any building or edifice; a dwelling; a household; a family; a legislative body of men; audience or attendance; a commercial establishment.—*vt.* (housing, housed). To put or receive into a house; to shelter.—*vi.* To take shelter; to take up abode.
**House-boat,** hous'bōt, *n.* A river boat supporting a wooden house.
**Housebreaker,** hous'brāk-ėr, *n.* One who breaks into a house; a burglar.
**Housebreaking,** hous'brāk-ing, *n.* Burglary.
**Household,** hous'hōld, *n.* Those who dwell under the same roof and compose a family.—*a.* Domestic.
**Householder,** hous'hōld-ėr, *n.* The chief of a household; one who keeps house with his family.
**Housekeeper,** hous'kēp-ėr, *n.* A householder; a female servant who has the chief care of the house or family.
**Housekeeping,** hous'kēp-ing, *n.* The care or management of domestic concerns.
**Housel,** hou'zel, *n.* The eucharist.
**Housemaid,** hous'mād, *n.* A female servant in a house.
**House-surgeon,** hous'sėr-jon, *n.* The resident medical officer in a hospital.
**House-warming,** hous'warm-ing, *n.* A feast on a family's entrance into a new house.
**Housewife,** hous'wif, *n.* The mistress of a family; a female manager of domestic affairs; a hussif (pronounced huz'if).
**Housewifery,** hous'wif-ri, *n.* The business of a housewife.
**Housing,** houz'ing, *n.* A horse-cloth; *pl.* the trappings of a horse.—*p.n.* Placing in houses; sheltering.
**Hovel,** ho'vel, *n.* A mean house; an open shed for cattle, etc.—*vt.* To put in a hovel.
**Hover,** ho'vėr, *vi.* To hang fluttering in the air; to be in doubt; to linger near.
**How,** hou, *adv.* In what manner; to what extent; for what reason; by what means; in what state.
**Howbeit,** hou-bē'it, *adv.* Be it as it may; nevertheless.
**Howdah,** hou'da, *n.* A seat on an elephant's back, usually covered overhead.
**However,** hou-ev'ėr, *adv.* In whatever manner or degree; in whatever state.—*conj.* Nevertheless; yet; still; though.
**Howitzer,** hou'its-ėr, *n.* A short piece of ordnance, designed for firing shells at a high angle.
**Howl,** houl, *vi.* To cry as a dog or wolf; to utter a loud mournful sound; to roar, as the wind.—*vt.* To utter or speak with outcry.—*n.* A loud protracted wail; cry of a wolf, etc.
**Howlet,** hou'let, *n.* An owl; an owlet.
**Howling,** houl'ing, *a.* Filled with howls or howling beasts; dreary.
**Howsoever,** hou-sō-ev'ėr, *adv.* In what manner soever; although.
**Hoyden,** hoi'dn, *n.* and *a. See* HOIDEN.
**Hub,** hub, *n.* The central cylindrical part of a wheel in which the spokes are set.
**Hubbub,** hub'bub, *n.* A great noise of many confused voices; tumult; uproar.
**Huckster,** huk'stėr, *n.* A retailer of small articles; a hawker.—*vi.* To deal in small articles; to higgle.—*vt.* To hawk.
**Huddle,** hud'l, *vi.* (huddling, huddled). To crowd or press together promiscuously.—*vt.* To throw or crowd together in confusion; to put on in haste and disorder.—*n.* A confused mass; confusion.
**Hue,** hū, *n.* Color; tint; dye; a shouting; outcry; alarm.
**Huff,** huf, *n.* A fit of peevishness or petulance; anger.—*vt.* To treat with insolence; to bully; to make angry.—*vi.* To swell up; to bluster; to take offense.
**Huffy,** huf'i, *a.* Petulant; angry.
**Hug,** hug, *vt.* (hugging, hugged). To press close in an embrace; to hold fast; to cherish; to keep close to.—*n.* A close embrace; a particular grip in wrestling.

H

**Huge,** hūj, *a.* Of immense bulk; enormous; prodigious.
**Hugely,** hūj'li, *adv.* Very greatly; vastly.
**Huguenot,** hū'ge-not, *n.* A French Protestant of the period of the religious wars in France in the 16th century.
**Hulk,** hulk, *n.* the body of an old vessel; anything bulky or unwieldy.
**Hulking, Hulky,** hul'king, hul'ki, *a.* Large and clumsy of body; loutish.
**Hull,** hul, *n.* The outer covering of anything, particularly of a nut or of grain; husk; frame or body of a ship.—*vt.* To strip off the hull or hulls; to pierce the hull of a ship with a cannon-ball.
**Hum,** hum, *vi.* (humming, hummed). To utter the sound of bees; to make an inarticulate, buzzing sound.—*vt.* To sing in a low voice; to sing or utter inarticulately.—*n.* The noise of bees or insects; a low, confused noise; a low, inarticulate sound.—*interj.* A sound with a pause, implying doubt and deliberation.
**Human,** hū'man, *a.* Belonging to man or mankind; having the qualities of a man.
**Humane,** hū-mān', *a.* Having the feelings and dispositions proper to man; compassionate; merciful; tending to refine.
**Humanitarian,** hū-man'i-tā''ri-an, *n.* A philanthropist; one who believes Christ to have been but a mere man; one who maintains the perfectibility of human nature without the aid of grace.
**Humanity,** hū-man'i-ti, *n.* The quality of being human or humane; mankind collectively; kindness; benevolence; classical and polite literature: generally plural, '*the humanities*.'
**Humanize,** hū'man-īz, *vt.* To render human or humane; to civilize; to soften.
**Human-kind,** hū'man-kīnd, *n.* The race of man; mankind.
**Humanly,** hū'man-li, *adv.* After the manner of men.
**Humble,** hum'bl, *a.* Of a low, mean, or unpretending character; lowly; modest; meek.—*vt.* (humbling, humbled). To make humble; to abase; to lower.
**Humble-pie,** hum'bl-pī, *n.* A pie made of the humbles.—**To eat humble-pie,** to have to take a humble tone; to apologize.
**Humbles,** hum'blz, *n.pl.* The heart, liver, kidneys, etc., of a deer.
**Humbling,** hum'bl-ing, *a.* Adapted to abase pride and self-dependence.
**Humbly,** hum'bli, *adv.* In an humble manner; meekly; submissively.
**Humbug,** hum'bug, *n.* A hoax; a cheat; a trickish fellow.—*vt.* (humbugging, humbugged). To impose on.
**Humdrum,** hum'drum, *a.* Commonplace; dull.—*n.* A droning tone; dull monotony.
**Humid,** hū'mid, *a.* Moist; damp.
**Humidity,** hū-mid'i-ti, *n.* State of being humid; moisture.
**Humiliate,** hū-mil'i-āt, *vt.* To humble; to depress; to mortify.
**Humiliating,** hū-mil'i-āt-ing, *a.* Tending to humiliate; mortifying.
**Humiliation,** hū-mil'i-ā''shon, *n.* Act of humbling; state of being humbled; cause of being humbled.
**Humility,** hū-mil'i-ti, *n.* Humbleness of mind; modesty; sense of insignificance.
**Humming-bird,** hum'ing-bėrd, *n.* A family of minute but richly-colored birds that make a humming sound with their wings.
**Hummock,** hum'ok, *n.* A rounded knoll.
**Humorist,** hū'mėr-ist or ū', *n.* One that makes use of a humorous style in speaking or writing; a wag.
**Humorous,** hū'mėr-us or ū', *a.* Containing humor; jocular; adapted to excite laughter.
**Humor,** hū'mėr or ū'mėr, *n.* Moisture or moist mater; fluid matter in an animal body, not blood; disposition; mood; a caprice; jocularity; a quality akin to wit, but depending for its effect less on point or brilliancy of expression.—*vt.* To comply with the inclination of; to soothe by compliance; to indulge.
**Hump,** hump, *n.* A protuberance, especially that formed by a crooked back; a hunch.
**Humpback,** hump'bak, *n.* A back with a hump; a humpbacked person; a kind of whale.
**Humus,** hū'mus, *n.* Vegetable mold.
**Hunch,** hunsh, *n.* A hump; a protuberance; a thick piece; a push or jerk with the fist or elbow.—*vt.* To bend so as to form a hump; to push with the elbow.
**Hunchback,** hunsh'bak, *n.* A humpbacked person.
**Hundred,** hun'dred, *a.* Ten times ten.—*n.* The sum of ten times ten; the number 100; a division or part of a county in England.
**Hundredweight,** hun'dred-wāt, *n.* A weight of a hundred and twelve pounds avoirdupois, twenty of which make a ton.
**Hungarian,** hung-gā'ri-an, *n.* A native of Hungary; the language of the Hungarians; Magyar.—*a.* Pertaining to Hungary.
**Hunger,** hung'gėr, *n.* An uneasy sensation occasioned by the want of food; a craving of food; a strong or eager desire.—*vi.* To feel the uneasiness occasioned by want of food; to desire with great eagerness.
**Hungry,** hung'gri, *a.* Feeling uneasiness from want of food; having an eager desire; lean; barren.
**Hunk,** hungk, *n.* A large lump; a hunch.
**Hunks,** hungks, *n.* A miser; a niggard.
**Hunt,** hunt, *vt.* To chase or search for, for the purpose of catching or killing; to follow closely; to use or manage, as hounds; to pursue animals over.—*vi.* To follow the chase; to search.—*n.* The chase of wild animals for catching them; pursuit; an association of huntsmen; a pack of hounds.
**Hunter,** hunt'ėr, *n.* One who hunts; a horse used in the chase; a kind of watch with a hinged case which protects the glass.
**Hunting,** hunt'ing, *n.* The act or practice of pursuing wild animals; the chase.
**Huntress,** hunt'res, *n.* A female that hunts or follows the chase.
**Huntsman,** hunts'man, *n.* One who practices hunting; the person whose office it is to manage the chase.
**Hurdle,** hėr'dl, *n.* A movable frame made of twigs or sticks, or of bars or rods.—*vt.* (hurdling, hurdled). To make up, cover, or close with hurdles.
**Hurdy-gurdy,** hėr'di-gėr-dl, *n.* A stringed instrument of music, whose sounds are produced by the friction of a wheel; a barrel-organ.
**Hurl,** hėrl, *vt.* To send whirling through the air; to throw with violence; to utter with vehemence.—*n.* Act of throwing with violence.
**Hurly-burly,** hėr'li-bėr'li, *n.* Tumult; bustle; confusion.
**Hurricane,** hu'ri-kān, *n.* A violent storm of wind traveling over 75 miles per hour.
**Hurried,** hu'rid, *p.a.* Characterized by hurry; done in a hurry; evidencing hurry.
**Hurriedly,** hu'rid-li, *adv.* In a hurried manner.
**Hurry,** hu'ri, *vt.* (hurrying, hurried). To drive or press forward with more rapidity; to urge to act with more celerity; to quicken.—*vi.* To move or act with haste; to hasten.—*n.* Act of hurrying; urgency; bustle.
**Hurry-skurry,** hu'ri-sku-ri, *adv.* Confusedly; in a bustle.—*n.* Bustle.
**Hurt,** hėrt, *n.* A wound; bruise; injury; harm.—*vt.* (pret. and pp. hurt). To cause physical pain to; to bruise; to harm; to impair; to injure; to wound the feelings of.
**Hurtful,** hėrt'ful, *a.* Causing hurt; tending to impair; detrimental; injurious.
**Hurtle,** hėr'tl, *vi.* (hurtling, hurtled). To meet in shock; to clash; to fly with threatening noise; to

resound.

**Husband,** huz'band, *n.* A married man; the correlative of wife; a good manager; a steward.—*vt.* To manage with frugality; to use with economy.

**Husbandman,** huz'band-man, *n.* A tiller of the ground; a farmer.

**Husbandry,** huz'band-ri, *n.* Farming; care of domestic affairs; thrift.

**Hush,** hush, *a.* Silent; still; quiet.—*n.* Stillness; quiet.—*vt.* To make quiet; to repress, as noise.—*vi.* To be still; to be silent.

**Hush-money,** hush'mu-ni, *n.* Money paid to hinder disclosure of facts.

**Husk,** husk, *n.* The covering of certain fruits or seeds.—*vt.* To strip the husk from.

**Husky,** husk'i, *a.* Abounding with husks; consisting of husks; resembling husks; rough, as sound; harsh; hoarse.

**Hussar,** hu-zär', *n.* A light-armed horse-soldier.

**Hussif,** hüz'if, *n.* A case for holding such things as needles, thimble, thread, etc.

**Hussy,** huz'i, *n.* A worthless woman; a jade; a pert, frolicsome wench; a quean.

**Hustle,** hus'l, *vt.* and *i.* (hustling, hustled). To shake or shuffle together; to push or crowd; to jostle.

**Hut,** hut, *n.* A small house, hovel, or cabin; a temporary building to lodge soldiers.—*vt.* (hutting, hutted). To place in huts, as troops.—*vi.* To take lodgings in huts.

**Hutch,** huch, *n.* A chest or box; a corn bin; a box for rabbits; a low wagon used in coal-pits; a measure of 2 bushels.

**Hyacinth,** hī'a-sinth, *n.* A flowering, bulbous plant, of many varieties; a red variety of zircon, tinged with yellow or brown: also applied to varieties of garnet, sapphire, and topaz.

**Hyacinthine,** hī-a-sinth'īn, *a.* Pertaining to, made of, or like hyacinth.

**Hyaline,** hī'al-in, *a.* Glassy; transparent.

**Hyalography,** hī-al-og'ra-fi, *n.* The art of engraving on glass.

**Hybrid,** hīb'rid, *n.* A mongrel; an animal or plant produced from the mixture of two species.—*a.* Mongrel.

**Hydatid,** hīd'a-tid, *n.* A larval form of tape-worm.

**Hydra,** hī'dra, *n.* A many-headed monster of Greek mythology.

**Hydrangea,** hī-dran'jē-a, *n.* An Asiatic shrub with beautiful flowers, cultivated in gardens.

**Hydrant,** hī'drant, *n.* A pipe with valves, etc., by which water is drawn from a main pipe.

**Hydrate,** hī'drāt, *n.* A chemical compound in which water or hydrogen is a characteristic ingredient.

**Hydraulic,** hī-dral'ik, *a.* Pertaining to fluids in motion, or the action of water utilized for mechanical purposes.

**Hydraulics,** hī-dral'iks, *n.* The science of fluids in motion, and the application of water in machinery.

**Hydrocarbon,** hī-drō-kär'bon, *n.* A chemical compound of hydrogen and carbon.

**Hydrocephalus,** hī-drō-sef'a-lus, *n.* Water in the head.

**Hydrogen,** hī'drō-jen, *n.* The gaseous elementary substance which combines with oxygen to form water.

**Hydrogenous,** hī-dro'jen-us, *a.* Pertaining to hydrogen.

**Hydrography,** hī-drog'ra-fi, *n.* The science of the measurements and representation by charts of seas, rivers, etc.

**Hydrology,** hī-drol'o-ji, *n.* The science of water, its properties and laws.

**Hydrometer,** hī-drom'et-ėr, *n.* An instrument for measuring the specific gravities of liquids, and the strength of spirituous liquors.

**Hydropathy,** hī-dro'pa-thi, *n.* A mode of treating diseases by the copious use of pure water, internally and externally.

**Hydrophobia,** hī-drō-fō'bi-a, *n.* A morbid dread of water; a disease produced by the bite of a mad animal, especially a dog.

**Hydrophyte,** hī'drō-fīt, *n.* A plant which lives and grows in water.

**Hydroponics,** hī drō-pon'iks, *n.* The cultivation of plants in chemical solutions without soil.

**Hydrostatic,** hī-drō-stat'ik, *a.* Relating to hydrostatics.

**Hydrostatics,** hī-drō-stat'iks, *n.* The science which treats of the weight, pressure, and equilibrium of fluids, particularly water, when in a state of rest.

**Hyena,** hī-ē'na, *n.* A carnivorous quadruped of Asia and Africa, feeding chiefly on carrion.

**Hygeian,** hī-jē'an, *a.* Relating to health, or the mode of preserving health.

**Hygiene,** hī'ji-ēn, *n.* A system of principles designed for the promotion of health; sanitary science.

**Hygienic,** hī-ji-en'ik, *a.* Relating to hygiene.

**Hygrometer,** hī-grom'et-ėr, *n.* An instrument for measuring the moisture of the atmosphere.

**Hygroscope,** hī'grō-skōp, *n.* An instrument for indicating the presence of moisture in the atmosphere.

H

**Hymen,** hī'men, *n.* The god of marriage.

**Hymeneal, Hymenean,** hī-men-ē'al, hī-men-ē'an, *a.* Pertaining to marriage.

**Hymn,** him, *n.* A song of praise; a song or ode in honor of God.—*vt.* To praise or celebrate in song.—*vi.* To sing in praise.

**Hymnal,** him'nal, *n.* A collection of hymns, generally for use in public worship.

**Hyoid,** hī'oid, *a.* Applied to a movable U-shaped bone between the root of the tongue and the larynx.

**Hyperbola,** hī-pėr'bō-la, *n.* A conic section, a curve formed by a section of a cone, when the cutting plane makes a greater angle with the base than the side of the cone makes.

**Hyperbole,** hī-pėr'bō-lē, *n.* Exaggeration; a figure of speech exceeding the truth.

**Hyperbolic, Hyperbolical,** hī-pėr-bol'ik, hī-pėr-bol'ik-al, *a.* Belonging to the hyperbola; containing hyperbole; exceeding the truth.

**Hyperborean,** hī-pėr-bō'rē-an, *a.* Being in the extreme north; arctic; frigid.—*n.* An inhabitant of the most northern regions.

**Hypercritic,** hī-pėr-krit'ik, *n.* One critical beyond measure; a captious censor.

**Hypercritical,** hī-pėr-krit'ik-al, *a.* Overcritical; excessively nice or exact.

**Hypercriticism,** hī-pėr-krit'i-sizm, *n.* Excessive rigor or nicety of criticism.

**Hyphen,** hī'fen, *n.* A character, thus (-), implying that two words or syllables are to be connected.

**Hypnotic,** hip-not'ik, *a.* Producing sleep.

**Hypnotism,** hip'no-tizm, *n.* A sleep-like condition caused by artificial means.

**Hypnotize,** hip'no-tīz, *vt.* To affect with hypnotism.

**Hypochondria,** hī-pō-kon'dri-a, *n.* An ailment characterized by exaggerated anxiety, mainly as to the health; low spirits.

**Hypochondriac,** hī-pō-kon'dri-ak, *a.* Pertaining to or affected with hypochondria.—*a.* One affected with hypochondria.

**Hypocrisy,** hi-pok'ri-si, *n.* A feigning to be what one is not; insincerity; a counterfeiting of religion.

**Hypocrite,** hi'pō-krit, *n.* One who feigns to be what he is not; a dissembler.

**Hypocritical,** hi-pō-krit'ik-al, *a.* Pertaining to or characterized by hypocrisy; insincere.

**Hypodermal, Hypodermic,** hī-pō-dėr'mal, hī-pō-dėr'mik, *a.* Pertaining to parts under the skin, or to the introduction of medicines under the skin.

**Hypotenuse,** hī-pot'ē-nūs, *n.* The side of a right-angled triangle opposite the right angle.

**Hypothec,** hī-poth'ek, *n.* In *Scots law,* a lien such as a landlord has over a tenant's furniture or crops.

**Hypothecate,** hī-poth'e-kāt, *vt.* To pledge in security for a debt, but without transfer; to mortgage.
**Hypothesis,** hī-poth'e-sis, *n.*; pl. **-ses,** -sēz. A supposition; something assumed for the purpose of argument; a theory assumed to account for what is not understood.
**Hypothetic, Hypothetical,** hī-po-thet'ik, hī-po-thet'ik-al, *a.* Relating to or characterized by hypothesis; conjectural.
**Hypsometer,** hip-som'et-ėr, *n.* An apparatus for measuring altitudes.
**Hyson,** hīs'on, *n.* A Chinese green tea.
**Hyssop,** his'sop, *n.* An aromatic plant possessing stimulating, stomachic, and carminative properties.
**Hysteria, Hysterics,** his-te'riks, *a.* Pertaining to hysterics or hysteria; affected by or subject to hysterics.
**Hysteric, Hysterical,** his-te'rik, hister'rik-al, *n.* A nervous affection chiefly attacking women, characterized by laughing and crying, convulsive struggling, sense of suffocation, etc.

# I

**I,** ī, *pron.* The pronoun of the first person in the nominative case; the word by which a speaker or writer denotes himself.
**Iamb,** ī-amb', *n.* An iambus.
**Iambic,** ī-am'bik, *a.* Pertaining to the iambus; consisting of an iambus or of iambi.—*n.* An iambic foot; a verse of iambi.
**Iambus,** ī-am'bus, *n.*; pl. **-buses** or **-bi.** A poetic foot of two syllables, the first short and the last long, as in *delight.*
**Iatric, Iatrical,** ī-at'rik, ī-at'rik-al, *a.* Relating to medicine or physicians.
**Iberian,** ī-be'ri-an, *a.* Spanish.—*n.* One of the primitive inhabitants of Spain, or their language.
**Ibex,** ī'beks, *n.* An animal of the goat family.
**Ibis,** ī'bis, *n.*; pl. **Ibises,** ī'bis-ez. A grallatorial bird allied to the stork.
**Ice,** īs, *n.* Water or other fluid congealed; ice-cream.—*vt.* (icing, iced). To cover with ice; to convert into ice; to cover with concreted sugar; to freeze.
**Iceberg,** īs'bėrg, *n.* A vast body of ice floating in the ocean.
**Ice-bound,** īs'bound, *a.* Totally surrounded with ice, as a ship.
**Ice-cream,** īs'krēm, *n.* A confection of cream, sugar, etc., frozen.
**Iced,** īst, *p.a.* Covered with ice; covered with concreted sugar.
**Ice-plant,** īs'plant, *n.* A plant whose leaves appear as if covered with frost.
**Ichneumon,** ik-nū'mon, *n.* A carnivorous Egyptian animal resembling a weasel, which hunts out crocodiles' eggs.
**Ichor,** ī'kor, *n.* In *mythology,* the ethereal juice that flowed in the veins of the gods; in *medicine,* a watery, acrid humor or discharge.
**Ichthyology,** ik-thi-ol'o ji, *n.* That part of zoology which treats of fishes.
**Ichthyosaurus,** ik'thi-ō-sa''rus, *n.* A fishlike lizard; an immense fossil marine reptile.
**Icicle,** īs'i-kl, *n.* A pendent, conical mass of ice.
**Iconoslast,** ī-kon'o-klast, *n.* A breaker of images; one who attacks cherished beliefs.
**Iconography,** ī-ko-nog'ra-fi, *n.* The knowledge of ancient statues, paintings, gems, etc.
**Icy,** īs'i, *a.* Abounding with ice; made of ice; resembling ice; chilling; frigid; destitute of affection or passion.
**Idea,** ī-dē'a, *n.* That which is seen by the mind's eye; an image in the mind; object of thought; notion; conception; abstract principle; ideal view.
**Ideal,** ī-dē'al, *a.* Existing in idea or fancy; visionary; imaginary; perfect.—*n.* An imaginary model of perfection.
**Idealism,** ī'dē'al-izm, *n.* The system that makes everything to consist in ideas, and denies the existence of material bodies, or which denies any ground for believing in the reality of anything but percipient minds and ideas.
**Idealist,** ī-dē'al-ist, *n.* One who holds the doctrine of idealism; a visionary.
**Ideality,** ī-dē-al'i-ti, *n.* Quality of being ideal; capacity to form ideals of beauty.
**Idealize,** ī-dē'al-iz, *vt.* To make ideal; to embody in an ideal form.
**Ideally,** ī-dē'al-li, *adv.* In an ideal manner; an idea; intellectually; mentally.
**Ideation,** ī-dē-ā-shon, *n.* The faculty for forming ideas; establishment of a distinct mental representation of an object.
**Identical,** ī-den'tik-al, *a.* The same.
**Identifiable,** ī-den'ti-fī-a-bl, *a.* That may be identified.
**Identification,** ī-den'ti-fi-kā''shon, *n.* Act of identifying.
**Identify,** ī-den'ti-fī, *vt.* To make to be the same; to consider as the same in effect; to ascertain or prove to be the same.
**Identity,** ī-den'ti-ti, *n.* Sameness, as distinguished from similitude and diversity; sameness in every possible circumstance.
**Ideograph, Ideogram,** id'ē-ō-graf, id'ē-ō-gram, *n.* A character, symbol, or figure which suggests the idea of an object; a hieroglyphic.
**Ideology,** ī-dē-ol'o-ji, *n.* The doctrine of ideas, or operations of the understanding.
**Ides,** īdz, *n.pl.* In the ancient Roman calendar the 15th day of March, May, July, and October, and the 13th day of the other months.
**Idiocy,** id'i-ō-si, *n.* State of being an idiot; hopeless insanity or madness.
**Idiograph,** id'ī-ō-graf, *n.* A private or trade mark.
**Idiom,** id'i-om, *n.* A mode of expression peculiar to a language; the genius or peculiar cast of a language; dialect.
**Idiomatic,** id'i-om-at''ik, *a.* Pertaining to the particular genius or modes of expression of a language.
**Idiomatically,** id'i-om-at''ik-al-li, *adv.* According to the idiom of a language.
**Idiopathy,** id-i-op'a-thi, *n.* A morbid state not produced by any preceding disease.
**Idiosyncrasy,** id'i-o-sin''kra-si, *n.* Peculiarity of temperament or constitution; mental or moral characteristic distinguishing an individual.
**Idiosyncratic,** id'i-o-sin-krat''ik, *a.* Of peculiar temper or disposition.
**Idiot,** i'di-ot, *n.* One void of understanding; one hopelessly insane.
**Idiotic, Idiotical,** id-i-ot'ik, id-i-ot'ik-al, *a.* Relating to or like an idiot; absurd.
**Idle,** I'dl, *a.* Not engaged in any occupation; inactive; lazy; futile; affording leisure; trifling; trivial.—*vi.* (idling, idled). To be idle; to lose or spend time in inaction.—*vt.* To spend in idleness.
**Idleness,** ī'dl-nes, *n.* Inaction; sloth; triviality; uselessness.
**Idly,** īd'li, *adv.* Lazily; carelessly; ineffectually; unprofitably.
**Idol,** ī'dol, *n.* An image or symbol of a deity consecrated as an object of worship; a person honored to adoration; anything on which we set our affections inordinately.
**Idolater,** ī-dol'at-ėr, *n.* A worshipper of idols; a pagan; a great admirer.
**Idolatrous,** ī-dol'at-rus, *a.* Pertaining to idolatry; consisting in or partaking of an excessive attachment or reverence.
**Idolatry,** ī-dol'at-ri, *n.* The worship of idols; excessive attachment to or veneration for any person or thing.
**Idolize,** ī'dol-īz, *vt.* To worship as an idol; to love or reverence to adoration.
**Idyl,** id'il or ī'dil, *n.* A short highly wrought descriptive poem; a short pastoral poem.

**Idyllic,** ī-dil'ik, *a.* Belonging to idylls; pastoral.
**If,** if, *conj.* Granting or supposing that; on condition that; whether; although.
**Igloo,** ig'lö, *n.* An Eskimo winter-hut, made of blocks of frozen snow.
**Igneous,** ig'nē-us, *a.* Pertaining to or consisting of fire; resembling fire; proceeding from the action of fire.
**Ignite,** ig-nīt', *vt.* (igniting, ignited). To set on fire.—*vi.* To take fire.
**Ignition,** ig-ni'shon, *n.* Act of setting on fire; act of catching fire; state of burning.
**Ignoble,** ig-nō'bl, *a.* Not noble; of low birth or family; base; dishonorable.
**Ignominious,** ig-nō-mi'ni-us, *a.* Shameful; dishonorable; infamous; despicable.
**Ignominy,** ig'nō-mi-ni, *n.* Public disgrace; loss of character or reputation; infamy; shame; contempt.
**Ignoramus,** ig-nō-rā'mus, *n.*; pl. **-muses.** An ignorant person.
**Ignorance,** ig-nō-rans, *n.* State of being illiterate, uninformed, or uneducated; want of knowledge.
**Ignorant,** ig'nō-rant, *a.* Wanting knowledge or information.
**Ignore,** ig-nōr', *vt.* (ignoring, ignored). To pass over or overlook as if ignorant of; to disregard.
**Iguana,** ig-wä'na, *n.* An American reptile of the lizard family.
**Iliac,** il'i-ak, *a.* Pertaining to the lower bowels.
**Ill,** il, *a.* Bad or evil; producing evil, unfortunate; cross; crabbed; sick or indisposed; impaired; ugly; unfavorable; rude.—*n.* Evil; misfortune; calamity; disease; pain.—*adv.* Not well; badly; with pain or difficulty.
**Ill-bred,** il-bred', *a.* Unpolite; rude.
**Illegal,** il-lē'gal, *a.* Not legal; contrary to law; prohibited; illicit.
**Illegality,** il-lē-gal'i-ti, *n.* State or quality of being illegal; unlawfulness.
**Illegible,** il-le'ji-bl, *a.* Not legible; that cannot be read.
**Illegitimacy,** il-lē-jit'i-ma-si, *n.* State of being illegitimate; bastardy.
**Illegitimate,** il-lē-jit'i-māt, *a.* Not legitimate; born out of wedlock; illogical; not authorized.—*vt.* To render illegitimate.
**Illiberal,** il-lib'ėr-al, *a.* Not liberal; not generous; narrow in scope; uncharitable.
**Illicit,** il-lis'it, *a.* Not permitted; unlawful; lawless.
**Illimitable,** il-lim'it-a-bl, *a.* That cannot be limited; boundless; infinite; vast.
**Illiteracy,** il-lit'ėr-a-si, *n.* State of being illiterate; want of education; ignorance.
**Illiterate,** il-lit'ėr-āt, *a.* Unlettered; ignorant of letters or books; not educated.
**Ill-mannered,** il-man'ėrd, *a.* Having bad manners; rude; boorish; impolite.
**Ill-nature,** il'nā-tūr, *n.* Bad temper; crossness; crabbedness.
**Illness,** il'nes, *n.* State or quality of being ill; ailment; malady; sickness.
**Illogical,** il-lo'jik-al, *a.* Not logical; contrary to logic or sound reasoning.
**Ill-tempered,** il'tem-pėrd, *a.* Of bad temper; morose; crabbed; sour.
**Ill-timed,** il'tīmd, *a.* Done or said at an unsuitable time.
**Illude,** il-lūd', *vt.* (illuding, illuded). To deceive; to mock; to make sport of.
**Illuminate,** il-lūm'in-āt, *vt.* (illuminating, illuminated). To light up; to adorn with festal lamps or bonfires; to enlighten intellectually; to adorn with colored pictures, etc., as manuscripts.
**Illuminati,** il-lū'mi-nā''tī, *n.pl.* A term applied to persons who affect to possess extraordinary knowledge.
**Illumination,** il-lūm'in-ā''shon, *n.* Act of illuminating; festive display of lights, etc.; splendor; infusion of intellectual or spiritual light; the adorning of manuscripts and books by hand with ornamental designs; such ornaments themselves.
**Illuminative,** il-lūm'in-āt-iv, *a.* Having the power of illuminating or giving light.
**Illusion,** il-lū'zhon, *n.* Deception; deceptive appearance; hallucination.
**Illusionist,** il-lū'zhon-ist, *n.* One given to illusion, or one who produces illusions, as by sleight of hand.
**Illusive,** il-lū'siv, *a.* Tending to cause illusion; deceptive; deceitful.
**Illusory,** il-lū'so-ri, *a.* Deceiving by false appearances; fallacious.
**Illustrate,** il-lus'trāt or il'lus-trāt, *vt.* (illustrating, illustrated). To make clear or obvious; to explain; to explain and adorn by means of pictures; drawings, etc.
**Illustration,** il-lus-trā'shon, Act of illustrating; that which illustrates; an example; design to illustrate the text of a book.
**Illustrative,** il-lus'trāt-iv or il'lus-trāt-iv, *a.* Having the quality of illustrating or elucidating.
**Illustrator,** il-lus'trāt-ėr or il'lus-trāt-ėr, *n.* One who illustrates; one who makes pictures for books.
**Illustrious,** il-lus'tri-us, *a.* Renowned; celebrated; noble; conferring honor or renown; glorious.
**Illwill,** il'wil, *n.* Unkind or hostile feeling; hatred; malevolence; malice.
**Image,** im'āj, *n.* A representative of any person or thing; a statue; an idol; embodiment; a picture drawn by fancy; the appearance of any object formed by the reflection or refraction of the rays of light.—*vt.* (imaging, imaged). To represent by an image; to mirror; to form a likeness of in the mind.
**Imagery,** im'āj-e-ri, *n.* Images in general; forms of the fancy; rhetorical figures.
**Imaginable,** im-aj'in-a-bl, *a.* That may or can be imagined.
**Imaginary,** im-aj'in-a-ri, *a.* Existing only in imagination; ideal; visionary.
**Imagination,** im-aj'in-ā''shon, *n.* The act of imagining; the faculty by which we form a mental image, or new combinations of ideas; mental image; a mere fancy; notion.
**Imaginative,** im-aj'in-āt-iv, *a.* That forms imaginations; owing existence to, or characterized by imagination.
**Imagine,** im-aj'in, *vt.* (imagining, imagined). To picture to oneself; to fancy; to contrive; to think; to deem.—*vi.* To conceive; to have a notion or idea.
**Imago,** im-ā'go, *n.* The last or perfect state of an insect.
**Imam, Imaum, Iman,** i-män', i-mam', i-män', *n.* A successor of Mohammed; the priest of a mosque.
**Imbecile,** im'be-sil, *a.* Destitute of strength; mentally feeble; fatuous; extremely foolish.—*n.* A poor, fatuous, or weak-minded creature.
**Imbed,** im-bed', *vt.* To lay in a bed; to lay in surrounding matter. Also *Embed.*
**Imbibe,** im-bīb', *vt.* (imbibing, imbibed). To drink in; to absorb; to admit into the mind.
**Imbitter, Imblazon, Imbody, Imbolden, Imbowel, Imbower.** *See* EMBITTER, etc.
**Imbricate, Imbricated,** im'bri-kāt, im'bri-kāt-ed, *a.* Bent and hollowed, like a roof tile; lapping over each other, like tiles.
**Imbrication,** im-bri-kā'shon, *n.* State of being imbricate; a hollow like that of a roof tile.
**Imbroglio,** im-brō'lyō, *n.* An intricate and perplexing state of affairs; a misunderstanding of a complicated nature.
**Imbue,** im-bū', *vt.* (imbuing, imbued). To tinge deeply; to dye; to inspire or impregnate (the mind).
**Imitable,** im'i-ta-bl, *a.* That may be imitated; worthy of imitation.
**Imitate,** im'i-tāt, *vt.* (imitating, imitated). To follow as a model or example; to copy; to mimic; to counterfeit.

I

**Imitation,** im-i-tā'shon, *n.* Act of imitating; that which is made or produced as a copy; resemblance; a counterfeit.
**Imitative,** im'i-tāt-iv, *a.* That imitates; inclined to imitate; exhibiting an imitation.
**Imitator,** im'i-tāt-ėr, *n.* One who imitates; one who takes another as pattern or model.
**Immaculate,** im-ma'kū-lāt, *a.* Without spot; undefiled; pure.
**Immanate,** im'ma-nāt, *vi.* To flow or issue in: said of something intangible.
**Immanent,** im'ma-nent, *a.* Remaining in or within; inherent and indwelling.
**Immaterial,** im-ma-tē'ri-al, *a.* Not consisting of matter; unimportant.
**Immaterialism,** im-ma-tē'ri-al-izm, *n.* The doctrine that all being may be reduced to mind and ideas in the mind.
**Immateriality,** im-ma-tē'ri-al''i-ti, *n.* Quality of being immaterial.
**Immature,** im-ma-tūr', *a.* Not mature; not perfect or completed; premature.
**Immaturity,** im-ma-tūr'i-ti, *n.* State or quality of being immature; crudity.
**Immeasurable,** im-me'zhūr-a-bl, *a.* That cannot be measured; immense.
**Immediate,** im-mē'di-āt, *a.* Without anything intervening; acting without a medium; direct; not acting by secondary causes; present; without intervention of time.
**Immediately,** im-mē'di-āt-li, *adv.* Without the intervention of anything; directly; without delay; instantly; forthwith.
**Immemorial,** im-me-mō'ri-al, *a.* Beyond memory; extending beyond the reach of record or tradition.
**Immense,** im-mens', *a.* Immeasurable; huge; prodigious; enormous.
**Immensity,** im-mens'i-ti, *n.* Condition or quality of being immense; that which is immense; infinity.
**Immerge,** im-merj', *vt.* (immerging, immerged). To dip or plunge; to immerse.—*vi.* To disappear by entering into any medium.
**Immerse,** im-mėrs', *vt.* (immersing, immersed). to plunge into water or other fluid; to overwhelm; to engage deeply.
**Immersion,** im-mėr'shon, *n.* Act of immersing; state of being overwhelmed or deeply engaged; disappearance of a celestial body behind another or into its shadow.
**Immesh,** im-mesh', *vt.* To entangle in the meshes of a net, etc.
**Immethodical,** im-me-thod'ik-al, *a.* Not methodical; without systematic arrangement; disorderly.
**Immigrant,** im'mi-grant, *n.* A person who immigrates into a country.
**Immigrate,** im'mi-grāt, *vi.* To come into a country for permanent residence.
**Immigration,** im-mi-grā'shon, *n.* Act of removing into a country for settlement.
**Imminence,** im'mi-nens, *n.* Quality or condition of being imminent.
**Imminent,** im'mi-nent, *a.* Hanging over; impending; threatening; near at hand.
**Imminently,** im'mi-nent-li, *adv.* In an imminent manner or degree.
**Immobile,** im-mōb'il, *a.* Not mobile; immovable; fixed; stable.
**Immobility,** im-mō-bil'i-ti, *n.* State or quality of being immobile; resistance to motion.
**Immoderate,** im-mo'dėr-āt, *a.* Exceeding just or usual bounds; excessive; intemperate.
**Immoderately,** im-mo'dėr-āt-li, *adv.* Excessively; unreasonably.
**Immodest,** im-mo'dest, *a.* Not modest; indelicate; indecent; lewd.
**Immodesty,** im-mo'des-ti, *n.* Want of modesty.
**Immolate,** im'mō-lāt, *vt.* (immolating, immolated). To sacrifice; to kill, as a victim offered in sacrifice; to offer in sacrifice.
**Immoral,** im-mo'ral, *a.* Not moral; wicked; depraved; licentious.
**Immorality,** im-mō-ral'i-ti, *n.* Quality of being immoral; any immoral act or practice; vice; licentiousness; depravity.
**Immortal,** im-mor'tal, *a.* Not mortal; everlasting; imperishable; not liable to fall into oblivion.—*n.* One who is exempt from death.
**Immortality,** im-mor-tal'i-ti, *n.* Condition or quality of being immortal; life destined to endure without end.
**Immortalize,** im-mor'tal-īz, *vt.* To render immortal; to make famous for ever.
**Immovability,** im-möv'a-bil''i-ti, *n.* State or quality of being immovable.
**Immovable,** im-möv'a-bl, *a.* That cannot be moved from its place; not to be moved from a purpose; fixed; unchangeable; unfeeling.
**Immovably,** im-möv'a-bli, *adv.* Unalterably; unchangeably.
**Immunity,** im-mū'ni-ti, *n.* Freedom from service or obligation; particular privilege or prerogative; state of not being liable.
**Immure,** im-mūr', *vt.* (immuring, immured). to inclose within walls; to imprison.
**Immutable,** im-mū'ta-bl, *a.* Unchangeable; unalterable; invariable.
**Immutably,** im-mu'ta-bli, *adv.* Unchangeably; unalterably.
**Imp,** imp, *n.* A young or little devil; a mischievous child.—*vt.* (imping, imped). To graft; to mend a deficient wing by the insertion of a feather; to strengthen.
**Impact,** im'pakt, *n.* A forcible touch; a blow; the shock of a moving body that strikes against another.
**Impair,** im-pār', *vt.* To make worse; to lessen in quantity, value, excellence, or strength.
**Impale,** im-pāl', *vt.* (impaling, impaled). To put to death by fixing on a stake; to join, as two coats of arms on one shield, with an upright line between.
**Impalpable,** im-pal'pa-bl, *a.* Not to be felt; so fine as not to be perceived by the touch; not easily or readily apprehended by the mind.
**Imparity,** im-pa'ri-ti, *n.* Inequality.
**Impart,** im-pärt', *vt.* To give, grant, or communicate; to bestow on another; to confer; to reveal; to disclose.
**Impartial,** im-pär'shal, *a.* Not partial; not biassed; equitable; just.
**Impartiality,** im-pär'shi-al''-ti, *n.* State or quality of being impartial; freedom from bias; equity.
**Impassable,** im-pas'a-bl, *a.* That cannot be passed or travelled over.
**Impassibility,** im-pas'i-bil''i-ti, *n.* State or quality of being impassible.
**Impassible,** im-pas'i-bl, *a.* Incapable of passion or suffering; not to be moved to passion or sympathy; unmoved.
**Impassion,** im-pa'shon, *vt.* To move or affect strongly with passion.
**Impassionable,** im-pash'on-a-bl, *a.* Easily excited; susceptible of strong emotion.
**Impassioned,** im-pa'shond, *p.a.* Actuated by passion; having the feelings warmed, as a speaker; expressive of passion, as a harangue.
**Impassive,** im-pas'iv, *a.* Not susceptible of pain or suffering; impassible; unmoved.
**Impatience,** im-pā'shens, *n.* Condition or quality of being impatient; uneasiness under pain, suffering, etc.
**Impatient,** im-pā'shent, *a.* Not patient; uneasy under given conditions and eager for change; not suffering quietly; not enduring delay.
**Impatiently,** im-pā'shent-li, *adv.* In an impatient manner.
**Impeach,** im-pēch', *vt.* To charge with a crime; to bring charges of maladministration against a minister of state, etc.; to call in question; to disparage.
**Impeachable,** im-pēch'a-bl, *a.* Liable to be impeached.
**Impeachment,** im-pēch'ment, *n.* Act of impeach-

ing; a calling in question; accusation brought by the House of Commons against some high official before the House of Lords, who act as judges.

**Impeccability,** im-pek'a-bil''i-ti, *n.* Quality of being impeccable.

**Impeccable,** im-pek'a-bl, *a.* Not peccable, or liable to sin.

**Impecunious,** im-pē-kū'ni-us, *a.* Not having money; without funds.

**Impede,** im-pēd', *vt.* (impeding, impeded). To entangle or hamper; to obstruct.

**Impediment,** im-ped'i-ment, *n.* That by which one is impeded; obstruction.

**Impel,** im-pel', *vt.* (impelling, impelled). To drive or urge forward; to press on; to instigate; to incite; to actuate.

**Impellent,** im-pel'ent, *a.* Having the quality of impelling.—*n.* A power that impels.

**Impend,** im-pend', *vi.* To hang over; to threaten; to be imminent.

**Impenetrability,** im-pe'ne-tra-bil''i-ti, *n.* Quality of being impenetrable; that quality of matter by which it excludes all other matter from the space it occupies.

**Impenetrable,** im-pe'ne-tra-bl, *a.* That cannot be penetrated; not admitting the entrance or passage of other bodies; impervious; obtuse or unsympathetic.

**Impenitence,** im-pe'ni-tens, *n.* Obduracy; hardness of heart.

**Impenitent,** im-pe'ni-tent, *a.* Not penitent; not repenting of sin; obdurate.

**Imperative,** im-pe'rat-iv, *a.* Expressive of command; obligatory; designating a mood of the verb which expresses command, etc.

**Imperatively,** im-pe'rat-iv-li, *adv.* In an imperative manner; authoritatively.

**Imperceptible,** im-pėr-sep'ti-bl, *a.* Not perceptible; not easily apprehended by the senses; fine or minute.

**Imperfect,** im-pėr'fekt, *a.* Not perfect; not complete; not perfect in a moral view; faulty; *imperfect tense,* a tense expressing an uncompleted action or state, especially in time past.

**Imperfection,** im-pėr-fek'shon, *n.* Want of perfection; defect; fault; failing.

**Imperfectly,** im-pėr'fekt-li, *adv.* In an imperfect manner; not fully.

**Imperforate,** im-pėr'fo-rāt, *a.* Not perforated or pierced; having no opening or pores.

**Imperial,** im-pē'ri-al, *a.* Pertaining to an empire or emperor; supreme; suitable for an emperor; of superior excellence.—*n.* A tuft of hair beneath a man's lower lip; a size of paper measuring 30 by 22 inches.

**Imperialism,** im-pē'ri-al-izm, *n.* State of being imperial; imperial power or authority.

**Imperialist,** im-pē'ri-al-ist, *n.* A subject or soldier of an emperor; one favorable to empire or imperial government.

**Imperil,** im-pe'ril, *vt.* (imperilling, imperilled). To bring into peril; to endanger.

**Imperious,** im-pē'ri-us, *a.* Commanding; haughty; domineering; arrogant; urgent; authoritative.

**Imperishable,** im-pe'rish-a-bl, *a.* Not perishable; indestructible; everlasting.

**Impermeable,** im-pėr'mē-a-bl, *a.* Not permeable; not permitting fluids to pass through; impervious.

**Impersonal,** im-pėr'son-al, *a.* Not having personal existence; not endued with personality; not referring to any particular person; *impersonal verb,* a verb (such as *it rains*) used only with an impersonal nominative.—*n.* That which wants personality; an impersonal verb.

**Impersonality,** im-pėr'son-al''i-ti, *n.* Condition of being impersonal.

**Impersonally,** im-pėr'son-al-li, *adv.* In an impersonal manner; as an impersonal verb.

**Impersonate,** im-pėr'son-āt, *vt.* To invest with personality; to assume the character of; to represent in character; as on the stage.

**Impertinence,** im-pėr'ti-nens, *n.* The quality of being impertinent; irrelevance; that which is impertinent; rudeness.

**Impertinent,** im-pėr'ti-nent, *a.* Not pertinent; irrelevant; petulant and rude; pert; intrusive.

**Impertinently,** im-pėr'ti-nent-li, *adv.* Irrelevantly; intrustively; rudely.

**Imperturbability,** im-pėr-tėrb'a-bil''i-ti, *n.* Quality of being imperturbable.

**Imperturbable,** im-pėr-tėrb'a-bl, *a.* That cannot be agitated; unmoved; calm.

**Impervious,** im-pėr'vi-us, *a.* Not pervious; impassable; impenetrable.

**Impetuosity,** im-pe'tū-os''i-ti, *n.* Quality of being impetuous; violence; vehemence; ardor and hurry of feelings.

**Impetuous,** im-pe'tū-us, *a.* Rushing with great force; forcible; precipitate; vehement of mind; hasty; passionate.

**Impetus,** im'pe-tus, *n.* The force with which any body is driven or impelled; momentum.

**Impiety,** im-pī'e-ti, *n.* Want of piety; irreverence toward the Supreme Being; ungodliness; an act of wickedness.

**Impinge,** im-pinj', *vi.* (impinging, impinged). To dash against; to clash.

**Impious,** im'pi-us, *a.* Destitute of piety; irreverent toward the Supreme Being; profane; tending to dishonor God or his laws.

**Impiously,** im'pi-us-li, *adv.* Profanely; wickedly; blasphemously.

**Impish,** imp'ish, *a.* Having the qualities of an imp.

**Implacability,** im-plā'ka-bil''i-ti, *n.* Quality of being implacable; irreconcilable enmity or anger.

**Implacable,** im-plā'ka-bl, *a.* Not to be appeased; inexorable; unrelenting.

**Implacably,** im-plā'ka-bli, *adv.* In an implacable manner; inexorably.

**Implant,** im-plant', *vt.* To set, fix, or plant; to insert; to instil; to infuse.

**Impleader,** im-plēd'ėr, *n.* One who impleads.

**Implement,** im'plē-ment, *n.* A tool, utensil, or instrument.—*vt.* To fulfil the conditions of; to perform.

**Implicate,** im'pli-kāt, *vt.* (implicating, implicated). To involve or bring into connection with; to prove to be connected or concerned, as in an offense.

**Implication,** im-pli-kā'shon, *n.* Act of implicating; state of being implicated; entanglement; a tacit inference; something to be understood though not expressed.

**Implicit,** im-pli'sit, *a.* Implied; fairly to be understood, though not expressed in words; trusting to another; unquestioning.

**Implicitly,** im-pli'sit-li, *adv.* In an implicit manner; with unreserved confidence.

**Implore,** im-plōr, *vt.* and *i.* (imploring, implored). To call upon or for, in supplication; to beseech, entreat.

**Imply,** im-plī', *vt.* (implying, implied). To involve or contain in substance or by fair inference; to signify indirectly; to presuppose.

**Impolicy,** im-po'li-si, *n.* Bad policy; inexpediency.

**Impolite,** im-pō-līt', *a.* Not polite; not of polished manners; uncivil.

**Impolitic,** im-po'lit-ik, *a.* Not politic; wanting policy or prudence; inexpedient.

**Imponderable,** im-pon'dėr-a-bl, *a.* Not having weight that can be measured.

**Import,** im-pōrt', *vt.* To bring into a place from abroad; to bear or convey, as the meaning; to signify; to imply; to be of moment or consequence to; to concern.—*n.* im'pōrt. That which is brought into a country from abroad; signification; purport; drift; importance.

**Importable,** im-pōrt'a-bl, *a.* That may be imported.

**Importance,** im-pōrt'ans, *n.* Quality of being important; weight; moment; rank or standing; weight in self-estimation.

**Important,** im-pōrt′ant, *a.* Full of import; momentous; influential; grave; consequential.
**Importantly,** im-pōr′tant-li, *adv.* In an important manner; weightily; forcibly.
**Importation,** im-pōrt-ā′shon, *n.* Act or practice of importing; a quantity imported.
**Importer,** im-pōrt′ėr, *n.* One who imports; a merchant who brings goods from abroad.
**Importune,** im-por-tūn′, *vt.* (importuning, importuned). To press with solicitation; to urge with frequent application.—*vi.* To solicit earnestly and repeatedly.
**Importunity,** im-por-tūn′i-ti, *n.* Pressing or frequent solicitation; application urged with troublesome frequency.
**Impose,** im-pōz′, *vt.* (imposing, imposed). To place, set, or lay on; to lay on, as a tax, penalty, duty, etc.; to lay on, as hands; to obtrude fallaciously; to palm or pass off.—*vi.* Used in phrase *to impose on* or *upon*, to deceive; to victimize.
**Imposing,** im-pōz′ing, *p.a.* Impressive in appearance; commanding; stately; majestic.
**Imposition,** im-pō-zi′shon, *n.* Act of imposing; act of laying on hands in the ceremony of ordination; that which is imposed; a tax, toll, duty, etc.; burden; imposture.
**Impossibility,** im-pos′i-bil″i-ti, *n.* State or character of being impossible; that which cannot be, or cannot be done.
**Impossible,** im-pos′i-bl, *a.* Not possible; that cannot be or be done.
**Impost,** im′pōst, *n.* That which is imposed by authority; tax or duty; point where an arch rests on a wall or column.
**Imposthume,** im-pos′tūm, *n.* An abscess.
**Imposter,** im-pos′tėr, *n.* One who imposes on others; a deceiver under a false character.
**Imposture,** im-pos′tūr, *n.* Imposition; fraud; deception.
**Impotence, Impotency,** im′pō-tens, im′pō-ten-si, *n.* State or quality of being impotent; want of ability or power; want of the power of procreation.
**Impotent,** im′pō-tent, *a.* Entirely wanting vigor of body or mind; feeble; destitute of the power of begetting children.
**Impotently,** im′pō-tent-li, *adv.* In an impotent manner; feebly; weakly.
**Impound,** im-pound′, *vt.* To confine in a pound or close pen; to confine; to take possession of for use when necessary.
**Impoverish,** im-po′vėr-ish, *vt.* To make poor; to reduce to indigence; to exhaust the strength or fertility of, as of soil.
**Impoverishment,** im-po′vėr-ish-ment, *n.* Act of impoverishing.
**Impracticability,** im-prak′ti-ka-bil″i-ti, *n.* State or quality of being impracticable.
**Impracticable,** im-prak′ti-ka-bl, *a.* Not practicable; unmanageable; stubborn; incapable of being passed.
**Imprecate,** im′prē-kāt, *vt.* (imprecating, imprecated). To invoke, as a curse or some evil.
**Imprecation,** im-prē-kā′shon, *n.* Act of imprecating; prayer that a curse or calamity may fall on anyone; malediction.
**Impregnability,** im-preg′na-bil″i-ti, *n.* State of being impregnable.
**Impregnable,** im-preg′na-bl, *a.* That cannot be taken by force; able to resist attack; invincible, as affection.
**Impregnably,** im-preg′na-bli, *adv.* In an impregnable manner or position.
**Impregnate,** im-preg′nāt, *vt.* To make pregnant; to imbue; to saturate.
**Impregnation,** im-preg-nā′shon, *n.* The act of impregnating: fecundation; infusion.
**Impress,** im-pres′, *vt.* To press into; to imprint; to stamp on the mind; to inculcate; to compel to enter into public service, as seamen; to take for public use.—*n.* im′press. That which is impressed; mark made by pressure; impression; character; act of compelling to enter into public service.
**Impressible,** im-pres′i-bl, *a.* That may be impressed; susceptible of impression; readily or easily affected.
**Impression,** im-pre′shon, *n.* Act of impressing; that which is impressed; mark; effect produced on the mind; an indistinct notion; idea; copy taken by pressure from type, etc.; edition; copies forming one issue of a book.
**Impressionable,** im-pre′shon-a-bl, *a.* Susceptible of impression.
**Impressionism,** im-pre′shon-izm, *n.* Views or practice of an impressionist.
**Impressionist,** im-pre′shon-ist, *n.* One who lays stress on impressions; an artist who depicts scenes by their most striking characteristics as they first impress the spectator.
**Impressive,** im-pres′iv, *a.* Making an impression; solemn; awe-inspiring.
**Impressment,** im-pres′ment, *n.* Act of impressing men into the public service.
**Imprimatur,** im-pri-mā′tėr, *n.* A license to print a book, etc.; mark of approval in general.
**Imprimis,** im-prī′mis, *adv.* In the first place.
**Imprint,** im-print′, *vt.* To impress; to stamp; to fix on the mind or memory.—*n.* im′print. The name of the printer or publisher of a book, etc., with place and time of publication.
**Imprison,** im-pri′zn, *vt.* To put into a prison; to confine; to deprive of liberty.
**Improbability,** im-pro′ba-bil″i-ti, *n.* Quality of being improbable; unlikelihood.
**Improbable,** im-pro′ba-bl, *a.* Not probable; not likely to be true; unlikely.
**Improbably,** im-pro′ba-bli, *adv.* In an improbable manner; without probability.
**Improbity,** im-prō-bi-ti, *n.* Dishonesty.
**Impromptu,** im-promp′tū, *n.* A saying, poem, etc., made off-hand; an extemporaneous composition.—*a.* Off-hand; extempore.—*adv.* Off-hand.
**Improper,** im-pro′pėr, *a.* Not proper; unfit; not decent; erroneous; wrong.
**Improperly,** im-pro′pėr-li, *adv.* In an improper manner; unsuitably; erroneously.
**Impropriety,** im-prō-prī′e-ti, *n.* Quality of being improper; that which is improper; an unsuitable act, expression, etc.
**Improvability,** im-pröv′a-bil″i-ti, *n.* State or quality of being improvable.
**Improvable,** im-pröv′a-bl, *a.* That may be improved; susceptible of improvement.
**Improve,** im-pröv′, *vt.* (improving, improved). To better; to ameliorate; to mend; to rectify; to use to good purpose; to apply to practical purposes.—*vi.* To grow better.
**Improvement,** im-pröv′ment, *n.* Act of improving; state of being improved; a change for the better; that which improves; a beneficial or valuable addition or alteration.
**Improvidence,** im-pro′vi-dens, *n.* Want of providence or foresight; wastefulness.
**Improvident,** im-pro′vi-dent, *a.* Not provident; wanting foresight or forethought; careless.
**Improving,** im-pröv′ing, *p.a.* Tending to improve; edifying; instructive.
**Improvise,** im-pro-vīz′, To form on the spur of the moment; to compose and recite, etc., without previous preparation.
**Imprudence,** im-prö′dens, *n.* Want of prudence; indiscretion; a rash act.
**Imprudent,** im-prö′dent, *a.* Not prudent; indiscreet; heedless; rash.
**Impudence,** im′pū-dens, *n.* The quality of being impudent; impudent language or behavior; effrontery; impertinence.
**Impudent,** im′pū-dent, *a.* Offensively forward in behavior; bold-faced; impertinent.
**Impugn,** im-pūn′, *vt.* To attack by words or arguments; to contradict; to call in question.
**Impulse,** im′puls, *n.* Force communicated instantaneously; effect of a sudden communication of motion; influence acting on the mind; motive;

sudden determination.

**Impulsive,** im-puls'iv, *a.* Having the power of impelling; actuated or governed by impulse.

**Impulsively,** im-puls'iv-li, *adv.* In an impulsive manner; by impulse.

**Impunity,** im-pū'ni-ti, *n.* Freedom from punishment or injury, loss, etc.

**Impure,** im-pūr', *a.* Not pure; mixed with extraneous substance; obscene; unchaste; lewd; defiled by sin or guilt; unholy.

**Impurely,** im-pūr'li, *adv.* In an impure manner; with impurity.

**Impurity,** im-pūr'i-ti, *n.* State or quality of being impure; foul matter; obscenity.

**Imputable,** im-pūt'a-bl, *a.* That may be imputed or charged to a person; chargeable.

**Imputation,** im-pū-tā'shon, *n.* The act of imputing; attribution; censure; reproach.

**Impute,** im-pūt', *vt.* (imputing, imputed). To set to the account of; to ascribe.

**In,** in, *prep.* Within; inside of; surrounded by; indicating presence or situation within limits, whether of place, time, circumstances, etc.—*adv.* In or within some place, state, circumstances, etc.; not out.

**Inability,** in-a-bil'i-ti, *n.* Want of ability; want of adequate means.

**Inaccessible,** in-ak-ses'i-bl, *a.* Not accessible; not to be obtained; forbidden access.

**Inaccuracy,** in-ak'kū-ra-si, *n.* The state of being inaccurate; an inaccurate statement; a mistake in a statement; an error.

**Inaccurate,** in-ak'kū-rāt, *a.* Not accurate; not exact or correct; erroneous.

**Inaccurately,** in-ak'kū-rāt-li, *adv.* In an inaccurate manner; incorrectly; erroneously.

**Inaction,** in-ak'shon, *n.* Want of action; forbearance of labor; idleness; rest.

**Inactive,** in-ak'tiv, *a.* Not active; not engaged in action; idle; indolent.

**Inactivity,** in-ak-tiv'i-ti, *n.* State or quality of being inactive.

**Inadequacy,** in-ad'ē-kwā-si, *n.* Quality of being inadequate; insufficiency.

**Inadequate,** in-ad'ē-kwāt, *a.* Not equal to the purpose; disproportionate; defective.

**Inadmissible,** in-ad-mis'i-bl, *a.* Not admissible; not proper to be admitted, allowed, or received.

**Inadvertence, Inadvertency,** in-ad-vėrt'ens, in-ad-vėrt'en-si, *n.* Quality of being inadvertent; any oversight or fault which proceeds from negligence or want of attention.

**Inadvertent,** in-ad-vėrt'ent, *a.* Not paying strict attention; heedless; unwary; negligent.

**Inadvertently,** in-ad-vėrt'ent-li, *adv.* In an inadvertent manner; from want of attention.

**Inalienable,** in-āl'yen-a-bl, *a.* Incapable of being alienated or transferred to another.

**Inalterable,** in-al'tėr-a-bl, *a.* Unalterable.

**Inamorata,** in-ā'mō-rä''tä, *n.* A female in love; a mistress.

**Inamorato,** in-ā'mō-rä''tō, *n.* A male lover.

**Inane,** in-ān', *a.* Empty; void; void of sense or intelligence.—*n.* Infinite void space.

**Inanimate,** in-an'i-māt, *a.* Not animate; destitute of animation or life; inactive; dull; spiritless.

**Inanition,** in-a-nis'hon, *n.* Vacuity; exhaustion from want of food.

**Inanity,** in-an'i-ti, *n.* The quality of being inane; vacuity; mental vacuity; silliness.

**Inapplicable,** in-ap'pli-ka-bl, *a.* Not applicable; not suitable; inappropriate.

**Inappreciable,** in-ap-prē'shi-a-bl, *a.* Not appreciable; so small as hardly to be noticed.

**Inapproachable,** in-ap-prōch'a-bl, *a.* Not approachable; unapproachable.

**Inappropriate,** in-ap-prō'pri-āt, *a.* Not appropriate; unsuited; not proper.

**Inapt,** in-apt', *a.* Unapt; unsuitable; unfit.

**Inaptitude,** in-apt'ti-tūd, *n.* Want of aptitude; unsuitableness.

**Inarch,** in-ärch', *vt.* To graft without separating (for a time) the scion from its parent tree.

**Inarticulate,** in-är-tik'ū-lāt, *a.* Not articulate; not jointed or articulated; not uttered distinctly.

**Inarticulately,** in-är-tik'ū-lāt-li, *adv.* Not with distinct syllables; indistinctly.

**Inartificial,** in-är'ti-fi''shal, *a.* Not artificial; simple; artless.

**Inartificially,** in-är'ti-fi''shal-li, *adv.* In an artificial or artless manner.

**Inasmuch,** in-az-much', *adv.* Seeing; seeing that; this being the fact.

**Inattention,** in-at-ten'shon, *n.* Want of attention; heedlessness; neglect.

**Inattentive,** in-at-tent'iv, *a.* Not attentive; regardless; thoughtless.

**Inattentively,** in-at-tent'iv-li, *adv.* Without attention; heedlessly.

**Inaudibility,** in-a'di-bil''i-ti, *n.* State or quality of being inaudible.

**Inaudible,** in-a'di-bl, *a.* Not audible; that cannot be heard.

**Inaudibly,** in-a'di-bli, *adv.* In a manner not to be heard.

**Inaugural,** in-a'gū-ral, *a.* Pertaining to inauguration.

**Inaugurate,** in-a'gū-rāt, *vt.* To induct into an office with suitable ceremonies; to perform initiatory ceremonies in connection with.

**Inauguration,** in-a'gū-rā''shon, *n.* Act of inaugurating; ceremonies connected with such an act.

**Inauspicious,** in-a-spi'shus, *a.* Not auspicious; ill-omened; unfavorable.

**Inauthoritative,** in-a-thor'i-tā-tiv, *a.* Having no authority.

**Inboard,** in'bōrd, *a.* Within a ship or other vessel.—*adv.* On board of a vessel.

**Inborn,** in'born, *a.* Born in; innate; implanted by nature; natural; inherent.

**Inbreathe,** in-brēᴛʜ', *vt.* To breathe in, or infuse by breathing.

**Inbred,** in'bred, *a.* Bred within; innate.

**Inca,** in'ka, *n.* A king or prince of Peru before its conquest by the Spaniards.

**Incage,** in-kāj', *vt.* To encage.

**Incalculable,** in-kal'kū-la-bl, *a.* Not calculable; very great.

**Incalculably,** in-kal'kū-la-bli, *adv.* In a degree beyond calculation.

**Incandescence,** in-kan-des'ens, *n.* Condition of being incandescent.

**Incandescent,** in-kan-des'ent, *a.* White or glowing with heat.—**Incandescent light,** a form of gas light; a form of electric light given forth from a filament of carbon inclosed in an airless glass globe.

**Incantation,** in-kan-tā'shon, *n.* The act of using certain words and ceremonies to raise spirits, etc.; the form of words so used; a magical charm or ceremony.

**Incapability,** in-kā'pa-bil''i-ti, *n.* Quality of being incapable.

**Incapable,** in-kā'pa-bl, *a.* Not capable; possessing inadequate power or capacity; not susceptible; incompetent; unqualified or disqualified.—*n.* One physically or mentally weak.

**Incapably,** in-kā'pa-bli, *adv.* In an incapable manner.

**Incapacitate,** in-ka-pa'si-tāt, *vt.* To render incapable; to deprive of competent power or ability; to disqualify.

**Incapacity,** in-ka-pa'si-ti, *n.* Want of capacity; incompetency; disqualification.

**Incarcerate,** in-kär'sė-rāt, *vt.* To imprison; to shut up or inclose.

**Incarceration,** in-kär'sė-rā''shon, *n.* Act of incarcerating; imprisonment.

**Incarnadine,** in-kär'na-dīn, *vt.* To tinge with the color of flesh; to dye red.

**Incarnate,** in-kär'nāt, *vt.* To clothe with flesh; to embody in flesh.—*a.* Invested with flesh; embodied in flesh.

**Incarnation,** in-kär-nā'shon, *n.* Act of taking on a human body and the nature of man; the state of

being incarnated; a vivid exemplification in person or act.
**Incase,** in-kās', *vt.* To inclose in a case.
**Incaution,** in-ka'shon, *n.* Want of caution.
**Incautious,** in-ka'shus, *a.* Not cautious; unwary; heedless; imprudent.
**Incautiously,** in-ka'shus-li, *adv.* In an incautious manner; unwarily; heedlessly.
**Incendiarism,** in-sen'di-a-rizm, *n.* Act or practice of maliciously setting fire to buildings.
**Incendiary,** in-sen'di-a-ri, *n.* A person who maliciously sets fire to property; one guilty of arson; one who inflames factions; a firebrand; small bomb dropped from an airplane and intended to cause a fire;—*a.* Relating to arson; tending to excite sedition or quarrels.
**Incense,** in'sens, *n.* Aromatic substance burned in religious rites; odors of spices and gums, burned in religious rites; flattery or agreeable homage.—*vt.* (incensing, incensed). To perfume with incense.
**Incense,** in-sens', *vt.* (incensing, incensed). To inflame to violent anger; to exasperate.
**Incentive,** in-sen'tiv, *a.* Inciting; encouraging.—*n.* That which incites; that which prompts to good or ill; motive; spur.
**Inception,** in-sep'shon, *n.* The act of beginning; first or initial stage.
**Inceptive,** in-sep'tiv, *a.* Pertaining to inception; beginning; applied to a verb which expresses the beginning of an action.—*n.* An inceptive verb.
**Inceptor,** in-sep'tėr, *n.* A beginner; one who is on the point of taking the degree of M.A. at an English university.
**Incertitude,** in-sėr'ti-tūd, *n.* Uncertainty.
**Incessant,** in-ses'ant, *a.* Unceasing; unintermitted; continual; constant.
**Incessantly,** in-ses'ant-li, *adv.* Without ceasing; continually.
**Incest,** in'sest, *n.* Sexual commerce between near blood relations.
**Incestuous,** in-sest'ū-us, *a.* Guilty of incest; involving the crime of incest.
**Inch,** insh, *n.* The twelfth part of a foot in length; a small quantity or degree.—*vt.* To drive or force by inches.
**Inch-meal,** insh'mēl, *adv.* By inches; by little and little.
**Inchoate,** in'kō-āt, *a.* Recently begun; incipient; rudimentary.
**Incidence,** in'si-dens, *n.* A falling or occurring; manner or direction of falling.
**Incident,** in'si-dent, *a.* Falling or striking; happening; liable to happen; appertaining to or following another thing.—*n.* That which happens; event; an appertaining fact.
**Incidental,** in-si-dent'al, *a.* Casual; occasional; appertaining and subsidiary.
**Incidentally,** in-si-dent'al-li, *adv.* Casually; beside the main design.
**Incinerate,** in-sin'ė-rāt, *vt.* To burn to ashes.
**Incipient,** in-si'pi-ent, *a.* Beginning.
**Incise,** in-sīz', *vt.* (incising, incised). To cut in or into; to carve; to engrave.
**Incision,** in-si'zhon, *n.* Act of cutting into; cut; gash; sharpness; trenchancy.
**Incisive,** in-sī'siv, *a.* Having the quality of cutting into anything; sharply and clearly expressive; trenchant.
**Incisor,** in-sīz'ėr, *n.* A front tooth which cuts or separates.
**Incite,** in-sīt', *vt.* (inciting, incited). To move to action by impulse or influence; to instigate; to encourage.
**Incitement,** in-sīt'ment, *n.* Act of inciting; that which incites; motive; impulse.
**Inclement,** in-kle'ment, *a.* Not clement; harsh; stormy; rigorously cold.
**Inclination,** in-klin-ā'shon, *n.* The act of inclining; deviation from a normal direction; a leaning of the mind or will; tendency; bent; bias; predilection; liking.
**Incline,** in-klīn', *vi.* (inclining, inclined). To deviate from a direction regarded as normal; to slope; to be disposed; to have some wish or desire.—*vt.* To cause to lean or bend towards or away from; to give a leaning to; to dispose.—*n.* An ascent or descent; a slope.
**Inclined,** in-klīnd', *p.a.* Having a leaning or inclination; disposed.
**Inclose,** in-klōz', *vt.* (inclosing, inclosed). To shut up or confine on all sides; to environ; to cover with a wrapper or envelope.
**Inclosure,** in-klō'zhūr, *n.* Act of inclosing; what is inclosed; a space inclosed or fenced; something inclosed with a letter, etc.
**Include,** in-klöd', *vt.* (including, included). To hold or contain; to comprise; to comprehend.
**Inclusion,** in-klö'zhon, *n.* Act of including.
**Inclusive,** in-klö'siv, *a.* Inclosing; comprehended in the number or sum; comprehending the stated limit.
**Inclusively,** in-klö'siv-li, *adv.* In an inclusive manner; so as to include something mentioned.
**Incognito,** in-kog'ni-tō, *pred.a.* or *adv.* In disguise.—*n.* (fem. being **Incognita**). One passing under an assumed name; assumption of a feigned character.
**Incognizable,** in-kog'ni-za-bl or in-kon'i-za-bl, *a.* Not cognizable.
**Incognizance,** in-kog'ni-zans or in-kon'i-zans, *n.* Failure to recognize or apprehend.
**Incognizant,** in-kog'ni-zant or in-kon'i-zant, *a.* Not cognizant.
**Incoherence, Incoherency,** in-kō-hēr'ens, in-kō-hēr'en-si, *n.* Quality of being incoherent; want of connection or agreement.
**Incoherent,** in-kō-hēr'ent, *a.* Not coherent; wanting rational connection, as ideas, language, etc.; rambling and unintelligible.
**Incoherently,** in-kō-hēr'ent-li, *adv.* In an incoherent manner.
**Incombustibility,** in-kom-bust'i-bil''i-ti, *n.* Quality of being incombustible.
**Incombustible,** in-kom-bust'i-bl, *a.* Not combustible; that cannot be burned.
**Income,** in'kum, *n.* Receipts or emoluments regularly coming in from property or employment; annual receipts; revenue.
**Income-tax,** in'kum-taks, *n.* A tax levied on incomes according to their amount.
**Incoming,** in'kum-ing, *p.a.* Coming in.
**Incommensurability,** in-kom-men'sūr-a-bil''i-ti, *n.* Quality or state of being incommensurable.
**Incommensurable,** in-kom-men'sūr-a-bl, *a.* Not commensurable; having no common measure.
**Incommensurably,** in-kom-men'sūr-a-bli, *adv.* So as not to admit of a common measure.
**Incommensurate,** in-kom-men'sūr-āt, *a.* Not commensurate; incommensurable; inadequate; insufficient.
**Incommode,** in-kom-mōd', *vt.* (incommoding, incommoded). To give trouble to; to inconvenience; to embarrass.
**Incommodious,** in-kom-mō'di-us, *a.* Not commodious; inconvenient.
**Incommunicable,** in-kom-mū'ni-ka-bl, *a.* Not communicable; not to be communicated.
**Incommunicative,** in-kom-mū'ni-kāt-ive, *a.* Not communicative; not inclined to impart information.
**Incomparable,** in-kom'pa-ra-bl, *a.* Not comparable; that admits of no comparison with others; matchless.
**Incomparably,** in-kom'pa-ra-bli, *adv.* Beyond comparison.
**Incompatibility,** in-kom-pat'i-bil''i-ti, *n.* State or quality of being incompatible; inconsistency; disposition or temper entirely out of harmony.
**Incompatible,** in-kom-pat'i-bl, *a.* Not compatible; inconsistent; irreconcilably different; that cannot be made to accord.
**Incompetence, Incompetency,** in-kom'pē-tens, in-kom'pē-ten-si, *n.* State or quality of being incompetent; want of suitable faculties, adequate

means, or proper qualifications.
**Incompetent,** in-kom'pē-tent, *a.* Not competent; incapable; wanting legal qualifications; not admissible.
**Incomplete,** in-kom-plēt', *a.* Not complete; imperfect; defective.
**Incomprehensibility,** in-kom'prē-hens'i-bil''i-ti, *n.* Quality of being incomprehensible.
**Incomprehensible,** in-kom'prē-hens''i-bl, *a.* Not comprehensible; beyond the reach of the human intellect.
**Incompressibility,** in-kom-pres'i-bil''i-ti, *n.* State or quality of being incompressible.
**Incompressible,** in-kom-pres'i-bl, *a.* Not compressible; resisting compression.
**Inconceivable,** in-kon-sēv'a-bl, *a.* Incapable of being conceived or thought of.
**Inconclusive,** in-kon-klös'iv, *a.* Not conclusive; not settling a point in debate.
**Inconclusively,** in-kon-klös'iv-li, *adv.* In an inconclusive manner.
**Incondensable,** in-kon-dens'a-bl, *a.* Not condensable; incapable of being condensed.
**Incondite,** in-kon'dīt, *a.* Rude; unpolished; said of literary compositions.
**Incongruent,** in-kong'gru-ent, *a.* Incongruous.
**Incongruity,** in-kong-gru'i-ti, *n.* Want of congruity; inconsistency; absurdity.
**Incongruous,** in-kong'gru-us, *a.* Not congruous; not such as to mingle well or unite in harmony; inconsistent.
**Inconsequence,** in-kon'sē-kwens, *n.* The condition or quality of being inconsequent; want of logical consequence.
**Inconsequent,** in-kon'sē-kwent, *a.* Not consequent; not having due relevance; not following from the logical premises.
**Inconsequential,** in-kon'sē-kwen''shal, *a.* Not consequential; not of importance.
**Inconsiderable,** in-kon-sid'ėr-a-bl, *a.* Not considerable; unimportant; insignificant.
**Inconsiderably,** in-kon-sid'ėr-a-bli, *adv.* In an inconsiderable degree; very little.
**Inconsiderate,** in-kon-sid'ėr-āt, *a.* Not considerate; hasty; thoughtless; injudicious.
**Inconsistence, Inconsistency,** in-kon-sist'ens, in-kon-sist'en-si, *n.* The condition or quality of being inconsistent; opposition or disagreement of particulars; self-contradiction; incongruity; discrepancy.
**Inconsistent,** in-kon-sist'ent, *a.* Not consistent; incompatible; discrepant; not exhibiting consistent sentiments or conduct.
**Inconsolable,** in-kon-sōl'a-bl, *a.* Not to be consoled; grieved beyond consolation.
**Inconspicuous,** in-kon-spik'ū-us, *a.* Not conspicuous; unobtrusive.
**Inconstancy,** in-kon'stan-si, *n.* The quality of being inconstant; instability of temper or affection; fickleness.
**Inconstant,** in-kon'stant, *a.* Not constant; subject to change of opinion or purpose; not firm in resolution; fickle.
**Inconstantly,** in-kon'stant-li, *adv.* In an inconstant manner.
**Incontestable,** in-kon-test'a-bl, *a.* Not contestable; not to be disputed; unquestionable.
**Incontestably,** in-kon-test'a-bli, *adv.* In a manner to preclude debate.
**Incontinent,** in-kon'ti-nent, *a.* Not continent; not restraining the passions or appetites; unchaste; unable to restrain discharges.
**Incontinently,** in-kon'ti-nent-li, *adv.* In an incontinent manner; unchastely; at once.
**Incontrovertible,** in-kon'trō-vėrt''i-bl, *a.* Not controvertible; too clear to admit of dispute.
**Inconvenience,** in-kon-vē'ni-ens, *n.* The quality of being inconvenient; annoyance; molestation; trouble; disadvantage.—*vt.* To put to inconvenience; to trouble.
**Inconvenient,** in-kon-vē'ni-ent, *a.* Not convenient; wanting due facilities; causing embarrassment; inopportune.
**Inconveniently,** in-kon-vē'ni-ent-li, *adv.* Unsuitably, unseasonably.
**Inconvertible,** in-kon-vėrt'i-bl, *a.* Not convertible; that cannot be changed into or exchanged for something else.
**Incorporate,** in-kor'pō-rāt, *vt.* To form into one body; to unite; to blend; to associate with another whole, as with a government; to form into a legal body or corporation.—*vi.* To unite; to grow into or coalesce.—*a.* Incorporated; united in one body.
**Incorporation,** in-kor'pō-rā''shon, *n.* Act of incorporating; state of being incorporated; union of different things; a body of individuals authorized to act as a single person.
**Incorporeal,** in-kor-pō'rē-al, *a.* Not corporeal; not consisting of matter; spiritual.
**Incorrect,** in-ko-rekt', *a.* Not correct; inaccurate; erroneous; faulty; untrue.
**Incorrectly,** in-ko-rekt'li, *adv.* Not in accordance with fact; inaccurately.
**Incorrigible,** in-ko'ri-ji-bl, *a.* That cannot be corrected; bad beyond correction or reform.
**Incorrigibly,** in-ko'ri-ji-bli, *adv.* In an incorrigible manner.
**Incorrodible,** in-ko-rōd'i-bl, *a.* That cannot be corroded.
**Incorrupt,** in-ko-rupt', *a.* Not corrupt; not marred by corruption or decay; pure; untainted; above the power of bribes.
**Incorruptibility,** in-ko-rupt'i-bil''i-ti, *n.* Quality of being incorruptible.
**Incorruptible,** in-ko-rupt'i-bl, *a.* Not corruptible; that cannot corrupt or decay; inflexibly just and upright.
**Incorruption,** in-ko-rup'shon, *n.* Exemption from corruption or decay.
**Increase,** in-krēs', *vi.* (increasing, increased). To become greater; to augment; to advance in any quality, good or bad; to multiply by the production of young.—*vt.* To make greater or larger; to add to.—*n.* in'krēs. A growing larger in size, quantity, etc.; augmentation; addition; increment; profit; interest; offspring.
**Increasingly,** in-krēs'ing-li, *adv.* In the way of increasing; by continual increase.
**Incredibility,** in-kred'i-bil''i-ti, *n.* Quality of being incredible; that which is incredible.
**Incredible,** in-kred'i-bl, *a.* Not credible; too improbable to admit of belief.
**Incredibly,** in-kred'i-bli, *adv.* In a manner to preclude belief.
**Incredulity,** in-krē-dū'li-ti, *n.* Quality of being incredulous; scepticism.
**Incredulous,** in-kred'ū-lus, *a.* Not credulous; refusing or withholding belief.
**Increment,** in'krē-ment, *n.* Act or process of increasing; increase; increase in the value of real property from adventitious causes.
**Incriminate,** in-krim'in-āt, *vt.* To bring an accusation against; to charge with a crime or fault.
**Incrust,** in-krust', *vt.* To cover with a crust or hard coat; to form a crust on.
**Incrustation,** in-krust-ā'shon, *n.* Act of incrusting; a crust or hard coat on the surface of a body; a covering or inlaying of marble or mosaic, etc.
**Incubate,** in'kū-bāt, *vi.* To brood or sit on eggs for hatching.
**Incubation,** in-kū-bā'shon, *n.* The act of incubating; the maturation of a contagious poison in the animal system.
**Incubator,** in'kū-bāt-ėr, *n.* One who or that which incubates; an apparatus for hatching eggs by artificial heat.
**Incubus,** in'kū-bus, *n.*; pl. **-buses** or **-bi.** A name of nightmare; something that weighs heavily on a person; burden or incumbrance; dead weight.
**Inculcate,** in-kul'kāt, *vt.* To press or urge forcibly and repeatedly; to teach.
**Inculcation,** in-kul-kā'shon, *n.* The act of inculcating.
**Inculpate,** in-kul'pāt, *vt.* To show to be in fault; to

I

impute guilt to; to incriminate.
**Incumbency,** in-kum'ben-si, *n*. State of being incumbent; state of holding a benefice or office.
**Incumbent,** in-kum'bent, *a*. Lying on; resting on a person, as duty or obligation.—*n*. One in possession of an ecclesiastical benefice or other office.
**Incunable, Incunabulum,** in-kū'na-bl, in-kū-nab'ū-lum, *n*.; pl. **-ula.** A book printed before the year 1500.
**Incur,** in-kėr', *vt*. (incurring, incurred). To expose oneself to; to become liable to; to bring on or contract, as expense.
**Incurable,** in-kūr'a-bl, *a*. That cannot be cured; not admitting remedy; irremediable.—*n*. A person diseased beyond cure.
**Incurious,** in-kū'ri-us, *a*. Not curious.
**Incursion,** in-kėr'shon, *n*. An entering into a territory with hostile intention; inroad.
**Incursive,** in-kėr'siv, *a*. Of the nature of an incursion; hostile; making an incursion.
**Incurvate, Incurve,** in-kėrv'āt, in-kėrv', *vt*. To bend or curve.
**Incurvate,** in-kėrv'āt, *a*. Curved inward or upward.
**Incurvature,** in-kėrv'a-tūr, *n*. An incurving or bending.
**Incuse,** in-kūz', *vt*. To impress by stamping.—*a*. Impressed by stamping.
**Indebted,** in-det'ed, *a*. Being in debt; obliged by something received.
**Indebtedness,** in-det'ed-nes, *n*. State of being indebted; amount of debt owed.
**Indecency,** in-dē'sen-si, *n*. The quality of being indecent; what is indecent in language, actions, etc.; indecorum; immodesty.
**Indecent,** in-dē'sent, *a*. Not decent; unseemly; immodest; obscene; filthy.
**Indecipherable,** in-dē-sī'fėr-a-bl, *a*. Incapable of being deciphered.
**Indecision,** in-dē-si'zhon, *n*. Want of decision; irresolution; hesitation.
**Indecisive,** in-dē-sis'iv, *a*. Not decisive; wavering; vacillating.
**Indeclinable,** in-dē-klīn'a-bl, *a*. Not declinable; not varied by terminations of case, etc.
**Indecomposable,** in-dē'kom-pōz''a-bl, *a*. Incapable of decomposition.
**Indecorous,** in-dē-kō'rus or in-de'kō-rus, *a*. Not decorous; unseemly; indecent; unbecoming.
**Indecorum,** in-dē-kō'rum, *n*. Want of decorum; unseemly conduct.
**Indeed,** in-dēd', *adv*. In reality; in fact; really; truly.
**Indefatigable,** in-dē-fat'ig-a-bl, *a*. That cannot be wearied; untiring; unremitting.
**Indefensible,** in-dē-fens'i-bl, *a*. Not defensible; untenable.
**Indefinable,** in-dē-fīn'a-bl, *a*. Incapable of being defined; not to be clearly explained.
**Indefinite,** in-def'i-nit, *a*. Not definite; not limited; not precise; uncertain; vague.
**Indefinitely,** in-def'i-nit-li, *adv*. In an indefinite manner; not precisely.
**Indelible,** in-de'li-bl, *a*. Not to be deleted or blotted out; that cannot be obliterated.
**Indelicate,** in-de'li-kāt, *a*. Wanting delicacy; offensive to modesty or nice sense of propriety; somewhat immodest.
**Indemnification,** in-dem'ni-fi-kā''shon, *n*. Act of indemnifying; reparation; reimbursement of loss or damage.
**Indemnify,** in-dem'ni-fī, *vt*. To make safe from loss or harm; to reimburse or compensate.
**Indemnity,** in-dem'ni-ti, *n*. Security given against loss, damage, or punishment; compensation for loss or injury sustained.
**Indent,** in-dent', *vt*. To notch; to cut into points or inequalities; to bind by indenture.—*n*. A cut or notch; an indentation.
**Indentation,** in-dent-ā'shon, *n*. Act of indenting; a cut in the margin of something; an angular depression in any border.
**Indented,** in-dent'ed, *p.a*. Notched; bound by indenture.
**Indenture,** in-den'tūr, *n*. That which is indented; a deed under seal between two or more parties, each having a duplicate.—*vt*. To indent; to bind by indenture.
**Independence,** in-dē-pend'ens, *n*. State of being independent; complete exemption from control; self-reliance; political freedom.
**Independent,** in-dē-pend'ent, *a*. Not dependent; not subject to control; moderately wealthy; not subject to bias or influence; free; bold; separate from; irrespective.—*n*. One who is independent; (with *cap*.) one who maintains that every congregation is an independent church.
**Indescribable,** in-dē-skrīb'a-bl, *a*. That cannot be described.
**Indestructible,** in-dē-strukt'i-bl, *a*. That cannot be destroyed; imperishable.
**Indeterminable,** in-dē-tėr'min-a-bl, *a*. That cannot be determined, ascertained, or fixed.
**Indeterminate,** in-dē-tėr'min-āt, *a*. Not determinate; not settled or fixed; uncertain.
**Indetermination,** in-dē-tėr'min-ā''shon, *n*. Want of determination; vacillation.
**Index,** in'deks, *n*.; pl. **Indexes** or **Indices,** in'dek-sez, in'di-sēz. Something that points out; the hand ☞ used by printers, etc.; a table of contents; list of books disapproved of by R. Catholic authorities; the forefinger; the figure denoting to what power any mathematical quantity is involved.—*vt*. To provide with an index; to place in an index.
**Indian,** in'di-an, *a*. Pertaining to India, or to the Indies, East or West; pertaining to the aborigines of America.
**India-paper,** in'di-a-pā-pėr, *n*. A delicate paper used for first proofs of engravings.
**Indicate,** in'di-kāt, *vt*. To point out; to show; to intimate; to suggest.
**Indication,** in-di-kā'shon, *n*. Act of indicating; what points out; mark; token; sign.
**Indicative,** in-dik'a-tiv, *a*. That serves to point out; serving as an indication; designating a mood of the verb that declares directly or asks questions.—*n*. The indicative mood.
**Indicator,** in'di-kāt-ėr, *n*. One who or that which indicates; a recording instrument of various kinds.
**Indicatory,** in'di-ka-to-ri, *a*. Serving to indicate or make known.
**Indict,** in-dīt', *vt*. To charge with a crime or misdemeanor in due form of law.
**Indictable,** in-dīt'a-bl, *a*. That may be indicted; subject to indictment.
**Indiction,** in-dik'shon, *n*. A cycle of fifteen fiscal or financial years.
**Indictment,** in-dīt'ment, *n*. The act of indicting; a formal charge; a written accusation of a crime or a misdemeanor.
**Indifference,** in-dif'ėr-ens, *n*. The state or quality of being indifferent; impartiality; unconcern; apathy; mediocrity.
**Indifferent,** in-dif'ėr-ent, *a*. Impartial; unconcerned; apathetic; immaterial or of little moment; middling; tolerable.
**Indifferentism,** in-dif'ėr-ent-izm, *n*. Systematic indifference; want of zeal.
**Indifferently,** in-dif'ėr-ent-li, *adv*. Impartially; without concern; tolerably.
**Indigence,** in'di-jens, *n*. State of being indigent; want; penury.
**Indigene,** in'di-jēn, *n*. A native.
**Indigenous,** in-di'jen-us, *a*. Native, as persons; not foreign or exotic, as plants.
**Indigent,** in'di-jent, *a*. Destitute of means of comfortable subsistence; needy.
**Indigested,** in-di-jest'ed, *a*. Not digested; not reduced to due form; crude.
**Indigestible,** in-di-jest'i-bl, *a*. Not digestible; digested with difficulty.
**Indigestion,** in-di-jest'yon, *n*. Incapability of or difficulty in digesting; dyspepsia.

**Indignant,** in-dig'nant, *a.* Affected with indignation; feeling the mingled emotions of wrath and scorn or contempt.
**Indignantly,** in-dig'nant-li, *adv.* In an indignant manner; without indignation.
**Indignation,** in-dig-nā'shon, *n.* A feeling of displeasure at what is unworthy or base; anger, mingled with contempt, disgust, or abhorrence; violent displeasure.
**Indignity,** in-dig'ni-ti, *n.* An insult; an affront; an outrage.
**Indigo,** in'di-go, *n.* A blue vegetable dye, from India and other places; the leguminous plant that produces the dye.
**Indirect,** in-di-rekt', *a.* Not direct; circuitous; not tending directly to a purpose or end; not straightforward; not resulting directly.
**Indirectly,** in-di-rekt'li, *adv.* In an indirect manner; not by direct means.
**Indiscreet,** in-dis-krēt', *a.* Not discreet; injudicious; inconsiderate.
**Indiscreetly,** in-dis-krēt'li, *adv.* In an indiscreet manner.
**Indiscretion,** in-dis-kre'shon, *n.* The condition or quality of being indiscreet; imprudence; an indiscreet act.
**Indiscriminate,** in-dis-krim'in-āt, *a.* Without discrimination; confused.
**Indispensable,** in-dis-pens'a-bl, *a.* Not to be dispensed with; necessary or requisite.
**Indispensably,** in-dis-pens'a-bli, *adv.* In an indispensable manner; unavoidably.
**Indispose,** in-dis-pōz', *vt.* To disincline; to disqualify; to affect with indisposition.
**Indisposed,** in-dis-pōzd', *p.a.* Not disposed; disinclined; averse; somewhat ill.
**Indisposition,** in-dis'pō-zi''shon, *n.* The state of being indisposed; slight ailment.
**Indisputable,** in-dis'pūt-a-bl, *a.* Not to be disputed; unquestionable; certain.
**Indissoluble,** in-dis'sō-lū-bl, *a.* Not capable of being dissolved; perpetually binding or obligatory; not to be broken.
**Indissolvable,** in-diz-zolv'a-bl, *a.* That cannot be dissolved; indissoluble.
**Indistinct,** in-dis-tingkt', *a.* Not distinct; faint; confused; imperfect or dim.
**Indistinctly,** in-dis-tingkt'li, *adv.* In an indistinct manner; dimly or obscurely.
**Indistinguishable,** in-dis-ting'gwish-a-bl, *a.* Incapable of being distinguished.
**Indite,** in-dīt', *vt.* and *i.* (inditing, indited). To compose or write; to direct or dictate.
**Inditement,** in-dīt'ment, *n.* Act of inditing.
**Individual,** in-di-vid'ū-al, *a.* Subsisting as one indivisible entity; pertaining to one only; peculiar to a single person or thing.—*n.* A being or thing forming one of its kind; a person.
**Individualism,** in-di-vid'ū-al-izm, *n.* The quality of being individual; self-interest; a system or condition in which each individual works for his own ends.
**Individuality,** in-di-vid'ū-al''i-ti, *n.* Quality or condition of being individual; separate existence; the sum of the traits peculiar to an individual.
**Individualize,** in-di-vid'ū-al-īz, *vt.* To single out; to distinguish by distinctive characters.
**Individually,** in-di-vid'ū-al-li, *adv.* In an individual manner; separately.
**Indivisibility,** in-di-viz'i-bil''i-ti, *n.* State or quality of being indivisible.
**Indivisible,** in-di-viz'i-bl, *a.* Not divisible; not separable into parts.—*n.* An elementary part or particle.
**Indocile,** in-dō'sīl or in-dos'il, *a.* Not docile or teachable; intractable.
**Indoctrinate,** in-dok'trin-āt, *vt.* To imbue with any doctrine; to teach; to instruct.
**Indolence,** in'dō-lens, *n.* Habitual love of ease; laziness; idleness.
**Indolent,** in'dō-lent, *a.* Habitually idle or lazy; slothful; idle; causing little or no pain.
**Indomitable,** in-dom'it-a-bl, *a.* Not to be tamed or subdued; irrepressible.
**Indoor,** in'dōr, *a.* Being within doors; being within the house.—**Indoors,** in'dōrz, *adv.* Within doors; inside a house.
**Indorse,** etc. *See* ENDORSE, etc.
**Indubitable,** in-dū'bit-a-bl, *a.* Not to be doubted; too plain to admit of doubt; evident.
**Induce,** in-dūs', *vt.* (inducing, induced). To lead by persuasion or argument; to prevail on; to actuate; to produce or cause.
**Inducement,** in-dūs'ment, *n.* Act of inducing; that which induces; motive; incentive.
**Inducible,** in-dūs'i-bl, *a.* That may be inferred by induction.
**Induct,** in-dukt', *vt.* To lead or bring into; to put in possession of an ecclesiastical living or office, with customary ceremonies.
**Inductile,** in-duk'tīl, *a.* Not ductile.
**Induction,** in-duk'shon, *n.* The act of inducting; introduction of a clergyman into a benefice, etc.; a prologue or prelude; method of reasoning from particulars to generals; the conclusion thus arrived at; process by which one body, having electrical or magnetic properties, causes like properties in another body without direct contact.
**Inductive,** in-dukt'iv, *a.* Relating to induction; proceeding by induction; employed in drawing conclusions by induction.
**Indue,** in-dū', *vt.* (induing, indued). To put on; to invest; to supply with.
**Indulge,** in-dulj', *vt.* (indulging, indulged). To give free course to; to gratify by compliance; to humor to excess.—*vi.* To indulge oneself; to practice indulgence.
**Indulgence,** in-dulj'ens, *n.* The act or practice of indulging; a favor; intemperance; gratification of desire; tolerance; remission of the penance attached to certain sins.
**Indulgent,** in-dulj'ent, *a.* Prone to indulge; disposed to leniency or forbearance.
**Indurate,** in'dū-rāt, *vi.* To grow hard.—*vt.* To make hard; to deprive of sensibility.
**Induration,** in-dū-rā'shon, *n.* Act of hardening; process of growing hard; obduracy.
**Industrial,** in-dus'tri-al, *a.* Pertaining to industry, or to the products of industry, art, or manufacture.
**Industrious,** in-dus'tri-us, *a.* Given to or characterized by industry; diligent; active.
**Industriously,** in-dus'tri-us-li, *adv.* In an industrious manner; diligently.
**Industry,** in'dus-tri, *n.* Habitual diligence; steady attention to business; the industrial arts generally, or any one of them; manufacture; trade.
**Indwell,** in'dwel, *vi.* To dwell or exist inwardly or within some place.
**Inebriant,** in-ē'bri-ant, *a.* Intoxicating.—*n.* Anything that intoxicates.
**Inebriate,** in-ē'bri-āt, *vt.* To make drunk; to intoxicate.—*n.* An habitual drunkard.
**Inebriation,** in'ē-bri-ā''shon, *n.* Act of inebriating; state of being inebriated.
**Ineffective,** in-ef-fekt'iv, *a.* Not effective; inefficient; useless; impotent.
**Ineffectual,** in-ef-fek'tū-al, *a.* Not effectual; inefficient; impotent; fruitless.
**Inefficacious,** in-ef'fi-kā''shus, *a.* Not producing the effect desired.
**Inefficacy,** in-ef'fi-ka-si, *n.* Want of efficacy; failure of effect.
**Inefficiency,** in-ef-fi'shen-si, *n.* Condition or quality of being inefficient; inefficacy.
**Inefficient,** in-ef-fi'shent, *a.* Not efficient; inefficacious; effecting nothing.
**Inelegance, Inelegancy,** in-el'ē-gans, in-el'ē-gan-si, *n.* Condition or quality of being inelegant; inelegant point or feature.
**Inelegant,** in-el'ē-gant, *a.* Not elegant; wanting elegance, beauty, polish, or refinement.
**Ineligibility,** in-el'i-ji-bil''i-ti, *n.* State or quality of being ineligible.

**Ineligible,** in-el'i-ji-bl, *a.* Not capable of being elected; not worthy to be chosen.
**Ineloquent,** in-el'ō-kwent, *a.* Not eloquent.
**Inept,** in-ept', *a.* Unsuitable; improper; foolish; silly; nonsensical.
**Ineptitude,** in-ept'i-tūd, *n.* Condition or quality of being inept; unfitness; silliness.
**Inequable,** in-ē'kwa-bl, *a.* Not equable.
**Inequality,** in-ē-kwol'i-ti, *n.* Condition of being unequal; want of equality; an elevation or depression in a surface; diversity.
**Inequitable,** in-ke'wit-a-bl, *a.* Not equitable.
**Ineradicable,** in-ē-rad'i-ka-bl, *a.* Incapable of being eradicated.
**Inert,** in-ėrt', *a.* Destitute of the power of moving itself, or of active resistance to motion impressed; lifeless; sluggish; inactive.
**Inertia,** in-ėr'shi-a, *n.* Passiveness; inactivity; the property of matter by which it tends to retain its state of rest or of uniform rectilinear motion.
**Inertly,** in-ėrt'li, *adv.* In an inert manner; sluggishly.
**Inessential,** in-es-sen'shal, *a.* Not essential.
**Inestimable,** in-es'tim-a-bl, *a.* That cannot be estimated; invaluable; priceless.
**Inestimably,** in-es'tim-a-bli, *adv.* In a manner not to be estimated.
**Inevitable,** in-ev'it-a-bl, *a.* Not to be avoided; unavoidable; certain to befall.
**Inevitably,** in-ev'it-a-bli, *adv.* Unavoidably.
**Inexact,** in-egz-akt', *a.* Not exact; not precisely correct or true.
**Inexcusable,** in-eks-kūz'a-bl, *a.* Not to be excused; unjustifiable; indefensible.
**Inexcusably,** in-eks-kūz'a-bli, *adv.* In an inxecusable manner; beyond excuse.
**Inexhaustible,** in-egz-ast'i-bl, *a.* Incapable of being exhausted; unfailing.
**Inexorable,** in-eks'ōr-a-bl, *a.* Not to be persuaded by entreaty or prayer; unbending; unrelenting; implacable.
**Inexorably,** in-eks'ōr-a-bli, *adv.* In an inexorable manner.
**Inexpedience, Inexpediency,** in-eks-pē'di-ens, in-eks-pē'di-en-si, *n.* The condition or quality of being inexpedient.
**Inexpedient,** in-eks-pē'di-ent, *a.* Not expedient; not advisable or judicious.
**Inexpensive,** in-eks-pen'siv, *a.* Not expensive.
**Inexperience,** in-eks-pē'ri-ens, *n.* Want of experience.
**Inexperienced,** in-eks-pē'ri-enst, *a.* Not having experience; unskilled.
**Inexplicable,** in-eks'pli-ka-bl, *a.* That cannot be explained or interpreted; unaccountable; mysterious.
**Inexplicably,** in-eks'pli'ka-bli, *adv.* In an inexplicable manner; unaccountably.
**Inexplicit,** in-eks-plis'it, *a.* Not explicit; not clear in statement.
**Inexplosive,** in-eks-plō'siv, *a.* Not liable to explode.—*n.* A substance not liable to explode.
**Inexpressible,** in-eks-pres'i-bl, *a.* Not to be expressed; unspeakable; indescribable.
**Inexpressibly,** in-eks-pres'i-bli, *adv.* In an inexpressible manner.
**Inexpressive,** in-eks-pres'iv, *a.* Not expressive; wanting in expression; inexpressible.
**Inextinguishable,** in-eks-ting'gwish-a-bl, *a.* That cannot be extinguished.
**Inextricable,** in-eks'tri-ka-bl, *a.* Not to be extricated or disentangled.
**Infallibility,** in-fal'i-bil''i-ti, *n.* Quality of being infallible; exemption from liability to error.
**Infallible,** in-fal'i-bl, *a.* Not fallible; not liable to fail; certain.
**Infallibly,** in-fal'i-bli, *adv.* In an infallible manner; to a certainty.
**Infamous,** in'fa-mus, *a.* Notoriously vile; detestable; branded with infamy.
**Infamously,** in'fa-mus-li, *adv.* In an infamous manner; scandalously.
**Infamy,** in'fa-mi, *n.* Total loss of reputation; public disgrace; qualities detested and despised; extreme vileness.
**Infancy,** in'fan-si, *n.* State of being an infant; early childhood; period from birth to the age of twenty-one; first age of anything.
**Infant,** in'fant, *n.* A very young child; one under twenty-one years of age.—*a.* Pertaining to infants.
**Infanta,** in-fan'ta, *n.* Formerly, in Spain and Portugal, any princess of the royal blood except the eldest.—**Infante,** in-fan'tā, *n.* Any son of the king except the eldest.
**Infanticide,** in-fant'i-sīd, *n.* Child murder; a slayer of infants.
**Infantile, Infantine,** in'fant-īl, in'fant-īn, *a.* Pertaining to infancy or an infant.
**Infantry,** in'fant-ri, *n.* The soldiers or troops that serve on foot.
**Infatuate,** in-fa'tū-āt, *vt.* To make foolish; to inspire with an extravagant passion.
**Infatuated,** in-fa'tū-āt-ed, *p.a.* Besotted; inspired with foolish passion.
**Infatuation,** in-fa'tū-ā''shon, *n.* Act of infatuating; state of being infatuated; foolish passion.
**Infect,** in-fekt', *vt.* To taint with disease; to communicate bad qualities to; to corrupt.
**Infection,** in-fek'shon, *n.* Act or process of infecting; communication of disease; contagion; the thing which infects.
**Infectious, Infective,** in-fek'shus, in-fek'tiv, *a.* Capable of infecting; contagious; easily diffused from person to person.
**Infectiously,** in-fek'shus-li, *adv.* By infection; in an infectious manner.
**Infelicitous,** in-fē-lis'it-us, *a.* Not felicitous; unhappy; unfortunate,
**Infelicity,** in-fē-lis'i-ti, *n.* Unhappiness.
**Infelt,** in'felt, *a.* Felt within or deeply.
**Infer,** in-fėr', *vt.* (inferring, inferred). To gather by induction or deduction; to deduce.
**Inferable,** in-fėr'a-bl, *a.* That may be inferred from premises; deducible; derivable.
**Inference,** in'fėr-ens, *n.* The act of inferring; that which is inferred; deduction.
**Inferential,** in-fėr-en'shal, *a.* Of or pertaining to an inference.
**Inferior,** in-fē'ri-ėr, *a.* Lower in place, station, age, value, etc.; subordinate.—*n.* A person lower in rank, importance, etc.
**Inferiority,** in-fē'ri-or''i-ti, *n.* State or quality of being inferior.
**Infernal,** in-fėr'nal, *a.* Pertaining to the lower regions or hell; very wicked and detestable; diabolical.—**Infernal machine,** an explosive apparatus contrived for assassination or other mischief.
**Infernally,** in-fėr'nal-li, *adv.* In an infernal way; detestably.
**Infertile,** in-fėr'tīl, *a.* Not fertile; barren.
**Infertility,** in-fėr-til'i-ti, *n.* Barrenness.
**Infest,** in-fest', *vt.* To attack; to molest; to annoy continually.
**Infidel,** in'fi-del, *n.* A disbeliever; a sceptic; one who does not believe in God or in Christianity.—*a.* Unbelieving; sceptical.
**Infidelity,** in-fi-del'i-ti, *n.* Want of faith or belief; scepticism; unfaithfulness in married persons; dishonesty; treachery.
**Infiltrate,** in-fil'trāt, *vi.* To enter by the pores or interstices; to percolate.
**Infiltration,** in-fil-trā'shon, *n.* Act or process of infiltrating; that which infiltrates.
**Infinite,** in'fi-nit, *a.* Not finite; without limits; not circumscribed in any way; vast.—*n.* The Infinite Being; infinite space.
**Infinitely,** in'fi-nit-li, *adv.* In an infinite manner; beyond all comparison.
**Infinitesimal,** in'fi-ni-tes''i-mal, *a.* Infinitely or indefinitely small.—*n.* An infinitely small quantity.
**Infinitive,** in-fin'it-iv, *a.* Designating a mood of the verb which expresses action without limitation of person or number, as, *to love.*—*n.* The in-

finitive mood.
**Infinity,** in-fin'i-ti, *n.* State or quality of being infinite; unlimited extent of time, space, quantity, etc.; immensity.
**Infirm,** in-fėrm', *a.* Not firm; weak; sickly; enfeebled; irresolute.
**Infirmary,** in-fėrm'a-ri, *n.* A place where the sick and injured are nursed; a hospital.
**Infirmity,** in-fėrm'i-ti, *n.* State of being infirm; unsound state of the body; weakness of mind or resolution; failing; malady.
**Infix,** in-fiks', *vt.* To fix or fasten in; to implant, as principles, etc.
**Inflame,** in-flām', *vt.* To set on fire; to kindle; to excite or increase; to incense; to make morbidly red and swollen.—*vi.* To grow hot, angry, and painful; to take fire.
**Inflammability,** in-flam'a-bil''i-ti, *n.* State or quality of being inflammable.
**Inflammable,** in-flam'a-bl, *a.* That may be inflamed; easily kindled; combustible.
**Inflammation,** in-flam-ā'shon, *n.* Act of inflaming; state of being inflamed; a redness and swelling attended with heat, pain, and feverish symptoms.
**Inflammatory,** in-flam'a-to-ri, *a.* Pertaining to inflammation; tending to excite anger, animosity, tumult, or sedition.
**Inflate,** in-flāt', *vt.* (inflating, inflated). To distend by injecting air; to puff up; to elate; to raise above the real or normal value.
**Inflated,** in-flāt'ed, *p.a.* Puffed up; turgid; bombastic; unduly raised in price.
**Inflation,** in-flā'shon, *n.* Act of inflating; state of being distended with air; state of being puffed up, as with vanity; over-issue of currency, tending to cause a general rise in prices.
**Inflatus,** in-flā'tus, *n.* A blowing or breathing in; inspiration.
**Inflect,** in-flekt', *vt.* To bend; to decline or conjugate; to modulate, as the voice.
**Inflection,** in-flek'shon, *n.* Act of inflecting; state of being inflected; grammatical variation of nouns, verbs, etc.; modulation of the voice; deflection or diffraction.
**Inflective,** in-flekt'iv, *a.* Having the power of inflecting; having grammatical inflection.
**Inflexed,** in-flekst', *a.* Curved; bent inward.
**Inflexibility,** in-fleks'i-bil''i-ti, *n.* Firmness of purpose; unbending pertinacity or obstinacy.
**Inflexible,** in-fleks'i-bl, *a.* That cannot be bent; firm in purpose; pertinacious; inexorable.
**Inflexibly,** in-fleks'i-bli, *adv.* In an inflexible manner; firmly; inexorably.
**Inflict,** in-flikt', *vt.* To cause to bear or suffer from; to impose, as pain, punishment, etc.
**Infliction,** in-flik'shon, *n.* Act of inflicting; punishment inflicted; calamity.
**Inflorescence,** in-flō-res'ens, *n.* A flowering; the manner in which blossoms are supported.
**Inflow,** in'flō, *n.* The act of flowing in or into; that which flows in; influx.
**Influence,** in'flu-ens, *n.* Agency or power serving to affect, modify, etc.; sway; effect; acknowledged ascendency with people in power.—*vt.* To exercise influence on; to bias; to sway.
**Influent,** in-flu-ent, *a.* Flowing in.
**Influential,** in-flu-en'shal, *a.* Exerting influence, physical or other; possessing power.
**Influenza,** in-flu-en'za, *n.* An epidemic catarrh or cold of an aggravated kind.
**Influx,** in'fluks, *n.* Act of flowing in; a coming in; importation in abundance; point at which one stream runs into another or into the sea.
**Infold,** in-fōld', *vi.* To fold in; to involve; to wrap up; to inclose; to embrace.
**Inform,** in-form', *vt.* To give form to; to give life to; to communicate knowledge to; to instruct, etc.—*vi.* To give information.
**Informal,** in-form'al, *a.* Not in the usual form or mode; not with the official or customary forms; without ceremony.
**Informality,** in-form-al'i-ti, *n.* Quality of being informal; want of regular form or order.
**Informally,** in-form'al-li, *adv.* In an informal manner; without the usual forms.
**Informant,** in-form'ant, *n.* One who informs.
**Information,** in-form-ā'shon, *n.* The act of informing; intelligence communicated or gathered; a charge or accusation before a magistrate.
**Informatory, Informative,** in-form'a-to-ri, in-form'a-tiv, *a.* Affording knowledge or information; instructive.
**Informer,** in-form'ėr, *n.* One who informs; one who makes a practice of informing against others for the sake of gain.
**Infraction,** in-frak'shon, *n.* Act of infringing; breach; violation; infringement.
**Infrangible,** in-fran'ji-bl, *a.* Not to be broken; not to be violated.
**Infra-red,** in'fra-red, *a.* Of the part of the spectrum beyond the red end of the visible spectrum.
**Infrequency,** in-frē'kwen-si, *n.* State of being infrequent; rareness.
**Infrequent,** in-frē'kwent, *a.* Not frequent; seldom happening; rare.
**Infrequently,** in-frē'kwent-li, *adv.* Not frequently; seldom, rarely.
**Infringe,** in-frinj', *vt.* (infringing, infringed). To break, as laws, agreements, etc.; to violate; to contravene.—*vi.* To encroach (with *on* or *upon*).
**Infringement,** in-frinj'ment, *n.* Breach; violation; encroachment.
**Infuriate,** in-fū'ri-āt, *vt.* To madden; to enrage.—*a.* Enraged; mad; raging.
**Infuse,** in-fūz', *vt.* (infusing, infused). To pour in, as a liquid; to instil, as principles; to steep in liquor without boiling, in order to extract solutions, etc.
**Infusible,** in-fūz'i-bl, *a.* Not fusible.
**Infusible,** in-fūz'i-bl, *a.* That may be infused.
**Infusion,** in-fū'zhon, *n.* Act or process of infusing; that which is infused; liquor obtained by infusing or steeping.
**Ingathering,** in'gaTH-ėr-ing, *n.* A gathering in; harvest.
**Ingenious,** in-jē'ni-us, *a.* Possessed of cleverness or ability; apt in contriving; contrived with ingenuity; witty or well conceived.
**Ingenuity,** in-jen-ū'i-ti, *n.* Quality of being ingenious; ready invention; skill in contrivance.
**Ingenuous,** in-jen'ū-us, *a.* Open, frank, or candid; free from reserve or dissimulation.
**Ingest,** in-jest', *vt.* To throw into the stomach.
**Inglorious,** in-glō'ri-us, *a.* Not glorious; not bringing honor or glory; disgraceful.
**Ingoing,** in'gō-ing, *n.* A going in; entrance.—*a.* Entering in.
**Ingot,** in'got, *n.* A mass of gold or silver cast in a mold; a mass of unwrought metal.
**Ingrate,** in'grāt, *n.* An ungrateful person.
**Ingratiate,** in-grā'shi-āt, *vt.* To get into another's good-will or confidence; to recommend; to insinuate; always *refl.*
**Ingratitude,** in-grat'i-tūd, *n.* Want of gratitude; unthankfulness.
**Ingredient,** in-grē'di-ent, *n.* That which is a component part of any mixture; an element, component, or constituent.
**Ingress,** in'gres, *n.* Entrance; power of entrance; means of entering.
**Inguinal,** in'gwin-al, *a.* Pertaining to the groin.
**Ingulf,** in-gulf', *vt.* To swallow up; to absorb; to overwhelm by swallowing.
**Inhabit,** in-ha'bit, *vt.* To live or dwell in; to occupy as a place of settled resident.—*vi.* To dwell; to live; to abide.
**Inhabitable,** in-ha'bit-a-bl, *a.* That may be inhabited; habitable.
**Inhabitant, Inhabiter,** in-hab'it-ant, in-ha'bit-ėr, *n.* One who inhabits; one who resides permanently in a place.
**Inhabitation,** in-ha'bi-tā''shon, *n.* The act of inhabiting; an abode.
**Inhalation,** in-ha-lā'shon, *n.* Act of inhaling; that

I

which is inhaled.
**Inhale,** in-hāl', *vt.* (inhaling, inhaled). To draw into the lungs; to suck in.
**Inhaler,** in-hāl'ėr, *n.* One who or that which inhales; an apparatus for inhaling vapors and volatile substances, as steam, vapor of chloroform, etc.; a respirator.
**Inharmonious,** in-här-mō'ni-us, *a.* Not harmonious; unmusical; discordant.
**Inherent,** in-hēr'ent, *a.* Naturally pertaining; innate.
**Inherit,** in-he'rit, *vt.* To come into possession of as an heir; to receive by nature from a progenitor; to hold as belonging to one's lot.—*vi.* To take or have possession of property.
**Inheritable,** in-he'rit-a-bl, *a.* Capable of being inherited.
**Inheritance,** in-he'rit-ans, *n.* Act of inheriting; that which is or may be inherited; what falls to one's lot; possession.
**Inheritor,** in-he'rit-ėr, *n.* One who inherits; an heir.
**Inhibit,** in-hib'it, *vt.* To hold in or back; to restrain; to forbid; to interdict.
**Inhibition,** in-hi-bis'hon, *n.* Act of inhibiting; a legal writ inhibiting a judge from further proceeding in a cause.
**Inhibitory,** in-hib'i-to-ri, *a.* Conveying an inhibition; prohibitory.
**Inhospitable,** in-hos'pit-a-bl, *a.* Not hospitable; wanting in hospitality; affording no entertainment to strangers.
**Inhospitality,** in-hos'pit-al''i-ti, *n.* Want of hospitality.
**Inhuman,** in-hū'man, *a.* Destitute of the kindness and tenderness that belong to a human being; cruel; merciless.
**Inhumanity,** in-hū-man'i-ti, *n.* Quality of being inhuman; cruelty.
**Inhumanly,** in-hū'man-li, *adv.* In an inhuman manner; cruelly; barbarously.
**Inhumation,** in-hūm-ā'shon, *n.* Interment.
**Inhume,** in-hūm', *vt.* (inhuming, inhumed). To bury; to inter (a dead body).
**Inimical,** in-im'ik-al, *a.* Unfriendly; hostile; adverse; hurtful; prejudicial.
**Inimitable,** in-im'it-a-bl, *a.* That cannot be imitated or copied; surpassing imitation.
**Inimitably,** in-im'it-a-bli, *adv.* To a degree beyond imitation.
**Iniquitous,** in-ik'wit-us, *a.* Characterized by iniquity; wicked; criminal.
**Iniquity,** in-ik'wi-ti, *n.* Want of equity; injustice; a sin or crime; wickedness.
**Initial,** in-i'shal, *a.* Placed at the beginning; pertaining to the beginning; beginning.—*n.* The first letter of a word; *pl.* the first letter in order of the words composing a name.—*vt.* (initialling, initialled). To put one's initials to; to mark by initials.
**Initiate,** in-i'shi-āt, *vt.* To begin; to be the first to practice or bring in; to instruct in rudiments; to introduce into any society or set; to let into secrets; to indoctrinate.
**Initiation,** in-i'shi-ā''shon, *n.* Act or process of initiating; beginning; formal introduction.
**Initiative,** in-i'shi-āt-iv, *a.* Serving to initiate.—*n.* An introductory step; first active procedure in any enterprise; power of taking the lead.
**Initiatory,** in-i'shi-a-to-ri, *a.* Serving to initiate; initiating; introductory.
**Inject,** in-jekt', *vt.* To throw, cast, or put in or into; to dart in; to cast or throw in.
**Injection,** in-jek'shon, *n.* Act of injecting; the throwing of a liquid medicine into the body by a syringe or pipe; that which is injected.
**Injector,** in-jekt'ėr, *n.* One who or that which injects; an apparatus for supplying the boilers of steam-engines with water.
**Injudicial,** in-jū-di'shal, *a.* Not judicial.
**Injudicious,** in-jū-di'shus, *a.* Not judicious; acting without judgment; indiscreet.
**Injudiciously,** in-jū-di'shus-li, *adv.* In an injudicious manner; indiscreetly.
**Injunction,** in-jungk'shon, *n.* Act of enjoining; a command; a precept; urgent advice; admonition.
**Injure,** in'jėr, *vt.* (injuring, injured). To do harm to; to hurt; to damage.
**Injurer,** in'jėr-ėr, *n.* One who or that which injures.
**Injurious,** in-jū'ri-us, *a.* Causing injury; tending to injure; hurtful; harmful.
**Injuriously,** in-jū'ri-us-li, *adv.* In an injurious or hurtful manner.
**Injury,** in'jū-ri, *n.* The doing of harm; harm or damage; mischief; detriment.
**Injustice,** in-just'is, *n.* Want of justice or equity; iniquity; wrong.
**Ink,** ingk, *n.* A colored liquid, usually black, for writing, printing, etc.—*vt.* To black or daub with ink.
**Ink-bag, Ink-sac,** ingk'bag, ingk'sak, *n.* A sac in some cuttle-fishes, containing a black viscid fluid.
**Inkling,** ingk'ling, *n.* A hint or whisper; a slight notion or idea.
**Inkstand,** ingk'stand, *n.* A vessel for holding ink.
**Inland,** in'land, *a.* Interior; remote from the sea; domestic, not foreign; confined to a country.—*adv.* In or towards the interior of a country.—*n.* The interior part of a country.
**Inlay,** in-lā', *vt.* (inlaying, inlaid). To lay in; to ornament by laying in thin slices of fine wood, ivory, etc., on some other surface.
**Inlaying,** in-lā'ing, *n.* Act or art of one who inlays; inlaid work.
**Inlet,** in'let, *n.* A passage for entrance; place of ingress; a narrow recess in a shore.
**Inmate,** in'māt, *n.* One who dwells in the same house with another; one of the occupants of hospitals, asylums, prisons, etc.
**Inmost,** in'mōst, *a.* Furthest within; remotest from the surface or external parts.
**Inn,** in, *n.* A house for the lodging and entertainment of travellers; a college of law professors and students.
**Innate,** in-nāt', *a.* Inborn; natural; native; inherent.
**Innately,** in-nāt'li, *adv.* In an innate manner; naturally.
**Innavigable,** in-na'vig-a-bl, *a.* That cannot be navigated.
**Inner,** in'ėr, *a.* Interior; further inward than something else; internal.—*n.* A shot which strikes the target between the bull's-eye and the innermost ring.
**Innermost,** in'ėr-mōst, *a.* Furthest inward; most remote from the outward part.
**Innervate,** in-nėr'vāt, *vt.* To supply with nervous strength or stimulus.
**Innervation,** in-nėr-vā'shon, *n.* Act of innerving; nervous stimulation.
**Inning,** in'ing, *n.* The ingathering of grain; *pl.* turn for using the bat in baseball, cricket, etc.
**Innkeeper,** in'kēp-ėr, *n.* One who keeps an inn or tavern.
**Innocence, Innocency,** in'nō-sens, in'nō-sen-si, *n.* Quality of being innocent; freedom from crime or guilt; simplicity of heart.
**Innocent,** in'nō-sent, *a.* Not noxious or hurtful; free from guilt; simple-hearted; guileless.—*n.* One free from guilt or harm; a natural or simpleton.
**Innocently,** in'nō-sent-li, *adv.* In an innocent manner.
**Innocuous,** in-nok'ū-us, *a.* Harmless; not injurious; producing no ill effect.
**Innominate,** in-nom'i-nāt, *a.* Having no name.
**Innovate,** in'nō-vāt, *vi.* To introduce novelties or changes.
**Innovation,** in-nō-vā'shon, *n.* The act of innovating; change made in anything established.—
**Innovator,** in'nō-vāt-ėr, *n.* One who innovates.
**Innoxious,** in-nok'shus, *a.* Free from mischievous qualities; innocent; harmless.

**Innuendo,** in-nū-en'dō, *n.*; pl. **Innuendos** or **-does,** dōz. An oblique hint; insinuation.
**Innumerable,** in-nū'mėr-a-bl, *a.* Incapable of being numbered for multitude; extremely numerous; countless.
**Innumerably,** in-nū'mėr-a-bli, *adv.* Without number.
**Innutrition,** in-nū-tri'shon, *n.* Want of nutrition; failure of nourishment.
**Innutritious,** in-nū-tri'shus, *a.* Not nutritious.
**Inobservant,** in-ob-zėrv'ant, *a.* Not observant; not keen in observation; heedless.
**Inobtrusive,** in-ob-trö'siv, *a.* Unobtrusive.
**Inoculate,** in-ok'ū-lāt, *vt.* To graft by inserting a bud; to communicate a disease to by morbid matter introduced into the blood; to infect; to contaminate.
**Inoculation,** in-ok'ū-lā''shon, *n.* The act or practice of inoculating; communication of a disease by matter introduced into the blood.
**Inodorous,** in-ō'dėr-us, *a.* Wanting odor or scent; having no smell.
**Inoffensive,** in-of-fens'iv, *a.* Giving no offense or annoyance; harmless.
**Inoffensively,** in-of-fens'iv-li, *adv.* In an inoffensive manner.
**Inofficial,** in-of-fi'shal, *a.* not official; not clothed with the usual forms of authority.
**Inoperative,** in-o'pe-rāt-iv, *a.* Not operative; not active; producing no effect.
**Inopportune,** in-op'por-tūn, *a.* Not opportune; inconvenient; unseasonable.
**Inopportunely,** in-op'por-tūn-li, *adv.* In an inopportune manner; unseasonably.
**Inordinacy,** in-or'din-a-si, *n.* The state or quality of being inordinate.
**Inordinate,** in-or'din-āt, *a.* Excessive; immoderate.
**Inordinately,** in-or'din-āt-li, *adv.* In an inordinate manner; excessively.
**Inorganic,** in-or-gan'ik, *a.* Not organic; devoid of the structure of a living being; pertaining to substances without carbon.
**Inosculate,** in-os'kū-lāt, *vi.* and *t.* To unite by apposition or contact, as arteries, nerves, etc.
**Inosculation,** in-os'kū-lā''shon, *n.* The act of inosculating; union by contact.
**In-patient,** in'pā'shent, *n.* A patient who is lodged as well as treated in a hospital.
**Inquest,** in'kwest, *n.* Inquiry; a judicial inquiry before a jury; the jury itself.
**Inquietude,** in-kwī'et-ūd, *n.* Want of quiet; uneasiness, either of body or mind.
**Inquire,** in-kwīr', *vi.* (inquiring, inquired). Often **enquire.** To ask a question; to seek for truth by discussion or investigation.—*vt.* To ask about; to seek by asking.
**Inquirer,** in-kwīr'ėr, *n.* One who inquires; one who seeks for knowledge or information.
**Inquiring,** in-kwīr'ing, *p.a.* Given to inquiry; disposed to investigation.
**Inquiry,** in-kwī'ri, *n.* Often **enquiry.** The act of inquiring; a question; research; investigation; examination.
**Inquisition,** in-kwi-zi'shon, *n.* The act of inquiring; inquiry; inquest; a R. Catholic court for the examination and punishment of heretics.
**Inquisitional, Inquisitionary,** in-kwi-zi'shon-al, in-kwi-zi'shon-a-ri, *a.* Pertaining to inquisition, or to the Inquisition.
**Inquisitive,** in-kwiz'i-tiv, *a.* Addicted to inquiry; given to pry; troublesomely curious.
**Inquisitively,** in-kwiz'i-tiv-li, *adv.* In an inquisitive manner.
**Inquisitor,** in-kwiz'i-tėr, *n.* One whose duty it is to inquire and examine; a member of the Inquisition.
**Inquisitorial,** in-kwiz'i-tō''ri-al, *a.* Pertaining to an inquisitor; making searching inquiry.
**Inroad,** in'rōd, *n.* A hostile incursion; an invasion; attack; encroachment.
**Insalubrious,** in-sa-lū'bri-us, *a.* Not salubrious; unfavorable to health.
**Insalubrity,** in-sa-lū'bri-ti, *n.* State or quality of being insalubrious.
**Insalutary,** in-sal'ū-ta-ri, *a.* Not salutary; unhealthy; productive of evil.
**Insane,** in-sān', *a.* Not sane; deranged in mind or intellect; intended for insane persons; senseless.
**Insanely,** in-sān'li, *adv.* In an insane manner; foolishly; without reason.
**Insanity,** in-san'i-ti, *n.* The state of being insane; derangement of intellect; lunacy.
**Insatiability,** in-sā'shi-a-bil''i-ti, *n.* The quality of being insatiable.
**Insatiable,** in-sā'shi-a-bl, *a.* Not satiable; incapable of being satisfied or appeased.
**Insatiate,** in-sā'shi-āt, *a.* Not satisfied; insatiable.
**Inscribe,** in-skrīb', *vt.* (inscribing, inscribed). To write down; to imprint on, as on the memory; to address or dedicate; to mark with letters or words; to draw a figure within another.
**Inscription,** in-skrip'shon, *n.* The act of inscribing; words engraved; address of a book, etc., to a person.
**Inscriptive,** in-skript'iv, *a.* Written as an inscription; bearing inscription.
**Inscrutability,** in-skrö'ta-bil''i-ti, *n.* Quality of being inscrutable.
**Inscrutable,** in-skrö'ta-bl, *a.* Unsearchable; that cannot be penetrated or understood by human reason.
**Insect,** in'sekt, *n.* One of those small animals that have three divisions of the body—head, thorax, and abdomen—and usually three pairs of legs and two pairs of wings, as flies, etc.; a puny, contemptible person.—*a.* Pertaining to insects; like an insect; mean.
**Insecticide,** in-sek'ti-sīd, *n.* One who or that which kills insects; the killing of insects.
**Insectivore,** in-sek'ti-vōr, *n.* An animal that eats insects.
**Insectivorous,** in-sek-tiv'ō-rus, *a.* Feeding on insects; belonging to the Insectivora.
**Insecure,** in-sē-kūr', *a.* Not secure; not confident of safety; unsafe.
**Insecurely,** in-sē-kūr'li, *adv.* In an insecure manner.
**Insecurity,** in-sē-kū'ri-ti, *n.* The state of being insecure; want of security.
**Insensate,** in-sens'āt, *a.* Destitute of sense or sensation; stupid; irrational.
**Insensibility,** in-sens'i-bil''i-ti, *n.* State or quality of being insensible; want of sensation; callousness; apathy.
**Insensible,** in-sens'i-bl, *a.* Not perceived or perceptible by the senses; void of feeling; unfeeling; callous; indifferent.
**Insensibly,** in-sens'i-bli, *adv.* In an insensible manner; by slow degrees.
**Insensitive,** in-sens'i-tiv, *a.* Not sensitive.
**Insentient,** in-sen'shi-ent, *a.* Not sentient.
**Inseparable,** in-sep'a-ra-bl, *a.* Not separable; not to be parted; always together.
**Insert,** in-sėrt', *vt.* To put, bring, or set in; to thrust in; to set in or among.
**Insertion,** in-sėr'shon, *n.* Act of inserting; thing inserted; place or mode of attachment of a part or organ to its support.
**Insessores,** in-ses-sō'rēz, *n.pl.* The order of passerine or perching birds.
**Insessorial,** in-ses-sō'ri-al, *a.* Belonging to the Insessores or perching birds.
**Inset,** in-set', *vt.* To set in; to implant.—*n.* in'set. That which is set in; insertion.
**Inshore,** in'shōr, *a.* or *adv.* Near the shore.
**Inside,** in'sīd, *n.* The interior side or part of a thing.—*a.* Interior; internal.—*prep.* In the interior of; within.
**Insidious,** in-sid'i-us, *a.* Treacherous; guileful; working evil secretly.
**Insight,** in'sīt, *n.* Sight into; thorough knowledge; discernment; penetration.
**Insignia,** in-sig'ni-a, *n.pl.* Badges or distinguishing marks of office or honor.

**Insignificance, Insignificancy,** in-sig-ni'fi-kans, in-sig-ni'fi-kan-si, *n*. Quality or state of being insignificant; triviality.
**Insignificant,** in-sig-ni'fi-kant, *a*. Not significant; void of signification; trivial or trifling; mean; contemptible.
**Insincere,** in-sin-sēr', *a*. Not sincere; wanting sincerity; hypocritical; deceitful.
**Insincerely,** in-sin-sēr'li, *adv*. In an insincere manner; without sincerity.
**Insincerity,** in-sin-ser'i-ti, *n*. Quality of being insincere; deceitfulness.
**Insinuate,** in-sin'ū-āt, *vt*. To introduce by windings or gently; to work gradually into favor; to introduce by gentle or artful means; to hint.—*vi*. To creep or wind; to make an insinuation; to wheedle.
**Insinuating,** in-sin'ū-āt-ing, *p.a*. Given to or characterized by insinuation; insensibly winning favor and confidence.
**Insinuation,** in-sin'ū-ā''shon, *n*. Act of insinuating; wheedling manner; hint or innuendo.
**Insipid,** in-sip'id, *a*. Destitute of taste; vapid; flat; dull; heavy; spiritless.
**Insipidity,** in-si-pid'i-ti, *n*. Quality of being insipid; want of life or spirit.
**Insist,** in-sist', *vi*. To rest or dilate on; to be urgent or peremptory.
**Insistence,** in-sis'tens, *n*. Act of insisting; persistency; urgency.
**Insnare,** in-snār', *vt*. To catch in a snare; to entrap; to entangle; to involve.
**Insobriety,** in-sō-brī'e-ti, *n*. Want of sobriety; intemperance; drunkenness.
**Insolate,** in'so-lāt, *vt*. To dry or prepare in the sun's rays.
**Insolation,** in-so-lā'shon, *n*. Exposure to the rays of the sun; sunstroke.
**Insolence,** in'sō-lens, *n*. State or quality of being insolent; insolent language or behavior.
**Insolent,** in'sō-lent, *a*. Showing haughty disregard of others; impudent; insulting.
**Insolently,** in'sō-lent-li, *adv*. In an insolent manner; haughty; rudely; saucily.
**Insolubility,** in-sol'ū-bil''i-ti, *n*. Quality of being insoluble.
**Insoluble,** in-sol'ū-bl, *a*. Incapable of being dissolved; not to be solved or explained.
**Insolvable,** in-sol'va-bl, *a*. Not solvable; not to be solved or explained.
**Insolvency,** in-sol'ven-si, *n*. State of being insolvent; inability to pay all debts.
**Insolvent,** in-sol'vent, *a*. Not solvent; not having money, etc., sufficient to pay debts.—*n*. One unable to pay his debts.
**Insomnia,** in-som'ni-a, *n*. Want of sleep; morbid or unnatural sleeplessness.
**Insomuch,** in-sō-much', *adv*. To such a degree; in such wise.
**Inspect,** in-spekt', *vt*. To view or examine to ascertain the quality or condition, etc.
**Inspection,** in-spek'shon, *n*. Act of inspecting; careful survey; official examination.
**Inspector,** in-spekt'ėr, *n*. One who inspects; a superintendent; an overseer.
**Inspiration,** in-spi-rā'shon, *n*. The act of inspiring; the drawing in of breath; the divine influence by which the sacred writers were instructed; influence emanating from any object; the state of being inspired; something conveyed to the mind when under extraordinary influence.
**Inspiratory,** in-spīr'a-to-ri, *a*. Pertaining to inspiration, or inhalation of air.
**Inspire,** in-spīr', *vt*. (inspiring, inspired). To breathe in; to breathe into; to communicate divine instructions to; to infuse ideas or poetic spirit into; to animate in general.—*vi*. To draw in breath; to inhale air into the lungs.
**Inspired,** in-spīrd', *p.a*. Having received inspiration; produced under the influence or direction of inspiration.
**Instability,** in-sta-bil'i-ti, *n*. Want of stability; inconstancy; fickleness.
**Install,** in-stal', *vt*. To place in a seat; to invest with any office with due ceremony.
**Installation,** in-stal-ā'shon, *n*. The act of installing.
**Installment,** in-stal'ment, *n*. Act of installing; a part of a whole produced or paid at various times; part payment of a debt.
**Instance,** in'stans, *n*. Act or state of being instant or urgent; urgency; an example; an occurrence.—*vt*. To mention as an instance, example, or case.
**Instant,** in'stant, *a*. Pressing or urgent; immediate; making no delay; present or current.—*n*. A moment.
**Instantaneous,** in-stant-ā'nē-us, *a*. Done or occurring in an instant.
**Instantaneously,** in-stant-ā'nē-us-li, *adv*. In an instant; in a moment.
**Instantly,** in'stant-li, *adv*. In an instant; immediately; with urgent importunity.
**Instate,** in-stāt', *vt*. (instating, instated). To set or place; to install.
**Instead,** in-sted', *adv*. In the place or room of; in place of that.
**Instep,** in'step, *n*. The fore part of the upper side of the foot, near its junction with the leg.
**Instigate,** in'sti-gāt, *vt*. To spur on; to urge; to incite; to impel.
**Instigation,** in-sti-gā'shon, *n*. Act of instigating; incitement; temptation.
**Instigator,** in'sti-gāt-ėr, *n*. One who instigates or incites another.
**Instil,** in-stil', *vt*. (instilling, instilled). To pour in, as by drops; to infuse by degrees; to insinuate imperceptibly.
**Instillation,** in-stil-ā'shon, *n*. Act of instilling.
**Instilment,** in-stil'ment, *n*. Instillation.
**Instinct,** in'stingkt, *n*. Spontaneous or natural impulse; the knowledge and skill which animals have without experience; intuitive feeling.—*a*. in-stingkt'. Animated or stimulated from within; inspired.
**Instinctive,** in-stingk'tiv, *a*. Prompted by instinct; spontaneous.
**Instinctively,** in-stingkt'iv-li, *adv*. In an instinctive manner; by force of instinct.
**Institute,** in'sti-tūt, *vt*. To set up or establish; to found; to begin; to appoint to an office; to invest with a benefice.—*n*. That which is instituted; established law; principle; a literary or scientific body; an institution; *pl*. a book of elements or principles.
**Institution,** in-sti-tū'shon, *n*. Act of instituting; something instituted; custom; a society for promoting any object; act of investing a clergyman with the care of souls.
**Institutional,** in-sti-tū'shon-al, *a*. Relating to institutions; instituted by authority; relating to elementary knowledge.
**Institutionary,** in-sti-tū'shon-a-ri, *a*. Relating to an institution or to institutions.
**Instruct,** in-strukt', *vt*. To impart knowledge to; to teach; to advise or give notice to.
**Instruction,** in-struk'shon, *n*. Act of instructing; information; education; authoritative direction; command.
**Instructive,** in-struk'tiv, *a*. Conveying instruction or a useful lesson.
**Instructor,** in-strukt'ėr, *n*. One who instructs; a teacher.
**Instructress,** in-strukt'res, *n*. A female who instructs.
**Instrument,** in'stru-ment, *n*. A tool; implement; one subservient to the execution of a plan; means used; any contrivance from which music is produced; a writing instructing one in regard to something agreed upon.
**Instrumental,** in-stru-ment'al, *a*. Conducive to some end; pertaining to or produced by instruments, as music.
**Instrumentalist,** in-stru-ment'al-ist, *n*. One who plays on a musical instrument.

**Instrumentality,** in'stru-men-tal'i-ti, *n.* State of being instrumental; agency.
**Instrumentation,** in'stru-men-tā''shon, *n.* The use of instruments; music for a number of instruments; art of arranging such music.
**Insubordinate,** in-sub-or'din-āt, *a.* Not submitting to authority; riotous.
**Insubordination,** in-sub-or'din-ā''shon, *n.* Quality or state of being insubordinate; resistance to lawful authority.
**Insuetude,** in'swē-tūd, *n.* State or quality of not being in use.
**Insufferable,** in-suf'ėr-a-bl, *a.* Not to be suffered; intolerable.
**Insufferably,** in-suf'ėr-a-bli, *adv.* Intolerably.
**Insufficiency,** in-suf-fi'shen-si, *n.* State of being insufficient; deficiency; inadequacy.
**Insufficient,** in-suf-fi'shent, *a.* Not sufficient; deficient; inadequate.
**Insufficiently,** in-suf-fi'shent-li, *adv.* In an insufficient manner; inadequately.
**Insular,** in'sū-lėr, *a.* Pertaining to an island; forming an island; narrow-minded.
**Insularity,** in-sū-la'ri-ti, *n.* State of being insular.
**Insulate,** in'sū-lāt, *vt.* To make into an island; to detach; to separate, as an electrified body, by interposition of non-conductors.
**Insulation,** in-sū-lā'shon, *n.* Act of insulating; state of being insulated.
**Insulator,** in'sū-lāt-ėr, *n.* One who or that which insulates; a body that interrupts the communication of electricity; non-conductor.
**Insulin,** ins'ū-lin, *n.* A substance extracted from the pancreas of animals, and found beneficial in diabetes.
**Insult,** in'sult, *n.* Any gross affront or indignity; act or speech of insolence or contempt.—*vt.* in-sult'. To treat with insult or insolence.—*vi.* To behave with insolent triumph.
**Insulting,** in-sult'ing, *p.a.* Containing or conveying insult.
**Insuperability,** in-sū'pėr-a-bil''i-ti, *n.* Quality of being insuperable.
**Insuperable,** in-sū'pėr-a-bl, *a.* That cannot be overcome; insurmountable.
**Insuperably,** in-sū'pėr-a-bli, *adv.* In an insuperable manner; insurmountably.
**Insupportable,** in-sup-pōrt'a-bl, *a.* That cannot be supported or borne; intolerable.
**Insuppressible,** in-sup-pres'i-bl, *a.* Not to be suppressed.
**Insurable,** in-shör'a-bl, *a.* That may be insured against loss or damage.
**Insurance,** in-shör'ans, *n.* Act of insuring against loss, etc.; a system of securing, by making certain payments, a certain sum of money at death, etc.
**Insure,** in-shör', *vt.* (insuring, insured). To make sure; to contract for the receipt of a certain sum in the event of loss, death, etc.
**Insurer,** in-shör'ėr, *n.* One who insures.
**Insurgent,** in-sėr'jent, *a.* Rising in opposition to lawful authority; rebellious.—*n.* One who rises in opposition to authority.
**Insurmountable,** in-sėr-mount'a-bl, *a.* That cannot be surmounted; insuperable.
**Insurrection,** in-sėr-rek'shon, *n.* A rising against authority; rebellion.
**Insurrectional, Insurrectionary,** in-sėr-rek'shon-al, in-sėr-rek'shon-a-ri, *a.* Pertaining to insurrection.
**Insusceptibility,** in-sus-sept'i-bil''i-ti, *n.* The quality of being insusceptible.
**Insusceptible,** in-sus-sept'i-bl, *a.* Not susceptible; not capable of being affected.
**Intact,** in-takt', *a.* Untouched; unimpaired.
**Intaglio,** in-tal'yō, *n.* Any figure engraved or cut into a substance; a gem with a figure or device sunk below the surface.
**Intangible,** in-tan'ji-bl, *a.* That cannot be touched; not perceptible to the touch.
**Integer,** in'ti-jer, *n.* A whole; whole number, in contradistinction to a fraction.
**Integral,** in'ti-gral, *a.* Whole; forming a necessary part of a whole; not fractional.—*n.* A whole; an entire thing.
**Integrate,** in'ti-grāt, *vt.* To make or form into one whole; to give the sum or total of.
**Integration,** in-ti-grā'shon, *n.* The act of integrating.
**Integrity,** in-teg'ri-ti, *n.* State of being entire; an unimpaired state; honesty; probity.
**Intellect,** in'tel-lekt, *n.* That mental faculty which receives ideas; the understanding; mental power; mind.
**Intellection,** in-tel-lek'shon, *n.* Act of understanding; simple apprehension of ideas.
**Intellectual,** in-tel-lek'tū-al, *a.* Relating or appealing to the intellect; having intellect.
**Intellectualism,** in-tel-lek'tū-al-izm, *n.* Intellectuality; the doctrine that knowledge is derived from pure reason.
**Intellectuality,** in-tel-lek'tū-al''i-ti, *n.* State of being intellectual; intellectual power.
**Intelligence,** in-tel'i-jens, *n.* The capacity to know; knowledge imparted or acquired; notice; an intelligent or spiritual being.
**Intelligent,** in-tel'i-jent, *a.* Endowed with the faculty of understanding or reason; endowed with a good intellect; well informed.
**Intelligently,** in-tel'i-jent-li, *adv.* In an intelligent manner.
**Intelligibility,** in-tel'i-ji-bil''i-ti, *n.* Quality or state of being intelligible.
**Intelligible,** in-tel'i-ji-bl, *a.* Capable of being understood; comprehensible; clear.
**Intemperate,** in-tem'pėr-ēt, *a.* Not temperate; addicted to an excessive use of alcoholic liquors; excessive or immoderate.—*n.* One not temperate.
**Intend,** in-tend', *vt.* To design; to purpose; to mean.
**Intended,** in-tend'ed, *p.a.* Purposed; betrothed.—*n.* An affianced lover.
**Intense,** in-tens', *a.* Closely strained; strict; extreme in degree; violent; severe.
**Intensely,** in-tens'li, *adv.* In an intense manner or degree.
**Intensify,** in-ten'si-fī, *vt.* To render intense or more intense; to aggravate.—*vi.* To become intense.
**Intension,** in-ten'shon, *n.* Act of intensifying; state of being strained; in *logic,* the qualities necessarily possessed by objects in virtue of their name.
**Intensity,** in-ten'si-ti, *n.* State of being intense; keenness; extreme degree; amount of energy.
**Intensive,** in-ten'siv, *a.* Serving to give emphasis.—*n.* Something giving emphasis.
**Intent,** in-tent', *a.* Having the mind bent on an object; sedulously applied.—*n.* Design or purpose; meaning; drift.
**Intention,** in-ten'shon, *n.* Act of intending; purpose; design; intension; method of treatment in surgery; a general concept.
**Intentional,** in-ten'shon-al, *a.* Done with design or purpose; intended.
**Intentionally,** in-ten'shon-al-li, *adv.* In an intentional manner; on purpose.
**Intently,** in-tent'li, *adv.* In an intent manner.
**Inter,** in-tėr', *vt.* (interring, interred). To bury; to inhume.
**Interact,** in'tėr-akt, *n.* Interval between two acts of a drama; any intermediate employment of time.—*vi.* To act reciprocally.
**Interaction,** in-tėr-ak'shon, *n.* Mutual or reciprocal action.
**Intercede,** in-tėr-sēd', *vi.* (interceding, interceded). To mediate; to plead in favor of one; to make intercession.
**Intercept,** in-tėr-sept', *vt.* To take or seize on by the way; to stop on its passage; to obstruct the progress of; to cut or shut off.
**Interception,** in-tėr-sep'shon, *n.* Act of intercepting.
**Intercession,** in-tėr-se'shon, *n.* Act of interceding;

I

mediation; prayer or solicitation to one party in favor of another.
**Intercessor,** in'tėr-ses-ėr, *n.* One who intercedes; a mediator.
**Interchange,** in-tėr-chānj', *vt.* To change, as one with the other; to exchange; to reciprocate.—*n.* in'tėr-chānj. Mutual change; exchange; alternate succession.
**Intercourse,** in'tėr-kōrs, *n.* Reciprocal dealings between persons or nations; fellowship; familiarity; sexual connection.
**Interdict,** in-tėr-dikt', *vt.* To forbid; to place under an interdict or prohibition.—*n.* in'tėr-dikt. A prohibition; a papal prohibition of the administration of religious rites.
**Interdiction,** in-tėr-dik'shon, *n.* Act of interdicting; prohibition.
**Interdictory,** in-tėr-dik'to-ri, *a.* Having power to interdict or prohibit.
**Interest,** in'tėr-est, *vt.* To concern; to engage the attention of.—*n.* Concern or regard; advantage; profit; profit per cent from money lent or invested; influence with a person.
**Interested,** in'tėr-est-ed, *p.a.* Having an interest; liable to be affected; chiefly concerned for one's private advantage.
**Interesting,** in'tėr-est-ing, *p.a.* Engaging the attention or curiosity.
**Interfere,** in-ter-fēr', *vi.* (interfering, interfered). To clash; to interpose; to take a part in the concerns of others.
**Interference,** in-tėr-fēr'ens, *n.* Act of interfering; clashing or collision.
**Interim,** in'tėr-im, *n.* The meantime; time intervening.—*a.* Belonging to an intervening time; temporary.
**Interior,** in-tē'ri-ėr, *a.* Internal; being within; inland.—*n.* The inner part of a thing; the inside; the inland part of a country, etc.
**Interject,** in-tėr-jekt', *vt.* To throw in between; to insert.
**Interjection,** in-tėr-jek'shon, *n.* Act of throwing between; a word thrown in between words to express some emotion; an exclamation.
**Interlace,** in-tėr-lās', *vt.* To weave together.—*vi.* To have parts intercrossing.
**Interleave,** in-tėr-lēv', *vt.* To insert, as blank leaves in a book between other leaves.
**Interline,** in-tėr-līn', *vt.* To put a line or lines between; to write or print in alternate lines or between lines.
**Interlinear, Interlineal,** in-tėr-lin'ē-ėr, in-tėr-lin'ē-al, *a.* Written or printed between lines; placed between lines; interlined.
**Interlineation,** in-tėr-lin'ē-ā''shon, *n.* Act of interlining; that which is interlined.
**Interlock,** in-tėr-lok', *vi.* and *t.* To unite or lock together by a series of connections.
**Interlocution,** in'tėr-lō-kū''shon, *n.* Dialogue; interchange of speech; an intermediate act or decree before final decision.
**Interlocutor,** in-tėr-lo'kūt-ėr, *n.* One who speaks in dialogue; *Scots law,* a judgment or order of any court of record.
**Interlocutory,** in-tėr-lo'kū-to-ri, *a.* Consisting of dialogue; not final or definitive.
**Interlope,** in-tėr-lōp', *vi.* To traffic without proper license; to intrude.
**Interloper,** in-tėr-lōp'ėr, *n.* An intruder.
**Interlude,** in'tėr-lūd, *n.* A short entertainment between the acts of a play, or between the play and the afterpiece; a piece of music between certain more important passages.
**Interlunar,** in-tėr-lū'nėr, *a.* Belonging to the time when the moon is invisible.
**Intermarriage,** in-tėr-ma'rij, *n.* Marriage between two families, tribes, etc.
**Intermarry,** in-tėr-ma'ri, *vi.* To become connected by marriage, as families.
**Intermeddle,** in-tėr-med'l, *vi.* To meddle in the affairs of others; to interfere.
**Intermeddler,** in-tėr-med'lėr, *n.* One who intermeddles.
**Intermediary,** in-tėr-mē'di-a-ri, *a.* Intermediate.—*n.* An intermediate agent.
**Intermediate,** in-tėr-mē'di-āt, *a.* Being between two extremes; intervening.
**Interment,** in-tėr'ment, *n.* Burial.
**Intermezzo,** in-tėr-met'zō, *n.* A short musical composition, generally of a light sparkling character; an interlude.
**Interminable,** in-tėr'min-a-bl, *a.* Admitting no limit; boundless; endless.
**Interminate,** in-tėr'min-āt, *a.* Unbounded; unlimited; endless.
**Intermingle,** in-tėr-ming'gl, *vt.* To mingle together.—*vi.* To be mixed or incorporated..
**Intermission,** in-tėr-mi'shon, *n.* Act or state of intermitting; pause; rest.
**Intermit,** in-tėr-mit', *vt.* (intermitting, intermitted). To cause to cease for a time; to suspend.—*vi.* To cease for a time.
**Intermittent,** in-tėr-mit'ent, *a.* Ceasing at intervals; ceasing and then returning, as certain fevers.—*n.* A fever which intermits.
**Intermix,** in-tėr-miks', *vt.* To mix together.—*vi.* To be mixed together.
**Intermixture,** in-tėr-miks'tūr, *n.* A mass formed by mixture; an admixture.
**Intern,** in-tėrn', *vt.* To send to and cause to remain in the interior of a country; to disarm and quarter in some place, as defeated troops.
**Internal,** in-tėrn'al, *a.* Inward; not external; domestic; not foreign.
**Internally,** in-tėrn'al-li, *adv.* Inwardly; mentally; spiritually.
**International,** in-tėr-na'shon-al, *a.* Relating to or mutually affecting nations; regularing the mutual intercourse between nations.
**Internecine,** in-tėr-nē'sīn, *a.* Marked by destructive hostilities; causing great slaughter.
**Internuncio,** in-tėr-nun'si-ō, *n.* A messenger; title of the pope's representative at republics and small courts.
**Interpellate,** in-tėr'pel-lāt, *vt.* To question; to interrupt by a queston.
**Interpellation,** in'tėr-pel-lā''shon, *n.* Act of interpellating; question put in legislative assembly to a member of the government.
**Interpolate,** in-tėr'pō-lāt, *vt.* To foist in; to add a spurious word or passage to.
**Interpolation,** in-tėr'pō-lā''shon, *n.* Act of interpolating; spurious word or passage inserted.
**Interpolator,** in-tėr'pō-lāt-ėr, *n.* One who interpolates.
**Interposal,** in-tėr-pōs'al, *n.* Act of interposing; interposition.
**Interpose,** in-tėr-pōz', *vt.* (interposing, interposed). to place between.—*vi.* To mediate; to put in or make a remark.
**Interposition,** in-tėr'pō-zi''shon, *n.* Act of interposing; intervention; mediation.
**Interpret,** in-tėr'pret, *vt.* To explain the meaning of; to expound; to construe; to represent artistically (as an actor).
**Interpretable,** in-tėr'pret-a-bl, *a.* That may be interpreted.
**Interpretation,** in-tėr'pret-ā''shon, *n.* Act of interpreting; explanation; representation of a character on the stage.
**Interpretative,** in-tėr'pret-āt-iv, *a.* Serving to interpret; containing explanation.
**Interpreter,** in-tėr'pret-ėr, *n.* One who interprets; a translator.
**Interregnum,** in-tėr-reg'num, *n.* The time between reigns; intermission or break in succession.
**Interrelation,** in'tėr-rē-lā''shon, *n.* Mutual or corresponding relation; correlation.
**Interrogate,** in-te'rō-gāt, *vt.* To question; to examine by asking questions.
**Interrogation,** in-te'rō-gā''shon, *n.* Act of interrogating; question put; a sign that marks a question, thus (?).
**Interrogative,** in-te-rog'at-iv, *a.* Denoting a question; expressed in the form of a question.—*n.* A

word used in asking questions, as *who? what?*
**Interrogator,** in-te'rō-gāt'ėr, *n*. One who interrogates or asks questions.
**Interrogatory,** in-te-rog'a-to-ri, *n*. A question.—*a*. Containing or expressing a question.
**Interrupt,** in-tėr-rupt', *vt*. To break in upon the progress of; to cause to stop in speaking.
**Interrupted,** in-tėr-rupt'ed, *p.a*. Having interruptions; broken; intermitted.
**Interruption,** in-tėr-rup'shon, *n*. Act of interrupting; a break or breach; obstruction or hindrance; cause of stoppage.
**Intersect,** in-tėr-sekt', *vt*. To cut in between; to divide; to cut or cross mutually.—*vi*. To meet and cut or cross each other.
**Intersection,** in-tėr-sek'shon, *n*. Act or state of intersecting; the point or line in which two lines or two planes cut each other.
**Intersperse,** in-tėr-spėrs', *vt*. To scatter or set here and there among other things.
**Interspersion,** in-tėr-spėr'shon, *n*. Act of interspersing.
**Interstellar, Interstellary,** in-tėr-stel'lėr, in-tėr-stel'la-ri, *a*. Intervening between the stars; situated beyond the solar system.
**Interstice,** in-tėrs'tis, *n*. A narrow space between things closely set; a chink.
**Intertwine,** in-tėr-twīn', *vt*. To unite by twining or twisting.—*vi*. To be interwoven.
**Interval,** in'tėr-val, *n*. A space between things; amount of separation between ranks, degrees, etc.; difference in gravity or acuteness between sounds.
**Intervene,** in-tėr-vēn', *vi*. (intervening, intervened). To come or be between; to interpose or interfere.
**Intervention,** in-tėr-ven'shon, *n*. Act of intervening; interposition; agency of persons between persons.
**Interview,** in'tėr-vū, *n*. A meeting between persons; a conference.—*vt*. To have an interview with to get information for publication.
**Interweave,** in-tėr-wēv', *vt*. To weave together; to unite intimately; to interlace.
**Intestable,** in-test'a-bl, *a*. Legally unqualified to make a will.
**Intestacy,** in-test'a-si, *n*. State of being intestate.
**Intestate,** in-test'āt, *a*. Dying without having made a will; not disposed of by will.—*n*. A person who dies without making a will.
**Intestinal,** in-tes'tin-al, *a*. Pertaining to the intestines.
**Intestine,** in-tes'tīn, *a*. Internal; domestic; not foreign. *n*. The canal extending from the stomach to the anus; *pl*. entrails or viscera in general.
**Intimacy,** in'ti-ma-si, *n*. State of being intimate; close friendship.
**Intimate,** in'ti-māt, *a*. Inward or internal; close in friendship; familiar; close.—*n*. An intimate or familiar friend.—*vt*. (intimating, intimated). To hint or indicate; to announce.
**Intimately,** in'ti-māt-li, *adv*. In an intimate manner; familiarly.
**Intimation,** in-ti-mā'shon, *n*. Act of intimating; a hint; announcement.
**Intimidate,** in-tim'id-āt, *vt*. To put in fear or dread; to cow; to deter with threats.
**Intimidation,** in-tim'id-ā''shon, Act of intimidating.
**Into,** in'tö, *prep*. In and to: expressing motion or direction towards the inside of, or a change of condition.
**Intolerable,** in-tol'ėr-a-bl, *a*. That cannot be borne; unendurable; insufferable.
**Intolerably,** in-tol'ėr-a-bli, *adv*. To a degree beyond endurance.
**Intolerance,** in-tol'ėr-ans, *n*. Quality of being intolerant; want of toleration.
**Intolerant,** in-tol'ėr-ant, *a*. That cannot bear; not enduring difference of opinion or worship; refusing to tolerate others.
**Intolerantly,** in-tol'ėr-ant-li, *adv*. In an intolerant manner.
**Intonate,** in'tōn-āt, *vi*. To sound the notes of the musical scale; to modulate the voice.—*vt*. To pronounce with a certain modulation.
**Intonation,** in-tōn-ā'shon, *n*. Act or manner of intonating; modulation of the voice; utterance with a special tone.
**Intone,** in-tōn', *vi*. To use a musical monotone in pronouncing.—*vt*. To pronounce with a muscial tone; to chant.
**Intoxicant,** in-toks'i-kant, *n*. That which intoxicates; an intoxicating liquor.
**Intoxicate,** in-toks'i-kāt, *vt*. To make drunk; to elate to enthusiasm or madness.—*vi*. To cause intoxication.
**Intoxicating,** in-toks'i-kāt-ing, *p.a*. Causing intoxication.
**Intoxication,** in-toks'i-kā''shon, *n*. Act of intoxicating; state of being drunk; delirious excitement; frenzy.
**Intractable,** in-trakt'a-bl, *a*. Not tractable; not to be governed or managed; refractory.
**Intrados,** in-trā'dos, *n*. The interior and lower line or curve of an arch.
**Intramural,** in-tra-mū'ral, *a*. Being within the walls, as of a town or university.
**Intransigent,** in-tran'si-jent, *a*. Irreconcilable.—*n*. An irreconcilable person.
**Intransitive,** in-trans'it-iv, *a*. Designating a verb which expresses an action or state limited to the subject.
**Intrench,** in-trensh', *vt*. To dig a trench around, as in fortification; to fortify with a ditch and parapet; to lodge within an intrenchment.—*vi*. To invade; to encroach.
**Intrenchment,** in-trensh'ment, *n*. Act of intrenching; a trench; any protection; encroachment.
**Intrepid,** in-tre'pid, *a*. Undaunted; fearless; bold; daring; courageous.
**Intrepidity,** in-tre-pid'i-ti, *n*. Quality of being intrepid; undaunted courage.
**Intricacy,** in'tri-ka-si, *n*. State of being intricate; complication; complexity.
**Intricate,** in'tri-kāt, *a*. Involved; complicated.
**Intrigue,** in-trēg', *n*. An underhand plot or scheme; plot of a play, etc.; an illicit intimacy between a man and woman.—*vi*. (intriguing, intrigued). To engage in an intrigue; to carry on forbidden love.
**Intriguing,** in-trēg'ing, *p.a*. Addicted to intrigue; given to secret machinations.
**Intrinsic, Intrinsical,** in-trin'sik, intrin'sik-al, *a*. Being within; inherent; essential.
**Introduce,** in-trō-dūs', *vt*. To lead or bring in; to insert; to bring to be acquainted; to present; to make known; to import; to bring before the public.
**Introduction,** in-trō-duk'shon, *n*. Act of introducing; act of making persons known to each other; act of bringing something into notice; a preliminary discourse.
**Introductory,** in-trō-duk'to-ri, *a*. Serving to introduce; prefatory; preliminary.
**Introspect,** in-trō-spekt', *vt*. To look into or within.
**Introspection,** in-trō-spek'shon, *n*. The act of looking inwardly; examination of one's own thoughts or feelings.
**Introvert,** in-trō-vėrt', *vt*. To turn inward.
**Intrude,** in-tröd', *vi*. (intruding, intruded). to thrust oneself in; to force an entry or way in without permission, right, or invitation; to encroach.—*vt*. To thrust in.
**Intrusion,** in-trö'zhon, *n*. Action of intruding; encroachment.
**Intrusive,** in-trö'siv, *a*. Apt to intrude; characterized by intrusion.
**Intrust,** in-trust', *vt*. To deliver in trust; to confide to the care of. Also *entrust*.
**Intuition,** in-tū-i'shon, *n*. A looking on; direct apprehension of a truth without reasoning.
**Intuitive,** in-tū'it-iv, *a*. Perceived by the mind immediately without reasoning; based on intuition; self-evident.

**Intuitively,** in-tū'it-iv-li, *adv.* In an intuitive manner; by intuition.
**Inundate,** in-un'dāt or in'-, *vt.* To spread or flow over; to flood; to overwhelm.
**Inundation,** in-un-dā'shon, *n.* Act of inundating; a flood.
**Inure,** in-ūr', *vt.* (inuring, inured). To accustom; to harden by use.—*vi.* To be applied.
**Invade,** in-vād', *vt.* (invading, invaded). To enter wiht hostile intentions; to make an inroad on; to encroach on; to violate.
**Invader,** in-vād'ėr, *n.* One who invades; an assailant; an encroacher.
**Invalid,** in-va'lid, *a.* Not valid; having no force or effect; void; null.
**Invalid,** in'va-lēd, *n.* One weak or infirm; a person disabled for active service.—*a.* In ill health; infirm; disabled.—*vt.* To render an invalid; to enrol on the list of invalids.
**Invalidate,** in-va'li-dāt, *vt.* To render of no force or effect.
**Invalidation,** in-va'li-dā''shon, *n.* Act of invalidating.
**Invalidity,** in-va-lid'i-ti, *n.* State of quality of being invalid; want of force or efficacy.
**Invaluable,** in-va'lū-a-bl, *a.* Precious above estimation; inestimable; priceless.
**Invaluably,** in-va'lū-a-bli, *adv.* Inestimably.
**Invar,** in'var, *n.* An alloy of nickel and steel which is practically unaffected by extremes of temperature.
**Invariable,** in-vā'ri-a-bl, *a.* Not variable; unchangeable; always uniform.
**Invariably,** in-vā'ri-a-bli, *adv.* Uniformly.
**Invasion,** in-vā'zhon, *n.* Act of invading; hostile entrance; infringement; violation.
**Invasive,** in-vā'siv, *a.* Making invasion; aggressive.
**Invective,** in-vek'tiv, *n.* Violent utterance of censure; railing language; vituperation.—*a.* Containing invectives; abusive.
**Inveigh,** in-vā', *vi.* To attack with invectives; to rail against; to reproach; to upbraid.
**Inveigle,** in-vē'gl, *vt.* To persuade to something evil; to entice; to seduce.
**Invent,** in-vent', *vt.* To devise or produce, as something new; to fabricate; to concoct.
**Invention,** in-ven'shon, *n.* Act of inventing; contrivance of that which did not before exist; device; power of inventing; ingenuity; faculty by which an author produces plots, etc.
**Inventive,** in-vent'iv, *a.* Able to invent; quick at contrivance; ready at expedients.
**Inventor,** in-vent'ėr, *n.* One who invents; a contriver.
**Inventory,** in'ven-to-ri, *n.* An account of catalogue of the goods and chattels of a deceased person; a catalogue of particular things.—*vt.* to make an inventory of.
**Inverse,** in'vėrs or in-vėrs', *a.* Opposite in order or relation; inverted.
**Inversely,** in-vėrs'li, *adv.* In an inverse order or manner; in inverse proportion.
**Inversion,** in-vėr'shon, *n.* Act of inverting; state of being inverted; change of order so that the last becomes first, and the first last; a turning backward.
**Invert,** in-vėrt', *vt.* To turn upside down; to place in a contrary position; to reverse.
**Invertebrate,** in-vėr'tē-brāt, *a.* Destitute of a backbone or vertebral column.—*n.* An animal (one of the invertebrata) in which there is no backbone.
**Inverted,** in-vėrt'ed, *p.a.* Turned upside down; changed in order.
**Invest,** in-vest', *vt.* To clothe; to array; to clothe with office or authority; to endow; to besiege; to lay out as money in some species of property.—*vi.* To make an investment.
**Investigate,** in-ves'ti-gāt, *vt.* To search into; to make careful examination of.
**Investigation,** in-ves'ti-gā''shon, *n.* Act of investigating, examination; search; scrutiny.
**Investigator,** in-ves'ti-gāt-ėr, *n.* One who investigates.
**Investiture,** in-ves'ti-tūr, *n.* Act of investing or giving possession of any manor, office, or benefice; clothing; covering.
**Investment,** in-vest'ment, *n.* Act of investing; act of besieging; money laid out for profit; that in which money is invested.
**Investor,** in-vest'ėr, *n.* One who invests.
**Inveteracy,** in-vet'ėr-a-si, *n.* State or quality of being inveterate; obstinacy of any quality or state acquired by time.
**Inveterate,** in-vet'ėr-āt, *a.* Long established; deep-rooted; obstinate; confirmed.
**Invidious,** in-vid'i-us, *a.* Envious; malignant; likely to incur hatred or to provoke envy.
**Invidiously,** in-vid'i-us-li, *adv.* In an invidious manner; malignantly.
**Invigorate,** in-vi'gor-āt, *vt.* To give vigor to; to give life and energy to.
**Invincible,** in-vin'si-bl, *a.* Not to be conquered or overcome; insurmountable.—*n.* One who is invincible.
**Invincibly,** in-vin'si-bli, *adv.* Unconquerably.
**Inviolability,** in-vī'ō-la-bil''i-ti, *n.* Quality or state of being inviolable.
**Inviolable,** in-vī'ō-la-bl, *a.* Not to be violated; that ought not to be injured or treated irreverently; not susceptible or hurt.
**Inviolably,** in-vī'ō-la-bli, *adv.* In an inviolable manner; without profanation.
**Inviolate,** in-vī'ō-lāt, *a.* Not violated; uninjured; unprofaned; unbroken.
**Invisibility,** in-vi'zi-bil''i-ti, *n.* State of being invisible.
**Invisible,** in-vi'zi-bl, *a.* Not visible; that cannot be seen; imperceptible.
**Invisibly,** in-vi'zi-bli, *adv.* In an invisible manner; imperceptible to the eye.
**Invitation,** in-vi-tā'shon, *n.* Act of inviting; bidding to an entertainment, etc.
**Invite,** in-vīt', *vt.* (inviting, invited). To ask to do something; to ask to an entertainment, etc.; to allure or attract.—*vi.* To give invitation; to allure.
**Inviting,** in-vīt'ing, *p.a.* Attractive.
**Invocate,** invō-kāt, *vt.* To invoke.
**Invocation,** in-vō-kā'shon, *n.* Act of invoking; the form or act of calling for the assistance of any being, particularly a divinity.
**Invoice,** in'vois, *n.* A written account of the merchandise sent to a person, with the prices annexed.—*vt.* (invoicing, invoiced). To make an invoice of; to enter in an invoice.
**Invoke,** in-vōk', *vt.* (invoking, invoked). To call upon; to address in prayer; to call on for assistance and protection.
**Involucre,** in-vō'lū'kėr, *n.* Any collection of bracts round a cluster of flowers.
**Involuntarily,** in-vo'lun-ta-ri-li, *adv.* In an involuntary manner.
**Involuntary,** in-vo'lun-ta-ri, *a.* Not voluntary; independent of will or choice.
**Involute,** in'vō-lūt, *n.* A curve traced by any point of a tense string when it is unwound from a given curve.—*a.* Involved; rolled inward from the edges.
**Involution,** in-vō-lū'shon, *n.* Act of involving; state of being involved; complication; the raising of a quantity to any power assigned.
**Involve,** in-volv', *vt.* (involving, involved). To roll up; to envelop to imply; to include; to implicate; to complicate; in algebra, etc., to raise a quantity to any assigned power.
**Invulnerable,** in-vul'nėr-a-bl, *a.* That cannot be wounded; incapable of receiving injury.
**Inward,** in'wėrd, *a.* Internal; being within; intimate; in the mind, soul, or feelings.—*adv.* Toward the inside; into the mind.—*n.pl.* The inner parts of an animal; the viscera.
**Iodide,** ī'ō-dīd, *n.* A compound of iodine and metal.
**Iodine,** ī'ō-dīn, ī'ō-dēn, *n.* A non-metallic element

chiefly extracted from the ashes of sea-weeds, and much used in medicine.

**Iodoform,** ī-od'ō-form, *n.* A compound of carbon, hydrogen, and iodine, an antiseptic.

**Ion,** ī'on, *n.* An electrified particle formed by the transfer of electrons when molecules of gas are broken up.

**Ionian,** ī-ō'ni-an, *a.* Pertaining to Ionia; Ionic.—*n.* One of an ancient Greek race.

**Ionic,** ī-on'ik, *a.* Relating to Ionia, or the Ionian Greeks; denoting an order of architecture distinguished by the volutes of its capital.

**Iota,** ī-ō'ta, *n.* The name of Greek letter *i*; an insignificant amount.

**I O U,** ī' ō ū, *n.* A signed paper having on it these letters and a sum of money borrowed, serving an an acknowledgment of a debt.

**Iranian,** i-rā'ni-an, *a.* Pertaning to *Iran*, the native name of Persia: applied to the Persian Zend, and cognate tongues.

**Irascibility,** ī-ras'i-bil''i-ti, *n.* Quality of being irascible.

**Irascible,** ī-ras'i-bl, *a.* Readily made angry; easily provoked; irritable.

**Irascibly,** ī-ras'i-bli, *adv.* In an irascible manner.

**Irate,** ī-rāt', *a.* Angry; enraged; incensed.

**Ire,** īr, *n.* Anger; wrath; rage.

**Iricism,** ī'ri-sizm, *n.* An Irish mode of expresson; any Irish peculiarity.

**Iridescence,** ī-rid-es'ens, *n.* Property of being iridescent; exhibition of colors like those of the rainbow.

**Iridescent,** ī-rid-es'ent, *a.* Exhibiting colors like the rainbow; shimmering wth rainbow colors.

**Iris,** ī'ris, *n.*; pl. **Irises,** ī'ris-ez. The rainbow; an appearance resembling the rainbow; the colored circle round the pupil of the eye; the flag-flower.

**Irish,** ī'rish, *a.* Pertaining to Ireland or its inhabitants.—*n.* Natives of Ireland; the Celtic language of the natives of Ireland.

**Irishism,** ī'rish-izm, *n.* An Iricism.

**Irk,** ėrk, *vt.* To weary; to annoy; to vex. (Used impersonally.)

**Irksome,** ėrk'sum, *a.* Wearisome; vexatious.

**Irksomely,** ėrk'sum-li, *adv.* Tediously.

**Iron,** ī'ėrn, *n.* The most common and useful metal; an instrument made of iron; a utensil for smoothing cloth; *pl.* fetters; chains; handcuffs.—*a.* Made of iron; consisting of or like iron; harsh; severe; binding fast; vigorous; inflexible.—*vt.* To smooth with an iron; to fetter; to furnish or arm with iron.

**Iron-clad,** ī'ėrn-klad, *a.* Covered with iron plates; armor-plated.—*n.* A war-ship covered with thick iron plates.

**Ironical,** ī-ron'ik-al, *a.* Containing irony; given to irony; expressing one thing and meaning the opposite.

**Ironically,** ī-ron'ik-al-li, *adv.* By way of iron; by the use of irony.

**Iron-mold,** ī'ėrn-mōld, *n.* A spot on cloth occassioned by iron rust.

**Iron-stone,** ī'ėrn-stōn, *n.* An ore of iron having a stony character.

**Ironware,** ī'ėrn-wār, *n.* Iron worked up into utensils, tools, etc.

**Irony,** ī'ėrn-i, *a.* Made of or like iron; hard.

**Irony,** ī'ron-i, *n.* A mode of speech which expresses a sense contrary to that conveyed by the words; a subtle kind of sarcasm.

**Irradiance, Irradiancy,** ir-rā'di-ans, ir-rā'di-an-si, *n.* Luster; splendor.

**Irrradiant,** ir-rā'di-ant, *a.* Emitting rays of light.

**Irradiate,** ir-rā'di-āt, *vt.* To send forth rays of light upon; to enlighten.—*vi.* To emit rays.

**Irradiation,** ir-rā'di-ā''shon, *n.* Act of irradiating; illumination; apparent enlargement of an object strongly illuminated.

**Irrational,** ir-ra'shon-al, *a.* Not rational; void of reason or understanding; foolish; in *mathematics*, surd.

**Irrationally,** ir-ra'shon-al-li, *adv.* In an irrational manner; without reason; absurdly.

**Irreconcilable,** ir-re'kon-sil''a-bl, *a.* Not reconcilable; inconsistent; incompatible.—*n.* One who is not to be reconciled; one who will not work in harmony with associates.

**Irrecoverable,** ir-rē-ku'vėr-a-bl, *a.* Not to be recovered or regained.

**Irredeemable,** ir-rē-dēm'-a-bl, *a.* Not redeemable; not subject to be paid at its nominal value.

**Irreducible,** ir-rē-dūs'i-bl, *a.* Not reducible; that cannot be reduced.

**Irrefutable,** ir-rē-fūt'a-bl or ir-ref'ūt-a-bl, *a.* That cannot be refuted; unanswerable.

**Irregular,** ir-re'gū-lėr, *a.* Not regular; not according to rule or custom; anomalous; vicious; crooked; variable; deviating from the common rules in its inflections.—*n.* A soldier not in regular service.

**Irregularity,** ir-re'gū-la''ri-ti, *n.* State or character of being irregular; want of regularity; that which is irregular; immoral action or behavior.

**Irregularly,** ir-re'gū-lėr-li, *adv.* In an irregular manner.

**Irrelevance, Irrelevancy,** ir-re'lē-vans, ir-re'lē-van-si, *n.* State or quality of being irrelevant.

**Irrelevant,** ir-rē'lē-vant, *a.* Not relevant; not applicable; not to the purpose.

**Irreligion,** ir-rē-li'jon, *n.* Want of religion, or contempt of it; impiety.

**Irreligious,** ir-rē-li'jus, *a.* Not religious; contrary to religion; impious; ungodly; profane.

**Irremediable,** ir-rē-mē'di-a-bl, *a.* Not to be remedied; incurable; irreparable.

**Irremissible,** ir-rē-mis'i-bl, *a.* Not to be remitted or pardoned; unpardonable.

**Irremovable,** ir-rē-möv'a-bl, *a.* Not removable; firmly fixed.

**Irreparable,** ir-rē'pa-ra-bl, *a.* Not reparable; irretrievable; irremediable.

**Irrepressible,** ir-rē-pres'i-bl, *a.* Not repressible; incapable of being repressed.

**Irreproachable,** ir-rē-prōch'a-bl, *a.* Incapable of being reproached; upright; faultless.

**Irreprovable,** ir-rē-pröv'a-bl, *a.* Not reprovable; blameless; upright; unblamable.

**Irresistance,** ir-rē-zis'tans, *n.* Non-resistance; passive submission.

**Irresistible,** ir-rē-zist'i-bl, *a.* Not resistible; that cannot be resisted; resistless.

**Irresolute,** ir-re'zō-lūt, *a.* Not resolute; not firm in purpose; undecided; wavering.

**Irresolvable,** ir-rē-zolv'a-bl, *a.* Not resolvable; that cannot be resolved.

**Irrespective,** ir-rē-spekt'iv, *a.* Having no respect to particular circumstances (with *of*).

**Irresponsible,** ir-rē-spons'i-bl, *a.* Not responsible; not liable to answer for consequences.

**Irresponsible,** ir-rēspons'iv, *a.* Not responsive.

**Irretrievable,** ir-rē-trēv'a-bl, *a.* That cannot be retrieved; irreparable.

**Irreverence,** ir-rev'ėr-ens, *n.* Want of reverence; want of veneration for the deity or for things sacred; want of due regard to a superior; irreverent conduct or action.

**Irreverent,** ir-rev'ėr-ent, *a.* Exhibiting or marked by irreverence; wanting in respect.

**Irreversible,** ir-rē-vėr'si-bl, *a.* Not reversible; not to be annulled.

**Irrevocable,** ir-re'vōk-a-bl, *a.* Not to be recalled, revoked, or annulled; irreversible.

**Irrigate,** ir'ri-gāt, *vt.* To bedew or sprinkle; to water by means of channels or streams.

**Irrigation,** ir-ri-gā'shon, *n.* Act or operation of irrigating.

**Irritability,** ir'rit-a-bil''i-ti, *n.* Quality or state of being irritable.

**Irritable,** ir'rit-a-bl, *a.* Susceptible of irritation; very liable to anger; easily provoked.

**Irritant,** ir'rit-ant, *a.* Irritating; producing inflammation.—*n.* That which irritates; a medical application that causes pain or heat.

**Irritate,** ir'rit-āt, *vt.* To rouse to anger; to provoke; to inflame.

**Irritating,** ir'rit-āt-ing, *p.a.* Causing irritation; annoying.
**Irritation,** ir-rit-ā'shon, *n.* Act of irritating; exasperation; annoyance; vital action in muscles or organs caused by some stimulus.
**Irruption,** ir-rup'shon, *n.* A bursting in; a sudden invasion or incursion.
**Irruptive,** ir-rup'tiv, *a.* Rushing in or upon.
**Is,** iz. The third pers. sing. of the verb *to be.*
**Isinglass,** ī'zing-glas, *n.* Fish-glue; a gelatinous substance prepared from the air-bladders of certain fishes.
**Islam,** is'lam, *n.* The religion of Mohammed; the whole body of those who profess it.
**Islamism,** is'lam-izm, *n.* Mohammedanism.
**Islamite,** is'lam-īt, *n.* A Mohammedan.
**Island,** ī'land, *n.* A piece of land surrounded by water; anything resembling an island.—*vt.* To cause to become or appear like an island; to dot, as with islands.
**Islander,** ī'land-ėr, *n.* An inhabitant of an island.
**Isle,** īl, *n.* An island.—*vt.* To island.
**Islet,** īl'et, *n.* A little isle.
**Isobar,** ī'sō-bär, *n.* A line on a map connecting places at which the mean height of the barometer at sea-level is the same.
**Isochronal, Isochronous,** ī-sok'ron-al, ī-sok'ron-us, *n.* Uniform in time; of equal time; performed in equal times.
**Isoclinal, Isoclinic,** ī-so-klī'nal, ī-sō-klin'ik, *a.* Of equal inclination or dip; applied to lines connecting places at which the dip of the magnetic needle is equal.
**Isolate,** ī'sō-lāt, *vt.* To place in or as in an island; to place by itself; to insulate.
**Isolation,** īs-ō-lā'shon, *n.* State of being isolated; insulation.
**Isolationist,** īs-ō-lā'shon-ist, *n.* One who favors keeping aloof from other countries politically.
**Isometric, Isometrical,** ī-sō-met'rik, ī-sō-met'rik-al, *a.* Pertaining to or characterized by equality of measure.
**Isosceles,** ī-sos'e-lēz, *a.* Having two legs or sides only that are equal (an *isosceles* triangle).
**Israelite,** iz'ra-el-īt, *n.* A descendant of *Israel* or Jacob; a Jew.
**Issuable,** ish'ū-a-bl, *a.* That may be issued.
**Issue,** ish'ū, *n.* The act of passing or flowing out; delivery; quantity issued at one time; event; consequence; progeny; offspring; an artifical ulcer to promote a secretion of pus; matter depending in a lawsuit.—*vi.* (issuing, issued). To pass or flow out; to proceed; to spring; to grow or accrue; to come to an issue in law; to terminate.—*vt.* To send out; to put into circulation; to deliver for use.
**Isthmus,** ist'mus or is'mus, *n.* A neck of land connecting two much larger portions.
**It,** it, *pron.* A pronoun of the neuter gender, third person, nominative or objective case.
**Italian,** i-ta'i-an, *a.* Pertaining to Italy.—*n.* A native of Italy; the language of Italy.
**Italic,** i-ta'lik, *a.* Pertaining to Italy; the name of a printing type sloping towards the right.—*n.* An italic letter or type.
**Italicize,** i-ta'li-sīz, *vt.* To print in italics.
**Itch,** ich, *n.* A sensation in the skin causing a desire to scratch; a constant teasing desire—*vi.* To feel an itch; to have a teasing sensation impelling to something.
**Itchy,** ich'i, *a.* Affected with itch.
**Item,** ī'tem, *adv.* Also.—*n.* A separate particular; a scrap of news.—*vt.* To make a note of.
**Iterate,** it'ėr-āt, *vt.* To repeat; to utter or do a second time.
**Iteration,** it-ėr-ā'shon, *n.* Act of repeating; recital or performance a second time.
**Itinerancy,** i- or ī-tin'ėr-an-si, *n.* A journeying; a passing from place to place.
**Itinerant,** i- or ī-tin'ėr-ant, *a.* Passing or travelling from place to place; not settled.—*n.* One who travels from place to place.
**Itinerary,** i- or ī-tin'ėr-a-ri, *n.* A work containing notices of places of a particular line of road; a travel route; plan of a tour.—*a.* Travelling; pertaining to a journey.
**Itinerate,** i- or ī-tin'ėr-āt, *vi.* To travel from place to place.
**Its,** its, *pron.* The possessive case singular of *it.*
**Itself,** it-self', *pron.* The neuter reflexive pronoun corresponding to *himself.*
**Ivory,** ī'vo-ri, *n.* The substance composing the tusks of the elephants, etc. something made of ivory.—*a.* Consisting or made of ivory.
**Ivy,** ī'vi, *n.* A plant which creeps along the ground, or climbs walls, trees, etc.

# J

**Jabber,** jab'ėr, *vi.* To gabble; to talk rapidly or indistinctly; to chatter.—*vt.* To utter rapidly with confused sounds.—*n.* Rapid and indistinct talk.
**Jacinth,** jā'sinth, *n.* The gem also called hyacinth.
**Jack,** jak, *n.* A name of various implements; a boot-jack; a contrivance for raising great weights by the action of screws; a contrivance for turning a spit; a coat serving as mail; a pitcher of waxed leather; a ball used for a mark in bowls; a flag on a bowsprit; the union flag; the male of certain animals; a young pike; the knave in a pack of cards.
**Jackal,** jak'äl, An animal resembling a fox, and closely akin to the dog.
**Jackass,** jak'as, *n.* The male of the ass; a dolt; a blockhead.
**Jack-boot,** jak'böt, *n.* A kind of large boot reaching up over the knee.
**Jackdaw,** jak'da, *n.* A small species of crow.
**Jacket,** jak'et, *n.* A short outer garment; a casing of cloth, felt, wood, etc.
**Jacobean,** ja-kō-bē'an, *a.* Pertaining to the time of James I. of England.
**Jacobin,** ja'kō-bin, *n.* One of a society of violent revolutionists in France during the first revolution; a politician of similar character.
**Jacobite,** ja'kō-bīt, *n.* A partisan of James II., king of England, after he abdicated the throne, and of his descendants.—*a.* Pertaining to the partisans of James II.
**Jactation, Jactitation,** jak-tā'shon, jak-ti-tā'shon, *n.* A restless tossing of the body; bragging; boastful display.
**Jade,** jād, *n.* A mean or poor horse; a low woman; a huzzy; a hard tenacious green stone of a resinous aspect when polished.—*vt.* (jading, jaded). To ride or drive severely; to weary or fatigue.—*vi.* To become weary; to sink.
**Jag,** jag, *vt.* (jagging, jagged). To cut into notches or teeth; to notch.—*n.* A notch; a ragged protuberance.
**Jagged,** jag'ed, *p.a.* Having notches or teeth; cleft; divided.
**Jaggery, Jagghery,** jag'ėr-i, *n.* Imperfectly granulated sugar; the inspissated juice of the palmyra-tree.
**Jaggy,** jag'i, *a.* Set with teeth; denticulated; uneven.
**Jaguar,** ja-gwär', *n.* The American tiger, a spotted carnivorous animal, the most formidable feline quadruped of the New World.
**Jail,** jāl, *n.* A prison; place of confinement.
**Jailer, Jailor,** jāl'ėr, *n.* The keeper of a jail.
**Jam,** jam, *n.* A conserve of fruits boiled with sugar and water.—*vt.* (jamming, jammed). To crowd; to squeeze tight; to wedge in.
**Jamb,** jam, *n.* The side-post or veritcal sidepiece of a door, window, etc.
**Jangle,** jang'gl, *vi.* (jangling, jangled). To sound harshly; to wrangle; to bicker.—*vt.* To cause to sound discordantly.—*n.* Prate; discordant sound.
**Janitor,** ja'ni-tor, *n.* A doorkeeper; one who looks after a public building.

**January,** ja'nū-a-ri, *n*. The first month of the year.
**Japan,** ja-pan', *n*. Work varnished and figured.—*vt*. (japanning, japanned). To cover with hard brilliant varnish, and embellish with figures; to varnish.
**Jar,** jär, *vi*. (jarring, jarred). To strike together discordantly; to clash; to interfere; to be inconsistent.—*vt*. To shake; to cause a short tremulous motion in.—*n*. A rattling vibration of sound; a harsh sound; contention; clash of interests or opinions; a vessel of earthenware or glass.
**Jardinière,** zhär-dēn-yār, *n*. An ornamental stand for plants and flowers.
**Jargon,** jär'gon, *n*. Confused, unintelligible talk; gibberish; phraseology peculiar to a sect, profession, etc.; a variety of zircon.
**Jargonelle,** jär-gon-el', *n*. A variety of pear.
**Jarrah,** jar'ra, *n*. A timber-tree of W. Australia, a species of eucalyptus.
**Jasmine,** jas'min, *n*. A fragrant shrub, bearing white or yellow flowers.
**Jasper,** jas'pėr, *n*. A variety of quartz, of red, yellow, and some dull colors.
**Jaundice,** jan'dis, *n*. A disease characterized by yellowness of the eyes and skin, loss of appetite, and general lassitude.—*vt*. To affect with jaundice, or with prejudice, envy, etc.
**Jaunt,** jänt, *vi*. To ramble here and there; to make an excursion.—*n*. A trip; a tour; an excursion; a ramble.
**Jauntily,** jän-ti-li, *adv*. Briskly; gaily.
**Jaunty,** jän'ti, *a*. Gay and easy in manner or actions; airy; sprightly; showy.
**Javelin,** jav'lin, *n*. A light spear thrown from the hand.
**Jaw,** ja, *n*. The bones of the mouth in which the teeth are fixed.
**Jay,** jā, *n*. A bird allied to the crows.
**Jazz,** jaz, *n*. Syncopated or rag-time music, originally of negro origin.
**Jealous,** je'lus, *a*. Uneasy through fear of, or on account of, preference given to another; suspicious in love; apprehensive of rivalry; anxiously fearful or careful.
**Jealously,** je'lus-li, *adv*. In a jealous manner; with jealousy; emulously.
**Jealousy,** je'lus-i, *n*. Quality of being jealous; painful suspicion of rivalry; suspicious fear or apprehension; solicitude for others.
**Jean,** jān, *n*. A twilled cotton cloth.
**Jeep,** jēp, *n*. Small 4-wheel drive military car for carrying army personnel.
**Jeer,** jēr, *vi*. To flout; to mock; to utter severe, sarcastic reflections.—*vt*. To treat with scoffs or derision.—*n*. A scoff; biting jest; jibe.
**Jeeringly,** jēr'ing-li, *adv*. With raillery; scornfully; contemptuously.
**Jehovah,** jē-hō'va, *n*. An old Hebrew name of the Supreme Being.
**Jelly,** je'li, *n*. Matter in a glutinous state; the thickened juice of fruit boiled with sugar; transparent matter obtained from animal substances by boiling.—*vi*. To become a jelly.
**Jelly-fish,** jel'i-fish, *n*. A gelatinous marine animal.
**Jennet,** jen'net, *n*. A small Spanish horse.
**Jenny,** jen'i, *n*. A machine for spinning, moved by water or steam.
**Jeopard,** je'pėrd, *vt*. To put in danger; to hazard.
**Jeopardize,** je'pėrd-iz, *vt*. To jeopard.
**Jeopardous,** je'pėrd-us, *a*. Hazardous.
**Jeopardy,** je'pėrd-i, *n*. Hazard; risk; exposure to death, loss, or injury.
**Jerboa,** jėr-bō'a, *n*. A small rodent resembling a mouse, but with long hind-limbs.
**Jeremiad,** jer-ē-mī'ad, *n*. A lamentation; a complaint; used in ridicule.
**Jerk,** jėrk, *vt*. To give a sudden pull, thrust, or push to; to throw with a quick motion.—*vi*. to make a sudden motion.—*n*. A sudden thrust, push, or twitch; a sudden spring; a spasmodic movement.
**Jerked,** jėrkt, *p.a*. Cut into thin slices, and dried, as beef.
**Jerkin,** jėr'kin, *n*. A jacket; a short coat; a close waistcoat.
**Jersey,** jėr'zi, *n*. A kind of close-fitting knitted woollen shirt.
**Jess,** jes, *n*. A short strap of leather tied round the legs of a hawk.
**Jessamine,** jes'a-min, *n*. *See* JASMINE.
**Jest,** jest, *n*. A joke; plesantry; object of laughter; a laughing-stock.—*vi*. To make merriment; to joke.
**Jester,** jest'ėr, *n*. One who jests; a buffoon; a merry-andrew.
**Jesuit,** je'zū-it, *n*. One of the Society of Jesus, so called, founded by Ignatius Loyola, in 1534; a crafty person; an intriguer.
**Jesuitic, Jesuitical,** je-sū-it'ik, je-zū-it'ik-al, *a*. Pertaining to the Jesuits; crafty.
**Jesuitism,** je'zū-it-izm, *n*. The principles and practices of the Jesuits; cunning.
**Jesus,** jē'zus, *n*. The Savior of men; Christ.
**Jet,** jet, *n*. A shooting forth or spouting; what issues from an orifice, as water, gas, etc.; a compact and very black species of coal, used for ornaments.—*vt*. (jetting, jetted). To emit in a jet.—*vi*. To issue in a jet.
**Jet-black,** jet'blak, *a*. Black as jet.
**Jet-propulsion,** jet-prō-pul'shon, *n*. Propulsion by the reaction to a jet of gas expelled from an engine.
**Jetsam, Jetson,** jet'sam, jet'sun, *n*. The throwing of goods overboard to lighten a ship in distress; goods so thrown away.
**Jettison,** jet'i-son, *n*. Jetsam.—*vt*. To throw overboard.
**Jetty,** jet'i, *n*. A kind of pier.—*a*. Made of jet, or black as jet.
**Jew,** jū, *n*. A Hebrew or Israelite.
**Jewel,** jū'el, *n*. A personal ornament of precious stones; a precious stone.—*vt*. (jewelling, jewelled). To adorn with jewels.
**Jeweller,** jū'el-ėr, *n*. One who makes or deals in jewels and other ornaments.
**Jewelry,** jū-el-ėr-i, jā'el-ri, *n*. Jewels in general.
**Jewess,** jū'es, *n*. A Hebrew woman.
**Jewish,** jū'ish, *a*. Pertaining to the Jews.
**Jewry,** jū'ri, *n*. The land of the Jews.
**Jew's-harp,** jūz'härp, *n*. A small musical instrument held between the teeth, sounding by the vibration of a steel tongue.
**Jib,** jib, *n*. The triangular foremost sail of a ship; the projecting arm of a crane.
**Jib, Jibe,** jib, jīb, *vt*. and *i*. (jibbed, jibed, jibd, jībd; jibbing, jibing, jib'ing, jīb'ing). To shift (as a fore-and-aft sail) from one side to the other; to pull against the bit, as a horse; to move restively.
**Jib-boom,** jib'böm, *n*. A spar which serves as a continuation of a bowsprit.
**Jiffy,** jif'i, *n*. A moment, an instant. (Colloq.)
**Jig,** jig, *n*. A quick tune; a light lively dance; a mechanical contrivance of various kinds.—*vi*. (jigging, jigged). to dance a jig; to jolt.—*vt*. To jerk; to jolt.
**Jilt,** jilt, *n*. A woman who gives her lover hopes and capriciously disappoints him.—*vt*. To deceive in love.—*vi*. To play the jilt.
**Jingle,** jing'gl, *vi*. and *t*. (jingling, jingled). To sound with a tinkling metallic sound; to clink.—*n*. A rattling or clinking sound.
**Jingo,** jing'go, *n*. An expletive used as a mild oath; a bellicose patriot; a Chauvinist.
**Jinricksha, Jinrikisha,** jin-rik'sha, jin-rik'i-sha, *n*. A small two-wheeled carriage drawn by one or more men, used in Japan, etc.
**Job,** job, *n*. A piece of work undertaken; a public transaction done for private profit.—*vt*. (jobbing, jobbed). To let out in separate portions or jobs; to let out for hire, as horses; to engage for hire; to peck or stab with something sharp.—*vi* To work at chance jobs; to buy and sell as a broker; to let or hire horses.

**Jobber,** job'ėr, *n.* One who jobs or works at jobs; one who lets or hires out carriages or horses; one who deals or dabbles in stocks.
**Jockey,** jok'i, *n.* A man who rides horses in a race; a dealer in horses; one who takes undue advantage in trade.—*vt.* To play the jockey to; to ride in a race; to jostle by riding against; to cheat.
**Jocose,** jōk-ōs', *a.* Given to jokes and jesting; facetious; merry; waggish.
**Jocular,** jok'ū-lėr, *a.* Given to jesting; jocose; humorous; sportive.
**Jocularity,** jok-ū-la'ri-ti, *n.* Quality of being jocular; merriment; jesting.
**Jocund,** jōk' or jok'und, *a.* Blithe; merry.
**Jog,** jog, *vt.* (jogging, jogged). To push with the elbow or hand; to excite attention by a slight push.—*vi.* To move at a slow trot; to walk or travel idly or slowly.—*n.* A push; a shake or push to awaken attention.
**Joggle,** jog'l, *vt.* (joggling, joggled). To shake slightly.—*vi.* To shake; to totter.—*n.* A kind of joint in masonry and carpentry.
**Jog-trot,** jog'trot, *n.* A slow easy trot; a slow routine.—*a.* Monotonous; humdrum.
**Join,** join, *vt.* To bind, unite, or connect; to unite in league or marriage; to associate; to add; to couple.—*vi.* To unite; to be close, or in contact; to unite with in marriage, league, etc.—*n.* Place, act, etc., of joining.
**Joiner,** join'ėr, *n.* A mechanic who does the woodwork of houses; a carpenter.
**Joinery,** join'ėr-i, *n.* Carpentry.
**Joining,** join'ing, *n.* A joint, junction.
**Joint,** joint, *n.* A joining; joining of two or more bones; articulation; a fissure in strata; part of an animal cut off by a butcher.—*a.* Joined; united; shared; acting in concert.—*vt.* To form with joints; to fit together; to divide into joints or pieces.—*vi.* To coalesce as by joints, or as parts fitted to each other.
**Jointed,** joint'ed, *p.a.* Having joints or articulations; formed with knots or nodes.
**Jointly,** joint'li, *adv.* In a joint manner; together; unitedly; in concert.
**Joint-stock,** joint'stok, *a.* Pertaining to stock or shares held in company.
**Jointure,** joint'ūr, *n.* Property settled on a woman at marriage to be used after her husband's decease.—*vt.* To settle a jointure upon.
**Joist,** joist, *n.* One of the pieces of timber to which the boards of a floor or the laths of a ceiling are nailed.—*vt.* To fit with joists.
**Joke,** jōk, *n.* A jest; something said to excite a laugh; raillery; what is not in earnest.—*vi.* (joking, joked). To jest; to sport.—*vt.* To cast jokes at; to rally.
**Joker,** jōk'ėr, *n.* One who jokes; a merry fellow; odd card in pack, used in some games as highest trump.
**Jokingly,** jōk'ing-li, *adv.* In a joking way.
**Jole, Joll,** jōl, *n.* Same as *Jowl.*
**Jolly,** jol'i, *a.* Merry; gay; mirthful; jovial; festive; plump and agreeable in appearance.
**Jolly-boat,** jol'i-bōt, *n.* A ship's boat, about 12 feet in length with a bluff bow.
**Jolt,** jōlt, *vi.* and *t.* To shake with sudden jerks.—*n.* A shake by a sudden jerk.
**Jonquil,** jon'kwil, *a.* A species of narcissus or daffodil.
**Jorum,** jō'rum, *n.* A term for a drinking vessel with liquor in it.
**Joss,** jos, *n.* A Chinese idol.
**Joss-stick,** jos'stik, *n.* In China, a small reed covered with the dust of odoriferous woods, and burned before an idol.
**Jostle,** jos'l, *vt.* (jostling, jostled). To push or knock against.—*vi.* To hustle.
**Jot,** jot, *n.* An iota; a tittle.—*vt.* (jotting, jotted). To set down in writing.
**Jotting,** jot'ing, *n.* A memorandum.
**Journal,** jėr'nal, *n.* A diary; an account of daily transactions, or the book containing such; a daily or periodical paper; a narrative of the transactions of a society, etc.; that part of an axle which moves in the bearings.
**Journalism,** jėr'nal-izm, *n.* Occupation of writing in, or conducting a journal.
**Journalist,** jėr'nal-ist, *n.* The writer of a journal; a newspaper editor or contributor.
**Journey,** jėr'ni, *n.* A travelling from one place to another; tour; excursion; distance travelled.—*vi.* To travel from place to place.
**Journeyman,** jėr'ni-man, *n.* A workman who has fully learned his trade.
**Joust,** jöst, *n.* A fight on horseback man to man with lances.—*vi.* To engage in fight with lances on horseback; to tilt.
**Jovial,** jō'vi-al, *a.* Gay; merry; jolly.
**Joviality,** jō-vi-al'i-ti, *n.* Festivity; merriment.
**Jovially,** jō'vi-al-li, *adv.* In a jovial manner.
**Jowl,** jōl, *n.* The cheek.—**Cheek by jowl,** with heads close together; side by side.
**Joy,** joi, *n.* Pleasure caused by the acquisition or expectation of good; delight; exultation; cause of joy or happiness.—*vi.* To rejoice; to be glad.—*vt.* To gladden.
**Joyful,** joi'ful, *a.* Full of joy, blithe; gleeful; joyous; happy; blissful; exulting.
**Joyfully,** joi'ful-li, *adv.* In a joyful manner; gladly.
**Joyous,** joi'us, *a.* Experiencing joy; causing joy; glad; gay; happy; delightful.
**Jubilant,** jū'bi-lant, *a.* Uttering songs of triumph; rejoicing; shouting with joy.
**Jubilation,** jū-bi-lā'shon, *n.* A rejoicing; exultation; feeling of triumph.
**Jubilee,** jū'bi-lē, *n.* Among the Jews, every fiftieth year; a season of great public joy; a celebration of a reign, marriage, etc., after it has lasted fifty years.
**Judaic, Judaical,** jū-dā'ik, jū-dā'ik-al, *a.* Pertaining to the Jews.
**Judaism,** jū'dā-izm, *n.* The religious doctrines and rites of the Jews; conformity to the Jewish rites and ceremonies.
**Judaize,** jū'dā-īz, *vi.* and *t.* To conform to the religious doctrines and rites of the Jews.
**Judas,** jū'das, *n.* A treacherous person.
**Judge,** juj, *n.* A civil officer who hears and determines causes in courts; one who has skill to decide on anything; a critic; a connoisseur.—*vi.* (judging, judged). To act as an judge; to pass sentence; to form an opinion; to estimate.—*vt.* To hear and determine; to examine into and decide; to try; to esteem.
**Judgeship,** juj'ship, *n.* Office of a judge.
**Judgment,** juj'ment, *n.* Act of judging; good sense; discernment; opinion or estimate; mental faculty by which man ascertains the relations between ideas; sentence pronounced; a calamity regarded as a punishment of sin; final trial of the human race.
**Judicative,** jū'di-kā-tiv, *a.* Having power to judge.
**Judicatory,** jū'di-kā-to-ri, *a.* Pertaining to the passing of judgment; dispensing justice.—*n.* A court of justice; administration of justice.
**Judicature,** jū'di-kā-tūr, *n.* Power of distributing justice; a court of justice; extent of jurisdiction of a judge or court.
**Judicial,** jū-di'shal, *a.* Pertaining to courts of justice; inflicted as a penalty or in judgment; enacted by law or statute.
**Judicially,** jū-di'shal-li, *adv.* In a judicial manner; by a court of justice.
**Judiciary,** jū-di'shi-a-ri, *a.* Relating to courts of justice.—*n.* The system of courts of justice in a government; the judges taken collectively.
**Judicious,** jū-di'shus, *a.* Prudent; sagacious.
**Judiciously,** jū-di'shus-li, *adv.* Discreetly.
**Jug,** jug, *n.* A vessel for liquors, generally with a handle; a mug; a pitcher.—*vt.* (jugging, jugged). To put in a jug; to cook by putting into a jug, and this into boiling water (*jugged* hare).
**Jugate,** jū'gāt, *a.* Coupled together, as leaflets in compound leaves.
**Juggernaut,** jug'ėr-nat, *n.* Any idea, custom, etc., to which one devotes himself or is ruthlessly

sacrificed.

**Juggle,** jug'l, *vi.* (juggling; juggled). To play tricks by sleight of hand; to practice imposture.—*vt.* To deceive by artifice.—*n.* A trick by legerdemain; an imposture.

**Juggler,** jug'lėr, *n.* One who juggles.

**Jugular,** jụ'gū-lėr, *a.* Pertaining to the throat or neck.

**Juice,** jūs, *n.* Sap of vegetables, especially fruit; fluid part of animal substances.

**Juicy,** jūs'i, *a.* Abounding with juice.

**Jujitsu,** jö-jit'sö, *n.* A style of Japanese wrestling based on a knowledge of muscular action.

**Jujube,** jū'jūb, *n.* The fruit of a piny shrub or small tree; the tree itself; a confection made with gum-arabic or gelatine.

**Julep,** jū'lep, *n.* A sweet drink.

**Julian,** jū'li-an, *a.* Pertaining to or derived from Julius Caesar.

**July,** jū-lī', *n.* The seventh month of the year.

**Jumble,** jum'bl, *vt.* (jumbling, jumbled). To mix in a confused mass.—*vi.* To meet, mix, or unite in a confused manner.—*n.* Confused mass; disorder; confusion.

**Jump,** jump, *vi.* To leap; to skip; to spring; to agree, tally, coincide.—*vt.* To pass over by a leap; to pass over hastily.—*n.* Act of jumping; leap; spring; bound.

**Jumper,** jump'ėr, *n.* One who or that which jumps; a long iron chisel; a loose blouse or jersey worn by women.

**Junction,** jungk'shon, *n.* Act or operation of joining; state of being joined; point of union; place where railways meet.

**Juncture,** jungk'tūr, *n.* A joining or uniting; line or point of joining; point of time; point rendered critical by circumstances.

**June,** jūn, *n.* The sixth month of the year.

**Jungle,** jung'gl, *n.* Land covered with trees, brushwood, etc., or coarse, reedy vegetation.

**Junior,** jū'ni-ėr, *a.* Younger; later or lower in office or rank.—*n.* A person younger than another or lower in standing.

**Juniper,** jū'ni-pėr, *n.* A coniferous shrub, the berries of which are used to flavor gin.

**Junk,** jungk, *n.* Pieces of old rope; salt beef supplied to vessels; a large flat-bottomed seagoing vessel used in China, a chunk.

**Junket,** jung'ket, *n.* Curds mixed with cream, sweetened and flavored; a sweetmeat; a feast.—*vi.* and *t.* To feast.

**Junta,** jun'ta, *n.* A meeting; a junto; a grand Spanish council of state.

**Junto,** jun'tō, *n.* A select council which deliberates in secret on any affair or government; a faction; a cabal.

**Jupiter,** jū'pi-tėr, *n.* The chief deity of the Romans; the largest and brightest planet.

**Jurassic,** jū-ras'ik, *a.* Of or belonging to the formation of the *Jura* Mountains; Oolitic.

**Juridical,** jū-rid'ik-al, *a.* Relating to the administration of justice or to a judge.

**Jurisconsult,** jū'ris-kon-sult, *n.* Anyone learned in jurisprudence; a jurist.

**Jurisdiction,** jū-ris-dik'shon, *n.* Judicial power; right of exercising authority; district within which power may be exercised.

**Jurisprudence,** jū-ris-prö'dens, *n.* The science of law; the knowledge of the laws, customs, and rights of men necessary for the due administration of justice.

**Jurist,** jū'rist, *n.* A man who professes the science of law; one versed in the law, or more particularly, in the civil law.

**Juror,** jū'rėr, *n.* One who serves on a jury.

**Jury,** jū'ri, *n.* A number of men selected according to law and sworn to declare the truth on the evidence; a body who jointly decides as to prizes.—*a.* In *ships*, applied to a temporary substitute, as a *jury*-mast.

**Just,** just, *a.* Right; acting rightly; upright, impartial; fair; due; merited; exact.—*adv.* Exactly; precisely; near or nearly; almost; merely; barely.

**Justice,** jus'tis, *n.* Quality of being just; rectitude; propriety; impartiality; fairness; just treatment; merited reward or punishment; a judge holding a special office.

**Justifiable,** just'i-fī-a-bl, *a.* That may be justified; warrantable; excusable.

**Justifiably,** just'i-fī-a-bli, *adv.* In a justifiable manner; rightly.

**Justification,** just'i-fi-kā''shon, *n.* Act of justifying; state of being justified; vindication; defense; remission of sin.

**Justificatory,** just-if'i-kā-to-ri, *a.* Tending to justify; vindicatory; defensory.

**Justify,** just'i-fī, *vt.* (justifying, justified). To prove or show to be just; to defend or maintain; to excuse; to judge rightly of; to adjust.

**Justly,** just'li, *adv.* Rightly; fairly; properly.

**Justness,** just'nes, *n.* Quality of being just; uprightness; equity.

**Jut,** jut, *vi.* (jutting, jutted). To project beyond the main body.—*n.* A projection.

**Jute,** jūt, *n.* A fibrous substance from an Indian plant of the linden family, used for carpets, bagging, etc.; the plant itself.

**Juvenescent,** jū-ve-nes'ent, *a.* Becoming young.

**Juvenile,** jū've-nīl, *a.* Young; youthful; pertaining to youth.—*n.* A young person.

**Juxtapose,** juks-ta-pōz', *vt.* To place near or next. Also **Juxtaposit**, jux-ta-poz'it.

**Juxtaposition,** juks'ta-pō-si''shon, *n.* A placeing or being placed near.



# K

**Kafir, Kaffir,** kaf'ėr, *n.* A member of the most improtant dark race in S. Africa.

**Kaftan,** kaf'tan, *n.* A kind of long vest with long hanging sleeves, tied at the waist with a girdle, worn in the East.

**Kail, Kale,** kāl, *n.* A kind of cabbage; colewort; cabbage or greens in general.

**Kaiser,** kī'zėr, *n.* An emperor.

**Kaleidoscope,** ka-lī'dos-kōp, *n.* An optical instrument which exhibits an endless variety of colored figures.

**Kangaroo,** kang'ga-rö, *n.* An Australian marsupial quadruped that moves forward by leaps.

**Karoo, Karroo,** ka-rö', *n.* An arid tract of clayey table-lands in S. Africa.

**Kedge,** kej, *n.* A small anchor.—*vt.* To warp (a ship) by a rope attached to a kedge.

**Keel,** kēl, *n.* The principal timber in a ship, extending from stem to stern at the bottom; the corresponding part in iron vessels; the whole ship; something resembling a keel; a coal-barge.—*vi.* To capsize.

**Keelhaul,** kēl'häl, *vt.* To punish by dropping into the sea on the one side of a ship and hauling up on the other.

**Keelson,** kēl'sun or kel'sun, *n.* An internal keel over the external keel.

**Keen,** kēn, *a.* Acute of mind; shrewd; sharp; eager; piercing; severe; bitter.

**Keenly,** kēn'li, *adv.* In a keen manner; eagerly; acutely; sharply; severely; bitterly.

**Keep,** kēp, *vt.* (keeping, kept). To hold; to preserve; to guard; to detain; to attend to; to continue any state, course, or action; to obey; to perform; to observe or solemnize; to confine to one's own knowledge; not to betray; to have in pay.—*vi.* To endure; not to perish or be impaired.—*n.* Care; guard; sustenance; a donjon or strong tower.

**Keeper,** kēp'ėr, *n.* One who has the care or custody of persons or things; a gamekeeper; a ring which keeps another on the finger.

**Keeping,** kēp'ing, *n.* A holding; custody; support; conformity; harmony.

**Keepsake,** kēp'sāk, *a.* Anything kept or given to be kept for the sake of the giver.

**Keeve,** kēv, *n.* A large vessel to ferment liquors in; a mashing-tub.
**Keg,** keg, *n.* A small cask or barrel.
**Kelp,** kelp, *n.* Large sea-weeds; alkaline substance yielded by sea-weeds when burned.
**Kelson,** kel'sun, *n.* Same as *Keelson.*
**Kelt, Keltic,** kelt, kel'tik, *See* CELT, CELTIC.
**Kelt,** kelt, *n.* A salmon in its spent state after spawning; a foul fish.
**Ken,** ken, *vt.* To know; to descry.—*n.* View; reach of sight; cognizance.
**Kennel,** ken'el, *n.* A house or cot for dogs; a pack of hounds; hole of a fox, etc.; a haunt; a gutter.—*vi.* and *t.* (kenneling, kenneled). To lodge in a kennel.
**Kerchief,** kėr'chif, *n.* A cloth to cover the head; any loose cloth used in dress.
**Kermes,** kėr'mēz, *n.* A scarlet dye-stuff consisting of the bodies of certain insects found on oak-trees round the Mediterranean.
**Kernel,** kėr'nel, *n.* The edible substance contained in the shell of a nut; the core; the gist.—*vi.* (kernelling, kernelled). To harden or ripen into kernels, as the seeds of plants.
**Kerosene,** ke'ro-sēn, *n.* A lamp-oil from petroleum, extensively used in America.
**Kersey,** kėr'zi, *n.* A species of coarse woollen cloth, usually ribbed.—*a.* Homespun; homely.
**Kerseymere,** kėr'zi-mēr, *n.* Cassimere.
**Kestrel,** kes'trel, *n.* A small British falcon.
**Ketch,** kech, *n.* A strongly built vessel, usually two-masted.
**Ketchup,** kech'up, *n.* A thick sauce for meat, fish, etc.: (**tomato ketchup**) of tomatoes: also **catsup, catchup.**
**Kettle,** ket'l, *n.* A vessel of iron or other metal, used for heating and boiling water, etc.
**Kettle-drum,** ket'l-drum, *n.* A drum made of a copper vessel covered with parchment.
**Key,** kē,*n.* An instrument for shutting or opening a lock; a little lever by which certain musical instruments are played on by the fingers; fundamental tone in a piece of music; that which serves to explain a cipher, etc.—*vt.* To furnish or fasten with a key.
**Key-board,** kē'bōrd, *n.* The series of levers in a keyed musical instrument upon which the fingers press.
**Keyed,** kēd, *a.* Furnished with keys; set to a key, as a tune.
**Keystone,** kē'stōn, *n.* The top stone of an arch, which, being the last put in, enters like a wedge, and fastens the work together.
**Khaki,** kä'ki, *a.* Of a brownish-yellow earth color.—*n.* A brownish-yellow earthy color; cloth of this color worn by soldiers.
**Khan,** kan, *n.* In Asia, a governor; a prince; a chief; an eastern inn; a caravansary.
**Kibble,** kib'l, *n.* A large bucket used in mining.
**Kick,** kik, *vt.* To strike with the foot; to strike in recoiling, as a gun.—*vi.* To strike with the foot or feet; to manifest opposition to restraint; to recoil.—*n.* A blow with the foot or feet; recoil of a firearm.
**Kickshaw,** kik'sha, *n.* Something fantastical; a light unsubstantial dish.
**Kid,** kid, *n.* A young goat; leather made from its skin; a small wooden tub.—*vt.* (kidding, kidded). To bring forth a kid.
**Kidnap,** kid'nap, *vt.* (kidnapping, kidnapped). To steal or forcibly abduct a human being.
**Kidney,** kid'ni, *n.* Either of the two glands which secret the urine; sort or character.
**Kilderkin,** kil'dėr-kin, *n.* A small barrel; the eighth part of a hogshead.
**Kill,** kil, *vt.* To deprive of life; to slay; to slaughter for food; to deaden (pain); to overpower.
**Killing,** kil'ing, *p.a.* Depriving of life; overpowering; dangerous.
**Kiln,** kil, *n.* A fabric of brick or stone, which may be heated to harden or dry anything.
**Kilogram,** kil'ō-gram, *n.* A French measure of weight, being 1000 grams or 2.2 lbs. avoir.
**Kiloliter,** kil'ō-lē-tr, *n.* A French measure, 1000 liters or 220.09 gallons.
**Kilometer,** kil'ō-mā-tr, *n.* A French measure; 1000 meters, about 5/8 of a mile or 1093.633 yards.
**Kilostere,** kil'ō-stār, *n.* A French solid measure equal to 35317.41 cubic feet.
**Kilt,** kilt, *n.* A kind of short petticoat worn by the Highlanders of Scotland in lieu of trousers.—*vt.* To tuck up or plait like a kilt.
**Kilted,** kilt'ed, *a.* Wearing a kilt.
**Kimono,** kim-ō'nō, *n.* A loose robe with short wide sleeves, worn by both sexes in Japan; a type of dressing-gown.
**Kin,** kin, *n.* Race; family; consanguinity or affinity; kindred.—*a.* Kindred; congenial.
**Kind,** kīnd, *n.* Race; genus; variety; nature; character.—**In kind,** to pay with produce or commodities.—*a.* Humane; having tenderness or goodness of nature; benevolent; friendly.
**Kindergarten,** kin'dėr-gär-tn, *n.* An infants' school in which amusements are systematically combined with instruction.
**Kindle,** kin'dl, *vt.* (kindling, kindled). To set on fire; to light; to rouse; to excite to action.—*vi.* To take fire; to be roused or exasperated.
**Kindly,** kīnd'li, *a.* Of a kind disposition; congenial; benevolent; mild.—*adv.* In a kind manner; favorably.
**Kindness,** kind'nes, *n.* Quality or state of being kind; benevolence; a kind act.
**Kindred,** kin'dred, *n.* Relationship by birth; affinity; relatives by blood.—*a.* Related; of like nature; cognate.
**Kine,** kīn, old *pl.* of *cow.*
**Kinematic,** ki-nē-mat'ik, *a.* Pertaining to kinematics. Also *Kinematical.*
**Kinematics,** ki-nē-mat'iks, *n.* That branch of mechanics which treats of motion without reference to the forces producing it.
**Kinetic,** ki-net'ik, *a.* Causing motion: applied to force actually exerted.
**Kinetics,** ki-net'iks, *n.* That branch of dynamics which treats of forces causing or changing motion in bodies.
**King,** king, *n.* The sovereign of a nation; monarch; a playing card having the picture of a king; chief piece in the game of chess; in draughts, a piece which has reached the opponent's base, and which can move backwards as well as forwards.
**Kingdom,** king'dum, *n.* The dominion of a king; realm; a primary division of natural objects (*e.g.* the mineral kingdom); place where anything prevails and holds sway.
**Kingfisher,** king'fish-ėr, *n.* A bird having splendid plumage which preys on fish.
**Kinglike,** king'lik, *a.* Like a king.
**Kingly,** king'li, *a.* LIke a king; belonging to a king; royal; regal; splendid.
**Kingship,** king'ship, *n.* The state, office, or dignity of a king; royalty.
**Kink,** kingk, *n.* A twist in a rope or thread; a crotchet.—*vi.* To twist or run into knots.
**Kinsfolk,** kinz'fōlk, *n.* People of the same kin; kindred; relations.
**Kinsman,** kinz'man, *n.* A man of the same kin; a relative.
**Kiosk,** ki-osk', *n.* A Turkish word signifying a kind of open pavilion or summer-house; a small roofed stall or booth.
**Kipper,** kip'ėr, *n.* A salmon at the spawning season; a fish split open, salted, and dried or smoked.—*vt.* To cure (fish) by splitting open, salting, and drying.
**Kirk,** kėrk, *n.* A church (Scot.).
**Kirtle,** kėr'tl, *n.* A short skirt.
**Kismet,** kis'met, *n.* Fate or destiny.
**Kiss,** kis, *vi.* To touch with the lips; to caress by joining lips; to touch gently.—*vi.* To join lips; to come in slight contact.—*n.* A salute given with the lips.
**Kit,** kit, *n.* A wooden tub for fish, butter, etc.; an outfit.

**Kit-cat,** kit'kat, *a.* and *n.* A term applied to any portrait about half-length in which the hands are shown.
**Kitchen,** ki'chen, *n.* The room of a house appropriated to cooking.
**Kitchen-garden,** ki'chen-gär-dn, *n.* A garden for raising vegetables for the table.
**Kitchen-range,** ki'chen-rānj, *n.* A kitchen-grate.
**Kite,** kīt, *n.* A bird of the falcon family; a light frame of wood and paper constructed for flying in the air.
**Kith,** kith, *n.* Relatives or friends collectively.
**Kitten,** kit'n, *n.* A young cat.—*vi.* To bring forth young, as a cat.
**Kleptomania,** klep-tō-mā'ni-a, *n.* An irresistible mania for pilfering.
**Knack,** nak, *n.* Facility of performance; dexterity.
**Knag,** nag, *n.* A knot in wood; a wart; the shoot of a deer's horn.
**Knaggy,** nag'i, *a.* Knotty; full of knots.
**Knap,** nap, *vt.* (knapping, knapped). To break short (as flints); to snap; to bite off.—*n.* A short sharp noise; a snap.
**Knapsack,** nap'sak, *n.* A bag for necessaries borne on the back by soldiers, etc.
**Knar, Knarl,** när, närl, *n.* A knot in wood.
**Knave,** nāv, *n.* A petty rascal; a dishonest man; a card with a soldier or servant on it.
**Knavery,** nāv'ė-ri, *n.* The practices of a knave; dishonesty; roguery.
**Knavish,** nāv'ish, *a.* Partaking of knavery; dishonest; roguish.
**Knead,** nēd, *vt.* To work into a mass or suitable consistency for bread, etc.
**Kneading-trough,** nēd'ing-trof, *n.* A trough in which dough is kneaded.
**Knee,** nē, *n.* The joint connecting the two principal parts of the leg; a similar joint; piece of bent timber or iron used in a ship, etc.
**Knee-breeches,** nē'brēch-ez, *n.pl.* Breeches that reach only to the knee.
**Knee-cap,** nē'kap, *n.* The movable bone covering the knee-joint in front.
**Kneed,** nēd, *a.* Having knees; having a bend like a knee.
**Kneel,** nēl, *vi.* (pret. and pp. kneeled and knelt). To bend the knee; to rest on the bended knees.
**Knell,** nel, *n.* The sound of a bell rung at a funeral; a death signal.—*vi.* To sound, as a funeral bell; to toll; to sound as a bad omen.
**Knickerbockers,** nik'ėr-bok-ėrz, *n.pl.* A kind of loosely fitting knee-breeches. Also **Knickers.**.
**Knick-knack,** nik'nak, *n.* A trinket.
**Knife,** nīf, *n.*; pl. **Knives,** nīvz. A cutting instrument consisting of a blade attached to a handle; cutting part of a machine.
**Knight,** nīt, *n.* Formerly one admitted to a certain military rank; now one who holds a dignity entitling him to have *Sir* prefixed to his name, but not hereditary; a champion; a piece in chess.—*vt.* To dub or create a knight.
**Knight-errant,** nīt-e'rant, *n.* A knight who travelled in search of adventures.
**Knighthood,** nīt'hud, *n.* The character, rank, or dignity of a knight; knightage.
**Knightly,** nīt'lī, *a.* Pertaining to a night.—*adv.* In a manner becoming a knight.
**Knit,** nit, *vt.* (knitting, knitted or knit). To tie in a knot; to form in a fabric by looping a continuous thread; to unite closely; to draw together; to contract.—*vi.* To interweave a continuous thread; to grow together.
**Knitting,** nit'ing, *n.* Formation of a fabric by knitting-needles; fabric thus formed.
**Knob,** nob, *a.* A hard protuberance; a boss; a round ball at the end of anything.
**Knobbed,** nobd, *p.a.* Containing knobs.
**Knobby,** nob'i, *a.* Full of knobs; hard.
**Knock,** nok, *vt.* To strike with something thick or heavy; to strike against; to clash.—*vi.* To strike.—*n.* A stroke; a blow; a rap.
**Knocker,** nok'ėr, *n.* One who knocks; something on a door for knocking.
**Knoll,** nōl, *n.* A little round hill; ringing of a bell; knell.—*vt.* and *i.* To sound, as a bell.
**Knot,** not, *n.* A complication of threads or cords; a tie; ornamental bunch of ribbon, etc.; hard protuberant joint of a plant; a knob; bunch; group; a difficult question; a natutical mile (= 1.151 ordinary mile).—*vt.* (knotting, knotted). To tie in a knot; to unite closely.—*vi.* To become knotted; to knit knots.
**Knotted,** not'ed, *p.a.* Full of knots.
**Knotty,** not'i, *a.* Full of knots; difficult; intricate.
**Knout,** nout, *n.* A powerful whip formerly used as an instrument of punishment in Russia.
**Know,** nō, *vt.* (pret. knew, pp. known). To perceive with certainty; to understand; to be aware of; to distinguish; to be acquainted with; to have experience of.—*vi.* To have knowledge; not to be doubtful.
**Knowable,** nō'a-bl, *a.* That may be known.
**Knowing,** nō'ing, *p.a.* Well informed; intelligent; significant; cunning.
**Knowingly,** nō'ing-li, *adv.* In a knowing manner; with knowledge; intentionally.
**Knowledge,** nol'ej, *n.* The result or condition of knowing; clear perception; learning; information; skill; acquaintance.
**Known,** nōn, *p.a.* Understood; familiar.
**Knuckle,** nuk'l, *n.* The joint of a finger, particularly at its base; knee-joint of a calf or pig.—*vt.* (knuckling, knuckled). To strike with the knuckles.—**To knuckle down,** or **under,** to yield.
**Koran,** kō'ran, *n.* The book regulating the faith and practice of Mohammedans, written by Mohammed.
**Kow-tow,** kou-tou', *n.* Formerly the mode of saluting the Emperor of China by prostrating oneself and touching the ground with the forehead nine times.—*vi.* To perform the kow-tow.
**Kraall,** kräl, *n.* A S. African native village.
**Kriegspiel,** krēg'spēl, *n.* A game played with pieces representing troops.
**Kudos,** kū'dos, *n.* Glory; fame; renown.
**Kyanize,** kī'an-īz, *vt.* To preserve (timber) from dry-rot by steeping in a solution of corrosive sublimate.

L

# L

**La,** la, *exclam.* Lo! look! see! behold!
**Laager,** lä'ger, *n.* In S. Africa, an encampment; a temporary defensive inclosure formed of wagons.—*vi.* To encamp.
**Label,** lā'bel, *n.* A slip of paper, etc., affixed to something and stating name, contents, etc.; a slip affixed to deeds to hold the seal.—*vt.* (labelling, labelled). To affix a label to.
**Labial,** lā'bi-al, *a.* Pertaining to the lips.—*n.* A vowel or consonant formed chiefly by the lips, as *b, m, p, o.*
**Labium,** lā'bi-um, *n.* A lip, especially the lower lip of insects.
**Laboratory,** lab-or'a-to-ri, *n.* A building or room for experiment in chemistry, physics, etc.; a chemist's work-room.
**Labor,** lā'bėr, *n.* Exertion, physical or mental; toil; work done or to be done; laborers in the aggregate; the pangs and efforts of childbirth.—*vi.* To engage in labor; to work; to proceed with difficulty; to be burdened.—*vt.* To cultivate; to prosecute with effort.
**Labored,** lā'bėrd, *p.a.* Produced with labor; bearing the marks of effort.
**Laborer,** lā'bėr-ėr, *n.* One who labors; a man who does work that requires little skill, as distinguished from an artisan.
**Laborious,** la-bō'ri-us, *a.* Full of labor; arduous; diligent; assiduous.
**Labrum,** lā'brum, *n.* An upper or outer lip.
**Laburnum,** la-bėr'num, *n.* A leguminous tree, with clusters of yellow flowers.
**Labyrinth,** lab'i-rinth, *n.* A place full of intrica-

cies; a maze; an inexplicable difficulty; a part of the internal ear.

**Lac**, lak, *n*. A resinous substance produced by insects on trees in Asia; in the East Indies.

**Lace**, lās, *n*. A cord used for fastening boots, etc.; ornamental cord or braid; a delicate fabric of interlacing threads.—*vt*. (lacing, laced). To fasten with a lace; to adorn with lace; to interlace; to mingle in small quantity.

**Lacerate**, la'sėr-āt, *vt*. To tear; to rend; to torture; to harrow.

**Laceration**, la-sėr-ā'shon, *n*. Act of lacerating; the breach made by rending.

**Laches**, lach'es or lash'ez, *n*. Neglect; negligence; remissness; inexcusable delay.

**Lachrymal**, lak'rim-al, *a*. Generating or secreting tears; pertaining to tears.

**Lachrymary**, lak'rim-a-ri, *a*. Containing tears.

**Lachrymatory**, lak'rim-a-to-ri, *n*. A small vessel found in ancient sepulchers, for holding the tears of a deceased person's friends.

**Lachrymose**, lak'rim-ōs, *a*. Full of tears; tearful in a sentimental way; lugubrious.

**Lacing**, lās'ing, *n*. A fastening with a lace or cord; a cord used in fastening.

**Lack**, lak, *vt*. To want; to be without; to need; to require.—*vi*. To be in want.—*n*. Want; deficiency; need; failure.

**Lackadaisical**, lak-a-dā'zik-al, *a*. Affectedly pensive; weakly sentimental.

**Lackey**, lak'i, *n*. A footboy or footman.—*vt*. and *i*. To attend as a lackey, or servilely.

**Lack-luster**, lak'lus-tėr, *a*. Wanting luster.

**Laconic, Laconical**, la-kon'ik, la-kon'ik-al, *a*. Expressing much in a few words; brief; sententious; pithy.

**Laconism, Laconicism**, la'kon-izm, la-kon'i-sizm, *n*. A concise style; a sententious expression.

**Lacquer**, lak'ėr, *n*. A varnish containing lac, etc.; ware coated with lacquer.—*vt*. To varnish or coat with lacquer.

**Lacros**, la-kros', *n*. A game at ball, played with a large battledore or *crosse*.

**Lactation**, lak-tā'shon, *n*. Act or time of giving suck; function of secreting milk.

**Lacteal**, lak'tē-al, *a*. Pertaining to milk; conveying chyle.—*n*. A vessel in animal bodies for conveying the chyle from the alimentary canal.

**Lactescent**, lak-tes'ent, *a*. Becoming milky; having a milky appearance or consistence.

**Lactic**, lak'tik, *a*. Procured from milk.

**Lactine, Lactose**, lak'tin, lak'tōs, *n*. Sugar of milk.

**Lactometer**, lak-tom'et-ėr, *n*. An instrument for ascertaining the quality of milk.

**Lacuna**, la-kū'na, *n*.; pl. **-nae**. A small depression; a blank space; gap; hiatus.

**Lacustrine, Lacustral**, la-kus'trīn, la-kus'tral, *a*. Pertaining to a lake.

**Lacy**, lās'i, *a*. Resembling lace.

**Lad**, lad, *n*. A stripling; a young man.

**Ladanum**, lad'a-num, *n*. The resinous juice which exudes from several species of cistus in Spain, Portugal, Crete, Syria, etc.

**Ladder**, lad'ėr, *n*. An article of wood, rope, etc., consisting of two long side-pieces connected by cross-pieces forming steps; means of rising to mienence; vertical flaw in stocking, etc.

**Lade**, lād, *vt*. (lading, pret. laded, pp. laded, laden). To load; to throw in or out (a fluid) with some utensil.

**Laden**, lād'n, *p.a*. Loaded; burdened.

**Lading**, lād'ing, *n*. That which constitutes a load or cargo; freight; burden.

**Ladle**, lā'dl, *n*. A utensil with a long handle for serving out liquor from a vessel.—*vt*. (lading, ladled). To serve with a ladle.

**Lady**, lā'di, *n*. A woman of rank or distinction, or of good breeding; a title given to a woman whose husband is not of lower rank than a knight; or whose father was not lower than an earl; the mistress of an estate.

**Lady-bird**, lā'di-bėrd, *n*. A small British beetle, the larva of which feeds on plant-lice.

**Lady-day**, lā'di-dā, *n*. The day of the annunciation of the Virgin Mary, March 25th.

**Lady-like**, lā'di-līk, *a*. Like a lady in manners.

**Ladyship**, lā'di-ship, *n*. Condition or rank of a lady; used as a title.

**Lag**, lag, *a*. Coming behind; sluggish; tardy.—*n*. Quantity of retardation of some movement.—*vi*. (lagging, lagged). To loiter, tarry.

**Lager-beer**, lä'gėr-bēr, *n*. A German beer stored for some months before use.

**Laggard**, lag'ärd, *a*. Slow; sluggish; backward.—*n*. One who lags; a loiterer.

**Lagoon, Lagune**, la-gön', *n*. A shallow lake connected with the sea or a river.

**Laic**, lā'ik, *a*. Belonging to the laity.—*n*. A layman.

**Laicize**, lā'i-sīz, *vt*. To make lay or laic; to deprive of clerical character.

**Lair**, lār, *n*. A place to lie or rest; the resting-place of a wild beast, etc.

**Laird**, lārd, *n*. In Scotland, a land-owner or house-proprietor.

**Laisser-faire**, lā-sā-fār', *n*. A letting alone, non-interference.

**Laity**, lā'i-ti, *n*. The people, as distinguished from the clergy; non-professional people.

**Lake**, lāk, *n*. A body of water wholly surrounded by land; a pigment of earthy substance with red (or other) coloring matter.

**Lama**, lā'mä, *n*. A priest of the variety of Buddhism in Tibet and Mongolia.

**Lamb**, lam, *n*. The young of the sheep; one as gentle or innocent as a lamb.—*vi*. To bring forth young, as sheep.

**Lambkin**, lam'kin, *n*. A little lamb.

**Lame**, lām, *a*. Crippled in a limb or limbs; disabled; limping; defective; not satisfactory; not smooth.—*vt*. (laming, lamed). To make lame; to render imperfect and unsound.

**Lamella**, la-mel'la, *n*.; pl. **Lamellae**. A thin plate or scale.

**Lamellar**, la-mel'lėr, *a*. Composed of thin plates.

**Lamellibranchiate**, la-mel'li-brang''ki-āt, *a*. Having lamellar gills and bivalve shells, as mussels, oysters, etc.

**Lamely**, lām'li, *adv*. In a lame manner; poorly; feebly.

**Lament**, la-ment', *vi*. To express sorrow; to weep; to grieve.—*vt*. To bewail; to deplore.—*n*. A lamentation; an elegy or mournful ballad.

**Lamentable**, la'ment-a-bl, *a*. To be lamented; doleful; miserable; wretched.

**Lamentably**, la'ment-a-bli, *adv*. In a lamentable manner.

**Lamentation**, la-ment-ā'shon, *n*. Act of lamenting; expression of sorrow; complaint.

**Lamina**, la'mi-na, *n*.; pl. **-nae**. A thin plate or scale; a layer lying over another; the blade of a leaf.

**Laminar**, la'mi-när, *a*. In thin plates.

**Lamination**, la-mi-nā'shon, *n*. State of being laminated; arrangement in laminae.

**Lammas**, lam'mas, *n*. The first day of August.

**Lamp**, lamp, *n*. A vessel for containing oil to be burned by means of a wick; any contrivance for supply artificial light.

**Lampblack**, lamp'blak, *n*. A pigment made from the fine soot of gas, oil, etc.

**Lampoon**, lam-pön', *n*. A scurrilous or personal satire in writing; a satiric attack.—*vt*. To write a lampoon against.

**Lamprey**, lam'prā, *n*. The name of eel-like, scaleless fishes with suctorial mouths, inhabiting fresh and salt waters.

**Lanate**, lā'nāt, *a*. Woolly.

**Lance**, lans, *n*. A weapon consisting of a long shaft with a sharp-pointed head; a long spear.—*vt*. (lancing, lanced). To pierce with a lance; to open with a lancet.

**Lanceolate**, lan'sē-o-lāt, *a*. Shaped like a lance-head.

**Lancer,** lans'ėr, *n.* One who lances; a cavalry soldier armed with a lance.
**Lancet,** lans'et, *n.* A sharp-pointed and two-edged instrument used in letting blood, etc.
**Lancet-window,** lans'et-win-dō, *n.* A high and narrow window pointed like a lancet.
**Lancinating,** lan'si-nāt-ing, *a.* Piercing: applied to a sharp shooting pain.
**Land,** land, *n.* The solid matter which constitutes the fixed part of the surface of the globe; soil; estate; country; people of a country or region.—*vt.* and *i.* To set or go on the land; to disembark.
**Landau,** lan-da', *n.* A kind of coach whose top may be opened and thrown back.
**Land-breeze,** land'brēz, *n.* A breeze setting from the land toward the sea.
**Landed,** land'ed, *p.a.* Having an estate in land; consisting in real estate or land.
**Landgrave,** land'grāv, *n.* Formerly a title of certain princes of the German empire.
**Landholder,** land'hōld-ėr, *n.* A holder or proprietor of land.
**Landing,** land'ing, *n.* Act of or place for going or setting on shore; level part of a staircase between the flights.
**Landlady,** land'lā-di, *n.* A woman who has property in land, and tenants holding from her; mistress of an inn, etc.
**Landlocked,** land'lokt, *a.* Inclosed by land, or nearly so, as a part of the sea.
**Landloper,** land'lōp-ėr, *n.* A vagrant.
**Landlord,** land'lord, *n.* The lord of land; owner of land or houses who has tenants under him; master of an inn, etc.
**Landlubber,** land'lub-ėr, *n.* A seaman's term of contempt for one not a sailor.
**Landmark,** land'märk, *n.* A mark to designate the boundary of land; an object on land that serves as a guide to seamen.
**Land-mine,** land'mīn, *n.* A bomb dropped by means of a parachute.
**Land-owner,** land'ōn-ėr, *n.* The owner or proprietor of land.
**Land-rail,** land'rāl, *n.* The corn-crake.
**Landscape,** land'skāp, *n.* A portion of land which the eye can comprehend in a single view; a country scene; picture representing a piece of country.
**Landslip, Landslide,** land'slip, land'slīd, *n.* A portion of a hill which slips down; the sliding down of a piece of land.
**Landsman,** landz'man, *n.* One who lives on the land; a raw inexperienced sailor.
**Land-steward,** land'stū-ėrd, *n.* A person who has the care of a landed estate.
**Land-surveying,** land'sėr-vā-ing, *n.* Act of surveying land; art of determining the boundaries and extent of land.
**Landward,** land'wėrd, *adv.* Toward the land.—*a.* Inland.
**Lane,** lān, *n.* A narrow way or street; a passage between lines of men.
**Language,** lang'gwāj, *n.* Human speech; speech peculiar to a nation; words especially used in any branch of knowledge; general style of expression; expresson of thought or feeling in any way.
**Languid,** lang'gwid, *a.* Wanting energy; listless; dull or heavy; sluggish.
**Languidly,** lang'gwid li, *adv.* Weakly; feebly.
**Languish,** lang'gwish, *vi.* To be or become faint, feeble or spiritless; to fade; to sink under sorrow or any continued passion; to look with tenderness.
**Languishing,** lang'gwish-ing, *p.a.* Looking softly and tenderly; pining.
**Languishment,** lang'gwish-ment, *n.* State of languishing.
**Languor,** lang'gėr, lang'gwėr, *n.* Languidness; lassitude; a listless or dreamy state.
**Languorous,** lang'gwėr-us, *a.* Characterized by languor
**Lank,** langk, *a.* Loose or lax; not plump; gaunt.
**Lanky,** lang'ki, *a.* Somewhat lank; lean.
**Lanoline,** lan'ō-lin, *n.* A greasy substance obtained from unwashed wool, used as an ointment.
**Lantern,** lan'tėrn, *n.* A case in which a light is carried; part of a lighthouse in which is the light; erection on the top of a dome, etc., to give light; a tower with the interior open to view.—*vt.* To provide with a lantern.
**Lanyard,** lan'yärd, *n.* A short piece of rope or line, used in ships.
**Lap,** lap, *n.* The loose lower part of a garment; the clothes on the knees of a person when sitting; the knees in this position; part of a thing that covers another; single round of a course in races; a lick, as with the tongue; sound as of water rippling on the beach.—*vt.* (lapping, lapped). To lap; to infold; to lick up; to wash gently against.—*vi.* To lie or be turned over; to lick up food; to ripple gently.
**Lapel,** la-pel', *n.* That part of the coat which laps over the facing, etc.
**Lapidary,** lap'i-da-ri, *n.* One who cuts and engraves precious stones.—*a.* Pertaining to the art of cutting stones.
**Lappet,** lap'et, *n.* A little lap or flap on a dress, especially on a head-dress.
**Lapse,** laps, *n.* A slipping or gradual falling; unnoticed passing; a slip; a failing in duty; deviation from rectitude.—*vi.* (lapsing, lapsed). To pass slowly; to glide; to slip in moral conduct; to fail in duty; to pass from one to another by some omission.
**Larceny,** lär'se-ni, *n.* Theft of goods or personal property.
**Larch,** lärch, *n.* A tall cone-bearing tree.
**Lard,** lärd, *n.* The fat of swine, after being melted and separated from the flesh.—*vt.* To apply lard to; to fatten; to stuff with bacon; to interlard.
**Larder,** lärd'ėr, *n.* A room, box, etc., where meat is kept before eating.
**Large,** lärj, *a.* Great in size, number, etc.; not small; copious; big; bulky; wide.—**At large,** without restraint; with all details.
**Large-hearted,** lärj'härt-ed, *a.* Liberal; munificent; generous.
**Largely,** lärj'li, *adv.* Widely; copiously; amply.
**Largess,** lärj-es', *n.* A present; a bounty bestowed.
**Larghetto,** lär-get'tō, *a.* and *adv.* In *music,* somewhat slow, but not so slow as *largo.*
**Largo,** lär'go, *a.* and *adv.* Slow; quicker than *adagio.*
**Lariat,** lä'ri-at, *n.* The lasso; a long cord or thong of leather with a noose used in catching wild horses, etc.
**Lark,** lärk, *n.* A small song-bird; a frolic.
**Larva,** lär'va, *n.*; pl. **Larvae.** An insect in the caterpillar or grub state.
**Larval,** lär'val, *a.* Belonging to a larva.
**Laryngeal, Laryngean,** la-rin-jē'al, la-rin-jē'an, *a.* Pertaining to the larynx.
**Larynx,** la'ringks, *n.*; pl. **Larynxes, Larynges,** la'ringks-ez, la-rin'jēz. The upper part of the windpipe, a cartilaginous cavity serving to modulate the sound of the voice.
**Lascivious,** las-si'vi-us, *a.* Wanton; lewd; lustful.
**Lash,** lash, *n.* The thong of a whip; a whip; a stroke with a whip; a stroke of satire; a cutting remark.—*vt.* To strike with a lash; to satirize; to dash against, as waves; to tie with a rope or cord.—*vi.* To ply the whip; to strike at.
**Lass,** las, *n.* A young woman; a girl.
**Lassitude,** las'i-tūd, *n.* Faintness; languor of body or mind.
**Lasso,** las'sō, *n.* A rope with a running noose, used for catching wild horses, etc.—*vt.* To catch with a lasso.
**Last,** läst, *a.* That comes after all the others; latest; final; next before the present; utmost.—*adv.* The last time; in conclusion.—*vi.* To continue in time; to endure; not to decay or perish.—*vt.* To form on or by a last.—*n.* A mold of the foot on

L

which boots are formed; a weight of 4000 lbs.

**Lasting,** läst'ing, *p.a.* Durable; permanent.—*n.* A species of stiff woollen stuff.

**Lastingly,** läst'ing-li, *adv.* Durably.

**Lastly,** läst'li, *adv.* In the last place; finally.

**Latch,** lach, *n.* A catch for fastening a door.—*vt.* To fasten with a latch.

**Latchet,** lach'et, *n.* The string that fastens a shoe (Archaic).

**Late,** lāt, *a.* Coming after the usual time; slow; not early; existing not long ago, but not now; deceased; recent; modern; last or recently in any place, office, etc.—*adv.* At a late time or period; recently.

**Lateen,** la-tēn', *a.* Said of a triangular sail having its fore edge fastened to an oblique yard.

**Lately,** lāt'li, *adv.* Not long ago; recently.

**Latency,** lā'ten-si, *n.* State of being latent.

**Latent,** lā'tent, *a.* Not apparent; under the surface.

**Lateral,** lat'ėr-al, *a.* Pertaining to or on the side; proceeding from the side.

**Lath,** läth, *n.* A long piece of wood nailed to the rafters to support tiles or plaster.—*vt.* To cover or line with laths.

**Lathe,** lāᴛʜ, *n.* A machine by which articles of wood, etc., are turned and cut into a smooth round form.

**Lather,** laᴛʜ'ėr, *n.* Foam or froth made by soap and water; foam or froth from profuse sweat, as of a horse.—*vt.* To spread over with the foam of soap.—*vi.* To become frothy.

**Lathing,** läth'ing, *n.* A covering made of laths; laths collectively.

**Latin,** laitin, *a.* Pertaining to the Latins, a people of Latium, in Italy; Roman.—*n.* The language of the ancient Romans.

**Latinism,** la'tin-izm, *n.* A Latin idiom.

**Latinist,** la'tin-ist, *n.* One skilled in Latin.

**Latinity,** la-tin'i-ti, *n.* Latin style or idiom; style of writing Latin.

**Latitude,** la'ti-tūd, *n.* Breadth; width; extent from side to side; scope; laxity; distance north or south of the equator, measured on a meridian; distance of a star north or south of the ecliptic.

**Latitudinarian,** la'ti-tūd-in-ā''ri-an, *a.* Indulging in latitude of opinion; lax in religious views.—*n.* One who indulges in latitude of opinion; one not strictly orthodox.

**Latrine,** la-trēn', *n.* A privy, especially one in an institution or camp.

**Latter,** lat'ėr, *a.* Later; opposed to former; mentioned the last of two; modern; lately done or past.

**Latterly,** lat'ėr-li, *adv.* Lately.

**Lattice,** lat'is, *n.* A structure of crossed laths or bars forming small openings like network; a window made of laths crossing like network.—*a.* Furnished with a lattice.—*vt.* To form with cross bars and open work.

**Laud,** lad, *n.* Praise; a hymn of praise; *pl.* a service of the church comprising psalms of praise.—*vt.* To praise; to celebrate.

**Laudable,** lad'a-bl, *a.* Deserving praise; praiseworthy; commendable.

**Laudanum,** la'da-num, *n.* Opium prepared in spirit of wine; tincture of opium.

**Laudation,** la-dā'shon, *n.* Act of lauding; praise.

**Laudatory,** lad'a-to-ri, *a.* Containing praise; tending to praise.—*n.* That which contains praise.

**Laugh,** läf, *vi.* To make the involuntary noise which sudden merriment excites; to treat with some contempt; to appear gay, bright, or brilliant.—*vt.* To express by laughing; to affect or effect by laughter.—*n.* The act of laughing; short fit of laughing.

**Laughable,** läf'a-bl, *a.* That may justly excite laughter; ridiculous; comical.

**Laughably,** läf'a-bli, *adv.* In a laughable manner; ludicrously.

**Laughingly,** läf'ing-li, *adv.* In a merry way; with laughter.

**Laughing-stock,** läf'ing-stok, *n.* An object of ridicule.

**Laughter,** läf'tėr, *n.* Act or sound of laughing, expression of mirth peculiar to man.

**Launch,** länsh or lansh, *vt.* To throw; to cause to slide into the water; to put out into another sphere of duty, etc.—*vi.* To glide, as a ship into the water; to enter on a new field of activity; to expatiate in language.—*n.* Act of launching; the largest boat carried by a man-of-war.

**Laundress,** län'dres or lan'dres, *n.* A female who washes and dresses linen, etc.

**Laundry,** län'dri or lan'dri, *n.* Place where clothes are washed and dressed.

**Laureate,** la're-āt, *a.* Decked or invested with laurel.—**Poet laureate,** in Great Britain, a poet specially appointed as the poet of the sovereign.—*n.* One crowned with laurel; a poet laureate.—*vt.* To crown with laurel; to honor with a degree, etc.

**Laureateship,** la'rē-āt-ship, *n.* Office of a laureate.

**Laurel,** la'rel, *n.* The bay-tree, a fragrant tree or shrub used in ancient times in making wreaths for victors, etc.; *pl.* a crown of laurel; honor; distinction.

**Lava,** la'va, *n.* Rock-matter that flows in a molten state from volcanoes.

**Lavatory,** lav'a-to-ri, *n.* A room or place for personal ablutions.

**Lave,** lāv, *vt.* (laving, laved). To wash; to bathe; to throw out, as water; to bale.—*vi.* To bathe; to wash oneself; to wash, as the sea on the beach.

**Lavender,** lav'en-dėr, *n.* An aromatic plant of the mint family, which yields an essential oil and a perfume; a pale blue color with a slight mixture of gray.

**Laver,** lā'vėr, *n.* A large basin.

**Lavish,** lav'ish, *a.* Profuse; liberal to a fault; extravagant; superabundant.—*vt.* To expend with profusion; to squander.

**Lavishly,** lav'ish-li, *adv.* Profusely; wastefully.

**Law,** la, *n.* A rule prescribed by authority; a statute; a precept; such rules or statues collectively; legal procedure; litigation; a principle deduced from practice or observation; a formal statement of facts observed in natural phenomena.

**Lawful,** la'ful, *a.* Agreeable to law; allowed by law; legal; rightful.

**Lawfully,** la'ful-li, *adv.* In a lawful manner; legally.

**Lawgiver,** la'giv-ėr, *n.* One who makes or enacts a law; a legislator.

**Lawless,** la'les, *a.* Not subject to law; contrary to law; illegal; capricious.

**Lawn,** lan, *n.* An open space between woods; a space of smooth level ground covered with grass; a fine linen or cambric.

**Lawn-tennis,** lan'ten-is, *n.* A game played with balls and rackets on a lawn.

**Lawsuit,** la'sūt, *n.* A suit in law for the recovery of a supposed right.

**Lawyer,** la'yėr, *n.* One versed in the laws, or a practitioner of law.

**Lax,** laks, *a.* Loose; flabby; soft; slack; vague; equivocal; not strict; remiss; having too frequent discharges from the bowels.

**Laxative,** laks'at-iv, *a.* Having the power of relieving from constipation.—*n.* A gentle purgative.

**Laxity,** laks'i-ti, *n.* State or quality of being lax; want of strictness; looseness.

**Lay,** lā, *vt.* (pret. and pp. laid). To place in a lying position; to set or place in general; to impose; to bring into a certain state; to settle; to allay; to place at hazard; to wager; to contrive.—*vi.* To bring forth eggs; wager.—*n.* A stratum; a layer; one rank in a series reckoned upward; a song; a narrative poem.—*a.* Not clerical; not professional.

**Layer,** lā'ėr, *n.* One who or that which lays; a stratum; a coat, as of paint; a row of masonry, etc.; a shoot of a plant, not detached from the stalk,

partly laid underground for growth.—*vt.* To propagate by bending a shoot into the soil.
**Lay-figure,** lā'fig-ūr, *n.* A jointed wooden figure used by artists to hold draperies, etc.
**Layman,** lā'man, *n.* One not a clergyman.
**Lazily,** lā'zi-li, *adv.* Sluggishly.
**Laziness,** lā'zi-nes, *n.* State or quality of being lazy; indolence; sloth.
**Lazy,** lā'zi, *a.* Disinclined to exertion; slothful; indolent; slow.
**Lea,** lē, *n.* A meadow; land under grass.
**Lead,** led, *n.* A soft and heavy metal; a plummet; a thin plate of type-metal, used to separate lines in printing; plumbago in pencils; *pl.* the leaden covering of a roof.—*a.* Made of lead; produced by lead.—*vt.* To cover with lead; to fit with lead.
**Lead,** lēd, *vt.* (pret. and pp. led). To guide or conduct; to direct and govern; to precede; to entice; to influence; to spend; to begin.—*vi.* To go before and show the way; to be chief or commander; to draw; to have a tendency.—*n.* Guidance; precedence.
**Leaded,** led'ed, *a.* Fitted with lead; set in lead; separated by leads.
**Leaden,** led'n, *a.* Made of lead; like lead; heavy; inert; dull.
**Leader,** lēd'ėr, *n.* One who leads; a guide; captain; head of a party; editorial article in a newspaper.
**Leadership,** lēd'ėr-ship, *n.* State or condition of a leader.
**Leading,** lēd'ing, *p.a.* Chief; principal.—**Leading question,** a question which suggests an answer that the questioner desires.
**Leaf,** lēf, *n.*; pl. **Leaves,** lēvz. One of the thin, expanded, deciduous growths of a plant; a part of a book containing two pages; a very thin plate; the movable side of a table; one side of a double door.—*vi.* To shoot out leaves; to produce leaves.
**League,** lēg, *n.* A combination between states for their mutual aid; an alliance; a compact; a measure of three miles or knots.—*vi.* (leaguing, leagued). To form a league; to confederate.
**Leagued,** lēgd, *p.a.* United in a league or mutual compact.
**Leaguer,** lēg'ėr, *n.* One who unites in a league; the camp of a besieging army; a siege.
**Leak,** lēk, *n.* A fissure in a vessel that admits water, or permits it to escape; the passing of fluid through an aperture.—*vi.* To let water in or out of a vessel through a crevice.
**Leakage,** lēk'āj, *n.* A leaking; quantity of a liquid that enters or issues by leaking; an allowance for the leaking of casks.
**Leaky,** lēk'i, *a.* Having a leak.
**Leal,** lēl, *a.* Loyal; true; faithful.
**Lean,** lēn, *vi.* (pret. and pp. leaned). To slope or slant; to incline; to tend; to bend so as to rest on something; to depend.—*vt.* To cause to lean; to support or rest.
**Lean,** lēn, *a.* Wanting flesh or fat on the body; meager; not fat; barren.—*n.* That part of flesh which consists of muscle without fat.
**Leanly,** lēn'li, *adv.* In a lean manner; meagerly; without fat or plumpness.
**Leap,** lēp, *vi.* (pret. and pp. leaped). To spring from the ground; to jump; to rush with violence; to bound.—*vt.* To pass over by leaping.—*n.* A jump; a spring; space passed by leaping; a sudden transition.
**Leap-frog,** lēp'frog, *n.* A game in which one stoops down and others leap over him.
**Leap-year,** lēp'yēr, *n.* A year containing 366 days: every fourth year.
**Learn,** lėrn, *vt.* (pret. and pp. learned). To gain knowledge of or skill in; to acquire by study.—*vi.* To gain knowledge; to receive instruction.
**Learned,** lėrn'ed, *a.* Having much knowledge; erudite; scholarly.
**Learnedly,** lėrn'ed-li, *adv.* In a learned manner; with much knowledge or erudition.
**Learner,** lėrn'ėr, *n.* One who learns; a pupil.
**Learning,** lėrn'ing, *n.* Acquired knowledge; erudition; scholarship; education.
**Lease,** lēs, *n.* A letting of lands, etc., for a rent; written contract for such letting; any tenure by grant or permission.—*vt.* (leasing, leased). To let; to grant by lease.
**Leaseholder,** lēs'hōld-ėr, *n.* A tenant under a lease.
**Leash,** lēsh, *n.* A thong or line by which a dog or hawk is held; three creatures of any kind.—*vt.* To bind by a leash.
**Leasing,** lēz'ing, *n.* Falsehood; lies.
**Least,** lēst, *a.* Smallest.—*adv.* In the smallest or lowest degree.—**At least, at the least,** to say no more; at the lowest degree.
**Leather,** leᴛʜ'ėr, *n.* The skin of an animal prepared for use; tanned hides in general.—*a.* Leathern.
**Leathern,** leᴛʜ'ėrn, *a.* Made of leather; consisting of leather.
**Leathery,** leᴛʜ'ėr-i, *a.* Like leather; tough.
**Leave,** lēv, *n.* Permission; liberty granted; a formal parting of friends.—*vt.* (leaving, left). To let remain; to have remaining at death; to bequeath; to quit; to abandon; to refer.—*vi.* To depart; to desist.
**Leave,** lēv, *vi.* (leaving, leaved). To leaf.
**Leaved,** lēvd, *a.* Furnished with leaves or foliage; made with leaves or folds.
**Leaven,** lev'n, *n.* A substance that produces fermentation, as in dough; yeast; barm.—*vt.* To mix with leaven; to excite fermentation in; to imbue.
**Leavings,** lēv'ingz, *n.pl.* Things left; relics; refuse; offal.
**Leavy,** lēv'i, *a.* Full of leaves.
**Lecher,** lech'ėr, *n.* A man given to lewdness.—*vi.* To practice lewdness; to indulge lust.
**Lecherous,** lech'ėr-us, *a.* Addicted to lewdness or lust; lustful; lewd.
**Lechery,** lech'ėr-i, *n.* Free indulgence of lust.
**Lectern,** lek'tėrn, *n.* A reading-desk in a church.
**Lection,** lek'shon, *n.* A reading; a difference or variety in a text.
**Lecture,** lek'tūr, *n.* A discourse on any subject; a reprimand; a formal reproof.—*vi.* (lecturing, lectured). To deliver a lecture or lectures.—*vt.* To reprimand; to reprove.
**Lecturer,** lek'tūr-ėr, *n.* One who lectures; one who delivers discourses to students.
**Lectureship,** lek'tūr-ship, *n.* The office of a lecturer.
**Ledge,** lej, *n.* A narrow shelf; a ridge or shelf of rocks.
**Ledger,** lej'ėr, *n.* The principal book of accounts among merchants and others.
**Lee,** lē, *n.* The quarter toward which the wind blows; shelter caused by an object keeping off the wind.—*a.* Pertaining to the side towards which the wind blows.
**Leech,** lēch, *n.* A blood-sucking wormlike animal.—*vt.* To treat or heal; to bleed by the use of leeches.
**Leek,** lēk, *n.* A culinary vegetable allied to the onion.
**Leer,** lēr, *n.* A side glance; an arch or affected glance.—*vi.* To give a leer; to look meaningly.—*vt.* To turn with a leer; to affect with a leer.
**Lees,** lēz, *n.pl.* The slime of liquor; dregs; sediment.
**Leeward,** lö'wėrd, *a.* Pertaining to the lee.—*adv.* Toward the lee.
**Leeway,** lē'wā, *n.* The drifting of a ship to the leeward.—**To make up leeway,** to overtake work in arrear.
**Left,** left, *a.* Denoting the part opposed to the right of the body.—*n.* The side opposite to the right.
**Left-hand,** left'hand, *a.* Relating to the left hand; on the left side.
**Left-handed,** left'hand-ed, *a.* Using the left hand and arm with more dexterity than the right; sinister; insincere; awkward.

L

**Left-off,** left'of, *a*. Laid aside; no longer worn.
**Leg,** leg, *n*. The limb of an animal; a lower or posterior limb; the long or slender support of anything.
**Legacy,** leg'a-si, *n*. A bequest; a particular thing given by last will.
**Legal,** lē'gal, *a*. According to, pertaining to, or permitted by law; lawful; judicial.
**Legality,** lē-gal'i-ti, *n*. Condition or character of being legal; conformity to law.
**Legalize,** lē'gal-īz, *vt*. To make legal or lawful; to authorize; to sanction.
**Legally,** lē'gal-li, *adv*. In a legal manner; lawfully; according to law.
**Legate,** le'gāt, *n*. An ambassador; the pope's ambassador to a foreign state.
**Legatee,** leg-a-tē', *n*. One to whom a legacy is bequeathed.
**Legation,** lē-gā'shon, *n*. An embassy; a diplomatic minister and his suite.
**Legator,** le-gä'tō, *a*. and *adv*. Played or sung in an even, smooth, gliding manner.
**Legend,** le'jend or lē'jend, *n*. A marvellous story handed down from early times; a nonhistorical narrative; an inscription.
**Legendary,** lej'end-a-ri or lē'jend-a-ri, *a*. Fabulous; traditional; mythical.
**Legerdemain,** lej'ėr-dē-mān'', *n*. Sleight of hand; an adroit trick.
**Legging,** leg'ing, *n*. A covering for the leg; a long gaiter; generally in *pl*.
**Legibility,** le-ji-bil'i-ti, *n*. Quality or state of being legible.
**Legible,** le'ji-bl, *a*. That may be read.
**Legibly,** le'ji-bli, *adv*. So as to be read.
**Legion,** lē'jon, *n*. A Roman body of infantry soldiers, in number from 3000 to above 6000; a military force; a great number.
**Legionary,** lē'jon-a-ri, *a*. Relating to, or consisting of, a legion.—*n*. A Roman soldier belonging to a legion.
**Legislate,** le'jis-lāt, *vi*. To make or enact a law or laws.
**Legislation,** le-jis-lā'shon, *n*. Act of making a law or laws; laws or statutes enacted.
**Legislative,** le'jis-lāt-iv, *a*. Capable of or pertaining to the enacting of laws.
**Legislator,** le'jis-lāt-ėr, *n*. A lawgiver; one who makes laws.
**Legislature,** le'jis-lāt-ūr, *n*. The body of men invested with power to make laws.
**Legist,** lē'jist, *n*. One skilled in the laws.
**Legitim,** le'ji-tim, *n*. In *Scots law*, the share of a father's movable property to which on his death his children are entitled by law.
**Legitimacy,** lē-jit'i-ma-si, *n*. State or quality of being legitimate; legality.
**Legitimate,** lē-jit'i-māt, *a*. Accordant with law; born in wedlock; genuine; following by logical or natural sequence; allowable; valid.—*vt*. To make legitimate.
**Legitimation,** lē-jit'i-mā-shon, *n*. Act of legitimating or rendering legitimate.
**Legitimist,** lē-jit'i-mist, *n*. One who believes in the sacredness of hereditary monarchies.
**Legitimize,** lē-jit'i-mīz, *vt*. To legitimate.
**Legume,** leg'ūm, le-gūm', *n*. A seed-vessel of two valves; a pod; *pl*. pulse, pease, beans, etc.
**Leguminous,** le-gū'min-us, *a*. Pertaining to legumes; consisting of pulse.
**Leisure,** lē'zhūr or lezh'ūr, *n*. Freedom from occupation; vacant time.—*a*. Not spent in labor; vacant.
**Leisurely,** lē'zhūr-li, *a*. Done at leisure; deliberate; slow.—*adv*. Slowly; at leisure.
**Lemma,** lem'ma, *n*. A subsidiary proposition in mathematics.
**Lemming,** lem'ing, *n*. A small rodent mammal.
**Lemon,** le'mon, *n*. An acid fruit of the orange kind; the tree that produces this fruit.
**Lemonade,** le-mon-ād', *n*. A beverage, usually aerated, consisting of lemon-juice mixed with water and sweetened.
**Lemur,** lē'mėr, *n*. A quadrumanous mammal, allied to monkeys and rodents.
**Lend,** lend, *vt*. (lending, lent). To furnish on condition of the thing being returned; to afford or grant; *refl*. to accommodate.
**Lender,** lend'ėr, *n*. One who lends.
**Length,** length, *n*. State or quality of being long; extent from end to end; extenstion; long duration; extent or degree.—**At length,** at full extent; at last.
**Lengthen,** length'n, *vt*. To make long or longer; to extend.—*vi*. To grow longer.
**Lengthily,** length'i-li, *adv*. In a lengthy manner.
**Lengthwise,** length'wīz, *adv*. In the direction of the length; longitudinally.
**Lengthy,** length'i, *a*. Somewhat long.
**Lenience, Leniency,** lē'ni-ens, lē'ni-en-si, *n*. Quality of being lenient; lenity; mildness.
**Lenient,** lē'ni-ent, *a*. Acting without rigor; gentle; clement.
**Leniently,** lē'ni-ent-li, *adv*. In a lenient manner; mercifully; mildly.
**Lenitive,** le'nit-iv, *a*. Softening; assuasive; emollient.—*n*. A medicine or application that eases pain.
**Lenity,** le'ni-ti, *n*. Gentleness; mildness; mercy.
**Leno,** lē'nō, *n*. A kind of cotton gauze.
**Lens,** lenz, *n*.; pl. **Lenses,** len'zes. A transparent substance, usually glass, by which objects appear magnified or diminished; one of the glasses of a telescope, etc.
**Lent,** lent, *n*. A fast of forty days, from Ash Wednesday till Easter.
**Lenten,** lent'en, *a*. Pertaining to Lent; used in Lent; sparing; plain.
**Lentil,** len'til, *n*. A pea-like plant, having seeds forming a very nutritious diet.
**Lento,** len'tō, *a*. and *adv*. A direction that music is to be performed slowly.
**Leo,** lē'ō, *n*. The Lion, the fifth sign of the zodiac.
**Leonine,** lē'ō-nīn, *a*. Belonging to a lion; resembling a lion; applied to a rhyming Latin measure of hexameter and pentameter verses.
**Leopard,** lep'ärd, *n*. A large carnivorous animal of the cat genus, with a spotted skin.
**Leper,** lep'ėr, *n*. One affected with leprosy.
**Lepidopterous,** lep-i-dop'tėr-us, *a*. Belonging to the order of insects called Lepidoptera, comprising butterflies and moths.
**Leporine,** lep'or-īn, *a*. Pertaining to or resembling the hare.
**Leprosy,** lep'rō-si, *n*. A foul cutaneous disease, characterized by dusky red or livid tubercles on the face or extremities.
**Leprous,** lep'rus, *a*. Infected with leprosy.
**Lesion,** lē'zhon, *n*. Injury; wound; derangement.
**Less,** les, *a*. Smaller; not so large or great.—*adv*. In a smaller or lower degree.—*n*. A smaller quantity.
**Lessee,** les-sē', *n*. The person to whom a lease is given.
**Lessen,** les'n, *vt*. To make less; to lower; to depreciate.—*vi*. To become less; to abate.
**Lesser,** les'ėr, *a*. Less; smaller.
**Lesson,** les'n, *n*. Portion which a pupil learns at one time; portion of Scripture read in divine service; something to be learned; severe lecture; truth taught by experience.
**Lest,** lest, *conj*. For fear that; in case.
**Let,** let, *vt*. (letting, let). To permit; to allow; to lease.—*vi*. To be leased or let.
**Let,** let, *vt*. To hinder; to impede.—*n*. A hindrance; impediment.
**Lethal,** lēth'al, *a*. Deadly; mortal; fatal.
**Lethargic,** le-thär'jik, *a*. Drowsy; morbidly inclined to sleep; dull.
**Lethargy,** le'thär-ji, *n*. Morbid drowsiness; profound sleep; dulness.
**Letter,** let'ėr, *n*. A mark used as the representative of a sound; a written message; an epistle; the literal meaning; in *printing*, a single type; *pl*. learning; erudition.—*vt*. To impress or form letters on.

**Lettered,** let'ėrd, *a.* Versed in literature or science; belonging to learning.
**Lettering,** let'ėr-ing, *n.* The act of impressing letters; the letters impressed.
**Letter-press,** let'ėr-pres, *n.* Letters printed by types, print.
**Lettuce,** let'is, *n.* An annual composite plant, used in salads.
**Leucoma,** lū-kō'ma, *n.* A white opacity of the cornea of the eye.
**Leucopathy,** lū-kop'a-thi, *n.* The condition of an albino.
**Levant,** le-vant', *n.* The eastern coasts of the Mediterranean.—*vi.* To run away without paying debts.
**Levanter,** lē-vant'ėr, *n.* A strong east wind in the Mediterranean; one who levants.
**Levantine,** lē-vant'īn, *a.* Pertaining to the Levant; designating a kind of silk cloth.
**Levee,** lev'ā or lev'ē, *n.* A morning reception of visitors held by a prince; in America, a river embankment.
**Level,** le'vel, *n.* An instrument for detecting variation from a horizontal surface; an instrument by which to find a horizontal line; a horizontal line or plane; a surface without inequalities; usual elevation; equal elevation with something else; horizontal gallery in a mine.—*a.* Horizontal; even; flat; having no degree of superiority.—*vt.* (leveling, leveled). To make level; to lay flat on the ground; to reduce to equality; to point, in taking aim.—*vi.* To point a gun, etc.; to aim.
**Leveller,** le'vel-ėr, *n.* One who levels; one who would destroy social distinctions.
**Levelling,** le'vel-ing, *n.* Act of one who levels; the art or practice of ascertaining the different elevations of objects.
**Lever,** lē'vėr, *n.* A bar used for raising weights, etc.; a kind of watch.
**Leverage,** lē'vėr-āj, *n.* Action or power of a lever; mechanical advantage gained by using a lever.
**Leviable,** le'vi-a-bl, *a.* That may be levied.
**Leviathan,** lē-vī'a-than, *n.* An immense seamonster.
**Levigate,** le'vi-gāt, *vt.* To grind to a fine impalpable powder; to make smooth.
**Levite,** lē'vīt, *n.* One of the tribe of Levi; a priest; a cleric.
**Levitical,** lē-vit'ik-al, *a.* Belonging to the Levites; priestly.
**Levity,** le'vi-ti, *n.* Lightness; inconstancy; giddiness; want of seriousness.
**Levy,** le'vi, *vt.* (levying, levied). To raise (troops); to collect (taxes); to being (war).—*n.* Act of raising troops or taxes; the troops or taxes raised.
**Lewd,** lūd, *a.* Lustful; sensual; vile.
**Lewdly,** lūd'li, *adv.* In a lewd manner.
**Lewis gun,** lō'is, gun, *n.* An automatic rifle, gas-operated and air-cooled, capable of firing forty-seven rounds without reloading.
**Lewisite,** lō'is-īt, *n.* A poison gas.
**Lexicographer,** leks-i-kog'ra-fėr, *n.* The author or compiler of a dictionary.
**Lexicographic, Lexicographical,** leks'i-kōgraf''ik, leks'i-kō-graf''ik-al, *a.* Pertaining to lexicography.
**Lexicography,** leks-i-kog'ra-fi, *n.* The act or art of compiling a dictionary.
**Lexicon,** leks'i-kon, *n.* A word-book; a dictionary; a vocabulary containing an alphabetical arrangement of the words in a language, with the definition of each.
**Liability,** lī-a-bil'i-ti, *n.* State of being liable; that for which one is liable; *pl.* debts.
**Liable,** lī'a-bl, *a.* Answerable for consequences; responsible; subject; exposed: with *to.*
**Liaison,** lē-ā-zōng, *n.* A bond of union; an illicit intimacy between a man and woman.
**Liar,** lī'ėr, *n.* One who utters falsehood.
**Lias,** lī'as, *n.* A series of strata in England, lying at the basis of the oolitic series.
**Libation,** lī-bā'shon, *n.* Act of pouring a liquor, usually wine, on the ground or on a victim in sacrifice, in honor of some deity; the wine or other liquor so poured.
**Libel,** lī'bel, *n.* A defamatory writing; a malicious publication; the written statement of a plaintiff's ground of complaint against a defendant.—*vt.* (libelling, libelled). To frame a libel against; to lampoon; to exhibit a charge against in court.
**Libeller,** lī'bel-ėr, *n.* One who libels.
**Libellous,** kī'bel-us, *a.* Containing a libel; defamatory.
**Liberal,** li'bėr-al, *a.* Generousl ample; profuse; favorable to reform or progress; not too literal or strict; free.—*n.* One who advocates great political freedom.
**Liberalism,** li'bėr-al-izm, *n.* Liberal principles; the principles or practice of liberals.
**Liberality,** li-bėr-al'i-ti, *n.* Largeness of mind; width of sympathy; generosity.
**Liberalize,** li'bėr-al-īz, *vt.* To render liberal; to free from narrow views.
**Liberally,** li'bėr-al-li, *adv.* In a liberal manner; bountifully; freely; not strictly.
**Liberate,** li'bėr-āt, *vt.* To free; to deliver; to set at liberty; to disengage.
**Liberation,** li-bėr-ā'shon, *n.* Act of liberating.
**Liberator,** li'bėr-āt-ėr, *n.* One who liberates.
**Libertine,** li'bėr-tīn, *n.* A freedman; one who indulges his lust without restraint; a debauchee.—*a.* Licentious; dissolute.
**Libertinism,** li'bėr-tin-izm, *n.* The conduct of a libertine or rake.
**Liberty,** li'bėr-ti, *n.* State or condition of one who is free; privilege; immunity; license; district within which certain exclusive privileges may be exercised; freedom of action or speech beyond civility or decorum; state of being disengaged.
**Libidinous,** li-bid'i-nus, *a.* Characterized by lust; lascivious; lewd.
**Libra,** lī'bra, *n.* The Balance, the seventh sign in the zodiac.
**Librarian,** lī-brā'ri-an, *n.* The keeper of a library or collection of books.
**Librarianship,** lī-brā'ri-an-ship, *n.* The office or post of a librarian.
**Library,** lī'bra-ri, *n.* A collection of books; edifice or apartment for holding books.
**Librate,** lī'brāt, *vt.* To poise; to balance.—*vi.* To move, as a balance; to be poised.
**Libration,** lī-brā'shon, *n.* Act of librating; state of being balanced.
**Libretto,** lī-bret'ō, *n.* The book of words of an opera, etc.
**Lice,** līs, *n.pl.* of *louse.*
**License,** lī'sens, *n.* Authority or liberty given to do any act; a certificate giving permission; excess of liberty; deviation from an artistic standard.—**License,** *vt.* (licensing, licensed). To grant a license to; to authorize to act in a particular character.
**Licensee,** lī-sens-ē', *n.* One to whom a license is granted.
**Licenser,** lī'sens-ėr, *n.* One who grants a license.
**Licentiate,** lī-sen'shi-āt, *n.* One who has a license to practice any art or to exercise a profession, as medicine or theology.
**Licentious,** lī-sen'shus, *a.* Characterized by license; profligate; libidinous.
**Lichen,** lī'ken or lich'en, *n.* A plant without stem and leaves, growing on the bark of trees, on rocks, etc.; an eruption of small red or white pimples.
**Licit,** li'sit, *a.* Lawful; legal; legitimate.
**Lick,** lik, *vt.* To draw the tongue over the surface of; to lap; to take in by the tongue; to beat.—*n.* A drawing of the tongue over anything; a slight smear or coat; a blow.
**Lickerish,** lik'ėr-ish, *a.* Nice in the choice of food; dainty; having keen relish.
**Licorice,** lik'or-is, *n.* Liquorice.
**Lictor,** lik'tėr, *n.* An officer who attended the Ro-

L

man magistrates, bearing an axe and rods.
**Lid,** lid, *n.* A movable cover of a vessel or box; eyelid.
**Lie,** lī, *vi.* (lying, lied). To utter falsehood with deceitful intention.—*n.* A falsehood; an intentional violation of truth.
**Lie,** lī, *vi.* (lying, pret. lay, pp. lain). To occupy a horizontal position; to rest on anything lengthwise; to be situated; to remain; to be incumbent; to exist; to depend; to be sustainable in law.—**To lie in,** to be in childbed.—**To lie to,** to stop and remain stationary.—*n.* Relative position of objects; general bearing or direction.
**Lief,** lēf, *a.* Beloved; agreeable; *poetical.*—*adv.* Gladly; willingly; readily.
**Liege,** lēj, *a.* Bound by a feudal tenure; subject; loyal; faithful.—*n.* A vassal; a lord or superior; a sovereign; a citizen in general; generally in *pl.*
**Lien,** lī'en, *n.* A legal claim; a right over the property of another until some claim or due is satisfied.
**Lieu,** lū, *n.* Place; stead: preceded by *in.*
**Lieutenancy,** lū-ten'an-si, *n.* Office or commission of a lieutenant; the collective body of lieutenants.
**Lieutenant,** lū-ten'ant, *n.* An officer who supplies the place of a superior in his absence; a commissioned army officer next in rank below a captain; commissioned naval officer below a lieutenant-commander.—**Lieutenant-colonel,** *n.* An army officer next in rank below a colonel.—**Lieutenant-commander,** *n.* A naval officer immediately below the rank of commander, and corresponding in rank to a major in the army.—**Lieutenant-general,** *n.* An army officer next in rank below a general.
**Life,** līf, *n.*; pl. **Lives,** līvz. State of animals and plants in which the natural functions are performed; vitality; present state of existence; time from birth to death; manner of living; animal being; spirit; vivacity; the living form; exact resemblance; rank in society; human affairs; a person; narrative of a life; eternal felicity.
**Life-belt,** līf'belt, *n.* A buoyant belt used to support the body in the water.
**Life-blood,** līf'blud, *n.* The blood necessary to life; vital blood.
**Life-boat,** līf'bōt, *n.* A boat for saving men in cases of shipwreck.
**Life-buoy,** līf'boi, *n.* A buoy to be thrown to a person in danger of drowning.
**Life-giving,** līf'giv-ing, *a.* Giving life; inspiriting; invigorating.
**Life-guard,** līf'gärd, *n.* A soldier that attends the person of a prince, etc.
**Lifeless,** līf'les, *a.* Deprived of life; dead; inanimate; dull; heavy; inactive.
**Lifelike,** līf'līk, *a.* Like a living person; true to the life.
**Lifelong,** līf'long, *a.* Lasting through life.
**Life-size,** līf'sīz, *a.* Of the size of the person or object represented.
**Lifetime,** līf'tīm, *n.* The time that life continues; duration of life.
**Lift,** lift, *vt.* To raise to a higher position; to hoist; to elevate; to raise in spirit; to collect when due.—*vi.* To raise; to rise.—*n.* Act of lifting; assistance; that which is to be raised; an elevator or hoist.
**Ligament,** li'ga-ment, *n.* That which unites one thing to another; a band; a substance serving to bind one bone to another.
**Ligan,** lī'gan, *n.* Goods sunk in the sea, but having something buoyant attached to mark their position.
**Ligation,** lī-gā'shon, *n.* Act of binding; ligature.
**Ligature,** li'ga-tūr, *n.* Anything that binds; a band or bandage.
**Light,** līt, *n.* That by which objects are rendered visible; day; that which gives or admits light; illumination of mind; knowledge; open view; explanation; point of view; situation; spiritual illumination.—*a.* Bright; clear; not deep, as color; not heavy; not difficult; easy to be digested; active; not laden; slight; moderate; unsteady; gay; trifling; wanton; sandy; having a sensation of giddiness; employed in light work.—*adv.* Lightly; cheaply.—*vt.* (pret. and pp. lighted or lit). To give light to; to enlighten; to ignite.—*vi.* To brighten; to descend, as from a horse, etc.; to alight; to come by chance.
**Lighten,** līt'n, *vi.* To become brighter; to shine; to flash, as lightning.—*vt.* To illuminate; to enlighten; to flash forth; to make less heavy; to alleviate; to cheer; to gladden.
**Lighter,** līt'ėr, *n.* One who or that which lights or kindles; a large flat-bottomed boat used in loading and unloading ships.
**Light-fingered,** līt'fing-gėrd, *a.* Thievish; addicted to petty thefts.
**Light-footed,** līt'fut-ed, *a.* Nimble; active.
**Light-headed,** līt'hed-ed, *a.* Thoughtless; unsteady; delirious; dizzy.
**Light-hearted,** līt'härt-ed, *a.* Free from grief or anxiety; gay; cheerful; merry.
**Light-horseman,** līt'hors-man, *n.* A light-armed cavalry soldier.
**Lighthouse,** līt'hous, *n.* A tower with a light on the top to direct seamen at night.
**Light-infantry,** līt'in-fant-ri, *n.* Infantry trained for rapid movement.
**Lightly,** līt'li, *adv.* With little weight; easily; cheerfully; nimbly; airily.
**Lightning,** līt'ning, *n.* The sudden and vivid flash that precedes thunder, produced by a discharge of atmospheric electricity.
**Lightning-rod,** līt'ning-rod, *n.* A metallic rod to protect buildings or vessels from lightning. Also **Lightning-conductor.**
**Lights,** līts, *n.pl.* The lungs of animals.
**Lightsome,** līt'sum, *a.* Bright; gay; cheering.
**Ligneous,** lig'nē-us, *a.* Woody; wooden.
**Lignify,** lig'ni-fī, *vt.* and *i.* To turn into wood.
**Lignite,** lig'nīt, *n.* Fossil wood or brown-coal.
**Lignum-vitae,** lig-num-vī'tē, *n.* A tropical tree having wood of extreme hardness.
**Like,** līk, *a.* Equal; similar; resembling; likely; feeling disposed.—*adv.* or *prep.* In the same manner; similarly; likely.—*vt.* (liking, liked). To be pleased with; to approve.—*vi.* To be pleased; to choose.—*n.* Some person or thing resembling another; a counterpart; a liking; a fancy.
**Likeable,** līk'a-bl, *a.* Such as to attract liking; lovable.
**Likelihood,** līk'li-hud, *n.* Probability; appearance of truth or reality.
**Likely,** līk'li, *a.* Probable; credible; suitable.—*adv.* Probably.
**Liken,** līk'en, *vt.* To compare; to represent as resembling or similar.
**Likeness,** līk'nes, *n.* Quality or state of being like; resemblance; similarity; one who resembles another; a portrait.
**Likewise,** līk'wiz, *adv.* In like manner; also; moreover; too.
**Liking,** līk'ing, *n.* Inclination; desire; preference; satisfaction.
**Lilac,** lī'lak, *n.* A shrub with flowers generally bluish or white.
**Lilliputian,** lil-i-pū'shan, *n.* A person of very small size.—*a.* Very small.
**Lilt,** lilt, *vt.* and *i.* To sing cheerfully; to give musical utterance.—*n.* A song; a tune.
**Lily,** lil'i, *n.* A bulbous plant with showy and fragrant flowers.
**Limb,** lim, *n.* The arm or leg, especially the latter; a branch of a tree; graduated edge of a quadrant, etc.; border of the disc of the sun, moon, etc.—*vt.* To supply with limbs; to tear off the limbs of.
**Limber,** lim'bėr, *a.* Flexible; pliant.—*n.* A carriage with ammunition boxes attached to the gun-carriage.—*vt.* and *i.* To attach the limber to the gun-carriage.
**Limbo,** lim'bo, *n.* A supposed region beyond this world for souls of innocent persons ignorant of

Christianity; any similar region; a prison of confinement.

**Lime,** līm, *n.* Any viscous substance; calcareous earth used in cement; mortar made with lime; the linden-tree; a tree producing an inferior sort of lemon.—*vt.* (liming, limed). To smear or manure with lime; to ensnare; to cement.

**Lime-juice,** līm'jūs, *n.* The juice of the lime-fruit, a specific against scurvy.

**Lime-kiln,** līm'kil, *n.* A furnace in which lime-stone is reduced to lime.

**Limerick,** lim'er-ik, *n.* A nonsense verse form of five lines, popularized by Edward Lear (1812-88) in his *Book of Nonsense* (1840).

**Limestone,** līm'stōn, *n.* A kind of stone consisting of varieties of carbonate of lime.

**Limit,** lim'it, *n.* Boundary; border; utmost extent; restraint; restriction.—*vt.* To bound; to circumscribe; to restrain; to restrict.

**Limitable,** lim'it-a-bl, *a.* That may be limited.

**Limitation,** lim-it-ā'shon, *n.* Act of limiting; state of being limited; restriction.

**Limited,** lim'it-ed, *a.* Narrow; circumscribed; confined; restricted.

**Limn,** lim, *vt.* To draw or paint, especially a portrait.

**Limner,** lim'nėr, *n.* One who limns; a portrait-painter.

**Limp,** limp, *vi.* To halt; to walk lamely.—*n.* A halt; act of limping.—*a.* Easily bent; pliant; flaccid.

**Limpid,** lim'pid, *a.* Clear; crystal; pellucid.

**Limy,** līm'i, *a.* Containing lime; resembling lime.

**Lin, Linn,** lin, *n.* A cataract or waterfall; the pool below a fall.

**Linch-pin,** linsh'pin, *n.* A pin to keep a wheel on the axle-tree.

**Line,** līn, *n.* A small rope or cord; a threadlike marking; a stroke or score; a row of soldiers, ships, words, etc.; a verse; an outline; a short written communication; course of procedure, etc.; connected series, as of descendants; series of public conveyances, as steamers; the twelfth part of an inch; the equator; the regular infantry of an army; *pl.* works covering extended positions and presenting a front in only one direction to the enemy.—*vt.* (lining, lined). To draw lines upon; to set with men or things in lines; to cover on the inside; to put in the inside of.

**Lineage,** lin'ē-āj, *n.* Descendants in a line from a common progenitor; race.

**Lineal,** lin'ē-al, *a.* Composed of or pertaining to lines; in a direct line from an ancestor; hereditary.

**Lineament,** lin'ē-a-ment, *n.* One of the lines which mark the features; feature; form.

**Linear,** lin'ē-ėr, *a.* Pertaining to a line; like a line; slender.

**Lineate, Lineolate,** lin'ē-āt, lin'ē-ō-lāt, *a.* In *botany,* marked longitudinally with lines.

**Linen,** lin'en, *n.* Cloth made of flax; under clothing.—*a.* Made of flax; resembling linen cloth.

**Liner,** līn'ėr, *n.* A vessel of a line of ocean going steamships.

**Linesman,** līnz'man, *n.* An infantryman.

**Ling,** ling, *n.* A fish of the cod family.

**Linger,** ling'gėr, *vi.* To delay; to loiter; to hesitate; to remain long.—*vt.* To spend wearily.

**Lingering,** ling'gėr-ing, *a.* Protracted; given to linger.

**Lingo,** ling'gō, *n.* Language; speech; contemptuous term for a peculiar language.

**Lingual,** ling'gwal, *a.* Pertaining to the tongue.—*n.* A sound pronounced with the tongue, as *l.*

**Linguist,** ling'gwist, *n.* A person skilled in languages.

**Linguistic,** ling-gwist'ik, *a.* Relating to language; philological.

**Linguistics,** ling-gwist'iks, *n.* The science of language; comparative philology.

**Liniment,** lin'i-ment, *n.* A species of soft ointment; an embrocation.

**Lining,** līn'ing, *n.* The covering of the inner surface of anything.

**Link,** lingk, *n.* A single ring of a chain; anything closed like a link; anything connecting; a measure of 7.92 inches; a torch.—*vi.* To be connected.—*vt.* To join or connect, as by links; to unite.

**Links,** lingks, *n.pl.* A stretch of uncultivated flat or undulating ground.

**Linseed,** lin'sēd, *n.* Flax-seed.

**Linsey-woolsey,** lin'si-wul-si, *n.* A fabric made of linen and wool.—*a.* Made of linen and wool; of different and unsuitable ingredients.

**Linstock,** lin'stok, *n.* A staff holding a lighted match, formerly used in firing cannon.

**Lint,** lint, *n.* Flax; linen scraped into a soft substance, and used for dressing wounds.

**Lintel,** lin'tel, *n.* The horizontal part of the door or window frame.

**Lion,** lī'on, *n.* A carnivorous animal of the cat family; a sign in the zodiac, Leo; an object of interest and curiosity.

**Lioness,** lī'on-es, *n.* The female of the lion.

**Lion-hearted,** lī'on-härt-ed, *a.* Having a lion's courage; brave and magnanimous.

**Lionize,** lī'on-īz, *vt.* To treat as an object of curiosity and interest.

**Lip,** lip, *n.* One of the two fleshy parts covering the front teeth in man, etc.; edge or border.—*vt.* (lipping, lipped). To touch as with the lip.

**Lipogram,** lī'pō-gram, *n.* A writing in which a particular letter is wholly omitted.

**Lipstick,** lip-stik, *n.* A cosmetic used by women for heightening the color of the lips.

**Liquate,** lī'kwāt, *vt.* and *t.* To melt; to separate by melting.

**Liquefaction,** lik-wē-fak'shon, *n.* Act or operation of melting; state of being melted.

**Liquefier,** lik'wē-fi-ėr, *n.* That which melts.

**Liquefy,** lik'wē-fi, *vt.* To melt; to dissolve by heat.—*vi.* To become liquid.

**Liquescent,** li-kwes'sent, *a.* Becoming liquid; melting.

**Liqueur,** li-kūr' or li-kör', *n.* An alcoholic beverage sweetened and containing some infusion of fruits or aromatic substances.

**Liquid,** lik'wid, *a.* Fluid; not solid; soft; smooth; devoid of harshness.—*n.* A fluid; a letter with a smooth flowing sound, as *l* and *r.*

**Liquidate,** lik'wid-āt, *vt.* To clear from obscurity; to adjust; to settle, adjust, and apportion, as a bankrupt's affairs.

**Liquidation,** lik-wid-ā'shon, *n.* Act of liquidating.

**Liquidity,** lik-wid'i-ti, *n.* State or quality of being liquid.

**Liquor,** lik'ėr, *n.* A liquid; spirituous fluids; drink.

**Liquorice,** lik'ėr-is, *n.* A plant of the bean family, the roots of which supply a sweet juice.

**Lira,** lē'rä, *n.*; pl. **Lire,** lē'rā. An Italian silver coin.

**Lisp,** lisp, *vi.* To pronounce the sibilant letters imperfectly, as in pronouncing *th* for *s*; to speak imperfectly, as a child.—*vt.* To pronounce with a lisp, or imperfectly.—*n.* The habit or act of lisping.

**Lissom,** lis'um, *a.* Supple; flexible; lithe; nimble; active.

**List,** list, *n.* The selvedge of cloth; a limit or border; a roll or catalogue; inclination to one side; *pl.* a field inclosed for a combat.—*vt.* To enroll; to enlist.—*vi.* To enlist, as in the army; to desire; to be disposed; to hearken.

**Listen,** lis'n, *vi.* To hearken; to give heed.—*vi.* To hear; to attend.

**Listless,** list'les, *a.* Having no wish; indifferent; uninterested; languid; weary.

**Listlessly,** list'les-li, *adv.* Without attention; heedlessly.

**Litany,** li'ta-ni, *n.* A solemn supplication; a collection of short supplications uttered by the priest and people alternately.

**Liter,** lē'tr, *n.* The French standard measure of capacity, equal to 61.028 cubic inches; the English

L

imperial gallon being fully 4½ liters.
**Literal,** li'tėr-al, *a*. According to the exact meaning; not figurative; expressed by letters.
**Literally,** li'tėr-al-li, *adv*. In a literal manner; not figuratively; word by word.
**Literary,** li'tėr-a-ri, *a*. Pertaining to letters or literature; versed in letters.
**Literate,** li'tėr-āt, *a*. Learned; literary.
**Literatim,** li-tėr-ā'tim, *adv*. Letter for letter.
**Literato,** li-tėr-ā'tō, *n*.; pl. **Literati,** li-tėr-ā'tī. A literary man; a litterateur.
**Literature,** li'tėr-a-tūr, *n*. Learning; literary knowledge; collective writings of a country or period; belles-lettres; the literary profession.
**Lith,** lith, *n*. A limb; a joint; a member.
**Litharge,** lith'ärj, *n*. An oxide of lead used in the arts.
**Lithe,** līTH, *a*. Pliant; flexible; limber.
**Lithesome,** līTH'sum, *a*. Pliant; nimble.
**Lithia,** lith'i-a, *n*. An oxide of lithium.
**Lithium,** lith'i-um, *n*. The lightest of all known solids.
**Lithoglyphics, Lithoglyptics,** lith-ō-glif'iks, lith-ō-glip'tiks, *n*. The art of engraving on precious stones, etc.
**Lithograph,** lith'ō-graf, *vt*. To draw on stone, and transfer to paper, etc., by printing.—*n*. A print from a drawing on stone.
**Lithographer,** li-tho'graf-ėr, *n*. One who practices lithography.
**Lithographic,** lith-ō-graf'ik, *a*. Pertaining to lithography; printed from stone.
**Lithography,** li-tho'gra-fi, *n*. The art of drawing with special pigments on a peculiar kind of stone, and of producing impressions of the designs on paper.
**Lithology,** li-thol'o-ji, *n*. The knowledge of rocks; study of the mineral structure of rocks.
**Lithotomy,** li-thot'ō-mi, *n*. The operation of cutting for stone in the bladder.
**Litigant,** li'ti-gant, *a*. Disposed to litigate; engaged in a lawsuit.—*n*. One engaged in a lawsuit.
**Litigate,** li'ti-gāt, *vt*. To contest in law.—*vi*. To carry on a suit by judicial process.
**Litigation,** li-ti-gā'shon, *n*. Act or process of litigating; a lawsuit.
**Litigious,** li-tij'us, *a*. Apt to go to law; disputable; contentious.
**Litmus,** lit'mus, *n*. A coloring matter procured from certain lichens, used as a chemical test.
**Litter,** lit'ėr, *n*. A frame supporting a bed in which a person may be borne; straw used as a bed for animals; the young produced at a birth by a quadruped; scattered rubbish; a condition of disorder.—*vt*. To furnish with bedding; to scatter in a slovenly manner; to bring forth.—*vi*. To lie in litter; to give birth to a litter.
**Little,** lit'l, *a*. Small in size or extent; short in duration; slight; mean.—*n*. A small quantity, space, etc.—**A little,** somewhat.—*adv*. In a small degree or quantity.
**Littoral,** lit'ō-ral, *a*. Pertaining to or inhabiting the shore.—*n*. A tract along a shore.
**Liturgic, Liturgical,** li-tėr'jik, li-tėr'jik-al, *a*. Pertaining to a liturgy.
**Liturgist,** li'tėr-jist, *n*. One who favors a liturgy, or is learned in liturgies.
**Liturgy,** li'tėr-ji, *n*. A ritual or established formulas for public worship.
**Live,** liv, *vi*. (living, lived). To exist; to be alive; to dwell; to conduct oneself in life; to feed or subsist; to acquire a livelihood; to be exempt from spiritual death.—*vt*. To lead, pass, or spend.
**Live,** līv, *a*. Having life; alive; not dead, ignited; vivid, as color.
**Lived,** livd or līvd, *a*. Having a life; as, long-*lived*.
**Livelihood,** līv'li-hud, *n*. Means of living; maintenance; sustenance.
**Livelong,** līv' or liv'long, *a*. That lives or endures long; lasting; tedious.
**Lively,** līv'li, *a*. Vivacious; active, gay; vivid.—*adv*. Briskly; vigorously.
**Liver,** liv'ėr, *n*. One who lives; the organ in animals which secretes the bile.
**Livery,** liv'ėr-i, *n*. State of a horse that is kept and fed at a certain rate; distinctive dress of male servants; distinctive garb worn by any body; the body or guild wearing such a garb.—*vt*. (liverying, liveried). To clothe in, or as in, livery.—*a*. Resembling the liver.
**Livid,** liv'id, *a*. Black and blue; of a lead color; discolored, as flesh by contusion.
**Living,** liv'ing, *p.a*. Having life; existing; in action or use.—*n*. Means of subsistence; manner of life; the benefice of a clergyman.
**Lixiviation,** lik-siv'i-ā''shon, *n*. The extraction of alkaline salts from ashes by pouring water on them.
**Lixivium,** lik-siv'i-um, *n*. Lye.
**Lizard,** li'zėrd, *n*. A four-footed, tailed reptile.
**Llama,** lā'mä or lyä'mä, *n*. A S. American ruminating animal allied to the camel, but smaller and without a hump.
**Llanos,** lan'ōz or lyä'nōz, *n.pl*. Vast grassy plains in S. America.
**Lloyd's,** loidz, *n*. A society in London for the collection and diffusion of maritime intelligence, the insurance, classification, and certification of vessels, etc.
**Load,** lōd, *vt*. To charge with a load; to burden; to encumber; to bestow in great abundance; to charge, as a gun.—*n*. A burden; cargo; a grievous weight; something that oppresses.
**Loading,** lōd'ing, *n*. A cargo; a burden; something added to give weight.
**Load-line,** lōd'līn, *n*. A line on the side of a vessel to show the depth to which she sinks when not overloaded.
**Loadstar, Lodestar,** lōd'stär, *n*. A star that serves to guide; the pole-star.
**Loadstone, Lodestone,** lōd'stōn, *n*. An ore of iron; the magnetic oxide of iron, which can attract iron; a magnet.
**Loaf,** lōf, *n*.; pl. **Loaves,** lōvz. A mass of bread formed by the baker; a conical lump of sugar.—*vi*. To lounge.—*vt*. To spend idly.
**Loafer,** lōf'ėr, *n*. A lounger; a low idler.
**Loam,** lōm, *n*. A rich species of earth or mold.—*vt*. To cover with loam.
**Loamy,** lōm'i, *a*. Consisting of or like loam.
**Loan,** lōn, *n*. Lending; that which is lent; a sum of money lent at interest.—*vt*. and *i*. To lend.
**Loath, Loth,** lōth, *a*. Disliking; unwilling; averse; not inclined; reluctant.
**Loathe,** lōTH, *vt*. (loathing, loathed). To feel disgust at; to abhor; to abominate.—*vi*. To feel nausea or abhorrence.
**Loathing,** lōTH'ing, *n*. Extreme disgust or aversion; abhorrence; detestation.
**Loathness,** lōTH'nes, *n*. Reluctance.
**Loathness,** lōTH'sum, *a*. Exciting disgust; disgusting; detestable; abhorrent.
**Lob,** lob, *n*. A dolt; a lout.—*vt*. (lobbing, lobbed). To throw or toss slowly.
**Lobar,** lō'bär, *a*. Pertaining to a lobe.
**Lobby,** lob'i, *n*. An apartment giving admission to others; an entrance-hall.
**Lobe,** lōb, *n*. A round projecting part of something; such a part of the liver, lungs, brain, etc.; the lower soft part of the ear.
**Lobster,** lob'stėr, *n*. A ten-footed crustacean with large claws, allied to the crab.
**Lobular,** lob'ū-lėr, *a*. Having the character of a lobule.
**Lobule,** lob'ūl, *n*. A small lobe.
**Local,** lō'kal, *a*. Pertaining to a particular place; confined to a spot or definite district.—*n*. A local item of news; a local railway train.
**Locale,** lō-käl', *n*. A locality.
**Localism,** lō'kal-izm, *n*. State of being local; word or phrase limited to a place.
**Locality,** lō-kal'i-ti, *n*. State of being local; position; situation; place.
**Localize,** lō'kal-īz, *vt*. To make local; to discover or detect the place of.

**Locally,** lō'kal-li, *adv.* In a local manner; with respect to place; in place.
**Locate,** lō'kāt, *vt.* (locating, located). To place; to settle.—*vi.* To reside.
**Location,** lō-kā'shon, *n.* Act of locating; situation with respect to place; place.
**Loch,** lo*ch*, *n.* A lake; a landlocked arm of the sea.
**Lock,** lok, *n.* An appliance for fastening doors, etc.; mechanism by which a firearm is discharged; a fastening together; inclosure in a canal, with gates at either end; a tuft or ringlet of hair.—*vt.* To fasten with a lock and key; to shut up or confine; to join firmly; to embrace closely.—*vi.* To become fast; to unite closely by mutual insertion.
**Lockage,** lok'āj, *n.* Works forming the locks on a canal; toll paid for passing the locks.
**Locker,** lok'ėr, *n.* A close receptable, as a drawer in a ship, closed with a lock.
**Locket,** lok'et, *n.* A little case worn as an ornament, often containing a lock of hair.
**Lock-jaw,** lok'ja, *n.* A spasmodic rigidity of the under jaw.
**Locksmith,** lok'smith, *n.* An artificer who makes or mends locks.
**Lock-up,** lok'up, *n.* A place in which persons under arrest are temporarily confined.
**Locomotion,** lō-kō-mō'shon, *n.* Act or power of moving from place to place.
**Locomotive,** lō-kō-mō'tiv, *a.* Moving from place to place.—*n.* A steam-engine placed on wheels, and employed in moving a train of carriages on a railway.
**Locust,** lō'kust, *n.* A large insect allied to the grasshopper; the locust-tree.
**Locust-tree,** lō'kust-trē, *n.* The carob; the name of certain American trees.
**Locution,** lō-kū'shon, *n.* A phrase; a mode of speech.
**Lode,** lōd, *n.* An open ditch; a metallic vein, or any regular mineral vein.
**Lodestar,** *n.* Same as *Loadstar.*
**Lodestone,** *n.* Same as *Loadstone.*
**Lodge,** loj, *n.* A small country house; a temporary abode; place where members of a society, as freemasons, meet; the society itself.—*vt.* (lodging, lodged). To furnish with temporary accommodation; to set or deposit for keeping; to beat down (growing crops).—*vi.* To have a temporary abode; to settle; to reside.
**Lodger,** loj'ėr, *n.* One who lodges; one who lives in a hired room or rooms.
**Lodging,** loj'ing, *n.* A temporary habitation; rooms let to another; usually in *pl.*
**Lodgment,** loj'ment, *n.* Act of lodging; state of being lodged; accumulation of something deposited; occupation of a position by the besieging party.
**Loft,** loft, *n.* The space below and between the rafters; a gallery raised within a larger apartment or in a church.
**Loftily,** loft'i-li, *adv.* In a lofty manner or position; proudly; haughtily.
**Lofty,** loft'i, *a.* Elevated in place; rising to a great height; proud; haughty; sublime; stately.
**Log,** log, *n.* A bulky piece of timber unhewed; a floating contrivance for measuring the rate of a ship's velocity; a log-book.
**Logan, Loggan,** log'an, *n.* A large stone so balanced as to be easily moved.
**Logan-berry,** lō'gan-be''ri, *n.* A cross between a blackberry and a raspberry.
**Logarithm,** log'a-rithm, *n.* In *mathematics,* the exponent of the power to which a given invariable number must be raised in order to produce another given number.
**Logarithmic, Logarithmical,** log-a-rith'mik, log-a-rith'mik-al, *a.* Pertaining to logarithms; consisting of logarithms.
**Log-book,** log'buk, *n.* Register of a ship's way, and of the incidents of the voyage.
**Log-cabin, Log-house, Log-hut,** log'ka-bin, log'h-ous, log'hut, *n.* A house made of logs laid on each other.
**Loggerhead,** log'ėr-hed, *n.* A blockhead; a dunce.—**At loggerheads,** quarrelling.
**Logic,** lo'jik, *n.* The science or art of reasoning; mode of arguing.
**Logical,** lo'jik-al, *a.* Pertaining to logic; skilled in logic; according to reason.
**Logically,** lo'jik-al-li, *adv.* In a logical manner.
**Logician,** lō-ji'shan, *n.* One skilled in logic.
**Logistic,** lō-jis'tik, *a.* Pertaining to judging, estimating, or calculating.
**Logogram,** log'ō-gram, *n.* A single type or symbol that forms a word.
**Log-rolling,** log'rōl-ing, *n.* The joining of a number of persons to collect logs; union for mutual assistance or praise.
**Logwood,** log'wud, *n.* A wood of a dark-red color, used as a dye-wood.
**Loin,** loin, *n.* The part of an animal on either side between the ribs and the haunch-bone.
**Loiter,** loi'tėr, *vi.* To be slow in moving; to spend time idly; to hang about.—*vi.* To waste carelessly; with *away.*
**Loiterer,** loi'tėr-ėr, *n.* One who loiters; a lingerer; an idler.
**Loll,** lol, *vi.* (lolling, lolled). To lean idly; to lie at ease; to hang out, as the tongue of a dog.—*vt.* To suffer to hang out.
**Lollipop,** lol'i-pop, *n.* A sugar confection which dissolves easily in the mouth.
**Lone,** lōn, *a.* Solitary; unfrequented; single.
**Lonely,** lōn'li, *a.* Unfrequented by men; retired; solitary.
**Lonesome,** lōn'sum, *a.* Solitary; secluded from society; lonely.
**Long,** long, *a.* Drawn out in a line; drawn out in time; tedious; protracted; late; containing much verbal matter.—*n.* Something that is long.—*adv.* To a great extent in space or in time; at a point of duration far distant.—*vi.* To desire eagerly; with *for.*
**Longevity,** lon-jev'i-ti, *n.* Great length of life.
**Longhand,** long'hand, *n.* Ordinary written characters, as distinguished from shorthand, etc.
**Longing,** long'ing, *p.a.* Earnestly desiring; manifesting desire.—*n.* An eager desire.
**Longingly,** long'ing-li, *adv.* With longing; with eager wishes or appetite.
**Longitude,** lon'ji-tūd, *n.* Length; distance on the surface of the globe east or west, measured by meridians.
**Longitudinal,** lon-ji-tūd'in-al, *a.* Pertaining to longitude; running lengthwise.
**Long-lived,** long'līvd, *a.* Having a long life or existence; lasting long.
**Longsome,** long'sum, *a.* Tiresome on account of length; tedious.
**Long-spun,** long'spun, *a.* Spun or extended to a great length; tedious.
**Long-suffering,** long'suf-ėr-ing, *a.* Patient; not easily provoked.—*n.* Patience of offense.
**Longways, Longwise,** long'wāz, long'wīz, *adv.* In the direction of length; lengthwise.
**Long-winded,** long'wind-ed, *a.* Not easily exhausted of breath; tedious.
**Loo,** lö, *n.* A game of cards.
**Loofah,** lö'fa, *n.* The dried fibrous interior of a kind of gourd, used as a flesh-brush.
**Look,** luk, *vi.* To direct the eye so as to see; to gaze; to consider; to expect; to heed; to face; to appear.—*vt.* To see; to express by a look.—*n.* Act of looking; sight; gaze; glance; mien; aspect.
**Looking-glass,** luk'ing-gläs, *n.* A mirror.
**Look-out,** luk-out', *n.* A careful watching for any object; place from which such observation is made; person watching.
**Loom,** löm, *n.* A frame or machine by which thread is worked into cloth; that part of an oar within the boat in rowing.—*vi.* To appear larger than the real dimensions, and indistinctly; to appear to the mind faintly.
**Loon,** lön, *n.* A worthless fellow; a rogue; a bird, the great northern diver.

**Loop,** löp, *n.* A noose; a doubling of a string, etc.; a small narrow opening.—*vt.* To form into or fasten with a loop.
**Loophole,** löp'hōl, *n.* A small opening in a fortification through which small-arms are discharged; a hole that affords means of escape; underhand method of evasion.
**Loose,** lös, *a.* Not attached; untied; not dense or compact; vague; careless; having lax bowels; unchaste.—*vt.* (loosing, loosed). To untie or unbind; to detach; to set free; to relax; to loosen.
**Loosely,** lös'li, *adv.* In a loose manner; laxly; slackly; carelessly; dissolutely.
**Loosen,** lös'n, *vt.* To make loose.—*vi.* To become loose.
**Loot,** löt, *n.* Booty; plunder, especially such as is taken in a sacked city.—*vt.* To plunder.
**Lop,** lop, *vt.* (lopping, lopped). To cut off; to trim by cutting.—*n.* That which is cut from trees.
**Lopping,** lop'ing, *n.* That which is lopped off; branches lopped.
**Lop-sided,** lop'sīd-ed, *a.* Heavier at one side than the other; inclining to one side.
**Loquacious,** lo-kwā'shus, *a.* Talkative; garrulous; babbling.
**Loquacity,** lo-kwas'i-ti, *n.* Quality of being loquacious; garrulity.
**Lorcha,** lor'cha, *n.* A light Chinese sailing vessel, carrying guns.
**Lord,** lord, *n.* A master; a ruler; proprietor of a manor; a nobleman; a British title applied to peers, sons of dukes and marquises, and the eldest sons of earls; honorary title of certain high officials; (with *cap.*) the Supreme Being.—*vi.* To act as a lord; to rule with arbitrary or despotic sway.
**Lordling,** lord'ling, *n.* A petty lord.
**Lordly,** lord'li, *a.* Becoming a lord; large; ample; proud; haughty.
**Lordship,** lord'ship, *n.* State or quality of being a lord; a title given to a lord; dominion; sovereignty.
**Lore,** lōr, *n.* Learning; erudition; space between the bill and the eye of a bird.
**Lorgnette,** lor-nyet', *n.* An opera-glass.
**Lorgnon,** lor-nyông, *n.* A double eye-glass fitting into a handle.
**Loricate,** lo'ri-kāt, *a.* Covered as with plates of mail.
**Lorn,** lorn, *a.* Undone; forsaken; lonely.
**Lorry,** lo'ri, *n.* A long four-wheeled wagon without sides.
**Lose,** löz, *vt.* (losing, lost). To cease to possess, as through accident; to fail to keep; to forfeit; not to gain or win; to miss; to cease or fail to see or hear; to misuse.—*vi.* To suffer loss; not to win.
**Losing,** löz'ing, *p.a.* Bringing or causing loss.
**Loss,** los, *n.* Act of losing; failure to gain; that which is lost; failure to utilize.
**Lost,** lost, *p.a.* Gone from our hold, view, etc.; not to be found; ruined; wasted; forfeited; perplexed; alienated.
**Lot,** lot, *n.* A person's part or share; fate which falls to one; part in life allotted to a person; a distinct portion; a considerable quantity or number; something used to decide what is yet undecided.—*vt.* (lotting, lotted). To assign by lot; to sort; to portion.
**Lothario,** lō-thā'ri-ō, *n.* A gay libertine.
**Lotion,** lō'shon, *n.* A wash for the complexion; a fluid applied externally in ailments.
**Lottery,** lot'è-ri, *n.* A scheme for the distribution of prizes by lot or chance.
**Lotus,** lō'tus, *n.* A tree, the fruit of which was fabled to cause forgetfulness of the past; also the Egyptian water-lily and other plants.
**Loud,** loud, *a.* Having a great sound; noisy; showy.—*adv.* Loudly.
**Loudly,** loud'li, *adv.* Noisily; clamorously.
**Loudspeaker,** loud-spē'kėr, *n.* A device for converting electrical energy into sounds capable of being heard at a distance.
**Lounge,** lounj, *vi.* (lounging, lounged). To loiter; to loll.—*n.* An idle gait or stroll; act of reclining at ease; a place for lounging.
**Lounger,** lounj'ėr, *n.* An idler.
**Louse,** lous, *n.*; pl. **Lice,** līs. A wingless insect, parasitic on man and other animals.
**Lousy,** louz'i, *a.* Infested with lice.
**Lout,** lout, *n.* A mean, awkward fellow.—*vt.* To bend or stoop down.
**Loutish,** lout'ish, *a.* Like a lout; clownish.
**Lovable,** luv'a-bl, *a.* Worthy of love; amiable.
**Love,** luv, *vt.* (loving, loved). To regard with affection; to like; to delight in.—*vi.* To be in love; to be tenderly attached.—*n.* Warm affection; fond attachment; the passion between the sexes; the object beloved; a word of endearment; Cupid, the god of love; the score of nothing at tennis, etc.
**Love-bird,** luv'bėrd, *n.* A small species of parrot.
**Loveless,** luv'les, *a.* Void of love; void of tenderness.
**Love-lorn,** luv'lorn, *a.* Forsaken by one's love; pining from love.
**Lovely,** luv'li, *a.* That may excite love; beautifu; charming; delightful.
**Lover,** luv'ėr, *n.* One who loves; a suitor; a wooer; one who likes strongly.
**Loving,** luv'ing, *p.a.* Fond; kind; affectionate; expressing love or kindness.
**Loving-kindness,** luv-ing-kīnd'nes, *n.* Tender regard; mercy; favor.
**Lovingly,** luv'ing-li, *adv.* With love; affectionately.
**Low,** lō, *a.* Depressed below any given surface or place; not high; deep; below the usual rate; not loud; wanting strength; mean; dishonorable; not sublime; plain.—*adv.* Not aloft; under the usual price; near the ground; not loudly.
**Low,** lō, *vi.* To bellow, as an ox or cow.
**Lower,** lō'ėr, *vt.* To make lower; to let down; to abase; to reduce.
**Lower,** lou'ėr, *vi.* To frown; to look sullen; to threaten a storm.
**Lowering,** lou'ėr-ing, *p.a.* Threatening a storm; cloudy; overcast.
**Lowing,** lō'ing, *n.* The bellow of cattle.
**Lowland,** lō'land, *n.* Land which is low with respect to the neighboring country; a low or level country.—**The Lowlands,** the southern or lower parts of Scotland.
**Lowly,** lō'li, *a.* Humble in position of life; meek; free from pride.—*adv.* In a low manner or condition.
**Low-water,** lō'wa-tėr, *n.* The lowest point of the ebb or receding tide.
**Loyal,** loi'al, *a.* Faithful to a government, plighted love, duty, etc.; constant to friends or associates.
**Loyalist,** loi'al-ist, *n.* One who adheres to his sovereign or constituted authority.
**Loyally,** loi'al-li, *adv.* In a loyal manner.
**Loyalty,** loi'al-ti, *n.* State or quality of being loyal; fidelity; constancy.
**Lozenge,** lo'zenj, *n.* A figure with four equal sides, having two acute and two obtuse angles; a small cake of sugar, etc.; a small diamond-shaped pane of glass.
**Lubber,** lub'ėr, *n.* A heavy, clumsy fellow.
**Lubberly,** lub'ėr-li, *a.* Like a lubber; clumsy.
**Lubricant,** lū'brik-ant, *n.* A substance for oiling or greasing.
**Lubricate,** lū-brik-āt, *vt.* To make smooth; to smear with oil, to diminish friction.
**Lubrication,** lū-brik-ā'shon, *n.* Act or process of lubricating.
**Lubricator,** lū-brik-āt-ėr, *n.* One who or that which lubricates; an oil-cup attached to a machine.
**Lubricity,** lū-bris'i-ti, *n.* Smoothness of surface; slipperiness; lasciviousness.
**Lucent,** lū'sent, *a.* Shining; resplendent.
**Lucerne, Lucern,** lū'sėrn, *n.* A leguminous plant valuable as fodder.
**Lucid,** lū'sid, *a.* Full of light; shining; bright; clear; not darkened or confused by delirium;

easily understood.
**Lucidity,** lū-sid'i-ti, *n.* The state or quality of being lucid; clearness; intelligibility.
**Lucifer,** lū'si-fėr, *n.* The morning-star; Satan; a match ignitible by friction.
**Luck,** luk, *n.* That which happens to a person; chance; hap; fortune; success.
**Luckily,** luk'i-li, *adv.* In a lucky manner; fortunately; by good fortune.
**Lucky,** luk'i, *a.* Meeting with good luck or success; fortunate; auspicious.
**Lucrative,** lū'krat-iv, *a.* Pertaining to gain; gainful; profitable.
**Lucre,** lū'kėr, *n.* Gain in money or goods; profit; emolument; pelf.
**Luculent,** lū'kū-lent, *a.* Full of light; clear.
**Ludicrous,** lū'di-krus, *a.* That serves for sport; laughable; droll; ridiculous.
**Luff,** luf, *n.* The weather part of a fore-and-aft sail.—*vi.* To put the helm so as to turn the ship toward the wind.
**Lug,** lug, *vt.* (lugging, lugged). To haul; to drag.—*n.* The ear; object resembling the ear, as the handle of a vessel.
**Luggage,** lug'āj, *n.* Anything cumbersome and heavy; a traveller's baggage.
**Lugger,** lug'ėr, *n.* A small vessel of two or three masts with lug-sails.
**Lug-sail,** lug'sāl, *n.* A square sail bent on a yard that hangs obliquely to the mast.
**Lugubrious,** lū-gū'bri-us, *a.* Mournful; indicating sorrow; doleful.
**Lugworm,** lug'wėrm, *n.* A worm which burrows in the muddy sand of the shore.
**Lukewarm,** lūk'warm, *a.* Moderately warm; tepid; not zealous; indifferent.
**Lull,** lul, *vt.* To sing to, as to a child; to soothe.—*vi.* To subside; to become calm.—*n.* A season of quiet or cessation.
**Lullaby,** lul'a-bī, *n.* A song to lull or quiet babes; that which quiets.
**Lumbago,** lum-bā'gō, *n.* A rheumatic affection of the muscles about the loins.
**Lumbar,** lum'bar, *n.* Pertaining to or near the loins.
**Lumber,** lum'bėr, *n.* Anything useless and cumbersome; in America, timber sawed orsplit for use.—*vt.* To fill with lumber; to heap together in disorder.—*vi.* To move heavily, as a vehicle; in America, to cut and prepare timber.
**Luminary,** lū'min-a-ri, *n.* Any body that gives light.
**Luminosity,** lū-min-os'i-ti, *n.* The quality of being luminous; brightness; clearness.
**Luminous,** lū'min-us, *a.* Shining; bright; giving light; clear; lucid.
**Lump,** lump, *n.* A small mass of matter; a mass of things.—*vt.* To throw into a mass; to take in the gross.
**Lumping,** lump'ing, *a.* Bulky; heavy; big.
**Lumpish,** lump'ish, *a.* Like a lump; heavy; dull; inactive.
**Lump-sugar,** lump'shug-ėr, *n.* Loaf-sugar in small lumps or pieces.
**Lumpy,** lump'i, *a.* Full of lumps; showing small irregular waves.
**Lunacy,** lū'na-si, *n.* Mental derangement; madness; insanity; craziness; mania.
**Lunar,** lū'nar, *a.* Pertaining to the moon; measured by the revolutions of the moon.
**Lunatic,** lū'nat-ik, *a.* Affected with lunacy; mad; insane.—*n.* A madman.
**Lunation,** lū-nā'shon, *n.* A lunar month; time from one new moon to the next.
**Lunch, Luncheon,** lunsh, lunsh'on, *n.* A slight repast between breakfast and dinner.—*vi.* To take a lunch.
**Lune,** lūn, *n.* Anything in the shape of a half-moon or a crescent.
**Lunette,** lū-net', *n.* A small fortified work with an angular front; window in a concave ceiling; crescent-shaped ornament.
**Lung,** lung, *n.* Either of the two organs of respiration in air-breathing animals.
**Lunge,** lunj, *n.* A sudden thrust or pass, as with a sword.—*vi.* (lunging, lunged). To make a thrust.
**Lunged,** lungd, *a.* Having lungs.
**Lunula, Lunule,** lū'nū-la, lū'nūl, *n.* Something in the shape of a crescent.
**Lunular,** lū'nū-lėr, *a.* Having the form of a small crescent.
**Lupine,** lū'pin, *n.* A leguminous flowering plant.—*a.* lū'pīn. LIke a wolf; wolfish.
**Lupulin, Lupuline,** lū'pū-lin, *n.* The bitter aromatic principle of the hop.
**Lupus,** lū'pus, *n.* A disease which eats away the flesh of the face.
**Lurch,** lėrch, *vi.* To lurk; to roll or sway to one side.—*n.* A sudden roll or stagger; a difficult or helpless position.
**Lurdan, Lurdane,** lėr'dan, lėr'dān, *a.* Lazy and useless.—*n.* A lazy, stupid fellow.
**Lure,** lūr, *n.* Something held out to call a trained hawk; a bait; any enticement.—*vt.* (luring, lured). To attract by a lure or bait; to entice.
**Lurid,** lū'rid, *a.* Pale yellow, as flame; ghastly pale; wan; gloomy; dismal.
**Lurk,** lėrk, *vi.* To lie hid; to lie in wait.
**Luscious,** lu'shus, *a.* Very sweet; delicious; sweet to excess.
**Lush,** lush, *a.* Fresh, succulent.
**Lust,** lust, *n.* Longing desire; carnal appetite; depraved affections.—*vi.* To desire eagerly; to have carnal desire.
**Luster,** lus'ter, *n.* Brightness; brilliancy; renown; a branched chandelier ornamented with cut glass; a glossy fabric for dress.
**Lustful,** lust'ful, *a.* Inspired by lust or the sexual appetite; lewd; libidinous.
**Lustily,** lust'i-li, *adv.* In a lusty manner; with vigor of body; stoutly.
**Lustral,** lus'tral, *a.* Used in purification; pertaining to purification.
**Lustrate,** lus'trāt, *vt.* To purify as by water.
**Lustration,** lus-trā'shon, *n.* A solemn ceremony of purifying; purification.
**Lustring,** lūs'tring, *n.* A glossy silk cloth.
**Lustrous,** lus'trus, *a.* Full of luster; bright; shining; luminous.
**Lustrum,** lus'trum, *n.*; pl. **-rums** or **-ra.** In ancient Rome, the quinquennial purification of the people; a period of five years.
**Lusty,** lust'i, *a.* Vigorous; robust; healthful; bulky; large; lustful.
**Lute,** lūt, *n.* A stringed instrument of the guitar kind; a composition of clay, etc.—*vt.* (luting, luted). To play on the lute; to close or coat with lute.
**Lutheran,** lū'thėr-an, *a.* Pertaining to Martin Luther, the reformer.—*n.* A follower of Luther.
**Lutheranism,** lū'thėr-an-izm, *n.* The doctrines of the Protestant church in Germany.
**Luxate,** luks'āt, *vt.* To put out of joint, as a limb; to dislocate.
**Luxation,** luks-ā'shon, *n.* The act of luxating; dislocation.
**Luxuriance,** luks-ū'ri-ans, *n.* State of being luxuriant; rank growth; exuberance.
**Luxuriant,** luks-ū'ri-ant, *a.* Exuberant in growth; abundant.
**Luxuriate,** luks-ū'ri-āt, *vi.* To grow exuberantly; to feed or live luxuriously; to indulge without restraint.
**Luxurious,** luks-ū'ri-us, *a.* Given to luxury; voluptuous; furnished with luxuries.
**Luxuriously,** luks-ū'ri-us-li, *adv.* In a luxurious manner; voluptuously.
**Luxury,** luks'ū-ri, *n.* Extravagant indulgence; that which gratifies a fastidious appetite; anything delightful to the senses.
**Lycanthropy,** lī-kan'thro-pi, *n.* A kind of insanity in which the patient supposes himself to be a wolf.
**Lyceum,** lī-sē'um, *n.* A literary institute; a higher school.
**Lycopod,** lī'kō-pod, *n.* A plant of an order betwee

L

mosses and ferns.

**Lyddite,** lid'īt, *n.* A powerful explosive substance.

**Lye,** lī, *n.* Water impregnated with alkaline salt imbibed from the ashes of wood; solution of an alkali.

**Lying-in,** lī'ing-in, *n.* and *a.* Childbirth.

**Lyingly,** lī'ing-li, *adv.* Falsely; by telling lies.

**Lymph,** limf, *n.* Water; a watery fluid; a colorless fluid in animal bodies.

**Lymphatic,** lim-fat'ik, *a.* Pertaining to lymph; phlegmatic; sluggish.—*n.* A vessel in animal bodies which contains or conveys lymph.

**Lynch,** linsh, *vt.* To inflict punishment upon, without the forms of law, as by a mob.

**Lynx,** lingks, *n.* A carnivorous animal resembling the cat, noted for its keen sight.

**Lyre,** līr, *n.* A stringed instrument of the harp kind much used by the ancients.

**Lyric, Lyrical,** li'rik, li'rik-al, *a.* Pertaining to a lyre; designating that species of poetry which has reference to the individual emotions of the poet, such as songs.—**Lyric,** li'rik, *n.* A lyric poem; an author of lyric poems.

**Lyrist,** lir'ist, *n.* One who plays on the lyre; a writer of lyrics or lyric poetry.

# M

**Macabre,** mak-a'br, *a.* Gruesome; terrible.

**Macaroni,** ma-ka-rō'ni, *n.* A paste of fine wheat flour made into small tubes; a kind of dandy in fashion in London about 1760.

**Marcaronic,** ma-ka-rō'nik, *a.* Pertaining to macaroni, or to a macaroni; applied to burlesque verse consisting of vernacular words Latinized or Latin words modernized.

**Macaroon,** ma-ka-rön', *n.* A small sweet-cake, containing almonds.

**Macaw,** ma-ka', *n.* A bird of the parrot tribe with long tail-feathers.

**Mace,** mās, *n.* A staff with a heavy metal head; an ensign of authority borne before magistrates; a spice, the dried covering of the seed of the nutmeg.

**Macer,** mās'ėr, *n.* A mace-bearer.

**Macerate,** ma'se-rāt, *vt.* To steep almost to solution; to make lean or cause to waste away.

**Maceration,** ma-se-rā'shon, *n.* Act or process of macerating.

**Machiavelian,** ma'ki-a-vēl''i-an, *a.* Pertaining to *Machiavelli,* or denoting his principles; cunning in political management.

**Machinate,** mak'i-nāt, *vt.* and *i.* To plot or plan; to form, as a plot or scheme.

**Machination,** mak'i-nā''shon, *n.* A plot; an artful design or scheme.

**Machine,** ma-shēn', *n.* Any contrivance which serves to regulate the effect of a given force or to produce or change motion; an organized system; a person who acts as the tool of another.—*vt.* To apply machinery to; to produce by machinery.

**Machine-gun,** ma-shēn'gun, *n.* A small-caliber fire-arm arranged to fire from a stand, carriage or tripod, and provided with mechanical devices to produce a very rapid rate of fire.

**Machinery,** ma-shēn'e-ri, *n.* The component parts of a complex machine; machines in general.

**Machinist,** ma-shēn'ist, *n.* A constructor of machines; one who works a machine.

**Mackerel,** mak'ėr-el, *n.* An edible sea fish.

**Mackintosh, Macintosh,** mak'in-tosh, *n.* A waterproof overcoat.

**Macrocosm,** mak'ro-kozm, *n.* The great world; the universe, analogous to the *microcosm.*

**Macula,** ma'kū-la, *n.*; pl. **-lae.** A spot, as on the skin.

**Maculate,** ma'kū-lāt, *vt.* To spot; to stain.—*a.* Marked with spots; impure.

**Mad,** mad, *a.* Disordered in intellect; insane; crazy; frantic; furious; infatuated.—*vt.* (madding, madded). To make mad.

**Madam,** ma'dam, *n.* My lady; a complimentary title given to ladies.

**Madcap,** mad'kap, *n.* and *a.* A flighty or hare-brained person; one who indulges in frolics.

**Madden,** mad'n, *vt.* To make mad.—*vi.* To become mad; to act as if mad.

**Madder,** mad'ėr, *n.* A climbing perennial plant, the root of which furnishes dyes and pigments.

**Madding,** mad'ing, *a.* Acting madly; wild.

**Made,** mād, pret. and pp. of *make.*

**Madeira,** ma-dē'ra, *n.* A rich wine made on the isle of Madeira.

**Mademoiselle,** mad-mwä-zel, *n.* Miss; a title given to young unmarried ladies in France.

**Mad-house,** mad'hous, *n.* A house where mad or insane persons are confined.

**Madly,** mad'li, *adv.* In a mad manner; frantically; furiously; rashly; wildly.

**Madman,** mad'man, *n.* A man who is mad; a maniac; a lunatic.

**Madness,** mad'nes, *n.* Lunacy; frenzy; extreme folly.

**Madonna,** ma-don'na, *n.* The Virgin Mary; a picture representing the Virgin.

**Madrepore,** ma'dre-pōr, *n.* A common branching variety of coral.

**Madrigal,** mad'ri-gal, *n.* A pastoral song; vocal composition in five or six parts.

**Maestoso,** mä-es-tō'zō, In *music,* with dignity.

**Maestro,** mä-es'trō, *n.* A master of any art; a musical composer.

**Magazine,** mag'a-zēn, *n.* A storehouse; a repository for ammunition or provisions; a serial publication.

**Magazine-rifle,** mag'a-zēn-rī-fl, *n.* A rifle that can fire a number of shots in rapid succession without reloading.

**Magdalen, Magdalene,** mag'da-len, mag'da-lēn, *n.* A reformed prostitute.

**Magenta,** ma-jen'ta, *n.* A brilliant blue-red color derived from coal-tar.

**Maggot,** ma'got, *n.* The larva of a fly or other insect; a grub; an odd fancy.

**Magi,** mā'jī, *n.pl.* The caste of priests among the ancient Medes and Persians; holy men or sages of the East.

**Magic,** ma'jik, *n.* The art of producing effects by superhuman means; sorcery; enchantment; power similar to that of enchantment.—*a.* Pertaining to magic; working or worked by or as if by magic.

**Magical,** ma'jik-al, *a.* Magic.

**Magically,** ma'jik-al-li, *adv.* In a magical manner; by enchantment.

**Magician,** ma-ji'shan, *n.* One skilled in magic; an enchanter.

**Magilp, Magilph,** ma-gilp', ma-gilf', *n.* A mixture of linseed-oil and mastic varnish used by artists as a vehicle for colors.

**Magisterial,** ma-jis-tē'ri-al, *a.* Pertaining to a master or magistrate; imperious; haughty; authoritative.

**Magistracy,** ma'jis-tra-si, *n.* The office or dignity of a magistrate; the body of magistrates.

**Magistrate,** ma'jis-trāt, *n.* A public civil officer, with executive or judicial authority.

**Magnanimity,** mag-na-nim'i-ti, *n.* Quality of being magnanimous; greatness of soul or mind.

**Magnanimous,** mag-nan'im-us, *a.* Great of soul or mind; elevated in sentiment; liberal and honorable; not selfish.

**Magnate,** mag'nāt, *n.* A great man; a person of rank or wealth.

**Magnesia,** mag-nē'si-a, *n.* Oxide of magnesium, a white slightly alkaline powder.

**Magnesian,** mag-nē'si-an, *a.* Pertaining to, containing, or resembling magnesia.

**Magnesium,** mag-nē'si-um, *n.* Metallic base of magnesia, a white malleable metal.

**Magnet,** mag'net, *n.* The loadstone, which has the property of attracting iron; a bar of iron or steel to which the properties of the loadstone have been imparted.

**Magnetic,** mag-net'ik, *a.* Pertaining to the magnet; possessing the properties of the magnet; attractive.

**Magnetically,** mag-net'ik-al-li, *adv.* In a magnetic manner; by magnetism.

**Magnetism,** mag'net-izm, *n.* A property of certain bodies whereby they naturally attract or repel one another; that branch of science which treats of magnetic phenomena; power of attraction.

**Magnetize,** mag'net-īz, *vt.* To give magnetic properties to.—*vi.* To acquire magnetic properties.

**Magneto-electricity,** mag-net'ō-ē-lek-tris'i-ti, *n.* Electricity evolved by the action of magnets.

**Magneto,** mag-nēt'ō, *n.* The igniting apparatus of a petrol engine.

**Magnific, Magnifical,** mag-nik'ik, mag-nif'ik-al, *a.* Grand; splendid; illustrious.

**Magnificence,** mag-nif'i-sens, *n.* Grandeur of appearance; splendor; pomp.

**Magnificent,** mag-nif'i-sent, *a.* Grand in appearance; splendid; showy.

**Magnificently,** mag-nif'i-sent-li, *adv.* In a magnificent manner.

**Magnifier,** mag'ni-fī-ėr, *n.* One who or that which magnifies.

**Magnify,** mag'ni-fī, *vt.* To make great or greater; to increase the apparent dimensions of; to extol; to exaggerate.—*vi.* To possess the quality of causing objects to appear larger.

**Magnitude,** mag'ni-tūd, *n.* Greatness; size; bulk; importance; consequence.

**Magnum,** mag'num, *n.* A bottle holding two English quarts.

**Magpie,** mag'pī, *n.* A chattering bird of the crow tribe with black and white plumage; a shot on the target between an inner and an outer.

**Magyar,** mag'yär, *n.* A Hungarian; the language of Hungary.

**Maharajah,** mä-hä-rä'ja, *n.* The title assumed by some Indian princes ruling over a considerable extent of territory.

**Mahdi,** mä'di, *n.* A name of some of the successors of Mohammed; one who is to spread Mohammedanism over the world.

**Mahl-stick,** mal'stik, *n.* A rod used by artists as a rest for the hand in painting.

**Mahogany,** ma-hog'a-ni, *n.* A tree of tropical America; its wood, reddish in color, used for cabinet work.

**Mahout,** ma-hout', *n.* An E. Indian elephant driver or keeper.

**Maid,** mād, *n.* A young unmarried woman; a girl; a virgin; a female servant.

**Maiden,** mād'n, *n.* A maid or virgin; an old Scottish instrument of capital punishment resembling the guillotine.—*a.* Pertaining to maidens; unpolluted; unused; first.

**Maidenhair,** mād'n-hār, *n.* An elegant fern found growing on rocks and walls.

**Maidenhead,** mād'n-hed, *n.* Virginity; the hymen.

**Maidenhood,** mād'n-hud, *n.* The state of being a maid; virginity.

**Maidenly,** mād'n-li, *a.* Like a maid; gentle; modest.

**Maid-servant** mād'sėr-vant, *n.* A female servant.

**Maigre,** mā'gr, *a.* A term applied to a preparation cooked merely with butter.

**Mail,** māl, *n.* A bag for conveying letters, etc.; letters conveyed; person or conveyance carrying the mail; armor of chain-work, etc.—*vt.* (mailing, mailed). To send by mail; to post; to arm with mail.

**Maim,** mām, *vt.* To mutilate; to disable.—*n.* An injury by which a person is maimed.

**Main,** mān, *a.* Chief, or most important; mighty; vast; directly applied; used with all one's might.—*n.* Strength; great effort; chief or main portion; the ocean; a principal gas or water pipe in a street; a hand at dice; a match at cock-fighting.

**Mainland,** mān'land, *n.* The principal land, as opposed to an isle; the continent.

**Mainly,** mān'li, *adv.* In the main; chiefly.

**Main-spring,** mān'spring, *n.* The principal spring of any piece of mechanism; the main cause of any action.

**Main-stay,** mān'stā, *n.* The stay extending from the top of a vessel's main-mast to the deck; chief support.

**Maintain,** mān-tān', *vt.* To hold or keep in any particular state; to sustain; to continue; to uphold; to vindicate; to assert.—*vi.* To affirm a position; to assert.

**Maintainable,** mān-tān'a-bl, *a.* That may be maintained; sustainable; defensible.

**Maintenance,** mān'ten-ans, *n.* Act of maintaining; means of support or livelihood; continuance.

**Maize,** māz, *n.* Indian corn.

**Majestic,** ma-jes'tik, *a.* Having majesty; august; sublime; lofty; stately.

**Majestically,** ma-jes'tik-al-li, *adv.* In a majestic manner.

**Majesty,** ma'jes-ti, *n.* Grandeur or dignity; a title of emperors, kings, and queens.

**Majolica,** ma-jol'i-ka, *n.* A kind of pottery richly colored and enameled.

**Major,** mā'jėr, *a.* The greater in number, quantity, or extent; the more important.—*n.* A military officer next above a captain; a person aged twenty-one years complete.

**Major-domo,** mā-jėr-dō'mo, *n.* A man who takes charge of a large household; a great officer of a palace.

**Major-general,** mā'jėr-jen'ėr-al, *n.* An army officer next in rank below a lieutenant-general.

**Majority,** ma-jo'ri-ti, *n.* The greater number; excess of one number over another; full age; rank or commission of a major.

**Majuscule,** ma-jus'kūl, *n.* A capital letter.

**Make,** māk, *vt.* (making, made). To produce or effect; to cause to be; to compose; to constitute; to perform; to cause to have any quality; to force; to gain; to complete; to arrive at; to have within sight.—*vi.* To act or do; to tend; to contribute; to flow toward land.—*n.* Form; structure; texture.

**Make-believe,** māk'bē-lēv, *n.* Pretense; sham.—*a.* Unreal; sham.

**Maker,** māk'ėr, *n.* One who makes; the Creator.

**Make-shift,** māk'shift, *n.* An expedient to serve a present purpose.

**Make-up,** māk'up, *n.* The manner in which one is dressed for a part in a play.

**Making,** māk'ing, *n.* Workmanship; what is made at one time; material; means of bringing successs in life; state of being made.

**Malachite,** mal'a-kit, *n.* Green carbonate of copper, used for many ornamental purposes.

**Malacology,** mal-a-kol'o-ji, *n.* The branch of zoology that treats of the mollusca.

**Maladjustment,** mal-ad-just'ment, *n.* A bad or wrong adjustment.

**Maladroit,** mal-a-droit', *a.* Awkward.

**Malady,** mal'a-di, *n.* Any disease of the human body; moral or mental disorder.

**Malar,** mā'lėr, *a.* Pertaining to the cheek or cheek-bone.

**Malaria,** ma-lā'ri-a, *n.* Noxious exhalations causing fever; fever produced by this cause.

**Malarial, Malarious,** ma-lā'ri-al, ma-lā'ri-us, *a.* Infected by malaria.

**Malay, Malayan,** ma-lā', ma-lā'yan, *n.* A native of the Malay Peninsula; their language.—*a.* Belonging to the Malays.

**Malcontent,** mal'kon-tent, *n.* A discontented person.—*a.* Discontented with the rule under which one lives.

**Male,** māl, *a.* Pertaining to the sex that begets young; masculine.—*n.* One of the sex that begets young; a plant which has stamens only.

**Malefactor,** mal-e-fak'tėr, *n.* A criminal; a culprit;

a felon.
**Malevolence,** ma-lev'ō-lens, *n.* Ill-will; personal hatred.
**Malevolent,** ma-lev'ō-lent, *a.* Having ill-will; evil-minded; spiteful; malicious.
**Malformation,** mal-form-ā'shon, *n.* Ill or wrong formation; deformity.
**Malic,** mā'lik, *a.* Pertaining to apples.
**Malice,** mal'is, *n.* A disposition to injure others; spite; ill-will; rancor.
**Malicious,** ma-li'shus, *a.* Evil-disposed; evil-minded; spiteful; rancorous.
**Malign,** ma-līn', *a.* Of an evil nature or disposition; malicious; pernicious.—*vt.* To defame; to villify.
**Malignance, Malignancy,** ma-lig'nans, ma-lig'nan-si, *n.* Extreme malevolence; virulence.
**Malignant,** ma-lig'nant, *a.* Having extreme malevolence; unpropitious; virulent; dangerous to life; extremely heinous.—*n.* A man of extreme enmity.
**Malignity,** ma-lig'ni-ti, *n.* Evil disposition of heart; rancor; virulence.
**Malinger,** ma-ling'gėr, *vi.* To feign illness in order to avoid military duty.
**Malingerer,** ma-ling'gėr-ėr, *n.* One who feigns himself ill.
**Malison,** mal'i-zn, *n.* A malediction; curse.
**Mall,** mal, *n.* A heavy wooden beetle or hammer; a public walk; a level shaded walk.
**Mallard,** mal'ard, *n.* The common wild duck.
**Malleability,** mal'lē-a-bil''i'ti, *n.* Quality of being malleable.
**Malleable,** mal'lē-a-bl, *a.* Capable of being beaten out with a hammer; easily persuaded.
**Mallet,** mal'et, *n.* A wooden hammer; a long-handled mallet is used in polo, croquet, etc.
**Mallow,** mal'ō, *n.* A plant with downy leaves.
**Malmsey,** mäm'zi, *n.* A kind of grape; a strong sweet white wine.
**Malnutrition,** mal-nū-tri'shon, *n.* Faulty feeding.
**Malpractice,** mal-prak'tis, *n.* Evil practice.
**Malt,** malt, *n.* Barley or other grain steeped in water till it germinates, then dried in a kiln and used in brewing.—*vt.* To make into malt.—*vi.* To become malt.
**Maltese,** mal-tēz', *n. sing.* and *pl.* A native or natives of Malta.—*a.* Belonging to Malta.
**Malting,** malt'ing, *n.* The act or process of making malt; ä work where malt is made.
**Malt-liquor,** malt'lik-ėr, *n.* A liquor prepared from malt by fermentation, as beer.
**Maltman, Maltster,** malt'man, malt'stėr, *n.* A man who makes malt.
**Maltreat,** mal-trēt, *vt.* To treat ill or roughly; to abuse.
**Maltreatment,** mal-trēt'ment, *n.* Ill-usage.
**Malversation,** mal-vėr-sā'shon, *n.* Fraudulent tricks; corruption in office.
**Mama, Mamma,** ma-mä', *n.* Mother.
**Mamma,** mam'ma, *n.* pl. **mae.** The breast; the organ that secretes the milk.
**Mammal,** mam'mal, *n.* An animal of the class Mammalia.
**Mammalia,** mam-mā'li-a, *n.pl.* The highest class in the animal kingdom, whose distinctive characteristic is that the female suckles the young.
**Mammilla,** mam-mil'la, *n.* A nipple, or something of this form.
**Mammillary,** mam'mil-a-ri, *a.* Pertaining to or resembling a nipple.
**Mammon,** mam'on, *n.* A Syrian god of riches; riches; wealth.
**Mammoth,** mam'oth, *n.* An extinct species of elephant.—*a.* Very large; gigantic.
**Man,** man, *n.*; pl. **Men,** men. A human being; a male adult of the human race; mankind; the male sex; a male servant; a piece in a game, as chess, etc.—*vt.* (manning, manned). To furnish with men; to guard with men; *refl.* to infuse courage into.
**Manacle,** man'a-kl, *n.* An instrument of iron for fastening the hands; a handcuff; used chiefly in the *plural*.—*vt.* (manacling, manacled). To put manacles on; to fetter.
**Manage,** man'āj, *vt.* (managing, managed). To wield; to direct in riding; to conduct or administer; to have under command; to treat with judgment.—*vi.* To conduct affairs.
**Manageable,** man'āj-a-bl, *a.* That may be managed; tractable.
**Management,** man'āj-ment, *n.* Act of managing; administration; manner of treating, body directing a business, etc.
**Manager,** man'āj-ėr, *n.* One who manages; one at the head of a business; a good economist.
**Manakin,** man'a-kin, *n.* A manikin; a small tropical American bird.
**Manatee,** man-a-tē', *n.* The sea-cow, an aquatic herbivorous mammal.
**Manchet,** man'shet, *n.* A small loaf of fine bread.—*a.* Fine and white.
**Manciple,** man'si-pl, *n.* A steward; a purveyor of a college or inn of court.
**Mandamus,** man-dā'mus, *n.* A writ requiring a person, corporation, or inferior court to do some specified act.
**Mandarin,** man-da-rēn', *n.* A Chinese public official; the court-language of China.
**Mandatary, Mandatory,** man'da-ta-ri, man'da-to-ri, *n.* One to whom a mandate is given.
**Mandate,** man'dāt', *n.* A command; written authority to act for a person.
**Mandatory,** man'da-to-ri, *a.* Containing a command; preceptive; directory.
**Mandible,** man'di-bl, *n.* An animal's jaw.
**Mandibular,** man-dib'ū-lėr, *a.* Belonging to the mandible or jaw.
**Mandoline, Mandolin,** man'dō-lin, *n.* A musical instrument of the guitar kind.
**Mandrake,** man'drāk, *n.* A narcotic plant with large thick roots.
**Mandrel, Mandril,** man'drel, man'dril, *n.* A bar or spindle, used variously.
**Mandrill,** man'dril, *n.* The great blue-faced or rib-nosed baboon.
**Mane,** mān, *n.* The long hair on the neck of a horse, lion, etc.
**Manège,** ma-nāzh', *n.* Horsemanship; a school for horsemanship.
**Manequin, Manikin,** man'i-kin, *n.* An artist's model of wood or wax.
**Manes,** mā'nēz, *n.pl.* Among the Romans the souls or shades of the dead.
**Maneuver,** ma-nū'vėr or ma-nö'vėr, *n.* A regulated movement, particularly of troops or ships; management with address; strategem.—*vi.* (maneuvering, maneuvered). To perform military or naval maneuvers; to employ stratagem; to manage with address.-*vt.* To cause to perform maneuvers.
**Manful,** man'ful, *a.* Having the spirit of a man; bold; honorable; energetic.
**Manfully,** man'ful-li, *adv.* Courageously.
**Manganese,** man̄-gan-ēz', *n.* A metal resembling iron.
**Manganite,** man'gan-īt, *n.* An ore of manganese, used in the manufacture of glass.
**Mange,** mānj, *n.* A skin disease of horses, cattle, dogs, etc.
**Manger,** mān'jėr, *n.* A trough in which food is placed for cattle and horses.
**Mangle,** mang'gl, *vt.* (mangling, mangled). To mutilate; to lacerate; to smooth, as linen.—*n.* A rolling press, or small calender, for smoothing cotton or linen.
**Mango,** mang'gō, *n.* The fruit of the mango-tree, a native of Asia.
**Mangosteen,** mang'gō-stēn, *n.* An E. Indian tree, with a delicious fruit.
**Mangrove,** man'grōv, *n.* A tropical tree growing on shores.
**Mangy,** mān'ji, *a.* Infected with the mange; scabby.
**Manhole,** man'hōl, *n.* A hole for admitting a man into a drain, steam-boiler, etc.

**Manhood,** man'hud, *a.* State of one who is a man; humanity; virility; manliness.
**Mania,** mā'ni-a, *n.* Insanity; madness; eager desire for anything; morbid craving.
**Maniac,** mā'ni-ak, *a.* Affected with mania; mad.—*n.* A madman.
**Maniacal,** ma-nī'ak-al, *a.* Affected with mania.
**Manicure,** man'i-kūr, *n.* One whose occupation is to trim the nails, etc., of the hand.
**Manifest,** man'i-fest, *a.* Clearly visible; evident; obvious.—*vt.* To make manifest; to display or exhibit.—*n.* A document stating a ship's cargo, destination, etc.
**Manifestation,** man'i-fest-ā''shon, *n.* Act of manifesting; exhibition; revelation; what serves to make manifest.
**Manifestly,** man'i-fest-li, *adv.* Evidently.
**Manifesto,** man-i-fest'ō, *n.* A public declaration; a proclamation.
**Manifold,** man'i-fōld, *a.* Numerous and various; of divers kinds.—*vt.* To multiply impressions of, as by a copying apparatus.
**Manikin,** man'i-kin, *n.* A little man; a dwarf; model of the human body.
**Manilla, Manila,** ma-nil'a, *n.* A kind of cheroot manufactured in *Manila.*
**Manipulate,** ma-nip'ū-lāt, *vt.* To treat with the hands; to handle; to operate upon so as to disguise.
**Manipulation,** ma-nip'ū-lā''shon, *n.* Act, art, or mode of manipulating.
**Manipulator,** ma-nip'ū-lāt-ėr, *n.* One who manipulates.
**Manis,** mā'nis, *n.* The pangolin or scaly anteater.
**Mankind,** man-kīnd', *n.* The species of human beings; the males of the human race.
**Manlike,** man'līk, *a.* Like a man; masculine; manly.
**Manliness,** man'li-nes, *n.* The best qualities of a man; manhood; bravery.
**Manly,** man'li, *a.* Having the qualities that best become a man; brave, resolute, etc.
**Manna,** man'na, *n.* A substance furnished as food for the Israelites in the wilderness; the sweet juice of a species of ash.
**Mannequin,** man'ē-kin, *n.* Person employed by dressmakers, etc., to wear and display costumes.
**Manner,** man'ėr, *n.* The mode in which anything is done; method; bearing or conduct; *pl.* carriage or behavior; civility in society; sort or kind.
**Mannered,** man'ėrd, *a.* Having manners of this or that kind.
**Mannerism,** man'ėr-izm, *n.* Adherence to the same manner; tasteless uniformity of style; peculiarity of personal manner.
**Mannerly,** man'ėr-li, *a.* Showing good manners; polite; respectful.
**Mannish,** man'ish, *a.* Characteristic of or resembling a man; bold or masculin.
**Man-of-war,** man'ov-war, *n.*; pl. **Men-of-war.** A war-vessel.
**Manometer,** ma-nom'et-ėr, *n.* An instrument to measure the elastic force of gases.
**Manor,** ma'nor, *n.* The land belonging to a lord; a lordship.
**Mansion,** man'shon, *n.* A large dwelling-house; abode; house of the lord of a manor.
**Manslaughter,** man'sla-tėr, *n.* Murder; the unlawful killing of a man without malice.
**Mantel, Mantel-piece,** man'tel, man'tel-pēs, *n.* The ornamental work above a fireplace; a narrow shelf or slab there.
**Mantelet, Mantlet,** man'tel-et, mant'let, *n.* A small mantle.
**Mantilla,** man-til'la, *n.* A mantle or hood; a Spanish lady's veil.
**Mantle,** man'tl, *n.* A kind of cloak worn over other garments; something that covers and conceals; incandescent hood for gas jet.—*vt.* (mantling, mantled). To cloak; to cover as with a mantle.—*vi.* To become covered with a coating; to cream; to display superficial changes of hue.
**Mantua,** man'tū-a, *n.* A lady's gown or mantle.
**Manual,** man'ū-al, *a.* Performed by the hand; used or made by the hand.—*n.* A small book; a compendium; the service-book of the R. Catholic Church; keyboard of an organ.
**Manufactory,** man-ū-fak'to-ri, *n.* A building in which goods are manufactured.
**Manufacture,** man-ū-fak'tūr, *n.* The process of making anything by hand or machinery; something made from raw materials.—*vt.* (manufacturing, manufactured). To fabricate from raw materials; to fabricate without real grounds.—*vi.* To be occupied in manufactures.
**Manufacturer,** man-ū-fak'tūr-ėr, *n.* One who manufactures; owner of a manufactory.
**Manufacturing,** man-ū-fak'tūr-ing, *p.a.* Pertaining to or occupied in manufactures.
**Manumit,** man-ū-mit', *vt.* (manumitting, manumitted). To release from slavery.
**Manure,** man-ūr', *vt.* (manuring, manured). To fertilize with nutritive substances.—*n.* Any substance added to soil to accelerate or increase the production of the crops.
**Manuscript,** man'ū-skript, *n.* A paper written with the hand: often contracted to *MS.*, pl. *MSS.*—*a.* Written with the hand.
**Manx,** mangks, *n.* The native language of the Isle of Man; *pl.* the natives of Man.—*a.* Belonging to the Isle of Man.
**Many,** me'ni, *a.* Forming or comprising a number; numerous.—**The many,** the great majority of people; the crowd.—**So many,** the same number of; a certain number indefinitely.
**Maori,** mä'o-ri, *n.* One of the native inhabitants of New Zealand.
**Map,** map, *n.* A representation of the surface of the earth or of any part of it.—*vt.* (mapping, mapped). To draw in a map; to plan.
**Maple,** mā'pl, *n.* A tree of the sycamore kind.
**Mar,** mär, *vt.* (marring, marred). To injure in any manner; to hurt, impair, disfigure, etc.
**Marabou,** ma'ra-bö, *n.* A large stork yielding valuable white feathers.
**Marasmus,** ma-ras'mus, *n.* A wasting of flesh without apparent disease; atrophy.
**Maraud,** ma-rad', *vi.* To rove in quest of plunder; to make an excursion for booty.
**Marauder,** ma-rad'ėr, *n.* A plunderer.
**Marble,** mär'bl, *n.* A calcareous stone of compact texture; a little hard ball used by boys in play; an inscribed or sculptured marble stone.—*a.* Made of or like marble.—*vt.* (marbling, marbled). To stain like marble.
**Marbling,** mär'bl-ing, *n.* Imitation of marble; veined coloring on the edges of a book.
**March,** märch, *vi.* To move by steps and in order, as soldiers; to walk in a stately manner; to progress; to be situated next.—*vt.* To cause to march.—*n.* The measured walk of a body of men; a stately walk; distance passed over; a musical composition to regulate the march of troops, etc.; a frontier or boundary (usually in *pl.*); the third month of the year.
**Marchpane,** märch'pān, *n.* A kind of sweet bread or biscuit.
**Mare,** mār, *n.* The female of the horse.
**Margarine,** mär'ga-rin, *n.* An imitation of butter, made from animal fat.
**Margin,** mär'jin, *n.* An edge, border, brink; edge of a page left blank; difference between the cost and selling price.—*vt.* To furnish with a margin; to enter in the margin.
**Marginal,** mär'jin-al, *a.* Pertaining to a margin; written or printed in the margin.
**Marigold,** ma'ri-gōld, *n.* A composite plant bearing golden-yellow flowers.
**Marine,** ma-rēn', *a.* Pertaining to the sea; found in the sea; used at sea; naval; maritime.—*n.* A soldier who serves on board of a man-of-war; collective shipping of a country; whole economy of naval affairs.
**Mariner,** ma'rin-ėr, *n.* A seaman; sailor.

M

**Mariolatry,** mā-ri-ol'a-tri, *n.* The adoration of the Virgin Mary.
**Marionette,** ma'ri-o-net'', *n.* A puppet moved by strings.
**Marital,** ma'ri-tal, *a.* Pertaining to a husband.
**Maritime,** ma'ri-tīm, *a.* Relating to the sea; naval; bordering on the sea; having a navy and commerce by sea.
**Marjoram,** mär'jō-ram, *n.* A plant of the mint family.
**Mark,** märk, *n.* A visible sign or impression on something; a distinguishing sign; indication or evidence; pre-eminence or importance; a characteristic; heed or regard; object aimed at; proper standard; extreme estimate; a German coin.—*vt.* To make a mark or marks on; to denote (often with *out*); to regard, observe, heed.—*vi.* To note; to observe critically; to remark.
**Marked,** märkt, *p.a.* Pre-eminent; outstanding; prominent; remarkable.
**Marker,** märk'ėr, *n.* One who marks; a counter used in card-playing.
**Market,** mär'ket, *n.* An occasion on which goods are publicly exposed for sale; place in which goods are exposed for sale; rate of purchase and sale; demand for commodities; privilege of keeping a public market.—*vi.* To deal in a market.—*vt.* To offer for sale in a market.
**Marketable,** mär'ket-a-bl, *a.* Fit for the market; that may be sold.
**Market-garden,** mär'ket-gär-dn, *n.* A garden growing vegetables, etc., for market.
**Marketing,** mär'ket-ing, *n.* Attendance upon a market; commodities purchased.
**Marking-ink,** märk'ing-ingk, *n.* Indelible ink, used for marking linen, etc.
**Marksman,** märks'man, *n.* One who is skilful to hit a mark; one who shoots well.
**Marl,** märl, *n.* A rich calcareous earth much used for manure.—*vt.* To manure with marl.
**Marlaceous,** märl-ā'shus, *a.* Resembling marl; partaking of the qualities of marl.
**Marline,** mär'lin, *n.* A small line of two strands, used for winding round ships' ropes.—*vt.* To wind marline round.
**Marlinespike,** mär'lin-spīk, *n.* An iron tool for opening the strands of rope.
**Marly,** märl'i, *a.* Consisting in or partaking of marl; resembling marl.
**Marmalade,** mär'ma-lād, *n.* A preserve made from various fruits, especially acid fruits, such as the orange.
**Marmorate,** mär'mo-rāt, *a.* Covered with marble; variegated like marble.
**Marmoreal,** mär-mō'rē-al, *a.* Pertaining to marble; made of marble.
**Marmot,** mär'mot, *n.* A hibernating rodent animal of northern latitudes.
**Maroon,** ma-rön, *n.* A fugitive slave in the W. Indies; a brownish crimson or claret color.—*vt.* To land and leave on a desolate island.
**Marque,** märk, *n.* Used in phrase *letter* or *letters of marque,* meaning a license to a private vessel to attack the ships, etc., of a public enemy.
**Marquee,** mär-kē', *n.* A large tent erected for a temporary purpose; an officer's field tent.
**Marquetry,** mär'ket-ri, *n.* Inlaid work.
**Marquis, Marquess,** mär'kwis, mär'kwes, *n.* A title of honor next below that of duke.
**Marriage,** ma'rij, *n.* The act or ceremony of marrying; matrimony; wedlock.
**Marriageable,** ma'rij-a-bl, *a.* Of an age suitable for marriage; fit to be married.
**Married,** ma'rid, *p.a.* Joined in marriage; conjugal; connubial.
**Marrow,** ma'rō, *n.* A soft substance in the cavities of bones; the best part; a kind of gourd, also called *vegetable marrow.*
**Marrow-bone,** ma'rō-bōn, *n.* A bone containing marrow.
**Marry,** ma'ri, *vt.* (marrying, married). To unite in wedlock; to dispose of in wedlock; to take for husband or wife.—*vi.* To take a husband or a wife.—*interj.* Indeed; forsooth.
**Mars,** märz, *n.* The god of war; a planet.
**Marsh,** märsh, *n.* A swamp; a tract of low wet land.—*a.* Pertaining to boggy places.
**Marshal,** mär'shal, *n.* One who regulates rank and order at a feast, procession, etc.; a military officer of the highest rank, generally called *field-marshal.*—*vt.* (marshalling, marshalled). To dispose in order; to array.
**Marshalling,** mär'shal-ing, *n.* Act of arranging in due order; arrangement of coats of arms on a shield.
**Marsh-mallow,** märsh'mal-ō, *n.* A plant of the hollyhock genus.
**Marshy,** märsh'i, *a.* Abounding in marshes; boggy; fenny; produced in marshes.
**Marsupial,** mär-sū'pi-al, *n.* and *a.* One of a large group of mammalians whose young are born in an imperfect condition and nourished in an external abdominal pouch.
**Mart,** märt, *n.* A market.
**Martello-tower,** mär-tel'ō-tou-ėr, *n.* A small round fort defending the sea-board.
**Marten,** mär'ten, *n.* A fierce kind of weasel, valued for its fur.
**Martial,** mär'shal, *a.* Pertaining to war; warlike.
**Martin,** mär'tin, *n.* A species of swallow.
**Martinet,** mär'ti-net, *n.* A precise, punctilious, or strict disciplinarian.
**Martingale,** mär'tin-gāl, *n.* A strap to prevent a horse from rearing; a short spar under the bowsprit.
**Martyr,** mär'tėr, *n.* One who suffers death or persecution on account of his belief; one greatly afflicted.—*vt.* To put to death for adhering to one's belief.
**Martyrdom,** mär'tėr-dom, *n.* The doom or death of a martyr.
**Marvel,** mär'vel, *n.* A wonder; something very astonishing.—*vi.* (marvelling, marvelled). To feel admiration or astonishment.
**Marvellous,** mär'vel-us, *a.* Exciting wonder or surprise; wonderful; astonishing.
**Marvellously,** mär'vel-us-li, *adv.* In a marvellous manner; wonderfully.
**Mascot,** mas'kot, *n.* A thing supposed to bring good luck to its owner.
**Masculine,** mas'kū-lin, *a.* Male; manly; robust; bold or unwomanly; designating nouns which are the names of male animals, etc.
**Mash,** mash, *n.* A mixture of ingredients beaten or blended together; a mixture of ground malt and warm water yielding wort.—*vt.* To mix; to beat into a confused mass.
**Mask,** mask, *n.* A cover for the face; a masquerade; a sort of play common in the 16th and 17th centuries; pretense.—*vt.* To cover with a mask; to disguise; to hide.
**Masked,** maskt, *a.* Having the face covered; wearing a mask; concealed; disguised.
**Masochism,** mas'ō-kism, *n.* Pathological sexual condition in which pleasure is derived from cruel treatment by the associate.
**Mason,** mā'sn, *n.* One who prepares stone, and constructs buildings; a freemason.
**Masonic,** ma-son'ik, *a.* Pertaining to the craft or mysteries of freemasons.
**Masonry,** mā'sn-ri, *n.* The art or occupation of a mason; stonework; the doctrines and practices of freemasons.
**Masquerade,** mas-kėr-ād', *n.* An assembly of persons wearing masks; a disguise.—*vi.* To assemble in masks; to go in disguise.
**Masquerader,** mas-kėr-ā'dėr, *n.* One who masquerades; one disguised.
**Mass,** mas, *n.* A body of matter; a lump; magnitude; an assemblage; collection; the generality; the communion service in the R. Catholic Church.—**The Masses,** the populace.—*vt.* and *i.* To form into a mass; to assemble in crowds.
**Massacre,** mas'sa-kėr, *n.* Ruthless, unnecessary, or indiscriminate slaughter.—*vt.* (massacring, massacred). To kill with indiscriminate vio-

lence; to slaughter.
**Massage,** ma-säzh′ or mas′āj, *n.* A process of kneading, rubbing, pressing, etc., parts of a person's body to effect a cure.—*vt.* (massaging, massaged). To treat by this process.
**Masseuse,** mas′öz, *n.* A female who practices massage.
**Masseur,** mas-ör, *n.* One who practices massage.
**Masseter,** mas-sē′tėr, *n.* Either of the pair of muscles which raise the under jaw.
**Massive,** mas′iv, *a.* Bulky and heavy; ponderous; pertaining to a mass; not local or special.
**Massy,** mas′i, *a.* Having the nature of a mass; massive.
**Mast,** mäst, *n.* A long upright timber in a vessel, supporting the yards, sails, and rigging; the fruit of the oak, beech, etc. (no *pl.*).—*vt.* To supply with a mast or masts.
**Masted,** mäst′ed, *a.* Furnished with a mast or masts.
**Master,** mäs′tėr, *n.* One who rules or directs; an employer; owner; captain of a merchant ship; teacher in a school; a man eminently skilled in some art; a word of address for men (written *Mr.* and pron. mis′tėr) and boys (written in full); a vessel having masts.—*vt.* To bring under control; to make oneself master of.—*a.* Belonging to a master; chief.
**Masterful,** mäs′tėr-ful, *a.* Inclined to exercise mastery; imperious; headstrong.
**Master-key,** mäs′tėr-kē, *n.* The key that opens many locks.
**Masterly,** mäs′tėr-li, *a.* Suitable to a master; most excellent; skilful.
**Masterpiece,** mäs′tėr-pēs, *n.* Chief performance; anything done with superior skill.
**Mastership,** mäs′tėr-ship, *n.* Office of a master; dominion; rule; mastery.
**Master-stroke,** mäs′tėr-strōk, *n.* A masterly act or achievement.
**Mastery,** mäs′tė-ri, *n.* Command; pre-eminence; victory; superior dexterity.
**Mast-head,** mäst′hed, *vt.* To send to the top of a mast and cause to remain there by way of punishment.
**Mastic, Mastich,** mas′tik, *n.* A resin from a tree of S. Europe, etc.; a kind of mortar.
**Masticate,** mas′ti-kāt, *vt.* To chew and prepare for swallowing.
**Mastication,** mas-ti-kā′shon, *n.* Act of masticating.
**Masticatory,** mas′ti-kā-to-ri, *a.* Adapted to masticate.—*n.* A substance to be chewed to increase the saliva.
**Mastiff,** mas′tif, *n.* A large heavy dog with deep and pendulous lips.
**Mastodon,** mas′to-don, *n.* An extinct quadruped like the elephant, but larger.
**Mat,** mat, *n.* An article of interwoven rushes, twine, etc., used for cleaning or protecting; anything growing thickly or closely interwoven.—*vt.* (matting, matted). To cover with mats; to entangle.—*vi.* To grow thickly together.
**Matador,** ma-ta-dōr′, *n.* The man appointed to kill the bull in bull-fights; a card in ombre and quadrille.
**Match,** mach, *n.* A person or thing equal to another; union by marriage; one to be married; a contest; a small body that catches fire readily or ignites by friction.—*vt.* To equal; to show an equal to; to set against as equal in contest; to suit; to marry.—*vi.* To be united in marriage; to suit; to tally.
**Matchless,** mach′les, *a.* That cannot be matched; having no equal; unrivalled.
**Matchlock,** mach′lok, *n.* Formerly the lock of a musket; containing a match for firing; the musket itself.
**Mate,** māt, *n.* A companion; a match; a husband or wife; second officer in a ship.—*vt.* (mating, mated). To equal; to match; to marry; to checkmate.
**Maté,** mä′tā, *n.* Paraguay tea; the leaves of the Brazilian holly used in S. America as a substitute for tea.
**Material,** ma-tē′ri-al, *a.* Consisting of matter; not spiritual; important; essential; substantial.—*n.* Anything composed of matter; substance of which anything is made.
**Materialism,** ma-tē′ri-al-izm, *n.* The doctrine of materialists.
**Materialist,** ma-tē′ri-al-ist, *n.* One who asserts that all existence is material.
**Materialistic,** ma-tē′ri-al-ist″ik, *a.* Relating to or partaking of materialism.
**Materialize,** ma-tē′ri-al-īz, *vt.* To reduce to a state of matter; to regard as matter.
**Materially,** ma-tē′ri-al-li, *adv.* In a material manner; in the state of matter; not formally; substantially; essentially.
**Maternal,** ma-tėr′nal, *a.* Motherly; pertaining to a mother; becoming a mother.
**Maternity,** ma-tėr′ni-ti, *n.* The state, character, or relation of a mother.
**Math,** math, *n.* A mowing; as in after-*math.*
**Mathematical, Mathematic,** ma-thē-mat′ik-al, ma-thē-mat′ik, *a.* Pertaining to mathematics.
**Mathematician,** ma′thē-ma-ti″shan, *n.* One versed in mathematics.
**Mathematics,** ma-thē-ma′tiks, *n.* The science of magnitude and number, comprising arithmetic, geometry, algebra, etc.
**Matinée,** mat′i-nā, *n.* An entertainment or reception held early in the day.
**Matrass,** mat′ras, *n.* A chemical vessel with a tapering neck used for evaporation, etc.
**Matricide,** mat′ri-sīd, *n.* The killing of a mother; the murderer of his or her mother.
**Matriculate,** ma-trik′ū-lāt, *vt.* To enroll; to admit to membership, particularly in a university.—*vi.* To be entered as a member.
**Matrimonial,** mat-ri-mō′ni-al, *a.* Pertaining to matrimony; nuptial.
**Matrimony,** mat′ri-mō-ni, *n.* Marriage; wedlock; the married or nuptial state.
**Matrix,** mā′triks, *n.*; pl. **Matrices** (mā′tri-sēz). The womb; a mold; substance in which a mineral, etc., is embedded.
**Matron,** mā′tron, *n.* An elderly married woman, or an elderly lady; head nurse or superintendent of a hospital, etc.
**Matronly,** mā′tron-li, *a.* Like or becoming a matron; elderly; sedate.
**Matte, Matt,** mat, *n.* Metal imperfectly smelted or purified.
**Matted,** mat′ed, *p.a.* Laid with mats; entangled.
**Matter,** mat′ėr, *n.* Not mind; body; that of which anything is made; substance as distinct from form; subject; business; circumstance; import; moment; pus.—*vi.* To be of importance; to signify; to form pus.
**Matter-of-fact,** mat′ėr-ov-fakt, *a.* Treating of facts; precise; prosaic.
**Matting,** mat′ing, *n.* Material for mats; mats collectively; coarse fabric for packing.
**Mattock,** mat′ok, *n.* A pick-axe with one or both of its ends broad.
**Mattress,** mat′res, *n.* A bed stuffed with hair, or other soft material, and quilted.
**Maturation,** ma-tur-ā′shon, *n.* Process of maturing; ripeness; suppuration.
**Maturative,** ma-tū′ra-tiv, *a.* Ripening; conducing to suppuration.
**Mature,** ma-tūr′, *a.* Ripe; perfect; completed; ready; having become payable.—*vt.* (maturing, matured). To make mature; to advance toward perfection.—*vi.* To become ripe or perfect; to become payable.
**Maturely,** ma-tūr′li, *adv.* In a mature manner; completely; with full deliberation.
**Maturity,** ma-tūr′i-ti, *n.* State of being mature; ripeness; time when a bill of exchange becomes due.
**Matutinal,** ma-tū-tīn′al, *a.* Pertaining to the morning.
**Maudlin,** mad′lin, *a.* Over-emotional; sickly sen-

timental; approaching to intoxication.
**Maugre,** ma'gėr, *adv.* In spite of; in opposition to; notwithstanding.
**Maul,** mal, *n.* A large hammer or mallet.—*vt.* To beat with a maul; to maltreat severely.
**Maul-stick,** mal'stik, *n. See* MAHL-STICK.
**Maunder,** man'dėr, *vi.* To speak with a beggar's whine; to drivel.
**Mausoleum,** ma-sō lē'um, *n.* A magnificent tomb or sepulchral monument.
**Mauve,** mōv, *n.* A purple dye obtained from aniline.
**Mavis,** mā'vis, *n.* The throstle or song-thrush.
**Maw,** ma, *n.* The stomach, especially of animals; paunch; crop of fowls.
**Mawkish,** mak'ish, *a.* Apt to cause satiety or loathing; insipid; sickly.
**Maxilla,** mak-sil'la, *n.*; pl. **ae.** A jaw-bone; a jaw.
**Maxillar, Maxillary,** mak-sil'lar, maks'il-la-ri, *a.* Pertaining to the jaw or jaw-bone.
**Maxim,** mak'sim, *n.* An established principle; axiom; aphorism; a light machine-gun.
**Maximum,** mak'sim-um, *n.* The greatest degree or quantity.—*a.* Greatest.
**May,** mā, *n.* The fifth month of the year; hawthorn blossom.—*vi.* To celebrate the festivities of May-day.—*v. aux.* (pret. might, mīt). Used to imply possibility, opportunity, permission, desire, etc.
**May-day,** mā'dā, *n.* The first day of May.
**Mayonnaise,** mā-on-āz, *n.* A sauce of yolks of eggs, oil, etc.
**Mayor,** mā'ėr, *n.* The chief magistrate of a city or borough.
**Mayoral,** mā'ėr-al, *a.* Pertaining to a mayor.
**Mayoralty,** mā'ėr-al-ti, *n.* Office of a mayor.
**May-pole,** mā'pōl, *n.* A pole to dance round on May-day.
**Mazarine,** maz-a-rēn', *n.* A deep blue color.
**Maze,** māz, *vt.* (mazing, mazed). To bewilder; to amaze.—*n.* Perplexed state of things; bewilderment; a labyrinth; a confusing network of paths or passages.
**Mazurka, Mazourka,** ma-zur'ka, *n.* A lively Polish dance; music written for it.
**Me,** mē, *pron. pers.* The objective of *I.*
**Mead,** mēd, *n.* A fermented liquor made from honey and water; a meadow: *poet.*
**Meadow,** me'dō, *n.* A low level tract of land under grass.—*a.* Belonging to a meadow.
**Meager,** mē'gėr, *a.* Thin; lean; poor; scanty.
**Meagerly,** mē'gėr-li, *adv.* Poorly; thinly; scantily.
**Meal,** mēl, *n.* Portion of food taken at one time; a repast; ground grain; flour.
**Mealy,** mēl'i, *a.* Having the qualities of meal; powdery; farinaceous.
**Mealy-mouthed,** mēl'i-mouᴛʜd, *a.* Unwilling to tell the truth in plain language; soft-spoken; inclined to hypocrisy.
**Mean,** mēn, *a.* Low in rank or birth; humble; base; comtemptible; occupying a middle position; middle; intermediate.—*n.* What is intermediate; average rate or degree; medium; *pl.* measure or measures adopted; agency (generally used as *sing.*); income or resources.—*vt.* (pret. and pp. *meant*). To have in the mind; to intend; to signify; to import.—*vi.* To have thought or ideas, or to have meaning.
**Meander,** mē-an'dėr, *n.* A winding course; a bend in a course; a labyrinth.—*vi.* To wind about; to be intricate.
**Meaning,** mēn'ing, *p.a.* Significant.—*n.* Design; signification; purport; force.
**Meaningless,** mēn'ing-les, *a.* Having no meaning.
**Meaningly,** mēn'ing-li, *adv.* Significantly.
**Meanly,** mēn'li, *adv.* In a mean manner; poorly; basely; shabbily.
**Meantime,** mēn'tīm, *adv.* During the interval; in the intervening time.—*n.* The interval between one period and another.
**Meanwhile,** mēn'whīl, *adv.* and *n.* Meantime.
**Measles,** mē'zlz, *n.* A contagious disease in man, characterized by a crimson rash.
**Measly, Measled,** mēz'li, mē'zld, *a.* Infected with measles or eruptions like measles.
**Measurable,** me'zhūr-a-bl, *a.* That may be measured; not very great; moderate.
**Measure,** me'zhūr, *n.* The extent or magnitude of a thing; a standard of size; a measuring rod or line; that which is allotted; moderation; just degree; course of action; legislative proposal; musical time; meter; a grave solemn dance; *pl.* beds or strata.—*vt.* (measuring, measured). To ascertain the extent or capacity of; to estimate; to value; to pass through or over; to proportion; to allot.—*vi.* To have a certain extent.
**Measured,** me'zhūrd, *p.a.* Deliberate and uniform; stately; restricted; moderate.
**Measurement,** me'zhūr-ment, *n.* Act of measuring; amount ascertained.
**Meat,** mēt, *n.* Food in general; the flesh of animals used as food; the edible portion of something (the *meat* of an egg).
**Meatus,** mē-ā'tus, *n.* A passage; a duct or passage of the body.
**Mechanic,** me-kan'ik, *a.* Mechanical.—*n.* An artisan; an artisan employed in making and repairing machinery.
**Mechanical,** me-kan'ik-al, *a.* Pertaining to mechanism or machinery; resembling a machine; done by the mere force of habit; pertaining to material forces; physical.
**Mechanically,** me-kan'ik-al-li, *adv.* In a mechanical manner; by the mere force of habit; by physical force or power.
**Mechanics,** me-kan'iks, *n.* The science which treats of motion and force.
**Mechanism,** mek'an-izm, *n.* A mechanical contrivance; structure of a machine.
**Mechlin,** mek'lin, *n.* A kind of fine lace.
**Medal,** med'al, *n.* A piece of metal in the form of a coin, stamped with some figure or device, as a memento or reward.
**Medallion,** me-dal'yon, *n.* A large antique medal; a circular or oval tablet.
**Medalist,** med'al-ist, *n.* An engraver or stamper of medals; one skilled in medals; one who has gained a medal.
**Meddle,** med'l, *vi.* (meddling, meddled). To interfere; to intervene officiously.
**Meddler,** med'lėr, *n.* One who meddles; an officious person; a busy-body.
**Meddlesome,** med'l-sum, *a.* Given to interfering; meddling; officiously intrusive.
**Meddling,** med'ling, *p.a.* Given to meddle; officious; busy in other men's affairs.
**Medial,** mē'di-al, *a.* Middle; mean; pertaining to a mean or average.
**Median,** mē'di-an, *a.* Situated in the middle; passing through or along the middle.
**Mediate,** mē'di-āt, *a.* Middle; intervening; acting as a means; not direct.—*vi.* (mediating, mediated). To negotiate between contending parties, with a view to reconciliation; to intercede.
**Mediately,** mē'di-āt-li, *adv.* Indirectly.
**Mediation,** mē-di-ā'shon, *n.* Act of mediating; intercession; entreaty for another.
**Mediative,** mē'di-āt-iv, *a.* Of or belonging to a mediator.
**Mediator,** mē'di-āt-ėr, *n.* One who mediates; an intercessor; an advocate.
**Mediatorial,** mē'di-a-tō''ri-al, *a.* Mediative.
**Medic, Medick,** mē'dik, *n.* A leguminous plant yielding fodder and allied to clover.
**Medicable,** med'ik-a-bl, *a.* That may be cured.
**Medical,** med'i-kal, *a.* Pertaining to the art of curing diseases; tending to cure.
**Medically,** med'i-kal-li, *adv.* According to the rules of medicine.
**Medicate,** med'i-kāt, *vt.* (medicating, medicated). To treat with medicine; to impregnate with anything medicinal.
**Medicative,** med'i-kā-tiv, *a.* Tending to cure or heal.
**Medicinal,** me-dis'in-al, *a.* Pertaining to medi-

cine; containing healing ingredients.
**Medicinally,** me-dis'in-al-li, *adv.* In a medicinal manner; with medicinal qualities.
**Medicine,** med'sin, *n.* Any substance used as a remedy for disease; a drug; the science and art of curing diseases.
**Medieval,** mē-di-ēv'al, *a.* Pertaining to the middle ages.
**Medievalism,** mē-di-ēv'al-izm, *n.* Medieval principles or practices.
**Mediocre,** mē'di-ō-kėr, *a.* Of moderate degree; middling.
**Mediocrity,** mē-di-ok'ri-ti, *n.* State of being mediocre; a moderate degree or rate; a person of mediocre talents or abilities.
**Meditate,** med'i-tāt, *vi.* (meditating, meditated). To dwell on anything in thought; to cogitate.—*vt.* To think on; to scheme; to intend.
**Meditation,** med-i-tā'shon, *n.* Act of meditating; serious contemplation.
**Meditative,** med'i-tāt-iv, *a.* Addicted to meditation; expressing meditation.
**Mediterranean,** med'i-te-rā'nē-an, *a.* Surrounded by land: now applied exclusively to the *Mediterranean* Sea.
**Medium,** mē'di-um, *n.*; pl. **-ia, -iums.** Something holding a middle position; a mean; means of motion or action; agency of transmission; instrumentality.—*a.* Middle; middling.
**Medlar,** med'lėr, *n.* A tree and its fruit, which resembles a small apple.
**Medley,** med'li, *n.* A mingled mass of ingredients; a miscellany; a jumble.
**Medoc,** me-dok', *n.* A kind of claret.
**Medulla,** me-dul'la, *n.* Marrow.
**Medullary, Medullar,** me-dul'la-ri, me-dul'lėr, *a.* Pertaining to, consisting of, or resembling marrow.
**Medusa,** me-dū'sa, *n.*; pl. **-ae.** A general name for the jelly-fishes or sea-nettles.
**Meed,** mēd, *n.* Reward; recompense.
**Meek,** mēk, *a.* Soft, gentle, or mild of temper; forbearing; humble; submissive.
**Meekly,** mēk'li, *adv.* Gently; humbly.
**Meerschaum,** mēr'shum, *n.* A silicate of magnesium, used for tobacco-pipes; a tobacco-pipe made of this.
**Meet,** mēt, *vt.* (meeting, met). To come face to face with; to come in contact with; to encounter; to light on; to receive; to satisfy.—*vi.* To come together; to encounter; to assemble.—*n.* A meeting, as of huntsmen.—*a.* Fit; suitable; proper.
**Meeting,** mēt'ing, *n.* A coming together; an interview; an assembly; encounter.
**Meeting-house,** mēt'ing-hous, *n.* A house of public worship for dissenters.
**Meetly,** mēt'li, *adv.* Fitly; suitably.
**Megalithic,** meg-a-lith'ik, *a.* Consisting of large stones.
**Megalosaurus,** meg'a-lō-sa''rus, *n.* A fossil carnivorous reptile 40 to 50 feet long.
**Megaphone,** meg'a-fōn, *n.* A cone-shaped speaking-trumpet.
**Megrim,** mē'grim, *n.* A neuralgic pain in the side of the head; *pl.* low spirits; whims or fancies.
**Melancholia,** mel-an-kō'li-a, *n.* Morbid melancholy.
**Melancholic,** mel'an-kol-ik, *a.* Disordered by melancholy; hypo chondriac; gloomy.
**Melancholy,** mel'an-ko-li, *n.* Mental alienation characterized by gloom and depression; hypochondria; dejection; sadness.—*a.* Gloomy; dejected; calamitous; somber.
**Melanic,** me-lan'ik, *a.* Black; belonging to a black type or class.
**Melanochroic,** mel'an-ō-krō''ik, *a.* A term applied to the dark-skinned white races of man.
**Mêlée,** mā-lā', *n.* A confused fight; an affray.
**Meliorate,** mē'lyor-āt, *vt.* To make better; to improve.—*vi.* To grow better.
**Mellifluence,** mel-if'lu-ens, *n.* A flow of honey or sweetness; a sweet smooth flow.
**Mellifluent, Mellifluous,** mel-if'lu̇-ent, mel-if'lu̇-us, *a.* Flowing with honey or sweetness; smooth; sweetly flowing.
**Mellow,** mel'ō, *a.* Soft with ripeness; soft to the ear, eye, or taste; toned down by time; half-tipsy.—*vt.* To make mellow; to soften.—*vi.* To become mellow.
**Melodeon,** me-lō'de-on, *n.* A wind-instrument of the accordion kind.
**Melodic,** me-lod'ik, *a.* Of the nature of melody; relating to melody.
**Melodious,** me-lō'di-us, *a.* Containing melody; musical; agreeable to the ear.
**Melodiously,** me-lō'di-us-li, *adv.* In a melodious manner; musically; sweetly.
**Melodist,** me'lō-dist, *n.* A composer or singer of melodies.
**Melodrama,** me-lō-dra'ma, *n.* Properly a musical drama; a serious play, with startling incidents, exaggerated sentiment, and splendid decoration.
**Melodramatic,** me'lō-dra-mat''ik, *a.* Pertaining to melodrama; sensational.
**Melody,** me'lō-di, *n.* An agreeable succession of sounds; sweetness of sound; the particular air or tune of a musical piece.
**Melon,** me'lon, *n.* A kind of cucumber and its large, fleshy fruit.
**Melt,** melt, *vt.* To reduce from a solid to a liquid state by heat; to soften; to overcome with tender emotion.—*vi.* To become liquid; to dissolve; to be softened to love, pity, etc.; to pass by imperceptible degrees.
**Melting,** melt'ing, *p.a.* Tending to soften; affecting; feeling or showing tenderness.
**Member,** mem'bėr, *n.* An organ or limb of an animal body; part of an aggregate; one of the persons composing a society, etc.; a representative in a legislative body.
**Membership,** mem'bėr-ship, *n.* State of being a member; the members of a body.
**Membrane,** mem'brān, *n.* A thin flexible texture in animal bodies; a similar texture in plants.
**Membranous,** mem'bra-nus, *a.* Belonging to or like a membrane; consisting of membranes.
**Memento,** mē-men'tō, *n.* That which reminds; a souvenir; a keepsake.
**Memoir,** mem'oir, mem'wär, *n.* A written account of events or transactions; a biographical notice; recollections of one's life (usually in the *pl.*).
**Memorabilia,** mem'or-a-bil''i-a, *n.pl.* Things worthy of remembrance or record.
**Memorable,** mem'or-a-bl, *a.* Worthy to be remembered; signal; remarkable; famous.
**Memorably,** mem'or-a-bil, *adv.* In a memorable manner.
**Memorandum,** mem-or-an'dum, *n.*; pl. **-dums** or **-da.** A note to help the memory; brief entry in a diary; formal statement.
**Memorial,** mē-mō'ri-al, *a.* Pertaining to memory or remembrance; serving to commemorate.—*n.* That which preserves the memory of something; a monument; memorandum; a written representation of facts, made as the ground of a petition.
**Memoralist,** mē-mō'ri-al-ist, *n.* One who writes, signs, or presents a memorial.
**Memorialize,** mē-mō'ri-al-īz, *vt.* To present a memorial to; to petition by memorial.
**Memorize,** mem'or-īz, *vt.* To cause to be remembered; to record.
**Memory,** mem'ō-ri, *n.* The faculty of the mind by which it retains knowledge or ideas; remembrance; recollection; the time within which a person may remember what is past; something remembered.
**Menace,** men'ās, *n.* A threat; indication of probable evil.—*vt.* (menacing, menaced). To threaten.
**Menacingly,** men'ās-ing-li, *adv.* In a menacing or threatening manner.
**Menage,** men-äzh', *n.* A household; housekeeping; household management.
**Menagerie,** me-naj'ėr-i, *n.* A collection of wild animals kept for exhibition.

**Mend,** mend, *vt.* To repair; to restore to a sound state; to amend.—*vi.* To advance to a better state; to improve.
**Mendacious,** men-dā'shus, *a.* Lying; false; given to telling untruths.
**Mendacity,** men-das'i-ti, *n.* Quality of being mendacious; deceit; untruth.
**Mender,** mend'ėr, *n.* One who mends.
**Mendicancy,** men'di-kan-si, *n.* State of being a mendicant; beggary.
**Mendicant,** men'di-kant, *a.* Begging.—*n.* A beggar; one who makes it his business to beg alms; a begging friar.
**Mendicity,** men-dis'i-ti, *n.* State of being a mendicant; the life of a beggar.
**Menhaden,** men-hā'den, *n.* A fish of the herring type.
**Menial,** mē'ni-al, *a.* Belonging to household servants; low with regard to employment.—*n.* A domestic servant (used mostly disparagingly).
**Meningitis,** men-in-jī'tis, *n.* Inflammation of the membranes of the brain or spinal cord.
**Menses,** men'sēz, *n.pl.* The monthly discharge of a woman.
**Menstrual,** men'stru-al, *a.* Monthly; pertaining to the menses of females.
**Menstruate,** men'stru-āt, *vi.* To discharge the menses.
**Menstruation,** men-stru-ā'shon, *n.* Act of menstruating; period of menstruating.
**Menstruum,** men'stru-um, *n.*; pl. **-uums** or **-ua.** Any fluid which dissolves a solid.
**Mensurable,** men'sūr-a-bl, *a.* Measurable.
**Mensuration,** men-sūr-ā'shon, *n.* The act, process, or art of measuring.
**Mental,** men'tal, *a.* Pertaining to the mind; performed by the mind; intellectual.
**Mentally,** men'tal-li, *adv.* In a mental manner; intellectually; in thought.
**Menthol,** men'thol, *n.* A white crystalline substance obtained from oil of peppermint.
**Mention,** men'shon, *n.* A brief notice or remark about something.—*vt.* To make mention of; to name.
**Mentionable,** men'shon-a-bl, *a.* That can or may be mentioned.
**Mentor,** men'tor, *n.* A friend or sage adviser.
**Menu,** men'ö, *n.* A list of dishes to be served at a dinner, etc.; a bill of fare.
**Mephitis,** me-fī'tis, *n.* Noxious exhalations.
**Mercantile,** mėr'kan-til, *a.* Pertaining to merchandise; trading; commercial.
**Mercenary,** mėr'se-na-ri, *a.* Hired; venal; that may be hired; greedy of gain; sordid.—*n.* One who is hired; a soldier hired into foreign service.
**Mercer,** mėr'sėr, *n.* One who has a shop for silks, woollens, linens, cottons, etc.
**Mercery,** mėr'sė-ri, *n.* The goods in which a mercer deals.
**Merchandise,** mėr'chand-īz, *n.* The goods of a merchant; objects of commerce; trade.
**Merchant,** mėr'chant, *n.* One who carries on trade on a large scale; a man who exports and imports goods.—*a.* Relating to trade; commercial.
**Merchantman,** mėr'chant-man, *n.* A ship engaged in commerce; a trading vessel.
**Merciful,** mėr'si-ful, *a.* Full of mercy; compassionate; tender; clement; mild.
**Mercifully,** mėr'si-ful-li, *adv.* In a merciful manner; tenderly; mildly.
**Merciless,** mėr'si-les, *a.* Destitute of mercy; pitiless; cruel; hard-hearted.
**Mercilessly,** mėr'si-les-li, *adv.* In a merciless manner.
**Mercurial,** mėr-kū'ri-al, *a.* Like the god Mercury; flighty; fickle; pertaining to or containing quicksilver.
**Mercurialize,** mėr-kū'ri-al-īz, *vt.* To affect or treat with mercury.
**Mercury,** mėr'kū-ri, *n.* Quicksilver, a heavy metal, liquid at all ordinary temperatures; the planet nearest the sun.
**Mercy,** mėr'si, *n.* Willingness to spare or forgive; clemency; pity; a blessing; benevolence; unrestrained exercise of authority.
**Mere,** mēr, *a.* This or that and nothing else; simple, absolute, entire, utter.—*n.* A pool or small lake; a boundary.
**Merely,** mēr'li, *adv.* For this and no other purpose; solely; simply; only.
**Meretricious,** me-rē-tri'shus, *a.* Pertaining to prostitutes; alluring by false show; gaudy.
**Merganser,** mėr-'gan'sėr, *n.* The goosander.
**Merge,** mėrj, *vt.* (merging, merged). To cause to be swallowed up or incorporated.—*vi.* To be sunk, swallowed, or lost.
**Meridian,** mē-rid'i-an, *n.* Pertaining to midday or noon; pertaining to the acme or culmination.—*n.* Mid-day; point of greatest splendor; any imaginary circle passing through both poles, used in marking longitude; a similar imaginary line in the heavens passing through the zenith of any place.
**Meridional,** mē-rid'i-on-al, *a.* Pertaining to the meridian; southern; southerly.
**Meringue,** mer-ang', *n.* A mixture of white of egg and pounded sugar; a light cake of this material with whipped cream in the center.
**Merino,** me-rē'no, *a.* Belonging to a Spanish variety of sheep with long and fine wool; made of the wool of the merino sheep.—*n.* A merino sheep; a woollen stuff twilled on both sides.
**Merit,** me'rit, *n.* What one deserves; desert; value; good quality.—*vt.* To deserve; to have a just title to; to incur.
**Meritorious,** me-rit-ō'ri-us, *a.* Having merit; praiseworthy.
**Merle,** mėrl, *n.* The blackbird.
**Merlin,** mėr'lin, *n.* A courageous species of hawk about the size of a blackbird.
**Mermaid,** mėr'mād, *n.* A fabled marine creature, having the upper part like a woman and the lower like a fish.
**Merrily,** me'ri-li, *adv.* In a merry manner; with mirth; with gaiety and laughter.
**Merriment,** me'ri-ment, *n.* Mirth; noisy gaiety; hilarity.
**Merry,** me'ri, *a.* Joyous; jovial; hilarious; gay and noisy; mirthful; sportive.
**Mésalliance,** mā-zal-yängs, *n.* A misalliance; an unequal marriage.
**Mesentery,** me'sen-te-ri, *a.* A membrane retaining the intestines in a proper position.
**Mesh,** mesh, *n.* The space between the threads of a net; something that entangles; implement for making nets.—*vt.* To catch in a net.
**Meshy,** mesh'i, *a.* Formed like net-work.
**Mesmeric,** mez-me'rik,*a.* Pertaining to mesmerism; hypnotic.
**Mesmerism,** mez'mėr-izm, *n.* The doctrine that some persons can exercise influence over the will and nervous system of others; animal magnetism; hypnotism.
**Mesmerist,** mez'mėr-ist, *n.* One who practices or believes in mesmerism.
**Mesmerize,** mez'mėr-īz, *vt.* To bring into a state of mesmeric or hypnotic sleep.
**Mesne,** mēn, *a.* In *law,* middle; intervening.
**Mesocephalic, Mesocephalous,** mes'o-se-fal''ik, mes-o-sef'a-lus, *a.* Applied to the human skull when of medium breadth.
**Mesozoic,** mes-o-zō'ik, *a.* In *geology,* pertaining to the secondary age, between the palaeozoic and cainozoic.
**Mess,** mes, *n.* A dish of food; food for a person at one meal; a number of persons who eat together, especially in the army or navy; a disorderly mixture; muddle.—*vi.* To take meals in common with others.
**Message,** mes'āj, *n.* A communication, written or verbal; an official written communication.
**Messenger,** mes'en-jėr, *n.* One who bears a message; a harbinger.
**Messiah,** mes-sī'a, *n.* The Anointed One; Christ,

the Anointed.
**Messieurs,** mes'yėrz, *n.* Sirs; gentlemen; the plural of *Mr.*, generally contracted into *Messrs.* (mes'ėrz).
**Metabolic,** me-ta-bol'ik, *a.* Pertaining to change or metamorphosis.
**Metabolism,** me-tab'ol-izm, *n.* Change or metamorphosis; chemical change of nutriment taken into the body.
**Metacenter,** me-ta-sen'tėr, *n.* That point in a floating body on the position of which its stability depends.
**Metal,** me'tal, *n.* An elementary substance, such as gold, iron, etc., having a peculiar luster and generally fusible by heat; the broken stone for covering roads.
**Metallic,** me-tal'ik, *a.* Pertaining to, consisting of, or resembling metal.
**Metalline,** me'tal'īn, *a.* Pertaining to, consisting of, or impregnated with metal.
**Metallist,** me'tal-ist, *n.* A worker in metals, or one skilled in metals.
**Metallurgic,** me-tal-ėr'jik, *a.* Pertaining to metallurgy.
**Metallurgy,** me'tal-ėr-ji, *n.* Art of working metals; art or operation of separating metals from their ores by smelting.
**Metamorphic,** me-ta-mor'fik, *a.* Pertaining to metamorphsis or metamorphism.
**Metamorphose,** me-ta-mor'fōs, *vt.* To change into a different form; to transform.
**Metamorphosis,** me-ta-mor'fos-is, *n.*; pl. **-ses.** Change of form or shape; transformation.
**Metaphor,** me'ta-for, *n.* A figure of speech founded on resemblance, as 'that man is a fox.'
**Metaphoric, Metaphorical,** me-ta-fo'rik, me-ta-fo'rik-al, *a.* Pertaining to metaphor; not literal; figurative.
**Metaphrase,** me'ta-frāz, *n.* A verbal translation from one language into another.
**Metaphrastic,** me-ta-frast'ik, *a.* Close or literal in translation.
**Metaphysic,** me-ta-fi'zik, *a.* Metaphysical.—*n.* Metaphysics.
**Metaphysical,** me-ta-fi'zik-al, *a.* Pertaining to metaphysics; according to rules or principles of metaphysics.
**Metaphysics,** me-ta-fi'ziks, *n.* The science of the principles and causes of all things existing; the philosophy of mind as distinguished from that of matter.
**Metathesis,** me-ta'the-sis, *n.* Transposition, as of the letters or syllables of a word.
**Mete,** mēt, *vt.* (meting, meted). To measure; to measure out; to dole.
**Metempsychosis,** me-temp'si-kō''sis, *n.* Transmigration of souls; passing of the soul after death into some other animal body.
**Meteor,** mē'tē-ėr, *n.* An atmospheric phenomenon; a transient luminous body; something that transiently dazzles.
**Meteoric,** mē-tē-or'ik, *a.* Pertaining to or consisting of meteors; proceeding from a meteor; transiently or irregularly brilliant.
**Meteorite,** mē'tē-ėr-īt, *n.* A meteorolite.
**Meterolite,** mē'tē-ėr-ō-līt, *n.* A meteoric stone; an aerolite.
**Meteorological,** mē'tē-ėr-ol-oj''ik-al, *a.* Pertaining to meteorology.
**Meterologist,** mē'tē-ėr-ol''o-jist, *n.* One versed or skilled in meteorology.
**Meteorology,** mē'tē-ėr-ol''o-ji, *n.* the science of atmospheric phenomena.
**Meter,** mē'tėr, *n.* One who or that which measures.
**Methinks,** mē-thingks', *v. impers.* (pret. methought). It seems to me; I think.
**Method,** me'thod, *n.* Mode or manner of procedure; system; classification.
**Methodic, Methodical,** me-thod'ik, me-thod'ik-al, *a.* Systematic; orderly.
**Methodism,** me'thod-izm, *n.* Observance of method or system; (with *cap.*) the doctrines and worship of the Methodists.
**Methodist,** me'thod-ist, *n.* One who observes method; (with *cap.*) one of a sect of Christians founded by John Wesley.
**Methodize,** me'thod-īz, *vt.* To reduce to method; to dispose in due order.
**Methought,** mē-that', pret. of *methinks.*
**Methyl,** meth'il, *n.* The hypothetical radical of wood-spirit and its combinations.
**Methylated,** meth'i-lāt-ed, *a.* Impregnated or mixed with methyl; containing wood-naphtha.
**Metonymy,** me-ton'i-mi, *n.* A figure of speech in which one word is put for another, as when we say, 'We read *Virgil*', meaning his *poetry.*
**Meter,** mē'tėr, *n.* Rhythmical arrangement of syllables into verses, etc.; rhythm; verse.
**Meter, Mèter,** mē'tėr, mā-tr, *n.* The French standard measure of length, equal to 39.37 English inches.
**Metric,** met'rik, *a.* Pertaining to the decimal system.
**Metric, Metrical,** met'rik, met'rik-al, *a.* Pertaining to rhythm; consisting of verse.
**Mettle,** met'l, *n.* Moral or physical constitution; spirit; courage; fire.
**Mettled,** met'ld, *a.* High-spirited; ardent.
**Mettlesome,** met'l-sum, *a.* Full of spirit; brisk; fiery.
**Mew,** mū, *n.* A sea-mew; a gull; moulting of a hawk; a coop for fowls; a place of confinement; the cry of a cat.—*vt.* To moult; to shut up, as in a cage.—*vi.* To moult; to cry as a cat.
**Mezzo,** med'zō, *a.* In *music,* middle; mean.
**Mezzo soprano,** a treble voice between soprano and contralto.
**Mezzotint,** mez'ō-tint or med'zō-tint, *n.* A manner of engraving on copper or steel in imitation of drawing in Indian ink.
**Miasma,** mī-az'ma, *n.*; pl. **Miasmata,** mī-az'ma-ta. The effluvia of any putrefying bodies; noxious emanation; malaria.
**Miasmatic,** mī-az-mat'ik, *a.* Producing, caused by, affected by miasma.
**Mica,** mī'ka, *n.* A mineral cleavable into thin shining elastic plates.
**Micaceous,** mī-kā'shus, *a.* Pertaining to, containing, like, or consisting of mica.
**Mice,** mīs, *n.pl.* of *mouse.*
**Microbe,** mī'krōb, *n.* A microscopic organism such as a bacillus or bacterium.
**Microcosm,** mī'krō-kozm, *n.* The little world; used for man, according to an old view an epitome of the *macrocosm.*
**Micrography,** mī-krog'ra-fi, *n.* The description of microscopic objects.
**Micrology,** mī-krol'o-ji, *n.* Attention to small or minute points.
**Micrometer,** mī-krom'et-ėr, *n.* An instrument for measuring small objects, spaces, or angles.
**Microphone,** mī'krō-fōn, *n.* An instrument to augment small sounds by means of electricity.
**Microphyte,** mī'krō-fīt, *n.* A microscopicplant, especially one that is parasitic.
**Microscope,** mī'krō-skōp, *n.* An optical instrument for magnifying.
**Miscroscopic, Microscopical,** mī-krō-skop'ik, mī-krō-skop'ik-al, *a.* Pertaining to a microscope; visible only by the aid of a microscope; very minute.
**Micturate,** mik'tūr-āt, *vi.* To pass urine.
**Mid,** mid, *a.*; no compar.; superl. midmost. Middle; intervening.
**Mid-air,** mid'ār, *n.* The middle of the sky; a lofty position in the air.
**Mid-day,** mid'dā, *n.* The middle of the day; noon.—*a.* Pertaining to noon.
**Middle,** mid'l, *a.*; no compar.; superl. middlemost. Equally distant from the extremes; intermediate; intervening.—**Middle ages,** the period from the fall of the Roman Empire to about 1450.—*n.* Point or part equally distant from the extremities; something intermediate.
**Middle-aged,** mid'l-ājd, *a.* Being about the mid-

dle of the ordinary age of man.
**Middle-class,** mid'l-kläs, *n.* The class of people holding a social position between the working-classes and the aristocracy.—*a.* Of or relating to the middle-classes.
**Middleman,** mid'l-man, *n.* An intermediary between two parties; an agent between producers and consumers.
**Middlemost,** mid'l-mōst, *a.* Being in the middle, or nearest the middle.
**Midnight,** mid'nīt, *n.* The middle of the night; twelve o'clock at night.—*a.* Pertaining to midnight; dark as midnight.
**Midriff,** mid'rif, *n.* The diaphragm.
**Midshipman,** mid'ship-man, *n.* A young officer in the navy, below a sub-lieutenant.
**Midst,** midst, *n.* The middle.—*prep.* Amidst: *poet.*
**Midsummer,** mid'sum-ėr, *n.* The middle of summer; the summer solstice, about June 21.
**Midway,** mid'wā, *n.* The middle of the way or distance.—*a.* and *adv.* In the middle of the way; half-way.
**Midwife,** mid'wīf, *n.* A woman that assists other women in childbirth.
**Midwifery,** mid'wif-ri, *n.* Obstetrics.
**Mien,** mēn, *n.* Look; bearing; carriage.
**Miff,** mif, *n.* A slight quarrel.
**Might,** mīt, *n.* Great power or ability to act; strength; force.—*v. aux.* Pret. of *may.*
**Mightily,** mīt'i-li, *adv.* In a mighty manner; with might; powerful; greatly.
**Mighty,** mīt'i, *a.* Having might; strong; powerful; potent; very great; vast.
**Migrant,** mī'grant, *n.* One who migrates; a migratory bird or other animal.
**Migrate,** mī'grāt, *vi.* (migrating, migrated). To remove to a distant place or country.
**Migration,** mī'grā-shon, *n.* Act of migrating; removal from one place to another.
**Migratory,** mī'grā-to-ri, *a.* Disposed to migrate; roving; passing from one climate to another, as birds.
**Mikado,** mi-kä'dō, *n.* The emperor of Japan.
**Milch,** milsh, *a.* Giving milk, as cows.
**Mild,** mīld, *a.* Gentle in temper or disposition; merciful; soft; bland; mellow.
**Mildew,** mil'dū, *n.* A minute parastic fungus that causes decay in vegetable matter; condition so caused.—*vt.* and *i.* To taint with mildew.
**Mildly,** mīld'li, *adv.* In a mild manner; softly; gently; tenderly.
**Mildness,** mīld'nes, *n.* State or quality of being mild; gentleness; clemency.
**Mile,** mīl, *n.* A measure of length or distance equal to 1760 yards.
**Mileage,** mīl'āj, *n.* Fees paid for travel by the mile; aggregate of miles travelled, etc.
**Milestone,** mīl'stōn, *n.* A stone or block set up to mark the miles on a road.
**Milfoil,** mil'foil, *n.* A common plant with finely divided leaves, and small, white or rose-colored flowers; yarrow.
**Militancy,** mil'i-tan-si, *n.* Warfare; combativeness.
**Militant,** mil'i-tant, *a.* Serving as a soldier; fighting; combative.
**Militarism,** mil'i-ta-rizm, *n.* The system that leads a nation to pay excessive attention to military affairs.
**Military,** mil'i-ta-ri, *a.* Pertaining to soldiers or war; martial; soldierly; belligerent.—*n.* The whole body of soldiers; the army.
**Militate,** mil'i-tāt, *vi.* (militating, militated). To stand arrayed; to have weight or influence.
**Militia,** mi-li'sha, *n.* A body of soldiers not permanently organized in time of peace.
**Militiaman,** mi-li'sha-man, *n.* One who belongs to the militia.
**Milk,** milk, *n.* A whitish fluid secreted in female animals, serving as nourishment for their young; what resembles milk; white juice of plants.—*vt.* To draw milk from.
**Milkman,** milk'man, *n.* A man that sells milk or carries milk to market.
**Milksop,** milk'sop, *n.* A piece of bread sopped in milk; one devoid of manliness.
**Milky,** milk'i, *a.* Pertaining to, resembling, yielding, or containing milk.
**Mill,** mil, *n.* A machine for making meal or flour; a machine for grinding, etc.; building that contains the machinery for grinding, etc.—*vt.* To pass through a mill; to stamp in a coining press; to throw, as silk; to full, as cloth.
**Milled,** mild, *p.a.* Passed through a mill; having the edge transversely grooved, as a coin.
**Millenarian,** mil-le-nā'ri-an, *a.* Consisting of a thousand years; millennial.—*n.* One who believes in the millennium.
**Millenary,** mil'le-na-ri, *a.* Pertaining to a thousand.—*n.* Period of a thousand years; commemoration of an event that happened a thousand years ago.
**Millennial,** mil-len'i-al, *a.* Pertaining to the millennium, or to a thousand years.
**Millennium,** mil-len'i-um, *n.* An aggregate of a thousand years; the thousand years of Christ's reign on earth.
**Milleped, Milliped,** mil'le-ped, mil'li-ped, *n.* A worm-like animal with many feet; a wood-louse.
**Miller,** mil'ėr, *n.* One who keeps or attends a mill for grinding grain.
**Millesimal,** mil-les'im-al, *a.* Thousandth; consisting of thousandth parts.
**Millet,** mil'et, *n.* A kind of small grain of various species used for food.
**Milliard,** mil-yärd', *n.* A thousand millions.
**Milligram,** mil'i-gram, *n.* The thousandth part of a gram.
**Millimèter,** mil-i-mā'tr, *n.* The thousandth part of a meter.
**Milliner,** mil'in-ėr, *n.* One who makes head-dresses, hats, etc., for females.
**Millinery,** mil'in-ė-ri, *n.* Articles made or sold by milliners; occupation of a milliner.
**Milling,** mil'ing, *n.* The process of grinding or passing through a mill; the transverse grooves on the edge of a coin.
**Million,** mil'yon, *n.* A thousand thousands; a very great number, indefinitely.
**Millionaire,** mil'yon-ār, *n.* One worth a million dollars, etc.; a very rich person.
**Millionth,** mil'yonth, *a.* The ten hundred thousandth.
**Mill-pond,** mil'pond, *n.* A pond furnishing water for driving a mill-wheel.
**Mill-race,** mil'rās, *n.* The stream of water driving a mill-wheel; channel in which it runs.
**Millstone,** mil'stōn, *n.* One of the stones used in a mill for grinding grain.
**Mill-wheel,** mil'whēl, *n.* A wheel used to drive a mill; a water-wheel.
**Mill-wright,** mil'rīt, *n.* A mechanic who constructs the machinery of mills.
**Milt,** milt, *n.* The spleen of an animal; the soft roe of fishes, or the spermatic organ of the males.
**Mime,** mīm, *n.* A species of ancient drama in which gestures predominated; an actor in such performances.
**Mimetic, Mimetical,** mī-met'ik, mī-met'ik-al, *a.* Apt to imitate; given to aping or mimicry; characterized by mimicry.
**Mimic,** mim'ik, *a.* Imitative; consisting of imitation.—*n.* One who imitates or mimics.—*vt.* (mimicking, mimicked). To imitate, especially for sport; to ridicule by imitation.
**Mimicry,** mim'ik-ri, *n.* Imitation, often for sport or ridicule.
**Mimosa,** mī-mō'sa, *n.* A leguminous plant.
**Minaret,** min'a-ret, *n.* A slender lofty turret on Mohammedan mosques, with one or more balconies; a small spire.
**Minatory,** min'a-to-ri, *a.* Threatening; menacing.
**Mince,** mins, *vt.* (mincing, minced). To cut or chop into very small pieces; to extenuate or palliate; to utter with affected softness; to clip, as

words.—*vi*. To walk with short steps; to speak with affected nicety.—*n*. Mince-meat.
**Mince-meat,** mins'mēt, *n*. A mixture of raisins and currants with chopped candied peel, suet, apples, etc.
**Mince-pie,** mins'pī, *n*. A pie made with mince-meat and other ingredients.
**Mincing,** mins'ing, *p.a*. Speaking or walking affectedly; affectedly elegant.
**Mind,** mīnd, *n*. The intellectual power in man; understanding; cast of thought and feeling; inclination; opinion; memory.—*vt*. To attend to; to observe; to regard.
**Minded,** mīnd'ed, *a*. Disposed; inclined.
**Mindful,** mīnd'ful, *a*. Bearing in mind; attentive; regarding with care; heedful.
**Mindless,** mīnd'les, *a*. Destitute of mind; unthinking; stupid; negligent; careless.
**Mine,** mīn, *adj. pron*. My; belonging to me.—*n*. A pit from which coal, ores, etc., are taken; an underground passage in which explosives may be lodged for destructive purposes; a contrivance floating on or near the surface of the sea, to destroy ships by explosion; a rich source or store of wealth.—*vi*. (mining, mined). To dig a mine; to dig for ores, etc.; to burrow.—*vt*. To undermine; to sap.
**Miner,** mīn'ėr, *n*. One who works in a mine.
**Mineral,** mi'ne-ral, *n*. An inorganic body existing on or in the earth.—*a*. Pertaining to or consisting of minerals; impregnated with mineral matter.
**Mineralogist,** mi-ne-ral'o-jist, *n*. One who is versed in the science of minerals.
**Mineralogy,** mi-ne-ral'o-ji, *n*. The science of the properties of mineral substances.
**Mingle,** ming'gl, *vt*. (mingling, mingled). To mix up together; to blend; to debase by mixture.—*vi*. To be mixed; to join.
**Miniature,** min'i-a-tūr, *n*. A painting of very small dimensions, usually in water-colors, on ivory, vellum, etc.; anything represented on a greatly reduced scale; a small scale.—*a*. On a small scale; diminutive.
**Minify,** min'i-fī, *vt*. To make little or less; opposite of *magnify*.
**Minikin,** min'i-kin, *n*. A darling; a favorite.—*a*. Small; diminutive.
**Minim,** min'im, *n*. Something exceedingly small; a dwarf; a note in music equal to two crochets; the smallest liquid measure; a single drop.
**Minimize,** min'i-mīz, *vt*. (minimizing, minimized). To reduce to a minimum; to represent as of little moment; to depreciate.
**Minimum,** min'i-mum, *n*. The least quantity assignable; the smallest amount or degree.
**Mining,** mīn'ing, *a*. Pertaining to mines.—*n*. The act or employment of digging mines.
**Minion,** min'yon, *n*. An unworthy favorite; a servile dependant; a minx; a small kind of printing type.
**Minish,** min-ish, *vt*. To diminish.
**Minister,** min'is-tėr, *n*. A servant; attendant; agent; a member of a government; a political representative or ambassador; the pastor of a church.—*vt*. To give; to supply.—*vi*. To perform service; to afford supplies; to contribute.
**Ministerial,** min-is-tē'ri-al, *a*. Pertaining to ministry, ministers of state, or ministers of the gospel.
**Ministerialist,** min-is-tē'ri-al-ist, *n*. A political supporter of the ministry.
**Ministering,** min'is-tėr-ing, *p.a*. Attending and serving as a subordinate agent.
**Ministrant,** min'is-trant, *a*. Performing service; acting as minister or attendant.
**Ministration,** min-is-trā'shon, *n*. Act of ministering; service; ecclesiastical function.
**Ministrative,** min'is-trāt-iv, *a*. Ministering; affording service.
**Ministry,** min'is-tri, *n*. The act of ministering; service; instrumentality; state of being a minister; profession of a minister of the gospel; the clergy; the administration.
**Minium,** min'i-um, *n*. Red oxide of lead; red-lead.
**Miniver,** min'i-ver, *n*. The fur of the Siberian squirrel; a fine white fur.
**Mink,** mingk, *n*. A quadruped allied to the pole-cat and weasel.
**Minnesinger,** min'ne-sing-ėr, *n*. One of a class of German lyric poets of the twelfth and thirteenth centuries.
**Minnow,** min'ō, *n*. A very small British fish inhabiting fresh-water streams.
**Minor,** mī'nor, *a*. Lesser; smaller; of little importance; petty; in *music*, less by a lesser semitone.—*n*. A person not yet 21 years of age.
**Minorite,** mī'nor-īt, *n*. A Franciscan friar.
**Minority,** mi-no'ri-ti, *n*. State of being a minor; period from birth until 21 years of age; the smaller number or a number less than half; the party that has the fewest votes.
**Minster,** min'stėr, *n*. A monastery; the church of a monastery; a cathedral church.
**Minstrel,** min'strel, *n*. A musician; a bard; a singer.
**Mint,** mint, *n*. The place where money is coined; a source of abundant supply; a herbaceous aromatic plant.—*vt*. To coin; to invent; to forge; to fabricate.
**Mintage,** mint'āj, *n*. That which is coined or stamped; duty paid for coining.
**Minuend,** mi'nū-end, *n*. The number from which another is to be subtracted.
**Minuet,** mi'nū-et, *n*. A slow graceful dance; the tune or air for it.
**Minus,** mī'nus, *a*. Less; less by so much; wanting; the sign (-).
**Minuscule,** mi-nus'kūl, *n*. A small sort of letter used in MSS. in the middle ages.
**Minute,** mi-nūt', *a*. Very small; precise; particular; exact.
**Minute,** mi'nit, *a*. The sixtieth part of an hour or degree; short sketch of an agreement, etc., in writing; a note to preserve the memory of anything.—*vt*. (minuting, minuted). To write down a concise state or note of.
**Minute-book,** mi'nit-buk, *n*. A book containing minutes or short notës.
**Minutely,** mi-nūt'li, *adv*. With minuteness; exactly; nicely.
**Minutiae,** mi-nū'shi-ē, *n.pl*. Small or minute things; minor or unimportant details.
**Minx,** mingks, *n*. A pert, forward girl.
**Miocene,** mī'ō-sēn, *a*. and *n*. The middle subdivision of the tertiary strata.
**Miracle,** mi'ra-kl, *n*. A marvel; a supernatural event; a miracle-play.
**Miracle-play,** mi'ra-kl-plā, *n*. Formerly a dramatic representation exhibiting the lives of the saints, or other sacred subjects.
**Miraculous,** mi-ra'kū-lus, *a*. Performed supernaturally; wonderful; extraordinary.
**Miraculously,** mi-ra'kū-lus-li, *adv*. By miracle; supernaturally; wonderfully.
**Mirage,** mi-räzh', *n*. An optical illusion, causing remote objects to be seen double, or to appear as if suspended in the air.
**Mire,** mīr, *n*. Wet, muddy soil; mud.—*vt*. and *i*. (miring, mired). To sink in mire; to soil with mud.
**Mirror,** mi'rėr, *n*. A looking-glass; any polished substance that reflects images; an exemplar.—*vt*. To reflect, as in a mirror.
**Mirth,** mėrth, *n*. The feeling of being merry; merriment; glee; hilarity.
**Mirthful,** mėrth'ful, *a*. Full of mirth; merry; jovial; amusing.
**Mirthless,** mėrth'les, *a*. Without mirth; joyless.
**Misadventure,** mis-ad-ven'tūr, *n*. An unlucky accident; misfortune; ill-luck.
**Misadvised,** mis-ad-vīzd', *a*. Ill-advised.
**Misalliance,** mis-al-lī'ans, *n*. Improper association; an unequal marriage.
**Misanthrope, Misanthropist,** mis'an-thrōp, mis-an'thrōp-ist, *n*. A hater of mankind.

M

**Misanthropic, Misanthropical,** mis-an-throp'ik, mis-an-throp'ik-al, *a.* Pertaining to a misanthrope; hating mankind.
**Misanthropy,** mis-an'thrō-pi, *n.* Hatred or dislike to mankind.
**Misapplication,** mis-ap'pli-kā''shon, *n.* The act of misapplying; a wrong application.
**Misapply,** mis-ap-plī', *vt.* To apply amiss; to apply to a wrong purpose.
**Misapprehend,** mis-ap'prē-hend'', *vt.* To misunderstand; to take in a wrong sense.
**Misapprehension,** mis-ap'prē'hen''shon, *n.* Act of misapprehending; mistake.
**Misappropriate,** mis-ap-prō'pri-āt, *vt.* To appropriate wrongly.
**Misarrange,** mis-a-rānj', *vt.* To arrange improperly.
**Misbecome,** mis-bē-kum', *vt.* Not to become; to suit ill.
**Misbecoming,** mis-bē-kum'ing, *p.* and *a.* Unbecoming.
**Misbegotten,** mis-bē-got'n, *p.a.* Unlawfully or irregularly begotten.
**Misbehave,** mis-bē-hāv', *vi.* To behave ill; to conduct oneself improperly.
**Misbehavior,** mis-bē-hāv'yėr, *n.* Ill behavior; misconduct.
**Misbelief,** mis-bē-lēf', *n.* Erroneous belief; false religion.
**Misbelieve,** mis-bē-lev', *vt.* To believe erroneously.
**Miscalculate,** mis-kal'kū-lāt, *vt.* To calculate erroneously.
**Miscalculation,** mis-kal'kū-lā''shon, *n.* Erroneous calculation.
**Miscall,** mis-kal', *vt.* To call by a wrong name; to revile or abuse.
**Miscarriage,** mis-ka'rij, *n.* Act of miscarrying; failure; act of bringing forth young before the time; abortion.
**Miscarry,** mis-ka'ri,*vi.* To fail to reach its destination; to fail of the intended effect; to bring forth young before the proper time.
**Miscellaneous,** mis-sel-lā'nē-us, *a.* Consisting of several kinds; promiscuous; producing written compositions of various sorts.
**Miscellany,** mis'sel-la-ni, *n.* A mixture of various kinds; a collection of various literary productions.
**Mischief,** mis'chif, *n.* Harm; injury; damage; vexatious affair; annoying conduct.
**Mischievous,** mis'chiv-us, *a.* Causing mischief; harmful; fond of mischief; troublesome in conduct.
**Misconceive,** mis-kon-sēv', *vt.* and *i.* To conceive erroneously; to misapprehend.
**Misconception,** mis-kon-sep'shon, *n.* An erroneous conception;; misapprehension.
**Misconduct,** mis-kon'dukt, *n.* Misbehavior; mismanagement.—*vt.* mis-kon-dukt'. To conduct amiss; *refl.* to misbehave.
**Misconstruction,** mis-kon-struk'shon, *n.* Wrong construction or interpretation.
**Misconstrue,** mis-kon'strö, *vt.* To construe or interpret erroneously.
**Miscount,** mis-kount', *vt.* and *i.* To mistake in counting.—*n.* An erroneous counting.
**Miscreant,** mis'krē-ant, *n.* A vile wretch; an unprincipled scoundrel.
**Misdate,** mis-dāt', *vt.* To date erroneously.—*n.* A wrong date.
**Misdeed,** mis-dēd', *n.* An evil action; transgression.
**Misdemean,** mis-dē-mēn', *vt.* To behave ill: used *refl.*
**Misdemeanant,** mis-dē-mēn'ant, *n.* One who commits a misdemeanor.
**Misdemeanor,** mis-dē-mēn'ėr, *n.* Ill behavior; an offense inferior to felony.
**Misdirect,** mis-di-rekt', *vt.* To direct to a wrong person or place.
**Misdirection,** mis-di-rek'shon, *n.* Act of misdirecting; wrong direction; error of a judge in charging a jury, in matters of law or of fact.
**Misdoubt,** mis-dout', *n.* Suspicion of crime or danger.—*vt.* To suspect of deceit or danger.
**Misemploy,** mis-em-ploi', *vt.* To employ amiss or to no purpose; to misuse.
**Miser,** mī'zėr, *n.* A niggard; one who in wealth acts as if suffering from poverty.
**Miserable,** miz'ėr-a-bl, *a.* Very unhappy; wretched; worthless; despicable.
**Miserably,** miz'ėr-a-bli, *adv.* In a miserable manner.
**Miserly,** mī'zėr-li, *a.* Like a miser in habits; penurious; sordid; niggardly.
**Misery,** miz'ėr-i, *n.* Great unhappiness; extreme distress; wretchedness.
**Misfeasance,** mis-fē'zans, *n.* In *law,* a wrong done; wrong-doing in office.
**Misfit,** mis-fit', *n.* A bad fit.—*vt.* To make (a garment, etc.) of a wrong size; to supply with something not suitable.
**Misfortune,** mis-for'tūn, *n.* Ill fortune; calamity; mishap.
**Misgive,** mis-giv', *vt.* To fill with doubt; to deprive of confidence; to fail.
**Misgiving,** mis-giv'ing, *n.* A failing of confidence; doubt; distrust.
**Misgovern,** mis-guv'ėrn, *vt.* To govern ill.
**Misgovernment,** mis-guv'ėrn-ment, *n.* Act of misgoverning; bad administration.
**Misguide,** mis-gīd', *vt.* To guide into error; to direct to a wrong purpose or end.
**Mishap,** mis-hap', *n.* A mischance; an unfortunate accident.
**Misinform,** mis-in-form', *vt.* To give erroneous information to.
**Misinterpret,** mis-in-tėr'pret, *vt.* To interpret erroneously.
**Misinterpretation,** mis-in-tėr'pre-tā''shon, *n.* Act of interpreting erroneously.
**Misjudge,** mis-juj', *vt.* To judge erroneously.—*vi.* To err in judgment.
**Mislay,** mis-lā', *vt.* To lay in a wrong place; to lay in a place not recollected.
**Mislead,** mis-lēd', *vt.* To lead astray; to cause to mistake; to deceive.
**Mislike,** mis-līk', *vt.* To dislike; to disapprove; to have aversion to.
**Mismanage,** mis-man'āj, *vt.* To manage ill; to administer improperly.
**Mismanagement,** mis-man'āj-ment, *n.* Bad management.
**Misname,** mis-nām', *vt.* To call by the wrong name.
**Misnomer,** mis-nō'mėr, *n.* A mistaken or inapplicable name or designation.
**Misogamist,** mi-sog'am-ist, *n.* A hater of marriage.
**Misogamy,** mi-sog'a-mi, *n.* Hatred of marriage.
**Misogynist,** mi-soj'in-ist, *n.* A woman-hater.
**Misogyny,** mi-soj'i-ni, *n.* Hatred of the female sex.
**Misplace,** mis-plās, *vt.* To put in a wrong place; to set on an improper object.
**Misplacement,** mis-plās'ment, *n.* Act of misplacing.
**Misprint,** mis-print', *vt.* To print wrongly.—*n.* A mistake in printing.
**Mispronounce,** mis-prō-nouns', *vt.* or *i.* To pronounce erroneously.
**Mispronunciation,** mis-prō-nun'si-ā''shon, *n.* Wrong pronunciation.
**Misquotation,** mis-kwōt-ā'shon, *n.* An erroneous quotation; act of quoting wrongly.
**Misquote,** mis-kwōt, *vt.* To quote erroneously; to cite incorrectly.
**Misreport,** mis-rē-pōrt', *vt.* To give an incorrect account of.—*n.* An erroneous report.
**Misrepresent,** mis-rep'rē-zent'', *vt.* To represent falsely.
**Misrepresentation,** mis-rep'rē-zent-ā''shon, *n.* False or incorrect account.
**Misrule,** mis-röl', *n.* Bad rule; misgovernment.—*vt.* To govern badly or oppressively.

**Miss,** mis, *vt.* To fail in hitting, obtaining, finding, etc.; to feel the loss of; to omit; to let slip.—*vi.* To fail to strike what is aimed at; to miscarry.—*n.* A failure to hit, obtain, etc.; loss; want; an unmarried woman.
**Missal,** mis'al, *n.* The R. Catholic mass-book.
**Misshape,** mis-shāp', *n.* A bad or incorrect form.—*vt.* To share ill.
**Misshapen,** mis-shāp'n, *a.* Ill-formed; ugly.
**Missile,** mis'īl, *a.* Capable of being thrown.—*n.* A weapon or projectile thrown with hostile intention, as an arrow, a bullet.
**Missing,** mis'ing, *p.a.* Not to be found; wanting; lost.
**Mission,** mi'shon, *n.* A sending or delegating; duty on which one is sent; destined end or function; persons sent on some political business or to propagate religion; a station of missionaries.
**Missionary,** mi'shon-a-ri, *n.* One sent to propagate religion.—*a.* Pertaining to missions.
**Missive,** mis'iv, *a.* Such as is sent; proceeding from some authoritative source.—*n.* A message; a letter or writing sent.
**Misspell,** mis-spel', *vt.* To spell wrongly.
**Misspelling,** mis-spel'ing, *n.* A wrong spelling.
**Misspend,** mis-spend', *vt.* To spend amiss; to waste.
**Misspent,** mis-spent', *p.a.* Ill-spent; wasted.
**Misstate,** mis-stāt', *vt.* To state wrongly; to misrepresent.
**Misstatement,** mis-stāt'ment, *n.* A wrong statement.
**Mist,** mist, *n.* Visible watery vapor; aqueous vapor falling in numerous but almost imperceptible drops; something which dims or darkens.
**Mistakable,** mis-tāk'a-bl, *a.* That may be mistaken.
**Mistake,** mis-tāk', *vt.* To misunderstand or misapprehend; to regard as one when really another.—*vi.* To err in opinion or judgment.—*n.* An error in opinion or judgment; blunder; fault.
**Mistaken,** mis-tāk'n, *p.a.* Erroneous; incorrect.
**Mister,** mis'tėr, *n. See* MASTER.
**Mistily,** mist'i-li, *adv.* In a misty manner; vaguely; darkly; obscurely.
**Mistime,** mis-tīm', *vt.* To time wrongly.
**Mistletoe,** mis'l-tō or miz'l-tō, *n.* A plant that grows parasitically on various trees, and was held in veneration by the Druids.
**Mistranslate,** mis-trans-lāt', *vt.* To translate erroneously.
**Mistress,** mis'tres, *n.* The female appellation corresponding to *master;* a woman who has authority, ownership, etc.; a female teacher; a concubine; a title of address applied to married women (written *Mrs.* and pronounced mis'iz).
**Mistrust,** mis-trust', *n.* Want of confidence or trust; suspicion.—*vt.* To distrust; to suspect; to doubt.
**Mistrustful,** mis-trust'ful, *a.* Full of mistrust; suspicious; wanting confidence.
**Misty,** mist'i, *a.* Overspread with mist; dim; obscure; clouded; hazy.
**Misunderstand,** mis-un'dėr-stand'', *vt.* To understand wrongly; to mistake.
**Misuse,** mis-ūz', *vt.* To use to a bad purpose; to abuse.—*n.* mis-ūs'. Improper use; misapplication.
**Mite,** mīt, *n.* A minute animal of the class Arachnida (cheese-*mite*, etc.); a very small coin formerly current; a very little creature.
**Mitigant,** mi'ti-gant, *a.* Softening; soothing.
**Mitigate,** mi'ti-gāt, *vt.* To make soft or mild; to assuage, lessen, abate, moderate.
**Mitigation,** mi-ti-gā'shon, *n.* Act of mitigating; alleviation.
**Miter,** mī'tėr, *n.* A high pointed cap worn by bishops.—*vt.* (mitering, mitered). To adorn with a miter.
**Mitered,** mī'tėrd, *p.a.* Wearing a miter; having the privilege of wearing a miter.
**Mitten,** mit'n, *n.* A covering for the hand without fingers, or without a separate cover for each finger.
**Mittimus,** mit'i-mus, *n.* A warrant of commitment to prison; a writ for removing records from one court to another.
**Mix,** miks, *vt.* (mixing, mixed). To unite or blend promiscuously; to mingle; to associate.—*vi.* To become united or blended; to join; to associate.
**Mixable,** miks'a-bl, *a.* Miscible.
**Mixed,** mikst, *p.a.* Promiscuous; indiscriminate; miscellaneous.
**Mixen,** mik'sn, *n.* A dunghill.
**Mixture,** miks'tūr, *n.* Act of mixing; state of being mixed; a compound; a liquid medicine of different ingredients.
**Mizzen, Mizen,** miz'n, *n.* A fore-and-aft sail on the aftermost mast of a ship, called the mizzen-mast.—*a.* Belonging to the mizzen.
**Mizzle,** miz'l, *vi.* (mizzling, mizzled). To rain in very fine drops.—*n.* Small rain.
**Mnemonic, Mnemonical,** nē-mon'ik, nē-mon'ik-al, *a.* Pertaining to to mnemonics.
**Mnemonics,** nē-mon'iks, *n.* The art of memory; rules for assisting the memory.
**Moan,** mōn, *vi.* To utter a low dull sound through grief or pain.—*vt.* To bewail or deplore.—*n.* A low dull sound due to grief or pain; a sound resembling this.
**Moanful,** mōn'ful, *a.* Expressing sorrow.
**Moat,** mōt, *n.* A deep trench round a castle or other fortified place.—*vt.* To surround with a ditch for defense.
**Mob,** mob, *n.* A crowd; disorderly assembly; rabble.—*vt.* (mobbing, mobbed). To attack in a disorderly crowd; to crowd round and annoy.
**Mobile,** mō'bil, *a.* Capable of being easily moved; changeable; fickle.
**Mobility,** mō-bil'i-ti, *n.* State of being mobile; susceptibility of motion; inconstancy.
**Mobilization,** mōb' or mob'il-i-zā''shon, *n.* The act of mobilizing.
**Mobilize,** mōb' or mob'il-īz, *vt.* To put (troops, etc.) in a state of readiness for active service.
**Moccasin,** mok'a-sin, *n.* A shoe of deer-skin or soft leather, worn by N. American Indians; a venomous serpent of the United States.
**Mock,** mok, *vt.* To mimic in contempt or derision; to flout; to ridicule; to set at naught; to defy.—*vi.* To use ridicule; to gibe or jeer.—*n.* A derisive word or gesture; ridicule; derision.—*a.* Counterfeit; assumed.
**Mocker,** mok'ėr, *n.* A scorner; a scoffer.
**Mockery,** mok'ė-ri, *n.* Derision; sportive insult; counterfeit appearance; vain effort.
**Mocking-bird,** mok'ing-bėrd, *n.* An American bird of the thrush family.
**Mockingly,** mok'ing-li, *adv.* By way of mockery or derision.
**Mode,** mōd, *n.* Manner; method; fashion; custom.
**Model,** mo'del, *n.* A pattern; an image, copy, facsimile; standard, plan, or type; a person from whom an artist studies his proportions, postures, etc.—*vt.* (modelling, modelled). To plan after some model; to form in order to serve as a model; to mold.—*vi.* To make a model.
**Modeller,** mo'del-ėr, *n.* One who models; one who makes figures in clay, etc.
**Modelling,** mo'del-ing, *n.* The making of a model; appearance of relief in painted figures.
**Moderate,** mo'dė-rāt, *vt.* To restrain from excess; to temper, lessen, allay.—*vi.* To become less violent or intense; to preside as a moderator.—*a.* Not going to extremes; temperate; medium; mediocre.—*n.* One not extreme in opinions.
**Moderately,** mo'de-rāt-li, *adv.* In a moderate manner or degree; not very.
**Moderation,** mo-de-rā'shon, *n.* Act of moderating; state or quality being moderate; act of presiding as a moderator.
**Moderator,** mo'de-rāt-ėr, *n.* One who or that which moderates; a president, especially of courts in Presbyterian churches.
**Modern,** mod'ėrn, *a.* Pertaining to the present time; of recent origin; late; recent.—*n.* A person

M

of modern times.
**Modernism,** mod'ėrn-izm, *n.* Modern practice, character, phrase, or mode of expression.
**Modernize,** mod'ėrn-īz, *vt.* To adapt to modern ideas, style, or language.
**Modest,** mod'est, *a.* Restrained by a sense of propriety; bashful; diffident; chaste; moderate; not excessive.
**Modestly,** mod'est-li, *adv.* With modesty; diffidently; not excessively.
**Modesty,** mod'es-ti, *n.* Quality of being modest; bashful reserve; chastity; freedom from excess.
**Modicum,** mod'i-kum, *n.* A little; a small quantity; small allowance or share.
**Modification,** mod'i-fi-kā''shon, *n.* Act of modifying; state of being modified; change.
**Modify,** mod'i-fī, *vt.* (modifying, modified). To qualify; to change or alter; to vary.
**Modillion,** mō-dil'yon, *n.* A carved bracket used in cornices of buildings.
**Modish,** mōd'ish, *a.* According to the mode or fashion; affectedly fashionable.
**Modiste,** mō-dēst', *n.* A woman who deals in articles of ladies' dress; dressmaker.
**Modulate,** mod'ū-lāt, *vt.* To proportion; to adjust; to vary (the voice) in tone; to transfer from one key to another.—*vi.* To pass from one key into another.
**Modulation,** mod-ū-lā'shon, *n.* Act of modulating; act of inflecting the voice; melodious sound; change from one scale to another.
**Modulator,** mod'ū-lāt-ėr, *n.* One who or that which modulates.
**Module,** mod'ūl, *n.* In *architecture,* a measure to regulate the proportions of a building.
**Modulus,** mod'ū-lus, *n.* In *mathematics,* etc., a constant quantity used in connection with some variable quantity.
**Modus,** mō'dus, *n.* A way, manner, or mode.
**Mogul,** mō-gul', *n.* A Mongolian.—**The Great Mogul,** the soverign of the Mongolian empire in Hindustan.
**Mohair,** mō'hār, *n.* The hair of the Angora goat; cloth made of this hair; an imitation wool and cotton cloth.
**Mohammedan,** mō-ham'med-an, *a.* Pertaining to Mohammed, or the religion founded by him.—*n.* A follower of Mohammed.
**Mohammedanism,** mō-ham'med-an-izm, *n.* The religion of Mohammed.
**Moil,** moil, *vi.* To labor; to toil.
**Moire,** mwär, *n.* A watered appearance on metals or cloths; watered silk.
**Moist,** moist, *a.* Moderately wet; damp.
**Moisten,** mois'n, *vt.* To make moist or damp; to wet in a small degree.
**Moisture,** mois'tūr, *n.* A moderate degree of wetness; humidity.
**Molar,** mō'lėr, *a.* Serving to grind the food in eating.—*n.* A grinding or double tooth.
**Molasses,** mō-las'ez, *n.sing.* A syrup from sugar in the process of making; treacle.
**Mold,** mōld, *n.* Fine soft earth; mustiness or mildew; dust from incipient decay; form in which a thing is cast; model; shape; character.—*vt.* To cause to contract mold; to cover with mold or soil; to model; to shape; to fashion.—*vi.* To become moldy.
**Molder,** mōld'ėr, *n.* One who molds or is employed making casting sin a foundry.—*vi.* To turn to mold or dust by natural decay.—*vt.* To convert into mold or dust.
**Molding,** mōld'ing, *n.* Anything cast in a mold; ornamental contour or form in wood or stone along an edge or a surface.
**Moldy,** mōld'i, *a.* Overgrown with mold; musty; decaying.
**Mole,** mōl, *n.* A small discolored protuberance on the human body; a mound or break-water to protect a harbor from the waves; a small burrowing insectivorous animal.
**Molecular,** mō-lek'ū-lėr, *a.* Belonging to or consisting of molecules.
**Molecule,** mo'le-kūl, *n.* A very minute particle of matter.
**Mole-hill,** mōl'hil, *n.* A little hillock of earth thrown up by moles; a very small hill.
**Moleskin,** mōl'skin, *n.* A strong twilled fustian or cotton cloth.
**Molest,** mō-lest', *vt.* To annoy; to disturb; to harass; to vex.
**Molestation,** mō-lest-ā'shon, *n.* Act of molesting; disturbance; annoyance.
**Mollification,** mol'i-fi-kā''shon, *n.* Act of mollifying, mitigating, or appeasing.
**Mollifier,** mol'i-fī-ėr, *n.* One who or that which mollifies.
**Mollify,** mol'i-fī, *vt.* (mollifying, mollified). To soften; to assuage; to appease; to reduce in harshness; to tone down.
**Mollusc, Mollusk,** mol'usk, *n.* An animal whose body is soft, as mussels, snails, cuttle-fish, etc.; one of the *Mollusca.*
**Molluscous,** mol-lus'kus, *a.* Pertaining to the mollusca; soft and flabby.
**Molten,** mōlt'n, old pp. of *melt.* Melted; made of melted metal.
**Moment,** mō'ment, *n.* A minute portion of time; a second; momentum; importance; gravity.
**Momentarily,** mō'ment-a-ri-li, *adv.* Every moment; for a moment.
**Momentary,** mō-ment-a-ri, *a.* Done in a moment; continuing only a moment.
**Momentous,** mō-ment'us, *a.* Of moment; important; weighty.
**Momentum,** mō-ment'um, *n.*; pl. **-ta.** The force possessed by a body in motion; impetus.
**Monachism,** mon'ak-izm, *n.* The monastic life or system.
**Monad,** mon'ad, *n.* An ultimate atom.
**Monadic,** mon-ad'ik, *a.* Having the nature or character of a monad.
**Monarch,** mon'ärk, *n.* A supreme governor of a state; a sovereign; one who or that which is chief of its kind.—*a.* Supreme; ruling.
**Monarchal,** mon-ärk'al, *a.* Pertaining to a monarch; suiting a monarch; sovereign.
**Monarchic, Monarchical,** mon-ärk'ik, mon-ärk'ik-al, *a.* Pertaining to monarchy; vested in a single ruler.
**Monarchist,** mon'ärk-ist, *n.* An advocate of monarchy.
**Monarchy,** mon'är-ki, *n.* Government in which the supreme power is lodged in a single person, actually or nominally; a kingdom.
**Monastery,** mon'as-te-ri, *n.* A house for monks, sometimes for nuns; abbey; priory; convent.
**Monastic,** mon-as'tik, *a.* Pertaining to monasteries or monks; recluse.—*n.* A monk.
**Monasticism,** mon-as'ti-sizm, *n.* Monastic life; the monastic system or condition.
**Monatomic,** mon-a-tom'ik, *a.* Said of an element one atom of which will combine with only one atom of another element.
**Monday,** mun'dā, *n.* The second day of the week.
**Monetary,** mo'ne-ta-ri, *a.* Relating to money; consisting in money.
**Monetize,** mon-et-īz', *vt.* To form into coin or money.
**Money,** mun'i, *n.* Coin; pieces of gold, silver, or other metal, stamped by public authority and used as the medium of exchange; a circulating medium; wealth; affluence.
**Moneyed,** mun'id, *a.* Having money; rich.
**Monger,** mung'gėr, *n.* A trader: now only in composition, as in iron*monger.*
**Mongol, Mongolian,** mon'gol, mon-gō'li-an, *n.* A native of Mongolia.—*a.* Belonging to Mongolia.
**Mongoose,** mong' or mung'gōs, *n.* A common ichneumon of India.
**Mongrel,** mung'grel, *a.* Of a mixed breed; hybrid.—*n.* An animal of a mixed breed.
**Monied,** mun'id, *a.* *See* MONEYED.
**Monism,** mon'izm, *n.* The doctrine that there is only a single principle from which everything is developed, this principle being either mind (*ide-*

*alistic monism*) or matter (*materialistic monism*).

**Monition,** mō-ni'shon, *n.* Admonition; warning; intimation.

**Monitor,** mo'ni-tėr, *n.* One who admonishes; one who warns of faults or informs of duty; a senior pupil in a school appointed to instruct and look after juniors; a lizard.

**Monitorial,** mo-ni-tō'ri-al, *a.* Relating to a monitor; conducted by monitors; admonitory.

**Monitory,** mo'ni-to-ri, *a.* Giving admonition.

**Monitress, Monitrix,** mon'i-tres, mon'i-triks, *n.* A female monitor.

**Monk,** mungk, *n.* A male inhabitant of a monastery, bound to celibacy.

**Monkey,** mung'ki, *n.* A long-tailed quadrumanous animal; a playful or mischievous youngster.

**Monkish,** mungk'ish, *a.* Like a monk, or pertaining to monks; monastic.

**Monochrome,** mon'ō-krōm, *n.* A painting in one color, but with light and shade.

**Monodrama,** mon'ō-dra-ma, *n.* A dramatic performance by a single person.

**Monody,** mon'ō-di, *n.* A poem in which a single mourner gives vent to his grief.

**Monogamist,** mon-og'a-mist, *n.* One who practices or upholds monogamy.

**Monogamous,** mon-og'a-mus, *a.* Upholding or practicing monogamy.

**Monogamy,** mon-og'a-mi, *n.* The practice or principle of marrying only once; the marrying of only one at a time.

**Monogram,** mon'ō-gram, *n.* A cipher composed of several letters interwoven.

**Monograph,** mon'ō-graf, *n.* An account of a single person, thing, or class of things.

**Monolith,** mon'ō-lith, *n.* A pillar, column, etc., consisting of a single stone.

**Monologue,** mon'ō-log, *n.* A speech uttered by one person alone; a soliloquy.

**Monomania,** mon-ō-mā'ni-a, *n.* Insanity in regard to a single subject or class of subjects; a craze.

**Monometallism,** mon-ō-met'al-izm, *n.* The having only one metal as the standard of coinage; the theory of a single metallic standard.

**Monopolist,** mo-nop'o-list, *n.* One that monopolizes or possesses a monopoly.

**Monopolize,** mo-nop'o-līz, *vt.* To obtain a monopoly of; to engross entirely.

**Monopoly,** mo-nop'o-li, *n.* An exclusive trading privilege; assumption of anything to the exclusion of others.

**Monosyllabic,** mon'ō-sil-lab''ik, *a.* Consisting of one syllable, or of words of one syllable.

**Monosyllable,** mon'ō-sil-la-bl, *n.* A word of one syllable.

**Monotheism,** mon'ō-thē-izm, *n.* The doctrine of the existence of one God only.

**Monotone,** mon'ō-tōn, *n.* A single tone; unvaried pitch of the voice.

**Monotonous,** mon-ot'on-us, *a.* Exhibiting monotony; wanting variety; unvaried.

**Monotony,** mon-ot'o-ni, *n.* Uniformity of sound; a dull uniformity; an irksome sameness or want of variety.

**Monsignore, Monsignor,** mon-sē-nyō'rā, mon-sēn'yor, *n.* A title of a bishop or high dignitary of the R. Catholic Church.

**Monsoon,** mon-sön', *n.* The trade-wind of the Indian seas, blowing from N.E. from November to March, and S.W. from April to October.

**Monster,** mon'stėr, *n.* An animal of unnatural form or of great size; one unnaturally wicked or evil.—*a.* Of inordinate size.

**Monstrance,** mon'strans, *n.* In the R. Catholic Church, a glass-faced shrine in which the consecrated host is presented for the adoration of the people.

**Monstrosity,** mon-stros'i-ti, *n.* State or quality of being monstrous; that which is monstrous.

**Monstrous,** mon'strus, *a.* Unnatural in form; enormous; huge; horrible.—*adv.* Exceedingly.

**Monstrously,** mon'strus-li, *adv.* In a monstrous manner; shockingly; terribly.

**Month,** munth, *n.* The period measured by the moon's revolution (the lunar month, about 29½ days); one of the twelve parts of the year (the calendar month, 30 or 31 days).

**Monthly,** munth'li, *a.* Done or happening once a month, or every month.—*n.* A publication appearing once a month.—*adv.* Once a month; in every month.

**Monument,** mon'ū-ment, *n.* Anything by which the memory of a person or of an event is preserved; a memorial; a singular or notable instance.

**Monumental,** mon-ū-ment'al, *a.* Pertaining to or serving as a monument; preserving memory; great and conspicuous.

**Moo,** mö, *vi.* (mooing, mooed). To low, as a cow.—*n.* The low of a cow.

**Mood,** möd, *n.* Temper of mind; disposition; a fit of sullenness; a form of verbs expressive of certainty, contingency, etc.; a form of syllogism.

**Moody,** möd'i, *a.* Subject to moods or humors; out of humor; gloomy; sullen.

**Moon,** mön, *n.* The changing luminary of the night; the heavenly body next to the earth, revolving round it in about 29½ days; a satellite of any planet; a month.

**Moonbeam,** mön'bēm, *n.* A ray of light from the moon.

**Moonlight,** mön'līt, *n.* The light afforded by the moon.—*a.* Illuminated by the moon; occurring during moonlight.—**Moon-lit,** mön'lit, *a.* Illuminated by the moon.

**Moonlighter,** mön'līt-ėr, *n.* One of those who in Ireland commit agrarian outrages by night.

**Moonlighting,** mön'līt-ing, *n.* The practices of moonlighters.

**Moonshine,** mön'shīn, *n.* The light of the moon; show without substance; pretense; illegally distilled corn whiskey.

**Moonstone,** mön'stōn, *n.* A translucent variety of felspar used in trinkets, etc.

**Moonstruck,** mön'struk, *a.* Affected by the influence of the moon; lunatic.

**Moony,** mön'i, *a.* Pertaining to or like the moon or moonlight; bewildered or silly.

**Moor,** mör, *n.* A tract of waste land, or of hilly ground on which game is preserved; a native of the northern coast of Africa.—*vt.* To secure a ship in a particular station, as by cables and anchors.—*vi.* To be confined by cables.

**Moorage,** mör'āj, *n.* A place for mooring.

**Mooring,** mör'ing, *n.* Act of one who moors; *pl.* the anchor, etc., by which a ship is moored; the place where a ship is moored.

**Moorish,** mör'ish, *a.* Pertaining to the Moors.

**Moorish, Moory,** mör'ish, mör'i, *a.* Having the character of a moor; moorland.

**Moorland,** mör'land, *n.* A waste, barren district; a moor.—Used also adjectively.

**Moose,** mös, *n.* The American variety of the elk.

**Moot,** möt, *vt.* To debate; to discuss.—*a.* Debatable; subject to discussion.

**Moot-point,** möt'point, *n.* A point debated or liable to be debated.

**Mop,** mop, *n.* A cloth or collection of yarns fastened to a handle, and used for cleaning; a grimace.—*vt.* (mopping, mopped). To rub with a mop; to wipe.—*vi.* To grimace.

**Mope,** mōp, *vi.* (moping, moped). To show a downcast air; to be spiritless or gloomy.—*n.* One who mopes.

**Mopet, Mopsey,** mop'et, mop'sē, *n.* A puppet made of cloth; a pet name of a little girl; a woolly variety of dog.

**Mopish, mōp'ish,** *a.* Inclined to mope; dull; spiritless; dejected.

**Moraine,** mō-rān', *n.* An accumulation of debris on glaciers or in the valleys at their foot.

**Moral,** mo'ral, *a.* Relating to morality or morals; ethical; virtuous; supported by reason and probability.—*n*. The practical lesson inculcated by any story; *pl*. general conduct as right or wrong; mode of life; ethics.

**Morale,** mō-räl′, *n*. Mental condition of soldiers, etc., as regards courage, zeal, hope.

**Moralist,** mo′ral-ist, *n*. One who teaches morals; a writer or lecturer on ethics; one who inculcates or practices moral duties.

**Morality,** mō-ral′i-ti, *n*. The doctrine of moral duties; ethics; moral character or quality; quality of an action in regard to right and wrong; an old form of drama in which the personages were allegorical representations of virtues, vices, etc.

**Moralize,** mo′ral-īz, *vt*. To apply to a moral purpose; to draw a moral from.—vi. To make moral reflections; to draw practical lessons from the facts of life.

**Morally,** mo′ral-li, *adv*. In a moral or ethical sense; virtuously; virtually.

**Morass,** mō-ras′, *n*. A tract of low, soft, wet ground; a marsh; a swamp; a fen.

**Morbid,** mor′bid, *a*. Diseased; sickly; not sound and healthful.

**Morbidly,** mor′bid-li, *adj*. In a morbid or diseased manner.

**Morbific,** mor-bif′ik, *a*. Causing disease.

**Mordacious,** mor-dā′shus, *a*. Biting; pungent; sarcastic.

**Mordacity,** mor-das′i-ti, *n*. Quality of being mordacious; pungency.

**Mordant,** mor′dant, *n*. A substance, such as alum, which fixes colors; matter by which gold-leaf is made to adhere.—*a*. Biting; severe.

**More,** mōr, *a*. *comp*. of *much* and *many*. Greater in amount, extent, degree, etc.; greater in number.—*adv*. In a greater degree, extent, or quantity; in addition.—*n*. A greater quantity or number; something further.

**Moreen,** mō-rēn′, *n*. A woollen, or woollen and cotton, fabric used for curtains, etc.

**Moreover,** mōr-ō′vėr, *adv*. Further; besides; likewisel

**Morganatic,** mor-ga-nat′ik, *a*. Applied to a kind of marriage with a female of lower rank, the offspring of which do not inherit the father's rank, though otherwise legitimate.

**Moribund,** mo′ri-bund, *a*. in a dying state.

**Morion,** mo′ri-on, *n*. A helmet without visor or beaver.

**Mormon,** mor′mon, *n*. A member of a sect founded in the United States in 1830, who practice polygamy; a Latter-day Saint. Also **Mormonite, Mormonist.**

**Morn,** morn, *n*. The morning: *poetic*.

**Morning,** morn′ing, *n*. The first part of the day; the time between dawn and the middle of the forenoon; the first or early part. Often used as an *adj*.

**Morning-star,** *n*. The planet Venus when it rises before the sun.

**Morning-tide,** morn′ing-tīd, *n*. Morning time; morning.

**Morocco,** mōrok′ō, *n*. A find kind of leather prepared from goat skin.

**Moron,** mo′ron, *n*. A feeble-minded or degenerate person.

**Morose,** mō-rōs′, *a*. Of a sour or sullen temper; gloomy; churlish; surly.

**Morosely,** mō-rōs′li, *adj*. In a morose manner; with sullenness.

**Morphia, Morphine,** mor′fi-a, mor′fin, *n*. The narcotic principle of opium, a powerful anodyne.

**Morphologist,** mor-fol′o-jist, *n*. One versed in morphology

**Morphology,** mor-fol′o-ji, *n*. The science which treats of the form and arrangement of the structures of plants and animals.

**Morris, Morrice,** mo′ris, *n*. A dance borrowed from the Moors; a fantastic dance formerly practiced in England.

**Morrow,** mo′rō, *n*. The day next after the present, or a specified day.

**Morsel,** mor′sel, *n*. A bite; a mouthful; a fragment; a little piece in general.

**Mortal,** mor′tal, *a*. Subject to death; deadly; fatal; human.—*n*. A being subject to death; a human being.

**Mortality,** mor-tal′i-ti, *n*. State of being mortal; actual death of great numbers of men or beasts; death-rate.

**Mortally,** mor′tal-li, *adv*. In a manner that must cause death; in the manner of a mortal.

**Mortar,** mor′tär, *n*. A vessel, in which substances are pounded with a pestle; a short piece of ordnance, thick and wide, for throwing shells, etc.; a mixture of lime and sand with water, used as a cement for building.

**Mortgage,** mor′gāj, *n*. A conveyance of land or house property as security for a debt; the deed effecting this conveyance.—*vt*. (mortgaging, mortgaged). To grant or assign on mortgage; to pledge.

**Mortgagee,** mor-ga-jē′, *n*. The person to whom an estate is mortgaged.

**Mortgager,** mor′gāj-ėr, *n*. The person who mortgages.

**Mortification,** mor′ti-fi-kā′′shon, *n*. Act of mortifying; condition of being mortified; death of a part of an animal body while the rest is alive; the subduing of the passions by penance, abstinence, etc.; chagrin.

**Mortify,** mor′ti-fī, *vt*. (mortifying, mortified). To affect with gangrene or mortification; to subdue by abstinence or rigorous severities; to humiliate; to chagrin.—*vi*. To lose vitality while yet a portion of a living body.

**Mortifying,** mor′ti-fī-ing, *p.a*. Humiliating; tending to mortify or humiliate.

**Mortise,** mor′tis, *n*. A hole cut in one piece of material to receive the tenon of another piece.—*vt*. To cut a mortise in; to join by a tenon and mortise.

**Mortuary,** mor′tū-a-ri, *n*. A place for the temporary reception of the dead.—*a*. Pertaining to the burial of the dead.

**Mosaic,** mō-zā′ik, *n*. Inlaid work of marble, precious stones, etc., disposed on a ground of cement so as to form designs.—*a*. Pertaining to or composed of mosaic.

**Mosaic, Mosaical,** mō-zā′ik, mō-zā′ik-al, *a*. Pertaining to Moses.

**Moselle,** mō-zel′, *n*. A species of white French and German wine.

**Moslem, moz′lem,** *n*. An orthodox Mohammedan.

**Mosque,** mosk, *n*. A Mohammedan place of worship.

**Mosquito,** mos-kē′tō, *n*. A sting gnat or fly.

**Moss,** mos, *n*. A small plant with simple branching stems and numerous small leaves; a bog; a place where peat is found,—*vt*. To cover with moss by natural growth.

**Mossy,** mos′i, *a*. Overgrown or abounding with moss; covered or bordered with moss.

**Most,** mōst, *a*. superl. of *more*. Greatest in any way.—*adv*. In the greatest degree, quantity, or extent; mostly; chiefly.—*n*. The greatest number; the majority; greatest amount; utmost extent, degree, etc.

**Mostly,** mōst′li, *adv*. For the most part; mainly; chiefly; generally speaking.

**Mote,** mōt, *n*. A small particle; anything proverbially small.

**Moth,** moth, *n*. The name of numerous nocturnal insects allied to the butterflies.

**Mother,** muTH′er, *n*. A female parent; a woman who has borne a child; source or origin; an abbess or other female at the head of a religious institution; a slimy substance that gathers in vinegar, etc.—*a*. Native; natural; inborn; vernacular.

**Mother-church,** muTH′ėr-chėrch, *n*. An original church; a metropolitan church.

**Mother-country,** muTH′ėr-kun-tri, *n*. A country

which has sent out colonies; a country as the producer of anything.

**Motherhood,** muTH'ėr-hụd, *n.* State of being a mother.

**Mother-in-law,** muTH'ėr-in-la, *n.* The mother of one's husband or wife.

**Motherly,** muTH'üėr-li, *a.* Like or becoming a mother; maternal; affectionate.

**Mother-of-pearl,** muTH'ėr-ov-pėrl, *n.* The hard silvery brilliant internal layer of several kinds of shells.

**Mothy,** moth'i, *a.* Full of moths.

**Motile,** mō'til, *a.* Having inherent power of motion.

**Motion,** mō'shon, *n.* Act or process of moving; power of moving; movement; internal impulse; proposal made; evacuation of the intestines.—*vi.* To make a significant gesture with the hand.

**Motionless,** mō'shon-les, *a.* Wanting motion; being at rest.

**Motive,** mō'tiv, *n.* That which incites to action; cause, inducement; purpose; theme in a piece of music; prevailing idea of an artist.—*a.* Causing motion.—*vt.* To supply a motive to or for; to prompt.

**Motivity,** mō-tiv'i-ti, *n.* Power of moving.

**Motley,** mot'li, *a.* Variegated in color; particolored; heterogeneous; diversified—*n.* A dress of various colors.

**Motor,** mō'tor, *n.* A moving power; force or agency that sets machinery in motion; a motor-car.—*a.* Imparting motion.

**Mottle,** mot'l, *n.* A blotched or spotted character of surface.—*vt.* (mottling, mottled). To mark with spots or blothes as if mottled.

**Mottled,** mot'ld, *p.a.* Spotted; marked with spots of different colors.

**Motto,** mot'tō, *n.*; pl. **-oes,** or **-os.** A short sentence or phrase, or a single word, adopted as expressive of one's guiding idea.

**Moult,** mōlt, *vi.* and *t.* To shed or cast the hair, feathers, skin, horns, etc., as birds and other animals.—*n.* Act or process of changing the feathers, etc.; time of moulting.

**Mound,** mound, *n.* An artificial elevation of earth; a bulwark, a rampart; the globe which forms part of the regalia.

**Mount,** mount, *n.* A hill; a mountain; that with which something is fitted; a setting, frame, etc.; opportunity or means of riding on horseback; a horse.—*vi.* To rise; to get on horseback or upon any animal; to amount.—*vt.* To raise aloft; to climb; to place oneself upon, as on horseback; to furnish with horses; to set in or cover with something; to set off to advantage.

**Mountain,** moun'tin, *n.* An elevated mass larger than a hill; anything very large.—*a.* Pertaining to a mountain; found on mountains.

**Mountain-ash,** moun'tin-ash, *n*, A British tree with scarlet berries; the rowan.

**Mountaineer,** moun-tin-ēr', *n.* An inhabitant of a mountainous district; a climber of mountains.—*vi.* To practice the climbing of mountains.

**Mountainous,** moun'tin-us, *a.* Full of mountains; large, as a mountain; huge.

**Mountebank,** moun'ti-bangk, *n.* One who mounts a bench or stage in a public place, and vends medicines or nostrums; a quack; any boastful and false pretender.

**Mounting,** mount'ing, *n.* Act of one who mounts; that with which an article is mounted or set off; trimming, setting, etc.

**Mourn,** mōrn, *vi.* To sorrow; to lament; to wear the customary habit of sorrow.—*vt.* To grieve for; to deplore.

**Mourner,** mōrn'ėr, *n.* One who mourns; one who attends a funeral.

**Mournful,** mōrn'ful, *a.* Expressing sorrow; sad; calamitous; sorrowful.

**Mournfully,** mōrn'ful-li, *adv.* In a mournful manner; with sorrow.

**Mourning,** mōrn'ing, *n.* Lamentation; dress worn by mourners.—*a.*. Employed to express grief.

**Mouse,** mous, *n.*; pl. **Mice,** mīs. A small rodent quadruped that infests houses, fields, etc.—*vi.* mouz (mousing, moused). To hunt for or catch mice.

**Mouser,** mouz'ėr, *n.* A cat good at catching mice.

**Moustache,** mus-tash', *n.* The long hair on the upper lip.

**Mouth,** mouth, *n.*; pl. **Mouths,** mouTHz. The opening in the head of an animal into which food is received, and from which voice is uttered; opening of anything hollow, as of a pitcher, or of a cave, pit, etc.; the part of a river, etc., by which it joins with the ocean.—*vt.* mouTH. To take into the mouth; to utter with a voice affectedly big.—*vi.* To speak with a loud, affected voice; to vociferate.

**Mouthful,** mouth'ful, *n.* As much as the mouth contains at once; a small quantity.

**Mouth-organ,** mouth-or'gan, *n.* A small popular wind-instrument, flat in shape, with openings for the various notes, which are produced by inhalation and exhalation.

**Mouth-piece,** mouth'pēs, *n.* The part of a wind-instrument to which the mouth is applied; a tube by which a cigar, etc., is held in the mouth; one who believes the opinions of others.

**Movable,** möv'a-bl, *a.* Capable of being moved; changing from one time to another.—*n.* Any part of a man's goods capable of being moved; *pl.* goods, commodities, furniture.

**Movably,** möv'a-bli, *adv.* In a movable manner or state.

**Move,** möv, *vt.* (moving, moved). To cause to change place, posture, or position; to set in motion; to affect; to rouse; to prevail on; to propose, as a resolution.—*vi.* To change place or posture; to stir; to begin to act; to shake; to change residence; to make a proposal to a meeting.—*n.* The act of moving; a movement; proceeding; action taken.

**Movement,** möv'ment, *n.* Act of moving; motion; change of position; manner of moving; gesture; an agitation to bring about some result desired; wheel-work of a clock.

**Mover,** mö'vėr, *n.* A person or thing that moves or gives motion; one who ofers a motion in an assembly.

**Moving,** *möv'ing, p.a.* Causing to move or act; pathetic; affecting.

**Mow,** mou or mō, *n.* A pile of hay or sheaves of grain deposited in a barn; part of a barn where they are packed; a wry face.—*vt.* To lay in a mow.—*vi.* To make mouths.

**Mow,** mō, *vt.* (pret. mowed, pp. mowed or mown). To cut down, as grass, etc.; to cut the grass from; to cut down in great numbers.—*vi.* To cut grass; to use the scythe.

**Mower,** mō'ėr, *n.* One who mows; a mowing-machine.

**Mowing-machine,** mō'ing-ma-shēn, *n.* A machine to cut down grass, grain, etc.

**Much,** much, *a.*; comp. *more,* superl. *most.* Great in quantity or amount; abundant.—*adv.* In a great degree; by far; greatly.—*n.* A great quantity; something strange or serious.

**Mucilage,** mū'si-lāj, *n.* A solution in water of gummy matter; a gummy substance found in certain plants.

**Mucilaginous,** mu-si-laj'in-us, *a.* Pertaining to or secreting mucilage; slimy.

**Muck** muk, *n.* Dung in a moist state; something mean, vile, or filthy.—*vt.* To manure with muck; to remove muck from.

**Muck-worm,** muk'wėrm, *n.* A worm that lives in muck; a miser.

**Mucous, Mucose,** mū'kus, *a.* Pertaining to mucus, or resembling it; slimy.—**Mucous membrane,** a membrane that lines all the cavities of the body which open externally, and secretes mucus.

**Mucus,** mū'kus, *n.* A viscid fluid secreted by the mucous membrane.

**Mud,** mud, *n.* Moist and soft earth; sediment

M

from turbid waters; mire.—*vt.* (mudding, mudded). To soil with mud; to make turbid.
**Muddle,** mud'l, *vt.* (muddling, muddled). To make muddy; to intoxicate partially; to confuse; to make a mess of.—*vi.* To become muddy; to act in a confused manner.—*n.* A mess; confusion; bewilderment.
**Muddy,** mud'i, *a.* Abounding in mud; miry; stupid; obscure.—*vt.* (muddying, muddied). To soil with mud; to cloud.
**Muezzin, Mueddin,** mu-ed'zin, mu-ed'in, *n.* A Mohammedan crier who proclaims from a minaret the summons to prayers.
**Muff,** muf, *n.* A warm cover for receiving both hands; a soft, useless fellow.
**Muffin,** muf'in, *n.* A light spongy cake.
**Muffle,** muf'l, *vt.* (muffling, muffled). To cover close, particularly the neck and face; to conceal; to deaden the sound of by wrapping cloth, etc., round.—*n.* The tumid and naked portion of the upper lip and nose of ruminants and rodents.
**Muffled,** muf'ld, *p.a.* Wrapped up closely; dulled or deadened: applied to sound.
**Muffler,** muf'lėr, *n.* A cover for the face or neck; a stuffed glove for lunatics.
**Mufti, Muftee,** muf'ti, muf'tē, *n.* A doctor of Mohammedan law; civilian dress.
**Mug,** mug, *n.* A small vessel of earthenware or metal for containing liquor; a jug.
**Muggy, Muggish,** mug'i, mug'ish, *a.* Damp and close; moist; moldy.
**Mulatto,** mū-lat'tō, *n.* A person who is the offspring of a white and a negro.
**Mulberry,** mul'be-ri, *n.* The berry of a tree, and the tree itself, cultivated to supply food for silkworms; a prefabricated harbor, used in the military operations of 1944.
**Mulch,** mulsh, *n.* Dungy material protecting the roots of newly-planted shrubs, etc.
**Mulct,** mulkt, *n.* A fine.—*vt.* To fine; to deprive.
**Mule,** mūl, *n.* The offspring of an ass and mare, or a horse and she-ass; a hybrid animal.
**Muleteer,** mūl-et-ēr', *n.* One who drives mules.
**Mulish,** mūl'ish, *a.* Like a mule; stubborn.
**Mull,** mul, *vt.* To heat, sweeten, and flavor with spices, as ale or wine.
**Mullet,** mul'et, *n.* A name for fishes of two different families, the gray mullets and the red mullets.
**Mulligatawny,** mul'i-ga-ta''ni, *n.* An E. Indian curry-soup.
**Mullion,** mul'yon, *n.* An upright division between the lights of windows, screens, etc., in Gothic architecture.
**Mullioned,** mul'yond, *a.* Having mullions.
**Multangular,** mul-tang'gū-lėr, *a.* Having many angles.
**Multifarious,** mul-ti-fā'ri-us, *a.* Having great diversity or variety.
**Multiform,** mul'ti-form, *a.* Having many forms, shapes, or appearances.
**Multilateral,** mul-ti-lat'ėr-al, *a.* Having many sides; many-sided.
**Multilineal,** mul-ti-lin'ē-al, *a.* Having many lines.
**Multipartite,** mul'ti-pär-tīt, *a* Divided into several or many parts.
**Multiped,** mul'ti-ped, *n.* An animal that has many feet.
**Multiple,** mul'ti-pl, *a.* Manifold; having many parts or divisions.—*n.* A number which contains another an exact number of times.
**Multiplex,** mul'ti-pleks, *a.* Manifold; complex.
**Multiplicand,** mul'ti-pli-kand'', *n.* A number to be multiplied by another.
**Multiplication,** mul'ti-pli-kā''shon, *n.* Act or process of multiplying; state of being multiplied; reproduction of animals.
**Multiplicative,** mul'ti-pli-kāt-iv, *a.* Tending to multiply.
**Multiplicity,** mul-ti-plis'i-ti, *n.* State of being multiplex or manifold; great number.
**Multiplier,** mul-ti-plī-ėr, *n.* One who or that which multiplies; the number by which another is multiplied.
**Multiply,** mul'ti-plī, *vt.* (multiplying, multiplied). To increase in number; to add to itself any given number of times.—*vi.* To increase in number, or to become more numerous by reproductive; to extend.
**Multitude,** mul'ti-tūd, *n.* State of being many; a great number, collectively or indefinitely; a crowd.—**The multitude,** the populace.
**Multitudinous,** mul-ti-tūd'in-us, *a.* Consisting of or pertaining to a multitude.
**Multivalve,** mul'ti-valv, *n.* An animal which has a shell of many valves or pieces.
**Multure,** mul'tūr, *n.* The grinding of grain.
**Mum,** mum, *a.* Silent.—*n.* A species of ale brewed from wheaten malt, etc.
**Mumble,** mum'bl, *vi.* (mumbling, mumbled). To mutter; to speak with mouth partly closed; to eat with the lips close.—*vt.* To utter with a low, inarticulate voice.
**Mumbler,** mum'blėr, *n.* One who mumbles or speaks with a low, inarticulate voice.
**Mummify,** mum'i-fī, *vt.* To make into a mummy; to embalm as a mummy.
**Mummy,** mum'i, *n.* A dead human body embalmed after the manner of the ancient Egyptians, with wax, balsams, etc.
**Mump,** mump, *vt.* or *i.* To mumble or mutter; to munch; to implore alms.
**Mumpish,** mump'ish, *a.* Dull; sullen; sour.
**Mumps,** mumps, *n.* Silent displeasure; sullenness; a disease consisting in an inflammation of the salivary glands.
**Munch,** munsh, *vt.* and *i.* To chew audibly.
**Mundane,** mun'dān, *a.* Belonging to this world; worldly· earthly.
**Municipal,** mū-ni'si-pal, *a.* Belonging to a corporation or city.
**Municipality,** mū-ni'si-pal''i-ti, *n.* A town possessed of local self-government; community under municipal jurisdiction.
**Munificence,** mū-ni'fi-sens, *n.* A bestowing liberally; liberality; generosity.
**Munificent,** mū-ni'fi-sent, *a.* Liberal in giving; bountiful; liberal; generous.
**Munificently,** mū-ni'fi-sent-li, *adv.* Liberally; generously.
**Muniment,** mū'ni-ment, *n.* Support; defense; a charter; a writing by which claims and rights are defended.
**Munition,** mū-ni'shon, *n.* Military stores; ammunition; material for any enterprise.
**Mural,** mū'ral, *a.* Pertaining to a wall; resembling a wall; perpendicular or steep.
**Murder,** mėr'dėr, *n.* Act of killing a human being with premeditated malice.—*vt.* To kill (a human being) with premeditated malice; to mar by bad execution.
**Murderer,** mėr'dėr-ėr, *n.* One who murders, or is guilty of murder.
**Murderess,** mėr'dėr-es, *n.* A female who commits murder.
**Murderous,** mėr'dėr-us, *a.* Pertaining to murder; guilty of murder; meditating murder; bloody.
**Muriatic,** mū-ri-at'ik, *a.* Pertaining to or obtained from brine or sea-salt; hydrochloric.
**Muricate, Muricated,** mū'ri-kāt, mū'ri-kāt-ed, *a.* Armed with sharp points or prickles.
**Murk,** mėrk, *n.* Darkness, gloom.
**Murky,** mėr'ki, *a.* Dark; obscure; gloomy.
**Murmur,** mėr'mėr, *n.* A low continued or repeated sound; a hum; a grumble or mutter.—*vi.* To utter a murmur or hum; to grumble.—*vt.* To utter indistinctly; to mutter.
**Murmurer,** mėr'mėr-ėr, *n.* One who murmurs.
**Murmuring,** mėr'mėr-ing, *n.* A continued murmur; a low confused noise.
**Murrain,** mu'rān, *n.* A deadly and infectious disease among cattle, etc.
**Muscadel, Muscatel, Muscadine,** mus'ka-del, mus'ka-tel, mus'ka-dīn, *a.* and *n.* A sweet and strong Italian or French wine; the grapes

which produce this wine; a delicious pear.
**Muscat,** mus'kat, *n.* A kind of grape, and the wine made from it. *See* MUSCADEL.
**Muscle,** mus'l *n.* A definite portion of an animal body consisting of fibers susceptible of contraction and relaxation, and thus effecting motion; a mussel.
**Muscled,** mus'ld, *a.* Having muscles.
**Muscovado,** mus-kō-vā'dō, *n.* or *a.* Unrefined sugar.
**Muscovite,** mus'kō-vit, *n.* A native of Muscovy, or Russia; common mica.
**Muscular,** mus'kū-lėr, *a.* Pertaining to or consisting of muscle; performed by a muscle; strong; brawny; vigorous.
**Muscularity,** mus-kū-la'ri-ti, *n.* State of being muscular.
**Muse,** mūz, *n.* One of the nine sister goddesses of the Greeks and Romans presiding over the arts; poetic inspiration; a fit of abstraction.—*vi.* (musing, mused). To ponder; to meditate in silence; to be absent in mind.—*vt.* To meditate on.
**Museum,** mū-zē'um, *n.* A repository of interesting objects connected with literature, art, or science.
**Mushroom,** mush'röm, *n.* An edible fungus; an upstart,—*a.* Pertaining to mushrooms; resembling mushrooms in rapidity of growth.
**Music,** mū'zik, *n.* Melody of harmony; the science of harmonious sounds; the written or printed score of a composition.
**Musical,** mū'zik-al, *a.* Belonging to music; producing music; melodious; harmonious; fond of or skilled in music.
**Musically,** mu'zik-al-li, *adv.* In a musical, melodious, or harmonious manner.
**Music-hall,** mū'zik-hal, *n.* A place of public entertainemnt in which the spectators are treated to singing, dancing, etc.
**Musician,** mū-zi'shan, *n.* One skilled in music.
**Musing,** mūz'ing, *n.* Meditation.
**Musk,** musk, *n.* A strong-scented substance obtained from the musk-deer; the animal itself; a musky smell; a plant giving out such a smell.—*vt.* To perfume with musk.
**Musk-deer,** musk'dēr, *n.* A deer of Central Asia, the male of which yields the perfume musk.
**Musket,** mus'ket, *n.* Early form of military handgun, with a smooth bore; a sparrow-hawk of inferior kind.
**Musketeer,** mus-ket-ēr', *n.* A soldier armed with a musket.
**Musketry,** mus'ket-ri, *n.* The fire of muskets; troops armed with muskets; the art or science of firing small-arms.
**Musky,** musk'i, *a.* Having the odor of musk; fragrant.
**Muslin,** muz'lin, *n.* A fine thin cotton cloth.—*a.* Made of muslin.
**Mussel,** mus'el, *n.* The common name of a genus of bivalve shell-fish.
**Must,** must, *vi.* without inflection, and present or past. A defective or auxiliary verb expressing obligation or necessity.—*n.* New wine unfermented.
**Mustard,** mus'tėrd, *n.* An annual plant cultivated for its pungent seeds; the condiment obtained from its seeds.
**Mustard gas,** mus'tėrd gas, *n.* A poisonous gas with a pungent smell resembling that of mustard.
**Muster,** mus'tėr, *vt.* To collect, as troops; to assemble or bring together—*vi.* To assemble; to meet in one place.—*n.* An assembling of troops; register of troops mustered; an array.
**Muster-roll,** mus'tėr-rōl, *n.* A roll or register of troops, or a ship's company.
**Musty,** mus'ti, *a.* Moldy; sour; stale.
**Mutability,** mū-ta-bil'i-ti, *n.* Quality or state of being mutable; inconstancy.
**Mutable,** mūta-bl, *a.* Changeable; inconstant; unstable; variable; fickle.
**Mutation,** mū-tā'shon, *n.* Act or process of changing; change; alteration, either in form or qualities; modification.
**Mute,** mūt, *a.* Silent; incapable of speaking; dumb; not pronounced, or having its sound checked by a contact of the vocal organs, as certain consonants (*t, p, k, etc.*).—*n.* A dumb person; a hired attendant at a funeral; a mute consonant.—*vi.* (muting, muted). To eject the contents of the bowels as birds.
**Mutely,** mūt'li, *adv.* In a mute manner; silently; without uttering words or sounds.
**Mutilate,** mū'ti-lāt, *vt.* To injure or disfigure by cutting a piece from; to maim; to render imperfect.
**Mutilation,** mū'ti-lā'shon, *n.* Act of mutilating; state of being mutilated; removal of some essential part.
**Mutineer,** mū-ti-nēr', *n.* One guilty of mutiny.
**Mutinous,** mū-ti-nus, *a.* Exciting or engaging in mutiny; seditious.
**Mutiny,** muti-ni, *n.* An insurrection of soldiers or seamen; revolt against constituted authority.—*vi.* (mutinying, mutinied). To rise against lawful authority.
**Mutter,** mut'ėr, *vi.* To utter words with compressed liips; to mumble; to murmur.—*vt.* To utter with a low, murmuring voice.—*n.* Murmur; obscure utterance.
**Muttering,** mut'ėr-ing, *n.* The sound made by one who mutters.
**Mutton,** mut'n, *n.* The flesh of sheep, raw or dressed for food.
**Mutton-chop,** mut-n-chop', *n.* A rib of mutton for broiling.
**Mutual,** mū'tū-al, *a.* Reciprocal; interchanged; given and received on both sides.
**Mutually,** mū'tū-al-li, *adv.* In a mutual manner; reciprocally.
**Muzzle,** muz'l, *n.* The projecting mouth and nose of an animal; the open end of a gun or pistol, etc.; a cover for the mouth which hinders an animal from biting.—*vt.* (muzzling, muzzled). To cover the mouth of to prevent biting or eating; to gag.
**My,** mī, *pron.* The possessive case sing. of *Iyopy; belonging to me.*
**Myalgia,** mī-al'ji-a, *n.* Cramp.
**Mycelium,** mī-sē'li-um, *n.*; pl. **-lia.** The cellular filamentous spawn of fungi.
**Mycology,** mī-kol'o-ji, *n.* That department of botany which investigates fungi.
**Myology,** mī-ol'o-ji, *n.* The science and description of the muscles.
**Myopia, Myopy,** mī-ō'pi-a, mī'o-pi, *n.* Short-sightedness; near-sightedness.
**Myriad,** mi'ri-ad, *n.* A countless number; the number of ten thousand collectively.—*a.* innumerable.
**Myrmidon,** mėr'mi-don, *n.* A soldier of a rough character; a ruffian under an unscrupulous leader.
**Myrrh,** mėr, *n.* An aromatic gum resin exuded by a spiny Arabian shrub.
**Myrtle,** mėr'tl, *n.* An evergreen shrub.
**Myself,** mī-self', *compd. pron.*; pl. **Ourselves,** our-selvz'. As a nominative it is used, generally after I, to express emphasis—I, and not another; in the objective often used reflexively and without any emphasis.
**Mysterious,** mis-tē'ri-us, *a.* Containing mystery; beyond human comprehension; untelligible; enigmatical.
**Mysteriously,** mis-tē'ri-us-li, *adv.* In a mysterious manner.
**Mystery,** mis'tėr-i, *n.* Something above human intelligence; a secret; an old form of drama in which the characters and events were drawn from sacred history; a trade craft, or calling.
**Mystic, Mystical,** mis'tik, mis'tik-al, *a.* Obscure to human comprehension; involving some secret meaning or import; mysterious; pertaining to mysticism.
**Mystic,** *n.* One who holds the doctrines of mysti-

M

cism.
**Mysticism,** mis'ti-sizm, *n.* Views in religion based on communication between man and God through spiritual perception; obscurity of doctrine.
**Mystification,** mis'ti-fi-kā''shon, *n.* The act of mystifying or state of being mystified.
**Mystify,** mis'ti-fi, *vt.* (mystifying, mystified). To perplex intentionally; to bewilder; to befog.
**Myth,** mith, *n.* A tradition or fable embodying the notions of a people as to their gods, origin early history etc.; an invented story.
**Mythic, Mythical,** mith'ik, mith'ik-al, *a.* Relating to myths; described in a myth; fabulous; fabled.
**Mythological, Mythologic,** mith-o-loj'ik-al, mith-o-loj'ik, *a.* Relating to or proceeding from mythology; fabulous.
**Mythologist, Mythologer,** mi-thol'o-jist, mi-thol'o-jer, *n.* One versed in mythology.
**Mythology,** mith-ol'o-ji, *n.* The science or doctrine of myths; the myths of a people collectively.
**Mythopoeic, Mythopoetic,** mith-ō-pē'ik, mith'ō-p-ō-et''ik, *a.* Myth-making; producing or tending to produce myths.

# N

**Nab,** nab, *vt.* (nabbing, nabbed). To catch or seize suddenly or unexpectedly.
**Nabob,** nā'bob, *n.* A provincial governor under a viceroy in the Mogul empire; European who has enriched himself in the East.
**Nacre,** nā'kėr, *n.* Mother-of-pearl.
**Nacreous,** nā'krē-us, *a.* Consisting of or resembling nacre.
**Nadir,** nā'dėr, *n.* That point of the lower hemisphere of the heavens directly opposite to the zenith; the lowest point.
**Nag,** nag, *n.* A small horse; a horse in general.—*t.* and *i.* (nagging, nagged). To find fault constantly.
**Naiad,** nā'yad, *n.* A water-nymph; a female deity that presides over rivers and springs.
**Naïf,** nä-ēf, *a.* Ingenuous; having a natural luster without being cut, as jewels.
**Nail,** nāl, *n.* The horny substance at the end of the human finger and toes; a claw; a small pointed piece of metal, to be driven into timber, etc.; a stud or boss; a measure of 2¼ inches.—*vt.* To fasten or stud with nails; to hold fast or make secure.
**Nainsook,** nān'suk, *n.* A kind of muslin.
**Naïve,** nä-ēv', *a.* Ingenuous; simple; artless.
**Naïvely,** nä-ēv'li, *adv.* In a naïve manner.
**Naïveté,** nā-ēv'tā, *n.* Native simplicity; unaffected ingenuousness.
**Naked,** nā'ked, *a.* Not having clothes on; bare; nude; open to view; mere, bare, simple; destitute; unassisted.
**Nakedly,** nā'ked-li, *adv.* In a naked manner; without covering.
**Nakedness,** nā'ked-nes, *n.* State of being naked; nudity; bareness.
**Namable, Nameable,** nām'a-bl, *a.* Capable or worthy of being named.
**Name,** nām, *n.* That by which a person or thing is designated; appellation; title; reputation; eminence; sound only; not reality; authority; behalf; a family.—*vt.* (naming, named). To give a name to; to designate; to style; to nominate; to speak of or mention as.
**Nameless,** nām'les, *a.* Without a name; not known to fame; inexpressible.
**Namely,** nām'li, *adv.* By name; particularly; that is to say.
**Namesake,** nam'sāk, *n.* One whose name has been given to him for the sake of another; one of the same name as another.
**Nankeen, Nankin,** nan-kēn', *n.* A species of cotton cloth usually of a yellow color; *pl.* breeches made of this material.
**Nap,** nap, *n.* The woolly substance on the surface of cloth, etc.; the downy substance on plants; a short sleep.—*vi.* (napping, napped). To have a short sleep; to drowse.
**Nape,** nāp, *n.* The prominent joint of the neck behind; the back part of the neck.
**Napery,** nā'pėr-i, *n.* A collective term for linen cloths used for domestic purposes.
**Naphtha,** naf'tha or nap', *n.* A volatile, limpid, bituminous liquid, of a strong peculiar odor and very inflammable.
**Napkin,** nap'kin, *n.* A sort of towel used at table; a handkerchief.
**Nappy,** nap'i, *a.* Having abudance of nap or down on the surface.
**Narcissus,** när-sis'us, *n.* An extensive genus of bulbous flowering plants.
**Narcotic,** när-kot'ik, *n.* A substance which relieves pain and produces sleep.—*a.* Having the properties of a narcotic.
**Nard,** närd, *n.* An aromatic plant, usually called spikenard; an unguent prepared from the plant.
**Nardine,** närd'in, *a.* Pertaining to nard; having the qualities of spikenard.
**Narial,** nā'ri-al, *a.* Pertaining to the nostrils; nasal.
**Narrate,** na-rāt' or nar', *vt.* (narrating, narrated). To tell or relate, orally or in writing.
**Narration,** na-rā'shon, *n.* Act of narrating; a narrative; relation; story.
**Narrative,** nar'a-tiv, *a.* Pertaining to narration.—*n.* That which is narrated or related; a relation orally or in writing.
**Narrator,** na-rāt'ėr or nar'rāt-ėr, *n.* One who narrates.
**Narrow,** na'rō, *a.* Of little breadth; not wide or broad; very limited; straitened; not liberal; bigoted; near; close; scrutinizing.—*n.* A narrow channel; a strait: usually in *pl.*—*vt.* To make narrow.—*vi.* To become narrow; to contract in breadth.
**Narrowly,** na'rō-li, *adv.* In a narrow manner; contractedly; closely; sparingly.
**Narrow-minded,** na'rō-mīnd-ed, *a.* Illiberal; of confined views or sentiments.
**Nasal,** nā'zal, *a.* Pertaining to the nose; formed or affected by the nose, as speech.—*n.* An elementary sound uttered partly through the nose.
**Nascent,** nas'ent, *a.* Arising; coming into being; springing up.
**Nastily,** nas'ti-li, *adv.* In a nasty manner.
**Nasturtium,** nas-tėr'shi-um, *n.* A genus of herbs, including the common water-cress.
**Nasty,** nas'ti, *a.* Filthy; dirty; indecent; disagreeable in taste or smell; troublesome.
**Natal,** nā'tal, *a.* Pertaining to birth; dating from one's birth; pertaining to the buttocks.
**Natant,** nā'tant, *a.* Floating; swimming.
**Natation,** na-tā'shon, *n.* Art or act of swimming.
**Natatores,** nā-ta-tō'rēz, *n.pl.* The order of swimming birds.
**Natatorial,** nā-ta-tō'ri-al, *a.* Swimming; adapted to swimming; belonging to the Natatores.
**Natatory,** nā'ta-to-ri, *a.* Enabling to swim; natatorial.
**Natch,** nach, *n.* The rump of an ox.
**Nation,** nā'shon, *n.* A body of people inhabiting the same country, or united under the same government; great number.
**National,** na'shon-al, *a.* Pertaining to a nation; public; attached to one's own country.
**Nationality,** na-shon-al'i-ti, *n.* Quality of being national; national character; strong attachment to one's own nation; a nation.
**Nationalize,** na'shon-al-īz, *vt.* To make the common property of the nation as a whole.
**Nationally,** na'shon-al-li, *adv.*. In a national manner; as a whole nation.
**Native,** nā'tiv, *a.* Pertaining to the place or cir-

cumstances of one's birth; indigenous; inborn; occurring in nature pure or unmixed.—*n*. One born in a place or country; an indigenous animal or plant; an oyster raised in an artificial bed.

**Natively,** nā'tiv-li, *adv*. In a native manner; by birth; naturally; originally.

**Nativity,** na-tiv'i-ti, *n*. Birth; time, place, and manner of birth.

**Natron,** nā'tron, *n*. Native carbonate of soda, or mineral alkali.

**Nattily,** nat'i-li, *adv*. Sprucely; tidily.

**Natty,** nat'i, *a*. Neat; tidy; spruce.

**Natural,** na'tūr-al, *a*. Pertaining to nature; produced or effected by nature; consistent with nature; not artificial; according to the life; not revealed; bastard; unregenerated.—*n*. An idiot; a fool.

**Naturalism,** na'tūr-al-izm, *n*. The doctrine that there is no interference of any supernatural power in the universe; realism in art.

**Naturalist,** na'tūr-al-ist, *n*. One versed in natural science or natural history.

**Naturaalization,** na'tūr-al-izā''shon, *n*. Act of investing an alien with the privileges of a native citizen.

**Naturalize,** na'tūr-al-iz, *vt*. To make natural; to confer the privileges of a native subject upon; to acclimatize.

**Naturally,** na'tūr-al-li, *adv*. In a natural manner; according to nature; without affection; according to life; spontaneously.

**Nature,** nā'tūr, *n*. The universe; the total of all agencies and forces in the creation; the inherent or essential qualities of anything; individual constitution; sort; natural human instincts; reality as distinct from that which is artificial.

**Naught,** nat, *n*. Nought; nothing.—**To set at naught,** tö slight or disregard.—*a*. Worthless.

**Naughtily,** na'ti-li, *adv*. In a naughty manner; mischievously.

**Naughty,** na'ti, *a*. Bad; mischievous.

**Nausea,** nā'shē-a, *n*. Sickness.

**Nauseate,** na'she-āt, *vi*. To feel nausea.—*vt*. To loathe; to affect with disgust.

**Nauseous,** na'shus, *a*. Loathsome; disgusting.

**Nautical,** na'tik-al, *a*. Pertaining to ships, seamen, or navigation; naval; marine.

**Nautilus,** n. A mollusc with a many-chambered shell in the form of a flat spiral.

**Naval,** nā'val, *a*. Pertaining to ships; pertaining to a navy; nautical; maritime.

**Nave,** nāv, *n*. The central block or hub of a wheel; middle part, lengthwise, of a church.

**Navel,** nā'vl, *n*. A depression in the center of the abdomen, the end of the umbilical cord.

**Navicert,** na'vi-sėrt, *n*. A certificate that a ship's cargo does not contravene contraband regulations in war-time.

**Navigable,** na'vi-ga-bl, *a*. That may be navigated; affording passage to ships.

**Navigate,** na'vi-gāt, *vi*. To conduct or guide a ship; to sail.—*vt*. To manage in sailing, as a vessel; to sail or guide a ship over.

**Navigation,** na-vi-gā'shon, *n*. Act of navigating; science or art of managing ships.

**Navigator,** na'vi-gāt-ėr, *n*. One who directs the course of a ship.

**Navvy,** nav'i, *n*. A laborer engaged in a making of canals, railways, etc.

**Navy,** nā'vi, *n*. All the ships of a certain class belonging to a country; the whole of the ships of war belonging to a mation.

**Nay,** nā, *adv*. No; not only so.—*n*. Denial; refusal.

**Nazarean, Nazarene,** naz'a-rē-an, naz-a-rēn', *n*. An inhabitant of Nazareth; a name given in contempt of Christ and the early Christians.

**Nazarite,** naz'a-rit, *n*. A Jew who bound himself to extraordinary purity of life.

**Nazi,** nä'tsi, *n*. A member of the German National Socialist party.

**Near,** nēr, *a*. Not distant in place, time, or degree; intimate; affecting one's interest or feelings; parsimonious; narrow; on the left of a horse; not circuitous.—*prep*. Close to; nigh.—*adv*. Almost; within a little; close to the wind.—*vt*. and *i*. To approach; to come near.

**Nearly,** nēr'li, *adv*. Closely; intimately; almost.

**Near-sighted,** nēr'sīted, *a*. Short-sighted.

**Neat,** nēt, *n*. Cattle of the bovine genus.—*a*. Pure; clean; trim; tidy; clever; smart; without water added.

**Neatly,** nēt'li, *adv*. Tidily; smartly; cleverly.

**Neb,** neb, *n*. The nose; the beak of a fowl.

**Nebula,** neb'ū-la, *n*. *pl*. **-ae.** Celestial objects like white clouds, generally clusters of stars.

**Nebular,** neb'ū-lėr, *a*. Pertaining to nebulae.

**Nebulous,** neb'ū-lus, *a*. Cloudy; hazy.

**Necessarily,** ne'ses-sa-ri-li, *adv*. In a necessary manner; by necessity; indispensably.

**Necessary,** ne'ses-sa-ri, *a*. Such as must be; inevitable; essential; acting from necessity.—*n*. Anything indispensably requisite.

**Necessitate,** nē-ses'si-tāt, *vt*. To make necessary; to render unavoidable; to compel.

**Necessitous,** nē-ses'sit-us, *a*. Wanting the necessaries of life; indigent; destitute.

**Necessity,** nē-ses'si-ti, *n*. Condition of being necessary; need; irresistible compulsion; what is absolutely requisite; extreme indigence.

**Neck,** nek, *n*. The part of an animal's body between the head and the trunk; a narrow tract of land; the slender part of a vessel, as a bottle.

**Neckcloth,** nek'kloth, *n*. A piece of linen or cotton cloth worn round the neck.

**Neckerchief,** nek'ėr-chif, *n*. A kerchief for the neck.

**Necklace,** nek'kās, *n*. A string of beads, precious stones, etc., worn round the neck.

**Necklet,** nek'let, *n*. A small chain worn round the neck for suspending a locket.

**Neck-tie,** nek'ti, *n*. A tie worn round the neck.

**Necrolatry,** nek-rol'a-tri, *n*. Excessive veneration for or worship of the dead.

**Necrology,** nek-rol'o-ji, *n*. A register of deaths; a collection of obituary notices.

**Necromancer,** nek'rō-man-sėr, *n*. One who practices necromancy; a sorcerer.

**Nocromancy,** nek'rō-man-si, *n*. The revealing of future events through pretended communication with the dead; sorcery.

**Necropolis,** nek-rō'po-lis, *n*. A city of the dead, a cemetery.

**Necrosis,** nek-rō'sis, *n*. Death or mortificatioon of a bone; a disease of plants.

**Nectar,** nek'tar, *n*. The fabled drink of the gods; any very sweet and pleasant drink; the honey of a flower.

**Nectareal, Nectarean, Nectareous,** nek-tā'-rē-al, nek-tā'rē-an, nek-tā'rē-us, *a*. Resembling nectar; very sweet and pleasant.

**Nectarine,** nek'ta-rīn, *a*. Sweet as nectar,—*n*. A variety of the common peach.

**Nectarous,** nek'tar-us, *a*. Sweet as nectar.

**Nectary,** nek'ta-ri, *n*. The part of a flower that contains or secretes the nectar.

**Née,** nā, *pp*. Born: a term indicating a married woman's maiden name.

**Need,** nēd. *n*. A state that requires supply or relief; urgent want; necessity; poverty; destitution.—*vt*. To have necessity or need for; to lack, require.—*vi*. To be necessary: used impersonally.

**Needful,** ned'ful, *a*. Needy; necessary; requisite.

**Needle,** nē'dl, *n*. An instrument for interweaving thread; a small steel instrument for sewing; a magnetized piece of steel in a compass attracted to the pole; anything in the form of a needle.

**Needless,** nēd'les, *a*. No needed or wanted; unnecessary; not requisite; useless.

**Needlessly,** nēd'les-li, *adv*. In a needless manner; without necessity.

**Needle-work,** nē'dl-wėrk, *n*. Work done with a needle; business of a seamstress.

**Needly,** nē'dl-i, *a*. Relating to or resembling a

N

needle.
**Needs,** nēdz, *adv*. Of necessity; necessarily; indispensably: generally with *must*.
**Needy,** nēd'i, *a*. Being in need; necessitous; indigent; very poor.
**Ne'er,** nār. A contradiction of *never*.
**Nefarious,** nē-fā'ri-us, *a*. Wicked in the extreme; infamous; atrocious.
**Negation,** nē-gā'shon, *n*. A denial; contradiction or contradictory condition.
**Negative,** neg'at-iv, *a*. That denies; implying denial or negation; implying absence; the opposite of positive.—*n*. A word which denies, as *not, no*; a proposition by which something is denied; a veto; a photographic picture on glass or celluloid, in which the lights and shades are the opposite of those in nature.—*vt*. To prove the contrary of; to reject by vote.
**Negatively,** neg'at-iv-li, *adv*. In a negative manner; with or by denial.
**Neglect,** neg-lekt', *vt*. To treat with no regard; to slight; to set at naught; to overlook.—*n*. Omission; slight; negligence.
**Neglectful,** neg-lekt'ful, *a*. Showing neglect; heedless; careless; inattentive.
**Negligé,** neg'lē-zhā, *n*. Easy or unceremonious dress; a loose gown—*a*. Carelessly arrayed; careless. Also *negligée*.
**Negligence,** neg'li-jens, *n*. Quality of being negligent; neglect; carelessness.
**Negligent,** neg'li-jent, *a* Characterized by neglect; apt to neglect; careless; neglectful.
**Negligently,** neg'li-jent-li, *adv*. In a negligent manner; carelessly; heedlessly.
**Negotiability,** nē-gō'shi-a-bil''i-ti, *n*. Quality of being negotiable.
**Negotiable,** nē-gō'shi-a-bl, *a*. That may be negotiated; that may be transferred by assignment or indorsement.
**Negotiate,** nē-gō'shi-āt, *vi*. To treat with another respecting purchase and sale; to hold diplomatic intercourse; to conduct communications in general.—*vt*. To procure or bring about by negotiation; to pass into circulation (as a bill of exchange).
**Negotiation,** nē-gō-shi-ā''shon, *n*. A negotiating; the treating with another regarding sale or purchase; diplomatic bargaining.
**Negotiator,** nē-gō'shi-āt-ėr, *n*. One who negotiates.
**Negress,** nē'gres, *n*. A femal negro.
**Negro,** nē'grō, *n*. A black man; a male of the African race.
**Negus,** nē'gus, *n*. A beverage of wine, hot water, sugar, nutmeg, and lemon-juice, or of wine, water, and sugar.
**Neigh,** nā, *vi*. To utter the cry of a horse; to whinny.—*n*. The voice of a horse.
**Neighbor,** nā'bėr, *n*. One who lives or dwells near, or on friendly terms with another; a fellow-being.—*vt*. To be near to; to adjoin.
**Neighborhood,** nā'bėr-hud, *n*. Condition of being neighbors; neighbors collectively; vicinity; locality.
**Neighboring,** nā'bėr-ing, *p.a*. Living or being near; adjoining.
**Neighborly,** nā'bėr-li, *a*. Like or becoming a neighbor; friendly; social.
**Neither,** nē'ᴛʜėr or nī'ᴛʜėr, *pron*. and *pron. adj*. Not either; not the one or the other.—*conj*. Not either; nor.
**Nematoid,** nem'a-toid, *n*. A round-worm; one of an order of entozoa or intestinal worms.—*a*. Pertaining to or resembling the nematoids.
**Nemesis,** nem'e-sis, *n*. A female Greek divinity personifying retributive justice; just retribution or punishment.
**Neo-Latin,** nē'ō-lat-in, *a*. and *n*. Applied to the Romance languages.
**Neolithic,** nē'ō-lith'ik, *a*. Belonging to a period in which implements of polished stone were used, the more recent of the two stone periods.
**Neologism,** nē-ol'o-jizm, *n*. A new word or phrase, or new use of a word.
**Neologist,** nē-ol'o-jist, *n*. One is given to neology; an introducer of new works; an innovator in theology.
**Neology,** nē-ol'o-ji, *n*. The introduction of a new word or of new words; novel doctrines; rationalistic views in theology.
**Neon,** nē'on, *n*. An inert gas present in small amount of air.
**Neophyte,** nē'ō-fīt, *n*. One newly implanted in the church; proselyte; novice; tyro.—*a*. Newly entered on some state.
**Neoteric,** nē-ō-te'rik, *a*. New; recent; modern.
**Nepenthe, Nepenthes,** nē-pen'thē, nē-pen'thēz, *n*. A potion supposed to make persons forget their sorrows; any draught or drug capable of removing pain or care.
**Nephew,** ne'vū. *n*. The son of a brother or sister.
**Nephritic,** ne-frit'ik, *a*. Pertaining to the kidneys.
**Nephritis,** nē-frī'tis, *n*. Inflammation of the kidneys.
**Nepotism,** nē'pot-izm, *n*. Undue patronage of relations; favoritism shown to nephews and other relatives.
**Neptune,** nep'tūn, *n*. The god of the sea; a planet, the remotest from the sun except Pluto.
**Neptunian,** nep-tū'ni-an, *a*. Pertaining to the ocean or sea; formed by water.
**Nereid,** nē'rē-id, *n*. A sea nymph; a marine annelid; a sea-centipede.
**Nerve,** nėrv, *n*. One of the fibrous threads in animal bodies whose function is to convey sensation and originate motion; fortitude; courage; energy; something resembling a nerve.—*vt*. (nerving, nerved). To give strength or vigor to; to steel.
**nerveless,** nėrv'les, *a*. Destitute of nerve or strength; weak; wanting strength of will.
**Nervous,** nėrv'us, *a*. Pertaining to the nerves; affecting the nerves; having the nerves easily affected; easily agitated; having nerve or bodily strength; vigorous; sinewy.
**Nervously,** nėrv'us-li, *adv*. In a nervous manner.
**Nervousness,** nėrv'us-nes, *n*. State or quality of being nervous.
**Nescience,** nē'shi-ens, *n*. Want of knowledge; ignorance.
**Ness,** nes, *n*. A promontory or cape.
**Nest,** nest, *n*. The place or bed formed by a bird for laying and hatching her eggs; a number of persons frequenting the same haunt; a snug abode.—*vi*. To build a nest; to nestle.
**Nestle,** nes'l, *vi*. (nestling, nestled). To make or occupy a nest; to lie close and snug.—*vt*. To shelter, as in a nest; to cherish.
**Nestling,** nes'ling, *n*. A young bird in the nest, or just taken from the nest.
**Net,** net, *n*. A texture of twine, etc., with meshes, commonly used to catch fish, birds, etc.; a snare.—*vt*. (netting, netted). To make into a net; to take in a net; to capture by wile.
**Net, Nett,** net, *a*. Being clear of all deductions; estimated apart from all expenses.—*vt*. (netting, netted). To gain as clear profit.
**Nether,** ne'ᴛʜėr, *a*. Lowest.
**Nethermost,** ne'ᴛʜėr-mōst, *a*. Lowest.
**Netting,** net'ing, *n*. A piece of net-work.
**Nettle,** net'l, *n*. A weed with stinging hairs.—*vt*. (nettling, nettled). To irritate or annoy somewhat; to pique.
**Net-work,** net'wėrk, *n*. Work formed like a net; an interlacement.
**Neural,** nū'ral, *a*. Pertaining to the nerves or nervous system.
**Neuralgia,** nū-ral'ji-a, *n*. Pain in a nerve.
**Neuralgic,** nū-ral'jik, *a*. Pertaining to neuralgia.
**Neurology,** nū-rol'o-ji, *n*. That branch of science which treats of the nerves.
**Neuropter, Neuropteran,** nū-rop'tėr, nū-rop'tėr-an, *n*. An insect (order Neuroptera) having naked wings, reticulated with veins, as the dragon-flies.
**Neurotic,** nū-rot'ik, *a*. Relating to the nerves; lia-

ble to nervous diseases; hysterical.

**Neuter,** nū'tėr, *a*. Neutral; neither masculine nor feminine; neither active nor passive, as a verb.—*n*. An animal or neither sex; a plant with neither stamens nor pistils; a noun of the neuter gender.

**Neutral,** nū'tral, *a*. Not siding with any party in a dispute; indifferent; neither acid nor alkaline.—*n*. A person or nation that takes no part in a contest between others.

**Neutrality,** nū-tral'i-ti, *n*. State of being neutral.

**Neutralize,** nū'tral-īz, *vt*. To render neutral or inoperative; to counteract.

**Neutron,** nū'tron, *n*. An uncharged particle of the same mass as a proton.

**Never,** nev'ėr, *adv*. Not ever; at no time; in no degree; not at all.

**Nevermore,** nev'ėr-mōr, *adv*. Never again; at no future time.

**Nevertheless,** nev'ėr-THė-les'', *adv*. Not the less; notwithstanding; yet; however.

**New,** nū, *a*. Recent in origin; novel; not before known; different; unaccustomed; fresh after any event; not second-hand.—*adv*. Newly; recently.

**Newel,** nū'el, *n*. The upright structure in a winding staircase supporting the steps.

**New-fangled,** nū'fang'gld, *a*. Fond of novelty; of new and unfamiliar fashion.

**Newfoundland,** nū-found'land or nū'found-land, *n*. A large dog, remarkable for sagacity and swimming powers.

**News,** nūz, *n*. Recent intelligence or information; tidings; a newspaper.

**Newsmonger,** nūz'mung-gėr, *n*. One who deals in news.

**Newspaper,** nūz'pā-pėr, *n*. A sheet of paper printed periodically for circulating news.

**Newt,** nūt, *n*. A small amphibian of lizard-like appearance.

**Next,** nekst, *a*. superl. of *nigh*. Nearest in place, time, rank, or degree.—*adv*. At the time or turn nearest.

**Nexus,** nek'sus, *n*. Tie; connection.

**Nib,** nib, *n*. The bill or beak of a bird; the point of anything, particularly of a pen.—*vt*. (nibbing, nibbed). To furnish with a nib; to mend the nib of, as a pen.

**Nibble,** nib'l, *vt*. and *i*. (nibbling, nibbled). To bite by little at a time; to bite at; to carp at.—*n*. A little bite.

**Nibbler,** nib'lėr, *n*. One who nibbles; a carper.

**Niblick,** nib'lik, *n*. A golf-club with a small heavy iron head.

**Nice,** nīs, *a*. Fastidious; punctilious; accurate; pleasant; delicate; dainty.

**Nicely,** nīs'li, *adv*. Fastidiously; exactly; finely; becomingly; pleasantly; satisfactorily.

**Nicety,** nīs'e-ti, *n*. State or quality of being nice; precision; a minute difference; *pl*. delicacies or dainties.

**Niche,** nich, n. A recess in a wall for a statue, a vase, etc.

**Nick,** nik, *n*. The exact point of time; the critical time; a notch; a score.—*vt*. To hit upon exactly; to make a nick in; to mark with nicks.

**Nickel,** nik'el, *n*. A valuable metal of a white color and great hardness, magnetic, and when pure malleable and ductile.

**Nickel-silver,** nik'el-sil-vėr, *n*. An alloy composed of copper, zinc, and nickel.

**Nick-nack,** nik'nak, *n*. A trinket; gimcrack; trifle. Also **Nick-knack, Knick-Knack.**

**Nickname,** nik'nām, *n*. A name given in contempt or jest.—*vt*. To give a nickname to.

**Nicotine,** nik'ō-tin, *n*. A volatile alkaloid from tobacco, highly poisonous.

**Nictate, Nictitate,** nik'tāt, nik'ti-tāt, *vi*. To wink.

**Nidificate, Nidify,** nid'i-fi-kāt, nid'i-fī, *vi*. To make a nest and bring out young.

**Nidor,** nī'dor, *n*. Scent; smell of cooked food.

**Nidus,** nī'dus, *n*. Any part of a living organism where a parasite finds nourishment; bodily seat of a zymotic disease.

**Niece,** nēs, *n*. The daughter of one's brother or sister.

**Niggard,** nig'ėrd, *n*. A miser; a stingy person; a sordid, parsimonious wretch.—*a*. Miserly; stingy; sordidly parsimonious.

**Niggardly,** nig'ėrd-li, *a*. Niggard.—*adv*. In a niggard manner.

**Niggling,** nig'gling, **adj. Known to be fastidious, fussy, or petty.**

**Nigh,** nī, *a*. Near; ready to aid.—*adv*. Near; almost.—*prep*. Near to.

**Night,** nīt, *n*. The daily period of darkness; the time from sunset to sunrise; a state or time of darkness, depression, etc.; ignorance; obscurity; death.

**Night-cap,** nīt'kap, *n*. A cap worn in bed; liquor taken before going to bed.

**Nightfall,** nīt'fal, *n*. The close of the day; evening.

**Nightingale,** nīt'in-gāl, *n*. A small insectivorous migratory bird that sings at night.

**Night-jar,** nīt'jär, *n*. The goat-sucker.

**Nightly,** nīt'li, *a*. Done by night or every night; nocturnal.—*adv*. By night; every night.

**Nightmare,** nīt'mār, *n*. A feeling of suffocation during sleep, accompanied by intense anxiety or horror; some oppressive or stupefying influence.

**Nightshade,** nīt'shād, *n*. A plant of the potato genus, etc., which possesses narcotic or poisonous properties.

**Night-walker,** nīt'wak-ėr, *n*. One who walks at night; a somnambūlist.

**Nightward,** nīt'wėrd, *a*. Approaching toward night.

**Night-watch,** nīt'woch, *n*. A guard in the night; a distinct period in the night.

**Nigrescent,** nī-gres'ent, *a*. Approaching to blackness.

**Nihilism,** nī'hil-izm, *n*. Nothingness; the doctrine that nothing can be known; principles of a Russian secret society of communists.

**Nihilist,** nī'hil-ist, *n*. One who holds the doctrine or principles of nihilism.

**Nil,** nil, *n*. Nothing.

**Nimble,** nim'bl, *a*. Quick in motion; moving with ease and celerity; agile; prompt.

**Nimbly,** nim'bli, *adv*. With agility.

**Nimbus,** nim'bus, *n*. A rain-cloud; a halo surrounding the head in representations of divine or sacred personages.

**Nincompoop,** nin'kom-pöp, n. A fool; a blockhead; a simpleton.

**Nine,** nīn, *a*. and *n*. One more than eight.

**Nine-fold,** nīn'fōld, *a*. Nine times.

**Nineteen,** nīn'tēn *a*. and *n*. Nine and ten.

**Nineteenth,** nīn'tēnth, *a*. The ordinal of nineteen.—*n*. A nineteenth part.

**Ninetieth,** nīn'ti-eth, *a*. The ordinal of ninety.—*n*. A ninetieth part.

**Ninety,** nīn'ti, *a*. and *n*. Nine times ten.

**Ninny,** nin'i, *n*. A fool; a simpleton.

**Ninth,** nīnth, *a*. The ordinal of nine.—*n*. A ninth part.

**Ninthly,** nīnth'li, *adv*. In the ninth place.

**Nip,** nip, *vt*. (nipping, nipped). To catch and compress sharply; to pinch; to snip or bite off; to blast, as by frost; to benumb.—*n*. A pinch as with the fingers; a blast by frost; a small drink.

**Nippers,** nip'ėrz, *n.pl*. Small pincers.

**Nipple,** nip'l, *n*. A teat; pap; something like a nipple; nozzle.

**Nit,** nit, *n*. The egg of a louse, etc.

**Niter,** nī'tėr, *n*. Nitrate of potassium or saltpeter, used for making gunpowder, in dyeing, medicine, etc.

**Nitrate,** nī'trāt, *n*. A salt of nitric acid.

**Nitric,** nī'trik, *a*. Pertaining to neter; containing nitrogent and oxygen.

**Nitrify,** nī'tri-fī, *vt*. To convert into niter.

**Nitrogen,** nī'tro-jen, *n*. The elementary unflammable gas constituting about four-fifths of the atmospheric air.

N

**Nitrogenous,** nī-troj'e-nus, *a.* Pertaining to or containing nitrogen.
**Nitro-glycerine,** nī-trō-glis'ėr-in, *n.* A powerful explosive produced by the action of nitric and sulphuric acids on glycerine.
**Nitrous,** nī'trus, *a.* Pertaining to niter; applied to compounds containing less oxygen than those called *nitric*.
**Nitwit,** nit'wit, *n.* A person of little intelligence.
**Nival,** nī'val, *a.* Snowy; growing among snow, or flowering during winter.
**No,** nō, *adv.* A word of denial or refusal; not in any degree; not.—*n.* A denial; a negative vote.—*a.* Not any; none.
**Nobility,** nō'bil'i-ti, *n.* State or quality of being noble; the peerage.
**Noble,** nō'bl, *a.* Of lofty lineage; belonging to the peerage; illustrious; lofty in character; magnanimous; magnificent; stately.—*n.* A person of rank; a peer; an old English gold coin.
**Nobleman,** nō'bl-man, *n.* A noble; a peer.
**Noblesse,** nō-bles' *n.* The nobility.
**Nobly,** nō'bli, *adv.* In a noble manner; heroically; with magnanimity; splendidly.
**Nobody,** nō'bo-di, *n.* No person; no one; a person of no standing or position.
**Noctambulist,** nok-tam'bū-list, *n.* A nightwalker or somnambulist.
**Nocturn,** nok'tėrn, *n.* A religious service formerly used in the R. Catholic Church at midnight, now a part of matins.
**Nocturnal,** nok'tėrn'ăl, *a.* Done or happening at night; nightly.
**Nocturne,** nok'tėrn, *n.* A painting or piece of music expressing some of the characteristic effects of night.
**Nod,** nod, *vi.* (nodding, nodded). To make a slight bow; to let the head sink from sleep; to incline the head, as in assent or salutation, etc.—*vt.* To incline; to signify by a nod.—*n.* A quick inclination of the head.
**Node,** nōd, *n.* A knot; a protuberance; a sort of knot on a stem where leaves arise; one of the two points in which two great circles of the celestial sphere intersect.
**Nodular,** nod'ū-lėr, *a.* Pertaining to or in the form of a nodule.
**Nodule,** nod'ūl, *n.* A little know or lump.
**Noetic,** nō-et'ik, *a.* Relating to the mind.
**Nog,** nog, *n.* A wooden pin.
**Noggin,** nog'in, *n.* A small wooden cup.
**Noise,** noiz, *n.* A sound of any kind; a din; clamor; frequent talk.—*vt.* (noising, noised). To spread by rumor or report.
**Noiseless,** noiz'les, *a.* Making no noise; silent.
**Noisily,** noiz'i-li, *adv.* In a noisy manner.
**Noisome,** noi'sum *a.* Noxious to health; offensive; disgusting; fetid.
**Noisy,** noiz'i, *a.* Making a loud noise; turbulent; obstreperous.
**Nomad,** nō'mad, *n.* One who leads a wandering of pastoral life.
**Nomadic,** nō-mad'ik, *a.* Pertaining to nomads; wandering for pasturage; pastoral.
**No Man's Land,** nō-manz-land, *n.* The ground between hostile trenches.
**Nomenclature,** no'men-kla-tūr, *n.* A system of names; vocabulary of terms appropriated to any branch of science
**Nominal,** no'mi-nal, *a.* Pertaining to a name; titular; not real; merely so called.
**Nominalist,** no'mi-nal-ist, *n.* One of a sect of philosophers who maintained that general notions (such as the notion of a tree) have no existence but as names: opposed to *realist*.
**Nominally,** no'mi-nal-li, *adv.* In a nominal manner; by name or in name only.
**Nominate,** no'mi-nāt, *vt.* To name; to designate or propose for an office.
**Nomination,** no-mi-nā'shon *n.* Act of nominating; power of appointing to office; state of being nominated.
**Nominative,** no'mi-nāt-iv, *a.* A term applied to the case of a noun or pronoun when subject of a sentence.—*n.* The nominative case; a nominative word.
**Nominator,** no'mi-nāt-ėr, *n.* One who nominates.
**Nominee,** no-mi-nē', *n.* A person nominated; one proposed to fill a place or office.
**Nonage,** non'āj, *n.* Minority in age.
**Nonagenarian,** non'a-je-nā''ri-an, *n.* One between ninety and a hundred years old.
**Nonagon,** non'a-gon, *n.* A plane figure having nine sides and nine angles.
**Nonchalance,** non'sha-lans, *n.* Indifference.
**Nonchalant,** non'sha-lant, *a.* Indifferent; careless; cool.
**Non-commissioned,** non-kom-mi'shond, *a.* Not having a commission; holding the rank of lance-corporal, corporal, or sergeant.
**Non-conductor,** non-kon-dukt'ėr, *n.* A substance which does not conduct, or transmits with difficulty, heat, electricity, etc.
**Nonconforming,** non-kon-form'ing, *a.* Not conforming to the established church.
**Nonconformist,** non-kon-form'ist, *n.* One who does not conform to the established church.
**Nonconformity,** non-kon-form'i-ti, *n.* Neglect or failure of conformity; refusal to unite with an established church.
**Non-content,** non-kon-tent', *n.* In the House of Lords, one who gives a negative vote.
**Nondescript,** non'dē-skript, *a.* That has not been described; abnormal; odd; indescribable.—*n.* A person or thing not easily described or classed.
**None,** nun, *n.* or *pron.* Not one; not any; not a part; not the least portion.
**Nonentity,** non-en'ti-ti, *n.* Non-existence; a thing not existing; a person utterly without consequence or importance.
**Nones,** nōnz, *n.pl.* The seventh day of March, May, July, and October, and the fifth of the other months.
**Nonesuch,** nun'such, n. A person or thing that has not its equal or parallel.
**Non-juring,** non-jūr'ing, *a.* Not swearing allegiance; pertaining to non-jurors.
**Non-juror,** non-jūr'ėr, *n.* One who refused to take the oath of allegiance to the crown of England at the Revolution of 1688.
**Nonpareil,** non-pa-rel', *n.* A person or thing having no equal; a nonesuch; a sort of apple; a very small printing type.
**Nonplus,** non'plus, *n.* A state in which one can say or do no more,—*vt.* (nonplussing, nonplussed). To bring to a stand; to puzzle.
**Non-residence,** non-re'zi-dens, *n.* Failure to reside where official duties require one to reside, or on one's own lands; residence by clergymen away from their cures.
**Nonsense,** non'sens, *n.* Words without meaning; absurdity; things of no importance.
**Nonsensical,** non-sens'ik-al, *a.* Destitue of sense; unmeaning; absurd; foolish.
**Nonsuit,** non'sūt, *n.* Stoppage of a suit at law by the plaintiff failing to make out a cause of action.—*vt.* To subject to a nonsuit.
**Noodle,** nö'dl, *n.* A simpleton.
**Nook,** nök, *n.* A corner; A secluded retreat.
**Noology,** nō-ol'o-ji, *n.* The science of intellectual facts or phenomena.
**Noon,** nön, *n.* The middle of the day; twelve o'clock; the prime.
**Noonday,** nön'dā, *n.* Mid-day; noon.—*a.* Pertaining to mid-day; meridional.
**Noontide,** nön'tīd, *n.* The time of noon; mid-day.—*a* Pertaining to noon.
**Noose,** nös or nöz, *n.* A running knot, which binds the closer the more it is drawn.—*vt.* (noosing, noosed). To tie or catch in a noose; to entrap.
**Nor,** nor, *conj.* A word used to render negative a subsequent member of a clause or sentence; correlative to *neither* or other negative; also equivalent to *and not*.
**Nordic,** nor'dik, *a.* Of or belonging to those peo-

ples of Northern Europe who are long-headed, tall, blue-eyed and fair-haired.
**Norm,** norm, *n.* A rule; a pattern; a type.
**Normal,** nor'mal, *a.* According to a rule; conforming with a certain type or standard; regular; perpendicular.—**Normal school,** a training-college for teachers.—*n.* A perpendicular.
**Norman,** nor'man, *n.* A native of Normandy.—*a.* Pertaining to Normandy or the Normans; denoting the round-arched stye of architecture.
**Norse,** nors, *n.* The language of Norway and Iceland.—*a.* Belonging to ancient Scandinavia.
**Norseman,** nors'man, *n.* A native of ancient Scandinavia.
**North,** north, *n.* One of the cardinal points, the opposite of *south*; a region opposite to the south.—*a.* Being in the north.
**North-east,** north-ēst', *n.* The point midway between the north and east.—*a.* Northeastern.—*adv.*. North-eastward.
**North-easter,** north-ēst'ėr, *n.* A wind from the north-east.
**North-easterly,** north-ēst'ėr-li, *a.* Toward or from the north-east.
**North-eastern,** north-ēst'ėrn, *a.* Pertaining to, from, toward, or in the north-east.
**North-eastward,** north-ēst'wėrd, *adv.* Toward the north-east.
**Northerly,** noᴛʜ'ėr-li, *a.* Pertaining to the north; northern; proceeding from the north.—*adv.* Toward the north.
**Northern,** noᴛʜ'ėrn, *a.* Being in the north; toward the north; proceeding from the north.—*n.* An inhabitant of the north.
**Northerner,** noᴛʜ'ėr-nėr, *n.* A native or inhabitant of a northern part.
**Northernmost,** noᴛʜ'ėrn-mōst, *a.* Situated at the point farthest north.
**Northward, Northwards,** north'wėrd north'wėrdz, *adv.* and *a.* Toward the north.
**Northwardly,** north'wėrd-li, *adv.* In a northern direction.
**North-west,** north-west', *n.* The point midway between the north and west.—*a.* North-western,—*adv.* North-westward.
**North-westerly,** north-west'ėr-li, *a.* Toward or from the north-west.
**North-western,** north-west'ėrn, *a.* Pertaining to, from, toward, or in the north-west.
**North-westward,** north-west'wėrd, *adv.* Toward the north-west.
**Norwegian,** nor-wē-jan, *a.* Belonging to Norway.—*n.* A native of Norway.
**Nose,** nōz, *n.* The organ of smell, employed also in respiration and speech; the power of smelling; scent; sagacity; a nozzle.—*vt.* and *i.* (nosing, nosed). To smell; to wange through the nose; to pry officiously.
**Nosegay,** nōz'gā, *n.* A bunch of flowers used to regale the sense of smell; a bouquet.
**Nosology,** no-sol'o-ji, *n.* Arrangment or classification of diseases.
**Nostalgia,** nos-tal'ji-a, *n.* Vehement desire to revisit one's native country; home-sickness.
**Nostril,** nos'tril, *n.* One of the two apertures of the nose.
**Nostrum,** nos'trum, *n.* A quack medicine, the ingredients of which are kept secret.
**Not,** not, *adv.* A word that expresses negation, denial, or refusal.
**Notability,** nōt-a-bil'i-ti, *n.* Notableness; a notable person or thing; a person of note.
**Notable,** nōt'a-bl, *a.* Worthy of note; remarkable; conspicuous.—*n.* A person or thing of note or distinction.
**Notably,** nōt'a-bli, *adv.* In a notable manner; remarkably; especially.
**Notarial,** nōt-ā'ri-al, *a.* Pertaining to a notary.
**Notary,** nōt'a-ri, *n.* An officer authorized to attest documents, to protest bills of exchange, etc.: called also *Notary Public.*
**Notation,** nōt-ā'shon, *n.* Act of recording anything by marks, or the marks employed, as in algebra, music, etc.
**Notch,** noch, *n.* An incision; nick; indentation.—*vt.* To cut a notch in; to indent.
**Note,** nōt, *n.* A mark, sign, or token; an explanatory or critical comment; a memorandum; a bill, account; a paper promising payment; a communication in writing; notice; reputation; distinction; a character representing a musical sound, or the sound itself.—*vt.* (noting, noted). To observe carefully; to mark; to set down in writing.
**Note-book,** nōt'buk, *n.* A book in which notes or memoranda are written.
**Noted,** nōt'ed, *p.a.* Celebrated; famous.
**Noteworthy,** nōt'wėr-ᴛʜi, *a.* Deserving notice; worthy of observation or notice.
**Nothing,** nu'thing, *n.* Not anything; nonexistence; a trifle; a cipher.—*adv.* In no degree.
**Notice,** nōt'is, *n.* Act of noting; regard; information; order; intimation; civility; a brief critical review.—*vt.* (noticing, noticed). To take note of; to perceive; to make observations on; to treat with attention.
**Noticeable,** nōt'is-a-bl, *a.* That may be noticed; worthy of observation.
**Notification,** nōt'i-fi-kā''shon, *n.* Act of notifying; intimation; the writing which communicates information.
**Notify,** nōt'i-fī, *vt.* To make known; to declare; to give notice to; to inform.
**Notion,** nō'shon, *n.* A mental conception; idea; opinion; slight feeling or inclination.
**Notoriety,** nō-tō-rī'e-ti, *n.* State of being notorious; discreditable publicity; one who is notorious.
**Notorious,** nō-tō'ri-us, *a.* Publicly known and spoken of; known to disadvantage.
**Notwithstanding,** not-wɪᴛʜ-stand'ing, *prep.* and *conj.* In spite of; nevertheless.
**Nought,** nat, *n.* Not anything; nothing; a cipher.
**Noumenon,** nou'men-on, *n.* An object conceived by the understanding, as opposed to *phenomenon.*
**Noun,** noun, *n.* A word that denotes any object of which we speak.
**Nourish,** nu'rish, *vt.* To feed; to supply with nutriment; to encourage; to foster.
**Nourisher,** nu'rish-ėr, *n.* A person or thing that nourishes.
**Nourishing,** nu'rish-ing, *p.a.* Helping to nourish; promoting growth; nutritious.
**Nourishment,** nu'rish-ment, *n.* Act of nourishing; nutrition; food; nutriment.
**Nous,** nous, *n.* Intellect; mind; talent.
**Novel,** no'vel, *a.* Of recent origin or introduction; new and striking; unusual.—*n.* A fictitious prose narrative picturing real life.
**Novelist,** no'vel-ist, *n.* A writer of novels.
**Novelty,** no'vel-ti, *n.* Quality of being novel; a new or strange thing.
**November,** nō-vem'bėr, *n.* The eleventh month of the year.
**Novice,** no'vis, *n.* One who is new in any business; a beginner; a tyro; a probationer.
**Novitiate,** nō-vi'shi-āt, *n.* State of being a novice; time of probation of a novice.
**Now,** nou, *adv.* and *conj.* At the present time; at that time; after this; things being so.—*n.* The present time.
**Nowadays,** nou'a-dāz, *adv.* In these days; in this age.
**Noway, Noways,** nō'wā, nō'wāz, *adv.* In no manner or degree; nowise.
**Nowhere,** nō'whār, *adv.* Not in any place or state.
**Noxious,** nok'shus, *a.* Hurtful; pernicious; unwholesome; corrupting to morals.
**Nozzle,** noz'l, *n.* The projecting spout of something; terminal part of a pipe.
**Nuance,** nu-ängs, *n.* A gradation of color; delicate degree in transitions.
**Nubile,** nū'bīl, *a.* Marriageable (used only of a

N

woman).
**Nuciferous,** nū-sif'ėr-us, *a.* Bearing or producing nuts.
**Nucleus,** nū'klē-us, *n.*; pl. **-lei.** A kernel or something similar; a mass about which matter is collected; body of a comet.
**Nude,** nūd, *a.* Naked; bare; undraped.
**Nudge,** nuj, *n.* A jog with the elbow.—*vt.* (nudging, nudged). To give a jog with the elbow.
**Nudity,** nūd'i-ti, *n.* State of being nude.
**Nugatory,** nū'ga-to-ri, *a.* Trifling; futile; worthless.
**Nugget,** nug'et, *n.* A lump, as of gold.
**Nuisance,** nū'sans, *n.* That which annoys or is offensive; a plague or pest; a bore.
**Null,** nul, *a.* Of no force or validity; of no importance or account.—*n.* A cipher.
**Nullify,** nul'i-fī, *vt.* (nullifying, nullified). To render null; to deprive of force.
**Nullity,** nul'i-ti, *n.* State or quality of being null; what is of no force or efficacy.
**Numb,** num, *a.* Benumbed; without sensation and motion; torpid.—*vt.* To make numb or torpid; to deaden.
**Number,** num'bėr, *n.* An aggregate of units, or a single unit; a numeral; many; one of a numbered series of things; part of a periodical; metrical arrangement of syllables; difference of form in a word to express unity or plurality.—*vt.* To reckon; to enumerate; to put a number on; to reach the number of.
**Numberless,** num'bėr-les, *a.* That cannot be numbered; countless; innumerable.
**Numbles,** num'blz, *n.pl.* The entrails of a deer; the humbles.
**Numerable,** nū'mėr-a-bl, *a.* That may be numbered.
**Numeral,** nū'mėr-al, *a.* Pertaining to number; consisting of or representing number.—*n.* A figure used to express a number.
**Numerary,** nū'mėr-a-ri, *a.* Belonging to number; numerical.
**Numerate,** nū'mėr-āt, *vt.* (numerating, numerated). To count; to enumerate.
**Numeration,** nū-mėr-ā'shon, *n.* Act or art of numbering.
**Numerator,** nū'mėr-āt-ėr, *n.* One who numbers; the number (above the line) in vulgar fractions which shows how many parts of a unit are taken.
**Numerical,** nū-me'rik-al, *a.* Belonging to number; consisting in numbers.
**Numerically,** nū-me'rik-al-li, *adv.* In numbers; with respect to number.
**Numerous,** nū'mėr-us, *a.* Consisting of a great number of individuals; many.
**Numismatic,** nū-mis-mat'ik, *a.* Pertaining to coins or medals.
**Numismatics,** nū-mis-mat'iks, *n.* The science or knowledge of coins and medals.
**Numismatist,** nū-mis'mat-ist, *n.* One versed in numismatics.
**Numskull,** num'skul, *n.* A blockhead; a dunce; a dolt; a stupid fellow.
**Nun,** nun, *n.* A woman devoted to religion who lives in a convent; a female monk.
**Nuncio,** nun'shi-o, *n.* An ambassador of the pope at the court of a sovereign.
**Nuncupative, Nuncupatory,** nun-kū'pat-iv, nun-kū'pa-to-ri, *a.* Orally pronounced; not written, as a will.
**Nunnery,** nun'ė-ri, *n.* A house in which nuns reside.
**Nuptials,** nup'shalz, *n.pl.* Marriage.
**Nuptial,** nup'shal, *a.* Pertaining to marriage.
**Nurse,** nėrs, *n.* One who suckles or nourishes a child; one who tends the young, sick, or infirm; an attendant in a hospital; one who or that which nurtures or protects.—*vt.* (nursing, nursed). To act as nurse to; to suckle; to rear; to tend in sickness or infirmity; to foment; to foster.
**Nursery,** nėr'sė-ri, *n.* The place in which children are nursed and taken care of; a place where trees, plants, etc., are propagated.
**Nurture,** nėr'tūr, *n.* Upbringing; education; nourishment.—*vt.* (nurturing, nurtured). To nourish; to educate; to bring or train up.
**Nut,** nut, *n.* A fruit containing a seed or kernel within a hard covering; a small block of metal or wood with a grooved hole, to be screwed on the end of a bolt.—*vi.* (nutting, nutted). To gather nuts.
**Nutation,** nū-tā'shon, *n.* A nodding, a slight gyratory movement of the earth's axis.
**Nut-cracker,** nut'krak-ėr, *n.* An instrument for cracking nuts; also pl. *Nut-crackers.*
**Nutmeg,** nut'meg, *n.* The aromatic kernel of the fruit of a tree of the Malay Archipelago.
**Nutrient,** nū'tri-ent, *a.* Nutritious.—*n.* Any substance which nourishes.
**Nutriment,** nū'tri-ment, *n.* That which nourishes; nourishment; food; aliment.
**Nutrition,** nū-tri'shon, *n.* Act or process of nourishing; that which nourishes; nutriment.
**Nutritious,** nū-tri'shus, *a.* Serving to nourish; containing or supplying nutriment.
**Nutritive,** nū'tri-tiv, *a.* Pertaining to nutrition; nutritious.
**Nut-shell,** nut'shel, *n.* The hard shell inclosing the kernel of a nut.
**Nutty,** nut'i, *a.* Abounding in nuts; flavored like a nut; resembling a nut.
**Nuzzle,** nuz'l, *vi.* and *t.* (nuzzling, nuzzled). To rub or work with the nose; to put a ring into the nose of; to lie snug; to nestle.
**Nylon,** nī'lon, *n.* A strong, synthetic textile material, used as a substitute for silk, etc.
**Nymph,** nimf, *n.* A goddess of the mountains, forests, meadow, or waters; a young and attractive woman; a maiden; the chrysalis of an insect.
**Nymphomania,** nim-fō-mā'ni-a, *n.* Morbid or unnatural sexual desire in women.

# O

**O,** ō. An exclamation used in earnest or solemn address; often distinguished from *Oh,* which is more strictly expressive of emotion.
**Oaf,** ōf, *n.* A fairy changeling; a dolt.
**Oafish,** ōf'ish, *a.* Stupid; dull; doltish.
**Oak,** ōk, *n.* A valuable tree of many species.
**Oaken,** ōk'n, *a.* Made or consisting of oak.
**Oakum,** ōk'um, *n.* Old ropes untwisted into loose fibers, employed for calking, etc.
**Oaky,** ōk'i, *a.* Like oak; firm; strong.
**Oar,** ōr, *n.* A long piece of timber used to propel a boat.—*vt.* To impel by rowing.
**Oared,** ōrd, *a.* Furnished with oars.
**Oarsman,** ōrz'man, *n.* One who rows at the oar.
**Oasis,** ō-ā'sis, *n.*; pl. **-ses.** A fertile spot where there is water in a desert.
**Oast,** ōst, *n.* A kiln to dry hops or malt.
**Oat,** ōt, *n.* A cereal plant valuable for its grain.
**Oath,** ōth, *n.* An appeal to God for the truth of what is affirmed; an imprecation.
**Oat-meal,** ōt'mēl, *n.* Meal of oats produced by grinding or pounding.
**Obduracy,** ob'dū-ra-si, *n.* State or quality of being obdurate; impenitence; obstinacy.
**Obdurate,** ob'dū-rāt, *a.* Hardened in heart; hardened against good; stubborn; inflexible.
**Obdurately,** ob'dū-rāt-li, *adv.* In an obdurate manner; stubbornly; inflexibly.
**Obedience,** ō-bē'di-ens, *n.* Act of obeying; quality of being obedient; submission to authority.
**Obedient,** ō-bē'di-ent, *a.* Submissive to authority; dutiful; compliant.
**Obediently,** ō-bē'di-ent-li, *adv.* In an obedient manner; dutifully; submissively.
**Obeisance,** ō-bā'sans, *n.* A bow or curtsy; act of reverence, deference, or respect.
**Obelisk,** o'be-lisk, *n.* A tall four-sided pillar, tapering as it rises, and terminating in a small

pyramid; a mark (†) used in printing.
**Obese,** ō-bēs', *a.* Excessively corpulent; fat.
**Obesity,** ō-bēs'i-ti, *n.* State or quality of being obese; excessive corpulency.
**Obey,** ō-bā', *vt.* To comply with, as commands or requirements; to be ruled by; to yield to.—*vi.* To submit to authority.
**Obfuscate,** ob-fus'kāt, *vt.* To darken; to confuse.
**Obituary,** ō-bit'ū-a-ri, *n.* An account of a person or persons deceased; list of the dead.—*a.* Relating to the decease of a person.
**Object,** ob'jekt, *n.* That about which any faculty of the mind is employed; end; purpose; a concrete reality; the word, clause, etc., governed by a transitive verb or by a preposition.—*vt.* objekt'. To oppose; to offer as an objection.—*vi.* To oppose in words or arguments.
**Objection,** ob-jek'shon, *n.* Act of objecting; adverse reason; fault found.
**Objectionable,** ob-jek'shon-a-bl, *a.* Justly liable to objections; reprehensible.
**Objective,** ob-jek'tiv, *a.* Pertaining to an object; relating to whatever is exterior to the mind (also pron. ob'jek-tiv); belonging to the case which follows a transitive verb or preposition.—*n.* The objective case; object, place, etc., aimed at.
**Objectivity,** ob-jek-tiv'i-ti, *n.* State or quality of being objective.
**Object-lesson,** ob'jekt-les-n, *n.* A lesson from actual examples.
**Objector,** ob-jekt'ėr, *n.* One who objects.
**Objuration,** ob-jū-rā'shon, *n.* Act of binding by oath.
**Objurgate,** ob-jėr'gāt, *vt.* and *i.* To chide, reprove, or reprehend.
**Objurgation,** ob-jėr-gā'shon, *n.* Act of objurgating; reproof.
**Oblate,** ob-lāt', *a.* Flattened or depressed at the poles, as a sphere or globe.
**Oblation,** ob-lā'shon, *n.* Anything offered in sacred worship; a sacrifice.
**Obligate,** ob'li-gāt, *vt.* To bring under some obligation; to oblige.
**Obligation,** ob-li-gā'shon, *n.* That which morally obliges; binding power of a promise, contract, or law; a favor bestowed and binding to gratitude; a bond with a condition annexed, and a penalty for non-fulfilment.
**Obligatory,** ob'li-ga-to-ri, *a.* Imposing an obligation; binding; requiring performance.
**Oblige,** ō-blij', *vt.* (obliging, obliged). To constrain; to bind by any restraint; to lay under obligation of gratitude; to render service or kindness to.
**Obliging,** ō-blij'ing, *p.a.* Having the disposition to oblige; civil; courteous; kind.
**Oblique,** ob-lēk', *a.* Neither perpendicular nor parallel; slanting; indirect; sinister.
**Obliterate,** ob-lit'ė-rāt, *vt.* To blot out; to efface; to cause to be forgotten.
**Obliteration,** ob-lit'ė-rā''shon, *n.* Act of obliterating; effacement; extinction.
**Oblivion,** ob-li'vi-on, *n.* State of being forgotten; forgetfulness; act of forgetting.
**Oblivious,** ob-li'vi-us, *a.* That easily forgets; forgetful; causing forgetfulness.
**Oblong,** ob'long, *a.* Rectangular, and longer than broad.—*n.* An oblong figure.
**Obloquy,** ob'lō-kwi, *n.* Censorious speech; contumely; odium; infamy.
**Obnoxious,** ob-nok'shus, *a.* Odious; offensive; hateful; unpopular.
**Oboe,** ō'bō, *n.* A musical wind-instrument made of wood; a hautboy.
**Obscene,** ob-sēn', *a.* Indecent; offensive to chastity and delicacy; inauspicious.
**Obscenely,** ob-sēn'li, *adv.* In an obscene manner; impurely; unchastely.
**Obscenity,** ob-sen'i-ti, *n.* State or quality of being obscene; ribaldry; lewdness.
**Obscurant, Obscurantist,** ob-skū'rant, ob-skū'rant-ist, *n.* One who labors to prevent enlightenment, inquiry, or reform.
**Obscure,** ob-skūr', *a.* Darkened; dim; not easily understood; abstruse; unknown to fame; indistinct.—*vt.* (obscuring, obscured). To darken; to make less visible, legible, or intelligible; to tarnish.
**Obscurely,** ob-skūr'li, *adv.* In an obscure manner; not clearly; indirectly.
**Obscurity,** ob-skū'ri-ti, *n.* State or quality of being obscure; darkness.
**Obsequies,** ob'se-kwiz, *n.pl.* Funeral rites and solemnities.
**Obsequious,** ob-sē'kwi-us, *a.* Promptly obedient or submissive; compliant; fawning.
**Observable,** ob-zėrv'a-bl, *a.* That may be observed; worthy of notice; remarkable.
**Observably,** ob-zėrv'a-bli, *adv.* In a manner worthy of observation.
**Observance,** ob-zėrv'ans, *n.* Act of observing; respect; performance of rites, etc.; rule of practice; thing to be observed.
**Observant,** ob-zėrv'ant, *a.* Observing; regardful; carefully attentive.
**Observantly,** ob-zėrv'ant-li, *adv.* In an observant manner.
**Observation,** ob-zėr-vā'shon, *n.* The act, power, or habit of observing; information or notion gained by observing; a remark; due performance.
**Observatory,** ob-zėr'va-to-ri, *n.* A place for astronomical observations; place of outlook.
**Observe,** ob-zėrv', *vt.* (observing, observed). To take notice of; to behold with attention; to remark; to keep religiously; to celebrate; to comply with; to practice.—*vi.* To remark; to be attentive.
**Observer,** ob-zėrv'ėr, *n.* One who observes; a spectator; one who observes phenomena for scientific purposes.
**Observing,** ob-zėrv'ing, *p.a.* Given to observation; attentive.
**Observingly,** ob-zėrv'ing-li, *adv.* With observation; attentively; carefully.
**Obsession,** ob-sesh'on, *n.* Act of besieging; persistent attack; state of being beset.
**Obsolescent,** ob-sō-les'ent, *a.* Becoming obsolete; passing into desuetude.
**Obsolete,** ob'sō-lēt, *a.* Antiquated; out of date; rudimentary.
**Obstacle,** ob'sta-kl, *n.* A stoppage; hindrance; obstruction; impediment.
**Obstetric, Obstetrical,** ob-stet'rik, ob-stet'rik-al, *a.* Pertaining to midwifery.
**Obstetrician,** ob-stet-rish'an, *n.* One skilled in obstetrics; an accoucheur.
**Obstetrics,** ob-stet'riks, *n.* The science or art of midwifery.
**Obstinacy,** ob'sti-na-si, *n.* State or quality of being obstinate; inflexibility; pertinacity.
**Obstinate,** ob'sti-nāt, *a.* Inflexible; stubborn; fixed firmly in opinion or resolution.
**Obstinately,** ob'sti-nāt-li, *adv.* In an obstinate manner; stubbornly; pertinaciously.
**Obstreperous,** ob-strep'ėr-us, *a.* Making a tumultuous noise; loud; noisy; clamorous.
**Obstruct,** ob-strukt', *vt.* To block up, as a way or passage; to impede; to hinder in passing; to retard; to interrupt.
**Obstruction,** ob-struk'shon, *n.* Act of obstructing; that which impedes progress; obstacle; impediment; check.
**Obstructionist,** ob-struk'shon-ist, *n.* One who practices obstruction; an obstructive.
**Obstructive,** ob-strukt'iv, *a.* Hindering; causing impediment.—*n.* One who hinders the transaction of business.
**Obstruent,** ob'stru-ent, *a.* Obstructing.—*n.* Anything that obstructs the natural passages in the body.
**Obtain,** ob-tān', *vt.* To get possession of; to acquire; to earn.—*vi.* To be received in common use; to prevail; to hold good.
**Obtainable,** ob-tān'a-bl, *a.* That may be ob-

tained, procured, or gained.

**Obtest,** ob-test', *vt.* To call upon earnestly; to implore; to supplicate.

**Obtestation,** ob-test'ā-shon, *n.* Entreaty.

**Obtrude,** ob-tröd', *vt.* (obtruding, obtruded). To thrust prominently forward; to offer with unreasonable importunity.—*vi.* To enter when not desired.

**Obtrusion,** ob-trö'zhon, *n.* Act of obtruding; a thrusting upon others by force or unsolicited.

**Obtrusive,** ob-trö'siv, *a.* Disposed to obtrude; forward.

**Obtrusively,** ob-trö'siv-li, *adv.* In an obtrusive manner.

**Obturate,** ob'tū-rāt, *vt.* To block or plug up, as a passage.

**Obtuse,** ob-tūs', *a.* Not pointed or acute; greater than a right angle; dull; stupid.

**Obverse,** ob'vėrs, *n.* and *a.* That side of a coin or medal which has the face or head or principal device on it.

**Obviate,** ob'vi-āt, *vt.* (obviating, obviated). To meet, as difficulties or objections; to get over; to remove.

**Obvious,** ob'vi-us, *a.* Easily discovered, seen, or understood; evident; manifest.

**Obviously,** ob'vi-us-li, *adv.* In an obvious manner; quite clearly; evidently.

**Obvolute,** ob'vo-lūt, *a.* Rolled or turned in.

**Ocarina,** ō-ka-rē'na, *n.* A small musical wind-instrument of terra cotta, etc.

**Occasion,** ok-kā'zhon, *n.* Occurrence; incident; opportunity; cause; need; juncture.—*vt.* To cause; to produce.

**Occasional,** ok-kā'zhon-al, *a.* Occurring at times; made as opportunity admits; incidental.

**Occasionally,** ok-kā'zhon-al-li, *adv.* At times; sometimes but not often; not regularly.

**Occident,** ok'si-dent, *n.* The west.

**Occidental,** ok-si-dent'al, *a.* Western.

**Occipital,** ok'si'pit-al, *a.* Pertaining to the occiput, or back part of the head.

**Occiput,** ok'si-put, *n.* That part of the skull which forms the hind part of the head.

**Occult,** ok-kult', *a.* Hidden; invisible and mysterious.—*vt.* To conceal by way of eclipse.

**Occultation,** ok-kult-ā'shon, *n.* A hiding or concealing; eclipse of a heavenly body.

**Occupancy,** ok'kū-pan-si, *n.* Act of occupying; a holding in possession; term during which one is occupant.

**Occupant,** ok'kū-pant, *n.* An occupier.

**Occupation,** ok-kū-pā'shon, *n.* Act of occupying; act of taking possession; tenure; business; employment; vocation.

**Occupy,** ok'kū-pī, *vt.* (occupying, occupied). To take possession of; to hold and use; to cover or fill; to employ; to engage: often *refl.*—*vi.* To be an occupant.

**Occur,** ok-kėr', *vi.* (occurring, occurred). To come to the mind; to happen; to be met with; to be found here and there.

**Occurrence,** ok-ku'rens, *n.* The act of occurring or taking place; any incident or accidental event; an observed instance.

**Ocean,** ō'shan, *n.* The vast body of water which covers more than three-fifths of the globe; the sea; one of the great areas into which the sea is divided; any immense expanse.—*a.* Pertaining to the great sea.

**Oceanic,** ō-shē-an'ik, *a.* Pertaining to the ocean; found or formed in the ocean.

**Ocellate, Ocellated,** ō-sel'lāt, ō-sel'lāt-ed, *a.* Resembling an eye; studded with little eyes.

**Ocellus,** ō-sel'lus, *n.*; pl. **-li.** One of the minute simple eyes of insects, spiders, etc.

**Ochlocracy,** ok-lok'ra-si, *n.* The rule of the mob or multitude.

**Ochre,** ō'kėr, *n.* A clay used as a pigment, of a pale-yellow or brownish-red color.

**Ochry, Ochreous,** ō'kėr-i, ō'krē-us, *a.* Consisting of, resembling, or containing ochre.

**Octagon,** ok'ta-gon, *n.* A plane figure having eight angles and sides.

**Octagonal,** ok-tag'on-al, *a.* Having eight angles and eight sides.

**Octahedral,** ok-ta-hed'ral, *a.* Having eight equal faces or sides.

**Octahedron,** ok-ta-hed'ron, *n.* A solid figure having eight faces or sides.

**Octangular,** ok-tang'gū-lėr, *a.* Having eight angles.

**Octave,** ok'tāv, *a.* Eighth; denoting eight.—*n.* An eighth; the eighth day or the eight days after a church festival; a stanza of eight lines; in *music,* an interval of seven degrees or twelve semitones.

**Octavo,** ok-tā'vō, *n.* A book in which the sheets are folded into eight leaves.—*a.* Having eight leaves to the sheet: written 8*vo.*

**Octennial,** ok-ten'i-al, *a.* Happening every eighth year; lasting eight days.

**October,** ok-tō'bėr, *n.* The tenth month of the year.

**Octogenarian,** ok'tō-je-nā''ri-an, *n.* One between eighty and ninety years of age.

**Octopus,** ok'tō-pus, *n.*; pl. **-puses.** A two-gilled cuttle-fish, having eight arms furnished with suckers.

**Octoroon,** ok-tō-rön', *n.* The offspring of a quadroon and a white person.

**Octosyllabic,** ok'tō-sil-lab''ik, *a.* Consisting of eight syllables.

**Ocular,** ok'ū-lėr, *a.* Pertaining to or depending on the eye; received by actual sight.

**Ocularly,** ok'ū-lėr-li, *adv.* In an ocular manner; by the eye, sight, or actual view.

**Oculist,** ok'ū-list, *n.* One skilled in diseases of the eyes.

**Odd,** od, *a.* Not even; not exactly divisible by 2; not included with others; incidental; casual; belonging to a broken set; queer.

**Oddfellow,** od'fel-ō, *n.* A member of a friendly society, modelled on freemasonry.

**Oddity,** od'i-ti, *n.* Singularity; a singular person or thing.

**Oddly,** od'li, *adv.* In an odd manner; not evenly; strangely; unusually; uncouthly.

**Oddment,** od'ment, *n.* A remnant.

**Odds,** odz, *n. sing.* or *pl.* Inequality; excess; difference in favor of one; advantage; amount by which one bet exceeds another.

**Ode,** ōd, *n.* A song; a short poem; a lyric poem of a lofty cast.

**Odious,** ō'di-us, *a.* Hateful; offensive; disgusting.

**Odiously,** ō'di-us-li, *adv.* Hatefully.

**Odium,** ō'di-um, *n.* Hatred; dislike; the quality that provokes hatred, blame, etc.

**Odontoid,** ō-don'toid, *a.* Tooth-like.

**Odontology,** ō-don-tol'o-ji, *n.* The science which treats of the teeth.

**Odoriferous,** ō-dor-if'ėr-us, *a.* Diffusing smell; perfumed; fragrant.

**Odorous,** ō'dor-us, *a.* Emitting a scent or odor; sweet of scent; fragrant.

**Odor,** ō'dor, *n.* Any scent or smell; fragrance; reputation.

**Odorless,** ō'dor-les, *a.* Free from odor.

**O'er,** ō'ėr, contracted from *over.*

**Of,** ov, *prep.* Denoting source, cause, motive, possession, quality, condition, material; concerning, relating to, about.

**Off,** of, *adv.* Away; distant; not on; from; not toward.—**Well off, ill off,** in good or bad circumstances. *a.* Distant; farther away; as applied to horses; right hand.—*prep.* Not on; away from; to seaward from.—*interj.* Begone!

**Offal,** of'al, *n.* The parts of an animal butchered which are unfit for use; refuse.

**Offense,** of-fens', *n.* Injury; an affront, insult, or wrong; displeasure; transgression of law; misdemeanor.

**Offend,** of-fend', *vt.* To displease; to shock; to cause to sin or neglect duty.—*vi.* To sin; to commit a fault; to cause dislike or anger.

**Offender,** of-fend'ėr, *n.* One who offends; a transgressor; a delinquent; a trespasser.

**Offensive,** of-fens'iv, *a*. Causing offense; causing displeasure or annoyance; disgusting; impertinent; used in attack; aggressive.—*n*. Act or posture of attack.
**Offensively,** of-fens'iv-li, *adv*. In an offensive manner; disagreeably; aggressively.
**Offer,** of'ėr, *vt*. To present for acceptance or rejection; to tender; to bid, as a price or wages.—*vi*. To present itself; to declare a willingness; to make an attempt.—*n*. Act of offering; act of bidding a price; the sum bid.
**Offering,** of'ėr-ing, *n*. Act of one who offers; that which is offered; a gift; oblation.
**Offertory,** of'ėr-to-ri, *n*. Sentences read or repeated in church while the alms or gifts are collecting; the alms collected.
**Off-hand,** of'hand, *a*. Done without thinking or hesitation; unpremeditated.—*adv*. On the spur of the moment; promptly.
**Office,** of'is, *n*. Special duty or business; high employment or position under government; function; service; a formulary of devotion; a place where official or professional business is done; persons intrusted with certain duties; persons who transact business in an office; *pl*. kitchens, outhouses, etc., of a mansion or farm.
**Office-bearer,** of'is-bār-ėr, *n*. One who holds office.
**Officer,** of'is-ėr, *n*. A person invested with an office; one who holds a commission in the army or navy.—*vt*. To furnish with officers.
**Official,** of-fi'shal, *a*. Pertaining to an office or public duty; made by virtue of authority.—*n*. One invested with an office of a public nature.
**Officially,** of-fi'shal-li, *adv*. In an official manner or capacity; by authority.
**Officiate,** of-fi'shi-āt, *vi*. To perform official duties; to act in an official capacity.
**Officinal,** of-fi'si-nal, *a*. Used in a shop, or belonging to it; used in the preparation of recognized medicines sold by apothecaries.
**Officious,** of-fi'shus, *a*. Troublesome in trying to serve; intermeddling.
**Officiously,** of-fi'shus-li, *adv*. In an officious manner; with forward zeal; meddlesomely.
**Offing,** of'ing, *n*. That part of the sea nearer to the horizon than to the shore.
**Offset,** of'set, *n*. A shoot or scion; a sum or amount set off against another as an equivalent; a contrast or foil.—*vt*. To set off, as one account against another.
**Offshoot,** of'shöt, *n*. A shoot of a plant; anything growing out of another.
**Offspring,** of'spring, *n*. *sing*. or *pl*. That which springs from a stock or parent; a child or children; progeny; issue.
**Oft,** oft, *adv*. Often: *poet*.
**Often,** of'n, *adv*. Frequently; many times.
**Oftentimes,** of'n-tīmz, *adv*. Often.
**Ofttimes,** oft'timz, *adv*. Frequently; often.
**Ogee,** ō-jē', *n*. An architectural molding, with an outline like the letter *s*.
**Ogham,** og'am, *n*. A kind of writing practiced by the ancient Irish.
**Ogle,** ō'gl, *vt*. (ogling, ogled). To view with side glances.—*n*. A side glance or look.
**Ogler,** ō'glėr, *n*. One who ogles.
**Ogre,** ō'gėr, *n*. A monster in fairy tales, who lived on human flesh; one like an ogre.
**Ogress,** ō'gres, *n*. A female ogre.
**Oh,** ō, *exclam*. (*See* O.) Denoting surprise, pain, sorrow, or anxiety.
**Ohm,** ōm, *n*. The unit of electric resistance.
**Oil,** oil, *n*. An unctuous inflammable liquid drawn from various animal and vegetable substances; a similar substance of mineral origin; an oil-color.—*vi*. To smear or rub over with oil.
**Oil-cloth,** oil'kloth, *n*. Painted canvas for floor-covering, etc.; floor-cloth.
**Oil-color,** oil'kul-ėr, *n*. A pigment made by grinding a coloring substance in oil.
**Oiler,** oil'ėr, *n*. One who oils; something used for oiling machinery.
**Oil-painting,** oil'pānt-ing, *n*. Art of painting with oil-colors; picture painted in oil-colors.
**Oil-skin,** oil'skin, *n*. Waterproof cloth.
**Oily,** oil'i, *a*. Consisting of, containing, or resembling oil; unctuous; hypocritically pious.
**Ointment,** oint'ment, *n*. Any soft, unctuous substance used for smearing the body or a diseased part; an unguent.
**Old,** ōld, *a*. Grown up to maturity and strength; aged; of some particular age; long made or used; not new or fresh; ancient; antiquated.—**Of old,** long ago; in ancient times.
**Old-fashioned,** ōld-fa'shond, *a*. Characterized by antiquated fashion; aping old people.
**Oleaginous,** ō-lē-a'jin-us, *a*. Oily; unctuous.
**Oleander,** ō-lē-an'dėr, *n*. An evergreen flowering shrub.
**Oleograph,** ō'lē-ō-graf, *n*. A picture produced in oils by a process analogous to lithographic printing.
**Olfactory,** ol-fak'to-ri, *a*. Pertaining to smelling; having the sense of smelling.—*n*. An organ of smelling.
**Oligarch,** o'li-gärk, *n*. One of a few persons in power; an aristocrat.
**Oligarchic, Oligarchical,** o-li-gärk'ik, o-li-gärk'ik-al, *a*. Pertaining to oligarchy.
**Oligarchy,** o'li-gär-ki, *n*. Government in which the supreme power is in a few hands; those who form such a class or body.
**Olio,** ō'li-o, *n*. A dish of meat boiled or stewed; medley; miscellany.
**Olive,** o'liv, *n*. An evergreen tree; its fruit, from which a valuable oil is expressed; the color of the olive; the emblem of peace.—*a*. Relating to, or of the color of the olive.
**Olympiad,** ō-lim'pi-ad, *n*. A period of four years reckoned from one celebration of the Olympic games to another, the first Olympiad beginning 776 B.C.
**Olympian, Olympic,** ō-lim'pi-an, ō-lim'pik, *a*. Pertaining to Olympus, or to Olympia, in Greece; relating to the Greek games celebrated at Olympia.
**Omega,** ō'me-ga or ō-me'ga, *n*. The last letter of the Greek alphabet, long *o*; the last, or the ending.
**Omelet,** o'me-let, *n*. A kind of pancake or fritter made with eggs, etc.
**Omen,** ō'men, *n*. An event thought to portend good or evil; an augury; presage.—*vi*. To augur; to betoken.—*vt*. To predict.
**Omened,** ō'mend, *p.a*. Containing an omen.
**Ominous,** o'min-us, *a*. Containing an omen, and especially an ill omen; inauspicious.
**Ominously,** o'min-us-li, *adv*. In an ominous manner; with ill omen.
**Omissible,** ō-mis'i-bl, *a*. Capable of being omitted.
**Omission,** ō-mi'shon, *n*. Act of omitting; neglect or failure to do something required; failure to insert or mention; something omitted.
**Omissive,** ō-mis'iv, *a*. Omitting; neglecting.
**Omit,** ō-mit', *vt*. (omitting, omitted). To pass over or neglect; not to insert or mention.
**Omnibus,** om'ni-bus, *n*. A large vehicle for conveying passengers; a book which contains a variety of items.
**Omnifarious,** om-ni-fā'ri-us, *a*. Of all varieties, forms, or kinds.
**Omnipotence,** om-nip'ō-tens, *n*. Almighty or unlimited power; an attribute of God.
**Omnipotent,** om-nip'ō-tent, *a*. All-powerful; almighty; possessing unlimited power.
**Omnipotently,** om-nip'ō-tent-li, *adv*. In an omnipotent manner.
**Omnipresence,** om-ni-prez'ens, *n*. Presence in every place at the same time.
**Omnipresent,** om-ni-prez'ent, *a*. Present in all places at the same time; ubiquitous.
**Omniscience, Omnisciency,** om-ni'shi-ens, om-ni'shi-en-si, *n*. The faculty of knowing all things; universal knowledge.

**Omniscient,** om-ni'shi-ent, *a.* Knowing all things; having universal knowledge.
**Omnisciently,** om-ni'shi-ent-li, *adv.* By omniscience.
**Omnivorous,** om-niv'or-us, *a.* All-devouring; eating food of every kind.
**Omphalic,** om-fal'ik, *a.* Pertaining to the navel.
**On,** on, *prep.* Above and touching; by contact with the surface or upper part; in addition to; at or near; immediately after and as a result; in reference or relation to; toward or so as to affect; at the peril of; among the staff of; pointing to a state, occupation, etc.—*adv.* Onward; in continuance; adhering; not off.
**Once,** wuns, *adv.* One time; formerly; immediately after; as soon as.—**At once,** all together; suddenly; forthwith.
**Oncoming,** on'kum-ing, *a.* Approaching; nearing.—*n.* Approach.
**One,** wun, *a.* Being but a single thing or a unit; closely united; forming a whole; single.—*n.* The first of the simple units; the symbol representing this (=1).—**At one,** in union or concord.—*pron.* Any single person; any man; any person; a thing; particular thing.
**Oneness,** wun'nes, *n.* State or quality of being one; singleness; individuality; unity.
**Onerary,** on'e-ra-ri, *a.* Fitted for the carriage of burdens; comprising a burden.
**Onerous,** on'ė-rus, *a.* Burdensome; heavy.
**Onerously,** on'ė-rus-li, *adv.* So as to burden or oppress.
**Oneself,** wun-self', *pron.* Oneself; one's own person.
**One-sided,** wun-sīd'ed, *a.* Having one side only; limited to one side; partial; unfair.
**Ongoing,** on'gō-ing, *n.* A going on; conduct; behavior; generally in *pl.*
**Onion,** un'yun, *n.* A plant with a bulbous root, used as an article of food.
**Onlooker,** on'luk-ėr, *n.* A spectator.
**Only,** ōn'li, *a.* Single; sole; alone.—*adv.* For one purpose alone; simply; merely; solely.—*conj.* But; excepting that.
**Onomatopeia,** on'o-ma-tō-pē''a, *n.* The formation of words by imitation of sounds.
**Onomatopoetic,** on'o-ma-tō-pō-et''ik, *a.* Pertaining to or formed by onomatopeia.
**Onrush,** on'rush, *n.* A rapid onset.
**Onset,** on'set, *n.* A violent attack; assault.
**Onslaught,** on'slat, *n.* An attack; onset.
**Ontology,** on-tol'o-ji, *n.* The doctrine of being; that part of metaphysics which treats of things or existences.
**Onus,** ō'nus, *n.* A burden.
**Onward, Onwards,** on'wėrd, on'wėrdz, *adv.* Forward; on; in advance.
**Onward,** *a.* Advanced or advancing; progressive; improved.
**Onyx,** o'niks, *n.* A semi-pellucid gem with variously-colored veins, a variety of quartz; an agate with layers of chalcedony.
**Oolite,** ō'ol-īt, *n.* A species of limestone; a series of strata, comprehending limestones, etc., which underlie the chalk formation.
**Oolitic,** ō-o-lit'ik, *a.* Pertaining to oolite; composed of oolite; resembling oolite.
**Oology,** ō-ol'o-ji, *n.* The study of birds' eggs.
**Ooze,** öz, *n.* A soft flow, as of water; soft mud or slime; liquor of a tan-vat.—*vi.* (oozing, oozed). To flow or issue forth gently; to percolate.—*vt.* To emit in the shape of moisture.
**Oozy,** öz'i, *a.* Miry; containing soft mud.
**Opacity,** ō-pas'i-ti, *n.* State or quality of being opaque.
**Opal,** ō-pal, *n.* A precious stone, which exhibits changeable reflections of green, blue, yellow, and red.
**Opalescent,** ō-pal-es'ent, *a.* Resembling opal; having the iridescent tints of opal.
**Opaline,** ō'pal-īn, *a.* Pertaining to or like opal.—*n.* A semi-translucent glass.
**Opaque,** ō-pāk', *a.* Not transparent.
**Ope,** ōp, *vt.* and *i.* To open: *poet.*
**Open,** ō'pn, *a.* Not shut, covered, or blocked; not restricted; accessible; public; spread out; free, liberal, bounteous; candid; clear; exposed; fully prepared; attentive; amenable; not settled; enunciated with a full utterance.—*n.* An open or clear space.—*vt.* To make open; to unclose; to cut into; to spread out; to begin; to make public; to declare open; to reveal.—*vi.* To unclose itself; to be parted; to begin.
**Open-hearted,** ō'pn-härt-ed, *a.* Candid; frank; generous.
**Opening,** ō'pn-ing, *a.* First in order; beginning.—*n.* Act of one who or that which opens; an open place; aperture; beginning; vacancy; opportunity of commencing a business, etc.
**Openly,** ō'pn-li, *adv.* In an open manner; publicly; candidly; plainly; evidently.
**Opera,** o'pe-ra, *n.* A dramatic composition set to music and sung and acted on the stage; a theater where operas are performed.
**Opera-glass,** o'pe-ra-gläs, *n.* A small binocular telescope used in theaters, etc.
**Operate,** o'pe-rāt, *vi.* (operating, operated). To work; to act; to produce effect; to exert moral power or influence.—*vt.* To act; to effect; to drive, as a machine.
**Operatic,** o-pe-rat'ik, *a.* Pertaining to the opera; resembling the opera.
**Operation,** o-pe-rā'shon, *n.* Act or process of operating; agency; action; process; surgical proceeding to which the human body is subjected; movements of troops or war-ships.
**Operative,** o'pe-rāt-iv, *a.* That operates; producing the effect; having to do with manual or other operations.—*n.* One who works or labors; an artisan.
**Operator,** o'pe-rāt-ėr, *n.* One who operates.
**Operculum,** ō-pėr'kū-lum, *n.* A little lid or cover, especially applied in zoology and botany.
**Operetta,** op-e-ret'ta, *n.* A short musical drama of a light character.
**Operose,** o'pe-rōs, *a.* Tedious; troublesome.
**Ophicleide,** o'fi-klīd, *n.* A large brass wind-instrument.
**Ophidian,** ō-fid'i-an, *a.* Pertaining to serpents.
**Ophiology,** of-i-ol'o-ji, *n.* That branch of zoology which treats of serpents.
**Ophthalmia,** of-thal'mi-a, *n.* Inflammation of the eye or its appendages.
**Ophthalmic,** of-thal'mik, *a.* Pertaining to the eye or to ophthalmia.
**Ophthalmist,** of-thal'mist, *n.* An oculist.
**Opiate,** ō'pi-āt, *n.* Any medicine that contains opium; a narcotic.
**Opine,** ō-pīn', *vi.* and *t.* To think; to suppose.
**Opinion,** ō-pin'yon, *n.* A judgment or belief; notion; persuasion; estimation.
**Opinionated,** ō-pin'yon-āt-ed, *a.* Stiff or obstinate in opinion; conceited.
**Opinionative,** ō-pin'yon-āt-iv, *a.* Unduly attached to one's own opinions; opinionated.
**Opium,** ō'pi-um, *n.* The inspissated juice of a kind of poppy, one of the most energetic of narcotics.
**Opossum,** ō-pos'um, *n.* The name of several marsupial mammals of America.
**Opponent,** op-pō'nent, *a.* Opposing; antagonistic; opposite.—*n.* One who opposes; an adversary; an antagonist.
**Opportune,** op-or-tūn', *a.* Seasonable; timely; well-timed; convenient.
**Opportunely,** op-or-tūn'li, *adv.* In an opportune manner; seasonably.
**Opportunist,** op-or-tūn'ist, *n.* One who waits upon favorable opportunities; a politician more influenced by place and power than principle.
**Opportunity,** op-or-tūn'i-ti, *n.* A fit or convenient time; favorable conjuncture.
**Oppose,** op-pōz', *vt.* (opposing, opposed). To place over against; to place as an obstacle; to act against; to resist; to check.—*vi.* To make objections; to act obstructively.

**Opposed,** op-pōzd', *p.a.* Adverse; hostile.
**Opposite,** op'pō-zit, *a.* Facing; adverse; contrary; inconsistent.—*n.* An adversary.
**Oppositely,** op'pō-zit-li, *adv.* So as to be opposite; adversely; against each other.
**Opposition,** op-pō-zi'shon, *n.* Act of opposing; attempt to check or defeat; contradiction; inconsistency; the collective body of opponents of a ministry.
**Oppositionist,** op-pō-zi'shon-ist, *n.* One who belongs to an opposition.
**Oppress,** op-pres', *vt.* To press or weigh down unduly; to harass; to overpower; to overburden.
**Oppression,** op-pres'shon, *n.* Act of oppressing; severity; hardship; dulness of spirits.
**Oppressive,** op-pres'iv, *a.* Burdensome; unjustly severe; tyrannical.
**Oppressor,** op-pres'ėr, *n.* One who oppresses; a cruel governor or taskmaster.
**Opprobrious,** op-prō'bri-us, *a.* Containing opprobrium; scurrilous; abusive.
**Opprobrium,** op-prō'bri-um, *n.* Scurrilous language; disgrace; scurrility; infamy.
**Oppugn,** op-pūn', *vt.* To attack by arguments or the like; to oppose or resist.
**Oppugnant,** op-pug'nant, *a.* Resisting; opposing; hostile.
**Optative,** op'tā-tiv, *a.* Expressing a desire; designating that mood of the verb in which desire is expressed.—*n.* The optative mood of a verb.
**Optic,** op'tik, *a.* Pertaining to sight; relating to the science of optics.—*n.* An organ of sight; an eye.
**Optical,** op'tik-al, *a.* Relating to the science of optics; optic.
**Optician,** op-ti'shan, *n.* A person skilled in optics; one who makes or sells optical instruments.
**Optics,** op'tiks, *n.* The science which treats of the nature and properties of light and vision, optical instruments, etc.
**Optimism,** op'tim-izm, *n.* The opinion or doctrine that everything is for the best; tendency to take the most hopeful view.
**Optimist,** op'tim-ist, *n.* One who believes in optimism.
**Optimistic,** op-tim-ist'ik, *a.* Relating to or characterized by optimism.
**Option,** op'shon, *n.* Choice; free choice; power of choosing.
**Optional,** op'shon-al, *a.* Left to one's own option or choice; depending on choice.
**Opulence,** op'ū-lens, *n.* Wealth; riches.
**Opulent,** op'ū-lent, *a.* Wealthy; rich.
**Opulently,** op'ū-lent-li, *adv.* In an opulent manner; richly.
**Opuscule, Opuscle,** ō-pus'kūl, ō-pus'l, *n.* A small work; a little book.
**Or,** or, *conj.* A particle that marks an alternative, and frequently corresponds with *either* and *whether.*—*adv.* Ere; before.—*n.* Heraldic name for gold.
**Oracle,** o'ra-kl, *n.* Among the Greeks and Romans, the answer of a god to an inquiry respecting some future event; place where the answers were given; the sanctuary of the ancient Jews; any person reputed uncommonly wise; a wise or authoritative utterance.
**Oracular,** ō-rak'ū-lėr, *a.* Pertaining to or like an oracle; uttering oracles; authoritative; sententious; ambiguous.
**Oracularly,** ō-rak'ū-lėr-li, *adv.* In an oracular manner; authoritatively.
**Oral,** ō'ral, *a.* Pertaining to the mouth; spoken, not written.
**Orally,** ō'ral-li, *adv.* In an oral manner; by word of mouth; verbally.
**Orange,** o'ranj, *n.* An evergreen fruit-tree, and also its fruit; the color of this fruit, a reddish yellow.—*a.* Belonging to an orange; colored as an orange.
**Orangeman,** o'ranj-man, *n.* A member of a society of Irish Protestants.
**Orange-peel,** o'ranj-pēl, *n.* The rind of an orange separated from the fruit; the peel of the bitter orange dried and candied.
**Orang-utan, Orang-outang,** o-rang'ö-tan, o-rang'ö-tang, *n.* One of the largest of the anthropoid or manlike apes.
**Orate,** ō'rāt, *vi.* (orating, orated). To make an oration; to talk loftily; to harangue.
**Oration,** ō-rā'shon, *n.* A formal public speech; an eloquent speech or address.
**Orator,** o'ra-tėr, *n.* A public speaker; a skilled or eloquent speaker.
**Oratorical,** o-ra-to'rik-al, *a.* Pertaining to an orator or to oratory; rhetorical.
**Oratorio,** o-ra-tō'ri-ō, *n.* A sacred musical composition.
**Oratory,** o'ra-to-ri, *n.* A small chapel; the art of public speaking; eloquence.
**Orb,** orb, *n.* A sphere; a heavenly body; a circular disc; a hollow globe.—*vt.* To encircle.
**Orbed,** orbd, *p.a.* Round; circular.
**Orbicular,** or-bik'ū-lėr, *a.* In the form of an orb; circular; spherical.
**Orbit,** or'bit, *n.* The path of a planet or comet; cavity in which the eye is situated.
**Orbital,** or'bit-al, *a.* Pertaining to an orbit.
**Orchard,** or'chėrd, *n.* An inclosure devoted to the culture of fruit-trees.
**Orchestra,** or'kes-tra, *n.* That part of the Greek theater allotted to the chorus; that part of a theater, etc., appropriated to the musicians; a body of musicians.
**Orchestral,** or-kes'tral, *a.* Pertaining to an orchestra; suitable for or performed in the orchestra.
**Orchestration,** or-kes-trā'shon, *n.* Arrangement of music for an orchestra; instrumentation.
**Orchid, Orchis,** or'kid, or'kis, *n.* A perennial plant with tuberous fleshy root and beautiful flowers.
**Ordain,** or-dān', *vt.* To establish authoritatively; to decree; to invest with ministerial or sacerdotal functions.
**Ordainment,** or-dān'ment, *n.* The act of ordaining; appointment.
**Ordeal,** or'dē-al, *n.* A trial by fire and water; severe trial or strict test.
**Order,** or'dėr, *n.* Regular disposition; proper state; established method; public tranquillity; command; instruction to supply goods or to pay money; rank, class, division, or dignity; a religious fraternity; division of natural objects; *pl.* clerical character, specially called holy orders.—**In order,** for the purpose.—*vt.* To place in order; to direct; to command; to give an order or commission for.—*vi.* To give command.
**Orderly,** or'dėr-li, *a.* In accordance with good order; well ordered; regular; on duty.—*n.* A private soldier or non-commissioned officer, who attends on a superior officer.—*adv.* According to due order.
**Ordinal,** or'din-al, *a.* Expressing order or succession.—*n.* A number denoting order (as *first*); a book containing an ordination service.
**Ordinance,** or'din-ans, *n.* That which is ordained; law, statute, edict, decree.
**Ordinarily,** or'din-a-ri-li, *adv.* In an ordinary manner: usually; generally.
**Ordinary,** or'din-a-ri, *a.* Conformable to order; regular; customary; common; of little merit.—*n.* An ecclesiastical judge; a judge who takes cognizance of causes in his own right; an eating-house where the prices are settled.—**In ordinary,** in actual and constant service; statedly attending, as a physician; but a ship *in ordinary* is one laid up.
**Ordinate,** or'din-āt, *a.* Regular; methodical.—*n.* In *geometry,* a line of reference determining the position of a point.
**Ordination,** or-din-ā'shon, *n.* Act of ordaining; act of conferring sacerdotal power; act of settling a Presbyterian clergyman in a charge.
**Ordnance,** ord'nans, *n.* Cannon or great guns

O

collectively; artillery.—**Ordnance survey,** the detailed survey of Britain.
**Ordure,** or'dūr, *n*. Dung; excrement.
**Ore,** ōr, *n*. A mineral substance from which metals are obtained by smelting; metal.
**Organ,** or'gan, *n*. An instrument or means; a part of an animal or vegetable by which some function is carried on; a medium of conveying certain opinions; a newspaper; the largest wind-instrument of music.
**Organic,** or-gan'ik, *a*. Pertaining to or acting as an organ; pertaining to the animal and vegetable worlds; organized; systematized.
**Organically,** or-gan'ik-al-li, *adv*. In an organic manner; by or with organs.
**Organism,** or'gan-izm, *n*. Organic structure; a body exhibiting organic life.
**Organist,** or'gan-ist, *n*. One who plays on the organ.
**Organization,** or'gan-i-zā''shon, *n*. Act or process of organizing; suitable disposition of parts for performance of vital functions.
**Organize,** or'gan-īz, *vt*. To give an organic structure to; to establish and systematize; to arrange so as to be ready for service.
**Orgasm,** or'gazm, *n*. Immoderate excitement or action.
**Orgy,** or'ji, *n*. A wild or frantic revel; a drunken party.
**Oriel,** ō'ri-el, *n*. A large projecting bay-window supported on brackets or corbels.
**Orient,** ō'ri-ent, *a*. Rising, as the sun;; eastern; oriental; bright.—*n*. The East; luster as that of a pearl.—*vt*. To define the position of; to cause to lie from east to west.
**Oriental,** ō-ri-ent'al, *a*. Eastern; from the east.—*n*. A native of some eastern country.
**Orientalism,** ō-ri-ent'al-izm, *n*. An eastern mode of thought or expression; erudition in oriental languages or literature.
**Orientalist,** ō-ri-ent'al-ist, *n*. One versed in the eastern languages and literature.
**Orientate,** ō-ri-ent'āt, *vt*. To orient.
**Orientation,** ōr'i-en-tā''shon, *n*. A turning towards the east; position east and west.
**Orifice,** o'ri-fis, *n*. The mouth or aperture of a tube, pipe, etc.; an opening; a vent.
**Origin,** o'ri-jin, *n*. Source; beginning; derivation; cause; root; foundation.
**Original,** ō-ri'jin-al, *a*. Pertaining to origin; primitive; first in order; having the power to originate; not copied.—*n*. Origin; source; first copy; model; that from which anything is translated or copied; a person of marked individuality.
**Originally,** ō-ri'jin-al-li, *adv*. In an original manner; primarily; at first.
**Originate,** ō-ri'jin-āt, *vt*. (originating, originated). To give origin to; to produce.—*vi*. To have origin; to be begun.
**Origination,** ō-ri'jin-ā''shon, *n*. Act or mode of originating; first production.
**Originator,** ō-ri'jin-āt-ėr, *n*. One who or that which originates.
**Oriole,** ō'ri-ōl, *n*. A bird with golden plumage.
**Orion,** ō-rī'on, *n*. A constellation near the equator.
**Ormolu,** or'mō-lū, *n*. A fine kind of brass made to imitate gold; gilt bronze.
**Ornament,** or'na-ment, *n*. That which adorns or embellishes; decoration.—*vt*. To decorate; to adorn.
**Ornamental,** or-na-ment'al, *a*. Serving to ornament; pertaining to ornament.
**Ornamentation,** or'na-men-tā''shon, *n*. Act of ornamenting; ornaments or decorations.
**Ornate,** or'nāt, *a*. Richly ornamented; adorned; of a florid character.
**Ornately,** or'nāt-li, *adv*. In an ornate manner.
**Ornithological,** or'ni-tho-loj''ik-al, *a*. Pertaining to ornithology.
**Ornithologist,** or-ni-thol'o-jist, *n*. A person who is skilled in ornithology.
**Ornithology,** or-ni-thol'o-ji, *n*. The science which treats of birds.
**Orographic, Orographical,** or-ō-graf'ik, or-ō-graf'ik-al, *a*. Relating to orography.
**Orography,** ō-rog'ra-fi, *n*. The scientific treatment of mountains; orology.
**Orotund,** ō'rō-tund, *a*. Characterized by fulness and clearness; rich and musical.
**Orphan,** or'fan, *n*. A child bereaved of father or mother, or of both.—*a*. Bereaved of parents.—*vt*. To reduce to being an orphan.
**Orphanage,** or'fan-āj, *n*. The state of an orphan; a home for orphans.
**Orphanhood,** or'fan-hud, *n*. The state of being an orphan.
**Orphean,** or-fē'an, *a*. Pertaining to Orpheus; melodious.
**Orpiment,** or'pi-ment, *n*. A yellow mineral consisting of sulphur and arsenic.
**Orris,** o'ris, *n*. A sort of gold or silver lace; a kind of iris.
**Ort,** ort, *n*. A scrap of food left; a fragment; a piece of refuse; commonly in *pl*.
**Orthodox,** or'thō-doks, *a*. Sound in opinion or doctrine; sound in religious doctrines; in accordance with sound doctrine.
**Orthodoxly,** or'thō-doks-li, *adv*. In an orthodox way; with soundness of faith.
**Orthodoxy,** or'thō-doks-i, *n*. Character or state of being orthodox; soundness of faith.
**Orthoepic, Orthoepical,** or-thō-ep'ik, or-thō-ep'ik-al, *a*. Pertaining to orthoepy.
**Orthoepist,** or'thō-ep-ist, *n*. One well skilled in pronunciation.
**Orthoepy,** or'thō-e-pi or or-thō'e-pi, *n*. Correct pronunciation of words.
**Orthographer,** or-thog'ra-fėr, *n*. One versed in orthography.
**Orthographic, Orthographical,** or-thō-graf'ik, or-thō-graf'ik-al, *a*. Pertaining to orthography.
**Orthography,** or-thog'ra-fi, *n*. The art of writing words with the proper letters; spelling.
**Orthopter, Orthopteran,** or-thop'tėr, or-thop'tėr-an, *n*. One of an order of insects including cockroaches, grasshoppers, and locusts.
**Ortolan,** or'tō-lan, *n*. A European bird of the bunting family, esteemed for the delicacy of its flesh.
**Oscillate,** os'sil-lāt, *vi*. To swing; to vibrate; to vary or fluctuate.
**Oscillation,** os-sil-lā'shon, *n*. Act or state of oscillating; vibration.
**Oscillatory,** os'sil-la-to-ri, *a*. Oscillating; swinging; vibrating.
**Oscitant,** os'si-tant, *a*. Yawning; gaping; drowsy; sluggish.
**Osculate,** os'kū-lāt, *vt*. and *i*. To kiss; to touch, as curves.
**Osculation,** o-skū-lā'shon, *n*. Act of kissing; a kiss; a coming in contact.
**Osier,** ō'zhi-ėr, *n*. The name of various species of willow, employed in basket-making.—*a*. Made of osier or twigs; like osier.
**Osmose,** os'mōs, *n*. The tendency of fluids to pass through porous partitions and mix.
**Osprey,** os'prā, *n*. A kind of hawk or eagle which feeds on fish; one of its feathers.
**Osseous,** os'ē-us, *a*. Bony; like bone.
**Ossicle,** os'i-kl, *n*. A small bone.
**Ossification,** os'i-fi-kā''shon, *n*. The process of changing into a bony substance.
**Ossifrage,** os'i-frāj, *n*. The sea-eagle or osprey.
**Ossify,** os'i-fī, *vt*. and *i*. To change into bone, or into a substance of the hardness of bone.
**Ostensible,** os-ten'si-bl, *a*. Put forth as having a certain character; apparent and not real; pretended; professed.
**Ostensibly,** os-ten'si-bli, *adv*. In an ostensible manner; professedly.
**Ostensive,** os-ten'siv, *a*. Showing; exhibiting.
**Ostentation,** os-ten-tā'shon, *n*. Ambitious display; vain show; parade; pomp.
**Ostentatious,** os-ten-tā'shus, *a*. Characterized by ostentation; showy.

**Osteology,** os-tē-ol'o-ji, *n.* The science which treats of the bones and bone-tissue.
**Osteopathy,** os-tē-op'a-thi, *n.* A system of medical treatment, based on the view that the proper adjustment of the vital mechanism is a more important factor than chemical intake in the maintenance of health.
**Ostracism,** os'tra-sizm, *n.* A mode of political banishment in ancient Athens effected by public vote; expulsion.
**Ostracize,** os'tra-sīz, *vt.* To banish by ostracism; to expel; to banish from society.
**Ostreaculture,** os'trē-a-kul''tūr, *n.* The artificial cultivation of oysters.
**Ostrich,** os'trich, *n.* A large running bird of Africa, Arabia, and S. America, the largest of existing birds.
**Other,** ᴜᴛʜ'ėr, *a.* and *pron.* Not the same; second of two; not this; opposite; often used reciprocally with *each.*
**Otherwise,** ᴜᴛʜ'ėr-wīz, *adv.* In a different manner; not so; by other causes; in other respects.—*conj.* Else; but for this.
**Otology,** ō-tol'o-ji, *n.* Knowledge of the ear and its diseases.
**Ottava-rima,** ot-tä'vä-rē-mä, *n.* A stanza of eight lines, the first six rhyming alternatively, the last two forming a couplet.
**Otter,** ot'ėr, *n.* An aquatic carnivorous animal resembling the weasel, but larger.
**Ottoman,** ot'tō-man, *a.* Pertaining to or derived from the Turks.—*n.* A Turk; a kind of couch introduced from Turkey.
**Oubliette,** ö'blē-et, *n.* A dungeon with an opening only at the top.
**Ouch,** ouch, *n.* The socket in which a precious stone is set; a brooch.
**Ought,** at, *n.* Aught.—*v.* To be held or bound in duty or moral obligation.
**Ounce,** ouns, *n.* The twelfth part of a pound troy, and the sixteenth of a pound avoirdupois; an Asiatic animal like a small leopard.
**Our,** our, *a.* or *pron.* Pertaining or belonging to us. **Ours** is used when no noun follows.
**Ourself,** our-self', *pron.* Used for *myself,* as a more dignified word, in the regal style.
**Ourselves,** our-selvz', *pron. pl.* We or us, not others; added to *we* by way of emphasis, but in the objective often without emphasis and reflexively.
**Oust,** oust, *vt.* To eject; to turn out.
**Out,** out, *adv.* On or towards the outside; not in or within; forth; beyond usual limits; not in proper place; public; exhausted; deficient; not in employment; loudly; in error; at a loss; having taken her place as a woman in society.—*n.* One who is out; a nook or corner.—*vt.* To put out.—*interj.* Away! begone!
**Out-and-out,** out'and-out, *a.* Thorough; thorough-paced; absolute; complete.
**Outbid,** out-bid', *vt.* To bid more than another.
**Outbreak,** out'brāk, *n.* A breaking forth; eruption; sudden manifestation as of anger, disease, etc.
**Outburst,** out'bėrst, *n.* A bursting or breaking out; an outbreak.
**Outcast,** out'käst, *p.a.* Cast out; rejected.—*n.* An exile; one driven from home or country.
**Outcome,** out'kum, *n.* The issue; result; consequence.
**Outcrop,** out'krop, *n.* Exposure of strata at the surface of the ground.
**Outcry,** out'krī, *n.* A loud cry; exclamation; clamor; noisy opposition.
**Outdistance,** out-dis'tans, *vt.* To excel or leave behind in any competition.
**Outdo,** out-dö', *vt.* To excel; to surpass.
**Outdoor,** out'dōr, *a.* In the open air; being without the house.
**Outdoors,** out'dōrz, *adv.* Abroad; in the open air.
**Outer,** out'ėr, *a.* Being on the outside; external.—*n.* That part of a target beyond the circles surrounding the bull's-eye; a shot which hits this part.
**Outermost,** out'ėr-mōst, *a.* Being farthest out; being on the extreme external part.
**Outfall,** out'fal, *n.* Mouth of a river, drain, etc.
**Outfit,** out'fit, *n.* A fitting out, as for a voyage; equipment of one going abroad.
**Outfitter,** out'fit-ėr, *n.* One who makes an outfit; clothier, etc.
**Outflank,** out-flangk', *vt.* To maneuver so as to attack in the flank; to get the better of.
**Outflow,** out'flō, *n.* Act of flowing out; efflux.
**Outgeneral,** out-jen'ė-ral, *vt.* To gain advantage over by superior military skill.
**Outgo,** out-gō', *vt.* To go beyond; to excel.—*n.* out'gō. Expenditure.
**Outgoing,** out-gō'ing, *n.* Act of going out; expenditure; outlay.—*a.* Going out.
**Outgrow,** out-grō', *vt.* To surpass in growth; to grow too great or old for anything.
**Outgrowth,** out'grōth, *n.* Excrescence; result.
**Out-house,** out'hous, *n.* A small house or building near the main one.
**Outing,** out'ing, *n.* A short excursion; an airing; short time spent out-of-doors.
**Outlandish,** out-land'ish, *a.* Foreign; strange; uncouth; bizarre.
**Outlast,** out-läst', *vt.* To last longer than.
**Outlaw,** out'la, *n.* A person excluded from the benefit of the law.—*vt.* To deprive of the benefit and protection of law; to proscribe.
**Outlawry,** out'la-ri, *n.* The putting of a man out of the protection of law.
**Outlay,** out'lā, *n.* Expenditure.
**Outlet,** out'let, *n.* Place by which anything is discharged; exit; a vent.
**Outline,** out'līn, *n.* The line by which a figure is defined; contour; general scheme.—*vt.* To draw the exterior line of; to sketch.
**Outlive,** out-liv', *vt.* To survive.
**Outlook,** out'luk, *n.* A looking out; vigilant watch; place of watch; prospect.
**Outlying,** out'lī-ing, *a.* Lying at a distance from the main body; being on the frontier.
**Outmaneuver,** out-ma-nö'vėr, or -nū'vėr, *vt.* To surpass in maneuvering.
**Outmarch,** out-märch', *vt.* To march so as to leave behind.
**Outmost,** out'mōst, *a.* Farthest outward.
**Outnumber,** out-num'bėr, *vt.* To exceed in number.
**Out-of-the-way,** out-ov-the-wā, *a.* Secluded; unusual; uncommon.
**Out-patient,** out'pā-shent, *n.* A patient not residing in a hospital, but who receives medical advice, etc., from the institution.
**Outpost,** out'pōst, *n.* A station at a distance from the main body of an army; troops placed at such a station.
**Outpour,** out-pōr', *vt.* To pour out.
**Output,** out'put, *n.* Quantity of material produced within a specified time.
**Outrage,** out'rāj, *vt.* (outraging, outraged). To do extreme violence or injury to; to abuse; to commit a rape upon.—*n.* Excessive abuse; injurious violence.
**Outrageous,** out-rā'jus, *a.* Characterized by outrage; furious; exorbitant; atrocious.
**Outrageously,** out-rā'jus-li, *adv.* In an outrageous manner; furiously; excessively.
**Outre,** ö-trā, *a.* Extravagant; bizarre.
**Outreach,** out-rēch', *vt.* To go or extend beyond.
**Outride,** out-rīd', *vt.* To pass by riding.
**Outrider,** out'rīd-ėr, *n.* A servant on horseback who attends a carriage.
**Outrigger,** out'rig-ėr, *n.* A structure of spars, etc., rigged out from the side of a sailing-boat; a projecting bracket on a boat, with the rowlock at the extremity; a light boat provided with such apparatus.
**Outright,** out'rīt, *adv.* Completely; utterly.
**Outrun,** out-run', *vt.* To exceed in running; to leave behind; to go beyond.
**Outset,** out'set, *n.* Beginning.

**Outshine,** out-shīn', *vi.* To shine out or forth.—*vt.* To excel in luster.
**Outside,** out'sīd, *n.* The external surface or superficies; exterior; the utmost; extreme estimate.—*a.* Exterior; superficial.—*prep.* On the outside of.
**Outsider,** out'sīd-ėr, *n.* One not belonging to a party, association or set; a horse which is not considered to have a chance of winning a race.
**Outskirt,** out'skėrt, *n.* Parts near the edge of an area; border; purlieu; generally in *pl.*
**Outspan,** out-span', *vt.* and *i.* To unyoke (a team of oxen) from a wagon.
**Outspoken,** out'spō-kn, *a.* Free or bold of speech; candid; frank.
**Outspread,** out-spred', *vt.* To spread out; to diffuse.—*a.* Extended; expanded.
**Outstanding,** out-stand'ing, *a.* Projecting outward; prominent; unpaid; undelivered.
**Outstrip,** out-strip', *vt.* To outgo; to outrun; to advance beyond; to exceed.
**Outvote,** out-vōt', *vt.* To exceed in the number of votes; to defeat by plurality of votes.
**Outwalk,** out-wak', *vt.* To walk farther, or faster than; to leave behind in walking.
**Outward,** out'wėrd, *a.* External; exterior; visible; adventitious.—*adv.* Tending toward the exterior; from a port or country.
**Outward-bound,** out'wėrd-bound, *a.* Bound to some foreign port; going seaward.
**Outwardly,** out'wėrd-li, *adv.* Externally; in appearance; not sincerely.
**Outwear,** out-wār', *vt.* To wear out; to last longer than.
**Outweigh,** out-wā', *vt.* To exceed in weight, value, etc.; to overbalance.
**Outwit,** out-wit', *vt.* (outwitting, outwitted). To overreach; to defeat by superior ingenuity.
**Outwork,** out'wėrk, *n.* Part of a fortification distant from the main fortress.
**Ova,** ō'va, *n.*; plural of *ovum.*
**Oval,** ō'val, *a.* Shaped like an egg; elliptical.—*n.* A figure shaped like an egg or ellipse.
**Ovarian,** ō-vā'ri-an, *a.* Belonging to the ovary.
**Ovariotomy,** ō-vā'ri-ot''o-mi, *n.* The operation of removing a tumor in the ovary.
**Ovary,** ō'va-ri, *n.* The female organ in which ova are formed.
**Ovate,** ō'vāt, *a.* Egg-shaped; oval.
**Ovation,** ō-vā'shon, *n.* A lesser triumph among the ancient Romans; triumphal reception; public marks of respect.
**Oven,** uv'n, *n.* A place built in closely for baking, heating, or drying.
**Over,** ō'vėr, *prep.* Above; denoting motive, occasion, or superiority; across; throughout; upwards of.—*adv.* From side to side; in width; on all the surface; above the top or edge; in excess; completely; too.—*a.* Upper; covering.—*n.* *(cricket)* The number of balls (six or eight) which the bowler delivers in succession from one end of the pitch, before a change is made to the other side.
**Overact,** ō-vėr-akt', *vt.* To perform to excess.
**Overalls,** ō'vėr-alz, *n.pl.* Loose trousers worn over others to protect them.
**Overbalance,** ō-vėr-bal'ans, *vt.* To weigh down; to exceed in importance; to destroy the equilibrium of.—*n.* Excess.
**Overbear,** ō-vėr-bār', *vt.* To bear down; to overpower; to domineer over.
**Overbearing,** ō-vėr-bār'ing, *a.* Haughty and dogmatical; imperious; domineering.
**Overboard,** ō'vėr-bōrd, *a.* Over the side of a ship; out of a ship.
**Overburden,** ō-vėr-ber'dn, *vt.* To load with too great weight; to overload.
**Overcast,** ō-vėr-käst', *vt.* To cloud; to darken; to sew coarsely over a rough edge.
**Overcharge,** ō-vėr-chärj', *vt.* To charge or burden to excess; to fill too numerously.—*n.* ō'vėr-chärj. An excessive charge.
**Overcloud,** ō-vėr-kloud', *vt.* To cover or overspread with clouds.
**Overcoat,** ō'vėr-kōt, *n.* An upper coat; top-coat.
**Overcome,** ō-vėr-kum', *vt.* To be victorious over; to master; to get the better of.—*vi.* To gain the superiority.
**Overcrowd,** ō-vėr-kroud', *vt.* To crowd to excess, especially with human beings.
**Overdo,** ō-vėr-dö', *vt.* To do to excess; to fatigue; to boil, bake, or roast too much.
**Overdose,** ō'vėr-dōs, *n.* Too great a dose.—*vt.* ō-vėr-dōs'. To dose excessively.
**Overdraw,** ō-vėr-dra', *vt.* To draw upon for a larger sum than is standing at one's credit; to exaggerate.
**Overdue,** ō'vėr-dū, *a.* Past the time of payment or arrival.
**Overflow,** ō-vėr-flō', *vt.* (pp. overflowed and overflown). To flow or spread over; to flood; to overwhelm.—*vi.* To be so full that the contents run over; to abound.—*n.* ō'vėr-flō. An inundation; superabundance.
**Overflowing,** ō-vėr-flō'ing, *p.a.* Abundant; copious; exuberant.
**Overgrow,** ō-vėr-grō', *vt.* To grow beyond; to cover with growth or herbage.—*vi.* To grow beyond the fit or natural size.
**Overgrowth,** ō'vėr-grōth, *n.* Exuberant or excessive growth.
**Overhand,** ō'vėr-hand, *a.* and *adv.* With the hand over the object.
**Overhang,** ō-vėr-hang', *vt.* and *i.* To hang, impend, jut, or project over.
**Overhaul,** ō-vėr-hal', *vt.* To examine thoroughly with a view to repairs; to re-examine; to gain upon or overtake.—*n.* ō'vėr-hal. Examination; inspection; repair.
**Overhead,** ō-vėr-hed', *adv.* Above; aloft.
**Overhear,** ō-vėr-hēr', *vt.* To hear by accident or stratagem.
**Overheat,** ō-vėr-hēt', *vt.* To heat to excess.
**Overhung,** ō-vėr-hung', *p.a.* Hung or covered over; adorned with hangings.
**Overissue,** ō'vėr-ish-ū, *n.* An excessive issue, as of coin or notes.—*vt.* To issue in excess.
**Overjoy,** ō-vėr-joi', *vt.* To give excessive joy to.—*n.* ō'vėr-joi. Joy to excess.
**Overland,** ō'vėr-land, *a.* Passing by land; made upon or across the land.
**Overlap,** ō-vėr-lap', *vt.* To lap or fold over.—*n.* ō'vėr-lap. The lapping of one thing over another.
**Overlay,** ō-vėr-lā', *vt.* To lay over; to coat or cover; to smother.
**Overleap,** ō-vėr-lēp', *vt.* To leap over; to pass by leaping.
**Overload,** ō-vėr-lōd', *vt.* To load too much; to overburden.
**Overlook,** ō-vėr-luk', *vt.* To oversee; to superintend; to view from a higher place; to pass by indulgently.
**Overlord,** ō'vėr-lord, *n.* One who is lord over another; a feudal superior.
**Overnight,** ō'vėr-nīt, *adv.* Through or during the night; in the night before.
**Overpass,** ō-vėr-päs', *vt.* To pass over; to overlook; to omit; to surpass.
**Overpower,** ō-vėr-pou'ėr, *vt.* To be too powerful for; to bear down by force; to overcome; to subdue; to crush.
**Overpowering,** ō-vėr-pou'ėr-ing, *p.a.* Excessive in degree or amount; irresistible.
**Over-production,** ō'vėr-prō-duk-shon, *n.* Production in excess of demand.
**Overrate,** ō-vėr-rāt', *vt.* To rate at too much; to regard too highly.
**Overreach,** ō-vėr-rēch', *vt.* To reach over or beyond; to deceive by artifice; to outwit.
**Override,** ō-vėr-rīd', *vt.* To ride over; to supersede; to set at naught.
**Overrule,** ō-vėr-röl', *vt.* To control; to govern with high authority; to disallow.
**Overrun,** ō-vėr-run', *vt.* To run or spread over; to ravage; to outrun.—*vi.* To overflow; to run over.

**Oversea,** ō'vėr-sē, *a.* Foreign; from beyond sea.—**Overseas,** ō-vėr-sēz, *adv.* Abroad.
**Oversee,** ō-vėr-sē', *vt.* To see or look over; to overlook; to superintend.
**Overseer,** ō-vėr-sēr', *n.* One who oversees or overlooks; a superintendent; an inspector.
**Overset,** ō-vėr-set', *vt.* To set over; to upset or capsize; to overthrow.—*vi.* To capsize.
**Overshadow,** ō-vėr-sha'dō, *vt.* To throw a shadow over; to shelter.
**Overshoe,** ō'vėr-shö, *n.* A shoe worn over another; an outer waterproof shoe.
**Overshoot,** ō-vėr-shöt', *vt.* To shoot over; to shoot beyond.
**Overshot,** ō-vėr-shot', *p.a.* Shot beyond; having the water flowing on to the top, as a waterwheel.
**Oversight,** ō'vėr-sīt, *n.* Superintendence; a mistake, error, omission, neglect.
**Overspread,** ō-vėr-spred', *vt.* To spread over; to cover over; to scatter over.
**Overstate,** ō-vėr-stāt', *vt.* To state in too strong terms; to exaggerate in statement.
**Overstep,** ō-vėr-step', *vt.* To step over or beyond; to exceed.
**Overstock,** ō-vėr-stok', *vt.* To stock to excess; to fill too full.
**Overt,** ō-vėrt, *a.* Open to view; manifest; not hidden; public; apparent.
**Overtake,** ō-vėr-tāk', *vt.* To come up with; to catch; to take by surprise.
**Overtax,** ō-vėr-taks', *vt.* To tax too heavily; to make too severe demands upon.
**Overthrow,** ō-vėr-thrō', *vt.* To throw or turn over; to overset; to defeat; to destroy.—*n.* ō'vėr-thrō. Ruin; defeat.
**Overtime,** ō-vėr-tīm, *n.* Time during which one works beyond the regular hours.
**Overtly,** ō'vėrt-li, *adv.* Openly; publicly.
**Overtop,** ō-vėr-top', *vt.* To rise above the top of; to excel; to surpass.
**Overture,** ō'vėr-tūr, *n.* A proposal; offer; a musical introduction to oratorios, operas, etc.
**Overturn,** ō-vėr-tėrn', *vt.* To overset or overthrow; to capsize; to subvert; to ruin.
**Overvalue,** ō-vėr-val'ū, *vt.* To value too highly; to rate at too high a price.
**Overweening,** ō-vėr-wēn'ing, *a.* Haughty; arrogant; proud; conceited.
**Overweigh,** ō-vėr-wā', *vt.* To outweigh.
**Overweight,** ō-vėr-wāt', *vt.* To overburden.—*n.* Excess of weight; preponderance.
**Overwhelm,** ō-vėr-whelm', *vt.* To whelm entirely; to swallow up; to submerge; to crush.
**Overwise,** ō'vėr-wīz, *a.* Wise to affectation.
**Overwork,** ō-vėr-wėrk', *vt.* To work beyond strength; to tire with labor.—*n.* ō'vėr-wėrk. Work done beyond one's strength or beyond the amount required.
**Overworn,** ō'vėr-wōrn, *a.* Worn to excess; worn out; trite; threadbare.
**Overwrought,** ō-vėr-rat', *p.a.* Wrought to excess; excited to excess; tasked beyond strength.
**Ovine,** ō'vīn, *a.* Pertaining to sheep; consisting of sheep.
**Oviparous,** ō-vip'a-rus, *a.* Bringing forth eggs; producing young from eggs.
**Ovoid,** ō'void, *a.* Egg-shaped.
**Ovoviviparous,** ō'vō-vi-vip''a-rus, *a.* Producing eggs which are hatched within the body (as is the case with vipers): opposed to *oviparous*.
**Ovule,** ō'vūl, *n.* A small ovum; a germinal vesicle of animals; a rudimentary seed.
**Ovum,** ō'vum, *n.*; pl. **ova.** A small vesicle within the ovary of a female, when impregnated becoming the embryo.
**Owe,** ō, *vt.* (owing, owed). To be indebted in; to be obliged or bound to pay; to be obliged for.
**Owing,** ō'ing, *ppr.* Required by obligation to be paid; ascribable; due.
**Owl,** oul, *n.* A nocturnal bird of prey.
**Owlet,** oul'et, *n.* An owl; a young owl.
**Owlish,** oul'ish, *a.* Resembling an owl.
**Own,** ōn, *a.* Belonging to: used, distinctively and emphatically, after a possessive pronoun, or a noun in the possessive.—*vt.* To hold or possess by right; to acknowledge or avow; to concede.
**Owner,** ōn'ėr, *n.* One who owns; the rightful possessor or proprietor.
**Ownership,** ōn'ėr-ship, *n.* State of being an owner; legal or just claim or title.
**Ox,** oks, *n.*; *pl.* **Oxen,** oks'en. Any animal of the bovine genus; a male of the bovine genus castrated.
**Oxidate,** oks'id-āt, *vt.* To oxidize.
**Oxidation,** oks-id-ā'shon, *n.* The operation or process of converting into an oxide.
**Oxide,** oks'īd, *n.* A compound of oxygen with another element.
**Oxidize,** oks'id-īz, *vt.* To convert into an oxide; to cause to combine with oxygen.—*vi.* To change into an oxide.
**Oxonian,** ok-sō'ni-an, *a.* Pertaining to Oxford.—*n.* A native of Oxford; a member of the University of Oxford.
**Oxygen,** oks'i-jen, *n.* A gaseous element, a component of atmospheric air and water, and essential to animal and vegetable life and combustion.
**Oxygenate,** oks'i-jen-āt, *vt.* To unite or cause to combine with oxygen.
**Oxygenize,** oks'i-jen-īz, *vt.* To oxygenate.
**Oxygenous,** oks-ij'en-us, *a.* Pertaining to, obtained from, or containing oxygen.
**Oyez,** ō'yes. The introduction to a proclamation by a public crier, repeated three times.
**Oyster,** ois'tėr, *n.* A bivalve shell-fish or mollusk.
**Oyster-bed,** ois'tėr-bed, *n.* A bed or breeding place of oysters.
**Ozocerite, Ozokerite,** ō-zō-sē'rīt, ō-zō-kē'rīt, *n.* A mineral wax or paraffin of a brown or brownish-yellow color.
**Ozone,** ō'zōn, *n.* A kind of gas with a peculiar odor, a modification of oxygen existing in the atmosphere.

# P



**Pabular,** pab'ū-lėr, *a.* Pertaining to food.
**Pabulum,** pab'ū-lum, *n.* Food; that which feeds either mind or body.
**Pace,** pās, *n.* A step; space between the two feet in walking; distance of 2½ feet or 5 feet; gait; rate of progress.—*vi.* (pacing, paced). To step; to walk slowly; to move by lifting the legs on the same side together; as a horse.—*vt.* To measure by steps; to accompany and set a proper rate of motion; to race.
**Pacer,** pās'ėr, *n.* One who paces; a horse trained to pace.
**Pachydermatous,** pak-i-dėr'ma-tus, *a.* Thick-skinned; not sensitive to ridicule, sarcasm, etc.
**Pacific,** pa-sif'ik, *a.* Suited to make peace; pacifying; calm.—**The Pacific Ocean,** the ocean between America, Asia, and Australia.
**Pacification,** pa'si-fi-kā''shon, *n.* Act of making peace; appeasement.
**Pacificator,** pa-sif'i-kāt-ėr, *n.* One who pacifies; a peacemaker.
**Pacificatory,** pa-sif'i-ka-to-ri, *a.* Tending to make peace; conciliatory.
**Pacifier,** pa'si-fī-ėr, *n.* One who pacifies.
**Pacify,** pa'si-fī, *vt.* (pacifying, pacified). To give peace to; to appease; to allay.
**Pack,** pak, *n.* A bundle; a bale; a set of playing-cards; a set of hounds or dogs; a gang.—*vt.* To make up into a bundle; to fill methodically with contents; to manipulate with fraudulent design; to dismiss without ceremony; to stuff.—*vi.* To make up bundles; to depart in haste (with *off* or *away*).
**Package,** pak'āj, *n.* A bundle or bale; a packet; charge for packing goods.
**Packer,** pak'ėr, *n.* One who packs or prepares

merchandise for transit.
**Packet,** pak'et, *n.* A small pack; a parcel; a vessel employed regularly, in carrying mails, goods and passengers.
**Pack-horse,** pak'hors, *n.* A horse employed in carrying goods and baggage on its back.
**Pack-ice,** pak'īs, *n.* An assemblage of large floating pieces of ice.
**Packing,** pak'ing, *n.* Act of one who packs; material used in packing; stuffing.
**Pack-man,** pak'man, *n.* One who carries a pack on his back; a pedlar.
**Pack-saddle,** pak'sad-l, *n.* The saddle of a pack-horse, made for bearing burdens.
**Packsheet,** pak'shēt, *n.* A strong coarse cloth for covering goods in bales.—Also *Packing-sheet.*
**Pact,** pakt, *n.* A contract; an agreement or covenant.
**Pad,** pad, *n.* An easy-paced horse; a robber who infests the road on foot; a soft saddle; a cushion; a quantity of blotting-paper.—*vi.* (padding, padded). To walk or go on foot; to rob on foot.—*vt.* To furnish with padding.
**Padding,** pad'ing, *n.* Act of stuffing; material used in stuffing; literary matter inserted in a book, etc., merely to increase the bulk.
**Paddle,** pad'l, *vi.* (paddling, paddled). To play in water with hands or feet; to row.—*vt.* To propel by an oar or paddle.—*n.* A broad short oar; a float-board of a paddle-wheel.
**Paddler,** pad'l-ėr, *n.* One who paddles.
**Paddle-wheel,** pad'l-whēl, *n.* A wheel with boards on its circumference, propelling a steamship.
**Paddock,** pad'ok, *n.* A toad or frog; an inclosure under pasture, usually adjoining a house.
**Paddy,** pad'i, *n.* Rice in the husk, whether in the field or gathered.
**Padlock,** pad'lok, *n.* A lock with a link to be fastened through a staple.—*vt.* To fasten or provide with a padlock.
**Padre,** päd'rā, *n.* A chaplain.
**Paean,** pē'an, *n.* A war-song; song of triumph.
**Pagan,** pā'gan, *n.* A heathen.—*a.* Heathenish; idolatrous.
**Paganism,** pā'gan-izm, *n.* Religious worship of pagans; heathenism.
**Paganize,** pā'gan-īz, *vt.* To convert to heathenism.
**Page,** pāj, *n.* A young male attendant on persons of distinction; one side of a leaf of a book; a written record.—*vt.* (paging, paged). To number the pages of.
**Pageant,** pa'jent, *n.* Something intended for pomp; a show, as at a public rejoicing.—*a.* Showy; pompous.
**Pageantry,** pa'jent-ri, *n.* Pageants collectively; show; pompous spectacle.
**Pagination,** pa-jin-ā'shon, *n.* Act of paging; figures indicating the number of pages.
**Pagoda.** pa-gō'da, *n.* A Hindu or Buddhist temple.
**Paideutics,** pā-dū'tiks, *n.* The science of teaching.
**Paigle,** pā'gl, *n.* The cowslip or primrose.
**Pail,** pāl, *n.* An open vessel for carrying liquids.
**Pailful,** pāl'ful, *n.* The quantity that a pail will hold.
**Paillasse,** pal-yas', *n.* An under bed of straw.
**Pain,** pān, *n.* A penalty; bodily suffering; distress; anguish; *pl.* The throes of childbirth; labor; diligent effort.—*vt.* To cause pain to; to afflict; to distress.
**Painful,** pān'ful, *a.* Full of pain; distressing; grievous; difficult.
**Painless,** pān'les, *a.* Free from pain.
**Painstaking,** pānz'tāk-ing, *a.* Giving close application; laborious and careful.—*n.* The taking of pains; careful labor.
**Paint,** pānt, *vt.* To represent by colors and figures; to cover with color; to portray; to delineate.—*vi.* To practice painting.—*n.* A substance used in painting; a pigment; rouge.
**Painter,** pānt'ėr, *n.* One whose occupation is to paint; one skilled in representing things in colors; a rope to fasten a boat.
**Painting,** pānt'ing, *n.* Art or employment of laying on colors; art of representing objects by colors; a picture; colors laid on.
**Pair,** pār, *n.* Two things of like kind, suited, or used together; a couple; a man and his wife; two members on opposite sides in parliament, etc., who agree not to vote for a time.—*vi.* To join in pairs; to mate.—*vt.* To unite in pairs.
**Pajamas,** pā-jäm-az, *n.pl.* A sleeping-suit.
**Palace,** pa'lās, *n.* The house in which an emperor, king, bishop, etc., resides, a splendid residence.
**Paladin,** pal'a-din, *n.* A knight attached to a sovereign's court; a knight-errant; a heroic champion; a hero.
**Paleography,** pal-ē-og'ra-fi, *n.* The art of deciphering ancient writing.
**Paleolith,** pal'ē-ō-lith, *n.* An unpolished stone implement of the earlier stone age.
**Paleolithic,** pal'ē-ō-lith''ik, *a.* Belonging to the earlier stone period, when rude unpolished stone implements were used.
**Paleontology,** pal'ē-on-tol''o-ji, *n.* The science of fossil organic remains.
**Paleozoic,** pal'ē-ō-zō''ik, *a.* In *geology,* applied to the lowest division of stratified groups.
**Palanquin, Palankeen,** pa-lan-kēn', *n.* A covered conveyance used in India, China, etc., borne on the shoulders of men.
**Palatable,** pa'lat-a-bl, *a.* Agreeable to the palate or taste; savory.
**Palatal,** pa'lat-al, *a.* Pertaining to the palate; uttered by the aid of the palate.—*n.* A sound pronounced by the aid of the palate, as that of *j.*
**Palate,** pa'lāt, *n.* The roof of the mouth; taste; relish; intellectual taste.
**Palatial,** pa-lā'shal, *a.* Pertaining to a palace; becoming a palace; magnificent.
**Palaver,** pa-la'vėr, *n.* A long or serious conference; idle talk.—*vt.* To flatter or humbug.—*vi.* To talk idly; to engage in a palaver.
**Pale,** pāl, *n.* A pointed stake; an inclosure; sphere or scope.—*vt.* (paling, paled). To inclose with pales; to fence in.—*vi.* To turn pale.—*a.* Whitish; wan; deficient in color; not bright; dim.
**Palea,** pā'lē-a, *n.*; pl. **-eae.** A bract between the florets of composite plants; an interior bract of the flowers of grasses.
**Palestra,** pa-les'tra, *n.* A place of wrestling; wrestling or other athletic exercises.
**Paletot,** pal'e-tō, *n.* A loose overcoat.
**Palette,** pa'let, *n.* A thin oval board on which a painter lays his pigments.
**Palfrey,** pal'fri, *n.* A riding horse; a small horse fit for ladies.
**Pali,** pä'lē, *n.* The sacred language of the Buddhists, not now spoken.
**Palimpsest,** pal'imp-sest, *n.* A parchment from which writing has been erased to make room for other writing, the first remaining faintly visible.
**Paling,** pāl'ing, *n.* A fence formed with pales, or vertical stakes or posts.
**Palingenesis,** pal-in-jen'e-sis, *n.* A transformation; a great geological change.
**Palinode,** pal'i-nōd, *n.* A recantation.
**Palisade,** pa-li-sād', *n.* A fence or fortification of pales or posts.—*vt.* (palisading, palisaded). To surround or fortify with stakes.
**Palish,** pāl'ish, *a.* Somewhat pale or wan.
**Pall,** pal, *n.* An outer mantle of dignity; a cloth thrown over a coffin at a funeral; a linen cloth to cover a chalice; a covering.—*vt.* To cover with a pall; to shroud; to make vapid; to cloy.—*vi.* To become vapid or cloying.
**Palladium,** pal-lā'di-um, *n.* A statue of the goddess Pallas; bulwark; safeguard; a grayish-white hard malleable metal.
**Pallet,** pal'et, *n.* A palette; a tool used by potters, etc.; a small rude bed.

**Palliate,** pal'i-āt, *vt.* To extenuate; to mitigate; to lessen, abate, alleviate.
**Palliation,** pal-i-ā'shon, *n.* Act of palliating; what serves to palliate.
**Palliative,** pal'i-āt-iv, *a.* Serving to palliate.—*n.* That which palliates.
**Pallid,** pal'id, *a.* Pale; wan.
**Pallium,** pal'i-um, *n.*; pl. **-ia.** A kind of ancient cloak; a vestment sent by the pope to metropolitans, etc.; the mantle of a mollusk.
**Pallor,** pal'or, *n.* Paleness.
**Palm,** päm, *n.* The inner part of the hand; a measure of 3 or 4 inches; a name of plants constituting an order of endogens; a branch or leaf of such a plant; victory; triumph.—*vt.* To conceal in the palm of the hand; to impose by fraud.
**Palmaceous,** pal-mā'shus, *a.* Belonging to the palm tribe.
**Palmate,** pal'māt, *a.* Having the shape of a hand; entirely webbed, as feet.
**Palmer,** päm'ėr, *n.* A pilgrim who returned from the Holy Land with a branch of palm; one who palms or cheats.
**Palmiped,** pä'mi-ped, *a.* Web-footed.
**Palmist,** päm'ist, *n.* One who deals in palmistry.
**Palmistry,** pam'is-tri, *n.* The art of telling fortunes by the hand.
**Palm-oil,** päm'oil, *n.* A fatty substance resembling butter, obtained from palms.
**Palm-Sunday,** päm'sun-dā, *n.* The Sunday next before Easter.
**Palmy,** päm'i, *a.* Abounding in palms; flourishing; prosperous; victorious.
**Palpable,** pal'pa-bl, *a.* Perceptible by the touch; plain; obvious.
**Palpably,** pal'pa-bli, *adv.* Plainly; obviously.
**Palpitate,** pal'pi-tāt, *vi.* (palpitating, palpitated). To pulsate rapidly; to throb; to tremble.
**Palpitation,** pal-pi-tā'shon, *n.* Act of palpitating; violent pulsation of the heart.
**Palsy,** pal'zi, *n.* Paralysis, especially of a minor kind.—*vt.* (palsying, palsied). To affect with palsy; to paralyze.
**Palter,** pal'tėr, *vi.* To act insincerely; to shift; to dodge.
**Paltry,** pal'tri, *a.* Mean and trivial; trifling; worthless; contemptible.
**Paludal,** pal'ū-dal, *a.* Pertaining to marshes. Also *paludine, palustral, palustrine.*
**Pampas,** pam'pas, *n.pl.* The immense grassy treeless plains of South America.
**Pamper,** pam'pėr, *vt.* To gratify to the full; to furnish with that which delights.
**Pamphlet,** pam'flet, *n.* A small book, stitched but not bound; a short treatise.
**Pamphleteer,** pam-flet-ėr', *n.* A writer of pamphlets; a scribbler.
**Pan,** pan, *n.* A broad and shallow vessel, of metal or earthenware; a pond for evaporating salt water to make salt; part of a gun-lock holding the priming; the skull; the Greek and Roman god of flocks and herds.
**Panacea,** pan-a-sē'a, *n.* A remedy for all diseases; a universal medicine.
**Pancake,** pan'kāk, *n.* A thin cake fried in a pan or baked on an iron plate.
**Pancreas,** pan'krē-as, *n.* A fleshy gland or organ between the bottom of the stomach and the vertebrae; the sweet-bread in cattle.
**Pancreatic,** pan-krē-at'ik, *a.* Pertaining to the pancreas.
**Pandean,** pan-dē'an, *a.* Pertaining to Pan. *Pandean pipes, Pan's pipes,* a musical wind-instrument composed of pipes of different lengths tied together; a syrinx.
**Pandemonium,** pan-dē-mō'ni-um, *n.* The abode of the evil spirits; any lawless, disorderly place or assemblage.
**Pander,** pan'dėr, *n.* A pimp; a male bawd.—*vi.* To act as agent for the lusts of others; to be subservient to lust or desire. Also *Pandar.*
**Pane,** pān, *n.* A plate of glass inserted in a window, door, etc.; a panel.
**Panegyric,** pa-ne-ji'rik, *n.* A laudatory speech; eulogy; encomium; laudation.
**Panel,** pa'nel, *n.* A surface distinct from others adjoining in a piece of work; a sunk portion in a door, etc.; a piece of wood on which a picture is painted; list of Health Insurance doctors for a district; a doctor's list of insured persons; list of those summoned to serve on a jury; in Scotland, the accused.—*vt.* (panelling, panelled). To form with panels.
**Panelling,** pa'nel-ing, *n.* Panelled work.
**Pang,** pang, *n.* A sharp and sudden pain; painful spasm; throe.
**Pangolin,** pan'gō-lin, *n.* The scaly ant-eater or manis.
**Panic,** pan'ik, *n.* A sudden fright; terror inspired by a trifling cause.—*a.* Extreme, sudden, or causeless: said of fright.
**Panicle,** pan'i-kl, *n.* A branching form of inflorescence, as in the lilac.
**Pannier,** pa'ni-ėr, *n.* A wicker-basket; a basket for a person's or beast's back.
**Panoplied,** pa'nō-plid, *a.* Wearing a panoply.
**Panoply,** pa'nō-pli, *n.* Complete armor of defense; a full suit of armor.
**Panorama,** pan-ō-rä'ma, *n.* A picture presenting from a central point a view of objects in every direction.
**Panoramic,** pan-ō-ram'ik, *a.* Belonging to or like a panorama.
**Pansy,** pan'zi, *n.* A garden variety of violet; heart's-ease.
**Pant,** pant, *vi.* To breathe quickly; to gasp; to desire ardently.—*n.* A gasp; a throb.
**Pantaloon,** pan'ta-lön, *n.* A character in the old Italian comedy; in harlequinades, a fatuous old man, the butt of the clown.
**Pantaloons,** pan'ta-lönz, *n.pl.* Tightly fitting trousers; trousers in general.
**Pantheism,** pan'thē-izm, *n.* The doctrine that the universe is God, or that all things are manifestations of God.
**Pantheist,** pan'thē-ist, *n.* One who believes in pantheism.
**Pantheistic,** pan-thē-ist'ik, *a.* Pertaining to pantheism.
**Pantheon,** pan'thē-on, *n.* A temple dedicated to all the gods; all the divinities collectively worshipped by a people.
**Panther,** pan'thėr, *n.* A spotted carnivorous animal, otherwise called the leopard.
**Pantograph,** pan'tō-graf, *n.* An instrument for copying maps, plans, etc., on any scale.
**Pantomime,** pan'tō-mīm, *n.* A representation in dumb-show; a Christmas stage entertainment of the burlesque kind.
**Pantry,** pan'tri, *n.* An apartment in which provisions are kept, or where plate and knives, etc., are cleaned.
**Panzer division,** pant'zėr di-vi'zhon, *n.* A German armored division, consisting of tanks, etc.
**Pap,** pap, *n.* A kind of soft food for infants; the pulp of fruit; a teat; a round hill.
**Papa,** pa-pä', *n.* A childish name for father.
**Papacy,** pā'pa-si, *n.* The office and dignity of the pope; the popes collectively; papal authority or jurisdiction; popedom.
**Papal,** pā'pal, *a.* Belonging to the pope.
**Paper,** pā'pėr, *n.* A substance formed into thin sheets used for writing, printing, etc.; a leaf, or sheet of this; a journal; an essay or article; promissory notes, bills of exchange, etc.—*a.* Made or consisting of paper; appearing merely in documents without really existing; slight.—*vt.* To cover with paper; to inclose in paper.
**Paper-hanger,** pā'pėr-hang-ėr, *n.* One who lines walls with paper-hangings.
**Paper-hangings,** pā'pėr-hang-ingz, *n.pl.* Paper for covering the walls of rooms, etc.
**Paper-money,** pā'pėr-mun-i, *n.* Bank-notes or the like circulated instead of coin.
**Papery,** pā'pėr-i, *a.* Like paper.
**Papier-mâché,** pap-yā-mä-shā, *n.* A material pre-

P

pared by pulping different kinds of paper into a mass, which is molded into various articles, dried, and japanned.

**Papillary,** pap'il-la-ri, *a.* Pertaining to or resembling the nipple. Also *papillose.*

**Papist,** pā'pist, *n.* A Roman Catholic.

**Papistic, Papistical,** pā-pis'tik, pā-pis'tik-al, *a.* Popish; pertaining to Popery.

**Papistry,** pā'pist-ri, *n.* Popery.

**Papyrus,** pa-pī'rus, *n.*; pl. **-ri.** An Egyptian sedge, the stems of which afforded an ancient writing material; a written scroll of papyrus.

**Par,** pär, *n.* State of equality; equality in condition or value; state of shares or stocks when they may be purchased at the original price.

**Parable,** pa'ra-bl, *n.* An allegorical representation of something real in life or nature, embodying a moral.

**Parabola,** pa-ra'bō-la, *n.* A conic section, shown when a cone is cut by a plane parallel to one of its sides; the curve described theoretically by a projectile.

**Parabolic, Parabolical,** pa-ra-bol'ik, pa-ra-bol'ik-al, *a.* Expressed by or pertaining to parable; belonging to a parabola.

**Parachute,** pa'ra-shöt, *n.* An apparatus like a large umbrella, enabling a safe drop to the ground from an aircraft.

**Paraclete,** pa'ra-klēt, *n.* One called to aid or support; the Holy Spirit.

**Parade,** pa-rād', *n.* Ostentation; show; military display; place where such display is held.—*vt.* (parading, paraded). To exhibit in ostentatious manner; to marshal in military order.—*vi.* To walk about for show; to go about in military procession.

**Paradigm,** pa'ra-dim, *n.* A pattern, model, or example.

**Paradise,** pa'ra-dīs, *n.* The garden of Eden; a place of bliss; heaven.

**Paradox,** pa'ra-doks, *n.* An assertion or proposition seemingly absurd, yet true in fact; a seeming contradiction.

**Paradoxical,** pa-ra-doks'ik-al, *a.* Having the nature of a paradox; inclined to paradox.

**Paraffin,** pa'ra-fin, *n.* A solid white substance obtained from the distillation of wood, bituminous coal or shale, etc.

**Paraffin-oil,** pa'ra-fin-oil, *n.* The oil obtained in the distillation of bituminous shale, used for illuminating and lubricating.

**Paragon,** pa'ra-gon, *n.* A model; a perfect example of excellence.

**Paragraph,** pa'ra-graf, *n.* The character ¶ used as a reference, etc.; a distinct section of a writing, distinguished by a break in the lines; a brief notice.

**Parakeet,** pa'ra-kēt, *n. See* PARRAKEET.

**Parallactic,** pa-ral-lak'tik, *a.* Pertaining to the parallax of a heavenly body.

**Parallax,** pa'ral-laks, *n.* The apparent change of position of an object when viewed from different points; the difference between the place of a heavenly body as seen from the earth's surface and its center at the same time.

**Parallel,** pa'ral-lel, *a.* Extended in the same direction, and in all parts equally distant, as lines or surfaces; running in accordance with something; equal in all essential parts.—*n.* A line which throughout its whole length is equidistant from another line; conformity in all essentials; likeness; comparison; counterpart.—*vt.* To place so as to be parallel; to correspond to; to compare.

**Parallelepiped,** pa-ral-lel'e-pip''ed, *n.* A regular solid comprehended under six parallelograms, the opposite ones being parallel and equal.

**Parallelism,** pa'ral-lel-izm, *n.* State of being parallel; resemblance; comparison.

**Parallelogram,** pa-ral-lel'ō-gram, *n.* A quadrilateral, whose opposite sides are parallel and equal.

**Paralogism,** pa-ral'o-jism, *n.* A fallacious argument; an illogical conclusion.

**Paralysis,** pa-ral'i-sis, *n.* A diseased state of nerves by which the power of action or sensation is lost.

**Paralytic,** pa-ra-lit'ik, *a.* Pertaining to or affected with paralysis.—*n.* A person affected with palsy.

**Paralyze,** pa'ra-līz, *vt.* (paralyzing, paralyzed). To affect with paralysis; to reduce to a helpless state.

**Paramount,** pa'ra-mount, *a.* Chief; superior to all others.

**Paramour,** pa'ra-mör, *n.* A lover; one who wrongfully holds the place of a spouse.

**Parapet,** pa'ra-pet, *n.* A wall or rampart breast-high; a wall on the edge of a bridge, quay, etc.

**Paraphernalia,** pa'ra-fėr-nā''li-a, *n.pl.* That which a bride brings besides her dowry, as clothing, jewels, etc.; personal attire; trappings.

**Paraphrase,** pa'ra-frāz, *n.* A statement giving the meaning of another statement; a loose or free translation; a sacred song based on a portion of Scripture.—*vt.* To make a paraphrase of; to explain or translate with latitude.

**Paraselene,** pa'ra-se-lē''nē, *n.*; pl. **-lenae.** A mock moon; a luminous ring round the moon.

**Parashot,** pa'ra-shot, *n.* Marksman trained to deal with paratroops.

**Parasite,** pa'ra-sīt, *n.* One who frequents the rich, and earns his welcome by flattery; a sycophant; an animal that lives upon or in another; a plant which grows on another.

**Parasitic, Parasitical,** pa-ra-sit'ik, pa-ra-sit'ik-al, *a.* Belonging to a parasite; living on some other body.

**Parasol,** pa'ra-sol, *n.* A small umbrella used to keep off the sun's rays.

**Paratroops,** pa'ra-tröps, *n.* Troops landed by means of parachutes.

**Paravane,** pa'ra-vān, *n.* A torpedo-shaped machine fitted with an apparatus for severing the moorings of sea-mines.

**Parboil,** pär'boil, *vt.* To boil partly.

**Parbuckle,** pär'buk-l, *n.* A purchase formed by a single rope round an object (as a barrel) for moving on an inclined plane.

**Parcel,** pär'sel, *n.* A portion of anything; a small bundle or package; a collection.—*vt.* (parcelling, parcelled). To divide into portions; to make up into packages.

**Parcel-post,** pär'sel-pōst, *n.* Department of a post-office by which parcels are sent.

**Parch,** pärch, *vt.* To dry to extremity; to scorch.—*vi.* To become very dry; to be scorched.

**Parchment,** pärch'ment, *n.* The skin of a sheep or goat dressed for writing on; a document written on this substance.

**Pardon,** pär'don, *vt.* To forgive; to forbear to exact a penalty for; to overlook; to excuse.—*n.* Forgiveness; remission of a penalty.

**Pardonable,** pär'dn-a-bl, *a.* That may be pardoned; venial; excusable.

**Pare,** pār, *vt.* (paring, pared). To trim by cutting; to dress; to cut away by little and little; to diminish.

**Paregoric,** pa-re-go'rik, *a.* Encouraging; soothing; assuaging pain.—*n.* An anodyne.

**Parent,** pā'rent, *n.* One who brings forth or begets; a father or mother; a progenitor; cause; origin.

**Parentage,** pā'rent-āj, *n.* Extraction; birth.

**Parental,** pa-rent'al, *a.* Pertaining to or becoming parents; tender; affectionate.

**Parenthesis,** pa-ren'the-sis, *n.*; pl. **-theses.** A sentence or words inserted in another sentence, usually in brackets, thus, ( ).

**Parenthetic, Parenthetical,** pa-ren-thet'ik, pa-ren-thet'ik-al, *a.* Pertaining to or of the nature of a parenthesis.

**Parer,** pār'ėr, *n.* One who or that which pares; an instrument for paring.

**Parget,** pär'jet, *n.* Plaster laid on roofs or walls, especially if ornamental.—*vt.* To cover with

parget.
**Pargeting, Parge-work,** pär'jet-ing, pärj'wėrk, *n.* Ornamental plaster-work.
**Parhelion,** pär-hē'li-on, *n.*; pl. **-lia.** A mock sun or meteor, appearing as a bright light near the sun.
**Pariah,** pā'ri-a, *n.* One of the lowest class of people in Hindustan; an outcast.
**Parian,** pā'ri-an, *a.* Pertaining to *Paros,* an isle in the Aegean Sea producing a fine marble.—*n.* A fine porcelain clay.
**Parietal,** pa-rī'et-al, *a.* Pertaining to a wall.
**Paring,** pār'ing, *n.* That which is pared off; rind; act of slicing off and burning the surface of grass-land.
**Parish,** pa'rish, *n.* An ecclesiastical division under the care of a priest or parson; a subdivision of a county for civil purposes.—*a.* Belonging to a parish; parochial.
**Parishioner,** pa-rish'on-ėr, *n.* One who belongs to a parish; a member of the parish church.
**Parisian,** pa-riz'i-an, *a.* Pertaining to *Paris.*—*n.* A native or resident of Paris.
**Parity,** pa'ri-ti, *n.* Equality; likeness; like state or degree; analogy.
**Park,** pärk, *n.* A piece of ground inclosed; ornamental ground adjoining a house; ground in a town for recreation; an assemblage of heavy ordnance.—*vt.* To inclose in a park; to bring together, as artillery; to draw up motorcars and leave them for a time in an inclosed space, or at the side of the road.
**Parka,** pär'ka, *n.* Hooded skin jacket of Eskimos.
**Parlance,** pär'lans, *n.* Conversation; talk; idiom.
**Parley,** pär'li, *vi.* To confer; to discuss orally.—*n.* Mutual discourse; conference with an enemy in war.
**Parliament,** pär'li-ment, *n.* An assembly of persons for deliberation, etc.; the legislature of Great Britain and Northern Ireland; any similar legislative assembly.
**Parliamentarian,** pär'li-ment-ā''ri-an, *n.* An adherent of parliament; one of those who adhered to the parliament in the time of Charles I.
**Parliamentary,** pär'li-ment''a-ri, *a.* Pertaining to, done by, or according to the rules and usages of parliament.
**Parlor,** pär'lėr, *n.* The sitting-room in a house which the family usually occupy.
**Parnassian,** pär-nas'i-an, *a.* Pertaining to *Parnassus,* the mountain in Greece sacred to Apollo and the Muses.
**Parochial,** pa-rō'ki-al, *a.* Belonging to a parish; narrow in views; provincial.
**Parodist,** pa'rod-ist, *n.* One who makes parodies.
**Parody,** pa'rod-i, *n.* An adaptation of the words of an author, etc., to a different purpose; a burlesque imitation.—*vt.* (parodying, parodied). To imitate in parody.
**Parole,** pa-rōl', *n.* Words or oral declarations; word of honor; a promise by a prisoner of war not to bear arms against his captors for a certain period, or the like; a military countersign.
**Paronomasia, Paronomasy,** pa-ron'om-ā''zi-a, pa-ron-om'a-si, *n.* A pun.
**Paroxysm,** pa'roks-izm, *n.* A violent access of feeling (as of rage); convulsion; spasm.
**Parquetry,** pär'ket-ri, *n.* Inlaid wood-work, principally used for floors.
**Parr,** pär, *n.* A young salmon.
**Parrakeet,** pa'ra-kēt, *n.* A small parrot of the eastern hemisphere.
**Parricide,** pa'ri-sīd, *n.* A person who murders his father or mother; the murder of a parent.
**Parrot,** pa'rot, *n.* A family of birds, including parrakeets, macaws, cockatoos, etc.; a bird which can imitate the human voice.
**Parry,** pa'ri, *vt.* and *i.* (parrying, parried). To ward off.
**Parsimonious,** pär-si-mō'ni-us, *a.* Niggardly; miserly; penurious.
**Parsimony,** pär'si-mō-ni, *n.* The habit of being sparing in expenditure of money; excessive frugality; miserliness; closeness.
**Parsley,** pärs'li, *n.* A garden vegetable, used for flavoring in cooking.
**Parsnip,** pärs'nip, *n.* An umbelliferous plant with a fleshy esculent root.
**Parson,** pär'sn, *n.* The priest or incumbent of a parish; a clergyman.
**Parsonage,** pär'sn-āj, *n.* The official dwelling-house of a parson.
**Part,** pärt, *n.* A portion or piece of a whole; a section; a constituent or organic portion; share; lot; party; duty; business; character assigned to an actor in a play; *pl.* faculties; superior endowments; regions; locality.—*vt.* To divide; to sever; to share; to distribute; to separate; to intervene.—*vi.* To become separated, broken, or detached; to quit each other; to depart.
**Partake,** pär-tāk', *vi.* (partaking, pret. partook, pp. partaken). To take or have a part with others; to share; to have something of the nature, claim, or right.—*vt.* To share.
**Partaker,** pär-tāk'ėr, *n.* One who partakes; a sharer; accomplice; associate.
**Partial,** pär'shal, *a.* Belonging to or affecting a part only; not general; biased to one party; having a fondness.
**Partiality,** pär'shi-al''i-ti, *n.* Unfair bias; undue favor shown; a liking or fondness.
**Partially,** pär'shal-li, *adv.* With undue bias; in part; to some extent.
**Partible,** pärt'i-bl, *a.* Divisible.
**Participate,** pär-tis'i-pāt, *vi.* and *t.* To partake, share.
**Participation,** pär-tis'i-pā''shon, *n.* Act of participating; a sharing with others.
**Participator,** pär-tis'i-pāt-or, *n.* One who participates or partakes; a partaker.
**Participial,** pär-ti-sip'i-al, *a.* Of the nature of, or formed from, a participle.—*n.* A word having the nature of a participle.
**Participle,** pär'ti-si-pl, *n.* A word having the properties of both an adjective and verb.
**Particle,** pär'ti-kl, *n.* An atom; a jot; a very small portion; a word not inflected.
**Particular,** pär-tik'ū-lėr, *a.* Pertaining to a single person or thing; private; special; exact; precise; circumstantial; notable; fastidious.—*n.* A single instance; detail; distinct circumstance.
**Particularity,** pär'tik'ū-la''ri-ti, *n.* State or quality of being particular; minuteness of detail; that which is particular.
**Particularize,** pär-tik'ū-lėr-īz, *vt.* To make particular mention of; to specify in detail.—*vi.* To be particular to details.
**Particularly,** pär-tik'ū-lėr-li, *adv.* In a particular manner; distinctly; specially.
**Parting,** pärt'ing, *p.a.* Serving to part or divide; given at separation; departing.—*n.* Division; separation; leave-taking.
**Partisan,** pär'ti-zan, *n.* An adherent of a party or faction; a party man.—*a.* Adhering to a faction.
**Partition,** pär-ti'shon, *n.* Act of parting or dividing; division; a division-wall; part where separation is made.—*vt.* To divide by partitions; to divide into shares.
**Partitive,** pär'ti-tiv, *a.* Denoting a part; referring to a part; distributive.
**Partlet,** pärt'let, *n.* A name for a hen.
**Partly,** pärt'li, *adv.* In part; in some measure.
**Partner,** pärt'nėr, *n.* One who shares with another; an associate in business; a husband or wife.
**Partnership,** pärt'nėr-ship, *n.* Fellowship; the association of two or more persons in any business; joint interest or property.
**Partridge,** pär'trij, *n.* A game bird of the grouse family.
**Parturient,** pär-tū'ri-ent, *a.* Bringing forth or about to bring forth young.
**Parturition,** pär-tū-ri'shon, *n.* The act of bringing forth young.
**Party,** pär'ti, *n.* A body of individuals; one of two litigants; a company made up for an occasion;

a single person; a detachment of troops.—*a*. Of or pertaining to a party.

**Party-colored,** pär'ti-kul-ėrd, *a*. Colored differently in different parts; motley.

**Party-wall,** pär'ti-wal, *n*. A wall that separates one house from the next.

**Parvenu,** pär've-nū, *n*. An upstart; a person who has newly risen to eminence.

**Parvis, Parvise,** pär'vis, *n*. Area round a church; a room above the church porch.

**Pas,** pä, *n*. A step; precedence.

**Paschal,** pas'kal, *a*. Pertaining to the passover or to Easter.

**Pasha,** pash'ä or pa-shä', *n*. A Turkish governor of a province, or military commander.

**Pasquil,** pas'kwil, *n*. A pasquin.

**Pasquin, Pasquinade,** pas'kwin, pas-kwin-ād', *n*. A lampoon; a satirical publication.—*vt*. To lampoon.

**Pass,** päs, *vi*. (pret. and pp. passed or past). To go by or past; to change; to die; to elapse; to be enacted; to be current; to thrust in fencing or fighting; to go successfully through an examination.—*vt*. To go past, beyond, or over; to cross; to live through; to undergo with success (as an examination); to circulate; to utter; to take no notice of; to enact; to thrust; to void, as feces.—*n*. A passage; a defile; a license to pass; a thrust; manipulation; condition; extremity.

**Passable,** pas'a-bl, *a*. That may be passed, travelled, or navigated; current; tolerable; allowable; pretty fair.

**Passably,** pas'a-bli, *adv*. Tolerably.

**Passage,** pas'āj, *n*. Act of passing; transit; a journey, especially by a ship; road; channel; a gallery or corridor; access; episode; part of a book, etc., referred to; enactment; an encounter.

**Passant,** pas'ant, *a*. In *heraldry*, said of an animal which appears to walk with head directed forward.

**Pass-book,** päs'bök, *n*. A book in which to enter articles bought on credit; bank-book.

**Passé, Passée,** pas-ā, *a*. Past; faded; past the hey-day of life.

**Passenger,** pas'en-jėr, *n*. A traveller; one who travels in a public conveyance; one who does not pull his weight in a crew or team.

**Passeres,** pas'ėr-ēz, *n.pl*. An extensive order of birds, also called insessorial or perching birds.

**Passerine,** pas'ėr-īn, *a*. Pertaining to the order Passeres.

**Passible,** pas'i-bl, *a*. Capable of feeling; susceptible of impressions.

**Passim,** pas'im, *adv*. Here and there.

**Passing,** päs'ing, *p.a*. Current; cursory; fleeting.—*adv*. Exceedingly; very.

**Passing-bell,** päs'ing-bel, *n*. A bell rung at the time of, or just after, a person's death.

**Passion,** pa'shon, *n*. A suffering or enduring; the last suffering of Christ; a strong feeling or emotion; violent anger; ardor; vehement desire; love.

**Passionate,** pa'shon-āt, *a*. Moved by passion; vehement; animated; irascible; hasty.

**Passionately,** pa'shon-āt-li, *adv*. In a passionate manner; vehemently; angrily.

**Passionless,** pa'shon-les, *a*. Void of passion; calm of temper.

**Passion-play,** pa'shon-plā, *n*. A play representing scenes in the passion of Christ.

**Passion-Sunday,** pa'shon-sun-dā, *n*. The fifth Sunday in Lent.

**Passion-week,** pa'shon-wēk, *n*. The week immediately preceding Easter.

**Passive,** pas'iv, *a*. Capable of feeling; suffering; not acting; unresisting; inert; in *grammar*, expressing that the nominative is the object of some action or feeling.

**Passively,** pas'iv-li, *adv*. In a passive manner; without action; unresistingly.

**Pass-key,** päs'kē, *n*. A key for several locks; a master-key; a latch-key.

**Passover,** päs'ō-vėr, *n*. A feast of the Jews commemorative of the deliverance in Egypt, when the destroying angel passed over the houses of the Israelites; the sacrifice offered.

**Passport,** päs'pōrt, *n*. A license empowering a person to travel; that which enables one to reach some desired object.

**Pass-word,** päs'wėrd, *n*. A secret word to distinguish a friend from a stranger.

**Past,** päst, *p.a*. Gone by or beyond; belonging to an earlier period; spent; ended.—*n*. Former time.—*prep*. Beyond; out of reach of; after.—*adv*. By; so as to pass.

**Paste,** pāst, *n*. A mass of a semi-fluid state; a mixture of flour, etc., used in cookery, or to cause substances to adhere; a mixture of clay for pottery; a brilliant glassy substance, used in making imitations of gems.—*vt*. (pasting, pasted). To unite or fasten with paste.

**Pasteboard,** pāst-bōrd, *n*. A thick paper formed of sheets pasted together; cardboard.

**Pastel,** pas'tel, *n*. A colored crayon; a drawing made with colored crayons; the art of drawing with colored crayons.

**Pastern,** pas'tėrn, *n*. The part of a horse's leg between the joint next the foot and the hoof.

**Pasteurization,** past'ūr-ī-zā''shun, *n*. Checking the activity of bacteria in milk, etc., by heating it to 60° or 70° C.

**Pastime,** pas'tīm, *n*. Recreation; diversion; sport; play.

**Pastor,** pas'tor, *n*. A minister of a church.

**Pastoral,** pas'tor-al, *a*. Pertaining to shepherds; rustic; rural; relating to the care of souls, or to a pastor.—*n*. A poem dealing with shepherds; a poem of rural life; a letter addressed by a bishop to the clergy and people of his diocese.

**Pastorate,** pas'tor-āt, *n*. Office or jurisdiction of a pastor; the body of pastors.

**Pastry,** pās'tri, *n*. Eatables made of paste; crust of pies, tarts, etc.

**Pasturage,** pas'tūr-āj, *n*. Grazing ground; growing grass for cattle.

**Pasture,** pas'tūr, *n*. Grass for the food of cattle; grazing ground; grass land.—*vt*. (pasturing, pastured). To feed on growing grass.—*vi*. To graze.

**Pasty,** pās'ti, *a*. Like paste.—*n*. A meat pie covered with paste.

**Pat,** pat, *n*. A light stroke with the fingers or hand; a tap; a small lump of butter beaten into shape.—*vt*. (patting, patted). To strike gently; to tap.—*a*. Hitting the mark; apt; convenient.—*adv*. Fitly; just in the nick.

**Patch,** pach, *n*. A piece of cloth sewn on a garment to repair it; a small piece of silk stuck on the face for adornment; a small piece of ground.—*vt*. To mend by sewing on a patch; to repair clumsily; to make hastily without regard to forms (with *up*).

**Patchwork,** pach'wėrk, *n*. Work composed of varied pieces sewn together; work composed of pieces clumsily put together.

**Patchy,** pach'i, *a*. Full of patches.

**Pate,** pāt, *n*. The head, or rather the top of the head.

**Patella,** pa-tel'la, *n*. A small pan, vase, or dish; the knee-pan.

**Paten,** pa'ten, *n*. A metallic flat dish; the plate on which the consecrated bread in the eucharist is placed.

**Patent,** pā'tent or pa'tent, *n*. A writing (called *letters patent*) granting a privilege, as a title of nobility; a similar writing, securing exclusive right to an invention or discovery.—*a*. Open; manifest; secured by patent; lacquered (leather).—*vt*. To secure, as the exclusive right of a thing to a person.

**Patentee,** pā'ten-tē or pa'ten-tē, *n*. One to whom a patent is granted.

**Paterfamilias,** pā'tėr-fa-mil''i-as, *n*. The head or father of a family.

**Paternal,** pa-tėr'nal, *a*. Fatherly; derived from the father; hereditary.

**Paternity,** pa-tėr'ni-ti, *n.* Fathership; relation of a father to his offspring; origin; authorship.
**Paternoster,** pa'tėr-nos-tėr, *n.* The Lord's prayer; a rosary; every tenth bead in a rosary.
**Path,** päth, *n.* A way beaten by the feet of man or beast; a footway; course or track; way or passage; course of life.
**Pathetic,** pa-thet'ik, *a.* Full of pathos; affecting; exciting pity, sorrow, etc.
**Pathetically,** pa-thet'ik-al-li, *adv.* In a pathetic manner; touchingly.
**Pathologic, Pathological,** path-o-loj'ik, path-o-loj'ik-al, *a.* Pertaining to pathology.
**Pathologist,** pa-thol'o-jist, *n.* One who is versed in or who treats of pathology.
**Pathology,** pa-thol'o-ji, *n.* That part of medicine which explains the nature of diseases, their causes and symptoms.
**Pathos,** pā'thos, *n.* Expression of strong or deep feeling; that quality which excites tender emotions, as pity, sympathy, etc.
**Patience,** pā'shens, *n.* Quality of being patient; endurance; composure; forbearance; a card game for one.
**Patient,** pā'shent, *a.* Enduring without murmuring; not easily provoked; persevering; not hasty.—*n.* A person or thing passively affected; a person under medical treatment.
**Patiently,** pā'shent-li, *adv.* In a patient manner; with patience; submissively.
**Patina,** pat'i-na, *n.* The fine green rust on ancient bronzes, copper coins, etc.
**Patois,** pat-wä, *n.* A rustic or provincial form of speech.
**Patriarch,** pā'tri-ärk, *n.* The chief of a race, tribe, or family; a dignitary above an archbishop in the Greek Church.
**Patriarchal,** pā-tri-ärk'al, *a.* Belonging to a patriarch; subject to a patriarch.
**Patrician,** pa-tri'shan, *a.* Belonging to the senators of ancient Rome; of noble birth.—*n.* A person of noble birth.
**Patrimonial,** pat-ri-mō'ni-al, *a.* Pertaining to a patrimony; inherited.
**Patrimony,** pat'ri-mo-ni, *n.* A paternal inheritance; a church estate or revenue.
**Patriot,** pā'tri-ot or pat', *n.* A person who loves his country, and zealously defends its interests.—*a.* Patriotic.
**Patriotic,** pā-tri-ot'ik or pat-, *a.* Actuated or inspired by the love of one's country; directed to the public welfare.
**Patriotism,** pā'tri-ot-izm or pat', *n.* The qualities of a patriot; love of one's country.
**Patristic,** pa-tris'tik, *a.* Pertaining to the fathers of the Christian church.
**Patrol,** pa-trōl', *n.* The marching round by a guard at night to secure the safety of a camp; the guard who go such rounds; on active service, a small party sent out to harass the enemy (fighting patrol), or to get information (reconnaissance patrol).—*vi.* (patrolling, patrolled). To go the rounds as a patrol.—*vt.* To pass round, as a guard.
**Patron,** pā'tron, *n.* A protector; one who supports or protects a person or a work; one who has the disposition of a church-living, professorship, or other appointment; a guardian saint.
**Patronage,** pat'ron-āj or pā', *n.* Act of patronizing; special support; guardianship, as of a saint; right of presentation to an ecclesiastical benefice.
**Patroness,** pā'tron-es, *n.* A female patron.
**Patronize,** pat'ron-īz or pā', *vt.* To act as patron of; to countenance or favor; to assume the air of a superior to.
**Patronizing,** pat'ron-īz-ing or pā', *p.a.* Assuming the airs of a patron; acting like one who condescends to patronize or favor.
**Patter,** pat'ėr, *vi.* To make a sound like that of falling drops; to move with quick steps; to mumble; to talk in a glib way.—*n.* A quick succession of small sounds; chatter; prattle.
**Pattern,** pat'ėrn, *n.* A model proposed for imitation; a sample; an ornamental design.
**Patty,** pat'i, *n.* A little pie; a pasty.
**Paucity,** pa'si-ti, *n.* Fewness; scarcity; smallness of quantity.
**Pauline,** pal'īn, *a.* Pertaining to St. *Paul,* or to his writings.
**Paunch,** pansh, *n.* The belly, and its contents; the abdomen.
**Paunchy,** pansh'i, *a.* Big-bellied.
**Pauper,** pa'pėr, *n.* A poor person; one dependent on the public for maintenance.
**Pauperism,** pa'pėr-izm, *n.* State of indigent persons requiring public support.
**Pauperize,** pa'pėr-īz, *vt.* To reduce to pauperism.
**Pause,** paz, *n.* A temporary cessation; cessation proceeding from doubt; suspense.—*vi.* (pausing, paused). To make a short stop; to delay; to deliberate; to hesitate.
**Pave,** pāv, *vt.* (paving, paved). To cover with stone, brick, etc., so as to make a level and solid surface for carriages or foot-passengers.
**Pavement,** pāv'ment, *n.* The solid floor of a street, courtyard, etc.; paved part of a road used by foot-passengers; material with which anything is paved.
**Pavilion,** pa-vil'yon, *n.* A tent; a small building having a tent-formed roof; a building of ornamental character for entertainments; the outer ear.—*vt.* To furnish with pavilions; to shelter with a tent.
**Paving,** pā'ving, *n.* Pavement.—*a.* Used for pavements.
**Pavonine,** pav'ō-nīn, *a.* Belonging to or like a peacock; iridescent.
**Paw,** pa, *n.* The foot of animals having claws.—*vi.* To draw the fore-foot along the ground.—*vt.* To scrape with the fore-foot; to handle roughly.
**Pawl,** pal, *n.* A short bar preventing a capstan, etc., from rolling back.
**Pawn,** pan, *n.* Something given as security for money borrowed; a pledge; state of being pledged; a pawnship; a man of the lowest rank in chess.—*vt.* To give in pledge; to pledge with a pawnbroker.
**Pawnbroker,** pan'brōk-ėr, *n.* A person licensed to lend money at a legally fixed rate of interest on goods deposited with him.
**Pay,** pā, *vt.* (paying, paid). To give money, etc., for goods received or service rendered; to reward; to discharge, as a debt; to give; to cover with tar or pitch.—*vi.* To make a payment; to be profitable or remunerative.—*n.* An equivalent for money due, goods, or services; salary; wages; reward.
**Payable,** pā'a-bl, *a.* That may or ought to be paid; justly due.
**Payee,** pā-ē', *n.* One to whom money is to be paid.
**Paymaster,** pā'mäs-tėr, *n.* An officer whose duty is to pay the men their wages.
**Payment,** pā'ment, *n.* Act of paying; what is given for service done; reward.
**Paynim,** pā'nim, *n.* A pagan; heathen.
**Pea,** pē, *n.*; pl. **Peas, Pease.** A well-known flowering plant cultivated for its seeds; one of the seeds of the plant.
**Peace,** pēs, *n.* A state of quiet; calm; repose; public tranquillity; freedom from war; concord.
**Peaceable,** pēs'a-bl, *a.* Disposed to peace; peaceful; pacific; calm.
**Peaceably,** pēs'a-bli, *adv.* In a peaceable manner; quietly.
**Peaceful,** pēs'ful, *a.* Free from war, noise, or disturbance; quiet; mild.
**Peacefully,** pēs'ful-li, *adv.* Quietly; calmly.
**Peace-maker,** pēs'māk-ėr, *n.* One who reconciles parties at variance.
**Peace-offering,** pēs'of-ėr-ing, *n.* Something offered to procure reconciliation.
**Peach,** pēch, *n.* A well-known tree and its fruit, allied to the almond.—*vi.* To betray one's accomplice.
**Peacock,** pē'kok, *n.* A large gallinaceous bird

P

with rich plumage; properly the male bird.
**Peahen,** pē'hen, *n.* The female of the peacock.
**Pea-jacket,** pē'jak-et, *n.* A thick woollen jacket worn by seamen, fishermen, etc.
**Peak,** pēk, *n.* A projecting point; the top of a mountain ending in a point; the upper corner of a sail extended by a yard; also, the extremity of the yard or gaff.—*vi.* To look sickly; to be emaciated.
**Peaked,** pēkt, *a.* Ending in a peak or point.
**Peal,** pēl, *n.* A series of loud sounds, as of bells, thunder, etc.; a set of bells tuned to each other; chime.—*vi.* To give out a peal.—*vt.* To cause to ring or sound.
**Pear,** pār, *n.* A well-known fruit-tree; one of the fruits of the tree.
**Pearl,** pėrl, *n.* A smooth lustrous whitish gem produced by certain mollusks; something resembling a pearl; a small printing type; what is choicest and best.—*a.* Relating to or made of pearl or mother-of-pearl.—*vt.* To set or adorn with pearls.
**Peasant,** pe'zant, *n.* A rustic; one whose business is rural labor.—*a.* Rustic.
**Peasantry,** pe'zant-ri, *n.* Peasants; rustics; the body of country people.
**Peat,** pēt, *n.* A kind of turf used as fuel; a small block of this cut and dried for fuel.
**Pebble,** peb'l, *n.* A stone rounded by the action of water; agate and rock-crystal used for glass in spectacles.
**Pebbly,** peb'li, *a.* Full of pebbles.
**Pecan, Pecan-nut,** pē-kan', pē-kan'nut, *n.* A species of hickory and its fruit.
**Peccable,** pek'a-bl, *a.* Liable to sin; apt to transgress the divine law.
**Peccadillo,** pek-a-dil'lō, *n.* A slight trespass or offense; a petty crime or fault.
**Peccant,** pek'ant, *a.* Sinning; criminal; morbid; bad; not healthy.
**Peccary,** pek'a-ri, *n.* A quadruped of America, allied to the swine.
**Peck,** pek, *n.* A dry measure of eight quarts.—*vt.* and *i.* To strike with the beak, or something pointed; to pick up, as food, with the beak.
**Pecker,** pek'ėr, *n.* One who or that which pecks; a woodpecker.
**Peckish,** pek'ish, *a.* Hungry.
**Pecten,** pek'ten, *n.* A marine bivalve mollusk having a shell with diverging furrows.
**Pectic,** pek'tik, *a.* Having the property of forming a jelly.
**Pectinal,** pek'tin-al, *a.* Pertaining to or resembling a comb.
**Pectinate,** pek'tin-āt, *a.* Toothed like a comb.
**Pectoral,** pek'to-ral, *a.* Pertaining to the breast.—*n.* A breastplate; a medicine for the chest and lungs.
**Peculate,** pe'kū-lāt, *vi.* To appropriate money or goods intrusted to one's care.
**Peculation,** pe-kū-lā'shon, *n.* Act of peculating; embezzlement.
**Peculator,** pe'kū-lāt-ėr, *n.* One who peculates.
**Peculiar,** pē-kū'li-ėr, *a.* One's own; characteristic; particular; unusual; odd.
**Peculiarity,** pē-kū'li-a''ri-ti, *n.* Quality of being peculiar; something peculiar to a person or thing.
**Peculiarly,** pē-kū'li-ėr-li, *adv.* In a peculiar manner; especially; singularly.
**Pecuniary,** pē-kū'ni-a-ri, *a.* Relating to or connected with money; consisting of money.
**Pedagogic,** ped-a-goj'ik, *a.* Resembling or belonging to a pedagogue.
**Pedagogics,** ped-a-goj'iks, *n.* The science or art of teaching.
**Pedagogue,** ped'a-gog, *n.* A teacher of children; a schoolmaster.
**Pedagogy,** ped'a-go-ji, *n.* The art or office of a pedagogue; the teaching profession.
**Pedal,** pēd'al, *a.* Pertaining to a foot or to a pedal.—*n.* pe'dal. A lever to be pressed by the foot; a part of a musical instrument acted on by the feet.
**Pedant,** pe'dant, *n.* One who makes a vain display of his learning; a narrow-minded scholar.
**Pedantic,** pe-dant'ik, *a.* Pertaining to or characteristic of a pedant.
**Pedantically,** pe-dant'ik-al-li, *adv.* In a pedantic manner.
**Pedantry,** pe'dant-ri, *n.* The qualities or character of a pedant; boastful display of learning; obstinate adherence to rules.
**Peddle,** ped'l, *vi.* and *t.* (peddling, peddled). To travel and sell small-wares; to trifle.
**Peddler,** ped'lėr, *n.* One who peddles; a pedlar.
**Pedestal,** pe'des-tal, *n.* The base or support of a column, pillar, statue, vase, etc.
**Pedestrian,** pe-des'tri-an, *a.* Going on foot; performed on foot.—*n.* One who journeys on foot; a remarkable walker.
**Pedestrianism,** pe-des'tri-an-izm, *n.* Practice of walking; art of a professional walker.
**Pedicel,** pe'di-sel, *n.* A small short foot-stalk of a leaf, flower, or fruit.
**Pedigree,** pe'di-grē, *n.* Lineage; line of ancestors; genealogy.
**Pediment,** pe'di-ment, *n.* The triangular mass resembling a gable at the end of buildings in the Greek style; a triangular decoration over a window, a door, etc.
**Pedlar, Pedler,** ped'lėr, *n.* A petty dealer who carries his wares with him.
**Pedometer,** pe-dom'et-ėr, *n.* An instrument which measures how far a person walks.
**Peduncle,** pē'dung-kl, *n.* The stem that supports the flower and fruit of a plant.
**Peel, Peel-tower,** pēl, pēl'tou-ėr, *n.* An old strong square fortress.
**Peel,** pēl, *vt.* To strip off, as bark or rind; to flay; to pare; to pillage.—*vi.* To lose the skin, bark or rind; to fall off, as bark or skin.—*n.* The skin or rind; a baker's wooden shovel.
**Peep,** pēp, *vi.* To chirp as a chicken; to begin to appear; to look through a crevice.—*n.* A chirp; a look through a small opening; first appearance.
**Peer,** pēr, *n.* One of the same rank; an equal; an associate; a nobleman (duke, marquis, earl, viscount, or baron).—*vi.* To appear; to peep out; to look narrowly.
**Peerage,** pēr'āj, *n.* The rank or dignity of a peer; the body of peers.
**Peeress,** pēr'es, *n.* A woman ennobled by descent, by creation, or by marriage.
**Peerless,** pēr'les, *a.* Matchless.
**Peevish,** pē'vish, *a.* Fretful; querulous; hard to please; froward.
**Peg,** peg, *n.* A piece of wood used in fastening things together; the pin of a musical instrument; a pin on which to hang anything.—*vt.* (pegging, pegged). To fasten with pegs.—*vi.* To work diligently.
**Pekoe,** pē'kō, *n.* A fine black tea.
**Pelagian,** pe-lā'ji-an, *n.* One who denies original sin, and asserts the doctrine of free-will and the merit of good works.—*a.* Pertaining to these doctrines or to Pelagius, their founder.
**Pelagic,** pe-laj'ik, *a.* Belonging to the ocean; inhabiting the open ocean.
**Pelargonium,** pel-är-gō'ni-um, *n.* A genus of ornamental plants, usually called *Geraniums.*
**Pelasgian, Pelasgic,** pe-las'ji-an, pe-las'jik, *a.* Pertaining to the Pelasgi, prehistoric inhabitants of Greece.
**Pelerine,** pel'ėr-in, *a.* A lady's long cape.
**Pelican,** pel'i-kan, *n.* A large web-footed bird with a very large bill.
**Pelisse,** pe-lēs', *n.* A coat for ladies or children.
**Pell,** pel, *n.* A skin; a roll of parchment.
**Pellet,** pel'et, *n.* A little ball; one of the globules of small shot.
**Pellicle,** pel'i-kl, *n.* A thin skin or film.
**Pell-mell,** pel'mel, *adv.* With confused violence; in utter confusion.
**Pellucid,** pel-lū'sid, *a.* Transparent; not opaque;

translucent.
**Pelt,** pelt, *n.* A raw hide; a blow; a heavy shower.—*vt.* To strike with something thrown.—*vi.* To throw missiles; to fall in a heavy shower.
**Peltate,** pel'tāt, *a.* In *botany,* fixed to the stalk by some point within the margin.
**Peltry,** pelt'ri, *n.* Undressed skins; furs in general.
**Pelvic,** pel'vik, *a.* Pertaining to the pelvis.
**Pelvis,** pel'vis, *n.* The bony cavity forming the framework of the lower part of the abdomen.
**Pen,** pen, *n.* An instrument for writing with ink; style or quality of writing; a small inclosure for cows, etc.; a fold.—*vt.* (penning, penned). To write; to compose; to coop or shut up.
**Penal,** pē'nal, *a.* Relating to, enacting, or incurring punishment.
**Penalty,** pen'al-ti, *n.* Punishment for a crime or offense; forfeit for non-fulfilment of conditions; sum to be forefeited; a fine.
**Penance,** pen'ans, *n.* An ecclesiastical punishment imposed for sin; voluntary suffering as an expression of penitence.
**Penates,** pē-nā'tēz, *n.pl.* Household gods.
**Penchant,** päng'shäng, *n.* Strong inclination; bias.
**Pencil,** pen'sil, *n.* A small brush used by painters; an instrument of black-lead, etc., for writing and drawing; a converging or diverging aggregate of rays of light.—*vt.* (pencilling, pencilled). To write or mark with a pencil.
**Pend,** pend, *vi.* To impend; to wait for settlement.
**Pendant,** pen'dant, *n.* Anything hanging down by way of ornament; a hanging apparatus for giving light, etc.; an appendix or addition; a flag borne at the mast-head.
**Pendent,** pen'dent, *a.* Hanging; pendulous; projecting.—*n.* Something hanging.
**Pending,** pend'ing, *p.a.* Hanging in suspense; undecided.—*pret.* During.
**Pendulate,** pen'dū-lāt, *vi.* To swing freely like a pendulum; to swing.
**Pendulous,** pen'dū-lus, *a.* Hanging; hanging so as to swing; swinging.
**Pendulum,** pen'dū-lum, *n.* A body suspended and swinging; the swinging piece in a clock which regulates its motion.
**Penetrable,** pen'e-tra-bl, *a.* That may be entered or pierced; susceptible of moral or intellectual impression.
**Penetrably,** pen'e-tra-bli, *adv.* In a penetrable manner; so as to be penetrable.
**Penetralia,** pen'e-trā''li-a, *n.pl.* The inner parts of a building; a sanctuary; hidden things.
**Penetrate,** pen'e-trāt, *vt.* and *i.* To enter or pierce, as into another body; to affect, as the mind; to cause to feel; to understand.
**Penetrating,** pen'e-trāt-ing, *p.a.* Sharp; subtle; acute; discerning.
**Penetration,** pen-e-trā'shon, *n.* Act of penetrating; sagacity; discernment.
**Penetrative,** pe'ne-trāt-iv, *a.* Piercing; sharp; subtle; acute; discerning.
**Penguin,** pen'gwin, *n.* A web-footed, flightless sea bird.
**Penicillin,** pen-i-sil'in, *n.* A bacteria-destroying substance derived from a mold.
**Peninsula,** pen-in'sū-la, *n.* A portion of land almost surrounded by water.
**Peninsular,** pen-in'sū-lėr, *a.* In the form of, pertaining to, or inhabiting a peninsula.
**Penis,** pē'nis, *n.* The male organ of generation.
**Penitence,** pe'ni-tens, *n.* State of being penitent; repentance; contrition.
**Penitent,** pe'ni-tent, *a.* Suffering sorrow on account of one's own sins; contrite.—*n.* One who repents of sin.
**Penitential,** pe-ni-ten'shal, *a.* Pertaining to or expressing penitence.—*n.* A Roman Catholic book of rules for penitents.
**Penitentiary,** pe-ni-ten'sha-ri, *a.* Relating to penance.—*n.* One who does penance; an office or official of the R. Catholic church connected with the granting of dispensations, etc.; a house of correction.
**Penknife,** pen'nīf, *n.* A small pocket-knife.
**Penman,** pen'man, *n.*; pl. **-men.** A writer.
**Penmanship,** pen'man-ship, *n.* The use of the pen; art or manner of writing.
**Pennant,** pen'ant, *n.* A small flag; a pennon; a pendant.
**Penniless,** pen'i-les, *a.* Without money.
**Pennon,** pen'on, *n.* A small pointed flag carried on spears or lances.
**Penny,** pen'i, *n.*; pl. **Pennies** or **Pence,** pen'iz, pens. (*Pennies* denotes the number of coins; *pence* the value.) A bronze coin; money.
**Penny-wise,** pen'i-wīz, *a.* Wise in saving small sums at the hazard of larger.
**Pennyworth,** pen'i-wėrth, *n.* As much as is bought for a penny; any purchase.
**Pensil,** pen'sīl, *a.* Hanging; suspended.
**Pension,** pen'shon, *n.* A stated yearly allowance in consideration of past services; a boarding-house on the Continent (pronounced päng-syong).—*vt.* To grant a pension to.
**Pensionary,** pen'shon-a-ri, *a.* Receiving a pension; consisting in a pension.—*n.* A pensioner.
**Pensioner,** pen'shon-ėr, *n.* One in receipt of a pension; a student at Cambridge, who pays for his board and other charges, as contrasted with a scholar, exhibitioner, or sizar.
**Pensive,** pen'siv, *a.* Thoughtful; expressing thoughtfulness with sadness.
**Pent,** pent, *p.a.* Shut up; confined (often with *up*).
**Pentagon,** pen'ta-gon, *n.* A plane figure having five angles and five sides.
**Pentagonal,** pen-tag'on-al, *a.* Having five corners or angles.
**Pentahedron,** pen-ta-hē'dron, *n.* A solid figure having five equal faces.
**Pentameter,** pen-tam'et-ėr, *n.* A poetic verse of five feet.
**Pentateuch,** pen'ta-tūk, *n.* The first five books of the Old Testament.
**Pentecost,** pen'tē-kost, *n.* A festival of the Jews on the fiftieth day after the Passover; Whitsuntide.
**Penthouse,** pent'hous, *n.* A shed standing aslope from the main wall or building; a roof sloping up against a wall.
**Pent-roof,** pent'röf, *n.* A sloping roof all of whose slope is on one side.
**Penult,** pēn'ult or pen'ult, *n.* The last syllable of a word except one.
**Penultimate,** pen-ul'ti-māt, *a.* The last but one.—*n.* The last syllable but one; penult.
**Penumbra,** pen-um'bra, *n.* The partial shadow on the margin of the total shadow in an eclipse; the point of a picture where the shade blends with the light.
**Penurious,** pe-nū'ri-us, *a.* Pertaining to penury; parsimonious; niggardly.
**Penury,** pe'nū-ri, *n.* Poverty; indigence; want of the necessaries of life.
**Peon,** pē'on, *n.* An attendant; a native constable; a day-laborer; a kind of serf.
**Peony,** pē'o-ni, *n.* A genus of plants of the ranunculus family, with large flowers.
**People,** pē'pl, *n.* The body of persons who compose a community, race, or nation; persons indefinitely.—*vt.* (peopling, peopled). To stock with inhabitants; to populate.
**Pepper,** pep'ėr, *n.*A plant and its aromatic pungent seed, much used in seasoning, etc.—*vt.* To sprinkle with pepper; to pelt with shot or missiles; to drub thoroughly.
**Pepper-corn,** pep'ėr-korn, *n.* The berry or fruit of the pepper plant.
**Peppermint,** pep'ėr-mint, *n.* A plant of the mint genus having a penetrating aromatic smell and a strong pungent taste.
**Pepsin, Pepsine,** pep'sin, *n.* The active principle of gastric juice.
**Peptic,** pep'tik, *a.* Promoting digestion; relating to digestion; digestive.

**Per,** pėr, *prep.* A Latin preposition used in the sense of *by* or *for,* chiefly in certain Latin phrases, as *per annum,* by or for the year.
**Perambulate,** pėr-am'bū-lāt, *vt.* To walk through or over; to traverse; to survey.
**Perambulation,** pėr-am'bū-lā''shon, *n.* Act of perambulating; survey or inspection.
**Perambulator,** pėr-am'bū-lāt-ėr, *n.* One who perambulates; a child's carriage propelled by hand from behind.
**Perceivable,** pėr-sēv'a-bl, *a.* That may be perceived; perceptible.
**Perceive,** pėr-sēv', *vt.* (perceiving, perceived). To apprehend by the organs of sense or by the mind; to observe; to discern.
**Percentage,** pėr-sent'āj, *n.* The allowance duty, rate of interest, proportion, etc., reckoned on each hundred.
**Perceptible,** pėr-sep'ti-bl, *a.* Perceivable.
**Perception,** pėr-sep'shon, *n.* Act, process, or faculty of perceiving; discernment.
**Perceptive,** pėr-sep'tiv, *a.* Relating to perception; having the faculty of perceiving.
**Perch,** pėrch, *n.* A spiny fresh-water fish; a roost for fowls; an elevated place or position; 5½ yards, also called a rod or pole; 30¼ square yards, a square rod.—*vi.* To sit on a perch; to light, as a bird.—*vt.* To place on a perch.
**Percipient,** pėr-sip'i-ent, *a.* Perceiving; having the faculty of perception.
**Percolate,** pėr'kō-lāt, *vt.* and *i.* To strain through; to filter.
**Percuss,** pėr-kus', *vt.* To strike against; to tap or strike in medical practice.
**Percussion,** pėr-ku'shon, *n.* Collision; impact; the act of striking the surface of the body to determine by sound the condition of the organs subjacent.
**Percussive,** pėr-kus'iv, *a.* Acting by percussion; striking against.
**Perdition,** pėr-di'shon, *n.* Entire ruin; utter destruction; eternal death.
**Perdu, Perdue,** pėr'dū or pėr-dū', *a.* Hid; in concealment; out of sight.
**Peregrinate,** pe're-grin-āt, *vi.* To travel from place to place; to wander.
**Peregrination,** pe're-grin-ā''shon, *n.* A travelling; a wandering.
**Peregrine,** pe're-grin, *n.* A kind of falcon.
**Peremptorily,** p'remp-to-ri-li, *adv.* In a peremptory manner; absolutely; positively.
**Peremptory,** pe'remp-to-ri, *a.* Such as to preclude debate; decisive; absolute.
**Perennial,** pe-ren'i-al, *a.* Lasting through the year; perpetual; unceasing.—*n.* A plant whose root remains alive more years than two.
**Perennially,** pe-ren'i-al-li, *adv.* In a perennial manner; continually.
**Perfect,** pėr'fekt, *a.* Finished; complete; fully informed; completely skilled; faultless; in *grammar,* denoting a tense which expresses an act completed.—*vt.* To accomplish; to make perfect; to make fully skilful.
**Perfectibility,** pėr-fek'ti-bil''i-ti, *n.* The quality of being perfectible.
**Perfection,** pėr-fek'shon, *n.* State of being perfect; an excellence perfect in its kind.
**Perfectly,** pėr'fekt-li, *adv.* In a perfect manner; consummately; completely; exactly.
**Perfidious,** pėr-fi'di-us, *a.* Guilty of or involving perfidy; treacherous; faithless.
**Perfidy,** pėr'fi-di, *n.* Act of breaking faith or allegiance; the violation of a trust reposed; treachery; disloyalty.
**Perforate,** pėr'fo-rāt, *vt.* To bore or penetrate through; to pierce with a pointed instrument.
**Perforation,** pėr-fo-rā'shon, *n.* Act of perforating; a hole bored.
**Perforator,** pėr'fo-rāt-ėr, *n.* One who or that which perforates.
**Perforce,** pėr-fōrs', *adv.* By force or violence; of necessity.
**Perform,** pėr-form', *vt.* To accomplish; to effect; to do; to act.—*vi.* To act a part; to play on a musical instrument, etc.
**Performable,** pėr-form'a-bl, *a.* That may be performed.
**Performance,** pėr-form'ans, *n.* Act of performing; deed; achievement; a literary work; exhibition on the stage; entertainment at a place of amusement.
**Performer,** pėr-form'ėr, *n.* One who performs, as an actor, musician, etc.
**Performing,** pėr-form'ing, *p.a.* Exhibiting performances or tricks.
**Perfume,** pėr'fūm or pėr-fūm', *n.* A pleasant scent or smell; fragrance.—*vt.* (perfuming, perfumed). To scent with perfume; to impregnate with a grateful odor.
**Perfumer,** pėr-fūm'ėr, *n.* One who or that which perfumes; one who sells perfumes.
**Perfumery,** pėr-fūm'ėr-i, *n.* Perfumes in general; the art of preparing perfumes.
**Perfunctory,** pėr-fungk'to-ri, *a.* Done carelessly or in a half-hearted manner; negligent.
**Perhaps,** pėr-haps', *adv.* It may be; peradventure; perchance; possibly.
**Peri,** pē'ri, *n.* In Persian belief, a fairy or spiritual being excluded from paradise till penance is accomplished.
**Pericardium,** pe-ri-kär'di-um, *n.* The membranous sac that incloses the heart.
**Peridot,** pe'ri-dot, *n.* A variety of the precious stone, chrysolite.
**Perigee,** pe'ri-jē, *n.* That point in the moon's orbit nearest the earth.
**Perihelion,** pe-ri-hēl'i-on, *n.* That point of the orbit of a planet or comet nearest the sun.
**Peril,** pe'ril, *n.* Risk; hazard; danger.—*vt.* (perilling, perilled). To hazard; to expose to danger.
**Perilous,** pe'ril-us, *a.* Dangerous; hazardous; full of risk.
**Perilously,** pe'ril-us-li, *adv.* Dangerously.
**Perimeter,** pe-rim'et-ėr, *n.* The outer boundary of a body or figure.
**Period,** pē'ri-od, *n.* The time taken up by a heavenly body in revolving round the sun; the time at which anything ends; end; an indefinite portion of any continued state or existence; a complete sentence; the point that marks the end of a sentence, thus (.).
**Periodic,** pē-ri-do'ik, *a.* Pertaining to period or revolution; happening by recurrence, at a stated time.
**Periodical,** pē-ri-od'ik-al, *n.* A magazine, newspaper, etc., published at regular periods.—*a.* Periodic.
**Peripatetic,** pe'ri-pa-tet''ik, *a.* Walking about; itinerant; pertaining to Aristotle's system of philosophy, taught while walking.—*n.* One who walks; a follower of Aristotle.
**Periphery,** pe-rif'ėr-i, *n.* The boundary line of a figure.
**Periphrasis,** pe-rif'ra-sis, *n.* A roundabout form of expression; circumlocution.
**Periphrastic,** pe-ri-fras'tik, *a.* Characterized by periphrasis; circumlocutory.
**Peripteral,** pe-rip'tėr-al, *a.* Surrounded by a single row of columns, as a temple.
**Periscope,** pe'ri-skōp, *n.* An apparatus or structure rising above the deck of a submarine vessel, giving by means of mirrors, etc., a view of outside surroundings, though the vessel itself remains submerged; a similar device used in trenches.
**Periscopic,** pe-ri-skop'ik, *a.* Viewing on all sides; applied to spectacles having concavo-convex lenses.
**Perish,** pe'rish, *vi.* To die; to wither and decay; to be destroyed; to come to nothing.
**Perishable,** pe'rish-a-bl, *a.* Liable to perish; subject to decay or destruction.
**Peristyle,** pe'ri-stīl, *n.* A range of surrounding columns.
**Peritoneum,** pe'ri-tō-nē''um, *n.* A membrane investing the internal surface of the abdomen,

and the viscera contained in it.
**Peritonitis,** per'i-tō-nī''tis, *n.* Inflammation of the peritoneum.
**Periwig,** pe'ri-wig, *n.* A small wig; a peruke.
**Periwinkle,** pe-ri-wing'kl, *n.* A univalve mollusk found abundantly on British rocks; a British under-shrub.
**Perjure,** pėr'jūr, *vt.* (perjuring, perjured). To forswear; wilfully to make a false oath when administered legally.
**Perjurer,** pėr'jūr-ėr, *n.* One who perjures himself.
**Perjury,** pėr'jū-ri, *n.* Act or crime of forswearing; act of violating an oath or solemn promise.
**Perk,** pėrk, *a.* Trim; spruce; pert.—*vi.* To hold up the head pertly.—*vt.* To make trim; to prank; to hold up (the head) pertly.
**Permanence, Permanency,** pėr'ma-nens, pėr'ma-nen-si, *n.* State or quality of being permanent; duration; fixedness.
**Permanent,** pėr'ma-nent, *a.* Lasting; durable; not decaying; abiding; fixed.
**Permeable,** pėr'mē-a-bl, *a.* That may be permeated or passed through, as solid matter.
**Permeate,** pėr'mē-āt, *vt.* (permeating, permeated). To pass through the pores or interstices of; to penetrate without rupture or displacement of parts.
**Permeation,** pėr-mē-ā'shon, *n.* Act of permeating.
**Permian,** pėr'mi-an, *a.* In *geology,* a term applied to a system of rocks lying beneath the trias and immediately above the carboniferous system.
**Permissible,** pėr-mis'i-bl, *a.* Allowable.
**Permission,** pėr-mi'shon, *n.* Act of permitting; allowance; authorization.
**Permissive,** pėr-mis'iv, *a.* That permits; granting persmision or liberty; allowing.
**Permit,** pėr-mit', *vt.* and *i.* (permitting, permitted). To allow; to grant; to suffer; to concede.—*n.* pėr'mit. A written permission or license given by competent authority.
**Permutation,** pėr-mū-tā'shon, *n.* Interchange; in *mathematics,* any of the ways in which a set of quantities can be arranged.
**Permute,** pėr-mūt', *vt.* To interchange.
**Pernicious,** pėr-ni'shus, *a.* Having the quality of destroying or injuring; destructive; deadly; noxious.
**Perorate,** pe'rō-rāt, *vi.* To make a peroration; to speechify; to spout.
**Peroxide,** pėr-ok'sid, *n.* The oxide of a given base which contains the greatest quantity of oxygen.
**Perpendicular,** pėr-pen-di'kū-lėr, *a.* Perfectly upright or vertical; being at right angles to a given line or surface.—*n.* A line at right angles to the plane of the horizon or to another line.
**Perpendicularly,** pėr-pen-di'kū-lėr-li, *adv.* Vertically; at right angles.
**Perpetrate,** pėr'pe-trāt, *vt.* To do in a bad sense; to be guilty of; to commit.
**Perpetual,** pėr-pe'tū-al, *a.* Continuing without end; permanent; everlasting.
**Perpetuate,** pėr-pe'tū-āt, *vt.* To make perpetual; to preserve from oblivion.
**Perpetuation,** pėr-pe'tū-ā''shon, *n.* Act of perpetuating or making perpetual.
**Perpetuity,** pėr-pe-tū'i-ti, *n.* State or quality of being perpetual; endless duration; something of which there will be no end.
**Perplex,** pėr-pleks', *vt.* To entangle or involve; to embarrass; to distract.
**Perplexing,** pėr-pleks'ing, *p.a.* Troublesome; embarrassing; difficult; intricate.
**Perplexity,** pėr-pleks'i-ti, *n.* State of being puzzled, or at a loss; bewilderment; state of being intricate or involved.
**Perquisite,** pėr'kwi-zit, *n.* Something in addition to regulr wages or salary.
**Persecute,** pėr'se-kūt, *vt.* (persecuting, persecuted). To harass with unjust punishment; to afflict for adherence to a particular creed.
**Persecution,** pėr-se-kū'shon, *n.* Act or practice of persecuting; state of being persecuted; continued annoyance.
**Persecutor,** pėr'se-kūt-ėr, *n.* One who persecutes.
**Perseverance,** pėr-se-vē'rans, *n.* Act or habit of persevering; continued diligence.
**Persevere,** pėr-se-vēr', *vi.* (persevering, persevered). To continue steadfastly in any business; to pursue steadily any design.
**Persevering,** pėr-se-vēr'ing, *p.a.* Given to persevere; constant in purpose.
**Persian,** pėr'shi-an, *a.* Pertaining to Persia, the Persians or their language.—*n.* A native of Persia; language spoken in Persia; a thin skin formerly used for lining.
**Persiflage,** pėr'sē-fläzh, *n.* Idle bantering talk.
**Persist,** pėr-sist', *vi.* To continue steadily in any business or course; to persevere; to continue in a certain state.
**Persistence, Persistency,** pėr-sist'ens, pėr-sist'en-si, *n.* Act or state of persisting; perseverance; continuance; obstinacy.
**Persistent,** pėr-sist'ent, *a.* Persisting; steady; tenacious.
**Persistently,** pėr-sist'ent-li, *adv.* In a persistent manner.
**Person,** pėr'son, *n.* An individual human being; each of the three beings of the Godhead; bodily form;; one of the three inflections of a verb.—In person, by oneself; not by representatives.
**Personable,** pėr'son-a-bl, *a.* Having a well-formed body; of good appearance.
**Personage,** pėr'son-āj, *n.* A person of importance; a man or woman of distinction.
**Personal,** pėr'son-al, *a.* Pertaining to a person; peculiar or proper to him or her; belonging to face and figure; denoting the person in a grammatical sense.
**Personality,** pėr-son-al'i-ti, *n.* State of being personal; that which constitutes an individual a distinct person; disparaging remark on one's conduct and character; in *law,* personal estate.
**Personally,** pėr'son-al-li, *adv.* In person; with respect to an individual; particularly.
**Personalty,** pėr'son-al-ti, *n.* Personal property, in distinction from real property.
**Personate,** pėr'son-āt, *vt.* To assume the character or appearance of; to act the part of.
**Personation,** pėr-son-ā'shon, *n.* The act of personating.
**Personification,** pėr-son'i-fi-kā''shon, *n.* Act of personifying; embodiment; a metaphor which represents inanimate objects as possessing the attributes of persons.
**Personify,** pėr-son'i-fī, *vt.* To represent with the attributes of a person; to impersonate.
**Personnel,** pėr-son-el', *n.* The body of persons employed in any occupation.
**Perspective,** pėr-spek'tiv, *n.* The art of representing objects on a flat surface so that they appear to have their natural dimensions and relations; a representation of objects in perspective; view.—*a.* Pertaining to the art of perspective.
**Perspicacious,** pėr-spi-kā'shus, *a.* Quick-sighted; of acute discernment.
**Perspicuous,** pėr-spi'kū-us, *a.* Clear to the understanding; lucid.
**Perspiration,** pėr-spi-rā'shon, *n.* Act of perspiring; exudation of sweat; sweat.
**Perspiratory,** pėr-spīr'a-to-ri, *a.* Pertaining to perspiration.
**Perspire,** pėr-spīr', *vi.* (perspiring, perspired). To emit the moisture of the body through the skin; to sweat; to exude.—*vt.* To emit through pores.
**Persuade,** pėr-swād', *vt.* (persuading, persuaded). To influence by argument, advice, etc.; to induce; to prevail on.
**Persuasion,** pėr-swā'zhon, *n.* Act of persuading; settled opinion or conviction; a creed or belief; a sect or party.
**Persuasive,** pėr-swā'siv, *a.* Having the power of persuading; calculated to persuade.—*n.* That which persuades; an incitement.
**Pert,** pėrt, *a.* Lively; brisk; saucy; bold.
**Pertain,** pėr-tān', *vi.* To belong; to relate; to concern; to regard.

P

**Pertinacious,** pėr-ti-nā'shus, *a.* Obstinate; inflexible; determined; persistent.
**Pertinacity,** pėr-ti-nas'i-ti, *n.* Obstinacy; resolution; constancy.
**Pertinence, Pertinency,** pėr'ti-nens, pėr'ti-nen-si, *n.* Quality or state of being pertinent; fitness; appositeness.
**Pertinent,** pėr'ti-nent, *a.* Related to the subject or matter in hand; apposite; fit.
**Pertinently,** pėr'ti-nent-li, *adv.* In a pertinent manner; appositely; to the purpose.
**Perturb,** pėr-tėrb', *vt.* To disturb; to agitate; to disquiet; to confuse.
**Perturbation,** pėr-tėrb-ā'shon, *n.* Act of perturbing; disorder; uneasiness; cause of disquiet.
**Perusal,** pe-rūz'al, *n.* Act of perusing or reading.
**Peruse,** pe-rūz', *vt.* (perusing, perused). To read through; to read with attention; to examine carefully.
**Peruvian,** pe-rū'vi-an, *a.* Pertaining to Peru.—*n.* A native of Peru.
**Pervade,** pėr-vād', *vt.* (pervading, pervaded). To pass or flow through; to permeate; to be diffused through.
**Pervasive,** pėr-vā'siv, *a.* Tending or having power to pervade.
**Perverse,** pėr-vėrs', *a.* Obstinate in the wrong; stubborn; untractable; petulant.
**Perversely,** pėr-vėrs'li, *adv.* Stubbornly; obstinately in the wrong.
**Perversion,** pėr-vėr'shon, *n.* A diverting from the true intent or object; misapplication.
**Perversity,** pėr-vėr'si-ti, *n.* State or quality of being perverse; disposition to thwart.
**Pervert,** pėr-vert', *vt.* To turn from truth or proper purpose; to corrupt; to misinterpret; to misapply.—*n.* pėr'vėrt. One who has been perverted.
**Pervious,** pėr'vi-us, *a.* That may be penetrated; permeable.
**Peseta,** pe-sē'ta, *n.* A Spanish coin.
**Pessimism,** pes'im-izm, *n.* The doctrine that the present state of things tends only to evil; the tendency always to look at the dark side of things.
**Pessimist,** pes'im-ist, *n.* One who believes in pessimism, or takes an unfavorable view of affairs.
**Pessimistic,** pes-im-is'tik, *a.* Pertaining to pessimism.
**Pest,** pest, *n.* A deadly epidemic disease; plague; pestilence; a mischievous person.
**Pester,** pes'tėr, *vt.* To plague; to trouble; to annoy with little vexations.
**Pestilence,** pes'ti-lens, *n.* Any contagious disease that is epidemic and fatal; something morally evil or destructive.
**Pestilent,** pes'ti-lent, *a.* Pestilential; mischievous; pernicious; troublesome.
**Pestilential,** pes-ti-len'shal, *a.* Partaking of the nature of a pestilence or the plague; destructive; pernicious.
**Pestle,** pes'l, *n.* An instrument for pounding substances in a mortar.—*vt.* and *i.* (pestling, pestled). To pound with a pestle.
**Pet,** pet, *n.* A darling; any little animal fondled and indulged; fit of peevishness.—*vt.* (petting, petted). To fondle; to indulge.
**Petal,** pe'tal, *n.* A flower leaf.
**Petard,** pe-tärd, *n.* An engine of war fixed on grates, barricades, etc., to destroy them by explosion.
**Petiole,** pe'ti-ol, *n.* The foot-stalk of a leaf.
**Petite,** pė-tēt', *a.* Small in figure; tiny.
**Petition,** pē-ti'shon, *n.* An entreaty, supplication, or prayer; a written application in legal proceedings.—*vt.* To supplicate; to solicit.
**Petitionary,** pē-ti'shon-a-ri, *a.* Supplicatory; containing a petition.
**Petitioner,** pē-ti'shon-ėr, *n.* One who petitions or presents a petition.
**Petrel,** pet'rel, *n.* A web-footed sea-bird often found far from land.
**Petrifaction,** pet-ri-fak'shon, *n.* the process of changing into stone; a fossil.
**Petrifactive,** pet-ri-fak'tiv, *a.* Having power to convert into stone.
**Petrify,** pet-ri-fī, *vt.* To turn into stone or a fossil; to paralyze or stupefy.—*vi.* To become stone, or of a stony hardiness.
**Petrol,** pet'rol, *n.* Petroleum spirit; refined petroleum used as the source of power for the internal-combustion engines of automobiles, airplanes, etc.
**Petroleum,** pe-trō'lē-um, *n.* Rock-oil; an inflammable liquid found in the earth.
**Petrology,** pe-trol'o-ji, *n.* The study of rocks.
**Petticoat,** pet'i-kōt, *n.* A loose under-garment worn by women.
**Petto,** pet'tō, *n.* The breast; hence, *in petto,* in secrecy.
**Petty,** pet'i, *a.* Small; little; trifling; trivial.
**Petulance, Petulancy,** pe'tū-lans, pe'tū-lan-si, *n.* Quality of being petulant; peevishness; pettishness; frowardness.
**Petulant,** pe'tū-lant, *a.* Irritable; peevish; fretful; saucy; pert; capricious.
**Pew,** pū, *n.* An inclosed seat in a church.
**Pewit,** pē'wit, *n.* The lapwing or peewit.
**Pewter,** pū'tėr, *n.* An alloy mainly of tin and lead; a vessel made of pewter.—*a.* Relating to or made of pewter.
**Pewterer,** pū'tėr-ėr, *n.* One who makes vessels and utensils of pewter.
**Pewtery,** pū'tė-ri, *a.* Belonging to or resembling pewter.
**Phaeton,** fā'ton, *n.* An open carriage on four wheels.
**Phalange,** fa-lanj', *n.* One of the small bones of the fingers and toes.
**Phalanx,** fal'angks, *n.*; pl. **-anges, anxes.** The heavy-armed infantry of an ancient Greek army; a body of troops in close array; a small bone of the fingers or toes.
**Phallic,** fal'lik, *a.* Pertaining to the phallus.
**Phallus,** fal'lus, *n.* The emblem of the generative power in nature, especially in certain religious usages.
**Phantasm,** fan'tazm, *n.* An apparition; a phantom; an idea, notion, or fancy.
**Phantasmagoria,** fan-tas'ma-gō''ri-a, *n.* An exhibition of figures by shadows, as by the magic lantern; illusive images.
**Phantasmal,** fan-taz'mal, *a.* Spectral; illusive.
**Phantom,** fan'tom, *n.* An apparition; a specter; a fancied vision; a phantasm.
**Pharisaic, Pharisaical,** fa-ri-sā'ik, fa-ri-sā'ik-al, *a.* Pertaining to or resembling the Pharisees; hypocritical.
**Pharisaism,** fa'ri-sā-izm, *n.* The notions, doctrines, and conduct of the Pharisees; formality and hypocrisy in religion.
**Pharisee,** fa'ri-sē, *n.* A Jew strict in religious observances; a hypocrite.
**Pharmaceutic, Pharmaceutical,** fär-ma-sū'tik, fär-ma-sū'tik-al, *a.* Pertaining to the knowledge or art of pharmacy.
**Pharmaceutics,** fär-ma-sū'tiks, *n.* Pharmacy.
**Pharmacology,** fär-ma-kol'o-ji, *n.* The science of drugs; the art of preparing medicines.
**Pharmacopeia,** fär'ma-kō-pē''a, *n.* A book describing the preparation of medicines.
**Pharmacy,** fär'ma-si, *n.* The art or practice of preparing medicines.
**Pharos,** fā'ros, *n.* A lighthouse.
**Pharynx,** fā'ringks, *n.* The muscular sac between the mouth and the esophagus.
**Phase,** fāz, *n.* A particular stage of the moon or a planet in respect to illumination; state of a varying phenomenon; one of the various aspects of a question.
**Phasis,** fā'siz, *n.*; pl. **phases,** fā'sēz. A phase: used in astronomy.
**Pheasant,** fe'zant, *n.* A bird commonly reared and preserved for sport and food.
**Pheasantry,** fe'zant-ri, *n.* A place for breeding, rearing, and keeping pheasants.

**Phenomenal,** fē-no'men-al, *a.* Pertaining to or constituted by a phenomenon; extremely remarkable; astounding.
**Phenomenon,** fē-no'me-non, *n.*; pl. **-mena.** An appearance; anything visible; an appearance whose cause is not immediately obvious; something extraordinary.
**Phial,** fī'al, *n.* A small glass bottle.
**Philander,** fi-lan'dėr, *vi.* To make love sentimentally to a lady; to flirt.
**Philanthropic, Philanthropical,** fī-lan-throp'ik, fī-lan-throp'ik-al, *a.* Relating to philanthropy; entertaining good-will towards all men; benevolent.
**Philanthropist,** fī-lan'throp-ist, *n.* One devoted to philanthropy; one who exerts himself in doing good to his fellowmen.
**Philanthropy,** fī-lan'thro-pi, *n.* The love of man or of mankind; benevolence towards the whole human family.
**Philatelist,** fi-lat'e-list, *n.* One who collects postage-stamps.
**Philately,** fi-lat'e-li, *n.* The practice of collecting postage-stamps.
**Philharmonic,** fil-här-mon'ik, *a.* Loving harmony; musical.
**Philippic,** fi-lip'ik, *n.* A discourse or declamation full of acrimonious invective.
**Philistine,** fi-lis'tīn or fil'is-tin, *n.* A person deficient in culture, and wanting in taste; a person of narrow views.
**Philistinism,** fil'is-tin-izm, *n.* Manner or modes of thinking of Philistines.
**Philological, Philologic,** fil-ō-loj'ik-al, fil-ō-loj'ik, *a.* Pertaining to philology.
**Philologist, Philologer,** fi-lol'o-jist, fi-lol'o-jėr, *n.* One versed in philology.
**Philology,** fi-lol'o-ji, *n.* The study of language; linguistic science.
**Philomel, Philomela,** fil'ō-mel, fil-ō-mē'la, *n.* The nightingale.
**Philosopher,** fi-los'o-fėr, *n.* A person versed in philosophy; one who studies moral or mental science.
**Philosophic, Philosophical,** fi-lō-sof'ik, fi-lō-sof'ik-al, *a.* Pertaining or according to philosophy; given to philosophy; calm; cool; temperate; rational.
**Philosophically,** fi-lō-sof'ik-al-li, *adv.* Calmly; wisely; rationally.
**Philosophize,** fi-los'o-fīz', *vi.* To act the philosopher; to reason like a philosopher; to formulate a philosophical theory.
**Philosophy,** fi-los'o-fi, *n.* The science which tries to account for the phenomena of the universe; metaphysics; the general principles underlying some branch of knowledge; practical wisdom.
**Philter,** fil'tėr, *n.* A love-charm; a potion supposed to excite love.
**Phlebitis,** flē-bī'tis, *n.* Inflammation of a vein.
**Phlebotomy,** flē-bot'o-mi, *n.* The act or practice of opening a vein; blood-letting.
**Phlegm,** flem, *n.* The viscid matter of the digestive and respiratory passages; bronchial mucus; coldness; indifference.
**Phlegmatic,** fleg-mat'ik, *a.* Abounding in or generating phlegm; cold; sluggish.
**Phlogistic,** flo-jis'tik, *a.* Pertaining to phlogiston; inflammatory.
**Phlogiston,** flo-jis'ton, *n.* A hypothetical element formerly thought to exist and to be pure fire or the principle of combustion.
**Phoenix,** fē-niks, *n.* A bird of ancient legend, said to live 500 years, when it burnt itself, and rose again from its ashes; an emblem of immotality; a paragon.
**Pholas,** fō-las, *n.* A marine mollusk which pierces rocks, wood, etc.
**Phonetic,** fō-net'ik, *a.* Pertaining to the voice; representing sounds.
**Phonetics,** fō-net'iks, *n.pl.* The doctrine or science of sounds, especially of the human voice; the representation of sounds.
**Phonograph,** fō'nō-graf, *n.* An instrument for registering and reproducing sounds; a predecessor of the gramophone.
**Phosgene,** fos'jēn, *n.* A poison gas, carbon oxychloride.
**Phosphate,** fos'fāt, *n.* A salt of phosphoric acid.
**Phosphorate,** fos'for-āt, *vt.* To combine or impregnate with phosphorus.
**Phosphoresce,** fos-for-es', *vi.* To give out a phosphoric light.
**Phosphorescence,** fos-for-es'ens, *n.* State of quality of being phosphorescent.
**Phosphorescent,** fos-for-es'ent, *a.* Shining with a faint light like that of phosphorus; luminous without sensible heat.
**Phosphoric,** fos-fo'rik, *a.* Pertaining to, or obtained from, or resembling phosphorus.
**Phosphorize,** fos'for-īz, *vt.* To phosphorate.
**Phosphorous,** fos'for-us, *a.* Pertaining to or obtained from phosphorus.
**Phosphorus,** fos'for-us, *n.* An elementary substance which undergoes slow combustion at common temperatures.
**Photograph,** fō-'tō-graf, *n.* A picture obtained by photography.—*vt.* To produce a representation of by photographic means.
**Photographer,** fō-tog'raf-ėr, *n.* One who takes pictures by means of photography.
**Photographic, Photographical,** fō-tō-graf'ik, fō-tō-graf'ik-al, *a.* Pertaining to photography.
**Photography,** fō-tog'ra-fi, *n.* The art or practice of producing representations of scenes and objects by the action of light on chemically prepared surfaces.
**Photogravure,** fō'tō-grav-ūr, *n.* A process by which an engraving is produced on a metal plate by light acting on a sensitive surface.
**Photology,** fō-tol'o-ji, *n.* The doctrine or science of light.
**Photometer,** fō-tom'et-ėr, *n.* An instrument for measuring the intensity of lights.
**Phrase,** frāz, *n.* A short sentence or expression; an idiom; style; diction.—*vt.* and *i.* (phrasing, phrased). To style; to express.
**Phraseology,** frā-zē-ol'o-ji, *n.* Manner of expression; peculiar words used in a sentence; diction; style.
**Phrenetic,** fre-net'ik, *a.* Having the mind disordered; frantic.—*n.* A frenzied person.
**Phrenic,** fren'ik, *a.* Belonging to the diaphragm.
**Phrenologist,** fre-nol'o-jist, *n.* One versed in phrenologyy.
**Phrenology,** fre-nol'o-ji, *n.* The doctrine that a person's endowments may be discovered by the configuration of the skull.
**Phthisical,** tiz'ik-al, *a.* Having or belonging to phthisis; consumptive.
**Phthisis,** thī'sis, *n.* A wasting disease of the lungs, commonly called consumption.
**Phylactery,** fi-lak'tėr-i, *n.* An amulet worn by the Jews, containing a strip of parchment inscribed with Old Testament texts.
**Physic,** fi'zik, *n.* The science of medicine; the art of healing; a medicine; a cathartic.—*vt.* (physicking, physicked). To treat with physic; to remedy.
**Physical,** fi'zik-al, *a.* Pertaining to nature or natural productions; bodily, as opposed to mental or moral; material; pertaining to physics.
**Physically,** fi'zik-al-li, *adv.* In a physical manner; as regards the material world; bodily.
**Physician,** fi-zi'shan, *n.* A person skilled in the art of healing; a doctor.
**Physicist,** fi'zi-sist, *n.* One skilled in physics; a natural philosopher.
**Physics,** fi'ziks, *n.* That branch of science which deals with mechanics, dynamics, light, heat, sound, electricity, and magnetism; natural philosophy.
**Physiognomist,** fi-zi-og'nō-mist, *n.* One who is skilled in physiognomy.
**Physiognomy,** fi-zi-og'no-mi, *n.* The art of perceiving a person's character by his counte-

nance; particular cast or expression of countenance.
**Physiography,** fi-zi-og'ra-fi, *n.* The science of the earth's physical features and phenomena; physical geography.
**Physiologic, Physiological,** fi'zi-ō-loj''ik, fi'zi-ō-loj''ik-al, *a.* Pertaining to physiology.
**Physiologist,** fi-zi-ol'o-jist, *n.* One who is versed in physiology.
**Physiology,** fi-zi-ol'o-ji, *n.* The science of the phenomena of life; the study of the functions of living beings.
**Physique,** fi-zēk', *n.* A person's physical or bodily structure or constitution.
**Phytoid,** fī'toid, *a.* Plant-like.
**Phytology,** fī-tol'o-ji, *n.* The science of plants; botany.
**Piacular,** pī-ak'ū-lär, *a.* Expiatory; having power to atone; requiring expiation.
**Pia-mater,** pī'a-mā-tėr, *n.* A membrane investing the surface of the brain.
**Pianist,** pi'an-ist, *n.* A performer on the piano.
**Piano,** pi-ä'nō, *a.* In *music,* soft.
**Piano,** pi-an'ō, *n.* A musical metal-stringed instrument with a key-board, sounded by hammers acting on the strings.
**Piazza,** pi-az'za, *n.* A rectangular open space surrounded by colonnades.
**Pibroch,** pē'broch, *n.* A species of music for the bagpipe.
**Pica,** pī'ka, *n.* A printing type having six lines in an inch, used as the standard size.
**Picador,** pik-a-dōr', *n.* A horseman with a lance who excites the bull in a bull-fight.
**Picaresque,** pik-a-resk', *a.* Pertaining to rogues; describing the fortunes of adventurers.
**Picaroon,** pik-a-rön', *n.* A rogue or cheat; one who lives by his wits.
**Piccolo,** pik'ko-lō, *n.* A small flute with shrill tones; an octave flute.
**Piceous,** pis'ē-us, *a.* Pitchy.
**Pick,** pik, *vt.* To strike at with something pointed; to peck at; to clean by the teeth, fingers, etc.; to select; to pluck; to gather.—*vi.* To eat slowly; to nibble; to pilfer.—*n.* A pointed tool; a pick-axe; choice; selection.
**Pickaxe,** pik'aks, *n.* A sharp-pointed iron tool used in digging, mining, etc.
**Picked,** pikt, *p.a.* Select; choice.
**Picker,** pik'ėr, *n.* One who picks; a name of tools or apparatus of many various shapes.
**Pickerel,** pik'ėr-el, *n.* A fresh-water fish of the pike family.
**Picket,** pik'et, *n.* A pointed stake used in fortification; a pale; an advanced guard or outpost; a game at cards.—*vt.* To fortify with pickets; to post as a guard of observation.
**Picking,** pik'ing, *n.* Act of one who picks; *pl.* perquisites not always honestly obtained.
**Pickle,** pik'l, *n.* Brine; a solution of salt and water for preserving flesh, fish, etc.; vegetables preserved in vinegar; a state of difficulty or disorder; a troublesome child.—*vt.* (pickling, pickled). To preserve in or treat with pickle.
**Pickpocket,** pik'pok-et, *n.* One who steals from the pocket of another.
**Picnic,** pik'nik, *n.* and *a.* A pleasure-party the members of which carry provisions with them.—*vi.* (picnicking, picnicked). To take part in a picnic party.
**Picric,** pik'rik, *a.* An acid used in dyeing.
**Pictorial,** pik-tō'ri-al, *a.* Pertaining to or forming pictures; illustrated by pictures.
**Pictorially,** pik-tō'ri-al-li, *adv.* In a pictorial manner; with pictures or engravings.
**Picture,** pik'tūr, *n.* A painting, drawing, etc., exhibiting the resemblance of anything; any resemblance or representation; *pl.* the moving photographs shown in cinematography; the cinema.—*vt.* To represent pictorially; to present an ideal likeness of; to describe in a vivid manner.
**Picturesque,** pik-tūr-esk', *a.* Forming, or fitted to form, a pleasing picture; abounding with vivid imagery; graphic.
**Piddle,** pid'l, *vi.* (piddling, piddled). To deal in trifles; to peddle.
**Pie,** pī, *n.* A paste baked with something in or under it; a mass of types unsorted; the magpie.
**Piebald,** pī'bald, *a.* Having spots or patches of various colors; pied; mongrel.
**Piece,** pēs, *n.* A portion of anything; a distinct part; a composition or writing of no great length; a separate performance; a picture; a coin; a single firearm.—*vt.* (piecing, pieced). To patch; to join.—*vi.* To unite or join on.
**Piecemeal,** pēs'mēl, *adv.* In or by pieces; in fragments; by little and little.
**Piecer,** pēs'ėr, *n.* One who pieces; one employed in a spinning factory to join threads.
**Piece-work,** pēs'wėrk, *n.* Word done by the piece or job; work paid by quantity.
**Pied,** pīd, *a.* Party-colored; spotted.
**Pier,** pēr, *n.* A mass of solid stonework for supporting an arch, bridge, etc.; a projecting wharf or landing-place.
**Pierce,** pērs, *vt.* (piercing, pierced). To stab or perforate with a pointed instrument; to penetrate; to move deeply.—*vi.* To enter; to penetrate.
**Piercer,** pērs'ėr, *n.* One who or that which pierces; an instrument that bores; that organ of an insect with which it pierces.
**Piercing,** pērs'ing, *p.a.* Penetrating; cutting; keen; sharp; severe.
**Piety,** pī'e-ti, *n.* Reverence or veneration towards God; godliness; devotion; religion.
**Pig,** pig, *n.* A young swine; a swine in general; an oblong mass of unforged metal.—*vt.* or *i.* (pigging, pigged). To bring forth pigs; to act like pigs.
**Pigeon,** pi'jon, *n.* A well-known bird of many varieties; a dove; a simpleton; a gull.
**Pigeon-hole,** pi'jon-hōl, *n.* A hole for pigeons to enter their dwelling; a division in a desk or case for holding papers.
**Pig-headed,** pig'hed-ed, *a.* Having a head like a pig; stupidly obstinate.
**Pig-iron,** pig'ī-ėrn, *n.* Iron in pigs, as it comes from the blast-furnace.
**Pigment,** pig'ment, *n.* Paint; any preparation used by painters, dyers, etc., to impart colors to bodies; coloring matter.
**Pig-skin,** pig'skin, *n.* The skin of a pig, especially when prepared for saddlery, etc.
**Pig-tail,** pig'tāl, *n.* The tail of a pig; the hair of the head tied behind in a tail.
**Pike,** pīk, *n.* A spike or pointed piece; a fork used in husbandry; a fresh-water fish with a pointed snout; a toll-bar.
**Pikeman,** pīk'man, *n.* A soldier armed with a pike.
**Pilaster,** pi-las'tėr, *n.* A square pillar, slightly projecting from a wall.
**Pilch,** pilch, *n.* A flannel cloth for an infant.
**Pilchard,** pil'shärd, *n.* A fish resembling the herring, but smaller.
**Pile,** pīl, *n.* A heap; a large mass of buildings; a galvanic or voltaic battery; hair; nap on cloth; a beam driven into the ground to support some superstructure; a heraldic figure like a wedge.—*vt.* (piling, piled). To heap; to amass; to drive piles into; to support with piles.
**Piles,** pīlz, *n.pl.* A disease of the rectum near the anus; hemorrhoids.
**Pilfer,** pil'fėr, *vi.* To steal in small quantities; to practice petty theft.—*vt.* To filch.
**Pilferer,** pil'fėr-ėr, *n.* One who pilfers.
**Pilgrim,** pil'grim, *n.* A wanderer; one who travels to visit a holy place or relics.
**Pilgrimage,** pil'grim-āj, *n.* A journey to some holy place; the journey of human life.
**Pill,** pil, *n.* A medicine in the form of a little ball; anything nauseous to be accepted.—*vt.* To dose with pills; to form into pills; to rob; to plunder.
**Pillage,** pil'āj, *n.* Act of plundering; plunder; spoil.—*vt.* (pillaging, pillaged). To rob by open

violence; to plunder.
**Pillager,** pil'āj-ėr, *n.* One who pillages.
**Pillar,** pil'ėr, *n.* A column; a perpendicular support; a supporter.
**Pill-box,** pil-boks, *n.* A small concrete blockhouse, used as a machine-gun emplacement.
**Pillion,** pil'yon, *n.* A cushion for a woman to ride on behind a person on horseback; the pad of a saddle.
**Pillory,** pil'o-ri, *n.* A frame of wood with movable boards and holes, through which were put the head and hands of an offender.—*vt.* (pillorying, pilloried). To punish with the pillory; to expose to ridicule, abuse, etc.
**Pillow,** pil'ō, *n.* A long soft cushion; something that bears or supports.—*vt.* To rest or lay on for support.
**Pillow-case, Pillow-slip,** pil'ō-kās, pil'ō-slip, *n.* The movable case or sack which is drawn over a pillow.
**Pilot,** pī'lot, *n.* One whose occupation is to steer ships; a guide; a director of one's course.—*vt.* To act as pilot of; to guide through dangers or difficulties.
**Pimp,** pimp, *n.* A man who provides gratifications for others' lusts; a procurer.—*vi.* To pander; to procure women for others.
**Pimpernel,** pim'pėr-nel, *n.* A little red-flowered annual found in British cornfields.
**Pimple,** pim'pl, *n.* A small elevation of the skin, with an inflamed base.
**Pimpled,** pim'pld, *a.* Having pimples; full of pimples.
**Pimply,** pim'pli, *a.* Pimpled.
**Pin,** pin, *n.* A longish piece of metal, wood, etc., used for a fastening, or as a support; a peg; a bolt.—*vt.* (pinning, pinned). To fasten with a pin or pins; to hold fast.—*vt.* To inclose, to pen or pound.
**Pinafore,** pin'a-fōr, *n.* A little apron.
**Pincers,** pin'sėrz, *n.pl.* An instrument for gripping anything; nippers; prehensile claws.
**Pinch,** pinsh, *vt.* To press hard or squeeze; to nip; to afflict.—*vi.* To press painfully; to be sparing.—*n.* A close compression, as with the fingers; a nip; a pang; straits; a strong iron lever; as much as is taken by the finger and thumb; a small quantity.
**Pinchbeck,** pinsh'bek, *n.* An alloy of copper and zinc resembling gold.—*a.* Sham; not genuine.
**Pincher,** pinsh'ėr, *n.* One who or that which pinches; *pl.* pincers.
**Pin-cushion,** pin'ku-shon, *n.* A small cushion in which pins are kept.
**Pindaric,** pin-da'rik, *a.* After the manner of Pindar, the Greek lyric poet.—*n.* An ode in imitation of Pindar; an irregular ode.
**Pine,** pīn, *n.* A valuable evergreen coniferous tree, furnishing timber, turpentine, pitch, and resin; the pine-apple.—*vi.* (pining, pined). To languish; to grow weakly with pain, grief, etc.
**Pineal,** pin'ē-al, *a.* Resembling a pine-cone in shape.
**Pineapple,** pīn'ap-l, *n.* A fruit like the cone of a pine-tree but different in character; the plant itself.
**Pinery,** pīn'ėr-i, *n.* A hot-house for pineapples; a place where pine trees grow.
**Piney, Piny,** pīn'i, *a.* Pertaining to pines; abounding with pines.
**Pinion,** pin'yon, *n.* A bird's wing; the joint of a wing remotest from the body; a large wing-feather; a small toothed wheel; a fetter for the arms.—*vt.* To bind the wings of; to cut off, as the first joint of the wing; to fetter.
**Pink,** pingk, *n.* A garden flower; a light rose-color or pigment; the flower or something supremely excellent.—*a.* Of a fine light rose-color.—*vt.* To work in eyelet-holes; to scallop; to stab.—*vi.* To wink or blink.
**Pink-eye,** pingk'ī, *n.* A disease attacking horses, a kind of influenza.
**Pink-eyed,** pingk'īd, *a.* Having small eyes.
**Pin-money,** pin'mun-i, *n.* A sum of money settled on a wife for her private expenses.
**Pinnace,** pin'ās, *n.* A small vessel navigated with oars and sails, usually with two masts; a boat with eight oars.
**Pinnacle,** pin'a-kl, *n.* A rocky peak; the summit; a minor structure or turret above a building.
**Pinnate,** pin'āt, *a.* Shaped or branching like a feather.
**Pint,** pīnt, *n.* The eighth part of a gallon.
**Pioneer,** pī-on-ēr', *n.* One whose business is to prepare the road for an army, make entrenchments, etc.; one who leads the way.—*vt.* To prepare a way for.—*vi.* To act as pioneer.
**Pious,** pī'us, *a.* Devout; godly; holy; proceeding from piety.
**Pip,** pip, *n.* The kernel or seed of fruit; a spot on cards; a disease of fowls.
**Pipe,** pīp, *n.* A wind-instrument of music; a long tube; a tube with a bowl at one end for tobacco; the windpipe; a call of a bird; a wine measure containing about 105 imperial gallons.—*vi.* (piping, piped). To play on a pipe; to whistle.—*vt.* To utter in a high tone; to call by a pipe or whistle.
**Pipe-clay,** pīp'kla, *n.* The purest kind of potter's-clay.—*vt.* To whiten with pipe-clay.
**Piper,** pīp'ėr, *n.* One who plays on a pipe; a bagpiper; a sea-urchin.
**Piping,** pīp'ing, *p.a.* Giving out a whistling sound; accompanied by the music of the pipe; boiling.—*n.* Pipes, as for water, etc.; a jointed stem for propagating plants.
**Pippin,** pip'in, *n.* An apple of various kinds.
**Pipy,** pīp'i, *a.* Resembling a pipe; tubular.
**Piquancy,** pē'kan-si, *n.* Quality of being piquant; sharpness; pungency.
**Piquant,** pē'kant, *a.* Making a lively impression; sharp; lively; interesting; pungent.
**Pique,** pēk, *n.* Irritation; offense taken; slight anger.—*vt.* (piquing, piqued). To nettle; to touch with envy, jealousy, etc.; to pride or value (oneself).—*vi.* To cause irritation.
**Piquet,** pik'et, *n.* A picket; a game at cards for two, with thirty-two cards.
**Piracy,** pī'ra-si, *n.* The act or practice of robbing on the high seas; infringement of the law of copyright.
**Pirate,** pī'rāt, *n.* A robber on the high seas; a ship engaged in piracy; one who publishes others' writings without permission.—*vi.* (pirating, pirated). To rob on the high-seas.—*vt.* To take without right, as writings.
**Piratical,** pī-rat'ik-al, *a.* Having the character of a pirate: pertaining to piracy.
**Piratically,** pī-rat'ik-al-li, *adv.* In a piratical manner; by piracy.
**Pirogue,** pi-rōg', *n.* A canoe made from a trunk of a tree hollowed out.
**Pirouette,** pi'rö-et, *n.* A turning about on the toes in dancing.—*vt.* To make a pirouette; to whirl about on the toes.
**Piscatorial, Piscatory,** pis-kā-tō'ri-al, pis'ka-to-ri, *a.* Related to fishing.
**Pisces,** pis'sēz, *n.pl.* The Fishes, a sign in the zodiac; the vertebrate animals of the class fishes.
**Pismire,** pis'mīr, *n.* The ant or emmet.
**Piss,** pis, *vi.* To discharge urine.—*vt.* To eject, as urine.
**Pistachio,** pis-tā'shi-ō, *n.* The nut of a small tree cultivated in S. Europe for its fruit; the tree itself, also called *pistacia*.
**Pistil,** pis'til, *n.* The seed-bearing organ of a flower.
**Pistillate,** pis'til-lāt, *a.* Having a pistil.
**Pistol,** pis'tol, *n.* A small firearm fired with one hand.—*vt.* (pistolling, pistolled). To shoot with a pistol.
**Pistole,** pis-tōl', *n.* An old gold coin of Spain, France.
**Piston,** pis'ton, *n.* a cylindrical piece of metal which fits exactly into a hollow cylinder, and works alternately in two directions.
**Piston-rod,** pis'ton-rod, *n.* A rod which connects

a piston to some other piece, and either moved by the piston or moving it.

**Pit,** pit, *n.* A hollow in the earth; the shaft of a mine; a vat in tanning, dyeing, etc.' a concealed hole for catching wild beasts; a small cavity or depression; part of the floor of a theater.—*vt.* (pitting, pitted). To lay in a pit or hole; to mark with little hollows; to set in competition.

**Pitch,** pich, *vt.* To thrust, as a pointed object; to fix; to set; to throw; to set the key-note of; to set in array; to smear or cover with pitch.—*vi.* To settle; to fall headlong; to fix choice; to encamp; to rise and fall, as a ship.—*n.* A throw; degree of elevation; highest rise; descent; elevation of a note; (cricket) prepared ground between wickets; a thick dark resinous substance obtained from tar.

**Pitch-dark,** pich'därk, *a.* Dark as pitch; very dark.

**Pitcher,** pich'ėr, *n.* A vessel with a spout, for holding liquors.

**Pitchfork,** pīch'fork, *n.* A fork used in throwing hay, etc.; a tuning-fork.—*vt.* To lift or throw with a pitchfork; to put suddenly into any position.

**Pitch-pipe,** pich'pīp, *n.* A small pipe used in finding or regulating the pitch of a tune.

**Piteous,** pi'tē-us, *a.* That may excite pity; sorrowful; sad; miserable; pitiful.

**Pitfall,** pit'fal, *n.* A pit slightly covered over, forming a kind of trap.

**Pith,** pith, *n.* The spongy substance in the center of exogenous plants; the spinal cord or marrow of an animal; strength or force; energy; cogency; essence.

**Pithily,** pith'i-li, *adv.* In a pithy manner; cogently; with energy.

**Pithy,** pith'i, *a.* Consisting of pith; terse and forcible; energetic; sententious.

**Pitiable,** pi'ti-a-bl, *a.* Deserving pity or compassion; lamentable; miserable.

**Pitiably,** pi'ti-a-bli, *adv.* Woefully.

**Pitiful,** pi'ti-ful, *a.* Full of pity; compassionate; woeful; to bë pitied; paltry; despicable.

**Pitiless,** pi'ti-les, *a.* Feeling no pity; hard-hearted; merciless; relentless; unmerciful.

**Pitman,** pit'man, *n.* One who works in a pit; a miner.

**Pit-saw,** pit'sa *n.* A large saw worked by two men, one of whom stands in a pit below.

**Pittance,** pit'ans, *n.* A very small portion allowed or assigned; a charity gift.

**Pity,** pi'ti, *n.* Sympathy or compassion; ground of pity; thing to be regretted.—*vt.* (pitying, pitied). To feel pain or grief for; to sympathize with.—*vi.* To be compassionate.

**Pivot,** pi'vot, *n.* A pin on which something turns; a turning-point; that on which important results depend.—*vt.* To place on or furnish with a pivot.

**Pix,** piks, *n. See* Pyx.

**Pixy, Pixie,** pik'si, *n.* A sort of English fairy.

**Placable,** pla'ka-bl, *a.* Readily appeased or pacified; willing to forgive.

**Placard,** plak'ėrd or pla-kärd', *n.* A written or printed bill posted in a public place; a poster.—*vt.* To post placards.

**Place,** plās, *n.* An open space in a town; a locality, spot, or site; position; room; an edifice; quarters; a passage in a book; rank; office; calling; ground or occasion; stead.—*vt.* (placing, placed). To put or set; to locate; to appoint or set in an office, rank, or condition; to invest; to lend.

**Placenta,** pla-sen'ta, *n.* The after-birth; an organ developed in mammals during pregnancy, connecting the mother and fetus; the part of the seed-vessel to which the seeds are attached.

**Placid,** pla'sid, *a.* Gentle; quiet; mild; unruffled; calm.

**Placidity,** pla-sid'i-ti, *n.* State or quality of being placid.

**Plagiarism,** plā'ji-a-rizm, *n.* The act of plagiarizing; literary theft.

**Plagiarist,** plā'ji-a-rist, *n.* One who plagiarizes the writings of another.

**Plagiarize,** plā'ji-a-rīz, *vt.* To purloin the published thoughts or words of another.

**Plagiary,** plā'ji-a-ri, *n.* One who purloins another's writings; a literary thief; plagiarism.

**Plague,** plāg, *n.* A stroke or calamity; severe trouble; a pestilential disease; a person who annoys or troubles.—*vt.* (plaguing, plagued). To vex; to scourge as with disease or any evil.

**Plaid,** plād, *n.* A large woollen cloth, frequently of tartan, worn as a wrap.

**Plain,** plān, *a.* Without elevations and depressions; smooth; level; clear; undisguised; artless; sincere; simple; mere; bare; evident; obvious.—*n.* A piece of level land.—*adv.* Distinctly.

**Plain-dealing,** plān'dēl-ing, *n.* Conduct free from stratagem or disguise; sincerity.—*a.* Dealing with sincerity.

**Plainly,** plān'li, *adv.* Distinctly; sincerely; clearly; bluntly.

**Plain-spoken,** plān'spōk-n, *a.* Speaking plainly or with bluntness.

**Plaintiff,** plānt'if, *n.* In *law,* the person who commences a suit before a tribunal for the recovery of a claim: opposed to *defendant.*

**Plaintive,** plānt'iv, *a.* Expressive of sorrow or grief; repining; mournful; sad.

**Plait,** plāt, *n.* A fold; a doubling of cloth, etc.; a braid, as of hair, etc.—*vt.* To fold; to double in narrow strips; to braid.

**Plaited,** plāt'ed, *p.a.* Folded; braided.

**Plan,** plan, *n.* The representation of anything on a flat surface; sketch; scheme; project; method; process.—*vt.* (planning, planned). To form a plan or representation of; to scheme.—*vi.* To form a scheme.

**Plane,** plān, *a.* Without elevations or depressions; perfectly level; even; flat.—*n.* A smooth or perfectly level surface; a joiner's tool, used ir paring or smoothing wood.—*vt.* To make level or smooth; to smooth by the use of a plane.

**Plane, Plane-tree,** plān, plān'trē, *n.* A forest tree with a straight smooth stem and palmate leaves; a kind of maple.

**Planet,** pla'net, *n.* A celestial body which revolves about the sun or other center.

**Planetary,** pla'net-a-ri, *a.* Pertaining to or produced by planets.

**Plangent,** plan'gent, *a.* Beating; dashing, as a wave; noisy; resonant.

**Planish,** pla'nish, *vt.* To make smooth, as wood; to smooth and toughen, as a metallic surface, by blows of a hammer; to polish.

**Planisphere,** pla'ni-sfēr, *n.* A sphere projected on a plane; a map exhibiting the circles of a sphere.

**Plank,** plangk, *n.* A flat broad piece of sawed timber.—*vt.* To cover or lay with planks.

**Plant,** plant, *n.* One of the living organisms of the vegetable kingdom; a herb; a shoot or slip; the machinery, etc., necessary to carry on a business.—*vt.* To set in the ground for growth; to set firmly; to establish; to furnish with plants; to set and direct, as cannon.—*vi.* To set plants in the ground.

**Plantain,** plan'tān, *n.* A species of herbs found in temperate regions.

**Plantar,** plan'tar, *a.* Pertaining to the sole of the foot.

**Plantation,** plan-tā'shon, *n.* The act of planting; the place planted; a wood or grove; a colony; an estate cultivated by non-European laborers.

**Planter,** plant'ėr, *n.* One who plants; one who owns a plantation abroad.

**Plantigrade,** plan'ti-grād, *a.* Walking on the sole of the foot and not on the toes.

**Plaque,** plak, *n.* An ornamental plate; a flat plate on which enamels are painted; a brooch; the plate of a clasp.

**Plasma,** plas'ma or plaz'ma, *n.* Formless matter; the simplest form of organized matter in the vegetable and animal body.

**Plasmic, Plasmatic,** plaz'mik, plaz-mat'ik, *a.* Pertaining to a plasma.
**Plaster,** pläs'tėr, *n.* An adhesive substance used in medical practice; a mixture of lime, water, sand, etc., for coating walls; calcined gypsum, used with water for finishing walls, for casts, cement, etc.—*vt.* To overlay with plaster; to lay on coarsely.
**Plasterer,** pläs'tėr-ėr, *n.* One who overlays with plaster.
**Plastering,** pläs'tėr-ing, *n.* The act of putting on plaster; a covering of plaster.
**Plastic,** plas'tik, *a.* Having the power to give form to matter; capable of being molded; applied to sculpture, as distinguished from painting, etc.—**Plastics,** plas'tiks, *n.* The science or craft of converting various resins into durable materials; the articles so made.
**Plasticity,** plas-tis'i-ti, *n.* The state or quality of being plastic.
**Plastron,** plas'tron, *n.* A breastplate; a protection for the chest used by fencers.
**Plat,** plat, *vt.* (platting, platted). To plait; to weave; to make a ground-plan of.—*n.* A plot of ground devoted to some special purpose.
**Platan, Platane,** plat'an, plat'ān, *n.* The plane-tree.
**Plate,** plāt, *n.* A flat piece of metal; gold and silver wrought into utensils; a shallow flattish dish for eatables; an engraved piece of metal for printing; a page of stereotype for printing.—*vt.* (plating, plated). To cover with a thin coating of metal, as of silver.
**Plate-armor,** plāt'är-mėr, *n.* Defensive armor consisting of plates of metal.
**Plateau,** pla-tō', *n.*; pl. **-teaux** or **-teaus** (-tōz). An elevated, broad, flat area of land; a table-land.
**Plate-glass,** plāt'gläs, *n.* A superior kind of thick glass used for mirrors, windows, etc.
**Plate-layer,** plāt'lā-ėr, *n.* A workman on railways whose occupation is to lay rails.
**Plate-mark,** plāt'märk, *n.* A mark on gold and silver articles to indicate their quality.
**Platform,** plat'form, *n.* A raised structure with a flat surface; the place where guns are mounted on a battery; the raised walk at a railway-station; a structure for speakers at public meetings; a declared system of policy.
**Plating,** plāt'ing, *n.* The art of covering articles with gold or silver; the coating itself.
**Platinum,** pla'tin-um, *n.* The heaviest of all metals, hard, ductile, malleable, and of a silvery color.
**Platinum-steel,** pla'tin-um-stēl, *n.* Steel alloyed with about 1=110th of platinum.
**Platitude,** pla'ti-tūd, *n.* A trite or stupid remark; a truism.
**Platitudinous,** pla-ti-tūd'i-nus, *a.* Of the nature of platitude.
**Platonic,** plā-ton'ik, *a.* Pertaining to Plato, or his philosophy, school, or opinions.
**Platoon,** pla-tön', *n.* A quarter of a company of infantry, usually 30 to 40 men, commanded by a subaltern.
**Platter,** plat'ėr, *n.* A large flat dish.
**Platting,** plat'ing, *n.* Slips of cane, straw, etc., platted or plaited, for hats, etc.
**Plaudit,** pla̤'dit, *n.* Applause; acclamation: usually in *pl.*
**Plauditory,** pla̤'di-to-ri, *a.* Applauding; commending.
**Plausibility,** pla̤z-i-bil'i-ti, *n.* Quality of being plausible; speciousness.
**Plausible,** pla̤z'i-bl, *a.* Apparently worthy of praise; apparently right; specious; fairspoken.
**Plausibly,** pla̤z'i-bli, *adv.* In a plausible manner; speciously.
**Play,** plā, *vi.* To do something for amusement; to sport; to gamble; to perform on an instrument of music; to act with free motion; to personate a character.—*vt.* To put in action or motion; to use, as an instrument of music; to act; to contend against; to perform.—*n.* Any exercise for diversion; sport; gaming; action; use; practice; a drama; motion; scope; swing.
**Play-bill,** plā'bil, *n.* A bill exhibited as an advertisement of a play.
**Play-book,** plā'bu̇k, *n.* A book of dramatic compositions.
**Player,** plā'ėr, *n.* An actor; musician; gamester.
**Playful,** plā'ful, *a.* Full of play; sportive; given to levity; indulging a sportive fancy.
**Playground,** plā'ground, *n.* A piece of ground set apart for open-air recreation.
**Play-house,** plā'hous, *n.* A theater.
**Playmate,** plā'māt, *n.* A play-fellow.
**Plaything,** plā'thing, *n.* A toy.
**Playwright,** plā'rīt, *n.* A maker of plays.
**Plea,** plē, *n.* A suit or action at law; that which is alleged in support, justification, or defense; an excuse; a pleading.
**Plead,** plēd, *vi.* (pleading, pleaded or pled). To argue in support of or against a claim; to present an answer to the declaration of a plaintiff; to supplicate with earnestness; to urge.—*vt.* To discuss and defend; to argue; to offer in excuse; to allege in a legal defense.
**Pleader,** plēd'ėr, *n.* One who pleads; a lawyer who argues in a court of justice.
**Pleading,** plēd'ing, *n.* The act of one who pleads; one of the written statements in a litigant's demand or defense.
**Pleasance,** ple'zans, *n.* Pleasure; part of a garden secluded by trees or hedges.
**Pleasant,** ple'zant, *a.* Pleasing; agreeable; grateful; humorous; sportive.
**Pleasantly,** ple'zant-li, *adv.* In a pleasant manner; pleasingly; agreeably; gaily.
**Pleasantry,** ple'zant-ri, *n.* Gaiety; humor; raillery; a jest; a frolic.
**Please,** plēz, *vt.* (pleasing, pleased). To excite agreeable sensations or emotions in; to delight; to gratify; to seem good to.—*vi.* To give pleasure; to be kind enough.
**Pleasing,** plēz'ing, *p.a.* Giving pleasure or gratification; agreeable; pleasant.
**Pleasurable,** ple'zhūr-a-bl, *a.* Pleasing; giving pleasure; affording gratification.
**Pleasurably,** ple'zhūr-a-bli, *adv.* In a pleasurable manner; with pleasure.
**Pleasure,** ple'zhūr, *n.* The gratification of the senses or of the mind; agreeable emotion; delight; joy; approbation; choice; will; purpose; command; arbitrary will or choice.
**Pleasure-ground,** ple'zhūr-ground, *n.* Ground laid out in an ornamental manner for recreation or amusement.
**Plebeian,** ple-bē'an, *a.* Pertaining to the common people; vulgar; common.—*n.* One of the lower ranks of men; one of the common people of ancient Rome.
**Plebiscite,** pleb'i-sit or pleb'i-sīt, *n.* A vote of a whole people or community.
**Plectrum,** plek'trum, *n.* A small instrument for striking the strings of a lyre, etc.
**Pledge,** plej, *n.* Personal property given in security of a debt; a pawn; a surety; a hostage; the drinking of another's health.—*vt.* (pledging, pledged). To deposit as a security; to engage solemnly; to drink a health to.
**Pledget,** plej'et, *n.* A compress or small flat mass of lint laid over a wound.
**Pleiad,** plī'ad, *n.*; pl. **Pleiads, Pleiades,** plī'adz, plī'ā-dēz. Any one of the cluster of seven stars situated in the neck of the constellation Taurus.
**Plenary,** plē'na-ri, *a.* Full; complete.
**Plenipotence, Plenipotency,** ple-nip'o-tens, ple-nip'o-ten-si, *n.* Fulness or completeness of power.
**Plenipotent,** ple-nip'o-tent, *a.* Possessing full power.
**Plenipotentiary,** ple'ni-pō-ten''shi-a-ri, *n.* A person with full power to act for another; an ambassador with full power.—*a.* Containing or invested with full power.
**Plenish,** ple'nish, *vt.* To replenish.

P

**Plenitude,** ple'ni-tūd, *n.* The state of being full or complete; plenty; abundance.
**Plenteous,** plen'tē-us, *a.* Abundant; copious; ample.
**Plentiful,** plen'ti-ful, *a.* Being in plenty or abundance; copious; ämple; abundant.
**Plentifully,** plen'ti-ful-li, *adv.* Copiously; abundantly.
**Plenty,** plen'ti, *n.* Abundance; copiousness; sufficiency.—*a.* Plentiful; abundant.
**Pleonasm,** plē'on-azm, *n.* A redundancy of words; use of more words than necessary.
**Pleonastic,** plē'on-as'tik, *a.* Pertaining to pleonasm; redundant.
**Plethora,** pleth'o-ra, *n.* Excess of blood; repletion; superabundance; a glut.
**Plethoric,** ple-thor'ik, *a.* Characterized by plethora; having a full habit of body.
**Pleura,** plū'ra, *n.*; pl. **-ae.** A thin membrane which covers the inside of the thorax, and invests either lung.
**Pleural,** plū'ral, *a.* Pertaining to the pleura.
**Pleurisy, Pleuritis,** plū'ri-si, plū-rī'tis, *n.* An inflammation of the pleura.
**Pleuritic,** plū-rit'ik, *a.* Pertaining to pleurisy.
**Pleuro-pneumonia,** plū'rō-nū-mō''ni-a, *n.* A disease of cattle, consisting in an inflammation of the pleura and lungs.
**Plexus,** plek'sus, *n.* A net-work of vessels, nerves, or fibers.
**Pliability,** plī-a-bil'i-ti, *n.* Pliancy.
**Pliable,** plī'a-bl, *a.* Easy to be bent; flexible; supple; liant; easily persuaded.
**Pliancy,** plī'an-si, *n.* The state or quality of being pliant or pliable.
**Pliant,** plī'ant, *a.* Pliable; readily yielding to force or pressure without breaking; flexible; plastic; limber.
**Plicate,** plī'kāt, *a.* Plaited; folded.
**Pliers,** plī'ėrz, *n.pl.* A small pair of pincers for bending wire, etc.
**Plight,** plīt, *vi.* To pledge, as one's word or honor; to give as a security; never applied to property or goods.—*n.* A pledge; a solemn promise; predicament; risky or dangerous state.
**Plighter,** plīt'ėr, *n.* One who plights.
**Plimsoll line,** plim'sol līn, *n.* Statutory loading line on British ships.
**Plinth,** plinth, *n.* A flat square slab, serving as the foundation of a column or pedestal.
**Pliocene,** plī'ō-sēn, *a.* and *n.* A term applied to the most modern division of the tertiary strata.
**Plod,** plod, *vi.* (plodding, plodded). To trudge or walk heavily; to toil; to drudge.—*vt.* To accomplish by toilsome exertion.
**Plodder,** plod'ėr, *n.* One who plods; a dull, heavy, laborious person.
**Plodding,** plod'ing, *p.a.* Given to plod; dilligent, but slow and laborious in execution.
**Plot,** plot, *n.* A small piece of ground; a plan, as of a field, etc., on paper; a scheme; a conspiracy; the story of a play, novel, etc.—*vt.* (plotting, plotted). To make a plan of; to devise.—*vi.* To conspire; to contrive a plan.
**Plotter,** plot'ėr, *n.* One who plots; a conspirator.
**Plover,** pluv'ėr, *n.* A grallatorial bird, as the golden plover, lapwing, etc.
**Plow,** plou, *n.* An instrument for turning up the soil.—*vt.* To turn up with the plow; to make grooves in; to run through, as in sailing.—*vi.* To turn up the soil with a plow; to use a plow.
**Plowshare,** plou'shār, *n.* The part of a plow which cuts the ground at the bottom of the furrow.
**Pluck,** pluk, *vt.* To pick or gaher; to pull sharply; to twitch; to strip by plucking; to reject as failing in an examination.—*n.* The heart, liver, and lights of a sheep, ox, etc.; courage or spirit.
**Pluckily,** pluk'i-li, *adv.* In a plucky manner; spiritedly.
**Plucky,** pluk'i, *a.* Spirited; courageous.
**Plug,** plug, *n.* A stopple or stopper; a bung; a peg; a quid of tobacco.—*vt.* (plugging, plugged). To stop with a plug; to make tight by stopping a hole.
**Plum,** plum, *n.* A fleshy fruit containing a kernel; the tree producing it; a raisin; a handsome sum or fortune generally.
**Plumage,** plöm'āj, *n.* The feathers of a bird.
**Plumb,** plum, *n.* A plummet; a perpendicular position.—*a.* Perpendicular.—*adv.* In a perpendicular direction.—*vt.* To set perpendicularly; to sound with a plummet; to ascertain the capacity of; to sound.
**Plumbago,** plum-bā'gō, *n.* Graphite or black-lead.
**Plumber,** plum'ėr, *n.* One who works in lead.
**Plumbery, Plummery,** plum'ė-ri, *n.* Manufactures in lead; place where plumbing is carried on; business of a plumber.
**Plumbing,** plum'ing, *n.* The art of casting and working in lead; plumber's work.
**Plumb-line,** plum'līn, *n.* A line with a weight attached, used to determine a perpendicular; a plummet.
**Plume,** plöm, *n.* The feather of a bird; a feather or feathers worn as an ornament; an ostrich's feather.—*vt.* (pluming, plumed). To pick and adjust, as feathers; to strip of feathers; to adorn with feathers; —*refl.* to pride.
**Plummet,** plum'et, *n.* A piece of lead, etc., attached to a line, used in sounding the depths of water; a plumb-line.
**Plumose, Plumous,** plöm'ōs, plöm'us, *a.* Feathery; resembling feathers.
**Plump,** plump, *a.* Fat; stout; chubby.—*vt.* To make plump; to dilate.—*vi.* To plunge or fall like a heavy mass; to fall suddenly; to vote for only one candidate.—*adv.* Suddenly; at once; flatly.
**Plumply,** plump'li, *adv.* Fully; roundly.
**Plunder,** plun'dėr, *vt.* To deprive of goods or valuables; to pillage; to spoil.—*n.* Robbery; pillage; spoil; booty.
**Plunderer,** plun'dėr-ėr, *n.* One who plunders.
**Plunge,** plunj, *vt.* (plunging, plunged). To thrust into water or other fluid; to immerse; to thrust or push; to cast or involve.—*vi.* To dive or rush into water, etc.; to pitch or throw oneself headlong; to throw the body forward and the hind-legs up, as a horse.—*n.* Act of plunging into water, etc.; act of throwing oneself headlong, like an unruly horse.
**Plunger,** plunj'ėr, *n.* One who or that which plunges; a diver; a solid cylinder used as a piston in pumps.
**Pluperfect,** plö'pėr-fekt, *a.* Applied to that tense of a verb which denotes that an action was finished at a certain period, to which the speaker refers.
**Plural,** plö'ral, *a.* Relating to, containing, or expressing more than one.—*n.* The number which designates more than one.
**Pluralist,** plö'ral-ist, *n.* A clergyman who holds more benefices than one.
**Plurality,** plö-ral'i-ti, *n.* State of being plural; two or more; majority; more than one benefice held by the same clergyman.
**Plurally,** plö'ral-li, *adv.* In a plural manner; in a sense implying more than one.
**Plus,** plus, *n.* A character (+) noting addition.—**Plus-fours,** *n.* Wide knickerbockers, with 4 in. overlap below the knee.
**Plush,** plush, *n.* A textile fabric with a velvet nap on one side.
**Plutocracy,** plö-tok'ra-si, *n.* The power or rule of wealth.
**Plutocrat,** plö'to-krat, *n.* A person possessing power on account of his riches.
**Plutonic,** plö-ton'ik, *a.* Pertaining to Pluto or to the regions of fire; volcanic; subterranean; dark.
**Plutonium,** plö-tōn'i-um, *n.* An element got from uranium by bombarding it with neutrons.
**Pluvial,** plö'vi-al, *a.* Relating to rain; rainy.
**Pluviometer,** plö-vi-om'et-ėr, *n.* A rain gauge.
**Ply,** plī, *vt.* (plying, plied). To employ with dili-

gence; to work at; to assail briskly; to beset; to press.—*vi.* To work steadily; to go in haste; to run regularly between any two ports, as a vessel.—*n.* A fold; a plait.

**Plyer,** plī'ėr, *n.* One who or that which plies; pl. same as *Pliers.*

**Pneumatic,** nū-mat'ik, *a.* Pertaining to air; moved or played by means of air; filled with or fitted to contain air.

**Pneumatically,** nū-mat'ik-al-li, *adv.* By pneumatic force; according to pneumatics.

**Pneumatics,** nū-mat'iks, *n.* That branch of physics which treats of the mechanical properties of elastic fluids and particularly of air.

**Pneumatology,** nū-ma-tol'o-ji, *n.* The branch of philosophy which treats of the mind or spirit; psycology.

**Pneumonia,** nū-mō'ni-a, *n.* An inflammation of the lungs.

**Poach,** pōch,*vt.* To cook (eggs) by breaking and pouring among boiling water; to pierce; to tread or stamp.—*vt.* To encroach on another's ground to steal game; to kill game contrary to law; to be or become swampy.

**Poacher,** pōch'ėr, *n.* One who steals game; one who kills game unlawfully.

**Poachy,** pōch'i, *a.* Wet and soft; easily penetrated by the feet of cattle, as land.

**Pock,** pok, *n.* A pustule raised on the skin in disease, especially in small-pox.

**Pocket,** pok'et, *n.* A small bag or pouch in a garment, a mass of rich ore.—*vt.* To put in the pocket; to take clandestinely.

**Pocket-book,** pok'et-buk, *n.* A small book for carrying papers in the pocket.

**Pocket-money,** pok'et-mun-i, *n.* Money for the pocket or for occasional expenses.

**Pocky,** pok'i, *a.* Having pocks or pustules.

**Pococurante,** pō'kō-kō-ran''tā, *n.* An apathetic, careless, indifferent person.

**Pod,** pod, *n.* The seed-vessel of certain plants, as peas, etc.—*vi.* (podding, podded). To produce pods; to swell and appear like a pod.

**Podagra,** pod-ag'ra, *n.* Gout in the foot.

**Podgy,** poj'i, *a.* Fat and short.

**Poem,** pō'em, *n.* A piece of poetry; a composition in verse.

**Poesy,** pō'e-si, *n.* The art of making or composing poems; poetry.

**Poet,** pō'et, *n.* The author of a poem; a peson distinguished for poetic talents.

**Poetaster,** pō'et-as-tėr, *n.* A petty poet; a pitiful rhymer or writer of verses.

**Poetess,** pō'et-es, *n.* A female poet.

**Poetic, poetical,** pō-et'ik, pō-et'ik-al, *a.* Pertaining or suitable to poetry; expressed in poetry or measure; possessing the peculiar beauties of poetry.

**Poetically,** pō-et'ik-al-li, *adv.* In a poetical manner.

**Poetics,** pō-et'iks, *n.* That branch of criticism which treats of the nature of poetry.

**Poetry,** pō'et-ri, *n.* The language of the imagination or emotions expressed rhythmically; the artistic expression of thought in emotional language; whatever appeals to the sense of ideal beauty; verse; poems.

**Poignancy,** poin'an-si, *n.* Quality of being poignant; severity; acuteness.

**Poignant,** poin'ant, *a.* Sharp to the taste; pointed; keen; bitter; severe; piercing.

**Poilu,** pwa-lu, *n.* A soldier in the French army.

**Point,** point, *n.* The sharp end of anything; a small headland; sting of an epigram; telling force of expression; exact spot; verge; stage; degree; a mark of punctuation; a mark or dot; end or purpose; characteristic; argument; (cricket) fielder square with wicket on off side; *pl.* The movable guiding rails at junctions on railways.—*vt.* To make pointed; to aim; to indicate; to punctuate; to fill the joints of with mortar.—*vi.* To direct the finger to an object; to indicate the presence of game, as dogs do; to show distinctly.

**Point-blank,** point-blangk, *a.* and *adv.* Having a horizontal direction; direct; express.

**Pointed,** point'ed, *p.a.* Having a sharp point; sharp; personal; epigrammatic.

**Pointedly,** point'ed-li, *adv.* In a pointed manner; with explicitness.

**Pointer,** point'ėr, *n.* One who or that which points; a kind of dog trained to point out game.

**Point-lace,** point'lās, *n.* A fine kind of lace.

**Pointless,** point'les, *a.* Having no point; blunt; without wit or application.

**Pointsman,** points'man, *n.* A man who has charge of the points on a railway.

**Poise,** poiz, *n.* Weight; balance; that which balances.—*vt.* (poising, poised). To balance in weight; to hold in equilibrium.—*vi.* To be balanced or suspended; to depend.

**Poison,** poi'zn, *n.* Any agent capable of producing a morbid effect on anything endowed with life.—*vi.* To infect with poison; to taint, impair, or corrupt.

**Poisonous,** poi'zn-us, *a.* Having the qualities of poison; venomous; deadly.

**Poke,** pōk, *n.* A bag or sack; a pouch; a gentle thrust.—*vt.* (poking, poked). To thrust or push against with something pointed; to stir; to jog.—*vi.* To grope; to search.

**Poker,** pōk'ėr, *n.* One who or that which pokes; an iron bar used in poking a fire; a game at cards.

**Polar,** pō'lėr, *a.* Pertaining to the pole or poles; situated near or proceeding from one of the poles; pertaining to the magnetic poles.

**Polarity,** pō-la'ri-ti, *n.* State of being polar; property of pointing towards the poles.

**Polarization,** pō'lėr-īz-ā''shon, *n.* Act of polarizing; state of having polarity.

**Polarize,** pō-lėr-īz, *vt.* To communicate polarity or polarization to.

**Pole,** pōl, *n.* A long piece of wood; a measure of $5^1/_2$ yards or $30^1/_4$ square yards; one of the extremities of the axis of the celestial sphere or the earth; the pole-star; one of the two points in a magnet in which the power seems concentrated; (with cap.) a native of Poland.—*vt.* (poling, poled). To furnish with poles; to impel by poles.

**Pole-axe,** pōl'aks, *n.* A battle-axe; an axe used in killing cattle.

**Pole-cat,** pōl'kat, *n.* A carnivorous animal, nearly allied to the weasel, distinguished by its offensive smell.

**Polemic,** pō-lem'ik, *a.* Pertaining to controversy; disputative.—*n.* A disputant.

**Polemical,** pō-lem'ik-al, *a.* Polemic.

**Polemics,** pō'lem'iks, *n.* Disputation; controversial writings.

**Pole-star,** pōl'stär, *n.* A star situated close to the North Pole; a lode-star.

**Police,** pō-lēs', *n.* The internal government of a community; a body of civil officers for enforcing order, cleanliness, etc.—*vt.* (policing, policed). To guard or regulate by police.

**Policeman,** pō-lēs'man, *n.* An ordinary member of a body of police.

**Policy,** po'li-si, *n.* The governing a city, state, or nation; line of conduct with respect to foreign or internal affairs; dexterity of management; pleasure-grounds around a mansion; contract of insurance.

**Poliomyelitis,** pol'i-ō-mī-el-it''is, *n.* Inflammation of the grey matter of the spinal cord; infantile paralysis.

**Polish,** po'lish, *vt.* To make smooth and glossy; to refine.—*vi.* To become smooth or glossy.—*n.* Gloss; elegance of manners.

**Polished,** po'lisht, *p.a.* Smooth and glossy; refined; polite.

**Polite,** pō-līt', *a.* Polished in manners; refined; urbane; elegant; well-bred.

**Politely,** pō-līt-li, *adv.* In a polite manner; courteously.

**Politic,** po'li-tik, *a.* Showing policy; adapted to

P

the public prosperity; sagacious; subtle; well devised.—**Body politic,** the citizens of a state.
**Political,** pō-lit'ik-al, *a.* Belonging or pertaining to a nation or state; public; derived from connection with government; politic; treating of politics.
**Politically,** pō-lit'ik-al-li, *adv.* In a political manner; with reference to politics.
**Politician,** po-li-ti'shan, *n.* One versed in or occupying himself with politics.
**Politics,** po'li-tiks, *n.* The science of government; political affairs, or the contests of parties for power.
**Polity,** po'li-ti, *n.* The form or system of civil government; method of government.
**Polka,** pōl'ka, *n.* A dance of Bohemian origin; the air played to the dance.
**Poll,** pōl, *n.* The head or the back part of the head; register of persons; the voting of electors; an election.—*vt.* To lop or clip; to enrol or register; to receive or give, as votes.
**Pollard,** pol'ėrd, *n.* A tree with its top cut off that it may throw out branches; a stag that has cast its horns; a coarse product of wheat.—*vt.* To make a pollard of.
**Polled,** pōld, *p.a.* Lopped, cropped, or clipped; having no horns or antlers.
**Pollen,** pol'en, *n.* The fecundating dust or male element of flowers.
**Pollenize,** pol'en-īz, *vt.* To supply or impregnate with pollen.
**Pollinate,** pol'i-nāt, *vt.* To pollenize.
**Poll-tax,** pōl'taks, *n.* A tax levied by the poll or head; a capitation-tax.
**Pollute,** pol-lūt', *vt.* (polluting, polluted). To defile; to profane; to taint morally; to debauch.
**Pollution,** pol-ū'shon, *n.* Act of polluting; defilement; uncleanness.
**Polo,** pō'lō, *n.* A game at ball resembling hockey, played on horseback.
**Polyandry,** po-li-an'dri, *n.* The practice of having more husbands than one at the same time.
**Polygamist,** po-lig'a-mist, *n.* A person who practices polygamy.
**Polygamy,** po-lig'a-mi, *n.* The practice of having more wives or husbands than one at the same time.
**Polyglot,** po'li-glot, *a.* Many-tongued; containing, speaking, or knowing several languages.—*n.* A book (as a Bible) printed in several languages in parallel columns.
**Polygon,** po'li-gon, *n.* A plane figure of many angles and sides.
**Polygraph,** po'li-graf, *n.* An instrument for multiplying copies of a writing.
**Polygraphy,** po-lig'ra-fi, *n.* The art of writing in various ciphers.
**Polygyny,** po-lij'i-ni, *n.* The practice of having more wives than one at the same time.
**Polyhedron,** po-li-hē'dron, *n.* A body or solid contained by many sides or planes.
**Polyp, Polype,** po'lip, *n.* The sea-anemone, or some allied animal.
**Polypetalous,** po-li-pe'tal-us, *a.* Having many petals, as a flower.
**Polypous,** po'li-pus, *a.* Pertaining to a polypus.
**Polypus,** po'li-pus, *n.*; pl. **Polypi,** po'li-pī. A polyp; a kind of tumor.
**Polysyllabic,** po'li-sil-lab''ik, *a.* Consisting of many syllables.
**Polysyllable,** po-li-sil'la-bl, *n.* A word of more syllables than three.
**Polysynthesis,** po-li-sin'the-sis, *n.* A compounding of several elements.
**Polysynthetic,** po'li-sin-thet''ik, *a.* Compounded of several elements, as words.
**Polytechnic,** po-li-tek'nik, *a.* Comprehending many arts; designating a school teaching many branches of art or science.—*n.* A school of instruction in arts.
**Polytheism,** po'li-thē-izm, *n.* The doctrine of a plurality of gods.
**Polytheist,** po'li-thē-ist, *n.* A person who believes in a plurality of gods.
**Pomace,** pom'ās, *n.* The substance of apples, etc., crushed by grinding.
**Pomaceous,** pō-mā'shus, *a.* Pertaining to or consisting of apples.
**Pomade,** pō-'mäd', *n.* Perfumed ointment; pomatum.
**Pomander,** pom'an-dėr, *n.* A perfume ball.
**Pomatum,** pō-mā'tum, *n.* A perfumed unguent for the hair.
**Pome,** pōm, *n.* A fruit of the character of the apple, pear, etc.
**Pomegranate,** pōm'gran-āt, *n.* A fruit of the size of an orange, containing numerous seeds; the tree producing the fruit.
**Pommel,** pum'el, *n.* A knob or ball; the knob on the hilt of a sword; the protuberant part of a saddle-bow.—*vt.* (pommelling, pommelled). To beat; to belabor.
**Pomology,** pō-mol'o-ji, *n.* The science of fruits; the cultivation of fruit-trees.
**Pomp,** pomp, *n.* A showy procession; display; pageantry; splendor; parade.
**Pomposity,** pom-pos'i-ti, *n.* Ostentation; vainglorious show.
**Pompous,** pomp'us, *a.* Displaying pomp; showy; ostentatious; high-flown.
**Pompously,** pomp'us-li, *adv.* In a pompous manner; ostentatiously.
**Pond,** pond, *n.* A body of water less than a lake, artificial or natural.
**Ponder,** pon'dėr, *vt.* To weigh in the mind; to consider.—*vi.* To deliberate.
**Ponderable,** pon'dėr-a-bl, *a.* That may be weighed.
**Ponderous,** pon'dėr-us, *a.* Heavy; weighty; massive.
**Pontiff,** pon'tif, *n.* A high-priest; applied particularly to the pope.
**Pontifical,** pon-tif'ik-al, *a.* Belonging to a high-priest or to the pope.—*n.* A book containing rites performable by a bishop; *pl.* the dress of a priest or bishop.
**Pontificate,** pon-tif'i-kāt, *n.* The dignity of a high-priest; papacy.
**Pontonier, Pontonnier,** pon-to-nėr', *n.* One who constructs pontoon-bridges.
**Pontoon,** pon-tön, *n.* A kind of boat for supporting temporary bridges; a water-tight structure to assist in raising submerged vessels.
**Pony,** pō'ni, *n.* A small horse.
**Poodle,** pö'dl, *n.* A small dog with long silky curling hair.
**Pooh,** pö, *interj.* An exclamation of contempt or disdain; poh.
**Pooh-pooh,** pö-pö', *vt.* To sneer at.
**Pool,** pöl, *n.* A small pond; a puddle; a hole in the course of a stream; the stakes at cards, etc.; a variety of play at billiards.
**Poop,** pöp, *vt.* The stern of a ship; the highest and aftmost deck of a ship.
**Poor,** pör, *a.* Needy; indigent; destitute of value or merit; infertile; mean; paltry; lean; weak; impotent; unhappy; wretched.
**Poorly,** pör'li, *adv.* In a poor manner or state; in poverty or indigence; insufficiently.—*a.* Somewhat ill; not in health.
**Pop,** pop, *n.* A small, smart sound.—*vi.* (popping, popped). To make a small, smart sound; to enter or issue forth suddenly.—*vt.* To offer with a quick sudden motion; to thrust or push suddenly.—*adv.* Suddenly.
**Pop-corn,** pop'korn, *n.* Parched maize.
**Pope,** pōp, *n.* The head of the Roman Catholic church.
**Popedom,** pōp'dum, *n.* The jurisdiction, office, or dignity of the pope; papal dignity.
**Popery,** pōp'ē-ri, *n.* The doctrins and practices of the Roman Catholic church (a Protestant term).
**Popinjay,** pop'in-jā, *n.* A parrot; the green woodpecker; a fop.
**Popish,** pōp'ish, *a.* Pertaining to the pope, or to the Roman Catholic church.

**Poplar,** pop'lėr, *n.* A tree of numerous species.
**Poplin,** pop'lin, *n.* A fabric made of silk and wool, of many varieties.
**Poppy,** pop'i, *n.* A plant with showy flowers and yielding opium.
**Populace,** po'pū-lās, *n.* The common people; the multitude; the mob.
**Popular,** po'pū-lėr, *a.* Pertaining to the common people; familiar; plain; liked by people in general; prevalent.
**Popularity,** po-pū-la'ri-ti, *n.* State or quality of being popular; favor of the people.
**Popularize,** po'pū-lėr-īz, *vi.* To make popular or suitable to the common mind; to spread among the people.
**Popularly,** po'pū'lėr-li, *adv.* In a popular manner; currently; commonly.
**Populate,** po'pū-lāt, *vt.* To people; to furnish with inhabitants.
**Population,** po-pū-lā'shon, *n.* Act or process of populating; number of people in a country, etc.; the inhabitants.
**Populous,** po'pū-lus, *a.* Abounding in people; full of inhabitants.
**Porbeagle,** por'bē'gl, *n.* A kind of shark.
**Porcelain,** pōr'se-lān, *n.* The finest species of pottery ware.
**Porch,** pōrch, *n.* A portico; covered approach at the entrance of buildings.
**Porcine,** pōr'sīn, *a.* Pertaining to swine; like a swine; hog-like.
**Porcupine,** por'kū-pīn, *n.* A rodent animal, about 2 feet long, with erectile spines.
**Pore,** pōr, *n.* A minute opening in the skin, through which the perspirable matter passes; a small interstice.—*vi.* (poring, pored). To look with steady attention; to read or examine with perseverance.
**Porgie, Porgy,** por'gi, *n.* A kind of fish.
**Pork,** pōrk, *n.* The flesh of swine, fresh or salted, used for food.
**Porker,** pōrk'ėr, *n.* A hog; a young pig for roasting.
**Pornography,** por-nog'ra-fi, *n.* Literature in which prostitutes figure.
**Porosity,** pōr-os'i-ti, *n.* Quality or state of being porous.
**Porous,** pōr'us, *a.* Having pores.
**Porphyry,** por'fi-ri, *n.* A reddish Egyptian stone like granite; a hard igneous rock containing crystals of felspar, etc.
**Porpoise,** por'pus, *n.* A small cetaceous mammal of the Northern Seas.
**Porridge,** po'rij, *n.* A kind of soup or broth; a dish of oatmeal boiled in water till thickened.
**Porringer,** po'rin-jėr, *n.* A small dish for porridge.
**Port,** pōrt, *n.* A harbor or haven; a gate; an opening in the side of a ship; a port-hole; the left side of a ship; mien; demeanor.—*vt.* To carry (as a rifle) slanting upwards towards the left; to turn to the left, as the helm.
**Port, Port-wine,** pōrt, pōrt'wīn, *n.* A kind of wine made in Portugal.
**Portable,** pōrt'a-bl, *a.* That may be carried; not bulky or heavy.
**Portage,** pōrt'āj, *n.* Act of carrying; carriage; freight.
**Portal,** pōrt'al, *n.* A door or gate; the main entrance of a cathedral, etc.—*a.* Belonging to a vein connected with the liver.
**Portcullis,** pōrt-kul'is, *n.* A sliding or falling grating of timber or iron at the gateway of a fortified place.
**Porte,** pōrt, *n.* The government of the Turkish empire.
**Portend,** por-tend', *vt.* To foretoken; to presage; to threaten.
**Portent,** pōr'tent, *n.* That which foretokens; an omen of ill.
**Portentous,** por-tent'us, *a.* Ominous; foreshowing ill; monstrous; wonderful.
**Porter,** pōr'tėr, *n.* A doorkeeper; a carrier; a dark brown malt liquor.
**Porterage,** pōr'tėr-āj, *n.* Charge for the carriage of burdens by a porter; carriage.
**Portfolio,** pōrt-fō'li-ō, *n.* A case for drawings, papers, etc.; office and functions of a minister of state.
**Port-hole,** pōrt'hōl, *n.* The embrasure of a ship of war.
**Portico,** pōr'ti-kō, *n.* A colonnade or covered walk; a porch.
**Portion,** pōr'shon, *n.* A part; a share or allotment; fate; final state.—*vt.* To parcel; to divide.
**Portioner,** pōr'shon-ėr, *n.* One who portions; in Scotland, the proprietor of a small feu.
**Portly,** pōrt'li, *a.* Of noble carriage or bearing; stately; rather tall, and inclining to stoutness.
**Portmanteau,** pōrt-man'tō, *n.* A bag for carrying clothes, etc., in travelling.
**Portrait,** pōr'trāt, *n.* A picture of a person; a vivid description.
**Portraiture,** pōr'trā-tūr, *n.* A portrait; the art or practice of making portraits, or describing vividly in words.
**Portray,** pōr-trā', *vt.* To delineate; to depict; to describe in words.
**Portrayal,** pōr-trā'al, *n.* The act of portraying; delineation; representation.
**Portuguese,** por'tū-gēz, *a.* Pertaining to Portugal.—*n.* The language of Portugal; the people of Portugal.
**Pory,** pō'ri, *a.* Porous; having pores.
**Pose,** pōz, *n.* Attitude or position; an artistic posture.—*vi.* (posing, posed). To attitudinize; to assume characteristic airs.—*vt.* To cause to assume a certain posture; to state or lay down; to perplex or puzzle.
**Poser,** pōz'ėr, *n.* One who poses; something that poses, puzzles, or puts to silence.
**Posit,** poz'it, *vt.* To lay down as a proposition or principle; to present as a fact.
**Position,** pō-zi'shon, *n.* State of being placed; place; posture; rank; state; principle laid down; thesis.
**Positive,** poz'it-iv, *a.* Definitely laid down; explicit; absolute; actual; confident; dogmatic; affirmative; noting the simple state of an adjective; applied to the philosophical system of Auguste Comte, which limits itself to human experience; applied to electricity produced by rubbing a vitreous substance.—*n.* That which is positive; the positive degree.
**Positively,** poz'it-iv-li, *adv.* Absolutely; not negatively; really; dogmatically.
**Positivism,** poz'it-iv-izm, *n.* The positive philosophy.
**Positivist,** poz'it-iv-ist, *n.* A believer in the doctrines of the positive philosophy.
**Posse,** pos'se, *n.* A small body of men; possibility.
**Possess,** po-zes', *vt.* To have and hold; to own; to affect by some power or influence; to pervade; to put in possession; to furnish or fill.
**Possession,** po-ze'shon, *n.* Act or state of possessing; ownership; occupancy; land, estate, or goods owned.
**Possessive,** po-zes'iv, *a.* Pertaining to possession; expressing or denoting possession.—*n.* The possessive case; a pronoun or other word denoting possession.
**Possessor,** po-zes'ėr, *n.* One who possesses; owner; master; occupant.
**Posset,** pos'et, *n.* a drink of hot milk curdled by wine or other liquor.
**Possibility,** pos-i-bil'i-ti, *n.* State or condition of being possible.
**Possible,** pos'i-bl, *a.* That may be or exist; that may be done; practicable; not impossible, though improbable.
**Possibly,** pos'i-bli, *adv.* In a possible manner; perhaps; perchance.
**Post,** pōst, *n.* A piece of timber, etc., set upright; a place assigned; a military or other station; office or employment; a carrier of letters, messages, etc.; a system for the public conveyance of letters, etc.; a post-office; a size of paper,

P

about 18 or 19 inches by 15.—*vt.* To travel with post-horses; to hasten on.—*vt.* To place; to place in the post-office; to transfer (accounts or items) to the ledger; to make master of full details; to fix up in some public place.—*a.* Used in travelling quickly.—*adv.* Travelling as a post; swiftly.

**Postage,** pōst'āj, *n.* The charge for conveying letters or other articles by post.

**Postal,** pōst'al, *a.* Relating to posts, or the carrying of mails.

**Post-card,** pōst'kärd, *n.* A card sent by post as a means of correspondence.

**Post-date,** pōst-dāt', *vt.* To inscribe with a later date than the real one.

**Poster,** pōst'ėr, *n.* One who posts; a courier; a large printed bill for advertising.

**Posterior,** pos-tē'ri-or, *a.* Later or subsequent; hinder.—*n.* A hinder part; *pl.* the hinder parts of an animal.

**Posterity,** pos-te'ri-ti, *n.* Descendants; succeeding generations.

**Postern,** post'ern, *n.* A back door; a private entrance; a covered passage under a rampart.

**Post-haste,** pōst-hāst', *n.* Haste or speed.—*adv.* With speed or expedition.

**Posthumous,** post'ū-mus, *a.* Born after the death of the father; published after the death of the author; existing after one's decease.

**Postilion,** (or **-ll-**), pos-til'yon, *n.* One who rides the near leading horse of a carriage and four, or the near horse of a pair.

**Postman,** pōst'man, *n.* A post or courier; a letter-carrier.

**Postmaster,** pōst'mäs-tėr, *n.* The officer who superintends a post-office.

**Postmeridian,** pōst-me-rid'i-an, *a.* After the meridian; being in the afternoon.

**Post-mortem,** pōst-mor'tem, *a.* After death.

**Post-obit,** pōst-ob'it, *n.* A bond which secures to a lender money on the death of some specified person.

**Post-office,** pōst'of-is, *n.* An office where letters are received for transmission; a government department that has the duty of conveying letters, etc.

**Postpone,** pōst-pōn, *vt.* (postponing, postponed). To put off to a later time; to set below something else in value.

**Postponement,** pōst-pōn'ment, *n.* Act of postponing.

**Post-prandial,** pōst-pran'di-al, *a.* Happening after dinner.

**Postscript,** pōst'skript, *n.* A paragraph added to a letter after it is signed; something added on to a book, etc., by way of supplement.

**Postulate,** pos'tū-lāt, *n.* Something assumed for the purpose of future reasoning; enunciation of a self-evident problem.—*vt.* To assume or take for granted.

**Posture,** pos'tūr, *n.* Attitude; relative position of parts; situation; condition.

**Posy,** pō'zi, *n.* A verse or motto inscribed on a ring, etc., or sent with a nosegay; a bouquet.

**Pot,** pot, *n.* A metallic or earthenware vessel more deep than broad; the quantity contained in a pot; a sort of paper of small-sized sheets.—*vt.* (potting, potted). To put in a pot; to preserve in pots; to plant in a pot of earth.

**Potable,** pō'ta-bl, *a.* Drinkable.

**Potash,** pot'ash, *n.* Vegetable alkali in an impure state, procured from the ashes of plants.—**Potash water,** an aerated drink of carbonic acid water with bicarbonate of potash superadded.

**Potassic,** pō-tas'ik, *a.* Relating to or containing potassium.

**Potassium,** pō-tas'si-um, *n.* The metallic basis of potash, a soft, white, light metal.

**Potation,** pō-tā'shon, *n.* A drinking or drinking bout; a draught.

**Potato,** pō-tā'tō, *n.*; pl. **-oes.** A well-known plant and its esculent tuber.

**Pot-boiler,** pot'boil-ėr, *n.* A work of art executed merely to earn money.

**Poteen,** po-tēn', *n.* Irish whisky, especially illicitly distilled whisky.

**Potency,** pō'ten-si, *n.* State or quality of being potent; might; force.

**Potent,** pō'tent, *a.* Mighty; strong; powerful; efficacious.

**Potentate,** pō'ten-tāt, *n.* One who possesses great power or sway; a monarch.

**Potential,** pō-ten'shal, *a.* Possible; latent; that may be manifested.

**Potentiality,** pō-ten'shi-al''i-ti, *n.* Quality of being potential; possibility; not actuality.

**Potentially,** pō-ten'shal-li, *adv.* In a potential manner; in possibility; not in act.

**Potently,** pō'tent-li, *adv.* Powerfully.

**Pother,** potH'ėr, *n.* Bustle; confusion; flutter.—*vi.* To make a pother or stir.—*vt.* To harass; to puzzle.

**Potion,** pō'shon, *n.* A draught; a liquid medicine; a dose to be drunk.

**Pot-luck,** pot'luk, *n.* What may be for a meal without special preparation.

**Pot-pourri,** pō-pö-rē, *n.* A mixed dish of meat and vegetables; a medley.

**Potsherd,** pot'shėrd, *n.* A piece or fragment of an earthenware pot.

**Pottage,** pot'āj, *n.* A food of meat boiled to softness in water; porridge.

**Potter,** pot'ėr, *n.* One who makes earthenware vessels or crockery.—*vi.* To busy oneself about trifles; to move slowly.

**Pottery,** pot'ė-ri, *n.* The ware made by potters; place where earthen vessels are made.

**Pottle,** pot'l, *n.* A measure of four pints; a large tankard; a small basket for fruit.

**Pouch,** pouch, *n.* A pocket; a small bag.—*vt.* To put into a pouch; to pocket.

**Poult,** pōlt, *n.* A young chicken, grouse, etc.

**Poulterer,** pōl'tėr-ėr, *n.* A dealer in poultry.

**Poultice,** pōl'tis, *n.* A soft composition applied to sores.—*vt.* (poulticing, poulticed). To apply a poultice to.

**Poultry,** pōl'tri, *n.* Domestic fowls.

**Pounce,** pouns, *n.* A fine powder to prevent ink from spreading on paper; the claw or talon of a bird.—*vt.* (pouncing, pounced). To sprinkle or rub with pounce.—*vi.* To fall on and seize with the pounces or talons; to fall on suddenly.

**Pound,** pound, *n.* A standard weight of 12 ounces troy or 16 ounces avoirdupois; a money of account; an inclosure for cattle.—*vt.* To confine in a public pound; to beat; to pulverize.

**Poundage,** pound'āj, *n.* A rate per pound; payment rated by the weight of a commodity; confinement of cattle in a pound.

**Pounder,** pound'ėr, *n.* One who or that which pounds; a thing denominated from a certain number of pounds, as a cannon, or a fish.

**Pour,** pōr, *vt.* To flow or issue forth in a stream.—*vt.* To let flow out or in; to emit; to throw in profusion.

**Pout,** pout, *vi.* To thrust out the lips; to look sullen; to be prominent.—*n.* Protrusion of the lips.

**Pouter,** pout'ėr, *n.* One who pouts; a kind of pigeon with a prominent breast.

**Poverty,** po'vėr-ti, *n.* State of being poor; indigence; want; defect; insufficiency.

**Powder,** pou'dėr, *n.* A dry substance of minute particles; dust; gunpowder.—*vt.* To reduce to fine particles; to sprinkle with powder; to corn, as meat.—*vi.* To fall to dust; to use powder for the hair or face.

**Powdery,** pou'dėr-i, *a.* Dusty; friable.

**Power,** pou'ėr, *n.* Ability to act or do; strength; influence; talent; command; authority; one who exercises authority; a state or government; warrant; a mechanical advantage or effect; product of the multiplication of a number by itself.

**Powerful,** pou'ėr-ful, *a.* Having great power; strong; potent; cogent; influential.

**Powerfully,** pou'ėr-fu-li, *adv.* In a powerful manner; with great force or energy.

**Powerless,** pou'ėr-les, *a.* Destitute of power;

weak; impotent.
**Pox,** poks, *n*. A disease characterized by pocks or pustules.
**Practicability,** prak'ti-ka-bil''i-ti, *n*. Quality or state of being practicable.
**Practicable,** prak'ti-ka-bl, *a*. That may be done or effected; feasible; passable.
**Practicably,** prak'ti-ka-bli, *adv*. In a practicable manner.
**Practical,** prak'ti-kal, *a*. Pertaining to practice, action, or use; not merely theoretical; skilled in actual work.
**Practically,** prak'ti-kal-li, *adv*. In a practical manner; by experience; in effect.
**Practice,** prak'tis, *n*. A doing or effecting; custom; habit; actual performance; exercise of any profession; medical treatment; training; drill; dexterity.
**Practice,** prak'tis, *vt*. (practicing, practiced). To put in practice; to do or perform frequently or habitually; to exercise, as any profession; to commit; to teach by practice.—*vi*. To perform certain acts frequently for instruction or amusement; to exercise some profession.
**Practitioner,** prak-ti'shon-ėr, *n*. One engaged in some profession, particularly law or medicine.
**Praetor,** pē'tor, *n*. A title of certain ancient Roman magistrates.
**Praetorian,** prē-tō'ri-an, *a*. Belonging to a praetor.—*n*. A soldier of the Praetorian guard.
**Pragmatic, Pragmatical,** prag-mat'ik, prag-mat'ik-al, *a*. Meddling; impertinently busy or officious.
**Prairie,** prā'ri, *n*. An extensive tract of grassy land, generally destitute of trees.
**Praise,** prāz, *n*. Approbation or admiration expressed; eulogy; honor; gratitude or homage to God, often in song; the object, ground, or reason of praise.—*vt*. (praising, praised). To extol; to commend; to honor.
**Praiseworthy,** prāz'wėr-ᴛʜi, *a*. Deserving of praise; commendable; laudable.
**Prance,** prans, *vt*. (prancing, pranced). To spring, leap, or caper, as a horse; to strut about ostentatiously.
**Prank,** prangk, *vt*. To adorn in a showy manner; to dress up.—*vi*. To have a showy appearance.—*n*. A merry trick; a caper.
**Prate,** prāt, *vi*. (prating, prated). To babble, chatter, tattle.—*vt*. To utter foolishly.—*n*. Trifling talk; unmeaning loquacity.
**Prating,** prāt'ing, *p.a*. Given to prate; loquacious.
**Prattle,** prat'l, *vi*. (prattling, prattled). To talk much and idly, like a child; to prate.—*n*. Trifling or puerile talk.
**Prawn,** pran, *n*. A small crustaceous animal of the shrimp family.
**Pray,** prā, *vi*. and *t*. To beg, supplicate, or implore; to address God.
**Prayer,** prā'ėr, *n*. One who prays; the act of praying; a petition; a solemn petition to God; a formula of worship, public or private; that part of a written petition which specifies the thing desired to be granted.
**Prayer-book,** prā'ėr-buk, *n*. A book containing prayers or forms of devotion.
**Prayerful,** prā'ėr-ful, *a*. Given to prayer; devotional; using much prayer.
**Praying,** prā'ing, *p.a*. Given to prayer.
**Preach,** prēch, *vi*. To deliver a sermon; to give earnest advice.—*vt*. To proclaim; to publish in religious discourses; to deliver in public, as a discourse.
**Preacher,** prēch'ėr, *n*. One who preaches; a person who delivers a sermon.
**Preaching,** prēch'ing, *n*. The act or profession of a preacher; a sermon.
**Preamble,** prē-am'bl or prē', *n*. An introduction; introductory part of a statute.
**Precarious,** prē-kā'ri-us, *a*. Depending on the will of another; uncertain; insecure.
**Precaution,** prē-ka'shon, *n*. Previous care; caution to prevent evil or secure good.—*vt*. To caution beforehand.
**Precede,** prē-sēd', *vt*. (preceding, preceded). To go before in time, rank, or importance; to preface.
**Precedence, Precedency,** prē-sed'ens, prē-sēd'en-si, *n*. Act or state of preceding; priority; order according to rank; superior importance.
**Precedent,** prē-sēd'ent, *a*. Preceding; going before in time; anterior.
**Precedent,** prē' or pre'sē-dent, *n*. Something done or said, serving as an example or rule.
**Precedented,** prē' or pre'sē-dent-ed, *a*. Authorized by or according with a precedent.
**Precentor,** prē-sen'tor, *n*. The leader of a choir in a cathedral or of the singing to a congregation.
**Precept,** prē'sept, *n*. Anything enjoined as an authoritative rule of action; injunction; doctrine; maxim.
**Preceptive,** prē-sep'tiv, *a*. Containing precepts; didactic.
**Preceptor,** prē-sep'tor, *n*. A teacher; an instructor; the teacher of a school.
**Precession,** prē-se'shon, *n*. Act of going before; advance.
**Precinct,** prē'singt, *n*. A bounding line; a part near a border; a minor territorial division.
**Precious,** pre'shus, *a*. Of great worth or value; costly; cherished; affected.
**Preciously,** pre'shus-li, *adv*. In a precious manner; valuably; exceedingly.
**Preciousness,** pre'shus-nes, *n*. Quality of being precious; literary affectation.
**Precipice,** pre'si-pis, *n*. A headlong declivity; a steep or overhanging cliff.
**Precipitance, Precipitancy,** prē-si'pi-tans, prē-si'pi-tan-si, *n*. Headlong hurry; rash or excessive haste.
**Precipitant,** prē-si'pi-tant, *a*. Falling or rushing headlong; precipitate.
**Precipitate,** prē'si'pi-tāt, *vt*. and *i*. To throw or hurl headlong; to hasten excessively; to cause to sink or to fall to the bottom of a vessel, as a substance in solution.—*a*. Headlong; overhasty.—*n*. A substance deposited from a liquid in which it has been dissolved.
**Precipitately,** prē-si'pi-tāt-li, *adv*. Headlong; too hastily; with rash haste.
**Precipitation,** prē-si'pi-tā''shon, *n*. Act or process of precipitating; state of being precipitated; rash, tumultuous haste.
**Precipitous,** prē-si'pi-tus, *a*. Very steep; headlong in descent.
**Précis,** prā-sē', *n*. A concise or abridged statement; a summary; an abstract.
**Precise,** prē-sīs', *a*. Sharply or exactly defined; exact; strictly accurate or correct; particular; formal; punctilious.
**Precisely,** prē-sīs'li, *adv*. In a precise manner; definitely; strictly; accurately.
**Precisian,** prē-si'zhan, *n*. One rigidly exact in the observance of rules.
**Precision,** prē-si'zhon, *n*. State of being precise; exactness; accuracy.
**Preclude,** prē-klöd', *vt*. (precluding, precluded). To shut out; to hinder; to render inoperative by anticipative action.
**Preclusive,** prē-klö'siv, *a*. Tending to preclude; hindering by previous obstacles.
**Precocious,** prē-kō'shus, *a*. Ripe before the natural time; acting like an adult though not grown up.
**Precocity,** prē-kos'i-ti, *n*. State or quality of being precocious; early development of the mental powers.
**Precognition,** prē-kog-ni'shon, *n*. Previous knowledge; preliminary examination, as of a witness befor a trial (*Scots law*).
**Preconceive,** prē-kon-sēv', *vt*. To form a conception or opinion of beforehand.
**Preconcert,** prē-kon-sėrt', *vt*. To arrange by previous agreement.—*n*. prē-kon'sėrt. A previous arrangement.
**Precursive,** prē-kėr'siv, *a*. Precursory.

**Precursor,** prē-kėr'sėr, *n*. A forerunner; a harbinger.
**Precursory,** prē-kėr'so-ri, *a*. Forerunning.
**Predaceous,** prē-dā'shus, *a*. Living by prey; given to prey on other animals.
**Predatory,** pred'a-to-ri, *a*. Plundering; pillaging; practicing rapine.
**Predecease,** prē-dē-sēs', *vt*. To die before.—*n*. The decease of one before another.
**Predecessor,** prē-dė-ses'ėr, *n*. One who has preceded another in any state, office, etc.
**Predestinarian,** prē-des'ti-nā''ri-an, *a*. Belonging to predestination.—*n*. One who believes in the doctrine of predestination.
**Predestinate,** prē-des'ti-nāt, *vt*. To foreordain.—*a*. Foreordained.
**Predestination,** prē-des'ti-nā''shon, *n*. The act of foredaining events; the doctrine that God has from eternity determined whatever comes to pass, and has preordained men to everlasting happiness or misery.
**Predestine,** prē-des'tin, *vt*. To decree beforehand; to foreordain.
**Predeterminate,** prē-dē-tėr'mi-nāt, *a*. Determined beforehand.
**Predetermination,** prē-dē-tėr'mi-nā''shon, *n*. Purpose formed beforehand.
**Predetermine,** prē-dē-tėr'min, *vt*. and *i*. To determine beforehand.
**Predial,** prē-di-al, *a*. Consisting of land or farms; landed; attached to land.
**Predicable,** pre'di-ka-bl, *a*. That may be attributed to something.—*n*. Anythng that may be affirmed of another.
**Predicament,** prē-dik'a-ment, *n*. Class or kind; condition; dangerous or trying state.
**Predicant,** pre'di-kant, *n*. One that affirms anything; a preaching friar; a Dominican.—*a*. Predicating; preaching.
**Predicate,** pre'di-kāt, *vt*. and *i*. To affirm one thing of another; to assert.—*n*. In *logic*, that which is affirmed or denied of the subject; in *grammar*, the word or words which express what is affirmed or denied of the subject.
**Predication,** pre-di'kā'shon, *n*. The act of predicating; affirmation; assertion.
**Predicative,** pre'di-kāt-iv, *a*. Expressing predication.
**Predict,** prē-dikt', *vt*. To foretell; to prophesy.
**Prediction,** prē-dik'shon, *n*. The act of predicting; a prophecy.
**Predictive,** prē-dik'tiv, *a*. Foretelling.
**Predictor,** prē-dik'tor, *n*. One who predicts.
**Predilection,** prē-di-lek'shon, *n*. A previous liking or preference; a prepossession of mind in favor of a person or thing.
**Predispose,** prē-dis-pōz', *vt*. To dispose beforehand; to fit or adapt previously.
**Predisposition,** prē-dis'pō-zi''shon, *n*. State of being predisposed; susceptibility from antecedent causes.
**Predominance, Predominancy,** prē-dom'i-nans, prē-dom'i-nan-si, *n*. Prevalence over others; superiority; ascendency.
**Predominant,** prē-dom'i-nant, *a*. Predominating; prevalent; ruling; controlling.
**Predominate,** prē-dom'i-nāt, *vi*. and *t*. To have surpassing power or authority; to rule.
**Pre-eminence,** prē-em'i-nens, *n*. State of being pre-eminent; superiority.
**Pre-eminent,** prē-em'i-nent, *a*. Eminent above others; surpassing or distinguished.
**Pre-emption,** prē-em'shon, *n*. The act or right of purchasing before others.
**Preen,** prēn, *vt*. To trim with the beak: said of birds dressing their feathers.
**Pre-engage,** prē-en-gāj', *vt*. To engage by previous agreement or influence.
**Pre-establish,** prē-es-tab'lish, *vt*. To establish beforehand.
**Pre-exist,** prē-egz-ist', *vi*. To exist beforehand, or before something else.
**Pre-existence,** prē-egz-ist'ens, *n*. Previous existence.
**Prefabricate,** prē-fab'ri-kāt, *vt*. To manufacture separately parts, of a building, etc., designed to be easily fitted together afterwards.
**Preface,** pre'fās, *n*. Introduction to a discourse or book, etc.—*vt*. (prefacing, prefaced). To introduce by preliminary remarks.
**Prefatory,** pre'fā-to-ri, *a*. Pertaining to or having the nature of a preface.
**Prefect,** prē'fekt, *n*. One placed over others; a governor, chief magistrate; a senior pupil entrusted with the maintenance of discipline.
**Prefecture,** prē'fekt-ūr, *n*. Office, jurisdiction, or official residence of a prefect.
**Prefer,** prē-fėr', *vt*. (preferring, preferred). To bring or lay before; to present, as a petition, etc.; to exalt; to set higher in estimation; to choose rather.
**Preferable,** pre'fėr-a-bl, *a*. Worthy to be preferred; more desirable.
**Preferably,** pre'fėr-a-bli, *adv*. Rather.
**Preference,** pre'fėr-ens, *n*. Act of preferring; state of being preferred; choice.
**Preferential,** pre-fėr-en'shal, *a*. Implying preference.
**Preferment,** prē-fėr'ment, *n*. Act of preferring; promotion; a superior office.
**Prefiguration,** prē-fig'ūr-ā''shon, *n*. Antecedent representation by similitude.
**Prefigure,** prē-fig'ūr, *vt*. To exhibit by antecedent representation; to foreshow.
**Prefix,** prē-fiks', *vt*. To put before or at the beginning of something.—*n*. prē'fiks, A letter, syllable, or word added at the beginning of a word.
**Pregnancy,** preg'nan-si, *n*. State of being pregnant; time of going with child.
**Pregnant,** preg'nant, *a*. Being with young; full of meaning or consequence.
**Prehensible,** prē-hen'si-bl, *a*. That may be seized.
**Prehensile,** prē-hen'sīl, *a*. Fitted for seizing or laying hold; grasping.
**Prehension,** prē-hen'shon, *n*. A taking hold of; apprehension.
**Prehistoric,** prē-his-tor'ik, *a*. Relating to a time anterior to written records.
**Prejudge,** prē-juj', *vt*. To judge beforehand; to condemn unheard.
**Prejudgment,** prē-juj'ment, *n*. Judgment without full examination.
**Prejudicate,** prē-jū'di-kāt, *vt*. and *i*. To prejudge; to judge with prejudice.
**Prejudice,** pre'jū-dis, *n*. An unwarranted bias; prepossession; detriment; injury.—*vt*. To blas the mind of; to do harm to.
**Prejudicial,** pre-jū-di'shal, *a*. Causing prejudice; hurtful; detrimental.
**Preliminary,** prē-lim'in-a-ri, *a*. Introductory; preparatory; prefactory.—*n*. Something introductory; preface; prelude.
**Prelude,** prel'ūd or prē-lūd', *vt*. (preluding, preluded). To introduce; to preface.—*vi*. To form a prelude.—*n*. prel'ūd or prē'lūd. Something preparatory; a musical introduction.
**Prelusive,** prē-lū'siv, *a*. Partaking of the nature of a prelude; introductory.
**Premature,** pre'ma-tūr, *a*. Happening, performed, etc., too early; untimely.
**Premeditate,** prē-me'di-tāt, *vt*. and *i*. To meditate upon beforehand; to contrive previously; to deliberate.
**Premeditation,** prē-me'di-tā''shon, *n*. Act of premeditating; previous deliberation.
**Premier,** pre'mi-ėr, *a*. First; chief.—*n*. The first minister of state; prime minister.
**Premise,** prē-mīz', *vt*. (premising, premised). To put forward by way of preface; to lay down, as antecedent to another statement.—*vi*. To make an introductory statement.
**Premise, Premiss,** pre'mis, *n*. A proposition laid down as a base of argument; *pl*. the portion of a legal document where articles of property to be transferred are described; a house and its ad-

juncts.

**Premium,** prē'mi-um, *n.* A reward or prize; a bonus; a bounty; sum paid for insurance; increase in value.

**Premonish,** prē-mon'ish, *vt.* To forewarn.

**Premonition,** prē-mō-ni'shon, *n.* Previous warning, notice, or information.

**Premonitory,** prē-mon'i-to-ri, *a.* Giving previous warning or notice.

**Prentice,** pren'tis,. Apprentice.

**Preoccupancy,** prē-ok'kū-pan-si, *n.* Preoccupation; previous occupancy.

**Preoccupation,** prē-ok'kū-pā''shon, *n.* Act of preoccupying; prior possession; state of being preoccupied.

**Preoccupied,** prē-ok'kū-pīd, *p.a.* Occupied beforehand; absorbed; abstracted.

**Preoccupy,** prē-ok'kū-pī, *vt.* To occupy before another; to engross before another; to engross beforehand.

**Preordain,** prē-or-dān', *vt.* To appoint beforehand; to foreordain.

**Preparation,** pre-pa-rā'shon, *n.* Act or operation of preparing; that which is prepared; state of being prepared.

**Preparative,** prē-pa'rat-iv, *a.* Tending to prepare; preparatory.—*n.* That which serves to prepare; preparation.

**Preparatory,** prē-pa'ra-to-ri, *a.* Serving to prepare; introductory; preliminary.

**Prepare,** prē-pār', *vt.* and *i.* (preparing, prepared). To make ready; to adjust; to provide; to procure as suitable.

**Prepay,** prē-pā', *vt.* To pay in advance.

**Prepayment,** prē-pā'ment, *n.* Act of prepaying; payment in advance.

**Prepense,** prē-pens', *a.* Premeditated.

**Preponderance,** prē-pon'dėr-ans, *n.* State of being preponderant.

**Preponderant,** prē-pon'dėr-ant, *a.* Superior in power, influence, or the like.

**Preponderate,** prē-pon'dėr-āt, *vi.* To outweigh; to exceed in influence or power.

**Preposition,** pre-pō-zi'shon, *n.* A word governing a noun, pronoun, or clause.

**Prepositional,** pre-pō-zi'shon-al, *a.* Pertaining to a preposition.

**Prepossess,** prē-po-zes', *vt.* To take possession of beforehand; to preoccupy; to prejudice.

**Prepossessing,** prē-po-zes'ing, *p.a.* Creating a favorable impression; attractive.

**Prepossession,** prē-po-ze'shon, *n.* Preconceived opinion; prejudice; bias.

**Preposterous,** prē-pos'tėr-us, *a.* Absurd; irrational; monstrous; utterly ridiculous.

**Prerogative,** prē-ro'ga-tiv, *n.* A prior claim or title; an exclusive privilege; an official and hereditary right.

**Presage,** prē'sāj or pres'āj, *n.* a presentiment; a prognostic, omen, or sign.—*vt.* and *i.* prē-sāj', (presaging, presaged). To betoken; to forebode; to predict.

**Presbyter,** pres'bi-tėr, *n.* An elder; a priest; a parson.

**Presbyterian,** pres-bi-tē'ri-an, *a.* Pertaining to presbyters; pertaining to ecclesiastical government by presbyteries.—*n.* A member of one of the Christian churches who vest church governments in presbyteries.

**Presbyterianism,** pres-bi-tē'ri-an-izm, *n.* The doctrines, principles, and ecclesiastical government of presbyterians.

**Presbytery,** pres'bi-te-ri, *n.* A body of presbyters; a church court consisting of the presbyterian pastors within a district, and one elder from each church.

**Prescience,** prē'shi-ens, *n.* Foreknowledge.

**Prescient,** prē'shi-ent, *a.* Foreknowing.

**Prescind,** prē-sind', *vt.* To consider apart from other ideas or notions.

**Prescribe,** prē-skrīb', *vt.* (prescribing, prescribed). To lay down authoritatively for direction; to appoint; to direct to be used as a remedy.—*vi.* To give directions; to give medical directions; to become of no validity through lapse of time.

**Prescription,** prē-skrip'shon, *n.* Act of prescribing; that which is prescribed; a claim or title based on long use; the loss of a legal right by lapse of time.

**Prescriptive,** prē-skrip'tiv, *a.* Consisting in or acquired by long use.

**Presence,** pre'zens, *n.* State of being present; existence in a certain place; company; sight; port; mien; the person of a great personage; an appearance or apparition; readiness.

**Present,** pre'zent, *a.* Being at hand, in view, or in a certain place; now existing; ready at hand; quick in emergency.—*n.* Present time; *pl.* term used in a legal document for the document itself.

**Present,** prē-zent', *vt.* To introduce to or bring before a superior; to show; to give or bestow; to nominate to an ecclesiastical benefice; to lay before a public body for consideration; to point or aim, as a weapon.—*n.* pre'zent. A donation; a gift.

**Presentable,** prē-zent'a-bl, *a.* That may be presented; in such trim as to be able to present oneself.

**Presentation,** pre-zent-ā'shon, *n.* Act of presenting; thing presented; the act or right of presenting a clergyman to a parish.

**Presently,** pre'zent-li, *adv.* Immediately; forthwith; speedily; soon.

**Presentment,** prē-zent'ment, *n.* Act of presenting; appearance; representation.

**Preservation,** pre-zėr-vā'shon, *n.* Act of preserving; state of being preserved; safety.

**Preservative,** prē-zėrv'at-iv, *a.* Tending to preserve.—*n.* That which preserves; a preventive of injury or decay.

**Preserve,** prē-zėrv', *vt.* (preserving, preserved). To save from injury; to keep in a sound state; to maintain; to restrict the hunting of, as game.—*n.* Something that is preserved, as fruit, vegetables, etc.; ground set apart for animals intended for sport or food.

**Preside,** prē-zīd', *vi.* (presiding, presided). To exercise authority or superintendence; to have the post of chairman.

**Presidency,** pre'zi-den-si, *n.* Act of presiding; the office, jurisdiction, or term of office of a president.

**President,** pre'zi-dent, *n.* One who presides; the head of a province or state; the highest officer of state in a republic.

**Presidential,** pre-zi-den'shal, *a.* Pertaining to a president.

**Press,** pres, *vt.* To bear or weigh heavily upon; to squeeze; to urge; to enforce; to emphasize; to solicit earnestly; to force into service.—*vi.* To bear heavily or with force; to crowd; to push with force.—*n.* A pressing; a crowd; an instrument for squeezing or crushing; a machine for printing; the art or business of printing; periodical literature; an upright cupboard; urgency.

**Pressing,** pres'ing, *p.a.* Urgent.

**Pressman,** pres'man, *n.* One who attends to a printing press; a journalist.

**Pressure,** pre'shūr, *n.* The act of pressing; the force of one body acting on another; moral force; distress or difficulty; urgency.

**Prestidigitation,** pres'ti-di'ji-tā''shon, *n.* Skill in legerdemain; juggling.

**Prestidigitator,** pres-ti-di'ji-tā-tėr, *n.* A juggler.

**Prestige,** pres'tij or pres-tēzh', *n.* Influence based on high character or conduct.

**Presto,** pres'tō, *adv.* Quickly; in a trice.

**Presumable,** prē-zūm'a-bl, *a.* That may be presumed.

**Presumably,** prē-zūm'a-bli, *adv.* As may be presumed.

**Presume,** prē-zūm', *vt.* (presuming, presumed). To take for granted; to take the liberty; to make bold.—*vi.* To infer; to act in a forward way.

P

**Presumption,** prē-zum'shon, *n.* Act of presuming; supposition; forwardness; arrogance.
**Presumptive,** prē-zum'tiv, *a.* Based on presumption or probability.
**Presumptuous,** prē-zum'tū-us, *a.* Taking undue liberties; arrogant; overweening.
**Presuppose,** prē-sup-pōz', *vt.* To suppose or imply as previous; to take for granted.
**Pretend,** prē-tend', *vt.* To feign; to simulate; to assume or profess to feel; use as a pretest.—*vi.* To assume a false character; to sham; to put in a claim.
**Pretended,** prē-tend'ed, *p.a.* Ostensible; feigned; assumed; hypocritical.
**Pretender,** prē-tend'ėr, *n.* One who pretends; one who lays claim to anything.
**Pretense,** prē-tens', *n.* Act of pretending; simulation; feint; pretext.
**Pretension,** prē-ten'shon, *n.* Claim true or false; an assumed right.
**Pretentious,** prē-ten'shus, *a.* Full of pretension; showy.
**Preterit, Preterite,** pre'tėr-it, *a.* Past.—*n.* The past tense.
**Pretermit,** prē-tėr-mit', *vt.* To omit; to overlook.
**Preternatural,** prē-tėr-na'tūr-al, *a.* Beyond what is natural; abnormal; anomalous.
**Pretext,** prē'tekst or prē-tekst', *n.* An ostensible reason or motive; a pretense.
**Prettily,** prit'i-li, *adv.* In a pretty manner.
**Pretty,** prit'i, *a.* Having diminutive beauty; of a pleasing form without dignity; comely; neatly arranged; affectedly nice; foppish.—*adv.* Moderately.
**Prevail,** prē-vāl', *vi.* To gain the victory or superiority; to be in force; to succeed; to gain over by persuasion.
**Prevailing,** prē-vāl'ing, *p.a.* Predominant; having superior influence; prevalent.
**Prevalence, Prevalency,** pre'va-lens, pre'va-len-si, *n.* State or quality of being prevalent; superiority.
**Prevalent,** pre'va-lent, *a.* Prevailing; predominant; extensively existing.
**Prevaricate,** prē-va'ri-kāt, *vi.* To act or speak evasively; to shuffle; to quibble.
**Prevarication,** prē-va'ri-kā''shon, *n.* Act of prevaricating; a shuffling or quibbling; misrepresentation by giving evasive evidence.
**Prevaricator,** prē-va'ri-kāt-or, *n.* One who prevaricates.
**Prevenient,** prē-vē'ni-ent, *a.* Going before; preventing; preventive.
**Prevent,** prē-vent', *vt.* To stop or intercept; to impede; to thwart.
**Prevention,** prē-ven'shon, *n.* The act of preventing; a hindering by previous action; measure of precaution.
**Preventive,** prē-vent'iv, *a.* Tending to prevent.—*n.* That which prevents; an antidote previously taken. Also *Preventitive.*
**Previous,** prē'vi-us, *a.* Antecedent; prior.
**Previously,** prē'vi-us-li, *adv.* In time previous; before; beforehand.
**Prevision,** prē-vi'zhon, *n.* Foresight.
**Prey,** prā, Property taken from an enemy; spoil; booty; a victim.—*vi.* To take prey or booty; to get food by rapine; to cause to pine away: with *on.*
**Price,** prīs, *n.* The value which a seller sets on his goods; cost; value; worthy.—*vt.* (pricing, priced). To set a price on; to ask the price of.
**Priceless,** prīs'les, *a.* Too valuable to admit of a price; invaluable; inestimable.
**Prick,** prik, *n.* A slender pointed thing that can pierce; a thorn; a puncture by a prick; a sting; tormenting thought.—*vt.* To pierce with a prick; to erect, as ears; to spur; to sting with remorse; to trace by puncturing.—*vi.* To spur on; to ride rapidly; to feel a prickly sensation.
**Pricking,** prik'ing, *n.* Act of piercing with a sharp point; a sensation of sharp pain, as if being pricked.
**Prickle,** prik'l, *n.* A small sharp-pointed shoot; a thorn; a small spine.—*vt.* To prick; to cause a prickly feeling in.
**Prickly,** prik'li, *a.* Full of small sharp points or prickles; pricking or stinging.
**Pride,** prīd, *n.* State or quality of being proud; inordinate self-esteem; a cause of pride; glory or delight; highest pitch; splendid show.—*vt.* To indulge pride; to value (oneself).
**Priest,** prēst, *n.* A man who officiates in sacred offices; a clergyman above a deacon and below a bishop.
**Priestcraft,** prēst'kraft, *n.* The craft or stratagems of priests.
**Priestess,** prēst'es, *n.* A female priest.
**Priesthood,** prēt'hud, *n.* The office or character of a priest; the order of priests.
**Priestlike,** prēst'lik, *a.* Resembling a priest; pertaining to a priest; sacerdotal.
**Priestly,** prēst'li, *a.* Resembling a priest; pertaining to a priest; sacerdotal.
**Priest-ridden,** prēst'rid-n, *a.* Entirely swayed or governed by priests.
**Prig,** prig, *n.* A conceited, narrow-minded fellow; one who affects superiority; a thief.—*vt.* (prigging, prigged). To steal.
**Prim,** prim, *a.* Formal; affectedly nice; demure.—*vt.* (primming, primmed). To deck with nicety.
**Primacy,** prī'ma-si, *n.* Position of chief rank; the office or dignity of primate or archbishop.
**Prima donna,** prē'ma don'na. The first or chief female singer in the opera.
**Prima facie,** prī'ma fā'shi-ē. At first view or appearance.
**Primal,** prī'mal, *a.* Primary; primitive.
**Primarily,** prī'ma-ri-li, *adv.* In a primary manner; originally; in the first place.
**Primary,** prī'ma-ri, *a.* First; chief; first in time; original; elementary; radical.—*n.* That which stands first or highest in importance; a large feather of a bird's wing.
**Primate,** prī'māt, *n.* A chief ecclesiastic; an archbishop.
**Prime,** prīm, *a.* Foremost; first; original; first in rank, excellence, or importance; not divisible by any smaller number.—*n.* The earliest stage; full health; strength; or beauty; the best part.—*vt.* (priming, primed). To make ready for action; to supply with powder for communicating fire to a charge; to instruct or prepare beforehand; to lay on the first color in painting.
**Primer,** prim'ėr, *n.* An elementary educational book; a size of printing-type.
**Primeval,** prīm-ē'val, *a.* Being of the earliest age or time; original; primitive.
**Priming,** prīm'ing, *n.* The powder used to ignite a charge; a first layer of paint; water carried over with the steam into the cylinder.
**Primitive,** prim'it-iv, *a.* Being the first or earliest of its kind; original; antiquated; primary; radical; not derived.—*n.* That which is original; an original word.
**Primitively,** prim'it-iv-li, *adv.* In a primitive manner; primarily; in antique style.
**Primordial,** prīm-or'di-al, *a.* First of all; first in order; original; earliest formed.—*n.* First principle or element.
**Primrose,** prim'rōz, *n.* An early flowering plant.—*a.* Resembling a yellow primrose in color; abounding with primroses.
**Prince,** prins, *n.* A chief ruler; the son of a king or emperor; the chief of any body of men.
**Princedom,** prins'dum, *n.* The jurisdiction, rank, or state of a prince.
**Princely,** prins'li, *a.* Pertaining to a prince; noble; august; magnificent.
**Princess,** prin'ses, *n.* A female of the rank of a prince; the consort of a prince.
**Principal,** prin'si-pal, *a.* First; chief; most important or considerable.—*n.* A chief or head; the president, governor, or chief in authority; one primarily engaged; a capital sum lent on interest.

**Principality,** prin-si-pal'i-ti, *n.* Sovereignty; territory of a prince; a prince.
**Principally,** prin'si-pal-li, *adv.* Chiefly; mainly.
**Principle,** prin'si-pl, *n.* Cause or origin; a general truth; a fundamental law; a rule of action; uprightness; an element.
**Principled,** prin'si-pld, *a.* Holding certain principles; fixed in certain principles.
**Print,** print, *vt.* To mark by pressure; to stamp; to form or copy by pressure; as from types, etc.—*vi.* To use or practice typography; to publish.—*n.* A mark made by pressure; an engraving, etc.; state of being printed; a newspaper; printed calico.
**Printer,** print'ėr, *n.* One who prints; more especially, the printer of letterpress.
**Printing,** print'ing, *n.* The act, art, or practice of impressing letters or figures on paper, cloth, etc.; typography.
**Printing-press,** print'ing-pres, *n.* A press for the printing of books, etc.
**Print-work,** print'wėrk, *n.* A place for printing calicoes.
**Prior,** prī'or, *a.* Preceding; earlier.—*adv.* Previously.—*n.* A monk next in dignity to an abbot.
**Prioress,** prī'or-es, *n.* A female prior.
**Priority,** prī-or'i-ti, *n.* State of being prior; preeminence; preference.
**Priory,** prī'o-ri, *n.* A convent of which a prior is the superior.
**Prise,** prīz, *vt.* (prising, prised). To raise as by means of a lever; to force up.
**Prism,** prizm, *n.* A solid whose ends are any similar, equal, and parallel plane figures, and whose sides are parallelograms.
**Prismastic,** priz-mat'ik, *a.* Pertaining to a prism; formed or exhibited by a prism.
**Prismoid,** priz'moid, *n.* A body that approaches to the form of a prism.
**Prison,** pri'zn, *n.* A place of confinement; a jail.—*vt.* To imprison.
**Prisoner,** pri'zn-ėr, *n.* One shut up in a prison; captive.
**Pristine,** pris'tīn, *a.* Original; first; earliest.
**Prithee,** pri'THē. A colloquial corruption of pray thee, I pray thee.
**Privacy,** priv'a-si, *n.* A state of being private; seclusion; secrecy.
**Private,** prī'vat, *a.* Separate from others; solitary; personal; secret; not having a public or official character.—**In private,** secretly.—*n.* A common soldier.
**Privateer,** prī-va-tēr', *n.* A private vessel licensed to seize or plunder the ships of an enemy.—*vi.* To engage in privateering.
**Privately,** prī'vat-li, *adv.* In a private or secret manner; not openly; personally.
**Privation,** prī-vā'shon, *n.* Act of depriving; state of being deprived; destitution; want; hardship.
**Privative,** pri'va-tiv, *a.* Causing deprivation.—*n.* A prefix to a word which gives it a contrary sense.
**Privet,** priv'et, *n.* A shrub much used for ornamental hedges.
**Privilege,** pri'vi-lej, *n.* A separate and personal advantage; a prerogative, immunity, or exemption.—*vt.* To grant some right or exemption to; to authorize.
**Privily,** pri'vi-li, *adv.* Privately; secretly.
**Privity,** pri'vi-ti, *n.* Privacy; joint knowledge of a private concern.
**Privy,** pri'vi, *a.* Private; assigned to private uses; secret; privately knowing (with *to*).—*n.* A water-closet or necessary house.
**Privy-council,** pri'vi-koun-sil, *n.* The council of state of the British sovereign.
**Prize,** prīz, *n.* That which is seized; that which is deemed a valuable acquisition; a reward.—*vt.* (prizing, prized). To value highly.
**Prize-fight,** prīz'fīt, *n.* A boxing-match for a prize.
**Prize-ring,** prīz'ring, *n.* An inclosed place for prize-fights; boxers collectively.
**Probability,** pro-ba-bil'i-ti, *n.* Likelihood; appearance of truth.
**Probable,** pro'bab-l, *a.* Likely; credible.
**Probably,** pro'ba-bli, *adv.* In a probable manner; as is probable; likely.
**Probate,** prō'bāt, *n.* The proceeding by which a person's will is established and registered; official proof of a will.
**Probation,** prō-bā'shon, *n.* Act of proving; proof; trial; period of trial; novitiate.
**Probationary,** prō-bā'shon-a-ri, *a.* Serving for probation or trial.
**Probationer,** prō-bā'shon-ėr, *n.* One who is on probation; a novice; in Scotland, a student in divinity licensed to preach.
**Probative, Probatory,** prō'bat-iv, prō-ba-to-ri, *a.* Serving for trial or proof.
**Probe,** prōb, *n.* A surgeon's instrument for examining a wound, ulcer, or cavity.—*vt.* (probing, probed). To apply a probe to; to examine thoroughly.
**Probity,** prō'bi-ti, *n.* Uprightness; honesty; rectitude; integrity.
**Problem,** prob'lem, *n.* A question proposed for solution; a knotty point to be cleared up.
**Problematic, Problematical,** prob-lem-at'ik, prob-lem-at'ik-al, *a.* Of the nature of a problem; questionable; doubtful.
**Proboscis,** prō-bos'is, *n.*; pl. **Proboscides,** prō-bos'i-dēz. The snout or trunk of an elephant, etc.; the sucking-tube of insects.
**Procedure,** prō-sēd'ūr, *n.* Act or manner of proceeding; conduct; management.
**Proceed,** prō-sēd,', *vi.* To go forth or forward; to issue, arise, emanate; to prosecute any design; to carry on a legal action; to take a university degree.
**Proceeding,** prō-sēd'ing, *n.* A going forward; transaction; procedure.
**Proceeds,** prō'sēdz, *n.pl.* Money brought in by some piece of business.
**Process,** prō'ses, *n.* A proceeding or moving forward; gradual progress; course; method of manipulation; lapse; course of legal proceedings; a projecting portion.
**Procession,** prō-se'shon, *n.* A marching forward; a train of persons moving with ceremonious solemnity.
**Processional,** prō-se'shon-al, *a.* Pertaining to a procession.—*n.* A service-book containing prayers, hymns, etc.
**Proclaim,** prō-klām', *vt.* To announce publicly; to promulgate; to publish.
**Proclamation,** pro-kla-mā'shon, *n.* Act of claiming; an official public announcement.
**Proclivity,** prō-kliv'i-ti, *n.* Inclination; propensity; tendency.
**Proclivous,** prō-kliv'us, *a.* Inclining forward; tending by nature.
**Proconsul,** prō-kon'sul, *n.* A Roman officer who acted in the place of a consul; the governor of a province.
**Procrastinate,** prō-kras'ti-nāt, *vt.* and *i.* To put off from day to day; to postpone.
**Procrastination,** prō-kras'ti-nā''shon, *n.* Act or habit of procrastinating; dilatoriness.
**Procreate,** prō'krē-āt, *vt.* To beget; to generate; to engender.
**Procreation,** prō-krē-ā'shon, *n.* Act of procreating or begetting.
**Proctor,** prok'tor, *n.* A legal practitioner in a civil or ecclesiastical court; an official in a university who sees that good order is kept.
**Procumbent,** prō-kum'bent, *a.* Lying down; prone; trailing on the ground.
**Procurable,** prō-kūr'a-bl, *a.* Obtainable.
**Procuration,** pro-kūr-ā'shon, *n.* Service rendered as procurator; agency.
**Procurator,** pro-kūr'āt-or, *n.* The manager of another's affairs as his representative; legal agent or prosecutor.
**Procure,** prō-kūr', *vt.* (procuring, procured). To

obtain; to cause, effect, contrive.—*vi*. To pimp.
**Procurement,** prō-kūr'ment, *n*. The act of procuring or obtaining.
**Procurer,** prō-kūr'ėr, *n*. A pimp.
**Procuress,** prō-kū'res or prok'ū-res, *n*. A female pimp; a bawd.
**Prod,** prod, *n*. A pointed instrument, as a goad; a stab.—*vt*. (prodding, prodded). To prick with a pointed instrument; to goad.
**Prodigal,** prod'i-gal, *a*. Lavish; wasteful.—*n*. A waster; a spendthrift.
**Prodigality,** prod-i-gal'i-ti, *n*. Extravagance in expenditure; profusion; waste.
**Prodigally,** prod'i-gal-li, *adv*. Lavishly.
**Prodigious,** prō-dij'us, *a*. Portentous; extraordinary; huge; enormous.
**Prodigiously,** prō-dij'us-li, *adv*. Enormously; astonishingly; excessively.
**Prodigy,** prod'i-ji, *n*. A portent; a wonder or miracle; a monster.
**Produce,** prō-dūs'v, *vt*. (producing, produced). To bring forward; to exhibit; to bring forth, bear, yield; to supply; to cause; to extend, as a line.—*n*. prō'dūs, What is produced; outcome; yield; agricultural products.
**Producer,** prō-dūs'ėr, *n*. One who produces.
**Producible,** prō-dūs'i-bl, *a*. That may be produced.
**Product,** pro'dukt, *n*. That which is produced; result; effect; number resulting from multiplication.
**Production,** prō-duk'shon, *n*. Act or process of producing; product; performance; literary composition.
**Productive,** prō-duk'tiv, *a*. Having the power of producing; fertile; causing to exist; producing commodities of value.
**Productivity,** prō-duk-tiv'i-ti, *n*. Power of producing.
**Proem,** prō'em, *n*. A prelude or preface; introduction.
**Profanation,** pro-fan-ā'shon, *n*. Act of violating sacred things; desecration.
**Profane,** prō-fān', *a*. Not sacred; secular; irreverent; blasphemous; impure.—*vt*. (profaning, profaned). To treat with irreverence; to desecrate.
**Profanely,** prō-fān'li, *adv*. In a profane manner; impiously; blasphemously.
**Profanity,** prō-fan'i-ti, *n*. Quality of being profane; profane language or conduct.
**Profess,** prō-fes', *vt*. To avow; to ackowledge; to declare belief in; to pretend; to declare oneself versed in.—*vi*. To declare openly.
**Professedly,** prō-fes'ed-li, *adv*. By profession or avowal; avowedly.
**Profession,** prō-fe'shon, *n*. Act of professing; declaration; vocation; such as medicine, law; etc.; the body of persons engaged in such calling.
**Professional,** prō-fe'shon-al, *a*. Pertaining to a profession.—*n*. A member of any profession; one who makes a living by arts, sports, etc., in which amateurs engage.
**Professor,** prō-fes'or, *n*. One who professes; a teacher of the highest rank in a university, etc.
**Professorial,** prō-fes'sō'ri-al, *a*. Pertaining to a professor.
**Professoriate,** prō-fes-sō'ri-āt, *n*. A body of professors; the teaching staff of professors.
**Professorship,** prō-fes'or-ship, *n*. The office or post of a professor.
**Proffer,** prof'ėr, *vt*. (proffering, proffered). To offer for acceptance.—*n*. An offer made.
**Proficiency, Proficience,** prō-fi'shen-si, prō-fe'shens, *n*. State of being proficient; skill and knowledge acquired.
**Proficient,** prō-fi'shent, *a*. Fully versed; competent.—*n*. An adept or expert.
**Proficiently,** prō-fi'shent-li, *adv*. In a proficient manner.
**Profile,** prō'fīl, *n*. An outline; an outline of the human face seen sideways; the side face.—*vt*. To draw in profile.
**Profit,** pro'fit', *n*. Any advantage, benefit, or gain; pecuniary gain.—*vt*. To benefit; to advance.—*vi*. To derive profit; to improve; to be made better or wiser.
**Profitable,** pro'fit-a-bl, *a*. Bringing profit or gain; lucrative; beneficial; useful.
**Profitably,** pro'fit-a-bli, *adv*. In a profitable manner; gainfully; advantageously.
**Profitless,** pro'fit-les, *a*. Void of profit, gain, or advantage.
**Profligacy,** pro'fli-ga-si, *n*. A profligate course of life; depravity; debauchery.
**Profligate,** pro'fli-gāt, *a*. Abandoned to vice; utterly dissolute.—*n*. A depraved man.
**Profound,** prō-found', *a*. Deep; deep in skill or knowledge; far-reaching; bending low; humble.—*n*. The ocean, the abyss.
**Profoundly,** prō-found'li, *adv*. In a profound manner; deeply; extremely.
**Profundity,** prō-fund'i-ti, *n*. State or quality of being profound; depth.
**Profuse,** prō-fūs', *a*. Lavish; exuberant.
**Profusely,** prō-fūs'li, *adv*. Lavishly.
**Profusion,** prō-fū'zhon, *n*. State or quality of being profuse; exuberant plenty.
**Progenitor,** prō-jen'i-tor, *n*. A forefather.
**Progeny,** pro'je-ni, *n*. Offspring; descendants.
**Prognathic, Prognathous,** prog-nath'ik, prog-nā'thus, *a*. Having projecting jaws.
**Prognosis,** prog-nō'sis, *n*. A forecast of the course of a disease.
**Prognostic,** prog-nos'tik, *a*. Foreshowing.—*n*. Omen; presage; token.
**Prognosticate,** prog-nos'tik-āt, *vt*. To foretell; to predict; to foreshow.—*vi*. To judge or pronounce from prognostics.
**Prognostication,** prog-nos'tik-ā''shon, *n*. Act of prognosticating; presage.
**Program,** prō'gram, *n*. A plan of proceedings; statement of the order of proceedings in any entertainment.
**Progress,** prō'gres, *n*. A going forward; a journey of state; a circuit; advance; development.—*vi*. prō-gres'. To advance; to improve.
**Progression,** prō-gre'shon, *n*. Act of progressing; progress; regular or proportional advance.
**Progressive,** prō-gres'iv, *a*. Making steady progress; advancing; advocating progress.
**Prohibit,** prō-hib'it, *vt*. To forbid; to interdict by authority; to prevent.
**Prohibition,** prō-hi-bi'shon, *n*. Act of prohibiting; an interdict; inhibition; the forbidding by law of the manufacture, importation, or sale of alcoholic liquors for ordinary use.
**Prohibitive, Prohibitory,** prō-hib'it-iv, prō-hib'i-to-ri, *a*. Implying prohibition; forbidding.
**Project,** prō-jekt', *vt*. To throw out or forth; to scheme; to delineate.—*vi*. To shoot forward; to jut.—*n*. pro'jekt. A scheme, plan.
**Projectile,** prō-jek'tīl, *a*. Throwing forward.—*n*. A body impelled forward; a missile from a gun.
**Projection,** prō-jek'shon, *n*. Act of projecting; a prominence; representation of something by lines, etc., drawn on a surface.
**Projector,** prō-jek'tor, *n*. One who plans; that which casts something forward.
**Prolapse, Prolapsus,** prō-laps', prō-lap'sus, *n*. A falling down of some internal organ from its proper position.
**Prolate,** prō'lat, *a*. Applied to a sphere projecting too much at the poles.
**Prolegomenon,** prō-le-gom'e-non, *n*.; pl. **-mena.** A preliminary observation; *pl*. an introduction.
**Prolepsis,** prō-lep'sis, *n*. Something of the nature of an anticipation; a rhetorical figure.
**Proleptic, Proleptical,** prō-lep'tik, prō-lep'tik-al, *a*. Pertaining to anticipation.
**Proletarian,** prō-le-tā'ri-an, *n*. and *a*. Applied to a member of the poorest class.
**Proletariat, Proletariate,** prō-le-tā'ri-āt, *n*. Proletarians collectively; the lower classes.
**Prolific,** prō-lif'ik, *a*. Fruitful; productive.
**Prolix,** prō'liks, *a*. Long and wordy; diffuse.
**Prolixity,** prō-liks'i-ti, *n*. State or quality of being

prolix.
**Prologue,** prō'log, *n.* A preface or introduction; address spoken before a dramatic performance.—*vt.* To preface.
**Prolong,** prō-long,' *vt.* To lengthen out; to protract; to postpone.
**Prolongation,** prō-long-gā'shon, *n.* Act of prolonging; part prolonged; extension.
**Prolusion,** prō-lū'zhon, *n.* A prelude; a preliminary trial.
**Promenade,** pro-me-näd', *n.* A walk for pleasure; a place set apart for walking.—*vi.* (promenading, promenaded). To walk for pleasure.
**Prominence,** pro'mi-nens, *n.* State of being prominent; projection; protuberance.
**Prominent,** pro'mi-nent, *a.* Jutting out; protuberant; eminent.
**Prominently,** pro'mi-nent-li, *adv.* Eminently; conspicuously.
**Promiscuous,** prō-mis'kū-us, *a.* Confused; indiscriminate; miscellaneous.
**Promise,** pro'mis, *n.* A statement binding the person who makes it; ground or basis of expectation; pledge.—*vt.* (promising, promised). To make a promise of; to afford reason to expect.—*vi.* To make a promise; to afford expectations.
**Promising,** pro'mis-ing, *p.a.* Giving promise or grounds for good hopes.
**Promissory,** pro'mis-o-ri, *a.* Containing a promise or binding declaration.
**Promontory,** pro'mon-to-ri, *n.* A headland; a cape.
**Promote,** prō-mōt', *vt.* (promoting, promoted). To forward or further; to advance; to encourage; to exalt; to form (a company).
**Promoter,** prō-mōt'ėr, *n.* One who or that which promotes; an encourager; one engaged in getting up a joint-stock company.
**Promotion,** prō-mō'shon, *n.* Act of promoting; advancement; encouragement.
**Prompt,** promt, *a.* Ready; unhesitating; done without delay.—*vt.* To incite to action; to tell a speaker words he forgets; to suggest.
**Prompter,** promt'ėr, *n.* One who prompts; anyone who suggests words to a speaker.
**Promptitude,** promt'i-tūd, *n.* State or quality of being prompt; cheerful alacrity.
**Promptly,** promt'li, *adv.* Readily.
**Promulgate,** prō-mul'gāt, *vt.* (promulgating, promulgated). To publish; to proclaim.
**Promulgation,** prō-mul-gā'shon, *n.* Act of promulgating; publication.
**Promulgator,** prō'mul-gāt-or, *n.* One who promulgates.
**Prone,** prōn, *a.* Bending forward; lying with the face downward; sloping; apt.
**Prong,** prong, *n.* A spike, as of a fork.
**Pronominal,** prō-nom'in-al, *a.* Belonging to or of the nature of a pronoun.
**Pronoun,** prō'noun, *n.* A word used instead of a noun.
**Pronounce,** prō-nouns', *vt.* and *i* (pronouncing, pronounced). To articulate by the organs of speech; to utter formally; to declare or affirm.
**Pronounceable,** prō-nouns'a-bl, *a.* That may be pronounced or uttered.
**Pronounced,** prō-nounst', *p.a.* Strongly marked or defined; decided; glaring.
**Pronounciation,** prō-nun'si-ā''shon, *n.* Act or mode of pronouncing; utterance.
**Proof,** prōf, *n.* Something which tests; trial; what serves to convince; evidence; firmness; a certain standard of strength in spirit; an impression in printing for correction; early impression of an engraving.—*a.* Impenetrable; able to resist.
**Prop,** prop, *n.* A body that supports a weight; a support.—*vt.* (propping, propped). To support by a prop; to sustain generally.
**Propaganda,** pro-pa-gan'da, *n.* An institution or system for propagating any doctrine.
**Propagandist,** prop-a-gan'dist, *n.* One who labors in spreading any doctrines.
**Propagate,** pro'pa-gāt, *vt.* To multiply by generation or reproduction; to diffuse; to increase.—*vi.* To have young or issue; to be multiplied by generation, etc.
**Propel,** prō-pel', *vt.* (propelling, proppeled). To drive, push, or thrust forward.
**Propeller,** prō-pel'ėr, *n.* One who or that which propels; a screw for propelling steamboats.
**Propense,** prō-pens', *a.* Naturally inclined; disposed; prone.
**Propensity,** prō-pens'i-ti, *n.* Bent of mind; natural tendency; disposition.
**Proper,** pro'pėr, *a.* One's own; peculiar: used as the name of a particular person or thing; adapted; correct; real.
**Properly,** pro'pėr-li, *adv.* In a proper manner; fitly; rightly; strictly.
**Property,** pro'pėr-ti, *n.* A peculiar quality or attribute; characteristic; ownership; the thing owned; estate; a stage requisite.
**Prophecy,** pro'fe-si, *n.* A foretelling; a prediction; inspired prediction or utterance.
**Prophesy,** pro'fe-sī, *vt.* To foretell; to predict.—*vi.* To utter prophecies.
**Prophet,** pro'fet, *n.* One who foretells future events.
**Prophetess,** pro'fet-es, *n.* A female prophet.
**Prophetic, Prophetical,** prō-fet'ik, prō-fet'ik-al, *a.* Pertaining to a prophet or prophecy; unfolding future events.
**Prophylactic,** prō-fi-lak'tik, *a.* Preventive of disease.—*n.* A medicine which preserves against disease.
**Propinquity,** prō-pin'kwi-ti, *n.* Nearness; vicinity; kindred.
**Propitiate,** prō-pi'shi-āt, *vt.* To make propitious; to appease.
**Propitiation,** prō-pi'shi-ā''shon, *n.* Act of propitiating or what propitiates; atonement.
**Propitiatory,** prō-pi'shi-a-to-ri, *a.* Having the power to make propitious; conciliatory.—*n.* Among the Jews, the mercy-seat.
**Propitious,** prō-pi'shus, *a.* Favorable; disposed to be gracious or merciful.
**Propitiously,** prō-pi'shus-li, *adv.* Favorably.
**Proportion,** pro-pōr'shon, *n.* Comparative relation; relative size and arrangement; symmetry; just or equal share; lot; that rule which enables us to find a fourth proportional to three numbers.—*vt.* To adjust in due proportion; to form with symmetry.
**Proportional,** pro-pōr'shon-al, *a.* Having a due proportion; relating to proportion.—*n.* A number or quantity proportioned.
**Proportionally,** pro-pōr'shon-al-li, *adv.* In proportion; in due degree.
**Proportionate,** pro-pōr'shon-āt, *a.* Proportional.—*vt.* To make proportional.
**Proposal,** prō-pōz'al, *n.* That which is proposed; offer; proposition.
**Propose,** prō-pōz', *vt.* (proposing, proposed). To offer for consideration.—*vi.* To make a proposal; to purpose; to offer oneself in marriage.
**Proposer,** prō-pōz'ėr, *n.* One who proposes.
**Proposition,** pro-pō-zi'shon, *n.* That which is proposed; a proposal; offer of terms; a form of speech in which something is affirmed or denied.
**Propound,** prō-pound', *vt.* To propose; to offer for consideration; to put, as a question.
**Proprietary,** prō-prī'e-ta-ri, *a.* Belonging to a proprietor.—*n.* A proprietor; a body of proprietors.
**Proprietor,** pro-prī'e-tor, *n.* An owner; one who has legal right to anything.
**Propriety,** prō-prī'e-ti, *n.* State of being proper; fitness; consonance with established principles or customs; justness.
**Propulsion,** prō-pul'shon, *n.* Act of propelling or of driving forward.
**Prosaic,** prō-zā'ik, *a.* Pertaining to prose; dull; commonplace.
**Proscribe,** prō-skrīb', *vt.* To outlaw; to condemn

P

as dangerous; to interdict.
**Proscription,** prō-skrip'shon, *n*. Act of proscribing; outlawry; utter rejection.
**Proscriptive,** prō-skrip'tiv, *a*. Pertaining to or consisting in proscription; proscribing.
**Prose,** prōz, *n*. Speech or language not in verse.—*vi*. (prosing, prosed). To write or speak in a dull, tedious, style.—*a*. Relating to prose; prosaic.
**Prosecute,** pro'se-kūt, *vt*. and *i* (prosecuting, prosecuted). To persist in; to carry on; to pursue at law.
**Prosecution,** pro-se-kū'shon, *n*. Act of prosecuting; the carrying on of a suit at law; the party by whom criminal proceedings are instituted.
**Prosecutor,** pro'se-kūt-or, *n*. One who prosecutes, especially in a criminal suit.
**Prosecutrix,** pro'sē-kūt-riks, *n*. A female 'who prosecutes.
**Proselyte,** pro'se-līt, *n*. A convert to the Jewish faith; a new convert.—*vt*. To make a convert of.
**Proselytism,** pro'se-līt-izm, *n*. The making of proselytes; conversion.
**Proselytize,** pro'se-līt-īz, *vt*. To make a proselyte of.—*vi*. To engage in making proselytes.
**Prosopopeia, Prosopopoeia,** pro'so-pō-pē''ya, *n*. A figure of rhetoric by which inanimate things are spoken as living; personification.
**Prospect,** pros'pekt, *n*. A distant view; sight; scene; outlook; exposure; expectation.—*vt*. and *i*. pros-pekt'. To make search for precious stones or metals.
**Prospective,** pros-pek'tiv, *a*. Looking forward; regarding the future.
**Prospectus,** pros-pek'tus, *n*. A statement of some enterprise proposed, as a literary work, a new company, etc.
**Prosper,** pros'pėr, *vi*. To increase in wealth or any good; to thrive.—*vt*. To make to succed.
**Prosperity,** pros-pe'ri-ti, *n*. Flourishing state; satisfactory progress; success.
**Prosperous,** pros'pėr-us, *a*. Successful; flourishing; fortunate; thriving.
**Prostitute,** pros'ti-tūt, *vt*. (prostituting, prostituted). To offer publicly for lewd purposes for hire; to devote to anything base.—*a*. Openly devoted to lewdness.—*n*. A female given to indiscrimate lewdness.
**Prostitution,** pros-ti-tū'shon, *n*. Practice of offering the body to indiscriminate intercourse with men; debasement.
**Prostrate,** pros'trāt, *a*. Lying with the body flat; lying at mercy.—*vt*. (prostrating, prostrated). To lay flat or prostrate; to bow in reverence; to overthrow; to ruin.
**Prostration,** pros-trā'shon, *n*. Act of prostrating; great depression of strength or spirits.
**Prostyle,** pros'tīl, *a*. Having pillars in front.
**Prosy,** prōz'i, *a*. Like prose; dull and tedious in discourse or writing.
**Protean,** prō'tē-an, *a*. Assuming different shapes; variable; changeable.
**Protect,** prō-tekt', *vt*. To shield from danger, injury, etc.; to guard against foreign competition by tariff regulations.
**Protection,** prō-tek'shon, *n*. Act of protecting; shelter; defence; the system of favoring articles of home production by duties on foreign articles.
**Protectionist,** prō-tek'shon-ist, *n*. One who favors the protection of some branch of industry; one opposed to free-trade.
**Protective,** prō-tekt'iv, *a*. Affording protection; sheltering; defensive.
**Protector,** prō-tekt'or, *n*. One who protects; a defender; a guardian; a preserver.
**Protectorate,** prō-tekt'or-āt, *n*. Government by a protector; a country protected by another.
**Protectress, Protectrix,** prō-tekt'res, prō-tekt'riks, *n*. A woman who protects..
**Protégé,** pro-tā-zhā; fem. **Protégée,** pro-tā-zhā, *n*. One under the care of another.
**Proteid,** prō'tē-id, *n*. A name of certain nitrogenous substances forming the soft tissues of the body, and found also in plants.
**Protest,** prō-test', *vi*. To affirm with solemnity; to make a formal declaration of opposition.—*vt*. To assert; to mark for non-payment, as a bill.—*n*. prō'test. A formal declaration of dissent; a declaration that payment of a bill has been refused.
**Protestant,** pro'test-ant, *n*. One of the party who adhered to Luther at the Reformation; a member of a reformed church.—*a*. Belonging to the religion of the Protestants.
**Protestantism,** pro'test-an-tizm, *n*. The principles or religion of Protestants.
**Protestation,** prō-test'-ā'shon, *n*. The act of protesting; a protest.
**Protocol,** prō'tō-kol, *n*. A diplomatic document serving as a preliminary to diplomatic transactions.
**Proton** prō'ton, *n*. A positively charged particle, the nucleus of a hydrogen atom.
**Protoplasm,** prō'tō-plazm, *n*. A substance constituting the basis of living matter in animals and plants..
**Prototype,** prō'tō-tīp, *n*. An original type or model; a pattern.
**Protract,** prō-trakt', *vt*. To prolong; to delay; to defer; to draw to a scale.
**Protraction,** prō-trak'shon, *n*. Act of protracting; act of laying down on paper the dimensions of a field, etc.
**Protractive,** prō-trakt'iv, *a*. Protracting.
**Protractor,** prō-trakt'or, *n*. One who or that which protracts; an instrument for surveying; a muscle which draws forward a part.
**Protrude,** prō-trōd', *vt*. and *i* (protruding, protruded). To thrust forward; to project.
**Protrusion,** prō-trō'zhon, *n*. State of being protruded; a thrusting forth.
**Protrusive,** prō-trō'siv, *a*. Protruding; prominent.
**Protuberance,** prō-tū'bėr-ans, *n*. A swelling or tumor; a prominence; a knob.
**Protuberant,** prō-tū'bėr-ant, *a*. Swelling; bulging out.
**Protuberate,** prō-tū'bėr-āt, *vi*. To bulge out.
**Proud,** proud, *a*. Having a high opinion of oneself; haughty; of fearless spirit; ostentatious; magnificent.—**Proud flesh,** an excessive granulation in wounds or ulcers.
**Proudly,** proud'li, *adv*. In a proud manner; haughtily; with lofty airs or mien.
**Provable,** prōv'a-bl, *a*. That may be proved.
**Prove,** prōv, *vt*. (proving, proved). To try by experiment; to test; to establish the truth or reaity of; to demonstrate; to obtain probate of.—*vi*. To be found by experience or trial; to turn out to be.
**Proven,** prō'vn, *pp*. Proved.
**Provenance,** prov'e-nans, *n*. Origin.
**Provender,** prov'en-dėr, *n*. Dry food or fodder for beasts; provisions; food.
**Proverb,** pro'vėrb, *n*. A popular saying, expressing a truth or common fact; an adage; a maxim; a by-word; a dark saying.
**Proverbial,** prō-vėrb'i-al, *a*. Pertaining to or like a proverb; commonly spoken of.
**Proverbially,** prō-vėrb'i-al-li, *adv*. In a proverbial style; by way of proverb.
**Provide,** prō-vīd', *vt*. and *i* (providing, provided). To procure beforehand; to prepare; to supply; to stipulate previously.
**Provided,** prō-vīd'ed, *conj*. On condition.
**Providence,** pro'vi-dens, *n*. Foresight; the care which God exercises over his creatures; God; a providential circumstance.
**Provident,** pro'vi-dent, *a*. Foreseeing and providing for wants; prudent; frugal.
**Providential,** pro-vi-den'shal, *a*. Effected by providence.
**Providentially,** pro-vi-den'shal-li, *adv*. By the intervention of providence.
**Providently,** pro'vi-dent-li, *adv*. In a provident manner; with prudent foresight.
**Province,** pro'vins, *n*. A territory at some distance from the metropolis; a large political divi-

sion; sphere of action; department.
**Provincial,** prō-vin'shal, *a.* Pertaining to or forming a province; characteristic of the people of a province; rustic.—*n.* A person belonging to a province.
**Provincialism,** prō-vin'shal-izm, *n.* A rustic idiom or word.
**Provision,** prō-vi'zhon, *n.* Act of providing; preparaton; stores provided; victuals; stipulation; proviso.—*vt.* To supply with provisions.
**Provisional,** prō-vi'zhon-al, *a.* Provided for present need; temporary.
**Provisionally,** prō-vi'zhon-al-li, *adv.* In a provisional manner; temporarily.
**Proviso,** prō-vī'zō *n.* An article or clause in any statute or contract; stipulation.
**Provisory,** prō-vī'zo-ri, *a.* Making temporary provision; temporary; conditional.
**Provocation,** pro-vō-kā'shon, *n.* Act of provoking; cause of resentment; incitement.
**Provocative,** prō-vok'a-tiv, *a.* Serving to provoke; exciting.—*n.* A stimulant.
**Provoke,** prō-vōk', vt (provoking, provoked). To incite; to stimulate; to incense; to irritate.—*vi.* To produce anger.
**Provoking,** prō-vōk'ing, *p.a.* Exciting resentment; annoying; vexatious.
**Provost,** pro'vost, *n.* The head of certain bodies, as colleges; chief dignitary of a cathedral; chief magistrate of a Scottish burgh.
**Provost-marshal,** pro'vo-mär-shal, *n.* A military officer who attends to offenses against discipline.
**Prow,** prou, *n.* The forepart of a ship.
**Prowess,** prou'es, *n.* Bravery; boldness and dexterity in war; gallantry.
**Prowl,** proul, *vi.* and *t.* To roam or wander stealthily.—*n.* Act of one who prowls.
**Proximity,** proks-im'i-ti, *n.* State of being proximate; immediate nearness.
**Proxy,** proks'i, *n.* Agency of a substitute; a deputy; a writing by which one authorizes another to vote in his stead.
**Prude,** pröd, *n.* A woman affecting great reserve and excessive delicacy.
**Prudence,** prö'dens, *n.* Quality of being prudent; caution; discretion.
**Prudent,** prö'dent, *a.* Provident; careful; discreet; judicious.
**Prudential,** prö-den'shal, *a.* Proceeding from or dictated by prudence; politic.
**Prudery,** pröd'ė-ri, *n.* The conduct of a prude; affected delicacy of feeling.
**Prudish,** pröd'ish, *a.* Like a prude; affecting excessive modesty or virtue.
**Prune,** prön, *vt.* (pruning, pruned). To trim; to cut or lop off; to clear from superfluities.—*n.* A plum, particularly a dried plum.
**Prurience, Pruriency,** prö'ri-ens, prö'ri-en-si, *n.* An itching desire for anything; tendency to lascivious thoughts.
**Prurient,** prö'ri-ent, *a.* Itching after something; inclined to lascivious thoughts.
**Pry,** prī, *vi.* (prying, pried). To peep narrowly; to look closely; to peer.—*n.* A keen glance.
**Prying,** prī'ing, *p.a.* Apt to pry; inspecting closely; looking into with curiosity.
**Psalm,** säm, *n.* A sacred song or hymn.
**Psalmist,** säm'ist, or sal'mist, *n.* A writer or composer of psalms.
**Psalter,** sal'tėr, *n.* The Book of Psalms; a book containing the Psalms separately.
**Psaltery,** sal'te-ri, *n.* A Hebrew stringed instrument of music; a kind of dulcimer.
**Pseudo-,** sū'dō. A prefix signifying false or spurious.
**Pseudonym,** sū'dō-nim, *n.* A false or feigned name; a name assumed by a writer.
**Psychiatry,** sī'ki-at-ri, *n.* Medical treatment of diseases of the mind.
**Psychic, Psychical,** sī'kik, sī'kik-al, *a.* Belonging to the soul; psychological; pertaining to that force by which spiritualists aver they produce "spiritual" phenomena.
**Psychologic, Psychological,** sī-ko-loj'ik, sī-ko-loj'ik-al, *a.* Pertaining to psychology or science of mind.
**Psychologist,** sī-kol'o-jist, *n.* One who is conversant with psychology.
**Psychology,** sī-kol'o-ji, *n.* That branch of knowledge which deals with the mind; mental science.
**Ptarmigan,** tär'mi-gan, *n.* The white grouse.
**Ptolemaic,** to-lē-mā'ik, *a.* Pertaining to Ptolemy, or to his system of the universe, in which the sun revolved round the earth.
**Ptomaine,** tō'mān, *n.* A name of certain substances generated during putrefaction or morbid conditions prior to death.
**Ptyalism,** tī'al-izm, *n.* Salivation.
**Puberty,** pū'bėr-ti, *n.* The age at which persons can beget or bear children.
**Pubescence,** pū-bes'ens, *n.* Puberty; the downy substance on plants.
**Pubescent,** pū-bes'ent, *a.* Arriving at puberty; covered with fine soft hairs.
**Public,** pub'lik, *a.* Not private; pertaining to a whole community; open or free to all; common; notorious.—*n.* The people, indefinitely.—**In public,** in open view.
**Publican,** pub'li-kan, *n.* A collector of public revenues; keeper of a public-house.
**Publication,** pub-li-kā'shon, *n.* Act of publishing; announcement; promulgation; act of offering a book, etc., to the public by sale; any book, etc., published.
**Public-house,** pub'lik-hous, *n.* An inn or shop for the retail of spirituous liquors.
**Publicist,** pub'li-sist, *n.* A writer on the current political topics.
**Publicity,** pub-lis'i-ti, *n.* State of being made public; notoriety; currency.
**Publicly,** pub'lik-li, *adv.* In a public manner; openly; without concealment.
**Publish,** pub'lish, *vt.* To make public; to proclaim, promulgate; to cause to be printed and offered for sale.
**Publisher,** pub'lish-ėr, *n.* One who publishes, especially books.
**Pucker,** puk'ėr, *vt.* and *i* To gather into small folds; to wrinkle.—*n.* A fold or wrinkle, or a collection of folds.
**Pudding,** pud'ing, *n.* An intestine; a sausage; a dish variously compounded, of flour, milk, eggs, fruit, etc.
**Puddle,** pud'l, *n.* A small pool of dirty water; clay worked into a mass impervious to water.—*vt.* (puddling, puddled). To make muddy; to make water-tight with clay; to convert pig-iron into wrought-iron.
**Puddling,** pud'ling, *n.* The operation of working clay so as to resist water; clay thus used; process of converting cast-iron into malleable iron.
**Pudgy,** puj'i, *a.* Fat and short.
**Puerperal,** pū-ėr'pėr-al, *a.* Pertaining to childbirth.
**Puff,** puf, *n.* A sudden emission of breath; a whiff; a short blast of wind; a puff-ball; piece of light pastry; a consciously exaggerated commendation.—*vi.* To give a quick blast with the mouth; to breathe hard after exertion.—*vt.* To drive with a blast; to inflate; to praise extravagantly.
**Puff-adder,** puf'ad-ėr, *n.* A venomous snake which swells out the upper part of its body.
**Puff-ball,** puf'bal, *n.* A ball-shaped fungus which when ripe discharges a fine powder.
**Puffin,** puf'in, *n.* A diving bird of the auk family.
**Puffy,** puf'i, *a.* Puffed out; turgid.
**Pug,** pug, *n.* A monkey; a dwarf variety of dog.
**Pugilism,** pū'jil-izm, *n.* The practice of boxing or fighting with the fist.
**Pugilist, pū'jil-ist,** *n.* One who fights with his fists.
**Pugilistic,** pū-jil-ist'ik, *a.* Pertaining to pugilism.
**Pugnacious,** pug-nā'shus, *a.* Disposed to fight;

P

quarrelsome.
**Pugnacity,** pug-nas'i-ti, *n.* Quality of being pugnacious; inclination to fight.
**Pug-nose,** pug'nōz, *n.* A nose turned up at the end; a snub-nose.
**Puisne,** pū'ni, *a.* Younger or inferior in rank.
**Puissance,** pū'is-ans, *n.* Power; might.
**Puissant,** pū'is-ant, *a.* Powerful; strong; mighty; forcible.
**Puke,** pūke, *vi.* and *t.* (puking, puked). To vomit.
**Pulchritude,** pul'kri-tūd, *n.* Beauty; comeliness.
**Pule,** pūl, *vi.* (puling, puled). To cry like a chicken; to whine; to whimper.
**Pulkha,** pul'ka, *n.* A Laplander's travelling sledge.
**Pull,** pul, *vt.* To draw towards one; to tug; to rend; to pluck; to gather.—*vi.* To draw; to tug.—*n.* Act of pulling; a twitch; act of rowing a boat; a drink; a struggle.
**Pullet,** pul'et, *n.* A young hen.
**Pulley,** pul'i, A small wheel in a block, used in raising weights.
**Pullman-car,** pul'man-kär, *n.* A luxuriously fitted up railway-carriage.
**Pull-over,** pul'ō-vėr, *n.* A knitted jersey without buttons, pulled over the head when put on.
**Pull-through,** pul'thrö, *n.* A cord with a weight at one end and a loop for a piece of oiled rag at the other, used for cleaning the barrel of a rifle.
**Pulmonary,** pul'mon-a-ri, *a.* Pertaining to or affecting the lungs.
**Pulp,** pulp, *n.* Moist, soft animal or vegetable matter.—*vt.* To make into pulp; to deprive of the pulp.
**Pulpit,** pul'pit, *n.* An elevated place for a preacher; preachers generally.
**Pulpy,** pul'pi, *a.* Like pulp; soft; fleshy.
**Pulsate,** pul'sāt, *vi.* To beat or throb.
**Pulsation,** pul-sā'shon, *n.* The beating of the heart or an artery; a throb.
**Pulse,** puls, *n.* The beating of the heart or an artery; vibration; leguminous plants or their seeds, as beans, etc.—*vi.* (pulsing, pulsed). To beat or throb.
**Pulverize,** pul'vėr-īz, *vt.* To reduce to dust or fine powder.
**Pulverulent,** pul-ver'ū-lent, *a.* Powdery.
**Puma,** pū'ma, *n.* A carnivorous quadruped of the cat kind; the cougar.
**Pumice,** pū'mis or pum'is, *n.* A light and spongy stone, used for polishing.
**Pumisceous,** pū-mi'shus, *a.* Pertaining to, consisting of or like pumice.
**Pump,** pump, *n.* A machine for raising water or extracting air; a shoe used in dancing.—*vi.* To work a pump.—*vt.* To raise with a pump; to free from liquid by a pump; to put artful questions to extract information.
**Pumpkin,** pump'kin, *n.* A plant and its fruit; a kind of gourd or vegetable marrow.
**Pun,** pun, *n.* A play on words like in sound, but different in meaning; a kind of quibble.—*vi.* (punning, punned) To make a pun or puns.
**Punch,** punsh, *n.* An instrument for driving holes in metal, etc.; a blow or thrust; a beverage of spirits, lemon-juice, water, etc.; a buffoon; a short-legged, barrel-bodied horse; a short fat fellow.—*vt.* To stamp or perforate with a punch; to hit with the fist.
**Puncheon,** pun'shon, *n.* A perforating or stamping tool; a punch; a cask containing from 84 to 120 gallons.
**Punchy,** punsh'i, *a.* Short and fat; squat.
**Punctual,** pungk'tū-al, *a.* Exact; made or done at the exact time.
**Punctuality,** pungk-tū-al'i-ti, *n.* Quality of being punctual; scrupulous exactness.
**Punctuate,** pungk'tū-āt, *vt.* To mark with the points necessary in writings.
**Punctuation,** pungk-tū-ā'shon, *n.* The act, art, or system of punctuating a writing.
**Puncture,** pungk'tūr, *n.* The act of pricking; a small hole thus made.—*vt.* (puncturing, punctured). To pierce with a small point.
**Pundit,** pun'dit, *n.* A learned Brahman; an Indian scholar; any learned man.
**Pungency,** pun'jen-si, *n.* State or quality of being pungent; sharpness; keenness.
**Pungent,** pun'jent, *a.* Biting; acrid; caustic; keen; stinging.
**Punic,** pū'nik, *a.* Pertaining to the Carthaginians; faithless.—*n.* The language of the Carthaginians; Phoenician.
**Punish,** pun'ish, *vt.* To inflict pain or any evil on, as a penalty; to chastise; to hurt.
**Punishable,** pun'ish-a-bl, *a.* Liable to punishment; capable of being punished.
**Punishment,** pun'ish-ment, *a.* Act of punishing; penalty.
**Punitive,** pū-ni-tiv, *a.* Pertaining to, awarding, or involving punishment.
**Punitory,** pū'ni-to-ri, *a.* Punitive.
**Punning,** pun'ing, *p.a.* Given to make puns; containing a pun or puns.
**Punster,** pun'stėr, *n.* One skilled in punning.
**Punt,** punt, *n.* A square-ended flat-bottomed boat.—*vt.* To convey in a punt; to propel (a boat) with a pole.
**Puny,** pūn'i, *a.* Small and weak; petty.
**Pup,** pup, *n.* A puppy.—*vi.* (pupping, pupped). To bring forth whelps.
**Pupa,** pū'pa, *n.*; pl. **-ae.** The chrysalis form of an insect.
**Pupil,** pū'pil, *n.* A young person under the care of a tutor; the aperture in the iris through which the rays of light pass.
**Pupilary,** (or **-ll-**), pū'pil-a-ri, *a.* Pertaining to a pupil or ward, or to the pupil of the eye.
**Puppet,** pup'et, *n.* A small figure in the human form mechanically worked; a person who is a mere tool.
**Puppy,** pup'i, *n.* A whelp; a young dog; a conceited, foppish fellow.
**Purchasable,** pėr'chās-a-bl, *a.* That may be purchased or bought.
**Purchase,** pėr'chās, *vt.* (purchasing, purchased). To buy; to obtain by labor, danger, etc.—*n.* Acquisition of anything by money; what is bought; mechanical advantage.
**Purchaser,** pėr'chās-ėr, *n.* A buyer.
**Pure,** pūr, *a.* Clean; clear; unmixed; spotless; chaste; genuine; sincere; absolute.
**Purely,** pūr'li, *adv.* Innocently; stainlessly; chastely; wholly; absolutely.
**Purgation,** pėr-gā'shon, *n.* Act or operation of purging.
**Purgative,** pėr'ga-tiv, *a.* Having the power of purging.—*n.* A medicine that purges.
**Purgatory,** pėr'ga-to-ri, *a.* Tending to purge or cleanse.—*n.* In the R. Catholic religion, a place in which souls after death are purified from sins; any place or state of temporary suffering.
**Purge,** pėrj, *vt.* and *i.* (purging, purged). To make pure or clean; to clear from accusation; to evacuate the bowels of.—*n.* The act of purging; a cathartic medicine.
**Purification,** pū'ri-fi-kā''shon, *n.* Act of purifying; a cleansing from guilt or sin.
**Purifier,** pū'ri-fī-ėr, *n.* One who or that which purifies or cleanses.
**Purify,** pū'ri-fī, *vt.* (purifying, purified). To make pure or clear; to free from admixture; to free from guilt.—*vi.* To become pure or clear.
**Purism,** pūr'izm, *n.* Practice of rigid purity; fastidious niceness in the use of words.
**Purist,** pūr'ist, *n.* One excessively nice in the use of words, etc.
**Puritan,** pūr'i-tan, *n.* One very strict in religious matters or in conduct; an early Protestant dissenter from the Church of England.—*a.* Pertaining to the Puritans.
**Puritanic, Puritanical,** pūr-i-tan'ik, pūr-i-tan'ik-al, *a.* Puritan; over rigid in religion.
**Purity,** pūr'i-ti, *n.* State or quality of being pure; cleanness; innocence; chastity.
**Purl,** pėrl, *n.* Spiced malt liquor; gentle murmur

of a stream.—*vi*. To murmur, as a stream; to reverse a stitch in knitting.
**Purlieu,** pėr'lū, *n*. Part lying adjacent; outskirts; generally in *pl*.
**Purloin,** pėr-loin', *vt*. To steal or pilfer; to filch; to take by theft or plagiarism.
**Purple,** pėr'pl, *n*. A color produced by mixing red and blue; a purple robe, the badge of the Roman emperors; regal power.—*a*. Of a color made of red and blue; dyed with blood.—*vt*. (purpling, purpled). To make purple.
**Purport,** pėr'pōrt, *n*. Meaning; import.—*vt*. To signify; to profess.
**Purpose,** pėr'pos, *n*. End or aim; design; intention; matter in question.—*vt*. and *i*. (purposing, purposed). To propose; to intend.
**Purposely,** pėr'pos-li, *adv*. By purpose or design; intentionally.
**Purr,** pėr, *vi*. To murmur, as a cat when pleased.—*n*. The sound of a cat when pleased.
**Purse,** pėrs, *n*. A small bag or receptacle for money; money collected as a prize or a present; finances.—*vt*. (pursing, pursed). To put in a purse; to pucker.
**Purser,** pėrs'ėr, *n*. A person belonging to a ship, who keeps accounts.
**Purslane,** pėrs'lān, *n*. A succulent plant, used as a pot-herb, and for salads, etc.
**Pursuance,** pėr-sū'ans, *n*. The pursuing or carrying out (of a design).
**Pursuant,** pėr-sū'ant, *a*. Done in prosecution of anything; conformable.
**Pursue,** pėr-sū', *vt*. (pursuing, pursued). To follow with a view to overtake; to chase; to use measures to obtain; to carry on.—*vi*. To go in pursuit; to act as prosecutor.
**Pursuer,** pėr-sū'ėr, *n*. One who pursues; the plaintiff.
**Pursuit,** pėr-sūt', *n*. Act of pursuing; chase; quest; business occupation.
**Pursuivant,** pėr'swi-vant, *n*. A state messenger; an attendant on heralds.
**Pursy,** pėr'si, *a*. Fat and short-winded.
**Purtenance,** pėr'te-nans, *n*. Appurtenance; the pluck of an animal.
**Purulence, Purulency,** pū'ru-lens, pū'ru-len-si, *n*. State of being purulent; pus.
**Purulent,** pū'ru-lent, *a*. Consisting or of the nature of pus.
**Purvey,** pėr-vā', *vt*. To provide.—*vi*. To supply provisions, especially for a number.
**Purveyance,** pėr-vā'ans, *n*. Act of purveying; the former royal prerogative of obtaining necessaries on easy terms.
**Purveyor,** pėr-vā'or, *n*. One who purveys; a caterer.
**Purview,** pėr'vū, *n*. The body of a statute; the scope of a statute; limit; sphere.
**Pus,** pus, *n*. The soft yellowish substance formed in suppuration; matter of a sore.
**Puseyism,** pū'zi-izm, *n*. The doctrines promulgated by Dr. *Pusey* and other divines; tractarianism.
**Push,** push, *vt*. To press against with force; to thrust or shove; to enforce; to urge; to prosecute energetically.—*vi*. To make a thrust or effort; to force one's way.—*n*. Act of pushing; vigorous effort; emergency; enterprise.
**Pushing,** push'ing, *p.a*. Pressing forward in business; enterprising; energetic.
**Pushto, Pushtoo,** push'tō, push'tö, *n*. The language of the Afghans.
**Pusillanimity,** pū'sil-la-nim''i-ti, *n*. Weakness of spirit; cowardice; timidity.
**Pusillanimous,** pū-sil-lan'im-us, *a*. Without strength of mind; timid; cowardly.
**Puss,** pus, *n*. A cat; a hare.
**Pussy,** pus'i, *n*. A diminutive of puss.
**Pustulate,** pus'tū-lāt, *vi*. To form into pustules.—*a*. Covered with pustule-like prominences.
**Pustule,** pus'tūl, *n*. A small blister; small elevation of the cuticle, containing pus.
**Put,** put, *vt*. (putting, put). To place in any position or situation; to apply; to propose or propound; to state in words.
**Put, Putt,** put, *vt*. (putting, putted). To throw (a heavy stone) from the shoulder; in golf, to play the ball into the hole.—*n*. A rustic; a silly fellow.
**Putrefaction,** pū-trē-fak'shon, *n*. Process or state of putrefying; decomposition.
**Putrefactive,** pū-trē-fak'tiv, *a*. Pertaining to or causing putrefaction.
**Putrefy,** pū'trē-fī, *vt*. (putrefying, putrefied). To render putrid.—*vi*. To decay; to rot.
**Putrescence,** pū-tres'ens, *n*. State of becoming rotten; a putrid state.
**Putrescent,** pū-tres'ent, *a*. Growing putrid.
**Putrid,** pū'trid, *a*. In a state of decay; rotten; corrupt.
**Putridity,** pū-trid'i-ti, *n*. State of being putrid; corruption.
**Putter,** put'ėr, *n*. One who puts, sets, or places; a kind of golfing club (pron. put'ėr).
**Putting-green,** put'ing-grēn, *n*. A smooth piece of sward round a hole in a gold course.
**Puttock,** put'ok, *n*. The common kite.
**Putty,** put'i, *n*. A paste made of whiting and linseed-oil.—*vt*. To cement or fill with putty.
**Puzzle,** puz'l, *vt*. (puzzling, puzzled). To perplex; to entangle.—*vi*. To be bewildered.—*n*. Perplexity; something to try ingenuity.
**Puzzle-headed,** puz'l-hed-ed, *a*. Having a head easily puzzled; bungling.
**Puzzlement,** puz'l-ment, *n*. The state of being puzzled; bewilderment.
**Puzzler,** puz'l-ėr, *n*. One who or that which puzzles.
**Puzzling,** puz'ling, *p.a*. Such as to puzzle; perplexing; embarrassing; bewildering.
**Pyemia,** pī-ē'mi-a, *n*. Blood-poisoning.
**Pygmy,** pig'mi, *n*. A dwarf; anything little.—*a*. Dwarfish; little.
**Pylorus,** pī-lō'rus, *n*. The lower orifice of the stomach.
**Pyramid,** pi'ra-mid, *n*. A solid body having triangular sides meeting in a point at the top.
**Pyramidal,** pi-ram'id-al, *a*. Formed like a pyramid; relating to a pyramid.
**Pyramidic, Pyramidical,** pi-ra-mid'ik, pi-ra-mid'ik-al, *a*. Having the form of a pyramid; relating to a pyramid.
**Pyre,** pīr, *n*. A heap of combustibles for burning a dead body; a funeral pile.
**Pyrethrum,** pi-reth'rum, *n*. A plant akin to the chrysanthemum.
**Pyretic,** pī-ret'ik, *n*. A medicine for fever.—*a*. Pertaining to fever; feverish.
**Pyrites,** pi-rī'tēz, *n*. A mineral combining sulphur with iron, copper, cobalt, etc.
**Pyrolatry,** pī-rol'a-tri, *n*. Fire-worship.
**Pyroligneous,** pī-rō-lig'nē-us, *a*. Generated by the distillation of wood.
**Pyrology,** pī-rol'o-ji, *n*. The science of heat.
**Pyrometer,** pī-rom'et-ėr, *n*. An instrument for measuring high degrees of heat.
**Pyrotechnic,** pī-rō-tek'nik, *a*. Pertaining to pyrotechny or fireworks. Also *Pyrotechnical*.
**Pyrotechnics, Pyrotechny,** pī-rō-tek'niks, pī-rō-tek'ni, *n*. The art of making fireworks; the use of fireworks.
**Pyrotechnist,** pī-rō-tek'nist, *n*. One skilled in pyrotechny.
**Pyrrhic,** pi'rik, *n*. and *a*. An ancient Grecian warlike dance; a metrical foot of two short syllables.—**Pyrrhic victory,** a victory like those of Pyrrhus of Epirus over the Romans, costing more to the victor than to the vanquished.
**Pythagorean,** pi-tha'gō-rē''an, *a*. Pertaining to Pythagoras or his philosophy, which taught the transmigration of souls.
**Python,** pī'thon, *n*. A large non-venomous serpent.
**Pythoness,** pī'thon-es, *n*. The priestess who gave oracular answers at Delphi; a female with a spirit of divination.
**Pyx,** piks, *n*. A vessel used in the R. Catholic

P

Church for holding the host; a box or chest for specimen coins at the British Mint; the metallic box containing the nautical compass-card.—**Trial of the Pyx,** the trial by weight and assay of the gold and silver coins of the United Kingdom.—*vt.* To test by weight and assay.

# Q

**Qua,** kwā, *adv.* In the quality or character of; as being; as.
**Quack,** kwak, *vi.* To cry like a duck; to boast; to practice quackery.—*n.* The cry of a duck; a pretender to skill or knowledge, especially medical.—*a.* Pertaining to quackery.
**Quackery,** kwak'ė-ri, *n.* Practice or boastful pretenses of a quack, particularly in medicine.
**Quackish,** kwak'ish, *a.* Like a quack.
**Quad,** kwod, *n.* A quadrangle or court.
**Quadragesima,** kwod-ra-je'si-ma, *n.* Lent.
**Quadrangle,** kwod-rang-gl, *n.* A plane figure, have four angles and sides; an inner square of a building.
**Quadrangular,** kwod-rang'gū-lėr, *a.* Having four angles and four sides.
**Quadrant,** kwod'rant, *n.* The fourth part of a circle or its circumference; an old instrument for taking altitudes and angles; an old form of sextant.
**Quadrat,** kwod'rat, *n.* A piece of type-metal for leaving a blank in printing.
**Quadrate,** kwod'rāt, *a.* Square.—*n.* A square surface or figure.—*vi.* To square with; to agree or suit.
**Quadratic,** kwod-rat'ik, *a.* In *algebra,* involving the square of an unknown quantity.
**Quadrennial,** kwod-ren'ni-al, *a.* Comprising four years; occurring once in four years.
**Quadrilateral,** kwod-ri-lat'ėr-al, *a.* Having four sides and four angles.—*n.* A plane figure having four sides and angles.
**Quadrillion,** kwod-ril'yon, *n.* The fourth power of a million; a number represented by a unit and 24 ciphers.
**Quadripartite,** kwod-ri-pär'tīt, *a.* Divided into or having four parts.
**Quadrisyllable,** kwod-ri-sil'la-bl, *n.* A word consisting of four syllables.
**Quadroon,** kwod-rön', *n.* The offspring of a mulatto by a white person.
**Quadrumana,** kwod-ru'ma-na, *n.pl.* An order of mammals comprising the monkey tribe, characterized by the four limbs terminating in prehensile hands.
**Quadrumanous,** kwod-ru'ma-nus, *a.* Pertaining to the Quadrumana; four-handed.
**Quadruped,** kwod'ru-ped, *n.* An animal with four legs or feet.
**Quadruple,** kwod'ru-pl, *a.* Fourfold.—*n.* Four times the sum or number.—*vt.* To make fourfold.—*vi.* To become fourfold.
**Quaff,** kwäf, *vt.* and *i.* To drain to the bottom; to drink coplously.
**Quagmire,** kwag'mīr, *n.* A piece of soft, wet, boggy land; a bog; a fen.
**Quail,** kwāl, *vi.* To shrink; to flinch; to cower.—*n.* A small bird allied to the partridge.
**Quaint,** kwānt, *a.* Fanciful; curious; odd and antique; singular; whimsical.
**Quaintly,** kwānt'li, *adv.* In a quaint manner; oddly; fancifully; whimsically.
**Quake,** kwāk, *vi.* (quaking, quaked). To shake; to tremble; to quiver.—*n.* A shake; tremulous agitation.
**Quaker,** kwāk'ėr, *n.* One who quakes; one of the religious sect called the *Society of Friends.*
**Quakerism,** kwāk'ėr-izm, *n.* The manners, tenets, or worship of the Quakers.
**Qualification,** kwo'li-fi-kā''shon, *n.* Act of qualifying; state of being qualified; suitable quality or characteristic; legal power; ability; modification; restriction.
**Qualified,** kwo'li-fīd, *p.a.* Having qualification; competent; limited; modified.
**Qualify,** kwo'li-fī, *vt.* (qualifying, qualified). To give proper or suitable qualities to; to furnish with the knowledge, skill, etc., necessary; to modify or limit; to soften or moderate; to dilute.—*vi.* To become qualified or fit.
**Qualitative,** kwo'li-tā-tiv, *a.* Relating to quality; estimable according to quality.
**Quality,** kwo'li-ti, *n.* Sort, kind, or character; a distinguishing property or characteristic; degree of excellence; high rank.
**Qualm,** kwäm, *n.* A sudden fit of nausea; a twinge of conscience; compunction.
**Quandary,** kwon-dā'ri or kwon'da-ri, *n.* A state of perplexity; a predicament.
**Quantify,** kwon'ti-fī, *vt.* To determine the quantity of; to modify with regard to quantity.
**Quantitative,** kwon'ti-tā-tiv, *a.* Relating to or having regard to quantity.
**Quantity,** kwon'ti-ti, *n.* That property in virtue of which a thing is measurable; bulk; measure; amount; metrical value of syllables.
**Quantum,** kwan'tum, *n.* A quantity; an amount; a sufficient amount.
**Quarantine,** kwo'ran-tīn, *n.* The period during which a ship suspected of being infected is obliged to forbear all intercourse with a port.—*vt.* To cause to perform quarantine.
**Quarrel,** kwo'rel, *n.* An angry dispute; a brawl; cause of dispute; a dart for a crossbow; a glazier's diamont.—*vi.* (quarrelling, quarelled). To dispute violently; to disagree.
**Quarrelsome,** kwo'rel-sum, *a.* Apt to quarrel; contentious; irascible; choleric.
**Quarrier,** kwo'ri-ėr, *n.* A worker at a quarry.
**Quarry,** kwo'ri, *n.* A place where stones are dug from the earth; any animal pursued for prey; game killed.—*vt.* (quarrying, quarried). To dig or take from a quarry.
**Quart,** kwart, *n.* The fourth part of a gallon; two pints.
**Quarter,** kwar'tėr, *n.* The fourth part of anything; 28 lbs; 8 bushels; any direction or point of the compass; a district; locality; division of a heraldic shield; proper position; mercy to a beaten foe; *pl.* shelter or lodging; encampment.—*vt.* To divide into four equal parts; to cut to pieces; to furnish with lodgings or shelter; to add to other arms on an heraldic shield.—*vi.* To lodge.
**Quarter-deck,** kwar'tėr-dek, *n.* The upper deck of a ship abaft the main-mast.
**Quartering,** kwar'tėr-ing, *n.* The conjoining of coats of arms in one shield; a compartment on a shield.
**Quarterly,** kwar'tėr-li, *a.* Recurring each quarter of the year.—*adv.* Once in a quarter of a year.—*n.* A periodical published quarterly.
**Quarter-master,** kwar'tėr-mäs-tėr, *n.* An officer who has charge of the barracks, tents, stores, etc., of a regiment; a petty officer in the navy, who steers, signals, etc.
**Quartern,** kwar'tėrn, *n.* The fourth part of a pint, peck, stone, etc.
**Quartet,** kwar-tet', *n.* A musical composition in four parts; the performers of such a composition.
**Quarto,** kwar'tō, *n.* A book in which the sheets are folded into four leaves.—*a.* Having four leaves to the sheet.
**Quartz,** kwartz, *n.* A pure variety of silica, a constituent of granite and other rocks.
**Quash,** kwosh, *vt.* To subdue or quell; to suppress; to annul or make void.
**Quantification,** kwon'ti-fi-kā''shon, *n.* The act or process of quantifying.
**Quasi,** kwā'sī. A prefix implying appearance without reality; sort of; sham.
**Quassia,** kwas'i-a, *n.* A bitter S. American plant, yielding a tonic used in medicine.
**Quatercentenary,** kwa-tėr-sen'te-na-ri, *n.* A four hundredth anniversary.

**Quaternary,** kwa-tėr'na-ri, *a.* Consisting of four; arranged in fours; applied to the strata above the tertiary.
**Quaternion,** kwa-tėr'ni-on, *n.* A set of four; a quantity employed in mathematics.
**Quatorzain,** kwa'tor-zān, *n.* A stanza or poem of fourteen lines.
**Quatrain,** kwot'rān, *n.* A stanza of four lines rhyming alternately.
**Quaver,** kwā'vėr, *vi.* To have a tremulous motion; to vibrate.—*vt.* To utter with a tremulous sound.—*n.* A shake or rapid vibration of the voice, or on a musical instrument; a musical note equal to half a crotchet.
**Quay,** kē, *n.* A built landing-place for vessels; a wharf.
**Quayage,** kē'āj, *n.* Money paid for the use of a quay.
**Quean,** kwēn, *n.* A worthless woman.
**Queasy** kwē'zi, *a.* Sick at the stomach; inclined to vomit; fastidious; squeamish.
**Queen,** kwēn, *n.* The wife of a king; a female sovereign; a pre-eminent woman; the sovereign of a swarm of bees; a playing-card; a piece at chess.
**Queenhood,** kwēn'hud, *n.* The rank, quality, or character of a queen.
**Queenly,** kwēn'li, *a.* Like a queen; becoming a queen; suitable to a queen.
**Queer,** kwēr, *a.* Odd; droll; peculiar.
**Quell,** kwel, *vt.* To subdue; to allay.
**Quench,** kwensh, *vt.* To put out, as fire; to allay or slake, as thirst; to repress.
**Quenchable,** kwensh'a-bl, *a.* That may be quenched or extinguished.
**Quenchless,** kwensh'les, *a.* That cannot be quenched; inextinguishable; irrepressible.
**Quercitron,** kwėr'sit-ron, *n.* The dyer's-oak, a tree of N. America; the dye-stuff itself.
**Querimonious,** kwe-ri-mō'ni-us, *a.* Apt to complain; complaining; querulous.
**Quern,** kwėrn, *n.* A stone hand-mill for grinding grain.
**Querulous,** kwe'rū-lus, *a.* Complaining; murmuring; peevish.
**Query,** kwē'ri, *n.* A question; the mark of interrogation (?).—*vi.* (querying, queried). To ask a question or questions.—*vt.* To question; to mark with a query.
**Quest,** kwest, *n.* Act of seeking; search; pursuit; inquiry; solicitation.
**Question,** kwest'yon, *n.* Act of asking; an interrogation; inquiry; discussion; subject of discussion.—*vi.* To ask a question; to doubt.—*vt.* To interrogate; to doubt; to challenge.
**Questionable,** kwest'yon-a-bl, *a.* That may be questioned; doubtful.
**Questionnaire,** kwest'yon-ār, kest-ē-on-ār', *n.* A list or series of questions designed to elicit information on a specific subject.
**Queue,** kū, *n.* The tail of a wig; a pigtail; a file of persons waiting, in the order of their arrival, to be served in a shop or admitted to a theater, etc.—*vi.* To join or wait in a queue.
**Quibble,** kwib'l, *n.* A turn of language to evade the point in question; a pun.—*vi.* (quibbling, quibbled). To evade the question or truth by artifice; to prevaricate; to pun.
**Quick,** kwik, *a.* Alive; brisk; swift; keen; sensitive; irritable.—*n.* A growing plant, usually hawthorn, for hedges; the living flesh; sensitiveness.—*adv.* Quickly; soon.
**Quicken,** kwik'n, *vt.* To revive or resuscitate; to cheer; to increase the speed of; to sharpen; to stimulate.—*vi.* To become alive; to move quickly or more quickly.
**Quick-hedge,** kwik'hej, *n.* A fence or hedge of growing plants.
**Quickline,** kwik'līm, *n.* Lime burned but not yet slaked with water.
**Quickly,** kwik'li, *adv.* In a quick manner; speedily; rapidly; soon; without delay.
**Quicksand,** kwik'sand, *n.* A movable sandbank under water; sand yielding under the feet; something treacherous.
**Quickset,** kwik'set, *n.* A plant set to grow, particularly for a hedge, as hawthorn.—*vt.* To plant with shrubs for a hedge.—*a.* Composed of living plants, as a hedge.
**Quicksilver,** kwik'sil-vėr, *n.* Mercury.
**Quid,** kwid, *n.* A piece of tobacco chewed and rolled about in the mouth.
**Quiddity,** kwid'i-ti, *n.* Essence or nature; a trifling nicety; quirk or quibble.
**Quidnunc,** kwid'nungk, *n.* One curious to know everything that passes; a newsmonger.
**Quiescence,** kwī-es'ens, *n.* Rest; repose.
**Quiescent,** kwī-es'ent, *a.* Resting; still; tranquil; silent.—*n.* A silent letter.
**Quiet,** kwī'et, *a.* At rest; calm; still; peaceful; patient; secluded; not glaring or showy.—*n.* Rest; repose; peace; security.—*vt.* To make quiet; to calm; to lull; to allay.
**Quietism,** kwī'et-izm, *n.* The practice of resigning onself to mental inactivity to bring the soul into direct union with God.
**Quietly,** kwī'et-li, *adv.* In a quiet manner; calmly; so as not to attract attention.
**Quietude,** kwī'et-ūd, *n.* Rest; quiet.
**Quietus,** kwī-ē'tus, *n.* A final discharge of an account; a finishing stroke.
**Quill,** kwil, *n.* The strong feather of a goose, etc.; a feather made into a pen; the spine of a porcupine; a piece of reed used by weavers; a plait of a ruffle.—*vt.* To plait.
**Quilt,** kwilt, *n.* A padded bed-cover.—*vt.* To form into a quilt; to sew pieces of cloth with soft substance between.
**Quilting,** kwilt'ing, *n.* The act of making a quilt; the material used for quilts.
**Quinary,** kwī'na-ri, *a.* Consisting of five; arranged by fives.
**Quince,** kwins, *n.* The fruit of a tree allied to the pear and apple; the tree itself.
**Quincentenary,** kwin-sen'te-na-ri, *n.* A five hundredth anniversary.
**Quincunx,** kwin'kungks, *n.* An arrangement of five objects in a square, one at each corner and one in the middle.
**Quinine,** kwin'ēn or kwin-īn', *n.* An alkaline substance obtained from the bark of trees of the cinchona genus.
**Quintessence,** kwint-es'ens, *n.* The fifth or highest essence of a natural body; the purest or most essential part of a thing.
**Quintet,** kwin-tet', *n.* A musical composition in five parts; the performers of such a composition.
**Quintuple,** kwin'tu-pl, *a.* Fivefold.—*vt.* To make fivefold.
**Quip,** kwip, *n.* A sharp sarcastic turn; a severe retort; a gibe.
**Quire,** kwīr, *n.* A chorus; a choir; part of a church where the singers sit; twenty-four sheets of paper.
**Quirk,** kwėrk, *n.* An artful turn for evasion; a shift; a quibble.
**Quit,** kwit, *a.* Discharged; released; free; clear.—*vt.* (quitting, quitted). To discharge; to rid; to acquit; to leave; to abandon.
**Quite,** kwīt, *adv.* Completely; wholly; entirely; altogether; very.
**Quiver,** kwi'vėr, *n.* A case or sheath for arrows.—*vi.* To shake with small rapid movements; to tremble; to shiver.
**Quixotic,** kwiks-ot'ik, *a.* Chivalrous to extravagance; aiming at visionary ends.
**Quiz,** kwiz, *n.* A hoax; a jest; one who quizzes; one liable to be quizzed; a game or test in which two or more persons or teams compete in answering questions.—*vt.* (quizzing, quizzed). To make fun of, as by obscure questions; to look at inquisitively; to tease; to test by questioning.
**Quizzical,** kwiz'i-kal, *a.* Addicted to quizzing or teasing; comical; humorously critical.

Q

**Quoad sacra,** kwō'ad sā'kra, *a.* So far as regards sacred matters.
**Quoin,** koin, *n.* An external solid angle, as of a building; a wedge.
**Quoit,** koit, *n.* A flattish ring of iron, thrown at a mark.—*vi.* To throw or play at quoits.
**Quondam,** kwon'dam, *a.* Former.
**Quorum,** kwō'rum, *n.* A number of the members of any body competent to transact business.
**Quota,** kwō'ta, *n.* A share or proportion assigned to each.
**Quotable,** kwōt'a-bl, *a.* That may be quoted.
**Quotation,** kwōt-ā'shon, *n.* Act of quoting; passage quoted; the naming of the price of commodities, or the price specified.
**Quote,** kwōt, *vt.* (quoting, quoted). To adduce or cite, as from some author; to name as the price of an article.
**Quotidian,** kwō-ti'di-an, *a.* Daily.—*n.* A fever whose paroxysms return every day.
**Quotient,** kwō'shent, *n.* The number obtained by dividing one number by another.

# R

**Rabbet,** rab'et, *vt.* To cut so as to make a joint along an edge.—*n.* The cut so made on an edge to form a joint.
**Rabbi,** rab'bī, *n.* A Jewish teacher or expounder of the law.
**Rabbinic, Rabbinical,** rab-bin'ik, rab-bin'ik-al, *a.* Pertaining to the Hebrew learning and teachers after Christ.
**Rabbit,** rab'it, *n.* A burrowing rodent allied to the hare.
**Rabble,** rab'l, *n.* A crowd of vulgar, noisy people; the mob; the lower class of people.
**Rabid,** ra'bid, *a.* Raving; furious; mad.
**Rabidly,** ra'bid-li, *adv.* Madly; furiously.
**Rabies,** rā'bi-ēs, *n.* A disease affecting certain animals, especially dogs, from which hydrophobia is communicated.
**Raccoon, Racoon,** ra-kön', *n.* An American carnivorous animal.
**Race,** rās, *n.* A body of individuals sprung from a common stock; a breed or stock; a running; a contest in speed; a course or career; a rapid current or channel.—*vi.* (racing, raced). To run swiftly; to contend in running.—*vt.* To cause to contend in speed.
**Race-course,** rās'kōrs, *n.* The ground or path on which races are run.
**Race-horse,** rās'hors, *n.* A horse bred or kept for racing.
**Racial,** rā'si-al, *a.* Pertaining to race or lineage; pertaining to the races of man.
**Racing,** rās'ing, *n.* Act of running in a race; the business of joining in horse-races.
**Rack,** rak, *vt.* To stretch unduly; to distort; to punish on the rack; to torture; to strain.—*n.* Something used for stretching; an instrument of torture; torment; anguish; a frame for fodder, etc.; a bar with teeth on one of its edges; flying broken clouds; wreck.
**Racket,** rak'et, *n.* A confused din; clamor; the bat used in tennis, etc.; *pl.* a game like tennis.—*vi.* To make a racket; to frolic.
**Racy,** rā'si, *a.* Strong and well-flavored; spirited; piquant.
**Radar,** rā'där, *n.* A method of finding the position of an object (ship, aircraft, etc.) by reflection of radio waves.
**Radial,** rā'di-al, *a.* Relating to a radius; grouped or appearing like radii or rays.
**Radiance,** rā'di-ans, *n.* Brightness shooting in rays; luster; brilliancy; splendor.
**Radiant,** rā'di-ant, *a.* Emitting rays of light or heat; issuing in rays; beaming.
**Radiate,** rā'di-āt, *vi.* To emit rays of light; to shine; to spread about as in rays.—*vt.* To emit in divergent lines; to enlighten.—*a.* Having rays or lines resembling radii.
**Radiation,** rā-di-ā'shon, *n.* Act of radiating; emission of rays; beamy brightness.
**Radical,** ra'di-kal, *a.* Pertaining to the root; original; thorough-going; native; underived; relating to radicals in politics.—*n.* A root; a simple, underived word; one who advocates extreme political reform.
**Radicalism,** ra'di-kal-izm, *n.* The principles of radicals in politics.
**Radically,** ra'di-kal-li, *adv.* In a radical manner; fundamentally; essentially.
**Radicle,** ra'di-kl, *n.* A small root; that part of the seed which becomes the root.
**Radio,** rā'di-ō, *n.* A combining form used in compound words as equivalent to *wireless*; also used as a noun for the wireless system of transmission.
**Radish,** ra'dish, *n.* A plant, the young root of which is eaten raw, as a salad.
**Radium,** rā'di-um, *n.* An intensely radio-active element extracted from pitchblende, and used in medicine.
**Radius,** rā'di-us, *n.*; pl. **-ii, -iuses.** A straight line from the center of a circle to the circumference; a bone of the forearm.
**Radix,** rā'diks, *n.* A root, as of a plant or a word; source; origin.
**Raff,** raf, *n.* Refuse; a worthless person; the rabble.
**Raffle,** raf'l, *n.* A kind of lottery.—*vi.* (raffling, raffled). To engage in a raffle.—*vt.* To dispose of by raffle.
**Raft,** räft, *n.* Logs fastened together and floated; a floating structure.
**Rafter,** räf'tėr, *n.* A large sloping piece of timber supporting a roof.
**Rag,** rag, *n.* A rough separate fragment; a tattered cloth; a shred; a tatter.
**Ragamuffin,** rag-a-muf'in, *n.* A paltry fellow; a mean wretch.
**Rage,** rāj, *n.* Violent anger; fury; enthusiasm; rapture.—*vi.* (raging, raged). To be furious with anger; to be violently agitated.
**Ragged,** rag'ed, *a.* Rent or worn into rags; tattered; rugged; wearing tattered clothes.
**Ragout,** ra-gö', *n.* A dish of stewed and highly seasoned meat and vegetables.
**Ragwort,** rag'wėrt, *n.* A British weed of the same genus as the groundsel.
**Raid,** rād, *n.* A hostile incursion; a foray.—*vi.* To engage in a raid.—*vt.* To make a raid on.
**Raider,** rād'ėr, *n.* One who makes a raid.
**Rail,** rāl, *n.* A horizontal bar of wood or metal; a connected series of posts; a railing; one of the parallel iron bars forming a track for locomotives, etc.; a railway; a grallatorial bird.—*vt.* To inclose with rails; to furnish with rails.-*vi.* To use abusive language; to scold; to inveigh.
**Railing,** rāl'ing, *n.* A fence; rails in general.
**Raillery,** rāl'ė-ri, *n.* Light ridicule or satire; banter; jesting language.
**Railroad,** rāl'rōd, *n.* A railway.
**Railway,** rāl'wā, *n.* A road having iron rails laid in parallel lines, on which carriages run; all the land, buildings, and machinery required for traffic on such a road.
**Raiment,** rā'ment, *n.* Clothing; vestments.
**Rain,** rān, *n.* The moisture of the atmosphere falling in drops; a shower of anything.—*vi.* To fall in drops from the clouds; to fall like rain.—*vt.* To pour or shower down.
**Rainbow,** rān'bō, *n.* An arc of a circle, consisting of all the prismatic colors, appearing in the heavens opposite the sun.
**Rainfall,** rān'fal, *n.* A fall of rain; the amount of water that falls as rain.
**Rain-gauge,** rān'gāj, *n.* An instrument for measuring the rainfall.
**Rainy,** rān'i, *a.* Wet; showery.
**Raise,** rāz, *vt.* (raising, raised). To cause to rise; to lift upward; to excite; to recall from death; to stir up; to construct; to levy; to breed; to origi-

nate; to give vent to; to inflate; to cause to be relinquished (a siege).

**Raisin,** rā'zn, *n.* A dried grape.

**Raisonné,** rā-zon-nā', *a.* Arranged and digested systematically.

**Rajah,** rä'jä, *n.* A Hindu king or ruler; a title of Hindus of rank.

**Rake,** rāk, *n.* An implement for collecting hay or straw, smoothing earth, etc.; a dissolute, lewd man; slope.—*vt.* (raking, raked). To apply a rake to; to gather with a rake; to ransack; to enfilade.—*vi.* To use a rake; to search minutely; to incline; to slope, aft, as masts.

**Raking,** rāk'ing, *n.* Act of using a rake; what is collected by a rake; severe scrutiny.

**Rakish,** rāk'ish, *a.* Like a rake; dissolute; debauched; sloping, as masts.

**Rally,** ral'i, *vt.* (rallying, rallied). To reunite, as disordered troops; to collect, as things scattered; to attack with raillery; to banter.—*vi.* To recover strength or vigor.—*n.* A stand made by retreating troops; recovery of strength.

**Ram,** ram, *n.* The male of the sheep; a battering-ram; the loose hammer of a pile-driving machine; a heavy steel beak of a war-vessel; an iron-clad ship with such a beak; one of the signs of the zodiac.—*vt.* (ramming, rammed). To strike with a ram; to batter; to cram.

**Ramble,** ram'bl, *vi.* (rambling, rambled). To roam carelessly about; to talk incoherently; to have parts stretching irregularly.—*n.* An irregular excursion.

**Rambler,** ram'blėr, *n.* One who rambles; an irregular wanderer; a rover.

**Rambling,** ram'bling, *p.a.* Roving; unsettled; straggling; irregularly formed.

**Ramification,** ra'mi-fi-kā''shon, *n.* The act or process of ramifying; a branch or set of branches; an offshoot.

**Ramify,** ra'mi-fī, *vt.* To divide into branches.—*vi.* To be divided; to branch out.

**Rammer,** ram'ėr, *n.* An instrument for driving down anything; a ramrod.

**Ramose, Ramous,** rā'mōs, rā'mus, *a.* Branched; branchy; full of branches.

**Ramp,** ramp, *vi.* To climb, as a plant; to rear on the hind-legs; to spring.—*n.* A spring or leap; a slope; a swindle; an attempt to get money under false pretenses.

**Rampage,** ram'pāj or ram-pāj', *vi.* To prance about; to rage and storm.—*n.* Violent conduct.

**Rampant,** ram'pant, *a.* Rank in growth; exuberant; unrestrained; in *heraldry,* standing up on the hind-legs.

**Rampart,** ram'pärt, *n.* A mound of earth round a place, capable of resisting cannon-shot; a bulwark; a defense.

**Ramrod,** ram'rod, *n.* A rod formerly used in ramming down the charge in a gun, pistol, etc.

**Ramson, Ramsons,** ram'zon, ram'zonz, *n.* A British species of wild garlic.

**Ranch,** ranch, *n.* In North America, a farming establishment for rearing cattle and horses.

**Rancid,** ran'sid, *a.* Having a rank or stinking smell; strong-scented; sour; musty.

**Rancor,** rang'kor, *n.* Deep-seated enmity; malice; malignity.

**Rancorous,** rang'kor-us, *a.* Characterized by rancor; malignant; malicious; virulent.

**Random,** ran'dum, *n.* Action without definite object; chance; caprice.—**At random,** in a haphazard manner.—*a.* Left to chance; done without previous calculation.

**Range,** rānj, *vt.* (ranging, ranged). To set in a row; to dispose systematically; to wander through or scour.—*vt.* To rank; to rove about; to fluctuate.—*n.* A row; a rank; compass or extent; a kitchen grate; distance to which a projectile is carried; a place for gun practice.

**Ranger,** rānj'ėr, *n.* One who ranges; an official connected with a forest or park.

**Rank,** rangk, *n.* A row; a line; a social class; comparative station; titled dignity.—*vt.* To place in a line; to classify.—*vi.* To belong to a class; to put in a claim against a bankrupt.—*a.* Luxuriant in growth;; strong-scented; utter; coarse; disgusting.

**Rankle,** rang'kl, *vi.* (rankling, rankled). To fester painfully; to continue to irritate.—*vt.* To irritate; to inflame.

**Rankly,** rangk'li, *adv.* In a rank manner; with vigorous growth; coarsely; grossly.

**Ransack,** ran'sak, *vt.* To plunder; to search thoroughly.

**Ransom,** ran'sum, *n.* Release from captivity by payment; price paid for redemption or pardon.—*vt.* To pay a ransom for; to buy off; to deliver.

**Rant,** rant, *vi.* To speak in extravagant language.—*n.* Boisterous, empty declamation; bombast.

**Ranter,** rant'ėr, *n.* One who rants; a boisterous preacher.

**Ranunculus,** ra-nun'kū-lus, *n.* A genus of flowering plants, the buttercup or crowfoot.

**Rap,** rap, *n.* A quick smart blow; a knock.—*vi.* (rapping, rapped). To strike a quick, sharp blow.—*vt.* To strike with a quick blow.

**Rapacious,** ra-pā'shus, *a.* Greedy of plunder; subsisting on prey; extortionate.

**Rapacity,** ra-pa'si-ti, *n.* Exorbitant greediness; extortionate practices.

**Rape,** rāp, *n.* A seizing by violence; carnal knowledge of a woman against her will; a plant of the cabbage kind, whose seeds yield an oil.—*vt.* (raping, raped). To carry off violently; to ravish.

**Rapid,** ra'pid, *a.* Very swift; speedy; hurried.—*n.* A swift current in a river.

**Rapidity,** ra-pid'i-ti, *n.* State or quality of being rapid; celerity; velocity.

**Rapidly,** ra'pid-li, *adv.* In a rapid manner; with great speed; swiftly.

**Rapier,** rā'pi-ėr, *n.* A long narrow sword; a sword used only in thrusting.

**Rapine,** ra'pīn, *n.* Act of plundering; violent seizure of goods; pillage.

**Rapparee, Raparee,** rap-a-rē', *n.* An armed Irish plunderer.

**Rapt,** rapt, *a.* Transported; enraptured.

**Raptorial,** rap-tō'ri-al, *a.* Pertaining to the birds of prey (Raptores).

**Rapture,** rap'tūr, *n.* Extreme joy or pleasure; ecstasy; transport; enthusiasm.

**Rare,** rār, *a.* Not dense or compact; sparse; not frequent; uncommon; very valuable; underdone, as meat.

R

**Rarefaction,** rā-rē-fak'shon, *n.* Act or process of rarefying; state of being rarefied.

**Rarefy,** rā'rē-fī, *vt.* and *i.* (rarefying, rarefied). To make or become less dense.

**Rarely,** rār'li, *adv.* In a rare degree or manner; seldom; not often.

**Rarity,** ra'ri-ti, *n.* State of being rare; a thing valued for its scarcity; tenuity.

**Rascal,** ras'kal, *n.* A scoundrel; a rogue.—*a.* Worthless; mean; low; base.

**Rascallion,** ras-kal'yun, *n.* A low mean person; a rascally wretch. Also *Rapscallion.*

**Rash,** rash, *a.* Precipitate; hasty; overbold; incautious.—*n.* An eruption on the skin.

**Rasher,** rash'ėr, *n.* A thin slice of bacon.

**Rashly,** rash'li, *adv.* In a rash manner; hastily; without due deliberation.

**Rasorial,** ra-sō'ri-al, *a.* Pertaining to the gallinaceous or scratching birds (Rasores).

**Rasp,** räsp, *vt.* To rub with something rough; to grate; to utter harshly.—*vi.* To rub or grate.—*n.* A coarse file; a raspberry.

**Raspberry,** räz'be-ri, *n.* The fruit of a plant allied to the bramble; the plant itself.

**Raspy,** räsp'i, *a.* Grating; harsh; rough.

**Rat,** rat, *n.* A small rodent; one who deserts his party.—*vi.* (ratting, ratted). To catch or kill rats; to desert one's party.

**Ratable,** rāt'a-bl, *a.* That may be rated or set at a certain value; liable to taxation.

**Ratafia,** rat-a-fē'a, *n.* A spirituous liquor flavored with the kernels of cherries, etc.
**Ratchet,** rach'et, *n.* A catch which abuts against the teeth of a wheel to prevent it running back.
**Ratchet-wheel,** rach'et-whēl, *n.* A wheel having teeth, into which a ratchet drops.
**Rate,** rāt, *n.* Proportion; standard; degree; degree of speed; price; a tax; assessment.—*vt.* (rating, rated). To fix the value, rank, or degree of; to appraise; to reprove; to scold.—*vi.* To be classed in a certain order.
**Ratel,** ra-tel', *n.* A carnivorous quadruped of the badger family.
**Rate-payer,** rāt'-pā-ėr, *n.* One who is assessed and pays a rate or tax.
**Rath, Rathe,** räth, rāthe, *a.* Early.—*adv.* Soon; early.
**Rather,** räᴛʜ'ėr, *adv.* More readily; preferably; more properly; somewhat.
**Ratification,** ra'ti-fi-kā''shon, *n.* Act of ratifying; confirmation; act of giving sanction.
**Ratify,** ra'ti-fī, *vt.* (ratifying, ratified). To confirm; to approve and sanction.
**Ratio,** rā'shi-ō, *n.* Relation or proportion; rate.
**Ratiocination,** ra-shi-os'i-nā''shon, *n.* The act or process of reasoning.
**Ration,** ra'shon, *n.* A daily allowance of provisions; allowance.—*vt.* To supply with rations.
**Rational,** ra'shon-al, *a.* Endowed with reason; agreeable to reason; judicious.
**Rationale,** ra-shon-ā'lē, *n.* Exposition of the principles of some process, action, etc.
**Rationalism,** ra'shon-al-izm, *n.* A system of opinions deduced from reason, as distinct from inspiration or opposed to it.
**Rationalist,** ra'shon-a-list, *n.* An adherent of rationalism; one who rejects the supernatural element in Scripture.
**Rationality,** ra-shon-al'i-ti, *n.* The quality of being rational; the power of reasoning.
**Rationally,** ra'shon-al-li, *adv.* In a rational manner; reasonably.
**Ratline, Ratlin,** rat'lin, *n.* One of the ropes forming ladders on a ship's shrouds.
**Rattan,** rat'an or rat-tan', *n.* An Asiatic palm; a walking-stick made from this.
**Rattle,** rat'l, *vi.* and *t.* (rattling, rattled). To clatter; to chatter fluently.—*n.* A rapid succession of clattering sounds; an instrument or toy which makes a clattering sound; one who talks much and rapidly.
**Rattlesnake,** rat'l-snāk, *n.* A venomous American snake, with horny pieces at the point of the tail which rattle.
**Raucous,** ra'kus, *a.* Hoarse; harsh.
**Ravage,** ra'vāj, *n.* Devastation; havoc.—*vt.* (ravaging, ravaged). To lay waste; to pillage.
**Rave,** rāv, *vi.* (raving, raved). To be delirious; to speak enthusiastically; to dote.
**Ravel,** ra'vel, *vt.* (ravelling, ravelled). To disentangle; to make intricate; to involve.
**Ravelin,** rav'lin, *n.* A detached triangular work in fortification.
**Raven,** rā'vn, *n.* A bird of prey of the crow kind, of a black color.
**Raven, Ravin,** rav'en, rav'in *n.* Prey; plunder.—*vi.* To prey with rapacity.—*vt.* To devour.
**Ravenous,** rav'en-us, *a.* Furiously voracious; hungry even to rage.
**Ravenously,** rav'en-us-li, *adv.* With raging voracity.
**Ravine,** ra-vēn', *n.* A long hollow formed by a torrent; a gorge or pass.
**Raving,** rāv'ing, *n.* Irrational, incoherent talk; delirious utterances.
**Ravish,** ra'vish, *vt.* To carry away by violence; to enrapture; to commit a rape upon.
**Ravishing,** ra'vish-ing, *p.a.* Delighting to rapture; transporting.
**Ravishment,** ra'vish-ment, *n.* Act of ravishing; rapture; transport; ecstasy.
**Raw,** ra, *a.* Not cooked or dressed; not manufactured; unfinished; not diluted; bare, as flesh; galled; sensitive; inexperienced; cold and damp.
**Ray,** rā, *n.* A line of light; a gleam of intellectual light; one of a number of diverging radii; a flatfish.—*vt.* and *i.* (raying, rayed). To shine forth; to radiate; to streak.
**Rayon,** rā'on, *n.* Artificial silk, made from cellulose.
**Raze,** rāz, *vt.* (razing, razed). To graze; to lay level with the ground; to efface.
**Razor,** rā'zor, *n.* A knife for shaving off hair.
**Reach,** rēch, *vt.* To extend; to hand; to extend or stretch from a distance; to arrive at; to gain.—*vi.* To extend; to stretch out the hand in order to touch; to make efforts at attainment.—*n.* Act or power of extending to; straight course of a river; scope.
**React,** rē-akt', *vi.* To act in return; to return an impulse; to act reciprocally upon each other.—*vt.* To perform anew.
**Reaction,** rē-ak'shon, *n.* A reacting; reciprocal action; tendency to revert to a previous condition; exhaustion consequent on activity, and *vice versa.*
**Reactionary,** rē-ak'shon-a-ri, *a.* Pertaining to or favoring reaction.—*n.* One who attempts to reverse political progress.
**Read,** rēd, *vt.* (reading, read). To peruse; to utter aloud, following something written or printed; to explain.—*vi.* To peruse; to study; to stand written or printed; to make sense.—*a.* red. instructed by reading; learned.
**Readable,** rēd'a-bl, *a.* That may be read, legible; fit or deserving to be read.
**Reader,** rēd'ėr, *n.* One who reads; one who reads aloud prayers, lectures, etc.; one who corrects for the press; a reading-book.
**Readily,** re'di-li, *adv.* In a ready manner; quickly; promptly; easily; cheerfully.
**Readiness,** re'di-nes, *n.* Quickness; promptitude; facility; aptitude; alacrity.
**Reading,** rēd'ing, *a.* Addicted to reading; studious.—*n.* Perusal; study of books; public or formal recital; form of a word or passage in a manuscript, etc.; rendering.
**Ready,** re'di, *a.* Prepared; in order; prompt; willing; inclined; at hand; opportune.
**Ready-made,** re'di-mād, *a.* Made beforehand; kept in stock ready for use or sale.
**Reaffirm,** rē-af-fėrm', *vt.* To affirm again.
**Reagent,** rē-ā'jent, *n.* Anything that produces reaction; a substance employed chemically to detect the presence of other bodies.
**Real,** rē'al, *a.* Actual; true; genuine; in *law,* pertaining to things fixed or immovable, as lands and houses.
**Realism,** rē'al-izm, *n.* The endeavor in art or literature to reproduce nature or describe life as it actually appears.
**Realist,** rē'al-ist, *n.* One who practices or believes in realism.
**Realistic,** rē-al-ist'ik, *a.* Pertaining to realism; representing scenes vividly.
**Reality,** rē-al'i-ti, *n.* State or quality of being real; actuality; fact; truth.
**Realize,** rē'al-īz, *vt.* (realizing, realized). To make real; to convert into money; to impress on the mind as a reality; to render tangible or effective; to acquire; to gain.
**Really,** rē'al-li, *adv.* Actually; in truth; in fact; indeed.
**Realm,** relm, *n.* The dominions of a sovereign; a region, sphere, or domain.
**Realty,** rē'al-ti, *n.* The fixed nature of property termed *real;* real property.
**Ream,** rēm, *n.* A package of paper, consisting generally of 20 quires, or 480 sheets.
**Reanimate,** rē-an'i-māt, *vt.* To animate again; to revive; to infuse new life into.
**Reap,** rēp, *vt.* and *i.* To cut with a scythe, etc., as grain; to gather; to clear of a grain crop; to receive as a reward of labor, etc.
**Reaper,** rēp'ėr, *n.* One who reaps; a machine for

reaping.
**Reappear,** rē-ap-pēr', *vi.* To appear a second time or anew.
**Reappoint,** rē-ap-point', *vt.* To appoint again.
**Rear,** rēr, *n.* The part behind; the part of an army behind the rest; the background.—*vt.* To raise; to bring up, as young; to breed, as cattle; to build up.—*vi.* To rise on the hind-legs, as horse; to become erect.
**Rear-guard,** rēr'gärd, *n.* The part of an army that marches in the rear.
**Rearmost,** rēr'mōst, *a.* Farthest in the rear; last of all.
**Rearrange,** rē'a-rānj, *vt.* To arrange again; to put in different order.
**Rearward,** rēr'ward, *n.* The rear-guard; the end.—*a.* At or towards the rear.
**Reason,** rē'zn, *n.* A motive or cause; explanation; faculty for logical operations; justice; equity; moderate demands.—*vi.* To exercise the faculty of reason; to argue; to discuss.—*vt.* To examine or discuss by arguments; to persuade by reasoning.
**Reasonable,** rē'zn-a-bl, *a.* Having the faculty of reason; rational; conformable to reason; moderate; fair; tolerable.
**Reasonably,** rē'zn-a-bli, *adv.* In a reasonable manner; moderately; tolerably.
**Reasoning,** rē'zn-ing, *n.* The act or process of exercising the faculty of reason; arguments employed.
**Reassemble,** rē-as-sem'bl, *vt.* and *i.* To assemble again.
**Reassert,** rē-as-sėrt', *vt.* To assert again.
**Reassurance,** rē-a-shör'ans, *n.* Act of reassuring; a second assurance against loss.
**Reassure,** rē-a-shör', *vt.* To assure anew; to free from fear or terror; to reinsure.
**Reave,** rēv, *vt.* (reaving, reaved or reft). To take away by violence; to bereave.
**Reaver,** rēv'ėr, *n.* One who reaves; a robber.
**Rebate,** rē-bāt', *vt.* (rebating, rebated). To blunt; to diminish; to make a discount from.
**Rebate, Rebatement,** rē-bāt', rē-bāt'ment, *n.* Abatement in price; deduction.
**Rebel,** re'bel, *n.* One who makes war against or opposes constituted authorities.—*a.* Rebellious; acting in revolt.—*vi.* rē-bel' (rebelling, rebelled). To oppose lawful authority; to revolt; to conceive a loathing.
**Rebellion,** rē-bel'yon, *n.* Act of rebelling; an armed rising against a government.
**Rebellious,** rē-bel'yus, *a.* Pertaining to rebellion; mutinous; insubordinate.
**Rebound,** rē-bound', *vi.* To spring or bound back; to recoil.—*n.* The act of flying back on collision; resilience.
**Rebuff,** rē-buf', *n.* A sudden check; a repulse; refusal.—*vt.* To beat back; to check; to repel the advances of.
**Rebuild,** rē-bild', *vt.* To build again.
**Rebuke,** rē-būk', *vt.* (rebuking, rebuked). To reprimand; to reprove sharply.—*n.* A direct and severe reprimand; reproof.
**Rebukingly,** rē-būk'ing-li, *adv.* In a rebuking manner; by way of rebuke.
**Rebus,** rē'bus, *n.* A set of words represented by pictures of objects; a kind of puzzle made up of such pictures.
**Rebut,** rē-but', *vt.* (rebutting, rebutted). To repel; to refute; in *law,* to oppose by argument, plea, or countervailing proof.
**Rebuttal,** rē-but'al, *n.* Refutation.
**Recalcitrant,** rē-kal'si-trant, *a.* Not submissive; refractory.
**Recalcitrate,** rē-kal'si-trāt, *vi.* To show resistance; to be refractory.
**Recall,** rē-kal', *vt.* To call or bring back; to revive in memory.—*n.* A calling back.
**Recant,** rē-kant', *vt.* To retract, as a declaration.—*vi.* To retract one's words.
**Recantation,** rē-kant-ā'shon, *n.* Act of recanting; retraction.
**Recapitulate,** rē-ka-pit'ū-lāt, *vt.* To give a summary of.—*vi.* To repeat briefly.
**Recapitulation,** rē-ka-pit'ū-lā''shon, *n.* Act of recapitulating; summary.
**Recapture,** rē-kap'tūr, *n.* Act of retaking; a prize retaken.—*vt.* To retake.
**Recast,** rē-kast', *vt.* To throw again; to mold anew.
**Recede,** rē-sēd', *vi.* (receding, receded). To go back; to withdraw.—*vt.* To cede back.
**Receipt,** rē-sēt', *n.* Act of receiving; that which is received; a written acknowledgment of something received; a recipe.—*vt.* To give a receipt for; to discharge, as an account.
**Receivable,** rē-sēv'a-bl, *a.* That may be received.
**Receive,** rē-sēv', *vt.* (receiving, received). To take, as a thing offered; to admit; to entertain; to contain; to be the object of; to take stolen goods.
**Receiver,** rē-sēv'ėr, *n.* One who receives; one who takes stolen goods from a thief.
**Recension,** rē-sen'shon, *n.* A revision of the text of an author; an edited version.
**Recent,** rē'sent, *a.* New; late; fresh.
**Recently,** rē'sent-li, *adv.* Lately.
**Receptacle,** rē-sep'ta-kl, *n.* A place or vessel in which anything is received; repository.
**Reception,** rē-sep'shon, *n.* Act or manner of receiving; welcome; a formal receiving of guests; admission or acceptance.
**Receptionist,** rē-sep'shon-ist, *n.* One who in a hotel, at a doctor's, etc., receives guests or patients.
**Receptive,** rē-sep'tiv, *a.* Such as to receive readily; able to take in or contain.
**Receptivity,** rē-sep-tiv'i-ti, *n.* The state or quality of being receptive.
**Recess,** rē-ses', *n.* A withdrawing; place or period of retirement; time during which business is suspended; a niche in a wall; an alcove.
**Recession,** rē-se'shon, *n.* Act of receding; withdrawal; a granting back.
**Rechauffé,** rā-shō-fā, *n.* A warmed-up dish; a concoction of old materials.
**Recherché,** rė-sher'shā, *a.* Much sought after; out of the common; exquisite.
**Recipe,** re'si-pē, *n.* A medical prescription; a statement of ingredients for a mixture.
**Recipient,** rē-si'pi-ent, *n.* One who or that which receives; a receiver.
**Reciprocal,** rē-sip'rō-kal, *a.* Reciprocating; alternate; done by each to the other; mutual; interchangeable.
**Reciprocally,** rē-sip'rō-kal-li, *adv.* In a reciprocal manner; mutually.
**Reciprocate,** rē-sip'rō-kāt, *vi.* To move backward and forward; to alternate.—*vt.* To exchange; to give in requital.
**Reciprocation,** rē-sip'rō-kā''shon, *n.* Act of reciprocating; a mutual giving.
**Reciprocity,** re-si-pros'i-ti, *n.* Reciprocation; interchange; reciprocal obligation; equal commercial rights mutually enjoyed.
**Recital,** rē-sīt'al, *n.* Act of reciting; narration; a musical entertainment.
**Recitation,** re-si-tā'shon, *n.* Recital; the delivery before an audience of the compositions of others.
**Recitative,** re'si-ta-tēv, *n.* A species of singing approaching ordinary speaking.
**Recite,** rē-sīt', *vt.* and *i.* (reciting, recited). To repeat aloud, as a writing committed to memory; to relate; to recapitulate.
**Reciter,** rē-sīt'ėr, *n.* One who recites; a book containing passages for recitation.
**Reck,** rek, *vt.* To heed; to regard.
**Reckless,** rek'les, *a.* Heedless; careless; rash.
**Recklessly,** rek'les-li, *adv.* Carelessly.
**Reckon,** rek'n, *vt.* and *i.* To count; to estimate; to account, consider.
**Reckoner,** rek'n-ėr, *n.* One who or that which reckons or computes.
**Reckoning,** rek'n-ing, *n.* Calculation; a statement of accounts with another; landlord's bill;

R

calculation of a ship's position.
**Reclaim,** rē-klām', *vt.* To claim back; to reform; to tame; to recover; to reduce to a state fit for cultivation.
**Reclaimable,** rē-klām'a-bl, *a.* That may be reclaimed, reformed, or tamed.
**Reclamation,** re-kla-mā'shon, *n.* Act of reclaiming; a claim made.
**Recline,** rē-klīn', *vt.* and *i* (reclining, reclined). To lean; to rest or repose.
**Recluse,** rē-klös', *a.* Retired; solitary.—*n.* A person who lives in seclusion; a hermit.
**Reclusion,** rē-klö'zhon, *n.* Seclusion.
**Recognition,** re-kog-ni'shon, *n.* Act of recognizing; avowal; acknowledgment.
**Recognizable,** re'kog-nīz-a-bl, *a.* That may be recognized.
**Recognizance,** rē-kog'niz-ans or rē-kon'i-zans, *n.* Recognition; an obligation, as to appear at the assizes, keep the peace, etc.
**Recognize,** re'kog-nīz, *vt.* (recognizing, recognized). To know again; to admit a knowledge of; to acknowledge formally; to indicate one's notice by a bow, etc.; to indicate appreciation of.
**Recoil,** rē-koil', *vi.* To move or start back; to retreat; to shrink; to rebound.—*n.* A starting or falling back; rebound, as of a gun.
**Recollect,** re'kol-lekt, *vt.* To remember; to recover composure of mind (with refl. pron.).
**Recollect,** rē-kol-lekt', *vt.* To collect again.
**Recollection,** re-kol-lek'shon, *n.* Act of recollecting; remembrance; something recalled to mind.
**Recommence,** rē-kom-mens', *vt.* To begin anew.
**Recommend,** re-kom-mend', *vt.* To praise to another; to make acceptable; to commit with prayers; to advise.
**Recommendation,** re'kom-mend-ā''shon, *n.* The act of recommending; a favorable representation; that which procures favor.
**Recommit,** rē-kom-mit', *vt.* To commit again; to refer again to a committee.
**Recommitment, Recommittal,** rē-kom-mit'ment, rē-kom-mit'al, *n.* Act of recommitting; a further commitment or reference.
**Recompense,** re'kom-pens, *vt.* (recompensing, recompensed). To compensate; to requite; to make amends for.—*n.* Compensation; reward; amends.
**Reconcilable,** re'kon-sil-a-bl, *a.* Capable of being reconciled.
**Reconcile,** re'kon-sīl, *vt.* (reconciling, reconciled). To make friendly again; to adjust or settle; to harmonize.
**Reconcilement,** re-kon-sīl'ment,*n.* Reconciliation; renewal of friendship.
**Reconciliation,** re'kon-si-li-ā''shon, *n.* Act of reconciling; renewal of friendship.
**Recondite,** rē-kon'dīt or re'kon-dīt, *a.* Abstruse; profound.
**Reconnaissance,** re-kon'nā-sans,*n.* The act or operation of reconnoitering.
**Reconnoiter,** re-kon-noi'tėr, *vt.* and *i.* (reconnoitering, reconnoitered). To make a preliminary survey of; to survey for military purposes.
**Reconsider,** rē-kon-si'dėr, *vt.* To consider again.
**Reconsideration,** rē-kon-si'dėr-ā''shon, *n.* Act of reconsidering; renewed consideration.
**Reconstruct,** rē-kon-strukt', *vt.* To construct again; to rebuild.
**Record,** rē-kord', *vt.* To preserve in writing; to register; to chronicle.—*n.* rek'ord. A written memorial; a register; a public document; memory; one's personal history; best results in contests.
**Recorder,** rē-kord'ėr, *n.* One who records; an official registrar; magistrate presiding over court of quarter sessions of borough; a kind of straight flute or flageolet; a registering apparatus.
**Recount,** rē-kount', *vt.* To relate in detail; to count again.—*n.* A second counting.
**Recoup,** rē-köp', *vt.* To recompense or compensate; to indemnify.
**Recourse,** rē-kōrs', *n.* A going to with a request, as for aid; resort in perplexity.
**Recover,** rē-kuv'ėr, *vt.* To get back; to regain; to revive; to rescue; to obtain in return for injury or debt.—*vi.* To grow well; to regain a former condition.
**Recoverable,** rē-kuv'ėr-a-bl, *a.* That may be recovered or regained.
**Recovery,** rē-kuv'ėr-i, *n.* Act of recovering; restoration from sickness, etc.; the obtaining of something by legal procedure.
**Recreant,** re'krē-ant, *a.* Craven; cowardly; apostate.—*n.* One who basely yields in combat; a cowardly wretch.
**Recreate,** re'krē-āt, *vt.* To revive; to enliven; to amuse.—*vi.* To take recreation.
**Re-create,** rē-krē-āt', *vt.* To create anew.
**Recreation,** re-krē-a'shon, *n.* Refreshment of the strength and spirits after toil; amusement; entertainment.
**Recreative,** re'krē-āt-iv, *a.* Serving to recreate; refreshing; diverting.
**Recrement,** re'krē-ment, *n.* Refuse; dross.
**Recriminate,** rē-krim'in-āt, *vi.* To return one accusation with another.—*vt.* To accuse in return.
**Recrimination,** rē-krim'in-ā''shon, *n.* Act of recriminating; a counter-accusation.
**Recriminative, Recriminatory,** rē-krim'in-āt-iv, rē-krim'in-ā-to-ri, *a.* Recriminating or retorting accusation.
**Recruit,** rē-kröt', *vt.* To repair; to supply with new soldiers.—*vi.* To gain new supplies of anything; to raise new soldiers.—*n.* A soldier newly enlisted.
**Rectangle,** rek'tang-gl, *n.* A quadrilateral having all its angles right angles.
**Rectangular,** rek-tang'gū-lėr, *a.* Right-angled.
**Rectification,** rek'ti-fi-kā''shon, *n.* Act or operation of rectifying; process of refining by repeated distillation.
**Rectifier,** rek'ti-fī-ėr, *n.* One who or that which rectifies; a refiner of alcohol.
**Rectify,** rek'ti-fī, *vt.* (rectifying, rectified). To correct; to refine by repeated distillation.
**Rectilineal, Rectilinear,** rek-ti-lin'ē-al, rek-ti-lin'ē-ėr, *a.* Consisting of straight lines.
**Rectitude,** rek'ti-tūd, *n.* Integrity; probity; uprightness; honesty.
**Rector,** rek'tor, *n.* A ruler; an Episcopal clergyman who has the cure of a parish; a head of certain institutions, chiefly academical.
**Rectorial,** rek-tō'ri-al, *a.* Pertaining to a rector or rectory.
**Rectorship, Rectorate,** rek'tor-ship, rek'tor-āt, *n.* Office or rank of a rector.
**Rectory,** rek'to-ri, *n.* A church or living held by a rector; a rector's house.
**Rectum,** rek'tum, *n.* The lowest part of the large intestine opening at the anus.
**Recumbent,** rē-kum'bent, *a.* Leaning; reclining; reposing; inactive.
**Recuperate,** rē-kū'pėr-āt, *vt.* and *i.* (recuperating, recuperated). To recover.
**Recuperation,** rē-kū'pėr-ā''shon, *n.* Recovery.
**Recuperative,** rē-kū'pėr-ā-tiv, *a.* Tending or pertaining to recovery.
**Recur,** rē-kėr', *vi.* (recurring, recurred). To return; to be repeated at a stated interval.
**Recurrence,** rē-ku'rens, *n.* Act of recurring; return; recourse.
**Recurrent,** rē-ku'rent, *a.* Recurring from time to time.
**Recusancy, Recusance,** re'kū-zan-si, re'kū-zans, *n.* Nonconformity.
**Recusant,** re'kū-zant, *a.* Obstinate in refusal; refusing to conform to the established church.—*n.* A nonconformist.
**Red,** red, *a.* Of a color resembling that of arterial blood.—*n.* A color resembling that of arterial blood; a red pigment.
**Redact,** rē-dakt', *vt.* To edit; to give a presentable literary form to.
**Redaction,** rē-dak'shon, *n.* Act of preparing for publication; the work thus prepared.

**Redactor,** rē-dakt'ėr, *n.* An editor.
**Redan,** rē-dan', *n.* A field fortification of two faces, forming an angle towards the enemy.
**Redargue,** red'är-gū, *vt.* To put down by argument; to refute.
**Redcoat,** red'kōt, *n.* A familiar name for a British soldier.
**Red-deer,** red'dēr, *n.* The common stag.
**Redden,** red'n, *vt.* To make red.—*vi.* To become red; to blush.
**Reddish,** red'ish, *a.* Somewhat red.
**Reeddition,** red-di'shon, *n.* A giving back; restitution.
**Reddle,** red'l, *n.* Red chalk; raddle.
**Redeem,** rē-dēm', *vt.* To buy back; to ransom; to rescue; to save; to atone for; to employ to the best purpose; to perform, as what has been promised.
**Redeemable,** rē-dēm'a-bl, *a.* That may be redeemed.
**Redeemer,** rē-dēm'ėr, *n.* One who redeems; Jesus Christ.
**Redeliver,** rē-dē-liv'ėr, *vt.* To deliver back or again.
**Redemption,** rē-dem'shon, *n.* The act of redeeming; state of being redeemed; ransom; release; deliverance.
**Red-handed,** red'hand-ed, *a.* With red or bloody hands; in the act.
**Red-hot,** red'hot, *a.* Red with heat; very hot.
**Redintegrate,** re-din'ti-grāt, *vt.* To make whole again.
**Red-lead,** red'led, *n.* An oxide of lead of a fine red color, used in painting, etc.; minium.
**Red-letter,** red'let-ėr, *a.* Having red letters; fortunate or auspicious.
**Redolence,** re'dō-lens, *n.* Quality of being redolent; fragrance; perfume; scent.
**Redolent,** re'dō-lent, *a.* Emitting an odor; having or diffusing a sweet scent.
**Redouble,** rē-du'bl, *vt.* To double again.—*vi.* To become twice as much.
**Redoubt,** rē-dout', *n. See* Redout.
**Redoubtable,** rē-dout'a-bl, *a.* Such as to cause dread; formidable; valiant.
**Redoubted,** rē-dout'ed, *a.* Redoubtable.
**Redound,** rē-dound', *vi.* To conduce; to contribute; to have effect.
**Redout, Redoubt,** rē-dout', *n.* A small inclosed fortification.
**Redraft,** rē-dräft', *vt.* To draft anew.—*n.* A second draft; a second order for money.
**Redraw,** rē-dra̤', *vt.* To draw again.—*vi.* To draw a new bill of exchange.
**Redress,** rē-dres', *vt.* To set right; to adjust; to repair; to relieve.—*n.* Relief; deliverance; reparation.
**Redshank,** red'shangk, *n.* A bird allied to the snipes, with red legs.
**Redskin,** red'skin, *n.* A Red Indian, or Indian of North America.
**Redstart, Redtail,** red'stärt, red'tāl, *n.* A bird with a red tail; a small singing bird.
**Red-tape,** red'tāp, *n.* Excessive official routine and formality.—*a.* Characterized by excessive routine or formality.
**Reduce,** rē-dūs', *vt.* (reducing, reduced). To bring down; to decrease; to degrade; to subdue; to bring under rules or within categories; to restore to its proper place.
**Reducible,** rē-dūs'i-bl, *a.* That may be reduced.
**Reduction,** rē-duk'shon, *n.* Act of reducing; diminution; conversion into another state or form; subjugation.
**Redundancy, Redundance,** rē-dun'dan-si, rē-dun'dans, *n.* Superfluity.
**Redundant,** rē-dun'dant, *a.* Superfluous; having more words than necessary.
**Reduplication,** rē-dū'pli-kā''shon, *n.* Act of reduplicating; the repetition of a root or initial syllable.
**Redwing,** red'wing, *n.* A species of thrush.
**Redwood,** red'wṳd, *n.* A name of various reddish timbers.
**Re-echo,** rē-e'kō, *vt.* and *i.* To echo back; to reverberate.—*n.* The echo of an echo.
**Reed,** rēd, *n.* A tall broad-leaved grass growing in marshy places, or its hollow stems; a musical instrument; a rustic pipe.
**Reed-pipe,** rēd'pīp, *n.* A musical pipe made of reed.
**Reedy,** rēd'i, *a.* Abounding with reeds; harsh and thin, as a voice.
**Reef,** rēf, *n.* The part of a sail which can be drawn together to expose a smaller area; a range of rocks in the sea near the surface; a vein containing gold.—*vt.* To take in a reef in; to reduce the extent of a sail.
**Reefer,** rēf'ėr, *n.* One who reefs; a midshipman.
**Reef-point,** rēf'point, *n.* One of the small pieces of line for tying up a sail when reefed.
**Reek,** rēk, *n.* Vapor; steam; exhalation; smoke.—*vi.* To smoke; to exhale.
**Reel,** rēl, *n.* A bobbin for thread; a revolving appliance for winding a fishing-line; a staggering motion; a lively Scottish dance.—*vt.* To wind upon a reel; to stagger.
**Re-elect,** rē-ē-lekt', *vt.* To elect again.
**Re-embark,** rē-em-bärk', *vt.* and *i.* To embark again.
**Re-enact,** rē-en-akt', *vt.* To enact again.
**Re-enforce,** rē-en-fōrs', *vt.* and *i.* To reinforce.
**Re-engage,** rē-en-gāj', *vt.* and *i.* To engage a second time.
**Re-enter,** rē-en'tėr, *vt.* and *i.* To enter again or anew.
**Re-establish,** rē-es-tab'lish, *vt.* To establish anew; to fix or confirm again.
**Reeve,** rēv, *n.* A bailiff; a steward; a peace officer.—*vt.* and *i.* (reeving, reeved). To pass a rope through any hole in a block, etc.; to pass through such hole.
**Re-examine,** rē-eg-zam'in, *vt.* To examine anew.
**Re-export,** rē-eks-pōrt', *vt.* To export after having been imported.—*n.* rē-eks'pōrt. Any commodity re-exported.
**Re-fashion,** rē-fa'shon, *vt.* To fashion or form into shape a second time.
**Refection,** rē-fek'shon, *n.* Refreshment after hunger or fatigue; a repast.
**Refectory,** rē-fek'to-ri, *n.* A room for refreshment or meals.
**Refer,** rē-fėr', *vt.* (referring, referred). To trace or carry back; to attribute; to appeal; to assign.—*vi.* To respect or have relation; to appeal; to apply; to allude.
**Referable,** ref'ėr-a-bl, *a.* That may be referred, assigned, attributed, etc.
**Referee,** ref-ėr-ē', *n.* One to whom a matter in dispute is referred for decision; an umpire.
**Reference,** re'fėr-ens, *n.* Act of referring; allusion; relation; one of whom inquiries may be made.
**Referendum,** ref-ėr-en'dum, *n.* The referring of a measure passed by a legislature to the people for final approval.
**Refill,** rē-fil', *vt.* To fill again.
**Refine,** rē-fīn', *vt.* (refining, refined). To increase the fineness of; to purify; to make elegant; to give culture to.—*vi.* To become purer; to indulge in hair-splitting.
**Refined,** rē-fīnd', *p.a.* Free from what is coarse, rude, etc.; polished; polite.
**Refinement,** rē-fīn'ment, *n.* Act of refining; elegance; culture; nicety.
**Refiner,** rē-fīn'ėr, *n.* One who refines, speciallyy metals, liquors, sugars, etc.
**Refinery,** rē-fīn'ėr-i, *n.* A place and apparatus for refining sugar, metals, etc.
**Refit,** rē-fit', *vt.* and *i* (refitting, refitted). To fit anew; to repair.—*n.* Repair.
**Reflect,** rē-flekt', *vt.* To cast back; to throw off, as light or heat, after striking the surface; to mirror.—*vi.* To throw back light or heat; to meditate; to bring reproach.
**Reflecting,** rē-flekt'ing, *p.a.* Serving to reflect; thoughtful; meditative.

**Reflection,** rē-flek'shon, *n.* Act of reflecting; that which is produced by being reflected; meditation; a censorious remark; reproach.
**Reflective,** rē-flekt'iv, *a.* Throwing back rays; meditating.
**Reflector,** rē-flekt'or, *n.* One who reflects; a polished surface for reflecting light, etc.
**Reflex,** rē'fleks, *a.* Bent or directed back; done involuntarily or unconsciously.—*n.* A reflection.
**Reflexible,** rē-fleks'i-bl, *a.* Capable of being reflected or thrown back.
**Reflexive,** rē-flek'siv, *a.* Reflective; having respect to something past; in *grammar,* having for its object a pronoun which stands for the subject; also applied to such pronouns.
**Refluent,** ref'lu-ent, *a.* Flowing back.
**Reflux,** rē'fluks, *n.* A flowing back; ebb.
**Refold,** rē-fōld, *vt.* To fold again.
**Reform,** rē-form', *vt.* and *i.* To change from worse to better; to amend; to form anew.—*n.* A beneficial change; amendment; a change in the regulations of parliamentary representation.
**Reformation,** re-for-mā'shon, *n.* Act of reforming; amendment; the Protestant revolution of the sixteenth century.
**Re-formation,** rē-for-mā'shon, *n.* The act of forming anew; a second forming.
**Reformatory,** rē-for'ma-to-ri, *n.* An institution for reclaiming young criminals.
**Reformed,** rē-formd', *a.* Restored to a good state; amended; having accepted the principles of the Reformation.
**Reformer,** rē-form'ėr, *n.* One who reforms; one who took a part in the Reformation; one who promotes political reform.
**Refract,** rē-frakt', *vt.* To bend back sharply; to deflect (a ray of light) on passing from one medium into another.
**Refraction,** rē-frak'shon, *n.* Act of refracting; a change of direction in rays on passing from one medium into another.
**Refractive,** rē-frakt'iv, *a.* Pertaining to refraction; having power to refract.
**Refractor,** rē-frakt'ėr, *n.* That which refracts; a refracting telescope.
**Refractory,** rē-frak'to-ri, *a.* Sullen in disobedience; stubborn; unmanageable; resisting ordinary treatment.
**Refrain,** rē-frān', *vt.* To restrain; to keep (oneself) from action.—*vi.* To forbear; to abstain.—*n.* The burden of a song; part repeated at the end of every stanza.
**Refresh,** rē-fresh', *vt.* To revive; to reanimate; to freshen.
**Refresher,** rē-fresh'ėr, *n.* One who or that which refreshes; additional fee paid to counsel in a long case.
**Refreshing,** rē-fresh'ing, *a.* Invigorating; reanimating; enlivening.
**Refreshment,** rē-fresh'ment, *n.* Act of refreshing; that which refreshes; *pl.* food and drink.
**Refrigerant,** rē-fri'jė-rant, *a.* Cooling.—*n.* A medicine which abates heat.
**Refrigerate,** rē-fri'jė-rāt, *vt.* To cool.
**Refrigeration,** rē-fri'jė-rā''shon, *n.* Act of refrigerating; abatement of heat.
**Refrigerator,** rē-frij'ė-rāt-ėr, *n.* That which refrigerates; an apparatus for cooling or for making ice; a refrigerant.
**Refrigent,** rē-frin'jent, *a.* Refractive; refracting.
**Refuge,** re'fūj, *n.* Protection from danger or distress; a retreat; a shelter; a device; contrivance; shift.—*vt.* and *i.* To shelter.
**Refugee,** re-fū-jē', *n.* One who flees for refuge; one who flees to another country or place for safety.
**Refulgence, Refulgency,** rē-ful'jens, rē-ful'jen-si, *n.* Splendor; brilliancy.
**Refulgent,** rē-ful'jent, *a.* Casting a bright light; shining; splendid.
**Refund,** rē-fund', *vt.* To pay back; to repay; to reimburse.
**Refurnish,** rē-fėr'nish, *vt.* To furnish anew.
**Refusal,** rē-fūz'al, *n.* Act of refusing; choice of taking or refusing.
**Refuse,** rē-fūz', *vt.* (refusing, refused). To deny, as a request or demand; to decline; to reject.—*vi.* To decline a request or offer.
**Refuse,** re'fūz, *a.* Rejected; worthless.—*n.* Waste matter; dregs.
**Refutable,** rē-fūt'a-bl or ref', *a.* That may be refuted or disproved.
**Refutation,** re-fūt-ā'shon, *n.* Act or process of refuting; disproof.
**Refute,** rē-fūt', *vt.* (refuting, refuted). To disprove; to overthrow by argument.
**Regain,** rē-gān', *vt.* To gain anew; to recover; to retrieve; to reach again.
**Regal,** rē'gal, *a.* Kingly; royal.
**Regale,** rē-gāl', *vt.* and *i.* (regaling, regaled). To refresh sumptuously; to feast.—*n.* A splendid feast; a treat.
**Regalia,** rē-gā'li-a, *n.pl.* Ensigns of royalty, as the crown, scepter, etc.
**Regality,** rē-gal'i-ti, *n.* Royalty; kingship.
**Regally,** rē'gal-li, *adv.* In a regal manner.
**Regard,** rē-gärd', *vt.* To notice carefully; to observe; to respect; to heed; to view in the light of; to relate to.—*n.* Look or gaze; respect; notice; heed; esteem; deference; *pl.* good wishes.
**Regardant,** rē-gärd'ant, *a.* Regarding; in *heraldry,* with the face turned backwards in an attitude of vigilance.
**Regardful,** rē-gärd'ful, *a.* Having or paying regard.
**Regarding,** rē-gärd'ing, *prep.* Respecting; concerning; relating to.
**Regardless,** rē-gärd'les, *a.* Without regard or heed; heedless; negligent; careless.
**Regatta,** rē-gat'a, *n.* A race in which yachts or boats contend for prizes.
**Regelation,** rē-je-lā'shon, *n.* The freezing together of pieces of moist ice.
**Regency,** rē'jen-si, *n.* Government of a regent; men intrusted with the power of a regent.
**Regeneracy,** rē-jen'ė-ra-si, *n.* State of being regenerated.
**Regenerate,** rē-jen'ė-rāt, *vt.* To generate anew; to bring into a better state.—*n.* Born anew; changed to a spiritual state.
**Regeneration,** rē-jen'ė-rā''shon, *n.* Act of regenerating; that change by which love to God is implanted in the heart.
**Regent,** rē'jent, *a.* Ruling.—*n.* A ruler; one who governs during the minority or disability of the king.
**Regicide,** re'ji-sīd, *n.* One who kills a king; the murder of a king.
**Regime,** rā-zhēm', *n.* Mode of management; administration; rule.
**Regimen,** re'ji-men, *n.* Orderly government; regulation of diet, exercise, etc.
**Regiment,** re'ji-ment, *n.* A body of troops under the command of a colonel.
**Regimental,** re-ji-ment'al, *a.* Belonging to a regiment.
**Regimentals,** re-ji-ment'alz, *n.pl.* Uniform of a regiment; articles of military dress.
**Region,** rē'jun, *n.* A tract of land; country; territory; portion of the body.
**Register,** re'jis-tėr, *n.* An official record; a roll; a book for special entries of facts; device for indicating work done by machinery; musical compass; a stop in an organ.—*vt.* To record; to insure (a letter).—*vi.* To enter one's name.
**Registered,** re'jis-tėrd, *p.a.* Enrolled; protected by enrolment; insured.
**Registrar,** re'jis-trär, *n.* An officer who keeps a public register or record.
**Registration,** re-jis-trā'shon, *n.* Act of registering; enrolment.
**Registry,** re'jis-tri, *n.* Registration; place where a register is kept; an entry.
**Regress,** rē'gres, *n.* Return; power of returning.—*vi.* rē-gres'. To go back.
**Regression,** rē-gre'shon, *n.* The act of passing

back or returning; retrogression.
**Regret,** rē-gret', *n.* Grief at something done or undone; remorse; penitence.—*vt.* (regretting, regretted). To be sorry for; to lament.
**Regretful,** rē-gret'ful, *a.* Full of regret.
**Regrettable,** rē-gret'a-bl, *a.* Admitting of or calling for regret.
**Regular,** re'gū-lėr, *a.* Conformed to a rule, law, or principle; normal; methodical; uniform; having the parts symmetrical; thorough.—*n.* A monk who has taken the vows in some order; a soldier of a permanent army.
**Regularity,** re-gū-la'ri-ti, *n.* State or character of being regular; steadiness or uniformity.
**Regularly,** re'gū-lėr-li, *adv.* In uniform order; at fixed periods; methodically.
**Regulate,** re'gū-lāt, *vt.* (regulating, regulated). To adjust by rule; to put or keep in good order; to direct.
**Regurgitate,** rē-gėr'jit-tāt, *vt.* and *i.* To pour or cause to surge back.
**Rehabilitate,** rē-ha-bil'i-tāt, *vt.* To restore to a former capacity or position; to re-establish in esteem.
**Rehearsal,** rē-hėrs'al, *n.* Act of rehearsing; recital; a trial performance.
**Rehearse,** rē-hėrs', *vt.* (rehearsing, rehearsed). To repeat; to recite; to relate; to repeat in private for trial.
**Reign,** rān, *vi.* To be sovereign; to rule; to prevail.—*n.* Royal authority; supremacy; time of a sovereign's supreme authority.
**Reimburse,** rē-im-bėrs', *vt.* To refund; to pay back.
**Reimport,** rē-im-pōrt', *vt.* To carry back to the country of exportation.—*n.* rē-im'pōrt. Something reimported.
**Rein,** rān, *n.* The strap of a bridle, by which a horse is governed; an instrument for restraining; restrait.—*vt.* To govern by a bridle; to restrain.—*vi.* To obey the reins.
**Reindeer,** rān'dēr, *n.* A deer of northern parts, with broad branched antlers.
**Reinforce,** rē-in-fōrs', *vt.* To strengthen by new assistance, as troops.—*n.* An additional thickness given to an object to strengthen it.
**Reinforcement,** rē-in-fōrs'ment, *n.* Act of reinforcing; additional troops or ships.
**Reinsert,** rē-in-sėrt', *vt.* To insert a second time.
**Reinstate,** rē-in-stāt', *vt.* To instate anew; to restore to a former position.
**Reinsurance,** rē-in-shör'ans, *n.* A renewed insurance; a contract by which an insurer devolves to another the risks he had undertaken himself; act of reinsuring.
**Reinvestment,** rē-in-vest'ment, *n.* A second or repeated investment.
**Reissue,** rē-ish'ū, *vt.* To issue a second time.—*n.* A second or repeated issue.
**Reiterate,** rē-it'ėr-āt, *vt.* To repeat again and again; to do or say repeatedly.
**Reject,** rē-jekt', *vt.* To cast off; to discard; to repel; to forsake; to decline.
**Rejoice,** rē-jois', *vi.* (rejoicing, rejoiced). To be glad; to exult.—*vt.* To gladden; to cheer.
**Rejoicing,** rē-jois'ing, *n.* Act of expressing joy; festivity.
**Rejoinder,** rē-join'dėr, *n.* An answer to a reply.
**Rejuvenate,** rē-jū'ven-āt, *vt.* To restore to youth; to make young again.
**Relapse,** rē-laps', *vi.* (relapsing, relapsed). To slip back; to return to a former state.—*n.* A falling back, either in health or morals.
**Relate,** rē-lāt', *vt.* (relating, related). To tell; to narrate; to ally by kindred.—*vi.* To refer; to stand in some relation.
**Related,** rē-lāt'ed, *p.a.* Connected by blood; standing in some relation.
**Relation,** rē-lā'shon, *n.* Act of relating; account; reference; connection; kindred; a relative; proportion.
**Relationship,** rē-lā'shon-ship, *n.* The state of being related; kinship.
**Relative,** re'lat-iv, *a.* Having relation or reference; not absolute or existing by itself; relevant.—*n.* Something considered in its relation to something else; one allied by blood; a word which relates to or represents another word or sentence.
**Relatively,** re'lat-iv-li, *adv.* In a relative manner; not absolutely; comparatively.
**Relator,** rē-lāt'ėr, *n.* One who relates.
**Relax,** rē-laks', *vt.* To slacken; to loosen or weaken; to unbend.—*vi.* To become loose, feeble, or languid; to abate in severity.
**Relaxation,** re-laks-ā'shon, *n.* Act of relaxing; abatement of rigor; recreation.
**Relay,** rē-lā', *n.* A supply of horses placed on the road to relieve others; a squad of men to relieve others; a supply stored up.—*vt.* To lay again; to lay a second time.
**Release,** rē-lēs', *vt.* (releasing, released). To liberate; to disengage; to acquit.—*n.* Liberation; discharge; acquittance.
**Re-lease,** rē-lēs', *vt.* To lease again.
**Relegate,** re'lē-gāt, *vt.* To consign to some remote destination; to banish.
**Relent,** rē-lent', *vi.* To soften in temper; to yield or become less severe.
**Relentless,** rē-lent'les, *a.* Unmerciful; implacable; pitiless.
**Relet,** rē-let', *vt.* To let anew, as a house.
**Relevance, Relevancy,** re'le-vans, re'le-van-si, *n.* State or quality of being relevant; pertinence.
**Relevant,** re'le-vant, *a.* Applicable; pertinent; to the purpose.
**Reliable,** rē-lī'a-bl, *a.* That may be relied on; trustworthy.
**Reliably,** rē-lī'a-bli, *adv.* In a reliable manner; so as to be relied on.
**Reliance,** rē-lī'ans, *n.* Act of relying; trust; confidence; dependence.
**Reliant,** rē-lī'ant, *a.* Confident; self-reliant.
**Relic,** re'lik, *n.* A remaining fragment; the body of a deceased person (usually in *pl.*); a memento or keepsake.
**Relief,** rē-lēf', *n.* Ease or mitigation of pain; succor; remedy; redress; assistance given to a pauper; one who relieves another by taking duty; prominence of figures above a plane surface in sculpture, carving, etc.; prominence or distinctness.
**Relieve,** rē-lēv', *vt.* (relieving, relieved). To remove or lessen, as anything that pains; to ease; to succor; to release from duty; to give variety to; to set off by contrast; to give the appearance of projection to.
**Religion,** rē-li'jon, *n.* An acknowledgment of our obligation to God; practical piety; devotion; any system of faith and worship.
**Religionist,** rē-li'jon-ist, *n.* A religious bigot; a formalist.
**Religiosity,** rē-li'ji-os''i-ti, *n.* A natural tendency of mind towards religion; weak superficial religious sentiment.
**Religious,** rē-li'jus, *a.* Pertaining to religion; teaching religion; used in worship; devout; scrupulously faithful.
**Religiously,** rē-li'jus-li, *adv.* Piously; reverently; strictly; conscientiously.
**Relinquish,** rē-ling'kwish, *vt.* To give up; to leave; to resign; to renounce.
**Relish,** re'lish, *vt.* To enjoy the taste of; to have a taste for; to give an agreeable taste to.—*vi.* To have a pleasing taste.—*n.* Taste, usually pleasing; fondness; flavor; something to increase the pleasure of eating.
**Relive,** rē-liv', *vi.* To live again.
**Reluctance, Reluctancy,** rē-luk'tans, rē-luk'tan-si, *n.* Aversion; unwillingness.
**Reluctant,** rē-luk'tant, *a.* Loath; averse; acting with slight repugnance.
**Rely,** rē-lī', *vt.* (relying, relied). To rest with confidence; to trust; with *on* or *upon*.
**Remain,** rē-mān', *vi.* To continue in a place or condition; to abide; to be left; to last.—*n.* That

R

which is left; *pl.* a dead body; literary works of one who is dead.

**Remainder,** rē-mān'dėr, *n.* That which remains; residue; remnant; an estate limited so as to be enjoyed after the death of the present possessor or otherwise.—*a.* Left over.

**Remake,** rē-māk', *vt.* To make anew.

**Remand,** rē-mand', *vt.* To call or send back; to send back to jail.

**Remanent,** rem'a-nent, *a.* Remaining.

**Remark,** rē-märk', *n.* Notice; an observation in words; a comment.—*vt.* To observe; to utter by way of comment.

**Re-mark,** rē-märk', *vt.* To mark anew.

**Remarkable,** rē-märk'a-bl, *a.* Worthy of remark; conspicuous; unusual; extraordinary.

**Remarkably,** rē-märk'a-bli, *adv.* Strikingly; singularly; surprisingly.

**Remarry,** rē-ma'ri, *vt.* and *i.* To marry again.

**Remediable,** re-mē'di-a-bl, *a.* Curable.

**Remedial,** re-mē'di-al, *a.* Affording a remedy; healing; intended for a remedy.

**Remedy,** re'me-di, *n.* That which cures a disease; that which counteracts an evil; redress.—*vt.* (remedying, remedied). To cure; to repair; to redress; to counteract.

**Remember,** rē-mem'bėr, *vt.* To have in the memory; to think of; to observe; to give a gratuity for service done.—*vi.* To have something in remembrance.

**Remembrance,** rē-mem'brans, *n.* The keeping of a thing in mind; memory; what is remembered; a memorial; a keepsake.

**Remembrancer,** rē-mem'brans-ėr, *n.* An officer in the exchequer; a recorder.

**Remind,** rē-mīnd', *vt.* To put in mind; to cause to remember.

**Reminder,** rē-mīnd'ėr, *n.* One who reminds; a hint that awakens remembrance.

**Reminiscence,** re-mi-nis'ens, *n.* Recollection; what is recalled to mind; account of past incidents within one's knowledge.

**Reminiscent,** re-mi-nis'ent, *a.* Having remembrance; calling to mind.

**Remiss,** rē-mis', *a.* Careless; negligent; heedless; slack.

**Remission,** rē-mi'shon, *n.* Act of remitting; relinquishment; abatement; pardon.

**Remissly,** rē-mis'li, *adv.* Carelessly; negligently; slackly.

**Remit,** rē-mit', *vt.* (remitting, remitted). To relax; to abate; to relinquish; to forgive; to transmit or send.—*vi.* To slacken; to abate in violence for a time.

**Remittance,** rē-mit'ans, *n.* Act of remitting; the sum or thing remitted.

**Remittent,** rē-mit'ent, *a.* Temporarily ceasing.—*n.* A remittent fever.

**Remnant,** rem'nant, *n.* That which is left; a scrap, fragment.—*a.* Remaining.

**Remonetize,** rē-mon'et-īz, *vt.* To make again a legal or standard money of account.

**Remonstrance,** rē-mon'strans, *n.* Act of remonstrating; expostulation; strong representation against something.

**Remonstrant,** rē-mon'strant, *a.* Remonstrating.

**Remonstrate,** rē-mon'strāt, *vi.* To present strong reasons against an act; to expostulate.

**Remora,** rem'o-ra, *n.* The sucking-fish.

**Remorse,** rē-mors', *n.* Reproach of conscience; compunction for wrong committed.

**Remorseful,** rē-mors'ful, *a.* Full of remorse; impressed with a sense of guilt.

**Remorseless,** rē-mors'les, *a.* Without remorse; ruthless; relentless; merciless.

**Remote,** rē-mōt', *a.* Distant in place or time; not immediate or direct; slight; inconsiderable.

**Remotely,** rē-mōt'li, *adv.* In a remote manner; distantly; slightly.

**Remount,** rē-mount', *vt.* and *i.* To mount again.—*n.* A fresh horse to mount.

**Removable,** rē-möv'a-bl, *a.* That may be removed.

**Removal,** rē-möv'al, *n.* Act of removing; a moving to another place.

**Remove,** rē-möv', *vt.* (removing, removed). To move from its place; to take away; to displace from an office; to banish or destroy.—*vi.* To be moved from its place; to change the place of residence.—*n.* A removal; departure.

**Removed,** rē-mövd', *p.a.* Remote.

**Remunerate,** rē-mū'nė-rāt, *vt.* To reward for service; to recompense.

**Remuneration,** rē-mū'nė-rā''shon, *n.* Act of remunerating; reward; compensation.

**Renaissance,** re-nā'sans, *n.* Revival; the revival of letters and arts in the fifteenth century.

**Renal,** rē'nal, *a.* Pertaining to the kidneys.

**Renard,** re'närd, *n.* A fox.

**Renascence,** rē-nas'ens, *n.* The state of being renascent; also same as *Renaissance*.

**Renascent,** rē-nas'ent, *a.* Springing into being again; reappearing; rejuvenated.

**Rencounter,** ren-koun'tėr, *n.* An abrupt meeting of persons; a casual combat; encounter.—*vi.* To meet an enemy unexpectedly.

**Rend,** rend, *vt.* (rending, rent). To force asunder; to tear away; to sever.—*vi.* To be or become torn; to split.

**Render,** ren'dėr, *vt.* To give in return; to give back; to present; to afford; to invest with qualities; to translate; to interpret; to clarify, as tallow.

**Rendering,** ren'dėr-ing, *n.* Version; translation; interpretation.

**Rendezvous,** ren'de-vö, *n.* A place of meeting.—*vi.* To meet at a particular place.

**Rendition,** ren-di'shon, *n.* A rendering; interpretation; translation; surrender.

**Renegade,** re'nē-gād, *n.* An apostate; a deserter.

**Renew,** rē-nū', *vt.* To make new again; to repair; to repeat; to grant anew; to transform.—*vi.* To grow or begin again.

**Renewal,** rē-nū'al, *n.* Act of renewing; a new loan on a new bill or note.

**Reniform,** rē'ni-form, *a.* Having the shape of the kidneys.

**Renitent,** rē-nī'tent, *a.* Resisting pressure; persistently opposed.

**Rennet,** ren'et, *n.* The prepared inner membrane of the calf's stomach, which coagulates milk; a kind of apple.

**Renounce,** rē-nouns', *vt.* (renouncing, renounced). To disown; to reject; to forsake.—*vi.* To revoke.

**Renovate,** re'nō-vāt, *vt.* To renew; to restore to freshness.

**Renovation,** re-nō-vā'shon, *n.* Act of renovating; renewal.

**Renown,** rē-noun', *n.* Fame; glory; reputation.—*vt.* To make famous.

**Renowned,** rē-nound', *a.* Famous; celebrated; eminent; remarkable.

**Rent,** rent, *n.* Money, etc., payable yearly for the use of lands or tenements; a tear; a schism.—*vt.* To let on lease; to hold on condition of paying rent.—*vi.* To be leased or let for rent.

**Rental,** rent'al, *n.* A roll or account of rents; gross amount of rents from an estate.

**Renter,** rent'ėr, *n.* The lessee or tenant who pays rent.—*vt.* To sew together finely; to fine-draw.

**Renunciation,** rē-nun'si-ā''shon, *n.* Act of renouncing; disavowal; abandonment.

**Reoccupy,** rē-ok'kū-pī, *vt.* To occupy anew.

**Reopen,** rē-ō'pen, *vt.* and *i.* To open again.

**Reorganize,** rē-or'gan-īz, *vt.* To organize anew.

**Rep, Repp,** rep, *n.* A dress fabric with a corded surface, the ribs being transverse.

**Repair,** rē-pār', *vt.* To restore; to refit; to mend; to retrieve.—*vi.* To betake oneself; to resort.—*n.* Restoration; supply of loss; state as regards repairing; a resorting; abode.

**Reparable,** re'pa-ra-bl, *a.* That may be repaired.

**Reparation,** re-pa-rā'shon, *n.* Act of repairing; restoration; satisfaction for injury; amends.

**Reparative,** re-pa'ra-tiv, *a.* Repairing; tending to

amend.—*n.* That which repairs or makes amends.

**Repartee,** re-pär-tē', *n.* A smart, ready, and witty reply.

**Repast,** rē-past', *n.* Act of taking food; food taken; a meal.—*vt.* and *i.* To feed.

**Repatriate,** rē-pā'tri-āt, *vt.* To restore to one's own country.

**Repay,** rē-pā', *vt.* To pay back or again; to refund; to requite.

**Repayable,** rē-pā-a-bl, *a.* That is to be or may be repaid.

**Repayment,** rē-pā'ment, *n.* Act of repaying; money repaid.

**Repeal,** rē-pēl', *vt.* To recall; to revoke; to abrogate, as a law.—*n.* Act of repealing; abrogation.

**Repeat,** rē-pēt', *vt.* To do or utter again; to recite; to recapitulate.—*n.* Repetition.

**Repeatedly,** rē-pēt'ed-li, *adv.* With repetition; again and again; indefinitely.

**Repeater,** rē-pēt'ėr, *n.* One who repeats; a watch that strikes the hours; an indeterminate decimal.

**Repeating,** rē-pēt'ing, *a.* Producing a like result several times in succession.

**Repel,** rē-pel', *vt.* (repelling, repelled). To drive back; to resist successfully.—*vi.* To cause repugnance; to shock.

**Repellence, Repellency,** rē-pel'ens, rē-pel'en-si, *n.* Quality of being repellent.

**Repellent,** rē-pel'ent, *a.* Having the effect of repelling; repulsive; deterring.

**Repent,** rē-pent', *vi.* To feel regret for something done or left undone; to be penitent.—*vt.* To remember with self-reproach or sorrow.

**Repent,** rē'pent, *a.* Creeping.

**Repentance,** rē-pent'ans, *n.* Act of repenting; sorrow for sin; penitence; contrition.

**Repentant,** rē-pent'ant, *a.* Repenting.

**Repercuss,** rē-pėr-kus', *vt.* To drive back (as sound or air); to make rebound.

**Repercussion,** rē-pėr-ku'shon, *n.* Act of driving back; reverberation.

**Repercussive,** rē-pėr-kus'iv, *a.* Having power of repercussion; causing to reverberate.

**Repertoire,** rep'ėr-twär, *n.* The aggregate of pieces that an actor or company performs.

**Repertory,** re'pėr-to-ri, *n.* A treasury; a magazine; a repository.

**Repetition,** re-pē-ti'shon, *n.* Act of repeating; recital; that which is repeated.

**Replace,** rē-plās', *vt.* (replacing, replaced). To put again in the former place; to put in the place of another; to take the place of.

**Replenish,** rē-plen'ish, *vt.* To fill again; to fill completely; to stock abundantly.

**Replete,** rē-plēt', *a.* Filled up; full; abounding; thoroughly imbued.

**Repletion,** rē-plē'shon, *n.* State of being replete; superabundant fulness; surfeit.

**Replevin, Replevy,** rē-plev'in, rē-plev'i, *n.* A personal action to recover goods.

**Replevy,** rē-plev'i, *vt.* (replevying, replevied). To reclaim (as goods wrongfully seized) upon giving security to try the cause in court.

**Replica,** rep'li-ka, *n.* A copy of a picture or a piece of sculpture made by the hand that executed the original; facsimile.

**Replication,** re-pli-kā'shon, *n.* An answer; a copy; a replica.

**Reply,** rē-plī', *vi.* and *t.* (replying, replied). To answer; to respond; to do something in return.—*n.* An answer; a response; a rejoinder.

**Report,** rē-pōrt', *vt.* and *i.* To bring back, as an answer; to relate; to give an official statement of; to take down from the lips of a speaker, etc.; to lay a charge against.—*n.* An account; rumor; repute; noise of explosion; official statement; account of proceedings.

**Reporter,** rē-pōrt'ėr, *n.* One who reports; one of a newspaper staff who gives accounts of public meetings, events, etc.

**Reposal,** rē-pōz'al, *n.* The act of reposing or resting with reliance.

**Repose,** rē-pōz', *vt.* (reposing, reposed). To lay at rest.—*vi.* To lie at rest; to rely.—*n.* A lying at rest; tranquillity; composure; absence of show of feeling.

**Reposeful,** rē-pōz'ful, *a.* Full of repose; affording repose or rest; trustful.

**Repoussé,** re-pös'sā, *a.* Embossed.

**Reprehend,** re-prē-hend', *vt.* To charge with a fault; to reprove; to censure.

**Reprehensible,** re-prē-hen'si-bl, *a.* Deserving reprehension; blamable.

**Reprehension,** re-prē-hen'shon, *n.* Act of reprehending; reproof; censure; blame.

**Reprehensive,** re-prē-hen'siv, *a.* Containing reprehension or reproof.

**Represent,** re-prē-zent', *vt.* To exhibit by a likeness of; to typify; to act the part of; to describe; to be a substitute for; to exemplify.

**Representable,** re-prē-zent'a-bl, *a.* That may be represented.

**Representation,** re'prē-zen-tā''shon, *n.* The act of representing; an image or likeness; dramatic performance; a remonstrance; the representing of a constituency.

**Representative,** re-prē-zent'a-tiv, *a.* Fitted or serving to represent; conducted by the agency of delegates; typical.—*n.* One who or that which represents; a person elected to represent a constituency.

**Repress,** rē-pres', *vt.* To press back; to check; to quell.

**Repressible,** rē-pres'i-bl, *a.* Capable of being repressed.

**Repression,** rē-pre'shon, *n.* Act of repressing or subduing; check; restraint.

**Repressive,** rē-pres'iv, *a.* Having power or tending to repress.

**Reprieve,** rē-prēv', *vt.* (reprieving, reprieved). To grant a respite to; to relieve temporarily.—*n.* Suspension of the execution of a criminal's sentence; respite.

**Reprimand,** rep'ri-mand, *n.* A severe reproof for a fault.—*vt.* rep-ri-mand'. To administer a sharp rebuke to.

**Reprint,** rē-print', *vt.* To print again.—*n.* rē'print. A second or new edition.

**Reprisal,** rē-prīz'al, *n.* Seizure from an enemy by way of retaliation; retaliation.

**Reproach,** rē-prōch', *vt.* To charge severely with a fault; to censure.—*n.* Censure; blame; source of blame; disgrace.

**Reproachable,** rē-prōch'a-bl, *a.* Deserving reproach.

**Reproachful,** rē-prōch'ful, *a.* Containing or expressing reproach; opprobrious.

**Reprobate,** re'prō-bāt, *a.* Morally abandoned; profligate.—*n.* A wicked, depraved wretch.—*vt.* To disapprove strongly; to reject.

**Reproduce,** rē-prō-dūs', *vt.* To produce again; to generate, as offspring; to portray or represent.

**Reproduction,** rē-prō-duk'shon, *n.* Act or process of reproducing; that which is produced anew; an accurate copy.

**Reproductive,** rē-prō-duk'tiv, *a.* Pertaining to or used in reproduction.

**Reproof,** rē-pröf', *n.* Words intended to reprove; rebuke.

**Reproval,** rē-pröv'al, *n.* Reproof.

**Reprove,** rē-pröv', *vt.* (reproving, reproved). To charge with a fault orally; to chide; to rebuke.

**Reptile,** rep'til, *a.* Creeping; grovelling.—*n.* An animal that moves on its belly, or by means of small short legs.

**Reptilian,** rep-til'i-an, *a.* Belonging to the class of reptiles.—*n.* A reptile.

**Republic,** rē-pub'lik, *n.* A commonwealth; a state in which the supreme power is vested in elected representatives.

**Republican,** rē-pub'lik-an, *a.* Pertaining to or consisting of a republic.—*n.* One who favors republican government.

**Repudiate,** rē-pū'di-āt, *vt.* (repudiating, repu-

R

diated). To divorce; to reject; to disavow.
**Repudiation,** rē-pū'di-ā''shon, *n.* Act of repudiating; rejection; disavowal.
**Repugnance,** rē-pug'nans, *n.* Aversion; reluctance; dislike; inconsistency.
**Repugnant,** rē-pug'nant, *a.* Opposed; inconsistent; inimical; offensive.
**Repulse,** rē-puls', *n.* Act of repelling; a check or defeat; refusal; denial.—*vt.* (repulsing, repulsed). To repel.
**Repulsion,** rē-pul'shon, *n.* Act of repelling; feeling of aversion.
**Repulsive,** rē-puls'iv, *a.* That repulses or repels; repellent; forbidding.
**Repurchase,** rē-pėr'chās, *vt.* To buy back.—*n.* Purchase again of what has been sold.
**Reputable,** re'pūt-a-bl, *a.* Held in esteem; estimable.
**Reputation,** re-pūt-ā'shon, *n.* Character derived from public opinion; repute; good name; honor; fame.
**Repute,** rē-pūt', *vt.* (reputing, reputed). To estimate; to deem.—*n.* Reputation; character; good character.
**Reputedly,** rē-pūt'ed-li, *adv.* In common repute.
**Request,** rē-kwest', *n.* An expressed desire; a petition; thing asked for; a state of being asked for.—*vt.* To ask; to beg.
**Requiem,** rē'kwi-em, *n.* A mass for the dead in the R. Catholic Church; music for this mass.
**Require,** rē-kwīr', *vt.* (requiring, required). To ask as of right; to demand; to have need for; to find it necessary.
**Requirement,** rē-kwīr'ment, *n.* Act of requiring; demand; an essential condition; something necessary.
**Requisite,** re'kwi-zit, *a.* Necessary; essential.—*n.* Something indispensable.
**Requisition,** re-kwi-zi'shon, *n.* Act of requiring; demand; a written call or invitation.—*vt.* To make a demand upon or for.
**Requital,** rē-kwīt'al, *n.* Act of requiting; reward; recompense; retribution.
**Requite,** rē-kwīt', *vt.* (requiting, requited). To repay; to reward; to retaliate on.
**Rescind,** rē-sind', *vt.* To abrogate; to annul; to repeal; to revoke.
**Rescission,** rē-si'zhon, *n.* Act of rescinding.
**Rescript,** rē'skript, *n.* Official decision; an edict or decree.
**Rescue,** res'kū, *vt.* (rescuing, rescued). To deliver from confinement, danger, or evil.—*n.* Act of rescuing; deliverance.
**Rescuer,** res'kū-ėr, *n.* One that rescues.
**Research,** rē-sėrch', *n.* A diligent seeking of facts or principles; investigation.—*vt.* To search again.
**Reseat,** rē-sēt', *vt.* To seat again; to furnish with a new seat.
**Reseize,** rē-sēz', *vt.* To seize again; to reinstate.
**Resemblance,** rē-zem'blans, *n.* Likeness; similarity; something similar; similitude.
**Resemble,** rē-zem'bl, *vt.* (resembling, resembled). To be like; to liken; to compare.
**Resent,** rē-zent', *vt.* To take ill; to consider as an affront; to be angry at.—*vi.* To feel resentment.
**Resentful,** rē-zent'ful, *a.* Full of resentment; of a vindictive temper.
**Resentment,** rē-zent'ment, *n.* Deep sense of injury; indignation; revengeful feeling.
**Reservation,** re-zėrv-ā'shon, *n.* Act of reserving; reserve; concealment; state of being treasured up; proviso.
**Reserve,** rē-zėrv', *vt.* (reserving, reserved). To keep in store; to retain.—*n.* Act of reserving; that which is retained; retention; habit of restraining the feelings; coldness towards others; shyness; troops kept for an exigency.
**Reserved,** rē-zėrvd', *a.* Showing reserve; not free or frank; restrained; cautious.
**Reservoir,** re'zėr-vwar, *n.* A place where anything is kept in store; an artificial lake to supply a town with water.
**Reset,** rē-set', *vt.* To set again.
**Reside,** rē-zīd', *vi.* (residing, resided). To have one's abode; to dwell; to inhere.
**Residence,** re'zi-dens, *n.* Act or state of residing; abode; home; dwelling.
**Residency,** re'zi-den-si, *n.* Residence; official residence of a British resident in India.
**Resident,** re'zi-dent, *a.* Residing.—*n.* One who resides; a dweller; a public minister at a foreign court.
**Residenter,** re'zi-dent-ėr, *n.* A resident.
**Residential,** re-zi-den'shal, *a.* Pertaining to or suitable for residence.
**Residual,** rē-zid'ū-al, *a.* Left after a part is taken.
**Residuary,** rē-zid'ū-a-ri, *a.* Pertaining to the residue.
**Residue,** re'zi-dū, *n.* That which remains after a part is taken; remainder.
**Resign,** rē-zīn', *vt.* To give up; to renounce; to submit, as to Providence.
**Resignation,** re-zig-nā'shon, *n.* Act of resigning; state of being resigned; habitual submission to Providence.
**Resigned,** rē-zīnd', *a.* Submissive; patient.
**Resilience, Resiliency,** rē-si'li-ens, rē-si'li-en-si, *n.* Act of resiling or rebounding; rebound from being elastic.
**Resilient,** rē-si'li-ent, *a.* Inclined to resile; rebounding.
**Resin,** re'zin, *n.* An inflammable vegetable substance; the hardened juice of pines.
**Resinous,** re'zin-us, *a.* Pertaining to, like, or obtained from resin.
**Resist,** rē-zist', *vt.* and *i.* To withstand; to oppose; to struggle against.
**Resistance,** rē-zist'ans, *n.* Act of resisting; check; quality of not yielding to force.
**Resistant, Resistent,** rē-zis'tent, *a.* Making resistance.—*n.* One who or that which resists.
**Resistible,** rē-zist'i-bl, *a.* That may be resisted.
**Resistless,** rē-zist'les, *a.* That cannot be resisted; that cannot resist.
**Resolute,** re'zō-lūt, *a.* Having fixedness of purpose; determined; steadfast.
**Resolutely,** re'zō-lūt-li, *adv.* In a resolute manner; steadily; determinedly.
**Resolution,** re-zō-lū'shon, *n.* Character of being resolute; determination; a formal decision; operation of separating the component parts; solution.
**Resolvable,** rē-zolv'a-bl, *a.* That may be resolved.
**Resolve,** rē-zolv', *vt.* (resolving, resolved). To separate the component parts of; to analyze; to solve; to determine; to decide.—*vi.* To separate into component parts; to melt; to determine; to decide.—*n.* Fixed purpose of mind; resolution.
**Resolvent,** rē-zolv'ent, *a.* Having power to resolve or to dissolve; causing solution.
**Resolver,** rē-zolv'ėr, *n.* One who or that which resolves; one who determines.
**Resonance,** re'zo-nans, *n.* State or quality of being resonant; act of resounding.
**Resonant,** re'zo-nant, *a.* Resounding; full of sounds.
**Resort,** rē-zort', *vi.* To have recourse; to go; to repair frequently.—*n.* Recourse; concourse; a haunt.
**Resound,** rē-zound', *vt.* To give back the sound of; to echo; to praise.—*vi.* To sound again; to echo; to be much praised.
**Resource,** rē-sōrs', *n.* Any source of aid or support; expedient; *pl.* funds; means.
**Respect,** rē-spekt', *vt.* To regard; to relate to; to honor; to have consideration for.—*n.* Regard; attention; due deference; bias; a point or particular; reference.
**Respectability,** rē-spekt'a-bil''i-ti, *n.* State or quality of being respectable.
**Respectable,** rē-spekt'a-bl, *a.* Worthy of respect; held in good repute; moderately good.
**Respectably,** rē-spekt'a-bli, *adv.* In a respectable manner; moderately; pretty well.
**Respectful,** rē-spekt'ful, *a.* Marked by respect;

civil; dutiful; courteous.
**Respecting,** rē-spekt'ing, *prep.* In regard to; regarding; concerning.
**Respective,** rē-spekt'iv, *a.* Relating severally each to each; relative.
**Respectively,** rē-spekt'iv-li, *adv.* In their respective relations; as each belongs to each.
**Respiration,** re-spi-rā'shon, *n.* Act of respiring or breathing.
**Respirator,** re'spi-rāt-ėr, *n.* An appliance covering the mouth, and serving to exclude cold air, dust, etc.; a device to prevent the breathing in of poison-gas.
**Respiratory,** re'spī-ra''to-ri, *a.* Serving for respiration; pertaining to respiration.
**Respire,** rē-spīr', *vi.* and *t.* (respiring, respired). To breathe; to recover one's breath.
**Respite,** res'pit, *n.* Temporary intermission; interval; a reprieve.—*vt.* (respiting, respited). To grant a respite to; to reprieve.
**Resplendence,** rē-splen'dens, *n.* Brilliant luster.
**Resplendent,** rē-splen'dent, *a.* Very bright; shining with brilliant luster.
**Respond,** rē-spond', *vi.* To answer; to suit.—*n.* A short anthem; response.
**Respondent,** rē-spond'ent, *a.* Answering; corresponding.—*n.* One who responds; one who answers in a lawsuit.
**Response,** rē-spons', *n.* An answer; reply.
**Responsibility,** rē-spons'i-bil''i-ti, *n.* State of being responsible; that for which one is responsible; ability to answer in payment.
**Responsible,** rē-spons'i-bl, *a.* Answerable; accountable; important.
**Responsive,** rē-spons'iv, *a.* Making reply; answering; correspondent; suited.
**Responsory,** rē-spon'so-ri, *a.* Containing response or answer.—*n.* A response.
**Rest,** rest, *n.* Cessation of action; peace; sleep; an appliance for support; a pause; remainder; the others.—*vi.* To cease from action; to lie for repose; to be supported; to be in a certain state; remain; to be left.—*vt.* To lay at rest; to place, as on a support.
**Restaurant,** res'tō-rong, *n.* An establishment for the sale of refreshments.
**Restaurateur,** res-tō'ra-tėr, *n.* The keeper of a restaurant.
**Restful,** rest'ful, *a.* Giving rest; quiet.
**Restitution,** rēs-ti-tū'shon, *n.* Act of restoring; reparation; amends.
**Restive,** res'tiv, *a.* Stubborn; fidgeting; impatient under restraint or opposition.
**Restless,** rest'les, *a.* Without rest; disturbed; uneasy; anxious.
**Restorable,** rē-stor'a-bl, *a.* Capable of being restored.
**Restoration,** re-stō-rā'shon, *n.* Act of restoring; replacement; recovery; the re-establishment of the English monarchy in 1660.
**Restorative,** rē-stōr'at-iv, *a.* Having power to renew strength.—*n.* A medicine which restores strength.
**Restore,** rē-stōr', *vt.* (restoring, restored). To make strong again; to repair; to cure; to re-establish; to give back.
**Restrain,** rē-strān', *vt.* To hold back; to curb; to check to repress; to restrict.
**Restraint,** rē-strānt', *n.* Act of restraining; hindrance; curb; limitation.
**Restrict,** rē-strikt', *vt.* To limit; to curb.
**Restriction,** rē-strik'shon, *n.* Act of restricting; limitation; a reservation.
**Restrictive,** rē-strikt'iv, *a.* Having the quality of restricting; imposing restraint.
**Result,** rē-zult', *vi.* To rise as a consequence; to issue; to ensue; to end.—*n.* Consequence; effect; issue; outcome.
**Resultant,** rē-zult'ant, *a.* Following as a result or consequence.
**Resumable,** rē-zūm'a-bl, *a.* That may be resumed.
**Resume,** rē-zūm', *vt.* (resuming, resumed). To take up again; to begin again.
**Résumé,** rā'zö-mā, *n.* A recapitulation; a summary.
**Resurgent,** rē-sėr'jent, *a.* Rising again.
**Resurrection,** re-zėr-rek'shon, *n.* A rising again; the rising of the dead at the general judgment.
**Resuscitate,** rē-sus'i-tāt, *vt.* and *i.* To revive.
**Resuscitation,** rē-sus'i-tā''shon, *n.* Act of resuscitating; restoration of life.
**Retail,** rē-tāl', *vt.* To sell in small quantities; to tell to many.—*n.* rē'tāl. The sale of commodities in small quantities; used also as *adj.*
**Retailer,** rē-tāl'ėr, *n.* One who retails.
**Retain,** rē-tān', *vt.* To hold back; to keep in possession; to detain; to hire; to engage.
**Retainer,** rē-tān'ėr, *n.* One who retains; an adherent or dependent; a fee to engage a counsel.
**Retake,** rē-tāk', *vt.* To take again or back.
**Retaliate,** rē-ta'li-āt, *vi.* and *t.* To return like for like; to repay; to take revenge.
**Retaliation,** rē-ta'li-ā''shon, *n.* The return of like for like; requital; reprisal.
**Retaliative, Retaliatory,** rē-ta'li-ā-tiv, rē-tal'i-ā-to-ri, *a.* Returning like for like.
**Retard,** rē-tärd', *vt.* To render slower; to impede; to delay; to postpone.
**Retardation,** rē-tärd-ā'shon, *n.* Act of retarding; diminution in speed; obstruction.
**Retch,** rech, *vi.* To make an effort to vomit; to strain, as in vomiting.
**Retention,** rē-ten'shon, *n.* Act or power of retaining; maintenance; memory.
**Retentive,** rē-ten'tiv, *a.* Characterized by retention; having power to retain ideas.
**Reticence,** re'ti-sens, *n.* Act or character of keeping silence; keeping of one's own counsel.
**Reticent,** re'ti-sent, *a.* Having a disposition to be silent; reserved.
**Reticular,** re-tik'ū-lėr, *a.* Having the form or character of a net.
**Reticulate, Reticulated,** re-tik'ū-lāt, re-tik'ū-lāt-ed, *a.* Resembling net-work.
**Reticulation,** re-tik'ū-lā''shon, *n.* Net-work.
**Reticule,** re'ti-kūl, *n.* A net-work bag.
**Retina,** re'ti-na, *n.* One of the coats of the eye, where visual impressions are received.
**Retinue,** re'ti-nū, *n.* A train of attendants; a suite.
**Retiral,** rē-tīr'al, *n.* Act of retiring.
**Retire,** rē-tīr', *vi.* (retiring, retired). To go back; to withdraw from business or active life; to go to bed.—*vt.* To remove from service; to pay when due, as a bill of exchange.
**Retired,** rē-tīrd', *a.* Secluded; private; having given up business.
**Retirement,** rē-tīr'ment, *n.* Act of retiring; retired life; seclusion.
**Retiring,** rē-tīr'ing, *a.* Reserved; unobtrusive; granted to one who retires from service.
**Retort,** rē-tort', *vt.* To retaliate; to throw back.—*vi.* To return an argument or charge.—*n.* A severe reply; a repartee; a chemical vessel for distilling.
**Retouch,** rē-tuch', *vt.* To improve by new touches, as a picture, etc.
**Retrace,** rē-trās', *vt.* To trace back; to trace over again.
**Retract,** rē-trakt', *vt.* To draw back; to recall.—*vi.* To unsay one's words.
**Retractable,** rē-trakt'a-bl, *a.* Capable of being retracted.
**Retractation,** rē-trak-tā'shon, *n.* Retraction.
**Retractile,** rē-trakt'īl, *a.* Capable of being drawn back, as claws.
**Retraction,** rē-trak'shon, *n.* Act of drawing back; recantation; retractation.
**Retractive,** rē-trakt'iv, *a.* Tending to retract.
**Retractor,** rē-trakt'ėr, *n.* One who retracts; a muscle that draws back some part.
**Retranslate,** rē-trans-lāt', *vt.* To translate back into the original tongue.
**Retreat,** rē-trēt', *n.* Act of retiring; seclusion; a shelter; the retiring of an army from an enemy.—*vi.* To draw back; to retire from an en-

R

emy.

**Retrench,** rē-trensh', *vt.* To lessen; to limit or restrict.—*vi.* To economize.

**Retrenchment,** rē-trensh'ment, *n.* Act of curtailing; economy; an interior rampart.

**Retribution,** re-tri-bū'shon, *n.* Act of rewarding; a requital for evil done.

**Retributive, Retributory,** rē-tri'būt-iv, rē-tri'bū-to-ri, *a.* Making retribution; entailing justly deserved punishment.

**Retrievable,** rē-trēv'a-bl, *a.* That may be retrieved or recovered.

**Retrieval,** rē-trēv'al, *n.* Act of retrieving.

**Retrieve,** rē-trēv', *vt.* (retrieving, retrieved). To recover; to regain; to repair.

**Retriever,** rē-trēv'ėr, *n.* A dog that brings in game which a sportsman has shot.

**Retroact,** rē-trō-akt' or ret'rō-akt, *vi.* To act backward, in opposition, or in return.

**Retrocede,** rē-trō-sēd' or ret', *vi.* To go back; to retire.—*vt.* To cede back.

**Retrocession,** rē-trō-se'shon or ret-, *n.* Act of going or of ceding back.

**Retrograde,** ret'rō-grād or rē', *a.* Going backward; appearing to move from east to west in the sky.—*vi.* To go backward.

**Retrogression,** rē-trō-gre'shon or ret-, *n.* Act of going backward.

**Retrogressive,** rē-trō-gres'iv or ret-, *a.* Going or moving backward; declining.

**Retrorse,** rē-trors', *a.* Turned or directed backwards, as a part of a plant.

**Retrospect,** ret'rō-spekt or rē', *n.* A view of things past; backward survey.

**Retrospection,** ret-rō-spek'shon or rē-, *n.* Act or faculty of looking on things past.

**Retrospective,** ret-rō-spekt'iv or rē-, *a.* Looking back; affecting things past.

**Retroussé,** rė-trö'sā, *a.* Turned up at the end, as a nose.

**Return,** rē-tėrn', *vi.* To come or go back; to recur.—*vt.* To send back; to repay; to report officially; to elect; to yield.—*n.* Act of returning; repayment; election of a representative; profit; an official statement; *pl.* tabulated statistics; a light tobacco.

**Returning-officer,** rē-tėrn'ing-of-is-ėr, *n.* The presiding officer at an election who declares the persons duly elected.

**Retuse,** rē-tūs', *a.* Having a rounded end, with a slight hollow or indentation, as a leaf.

**Reunion,** rē-ūn'yon, *n.* Union after separation; a meeting for social purposes.

**Reunite,** rē-ū-nīt', *vt.* and *i.* To unite again; to reconcile after variance.

**Reveal,** rē-vēl', *vt.* To disclose; to divulge; to make known by divine means.

**Reveille,** re-vel'ye, *n.* A bugle-call sounded at sun-rise.

**Revel,** re'vel, *n.* A feast with noisy jollity.—*vi.* (revelling, revelled). To carouse; to delight.

**Revelation,** re-ve-lā'shon, *n.* Act of revealing; that which is revealed; divine communication; the Apocalypse.

**Revenge,** rē-venj', *vt.* and *i.* (revenging, revenged). To take vengeance for; to avenge.—*n.* Act of revenging; retaliation; deliberate infliction of injury in return for injury; vindictive feeling.

**Revengeful,** rē-venj'fụl, *a.* Full of revenge; vindictive; resentful.

**Revenue,** re've-nū, *n.* Income; the annual income of a state.

**Reverberate,** rē-vėr'bė-rāt, *vt.* and *i.* To return, as sound; to echo; to reflect, as heat or light.

**Revere,** rē-vēr', *vt.* (revering, revered). To regard with awe and respect; to venerate.

**Reverence,** rev'ėr-ens, *n.* Awe combined with respect; veneration; an obeisance; a reverend personage; a title of the clergy.—*vt.* To revere; to pay reverence to.

**Reverend,** rev'ėr-end, *a.* Worthy of reverence; a title given to clergymen.

**Reverent,** rev'ėr-ent, *a.* Expressing reverence; humble; impressed with reverence.

**Reverie,** re'vėr-i, *n.* A loose train of thoughts; a day-dream; a visionary project.

**Reversal,** rē-vėrs'al, *n.* Act of reversing; a change or overthrowing.

**Reverse,** rē-vėrs', *vt.* (reversing, reversed). To alter to the opposite; to annul.—*n.* A reversal; a complete change or turn; a check; a defeat; the contrary; the back or under-surface.—*a.* Turned backward; opposite.

**Reversible,** rē-vėrs'i-bl, *a.* That may be reversed, turned outside in, or the like.

**Reversion,** rē-vėr'shon, *n.* A reverting or returning; succession to an office after the present holder's term; a return towards some ancestral type; return of an estate to the grantor or his heirs.

**Revert,** rē-vėrt', *vt.* To reverse.—*vi.* To return to a former position, habit, statement, etc.; to return to the donor.

**Revertible,** rē-vėrt'i-bl, *a.* That may revert, as an estate.

**Revet,** rē-vet', *vt.* (revetting, revetted). To face (an embankment) with mason-work, etc.

**Revetment,** rē-vet'ment, *n.* A facing to a wall or bank; a retaining wall.

**Review,** rē-vū', *vt.* To view again; to reconsider; to write a critical notice of; to inspect.—*vi.* To write reviews.—*n.* A re-examination; a criticism; a periodical containing criticisms; official inspection of troops.

**Reviewer,** rē-vū'ėr, *n.* One who writes reviews.

**Revile,** rē-vīl', *vt.* (reviling, reviled). To vilify; to upbraid; to abuse.

**Revisal,** rē-vīz'al, *n.* Revision.

**Revise,** rē-vīz', *vt.* (revising, revised). To go over with care for correction.—*n.* A revision; a second proof-sheet in printing.

**Reviser,** rē-vīz'ėr, *n.* One who revises.

**Revision,** rē-vi'zhon, *n.* Act of revising; revisal; what is revised.

**Revisit,** rē-vi'zit, *vt.* To visit again.

**Revival,** rē-vīv'al, *n.* Act of reviving; restoration from neglect or depression; religious awakening.

**Revive,** rē-vīv', *vi.* (reviving, revived). To return to life; to recover new vigor.—*vt.* To bring again to life; to refresh; to bring again intouse or notice.

**Revivify,** rē-viv'i-fī, *vt.* To recall to life.

**Revocable,** re'vōk-a-bl, *a.* That may be revoked.

**Revocation,** re-vōk-ā'shon, *n.* Act of revoking; annulment; repeal.

**Revoke,** rē-vōk', *vt.* (revoking, revoked). To repeal; to annul.—*vi.* In *card playing,* to neglect to follow suit.

**Revolt,** rē-vōlt', *vi.* To renounce allegiance; to rebel; to be disgusted: with *at.*—*vt.* To shock.—*n.* Rebellion; mutiny.

**Revolting,** rē-vōlt'ing, *a.* Exciting extreme disgust; shocking.

**Revolution,** re-vō-lū'shon, *n.* Acto of revolving; rotation; a turn; circuit; a cycle of time; a radical change; overthrow of existing political institutions.

**Revolutionary,** re-vō-lū'shon-a-ri, *a.* Pertaining to or tending to produce a revolution.—*n.* A revolutionist.

**Revolutionist,** re-vō-lū'shon-ist, *n.* The favorer of revolution.

**Revolutionize,** re-vō-lū'shon-īz, *vt.* To bring about a complete change in.

**Revolve,** rē-volv', *vi.* (revolving, revolved). To turn round an axis or center.—*vt.* To cause to turn round; to consider attentively.

**Revolver,** rē-volv'ėr, *n.* A pistol having a revolving set of cartridge chambers, so constructed as to discharge several shots in quick succession without being reloaded.

**Revue,** rē-vū', *n.* A loosely-constructed and spectacular theatrical exhibition, depending on music and scenic and staging effects.

**Revulsion,** rē-vul'shon, *n.* A violent drawing away; a violent change, especially of feeling.
**Reward,** rē-wạrd', *n.* What is given in return for good done; recompense; punishment.—*vt.* To repay; to requite.
**Rhapsodic, Rhapsodical,** rap-sod'ik, rap-sod'ik-al, *a.* Pertaining to rhapsody.
**Rhapsodist,** rap'sod-ist, *n.* One who writes or sings rhapsodies or extravagant matter.
**Rhapsody,** rap'so-di, *n.* A short epic poem, or portion of an epic; a confused series of extravagantly enthusiastic statements.
**Rhetoric,** re'to-rik, *n.* The art of using language effectively; the art which teaches oratory; eloquence; flashy oratory; declamation.
**Rhetorical,** re-to'rik-al, *a.* Pertaining to, exhibiting, or involving rhetoric.
**Rhetorician,** re-to-ri'shan, *n.* One who teaches or is versed in rhetoric; a declaimer.
**Rheum,** rūm, *n.* A thin serous fluid secreted by the mucous glands, etc.
**Rheumatic,** rū-mat'ik, *a.* Pertaining to or like rheumatism; subject to rheumatism.
**Rheumatism,** rū'mat-izm, *n.* A painful disease of the muscles and joints.
**Rheumy,** rūm'i, *a.* Pertaining to, like, or affected with rheum.
**Rhinal,** rī'nal, *a.* Pertaining to the nose.
**Rhinoceros,** ri-nos'e-ros, *n.* A large hoofed animal, allied to the hippopotamus, with one or two horns on the nose.
**Rhododendron,** rō-dō-den'dron, *n.* An evergreen shrub with large brilliant flowers.
**Rhomb, Rhombus,** rom, rom'bus, *n.* A quadrilateral whose sides are equal, but the angles not right angles.
**Rhombic,** rom'bik, *a.* Having the figure of a rhomb.
**Rhomboid,** rom'boid, *n.* A quadrilateral whose opposite sides only are equal, and whose angles are not right angles.
**Rhomboidal,** rom-boid'al, *a.* Having the shape of a rhomboid.
**Rhubarb,** rö'bärb, *n.* A plant of which the leafstalks are used in cookery, and the roots of some species in medicine.
**Rhyme,** rīm, *n.* A correspondence of sound in the ends of words or verses; a short poem; a word rhyming with another.—*vi.* (rhyming, rhymed). To make verses; to accord in sound.—*vt.* To put into rhyme.
**Rhythm,** rithm, *n.* Periodical emphasis in verse or music; metrical movement; harmony; rhyme; meter; verse.
**Rhythmic, Rhythmical,** rith'mik, rith'mik-al, *a.* Pertaining to or having rhythm.
**Rib,** rib, *n.* One of the curved bones springing from the backbone; something resembling a rib; a long ridge on cloth.—*vt.* (ribbing, ribbed). To furnish with ribs; to inclose with ribs.
**Ribald,** ri'bald, *n.* A low, lewd fellow.—*a.* Low; obscene.
**Ribbon,** ri'bon, *n.* A narrow band of silk, satin, etc.
**Rice,** rīs, *n.* A cereal plant, whose seed forms a light nutritious food.
**Rich,** rich, *a.* Having abundant possessions; wealthy; costly; valuable; fertile; plentiful; bright; mellow; highly flavored; highly provocative of amusement.
**Riches,** rich'ez, *n.* Wealth; opulence; affluence.
**Richly,** rich'li, *adv.* In a rich manner; abundantly; splendidly; amply.
**Richness,** rich'nes, *n.* Wealth; fertility; brilliancy; sweetness.
**Rick,** rik, *n.* A stack or pile of grain or hay.—*vt.* To pile up in ricks, as hay.
**Rickets,** rik'ets, *n.pl.* A disease of children in which there is usually some distortion of the bones.
**Rickety,** rik'et-i, *a.* Affected with rickets; feeble; shaky.
**Ricochet,** rik'o-shet, *n.* A rebounding from a flat, horizontal surface.—*vt.* and *i.* rik-o-shet'. To operate upon by ricochet firing; to rebound.
**Rid,** rid, *vt.* (ridding, rid). To make free; to clear; to disencumber.—*a.* Free; clear.
**Riddance,** rid'ans, *n.* Act of ridding; disencumbrance.
**Riddle,** rid'l, *n.* A puzzling question; an enigma; a coarse sieve.—*vt.* (riddling, riddled). To solve; to sift; to make many holes in.
**Riddlings,** rid'lingz, *n.pl.* That which is separated out by riddling.
**Ride,** rīd, *vi.* (riding, pret. rode, pp. ridden). To be borne on horseback, in a vehicle, etc.; to have ability as an equestrian; to be at anchor.—*vt.* To sit on, so as to be carried; to go over in riding; to domineer over.—*n.* An excursion on horseback, or in a vehicle; a road for the amusement of riding.
**Rider,** rīd'ėr, *n.* One who rides; one who manages a horse; a supplement or amendment; subsidiary problem.
**Ridge,** rij, *n.* A long narrow prominence; strip thrown up by a plow; a long crest of hills; upper angle of a roof.—*vt.* (ridging, ridged). To form into ridges.
**Ridicule,** ri'di-kūl, *n.* Laughter with contempt; mockery; satire.—*vt.* To treat with ridicule; to make sport of.
**Ridiculous,** ri-dik'ū-lus, *a.* Worthy of or fitted to excite ridicule; droll; absurd.
**Riding,** rīd'ing, *p.a.* Used in riding; pertaining to riding.
**Riding-habit,** rīd'ing-ha-bit, *n.* A garment worn by ladies on horseback.
**Rife,** rīf, *a.* Abundant; prevalent; replete.
**Riffraff,** rif'raf, *n.* Refuse; the rabble.
**Rifle,** rī'fl, *n.* A gun the inside of whose barrel is grooved; *pl.* a body of troops with rifles.—*vt.* (rifling, rifled). To groove spirally the bore of; to rob; to plunder.
**Rifleman,** rī'fl-man, *n.* One of a body of troops armed with rifles.
**Rift,** rift, *n.* An opening; a cleft; a fissure.—*vt.* and *i.* To cleave; to split.
**Rig,** rig, *vt.* (rigging, rigged). To clothe; to accoutre; to fit with tackling.—*n.* Dress; style of the sails and masts of a ship.
**Rigadoon,** rig-a-dön', *n.* A gay brisk dance performed by one couple.
**Rigger,** rig'ėr, *n.* One whose occupation is to fit up the rigging of a ship.
**Rigging,** rig'ing, *n.* The ropes which support the masts, extend the sails, etc., of a ship.
**Right,** rīt, *a.* Straight; upright; just; suitable; proper; real; correct; belonging to that side of the body farther from the heart; to be worn outward; perpendicular; formed by one line perpendicular to another.—*adv.* Justly; correctly; very; directly; to the right hand.—*n.* What is right; rectitude; a just claim; authority; side opposite to the left.—*vt.* To put right; to do justice to; to restore to an upright position.—*vi.* To resume a vertical position.
**Righteous,** rīt'yus, *a.* Upright; pious; just; honest; virtuous; equitable.
**Righteously,** rīt'yus-li, *a.* Uprightly.
**Righteousness,** rīt'yus-nes, *n.* Integrity; purity of heart and rectitude of life; justice.
**Right-hand,** rīt'hand, *a.* Belonging to or on the side next the right hand; essentially needful or serviceable.
**Right-handed,** rīt'hand-ed, *a.* Using the right hand more easily than the left.
**Rightly,** rīt'li, *adv.* In a right manner; properly; fitly; justly; correctly.
**Rigid,** ri'jid, *a.* Stiff; unyielding; not pliant; strict; stern; rigorous.
**Rigidity,** ri-jid'i-ti, *n.* State or quality of being rigid; stiffness; severity; harshness.
**Rigidly,** ri'jid-li, *adv.* Stiffly; strictly.
**Rigmarole,** rig'ma-rōl, *n.* A succession of confused statements.
**Rigor,** rī'gor, *n.* A sudden coldness attended by

shivering.
**Rigor,** rig'or, *n.* Stiffness; strictness; austerity; severity; intense cold.
**Rigorous,** rig'or-us, *a.* Characterized by rigor; severe; stringent.
**Rigorously,** rig'or-us-li, *adv.* Strictly; rigidly.
**Rilievo,** re-lē-ä'vō, *n.* Relief, in *carving,* etc.
**Rill,** ril, *n.* A small brook.
**Rim,** rim, *n.* The border or edge of a thing; brim.—*vt.* (rimming, rimmed). To put a rim round.
**Rime,** rīm, *n.* White or hoar frost; a chink; rhyme.
**Rimose, Rimous,** rī'mōs, rī'mus, *a.* Full of chinks and fissures.
**Rimy,** rīm'i, *a.* Abounding with rime; frosty.
**Rind,** rīnd, *n.* The outward coat of trees, fruits, etc.; bark; peel.
**Ring,** ring, *n.* Anything in the form of a circle; a circle of gold, etc., worn on the finger; an area in which games, etc., are performed; a group of persons; sound of a bell; a metallic sound.—*vt.* To encircle; to cause to sound; to repeat often or loudly.—*vi.* To sound; to resound; to tingle.
**Ringleader,** ring'lēd-ėr, *n.* The leader of a circle of persons engaged in any evil course.
**Ringlet,** ring'let, *n.* A small ring; a curl.
**Ringworm,** ring'wėrm, *n.* A contagious skin disease forming discolored rings.
**Rink,** ringk, *n.* A portion of a sheet of ice marked off for curling; a smooth flooring for skating on with roller-skates.
**Rinse,** rins, *vt.* (rinsing, rinsed). To wash by laving water over; to cleanse the interior by the introduction of any liquid.
**Riot,** rī'ot, *n.* An uproar; a tumult; wild and loose festivity; revelry.—*vi.* To engage in a riot; to revel.
**Rioter,** rī'ot-ėr, *n.* One who engages in a riot.
**Riotous,** rī'ot-us, *a.* Indulging in riot or revelry; tumultuous; seditious; excessive.
**Rip,** rip, *vt.* (ripping, ripped). To tear or cut open; to take out by cutting or tearing.—*n.* A rent; a scamp.
**Riparian,** rī-pā'ri-an, *a.* Pertaining to the bank of a river.
**Ripe,** rīp, *a.* Brought to perfection in growth; mature; complete; ready for action or effect.—*vt.* and *i.* (riping, riped). To mature.
**Ripen,** rīp'n, *vi.* To grow or become ripe; to become ready.—*vt.* To mature.
**Ripple,** rip'l, *vi.* (rippling, rippled). To show a ruffled surface, as water; to make a gentle sound, as running water.—*vt.* To clean the seeds from, as flax.—*n.* A ruffle of the surface of water; a comb for separating the seeds from flax.
**Rise,** rīz, *vi.* (rising, pret. rose, pp. risen). To pass to a higher position; to stand up; to bring a session to an end; to arise; to swell by fermentation; to slope upwards; to become apparent; to come into existence; to rebel.—*n.* Act of rising; ascent; elevation; origin; beginning; appearance above the horizon; increase; advance.
**Rising,** rīz'ing, *p.a.* Increasing in power, etc.; advancing to adult years.—*n.* Act of one who or that which rises; appearance above the horizon; resurrection; an insurrection; a prominence.
**Risk,** risk, *n.* Hazard; peril; jeopardy.—*vt.* To hazard; to dare to undertake.
**Risky,** risk'i, *a.* Dangerous; full of risk.
**Rissole,** ris'ōl, *n.* A dish of minced meat or fish covered with a paste and fried.
**Rite,** rīt, *n.* A formal act of religion, etc.; form; ceremony; observance; usage.
**Ritual,** rit'ū-al, *a.* Pertaining to rites.—*n.* A book containing the rites of a church; a system of rights; ceremonial.
**Ritualism,** rit'ū-al-izm, *n.* Observance of prescribed forms in religion.
**Ritualist,** rit'ū-al-ist, *n.* One skilled in ritual; one who favors an elaborate ritual.
**Rival,** rī'val, *n.* One who pursues the same object as another; a competitor.—*a.* Having the same pretensions or claims; competing.—*vt.* (rivalling, rivalled). To strive to excel; to compete with.
**Rivalry,** rī'val-ri, *n.* Act of rivalling; competition; emulation.
**Rive,** rīv, *vt.* and *i* (riving, rived, pp. rived and riven). To tear or rend; to split; to cleave.
**Rivel,** riv'l, *vt.* and *i* (rivelling, rivelled). To wrinkle; to corrugate.
**River,** ri'vėr, *n.* A large stream of water on land; a copious flow; abundance.
**Rivet,** ri'vet, *n.* A metallic bolt whose end is hammered broad after insertion.—*vt.* (riveting, riveted). To fasten with rivets; to clinch; to make firm.
**Riveter,** ri'vet-ėr, *n.* One who rivets; a workman employed in fixing rivets.
**Rivulet,** ri'vū-let, *n.* A small stream.
**Roach,** rōch, *n.* A fresh-water fish of the carp family.
**Road,** rōd, *n.* An open way or public passage; a highway; a means of approach; a roadstead (usually in *plural*).
**Roadstead,** rōd'sted, *n.* A place where ships may ride at anchor off a shore.
**Roadway,** rōd'wā, *n.* The part of a road travelled by horses and carriages; highway.
**Roam,** rōm, *vi.* To wander; to rove; to ramble.
**Roan,** rōn, *a.* Of a mixed color with a shade of red predominant.—*n.* A roan color, or horse of this color; a leather prepared from sheep-skin.
**Roar,** rōr, *vi.* To cry with a full, loud sound; to bellow; to bawl or squall.—*vt.* To cry out aloud.—*n.* A full, loud sound of some continuance; cry of a beast.
**Roaring,** rōr'ing, *n.* Loud, continued sound; a bronchial disease in horses.—*a.* Characterized by noise; disorderly; very brisk.
**Roast,** rōst, *vt.* To cook by exposure to a fire; to parch by heat; to banter severely.—*vi.* To become roasted.—*n.* Roasted meat; part selected for roasting.—*a.* Roasted.
**Rob,** rob, *vt.* (robbing, robbed). To strip unlawfully and by force; to deprive by stealing; to deprive.
**Robber,** rob'ėr, *n.* One who robs.
**Robbery,** rob'ėr-i, *n.* Act or practice of robbing; theft.
**Robe,** rōb, *n.* A gown, or long, loose garment, worn over other dress; an elegant dress.—*vt.* (robing, robed). To put a robe upon; to invest.
**Robin,** rob'in, *n.* The European bird called also redbreast.
**Roborant,** rob'o-rant, *a.* Strengthening.—*n.* A tonic.
**Robot,** rōb'ot, *n.* Any mechanical contrivance designed to perform work normally requiring the exercise of human intelligence.
**Robust,** rō-bust', *a.* Sturdy; vigorous; muscular.
**Rocambole,** rok'am-bōl, *n.* A kind of garlic.
**Rochet,** roch'et, *n.* A sort of short surplice, with tight sleeves, worn by bishops.
**Rock,** rok, *vt.* To move backwards and forwards without displacing; to swing.—*vi.* To sway; to reel.—*n.* A large mass of stone; defense; source of peril or disaster; a kind of solid sweetmeat.
**Rock-crystal,** rok'kris-tal, *n.* Crystallized quartz.
**Rocker,** rok'ėr, *n.* One who rocks; a curving piece on which a cradle, etc., rocks; a trough for washing ore by agitation.
**Rockery,** rok'ėr-i, *n.* An ornamented mound formed of fragments of rock, for ferns, etc.
**Rocket,** rok'et, *n.* A projectile firework; a similar device used as a lethal weapon; a garden plant.
**Rocking-horse,** rok'ing-hors, *n.* A wooden horse mounted on rockers; a hobby-horse.
**Rock-salt,** rok'salt, *n.* Mineral salt; common salt found in masses in the earth.
**Rocky,** rok'i, *a.* Full or rocks; resembling a rock; stony; obdurate.
**Rococo,** ro-kō'kō, *n.* and *a.* A meaninglessly decorative style of ornamentation of the time of Louis XIV and XV.

**Rod,** rod, *n.* A straight slender stick; a badge of office; an enchanter's wand; a fishing-rod; a measure of 5½ lineal yards.
**Rodent,** rō'dent, *a.* Gnawing; belonging to the gnawing animals (Rodentia).—*n.* An animal that gnaws, as the squirrel.
**Rodeo,** rōd-ā'o, *n.* A public exhibition of horse-breaking, lariat-throwing, etc.
**Rodomontade,** rod'ō-mon-tād'', *n.* Vain boasting; empty bluster; rant.
**Roe,** rō, *n.* The spawn of fishes; female of the hart.
**Roebuck, Roe-deer,** rō'buk, rō'dēr, *n.* A small species of European deer of elegant shape and remarkably nimble.
**Rogation,** rō-gā'shon, *n.* A supplication; the litany.
**Rogue,** rōg, *n.* A knave; a wag; a sly fellow.
**Roguery,** rōg'ėr-i, *n.* Knavish tricks; fraud; waggery; mischievousness.
**Roguish,** rōg'ish, *a.* Pertaining to or like a rogue; knavish; waggish.
**Roil,** roil, *vt.* To render turbid by stirring.
**Roister,** rois'tėr, *vi.* To bluster; to swagger.
**Rôle,** rōl, *n.* A part represented by an actor; any conspicuous part or function.
**Roll,** rōl, *vt.* To turn on its surface; to wrap on itself by turning; to involve in a bandage or the like; to press with a roller.—*vi.* To turn over and over; to run on wheels; to be tossed about; to sound with a deep prolonged sound.—*n.* Act of rolling; something rolled up; an official document; a catalogue; a cake of bread; a roller; a prolonged deep sound.
**Roll-call,** rōl'kal, *n.* The calling over a list of names, as of soldiers.
**Roller,** rōl'ėr, *n.* One who or that which rolls; a cylinder for smoothing, crushing, etc.; that on which something may be rolled up; a long, heavy, swelling wave.
**Roller-skate,** rōl'ėr-skāt, *n.* A skate mounted on small wheels or rollers.
**Rollick,** rol'ik, *vt.* To move with a careless swagger; to be jovial.
**Rolling,** rōl'ing, *p.a.* Revolving; making a continuous noise; undulating.
**Rolling-pin,** rōl'ing-pin, *n.* A round piece of wood with which dough is rolled out.
**Rolling-stock,** rōl'ing-stok, *n.* The carriages, vans, engines, etc., of a railway.
**Rollock,** rol'ok, *n.* Same as *Rowlock*.
**Roly-poly,** rō'li-pō-li, *n.* Paste spread with jam and rolled into a pudding.
**Romaic,** rō-mā'ik, *n.* and *a.* The vernacular language of modern Greece.
**Roman,** rō'man, *a.* Pertaining to Rome or its people and to the Roman Catholic religion; applied to the common upright letter in printing.
**Romance,** rō-mans', *n.* A tale in verse in a Romance dialect; a popular epic or tale in prose or verse of some length; a tale of extraordinary adventures; tendency to the wonderful or mysterious; a fiction.—*a.* (with *cap.*). A term applied to the languages sprung from the Latin.—*vi.* To tell fictitious stories.
**Romancer,** rō'mans'ėr, *n.* One who romances; a writer of romance.
**Romancist,** rō-mans'ist, *n.* A romancer.
**Romanesque,** rō-man-esk', *a.* and *n.* Applied to the debased style of architecture that prevailed in later Roman Empire.
**Romanism,** rō'man-izm, *n.* The tenets of the Church of Rome.
**Romantic,** rō-man'tik, *a.* Pertaining to romance; fanciful; extravagant; wildly picturesque.
**Romanticism,** rō-man'ti-sizm, *n.* State or quality of being romantic; a reaction in literature or art from classical to mediaeval or modern qualities; romantic feeling.
**Romanticist,** rō-man'ti-sist, *n.* One imbued with romanticism.
**Romany, Rommany,** rom'a-ni, *n.* A Gypsy; the language spoken by the Gypsies.
**Romp,** romp, *n.* Rude play or frolic; a boisterous girl.—*vi.* To play boisterously; to frisk about.
**Rondeau,** ron'dō, *n.* A poem of thirteen lines, with two rhymes, and a refrain occurring twice; a piece of three strains.
**Rondel,** ron'del, *n.* A poem like the rondeau.
**Rood,** röd, *n.* A cross or crucifix; the fourth part of an acre; a measure of 5½ lineal yards.
**Roof,** röf, *n.* The cover of any building; a canopy; the palate; a house.—*vi.* To cover with a roof; to shelter.
**Roofing,** röf'ing, *n.* Act of covering with a roof; materials of a roof; the roof itself.
**Rook,** ruk, *n.* A kind of crow; a cheat; a piece in chess.—*vi.* and *t.* To cheat; to rob.
**Rookery,** ruk'ėr-i, *n.* A grove used for nesting-places by rooks; a resort of thieves, etc.
**Rooky,** ruk'i, *a.* Inhabited by rooks.
**Room,** röm, *n.* Space; scope; opportunity; stead; apartment in a house; chamber.
**Roomy,** röm'i, *a.* Spacious; wide; large.
**Roost,** röst, *n.* The pole on which birds rest at night; a collection of fowls resting together.—*vi.* To occupy a roost; to settle.
**Rooster,** röst'ėr, *n.* The male of the domestic fowl; a cock.
**Root,** röt, *n.* That part of a plant which fixes itself in the earth; lower part of anything; origin; a form from which words are derived.—*vi.* To fix the root; to be firmly fixed.—*vt.* To plant deeply; to impress durably; to tear up or out; to eradicate.
**Rooted,** röt'ed, *a.* Fixed; deep; radical.
**Rope,** rōp, *n.* A cord or line of some thickness; a row or string of things united.—*vi.* (roping, roped). To draw out in threads.—*vt.* To pull by a rope; to fasten or inclose with a rope.
**Ropery,** rōp'ėr-i, *n.* A place where ropes are made.
**Ropy,** rōp'i, *a.* Stringy; viscous; glutinous.
**Rorqual,** ror'kwal, *n.* A large whale of several species.
**Rosaceous,** rōz-ā'shus, *a.* Rose-like; relating to roses.
**Rosary,** rōz'a-ri, *n.* A garland of roses; an anthology; a string of beads on which R. Catholics number their prayers.
**Rose,** rōz, *n.* A plant and its flower, of many species; an ornamental knot of ribbon; a perforated nozzle of a spout, etc.—*a.* Of a purplish-red color.
**Roseate,** rōz'ē-āt, *a.* Rosy; blooming.
**Rosemary,** rōz'ma-ri, *n.* An evergreen shrub, yielding a fragrant essential oil.
**Rosery,** rōz'ėr-i, *n.* A place where roses grow; a nursery of rose bushes.
**Rosette,** rō-zet', *n.* An ornamental knot of ribbons; an architectural ornament.
**Rose-water,** rōz'wa-tėr, *n.* Water tinctured with roses by distillation.
**Rosewood,** rōz'wud, *n.* The wood of a tree used in cabinet-work, when freshly cut having a faint smell of roses.
**Rosin,** ro'zin, *n.* The resin left after distilling off the volatile oil from turpentine; resin in a solid state.—*vt.* To rub with rosin.
**Roster,** ros'tėr, *n.* A list showing the rotation in which individuals, regiments, etc., are called on to serve.
**Rostrum,** ros'trum, *n.*; pl. **-tra.** The beak or bill of a bird; the ram of an ancient ship; *pl.* a platform or pulpit.
**Rosy,** rōz'i, *a.* Like a red rose in color; blooming; blushing; cheering; hopeful.
**Rot,** rot, *vi.* (rotting, rotted). To become rotten; to decay.—*vt.* To make rotten.—*n.* Putrid decay; a fatal distemper of sheep; a disease injurious to plants; nonsense.
**Rotary,** rō'ta-ri, *a.* Turning, as a wheel on its axis.
**Rotate,** rō'tāt, *vi.* (rotating, rotated). To revolve round a center or axis, like a wheel; to act in turn.—*vt.* To cause to turn like a wheel.
**Rotation,** rō-tā'shon, *n.* Act of rotating; the turn-

R

ing of a wheel or solid body on its axis; succession in a series.

**Rotatory,** rō'ta-to-ri, *a.* Pertaining to, exhibiting, or producing rotation; rotary.

**Rote,** rōt, *n.* Repetition of words by memory; mere effort of memory.

**Rotten,** rot'n, *a.* Decomposed; decaying; putrid; unsound; corrupt; fetid.

**Rotund,** rō-tund', *a.* Round; spherical.

**Rotunda,** rō-tun'da, *n.* A round building.

**Rouble,** rö'bl, *n.* The unit of the Russian money system.

**Roué,** rö-ā, *n.* A man devoted to pleasure and sensuality; a licentious man; a rake.

**Rouge,** rözh, *n.* A cosmetic to impart ruddiness to the complexion.—*vt.* and *i* (rouging, rouged). To paint with rouge.

**Rough,** ruf, *a.* Not smooth; rugged; boisterous; harsh; rude; cruel; vague; hasty.—*vt.* To make rough; to rough-hew.—**To rough it,** to submit to hardships.—*n.* State of being rough or unfinished; a rowdy.

**Rough-cast,** ruf'kast, *vt.* To form roughly; to cover with a coarse plaster.—*n.* A first plan or model; a coarse plastering.

**Roughen,** ruf'n, *vt.* To make rough.—*vi.* To become rough.

**Rough-hew,** ruf'hū, *vt.* To hew without smoothing; to give the first form to a thing.

**Roughly,** ruf'li, *adv.* Coarsely; without finish; harshly; approximately.

**Rough-shod,** ruf'shod, *a.* Shod with shoes armed with points.

**Roulade,** rö-läd, *n.* In *music*, a rapid run of notes, introduced as an embellishment.

**Rouleau,** rö-lō', *n.*; pl. **-leaus** (-lōz) or **-leaux** (-lōz). A little roll; a roll of coin in paper.

**Roulette,** rö-let', *n.* A game of chance; an engraver's tool with a toothed wheel.

**Round,** round, *a.* Circular; spherical; large; open; candid; brisk, as a trot; not minutely accurate, as a number.—*n.* That which is round; rung of a ladder; a circular course or series; circuit made by one on duty; a vocal composition in parts; ammunition for firing once; a turn or bout.—*vt.* To make round; to encircle; to make full and flowing; to pass round.—*vi.* To become round or full; to make a circuit.—*adv.* In a circle; around; not directly.—*prep.* About; around.

**Roundabout,** round'a-bout, *a.* Indirect; circuitous.—*n.* A revolving structure on which children ride.

**Roundelay,** round'ē-lā, *n.* A poem of thirteen verses, eight in one rhyme and five in another; a short and lively rural strain; a rural dance.

**Rounder,** roun'dėr, *n.* One who rounds; *pl.* a game played with a bat and ball by two sides.

**Roundhead,** round'hed, *n.* A member of the Puritan or parliamentary party in the English Civil War.

**Roundish,** round'ish, *a.* Somewhat round.

**Roundly,** round'li, *adv.* In a round manner; openly; plainly; vigorously.

**Round-robin,** round-rob'in, *n.* A written petition signed by names in a circle.

**Rouse,** rouz, *vt.* (rousing, roused). To arouse; to awaken; to stir up.—*vi.* To awake; to arise.—*n.* A carousal; a drinking frolic.

**Rousing,** rouz'ing, *a.* Having power to rouse or excite; very active or busy.

**Rout,** rout, *n.* A crowd; a rabble; a fashionable evening assembly; total defeat of troops; confusion of troops defeated.—*vt.* To defeat and throw into confusion; to overthrow; to rouse or drive out.

**Route,** röt, *n.* A course or way.

**Routine,** rö-tēn', *n.* A round of business or pleasure; regular course.

**Rove,** rōv, *vt.* (roving, roved). To move about aimlessly; to roam; to ramble.—*vt.* To wander over; to card into flakes, as wool.

**Rover,** rōv'ėr, *n.* One who roves; a pirate.

**Row,** rō, *n.* A series in a line; a rank; a line of houses; an excursion in a boat with oars.—*vt.* To impel by oars, as a boat; to transport by rowing.—*vi.* To work with the oar.

**Row,** rou, *n.* A noisy disturbance; a riot.—*vt.* To scold.

**Rowdy,** rou'di, *n.* A turbulent fellow; a rough.—*a.* Disreputable; blackguardly.

**Rowel,** rou'el, *n.* The little wheel of a spur, formed with sharp points.

**Rowlock,** rō'lok, *n.* A contrivance on a boat's gunwale to support the oar.

**Royal,** roi'al, *a.* Pertaining to a king; regal; kingly; august.—*n.* A large kind of paper; a shoot of a stag's antlers.

**Royalist,** roi'al-ist, *n.* An adherent to a king or kingly government.

**Royally,** roi'al-li, *adv.* In a royal or kingly manner; like a king; as becomes a king.

**Royalty,** roi'al-ti, *n.* State or character of being royal; a royal personage; share paid to a superior, inventor, or author.

**Rub,** rub, *vt.* (rubbing, rubbed). To move something along the surface of with pressure; to scour; to remove by friction; to chafe.—*vi.* To move along with pressure; to fret.—*n.* Act of rubbing; friction; obstruction; difficulty; a gibe.

**Rubber,** rub'ėr, *n.* One who rubs; thing used in polishing or cleaning; india-rubber; obstruction or difficulty; contest of three games in whist.

**Rubbish,** rub'ish, *n.* Refuse; debris; trash.

**Rubble,** rub'l, *n.* Broken stones of irregular shapes; masonry of such stones.

**Rubescent,** rö-bes'ent, *a.* Becoming red; blushing.

**Rubicund,** rö'bi-kund, *a.* Red or highly colored, as the face; ruddy.

**Rubric,** rö'brik, *n.* Important words in a manuscript, etc., colored red; a heading or title; direction in a prayer-book.

**Ruby,** rö'bi, *n.* A very valuable gem or precious stone of various shades of red; a fine red color; a blotch on the face; a small printing type.—*vt.* To make red.—*a.* Red.

**Ruck,** ruk, *vt.* To wrinkle; to crease.—*n.* A wrinkle; an undistinguished crowd; those of no special merit.

**Rucksack,** ruk'sak, *n.* A bag made to strap on the shoulders, and used by walkers, climbers, etc.

**Rud, Rudd,** rud, *n.* Red ochre.

**Rudd,** rud, *n.* A fresh-water fish.

**Rudder,** rud'ėr, *n.* The instrument by which a ship is steered.

**Ruddle,** rud'l, *n.* A species of red earth, used for marking sheep.—*vt.* (ruddling, ruddled). To mark with ruddle.

**Ruddoc, Ruddock,** rud'ok, *n.* The robin-redbreast.

**Ruddy,** rud'i, *a.* Of a red color; reddish; of a lively flesh color.—*vt.* (ruddying, ruddied). To make red or ruddy.

**Rude,** röd, *a.* Unformed by art or skill; rough; uncivilized; uncivil; impudent; violent.

**Rudely,** röd'li, *adv.* In a rude manner; violently; coarsely; unskilfully.

**Rudiment,** rö'di-ment, *n.* The original of anything; a first principle; an undeveloped organ; *pl.* first elements of a science or art.

**Rudimentary,** rö-di-ment'a-ri, *a.* Pertaining to rudiments; consisting in first principles; initial; in an undeveloped state.

**Rue,** rö, *vt.* (ruing, rued). To repent of; to regret.—*vi.* To become sorrowful or repentant.—*n.* An acrid ill-smelling plant.

**Rueful,** rö'ful, *a.* Woeful; mournful; piteous; expressing or suggesting sorrow.

**Ruff,** ruf, *n.* A plaited collar or frill; a ruffle; act of trumping at cards.—*vt.* To trump instead of following suit at cards.

**Ruffian,** ruf'i-an, *n.* A boisterous brutal fellow.—*a.* Like a ruffian; brutal.

**Ruffianism,** ruf'i-an-izm, *n.* The character or conduct of a ruffian.

**Ruffianly,** ruf'i-an-li, *a.* Like a ruffian; violent.
**Ruffle,** ruf'l, *vt.* (ruffling, ruffled). To rumple; to derange; to disturb.—*vi.* To bluster.—*n.* A plaited cambric, etc., attached to one's dress; frill; state of being agitated; low vibrating beat of a drum.
**Rufous,** rö'fus, *a.* Reddish; of a dull or brownish red.
**Rug,** rug, *n.* A heavy fabric used to cover a bed, protect a carpet, etc.; a mat.
**Ruga,** rö'ga, *n.*; pl. **-ae.** A wrinkle.
**Rugby,** rug'bi, *n.* One of the two principal varieties of football, played by fifteen men a side, with an oval ball, handling being permitted.
**Rugged,** rug'ed, *a.* Full of rough projections; rough; harsh; crabbed.
**Rugose, Rugous,** rö'gōs, rö'gus, *a.* Wrinkled.
**Ruin,** rö'in, *n.* Destruction; fall; overthrow; anything in a state of decay; that which destroys; *pl.* remains of a city, house, etc.; state of being destroyed.—*vt.* To bring to ruin; to destroy; to impoverish.
**Ruinate,** rö-i-nāt,. *vt.* To ruin.—*a.* In ruins.
**Ruination,** rö'i-nā'shon, *n.* Act of ruinating; overthrow; demolition.
**Ruinous,** rö'in-us, *a.* Fallen to ruin; dilapidated; destructive; baneful.
**Rule,** röl, *n.* A ruler or measure; a guiding principle or formula; a precept, law, maxim; government; control; regulation; order; method.—*vt.* (ruling, ruled). To govern; to manage; to decide; to mark with lines by a ruler.—*vi.* To exercise supreme authority; to maintain a level, as the market price; to settle, as a rule of court.
**Ruler,** röl'ėr, *n.* One who rules or governs; an instrument by which lines are drawn.
**Ruling,** röl'ing, *a.* Having control; reigning; predominant.—*n.* A point settled by a judge, chairman, etc.
**Rum,** rum, *n.* Spirit distilled from cane-juice or molasses.—*a.* Odd; queer.
**Rumble,** rum'bl, *vi.* (rumbling, rumbled). To make a dull, continued sound.—*n.* A low, heavy, continued sound; a seat for servants behind a carriage.
**Ruminant,** rö'min-ant, *a.* Chewing the cud.—*n.* An animal that chews the cud; a hoofed ruminating animal.
**Ruminate,** rö'min-āt, *vi.* To chew the cud; to meditate.—*vt.* To meditate on.
**Rumination,** rö-min-ā'shon, *n.* Act of ruminating; meditation or reflection.
**Rummage,** rum'āj, *vt.* (rummaging, rummaged). To search narrowly but roughly; to ransack.—*n.* A careful search; turning about of things.
**Rumor,** rö'mėr, *n.* A current story; a mere report.—*vt.* To report; to spread abroad.
**Rump,** rump, *n.* End of an animal's backbone; buttocks; fag-end of something.
**Rumpus,** rum'pus, *n.* A great noise; disturbance.
**Run,** run, *vi.* (running, pret. ran, pp. run). To move by using the legs more quickly than in walking; to take part in a race; to flee; to spread; to ply; to move or pass; to become fluid; to continue in operation; to have a certain direction; to have a certain purport; to be current; to continue in time.—*vt.* To cause to run; to pursue, as a course; to incur; to break through (a blockage); to smuggle; to pierce; to melt; to carry on.—*n.* Act of running; course or distance run; a trip; course, tenor, etc.; general demand, as on a back; place where animals may run; generality.
**Runaway,** run'a-wā, *n.* One who flies from danger or restraint; deserter; fugitive.—*a.* Effected by running away or eloping.
**Rune,** rön, *n.* One of a set of alphabetic characters peculiar to the ancient northern nations of Europe.
**Rung,** rung, *n.* A heavy staff; the round or step of a ladder.
**Runlet, Rundlet,** run'let, rund'let, *n.* A small barrel of no certain capacity.
**Runnel,** run'l, *n.* A rivulet or small brook.
**Runner,** run'ėr, *n.* One who runs; a messenger; a bird of the order Cursores; a stem running along the ground and taking root; that on which something runs or slides.
**Running,** run'ing, *a.* Kept for the race; continuous; in succession; discharging pus.
**Runt,** runt, *n.* A dwarfed animal; a variety of pigeon; stalk of a cabbage.
**Rupee,** rö-pē', *n.* A silver coin, the unit of value in India.
**Rupture,** rup'tūr, *n.* Act of breaking or bursting; fracture; breach; open hostility; hernia.—*vt.* (rupturing, ruptured). To cause a rupture in; to break.
**Rural,** rö'ral, *a.* Pertaining to the country; rustic.
**Ruse,** röz, *n.* Artifice; trick; deceit.
**Rush,** rush, *vi.* To move with great speed; to enter over-hastily.—*n.* A violent motion or course; an eager demand; a plant found in damp places; a reed.
**Rusk,** rusk, *n.* A light hard cake browned in the oven.
**Russet,** rus'et, *a.* Of a reddish-brown color; coarse; homespun; rustic.—*n.* A reddish-brown color; coarse country cloth; a kind of winter apple.
**Russian,** ru'shi-an, *a.* Pertaining to Russia.—*n.* A native of Russia; the language of Russia.
**Rust,** rust, *n.* The red coating formed on iron exposed to moisture; a parasitic fungus; loss of power by inactivity.—*vi.* To contract rust; to degenerate in idleness.—*vt.* To make rusty.
**Rustic,** rus'tik, *a.* Pertaining to the country; rural; homely; unpolished.—*n.* A country-man, a peasant; a clown.
**Rustle,** rus'l, *vi.* and *t.* (rustling, rustled). To make the noise of things agitated, as straw, leaves, etc.—*n.* The noise of things that rustle; a slight sibilant sound.
**Rusty,** rust'i, *a.* Covered with rust; impaired by inaction; rough; grating.
**Rut,** rut, *n.* The track of a wheel; a line cut with a spade; line of routine; time during which certain animals are under sexual excitement.—*vt.* (rutting, rutted). To cut in ruts.—*vi.* To be in heat, as deer.
**Ruthenium,** rö-thē'ni-um, *n.* A rare metal occurring in platinum ore.
**Ruthless,** röth'les, *a.* Cruel; pitiless.
**Ruttish,** rut'ish, *a.* Lustful.
**Rye,** rī, *n.* A cereal plant and it seed.
**Rye-grass,** rī'gräs, *n.* A kind of grass much cultivated for cattle and horses.
**Ryot,** rī'ot, *n.* A Hindu cultivator of the soil.

S

# S

**Sabaism,** sa-bā'izm, *n.* The worship of the heavenly bodies.
**Sabaoth,** sa-bā'oth, *n.* Armies; hosts.
**Sabbatarian,** sa-ba-tā'ri-an, *n.* A strict observer of the Sabbath.—*a.* Pertaining to the Sabbath.
**Sabbath,** sa'bath, *n.* The day of rest; Sunday.
**Sabbatic, Sabbatical,** sa-bat'ik, sa-bat'ik-al, *a.* Pertaining to the Sabbath; pertaining to a recurrence by sevens.
**Saber,** sā'bėr, *n.* A sword with one edge; a cavalry sword.—*vt.* (sabering, sabered). To strike or kill with a saber.
**Sabertache, Sabertash,** sā'bėr-tash, *n.* A leathern pocket worn by cavalry, suspended from the sword-belt.
**Sable,** sā'bl, *n.* A small animal of the weasel family; the fur of the sable; black.—*a.* Black; dark.
**Sabot,** sä-bō', *n.* A wooden shoe worn by continental peasants.
**Sabotage,** sä-bō-täzh, *n.* Malicious destruction of employers, property or national plant by employees on strike or during war-time.
**Sac,** sak, *n.* A bag; receptacle for a liquid.

**Saccharin,** sak'a-rin, *n.* A substance of great sweetness obtained from coal-tar.
**Saccharine,** sak'ka-rīn, *a.* Pertaining to or of the nature of sugar; sugary.
**Saccharose,** sak'a-rōs, *n.* A chemical name for pure or crystalline sugar.
**Sacerdotal,** sa-sėr-dōt'al, *a.* Pertaining to priests or the priesthood; priestly.
**Sachem,** sā'chem, *n.* A chief among some of the American Indian tribes.
**Sachet,** sä-shā, *n.* A small bag for odorous substances.
**Sack,** sak, *n.* A bag for flour, wool, etc.; that which a sack holds; a sort of jacket; a dry wine; pillage of a town.—*vt.* To put in sacks; to pillage, as a town.
**Sackbut,** sak'but, *n.* A musical instrument of the trumpet or trombone kind.
**Sackcloth,** sak'kloth, *n.* Cloth of which sacks are made.
**Sacking,** sak'ing, *n.* The material of which sacks are made, a cloth of flax or hemp.
**Sacral,** sā'kral, *a.* Pertaining to the sacrum.
**Sacrament,** sa'kra-ment, *n.* A solemn religious ordinance observed by Christians, as baptism or the Lord's Supper.
**Sacramental,** sa-kra-ment'al, *a.* Constituting or pertaining to a sacrament.
**Sacred,** sā'kred, *a.* Set apart for a holy purpose; consecrated; religious; set apart to some one in honor; venerable.
**Sacredly,** sā'kred-li, *adv.* In a sacred manner; religiously; inviolably; strictly.
**Sacrifice,** sa'kri-fīs, *n.* The offering of anything to God; anything offered to a divinity; surrender made in order to gain something else.—*vt.* (sacrificing, sacrificed). To make an offering or sacrifice of.—*vi.* To offer up a sacrifice to some deity.
**Sacrificial,** sa-kri-fi'shal, *a.* Pertaining to sacrifice; performing sacrifices.
**Sacrilege,** sa'kri-lej, *n.* Violation of sacred things.
**Sacrilegious,** sa-kri-lē'jus, *a.* Relating to or implying sacrilege; profane; impious.
**Sacring,** sā'kring, *n.* Consecration.
**Sacrist,** sā'krist, *n.* A sacristan.
**Sacristan,** sa'krist-an, *n.* A church officer who has the care of the sacred utensils.
**Sacristy,** sa'krist-i, *n.* An apartment in a church where the sacred utensils, vestments, etc., are kept; the vestry.
**Sacrosanct,** sa'krō-sangt, *a.* Sacred and inviolable; holy and venerable.
**Sacrum,** sā'krum, *n.* The bone forming the lower extremity of the vertebral column.
**Sad,** sad, *a.* Sorrowful; affected with grief; gloomy; distressing; calamitous.
**Sadden,** sad'n, *vt.* To make sad.—*vi.* To become sad.
**Saddle,** sad'l, *n.* A seat for a rider on a horse's back; something like a saddle in shape or use.—*vt.* (saddling, saddled). To put a saddle on; to burden.
**Saddle-cloth,** sad'l-kloth, *n.* A cloth to be placed under a saddle; a housing.
**Saddler,** sad'lėr, *n.* One whose occupation is to make saddles or harness in general.
**Saddlery,** sad'lėr-i, *n.* The articles sold by a saddler; the trade of a saddler.
**Sadducee,** sad'ū-sē, *n.* One of a sect among the Jews who denied the resurrection and the existence of angels or spirits.
**Sadism,** säd'ism, *n.* A form of sexual perversion, in which pleasure is taken in the cruel treatment of the companion.
**Safe,** sāf, *a.* Secure; free from danger; unharmed; no longer dangerous; trustworthy.—*n.* A strong box or chamber for securing valuables; a cool receptacle for meat.
**Safeguard,** sāf'gärd, *n.* One who or that which guards; a defense; protection; a passport.—*vt.* To guard.
**Safely,** sāf'li, *adv.* In a safe manner; without injury; securely.
**Safety,** sāf'ti, *n.* State of being safe; freedom from danger, hurt, or loss.
**Safety-match,** sāf'ti-mach, *n.* A match which lights only on a special substance.
**Safety-valve,** sāf'ti-valv, *n.* A valve on a boiler, which lets the steam escape when the pressure becomes too great.
**Saffron,** saf'ron, *n.* A bulbous plant allied to the crocus, with flowers of a rich orange color.—*a.* Of a deep yellow.
**Sag,** sag, *vi.* (sagging, sagged). To sink in the middle; to yield under care, difficulties, etc.
**Saga,** sä'ga, *n.* An ancient Scandinavian legend of some length.
**Sagacious,** sa-gā'shus, *a.* Quick of perception; shrewd; sage.
**Sagaciously,** sa-gā'shus-li, *adv.* With discernment or penetration.
**Sagacity,** sa-gas'i-ti, *n.* Quickness of discernment; shrewdness; high intelligence.
**Sage,** sāj, *a.* Wise; sagacious; well-judged; grave.—*n.* A wise man; a man venerable for years, and of sound judgment; a labiate plant.
**Sagely,** sāj'li, *adv.* Wisely; sapiently.
**Sagittarius,** sa-ji-tā'ri-us, *n.* The archer, a sign of the zodiac.
**Sagittate,** sa'ji-tāt, *a.* Shaped like the head of an arrow.
**Sago,** sā'gō, *n.* A starchy substance much used as food, prepared from the pith of several species of palms.
**Sahib,** sä'ib, *n.* An Eastern term of respect, much the same as "Sir" or "Mr."
**Sail,** sāl, *n.* A piece of cloth to catch the wind and so move a ship; a ship; a passage in a ship.—*vi.* To be carried over the water by sails or steam, etc.; to begin a voyage; to glide.—*vt.* To pass over by means of sails; to navigate.
**Sail-cloth,** sāl'kloth, *n.* Canvas used in making sails for ships.
**Sailing,** sāl'ing, *p.a.* Moved by sails and not by steam.—*n.* Act of setting sail; art or rules of navigation.
**Sailor,** sāl'or, *n.* A seaman; a mariner.
**Saint,** sānt, *n.* One eminent for piety and virtue; one of the blessed; a person canonized—*vt.* To canonize.
**Sainted,** sānt'ed, *a.* Holy; sacred; canonized; gone to heaven; dead.
**Saintly,** sānt'li, *a.* Like a saint.
**Sake,** sāk, *n.* Cause; purpose; regard.
**Saker,** sā'kėr, *n.* A species of hawk or falcon; an ancient small piece of artillery.
**Sal,** sal, *n.* Salt.
**Sal,** säl, *n.* A valuable timber tree of India.
**Salaam,** sa-läm', *n.* A ceremonious salutation or obeisance among orientals.—*vt.* and *i.* To salute with a salaam.
**Salacious,** sa-lā'shus, *a.* Lustful.
**Salacity,** sa-las'i-ti, *n.* Lust; lecherousness.
**Salad,** sa'lad, *n.* A dish of certain vegetables, as lettuce, cress, etc., dressed and eaten raw.
**Salamander,** sa-la-man'dėr, *n.* A small harmless amphibian; a kind of lizard formerly believed able to live in fire.
**Salaried,** sa'la-rid, *p.a.* Having a salary.
**Salary,** sa'la-ri, *n.* A stipulated recompense for services; stipend; wages.
**Sale,** sāl, *n.* Act of selling; power or opportunity of selling; market; auction; state of being to be sold.
**Saleable,** sāl'a-bl, *a.* That may be sold; being in demand.
**Salesman,** sālz'man, *n.* One employed to sell goods.
**Salic,** sal'ik, *a.* Belonging to the Salian Franks; usually applied to a clause in their code of laws which excluded females from the throne.
**Salicin, Salcine,** sal'i-sin, sal'i-sēn, *n.* A bitter crystallizable substance extracted from willow and poplar bark, a valuable tonic.

**Salicylic,** sal-i-sil'ik, *n.* An acid used as an antiseptic, etc.
**Salience,** sā'li-ens, *n.* Projection; protrusion.
**Salient,** sā'li-ent, *a.* Springing; darting; projecting, conspicious.
**Salina,** sa-lī'na, *n.* A salt marsh; a salt-work.
**Saline,** sa-līn', *a.* Consisting of salt; salt.—*n.* A salt spring.
**Saliva,** sa-lī'va, *n.* The fluid secreted by certain glands, which moistens the mouth and assists digestion.
**Salivant,** sa'li-vant, *a.* Exciting salivation.—*n.* That which produces salivation.
**Salivary,** sa'li-va-ri, *a.* Pertaining to the saliva; secreting or conveying saliva.
**Salivate,** sa'li-vāt, *vt.* To produce an unusual secretion and discharge of saliva.
**Salivation,** sa-li-vā'shon, *n.* Act of salivating; excessive secretion of saliva.
**Sallow,** sal'ō, *a.* Having a pale, sickly, yellowish color.—*n.* A kind of willow.
**Sally,** sal'i, *n.* A leaping forth; a rush of troops from a besieged place; a dart of intellect, fancy, etc.; frolic.—*vi.* (sallying, sallied). To leap forth; to issue suddenly.
**Salmagundi, Salmagundy,** sal-ma-gun'di, *n.* A dish of chopped meat, eggs, anchovies, cabbage, etc.; a miscellany.
**Salmi, Salmis,** säl'mē, *n.* A ragout of woodcocks, larks, thrushes, etc.
**Salmon,** sa'mun, *n.* A large fish highly valued as food.
**Salmon-trout,** sa'mun-trout, *n.* The seatrout, like the salmon in form and color.
**Salon,** sä-long, *n.* An apartment for the reception of company; a saloon.
**Saloon,** sa-lön', *n.* A sapcious apartment; a large public room; main cabin of a steamer.
**Salse,** säls, *n.* A mud volcano.
**Salsify,** sal'si-fi, *n.* A plant cultivated for its edible root.
**Salt,** salt, *n.* A sbustance for seasoning and preserving food; a compound produced by the combination of a base with an acid; taste; savor; piquancy; an old sailor.—*a.* Impregnated with salt; pungent.—*vt.* To sprinkle or season with salt.
**Saltant,** sal'tant, *a.* Leaping; dancing.
**Saltation,** sal-tā'shon, *n.* A leaping; beating or palpitation.
**Saltatory,** sal'ta-to-ri, *a.* Leaping; used in leaping.
**Salt-cellar,** salt'sel-lėr, *n.* A small vessel used at table for holding salt.
**Saltern,** salt'ėrn, *n.* A salt-work.
**Saltire, Saltier,** sal'tėr, *n.* A heraldic figure formed by the crossing of two diagonal bands.
**Saltish,** salt'ish, *a.* Somewhat salt.
**Salt-mine,** salt'mīn, *n.* A mine where rocksalt is obtained.
**Salt-pan, Salt-pit,** salt'pan, salt'pit, *n.* A place where salt is obtained by evaporation.
**Saltpeter,** salt'pē-tėr, *n.* Niter.
**Salts,** salts, *n.pl.* Salt used as a medicine.
**Salt-water,** salt'wa-tėr, *n.* Water impregnated with salt; sea-water.
**Salubrious,** sa-lū'bri-us, *a.* Healthful.
**Salutary,** sa'lū-ta-ri, *a.* Healthful; wholesome; beneficial; profitable.
**Salutation,** sa-lū-tā'shon, *n.* Act of saluting; a greeting; a salute.
**Salute,** sa-lūt', *vt.* (saluting, saluted). To greet; to greet by a bow, etc.; to kiss; to honor.—*vi.* To perform a salutation; to greet each other.—*n.* Act of saluting; greeting; a kiss; a bow; discharge of artillery, etc.
**Salvable,** sal'va-bl, *a.* That may be saved; admitting of salvation.
**Salvage,** sal'vāj, *n.* Act of saving a ship or goods from shipwreck, fire, etc.; an allowance for the saving of property; goods thus saved.
**Salvation,** sal-vā'shon, *n.* Act of saving; redemption of man from sin; that which saves.
**Salve,** salv, *vt.* (salving, salved). To save a ship or goods from wreck, fire, etc.
**Salve,** salv or säv, *n.* A healing ointment; remedy.—*vt.* (salving, salved). To apply salve to; to remedy.
**Salver,** sal'vėr, *n.* A tray on which articles are presented.
**Salvo,** sal'vō, A reservation; excuse; salute of guns; a shouting or cheering.
**Salvor,** sal'vor, *n.* One who saves a ship or goods from wreck or destruction.
**Sambo,** sam'bō, *n.* The offspring of a black person and a mulato.
**Same,** sām, *a.* Identical; not different or other; of like kind; just mentioned.—**All the same,** nevertheless.
**Sameness,** sām'nes, *n.* Similarity; identity; monotony.
**Samite,** sā'mīt, *n.* An old rich silk stuff interwoven with gold or embroidered.
**Samlet,** sam'let, *n.* A little salmon.
**Samphire,** sam'fīr, *n.* Saint Peter's wort; sea-fennel.
**Sample,** sam'pl, *n.* A specimen; a part presented as typical of the whole.—*vt.* (sampling, sampled). To take a sample of.
**Sampler,** sam'plėr, *n.* One who samples; one who exhibits samples of goods; a piece of fancy sewed or embroidered work.
**Sanable,** san'a-bl, *a.* Curable.
**Sanative,** san'a-tiv, *a.* Healing.
**Sanatorium,** san-a-tō'ri-um, *n.* A place to which people go for the sake of health.
**Sanatory,** san'a-to-ri, *a.* Conducive to health; healing.
**Sanctification,** sangk'ti-fi-kā''shon, *n.* Act of sanctifying; consecration.
**Sanctified,** sangk'ti-fīd, *p.a.* Made holy; consecrated; sanctimonious.
**Sanctify,** sangk'ti-fī, *vt.* (sanctifying, sanctified). To make holy; to hallow; to make pure from sin.
**Sanctimonious,** sangk-ti-mō'ni-us, *a.* Making a show of sanctity; hypocrtical.
**Sanction,** sangk'shon, *n.* Confirmation; ratification; authority.—*vt.* To ratify; to authorize; to countenance.
**Sanctity,** sangk'ti-ti, *n.* State of being sacred; holiness; inviolability.
**Sanctuary,** sangk'tū-a-ri, *n.* A sacred place; a place of worship; part of a church where the altar is placed; a place of protection to criminals, debtors, etc.; shelter.
**Sanctum,** sangk'tum, *n.* A sacred place; a private room.
**Sand,** sand, *n.* Fine particles of stone; *pl.* tracts of sand on the sea-shore, etc.—*vt.* To sprinkle or cover with sand.
**Sandal,** san'dal, *n.* A kind of shoe consisting of a sole fastened to the foot.
**Sandal-wood,** san'dal-wud, *n.* The fragrant wood of certain E. Indian trees.
**Sand-blast,** sand'blast, *n.* Sand driven by a blast of steam or air, and used in engraving and cutting glass, etc.
**Sandiver,** san'di-vėr, *n.* The scum of glass in fusion, used, when pulverized, as a polishing substance.
**Sandix, Sandyx,** san'diks, *n.* A kind of red-lead used as a pigment.
**Sand-martin,** sand'mär-tin, *n.* A British swallow which nests in sandy banks.
**Sand-paper,** sand'pā-pėr, *n.* Paper coated with fine sand, used to smooth and polish.
**Sandpiper,** sand'pī-pėr, *n.* A grallatorial bird allied to the snipe, plover, etc.
**Sandstone,** sand'stōn, *n.* A stone composed of agglutinated grains of sand.
**Sandwich,** sand'wich, *n.* Slices of bread, with meat or something savory between.—*vt.* To insert like the meat in a sandwich; to fit between two other pieces.
**Sandy,** sand'i, *a.* Abounding with sand; like sand; yellowish red; arid or dry.

**Sane,** sān, *a.* Sound in mind; discreet.
**Sangaree,** sang'ga-rē, *n.* Wine and water sweetened and spiced.
**Sang-froid,** sang'frwä, *n.* Coolness; imperturbable calmness.
**Sanguinary,** sang'gwin-a-ri, *a.* Bloody; murderous; savage; cruel.
**Sanguine,** sang'gwin, *a.* Consisting of blood; full of blood; of the color of blood; cheerful; confident.
**Sanguineous,** sang-gwin'ē-us, *a.* Bloody; abounding with blood; sanguine.
**Sancile,** san'i-kl, *n.* An umbelliferous plant of several species.
**Sanies,** sā'ni-ēz, *n.* A thin reddish discharge from wounds or sores.
**Sanitary,** san'i-ta-ri, *a.* Pertaining to or designed to secure health; hygienic.
**Sanitation,** san-i-tā'shon, *n.* The adoption of sanitary measures for the health of a community.
**Sanity,** san'i-ti, *n.* State of being sane; soundness of mind.
**Sans,** sanz, *prep.* Without; deprived of.
**Sans-culotte, Sans-culottist,** sanz-kū-lot', sanz-kū-lot'ist, *n.* A rabid republican.
**Sanskrit, Sanscrit,** san'skrit, *n.* and *a.* The ancient language of the Hindus.
**Sap,** sap, *vt.* (sapping, sapped). To undermine; to destroy by some invisible process.—*vi.* To proceed by undermining.—*n.* A trench; vital juice of plants.
**Sapajou, Sajou,** sap'a-jö, sä'jö, *n.* A South American prehensile-tailed monkey.
**Sapient,** sā'pi-ent, *a.* Wise; sage; discerning; now generally ironic.
**Sapless,** sap'les, *a.* Withered; dry.
**Sapling,** sap'ling, *n.* A young tree.
**Saponaceous,** sa-pon-ā'shus, *a.* Soapy.
**Saponify,** sa-pon'i-fī, *vt.* To convert into soap by combination with an alkali.
**Sapor,** sā'por, *n.* Taste; savor; relish.
**Sapper,** sap'ėr, *n.* One who saps; a soldier employed to dig saps or trenches; a member of the Royal Engineers (applied to all ranks).
**Sapphic,** saf'fik, *a.* Pertaining to *Sappho,* a Grecian poetess, or to a kind of verse invented by her.—*n.* A Sapphic verse.
**Sapphire,** saf'fīr, *n.* A precious stone of very great hardness, and of various shades of blue; a rich blue color; blue.
**Sappy,** sap'i, *a.* Abounding with sap; juicy; succulent; young and soft.
**Saraband,** sa'ra-band, *n.* A slow Spanish dance; a piece of music for the dance.
**Saracen,** sa'ra-sen, *n.* A Mussulman of the early and proselytizing period.
**Sarcasm,** sär'kazm, *n.* A bitter cutting jest; a severe gibe; keen irony.
**Sarcastic,** sär-kas'tik, *a.* Containing sarcasm; scornfully severe; taunting.
**Sarcastically,** sär-kas'tik-al-li, *adv.* In a sarcastic manner; with sarcasm.
**Sarcenet, Sarsenet,** särs'net, *n.* A fine thin silk used for linings, etc.
**Sarcode,** sär'kōd, *n.* Structureless gelatinous matter forming the bodies of animals belonging to the protozoa.
**Sarcoid,** sär'koid, *a.* Resembling flesh.
**Sarcophagus,** sär-kof'a-gus, *n.*; pl. **-gi** and **-guses.** A coffin of stone.
**Sard, Sardine,** särd, sär'dīn, *n.* A variety of carnelian of a deep blood-red color.
**Sardine,** sär'dēn, *n.* Pilchars and other small fish preserved in olive oil and tinned.
**Sardonic,** sär-don'ik, *a.* Forced, as a laugh; bitterly ironical; sarcastic.
**Sardonyx,** sär'dō-niks, *n.* A precious stone, a variety of onyx, with layers of sard.
**Sark,** särk, *n.* A shirt.
**Sarmentum,** sär-men'tum, *n.*; pl. **-ta.** A running stem giving off leaves or roots at intervals.
**Sarsaparilla,** sär'sa-pa-ril''la, *n.* The rhizome of several tropical plants yielding a demulcent medicine.
**Sartorial,** sär-tō'ri-al, *a.* Pertaining to a tailor.
**Sash,** sash, *n.* A long band or scarf worn for ornament; the frame of a window; a frame for a saw.—*vt.* To furnish with sashes or sash windows.
**Sasin,** sä'sin, *n.* An Indian antelope, remarkable for swiftness and beauty.
**Sasine,** sā'sin, *n.* In *Scots law,* the act of giving possession of feudal property, or the instrument by which the fact is proved.
**Sassafras,** sas'a-fras, *n.* A kind of laurel, the root of which has medicinal virtues.
**Sassenach,** sas'en-ach, *n.* A name applied by British Celts to Saxons.
**Satan,** sā'tan, *n.* The devil or prince of darkness; the chief of the fallen angels.
**Satanic,** sā-tan'ik, *a.* Having the qualities of Satan; devilish; infernal.
**Satchel,** sa'chel, *n.* A little sack or bag; a bag for a school-boy's books.
**Sate,** sāt, *vt.* (sating, sated). To satiate; to satisfy the appetite of; to glut.
**Sateen,** sa-ten', *n.* A glossy fabric like satin, but with a woollen or cotton face.
**Satellite,** sa'tel-līt, *n.* An attendant; an obsequious dependant; a small planet revolving round another.
**Satiable,** sā'shi-a-bl, *a.* That may be satiated.
**Satiate,** sā'shi-āt, *vt.* (satiating, satiated). To fully satisfy the desire of; to surfeit; to glut.—*a.* Filled to satiety.
**Satiety,** sa-tī'e-ti, *n.* State of being satiated; repletion; surfeit.
**Satin,** sa'tin, *n.* A glossy close-woven silk cloth.—*a.* Belonging to or made of satin.
**Satinet,** sa'ti-net, *n.* A thin species of satin; a cloth made in imitation of satin, having a cotton warp and woollen filling.
**Satin-wood,** sa'tin-wud, *n.* The wood of an Indian tree, heavy and durable.
**Satiny,** sa'tin-i, *a.* Resembling satin.
**Satire,** sa'tīr, *n.* A writing ridiculing vice or folly; an invective poem; sarcastic or contemptuous ridicule.
**Satiric, Satirical,** sa-ti'rik, sa-ti'rik-al, *a.* Belonging to satire; given to satire; sarcastic.
**Satirist,** sa'ti-rist, *n.* One who satirizes.
**Satirize,** sa'ti-rīz, *vt.* To expose by satire; to censure in a satiric manner.
**Satisfaction,** sa-tis-fak'shon, *n.* Act of satisfying; gratification of desire; contentment; payment; compensation.
**Satisfactorily,** sa-tis-fak'to-ri-li, *adv.* So as to give satisfaction.
**Satisfactory,** sa-tis-fak'to-ri, *a.* Giving satisfaction; making amends.
**Satisfy,** sa'tis-fī, *vt.* and *i.* (satisfying, satisfied). To gratify fully; to content; to fulfil the claims of; to answer; to free from doubt.
**Satrap,** sā'trap or sat'rap, *n.* A governor of a province of ancient Persia; a viceroy.
**Saturable,** sa'tūr-a-bl, *a.* That may be saturated.
**Saturate,** sa'tūr-āt, *vt.* To imbue till no more can be received; to soak thoroughly.
**Saturation,** sa-tūr-ā'shon, *n.* Act of saturating; complete impregnation.
**Saturday,** sa'tėr-dā, *n.* The seventh day of the week.
**Saturn,** sa'tėrn, *n.* An ancient Roman diety; a planet.
**Saturnalia,** sa-tėr-na'li-a, *n.pl.* The Roman festival of Saturn; noisy revelry.
**Saturnalian,** sa-tėr-na'li-an, *a.* Loose; dissolute.
**Saturnine,** sa'tėrn-īn, *a.* Morose; gloomy; phlegmatic.
**Satyr,** sa'tėr, *n.* A sylvan deity of the ancient Greeks and Romans, part man and part goat, and extremely wanton.
**Sauce,** sas, *n.* A liquid to be eaten with food to give it relish; pertness.—*vt.* To make savory with sauce; to be pert to.
**Sauce-pan,** sas'pan, *n.* A small metallic vessel

for boiling or stewing.

**Saucer,** sa'sėr, *n.* A piece of china, etc., in which a cup is set.

**Saucily,** sas'i-li, *adv.* Pertly; petulantly.

**Saucy,** sas'i, *a.* Showing impertinent boldness; pert; impudent; rude.

**Saunter,** san'tėr, *vi.* To stroll about idly; to loiter.—*n.* A stroll; a leisurely pace.

**Saurian,** sa'ri-an, *a.* Pertaining to the lizards.—*n.* A scaly reptile, as the lizard.

**Sausage,** sa'sāj, *n.* The prepared intestine of an ox, etc., stuffed with minced meat.

**Savage,** sa'vāj, *a.* wild; uncultivated; barbarous; brutal.—*n.* One who is uncivilized; a barbarian.

**Savagely,** sa'vāj-li, *adv.* Barbarously.

**Savagery,** sa'vāj-ri, *n.* State of being savage; cruelty; barbarity.

**Savant,** sä-väng', A man of learning; a man eminent for his scientific acquirements.

**Save,** sāv, *vt.* (saving, saved). To preserve; to protect; to rescue; to spare; to keep from doing or suffering; to reserve; to obviate.—*vi.* To be economical.—*prep.* Except.

**Savin, Savine,** sav'in, *n.* A tree or shrub of the juniper kind.

**Saving,** sāv'ing, *a.* Thrifty; that secures from evil; containing some reservation.—*n.* What is saved; sums accumulated by economy: generally *pl.*—*prep.* Excepting.

**Savior,** sāv'yėr, *n.* One who saves from evil, destruction, or danger; Christ.

**Savor,** sā'vor, *n.* Taste; flavor; odor; distinctive quality.—*vi.* To have a particular taste; to partake of some characteristic of something else.—*vt.* To taste or smell with pleasure; to like.

**Savory,** sā'vo-ri, *a.* Having a good savor; palatable; agreeable.

**Savory,** sā'vėr-i, *n.* A labiate plant used to flavor dishes, etc.

**Savoy,** sav'oi, *n.* A variety of cabbage with crisp leaves for winter use.

**Saw,** sa, *n.* A instrument consisting of a thin blade of steel with a toothed edge; a saying or maxim.—*vt.* and *i.* To cut with a saw.

**Sawdust,** sa'dust, *n.* Small fragments of wood produced by the action of a saw.

**Saw-fish,** sa'fish, *n.* A fish allied to the sharks, with a long serrated bony snout.

**Saw-mill,** sa'mil, *n.* A mill for sawing timber, driven by water, steam, etc.

**Sawyer,** sa'yėr, *n.* One who saws timber.

**Saxon,** saks'on, *n.* An Anglo-Saxon; one of English race; a native of modern Saxony.—*a.* Pertaining to the Saxons or to modern Saxony; Anglo-Saxon.

**Saxophone,** saks'ō-fōn, *n.* A wind-instrument similar to the sax-horn, with a clarinet mouthpiece.

**Say,** sā, *vt.* (saying, said). To utter in words; to speak; to declare; to assume.—*vi.* To speak; to relate.—*n.* A speech; statement.

**Saying,** sā'ing, *n.* Something said; speech; an adage; a maxim; a proverb.

**Scab,** skab, *n.* An incrusted substance over a sore in healing; a disease of sheep; the mange in horses.

**Scabbard,** skab'ard, *n.* The sheath of a sword.

**Scabbed,** skabd, or skab'ed, *a.* Abounding with scabs; scabby.

**Scabby,** skab'i, *a.* Affected with scab or scabs; mangy; mean; worthless.

**Scabious,** skā'bi-us, *a.* Consisting of scabs; rough; itchy; leprous.

**Scaffold,** skaf'old, *n.* A temporary platform for workmen; an elevated platform for the execution of a criminal.—*vt.* To furnish with a scaffold.

**Scaffolding,** skaf'old-ing, *n.* A structure for support of workmen in building.

**Scagliola,** skal-yō-'la, *n.* A composition gypsum, splinters of marble, etc., imitative of marble, and used in decoration.

**Scald,** skald, *vt.* To burn or injure with hot liquor; to expose to a boiling or violent heat.—*n.* An injury caused by a hot liquid.—*a.* Covered with scurf; scabby; paltry.

**Sçald,** skald or skäld, *n.* An ancient Scandinavian bard.

**Sçaldic,** skald'ik or skäld'ik, *a.* Pertaining to the scalds.

**Sçale,** skāl, *n.* A thin flake on the skin of an animal; dish of a balance; balance itself (generally *pl.*); anything graduated used as a measure; series of steps or ranks; relative dimensions; succession of notes; gamut.—*vt.* (scaling, scaled). To weigh, as in scales; to strip of scales; to clean; to climb, as by a ladder.—*vi.* To come off in thin layers.

**Scalene,** skā'lēn, *a.* A term applied to a triangle of which the three sides are unequal.

**Scall,** skal, *n.* Scab, scabbiness.

**Scalled,** skald, *a.* Scurvy; scabby.

**Scallion,** skal'yun, *n.* A shallot.

**Scallop,** skal'op or skol'op, *n.* An edible bivalve of the oyster family; a curving on the edge of anything.—*vt.* To cut the edge of into scallops or segmets of circles.

**Scalloped,** skal'opt, *p.a.* Cut at the edge into segments of circles.

**Scalp,** skalp, *n.* The skin of the top of the head, with the hair on it.—*vt.* To deprive of the scalp.

**Scapel,** skal'pel, *n.* A knife used in anatomical dissections.

**Scaly,** skāl'i, *a.* Covered with scales; resembling scales, laminae, or layers.

**Scammony,** skam'o-ni, *n.* A gum-resin obtained from a species of convolvulus, used as a drastic purge; the plant itself.

**Scamp,** skamp, *n.* A knave; swindler; rogue.—*vt.* To do in a perfunctory manner.

**Scamper,** skam'pėr, *vi.* To run with speed; to scurry.—*n.* A hurried run.

**Scan,** skan, *vt.* (scanning, scanned). To measure by the metrical feet, as a verse; to scrutinize; to eye.

**Scandal,** skan'dal, *n.* Public reproach; shame; defamatory talk; slander.

**Scandalize,** skan'dal-īz, *vt.* To offend by some action deemed disgraceful; to shock.

**Scandalous,** skan'dal-us, *a.* Causing scandal; shameful; defamatory; slanderous.

**Scandalously,** skan'dal-us-li, *adv.* In a scandalous manner; disgracefully.

**Scandent,** skan'dent, *a.* Climbing.

**Scansorial,** skan-sō'ri-al, *a.* Adapted to climbing; belonging to the climbing birds (Scansores).

**Scant,** skant, *a.* Not full; scarcely sufficient; scarce.—*vt.* To limit; to stint; to grudge.—*adv.* Scarcely; hardly.

**Scantily, Scantly,** skant'i-li, skant'li, *adv.* In a scant or scanty manner.

**Scanty,** skant'i, *a.* Scant; insufficient.

**Scape,** skāp, *n.* A stem rising directly from a root and bearing the fructification without leaves; the shaft of a feather or column.—*vt.* and *i.* To escape.

**Scape-goat,** skāp'gōt, *n.* One made to bear the blame of others.

**Scapula,** skap'ū-la, *n.* The shoulder-blade.

**Scapular,** skap'ū-lėr, *a.* Pertaining to the shoulder, or to the shoulder-blade.

**Scapular, Scapulary,** skap'ū-lėr, skap'ū-la-ri, *n.* A monastic garment resting on the shoulders, with a flap hanging down in front and another behind.

**Scapus,** skā'pus, *n.*; pl. **-pi.** The shaft of a column.

**Scar,** skär, *n.* The mark of a wound or ulcer; a cicatrix; a cliff; a bare place on the side of a hill.—*vt.* (scarring, scarred). To mark with a scar; to wound.

**Scarab, Scarabee,** skaāab, ska'ra-bē, *n.* The sacred beetle of the Egyptians.

**Scaramouch,** ska'ra-mouch, *n.* A buffoon; a poltroon or braggadocio.

**Scarce,** skārs, *n.* Not plentiful; deficient; uncommon.
**Scarce, Scarcely,** skārs, skārs'li, *adv.* Hardly; scantly; barely; with difficulty.
**Scarcity,** skārs'i-ti, *n.* State or condition of being scarce; deficiency; dearth.
**Scare,** skār, *vt.* (scaring, scared). To strike with sudden terror; to frighten.—*n.* A sudden fright, a causeless alarm.
**Scarecrow,** skār'krō, *n.* Anything set up to scare birds from crops; anything terrifying without danger; a ragged or very odd-looking person.
**Scarf,** skärf, *n.*; pl. **Scarfs,** skärfs, and **Scarves,** skärvz. A light article of dress worn round the neck, etc.; a joint in timber.—*vt.* To unite (timber) by means of a scarf.
**Scarify,** ska'ri-fī, *vt.* (scarifying, scarified). To make small superficial incisions in the skin; to remove the flesh about a tooth.
**Scarlatina,** skar-la-tē'na, *n.* A malady characterized by fever and a red rash.
**Scarlet,** skär'let, *n.* A bright-red color.—*a.* Of a bright-red color.
**Scarlet-fever,** skär'let-fē-vėr, *n.* Same as *Scarlatina.*
**Scarp,** skärp, *n.* The interior slope of a ditch.—*vt.* To cut down like a scarp.
**Scathe,** skāth, *n.* Damage; injury.—*vt.* (scathing, scathed). To injure; to harm.
**Scathing,** skāth'ing, *p.a.* Injuring; harming; blasting.
**Scatter,** skat'ėr, *vt.* To disperse; to spread; to strew; to disunite.—*vi.* To be dispersed; to straggle apart.
**Scatter-brain,** skat'ėr-brān, *n.* A thoughtless person.
**Scattered,** skat'ėrd, *p.a.* Thinly spread; loose and irregular in arrangement.
**Scaup,** skap, *n.* A bed of shell-fish; a species of duck which feeds on mollusks, etc.
**Scaur,** skar, *n.* A scar or cliff.
**Scavenger,** ska'ven-jėr, *n.* One employed to clean the streets.
**Scene,** sēn, *n.* A stage; a distinct part of a play; a painted device on the stage; place of action or exhibition; general appearance of any action; a view; display of emotion.
**Scenery,** sēn'ė-ri, *n.* The painted representations on the stage; pictorial features; landscape characteristics.
**Scenic, Scenical,** sēn'ik, sēn'ik-al;, *a.* Pertaining to the stage; dramatic; theatrical.
**Scent,** sent, *n.* That which causes the sensation of smell; odor; fragrance; power of smelling; chase followed by the scent; track.—*vt.* To perceive by the sense of smell; to imbue with odor.
**Scentless,** sent'les, *a.* Having no scent; inodorous; destitute of smell.
**Sceptic,** skep'tik, *n.* One who doubts or disbelieves.—*a.* Sceptical.
**Sceptical,** skep'tik-al, *a.* Doubting; doubting the truth of revelation.
**Scepticism,** skep'ti-sizm, *n.* Doubt; incredulity.
**Scepter,** sep'tėr, *n.* A staff or baton carried by a ruler as a symbol of authority.
**Sceptered,** sep'tėrd, *a.* Invested with a scepter; having royal power; regal.
**Schedule,** shed'ūl, sed'ūl, *n.* A paper containing a list, and annexed to a larger writing, as to a will, deed, etc.; an inventory.—*vt.* (scheduling, scheduled). To place in a schedule.
**Scheme,** skēm, *n.* A combination of things adjusted by design; a system; project; diagram.—*vt.* and *i.* (scheming, schemed). To plan, contrive, project.
**Schemer,** skēm'ėr, *n.* A contriver; plotter.
**Scheming,** skēm'ing, *a.* Intriguing.
**Scherzo,** skert'so, *n.* A passage of a sportive character in musical pieces.
**Schiedam,** skē-dam', *n.* Holland gin.
**Schism,** sizm, *n.* A separation; breach among people of the same religious faith.
**Schismatic, Schismatical,** siz-mat'ik, siz-mat'ik-al, *a.* Pertaining to schism; implying schism; tending to schism.
**Schismatic,** siz-mat'ik, *n.* One who practices or promotes schism.
**Schist,** shist, *n.* A rock of a slaty structure.
**Schistose, Shistous,** shis'tōz, shis'tus, *a.* Having the character of schist.
**Scholar,** skol'ėr, *n.* One who attends a school; a pupil; a learned person; a junior member of an English university who is aided by college revenues.
**Scholarly,** skol'ėr-li, *a.* Like a scholar; becoming a scholar or man of learning.
**Scholarship,** skol'ėr-ship, *n.* Erudition; a foundation for the support of a student.
**Scholastic,** skō-las'tik, *a.* Pertaining to a scholar or school; pertaining to the schoolmen; pedantic; needlessly subtle.
**Scholasticism,** skō-las'ti-sizm, *n.* The philosophy of the schoolmen.
**Scholium,** skō'li-um, *n.*; pl. **-ia** or **-iums.** A marginal note; comment.
**School,** sköl, *n.* A place of instruction; a body of pupils; disciples; sect or body; a system or custom; a shoal (of fishes).—*a.* Relating to a school; scholastic.—*vt.* To instruct; to reprove.
**School-house,** sköl'hous, *n.* A house used as a school; a schoolmaster's house.
**Schooling,** sköl'ing, *n.* Instruction in school; tuition; reproof; reprimand.
**Schooner,** skön'ėr, *n.* A vessel with two or more masts, her chief sails fore-and-aft.
**Schottische,** shot-tish', *n.* A dance resembling a polka; the music for such a dance.
**Sciagraphy,** sī-ag'ra-fi, *n.* The art or representing or delineating shadows.
**Sciatic, Sciatical,** sī-at'ik, sī-at'ik-al, *a.* Pertaining to the hip or to sciatica.
**Sciatica,** sī-at'i-ka, *n.* Neuralgia or inflammation of the sciatic never or great nerve of the thigh.
**Science,** sī'ens, *n.* Knowledge reduced to a system; the facts pertaining to any department of mind or matter in their due connections; skill resulting from training.
**Sciential,** sī-en'shal *a.* Pertaining to science.
**Scientific,** sī-en-tif'ik, *a.* Pertaining to science; versed in science; according to the rules or principles of science.
**Scientifically,** sī-en-tif'ik-al-li, *adv.* In a scientific manner.
**Scientist,** sī'ent-ist, *n.* One versed in science; a scientific man.
**Scilicet,** sī'li-set. To wit; namely; abbreviated to *Scil.* or *Sc.*
**Scimitar,** si'mi-tėr, *n.* A short curved sword.
**Scintilla,** sin-til'la, *n.* A spark; glimmer; trace.
**Scintillate,** sin'til-lāt, *vi.* To emit sparks; to sparkle, as the fixed stars.
**Scintillation,** sin-til-lā'shon, *n.* Twinkling; coruscation.
**Sciolism,** sī'ol-izm, *n.* Superficial knowledge.
**Sciolist,** sī'ol-ist, *n.* One who knows things superficially; a smatterer.
**Sciomachy, Sciamachy,** sī-om'ak-i, sī-am'ak-i, *n.* A fighting with a shadow.
**Scion,** sī'on, *n.* A cutting or twig; a young shoot; a descendant; an heir.
**Scirrhosity, Scirrosity,** ski-ros'i-ti, si-ros'i-ti, *n.* Stae of being scirrhous; a scirrhus.
**Scirrhous,** ski'rus or si'rus, *a.* Pertaining to or proceeding from a scirrhus.
**Scirrhus, Scirrhosis,** ski'rus or si'rus, ski-rō'sis or si-rō'sis, *n.* A hard tumor.
**Scissel, Scissil,** sis'sel, sis'sil, *n.* Clippings or shreds of metal, as in coining.
**Scission,** si'zhon, *n.* Act of cutting; state of being cut; division.
**Scissors,** siz'ėrz, *n.pl.* A cutting instrument consisting of two blades.
**Scleroma, Sclerosis,** sklē-rō'ma, sklē-rō'sis, *n.* Induration of the cellular tissue.
**Scoff,** skof, *n.* An expression of derision or scorn; a gibe.—*vi.* To utter contemptuous language; to

jeer; to mock.—*vt.* To mock at.
**Scoffer,** skof'ėr, *n.* One who scoffs.
**Scoffingly,** skof'ing-li, *adv.* In a scoffing manner; by way of derision.
**Scold,** skōld, *vi.* To find fault with rude clamor; to utter harsh, rude rebuke.—*vt.* To reprimand loudly; to chide.—*n.* A clamorous, foul-mouthed woman.
**Scolding,** skōld'ing, *n.* Act of one who scolds; railing language; a rating.
**Scolecida,** skō-lē'si-da, *n.pl.* The tape-worms and allied animals.
**Scollop,** skol'op, *n.* A scallop.
**Sconce,** skons, *n.* A case or socket for a candle; a projecting candlestick; a detached fort; a head-piece; the skull.—*vt.* To ensconce.
**Scoop,** sköp, *n.* An implement for liting things; an instrument for hollowing out; the act of scooping.—*vt.* To take out with a scoop; to lade out; to hollow out.
**Scope,** skōp, *n.* An aim or end; intention; amplitude or range; space; sweep.
**Scorbutic,** skor-būt'ik, *a.* Pertaining to or diseased with scurvy.
**Scorch,** skorch, *vt.* To burn superficially; to singe; to parch.—*vi.* To be as hot as to burn a surface; to be dried up; to ride a cycle at excessive speed.
**Score,** skōr, *n.* A notch; a long scratch or mark; an account or reckoning; the number twenty; a debt; the number of points made in certain games; motive; ground; draft of a musical composition.—*vt.* (scoring, scored). To make scores or scratches on; to record; to get for oneself, as points, etc., in games.
**Scorer,** skōr'ėr, *n.* One who keeps the scores of competitors, or the like; an instrument to mark numbers, etc., on trees.
**Scoria,** skō'ri-a, *n.*; pl. **-ae.** Dross; cinder; the cellular, slaggy lavas of a volcano.
**Scorn,** skorn, *n.* Extreme contempt; subject of contempt.—*vt.* To hold in extreme contempt; to despise.—*vi.* To feel or show scorn.
**Scorner,** skorn'ėr, *n.* One who scorns; a scoffer.
**Scornful,** skorn'ful, *a.* Filled with or expressing scorn; contemptuous.
**Scornfully,** skorn'ful-li, *adv.* In a scornful manner.
**Scorpion,** skor'pi-on, *n.* An animal of the class Arachnida, with a jointed tail terminating with a venomous sting; a sign of the zodiac.
**Scot,** skot, *n.* A native of Scotland; a tax or contribution.
**Scotch,** skoch, *a.* Pertaining to Scotland or its inhabitants; Scottish.—*n.* The dialect of Scotland; the people of Scotland.
**Scotch,** skoch, *vt.* To cut with shallow incisions; to notch.—*n.* A slight cut.
**Scotchman,** skoch'man, *n.* A native of Scotland.
**Scot-free,** skot'frē, *a.* Free from payment of scot; untaxed; unhurt; clear; safe.
**Scotia,** skō'ti-a, *n.* A hollow molding in the base of a column.
**Scots,** skots, *a.* Scottish.—*n.* The Scottish language.
**Scotsman,** skots'man, *n.* A native of Scotland.
**Scottice,** skot'ti-sē, *adv.* In the Scottish manner or language.
**Scotticism,** skot'i-sizm, *n.* An idiom or expression peculiar to Scots.
**Scottish,** skot'ish, *a.* Pertaining to Scotland, its inhabitants, or language.
**Scoundrel,** skoun'drel, *n.* A mean, worthless fellow; a rascal.—*a.* Base; unprincipled.
**Scoundrelism,** skoun'drel-izm, *n.* The practices of a scoundrel; rascality.
**Scoundrelly,** skoun'drel-li, *a.* Base; mean.
**Scour,** skour, *vt.* and *i.* To clean by rubbing; to purge violently; to range for the purpose of finding something; to pass swiftly over.
**Scourer,** skour'ėr, *n.* One who or that which scours.
**Scourge,** skėrj, *n.* A lash; a whip; an affliction sent for punishment; one who harasses.—*vt.* (scourging, scourged). To lash; to chastise; to harass.
**Scout,** skout, *n.* A person sent to obtain intelligence regarding an enemy; a college servant.—*vi.* To act as a scout.—*vt.* To watch closely; to treat with disdain.
**Scout-master,** skout-mäs'tėr, *n.* The leader of a troop of Boy Scouts.
**Scow,** skou, *n.* A flat-bottomed boat.
**Scowl,** skoul, *vi.* To wrinkle the brows, as in displeasure; to frown.—*n.* A deep angry frown; gloom.
**Scrabble,** skrab'l, *vi.* and *t.* To scrawl; to scribble.—*n.* A scribble.
**Scrag,** skrag, *n.* Something dry, or lean with roughness.
**Scragged,** skrag'ed, *a.* Like a scrag; scraggy.
**Scraggy,** skrag'i, *a.* Rough or rugged; scragged; lean and bony.
**Scramble,** skram'bl, *vi.* (scrambling, scrambled). To move or climb on all-fours; to push rudely in eagerness for something.—*n.* Act of scrambling; eager contest.
**Scrambling,** skram'bling, *a.* Irregular; straggling.
**Scranne,** skran'el, *a.* Slight; slender.
**Scrap,** skrap, *n.* A small piece; a fragment; a little picture for ornamenting screens, etc.
**Scrap-book,** skrap'buk, *n.* A book for preserving extracts, drawings, prints, etc.
**Scrape,** skrāp, *vt.* (scraping, scraped). To rub with something hard; to clean by a sharp edge; to act on with a grating noise; to erase; to collect laboriously.—*vi.* To roughen or remove a surface by rubbing; to make a grating noise.—*n.* Act of scraping; an awkward bow; an awkward predicament.
**Scraper,** skrāp'ėr, *n.* One who or that which scrapes; an instrument for scraping or cleaning.
**Scraping,** skrāp'ing, *n.* What is scraped from a substance, or is collected by scraping.
**Scrappy,** skrap'i, *a.* Consisting of scraps; incomplete; disjointed.
**Scratch,** skrach, *vt.* and *i* To mark or wound with something sharp; to tear with the nails; to withdraw from the list of competitors.—*n.* A score in a surface; a slight wound; a line from which runners start, etc.; one most heavily handicapped in a contest.—*a.* Taken at random; hastily collected.
**Scratcher,** skrach'ėr, *n.* One who or that which scratches; a gallinaceous bird.
**Scrawl,** skral, *vt.* and *i* To write or draw carelessly or äwkwardly.—*n.* Inelegant or hasty writing.
**Screak,** skrēk, *vi.* To screech; to creak.
**Scream,** skrēm, *vi.* To shriek; to utter a shrill cry.—*n.* A sharp, shrill cry.
**Screamer,** skrēm'ėr, *n.* One that screams; a name of certain birds.
**Screaming,** skrēm'ing, *a.* Crying out with a scream; causing screams of laughter.
**Screech,** skrēch, *vi.* To scream; to shriek.—*n.* A sharp, shrill cry.
**Screech-owl,** skrēch-oul, *n.* An owl that screeches, in opposition to one that hoots.
**Screed,** skrēd, *n.* A strip of cloth; a lengthy statement; a harangue.
**Screen,** skrēn, *n.* An article to intercept heat, cold, etc.; a shelter; a kind of sieve; an ornamental partition in a church.—*vt.* To shelter; to conceal; to sift.
**Screenings,** skren'ingz, *n.pl.* The refuse matter left after sifting coal, etc.
**Screes,** skrēz, *n.pl.* Debris of rocks; shingle.
**Screw,** skrö, *n.* A cylinder with a sprial ridge which enables it when turned to enter another body; a screw-propeller; a twist or turn; a niggard.—*vt.* To fasten by a screw; to twist; to oppress.
**Screw-driver,** skrö'drīv-ėr, *n.* An instrument for

S

turning screw-nails.
**Screw-key,** skrö'kē, *n.* An instrument for turning large screws or their nuts.
**Screw-nail,** skrö'nāl, *n.* A nail grooved like a screw.
**Screw-propeller,** skrö'prō-pel-ėr, *n.* An apparatus on the principle of the common screw, for propelling boats and ships.
**Scribble,** skrib'l, *vt.* and *i.* (scribbling, scribbled). To write with haste or without care; to tease coarsely, as cotton or wool.—*n.* Careless writing; a scrawl.
**Scribbler,** skrib'lėr, *n.* One who writes carelessly or badly; a machine which teases cotton or wool.
**Scribe,** skrīb, *n.* A writer; notary; copyist; doctor of the law among the Jews.
**Scrimmage,** skrim'āj, *n.* A tussle; a confused, close struggle in football.
**Scrimp,** skrimp, *vt.* To make too small or short; to scant; to limit.—*a.* Scanty.
**Scrip,** skrip, *n.* A small bag; a wallet; a small writing; a certificate of stock.
**Script,** skript, *n.* Handwriting; printing type resembling handwriting.
**Scriptorium,** skrip-tō'ri-um, *n.* A room set apart for writing or copying.
**Scriptural,** skrip'tūr-al, *a.* Contained in or according to the Scriptures; biblical.
**Scripturally,** skrip'tūr-al-li, *adv.* In a scriptural manner.
**Scripture,** skrip'tūr, *n.* The Old and New Testaments; the Bible: often *pl.*—*a.* Scriptural.
**Scrivener,** skri'ven-ėr, *n.* An old name for a notary; a money-broker; a writer; a poor author.
**Scrofula,** skro'fū-la, *n.* A disease, a variety of consumption, often showing itself by glandular tumors in the neck which suppurate.
**Scrofulous,** skro'fū-lus, *a.* Pertaining to scrofula; diseased or affected with scrofula.
**Scroll,** skrōl, *n.* A roll of paper or parchment; a draft or first copy; a spiral ornament; a flourish added to a person's name.
**Scrotum,** skrō'tum, *n.* The bag which contains the testicles.
**Scrub,** skrub, *vt.* (scrubbing, scrubbed). To rub hard with something rough, to make clean or bright.—*vi.* To be diligent and penurious.—*n.* One who labors hard and lives sparingly; a mean fellow; a worn-out brush; low underwood.—*a.* Mean.
**Scrubby,** skrub'i, *a.* Small and mean; stunted in growth; niggardly; shabby.
**Scrunsh,** skrunsh, *vt.* To crunch.
**Scruple,** skrö'pl, *n.* A weight of 20 grains; doubt; hesitation; backwardness.—*vi.* (scrupling, scrupled). To doubt; to hesitate.
**Scrupulosity,** skrö-pū-los'i-ti, *n.* Quality or state of being scrupulous; preciseness.
**Scrupulous,** skrö'pū-lus, *a.* Having scruples; cautious; conscientious; exact.
**Scrupulously,** skrö'pū-lus-li, *adv.* In a scruplous manner; carefully; exactly.
**Scrutineer,** skrö'ti-nēr, *n.* One who scrutinizes, as votes at an election.
**Scrutinize,** skrö'ti-nīz, *vt.* and *i.* To examine closely; to investigate.
**Scrutinous,** skrö'tin-us, *a.* Given to scrutiny; closely inquiring or examining.
**Scrutiny,** skrö'ti-ni, *n.* Close search; careful investigation; an authoritive examination of votes given at an election.
**Scud,** skud, *vi.* (scudding, scudded). To run quickly; to run before a strong wind with little or no sail.—*vt.* To pass over quickly.—*n.* Act of scudding; loose, vapory clouds.
**Scuffle,** skuf'l, *n.* A confused struggle.—*vi.* (scuffling, scuffled). To strive confusedly at close quarters.
**Scull,** skul, *n.* A short oar, used in pairs.—*vt.* To propel by sculls, or by moving an oar at the stern.
**Sculler,** skul'ėr, *n.* One who rows with a scull or sculls; a boat rowed by sculls.
**Scullery,** skul'ė-ri, *n.* A place where culinary utensils are cleaned and kept.
**Scullion,** skul'yon, *n.* A servant of the scullery; a low, worthless fellow.
**Sculptor,** skulp'tor, *n.* One who works in sculpture; an artist who carves or models figures.
**Sculptural,** skulp'tūr-al, *a.* Pertaining to sculpture.
**Sculpture,** skulp'tūr, *n.* The art of carving wood or stone into images; an image in stone, etc.—*vt.* (sculpturing, sculptured). To carve; to form, as images on stone, etc.
**Scum,** skum, *n.* Impurities which rise to the surface of liquors; refuse.—*vt.* (scumming, scummed). To take the scum from.—*vi.* To throw up scum.
**Scumble,** skum'bl, *vt.* To cover thinly with opaque colors to modify the effect.
**Scummings,** skum'ingz, *n.pl.* The matter skimmed from boiling liquors.
**Scummy,** skum'i, *a.* Covered with scum.
**Scupper,** skup'ėr, *n.* A hole for carrying off water from the deck of a ship.
**Scurf,** skėrf, *n.* Dry scales or flakes on the skin; matter adhering to a surface.
**Scurfy,** skėrf'i, *a.* Having scurf; covered with scurf; resembling scurf.
**Scurrility,** sku-ril'i-ti, *n.* Scurrilous language; low abuse; insolence.
**Scurrilous,** sku'ril-us, *a.* Foul-mouthed; abusive; obscenely jocular.
**Scurry,** sku'ri, *vt.* (scurrying, scurried). To run rapidly; to hurry.—*n.* Hurry; haste.
**Scurvily,** skėr'vi-li, *adv.* In a scurvy manner; basely; meanly; shabbily.
**Scurvy,** skėr'vi, *n.* A disease caused by insufficiency of vegetable food.—*a.* Vile; mean; malicious.
**Scutage,** skū'tāj, *n.* A tax on feudal tenants.
**Scutch,** skuch, *vt.* To dress by beating, as flax.
**Scutcheon,** skuch'on, *a.* A shield for armorial bearings; an escutcheon.
**Scute,** skūt, *n.* A scale, as of a reptile.
**Scuttle,** skut'l, *n.* A broad basket; a pail for coals; a hatchway in a ship's deck; a short run; a quick pace.—*vt.* (scuttling, scuttled). To sink by making holes in (a ship).—*vi.* To scurry.
**Scye,** sī, *n.* The curve in a piece of a garment to receive the sleeve.
**Scythe,** sīth, *n.* An implement for mowing grass, etc.—*vt.* To cut with a scythe.
**Sea,** sē, *n.* The mass of salt water covering most of the earth; some portion of this; a name of certain lakes; a large wave; a surge; a flood.
**Sea-anemone,** sē'a-nem'o-nē, *n.* A beautiful seashore, plant-like animal.
**Sea-board,** sē'bōrd, *n.* The sea-coast or seashore.—*a.* Bordering on the sea.
**Sea-breeze,** sē'brēz, *n.* A wind or current of air blowing from the sea upon land.
**Sea-calf,** sē'käf, *n.* The common seal.
**Sea-coast,** sē'kōst, *n.* The land adjacent to the sea or ocean.
**Sea-dog,** sē'dog, *n.* The dog-fish; the common seal; a sailor who has been long afloat.
**Seafarer,** sē'fār-ėr, *n.* One who fares or travels by sea; a mariner; a seaman.
**Seafaring, sē'fār-ing,** *a.* Going to sea; employed in seamanship.
**Sea-going,** sē'gō-ing, *a.* Travelling by sea, as a vessel which trades with foreign ports.
**Sea-horse,** sē'hors, *n.* The walrus; a small fish with head shaped like a horse's.
**Seal,** sēl, *n.* A hard substance bearing some device, used to make impressions; the wax stamped with a seal; assurance; that which makes fast; a carnivorous marine mammal.—*vt.* To set a seal to; to confirm; to fasten; to shut or keep close.
**Sea-legs,** sē'legz, *n.pl.* The ability to walk on a ship's deck when pitching or rolling.
**Sealer,** sēl'ėr, *n.* One who seals; an officer in

Chancery who seals writs, etc.; one engaged in the seal-fishery.

**Sea-level,** sē'le-vel, *n.* The level of the surface of the sea.

**Sealing,** sēl'ing, *n.* The operation of taking seals and curing their skins.

**Sealing-wax,** sēl'ing-waks, *n.* A resinous compound used for sealing letters, etc.

**Sea-lion,** sē'lī-on, *n.* The name of several large seals.

**Seam,** sēm, *n.* The joining of two edges of cloth; a line of juncture; a vein of metal, coal, etc.; a scar.—*vt.* To unite by a seam; to scar.

**Seaman,** sē'man, *n.* A sailor; a mariner.

**Seamanship,** sē'man-ship, *n.* The art or skill of a seaman; art of managing a ship.

**Seamstress,** sēm'stres, *n.* A woman whose occupation is sewing; a sempstress.

**Seamy,** sēm'i, *a.* Having a seam; showing seams; showing the worst side; disagreeable.

**Séance,** sā-angs, *n.* A session, as of some public body; a sitting with the view of evoking spiritual manifestations.

**Seaplane,** sē'plān, *n.* An airplane fitted with floats to enable it to take off from and land on water.

**Sea-port,** sē'pōrt, *n.* A harbor on the seacoast; a town on or near the sea.

**Sear,** sēr, *vt.* To wither; to dry; to cauterize; to deaden.—*a.* Dry; withered.

**Sear,** sēr, *n.* A catch in the mechanism of a rifle which holds back the cocking-piece.

**Search,** sėrch, *vt.* To look through to find something; to examine.—*vi.* To seek diligently; to inquire.—*n.* Act of searching; examination; inquiry.

**Searchable,** sėrch'a-bl, *a.* That may be searched or explored.

**Searcher,** sėrch'ėr, *n.* One who or that which searches; an investigator.

**Searching,** sėrch'ing, *a.* Penetrating; trying; closely scrutinizing.

**Searchless,** sėrch'les, *a.* Inscrutable.

**Sea-scape,** sē'skāp, *n.* A picture representing a scene at sea; a sea-piece.

**Sea-serpent,** sē'sėr-pent, *n.* An enormous marine animal resembling a serpent, the existence of which is doubtful.

**Sea-shore,** sē'shōr, *n.* The shore of the sea; ground between high and low water mark.

**Sea-sick,** sē'sik, *a.* Affected with sickness caused by the motion of a vessel at sea.

**Season,** sē'zn, *n.* A division of the year; a suitable time; a time; time of the year marked by special activity; seasoning.—*vt.* To accustom; to acclimatize; to flavor.—*vi.* To become suitable by time.

**Seasonable,** sē'zn-a-bl, *a.* Natural to the season; opportune; timely.

**Seasoning,** sē'zn-ing, *n.* Something added to food to give it relish; relish; condiment.

**Seat,** sēt, *n.* That on which one sits; a chair; stool, etc.; place of sitting; a right to sit; residence; station.—*vt.* To place on a seat; to settle; to locate; to assign seats to; to fit up with seats.

**Seaward,** sē'wėrd, *a.* and *adv.* Toward the sea.

**Sea-weed,** sē'wēd, *n.* A marine plant.

**Sea-worthy,** sē'wėr-THi, *a.* Fit to go to sea; fit for a voyage.

**Sebaceous,** sē-bā'shus, *a.* Made of, containing, or secreting fatty matter.

**Sebiferous,** sē-bif'ėr-us, *a.* Producing fat.

**Secant,** sē'kant, *a.* Cutting.—*n.* A straight line that cuts a curve or figure.

**Secede,** sē-sēd', *vi.* (seceding, seceded). To withdraw from fellowship or association.

**Seceder,** sē-sēd'ėr, *n.* One who secedes.

**Secern,** sē-sėrn', *vt.* To separate; to distinguish; to secrete.

**Secernent,** sē-sėr'nent, *n.* That which promotes secretion; a secreting vessel.—*a.* Secreting.

**Secession,** sē-se'shon, *n.* Act of seceding.

**Secessionist,** sē-se'shon-ist, *n.* One who advocates or engages in a secession.

**Seclude,** sē-klöd', *vt.* (secluding, secluded). To shut up apart; to separate; *refl.* to withdraw into solitude.

**Secluded,** sē-klöd'ed, *a.* Separated from others; retired; sequestered.

**Seclusion,** sē-klö'zhon, *n.* Act of secluding: retired mode of life; privacy.

**Seclusive,** sē-klö'sive, *a.* Tending to seclude or keep in retirement.

**Second,** se'kund, *a.* Next after the first; repeated again; inferior; other.—*n.* One who or that which comes next a first; one who supports another; attendant in a duel; sixtieth part of a minute; a lower part in music; *pl.* a coarse kind of flour.—*vt.* To follow in the next place; to support; to join with in proposing some measure.

**Secondarily,** se'kun-da-ri-li, *adv.* In a secondary manner; secondly.

**Secondary,** se'kun-da-ri, *a.* Of second place; subordinate; not elementary.

**Second-cousin,** se'kund-ku-zn, *n.* The child of a parent's first-cousin.

**Seconder,** se'kund-ėr, *n.* One who supports what another attempts, affirms, or proposes.

**Second-hand,** se'kund-hand, *a.* Received not from the original possessor; not new.

**Secondly,** se'kund-li, *adv.* In the second place.

**Second-rate,** se'kund-rāt, *n.* The second order in size, dignity, or value.

**Second-sight,** se'kund-sīt, *n.* The power of seeing things future; prophetic vision.

**Secrecy,** sē'kre-si, *n.* State or character of being secret; seclusion; fidelity to a secret.

**Secret,** sē'kret, *a.* Hidden; concealed; private; unseen.—*n.* Something hidden or not to be revealed; a mystery.

**Secretarial,** se-krē-tā'ri-al, *a.* Pertaining to a secretary.

**Secretariate,** se-krē-tā'ri-āt, *n.* The position or business of a secretary.

**Secretary,** se'krē-ta-ri, *n.* A person employed to write orders, letters, etc.; an escritoire; one who manages the affairs of a department of government.

**Secrete,** sē-krēt', *vt.* (secreting, secreted). To hide; to separate from the blood in animals or from the sap in vegetables.

**Secretion,** sē-krē'shon, *n.* Act or process of secreting; matter secreted, as bile, etc.

**Secretive,** sē-krēt'iv, *a.* Causing secretion; secretory; given to secrecy; reticent.

**Secretly,** sē'kret-li, *adv.* In a secret manner; privately; privily; not openly.

**Secretory,** sē-krē'to-ri, *a.* Performing the office of secretion; secreting.

**Sect,** sekt, *n.* A body of persons united in tenets, chiefly in religion or philosphy; a school; a denomination.

**Sectarian,** sek-tā'ri-an, *a.* Pertaining to a sect or sectary.—*n.* One of a sect.

**Sectarianism,** sek-tā'ri-an-izm, *n.* State or quality of being sectarian; rigid devotion to a party, chiefly in religion.

**Sectary,** sek'ta-ri, *n.* One that belongs to a sect; a schismatic; a sectarian.

**Sectile,** sek'tīl, *a.* Capable of being cut in slices with a knife.

**Section,** sek'shon, *n.* Act of cutting; a distinct part; subdivision of a chapter, etc.; representation of an object as if cut asunder by an intersecting plane; a quarter of a platoon of infantry, the normal fire-unit.

**Sectional,** sek'shon-al, *a.* Pertaining to a section; composed of independent sections.

**Sector,** sek'tor, *n.* A part of a circle between two radii; a mathematical instrument useful in making diagrams.

**Secular,** se'kū-lėr, *a.* Pertaining to things not spiritual or sacred; worldly; temporal; coming once in a century.

**Secularism,** sek'ū-lėr-izm, *n.* The elimination of the religious element from life.

**Secularist,** sek'ū-lėr-ist, *n.* An upholder of secularism; one who theoretically rejects every form of religious faith.
**Secularize,** se'kū-lėr-īz, *vt.* To make secular; to convert from sacred to secular use.
**Securable,** sē-kūr'a-bl, *a.* That may be secured.
**Secure,** sē-kūr', *a.* Free from care or danger; heedless; undisturbed; safe; confident.—*vt.* (securing, secured). To make safe or certain; to seize and confine; to guarantee; to fasten.
**Securely,** sē-kūr'li, *adv.* In a secure manner; in security; safely.
**Security,** sē-kū'ri-ti, *n.* Safety; confidence; protection; a guarantee; a surety; an evidence of property, as a bond, a certificate of stock, etc.
**Sedan,** sē-dan', *n.* A kind of covered chair for a single person, borne on poles by two men; an enclosed automobile.
**Sedate,** sē-dāt', *a.* Composed in manner; staid; placid; sober; serious.
**Sedately,** sē-dāt'li, *adv.* In a sedate manner; calmly; tranquilly.
**Sedative,** se'da-tiv, *a.* Tending to soothe; assuaging pain.—*n.* A medicine which assuages pain, etc.
**Sedentary,** se'den-ta-ri, *a.* Accustomed to sit much; requiring much sitting.
**Sederunt,** se-dē'runt, *n.* A sitting of a court or the like; a formal meeting.
**Sedge,** sej, *n.* A coarse grass-like plant growing mostly in marshes and swamps.
**Sedgy,** sej'i, *a.* Abounding in sedge.
**Sediment,** se'di-ment, *n.* That which settles at the bottom of liquor; lees.
**Sedimentary,** se-di-ment'a-ri, *a.* Pertaining to sediment; formed of sediment.
**Sedition,** sē-di'shon, *n.* A commotion in a state; insurrection; civic discord.
**Seditious, sē-di'shus,** *a.* Pertaining to sedition; stirring up sedition; inflammatory.
**Seduce,** sē-dūs', *vt.* (seducing, seduced).To lead astray; to corrupt; to entice to a surrender of chastity.
**Seducer,** sē-dūs'ėr, *n.* One who seduces.
**Seducible,** sē-dūs'i-bl, *a.* Capable of being seduced.
**Seduction,** sē-duk'shon, *n.* Act of seducing; allurement; the persuading of a female to surrender her chastity.
**Seductive,** sē-duk'tiv, *a.* Tending to seduce; enticing; alluring.
**Sedulity,** se-dū'li-ti, *n.* Unremitting industry; diligence; assiduity.
**Sedulous,** se'dū-lus, *a.* Assiduous; diligent; industrious.
**See,** sē, *vt.* (seeing, pret, saw, pp. seen). To perceive by the eye; to notice; to discover; to understand; to receive; to experience; to attend.—*vi.* To have the power of sight; to understand; to consider.—*interj.* Lo! look!—*n.* A seat of episcopal power; a diocese.
**Seed,** sēd, *n.* That product of a plant which may produce a similar plant; seeds collectively; the semen; first principle; offspring.—*vi.* To produce seed; to shed the seed.—*vt.* To sow; to supply with seed.
**Seeded,** sēd'ed, *a.* Sown; sprinkled or covered with seed; bearing seed.
**Seedling,** sēd'ling, *n.* A plant reared from the seed.
**Seedsman,** sēdz'man, *n.* A person who deals in seeds; a sower.
**Seed-time,** sēd'tīm, *n.* The season proper for sowing.
**Seedy,** sēd'i, *a.* Abounding with seeds; run to seed; shabby; feeling or appearing wretched.
**Seeing,** sē'ing, *conj.* Since; inasmuch as.
**Seek,** sēk, *vt.* and *i* (seeking, sought). To search for; to solicit; to have recourse to.
**Seem,** sēm, *vi.* To appear; to look as if; to imagine; to feel as if.
**Seeming,** sēm'ing, *p.a.* Appearing; specious.—*n.* Appearance; semblance.
**Seemingly,** sēm'ing-li, *adv.* Apparently.
**Seemly,** sēm'li, *a.* Becoming; suitable; decorous.—*adv.* In a suitable manner.
**Seer,** sēr, *n.* One who sees into futurity; a prophet.
**See-saw,** sē'sa, *n.* A swinging movement up and down; a game in which children swing up and down on the two ends of a balanced piece of timber.—*vi.* and *t.* To move up and down or to and fro.
**Seethe,** sēᴛʜ, *vt.* (seething, seethed). To boil; to soak.—*vi.* To be in a state of ebullition; to be hot.
**Seggar,** seg'är, *n.* A case of fire-clay in which fine stoneware is inclosed while baked in the kiln.
**Segment,** seg'ment, *n.* A part cut off; a section; a natural division of a body (as an orange).
**Segregate,** se'grē-gāt, *vt.* To set apart or separate.
**Segregation,** se-grē-gā'shon, *n.* Act of segregating; separation.
**Seignoir, Seigneur,** sēn'yėr, *n.* A lord or great man; a feudal superior.
**Seigniorage, Seignorage,** sēn'yėr-āj, *n.* Something claimed by the sovereign or a superior as a prerogative, a royalty.
**Seine, Sein,** sēn or sān, *n.* A large fishing net.—*vt.* (seining, seined). To catch with a seine.
**Seismic, Seismal,** sīs'mik, sīs'mal, *a.* Pertaining to earthquakes.
**Seismograph,** sīs'mō-graf, *n.* An instrument to register shocks of earthquakes.
**Seismology,** sīs-mol'o-ji, *n.* The science of earthquakes.
**Seizable,** sēz'a-bl, *a.* Liable to be taken.
**Seize,** sēz, *vt.* (seizing, seized). To lay hold of suddenly; to take by force or legal authority; to attack, as a disease, fear, etc.; to comprehend; to put in possession.—*vi.* To take hold or possession.
**Seizure,** sēz'ūr, *n.* Act of seizing; thing taken or seized; a sudden attack.
**Sejant, Sejeant,** sē'jant, *a.* Sitting.
**Seldom,** sel'dom, *adv.* Rarely; not often.
**Select,** sē-lekt', *vt.* To choose; to pick out; to cull.—*a.* Chosen; choice; exclusive.
**Selection,** sē-lek'shon, *n.* Act of selecting; a collection of things selected.
**Selective,** sē-lek'tiv, *a.* Pertaining to selection; selecting; tending to select.
**Selenite,** sel'en-īt, *n.* Foliated or crystallized sulphate of lime, somewhat resembling mica.
**Selenium,** se-lē'ni-um, *n.* A non-metallic element akin to sulphur and tellurium.
**Selenology,** sel-ē-nol'o-ji, *n.* That branch of astronomy which treats of the moon.
**Self,** self, *n.*; pl. **Selves,** selvz. One's individual person; personal interest; a blossom of a uniform color (with *pl.* **Selfs**).—*a.* or *pron.* Same. Affixed to pronouns and adjectives to express emphasis or distinction, or reflexive usage.
**Self-acting,** self'akt-ing, *a.* Acting of itself; automatic.
**Self-command,** self-kom-mand' *a.* Command of one's powers or feelings; coolness.
**Self-conceit,** self-kon-sēt', *n.* A high opinion of oneself; vanity; self-suffciency.
**Self-confident,** self-kon'fi-dent, *a.* Confident of one's own strength or abilities.
**Self-conscious,** self-kon'shus, *a.* Conscious of one's personal states or acts; apt to think of how oneself appears.
**Self-contained,** self-kon-tānd', *a.* Wrapped up in oneself; reserved.
**Self-control,** self-kon-trōl', *n.* Control exercised over oneself; self-command.
**Self-denial,** self-dē-nī'al, *n.* The forebearing to gratify one's own desires.
**Self-denying,** self-dē-nī'ing, *a.* Denying oneself; forbearing to indulge one's own desires.
**Self-educated,** self-ed'ū-kāt-ed, *a.* Educated by one's own efforts.
**Self-esteem,** self-es-tēm', *n.* The esteem or good opinion of oneself; vanity.
**Self-evident,** self-ev'i-dent, *a.* Evident in its own

nature; evident without proof.
**Self-government,** self-gu'vėrn-ment, *n.* The government of oneself; government by rulers appointed by the people.
**Self-important,** self-im-pōrt'ant, *a.* Important in one's own esteem; pompous.
**Self-imposed,** self'im-pōzd, *a.* Imposed or voluntarily taken on oneself.
**Selfish,** self'ish, *a.* Devoted unduly to self; influenced by a view to private advantage.
**Self-made,** self'mād, *a.* Made by oneself; risen in the world by one's exertions.
**Self-respect,** self'rē-spekt, *n.* Respect for oneself; proper pride.
**Self-righteous,** self-rīt'yus, *a.* Righteous in one's own esteem; sanctimonious.
**Self-same,** self'sām, *a.* Exactly the same; the very same; identical.
**Self-seeking,** self'sēk-ing, *a.* Selfish.
**Self-styled,** self'stīld, *a.* Called by a title assumed without warrant.
**Self-sufficient,** self-suf-fi'shent, *a.* Having too much confidence in oneself; conceited; assuming; overbearing.
**Self-willed,** self'wild, *a.* Wilful; obstinate.
**Sell,** sel, *vt.* (selling, sold). To give in exchange for money, etc.; to betray.—*vi.* To practice selling; to be sold.
**Seller,** sel'ėr, *n.* The person who sells.
**Selvedge, Selvage,** sel'vej, sel'vāj, *n.* The edge of cloth; border of close work.
**Selvedged, Selvaged,** sel'vejd, sel'vājd, *a.* Having a selvedge.
**Semaphore,** se'ma-fōr, *n.* An apparatus for signalling at a distance, usually a pole supporting a movable arm.
**Semblance,** sem'blans, *n.* Similarity; resemblance; image; appearance.
**Semeiology,** sē-mī-ol'o-ji, *n.* The doctrine of signs; semeiotics.
**Semeiotics,** sē-mī-ot'iks, *n.* The science of signs; the doctrine of symptoms of disease.
**Semen,** sē'men, *n.* The seed or fecundating fluid of male animals; sperm.
**Semibreve,** se'mi-brēv, *n.* A note in music equivalent to two minims.
**Semicircle,** se'mi-sėr-kl, *n.* The half of a circle.
**Semicircular,** se-mi-sėr'kū-lėr, *a.* Forming a semicircle.
**Semicolon,** se'mi-kō-lon, *n.* The point (;), marking a greater break than a comma.
**Semi-detached,** se'mi-dē-tacht'', *a.* Partly separated; joined on to another house, but the two detached from other buildings.
**Seminal,** se'min-al, *a.* Pertaining to seed; germinal; rudimental.
**Seminary,** se'min-a-ri, *n.* A school or academy; a place for educating for the priesthood.
**Semination,** se-min-ā'shon, *n.* Act of sowing; the natural dispersion of seeds.
**Semiquaver,** se'mi-kwā-vėr, *n.* Half a quaver in music.
**Semite,** sem'īt, *n.* A descendant of Shem; one of the Semitic race; a Shemite.
**Semitic,** sem-it'ik, *a.* Pertaining to the Semites; Hebrew.
**Semitone,** se'mi-tō, *n.* Half a tone in music.
**Semi-vowel,** se'mi-vou-el, *n.* A sound partaking of the nature of both a vowel and a consonant, as *l, m, r.*
**Semolina,** se-mō-lī'na, *n.* The large hard grains of flour, separated from the fine flour.
**Sempiternal,** sem-pi-tėrn'al, *a.* Everlasting.
**Sempstress,** semp'stres, *n.* A woman who lives by needlework; a seamstress.
**Senary,** sē'na-ri, *a.* Of six; belonging to six, containing six.
**Senate,** se'nāt, *n.* The legislative body in ancient Rome; the upper branch of a legislature; the governing body of a university, etc.
**Senator,** se'nat-or, *n.* A member of a senate.
**Senatorial,** se-na-tō'ri-al, *a.* Pertaining to a senate.
**Senatus,** se-nā'tus, *n.* A senate; the governing body in certain universities.
**Send,** send, *vt.* (sending, sent). To cause to go or be carried; to transmit; to direct to go and act; to make befall.—*vi.* To dispatch an agent or message.
**Sendal,** sen'dal, *n.* A thin silk stuff.
**Senescence,** sē-nes'ens, *n.* State of growing old.
**Senescent,** sē-nes'ent, Growing old.
**Seneschal,** se'ne-shal, *n.* A kind of steward in the houses of princes, etc.
**Senile,** sē'nīl, *a.* Pertaining to old age; characterized by the failings of old age.
**Senility,** sē-nil'i-ti, *n.* State of being old; dotage.
**Senior,** sē'ni-or, sēn'yor, *a.* Older; older or more advanced in office.—*n.* One older in age or office.
**Seniority,** sē-ni-or'i-ti, *n.* State of being senior; superiority in office.
**Senna,** sen'na, *n.* The dried leaves of certain plants used as a purgative; the plant iself.
**Sennite,** sen'it, *n.* A sort of flat braided cordage used on ships.
**Señor,** sen-yōr, *n.* A Spanish form of address, corresponding to Mr. or Sir; a gentleman.
**Señora,** sen-yō'ra, *n.* Madame or Mrs.; a lady.
**Señorita,** sen-yō-rē'tä, *n.* Miss; a young lady.
**Sensation,** sen-sā'shon, *n.* Impression made through the senses; feeling; power of feeling; what produces excited interest.
**Sensational,** sen-sā'shon-al, *a.* Relating to sensation; producing excited interest.
**Sensationalism,** sen-sā'shon-al-izm, *n.* The doctrine that all ideas are derived through our senses; senational writing.
**Sense,** sens, *n.* The faculty of receiving impressions; a separate faculty of perception; sight; hearing, taste, smell, or touch; consciousness; discernment; understanding; good judgment; meaning.
**Senseless,** sens'les, *a.* Wanting sense; unfeeling; unreasonable; foolish.
**Senselessly,** sens'les-li, *adv.* Stupidly.
**Sensibility,** sens-i-bil'i-ti, *n.* State or quality of being sensible; acuteness of perception; delicacy of feeling.
**Sensible,** sens'i-bl, *a.* That may be perceived by the senses; perceptible; sensitive; easily affected; cognizant; reasonable.
**Sensibly,** sens'i-bli, *adv.* In a sensible manner; appreciably; judiciously.
**Sensitive,** sens'i-tiv, *a.* Having the capacity of receiving impressions; easily affected; having the feelings easily hurt.
**Sensitively,** sens'i-tiv-li, *adv.* In a sensitive manner.
**Sensitize,** sens'i-tīz, *vt.* To render sensitive; to make capable of being acted on by the rays of the sun.
**Sensorial,** sen-sō'ri-al, *a.* Sensory.
**Sensorium,** sen-sō'ri-um, *n.* The common center at which all the impressions of sense are received; the brain.
**Sensory,** sen'so-ri, *a.* Relating to the sensorium; conveying sensation.
**Sensual,** sens'ū-al, *a.* Pertaining to the senses, as distinct from the mind; carnal; voluptuous; indulging in lust.
**Sensualism,** sens'ū-al-izm, *n.* Sensuality; sensationalism.
**Sensualist,** sens'ū-al-ist, *n.* A person given to sensuality; a voluptuary.
**Sensuality,** sens-ū-al'i-ti, *n.* Quality of being sensual; indulgence in lust.
**Sensuous,** sens'ū-us, *a.* Pertaining to the senses; readily affected through the senses.
**Sentence,** sen'tens, *n.* Opinion; a maxim; a judgment; a number of words containing complete sense.—*vt.* (sentencing, sentenced). To pass sentence upon; to condemn.
**Sentential,** sen-ten'shal, *a.* Comprising sentences; pertaining to a sentence.
**Sententious,** sen-ten'shus, *a.* Abounding in max-

ims; terse; gravely judicial.
**Sentient,** sen'shi-ent, *a.* Having the capacity of sensation; perceptive; sensible.
**Sentiment,** sen'ti-ment, *n.* Thought prompted by emotion; tenderness of feeling; sensibility; a thought or opinion.
**Sentimental,** sen-ti-men'tal, *a.* Having sentiment; apt to be swayed by emotional feelings; mawkishly tender.
**Sentimentalist,** sen-ti-men'tal-ist, *n.* One who affects sentiment.
**Sentimentality,** sen'ti-men-tal''i-ti, *n.* State or quality of being sentimental.
**Sentinel,** sen'ti-nel, *n.* One who is set to keep watch; a sentry (now archaic or poetical).
**Sentry,** sen'tri, *n.* A soldier placed on guard; guard; watch; sentinel's duty.
**Sentry-box,** sen'tri-boks, *n.* A box or small shed to shelter a sentinel at his post.
**Sepal,** sē'pal or sep'al, *n.* The leaf of a calyx.
**Separable,** se'pa-ra-bl, *a.* That may be separated; capable of separation.
**Separate,** se'pa-rāt, *vt.* (separating, separated). To put or set apart; to disjoin.—*vi.* To go apart; to cleave or split.—*a.* Detached; distinct; individual.
**Separately,** se'pa-rāt-li, *adv.* In a separate state; apart; distinct; singly.
**Separation,** se-pa-rā'shon, *n.* Act of separating; disunion; incomplete divorce.
**Separatist,** se'pa-rāt-ist, *n.* One who advocates separation; a seceder.
**Separator,** se'pa-rāt-ėr, *n.* One who or that which separates.
**Separatory, Separative,** se'pa-ra-to-ri, se'pa-ra-tiv, *a.* Tending to separate; causing or used in separation.
**Sepia,** sē'pi-a, *n.* The cuttle-fish; a brown pigment obtained from the cuttle-fish.
**September,** sep-tem'bėr, *n.* The ninth month of the year.
**Septenary,** sep'ten-a-ri, *a.* Consisting of or proceeding by sevens; lasting seven years.
**Septennial,** sep-ten'ni-al, *a.* Lasting seven years; happening every seven years.
**Septet, Septette,** sep-tet', *n.* A muscial composition for seven voices or instruments.
**Septic,** sep'tik, *a.* Promoting or causing putrefaction.—*n.* A substance causing putrefaction.
**Septicemia,** sep-ti-sē'mi-a, *n.* Blood-poisoning by absorption of putrid matter.
**Septuagenarian,** sep'tū-a-jen-ā''ri-an, *n.* A person seventy years of age.
**Septuagesima,** sep'tū-a-jes''i-ma, *n.* The third Sunday before Lent.
**Septuagint,** sep'tū-a-jint, *n.* A Greek version of the Old Testament, finished about 200 B.C.
**Septum,** sep'tum, *n.*; pl. **-ta.** A wall separating cavities, as in animals or plants.
**Sepulchral,** sē-pul'kral, *a.* Pertaining to a sepulcher; grave; hollow, as a voice.
**Sepulcher,** se'pul-kėr, *n.* A tomb.—*vt.* To bury.
**Sepulture,** se'pul-tūr, *n.* Burial.
**Sequacious,** sē-kwā'shus, *a.* Following; logically consistent; consecutive.
**Sequel,** sē'kwel, *n.* That which follows; a succeeding part; result; issue.
**Sequence,** sē'kwens, *n.* A coming after; succession; arrangement; series.
**Sequent, Sequential,** sē'kwent, sē-kwen'shal, *a.* Following; succeeding.
**Sequester,** se-kwes'tėr, *vt.* To set apart; *refl.* to retire into seclusion; in *law,* to separate from the owner until the claims of creditors be satisfied; to appropriate.
**Sequestered,** se-kwes'tėrd, *a.* Secluded.
**Sequestrate,** se-kwes'trāt, *vt.* To set apart; to divide among creditors.
**Seraglio,** se-räl'yō, *n.* Originally the old palace of the Turkish sultan at Constantinople; so a harem.
**Serai,** se-rī', *n.* In Eastern countries, a place for the accommodation of travellers.
**Seraph,** se'raf, *n.*; pl. **-phs** or **phim.** An angel of the highest rank or order.
**Seraphic,** se-raf'ik, *a.* Pertaining to a seraph; celestial; pure.
**Serenade,** se-rē-nād', *n.* Music played at night under the windows of ladies.—*vt.* (serenading, serenaded). To entertain with a serenade.—*vi.* To perform a serenade.
**Serene,** sē-rēn', *a.* Clear; bright; calm; unruffled; formerly a form of address for princes, etc., in Germany and Austria.—*n.* Serenity; what is serene.
**Serenely,** sē-rēn'li, *adv.* In a serene manner; calmly; quietly; coolly.
**Serenity,** sē-ren'i-ti, *n.* State of being serene; peace; calmness; coolness.
**Serf,** sėrf, *n.* A villein; a forced laborer attached to an estate; a bondman.
**Serfdom,** sėrf'dom, *n.* The state or condition of serfs.
**Serge,** sėrj, *n.* A tough twilled worsted cloth; a twilled silken fabric.
**Sergeant,** sär'jant, *n.* A noncommissioned officer above corporal; a police officer.
**Sergeantcy,** sär'jant-si, *n.* The office of a sergeant.
**Sergeantship,** sär'jant-ship, *n.* The office of a sergeant.
**Serial,** sē'ri-al, *a.* Pertaining to a series; forming a series.—*n.* A written composition issued in numbers.
**Seriatim,** sē-ri-ā'tim, *adv.* In regular order; one after the other.
**Sericeous,** sē-ri'shus, *a.* Pertaining to silk; silky.
**Sericulture,** sē'ri-kul-tūr, *n.* The breeding and treatment of silk-worms.
**Series,** sē'ri-ēz or sē'rēz, *n.*; pl. the same. A succession of things; sequence; course.
**Serious,** sē'ri-us, *a.* Grave; earnest; momentous; attended with danger.
**Seriously,** sē'ri-us-li, *adv.* Gravely; earnestly; in an important degree.
**Sermon,** sėr'mon, *n.* A religious discourse by a clergyman; a homily.—*vt.* To tutor; to lecture.
**Sermonize,** sėr'mon-īz, *vi.* To preach; to inculcate rigid rules; to harangue.
**Seroon,** se-rön', *n.* A hamper of certain kinds of goods, as raisins or almonds.
**Serosity,** sē-ros'i ti, *n.* State of being serous.
**Serous,** sēr'us, *a.* Pertaining to serum; thin; watery; like whey; secreting serum.
**Serpent,** sėr'pent, *n.* A scaly reptile without feet; a bass musical instrument of wood; a firework.—*a.* Pertaining to a serpent.
**Serpentine,** sėr'pent-īn, *a.* Resembling or pertaining to a serpent; spiral.—*n.* A rock resembling a serpent's skin in appearance, used for decoration.—*vi.* To wind like a serpent.
**Serpigo,** sėr-pī'go, *n.* Ring-worm.
**Serrate, Serrated,** ser'rāt, ser'rāt-ed, *a.* Notched on the edge like a saw; toothed.
**Serration,** ser-rā'shon, *n.* Formation in the shape of a saw.
**Serrature,** ser'ra-tūr, *n.* A notching in the edge of anything, like a saw; serration.
**Serried,** se'rid, *a.* Crowded; in close order.
**Serum,** sē'rum, *n.* The watery part of curdled milk; whey; the thin part of the blood, etc.
**Serval,** sėr'val, *n.* A small S. African leopard.
**Servant,** sėrv'ant, *n.* One who serves; an attendant in a household; a drudge.
**Serve,** sėrv, *vt.* (serving, served). To work for and obey; to minister to; to set on a table for a meal; to conduce to; to be sufficient for; to manage or work; to deliver or transmit to; to perform the conditions of.—*vi.* To perform offices for another; to perform duties; to suffice; to suit.
**Server,** sėrv'ėr, *n.* One who or that which serves; a salver.
**Service,** sėrv'is, *n.* Act of one who serves; employment; kind office; military or naval duty; period of such duty; usefulness; public religious wor-

ship; liturgy; set of dishes for the table; supply of things regularly provided.
**Serviceable,** sėrv'is-a-bl, *a.* That renders service; useful; beneficial.
**Service-book,** sėrv'is-buk, *n.* A book used in church service; a prayer-book.
**Service-tree,** sėrv'is-trē, *n.* A European tree of the pear family.
**Serviette,** sėr-vi-et', *n.* A table-napkin.
**Servile,** sėr'vīl, *a.* Slavish; mean; dependent; fawning; meanly submissive.
**Servilely,** sėr'vīl-li, *adv.* In a servile manner; slavishly; meanly.
**Servility,** sėr-vil'i-ti, *n.* State of being servile; mean submission.
**Servitor,** sėrv'i-tor, *n.* A male servant.
**Servitude,** sėrv'i-tūd, *n.* State of a slave; slavery; compulsory labor.
**Sesame,** ses'a-me, *n.* An annual herbaceous plant, the seeds of which yield a fine oil.
**Sesquipedalian, Sesquipedal,** ses'kwi-pē-dā''li-an, ses'kwi-pē-dal, *a.* Containing a foot and a half: applied to long words; using long words.
**Sessile,** ses'īl, *a.* Attached without any sensible projecting support; having no stalk.
**Session,** se'shon, *n.* The sitting of a court, etc., for business; time or term of sitting.—**Court of Session,** the hghest civil court of Scotland.
**Sessional,** se'shon-al, *a.* Relating to sessions.
**Sestet, Sestette,** ses'tet, ses-tet', *n.* A musical composition for six voices or six instruments; the last six lines of a sonnet.
**Set,** set, *vt.* (setting, set). To put or dispose in a certain place or position; to fix; to appoint; to estimate; to regulate or adjust; to fit to music; to adorn; to intersperse; to incite.—*vi.* To disappear below the horizon; to solidify; to tend; to point out game; to apply oneself.—*p.a.* Placed, fixed, etc.; determined; established.—*n.* The descent of the sun, etc.; attitude, position; turn or bent; number of things combining to form a whole; a complete assortment; a clique.
**Seta,** sē'ta, *n.*; pl. **-ae.** A bristle or sharp hair.
**Setaceous,** se-tā'shus, *a.* Bristly.
**Set-off,** set'of, *n.* Any counterbalance; and equivalent; a counter claim.
**Seton,** sē'ton, *n.* A twist of silk or cotton drawn under the skin to keep up an issue.
**Setose,** sē'tōs, *a.* Bristly.
**Settee,** set-tē', *n.* A long seat with a back to it; a kind of sofa.
**Setter,** set'ėr, *n.* One who or that which sets; a sporting dog.
**Setting,** set'ing, *n.* Act of sinking below the horizon; that in which something, as a jewel, is set; music set for certain words.
**Settle,** set'l, *n.* A bench with a high back and arms.—*vt.* (settling, settled). To place in a more or less permanent position; to establish; to quit; to determine; to reconcile; to pay; to square or adjust; to colonize.—*vi.* To become fixed; to fix one's abode; to subside; to become calm; to adjust differences or accounts.
**Settled,** set'ld, *p.a.* Established; steadfast; stable; methodical.
**Settlement,** set'l-ment, *n.* Act of settling; establishment in life; colonization; a colony; adjustment; liquidation; arrangement; settling of property on a wife.
**Settler,** set'lėr, *n.* One who settles; a colonist; that which decides anything.
**Settling,** set'ling, *n.* Act of one who settles; payment, as of an account; *pl.* dregs.
**Set-to,** set-tö', *n.* A sharp contest.
**Seven,** se'ven, *a.* and *n.* One more than six.
**Sevenfold,** se'ven-fōld, *a.* Repeated seven times.—*adv.* Seven times as much or often.
**Seventeen,** se'ven-tēn, *a.* and *n.* Seven and ten.
**Seventeenth, se'ven-tēnth,** *a.* and *n.* The next in order after the sixteenth; one of seventeen equal parts.
**Seventh,** se'venth, *a.* Next after the sixth; containing or being one part in seven.—*n.* One part in seven.
**Seventieth,** se'ven-ti-eth, *a.* and *n.* The next after sixty-ninth; one of seventy equal parts.
**Seventy,** se'ven-ti, *a.* and *n.* Seven times ten.
**Sever,** se'vėr, *vt.* To separate by violence; to keep distinct.—*vi.* To separate.
**Severable,** se'vėr-a-bl, *a.* Capable of being severed.
**Several,** se'vėr-al, *a.* Separate; distinct; more than two, but not very many.
**Severally,** se'vėr-al-li, *adv.* Separately.
**Severalty,** se'vėr-al-ti, *n.* A state of separation from the rest, or from all others.
**Severance,** se'vėr-ans, *n.* Act of severing; separation.
**Severe,** sē-vēr', *a.* Serious; grave; harsh; stern; austere; rigidly exact; keen.
**Severely,** sē-vēr'li, *adv.* Harshly; strictly.
**Severity,** sē-ve'ri-ti, *n.* State or quality of being severe; rigor; intensity; austerity.
**Sevres,** sā-vr, *n.* A kind of beautiful porcelain, made of *Sèvres,* near Paris.
**Sew,** sō, *vt.* and *i.* To unite or make by needle and thread.
**Sewage,** sū'āj, *n.* The filthy matter which passes through sewers.
**Sewer,** sū'ėr, *n.* A subterranean drain, as in a city, to carry off water, filth, etc.
**Sewer,** sō'ėr, *n.* One who sews.
**Sewerage,** sū'ėr-āj, *n.* The system of sewers as in a city; sewage.
**Sewing,** sō'ing, *n.* Act of using a needle; that which is sewed; stitches made.
**Sex,** seks, *n.* That character by which an animal is male or female.
**Sexagenarian,** seks-a'jen-ā''ri-an, *n.* A person sixty years of age.—*a.* Sixty years old.
**Sexagenary,** seks-a'jen-a-ri, *a.* Pertaining to the number sixty.—*n.* A person sixty years old.
**Sexagesima,** seks-a-jes'i-ma, *n.* The second Sunday before Lent.
**Sexennial,** seks-en'ni-al, *a.* Lasting six years, or happening once in six years.
**Sextain,** seks'tān, *n.* A stanza of six lines.
**Sextant,** seks'tant, *n.* The sixth part of a circle; an instrument for measuring the angular distances of objects by reflection.
**Sexto-decimo,** seks-tō-des'i-mō, *n.* The size of a book when each sheet makes sixteen leaves: usually written 16mo (*sixteenmo*).
**Sexton,** seks'ton, *n.* An under officer of a church who takes care of the sacred vessels, acts as janitor, etc.
**Sextuple,** seks'tū-pl, *a.* Sixfold.
**Sexual,** seks'ū-al, *a.* Pertaining to, proceeding from, characterized by sex.
**Sexuality,** seks'ū-al'i-ti, *n.* State of being sexual.
**Sexually,** seks'ū-al-li, *adv.* In a sexual manner.
**Sforzando,** sfor-tsän'dō. A musical term marking notes that are to be emphasized, contracted *sf.*
**Shabbily,** shab'i-li, *adv.* In a shabby manner; with shabby clothes; meanly.
**Shabby,** shab'i, *a.* Poor in appearance; threadbare; mean; paltry; stingy.
**Shackle,** shak'l, *n.* A fetter; a manacle; that which obstructs free action.—*vt.* (shackling, shackled). To bind with shackles; to hamper.
**Shad,** shad, *n. sing.* and *pl.* A fish of the herring family.
**Shade,** shād, *n.* Obscurity caused by the interception of light; obscure retreat; twilight dimness; a screen; darker part of a picture; gradation of light; a scarcely perceptible degree or amount; a ghost.—*vt.* (shading, shaded). To screen from light; to obscure; to protect; to darken; to mark with gradations of color.
**Shading,** shād'ing, Act of making shade; light and shade in a picture.
**Shadoof,** sha-döf', *n.* An oriental contrivance for raising water, consisting of a long pole working on a post and weighted at one end, the other end having a bucket attached.

**Shadow,** sha'dō, *n.* A figure projected by the interception of light; shade; an inseparable companion; an imperfect representation; a spirit; protection.—*vt.* To shade; to cloud; to screen; to represent faintly; to follow closely.
**Shadowy,** sha'dō-i, *a.* Full of shadow; shady; dark; dim; unsubstantial.
**Shady,** shād'i, *a.* Abounding in shade; affording shade; of dubious morality.
**Shaft,** shäft, *n.* The long part of a spear or arrow; body of a column; spire of a steeple, etc.; pole of a carriage; a kind of large axle; a narrow passage, as into a mine.
**Shafting,** shäft'ing, *n.* A system of shafts communicating motion in machinery.
**Shag,** shag, *n.* Coarse hair or nap; cloth with a coarse nap; tobacco leaves shredded for smoking.—*vt.* (shagging, shagged). To make shaggy.
**Shaggy,** shag'i, *a.* Covered with shag; rough; rugged.
**Shagreen,** sha-grēn', *n.* A leather with a granulated surface prepared without tanning from the skins of horses, sharks, etc.
**Shah,** shä, *n.* A title given by Europeans to the monarch of Persia.
**Shake,** shāk, *vt.* (shaking, pret, shook, pp. shaken). To cause to move with quick vibrations; to agitate; to move from firmness; to cause to waver; to trill.—*vi.* To tremble; to shiver; to quake.—*n.* A wavering or rapid motion; tremor; shock; a trill in music; a crack in timber.
**Shake-down,** skāk'doun, *n.* A temporary substitute for a bed, formed on the floor.
**Shaker,** shāk'ėr, *n.* A person or thing that shakes; a member of a religious sect.
**Shako,** shak'ō, *n.* A stiff military cap with a peak in front.
**Shaky,** shāk'i, *a.* Apt to shake or tremble; unsteady; feeble.
**Shale,** shāl, *n.* A fine-grained rock; a clay rock having a slaty structure.
**Shall,** shal, *verb auxiliary*; pret. *should*, shud. In the first person it forms part of the future tense; in the second and third persons it implies authority.
**Shalli,** shal'i, *n.* A kind of twilled cloth made from Angora goat's hair.
**Shalloon,** sha-lön', *n.* A slight woollen stuff.
**Shallop,** shal'op, *n.* A small light boat.
**Shallot,** sha-lot', *n.* A species of onion.
**Shallow,** shal'ō, *a.* Not deep; superficial; simple; silly.—*n.* A place where the water is not deep; a shoal.
**Shallowly,** shal'ō-li, *adv.* In a shallow manner; superficially.
**Shaly,** shāl'i, *a.* Pertaining to shale; partaking of the qualities of shale.
**Sham,** sham, *n.* That which appears to be what it is not; imposture; humbug.—*a.* False; counterfeit.—*vt.* and *i.* (shamming, shammed). To feign, pretend.
**Shamanism,** shä'man-izm, *n.* An idolatrous religion of Northern Asia, etc., characterized by a belief in sorcery and in demons who require to be propitiated.
**Shamble,** sham'bl, *vi.* (shambling, shambled). To walk awkwardly, as if the knees were weak.—*n.* The gait of one who shambles.
**Shambles,** sham'blz, *n.pl.* A flesh-market; a slaughter-house; a place of butchery.
**Shambling,** sham'bling, *p.a.* Walking with an irregular, clumsy pace.
**Shame,** shām, *n.* A painful sensation excited by guilt, disgrace, etc.; reproach; disgrace.—*vt.* (shaming, shamed). To make ashamed; to disgrace.
**Shamefaced,** shām'fāst, *a.* Easily put out of countenance; modest; bashful.
**Shameful,** shām'ful, *a.* Full of shame; disgraceful; scandalous; infamous.
**Shameless,** shām'les, *a.* Destitute of shame; immodest; unblushing.
**Shammy, Shamoy,** sham'i, sham'oi, *n.* A soft leather for polishing, prepared originally from the skin of the chamois.
**Shampoo,** sham-pö', *vt.* (shampooing, shampooed). To press and rub the body after a hot bath; to wash and rub thoroughly the head.
**Shamrock,** sham'rok, *n.* A trefoil plant, the national emblem of Ireland.
**Shandry, Shandrydan,** shan'dri, shan'dri-dan, *n.* A one-horse Irish conveyance.
**Shank,** shangk, *n.* The leg; the shin-bone; the part of a tool connecting the acting part with a handle; the stem of an anchor.
**Shanty,** shan'ti, *n.* A hut or mean dwelling; song sung by sailors working together.
**Shape,** shāp, *vt.* (shaping, shaped). To form; to mold; to adjust.—*vi.* To suit.—*n.* Form or figure; make; a model; a dish of blancmange, etc.
**Shapeless,** shāp'les, *a.* Destitute of any regular form; deformed.
**Shapely,** shāp'li, *a.* Well-formed; symmetrical; handsome.
**Shard,** shärd, *n.* A fragment of an earthen vessel; the wing-case of a beetle.
**Share,** shār, *n.* A part bestowed or contributed; lot or portion; a plow-share.—*vt.* (sharing, shared). To part among two or more; to participate in.—*vi.* To have part.
**Share-broker,** shār'brōk-ėr, *n.* A dealer in the shares and securities of joint-stock companies and the like.
**Shareholder,** shār'hōld-ėr, *n.* One who holds shares in a joint property.
**Sharer,** shār'ėr, *n.* One who shares.
**Shark,** shärk, *n.* A voracious sea-fish; an unscrupulous person; a sharper.
**Sharp,** shärp, *a.* Having a very thin edge or fine point; keen; abrupt; not blurred; shrewd; acid; shrill; fierce; short and rapid; biting; barely honest; in *music*, raised a semitone.—*n.* A note raised a semitone, marked by the sign (♯); the sign itself; *pl.* the hard parts of wheat.—*vt.* To sharpen.—*adv.* Sharply; exactly; rapidly.
**Sharpen,** shärp'n, *vt.* To make sharp or sharper; to whet.—*vi.* To become sharp.
**Sharpener,** shärp'nėr, *n.* One who or that which sharpens; a tool for sharpening.
**Sharper,** shärp'ėr, *n.* One who lives by sharp practices; a tricky fellow; a cheat; a sharpener.
**Sharply,** shärp'li, *adv.* In a sharp manner; severely; keenly; acutely; abruptly.
**Sharpness,** shärp'nes, *n.* Keenness; pungency; acuteness.
**Sharp-shooter,** shärp'shöt-ėr, *n.* A soldier skilled in shooting with exactness.
**Sharp-sighted,** shärp'sīt-ed, *a.* Having quick sight; having acute discernment.
**Shaster, Shastra,** shäs'tėr, shäs'tra, *n.* A book of laws or precepts among the Hindus.
**Shatter,** shat'ėr, *vt.* To break into many pieces; to overthrow, destroy.—*vt.* To be broken into fragments.—*n.* A fragment.
**Shattery,** *a.* Easily shattered; brittle; loose of texture.
**Shave,** shāv, *vt.* (shaving, shaved). To cut off the hair from the skin with a razor; to cut off thin slices from; to skim along; to fleece.—*vi,* To cut off the beard with a razor.—*n.* A cutting off of the beard; a thin slice; an exceedingly narrow escape.
**Shaver,** shāv'ėr, *n.* A barber; one who fleeces; a small boy.
**Shaving,** shāv'ing, *n.* Act of one who shaves; a thin slice pared off.
**Shaw,** sha, *n.* A grove or thicket.
**Shawl,** shal, *n.* An article of dress, used mostly as a loose covering for the shoulders.
**She,** shē, *pron. nominative.* The feminine pronoun of the third person.
**Shea,** shē'a, *n.* A tree of tropical Asia and Africa, called also *butter-tree.*
**Sheaf,** shēf, *n.*; pl. **Sheaves,** shēvz, A bundle of

the stalks of wheat, oats, etc.; any similar bundle.—*vt.* To make into sheaves.—*vi.* To make sheaves.

**Sheafy,** shēf'i, *a.* Pertaining to or consisting of sheaves.

**Shealing, Sheal,** shēl'ing, shēl, *n.* A hut or shed. Also *Sheiling, Shieling.*

**Shear,** shēr, *vt.* and *i.* (pret. sheared or shore, pp. sheared or shorn). To cut with shears; to clip the wool from; to cut from a surface; to fleece.

**Shearer,** shēr-ėr, *n.* One who shears.

**Shearing,** shēr'ing, *n.* Act of shearing; the result of the operation of clipping.

**Shears,** shērz, *n.pl.* An instrument of two blades for cutting.

**Shear-steel,** shēr'stēl, *n.* Steel prepared from bars of common steel, heated, beaten together, and drawn out.

**Sheath,** shēth, *n.* A case for a sword, etc.; a scabbard; wing-case of an insect.

**Sheathe,** shēTH, *vt.* (sheathing, sheathed). To put into a sheath; to protect by a casing.

**Sheathed,** shēTHd, *p.a.* Put in or having a sheath; covered with sheathing.

**Sheathing,** shēTH'ing, *n.* Act of one who sheathes; that which sheathes; covering of metal to protect a ship's bottom.

**Sheave,** shēv, *n.* A small grooved wheel on which a rope works; the wheel of a pulley.

**Shed,** shed, *vt.* (shedding, shed). To cast or throw off; to emit or diffuse; to let fall in drops; to spill.—*vi.* To let fall seed, a covering, etc.—*n.* A watershed; the opening betweem threads in a loom through which the shuttle passes; a penthouse; a hut; a large open structure.

**Sheen,** shēn, *n.* Brightness; splendor.—*a.* Bright; shining: *poetical.*

**Sheep,** shēp, *sing.* and *pl.* A ruminant animal valued for its wool and flesh; a silly or timid fellow.—**Sheep's eye,** a loving or wistful glance.

**Sheepfold,** shēp'fōld, *n.* A fold or pen in which sheep are collected or confined.

**Sheepish,** shēp'ish, *a.* Like a sheep; foolish; bashful; over-modest or diffident.

**Sheep-skin,** shēp'skin, *n.* The skin of a sheep prepared with the wool on; leather prepared from it.

**Sheer,** shēr, *a.* Mere; downright; precipitous.—*vi.* To deviate from the proper course.—*n.* The upward bend of a ship at stem or stern.

**Sheers,** shērz, *n.pl.* A hoisting apparatus of two or more poles fastened near the top, from which depends the necessary tackle.

**Sheet,** shēt, *n.* A broad, thin piece of anything; broad expanse; piece of linen or cotton spread on a bed; piece of paper; a rope fastened to the lower corner of a sail.—*vt.* To furnish with sheets; to shroud.

**Sheeting,** shēt'ing, *n.* Linen or cotton cloth for making bed-sheets.

**Sheet-lightning,** shēt'līt-ning, *n.* Lightning appearing in wide expanded flashes.

**Sheikh,** shēk, *n.* An Arab chief; a title of dignity among the Arabs.

**Sheil, Sheiling,** shēl, shēl'ing, *n.* *See* SHEALING.

**Shekel,** she'kel, *n.* An ancient Jewish weight of about half an ounce.

**Shelf,** shelf, *n.*; pl. **Shelves,** shelvz. A board fixed along a wall to support articles; a ledge; a ledge of rocks in the sea.

**Shelfy,** shelf'i, *a.* Full of rocky shelves.

**Shell,** shel, *n.* A hard outside covering; an outside crust; framework; any slight hollow structure; a projectile contaiing a bursting charge.—*vt.* To strip off the shell of; to throw bomb-shells into or among.—*vi.* To cast the exterior covering.

**Shellac,** shel-lak', *n.* Lac melted and formed into thin cakes.

**Shell-fish,** shel'fish, *n. sing.* and *pl.* A mollusk or a crustacean whose external covering consists of a shell.

**Shell-shock,** shel'shok, *n.* Neurosis caused by shell-fire.

**Shelly,** shel'i, *a.* Abounding with shells; consisting of shells.

**Shelter,** shel'tėr, *n.* A protection; asylum; refuge; security.—*vt.* To protect; to screen.—*vi.* To take shelter.

**Shelve,** shelv, *vt.* (shelving, shelved). To place on a shelf; to dismiss from use or attention; to furnish with shelves.—*vi.* To slope.

**Shelving,** shelv'ing, *n.* The operation of fixing up shelves; shelves collectively.

**Shelvy,** shelv'i, *a.* Full of shelves of rock.

**Shepherd,** shep'ėrd, *n.* One who tends sheep.

**Sherbet,** sher'bet, *n.* An Eastern drink of water, the juice of fruits, and sugar.

**Sherd,** sherd, *n.* A fragment; a shard.

**Shereef, Sheriff, Sherif,** she-rēf', *n.* A descendant of Mohammed through his daughter Fatima; chief magistrate of Mecca.

**Sheriff,** she'rif, *n.* An officer in each county to whom is entrusted the administration of the law; in Scotland, the chief judge of a county.

**Sherry,** she'ri, *n.* A wine of southern Spain.

**Shibboleth,** shib'bō-leth, *n.* The watchword of a party; a cry or motto.

**Shield,** shēld, *n.* A broad piece of armor carried on the arm; protection; an escutcheon with a coat of arms.—*vt.* To cover, as with a shield; to protect.

**Shieling,** shēl'ing, *n.* *See* SHEALING.

**Shift,** shift, *vi.* To change; to change place or direction; to manage; to practice indirect methods.—*vt.* To remove; to alter; to dress in fresh clothes.—*n.* A change; expedient; evasion; an under garment; a squad of workmen; the working time of a relay of men; the spell of work.

**Shiftless,** shift'les, *a.* Destitute of expedients; wanting in energy or effort.

**Shifty,** shift'i, *a.* Full of shifts; fertile in expedients or evasions; tricky.

**Shillelah,** shil-lel'a, *n.* An Irish name for an oaken or blackthorn sapling used as a cudgel.

**Shilling,** shil'ing, *n.* An old English silver coin equal to twelve old pence.

**Shilly-shally,** shil'i-shal-ī, *vi.* To hesitate.—*n.* Foolish trifling; irresolution.

**Shimmer,** shim'ėr, *vi.* To emit a faint or tremulous light; to glisten.—*n.* A glistening.

**Shin,** shin, *n.* The fore-part of the leg, between the ankle and the knee.

**Shine,** shīn, *vi.* (shining, shone). To give out a steady brilliant light; to be lively, bright, or conspicuous.—*vt.* To cause to shine.—*n.* Brightness; fair weather.

**Shingle,** shing'gl, *n.* A thin piece of wood used in covering roofs; loose gravel and pebbles.—*vt.* To cover with shingles; to hammer so as to expel slag or scoriae from in puddling iron.

**Shingles,** shing'glz, *n.* An eruptive disease which spreads around the body.

**Shingling,** shing'gling, *n.* A covering of shingles; a process in reducing iron from the cast to the malleable state.

**Shingly,** shing'gli, *a.* Abounding with shingle or gravel.

**Shining,** shīn'ing, *a.* Bright; illustrious.

**Shinto, Shintoism,** shin'to, shin'to-izm, *n.* The ancient religion of Japan.

**Shinty,** shin'ti, *n.* Hockey.

**Shiny,** shīn'i, *a.* Bright; brilliant; clear.

**Ship,** ship, *n.* A vessel of some size adapted to navigation; a three-masted, square-rigged vessel.—*vt.* (shipping, shipped). To put on board of a ship; to transport in a ship; to hire for service in a ship; to fix in its place.—*vi.* To engage for service on a ship; to embark.

**Shipboard,** ship'bōrd, *n.* The deck or interior of a ship: used in *on shipboard.*

**Ship-broker,** ship'brō-kėr, *n.* A broker who procures insurance, etc., for ships.

**Ship-builder,** ship'bild-ėr, *n.* One who builds ships; a naval architect; a shipwright.

**Ship-chandler,** ship'chand-lėr, *n.* One who deals

in cordage, canvas, etc., for ships.
**Ship-master,** ship'mas-tėr, *n*. The master, captain, or commander of a ship.
**Shipmate,** ship'māt, *n*. One who serves in the same ship; a fellow-sailor.
**Shipment,** ship'ment, *n*. Act of putting goods on board of a ship; goods shipped.
**Shippen, Shippon,** ship'n, *n*. A house or shed for cattle or sheep.
**Shipper,** ship'ėr, *n*. One who sends goods on board a ship for transportation.
**Shipping,** ship'ing, *n*. Ships in general; aggregate tonnage.
**Ship-shape,** ship'shāp, *a*. Having a seamanlike trim; well arranged.
**Shipwreck,** ship'rek, *n*. The wreck or loss of a ship; destruction; ruin.—*vt*. To wreck; to cast away; to ruin.
**Shipwright,** ship'rīt, *n*. A builder of ships or other vessels; a ship-carpenter.
**Ship-yard,** ship'yärd, *n*. A yard or place in which ships are constructed.
**Shire,** shīr (but shir in county names), *n*. A county.
**Shirk,** shėrk, *vt*. and *i* To avoid unfairly; to seek to avoid duty.
**Shirt,** shėrt, *n*. A man's loose under garment of linen, etc.; a lady's blouse.—*vt*. To clothe with a shirt.
**Shirting,** shėrt'ing, *n*. Cloth for shirts.
**Shittah-tree,** shit'ta-trē, *n*. A species of acacia.
**Shittim-wood,** shit'tim-wud, *n*. The hard and durable wood of the shittah-tree.
**Shive,** shīv, *n*. A slice; a fragment.
**Shiver,** shi'vėr, *vt*. To shatter.—*vi*. To fall into many small pieces; to tremble, as from cold; to shudder.—*n*. A small fragment; a shaking fit; shudder.
**Shivery,** shi'vėr-i, *a*. Pertaining to shivering; characterized by shivering.
**Shoal,** shōl, *n*. A multitude; a crowd; a sandbank or bar; a shallow.—*vi*. To become more shallow.—*a*. Shallow.
**Shoaly,** shōl'i, *a*. Full of shoals
**Shock, shok, *n*. A violent striking against; violent onset; a sudden disturbing emotion; a stook; a thick mass of hair.—*vt*. To give a shock to; to encounter violently; to disgust; to make up into shocks or stooks.**
**Shocking,** shok'ing, *a*. Serving to shock; dreadful; disgusting; offensive.
**Shock troops,** shok tröps, *n*. Picked soldiers specially trained for offensive action.
**Shod,** shod, pret. and pp. of *shoe*.
**Shoddy,** shod'i, *n*. Fiber obtained from old woollen fabrics mixed with fresh wool and manufactured anew; inferior cloth made from this.—*a*. Made of shoddy; trashy.
**Shoe,** shö, *n*. A covering for the foot; a plate of iron nailed to the hoof of a horse, etc.—*vt*. (shoeing, shoed). To furnish with shoes.
**Shoeblack,** shö'blak, *n*. A person that cleans shoes.
**Shoe-horn, Shoeing-horn,** shö'horn, shö'ing-horn, *n*. A curved implement used to aid in putting on shoes.
**Shoemaker,** shö'māk-ėr, *n*. One who makes shoes.
**Shone,** shon, pret. and pp. of *shine*.
**Shook,** shuk, pret. and pp. of *shake*.—*n*. The staves for a single barrel made into a package.
**Shoot,** shöt, *vt*. (shooting, shot). To cause to fly forth; to discharge; to hit or kill with a missile; to empty out suddenly; to thrust forward; to pass rapidly under, over, etc.—*vi*. To charge a missile; to dart along; to sprout; to project.—*n*. A shooting; a young branch; a sloping trough; a place for shooting rubbish.
**Shooting,** shöt'ing, *n*. Sport of killing game with firearms; tract over which game is shot; sensation of a darting pain.—*a*. Pertaining to one who shoots.
**Shop,** shop, *n*. A place where goods are sold by retail; a building in which mechanics work; one's special business.—*vi*. (shopping, shopped). To visit shops for purchasing goods.
**Shopkeeper,** shop'kēp-ėr, *n*. One who keeps a shop; one who sells goods by retail.
**Shop-lifter,** shop'lift-ėr, *n*. One who steals in a shop on pretense of buying.
**Shore,** shōr, *n*. Land along the edge of the sea; the coast; a prop.—*vt*. To support by props: pret. of *shear*.
**Shorn,** shōrn, pp. of *shear*.
**Short,** short, *a*. Not long or tall; scanty; deficient; concise; snappish; severe; brittle.—*adv*. Abruptly; insufficiently.—*n*. Something short; *pl*. garments resembling trousers, but ending above the knee.—**In short,** in few words; briefly.
**Shortage,** short'āj, *n*. Amount short or deficient; deficit.
**Shortcoming,** short'kum-ing, *n*. A failing of the usual quantity; a delinquency.
**Short-dated,** short'dāt-ed, *a*. Having little time to run.
**Shorten,** short'n, *vt*. To make short or shorter; to deprive.—*vi*. To contract.
**Shorthand,** short'hand, *n*. A shorter mode of writing than is usually employed.
**Short-handed,** short'hand-ed, *a*. Not having the usual number of assistants.
**Short-horn,** short'horn, *n*. One of a breed of cattle with very short horns.
**Short-lived,** short'līvd, *a*. Not living or lasting long; of short continuance.
**Shortly,** short'li, *adv*. Quickly; soon; briefly.
**Short-sighted,** short'sīt-ed, *n*. Unable to see far; myopic; wanting foresight.
**Short-winded,** short'wind-ed, *a*. Affected with shortness of breath.
**Shot,** shot, *n*. Act of shooting; a projectile; a bullet; bullets collectively; range or reach; a marksman; the number of fish caught in one haul; a reckoning.—*vt*. (shotting, shotted). To load with shot.—*a*. Having a changeable color, as silk; interwoven.
**Should,** shud, the pret. of *shall*, denoting present or past duty or obligation, or expressing a hypothetical case.
**Shoulder,** shōl'dėr, *n*. The joint by which the arm or the fore-leg is connected with the body; a projection; support.—*vt*. To push with the shoulder; to put upon the shoulder.—*vi*. To push forward.
**Shoulder-blade,** shōl'dėr-blād, *n*. The bone of the shoulder; scapula.
**Shoulder-knot,** shōl'dėr-not, *n*. An ornamental knot of ribbon or lace on the shoulder.
**Shoulder-strap,** shōl'dėr-strap, *n*. A strap worn on the shoulder, either to support dress, or as a badge of distinction.
**Shout,** shout, *vi*. To utter a loud and sudden cry.—*vt*. To utter with a shout.—*n*. A loud sudden cry.
**Shove,** shuv, *vt*. and *i* (shoving, shoved). To push forward; to press against; to jostle.—*n*. Act of shoving; a push.
**Shovel,** shu'vel, *n*. An instrument with a broad shallow blade, for lifting earth, etc.—*vt*. (shovelling, shovelled). To throw with a shovel.
**Shovelful,** shu'vel-ful, *n*. As much as a shovel will hold.
**Shovel-hat,** shu'vel-hat, *n*. A clergyman's hat with a broad brim, turned up at the sides.
**Show,** shō, *vt*. (pret. showed, pp. shown or showed). To display to the view of others; to let be seen; to make known; to prove; to bestow, afford.—*vi*. To appear.—*n*. Act of showing; exhibition; appearance; pretense; pageant; things exhibited for money.
**Shower,** shō'ėr, *n*. One who shows.
**Shower,** shou'ėr, *n*. A fall of rain, etc.; a copious supply.—*vt*. To water with a shower; to bestow liberally.—*vi*. To rain in showers.
**Showery,** shou'ėr-i, *a*. Raining in showers; abounding with frequent falls of rain.
**Showily,** shō'i-li, *adv*. In a showy manner.

**Showman,** shō'man, *n*. One who exhibits a show; the owner of a travelling show.
**Show-room,** shō'röm, *n*. A room in which a show is exhibited; an apartment where goods are displayed.
**Showy,** shō'i, *a*. Making a great show; ostentatious; gorgeous; gaudy.
**Shrapnel,** shrap'nel, *n*. A shell filled with bullets, timed to burst at any given point.
**Shred,** shred, *vt*. (shredding, shred or shredded). To tear into small pieces.—*n*. A long, narrow piece cut off; a tatter.
**Shreddy,** shred'i, *a*. Consisting of shreds.
**Shrew,** shrö, *n*. A peevish, ill-tempered woman; a scold; a shrew-mouse.
**Shrewd,** shröd, *a*. Astute; sagacious; discerning; sharp.
**Shrewdly,** shröd'li, *adv*. Astutely.
**Shrewish,** shrö'ish, *a*. Having the qualities of a shrew; peevish; vixenish.
**Shrew-mouse,** shrö'mous, *n*. A small insectivorous animal resembling a mouse.
**Shriek,** shrēk, *vi*. To cry out shrilly; to scream.—*n*. A shrill cry; a scream.
**Shrift,** shrift, *n*. The act of shriving or being shriven; confession to a priest; absolution.
**Shrike,** shrīk, *n*. An insessorial bird which feeds on insects, small birds, etc.; a butcher-bird.
**Shrill,** shril, *a*. Sharp or piercing in sound; uttering an acute sound.—*vi*. and *t* To utter an acute piercing sound.
**Shrilly,** shril'li, *adv*. In a shrill manner; acutely.—*a*. shril'i. Somewhat shrill.
**Shrimp,** shrimp, *n*. A small crustacean allied to the lobster; a mannikin.
**Shrimper,** shrimp'ėr, *n*. A fisherman who catches shrimps.
**Shrine,** shrīn, *n*. A case, as for sacred relics; a tomb; altar; a place hallowed from its associations.—*vt*. (shrining, shrined). To enshrine.
**Shrink,** shringk, *vi*. (pret. shrank or shrunk, pp. shrunk or shrunken). To contact spontaneously; to shrivel; to withdraw, as from danger; to flinch.—*vt*. To cause to contract.—*n*. Contraction.
**Shrinkage,** shringk'āj, *n*. A shrinking; diminution in bulk or quantity; reduction.
**Shrive,** shrīv, *vt*. (shriving, pret. shrove or shrived, pp. shriven or shrived). To hear the confession of; to confess and absolve.
**Shrivel,** shri'vel, *vi*. and *t* (shrivelling, shrivelled). To shrink into wrinkles; to shrink and form corrugations.
**Shroud,** shroud, *n*. That which clothes or covers; a winding-sheet; one of the large ropes in a ship supporting the mast.—*vt*. To cover; to dress for the grave; to screen.
**Shrove-tide,** shrōv'tīd, *n*. Confession time before Lent.
**Shrove-Tuesday,** shrōv'tūz-dā, *n*. The Tuesday before the first day of Lent.
**Shrub,** shrub, *n*. A woody plant less than a tree; a plant with several woody stems from the same root; a beverage containing the juice of fruit, etc.
**Shrubbery,** shrub'ėr-i, *n*. An ornamental plantation of shrubs; shrubs collectively.
**Shrubby,** shrub'i, *a*. Full of shrubs; resembling a shrub; consisting of brushwood.
**Shrug,** shrug, *vt*. and *i* (shrugging, shrugged). To draw up or to contract, as the shoulders.—*n*. A drawing up of the shoulders.
**Shrunken,** shrungk'n, *p.a*. Having shrunk; shrivelled; contracted.
**Shuck,** shuk, *n*. A shell or husk.
**Shudder,** shud'ėr, *vi*. To tremble with fear, horror, etc.; to quake.—*n*. A tremor.
**Shuffle,** shuf'l, *vt*. (shuffling; shuffled). To shove one way and the other; to confuse; to change the position of cards.—*vi*. To change position; to quibble; to move with a dragging gait; to scrape the floor in dancing.—*n*. An evasion; mixing cards; scraping movement in dancing.
**Shuffler,** shuf'lėr, *n*. One who shuffles; one who prevaricates; one who plays tricks.
**Shun,** *vt*. (shunning, shunned). To avoid; to refrain from; to neglect.
**Shunt,** shunt, *vi*. and *t*. In railways; to turn from one line of rails into another; to free oneself of.
**Shut,** shut, *vt*. (shutting, shut). To close or stop up; to bar; to preclude; to exclude; to confine.—*vi*. To close itself; to be closed.—*a*. Made close; closed; not resonant.
**Shutter,** shut'ėr, *n*. One who shuts; a moveable covering for a window or aperture.
**Shuttle,** shut'l, *n*. An instrument used by weavers for shooting the thread of the woof between the threads of the warp.
**Shuttle-cock,** shut'l-kok, *n*. A cork stuck with feathers, and struck by a battledore.—*vt*. To throw backwards and forwards.
**Shy,** shī, *a*. Timid; retiring; reserved; coy; cautious; wary.—*vi*. (shying, shied). To start suddenly aside, as a horse.—*vt*. To throw.—*n*. The starting suddenly aside of a horse.
**Shyly,** shī'li, *adv*. In a shy or timid manner; not familiarly; diffidently.
**Shyness,** shī'nes, *n*. Quality or state of being shy; reserve; coyness.
**Siamese,** sī-a-mēz', *n. sing.* and *pl.* A native of Siam; the language of Siam.
**Sibilant,** si'bi-lant, *a*. Hissing.—*n*. A letter uttered with a hissing, as *s* and *z*.
**Sibilate,** si'bi-lāt, *vt*. To pronounce with a hissing sound.
**Sibilation,** si-bi-lā'shon, *n*. The act of sibulating; a hiss.
**Sibyl,** si'bil, *n*. A prophetess; sorceress.
**Sibylline,** si'bil-līn, *a*. Pertaining to the sibyls; like the productions of the sibyls; prophetical.
**Sic,** sik, *adv*. Thus; it is so: often used within brackets in quoting, to note that a peculiarity in the quotation is literally exact.
**Siccate,** sik'āt, *vt*. To dry.
**Siccative,** sik'a-tiv, *a*. Drying; causing to dry.
**Siccity,** sik'si-ti, *n*. Dryness, aridity.
**Sick,** sik, *a*. Affected with disease of any kind; ill; inclined to vomit; disgusted or weary; pertaining to those who are sick.
**Sick-bay,** sik'bā, *n*. A ship's hospital.
**Sicken,** sik'n, *vt*. To make sick; to disgust.—*vi*. To become sick; to be disgusted; to languish.
**Sickening,** sik'n-ing, *a*. Making sick; disgusting.
**Sickish,** sik'ish, *a*. Somewhat sick.
**Sickle,** sik'l, *n*. An instrument for cutting grain, used with one hand; a reaping-hook.
**Sickly,** sik'li, *a*. Affected with sickness; not healthy; ailing; languid; faint.—*adv*. In a sick manner or condition.
**Sickness,** sik'nes, *n*. Disease; ill-health; illness; nausea.
**Sick-room,** sik'röm, *n*. The apartment where one lies ill.
**Side,** sīd, *n*. The broad or long surface of a body; edge, border; right or left half of the body; part between the top and bottom; any party or interest opposed to another.—*a*. Being on, from, or toward the side; indirect.—*vi*. (siding, sided). To embrace the opinions of one party.
**Side-arms,** sīd'ärmz, *n.pl.* Arms carried by the side, as sword, bayonet, etc.
**Sideboard,** sīd'bōrd, *n*. A piece of furniture used to hold dining utensils, etc.
**Sided,** sīd'ed, *p.a.* Having a side or sides; used in composition.
**Side-light,** sīd'līt, *n*. A light at a side; information thrown indirectly on a subject.
**Sidelong,** sīd'long, *adv*. Laterally; obliquely.—*a*. Lateral; oblique.
**Sidereal,** sī-dē'rē-al, *a*. Pertaining to stars; measured by the motion of the stars.
**Siderite,** sid'ėr-iīt, *n*. Magnetic iron ore or loadstone.
**Siderography,** sid-ėr-og'ra-fi, *n*. The art or practice of engraving on steel.

S

**Siderolite,** sid'ėr-ō-līt, *n.* A meteoric stone chiefly consisting of iron.
**Side-saddle,** sīd'sad-l, *n.* A saddle for a woman.
**Sidewalk,** sīd'wak, *n.* A raised walk for footpassengers by the side of a street or road.
**Sidewise,** sīd'wīz, *adv.* Toward one side; laterally; on one side.
**Siding,** sīd'ing, *n.* A short additional line of rails laid for the purpose of shunting.
**Sidle,** sīd'l, *vi.* (sidling, sidled). To go or move side foremost; to move to one side.
**Siege,** sēj, *n.* A regular attack on a fortified place; continued endeavor to gain possession.
**Siege-train,** sēj'trān, *n.* The artillery, carriages, ammunition, etc., carried with an army for attacking fortified places.
**Sienna,** sē-en'na, *n.* An earth of a fine yellow color, used as a pigment.
**Siesta,** sē-es'ta, *n.* A sleep or rest in the hottest part of the day.
**Sieve,** siv, *n.* A utensil for separating the smaller particles of a loose substance.
**Sift,** sift, *vt.* To separate by a sieve; to examine minutely.—*vi.* To pass as if through a sieve.
**Sifter,** sift'ėr, *n.* One who sifts; a sieve.
**Sigh,** sī, *vi.* To make a long breath audibly, as from grief; to make a melancholy sound.—*n.* A long breath made audibly, as in grief.
**Sight,** sīt, *n.* Act or power of seeing; view; vision; visibility; estimation; a show; an appliance for guiding the eye.—*vt.* To see; to descry; to give the proper elevation and direction to, as a piece of ordnance.
**Sighted,** sīt'ed, *a.* Having sight; seeing in a particular manner; having sights, as a rifle.
**Sightless,** sīt'les, *a.* Wanting sight; blind.
**Sightly,** sīt'li, *a.* Pleasing to the sight or eye; agreeable to look on.
**Sight-seeing,** sīt'sē-ing, *n.* The act of seeing sights or visiting scenes of interest.
**Sight-seer,** sīt'sē-ėr, *n.* One who goes to see sights or curiosities.
**Sigillaria,** sij-il-lā'ri-a, *n.* A large fossil plant of the coal formation.
**Sign,** sīn, *n.* A mark or stamp indicative of something; a token; indication; emblem; a symbol or character.—*vt.* To express by a sign; to affix a signature to.—*vi.* To make a sign or signal.
**Signal,** sig'nal, *n.* A sign to communicate intelligence, orders, etc., at a distance.—*a.* Worthy of note; remarkable.—*vt.* or *i.* (signalling, signalled). To communicate by signals.
**Signal-box,** sig'nal-boks, *n.* A small house from which railway signals are worked.
**Signalize,** sig'nal-īz, *vt.* To make remarkable; to distinguish by some fact or exploit.
**Signally,** sig'nal-li, *adv.* In a signal manner; eminently; remarkably; memorably.
**Signal-man,** sig'nal-man, *n.* A man who works signals.
**Signatory, Signatary,** sig'na-to-ri, sig'na-ta-ri, *a.* Relating to the signing of documents.—*n.* One who signs; a state representative who signs a public document.
**Signature,** sig'na-tūr, *n.* A mark impressed; the name of a person written by himself; in *printing*, a distinctive letter or mark at the bottom of the first page of each sheet.
**Sign-board,** sīn'bōrd, *n.* A board on which one sets a notice of his occupation or of articles for sale.
**Signer,** sīn'ėr, *n.* One who signs.
**Signet,** sig'net, *n.* A seal; seal used by the sovereign in sealing private letters.
**Signet-ring,** sig'net-ring, *n.* A ring containing a signet or private seal.
**Signifiable,** sig-ni-fī'a-bl, *a.* That may be signified.
**Significance, Significancy,** sig-ni'fi-kans, sig-ni'fi-kan-si, *n.* Meaning; import.
**Significant,** sig-ni'fi-kant, *a.* Signifying something; indicative; important.
**Significantly,** sig-ni'fi-kant-li, *adv.* In a significant manner; meaningly; expressively.
**Signification,** sig'ni-fi-kā''shon, *n.* Act of signifying; meaning; import; sense.
**Signify,** sig'ni-fī, *vt.* (signifying, signified). To make known either by signs or words; to betoken; to mean; to imply; to import.
**Signitary,** sig'ni-ta-ri, *a.* *See* SIGNATORY.
**Signor, Signior,** sēn'yor, *n.* An English form of Italian *Signore*, Spanish *Señor*, equivalent to *Sir* or *Mr.*; a gentleman.
**Signora,** sēn-yō'ra, *n.* *Madam* or *Mrs.*; a lady.
**Signorina,** sēn-yō-rē'na, *n.* *Miss*; a young lady.
**Sign-post,** sīn'pōst, *n.* A post on which a sign hangs; a finger-post.
**Silence,** sī'lens, *n.* State of being silent; quiet; secrecy; absence of mention.—*vt.* To put to silence; to quiet; to cause to cease firing.
**Silent,** sī'lent, *a.* Not speaking; mute; dumb; taciturn; making no noise.
**Silently,** sī'lent-li, *adv.* In a silent manner.
**Silhouette,** sil'ö-et, *n.* A profile portrait filled in with a dark color.
**Silica, Silex,** sil'i-ka, sī'leks, *n.* Oxide of silicon, the chief constituent of quartz, flint, etc.
**Silicate,** sil'i-kāt, *n.* A compound of silica with certain bases.
**Siliceous, Silicious,** si-lish'us, *a.* Pertaining to, containing, or like silica.
**Silicon, Silicium,** sil'i-kon, si-lis'i-um, *n.* The nonmetallic element of which silica is the oxide.
**Silicosis,** si-li-kō'sis, *n.* A disease of the lungs caused by inhaling small particles of silica.
**Siliqua,** sil'i-kwa, *n.*; pl. **-quae,** The long pod of such cruciferous plants as wallflower; a weight for gold or gems; a carat.
**Silk,** silk, *n.* The fine thread produced by various caterpillars, particularly the silk-worm; cloth made of silk; garment made of this cloth.—*a.* Pertaining to silk; silken.
**Silken,** silk'en, *a.* Made of silk; silky.
**Silk-worm,** silk'wėrm, *n.* A worm which produces silk; the larva of various moths which spin a silken cocoon for the chrysalis.
**Silky,** silk'i, *a.* Made of silk; like silk; soft and smooth to the touch.
**Sill,** sil, *n.* The timber or stone at the foot of a door or window; the threshold; the floor of a gallery in a mine.
**Sillabub,** sil'la-bub, *n.* A liquor made by mixing wine or cider with milk.
**Silly,** sil'li, *a.* Weak in intellect; foolish; unwise.
**Silo,** sī'lō, *n.* The pit in which green fodder is preserved in the method of ensilage.
**Silt,** silt, *n.* A deposit of fine earth from running or standing water.—*vt.* To fill with silt.
**Silurian,** sī-lū'ri-an, *a.* Applied to the lowest division of the paleozoic strata.
**Silver,** sil'vėr, *n.* A precious metal of a white color; money; plate made of silver.—*a.* Made of silver; silvery.—*vt.* and *i.* To cover with a coat of silver; to tinge with gray.
**Silverside,** sil'vėr-sīd, *n.* A cut of beef from the underside of the rump, often salted.
**Silversmith,** sil'vėr-smith, *n.* One whose occupation is to work in silver.
**Silver-tongued,** sil'vėr-tungd, *a.* Having a smooth tongue or speech.
**Silvery,** sil'vėr-i, *a.* Like silver; covered with silver; clear as the sound of a silver bell.
**Simian, Simious,** si'mi-an, si'mi-us, *a.* Pertaining to apes or monkeys; ape-like.
**Similar,** si'mi-lėr, *a.* Like; resembling; having like parts and relations but not of the same magnitude.
**Similarity,** si-mi-la'ri-ti, *n.* State of being similar; likeness; resemblance.
**Similarly,** si'mi-lėr-li, *a.* In a similar or like manner; with resemblance.
**Simile,** si'mi-lē, *n.* A figure of speech consisting in likening one thing to another.
**Similitude,** si-mil'i-tūd, *n.* Likeness; resemblance; comparison.
**Simmer,** si'mėr, *vi.* To boil gently.

**Simoom,** si-möm', *n.* A hot suffocating wind in Africa and Arabia.
**Simper,** sim'pėr, *vi.* To smile in a silly manner.—*n.* A silly or affected smile.
**Simple,** sim'pl, *a.* Not complex; single; not involved; clear; artless; mere; plain; sincere; silly.—*n.* Something not mixed; a medicinal herb.
**Simpleton,** sim'pl-ton, *n.* A simple or silly person; one easily deceived.
**Simplicity,** sim-plis'i-ti, *n.* State or quality of being simple; singleness; artlessness; sincerity; plainness; foolishness.
**Simplify,** sim'pli-fī, *vt.* To make simple; to make plain or easy.
**Simply,** sim'pli, *adv.* In a simple manner; artlessly; plainly; merely; foolishly.
**Simulacrum,** sim-ū-lā'krum, *n.*; pl. **-cra.** An image or likeness; a phantom.
**Simulate,** sim'ū-lāt, *vt.* To counterfeit; to feign.
**Simulation,** sim-ū-lā'shon, *n.* Act of simulating; pretense.
**Simulator,** sim'ū-lāt-or, *n.* One who feigns.
**Simultaneous,** si-mul-tā'nē-us, *a.* Taking place or done at the same time.
**Sin,** sin, *n.* A transgression of the divine law; moral depravity; an offense in general.—*vi.* (sinning, sinned). To violate the divine law or any rule of duty.
**Sinapism,** sin'a-pizm, *n.* A mustard poultice.
**Since,** sins, *adv.* From that time; from then till now; ago.—*prep.* Ever from the time of; after.—*conj.* From the time when; because that.
**Sincere,** sin-sēr', *a.* Pure; unmixed; real; genuine; guileless; frank; true.
**Sincerely,** sin-sēr'li, *adv.* In a sincere manner; unfeignedly; genuinely; really.
**Sincerity,** sin-se'ri-ti, *n.* Honesty of mind or intention; freedom from hypocrisy.
**Sinciput,** sin'si-put, *n.* The fore part of the skull.
**Sine,** sīn, *n.* A geometrical line drawn from one end of an arc perpendicular to the diameter through the other end.
**Sinecure,** sī'nē-kūr, *n.* An ecclesiastical benefice without cure of souls; a paid office without employment.
**Sinew,** si'nū, *n.* The fibrous cord which unites a muscle to a bone; a tendon; strength.—*vt.* To bind, as by sinews; to strengthen.
**Sinewy,** si'nū-i, *a.* Consisting of a sinew or sinews; brawny; vigorous; firm.
**Sinful,** sin'ful, *a.* Full of sin; wicked; iniquitous; wrong.
**Sing,** sing, *vi.* (pret. sang, sung, pp. sung). To utter sounds with melodious modulations of voice; to have a ringing sensation.—*vt.* To utter with musical modulations of voice, to celebrate in song; to tell.
**Singe,** sinj, *vt.* (singeing, singed). To burn slightly; to burn the surface of.—*n.* A burning of the surface.
**Singer,** sing'ėr, *n.* One who sings; a bird that sings.
**Single,** sing'gl, *a.* Being one or a unit; individual; unmarried; performed by one person; simple; sincere.—*vt.* (singling, singled). To select individually; with *out.*
**Single-entry,** sing'gl-en-tri, *n.* A system of book-keeping in which each entry appears only once on one side or other of an account.
**Single-handed,** sing'gl-hand-ed, *a.* Unassisted; by one's own efforts.
**Single-minded,** sing'gl-mīnd-ed, *a.* Free from guile; honest; straightforward.
**Singly,** sing'gli, *adv.* In a single manner; individually; separately; sincerely.
**Sing-song,** sing'song, *n.* A drawling tone; repetition of similar words or tones.
**Singular,** sing'gū-lėr, *a.* That is single; expressing one person or thing; remarkable; rare; odd.—*n.* The singular number.
**Singularity,** sing-gū-la'ri-ti, *n.* Peculiarity; eccentricity.
**Singularly,** sing'gū-lėr-li, *adv.* Peculiarly; remarkably; oddly; so as to express one.
**Sinister,** si'nis-tėr, *a.* Left; evil; baneful; malign; unlucky.
**Sinistral,** si'nis-tral, *a.* Belonging to the left hand or side; sinistrous.
**Sinistrorse,** si'nis-trors, *a.* Directed to the left.
**Sink,** singk, *vi.* (pret. sank or sunk, pp. sunk). To descend in a liquid; to subside; to enter; to decline in worth, strength, etc.—*vt.* To immerse; to submerge; to make by digging; to depress; to degrade.—*n.* A receptacle for liquid filth; a sewer; place where iniquity is gathered.
**Sinker,** singk'ėr, *n.* One who sinks; a weight on some body to sink it.
**Sinking,** singk'ing, *a.* Causing to sink; depressing; set apart from the reduction of a debt.
**Sinless,** sin'les, *a.* Free from sin; innocent.
**Sinner,** sin'ėr, *n.* One who sins; a transgressor; offender; criminal.
**Sinn Fein,** shin fān, *n.* An Irish republican party, aiming at complete independence and separation, with the restoration of the old Irish tongue.
**Sinologue,** sin'o-log, *n.* A student of the Chinese language, literature, history, etc.
**Sinology,** si-nol'o-ji, *n.* The knowledge of the Chinese language, etc.
**Sinter,** sin'tėr, *n.* Stony matter precipitated by springs.
**Sinuate,** sin'ū-āt, *a.* Winding.
**Sinuosity,** sin-ū-os'i-ti, *n.* Quality of being sinuous; a curving; a wavy line.
**Sinuous,** sin'ū-us, *a.* Bending or curving in and out; crooked.
**Sinus,** sī'nus, *n.* A curved opening; a bay; a cavity containing pus; a fistula.
**Sinusitis,** sī-nū-zī'tis, *n.* Inflammation of one of the air-cavities of the skull connecting with the nose.
**Sip,** sip, *vt.* (sipping, sipped). To drink in small quantities; to drink out of.—*vi.* To take a fluid with the lips.—*n.* A small quantity of liquid taken with the lips.
**Siphon,** sī'fon, *n.* A bent tube used for drawing off liquids, as from a cask, etc.
**Siphon-bottle,** sī'fon-bot-l, *n.* A bottle for aerated waters, discharged through a bent tube by the pressure of the gas within.
**Sippet,** sip'et, *n.* A small sip; a small piece of bread served with soup, etc.
**Sir,** sėr, *n.* A word of respect used to men; title distinctive of knights and baronets.
**Sire,** sīr, *n.* A respectful word of address to a king; a father; male parent of a horse, etc.
**Siren,** sī'ren, *n.* A sea-nymph who enticed seamen by songs, and then slew them; a woman dangerous from her fascinations; a fog-signal; a signal used as an air-raid warning.—*a.* Bewitching.
**Sirius,** si'ri-us, *n.* The Dog-star.
**Sirloin,** sėr'loin, *n.* The upper part of a loin of beef; a loin of beef.
**Sirocco,** si-rok'kō, *n.* An oppressive south or south-east wind in Italy.
**Siskin,** sis'kin, *n.* A greenish European song-bird of the finch family.
**Sist,** sist, *vt.* In *Scots law,* to stop; to cite or summon.
**Sister,** sis'tėr, *n.* A female born of the same parents; a female of the same kind, society, etc.; a senior hospital nurse.
**Sisterhood,** sis'tėr-hud, *n.* State or condition of a sister; a society of females.
**Sister-in-law,** sis'tėr-in-la, *n.* A husband or wife's sister.
**Sisterly,** sis'tėr-li, *a.* Becoming a sister; affectionate.
**Sistrum,** sis'trum, *n.* A jingling metallic instrument used by the ancient Egyptians in the religious ceremonies.
**Sit,** sit, *vi.* (sitting, sat). To rest on the lower extremity of the body; to incubate; to remain; to be placed; to suit; to have a seat in Parliament,

S

etc.; to hold a session.—*vt*. To keep the seat upon (a horse, etc.).
**Site,** sīt, *n*. Situation; a plot of ground for building on.
**Sitology,** sī-tol'o-ji, *n*. Dietetics.
**Sitter,** sit'ėr, *n*. One who sits; one who sits for his portrait; a bird that incubates.
**Sitting,** sit'ing, *n*. Act of one who sits; occasion on which one sits for a portrait; session; seat in a church pew.
**Sitting-room,** sit'ing-röm, *n*. An apartment for sitting in; sufficient space for sitting in.
**Situate,** sit'ū-āt, *a*. Placed with respect to any other object.
**Situated,** sit'ū-āt-ed, *a*. Having a site or position; situate; circumstanced.
**Situation,** sit-ū-ā'shon, *n*. Position; station; plight; post or engagement.
**Sitz-bath,** sits-bäth, *n*. A bath in which one can bathe sitting; a bath taken in a sitting posture.
**Six,** siks, *a*. and *n*. One more than five.
**Sixfold,** siks'fōld, *a*. and *adv*. Six times.
**Sixpence,** siks'pens, *n*. An English silver coin.
**Sixpenny,** siks'pen-i, *a*. Worth sixpence.
**Sixteen,** siks'tēn, *a*. and *n*. Six and ten.
**Sixtennmo,** siks'tēn-mō, *n*. Sexto-decimo.
**Sixteenth,** siks'tēnth, *a*. The sixth after the tenth.—*n*. One of sixteen equal parts.
**Sixth,** siksth, *a*. Next after the fifth.—*n*. One part in six.
**Sixthly,** siksth'li, *adv*. In the sixth place.
**Sixtieth,** siks'ti-eth, *a*. and *n*. The next after fifty-ninth; one of sixty equal parts.
**Sixty,** siks'ti, *a*. and *n*. Six times ten.
**Sizable, Sizeable,** sīz'a-bl, *a*. Of considerable bulk; of reasonable size.
**Size,** sīz, *n*. Comparative magnitude; bigness; bulk; a glutinous substance used by painters, etc.—*vt*. (sizing, sized). To arrange according to size; to take the size of; to cover with size.
**Sized,** sīzd, *a*. Having a particular size.
**Sizer,** sīz'ėr, *n*. One who or that which sizes; a kind of gauge.
**Sizing,** sīz'ing, *n*. Size or weak glue; act of covering with size.
**Sizy,** sīz'i, *a*. Glutinous; ropy.
**Skain,** skān, *n*. A skein.
**Skate,** skāt, *n*. A narrow steel bar fastened under the foot, for moving rapidly on ice; a flat fish.—*vi*. (skating, skated). To slide on skates.
**Skater,** skāt'ėr, *n*. One who skates on ice.
**Skating-rink,** skāt'ing-ringk, *n*. A rink or prepared area for skating.
**Skein,** skān, *n*. A small hank of thread.
**Skeleton,** ske'le-ton, *n*. The bony framework of an animal; general structure or frame; outline.—*a*. Resembling a skeleton.
**Skeleton-key,** ske'le-ton-kē, *n*. A thin light key that opens various locks.
**Skerry,** ske'ri, *n*. A rocky isle; a rock.
**Sketch,** skech, *n*. An outline or general delineation; a first rough draft.—*vt*. To draw a sketch of; to give the chief points of; to plan.—*vi*. To practice sketching.
**Sketcher,** skech'ėr, *n*. One who sketches.
**Sketchy,** skech'i, *a*. Having the nature of a sketch; unfinished; incomplete.
**Skew,** skū, *a*. Oblique.—*adv*. Awry; obliquely.—*vt*. To put askew.
**Skew-bridge,** skū'brij, *n*. A bridge set obliquely over a road, etc.
**Skewer,** skū'ėr, *n*. A pin for fastening meat.—*vt*. To fasten with skewers.
**Ski,** skē, *n*. A long, narrow snow-shoe for running or travelling over snow.
**Skid,** skid, *n*. A drag for the wheels of a vehicle.—*vt*. (skidding, skidded). To check with a skid.—*vi*. To slip sideways on mud, ice, etc., as a cycle.
**Skiff,** skif, *n*. A small light boat.
**Skilful,** skil'ful, *a*. Skilled; dexterous; expert; clever.
**Skilfully,** skil'ful-li, *adv*. In a skilful manner; dexterously.
**Skill,** skil, *n*. Ability; knowledge united with dexterity; aptitude.
**Skilled,** skild, *a*. Having skill; expert.
**Skillet,** skil'et, *n*. A small vessel of metal, with a long handle, for heating water, etc.
**Skim,** skim, *vt*. (skimming, skimmed). To remove the scum from; to take off from a surface; to pass lightly over; to glance over superficially.—*vi*. To glide along.
**Skimmer,** skim'ėr, *n*. A utensil for skimming liquors; an aquatic swimming bird.
**Skim-milk,** skim'milk, *n*. Milk from which the cream has been taken.
**Skimming,** skim'ing, *n*. Act of one who skims a liquid; scum removed.
**Skin,** skin, *n*. The natural outer coating of animals; a hide; bark; rind.—*vt*. (skinning, skinned). To strip the skin from; to cover superficially.—*vi*. To be covered with skin.
**Skin-deep,** skin'dēp, *a*. Superficial; slight.
**Skinflint,** skin'flint, *n*. A niggard.
**Skink,** skingk, *n*. A small lizard of Egypt, etc.
**Skinner,** skin'ėr, *n*. One who skins; one who deals in skins, pelts, or hides; a furrier.
**Skinny,** skin'i, *a*. Consisting of skin or nearly so; wanting flesh.
**Skip,** skip, *vi*. (skipping, skipped). To leap lightly; to bound; to spring.—*vt*. To pass with a bound; to omit.—*n*. A light leap; a large basket on wheels, used in mines.
**Skipper,** skip'ėr, *n*. The master of a merchant vessel; a sea-captain; the cheese maggot.
**Skipping,** skip'ing, *a*. Frisky; bounding.
**Skipping-rope,** skip'ing-rōp, *n*. A small rope swung by young persons under their feet and over their heads in play.
**Skirmish,** skėr'mish, *n*. A slight battle; a brief contest.—*vi*. To fight in short contests or in small parties.
**Skirt,** skėrt, *n*. The lower and loose part of a garment; border; a woman's garment like a petticoat.—*vt*. To border.—*vi*. To be on the border.
**Skit,** skit, *n*. A satirical or sarcastic attack; a pasquinade; a squib.
**Skittish,** skit'ish, *a*. Timorous; wanton; frisky; hasty; fickle.
**Skittles,** skit'lz, *n.pl*. A game with nine pins set upright, to be knocked down with as few throws as possible of a ball.
**Skiver,** skī'vėr, *n*. An inferior leather made of split sheep-skin.
**Skulk,** skulk, *vi*. To lurk; to sneak out of the way; to shun doing one's duty.
**Skulk, Skulker,** skulk, skulk'ėr, *n*. A person who skulks or avoids duties.
**Skull,** skul, *n*. The bony case which contains the brain.
**Skull-cap,** skul'kap, *n*. A cap fitting closely to the head.
**Skunk,** skungk, *n*. An animal of the weasel family, with glands that emit a fetid fluid.
**Sky,** skī, *n*. The apparent arch of the heavens; the region of clouds; climate.
**Skylark,** skī'lärk, *n*. The common lark that mounts and sings as it flies.
**Skylarking,** skī'lärk-ing, *n*. Gambols in the rigging of a ship; frolicking of any kind.
**Sky-light,** skī'līt, *n*. A window in the roof of a building.
**Skyward,** skī'wėrd, *a*. and *adv*. Toward the sky.
**Slab,** slab, *n*. A thin flat piece of anything, as marlbe.—*a*. Thick and slimy.
**Slack,** slak, *a*. Not tight or tense; loose; remiss; backward; not busy.—*adv*. In a slack manner; partially; insufficiently.—*n*. The part of a rope that hangs loose; small broken coal.—*vt*. and *i*. To slacken; to slake.
**Slacken,** slak'n, *vi*. To become slack; to abate; to flag.—*vt*. To lessen the tension of; to relax.
**Slackly,** slak'li, *adv*. In a slack manner; loosely; negligently; remissly.
**Slag,** slag, *n*. The scoria from a smelting furnace

or volcano; fused dross of metal.
**Slaggy,** slag'i, *a.* Pertaining to or like slag.
**Slake,** slāk, *vt.* (slaking, slaked). To quench, as thirst or rage; to extinguish.—*vi.* To abate; to become extinct.—*n.* A muddy tract adjoining the sea.
**Slam,** slam, *vt.* and *i.* (slamming, slammed). To shut with violence; to bang.—*n.* A violent shutting of a door.
**Slander,** slan'dėr, *n.* A false report maliciously uttered; defamation.—*vt.* To defame; to calumniate.
**Slanderer,** slan'dėr-ėr, *n.* One who slanders; a defamer; a calumniator.
**Slanderous,** slan'dėr-us, *a.* Containing slander; that utters slander; defamatory.
**Slang,** slang, *n.* and *a.* A class of expressions not generally approved of, as being inelegant or undignified.—*vt.* To address with slang; to abuse vulgarly.
**Slant,** slant, *a.* Sloping.—*vt.* and *i.* To turn from a direct line; to slope; to incline.—*n.* A slope.
**Slap,** slap, *n.* A blow with the open hand, or something broad.—*vt.* (slapping, slapped). To strike with the open hand.—*adv.* With a sudden and violent blow.
**Slap-dash,** slap'dash, *adv.* All at once; offhand; at random.
**Slash,** slash, *vt.* To cut by striking violently and at random.—*vi.* To strike violently and at random with a cutting instrument.—*n.* A long cut; a cut made at random.
**Slashed,** slasht', *p.a.* Cut with a slash; having long narrow openings, as a sleeve.
**Slat,** slat, *n.* A narrow strip of wood.
**Slate,** slāt, *n.* Rock which splits into thin layers; a slab of smooth stone for covering buildings; a tablet for writing upon.—*vt.* (slating, slated). To cover with slates; to criticize severely.
**Slating,** slāt'ing, *n.* Act of covering with slates; the cover thus put on; severe criticism.
**Slattern,** slat'ėrn, *n.* A female who is not tidy; a slut.—*a.* Slatternly.
**Slatternly,** slat'ėrn-li, *a.* Like a slattern; slovenly; sluttish.
**Slaughter,** sla'tėr, *n.* A slaying; carnage; massacre; a killing of beasts for market.—*vt.* To slay; to kill for the market.
**Slaughter-house,** sla'tėr-hous, *n.* A place where beasts are killed for the market.
**Slaughterous,** sla'tėr-us, *a.* Murderous.
**Slav, Slavonian,** släv, sla-vō'ni-an, *n.* One of a race of Eastern Europe, comprising the Russians, Poles, Bohemians, Bulgarians, etc.
**Slave,** slāv, *n.* A person wholly subject to another; a bondman; drudge.—*vi.* (slaving, slaved). To labor as a slave.
**Slave-driver,** slāv'drīv-ėr, *n.* An overseer of slaves; a severe or cruel master.
**Slaver,** slā'vėr, *n.* A person or vessel engaged in the slave-trade.
**Slaver,** sla'vėr, *n.* Saliva drivelling from the mouth; drivel.—*vi.* To suffer the saliva to issue from the mouth.—*vt.* To smear with saliva.
**Slaverer,** sla'vėr-ėr, *n.* One who slavers; a driveller.
**Slavery,** slāv'ė-ri, *n.* State of a slave; bondage; servitude; drudgery.
**Slave-trade,** slāv'trād, *n.* The business of purchasing or kidnapping men and women, and selling them for slaves.
**Slavic, Slavonic, Slavonian,** slav'ik, sla-von'ik, sla-vō'ni-an, *a.* Pertaining to the Slavs, or to their language.
**Slavish,** slāv'ish, *a.* Pertaining to slaves; servile; mean; oppressively laborious.
**Slavishly,** slāv'ish-li, *adv.* In a slavish manner; servilely; meanly.
**Slay,** slā, *vt.* (pret. slew, pp. slain). To kill by violence; to murder; to destroy.
**Slayer,** slā'ėr, *n.* One who slays; murderer.
**Sleazy,** slē'zi, *a.* Thin; flimsy; wanting firmness of texture, as silk. Also *Sleezy.*
**Sled,** sled, *n.* A sledge.—*vt.* (sledding, sledded). To convey on a sled.
**Sledge, Sledge-hammer,** slej, slej'ham-ėr,*n.* A large, heavy hammer, used by iron-workers.
**Sledge,** slej, *n.* A vehicle on runners used over snow or ice; a sleigh.—*vt.* and *i.* To convey or travel in a sledge.
**Sleek,** slēk, *a.* Smooth and glossy.—*vt.* To make smooth and glossy.
**Sleeky,** slēk'i, *a.* Of a sleek appearance.
**Sleep,** slēp, *vi.* (sleeping, slept). To take rest by a suspension of voluntary exercise of the powers of body and mind; to be dormant or inactive.—*vt.* To pass in sleeping; to get rid of by sleeping; with *off.*—*n.* That state in which volition is suspended; slumber; death; dormant state.
**Sleeper,** slēp'ėr, *n.* One that sleeps; a timber supporting a weight; in railways, a beam of wood supporting the rails.
**Sleeping,** slēp'ing, *a.* Reposing in sleep; pertaining to sleep; causing sleep.—**Sleeping sickness,** *n.* A tropical African disease due to microscopic animals introduced into the blood by the bites of tsetse flies.
**Sleepless,** slēp'les, *a.* Without sleep; wakeful; having no rest; perpetually agitated.
**Sleepy,** slēp'i, *a.* Inclined to sleep; drowsy; lazy; sluggish.
**Sleet,** slēt, *n.* Hail or snow mingled with rain.—*vi.* To snow or hail with rain.
**Sleety,** slēt'i, *a.* Consisting of or like sleet.
**Sleeve,** slēv, *n.* That part of a garment covering the arm.—*vt.* (sleeving, sleeved). To furnish with sleeves.
**Sleeveless,** slēv'les, *a.* Having no sleeves; wanting a pretext; bootless.
**Sleigh,** slā, *n.* A vehicle on runners for transporting persons on snow or ice.
**Sleight,** slīt, *n.* A sly artifice; an artful trick; dexterity.
**Slender,** slen'dėr, *a.* Thin; slim; slight; feeble; meager; scanty.
**Slew,** slö, *vt.* To slue. Pret. of *slay.*
**Sley,** slā, *n.* A weaver's reed.
**Slice,** slīs, *vt.* (slicing, sliced). To cut into thin pieces; to divide.—*n.* A thin, broad piece cut off; a broad flat utensil.
**Slide,** slīd, *vi.* (sliding, pret. slid, pp. slid, slidden). To move along a surface by slipping; to pass smoothly or gradually.—*vt.* To thrust smoothly along a surface.—*n.* A smooth and easy passage; that part of an apparatus which slides into place.
**Slider,** slīd'ėr, *n.* One who slides; part of an instrument that slides.
**Sliding,** slīd'ing, *a.* Make so as to slide freely; fitted for sliding.—*n.* The act of one who slides; lapse; backsliding.
**Sliding-scale,** slīd'ing-skāl, *n.* A sliding-rule; a varying rate of payment.
**Slight,** slīt, *a.* Small; trifling; not thorough; slender; frail.—*n.* Intentional disregard.—*vt.* To disregard; to treat with disrespect.
**Slightly,** slīt'li, *adv.* In a slight manner or measure; but little; somewhat; slenderly.
**Slim,** slim, *a.* Slight; slender; thin; flimsy; cunning.—*vi.* To reduce weight by means of dieting.
**Slime,** slīm, *n.* A soft or glutinous substance; moist earth or mud; viscous substance exuded by certain animals.—*vt.* (sliming, slimed). To cover with slime; to make slimy.
**Slimy,** slīm'i, *a.* Abounding with slime; consisting of slime; viscous; glutinous.
**Sling,** sling, *vt.* (slinging, slung). To throw; to hang so as to swing; to place in a sling.—*n.* An instrument for throwing stones; a bandage to support a wounded limb; a rope for raising heavy articles.
**Slinger,** sling'ėr, *n.* One who uses the sling.
**Slink,** slingk, *vi.* (slinking, slunk). To sneak; to steal away.—*vt.* To cast prematurely.—*n.* A premature calf.

**Slip,** slip, *vi.* (slipping, slipped). To move smoothly along; to glide; to depart secretly; to have the feet slide; to err; to escape insensibly.—*vt.* To put or thrust secretly; to omit; to disengage oneself from; to make a slip of for planting.—*n.* A sliding of the feet; an unintentional error; a twig cut for planting or grafting; a long narrow piece; a leash by which a dog is held; a long strip of printed matter; a loose covering; an inclined plane upon which a ship is built.

**Slipper,** slip'ėr, *n.* One who slips or lets slip; a loose light shoe for household wear.

**Slippery,** slip'ėr-i, *a.* So smooth as to cause slipping; untrustworthy; uncertain.

**Slipshod,** slip'shod, *a.* Shod with slippers; having shoes down at heel; slovenly.

**Slipslop,** slip'slop, *n.* Bad liquor; feeble composition.—*a.* Feeble; poor; jejune.

**Slit,** slit, *vi.* (slitting, slit or slitted). To cut lengthwise; to cut into long strips.—*n.* A long cut or opening.

**Slitter,** slit'ėr, *n.* One who or that which slits.

**Sliver,** sli'vėr, or slī'vėr, *vt.* To cleave; to cut into long thin pieces.—*n.* A long piece cut off; a splinter.

**Slobber,** slob'ėr, *vi.* and *t.* To slaver; to slabber.—*n.* Slaver; liquor spilled.

**Slobbery,** slob'ėr-i, *a.* Moist; sloppy.

**Sloe,** slō, *n.* A British shrub of the plum genus, the blackthorn; also its fruit.

**Slogan,** slō'gan, *n.* A war-cry; a watchword.

**Sloop,** slöp, *n.* A vessel with one mast, hardly different from a cutter.

**Slop,** slop, *vt.* (slopping, slopped). To soil by liquid; to spill.—*n.* Water carelessly thrown about; a smock-frock; *pl.* mean liquid food; waste dirty water; wide breeches; ready-made clothing.

**Slope,** slōp, *n.* An oblique direction; a declivity.—*vt.* and *i.* (sloping, sloped). To form with a slope; to incline.

**Sloppy,** slop'i, *a.* Muddy; plashy; slovenly.

**Slopy,** slōp'i, *a.* Sloping.

**Slot,** slot, *n.* A bolt or bar; an oblong hole; track of a deer.—*vt.* (slotting, slotted). To make a slot in.

**Sloth,** slōth or sloth, *n.* Indolence; laziness; idleness; a South American mammal.

**Slothful,** slōth'ful or sloth', *a.* Addicted to sloth; sluggish; lazy; indolent.

**Slouch,** slouch, *n.* A stoop in walking; an ungainly gait; a droop.—*vi.* To hang down; to have a drooping gait.—*vt.* To cause to hang down.

**Slouch-hat,** slouch'hat, *n.* A hat with a hanging brim; a soft hat.

**Slouching,** slouch'ing, *a.* Drooping downward; walking heavily and awkwardly.

**Slough,** slou, *n.* A place of deep mud; a hole full of mire.

**Slough,** sluf, *n.* The cast-off skin of a serpent, etc.; the dead flesh that separates from living parts in a wound, etc.—*vi.* To come off as a slough from the living parts.

**Sloughy,** sluf'i, *a.* Resembling dead matter separating from a wound.

**Sloven,** slu'ven, *n.* A man habitually negligent of neatness and order.

**Slovenly,** slu'ven-li, *a.* Disorderly; not neat or tidy.—*adv.* In a negligent manner.

**Slow,** slō, *a.* Moving little in a long time; not rapid; dilatory; heavy in wit; dull; behind in time.—*vt.* and *i.* To delay; to slacken in speed.

**Slowly,** slō'li, *adv.* In a slow manner; tardily; gradually.

**Sloyd,** sloid, *n.* A system of manual training for schools, originating in Sweden.

**Slub,** slub, *n.* A roll of wool drawn out and slightly twisted by spinning machinery.

**Slubber,** slub'ėr, *vt.* To slobber; to soil; to do lazily or carelessly.

**Sludge,** sluj, *n.* Mire; soft mud.

**Sludgy,** sluj'i, *a.* Miry; slushy.

**Slue,** slö, *vt.* (sluing, slued). To turn or swing round (as the yard of a ship).

**Slug,** slug, *n.* A sluggard; a shell-less snail injurious to plants; a piece of metal used for the charge of a gun.

**Sluggard,** slug'ärd, *n.* A person habitually lazy; a drone.—*a.* Sluggish.

**Sluggish,** slug'ish, *a.* Lazy; slothful; inert; not quick.

**Sluice,** slös, *n.* A contrivance to control the flow of water in a river, dam, etc.; a trough to separate gold from sand, etc.; flood-gate.—*vt.* (sluicing, sluiced). To wet abundantly; to cleanse by means of sluices.

**Slum,** slum, *n.* A low, dirty street of a city.—*vi.* (slumming, slummed). To visit slums from benevolent motives.

**Slumber,** slum'bėr, *vi.* To sleep; to be inert or inactive.—*n.* Light sleep; repose.

**Slumberous, Slumbrous,** slum'bėr-us, slum'brus, *a.* Inviting or causing sleep.

**Slump,** slump, *n.* The whole number taken in one lot; a sudden fall in prices or values.—*vt.* To throw into one lot.—*vi.* To sink in walking, as in snow.

**Slung,** slung, pret. & pp. of *sling.*

**Slunk,** slungk, pret. & pp. of *slink.*

**Slur,** slėr, *vt.* (slurring, slurred). To soil; to traduce; to pass lightly over; to pronounce in a careless indistinct manner.—*n.* A slight reproach; a stain or stigma.

**Slush,** slush, *n.* Sludge or soft mud; wet, half-melted snow.

**Slushy,** slush'i, *a.* Consisting of slush; resembling slush.

**Slut,** slut, *n.* A woman negligent of tidiness and dress; a slattern.

**Sluttish,** slut'ish, *a.* Not neat or cleanly.

**Sly,** slī, *a.* Cunning; crafty; wily; shrewd.

**Slyly,** slī'li, *adv.* Cunningly; craftily.

**Slyness,** slī'nes, *n.* Artful secrecy; cunning; craftiness.

**Smack,** smak, *vi.* To make a sharp noise with the lips; to taste; to savor.—*vt.* To make a sharp noise with; to slap.—*n.* A loud kiss; a sharp noise; a smart blow; a slap; a slight taste; a smattering; a fishing-vessel.

**Small,** smal, *a.* Little; petty; short; weak; gentle; not loud; narrow-minded; mean.—*n.* The small part of a thng; *pl.* small-clothes.

**Small-arms,** smal'ärmz, *n.pl.* A general name for rifles, pistols, etc., as distinguished from cannon.

**Small-pox,** smal'poks, *n.* A contagious eruptive disease.

**Smalt,** smalt, *n.* Common glass tinged to a fine deep-blue by cobalt.

**Smart,** smärt, *n.* A quick, keen pain; pungent grief.—*a.* Keen; quick; sharp; brisk; witty; spruce; well dressed.—*vt.* To feel a sharp pain; to be acutely painful; to be punished.

**Smarten,** smärt'n, *vt.* To make smart.

**Smartly,** smärt'li, *adv.* Keenly; briskly; sharply; wittily; sprucely.

**Smash,** smash, *vt.* To dash to pieces.—*vi.* To go to pieces.—*n.* A breaking to pieces; ruin; bankruptcy.

**Smatter,** smat'ėr, *vi.* To have a slight knowledge; to talk superficially.—*n.* A superficial knowledge.

**Smatterer,** smat'ėr-ėr, *n.* One who has only a superficial knowledge.

**Smattering,** smat'ėr-ing, *n.* A superficial knowledge.

**Smear,** smēr, *vt.* To overspread with anything adhesive; to daub; to soil.

**Smell,** smel, *vt.* (smelling, smelled ). To perceive by the nose; to perceive the scent of; to detect.—*vi.* To give out an odor.—*n.* The faculty by which odors are perceived; scent; perfume.

**Smelling,** smel'ing, *n.* The sense of smell.

**Smelling-salts,** smel'ing-saltz, *n.pl.* Volatile salts used as a stimulant.

**Smelt,** smelt, *vt.* To melt, as ore, to separate the metal.—*n.* A small fish allied to the salmon.

**Smelter,** smelt'ėr, *n.* One who smelts ore.
**Smeltery,** smelt'ė-ri, *n.* A place for smelting ores.
**Smew,** smū, *n.* A swimming bird of the merganser family.
**Smile,** smīl, *vi.* (smiling, smiled). To show pleasure, sarcasm, pity, etc., by a look; to appear propitious.—*vt.* To express by a smile; to affect by smiling.—*n.* A set of the features expressing pleasure, scorn, etc.; favor.
**Smiling,** smīl'ing, *p.a.* Wearing a smile; gay in aspect.
**Smirch,** smėrch, *vt.* To stain; to smudge.
**Smirk,** smėrk, *vi.* To smile affectedly or pertly.—*n.* An affected smile.
**Smite,** smīt, *vt.* (smiting, pret. smote, pp. smit, smitten). To strike; to slay; to blast; to afflict; to affect with love, etc.—*vi.* To strike; to clash together.
**Smith,** smith, *n.* One who works in metals.
**Smithery,** smith'ė-ri, *n.* The workshop of a smith; a smithy; work done by a smith.
**Smithy,** smith'i, *n.* The shop of a smith.
**Smock,** smok, *n.* A chemise; a smock-frock.—*vt.* To clothe with a smock; to pucker diagonally.
**Smocking,** smok'ing, *n.* An ornamental diagonal puckering, in form of a honey-comb, and capable of being expanded.
**Smoke,** smōk, *n.* The exhalation from a burning substance; vapor; idle talk; nothingness; a drawing in and puffing out of tobacco fumes.—*vi.* (smoking, smoked). To emit smoke; to use tobacco.—*vt.* To apply smoke to; to befoul by smoke; to fumigate; to use in smoking.
**Smokeless,** smōk'les, *a.* Having no smoke.
**Smoker,** smōk'ėr, *n.* One who smokes; one who uses tobacco.
**Smoking,** smōk'ing, *n.* Act of one who or that which smokes; the use of tobacco.—*a.* Pertaining to smoking.
**Smoky,** smōk'i, *a.* Emitting smoke; filled or tarnished with smoke; like smoke.
**Smolt,** smōlt, *n.* A salmon a year or two old, when it has acquired its silvery scales.
**Smooth,** smōTH, *a.* Even on the surface; glossy; moving equably; not harsh; bland.—*n.* Smooth part of anything.—*vt.* To make smooth; to level; to make easy; to palliate; to soothe.
**Smoothen,** smōTH'n, *vt.* To make smooth.
**Smoothly,** smōTH'li, *adv.* Evenly; not roughly; blandly; with insinuating language.
**Smote,** smōt, pret. of *smite.*
**Smother,** smuTH'ėr, *n.* Stifling smoke; suffocating dust.—*vt.* To stifle; to suffocate; to suppress.—*vi.* To be suffocated or suppressed; to smoulder.
**Smothery,** smuTH'ėr-i, *a.* Tending to smother; stifling; full of smother or dust.
**Smoulder,** smōl'dėr, *vi.* To burn and smoke without flame; to exist in a suppressed state.
**Smudge,** smuj, *vt.* (smudging, smudged). To stain with dirt or filth; to smear.—*n.* A stain; a smear.
**Smug,** smug, *a.* Neat; spruce; affectedly nice.—*vt.* (smugging, smugged). To make smug.
**Smuggle,** smug'l, *vt.* (smuggling, smuggled). To import or export secretly and in defiance of law; to convey clandestinely.
**Smuggler,** smug'lėr, *n.* One who smuggles; a vessel employed in smuggling goods.
**Smuggling,** smug'ling, *n.* The importing or exporting secretly goods subject to duty.
**Smut,** smut, *n.* A spot or stain; a spot of soot, etc.; a disease in grain; obscene language.—*vt.* and *i.* (smutting, smutted). To stain with smut; to tarnish.
**Smutch,** smuch, *vt.* To smudge.—*n.* A foul spot; a smudge.
**Smutty,** smut'i, *a.* Soiled with smut; affected with mildew; obscene.
**Snack,** snak, *n.* A small portion of food; a hasty repast; a bite; a share.
**Snaffle,** snaf'l, *n.* A bridle consisting of a slender bitmouth without a curb.—*vt.* To bridle; to manage with a snaffle.
**Snag,** snag, *n.* A short projecting stump; a shoot; the tine of a deer's antler; a tree in a river dangerous to vessels.
**Snail,** snāl, *n.* A slimy, slow-creeping mollusk; a slug; a sluggard.
**Snake,** snāk, *n.* A serpent.
**Snaky,** snāk'i, *a.* Pertaining to a snake; cunning; insinuating; infested with snakes.
**Snap,** snap, *vt.* (snapping, snapped). To bite or seize suddenly; to break with a sharp sound; to break short.—*vi.* To try to seize with the teeth; to break suddenly or without bending.—*n.* A quick eager bite; a sudden breaking; a sharp noise; a kind of biscuit.
**Snap-shot,** snap'shot, *n.* A hasty shot at a moving animal; a photograph taken hastily with a hand camera.
**Snare,** snār, *n.* A line with a noose for catching animals; anything that entraps.—*vt.* (snaring, snared). To catch with a snare; to ensnare.
**Snarl,** snärl, *vi.* To growl, as an angry dog; to talk in rude murmuring terms.—*vt.* To entangle.—*n.* A sharp angry growl; a knot; embarrassment.
**Snarling,** snärl'ing, *a.* Given to snarl; growling; snappish; peevish.
**Snary,** snār'i, *a.* Tending to ensnare.
**Snatch,** snach, *vt.* To seize hastily or abruptly.—*vi.* To make a grasp.—*n.* A hasty catch; a short fit or turn; a small portion; a snack.
**Sneak,** snēk, *vt.* To creep privately; to go furtively; to crouch.—*n.* A mean fellow; one guilty of underhand work.
**Sneaking,** snēk'ing, *p.a.* Pertaining to a sneak; mean; servile; underhand.
**Sneaky,** snēk'i, *a.* Mean; underhand.
**Sneer,** snēr, *vi.* To show contempt by a look; to jeer; to speak derisively.—*n.* A look or grin of contempt; a scoff; a jeer.
**Sneeze,** snēz, *vi.* (sneezing, sneezed). To emit air through the nose, etc., by a kind of involuntary convulsive effort.—*n.* A single act of sneezing.
**Snick,** snik, *vt.* To cut; to clip; to snip.
**Sniff,** snif, *vi.* To draw air audibly up the nose; to snuff.—*n.* A slight smell; snuff.
**Snigger,** snig'ėr, *vi.* To laugh in a suppressed manner.—*n.* A suppressed laugh; a giggle.
**Snip,** snip, *vt.* (snipping, snipped). To cut off at a stroke with shears; to clip.—*n.* A single cut with shears; a bit cut off.
**Snipe,** snīp, *n.* A grallatorial bird with a long bill; a simpleton.—*vi.* To shoot singly at the enemy, generally from specially constructed cover and with a specially sighted rifle.
**Snippet,** snip'et, *n.* A small part or share.
**Snivel,** sni'vel, *vi.* (snivelling, snivelled). To run at the nose; to whimper.—*n.* Whimpering; maudlin sentiment.
**Snivelling,** sni'vel-ing, *p.a.* Apt to snivel or whine; tearful; weakly sentimental.
**Snivelly,** sni'vel-i, *a.* Running at the nose; pitiful; whining.
**Snob,** snob, *n.* A shoemaker; one who apes gentility; a would-be aristocrat.
**Snobbery,** snob'ėr-i, *n.* The quality of being snobbish.
**Snobbish, Snobby,** snob'ish, snob'i, *a.* Like a snob; pretending to gentility.
**Snobbism,** snob'izm, *n.* The manners of a snob; state or habit of being snobbish.
**Snood,** snöd, *n.* A fillet or ribbon for the hair.
**Snooze,** snöz, *n.* A nap or short sleep.—*vi.* (snoozing, snoozed). To take a short nap.
**Snore,** snōr, *vi.* (snoring, snored). To breathe with a rough, hoarse noise in sleep.—*n.* A breathing with a hoarse noise in sleep.
**Snort,** snort, *vi.* To force air with violence through the nose.—*n.* A loud sound produced by forcing the air through the nostrils.
**Snout,** snout, *n.* The projecting nose of a beast; muzzle; nozzle.
**Snow,** snō, *n.* Watery particles congealed in the air, and falling in flakes.—*vi.* To fall in snow; used impersonally.—*vt.* To scatter like snow.
**Snow-ball,** snō'bal, *n.* A ball of snow.—*vt.* To pelt

with snow-balls.—*vi.* To throw snow-balls.
**Snowberry,** snō'be-ri, *n.* A shrub bearing fruits of snow-white berries.
**Snowdrop,** snō'drop, *n.* An early plant with white drooping flowers.
**Snow-plow,** snō'plou, *n.* An implement for clearing away the snow from roads, etc.
**Snow-shoe,** snō'shö, *n.* A light frame worn on each foot to keep the wearer from sinking in snow; a snow-boot.
**Snub,** snub, *vt.* (snubbing, snubbed). To stop or rebuke with a tart, sarcastic remark; to slight designedly.—*n.* A check; a rebuke.
**Snub-nose,** snub'nōz, *n.* A flat nose.
**Snuff,** snuf, *vt.* To draw up through the nose; to smell; to crop, as the snuff of a candle.—*vi.* To draw up air or tobacco through the nose; to take offense.—*n.* A drawing up through the nose; resentment; burned wick of a candle; pulverized tobacco.
**Snuffer,** snuf'ėr, *n.* One who snuffs; *pl.* instrument for removing the snuff of a candle.
**Snuffle,** snuf'l, *vi.* (snuffling, snuffled). To speak through the nose; to breathe hard through the nose.—*n.* A sound made by air drawn through the nostrils; nasal twang; *pl.* an ailment accompanied by snuffling with the nose.
**Snuffy,** snuf'i, *a.* Pertaining to or like snuff; soiled with snuff.
**Snug,** snug, *a.* Neat; trim; cozy.
**Snuggery,** snug'ė-ri, *n.* A snug place.
**Snuggle,** snug'l, *vi.* (snuggling, snuggled). To lie close for convenience or warmth; to nestle.
**Snugly,** snug'li, *adv.* Comfortably; safely.
**So,** sō, *adv.* In this or that manner; to that degree; thus; extremely; very; the case being such; thereby.—*conj.* Provided that; in case that; therefore; accordingly.
**Soak,** sōk, *vt.* To let lie in a fluid till the substance has imbibed all that it can; to steep; to wet thoroughly.—*vi.* To steep; to enter by pores; to tipple.
**Soaker,** sōk'ėr, *n.* One who soaks; a hard drinker.
**Soaking,** sōk'ing, *p.a.* Such as to soak; that wets thoroughly; drenching.
**Soaky,** sōk'i, *a.* Moist on the surface; steeped in or drenched with water.
**So-and-so,** sō'and-sō, *n.* A certain person not named; an indefinite person or thing.
**Soap,** sōp, *n.* A compound of oil or fat with an alkali, used in washing.—*vt.* To rub or cover with soap.
**Soapy,** sōp'i, *a.* Resembling soap; smeared with soap; unctuous.
**Soar,** sōr, *vi.* To mount upon the wing; to rise high; to tower.—*n.* A towering flight; a lofty ascent.
**Sob,** sob, *vi.* (sobbing, sobbed). To sigh or weep convulsively; to make a similar sound.—*n.* A convulsive catching of the breath in weeping or sorrow.
**Sober,** sō'bėr, *a.* Temperate; not drunk; calm; cool; staid; grave; dull-looking.—*vt.* To make sober.—*vi.* To become sober.
**Soberly,** sō'bėr-li, *adv.* Temperately; coolly; gravely.
**Sobriety,** sō-brī'e-ti, *n.* Temperance; abstemiousness; moderation; saneness; sedateness; gravity.
**Sobriquet,** so-brē-kā, *n.* A nickname.
**Sociability,** sō'shi-a-bil''i-ti, *n.* Quality of being sociable.
**Sociable,** sō'shi-a-bl, *a.* Fond of companions; inclined to mix in society; social.
**Sociably,** sō'shi-a-bli, *adv.* In a sociable manner; conversably; familiarly.
**Social,** sō'shal, *a.* Pertaining to society; sociable; consisting in union or mutual converse; living in communities.
**Socialism,** sō'shal-izm, *n.* A theory of social organization aiming at co-operative action and community of property.
**Socialist,** sō'shal-ist, *n.* One who advocates socialism; a collectivist.
**Socialistic,** sō-shal-is'tik, *a.* Pertaining to socialism.
**Sociality,** sō-shal'i-ti, *n.* Sociability.
**Socialize,** sō'shal-īz, *vt.* To render social; to regulate according to socialism.
**Socially,** sō'shal-li, *adv.* In a social manner or way; in regard to social position.
**Society,** sō-sī'e-ti, *n.* Fellowship; company; a body of persons united for some object; persons living in the same circle; those who take the lead in social life.
**Socinian,** sō-sin'i-an, *n.* One who rejects the doctrine of the Trinity, the deity of Christ, and the atonement, etc.
**Sociologist,** sō-shi-ol'o-jist, *n.* One versed in sociology.
**Sociology,** sō-shi-ol'o-ji, *n.* The science which treats of society, its development, the progress of civilization, etc.
**Sock,** sok, *n.* The shoe of the ancient actors of comedy; a short woven covering for the foot.
**Socket,** sok'et, *n.* A cavity into which anything is fitted.
**Socle,** so'kl, *n.* A plain, low pedestal; a plain face or plinth at the lower part of a wall.
**Sod,** sod, *n.* That layer of earth which is covered with grass; piece of turf.
**Soda,** sō'da, *n.* The alkali carbonate of sodium used in washing, glass-making, etc., and extensively made from salt.
**Sodality,** sō-dal'i-ti, *n.* A fellowship or fraternity.
**Soda-water,** sō'da-wa'tėr, *n.* An effervescent drink generally consisting of water into which carbonic acid has been forced.
**Sodden,** sod'n, *a.* Seethed; saturated; soaked and soft; not well baked; doughy.
**Soddy,** sod'i, *a.* Turfy; covered with sod.
**Sodium,** sō'di-um, *n.* A soft light silvery metal.
**Sodomite,** sod'om-īt, *n.* One guilty of sodomy.
**Sodomy,** sod'om-i, *n.* A carnal copulation against nature.
**Sofa,** sō'fa, *n.* A long seat with a stuffed bottom, back, and ends.
**Soffit,** sof'it, *n.* The lower surface of an arch, architrave, or overhanging cornice, etc.
**Soft,** soft, *a.* Easily yielding to pressure; delicate; mild; effeminate; not loud or harsh; not strong or glaring.—*adv.* Softly.—*interj.* Be soft; stop; not so fast.
**Soften,** sof'n, *vt.* To make soft or more soft; to mollify; to alleviate; to tone down.—*vi.* To become soft; to relent; to become milder.
**Softening,** sof'n-ing, *n.* Act of making or becoming more soft or softer.
**Softly,** soft'li, *adv.* In a soft manner; gently; quietly; mildly; tenderly.
**Soft-spoken,** soft'spō-kn, *a.* Speaking softly; mild; affable.
**Soho,** sō-hō', *interj.* A word used in calling; a sportman's halloo.
**Soi-disant,** swa-dē-zäng, *a.* Self-styled; pretended; would-be.
**Soil,** soil, *vt.* To sully; to tarnish; to manure; to feed (cattle) indoors with green fodder.—*vi.* To tarnish.—*n.* Dirt; ordure; tarnish; the upper stratum of the earth; mould; loam; earth; land; country.
**Soiree,** swa'rā, *n.* A meeting of some body at which there are tea and other refreshments, with music, speeches, etc.
**Sojourn,** sō'jėrn, *vi.* To reside for a time.—*n.* A temporary residence or stay.
**Sojourner,** sō'jėrn-ėr, *n.* One who sojourns; a temporary resident.
**Solace,** so'lās, *vt.* (solacing, solaced). To cheer or console; to allay.—*n.* Consolation; comfort; relief; recreation.
**Solar,** sō'lėr, *a.* Pertaining to the sun, or proceeding from it; sunny; measured by the progress of the sun.
**Solatium,** sō-lā'shi-um, *n.* A compensation in money.
**Solder,** sol'dėr, *vt.* To unite metals by a fused me-

tallic substance; to patch up.—*n*. A metallic cement.

**Soldier,** sōl'jėr, *n*. A man in military service; a man of distinguished valor.

**Soldiering,** sōl'jėr-ing, *n*. The occupation of a soldier.

**Soldier-like, Soldierly,** sōl'jėr-līk, sōl'jėr-li, *a*. Like or becoming a soldier; brave.

**Soldiery,** sōl'jė-ri, *n*. Soldiers collectively; the body of military men.

**Sole,** sōl, *n*. The under side of the foot; the bottom of a shoe; a marine fish allied to the flounder.—*vt*. (soling, soled). To furnish with a sole, as a shoe.—*a*. Single; individual; only; alone.

**Solecism,** so'le-sizm, *n*. A grammatical error; deviation from correct idiom.

**Solecize,** so'le-sīz, *vi*. To commit solecism.

**Solely,** sōl'li, *adv*. Singly; alone; only.

**Solemn,** so'lem, *a*. Marked with religious gravity or sanctity; impressive; earnest; affectedly grave.

**Solemnity,** so-lem'ni-ti, *n*. Gravity; impressiveness; a solemn ceremony.

**Solemnize,** so'lem-nīz, *vt*. To honor by solemn ceremonies; to celebrate; to make grave.

**Solemnly,** so'lem-li, *adv*. With solemnity; religiously; with formal gravity.

**Sol-fa,** sol'fä, *vi*. and *t*. (sol-faing, sol-faed). To sing the notes of the scale, using the syllables *do* (or *ut*), *re, mi, fa, sol, la, si*.

**Solfeggio,** sol-fej'i-ō, *n*. and *a*. In *music*, a system of arranging the scale by the names *do* (or *ut*), *re, mi, fa, sol, la, si*.

**Solicit,** sō-lis'it, *vt*. and *i*. To ask earnestly; to beg; to invite; to disquiet; to incite.

**Solicitant,** sō-lis'it-ant, *n*. One who solicits.

**Solicitation,** sō-lis'it-ā''shon, *n*. Earnest request; supplication; entreaty.

**Solicitor,** sōlis'it-ėr, *n*. One who solicits; an attorney; a law-agent.

**Solicitor-general,** sō-lis'it-ėr-jen-ė-ral, *n*. An officer of the British crown next in rank to the attorney-general, or in Scotland to the lord-advocate.

**Solicitous,** sō-lis'it-us, *a*. Anxious; very desirous; concerned; apprehensive.

**Solicitude,** sō-lis'i-tūd, *n*. State of being solicitous; carefulness; concern; anxiety.

**Solid,** so'lid, *a*. Resisting pressure; not liquid or gaseous; not hollow; cubic; sound; not frivolous.—*n*. A body that naturally retains the same shape.

**Solidarity,** so-li-dar'i-ti, *n*. Unity or communion of interests and responsibilities.

**Solidification,** so-lid'i-fi-kā''shon, *n*. Act or process of solidifying.

**Solidify,** so-lid'i-fī, *vt*. (solidifying, solidified). To make solid.—*vt*. To become solid.

**Solidity,** so-lid'i-ti, *n*. State or quality of being solid; density; firmness; soundness.

**Solidly,** so'lid-li, *adv*. In a solid manner; firmly; compactly; on firm grounds.

**Soliloquize,** sō-lil'ō-kwīz, *vi*. To utter a soliloquy.

**Soliloquy,** sō-lil'ō-kwi, *n*. A speaking to oneself; discourse of a person alone.

**Solitaire,** so'li-tār, *n*. A solitary; an article of jewelry in which a single gem is set; a game for a single person.

**Solitarily,** so'li-ta-ri-li, *adv*. In a solitary manner; in solitude; alone.

**Solitary,** so'li-ta-ri, *a*. Being alone; lonely; retired; not much frequented; shared by no companions; single; sole.—*n*. A hermit; a recluse.

**Solitude,** so'li-tūd, *n*. State of being alone; a lonely life; a lonely place.

**Solmization, Solmisation,** sol-mī-zā'shon, *n*. Solfeggio; act of sol-faing.

**Solo,** sō'lō, *n*. A tune or air for a single instrument or voice.

**Soloist,** sō'lō-ist, *n*. A solo singer or performer.

**Solstice,** sol'stis, *n*. The time when the sun arrives at the point farthest north or south of the equator, namely 21st June and 22nd Dec.; either of the two points in the ecliptic where the sun then appears to be.

**Solstitial,** sol-sti'shal, *a*. Pertaining to a solstice; happening at a solstice.

**Solubility,** so-lū-bil'i-ti, *n*. Quality of being soluble.

**Soluble,** so'lū-bl, *a*. Susceptible of being dissolved in a fluid; capable of being solved, as a problem.

**Solution,** so-lū'shon, *n*. A dissolving; preparation made by dissolving a solid in a liquid; act of solving; explanation; termination or crisis of a disease.

**Solvable,** solv'a-bl, *a*. Soluble.

**Solve,** solv, *vt*. (solving, solved). To explain; to make clear; to unravel; to work out.

**Solvency,** sol'ven-si, *n*. Ability to pay debts.

**Solvent,** sol'vent, *a*. Having the power of dissolving; able to pay all debts.—*n*. A fluid that dissolves any substance.

**Somatic,** sō-mat'ik, *a*. Corporeal; bodily.

**Somatology,** sō-ma-tol'o-ji, *n*. The doctrine of living bodies; the science of matter.

**Somber,** som'bėr, *a*. Dark; gloomy; dismal.—*vt*. (sombring, sombred). To make somber.

**Sombrero,** som-brār'ō, *n*. A broad-brimmed hat.

**Sombrous,** som'brus, *a*. Somber; gloomy.

**Some,** sum, *a*. A certain; a; a little; indefinite and perhaps considerable; about or near.—*pron*. An indefinite part, quantity, or number; certain individuals.

**Somebody,** sum'bo-di, *n*. A person indeterminate; a person of consideration.

**Somehow,** sum'hou, *adv*. In some way not yet known; one way or another.

**Somersault, Somerset,** sum'ėr-salt, sum'ėr-set, *n*. A leap in which the heels turn over the head; a turn of the body in the air.

**Something,** sum'thing, *n*. A thing, quantity, or degree indefinitely; a person or thing of importance.—*adv*. Somewhat.

**Sometime,** sum'tīm, *adv*. Once; formerly; by and by.—*a*. Former; whilom.

**Sometimes,** sum'tīmz, *adv*. At some or certain times; not always; now and then.

**Somewhat,** sum'whot, *n*. Something; more or less.—*adv*. In some degree; a little.

**Somewhere,** sum'whār, *adv*. In some place; to some place.

**Somite,** sō'mīt, *n*. A single segment in the body of an articulated animal.

**Somnambulate,** som-nam'bū-lāt, *vi*. and *t*. To walk or walk over in sleep.

**Somnambulism,** som-nam'bū-lizm, *n*. The act or practice of walking in sleep.

**Somnambulist,** som-nam'bū-list, *n*. One who walks in his sleep.

**Somniferous,** som-nif'ėr-us, *a*. Bringing or causing sleep; soporific.

**Somnific,** som-nif'ik, *a*. Causing sleep.

**Somniloquence, Somniloquism,** som-nil'ō-kwens, som-nil'ō-kwizm, *n*. The act of talking in sleep.

**Somnolence,** som'nō-lens, *n*. Sleepiness.

**Somnolent,** som'nō-lent, *a*. Sleepy; drowsy.

**Son,** sun, *n*. A male child.

**Sonant,** sō'nant, *a*. Sounding; uttered with voice and not breath merely.—*n*. A sonant letter.

**Sonata,** sō-nä'tä, *n*. A musical composition of several movements for a solo instrument.

**Song,** song, *n*. That which is sung; vocal music or melody; a poem to be sung; a lyric; poetry; a trifle.

**Songstress,** song'stres, *n*. A female singer.

**Son-in-law,** sun'in-la, *n*. A man married to one's daughter.

**Sonnet,** son'et, *n*. A poem of fourteen pentameter lines.

**Sonneteer,** son-et-ēr', *n*. A composer of sonnets; a petty poet.

**Sonorous,** sō-nō'rus, *a*. Giving sound when struck; resonant; high-sounding.

**Sonship,** sun'ship, *n*. State of being a son; filia-

S

tion; the character of a son.

**Soon,** sön, *adv.* In a short time; shortly; early; quickly; promptly; readily; gladly.

**Soot,** söt, *n.* A black substance formed from burning matter.—*vt.* To cover or foul with soot.

**Sooth,** söth, *a.* True.—*n.* Truth; reality.

**Soothe,** SÖTH, *vt.* (soothing, soothed). To please with soft words; to flatter; to pacify; to assuage; to soften.

**Soothing,** SÖTH'ing, *p.a.* Serving to soothe, calm, or assuage; mollifying.

**Soothsayer,** söth'sā-ėr, *n.* One who foretells or predicts; a prophet.

**Soothsaying,** söth'sā-ing, *n.* A foretelling; a prediction; divination.

**Sooty,** söt'i, *a.* Producing soot; consisting of soot; foul with soot; dusky; dark.

**Sop,** sop, *n.* Something dipped in broth or liquid food; anything given to pacify.—*vt.* (sopping, sopped). To steep in liquor.

**Sophism,** sof'izm, *n.* A specious but fallacious argument; a subtlety in reasoning.

**Sophist,** sof'ist, *n.* A captious or fallacious reasoner.

**Sophistic, Sophistical,** sō-fist'ik, sō-fist'ik-al, *a.* Pertaining to sophistry; fallaciously subtle; not sound in reasoning.

**Sophisticate,** sō-fist'ik-āt, *vt.* To pervert by sophistry; to adulterate.

**Sophistication,** sō-fis'ti-kā''shon, *n.* Adulteration; act or art of quibbling; a quibble.

**Sophistry,** sof'ist-ri, *n.* Fallacious reasoning.

**Soporiferous,** sō-pō-rif'ik, *a.* Causing sleep.—*n.* A drug or anything that induces sleep.

**Soppy,** sop'i, *a.* Soaked; wet.

**Soprano,** sō-prä'nō, *n.* The highest female voice; a singer with such a voice.

**Sorb,** sorb, *n.* The service-tree or its fruit.

**Sorcerer,** sōr'sėr-ėr, *n.* A wizard; an enchanter; a magician.

**Sorceress,** sōr'sėr-es, *n.* A female sorcerer.

**Sorcery,** sōr'sėr-i, *n.* Magic; enchantment; witchcraft.

**Sordid,** sor'did, *a.* Dirty; foul; vile; base; niggardly; covetous.

**Sordidly,** sor'did-li, *adv.* Basely; covetously.

**Sore,** sōr, *a.* Painful; severe; distressing; tender; galled.—*n.* An ulcer, wound, etc.—*adv.* Severely; sorely.

**Sorely,** sōr'li, *adv.* In a sore manner; grievously; greatly; violently; severely.

**Sorghum,** sor'gum, *n.* A kind of millet.

**Sororal,** sō-rō'ral, *a.* Sisterly.

**Sorrel,** so'rel, *n.* A plant allied to the docks; a reddish or yellow-brown color.—*a.* Of a reddish color.

**Sorrily,** so'ri-li, *adv.* In a sorry manner; meanly; pitiably; wretchedly.

**Sorrow,** so'rō, *n.* Affliction or distress of mind; grief; regret.—*vi.* To feel sorrow; to grieve.

**Sorrowful,** so'rō-ful, *a.* Full of sorrow; sad; mournful; dejected.

**Sorry,** so'ri, *a.* Feeling sorrow; grieved; sorrowful; wretched; pitiful.

**Sort,** sort, *n.* Nature or character; kind; species; manner; a set.—*vt.* To assort; to arrange; to reduce to order.—*vi.* To consort; to agree.

**Sorter,** sort'ėr, *n.* One who sorts; one who separates and arranges.

**Sortie,** sor'tē, *n.* The issuing of troops from a besieged place; a sally.

**Sortilege,** sor'ti-lej, *n.* Act or practice of drawing lots; divination by lots.

**Sortment,** sort'ment, *n.* Act of sorting; assortment.

**So-so,** sō'sō, *a.* Middling.

**Sot,** sot, *n.* A dolt or blockhead; an habitual drunkard.

**Sottish,** sot'ish, *a.* Like a sot; foolish; given to drunkenness.

**Sou,** sö, *n.* A French copper coin, worth about a halfpenny.

**Soubrette,** sö-bret', *n.* An intriguing servant-girl in a comedy.

**Soufflé,** söf-la, *n.* A light dish, partly composed of white of eggs.

**Sough,** suf, *vi.* To emit a rushing or roaring sound like wind; to sound like the sea.—*n.* A rushing sound; a deep sigh.

**Soul,** sōl, *n.* The spiritual principle in man; the moral and emotional part of man's nature; elevation of mind; fervor; essence; an inspirer or leader; a person.

**Souled,** sōld, *a.* Instinct with soul or feeling.

**Soulless,** sōl'les, *a.* Without a soul; without nobleness of mind; mean; spiritless.

**Sound,** sound, *a.* Not in any way defective; healthy; valid; free from error; orthodox; just; heavy.—*n.* A narrow channel of water; a strait; air-bladder of a fish; that which is heard; noise.—*vt.* To measure the depth of; to examine medically; to try to discover the opinion, etc., of; to cause to give out a sound; to pronounce.—*vi.* To give out a sound; to appear on narration; to be spread or published.

**Sounding,** sound'ing, *a.* Causing sound; sonorous; having a lofty sound; bombastic.

**Sounding-board,** sound'ing-bōrd, *n.* A canopy over a platform, etc., to direct the sound of a speaker's voice to the audience.

**Sounding-line,** sound'ing-līn, *n.* A line for ascertaining the depth of water.

**Soundings,** sound'ingz, *n.pl.* The depths of water in rivers, harbors, etc.

**Soundless,** sound'les, *a.* That cannot be fathomed; noiseless.

**Soundly,** sound'li, *adv.* Healthily; validly; thoroughly; with heavy blows.

**Soundness,** sound'nes, *n.* Healthiness; solidity; validity; orthodoxy.

**Soup,** söp, *n.* A liquid food made generally from flesh and vegetables.

**Sour,** sour, *a.* Acid or sharp to the taste; tart; peevish; morose.—*vt.* To make sour; to make cross or discontented; to embitter.—*vi.* To become sour or peevish.

**Source,** sōrs, *n.* That from which anything rises; the spring, etc., from which a stream proceeds; first cause; origin.

**Sourly,** sour'li, *adv.* Acidly; peevishly.

**Souse,** sous, *n.* Pickle; the ears, feet, etc., of swine pickled; a swoop.—*vt.* (sousing, soused). To steep in pickle; to plunge into water.—*vi.* To swoop.—*adv.* With sudden descent or plunge.

**South,** south, *n.* The region in which the sun is at mid-day.—*a.* Being in or toward the south; pertaining to or from the south.—*adv.* Toward the south.

**South-east,** south'ēst, *n.* The point midway between the south and east.—*a.* Pertaining to or from the south-east.—*adv.* Toward the south-east.

**South-easter,** south-ēst'ėr, *n.* A wind from the south-east.

**Southerner,** SUTH'ėr-nėr, *n.* An inhabitant or native of the south.

**Southmost,** south'mōst, *a.* Farthest toward the south.

**South-west,** south'west, *n.* The point mid-way between the south and west.—*a.* Pertaining to or from the south-west.—*adv.* Toward the south-west.

**South-wester,** south-west'ėr, *n.* A strong south-west wind; a waterproof hat with a flap hanging over the neck, often *Sou'wester.*

**South-western,** south-west'ėrn, *a.* Pertaining to or toward the south-west.

**Souvenir,** sö-ve-nēr', *n.* A keepsake.

**Sovereign,** so've-rin, *a.* Supreme in power; chief.—*n.* A monarch; the standard British gold coin.

**Sovereignty,** so've-rin-ti, *n.* Supreme power; dominion.

**Soviet,** sov'i-et, *n.* The method of government in Russia since the Revolution, local soviets (elected councils) sending delegates to larger

bodies, and these, in their turn, to the Supreme Congress, which elects the Supreme Council.
**Sovran,** sov'ran, *n.* and *a.* Sovereign.
**Sow,** sou, *n.* The female of the swine.
**Sow,** sō, *vt.* (pret. sowed, pp. sowed or sown). To scatter seed over; to spread abroad.—*vi.* To scatter seed for growth.
**Sowar,** sou'ar, *n.* An Indian cavalry soldier.
**Sower,** sō'ėr, *n.* One who sows.
**Soy,** soi, *n.* A sauce prepared in China and Japan from a bean; the plant producing the bean.
**Spa,** spa, *n.* A place to which people go on account of a spring of mineral water.
**Space,** spās, *n.* Extension; room; interval between points or objects; quantity of time; a while.—*vt.* (spacing, spaced). To arrange at proper intervals; to arrange the spaces in.
**Spacial,** Same as *Spatial.*
**Spacious,** spā'shus, *a.* Roomy; widely extended; ample; capacious.
**Spade,** spād, *n.* An instrument for digging; a playing card of a black suit.—*vt.* (spading, spaded). To dig with a spade; to use a spade on.
**Spadeful,** spād'ful, *n.* As much as a spade will hold.
**Spake,** spāk, A preterit of *speak.*
**Span,** span, *n.* Reach or extent in general; space between the thumb and little finger; nine inches; a short space of time; the stretch of an arch; a yoke of animals.—*vt.* (spanning, spanned). To extend across; to measure with the hand with the fingers extended.
**Spandrel,** span'drel, *n.* The triangular space between the curve of an arch and the rectangular part inclosing it.
**Spangle,** spang'gl, *n.* A small glittering metal ornament; a small sparkling object.—*vt.* (spangling, spangled). To adorn with spangles.
**Spangly,** spang'gli, *a.* Like a spangle or spangles; glittering; glistening.
**Spaniard,** Span'yėrd, *n.* A native of Spain.
**Spaniel,** span'yel, *n.* A dog of several breeds; a cringing, fawning person.
**Spanish,** span'ish, *a.* Pertaining to Spain.—*n.* The language of Spain.
**Spank,** spangk, *vi.* To move or run along quickly.—*vt.* To slap or smack.
**Spanker,** spangk'ėr, *n.* One that spanks; a large fore-and-aft sail on the mizzen-mast.
**Spanking,** spangk'ing, *a.* Moving quickly; dashing; free-going.
**Spanner,** span'ėr, *n.* A screw-key.
**Spar,** spär, *n.* A long piece of timber; a pole; a crystalline mineral; boxing-match; flourish of the fists.—*vi.* (sparring, sparred). To fight in show; to box; to bandy words.
**Sparable,** spar'a-bl, *n.* A nail driven into the soles of shoes and boots.
**Spare,** spār, *a.* Scanty; thin; sparing or chary; superfluous; held in reserve.—*vt.* (sparing, spared). To use frugally; to dispense with; to omit; to use tenderly; to withhold from.—*vi.* To be frugal; to use mercy or forbearance.
**Sparely,** spār'li, *adv.* Sparingly.
**Sparing,** spār'ing, *a.* Saving; economical.
**Sparingly,** spār'ing-li, *adv.* Frugally; not lavishly; seldom; not frequently.
**Spark,** spärk, *n.* A particle of ignited substance, which flies off from burning bodies; a small transient light; a gay man; a lover.—*vi.* To emit particles of fire; to sparkle.
**Sparkish,** spärk'ish, *a.* Gay; gallant.
**Sparkle,** spär'kl, *n.* A little spark; luster.—*vi.* (sparkling, sparkled). To emit sparks; to glitter; to be animated.
**Sparkling,** spärk'ling, *a.* Emitting sparks; glittering; lively.
**Sparrow,** spa'rō, *n.* A bird of the finch family.
**Sparse,** spärs, *a.* Thinly scattered; not thick or close together.
**Sparsely,** spärs'li, *adv.* Thinly.
**Spartan,** spär'tan, *a.* Pertaining to ancient Sparta; hardy; undaunted; enduring.
**Spasm,** spazm, *n.* A violent contraction of a muscle; a convulsive fit.
**Spasmodic,** spaz-mod'ik, *a.* Relating to spasm; convulsive; overstrained in expression or style.
**Spastic,** spas'tik, *a.* Spasmodic.
**Spat,** spat, *n.* The spawn of shell-fish.—*vi.* (spatting, spatted). To emit spawn or spat.
**Spate, Spait,** spāt, *n.* A sudden heavy flood, especially in mountain streams.
**Spatial,** spā'shal, *a.* Pertaining to space; existing in space.
**Spatter,** spat'ėr, *vt.* To scatter a liquid substance on; to sprinkle; to asperse.—*n.* Act of spattering; something sprinkled.
**Spatula,** spat'ū-la, *n.* A broad thin flexible blade, used by painters, apothecaries, etc.
**Spavin,** spa'vin, *n.* A disease of horses affecting the joint of the hind-leg between the knee and the fetlock, and causing lameness.
**Spawn,** span, *n.* The eggs or ova of fish, frogs, etc., when ejected; offspring, in contempt.—*vt.* and *i.* To eject or deposit as spawn.
**Spawner,** span'ėr, *n.* A female fish.
**Spay,** spā, *vt.* To destroy the ovaries of, as is done to female animals.
**Speak,** spēk, *vi.* (pret. spoke, spake, pp. spoken). To utter words; to talk; to deliver a speech; to argue; to plead; to be expressive.—*vt.* To utter with the mouth; to pronounce; to accost; to express.
**Speakable,** spēk'a-bl, *n.* That can be spoken.
**Speaker,** spēk'ėr, *n.* One who speaks; the person who presides in a deliberative assembly, as the House of Commons.
**Speaking,** spēk'ing, *p.a.* Used to convey speech; forcibly expressive; vivid in resemblance; extending to phrases of civility.
**Spear,** spēr, *n.* A long, pointed weapon; a lance.—*vt.* To pierce or kill with a spear.
**Special,** spe'shal, *a.* Pertaining to a species; particular; distinctive; having a particular purpose or scope.
**Specialism,** spe'shal-izm, *n.* Devotion to a particular branch of knowledge.
**Specialist,** spe'shal-ist, *n.* One who devotes himself to some particular subject.
**Speciality,** spe-shi-al'i-ti, *n.* Special characteristic; that in which a person is specially versed.
**Specialize,** spe-shal-īz, *vt.* To assign a specific use to.—*vi.* To apply oneself to a particular subject.
**Specially,** spe'shal-li, *adv.* Especially; for a particular purpose or occasion.
**Specialty,** spe'shal-ti, *n.* Special characteristic; a special pursuit; a special product.
**Specie,** spē'shi, *n.* Metallic money; coin.
**Species,** spē'shēz, *n. sing.* and *pl.* Outward appearance; a kind, sort, or variety; a class.
**Specific,** spe-sif'ik, *a.* Pertaining to, designating or constituting a species; definite; precise.—*n.* A remedy which exerts a special action in the cure of a disease; an infallible remedy.
**Specifically,** spe-sif'ik-al-li, *adv.* In a specific manner; definitely; particularly.
**Specification,** spe'si-fi-kā''shon, *n.* The act of specifying; details of particulars; particular mention; statement.
**Specify,** spe'si-fī, *vt.* (specifying, specified). To make specific; to state in detail.
**Specimen,** spe'si-men, *n.* A sample; a part intended to typify the whole.
**Specious,** spē'shus, *a.* Superficially correct; appearing well at first view; plausible.
**Speciously,** spē'shus-li, *adv.* Plausibly.
**Speck,** spek, *n.* A small spot; a stain; a flaw; an atom.—*vt.* To spot.
**Speckle,** spek'l, *n.* A speck; a small colored marking.—*vt.* (speckling, speckled). To mark with small specks.
**Speckled,** spek'ld, *p.a.* Marked with specks; spotted.
**Spectacle,** spek'ta-kl, *n.* A show; a sight; an exhibition; a pageant; *pl.* glasses to assist or correct

defective vision.

**Spectacular,** spek-tak'ū-ler, *a.* Pertaining to or of the nature of a show.

**Spectator,** spek-tā'tor, *n.* A looker-on; a beholder; an eye-witness.

**Spectral,** spek'tral, *a.* Pertaining to a specter; ghostly; pertaining to spectra.

**Specter,** spek'tėr, *n.* An apparition; a ghost; a phantom.

**Spectroscope,** spek'trō-skōp, *n.* The instrument employed in spectrum analysis.

**Spectrum,** spek'trum, *n.*; pl. **-tra.** An image seen after the eyes are closed; the colored band of light, showing prismatic colors, produced when a beam of light is subjected to analysis by a spectroscope.

**Specular,** spek'ū-lär, *a.* Having a smooth reflecting surface.

**Speculate,** spek'ū-lāt, *vi.* (speculating, speculated). To meditate; to engage in risky financial transactions with a view to profit.

**Speculation,** spek-ū-lā'shon, *n.* Contemplation; theory; hazardous financial transactions.

**Speculative,** spek'ū-lāt-iv, *a.* Given to speculation; theoretical; adventurous in business.

**Speculator,** spek'ū-lāt-or, *n.* A theorizer; one who speculates in business.

**Speculum,** spek'ū-lum, *n.*; pl. **-la** or **-lums.** A mirror; a metallic reflector.

**Speech,** spēch, *n.* The faculty of speaking; language; talk; a formal discourse; oration.

**Speechify,** spēch'i-fī, *vi.* To make a speech; to harangue.

**Speechless,** spēch'les, *a.* Destitute of the faculty of speech; dumb; mute; silent.

**Speed,** spēd, *n.* Success; velocity; haste.—*vi.* (speeding, sped). To make haste; to prosper.—*vt.* To dispatch in haste; to help forward; to dismiss with good wishes.

**Speedily,** spēd'i-li, *adv.* In a speedy manner; quickly; with haste; soon.

**Speedometer,** spēd-om'et-ėr, *n.* A speed-indicator.

**Speedway,** spēd'wā, *n.* The track on which automobile and motor-cycle races are run.

**Spell,** spel, *n.* An incantation; a charm; fascination; a turn of work; a period.—*vt.* (pret. and pp. spelled or spelt). To give the letters of in order; to read; to import.—*vi.* To form words with the proper letters.

**Spelling,** spel'ing, *n.* Act of one who spells; orthography; letters that form a word.

**Spelling-book,** spel'ing-buk, *n.* A book for teaching children to spell and read.

**Spelter,** spel'tėr, *n.* Zinc, commonly impure.

**Spencer,** spen'sėr, *n.* A man's or woman's outer coat or jacket.

**Spend,** spend, *vt.* (spending, spent). To lay out, as money; to squander; to pass, as time; to exhaust of force.—*vi.* To spend money; to be dissipated.

**Spendthrift,** spend'thrift, *n.* and *a.* One who spends improvidently; a prodigal.

**Spent,** spent, *p.a.* Wearied; exhausted; having deposited spawn.

**Sperm,** spėrm, *n.* The seminal fluid of animals.

**Spermaceti,** spėr-ma-se'ti, *n.* A fatty material obtained from a species of whale.

**Spermatic,** spėr-mat'ik, *a.* Seminal.

**Spermatozoon,** spėr'ma-to-zō''on, *n.*; pl. **-oa.** One of the microscopic bodies in the semen of animals essential to impregnation.

**Sperm-whale,** spėrm'whāl, *n.* The spermaceti whale or cachalot.

**Spew,** spū, *vt.* To vomit; to cast out with abhorrence.—*vi.* To vomit.

**Sphenoid,** sfē'noid, *a.* Resembling a wedge.—*n.* A wedge-shaped body.

**Spheral,** sfēr'al, *a.* Pertaining to the spheres; rounded like a sphere.

**Sphere,** sfēr, *n.* An orb; a ball; a globe; a sun, star, or planet; circuit of motion, action, etc.; range; province; rank.—*vt.* (sphering, sphered). To place in a sphere or among the spheres.

**Spheric, Spherical,** sfe'rik, sfe'rik-al, *a.* Pertaining to a sphere; globular.

**Spherically,** sfe'rik-al-li, *adv.* In the form of a sphere.

**Spheroid,** sfēr'oid, *n.* A body like a sphere, but not perfectly spherical.

**Spheroidal,** sfēr-oid'al, *a.* Having the form of a spheroid.

**Sphincter,** sfingk'tėr, *n.* A ring-like muscle closing the external orifices of organs, as the mouth or anus.

**Sphinx,** sfingks, *n.* A monster or figure with the bust of a woman on the body of a lioness, said to have proposed a riddle; a person who puts puzzling questions.

**Sphragistics,** sfra-jis'tiks, *n.* The science of seals.

**Sphygmograph,** sfig'mō-graf, *n.* An instrument to indicate the nature of the pulse.

**Spicate,** spī'kāt, *a.* Eared like corn.

**Spice,** spīs, *n.* A vegetable production, aromatic to the smell and pungent to the taste; something piquant; flavor; smack.—*vt.* (spicing, spiced). To season with spice; to flavor.

**Spicery,** spīs'ė-ri, *n.* Spices in general; a repository of spices; spiciness.

**Spicily,** spīs'i-li, *adv.* In a spicy manner; pungently; with flavor.

**Spick-and-span,** spik'and-span, *a.* Trim; flawless.—*adv.* Quite (with *new*).

**Spicule,** spik'ūl, *n.* A little spike; a little sharp needle-shaped body.

**Spicy,** spīs'i, *a.* Producing or abounding with spice; pungent; piquant; racy.

**Spider,** spī'dėr, *n.* An animal that spins webs for taking its prey.

**Spigot,** spi'got, *n.* A peg to stop a faucet or cask.

**Spike,** spīk, *n.* A piece of pointed iron; an ear of corn, etc.—*vt.* (spiking, spiked). To fasten or set with spikes; to stop the vent of a cannon with a nail, etc.; to fix upon a spike.

**Spikenard,** spīk'närd, *n.* An aromatic plant of the East Indies; a fragrant essential oil; an ancient unguent.

**Spile,** spīl, *n.* A spigot.—*vt.* To supply with a spile or spigot.

**Spill,** spil, *vt.* (pret. and pp. spilled or split). To suffer to fall, flow over, etc.; to shed.—*vi.* To be shed; to be suffered to fall, be lost, or wasted.—*n.* A spigot; piece of wood or paper used to light a lamp, etc.; a fall.

**Spin,** spin, *vt.* (spinning, spun). To draw out and twist into threads; to protract; to whirl; to make threads, as a spider.—*vi.* To work at drawing and twisting threads; to rotate; to go quickly.—*n.* Act of spinning; a rapid run.

**Spinach, Spinage,** spin'āj, *n.* A culinary vegetable.

**Spinal,** spīn'al, *a.* Pertaining to the spine.

**Spindle,** spin'dl, *n.* A pin carrying a bobbin in a spinning machine; a small axis; a long, slender stalk; a measure of yarn.—*vi.* To grow in a long slender stalk.

**Spindle-legs, Spindle-shanks,** spin'dl-legz, spin'dl-shangks, *n.* Long slender legs, or a person having such.

**Spine,** spīn, *n.* A prickle; a thorn; a thin, pointed spike in animals; the backbone or spinal column.

**Spined,** spīnd, *a.* Having spines.

**Spinel, Spinelle,** spi-nel', *n.* A kind of gem or hard stone.

**Spinet,** spin'et, *n.* An old instrument of music resembling a harpsichord.

**Spinnaker,** spin'a-kėr, *n.* A triangular sail carried by yachts on the opposite side to the mainsail in running before the wind.

**Spinner,** spin'ėr, *n.* One who spins; a contrivance for spinning; a spider.

**Spinney, Spinny,** spin'i, *n.* A small wood; a clump of trees.

**Spinose, Spinous,** spīn'ōs, spīn'us, *a.* Full of spines; thorny.

**Spinster,** spin'stėr, *n.* A woman who spins; an un-

married woman; an old maid.
**Spiny,** spīn'i, *a.* Thorny; difficult.
**Spiracle,** spi'ra-kl or spī'ra-kl, *n.* Any aperture in animals for breathing.
**Spirea,** spī-rē'a, *n.* A genus of flowering plants.
**Spiral,** spī'ral, *a.* Pertaining to a spire; winding like a screw.—*n.* A curve winding like a screw.
**Spirally,** spī'ral-li, *adv.* In a spiral form or direction; in the manner of a screw.
**Spire,** spīr, *n.* A winding line like a screw; a spiral; a wreath; a convolution; a steeple; a stalk or blade of grass, etc.—*vi.* (spiring, spired). To taper up.
**Spirit,** spi'rit, *n.* The breath of life; the soul; a spectre; vivacity; courage; mood; essence; real meaning; intent; a liquid obtained by distillation; *pl.* alcoholic liquor.—*vt.* To infuse spirit into; to encourage.
**Spirited,** spi'rit-ed, *p.a.* Showing spirit; animated; lively; bold; courageous.
**Spiritless,** spi'rit-les, *a.* Destitute of life or spirit; dejected; depressed.
**Spirit-level,** spi'rit-le-vel, *n.* A glass tube nearly filled with spirit, for determining when a thing is horizontal by the central position of an air-bubble.
**Spiritual,** spi'rit-ū-al, *a.* Pertaining to spirit; not material; mental; intellectual; divine; pure; ecclesiastical.
**Spiritualism,** spi'rit-ū-al-izm, *n.* State of being spiritual; doctrine of the existence of spirit distinct from matter; belief that communication can be held with departed spirits.
**Spiritualist,** spi'rit-ū-al-ist, *n.* One who professes a regard for spiritual things only; one who believes in spiritualism.
**Spiritualistic,** spi'rit-ū-a-lis''tik, *a.* Relating to spiritualism.
**Spirituality,** spi'rit-ū-al''i-ti, *n.* Quality or state of being spiritual; spiritual nature or character.
**Spiritualize,** spi'rit-ū-al-īz, *vt.* To render spiritual; to convert to a spiritual meaning.
**Spiritually,** spi'rit-ū-al-li, *adv.* In a spiritual manner.
**Spirituous,** spi'rit-ū-us, *a.* Alcoholic; ardent.
**Spirt,** spėrt, *vt.* To force out in a jet; to squirt.—*vi.* To gush out in a jet.—*n.* A jet of fluid.
**Spiry,** spīr'i, *a.* Of a spiral form; tapering to a point; abounding in steeples.
**Spit,** spit, *n.* A prong on which meat is roasted; low land running into the sea.—*vt.* (spitting, spitted). To put on a spit; to pierce.
**Spit,** spit, *vt.* and *i.* (spitting, spat). To eject from the mouth, as saliva.—*n.* What is ejected from the mouth; spittle.
**Spitchcock,** spich'kok, *n.* An eel split and broiled.—*vt.* To split (an eel) and broil it.
**Spite,** spīt, *n.* A feeling of ill-will; malice; rancour.—**In spite of,** notwithstanding.—*vt.* (spiting, spited). To mortify or chagrin; to thwart.
**Spiteful,** spīt'ful, *a.* Having a desire to annoy or injure; malignant; malicious.
**Spitfire,** spit'fīr, *n.* A violent or passionate person; one who is irascible or fiery.
**Spittle,** spit'l, *n.* Saliva; the moist matter ejected from the mouth.
**Spittoon,** spit-tön', *n.* A vessel to receive discharges of spittle.
**Splanchnic,** splangk'nik, *a.* Belonging to the viscera or entrails.
**Splash,** splash, *vt.* and *i.* To bespatter with liquid matter.—*n.* A quantity of wet matter thrown on anything; a noise from water dashed about; a spot of dirt.
**Splash-board,** splash'bōrd, *n.* A board in front of a vehicle to ward off dirt thrown by the horses' heels.
**Splay,** splā, *vt.* To slope or form with an angle.—*n.* A sloped surface.—*a.* Turned outward, as a person's feet.
**Splay-footed,** splā'fut-ed, *a.* Having the feet turned outward; having flat feet.
**Spleen,** splēn, *n.* The milt, an organ in the abdomen connected with digestion; spite; ill-humor; low spirits.
**Splendent,** splen'dent, *a.* Shining; gleaming; illustrious.
**Splendid,** splen'did, *a.* Brilliant; magnificent; famous; celebrated.
**Splendidly,** splen'did-li, *adv.* Brilliantly; magnificently; richly.
**Splendor,** splen'dėr, *n.* Brilliancy; magnificence; display; pomp; grandeur.
**Splice,** splīs, *vt.* (splicing, spliced). To unite, as two ropes, by interweaving the strands; to unite by overlapping, as timber.—*n.* Union of ropes by interweaving; piece added by splicing.
**Splint,** splint, *n.* A splinter; piece of wood to confine a broken bone when set.
**Splinter,** splint'ėr, *n.* A piece of wood, or other solid substance, split off.—*vt.* To split into splinters; to shiver.
**Splintery,** splint'ėr-i, *a.* Liable to splinter; consisting of splinters.
**Split,** split, *vt.* (splitting, split). To divide lengthwise; to cleave; to rend; to burst.—*vi.* To part asunder; to burst; to crack; to differ in opinion.—*n.* A rent; fissure; breach or separation.—*a.* Divided; rent; deeply cleft.
**Splotch,** sploch, *n.* A spot; smear.
**Splutter,** splut'ėr, *n.* A bustle; a stir.—*vi.* To speak confusedly; to sputter.
**Spode,** spōd, *n.* A material composed of calcined ivory, of which vases, etc., are made.
**Spoil,** spoil, *n.* Pillage; booty; plunder.—*vt.* To plunder; to impair; to ruin; to injure by over-indulgence.—*vi.* To grow useless; to decay.
**Spoiler,** spoil'ėr, *n.* One who spoils; a plunderer.
**Spoke,** spōk, *n.* A bar of a wheel; the round of a ladder; a bar.—*vt.* (spoking, spoked). To furnish with spokes. Pret. of *speak*.
**Spoken,** spōk'n, *p.a.* Oral; speaking (as in fair-spoken).
**Spokesman,** spōks'man, *n.* One who speaks for another.
**Spoliate,** spō-li-āt, *vt.* To spoil; to plunder.
**Spondee,** spon'dē, *n.* A metrical foot of two long syllables.
**Sponge,** spunj, *n.* A soft porous marine substance which readily imbibes liquids; a mean parasite.—*vt.* (sponging, sponged). To wipe with a sponge; to wipe out completely; to harass by extortion; to get by mean arts.—*vi.* To imbibe; to act as a hanger-on.
**Spongy,** spunj'i, *a.* Soft and full of cavities; soaked and soft.
**Sponsion,** spon'shon, *n.* A solemn promise; act of becoming surety.
**Sponsor,** spon'sor, *n.* A surety or guarantor; a godfather or godmother.
**Spontaneity,** spon-ta-nē'i-ti, *n.* Self-originated activity; readiness.
**Spontaneous,** spon-tā'nē-us, *a.* Voluntary; self-originated; acting by its own impulse.
**Spontaneously,** spon-tā'nē-us-li, *adv.* Of one's own accord.
**Spook,** spök, *n.* A ghost; an apparition.
**Spool,** spöl, *n.* A reel to wind thread or yarn on.
**Spoon,** spön, *n.* A domestic utensil for taking up liquids, etc., at table.—*vt.* To take up with a spoon.
**Spoonerism,** spön'ėr-izm, *n.* An inadvertent and usually amusing transposition of sounds, e.g. *half-warmed fish* for *half-formed wish*.
**Spoonful,** spön'ful, *n.* As much as a spoon contains.
**Spoony, Spooney,** spön'i, *a.* Weak-minded; foolishly fond.—*n.* A silly fellow.
**Spoor,** spör, *n.* The track or trail of an animal.
**Sporadic,** spō-rad'ik, *a.* Scattered; occurring here and there in a scattered manner.
**Spore,** spōr, *n.* The reproductive germ of a cryptogamic plant; a germ of certain animal organisms.
**Sporran, Sporan,** spo'ran, *n.* The fur pouch worn

S

in front of the kilt.
**Sport,** spōrt, *n.* A game; a merry-making; out-of-door recreation, as shooting, horse-racing, etc.; jest; object of mockery; a plant or animal that differs from the normal type.—*vt.* To divert (oneself); to wear in public.—*vi.* To play; to frolic; to practise the diversions of the field.
**Sportful,** spōrt'ful, *a.* Sportive.
**Sporting,** spōrt'ing, *a.* Indulging in sport; belonging to sport.
**Sportive,** spōrt'iv, *a.* Full of sport; gay; playful; frolicsome; jocular.
**Sportsman,** spōrts'man, *n.* One who engages in shooting, fishing, etc.
**Spot,** spot, *n.* A place discolored; a speck; a blemish; a flaw; a locality.—*vt.* (spotting, spotted). To make a spot on; to stain; to catch with the eye.—*vi.* To act as observer of enemy's position, of effect of gunfire, or of approach of hostile aircraft.
**Spotless,** spot'les, *a.* Free from spots; unblemished; pure; immaculate.
**Spotted,** spot'ed, *a.* Marked with spots; speckled.
**Spotty,** spot'i, *a.* Full of spots; spotted.
**Spousal,** spouz'al, *a.* Nuptial; connubial.
**Spouse,** spouz, *n.* A husband or wife.
**Spout,** spout, *n.* A nozzle, or projecting mouth of a vessel; a water-spout; a jet or gush of water.—*vt.* and *i.* To discharge in a jet and with some force; to mouth or utter pompously.
**Spouter,** spout'ėr, *n.* One who spouts; one who speaks in a pompous manner.
**Sprain,** sprān, *vt.* To overstrain, as the muscles or ligaments of a joint.—*n.* A violent strain of a joint without dislocation.
**Sprat,** sprat, *n.* A small fish of the herring family.
**Sprawl,** spral, *vi.* To struggle or show convulsive motions; to lie or crawl with the limbs stretched.
**Spray,** sprā, *n.* A twig; collection of small branches; water or any liquid flying in small drops or particles.—*vt.* To cause to take the form of spray; to treat with spray.
**Spread,** spred, *vt.* (spreading, spread). To stretch or expand; to overspread; to disseminate; to emit; to diffuse.—*vi.* To stretch out; to be diffused.—*n.* Extent; diffusion; a meal or banquet.
**Spread-eagle,** spred'ē-gl, *n.* The figure of an eagle with the wings and legs extended.—*a.* Pretentious; defiantly bombastic.
**Spree,** sprē, *n.* A merry frolic; a carousal.
**Sprig,** sprig, *n.* A small shoot or twig; a spray; a scion; a small square brad.
**Sprightly,** sprīt'li, *a.* Full of spirit; lively; brisk; gay; vivacious.
**Spring,** spring, *vi.* (pret. sprang or sprung, pp. sprung). To leap; to start up; to dart; to warp; to become cracked; to originate.—*vt.* To start or rouse; to propose on a sudden; to crack; to jump over.—*n.* A leap; resilience; an elastic body, made of various materials, especially steel; cause; an issue of water; source of supply; season of the year when plants begin to grow; a crack in timber.
**Spring-board,** spring'bōrd, *n.* An elastic board used in vaulting, etc.
**Spring-tide,** spring'tīd, *n.* The high tide which happens at the new and full moon.
**Spring-time,** spring'tīm, *n.* The spring.
**Spring-water,** spring'wa-tėr, *n.* Water issuing from a spring.
**Springy,** spring'i, *a.* Elastic; light of foot; abounding with springs; wet; spongy.
**Sprinkle,** spring'kl, *vt.* and *i.* (sprinkling, sprinkled). To scatter in small drops; to bedew.—*n.* A small quantity scattered in drops.
**Sprinkling,** spring'kling, *n.* Act of one who sprinkles; a sprinkle; a small quantity distributed in a scattered manner.
**Sprint,** sprint, *n.* A short swift foot-race; a spurt.
**Sprit,** sprit, *n.* A small spar which crosses a sail to extend and elevate it.
**Sprite,** sprīt, *n.* A spirit; a kind of goblin.
**Sprout,** sprout, *vi.* To bud; to push out new shoots.—*n.* A shoot of a plant; *pl.* young coleworts; Brussels sprouts.
**Spruce,** sprös, *a.* Neat in dress; trim; smug.—*n.* A pine-tree yielding valuable timber.
**Sprucely,** sprös'li, *adv.* In a spruce manner; with extreme or affected neatness.
**Spry,** sprī, *a.* Nimble; active; lively.
**Spud,** spud, *n.* A small spade for cutting the roots of weeds.
**Spume,** spūm, *n.* Froth; foam.—*vi.* To froth.
**Spumescent,** spūm-es'ent, *a.* Frothy.
**Spun,** spun, pret. & pp. of *spin*.
**Spunk,** spungk, *n.* Touchwood; tinder; mettle; pluck; courage.
**Spur,** spėr, *n.* An instrument with sharp points, worn on horsemen's heels; incitement; stimulus; a sharp outgrowth; a mountain mass that shoots from another.—*vt.* (spurring, spurred). To prick with a spur; to incite; to put spurs on.—*vi.* To travel with great expedition.
**Spurgall,** spėr'gal, *n.* A place galled by the spur.—*vt.* To gall with the spurs.
**Spurious,** spū'ri-us, *a.* Bastard; not genuine; counterfeit; false.
**Spurn,** spėrn, *vt.* To drive away, as with the foot; to reject with disdain; to treat with contempt.—*vi.* To kick up the heels; to manifest disdain.
**Spurrier,** spėr'i-ėr, *n.* One who makes spurs.
**Spurt,** spėrt, *vt.* and *i.* To spirt.—*n.* A gush of liquid; sudden effort for an emergency; sudden increase of speed.
**Spur-wheel,** spėr'whēl, *n.* A cog-wheel with teeth perpendicular to the axis.
**Sputter,** sput'ėr, *vi.* To emit saliva in speaking; to throw out moisture; to speak hastily and indistinctly.
**Spy,** spī, *vt.* (spying, spied). To gain sight of; to gain knowledge of by artifice; to explore.—*vi.* To pry.—*n.* One who keeps watch on the actions of others; a secret emissary.
**Spy-glass,** spī'gläs, *n.* A small telescope.
**Squab,** skwob, *a.* Short and fat; plump; unfeathered.—*n.* A short, fat person; an unfledged bird; a kind of couch.
**Squabble,** skwob'l, *vi.* (squabbling, squabbled). To dispute noisily; to wrangle.—*n.* A scuffle; a brawl.
**Squad,** skwod, *n.* A small party of men assembled for drill; any small party.
**Squadron,** skwod'ron, *n.* The principal division of a regiment of cavalry, usually from 100 to 200 men; a division of a fleet; a group of some twelve or so military airplanes.
**Squalid,** skwo'lid, *a.* Foul; filthy.
**Squall,** skwal, *vi.* To cry out; to scream violently.—*n.* A loud scream; a violent gust of wind; a brief storm of wind.
**Squally,** skwal'i, *a.* Abounding with squalls.
**Squalor,** skwol'ėr, *n.* Foulness; filthiness.
**Squama,** skwā'ma, *n.*; pl. **-mae.** A scale or scaly part of plants or animals.
**Squamose, Squamous,** skwa-mōs', skwā'mus, *a.* Covered with or consisting of scales.
**Squander,** skwon'dėr, *vt.* To spend lavishly; to fling away; to waste.
**Square,** skwār, *a.* Having four equal sides and four right angles; forming a right angle; just; honest; even; suitable.—*n.* A figure having four equal sides and right angles; any similar figure or area; an instrument having one edge at right angles to another; product of a number multiplied by itself; level; equality.—*vt.* (squaring, squared). To make square; to form to right angles; to adjust; to fit; to settle (accounts); to multiply a number by itself.—*vi.* To suit; to spar (colloq.).
**Squarely,** skwār'li, *adv.* In a sqaure form; directly; fairly; honestly.
**Squash,** skwosh, *vt.* To crush; to beat or press into pulp or a flat mass.—*n.* Something easily crushed; sudden fall of a heavy soft body; a

kind of gourd.

**Squat,** skwot, *vi.* (squatting, squatted). To sit upon the hams or heels; to cover; to settle on land without any title.—*a.* Cowering; short and thick.—*n.* The posture of one who squats.

**Squatter,** skwot'ėr, *n.* One that settles on unoccupied land without a title; in Australia, one who occupies a large are of pasturage.

**Squaw,** skwa, *n.* Among American Indians, a female or wife.

**Squawk,** skwak, *vi.* To cry with a harsh voice.

**Squeak,** skwēk, *vi.* To utter a sharp, shrill sound.—*n.* A sharp, shrill sound.

**Squeal,** skwēl, *vi.* To cry with a sharp, shrill voice.—*n.* A shrill, sharp cry.

**Squeamish,** skwēm'ish, *a.* Having a stomach easily turned; fastidious.

**Squeeze,** skwēz, *vt.* (squeezing, squeezed). To subject to pressure; to harass by extortion; to hug.—*vi.* To press; to crowd.—*n.* An application of pressure; compression.

**Squelch,** skwelch, *vt.* To crush; to destroy.—*vi.* To be crushed.—*n.* A flat heavy fall.

**Squib,** skwib, *n.* A small firework; a lampoon; a skit.—*vi.* (squibbing, squibbed). To throw squibs; to utter sarcastic reflections.

**Squid,** skwid, *n.* A cuttle-fish.

**Squinch,** skwinsh, *n.* An arched structure formed across an angle to support the masonry above it.

**Squint,** skwint, *a.* Looking obliquely or different ways.—*n.* An oblique look; an affection in which the optic axes do not coincide.—*vi.* To look obliquely.

**Squire,** skwīr, *n.* A gentleman next in rank to a knight; a country gentleman; a beau.—*vt.* (squiring, squired). To attend as a squire or beau; to escort.

**Squirm,** skwėrm, *vi.* To wriggle; to writhe.—*n.* A wriggling motion.

**Squirrel,** skwi'rel, *n.* A rodent with a long bushy tail, living in trees.

**Squirt,** skwėrt, *vt.* To eject out of an orifice in a stream.—*vi.* To spurt.—*n.* An instrument which ejects a liquid in a stream; a syringe; a small jet; a spurt.

**Stab,** stab, *vt.* and *i.* (stabbing, stabbed). To pierce or kill with a pointed weapon; to wound figuratively; to injure secretly.—*n.* A thrust or wound with a pointed weapon; underhand injury; poignant pain.

**Stability,** sta-bil'i-ti, *n.* State or quality of being stable; steadfastnesss; firmness.

**Stable,** stā'bl, *a.* Firm; firmly established; steadfast.—*n.* A house for horses, etc.—*vt.* (stabling, stabled). To put or keep in a stable.—*vi.* To dwell in a stable.

**Staccato,** stak-kä'tō, *a.* In *music,* a direction to perform notes in a detached or pointed manner.

**Stack,** stak, *n.* A large, regularly built pile of hay, grain, etc.; a number of chimneys standing together; a single tall chimney; a high rock detached.—*vt.* To build into a stack; to pile together.

**Staddle,** stad'l, *n.* A frame supporting a stack; a tree left uncut when others are cut down.

**Stadium,** stā'di-um, *n.* A Greek measure equal to 606 feet 9 inches; a large arena for sports.

**Staff,** stäf, *n.*; pl. **Staves** or **Staffs,** stāvz, stäfs. A stick or rod; a prop or support; a baton; the five parallel lines on which musical characters are written; a body of officers attached to an army as a whole (pl. *staffs*); a body of persons assisting in any undertaking.

**Staff-officer,** stäf'of-is-ėr, *n.* An officer upon the staff of an army or regiment.

**Stag,** stag, *n.* A male animal, especially the male red-deer; a hart.

**Stage,** stāj, *n.* An elevated platform; the platform on which theatrical performances are exhibited; place of action; a halting-place; distance between two stopping-places; degree of progression; point reached.—*vt.* To put upon the theatrical stage.

**Stage-coach,** stāj'kōch, *n.* Formerly a coach running regularly for the conveyance of passengers.

**Stager,** stāj'ėr, *n.* One that has long acted on the stage of life; a person of experience.

**Stage-struck,** stāj'struk, *a.* Seized by a passionate desire to become an actor.

**Stagger,** stag'ėr, *vi.* To reel; to totter; to waver.—*vt.* To cause to waver; to amaze; to arrange working hours so that employees enter and leave their place of work at intervals in batches, instead of simultaneously.—*n.* A sudden swaying of the body; *pl.* a disease of cattle, etc., attended with giddiness.

**Stag-hound,** stag'hound, *n.* A large hound used in hunting the stag or red-deer.

**Staging,** stāj'ing, *n.* A temporary structure for support; scaffolding.

**Stagnant,** stag'nant, *a.* Not flowing; motionless; still; dull; not brisk.

**Stagnate,** stag'nāt, *vi.* (stagnating, stagnated). To cease to flow; to become motionless or dull.

**Stagnation,** stag-nā'shon, *n.* State of being or becoming stagnant.

**Staid,** stād, *a.* Sober; grave; sedate.

**Stain,** stān, *vt.* To mark or spot; to discolor; to soil; to disgrace; to tinge with color.—*vi.* To take stains; to become stained.—*n.* A discoloration; a spot; disgrace; a color.

**Stainless,** stān'les, *a.* Free from stains; untarnished; unblemished.

**Stair,** stār, *n.* One of a set of steps to go up or down by; a series of connected steps.

**Staircase,** stār'kās, *n.* The part of a building which contains the stairs.

**Stake,** stāk, *n.* A sharpened piece of wood; a post; that which is pledged or wagered; hazard (preceded by *at*).—*vt.* (staking, staked). To support, defend, or mark with stakes; to pledge; to wager.

**Stalactite,** sta-lak'tīt, *n.* A mass of calcareous matter attached, like an icicle, to the roof of a cavern.

**Stalagmite,** sta-lag'mīt, *n.* A deposit of stalactitic matter on the floor of a cavern.

**Stale,** stāl, *a.* Vapid; tasteless; not new; musty; trite.—*vt.* (staling, staled). To make stale.—*vi.* To discharge urine, as cattle.—*n.* Urine of horses and cattle.

**Stalk,** stak, *n.* The stem of a plant; part that supports a flower, leaf, fruit, etc.; a stately step or walk.—*vi.* To walk in a dignified manner.—*vt.* To watch and follow warily, as game, for the purpose of killing.

**Stalker,** stak'ėr, *n.* One who stalks; a kind of fishing-net.

**Stall,** stal, *n.* A place where a horse or ox is kept and fed; division of a stable; a bench or shed where anything is exposed to sale, etc.; the seat of a clerical dignitary in the choir; a seat in a theatre.—*vt.* To put into a stall; to plunge into mire.

**Stallion,** stal'yun, *n.* A horse not castrated.

**Stalwart, Stalworth,** stal'wėrt, stal'wėrth, *a.* Stout-hearted; tall and strong.

**Stamen,** stā'men., *n.* The male organ of fructification in plants.

**Stamina,** sta'mi-na, *n.pl.* Whatever constitutes the principal strength; robustness; power of endurance.

**Stammer,** stam'ėr, *vt.* and *t.* To make involuntary breaks in utterance; to stutter.—*n.* Defective utterance; a stutter.

**Stamp,** stamp, *vt.* To strike by thrusting the foot down; to impress; to imprint; to affix a postage-stamp to; to coin; to form.—*vi.* To strike the foot forcibly downward.—*n.* Act of stamping; an instrument for crushing or for making impressions; mark imprinted; a postage-stamp; character; sort.

**Stampede,** stam-pēd', *n.* A sudden fright and flight, as of horses.—*vi.* (stampeding, stampeded). To take sudden flight.—*vt.* To cause to break off in a stampede.

**Stanch, Staunch,** stänsh, stansh, *vt.* To stop from running, as blood; to stop the flow of blood from.—*vi.* To cease to flow.—*a.* Strong and tight; constant and zealous; loyal.

**Stanchion,** stan'shon, *n.* A prop or support; a post of timber or iron.

**Stand,** stand, *vi.* (standing, stood). To be upon the feet in an upright position; to be on end; to have locality; to stop; to endure; to persevere; to be as regards circumstances; to be equivalent; to become a candidate; to hold a certain course; to be valid.—*vt.* To set on end; to endure.—*n.* Act of standing; a stop; a halt; a station; a small table or frame; platform for spectators at gatherings.

**Standard,** stan'därd, *n.* A flag of war; a banner; a rule or measure; criterion; test; a certain grade in schools; an upright support.—*a.* Serving as a standard; satisfying certain legal conditions; not trained on a wall, etc., but standing by itself.

**Standard-bearer,** stan'därd-bãr-ėr, *n.* An officer who bears a standard.

**Standing,** stand'ing, *a.* Upright; erect; established; permanent; stagnant.—*n.* Act of one who stands; duration; place to stand in; power to stand; rank.

**Standish,** stan'dish, *n.* A case for pen and ink.

**Stand-point,** stand'point, *n.* A fixed point or station; point of view from which a matter is considered.

**Stand-still,** stand'stil, *n.* A stop.

**Stannary,** stan'a-ri, *n.* A tin mine.—*a.* Relating to the tin mines or works.

**Stannic,** stan'ik, *a.* Pertaining to tin.

**Stanniferous,** stan-if'ėr-us, *a.* Containing or affording tin.

**Stanza,** stan'za, *n.* A verse or connected number of lines of poetry.

**Stanzaic,** stan-zā'ik, *a.* Consisting of or relating to stanzas; arranged as a stanza.

**Staple,** stā'pl, *n.* An emporium; a principal commodity; chief constitutent; thread or pile of wool, cotton, or flax; raw material; an iron loop with two points.—*a.* Chief; principal; established in commerce.—*vt.* (stapling, stapled). To adjust the staples of, as wool.

**Stapler,** stā'pl-ėr,*n.* A dealer in staple commodities; one who assorts wool.

**Star,** stär, *n.* Any celestial body except the sun and moon; a heavenly body similar to our sun; a figure with radiating points; a badge of honor; an asterisk, thus *; a brilliant theatrical performer.—*vt.* (starring, starred). To adorn with stars; to bespangle.—*vi.* To shine as a star; to appear as an eminent actor among inferior players.

**Starboard,** stär'bōrd, *n.* and *a.* The right-hand side of a ship.

**Starch,** stärch, *n.* A vegetable substance, employed for stiffening linen, etc.; stiffness of behavior.—*vt.* To stiffen with starch.

**Starched,** stärcht, *p.a.* Stiffened with starch; precise; formal.

**Starchy,** stärch'i, *a.* Consisting of starch; resembling starch; stiff; precise.

**Star-crossed,** stär'krost, *a.* Not favored by the stars; ill-fated.

**Stare,** stãr, *vi.* (staring, stared). To look with fixed eyes wide open; to gaze; to stand out stiffly.—*vt.* To affect or abash by staring.—*n.* A fixed look with the eyes; a starling.

**Star-fish,** stär'fish, *n.* A marine animal like a star with five or more rays.

**Stark,** stärk, *a.* Stiff; rigid; strong; mere; downright.—*adv.* Wholly.

**Starling,** stär'ling, *n.* A bird allied to the crows, capable of being taught to whistle.

**Start,** stärt, *vi.* To move with sudden quickness; to wince; to deviate; to set out; to begin; to move from its place.—*vt.* To rouse suddenly; to startle; to originate; to dislocate.—*n.* A sudden motion; a twitch; outset; a handicap.

**Starter,** stärt'ėr, *n.* One who starts; one who sets persons or things in motion.

**Startle,** stärt'l, *vi.* (startling, startled). To move suddenly.—*vt.* To cause to start; to frighten.—*n.* A start, as from fear.

**Startling,** stärt'ling, *a.* Such as to startle; surprising; alarming.

**Starvation,** stär-vā'shon, *n.* Act of starving; keen suffering from hunger or cold.

**Starve,** stärv, *vi.* (starving, starved). To perish with cold; to suffer from hunger; to be very indigent.—*vt.* To kill or distress with hunger or cold; to make inefficient through insufficient expenditure.

**State,** stāt, *n.* Condition; situation; rank; pomp; grandeur; an estate (of the realm); a commonwealth; a nation; civil power.—*a.* National; public; governmental.—*vt.* (stating, stated). To express the particulars of; to narrate.

**Stated,** stāt'ed, *p.a.* Established; regular.

**Stately,** stāt'li, *a.* Such as pertains to state; august; grand; lofty; dignified.

**Statement,** stāt'ment, *n.* Expression of a fact or opinion; narrative.

**State-room,** stāt'röm, *n.* A magnificent room; separate cabin in a steamer.

**Statesman,** stāts'man, *n.* A man versed in state affairs or in the arts of government.

**Static,** stat'ik, *a.* Statical.

**Statical,** stat'ik-al, *a.* Pertaining to bodies at rest or in equilibrium.

**Station,** stā'shon, *n.* Place where anything stands; post assigned; situation; social position; a regular stopping-place, as on railways, etc.—*vt.* To assign a position to; to post.

**Stationary,** stā'shon-a-ri, *a.* Fixed; not moving; not appearing to move.

**Stationer,** stā'shon-ėr, *n.* One who sells paper, pens, ink, pencils, etc.

**Stationery,** stā'shon-ė-ri, *n.* and *a.* Articles sold by stationers, as paper, ink, etc.

**Station-master,** stā'shon-mäs-tėr, *n.* The official in charge of a railway-station.

**Statist,** stat'ist, *n.* A statistician.

**Statistical, Statistic,** sta-tis'tik-al, sta-tis'tik, *a.* Pertaining to statistics.

**Statistician,** stat-is-ti'shan, *n.* One versed in statistics.

**Statistics,** sta-tist'iks, *n.* A collection of facts, tabulated numerically; the science of subjects as elucidated by facts.

**Statuary,** stat'ū-a-ri, *n.* One who carves statues; the art of carving statues; statues regarded collectively.

**Statue,** stat'ū, *n.* An image of a human figure or animal in marble, bronze, or other solid substance.

**Statuesque,** stat-ū-esk', *a.* Partaking of or having the character of a statue.

**Statuette,** stat-ū-et', *n.* A small statue.

**Stature,** stat'ūr, *n.* The height of anyone standing; bodily tallness.

**Status,** stā'tus, *n.* Social position; rank; condition; position of affairs.

**Statute,** stat'ūt, *n.* A law passed by the legislature of a state; an enactment; a fundamental or permanent rule or law.

**Statutory,** stat'ū-to-ri, *n.* Enacted by statute.

**Stave,** stāv, *n.* A pole; one of the pieces of timber of casks, etc.; a stanza, in *music*, the staff.—*vt.* (staving, staved). To break in a stave of; to break a hole in (pret. & pp. also *stove*).—**To stave off,** to put off; to delay.

**Stay,** stā, *vt.* (pret. & pp. stayed or staid). To prop; to stop; to delay; to await.—*vi.* To remain; to reside; to delay; to forbear to act; to stop.—*n.* Sojourn; stop; obstacle; a prop; a rope to support a mast; *pl.* a stiffened bodice worn by females; a corset.—**To miss stays,** to fail in the attempt to tack about.

**Stead,** sted, *n.* Place or room which another had or might have; assistance: preceded by *in*.—*vt.*

To be of use to.
**Steadfast,** sted'fäst, *a*. Firm; constant; resolute; steady.
**Steadily,** sted'i-li, *adv*. In a steady manner; without shaking or tottering; assiduously.
**Steady,** sted'i, *a*. Firm; stable; constant; regular; equable.—*vt*. (steadying, steadied). To make or keep firm.
**Steak,** stāk, *n*. A slice of beef, etc., broiled or cut for broiling.
**Steal,** stēl, *vt*. (pret. stole, pp. stolen). To take feloniously; to pilfer; to gain by address or imperceptibly; to perform secretly.—*vi*. To pass silently or privily; to practice theft.
**Stealing,** stēl'ing, *n*. Theft.
**Stealth,** stelth, *n*. A secret method of procedure; a proceeding by secrecy.
**Stealthy,** stel'thi, *a*. Done by stealth; furtive; sly.
**Steam,** stēm, *n*. The vapor of water; aeriform fluid generated by the boiling of water.—*vi*. To give out steam; to rise in vaporous form; to sail by means of steam.—*vt*. To expose to steam; to apply steam to.
**Steam-boat, Steam-vessel,** stēm'bōt, stēm'vesel, *n*. A vessel propelled by steam.
**Steam-engine,** stēm'en-jin, *n*. An engine worked by steam.
**Steamer,** stēm'ėr, *n*. A steam-boat; a vessel in which articles are subjected to steam.
**Steam-power,** stēm'pou-ėr, *n*. The power of steam mechanically applied.
**Steam-ship,** stēm'ship, *n*. A steam-boat.
**Steam-whistle,** stēm'whis-l, *n*. A whistle sounded by steam passing through.
**Stearine, Stearin,** stē'a-rin, *n*. The chief and harder ingredient of animal fats.
**Steatite,** stē'a-tīt, *n*. A mineral consisting of magnesia and alumina.
**Steed,** stēd, *n*. A horse; a horse of high mettle, for state or war.
**Steel,** stēl, *n*. A very hard form or iron, produced by addition of carbon; weapons, swords, etc.; a knife-sharpener; sternness; rigor.—*a*. Made of or like steel; unfeeling; rigorous.—*vt*. To furnish with steel; to harden.
**Steely,** stēl'i, *a*. Made of or like steel; hard.
**Steelyard,** stēl'yärd, *n*. A kind of balance for weighing, with unequal arms.
**Steep,** stēp, *a*. Sloping greatly; precipitous.—*n*. A precipitous place; a cliff; process of steeping; liquid in which something is steeped.—*vt*. To soak; to imbue.
**Steeple,** stē'pl, *n*. A lofty erection attached to a church, etc.; spire.
**Steeple-chase,** stē'pl-chās, *n*. A horse-race across country and over obstacles.
**Steer,** stēr, *vt*. and *i*. To direct and govern, as a ship; to guide; to pursue a course in life.—*n*. A young ox; a bullock.
**Steerage,** stēr'āj, *n*. The steering of a ship; part of a ship allotted to inferior passengers, usually in the fore part.
**Steeve,** stēv, *vi*. To rise up from the bows at an angle: said of a bowsprit.
**Stela, Stele,** stē'la, stē'lē, *n*.; pl. **-lae.** A small column serving as a monument.
**Stellar, Stellary,** stel'ėr, stel'a-ri, *a*. Pertaining to stars; astral; starry.
**Stellate,** stel'lāt, *a*. Resembling a star; radiated.
**Stelliform,** stel'li-form, *a*. Radiated.
**Stellular, Stellulate,** stel'ū-lėr, stel'ū-lāt, *a*. Like stars; having marks like stars.
**Stem,** stem, *n*. The principal body of a tree, shrub, etc.; the stalk; stock or branch of a family; the prow of a vessel—*vt*. (stemming, stemmed). To make way against; to press forward through; to dam up; to check.
**Stench,** stensh, *n*. An ill smell; stink.
**Stencil,** sten'sil, *n*. A thin plate with a pattern cut through it, brushed over with color to mark a surface below.—*vt*. (stenciling, stenciled). To form by a stencil; to color with stencils.
**Sten gun,** sten gun, *n*. A machine carbine suitable for use at short range (up to 200 yards) and capable of firing 96 rounds (three magazines) per minute. The name is derived from the initials of the two patentees, Saltoun and Thornton, and from Enfield, the place of patent.
**Stenograph,** sten'ō-graf, *n*. A writing in shorthand; a kind of typewriter.
**Stenographer, Stenographist,** ste-nog'ra-fėr, sten-nog'ra-fist, *n*. One who is skilled in stenography or shorthand.
**Stenographic, Stenographical,** sten-ō-graf'ik, sten-ō-graf'ik-al, *a*. Pertaining to or expressed in shorthand.
**Stenography,** ste-nog'ra-fi, *n*. The art of writing in shorthand; shorthand.
**Stentorian,** sten-tō'ri-an, *a*. Extremely loud; able to utter a loud and deep sound.
**Step,** step, *vi*. (stepping, stepped). To move the leg and foot in walking; to walk.—*vt*. To set (the foot); to fix the foot of, as of a mast.—*n*. A pace; a small space; a grade; a rise; footprint; gait; footfall; action adopted; something to support the feet in ascending; round of a ladder; *pl*. a step-ladder.
**Stepbrother,** step'bruᴛʜ-ėr, *n*. A father's or mother's son by another marriage.—Also *stepsister*.
**Stepfather,** step'fä-ᴛʜėr, *n*. A mother's second or subsequent husband.—Also *stepmother*.
**Step-ladder,** step'lad-ėr, *n*. A portable self-supporting ladder.
**Steppe,** step, *n*. An extensive treeless plain in Russia or Siberia.
**Stepping-stone,** step'ing-stōn, *n*. A stone to raise the feet above a stream or mud; a means of progress or advancement.
**Stepson,** step'sun, *n*. The son of a husband or wife by a former marriage.—Also *stepdaughter, stepchild*.
**Stère,** stār, *n*. The French unit for solid measure, equal to a cubic meter or 35.3156 cubic feet.
Relating to stereography.
**Stereography,** ste-rō-og'ra-fi, *n*. The art of delineating solid bodies on a plane.
**Stereoscope,** ste'rē-ō-skōp, *n*. An optical instrument by which two pictures taken under a small difference of angular view and placed side by side appear as one, the objects seeming solid and real.
**Stereoscopic,** ste'rē-ō-skop''ik, *a*. Pertaining to the stereoscope.
**Stereotype,** ste'rē-ō-tīp, *n*. and *a*. A metal plate presenting a facsimile of a page of type; an electrotype plate.—*vt*. To make a stereotype of; to fix unchangeably.
**Sterile,** ste'ril, *a*. Barren; unfruitful; incapable of reproduction; barren of ideas.
**Sterility,** ste-ril'i-ti, *n*. Quality or state of being sterile; unproductiveness.
**Sterlize,** ste'ril-īz, *vt*. To make sterile; to render free from bacteria or germs.
**Sterilizer,** ste'ril-īz-ėr, *n*. One who sterilizes; an apparatus to destroy bacilli, etc.
**Sterlet,** stėr'let, *n*. A species of sturgeon.
**Sterling,** stėr'ling, *a*. An epithet distinctive of English money; genuine; of excellent quality.
**Stern,** stėrn, *a*. Austere; harsh; rigid; stringent.—*n*. The hind part of a ship.
**Sternal,** stėr'nal, *a*. Pertaining to the sternum.
**Stern-chaser,** stėrn'chās-ėr, *n*. A cannon placed in a ship's stern, pointed backward.
**Sternly,** stėrn'li, *adv*. In a stern manner.
**Sternum,** stėr'num, *n*. The breast-bone.
**Stertorous,** stėr'to-rus, *a*. Characterized by deep snoring.
**Stethoscope,** ste'thō-skōp, *n*. An instrument for sounding the chest, lungs, etc.
**Stevedore,** stē've-dōr, *n*. One who loads or unloads vessels.
**Stew,** stū, *vt*. To boil slowly in a closed vessel.—*vi*. To be cooked slowly.—*n*. Meat stewed; a bathing house with hot baths; a brothel; a state of excitement.

S

**Steward,** stū'ėrd, *n.* One who manages affairs for another; one who helps to manage a public function; an officer on a vessel who attends to passengers, etc.
**Stewardess,** stū'ärd-es, *n.* A female steward.
**Stick,** stik, *vt.* (sticking, stuck). To pierce or stab; to fasten by piercing, gluing, etc.; to fix; to set.—*vi.* To adhere; to abide firmly; to be brought to a stop; to scruple.—*n.* A rod or wand; a staff; a stiff, awkward person.
**Stickler,** stik'lėr, *n.* One who stickles; an obstinate contender about trifles.
**Stiff,** stif, *a.* Rigid; tense; not moving easily; thick; not natural and easy; formal in manner; stubborn; difficult; strong.
**Stiffen,** stif'n, *vt.* To make stiff.—*vi.* To become stiff or stiffer.
**Stiffening,** stif'n-ing, *n.* Something used to make a substance more stiff; starch, etc.
**Stiffly,** stif'li, *adv.* In a stiff manner; firmly; rigidly; obstinately; formally.
**Stiff-necked,** stif'nekt, *a.* Stubborn; inflexibly obstinate; contumacious.
**Stiffness,** stif'nes, *n.* Want of pliancy; rigidity; viscidness; stubbornness; formality.
**Stifle,** stī'fl, *vt.* and *i.* (stifling, stifled). To suffocate; to smother; to suppress.—*n.* The joint of a horse next to the buttock.
**Stigma,** stig'ma, *n.*; pl. **-mas** or **-mata.** A brand made with a red-hot iron; any mark of infamy; part of a flower pistil which receives the pollen; pl. *stigmata,* bodily marks like Christ's wounds impressed supernaturally.
**Stigmatic,** stig-mat'ik, *a.* Pertaining to stigmas or stigmata.—*n.* A person marked with stigmata.
**Stigmatize,** stig'mat-īz, *vt.* To characterize by some opprobrious epithet.
**Stile,** stīl, *n.* A step or steps to aid persons in getting over a fence or wall.
**Stiletto,** sti-let'tō, *n.* A small strong dagger; a pointed instrument for making eyelet-holes.—*vt.* (stilettoing, stilettoed). To stab or pierce with a stiletto.
**Still,** stil, *a.* At rest; calm; silent; not loud; soft; not effervescing.—*vt.* To make still; to check; to appease or allay.—*adv.* To this time; always; nevertheless; yet.—*n.* A vessel or apparatus for distilling; a distillery.
**Still-born,** stil'born, *a.* Dead at the birth; abortive; produced unsuccessfully.
**Stilt,** stilt, *n.* Either of a pair of poles, with a rest for the foot, used for raising the feet in walking.
**Stilted,** stilt'ed, *a.* Elevated as if on stilts; stiff and bombastic; jerky.
**Stimulant,** stim'ū-lant, *a.* Serving to stimulate.—*n.* An agent which produces an increase of vital energy; an intoxicant.
**Stimulate,** stim'ū-lāt, *vt.* To rouse up; to incite; to excite greater vitality in.
**Stimulating,** stim'ū-lāt-ing, *p.a.* Serving to stimulate or rouse; rousing; stirring.
**Stimulation,** stim-ū-lā'shon, *n.* Act of stimulating; incitement; use of a stimulus.
**Stimulus,** stim'ū-lus, *n.* pl. **-li.** Something that stimulates; an incitement.
**Sting,** sting, *vt.* (stinging, stung). To pierce, as wasps, etc.; to prick, as a nettle; to pain acutely.—*n.* A sharp-pointed defensive organ of certain animals; the thrust of a sting into the flesh; something that gives acute pain; the biting effect of words.
**Stingily,** stin'ji-li, *adv.* In a stringy or niggardly manner; meanly; shabbily.
**Stinging,** sting'ing, *p.a.* Furnished with a sting; goading; sharp; keen.
**Stingy,** stin'ji, *a.* Very niggardly; meanly avaricious; scanty.
**Stink,** stingk, *vi.* (stinking, stunk). To emit a strong offensive smell; to be in disrepute.—*n.* A strong offensive smell.
**Stint,** stint, *vt.* To restrict; to make scanty.—*vi.* To cease; to desist from.—*n.* Limit; restraint; restriction.
**Stipe, Stipes,** stīp, stī'pēz, *n.* A stalk or stem.
**Stipend,** stī'pend, *n.* Yearly allowance; salary.
**Stipendiary,** sti-pend'i-a-ri, *a.* Receiving stipend.—*n.* A paid magistrate in a town; one who performs services for a stipend.
**Stipple,** stip'l, *vt.* (stippling, stippled). To engrave by means of dots.—*n.* A process of engraving by means of dots.
**Stipulate,** stip'ū-lāt, *vi.* (stipulating, stipulated). To make an agreement; to contract; to settle terms.
**Stipulaton,** stip-ū-lā'shon, *n.* Act of stipulating; a contract;; item in a contract.
**Stir,** stėr, *vt.* (stirring, stirred). To put into motion; to agitate; to rouse; to provoke; to disturb.—*vi.* To move oneself; not to be still; to be awake or out of bed.—*n.* Commotion; bustle; disorder.
**Stirrup,** sti'rup, *n.* A metal loop, suspended by a strap, to support the foot in riding.
**Stitch,** stich, *n.* A sharp pain; one complete movement of a needle in sewing; a complete turn or link in knitting, netting, etc.—*vt.* and *i.* To sew by making stitches in; to unite by stitches.
**Stitching,** stich'ing, *n.* Act signified by the verb to stitch; work done by stitching.
**Stiver,** stī'vėr, *n.* An old Dutch coin; something insignificant.
**Stoa,** stō'a, *n.* A porch or portico.
**Stoat,** stōt, *n.* The ermine in its summer fur.
**Stock,** stok, *a.* A post; a lifeless mass; stem of a tree; wooden piece of a rifle; a stiff cravat; an original progenitor; lineage; capital invested in any business; money funded in government securities; store; animals belonging to a farm; liquor used to form a foundation for soups and gravies; a sweet-smelling garden-plant; *pl.* an instrument of punishment confining the offender's ankles or wrists; timbers on which a ship is supported while building.—*vt.* To provide with a stock; to lay up in store.—*a.* Kept in stock; standing; permanent.
**Stockade,** stok-ād', *n.* A defense of strong posts stuck close to each other; an enclosure made with posts.—*vt.* (stockading, stockaded). To fortify with posts fixed in the ground.
**Stockbroker,** stok'brō-kėr, *n.* A broker who buys and sells stocks or shares for others.
**Stock-exchange,** stok'eks-chānj, *n.* The place where stocks or shares are bought and sold; an organized association of stockbrokers.
**Stockholder,** stok'hōld-ėr, *n.* A shareholder or proprietor of stock.
**Stocking,** stok'ing, *n.* A close-fitting knitted covering for the foot and leg.
**Stodgy,** stoj'i, *a.* Crammed together roughly; crude and indigestible.
**Stoic,** stō'ik, *n.* One of an Athenian sect of philosophers, who held that men should strive to be unmoved by joy or grief, regarding virtue alone as the highest good; an apathetic person; one indifferent to pleasure or pain.
**Stoical,** stō'ik-al, *a.* Like a stoic; manifesting indifference to pleasure or pain.
**Stoicism,** stō'i-sizm, *n.* Indifference to pleasure or pain.
**Stoke,** stōk, *vt.* (stoking, stoked). To keep supplied with fuel, as a fire.
**Stoker,** stōk'ėr, *n.* One who attends to a furnace or large fire.
**Stole,** stōl, *n.* A long and narrow scarf worn round the neck, with the ends hanging down, by clergymen of the Anglican and Roman Catholic churches.
**Stolid,** stol'id, *a.* Dull; foolish; stupid.
**Stolidity,** sto-lid'i-ti, *n.* Dullness of intellect; stupidity.
**Stolon,** stō'lon, *n.* In *botany,* a sucker.
**Stoma,** stō'ma, *n.*; pl. **-ata.** A minute orifice or pore in plants or animals.
**Stomach,** stum'ak, *n.* A membranous sac, the principal organ of digestion; appetite; inclination.—*vt.* To brook; to put up with.

**Stomacher,** stum'a-chėr, *n.* An ornamental article of dress worn by females on the breast.
**Stomachic,** stō-mak'ik, *a.* Pertaining to the stomach.—*n.* A medicine for the stomach.
**Stone,** stōn, *n.* A hard mass of earthy or mineral matter; a pebble; a precious stone; concretion in the kidneys or bladder; a testicle; the nut of a fruit; a measure of 14 lbs. avoirdupois.—*a.* Made of stone; like stone.—*vt.* (stoning, stoned). To pelt with stones; to free from stones; to provide with stones.
**Stone-cutter,** stōn'kut-ėr, *n.* One whose occupation is to cut or hew stones.
**Stone-dresser,** stōn'dres-ėr, *n.* One who smooths and shapes stone for building.
**Stone-ware,** stōn'wār, *n.* Common glazed pottery ware.
**Stony,** stōn'i, *a.* Pertaining to, abounding in, or like stone; hard; pitiless; frigid.
**Stony-hearted,** stōn'i-härt-ed, *a.* Hard-hearted; cruel; pitiless; unfeeling.
**Stook,** stuk, *n.* A set of sheaves of corn, etc., set on end.—*vt.* To set up in stooks.
**Stool,** stöl, *n.* A portable seat without a back for one person; the seat used in evacuating the bowels; a discharge from the bowels.
**Stoop,** stöp, *vi.* To bend the body forward and downward; to yield; to deign; to pounce.—*n.* Act of stooping; bend of the back or shoulders; a condescension; swoop.
**Stooping,** stöp'ing, *p.a.* Having a stoop; in act to stoop; bowed, as the shoulders.
**Stop,** stop, *vt.* (stopping, stopped). To stuff up; to close; to arrest the progress of; to put an end to; to regulate the sounds of musical strings by the fingers, etc.—*vi.* To cease from any motion; to come to an end; to stay; to remain.—*n.* Obstruction; interruption; pause; a series of pipes in an organ giving distinctive sounds; a point in writing.
**Stop-gap,** stop'gap, *n.* That which fills up a gap; a temporary expedient.
**Stopper,** stop'ėr, *n.* One who or that which stops; a stopple.—*vt.* To close with a stopper.
**Stopple,** stop'l, *n.* That which closes the mouth of a vessel; a plug.—*vt.* (stoppling, stoppled). To close with a stopple.
**Stop-watch,** stop'woch, *n.* A watch one of the hands of which can be stopped instantaneously so as to mark with accuracy any point of time.
**Storage,** stōr'āj, *n.* Act of storing; charge for keeping goods in a store.
**Store,** stōr, *n.* A large quantity for supply; abundance; a place where goods are kept; a shop; *pl.* necessary articles laid up for use.—*a.* Pertaining to a store; kept in store.—*vt.* (storing, stored). To amass; to supply; to reposit in a store for preservation.
**Storehouse,** stōr'hous, *n.* A place in which things are stored; a repository.
**Store-room,** stōr'röm, *n.* A room for the reception of stores.
**Storied,** stō'rid, *a.* Having stories or tales associated with it; celebrated in story.
**Stork,** stork, *n.* A large grallatorial or wading bird resembling the heron.
**Storm,** storm, *n.* A violent disturbance of the atmosphere; a tempest; an outbreak; assault on a strong position.—*vt.* To take by assault; to attack.—*vi.* To be in violent agitation; to rage.
**Storm-glass,** storm'gläs, *n.* A weather-glass consisting of a tube containing a chemical solution sensible to atmospheric changes.
**Stormy,** storm'i, *a.* Abounding with storms; boisterous; passionate; angry.
**Story,** stō'ri, *n.* A narrative; an account; a tale; a fiction; a falsehood.
**Story, Storey,** stō'ri, *n.* A state or floor of a building.
**Stoup,** stöp or stoup, *n.* A basin for holy water in R. Catholic church; a flagon.
**Stout,** stout, *a.* Bold; valiant; sturdy; bulky; corpulent.—*n.* A dark-brown malt liquor.
**Stoutly,** stout'li, *adv.* Boldly; lustily.
**Stove,** stōv, *n.* An apparatus for warming a room, cooking, etc.—*vt.* (stoving, stoved). To heat in a stove. Pret. of *stave.*
**Stow,** stō, *vt.* To put in a suitable place; to pack; to compactly arrange anything in.
**Stowage,** stō'āj, *n.* Act of stowing; room for things to be packed away; charge for stowing goods.
**Stowaway,** stō'a-wā, *n.* One who hides himself on a ship to obtain a free passage.
**Straddle,** strad'l, *vt.* and *t.* (straddling, straddled). To spread the legs wide; to sit astride; to stride across; to drop bombs along or across a target so as to cover a large area.
**Straggle,** strag'l, *vi.* (straggling, straggled). To rove; to wander in a scattered way; to occur at intervals.
**Straight,** strāt, *a.* Stretched tight; direct; correct; upright.—*n.* A straight part or piece; straight direction.—*adv.* Immediately; directly.—*vt.* To straighten.
**Straight-edge,** strāt'ej, *n.* An implement with a perfectly straight edge for testing surfaces or drawing straight lines.
**Straighten,** strāt'n, *vt.* To make straight.
**Straightforward,** strāt'for-wėrd, *a.* Proceeding in a straight course; candid; honest; frank; open.—*adv.* Directly forward.
**Strain,** strān, *vt.* To stretch tightly; to exert to the utmost; to overtask; to sprain; to carry too far; to wrest; to filter.—*vi.* To exert oneself; to filter.—*n.* Violent effort; excessive stretching or exertion; tenor; theme; a lay; tune; race; family blood; tendency.
**Strained,** strānd, *a.* Stretched to the utmost; forced or unnatural.
**Strainer,** strān'ėr, *n.* One who strains; an instrument for filtration.
**Strait,** strāt, *a.* Confined; narrow; close; strict.—*n.* A narrow passage; a narrow stretch of water (often *pl.*); a position of hardship or difficulty.
**Straiten,** strāt'n, *vt.* To make strait; to distress; to hamper.
**Strait-laced,** strāt'lāst, *a.* Laced tightly; excessively strict or scrupulous.
**Straitly,** strāt'li, *adv.* Narrowly; closely; strictly.
**Strake,** strāk, *n.* A continuous line of planking or plates on a ship's side.
**Stramineous,** stra-min'ē-us, *a.* Consisting of or like straw.
**Stramonium,** stra-mō'ni-um, *n.* The thorn-apple; a drug obtained from it.
**Strand,** strand, *n.* The shore of a sea or lake; one of the twists of a rope.—*vt.* and *i.* To drive or be driven ashore.
**Strange,** strānj, *a.* Foreign; wonderful; odd; not familiar.
**Strangely,** strānj'li, *adv.* In a strange manner; wonderfully; remarkably.
**Stranger,** strān'jėr, *n.* A foreigner; an alien; one unknown; a visitor.
**Strangle,** strang'gl, *vt.* (strangling, strangled). To choke; to throttle; to suppress or stifle.
**Strangulate,** strang'gū-lāt, *vt.* To strangle; to stop vital action in by compression.
**Strangury,** strang'gū-ri, *n.* A disease in which there is pain in passing the urine, which is excreted in drops.
**Strap,** strap, *n.* A long narrow slip of leather, etc.; a plate or strip of metal.—*vt.* (strapping, strapped). To beat with a strap; to fasten with a strap.
**Strapper,** strap'ėr, *n.* One who uses a strap; a kind of groom or attendant on horses.
**Strapping,** strap'ing, *a.* Tall and well made; handsome.
**Strass,** stras, *n.* A variety of flint-glass or paste used to make artificial gems.
**Stratagem,** stra'ta-jem, *n.* A piece of generalship; an artifice in war; a wile.
**Strategic, Strategical,** stra-tej'ik, stra-tej'ik-al, *a.*

S

Pertaining to strategy; effected by strategy.

**Strategist,** stra'te-jist, *n.* One skilled in strategy.

**Strategy,** stra'te-ji, *n.* The science of military operations; generalship.

**Stratification,** stra'ti-fi-kā''shon, *n.* Arrangement in strata or layers.

**Stratify,** stra'ti-fī, *vt.* To form into a stratum or strata; to lay in strata.

**Stratosphere,** stra'tō-sfēr, *n.* The upper region of the earth's atomosphere.

**Stratum,** strā'tum, *n.*; pl. **-ta.** A layer of any substance, as sand, clay, etc., especially when one of a number.

**Stratus,** strā'tus, *n.* A low horizontal cloud.

**Straw,** stra, *n.* The dry stalk of grain, pulse, etc.—*a.* Made of straw.

**Strawberry,** stra'be-ri, *n.* A herbaceous plant and its succulent fruit.

**Stray,** strā, *vi.* To go astray; to err; to roam.—*a.* Having gone astray; straggling.—*n.* Any domestic animal that wanders at large, or is lost.

**Streak,** strēk, *n.* A long mark; a stripe; appearance of a mineral when scratched.—*vt.* To form streaks in.

**Streaky,** strēk'i, *a.* Striped; variegated with streaks.

**Stream,** strēm, *n.* A river or brook; a current; drift.—*vi.* and *t.* To move in a stream; to stretch in a long line; to float at full length in the air.

**Streamer,** strēm'ėr, *n.* That which streams out; a long pennon; a luminous beam or column.

**Streamline,** strēm-līn', *vt.* To shape so as to reduce resistance to air and water.

**Streamy,** strēm'i, *a.* Abounding with streams; beaming.

**Street,** strēt, *n.* A road in a town or village; the roadway and houses together.

**Strength,** strength, *n.* Property of being strong; force or energy; power; support; vigor; intensity; amount or numbers of an army, fleet, or the like.—**On the strength of,** in reliance upon, on the faith of.

**Strengthen,** strength'en, *vt.* and *i.* To make or become strong or stronger.

**Strenuous,** stren'ū-us, *a.* Energetic; vigorous; zealous; ardent; earnest.

**Stress,** stres, *vt.* To put in difficulties; to subject to emphasis.—*n.* Constraint; pressure; weight; violence, as of weather; emphasis.

**Stretch,** strech, *vt.* To draw out tight; to extend; to straighten; to strain; to exaggerate.—*vi.* To reach or extend; to spread; to have elasticity.—*n.* Strain; extent; scope; expanse; a turn or spell.

**Stretcher,** strech'ėr, *n.* One who stretches; a contrivance for stretching things; a litter for carrying persons.

**Strew,** strö or strō, *vt.* (pp. strewed or strewn). To scatter or sprinkle; to cover by scattering; to besprinkle.

**Stria,** strī'a, *n.*; pl. **-iae.** A term for fine streaks on surfaces of minerals, plants, etc.

**Stricken,** strik'n, pp. of *strike.* Struck; smitten; advanced in age.

**Strict,** strikt, *a.* Tight; tense; exact; severe; rigorous; not loose or vague.

**Strictly,** strikt'li, *adv.* In a strict manner; correctly; definitely; rigorously; severely.

**Stricture,** strik'tūr, *n.* A contraction of any canal of the body; a critical remark; censure.

**Stride,** strīd, *vi.* (striding, pret. strode, pp. stridden). To walk with long steps; to straddle.—*vt.* To pass over at a step.—*n.* A long step; a measured tread.

**Strident,** strī'dent, *a.* Harsh; grating.

**Strife,** strīf, *n.* Act of striving; struggle; contest; discord; conflict; quarrel or war.

**Strike,** strīk, *vi.* (striking, pret. struck, pp. struck, stricken). To move or turn aside rapidly; to light (upon); to make a blow; to hit; to be stranded; to yield; to quit work to compel better terms.—*vt.* To smite; to mint; to thrust in; to notify by sound; to occur to; to impress strongly; to effect at once; to lower, as the flag or sails of a vessel.—*n.* Act of workmen who quit work to force their employer to give better terms; a strickle.

**Striker,** strīk'ėr, *n.* One who or that which strikes; one who engages in a strike.

**Striking,** strīk'ing, *p.a.* Surprising; remarkable; notable; impressive.

**String,** string, *n.* A small cord; a piece of twine; a line with the things on it; chord of a musical instrument; a series.—*vt.* (stringing, strung). To furnish with string; to put on a string; to make tense.

**Stringent,** strin'jent, *a.* Strict; rigorous; rigid.

**Strip,** strip, *vt.* (stripping, stripped). To deprive of a covering; to skin; to deprive; to pillage.—*vi.* To take off the covering or clothes.—*n.* A long narrow piece.

**Stripe,** strīp, *n.* A long narrow division or marking; a streak; a strip; a stroke with a lash; a wale or weal.—*vt.* (striping, striped). To form or variegate with stripes.

**Strive,** strīv, *vi.* (striving, pret. strove, pp. striven). To endeavor; to make efforts; to struggle; to vie.

**Stroke,** strōk, *n.* A blow; calamity; attack; striking of a clock; touch; a masterly effort; a dash in writing or printing; a touch of the pen; a line; a gentle rub; the sweep of an oar; a stroke-oar.—*vt.* (stroking, stroked). To rub gently with the hand.

**Stroll,** strōl, *vi.* To ramble; to rove; to roam.—*n.* A short leisurely walk.

**Strong,** strong, *a.* Having power or force; robust; not easily broken; firm; effectual; earnest; containing much alcohol; glaring; forcible; tending upwards in price; effecting inflection by internal vowel change.

**Stronghold,** strong'hōld, *n.* A place of strength or security; a fortified place.

**Strongly,** strong'li, *adv.* With strength or power; forcibly; firmly; greatly.

**Strong-room,** strong'röm, *n.* A room in which valuables are kept.

**Strontia,** stron'shi-a, *n.* An oxide of strontium.

**Strontium,** stron'shi-um, *n.* A metal of a yellow color, somewhat harder than lead.

**Strop,** strop, *n.* A strip of leather, etc., for sharpening razors.—*vt.* (stropping, stropped). To sharpen on a strop.

**Strophe,** strō'fē, *n.* The former of two corresponding stanzas in an ode.

**Strove,** strōv, pret. of *strive.*

**Strow,** strō. *See* STREW.

**Struck,** struk, pret. and pp. of *strike.*

**Structural,** struk'tūr-al, *a.* Pertaining to structure.

**Structure,** struk'tūr, *n.* A building of any kind; manner of building; make; organization.

**Struggle,** strug'l, *vi.* (struggling, struggled). To make great efforts; to strive; to contend.—*n.* A violent effort of the body; forcible effort; contest; strife.

**Strum,** strum, *vi.* and *t.* (strumming, strummed). To play unskilfully on a stringed instrument; to thrum.

**Struma,** strö'ma, *n.*; pl. **-mae.** A scrofulous swelling or tumor; scrofula.

**Strumose, Strumous,** strö'mōs, strö'mus, *a.* Scrofulous.

**Strumpet,** strum'pet, *n.* A prostitute.

**Strut,** strut, *vi.* (strutting, strutted). To walk with affected dignity.—*n.* A lofty, proud step or walk; a strengthening piece placed diagonally in a framework.

**Strychnia, Strychinine,** strik'ni-a, strik'nīn, *n.* A vegetable alkaloid poison obtained from the seeds of nux-vomica.

**Stub,** stub, *n.* The stump of a tree; a remaining part of anything.—*vt.* (stubbing, stubbed). To grub up by the roots.

**Stubble,** stub'l, *n.* The stumps of a grain crop left in the ground after reaping.

**Stubbly,** stub'li, *a.* Covered with stubble; resem-

bling stubble; short and stiff.
**Stubborn,** stub'orn, *a.* Not to be moved or persuaded; obstinate; intractable.
**Stubby,** stub'i, *a.* Abounding with stubs; short and thick.
**Stucco,** stuk'kō, *n.* A fine plaster; work made of stucco; plaster of Paris or gypsum.—*vt.* (stuccoing, stuccoed). To overlay with stucco.
**Stuck-up,** stuk'up, *a.* Giving oneself airs of importance; proud; pompous.
**Stud,** stud, *n.* A post; a prop; a nail with a large head; an ornamental button; a set of breeding horses; a person's horses collectively.—*vt.* (studding, studded). To adorn with studs; to set thickly, as with studs.
**Studding-sail,** stud'ing-sāl, *n.* A sail set on the outer edge of a principal sail during a light wind.
**Student,** stū'dent, *n.* One who studies; a scholar; a bookish person.
**Stud-horse,** stud'hors, *n.* A breeding horse.
**Studied,** stu'did, *a.* Made the object of study; qualified by study; premeditated.
**Studio,** stū'di-ō, *n.* The work-place of a painter or sculptor.
**Studious,** stū'di-us, *a.* Given to study; mindful; earnest; careful; deliberate.
**Studiously,** stū'di-us-li, *adv.* Diligently; carefully; deliberately.
**Study,** stu'di, *n.* Earnest endeavor; application to books, etc.; subject which one studies; apartment devoted to study; a reverie; a preparatory sketch.—*vt.* and *i.* (studying, studied). To apply the mind to; to investigate; to have careful regard to.
**Stuff,** stuf, *n.* Substance indefinitely; material; cloth; a light woollen fabric; goods; trash.—*vt.* To pack; to thrust in; to fill, as meat with seasoning; to fill, as an animal's skin to preserve the form.—*vi.* To cram; to feed gluttonously.
**Stuffing,** stuf'ing, *n.* That which is used to fill anything, as a cushion; substance put into a fowl for cooking.
**Stuffy,** stuf'i, *a.* Difficult to breathe in; close; stifling.
**Stultify,** stul'ti-fi, *vi.* To prove foolish; to cause to seem absurd; to make a fool of.
**Stumble,** stum'bl, *vi.* (stumbling, stumbled). To trip in moving; to walk unsteadily; to fall into error; to light by chance (with *on*).—*n.* A trip in walking or running; a blunder.
**Stumbling-block, Stumbling-stone,** stum'bling-blok, stum'bling-stōn, *n.* Any cause of stumbling or erring.
**Stump,** stump, *n.* The part of a tree, limb, etc., left after the rest is cut off or destroyed; a worn-down tooth; a wicket in cricket.—*vt.* To lop, as trees; to make a tour through, delivering speeches; to put out of play in cricket by knocking down a stump.—*vi.* To walk stiffly or noisily.
**Stumpy,** stump'i, *a.* Full of stumps; short and thick.
**Stun,** stun, *vt.* (stunning, stunned). To overpower the sense of hearing of; to stupefy; to make senseless with a blow; to surprise completely.
**Stunning,** stun'ing, *p.a.* Such as to stun; first-rate; excellent.
**Stunt,** stunt, *vt.* To stop the growth of; to dwarf.—*n.* A check in growth.
**Stunted,** stunt'ed, *a.* Hindered from growth; dwarfish in growth or size.
**Stupe,** stūp, *n.* Flannel, flax, etc., wrung out of hot water, applied to a sore.
**Stupefaction,** stū-pē-fak'shon, *n.* State of being stupefied; insensibility; stupidity.
**Stupefy,** stū'pē-fi, *vt.* (stupefying, stupefied). To deprive of sensibility.
**Stupendous,** stū-pen'dus, *a.* Of astonishing magnitude; grand or awe-inspiring.
**Stupid,** stū'pid, *a.* Struck senseless; foolish; dull in intellect; nonsensical.
**Stupidity,** stū-pid'i-ti, *n.* Extreme intellectual dullness; senselessness.
**Stupor,** stū'por, *n.* A condition in which the faculties are deadened; torpor; insensibility.
**Stuprate,** stū'prāt, *vt.* To ravish; to debauch.
**Sturdily,** stėr'di-li, *adv.* Hardily; stoutly; lustily.
**Sturdy,** stėr'di, *a.* Stout; strong; hardy; firm; robust; vigorous.
**Sturgeon,** stėr'jon, *n.* A genus of large fishes having flesh valuable as food.
**Stutter,** stut'ėr, *vi.* To stammer.—*n.* A stammer; broken utterance of words.
**Sty,** stī, *n.* An inclosure for swine; a pig-sty; any filthy hovel or place.—*vt.* (stying, stied). To shut up in a sty.
**Stye,** stī, *n.* A small inflammatory tumor on the edge of the eyelid.
**Stygian,** stij'i-an, *a.* Pertaining to Styx, a fabled river of hell over which the shades of the dead passed; dark and gloomy; infernal.
**Style,** stīl, *n.* A burin; pin of a sun-dial; manner of writing with regard to language; a characteristic mode in the fine arts; type; external manner, mode, or fashion; title; in *botany,* a slender prolongation of the ovary supporting the stigma.—*vt.* (styling, styled). To term; to designate.
**Stylet,** stīl'et, *n.* In *surgery,* a probe.
**Stylish,** stīl'ish, *a.* In the mode; fashionable.
**Stylist,** stīl'ist, *n.* A writer or speaker careful of his style; a master of style.
**Stylite,** stī'līt, *n.* An ascetic who lived on the top of high columns or pillars.
**Stylobate,** stī'lō-bāt, *n.* A continuous pedestal on which a row of columns stands.
**Stylus,** stī'lus, *n.* A style or pointed instrument.
**Styptic,** stip'tik, *a.* Able to stop bleeding.—*n.* A substance which stops a flow of blood.
**Suave,** swāv, *a.* Gracious in manner; blandly polite; pleasant.
**Sub,** sub, *n.* A contraction for *subordinate.*
**Subaquatic, Subaqueous,** sub-a-kwat'ik, sub-ak'wē-us, *a.* Being under water; in *geol.* formed or deposited under water.
**Subclass,** sub'klas, *n.* A subdivision of a class.
**Subcommittee,** sub-kom-mit'tē, *n.* An under committee; a division of a committee.
**Subcutaneous,** sub-kū-tā'nē-us, *a.* Situated immediately under the skin.
**Subdivide,** sub-di-vīd', *vt.* To divide part of into more parts.—*vi.* To be subdivided; to separate.
**Subdue,** sub-dū', *vt.* (subduing, subdued). To subjugate; to overpower; to tame; to soften; to tone down.
**Subdued,** sub-dūd', *a.* Toned down; reduced in intensity; low in tone.
**Subject,** sub'jekt, *a.* Ruled by another; liable; prone; submissive.—*n.* One who owes allegiance to a ruler or government; matter dealt with; theme; topic; the nominative of a verb; the thinking agent or principle.—*vt.* sub-jekt'. To subdue; to make liable; to cause to undergo.
**Subjection,** sub-jek'shon, *n.* Act of subjecting; subjugation; enthralment.
**Subjective,** sub-jekt'iv or sub'jekt-iv, *a.* Relating to the subject; belonging to ourselves, the conscious subject; exhibiting strongly the personality of the author.
**Subject-matter,** sub'jekt-mat-ėr, *n.* The matter or theme presented for consideration.
**Subjoin,** sub-join', *vt.* To add at the end; to affix; to annex; to attach.
**Subjugate,** sub'jū-gāt, *vt.* To subdue; to conquer and compel to submit.
**Subjugation,** sub-jū-gā'shon, *n.* Act of subjugating or subduing; subdual; subjection.
**Subjunctive,** sub-jungk'tiv, *a.* and *n.* Applied to a mood of verbs that expresses condition, hypothesis, or contingency.
**Sublease,** sub'lēs, *n.* A lease granted to a subtenant.
**Sublet,** sub-let', *vt.* To let to another person, the party letting being himself a lessee.
**Sublimate,** sub'li-māt, *vt.* To raise by heat into vapor, as a solid, which, on cooling, returns again to the solid state; to refine; to elevate.—*n.* The

S

product of sublimation.
**Sublimation,** sub-li-mā'shon, *n.* The process or operation of sublimating; exaltation; a highly refined product.
**Sublimatory,** sub'li-ma-to-ri, *n.* A vessel used in sublimation.—*a.* Used in sublimation.
**Sublime,** sub-līm', *a.* High in place or excellence; affecting the mind with a sense of grandeur; noble; majestic.—**The sublime,** the grand in the works of nature or of art; grandeur of style; highest degree.—*vt.* (subliming, sublimed). To render sublime; to sublimate.—*vi.* To be susceptible of sublimation.
**Sublimely,** sub-līm'li, *adv.* In a sublime manner; grandly; majestically; loftily.
**Submarine,** sub-ma-rēn', *a.* Being under the surface of the sea.—*n.* A vessel which can be submerged at will and which can travel under the water.
**Submerge,** sub-mėrj', *vt.* and *i.* (submerging, submerged). To put under or cover with water; to drown; to sink.
**Submerse, Submersed,** sub-mėrs', sub-mėrst', *a.* Being or growing under water.
**Submersion,** sub-mėr'shon, *n.* Act of submerging; state of being under fluid; a dipping or plunging.
**Submission,** sub-mi'shon, *n.* Act of submitting; surrender; humble behavior; obedience; resignation.
**Submissive,** sub-mis'iv, *a.* Yielding; obedient; compliant; humble; modest.
**Submissively,** sub-mis'iv-li, *adv.* In a submissive manner; obediently; humbly.
**Submit,** sub-mit', *vt.* (submitting, submitted). To yield or surrender; to refer; to state, as a claim.—*vi.* To surrender; to acquiesce; to suffer without complaint.
**Subordinacy, Subordinance,** sub-or'di-na-si, sub-or'di-nans, *n.* State of being subordinate.
**Subordinate,** sub-or'din-āt, *a.* Inferior; occupying a lower position.—*n.* One who stands in rank, power, etc., below another.—*vt.* To place in a lower order or rank.
**Suborn,** sub-orn', *vt.* To bribe to commit perjury; to bribe to some wickedness.
**Subpoena,** sub-pē'na, *n.* A writ summoning a witness under a penalty.—*vt.* (subpoenaing, subpoenaed). To serve with a writ of subpoena.
**Subscribe,** sub-skrīb', *vt.* and *i.* (subscribing, subscribed). To append one's own signature to; to promise to contribute (money) by writing one's name; to assent.
**Subscriber,** sub-skrīb'ėr, *n.* One who subscribes.
**Subscript,** sub'skript. *a.* Underwritten; written below something.
**Subscription,** sub-skrip'shon, *n.* Act of subscribing; signature; attestation; a sum subscribed.
**Subsection,** sub'sek-shon, *n.* The part or division of a section.
**Subsequence,** sub'sē-kwens, *n.* The state of being subsequent.
**Subsequent,** sub'sē-kwent, *a.* Following in time; succeeding; next.
**Subsequently,** sub'sē-kwent-li, *adv.* At a later time; after something else in order.
**Subside,** sub-sīd', *vt.* (subsiding, subsided). To sink or fall to the bottom; to settle down; to abate.
**Subsidence,** sub-sīd'ens or sub'si-dens, *n.* Act or process of subsiding.
**Subsidiary,** sub-si'di-a-ri, *a.* Pertaining to a subsidy; aiding; assistant; subordinate.—*n.* An assistant.
**Subsidize,** sub'si-dīz, *vt.* (subsidizing, subsidized). To furnish with a subsidy; to purchase the assistance of another by a subsidy.
**Subsidy,** sub'si-di, *n.* A sum of money granted for a purpose; a sum given by a government to meet expenses.
**Subsist,** sub-sist', *vi.* To have existence; to live; to inhere.
**Subsistence,** sub-sist'ens, *n.* Existence; real being; livelihood; sustenance.
**Subsistent,** sub-sist'ent, *a.* Having being or existence; inherent.
**Subsoil,** sub'soil, *n.* The bed or stratum of earth below the surface soil.
**Subspecies,** sub'spē-shēz, *n.* A subdivision of a species.
**Substance,** sub'stans, *n.* That of which a thing consists; material; a body; essence; purport; means and resources.
**Substantial,** sub-stan'shal, *a.* Actually existing; real; solid; strong; moderately wealthy.
**Substantiality,** sub-stan'shi-al''i-ti, *n.* State of being substantial.
**Substantially,** sub-stan'shal-li, *adv.* With reality of existence; strongly; in substance; in the main.
**Substantiate,** sub-stan'shi-āt, *vt.* To give substance to; to prove.
**Substantiation,** sub-stan'shi-ā''shon, *n.* Act of substantiating; evidence; proof.
**Substantive,** sub'stan-tiv, *a.* Expressing existence; independent; real; of the nature of a noun.—*n.* A noun.
**Substitute,** sub'sti-tūt, *vt.* (substituting, substituted). To put in the place of another; to exchange.—*n.* A person or thing in the place of another; a deputy.
**Substitution,** sub-sti-tū'shon, *n.* Act of substituting; state of being substituted.
**Substratum,** sub'strā-tum, *n.*; pl. **-ta.** A layer or stratum under another.
**Substructure,** sub'struk-tūr, *n.* An under structure; a foundation.
**Subsume,** sub-sūm', *vt.* (subsuming, subsumed). In *logic,* to include under a more general category.
**Subtenant,** sub-te'nant, *n.* One who rents land or houses from a tenant.
**Subtend,** sub-tend', *vt.* To stretch or extend under, or be opposite to.
**Subterfuge,** sub'tėr-fūj, *n.* An artifice to escape or justify; evasion; a dishonest shift.
**Subterranean, Subterraneous,** sub-te-rā'nē-an, sub-te-rā'nē-us, *a.* Being under the surface of the earth.
**Subtle,** sut'l, *a.* Thin or tenuous; acute; sly; cunning; artful.
**Subtlety,** sut'l-ti, *n.* Quality of being subtle; delicacy; craft; cunning; acuteness; nicety of distinction; something subtle.
**Subtly,** sut'li, *adv.* Artfully; cunningly; nicely.
**Subtract,** sub-trakt', *vt.* To withdraw or take from; to deduct.
**Subtraction,** sub-trak'shon, *n.* The taking of a number or quantity from a greater.
**Subulate,** sū'bū-lāt, *a.* Slender or gradually tapering toward the point.
**Suburb,** sub'ėrb, *n.* An outlying part of a city or town.
**Suburban,** sub-ėrb'an, *a.* Relating to the suburbs; being in the suburbs of a city.
**Subversion,** sub-vėr'shon, *n.* Act of subverting; overthrow; destruction; ruin.
**Subversive,** sub-vėrs'iv, *a.* Tending to subvert, overthrow, or ruin: with *of.*
**Subvert,** sub-vėrt', *vt.* To ruin utterly; to overturn; to pervert.
**Subway,** sub'wā, *n.* An underground passage.
**Succedaneous,** suk-sē-dā'nē-us, *a.* Supplying the place of something else.
**Succedaneum,** suk-sē-dā'nē-um, *n.*; pl. **-nea.** A substitute.
**Succeed,** suk-sēd', *vt.* To follow in order; to take the place of; to come after.—*vi.* To follow in order; to ensue; to become heir; to obtain the end or object desired; to prosper.
**Success,** suk-ses', *n.* Issue; favorable result; good fortune; prosperity; something that succeeds.
**Successful,** suk-ses'ful, *a.* Accompanied by or attaining success; having the desired effect; prosperous; fortunate.
**Successfully,** suk-ses'ful-li, *adv.* Prosperously;

fortunately; favorably.
**Succession,** suk-se'shon, *n.* A following of things in order; series of things; lineage; right of inheriting; act or right of succeeding to an office, rank, etc.
**Successional,** suk-se'shon-al, *a.* Pertaining to succession; consecutive.
**Successive,** suk-ses'iv, *a.* Coming in succession; consecutive.
**Successor,** suk-ses'or, *n.* One who succeeds or follows another.
**Succinct,** suk-singkt', *a.* Compressed into few words; brief; concise.
**Succinic,** suk-sin'ik, *a.* Pertaining to amber; obtained from amber.
**Succor,** suk'ėr, *vt.* To help when in difficulty; to aid; to relieve.—*n.* Aid; help; assistance given in distress; the person or thing that brings relief.
**Succulence, Succulency,** suk'kū-lens, suk'kū-len-si, *n.* Juiciness.
**Succulent,** suk'kū-lent, *a.* Full of sap or juice; sappy; juicy.
**Succumb,** suk-kum', *vt.* To yield; to submit; to sink unresistingly.
**Such,** such, *a.* Of like kind or degree; similar; like; the same as mentioned.
**Suchwise,** such'wīz, *adv.* In such a manner.
**Suck,** suk, *vt.* and *i.* To draw with the mouth; to draw milk from with the mouth; to imbibe; to absorb.—*n.* Act of sucking; milk drawn from the breast.
**Sucker,** suk'ėr, *n.* One who or that which sucks; an organ in animals for sucking; piston of a pump; shoot of a plant; the sucking-fish.
**Suckle,** suk'l, *vt.* (suckling, suckled). To give suck to; to nurse at the breast.
**Suckling,** suk'ling, *n.* A young child or animal nursed by the mother's milk.
**Sucrose,** sū'krōs, *n.* A name for the sugars identical with cane-sugar.
**Suction,** suk'shon, *n.* Act of sucking; the sucking up of a fluid by the pressure of the external air.
**Suctorial,** suk'tō-ri-al, *a.* Adapted for sucking; living by sucking; adhering by sucking.
**Sudden,** sud'en, *a.* Happening without warning; abrupt; quick; hasty; violent.
**Suddenly,** sud'en-li, *adv.* Unexpectedly; hastily; without preparation; all at once.
**Sudoriferous,** sū-do-rif'ėr-us, *a.* Producing sweat; secreting perspiration.
**Sudorific,** sū-do-rif'ik, *a.* Causing sweat.—*n.* A medicine that produces sweat.
**Suds,** sudz, *n.pl.* Water impregnated with soap and forming a frothy mass.
**Sue,** sū, *vt.* (suing, sued). To seek justice from by legal process; to seek in marriage.—*vi.* To woo; to prosecute a suit at law; to petition.
**Suet,** sū'et, *n.* The harder fat of an animal about the kidneys and loins.
**Suffer,** suf'ėr, *vt.* To endure; to undergo; to be affected by; to permit.—*vi.* To undergo pain; to be injured.
**Sufferable,** suf'ėr-a-bl, *a.* That may be tolerated, permitted, endured, or borne.
**Sufferance,** suf'ėr-ans, *n.* Endurance; pain endured; passive consent; allowance.
**Sufferer,** suf'ėr-ėr, *n.* One who endures pain; one who permits or allows.
**Suffering,** suf'ėr-ing, *n.* The bearing of pain; pain endured; distress.
**Suffice,** suf'fīs, *vi.* (sufficing, sufficed). To be sufficient.—*vt.* To satisfy; to content.
**Sufficiency,** suf-fi'shen-si, *n.* State of being sufficient; competence; ability; conceit.
**Sufficient,** suf-fi'shent, *a.* Adequate; enough; competent; fit; able.
**Suffix,** suf'fiks, *n.* A letter or syllable added to the end of a word.—*vt.* To add a letter or syllable to a word.
**Suffocate,** suf'fō-kāt, *vi.* (suffocating, suffocated). To stifle; to choke by stopping respiration; to kill by depriving of oxygen.
**Suffocation,** suf-fō-kā'shon, *n.* Act of suffocating; condition of being suffocated.
**Suffocative,** suf'fō-kāt-iv, *a.* Tending or able to suffocate, choke, or stifle.
**Suffrage,** suf'frāj, *n.* A vote; assent; right of voting for a representative.
**Suffuse,** suf-fūz', *vt.* (suffusing, suffused). To overspread, as with a fluid or a color.
**Suffusion,** suf-fū'zhon, *n.* Act of suffusing; state of being suffused; that which is suffused.
**Sugar,** shu'gėr, *n.* A sweet granular substance, manufactured from sugar-cane, maple, beet, etc.; something sweet like sugar.—*a.* Belonging to or made of sugar.—*vt.* To season, mix, etc., with sugar; to sweeten.
**Sugar-cane,** shu'gėr-kān, *n.* The cane or plant from whose juice much sugar is obtained.
**Sugar-loaf,** shu'gėr-lōf, *n.* A conical mass of refined sugar; something of like shape.
**Sugar-plum,** shu'gėr-plum, *n.* A comfit made of boiled sugar; a bon-bon.
**Sugary,** shu'gėr-i, *a.* Like sugar; containing sugar; sweet; flattering.
**Suggest,** su-jest' or sug-jest', *vt.* To hint; to insinuate; to propose; to intimate.
**Suggestion,** su-jest'yon, *n.* A hint; a tentative proposal; insinuation; intimation.
**Suggestive,** su-jest'iv, *a.* Containig a suggestion; suggesting what does not appear on the surface.
**Suicidal,** sū-i-sīd'al, *a.* Pertaining to or partaking of the crime of suicide.
**Suicide,** sū'i-sīd, *n.* Self-murder; one guilty of self-murder.
**Suit,** sūt, *n.* Act of suing; a request; courtship; a suing at law; a set of things.—*vt.* and *i.* To adapt; to fit; to be agreeable to; to agree.
**Suitability,** sūt-a-bil'i-ti, *n.* State or quality of being suitable; fitness.
**Suitable,** sūt'a-bl, *a.* That suits; fitting; proper; appropriate; becoming.
**Suitably,** sūt'a-bli, *adv.* In a suitable manner; fitly; agreeably; with propriety.
**Suite,** swēt, *n.* A company of attendants; a retinue; a connected series, as of apartments.
**Suitor,** sūt'or, *n.* One who sues; one who prosecutes a suit at law; a wooer.
**Sulcate, Sulcated,** sul'kāt, sul'kāt-ed, *a.* Furrowed; grooved; channelled.
**Sulk,** sulk, *vi.* To indulge in a sulky or sullen fit or mood.
**Sulks,** sulks, *n.pl.* Sulky fit or mood.
**Sulky,** sulk'i, *a.* Sullen; morose.—*n.* A light two-wheeled carriage for one person.
**Sullen,** sul'en, *a.* Gloomily angry and silent; morose; sour; dismal; somber.
**Sullenly,** sul'en-li, *adv.* In a sullen manner; gloomily; with sulky moroseness.
**Sully,** sul'i, *vt.* (sullying, sullied). To soil; to tarnish; to stain or pollute.—*vi.* To be soiled.—*n.* Soil; tarnish; spot.
**Sulphate,** sul'fāt, *n.* A salt of sulphuric acid.
**Sulphide,** sul'fīd, *n.* A combination of sulphur with another element.
**Sulphite,** sul'fīt, *n.* A salt composed of sulphurous acid with a base.
**Sulphur,** sul'fėr, *n.* Brimstone; a simple mineral substance of a yellow color which burns with a pale-blue flame.
**Sulphurate,** sul'fū-rāt, *vt.* To combine with sulphur; to subject to the action of sulphur.
**Sulphuret,** sul'fū-ret, *n.* A sulphide.
**Sulphuretted,** sul'fū-ret-ed, *a.* Having sulphur in combination.
**Sulphuric,** sul-fū'rik, *a.* Pertaining to sulphur.
**Sulphurous,** sul'fėr-us, *a.* Impregnated with or containing sulphur; like sulphur.
**Sultan,** sul'tan, *n.* A Mohammedan sovereign; formerly, the ruler of Turkey.
**Sultry,** sul'tri, *a.* Very hot; oppressive; close and heavy.
**Sum,** sum, *n.* The whole; aggregate; essence or substance; a quantity of money; an arithmetical problem.—*vt.* (summing, summed). To add

S

into one whole; to reckon up; to recapitulate.

**Sumac, Sumach,** sū'mak, *n.* A shrub the leaves of which are used for tanning.

**Summarily,** sum'a-ri-li, *adv.* In a summary manner; briefly; promptly.

**Summarize,** sum'a-rīz, *vt.* To make a summary, abstract, or abridgment of.

**Summary,** sum'a-ri, *a.* Concise; brief; intended to facilitate dispatch.—*n.* An abridged account; an abstract.

**Summation,** sum-ā'shon, *n.* Act or process of summing; addition; aggregate.

**Summer,** sum'ėr, *n.* The warmest season of the year; a lintel; a girder.—*a.* Relating to summer.—*vi.* To pass the summer.—*vt.* To keep or carry through the summer.

**Summit,** sum'it, *n.* The top; highest point; highest degree; acme.

**Summon,** sum'un, *vt.* To call by authority to appear at a place, especially a court of justice; to send for; to call up.

**Summoner,** sum'un-ėr, *n.* One who summons or cites by authority.

**Summons,** sum'unz, *n.* A call by authority to appear; a citation; document containing such citation; an earnest call.

**Sump,** sump, *n.* A pond of water for use in salt-works; a reservoir.

**Sumptuary,** sump'tū-a-ri, *a.* Relating to expense; regulating expenditure.

**Sumptuous,** sump'tū-us, *a.* Very expensive or costly; splendid; magnificent.

**Sumptuously,** sump'tū-us-li, *adv.* In a sumptuous manner; splendidly.

**Sun,** sun, *n.* The self-luminous orb which gives light and heat to all the planets; sunshine or sunlight; sunny position; chief source of light, glory, etc.; a year.—*vt.* (sunning, sunned). To expose to the sun's rays.

**Sunbeam,** sun'bēm, *n.* A ray of the sun.

**Sun-bonnet,** sun'bon-et, *n.* A bonnet for protecting the face and neck from the sun.

**Sun-burn,** sun'bėrn, *vt.* To discolor or scorch by the sun; to tan.

**Sunday,** sun'dā, *n.* The Christian Sabbath; the first day of the week.—*a.* Belonging to the Christian Sabbath.

**Sunder,** sun'dėr, *vt.* To part; to separate; to disunite in any manner.

**Sun-dial,** sun'dī-al, *n.* An instrument to show the time by a shadow cast by the sun.

**Sundry,** sun'dri, *a.* Several; divers; various; a few.

**Sunflower,** sun'flou-ėr, *n.* A plant with a large yellow flower.

**Sunken,** sungk'en, *p.a.* Sunk; covered with water; below the general surface.

**Sunlit,** sun'lit, *a.* Lit by the sun.

**Sunnite,** sun'īt, *n.* An orthodox Mohammedan who receives the *sunna* or traditionary law as of equal importance with the Koran.

**Sunny,** sun'i, *a.* Like the sun; brilliant; exposed to the sun; having much sunshine; bright or cheerful.

**Sunrise, Sunrising,** sun'rīz, sun'rīz-ing, *n.* The first appearance of the sun in the morning; time of such appearance; the east.

**Sunset, Sunsetting,** sun'set, sun'set-ing, *n.* The descent of the sun below the horizon; evening; close or decline; the west.

**Sunshine,** sun'shīn, *n.* The light of the sun; warmth; brightness; cheerfulness.

**Sunstroke,** sun'strōk, *n.* A bodily affection produced by exposure to the sun.

**Sup,** sup, *vt.* (supping, supped). To take into the mouth with the lips, as a liquid.—*vi.* To take supper.—*n.* A sip; a small mouthful.

**Superable,** sū'pėr-a-bl, *a.* That may be overcome or surmounted.

**Superabound,** sū'pėr-a-bound'', *vi.* To abound to excess; to be superabundant.

**Superabundance,** sū'pėr-a-bun''dans, *n.* Excessive abundance; more than enough.

**Superabundant,** sū'pėr-a-bun''dant, *a.* Abounding to excess; more than sufficient.

**Superannuate,** sū-pėr-an'nū-āt, *vt.* To pension off on account of old age.—*vi.* To retire on a pension.

**Superannuated,** sū-pėr-an'nū-āt-ed, *a.* Impaired or disabled by old age; having received a retiring allowance for long service.

**Superb,** sū-pėrb', *a.* Magnificent; sumptuous; splendid; august; grand.

**Superbly,** sū-pėrb'li, *adv.* In a superb, magnificent, or splendid manner.

**Superciliary,** sū-pėr-sil'i-a-ri, *a.* Pertaining to the eyebrow; being above the eyelid.

**Supercilious,** sū-pėr-sil'i-us, *a.* Lofty with pride; haughty; overbearing.

**Supererogation,** sū-pėr-e'rō-gā''shon, *n.* Giving more than enough; performance of more than duty requires.

**Superficial,** sū-pėr-fi'shal, *a.* Being on the surface; shallow; not thorough.

**Superficially,** sū-pėr-fi'shal-li, *adv.* Without going deep; slightly; not thoroughly.

**Superficies,** sū-pėr-fi'shēz, *n.* Surface; the exterior part.

**Superfine,** sū-pėr-fīn', *a.* Very fine; excessively subtle.

**Superfluity,** sū-pėr-flu'i-ti, *n.* Superabundance; something beyond what is necessary.

**Superfluous,** sū-pėr'flu-us, *a.* Being more than is wanted; redundant; unnecessary.

**Superhuman,** sū-pėr-hū'man, *a.* Above or beyond what is human; divine.

**Superimpose,** sū'pėr-im-pōz'', *vt.* To lay or impose on something else.

**Superincumbent,** sū'pėr-in-kum''bent, *a.* Lying or pressing on something else.

**Superinduce,** sū'pėr-in-dūs'', *vt.* To bring in or on as an addition to something.

**Superintend,** sū'pėr-in-tend'', *vt.* To have the charge and oversight of; to direct or manage; to take care of with authority.

**Superintendent,** sū'pėr-in-tend''ent, *n.* One who manages and directs; an overseer.—*a.* Overlooking others with authority.

**Superior,** sū-pē'ri-or, *a.* Higher; higher in rank or dignity; greater in excellence.—*n.* One who is superior to another; chief of a monastery, convent, or abbey.

**Superiority,** sū-pē'ri-o''ri-ti, *n.* Quality of being superior; pre-eminence; advantage.

**Superlative,** sū-pėr'lat-iv, *a.* Highest in degree; supreme.—*n.* That which is superlative; the highest degree of adjectives or adverbs.

**Superlatively,** sū-pėr'lat-iv-li, *adv.* In a superlative manner; in the highest degree.

**Supernaculum,** sū-pėr-nak'ū-lum, *n.* Wine or other liquor of great excellence.

**Supernal,** sū-pėr'nal, *a.* Relating to things above; celestial; heavenly.

**Supernatant,** sū-pėr-nā'tant, *a.* Swimming above; floating on the surface.

**Supernatural,** sū-pėr-na'tūr-al, *a.* Being above or beyond nature; miraculous.

**Supernumerary,** sū-pėr-nū'me-ra-ri, *a.* Exceeding the number stated, necessary, or usual.—*n.* A person or thing beyond a number stated, but required on an emergency.

**Superscribe,** sū-pėr-skrīb', *vt.* To write upon or over; to put an inscription on.

**Superscription,** sū-pėr-skrip'shon, *n.* Act of superscribing; that which is written or engraved above or on the outside; address on a letter, etc.

**Supersede,** sū-pėr-sēd', *vt.* (superseding, superseded). To set aside; to take the place of; to supplant.

**Supersensitive,** sū-pėr-sens'i-tiv, *a.* Excessively sensitive.

**Supersonic,** sū-pėr-son'ik, *a.* Faster than sound; above the audible limit.

**Superstition,** sū-pėr-sti'shon, *n.* Groundless belief in supernatural agencies; a popular belief held without reason.

**Superstitious,** sū-pėr-sti'shus, *a.* Addicted to superstition; proceeding from or manifesting superstition.
**Superstructure,** sū-pėr-struk'tūr, *n.* Any structure raised on something else.
**Supervene,** sū-pėr-vēn', *vi.* (supervening, supervened). To come, as something extraneous; to happen.
**Supervention,** sū-pėr-ven'shon, *n.* Act of supervening.
**Supervise,** sū-pėr-vīz', *vt.* (supervising, supervised). To oversee and direct; to superintend; to inspect.
**Supervision,** sū-pėr-vi'zhon, *n.* Act of supervising; superintendence; direction.
**Supervisor,** sū-pėr-vī'zor, *n.* One who supervises; a superintendent; an overseer.
**Supine,** sū-pīn', *a.* Lying on the back; indolent; careless.—*n.* sū'pīn. A part of the Latin verb.
**Supinely,** sū-pīn'li, *adv.* In a supine manner; carelessly; indolently; listlessly.
**Supper,** sup'ėr, *n.* The last meal of the day; the evening meal.
**Supplant,** sup-plant', *vt.* To take the place of, usually by stratagem.
**Supple,** sup'l, *a.* Pliant; flexible; yielding.—*vt.* (suppling, suppled). To make supple.—*vi.* To become supple.
**Supplement,** sup'lē-ment, *n.* An addition; an appendix.—*vt.* sup-lē-ment'. To increase or complete by a supplement.
**Supplemental, Supplementary,** sup-lē-ment'al, sup-lē-ment'a-ri, *a.* Of the nature of a supplement; serving to supplement.
**Suppliance,** sup'li-ans, *n.* The act of supplicating; supplication; entreaty.
**Suppliant,** sup'li-ant, *a.* Supplicating; entreating earnestly; beseeching.—*n.* A supplicant; a humble petitioner.
**Supplicant,** sup'li-kant, *a.* Suppliant.—*n.* One who supplicates; a suppliant.
**Supplicate,** sup'li-kāt, *vt.* (supplicating, supplicated). To beg humbly for; to entreat; to address in prayer.—*vi.* To beg; to petition; to beseech.
**Supplication,** sup-li-kā'shon, *n.* Humble and earnest prayer; entreaty.
**Supplicatory,** sup'li-kā-to-ri, *a.* Containing supplication; suppliant.
**Supply,** sup-plī', *vt.* (supplying, supplied). To furnish; to provide; to satisfy.—*n.* Act of supplying; quantity supplied; store; *pl.* stores or articles necessary; money provided for government expenses.
**Support,** sup-pōrt', *vt.* To rest under and bear; to prop; to endure; to assist; to second; to maintain; to provide for.—*n.* Act of supporting; a prop; help; sustenance; maintenance.
**Supporter,** sup-pōrt'ėr, *n.* One who or that which supports; a defender; adherent; prop; figure on each side of a heraldic shield.
**Supposable,** sup-pōz'a-bl, *a.* That may be supposed or imagined to be or exist.
**Suppose,** sup-pōz', *vt.* (supposing, supposed). To lay down or regard as matter of fact; to take for granted; to imagine; to imply.—*vi.* To think; to imagine.
**Supposition,** sup-po-zi'shon, *n.* Act of supposing; hypothesis; assumption; surmise.
**Suppositional,** sup-po-zi'shon-al, *a.* Based on supposition; hypothetical.
**Suppress,** sup-pres', *vt.* To put down; to crush; to quell; to check; to conceal.
**Suppression,** sup-pre'shon, *n.* Act of suppressing; concealment; morbid retention of discharges; ellipsis.
**Suppressive,** sup-pres'iv, *a.* Suppressing or tending to suppress.
**Suppurate,** sup'pū-rāt, *vi.* (suppurating, suppurated). To form or generate pus; to fester.
**Suppuration,** sup-pū-rā'shon, *n.* Process or state of suppurating.
**Supramundane,** sū-pra-mun'dān, *a.* Being above the world; celestial.
**Supremacy,** sū-prem'a-si, *n.* State or character of being supreme; supreme authority.
**Supreme,** sū-prēm', *a.* Highest in authority; utmost; greatest possible.
**Supremely,** sū-prēm'li, *adv.* In a supreme manner or degree; to the utmost extent.
**Sural,** sū'ral, *n.* Pertaining to the calf of the leg.
**Surcease,** sėr-sēs', *vi.* To cease; to leave off.—*n.* Cessation; stop: *poetical.*
**Surcharge,** sėr-chärj', *vt.* To overload.—*n.* An excessive load; an overcharge.
**Surcingle,** sėr'sing-gl, *n.* A belt, band, or girth for a horse.
**Surcoat,** sėr'kōt, *n.* An outer garment; a loose garment worn over mail.
**Sure,** shör, *a.* Certain; positive; unfailing; stable; secure.—*adv.* Certainly.
**Surely,** shör'li, *adv.* In a sure manner; firmly; stably; certainly; presumably.
**Surety,** shör'ti, *n.* State of being sure; certainty; security; one who gives security; a bail.
**Surf,** sėrf, *n.* The swell of the sea which breaks on the shore, rocks, etc.
**Surface,** sėr'fās, *n.* The exterior part of anything that has length and breadth; outside; external appearance.—*a.* Pertaining to the surface; superficial.
**Surfeit,** sėr'fit, *n.* An overloading of the stomach; disgust caused by excess; satiety.—*vt.* and *i.* To feed to excess; to nauseate; to cloy.
**Surge,** sėrj, *n.* The swelling of a wave; a large wave; a rolling swell of water.-*vi.* (surging, surged). To swell; to rise high and roll, as waves.
**Surgeon,** sėr'jon, *n.* A medical man who treats diseases or injuries of the body by manual operation.
**Surgery,** sėr'je-ri, *n.* The operative branch of medical practice; a doctor's consulting room and dispensary.
**Surgical,** sėr'ji-kal, *a.* Pertaining to surgeons or surgery.
**Surly,** sėr'li, *a.* Gloomily sour or morose; churlish; boisterous; dismal.
**Surmise,** sėr-mīz', *n.* A supposition; conjecture; speculation.—*vt.* (surmising, surmised). To guess; to imagine; to suspect.
**Surmount,** sėr-mount', *vt.* To mount or rise above; to overcome.
**Surname,** sėr'nām, *n.* The family name of an individual.—*vt.* To give a surname to.
**Surpass,** sėr-päs', *vt.* To go beyond; to excel; to outdo.
**Surpassable,** sėr-päs'a-bl, *a.* Capable of being surpassed.
**Surpassing,** sėr-päs'ing, *a.* Excellent in an eminent degree; exceeding others.
**Surplice,** sėr'plis, *n.* A loose white garment worn by clergy and choristers.
**Surplus,** sėr'plus, *n.* and *a.* Excess beyond what is required; balance.
**Surprisal,** sėr-prz'al, *n.* Act of surprising; a taking unawares; a surprise.
**Surprise,** sėr-prīz', *n.* Act of coming upon unawares, or of taking suddenly; emotion excited by something unexpected; astonishment.—*vt.* (surprising, surprised). To fall upon unexpectedly; to take unawares; to astonish.
**Surprising,** sėr-prīz'ing, *a.* Exciting surprise; wonderful; extraordinary.
**Surrealism,** sėr-ē'al-izm, *n.* A form of art which claims to express the unconscious mind.
**Surrebutter,** sėr-rē-but'ėr, *n.* The plaintiff's reply in pleading to a defendant's rebutter.
**Surrejoinder,** sėr-rē-join'dėr, *n.* The plaintiff's reply to a defendant's rejoinder.
**Surrender,** sėr-ren'dėr, *vt.* To deliver up; to yield to another; to resign; to relinquish.—*vi.* To yield.—*n.* Act of surrendering; a yielding or giving up.
**Surreptitious,** sėr-rep-ti'shus, *a.* Done by stealth; clandestine; underhand.
**Surrogate,** su'rō-gāt, *n.* The deputy of a bishop or his chancellor.

S

**Surround,** sėr-round', *vt.* To be round about; to encompass; to invest.
**Surrounding,** sėr-round'ing, *n.* An environment; generally in *pl.*
**Surtax,** sėr'taks, *n.* A tax heightened for a particular purpose; an extra tax.
**Surveillance,** sėr-vāl'yans, *n.* A keeping watch over; superintendence; oversight.
**Survey,** sėr-vā', *vt.* To oversee; to examine; to measure and value, as land, etc.; to determine the boundaries, natural features, etc., of.—*n.* sėr'vā or sėr-vā'. A general view; examination; determination or account of topographical particulars.
**Surveying,** sėr-vā'ing, *n.* The art or practice of measuring and delineating portions of the earth's surface.
**Surveyor,** sėr-vā'or, *n.* One who surveys; an overseer; inspector.
**Survival,** sėr-vīv'al, *n.* A living beyond the life of another person, thing, or event; old habit, belief, etc., existing merely from custom.
**Survive,** sėr-vīv', *vt.* (surviving, survived). To outlive; to live beyond the life of; to outlast.—*vi.* To live after another or after anything else.
**Survivor,** sėr-vīv'or, *n.* One who survives; the longer liver of two persons.
**Susceptibility,** sus-sep'ti-bil''i-ti, *n.* Quality of being susceptible.
**Susceptible,** sus-sep'ti-bl, *a.* Capable of admitting any change of influence; impressible; sensitive.
**Susceptive,** sus-sep'tiv, *a.* Susceptible.
**Suspect,** sus-pekt', *vt.* To imagine as existing; to mistrust; to imagine to be guilty; to doubt.—*vi.* To have suspicion.—*n.* sus'pekt. A suspected person.
**Suspend,** sus-pend', *vt.* To hang; to cause to cease for a time; to debar temporarily; to stay.
**Suspender,** sus-pend'ėr, *n.* One who suspends; *pl.* braces.
**Suspense,** sus-pens', *n.* State of being uncertain; indecision; cessation for a time.
**Suspensible,** sus-pen'si-bl, *a.* Capable of being suspended or held from sinking.
**Suspension,** sus-pen'shon, *n.* Act of suspending; intermission; abeyance; deprivation of office or privileges for a time.
**Suspension-bridge,** sus-pen'shon-brij, *n.* A bridge of chains, wire-ropes, or the like.
**Suspensive,** sus-pen'siv, *a.* Suspensory.
**Suspicion,** sus-pi'shon, *n.* Act of suspecting; fear of something wrong; mistrust.
**Suspicious,** sus-pi'shus, *a.* Mistrustful; inclined to suspect; apt to raise suspicion; doubtful.
**Suspiciously,** sus-pi'shus-li, *adv.* With suspicion; so as to excite suspicion.
**Sustain,** sus-tān', *vt.* To rest under and bear up; to support; to aid effectually; to undergo; to endure; to hold valid; to confirm; to continue.
**Sustenance,** sus'ten-ans, *n.* Act of sustaining; support; maintenance; food.
**Sutler,** sut'lėr, *n.* One who follows an army and sells provisions to the troops.
**Sutling, Suttling,** sut'ling, *n.* The occupation of a sutler.
**Suttee,** sut-tē', *n.* A Hindu widow burnt on the funeral pile of her husband; self-immolation of Hindu widows.
**Suture,** sū'tūr, *n.* A sewing together; a seam; the uniting of the parts of a wound by stitching; seam or joint of the skull.
**Swab,** swob, *n.* A mop for cleaning floors, decks, etc.—*vt.* (swabbing, swabbed). To clean with a swab.
**Swaddle,** swod'l, *vt.* (swaddling, swaddled). To swathe; to bind tight with clothes.—*n.* A swaddling-band.
**Swaddling-band,** swod'ling-band, *n.* A band of cloth to swaddle an infant.
**Swag,** swag, *vi.* (swagging, swagged). To sway, as something heavy and pendent; to sag.
**Swagger,** swag'ėr, *vt.* To strut; to bluster.—*n.* Pretentious strut; bluster.
**Swaggering,** swag'ėr-ing, *p.a.* Apt to swagger; exhibiting an insolent bearing.
**Swain,** swān, *n.* A peasant or rustic; a hind; a country gallant; a wooer.
**Swallow,** swol'ō, *vt.* To receive through the gullet into the stomach; to ingulf; to absorb; to believe readily; to put up with.—*n.* The gullet; voracity; capacity of swallowing; a small migratory bird.
**Swamp,** swomp, *n.* A piece of wet spongy land; a fen; a bog.—*vt.* To sink in a swamp; to overwhelm; to overset or fill, as a boat in water.
**Swan,** swon, *n.* A long-necked web-footed bird of the duck family.
**Swan's-down,** swonz'doun, *n.* The down of the swan; a kind of soft thick cloth.
**Swap,** swop, *vt.* (swapping, swapped). To barter; to exchange.—*n.* An exchange.
**Sward,** sward, *n.* The grassy surface of land; turf; sod.—*vt.* To cover with sward.
**Swarm,** swarm, *n.* A large body of small insects; a multitude.—*vi.* To depart from a hive in a body; to crowd; to abound; to climb a tree, pole, etc., by clasping it with the arms and legs.
**Swarthy,** swarth'i, *a.* Being of a dark hue or dusky complexion; tawny; black.
**Swash,** swosh, *vt.* To splash or dash, as water; to bluster.
**Swash-buckler,** swosh-buk-lėr, *n.* A swaggering fellow; a bravo; a bully.
**Swastika,** swas'tik-a, *n.* An ancient Aryan symbol adopted by Nazi Germany. It consists of a cross with arms of equal length, each arm having a prolongation at right angles. It was intended to represent the sun.
**Swath,** swath or swäth, *n.* A line of mown grass or grain; track formed by mowing; sweep of a scythe in mowing.
**Swathe,** swāᴛʜ, *vt.* (swathing, swathed). To bind with a bandage; to swaddle.—*n.* A bandage.
**Sway,** swā, *vi.* To swing or vibrate; to incline; to govern.—*vt.* To swing; to wield; to bias; to influence; to rule.—*n.* Swing or sweep; preponderance; power; rule; ascendency.
**Swear,** swār, *vt.* and *t.* (swearing, pret. swore, pp. sworn). To make a solemn declaration, with an appeal to God for its truth; to make promise upon oath; to cause to take an oath; to curse.
**Sweat,** swet, *n.* The moisture which comes out upon the skin; labor; moisture resembling sweat.—*vi.* (pret. and pp. sweated or sweat). To emit sweat or moisture; to toil.—*vt.* To exude; to cause to perspire; to employ at starvation wages.
**Sweater,** swet'ėr, *n.* A heavy woollen jersey.
**Swede,** swēd, *n.* A native of Sweden; a Swedish turnip.
**Swedish,** swēd'ish, *a.* Pertaining to Sweden.—*n.* The language used in Sweden.
**Sweep,** swēp, *vt.* (sweeping, swept). To rub over with a brush; to carry with a long swinging motion; to drive off in numbers at a stroke.—*vi.* To pass with swiftness and violence; to pass with pomp; to move with a long reach.—*n.* Reach of a stroke, etc.; range; rapid survey; a curve; one who sweeps chimneys.
**Sweeping,** swēp'ing, *a.* Wide and comprehensive in scope.
**Sweepings,** swep'ingz, *n.pl.* Things collected by sweeping; rubbish.
**Sweepstake, Sweepstakes,** swēp'stāk, swēp'stāks, *n.* A prize made up of several stakes.
**Sweet,** swēt, *a.* Agreeable to the taste or senses; having the taste of honey or sugar; fragrant; melodious; beautiful; not salt or sour; gentle.—*n.* A sweet substance; a bonbon; a word of endearment.
**Sweeten,** swēt'n, *vt.* To make sweet.—*vi.* To become sweet.
**Sweetening,** swēt'n-ing, *n.* Act of making sweet; that which sweetens.
**Sweetheart,** swēt'härt, *n.* A lover, male or female.

**Sweetly,** swēt'li, *adv*. In a sweet manner; gratefully; harmoniously.
**Sweetmeat,** swēt'mēt, *n*. A confecton made of sugar; fruit preserved with sugar.
**Sweet-pea,** swēt'pē, *n*. A pea-like plant with showy sweet-scented flowers.
**Sweet-william,** swēt-wil'yam, *n*. A plant, a species of pink.
**Swell,** swel, *vi*. (pp. swelled or swollen). To grow larger; to heave; to bulge out; to increase.—*vt*. To expand or increase; to puff up.—*n*. Act of swelling; gradual increase; a rise of ground; a wave or surge; an arrangement in an organ for regulating the intensity of the sound; an important person; a dandy.
**Swelling,** swel'ing, *a*. Tumid; turgid.—*n*. A tumor; a protuberance.
**Swelter,** swel'tėr, *vi*. To be overcome with heat; to perspire.—*vt*. To oppress with heat.
**Sweltry,** swel'tri, *a*. sultry.
**Swerve,** swėrv, *vi*. (swerving, swerved). To deviate; to turn aside; to waver.
**Swift,** swift, *a*. Speedy; rapid; fleet; ready; prompt.—*n*. A bird like the swallow.
**Swiftly,** swift'li, *adv*. Speedily; fleetly.
**Swig,** swig, *vt*. and *i*. (swigging, swigged). To drink in large gulps.—*n*. A large draft.
**Swill,** swil, *vi*. To swallow large drafts; to drink greedily.—*n*. Drink taken in large quantities; liquid food given to swine.
**Swim,** swim, *vi*. (swimming, pret. swam, swum, pp. swum). To float; to move through water by the motion of the limbs or fins; to be flooded; to be dizzy.—*vt*. To pass by swimming.—*n*. Act of swimming; distance swum; air-bladder of fishes.
**Swimmer,** swim'ėr, *n*. One who swims; a bird or other animal that swims.
**Swimming,** swim'ing, *n*. The act or art of moving on the water by means of the limbs; a dizziness or giddiness in the head.
**Swimmingly,** swim'ing-li, *adv*. Smoothly; without obstruction; with great success.
**Swindle,** swin'dl, *vt*. (swindling, swindled). To cheat; to defraud deliberately.—*n*. A scheme to dupe people out of money; fraud.
**Swindler,** swin'dlėr, *n*. One who swindles; a cheat; one who defrauds people grossly.
**Swine,** swīn, *n. sing*. and *pl*. A hog; a pig; a sow or boar; *pl*. hogs collectively.
**Swing,** swing, *vi*. (swinging, swung). To move to and fro, as a body suspended; to turn round at anchor; to be hanged.—*vt*. To make to oscillate; to brandish.—*n*. Sweep of a body; swinging gait; apparatus for persons to swing in; free course.
**Swinge,** swingj, *vt*. (swingeing, swinged). To beat soundly; to whip; to chastise.
**Swingeing,** swinj'ing, *a*. Great; large; excessive.
**Swingle-tree, Swing-tree,** swing'gl-trē, swing'trē, *n*. A cross-bar by which a horse is yoked to a carriage, plow, etc.
**Swinish,** swīn'ish, *a*. Like swine; gross.
**Swink,** swingk, *vi*. To labor; to toil.
**Swipe,** swīp, *vt*. and *i*. (swiping, swiped). To strike with a sweeping blow.—*n*. A sweeping blow.
**Swirl,** swėrl, *vi*. To form eddies; to whirl in eddies.—*n*. An eddy.
**Swish,** swish, *vt*. To swing or brandish; to lash.—*n*. A sound as of a switch in the air, a scythe in cutting grass, etc.
**Swiss,** swis, *n. sing*. or *pl*. A native of Switzerland.—*a*. Belonging to the Swiss.
**Switch,** swich, *n*. A small flexible twig or rod; a movable rail at junctions; a device for changing the course of an electric current.—*vt*. To strike with a switch; to shunt.
**Switzer,** swit'zėr, *n*. A Swiss.
**Swivel,** swi'vel, *n*. A link in a chain partly consisting of a pivot turning in a hole in the next link; a fastening that allows the thing fastened to turn round freely.—*vi*. (swivelling, swivelled). To turn on a swivel.
**Swollen,** swōln, *p*. and *a*. Swelled.
**Swoon,** swön, *vi*. To faint.—*n*. A fainting fit; a faint; syncope.
**Swoop,** swöp, *vi*. To dart upon prey suddenly; to stoop.—*vt*. To take with a swoop.—*n*. The pouncing of a bird on its prey; a falling on and seizing.
**Sword,** sörd, *n*. A military weapon consisting of a long steel blade and a hilt, used for thrusting or cutting; the emblem of justice, authority, war, or destruction; the military profession.
**Sword-arm,** sōrd'ärm, *n*. The right arm.
**Sword-fish,** sōrd'fish, *n*. A large fish allied to the mackerel having the upper jaw elongated so as to somewhat resemble a sword.
**Sword-play,** sōrd'plā, *n*. Fencing or fighting with swords.
**Swordsman,** sōrdz'man, *n*. A man who carries a sword; a man skilled in the sword.
**Sworn,** swōrn, *p.a*. Bound by oath; having taken an oath; closely bound.
**Sybarite,** sib'a-rīt, *n*. A person devoted to luxury and pleasure.
**Sycamore,** si'ka-mōr, *n*. A fruit-tree of the fig family; a maple naturalized in Britain; the plane-tree of America.
**Sycophancy,** si'kō-fan-si, *n*. Obsequious flattery; servility.
**Sycophant,** si'kō-fant, *n*. A servile hanger-on of great people; a parasite; mean flatterer.
**Sycophantic,** si-kō-fant'ik, *a*. Obsequiously flattering; meanly parasitic.
**Syenite,** sī'en-īt, *n*. A granitic rock composed of quartz, hornblende, and felspar.
**Syllabary,** sil'a-ba-ri, *n*. A catalogue of the primitive syllables of a language.
**Syllabic, Syllabical,** sil-lab'ik, sil-lab'ik-al, *a*. Pertaining to a syllable or syllables.
**Syllabicate, Syllabify,** sil-lab'i-kāt, sil-lab'i-fī, *vt*. To form into syllables.
**Syllable,** sil'la-bl, *n*. A sound or combination of sounds uttered with one effort; the smallest expressive element of language.—*vt*. To articulate.
**Sylph,** silf, *n*. A fabulous aerial spirit; a woman of graceful and slender proportions.
**Sylphid,** silf'id, *n*. A diminutive sylph.
**Sylphine,** silf'in, *a*. Like or relating to a sylph.
**Sylva, Silva,** sil'va, *n*. The forest trees of any region or country collectively.
**Sylvan,** sil'van, *a*. Pertaining to a wood; wooded; rural.
**Sylviculture,** sil-vi-kul'tūr, *n*. The culture of forest trees; arboriculture.
**Symbol,** sim'bol, *n*. A sign; an emblem; a type; a figure; an attribute; a creed or summary of articles of religion.
**Symbolic, Symbolical,** sim-bol'ik, sim-bol'ik-al, *a*. Serving as a symbol; representative; figurative; typical.
**Symbolism,** sim'bol-izm, *n*. The attributing to things a symbolic meaning; meaning expressed by symbols; use of symbols.
**Symbolist,** sim'bol-ist, *n*. One who symbolizes; one addicted to using symbols.
**Symbolize,** sim'bol-īz, *vt*. To represent by a symbol; to typify; to treat as symbolic.—*vi*. To express or represent in symbols.
**Symbology, Symbolology,** sim-bol'o-ji, sim-bol-ol'o-ji, *n*. The doctrine of symbols; symbols collectively.
**Symmetrical,** sim-met'rik-al, *a*. Having symmetry; proportional in all its parts; finely or regularly made.
**Symmetrize,** sim'me-trīz, *vt*. To make symmetrical; to reduce to symmetry.
**Symmetry,** sim'me-tri, *n*. Due proportion of parts or elements; harmony; correspondence of arrangement.
**Sympathetic, Sympathetical,** sim-pa-thet'ik, sim-pa-thet'ik-al, *a*. Able to participate in the sorrows and joy of others; compassionate.
**Sympathize,** sim'pa-thīz, *vi*. (sympathizing, sym-

S

pathized). To have sympathy; to feel in consequence of what another feels; to condole; to harmonize.

**Sympathy,** sim'pa-thi, *n.* Fellow-feeling; compassion; agreement of inclinations; correspondence of sensations or affections.

**Symphonic,** sim-fon'ik, *a.* Pertaining to a symphony.

**Symphonious,** sim-fō'ni-us, *a.* Agreeing in sound; harmonious.

**Symphonist,** sim-fō'nist, *n.* A composer of symphonies.

**Symphony,** sim'fō-ni, *n.* Unison of sound; a musical composition for a full orchestra.

**Symposium,** sim-pō'zi-um, *n.*; pl. **-ia.** A merry feast; a convivial party; a discussion by different writers in a periodical.

**Symptom,** sim'tom, *n.* That which indicates the existence and character of something else; a mark, sign, or token.

**Symptomatic,** sim-tom-at'ik, *a.* Pertaining to symptoms; serving as a symptom.

**Synagogue,** sin'a-gog, *n.* A congregation of Jews met for worship; a Jewish place of worship.

**Synchronal,** sin'kron-al, *a.* Synchronous.

**Synchronism,** sin'kron-izm, *n.* Concurrence of events in time; tabular arrangement of history according to dates.

**Synchronize,** sin'kron-īz, *vi.* To agree in time.—*vt.* To make to agree in time.

**Synchronous,** sin'kron-us, *a.* Happening at the same time; simultaneous.

**Synchrony,** sin'kron-i, *a.* Synchronism.

**Synclinal,** sin-klī'nal, *a.* In *geology,* dipping in opposite directions toward a common line or plane.

**Syncopate,** sin'ko-pāt, *vt.* To contract by omission of letters from the middle; to prolong a note in music.

**Syncopation,** sin-ko-pā'shon, *n.* Act of syncopating; contraction of a word; interruption of the regular measure in music.

**Syncretism,** sin'krēt-izm, *n.* The attempted blending of irreconcilable principles, as in philosophy or religion.

**Syndesmology,** sin-des-mol'o-ji, *n.* The department of anatomy that deals with the ligaments.

**Syndic,** sin'dik, *n.* A magistrate; one chosen to transact business for others.

**Syndicalism,** sin'dik-al-izm, *n.* A policy involving ownership of the means of production in each trade by a union of the workers in that trade, such policy to be brought about by means of the general strike and other violent methods.

**Syndicate,** sin'di-kāt, *n.* A body of syndics; office of a syndic; body of persons associated to promote some enterprise.—*vt.* To form a syndicate or body for the use of.

**Synecdoche,** sin-ek'do-kē, *n.* A rhetorical figure by which the whole of a thing is put for a part, or a part for the whole.

**Syneresis,** si-nē're-sis, *n.* The contraction of two syllables into one.

**Synod,** sin'od, *n.* A council or meeting of ecclesiastics; an ecclesiastical court; a meeting or council in general.

**Synodic, Synodical,** sin-od'ik, sin-od'ik-al, *a.* Pertaining to a synod; pertaining to conjunction of heavenly bodies.

**Synonym,** sin'ō-nim, *n.* A word having the same signification as another.

**Synonymous,** sin-on'im-us, *a.* Having the same meaning.

**Synonymy,** sin-on'im-i, *n.* Quality of being synonymous; synonyms collectively.

**Synopsis,** sin-op'sis, *n.*; pl. **-ses.** A summary; brief statement of topics; conspectus.

**Synoptic, Synoptical,** sin-op'tik, sin-op'tik-al, *a.* Affording a synopsis or general view.

**Syntactic, Syntactical,** sin-tak'tik, sin-tak'tik-al. *a.* Pertaining to syntax.

**Syntax,** sin'taks, *n.* The construction of sentences in grammar; due arrangement of words in sentences.

**Synthesis,** sin'the-sis, *n.*; pl. **-ses.** The putting of things together to form a whole; composition or combination.

**Synthetic, Synthetical,** sin-thet'ik, sin-thet'ik-al, *a.* Pertaining to synthesis; consisting in synthesis.

**Syphilis,** sif'i-lis, *n.* A contagious and hereditary venereal disease.

**Syphilitic,** sif-i-lit'ik, *a.* Pertaining to or infected with syphilis.

**Syrian,** si'ri-an, *a.* Pertaining to Syria.—*n.* A native of Syria.

**Syringe,** si'rinj, *n.* A tube and piston serving to draw in and expel fluid.—*vt.* (syringing, syringed). To inject by a syringe; to cleanse by injections from a syringe.

**Syrinx,** sī'ringks, *n.* The Pandean pipes; the organ of voice in birds.

**Syrup,** si'rup, *n.* A strong solution of sugar in water; any sweet thick fluid; the uncrystallizable fluid separated from crystallized sugar in refining.

**Syrupy,** si'rup-i, *a.* Like syrup.

**System,** sis'tem, *n.* An assemblage of things forming a connected whole; a complex but ordered whole; the body as a functional unity; a plan or scheme; method.

**Systematic, Systematical,** sis-tem-at'ik, sis-tem-at'ik-al, *a.* Pertaining to system; methodical.

**Systematize,** sis'tem-at-īz, *vt.* To reduce to a system or regular method.

**Systemic,** sis-tem'ik, *a.* Pertaining to a system, or to the body as a whole.

**Systole,** sis'to-lē, *n.* The contraction of the heart and arteries for driving onwards the blood and carrying on the circulation.

**Systolic,** sis-tol'ik, *a.* Relating to systole.

**Sythe,** sīTH, *n.* A scythe.

**Syzygy,** siz'i-ji, *n.* The conjuction or opposition of any two heavenly bodies.

# T

**Tab,** tab, *n.* A small flap or projecting piece.

**Tabaret,** tab'a-ret, *n.* A satin-striped silk used for furniture.

**Tabby,** tab'i, *n.* A rich watered silk or other stuff; a cat of a brindled color; a female cat.—*vt.* To water or cause to look wavy.

**Tabefaction,** tā-bē-fak'shon, *n.* A wasting away; gradual loss of flesh by disease.

**Tabernacle,** tab'ėr-na-kl, *n.* A booth; a temporary habitation; a place of worship; a repository for holy things.—*vi.* To sojourn.

**Tabes,** tā'bēz, *n.* A wasting disease.

**Tabid,** ta'bid, *a.* Relating to tabes; wasted by disease; emaciated.

**Tabinet,** tab'i-net, *n.* A fabric of silk and wool used for curtains.

**Table,** tā'bl, *n.* A thing with a flat surface; an article of furniture having a flat surface; fare or eatables; persons sitting at a table; a syllabus; index; list.—*vt.* (tabling, tabled). To tabulate; to lay on the table.—*a.* Appertaining to a table.

**Tableau,** tab-lō', *n.*; pl. **Tableaux,** tab-loz'. A picture; a striking group or dramatic scene.

**Table-cloth,** tā'bl-kloth, *n.* A cloth for covering a table, particularly at meals.

**Table d'hôte,** tä'bl-dōt, *n.* A common table for guests at a hotel.

**Tablet,** tab'let, *n.* A small slab for writing on; a slab bearing an inscription; a small flattish cake, as of soap, etc.

**Taboo,** ta-bö', *n.* The setting of something apart from human contact; prohibition of contact or intercourse.—*vt.* (tabooing, tabooed). To interdict approach to or contact with.

**Tabor,** tā'bor, *n.* A small drum.—*vt.* To play on a tabor.

**Taboret,** tā'bor-et, *n.* A small tabor; a frame for embroidery.
**Tabret,** tā'bret, *n.* A small tabor.
**Tabular,** ta'bū-lėr, *a.* In form of a table; having a flat surface; set in columns.
**Tabulate,** ta'bū-lāt, *vt.* (tabulating, tabulated). To set down in a table of items.—*a.* Tabular.
**Tacit,** ta'sit, *a.* Implied, but not expressed in words; silent; unspoken.
**Tacitly,** ta'sit-li, *adv.* In a tacit manner; silently; by implication; without words.
**Taciturn,** ta'si-tėrn, *a.* Habitually silent; not apt to talk or speak.
**Tack,** tak, *n.* A small nail; a slight fastening; a rope for certain sails; course of a ship as regards the wind; in *Scots law,* a lease.—*vt.* To fasten by tacks; to attach slightly; to append.—*vi.* To change the course of a ship so as to have the wind acting from the other side.
**Tackle,** tak'l, *n.* Gear or apparatus; pulleys and ropes for moving weights; ropes and rigging, etc., of a ship.—*vt.* (tackling, tackled). To supply with tackle; to set vigorously to work upon; to seize.
**Tackling,** tak'ling, *n.* Tackle; gear; rigging; harness, or the like.
**Tact,** takt, *n.* Touch; nice perception or discernment; adroitness in words or actions.
**Tactic, Tactical,** tak'tik, tak'tik-al, *a.* Pertaining to tactics.
**Tactician,** tak-ti'shan, *n.* One versed in tactics.
**Tactics,** tak'tiks, *n.pl.* The science and art of disposing forces in order for battle, and performing evolutions.
**Tactile,** tak'tīl, *a.* Capable of being touched or felt; pertaining to the sense of touch.
**Taction,** tak'shon, *n.* Act of touching; touch; contact.
**Tactless,** takt'les, *a.* Destitute of tact.
**Tactual,** tak'tu-al, *a.* Pertaining to touch.
**Tadpole,** tad'pōl, *n.* The young of the frog in its first state from the spawn.
**Taffeta, Taffety,** taf'e-ta, taf'e-ti, *n.* A silk fabric, or a mixed fabric of silk and wool.
**Taffrail, Tafferel,** taf'rāl, taf'e-rel, *n.* The rail at the stern of a ship.
**Tag,** tag, *n.* A metallic point to the end of a string; an appendage; catch-word of an actor's speech.—*vt.* (tagging, tagged). To fit with a tag; to tack or join.
**Tail,** tāl, *n.* The projecting termination of an animal behind; the hinder or inferior part; the reverse of a coin; limited ownership.
**Tailor,** tā'lor, *n.* One who makes men's outer garments.—*vi.* To practice making men's clothes.
**Taint,** tānt, *vt.* To defile; to infect; to vitiate.—*vi.* To be infected or corrupted.—*n.* Infection; corruption; a stain; a blemish on reputation.
**Take,** tāk, *vt.* (taking, pret. took, pp. taken). To receive or accept; to capture; to captivate; to understand; to feel concerning; to employ; to need; to form or adopt; to assume; to note down; to be infected or seized with; to bear; to conduct, carry; to leap over.—*vi.* To direct one's course; to please; to have the intended effect; to admit of being made a portrait of.
**Taking,** tāk'ing, *a.* Alluring; attracting.—*n.* A seizing; apprehension; agitation.
**Talc,** talk, *n.* A magnesian mineral, unctuous to the touch.—*vt.* To rub with talc.
**Talcky, Talcose, Talcous,** talk'i, talk'ōs, talk'us, *a.* Like talc; consisting of talc.
**Tale,** tāl, *n.* Number counted; reckoning; a story; a narrative.
**Talent,** ta'lent, *n.* An ancient weight and denomination of money; a special faculty; general mental power; people of high abilities collectively.
**Talented,** ta'lent-ed, *a.* Furnished with talents or great intellectual power.
**Talion,** tā'li-on, *n.* The law of retaliation or punishment of like for like.
**Talisman,** ta'lis-man, *n.* A charm; a magical figure cut or engraved on stone or metal; something producing extraordinary effects.
**Talk,** tak, *vi.* To utter words; to converse.—*vt.* To speak; to gain over by persuasion; to discuss.—*n.* Familiar conversation; report; rumor; subject of discourse; discussion.
**Talkative,** tak'a-tiv, *a.* Given to much talking; loquacious; garrulous; prating.
**Talker,** tak'ėr, *n.* One who talks; a loquacious person; a prattler.
**Tall,** tal, *a.* High in stature; lofty; remarkable; extravägant.
**Tallow,** tal'ō, *n.* The fat of oxen, sheep, etc., melted and separated from the fibrous matter.—*vt.* To smear with tallow.
**Tallowy,** tal'ō-i, *a.* Greasy.
**Tally,** tal'i, *n.* A piece of wood on which notches are cut to keep accounts; anything made to suit another.—*vt.* (tallying, tallied). To record on a tally; to make to correspond.—*vi.* To correspond or agree exactly.
**Tally-ho,** tal'i-hō'', *interj.* and *n.* A huntsman's cry to urge on his hounds.
**Talmud,** tal'mud, *n.* The Hebrew civil and canonical laws, traditions, etc.
**Talon,** ta'lon, *n.* The claw of a bird of prey.
**Talus,** tā'lus, *n.* The ankle; slope; a sloping heap of broken rocks.
**Tamable, Tameable,** tām'a-bl, *a.* That may be tamed.
**Tamarind,** tam'a-rind, *n.* A tropical leguminous tree and its fruit.
**Tamarisk,** tam'a-risk, *n.* A shrub or small tree of S. Europe and Asia.
**Tambour,** tam'bör, *n.* A drum; a cylindrical stone, as in a column; a circular frame for embroidery.—*vt.* and *i.* To embroider with a tambour; to work on a tambour frame.
**Tambourine,** tam-bö-rēn', *n.* A musical instrument of the drum species played on with the hand, and having jingles attached.
**Tame,** tām, *a.* Having lost its natural wildness; domesticated; spiritless; insipid.—*vt.* (taming, tamed). To make tame; to subdue; to depress.
**Tameless,** tām'les, *a.* Untamable.
**Tamely,** tām'li, *adv.* In a tame manner; submissively; meanly; without spirit.
**Tamil,** tam'il, *n.* One of a Dravidian race of S. India; their language.
**Tamine, Taminy,** tam'in, tam'i-ni, *n.* A glazed woollen or worsted stuff; a strainer of hair or cloth.
**Tamis, Tammy,** tam'i, *n.* A sieve.
**Tamp,** tamp, *vt.* To ram tight with clay, etc.; to stamp or make firm.
**Tamper,** tam'pėr, *vi.* To meddle or interfere; to influence secretly.
**Tampion, Tompion,** tam'pi-on, tom'pi-on, *n.* The stopper of a cannon; a plug.
**Tan,** tan, *vt.* (tanning, tanned). To convert into leather, as skins; to make sunburnt; to flog.—*vi.* To become tanned.—*n.* Bark used for tanning; a yellowish-brown color.—*a.* Like tan in color; tawny.
**Tandem,** tan'dem, *adv.* With two horses harnessed singly one before the other.—*n.* A wheeled carriage so drawn; a cycle for two persons, one behind the other.
**Tang,** tang, *n.* A taste; characteristic flavor or property; part of a tool which fits into the handle; tongue of a buckle.
**Tangent,** tan'jent, *n.* A straight line which touches a circle or curve, but which, when produced, does not cut it.
**Tangential,** tan-jen'shal, *a.* Pertaining to a tangent; in the direction of a tangent.
**Tangibility,** tan-ji-bil'i-ti, *n.* Quality of being tangible or perceptible by touch.
**Tangible,** tan'ji-bl, *a.* That may be touched; real actual; evident.
**Tangle,** tang'gl, *vt.* (tangling, tangled). To unite confusedly; to involve; to complicate.—*n.* A confused knot of threads, etc.; an embarrassment;

T

a species of sea-weed.

**Tanist,** tan'ist, *n.* An elective prince among the ancient Irish.

**Tanistry,** tan'ist-ri, *n.* An Irish custom, according to which the prince was elected by the family to which he belonged.

**Tank,** tangk, *n.* A storage vessel to contain liquids or gas; a reservoir; an armored car with caterpillar wheels, protected by guns fired from inside.

**Tankard,** tang'kärd, *n.* A large drinking vessel, often with a cover.

**Tanner,** tan'ėr, *n.* One who tans hides, or converts them into leather by the use of tan.

**Tannery,** tan'ėr-i, *n.* A place where tanning is carried on; art or process of tanning.

**Tannic,** tan'ik, *a.* Applied to an acid in oak, gall-nuts, etc., the efficient substance in tanning.

**Tannin,** tan'in, *n.* Tannic acid.

**Tanning,** tan'ing, *n.* The converting of hides into leathe by the use of tan or other substances; leather manufacture.

**Tansy,** tan'zi, *n.* An aromatic and bitter herb with yellow flowers; a dish made of eggs, cream, sugar, the juice of tansy, etc.

**Tantalize,** tan'ta-līz, *vt.* (tantalizing, tantalized). To torment by presenting something desirable which cannot be attained; to excite by hopes that are never realized.

**Tantamount,** tan'ta-mount, *a.* Equal; equivalent in value, force, or effect.

**Tantivy,** tan-ti'vi, *n.* A violent gallop in the hunting-field; a hunting-cry inciting to speed.—*a.* Swift; hasty.—*adv.* Swiftly; at full speed.

**Tantrum,** tan'trum, *n.* A fit of ill-humor; display of temper; chiefly in *pl.*

**Tap,** tap, *n.* A plug to stop a hole in a cask; a spigot; a faucet; a gentle blow; a pat.—*vt.* (tapping, tapped). To broach, as a cask; to draw liquid from; to strike gently.—*vi.* To strike a gentle blow.

**Tape,** tāp, *n.* A narrow strip of woven work, used for strings and the like.

**Tape-line, Tape-measure,** tāp'līn, tāp'me-zhūr, *n.* A tape marked with feet, inches, etc., used in measuring.

**Taper,** tā'pėr, *n.* A long wick coated with wax; a small light; tapering form; gradual diminution of thickness.—*vi.* To become gradually smaller.—*vt.* To cause to taper.

**Tapestry,** ta'pes-tri, *n.* A kind of rich woven hangings of wool and silk, with pictorial representations.—*vt.* To adorn with tapestry.

**Tape-worm,** tāp'wėrm, *n.* A parastic worm found in the intestines of animals.

**Tapioca,** tap-i-ō'ka, *n.* A farinaceous substance prepared from cassava meal.

**Tapir,** tā'pir, *n.* A hoofed animal allied to the rhinoceros, with a nose resembling a small proboscis.

**Tapping,** tap'ing, *n.* The surgical operation of letting out fluid, as in dropsy.

**Tap-room,** tap'röm, *n.* A room in which beer is served from the tap.

**Tap-root,** tap'röt, *n.* Main root of a plant.

**Tar,** tär, *n.* A thick, dark, viscid substance obtained from pine or fir, coal, shale, etc.; a sailor.—*vt.* (tarring, tarred). To smear with tar.

**Tarantella,** tar-an-tel'la, *n.* A whirling Italian dance; music for the dance.

**Tarantula,** ta-ran'tū-la, *n.* A kind of spider found in S. Italy; the dance tarantella.

**Tardigrade,** tär'di-grād, *a.* Slow-paced; pertaining to the tardigrades.—*n.* One of a family of mammals comprising the sloths.

**Tardily,** tär'di-li, *adv.* Slowly.

**Tardy,** tär'di, *a.* Slow; dilatory; late; backward; reluctant.

**Tare,** tãr, *n.* A leguminous plant; vetch; allowance for the weight of the package of a commodity.

**Targe,** tärj, *n.* A target or shield.

**Target,** tär'get, *n.* A small circular shield; a mark shot at in rifle practice, etc.

**Targeteer, Targetier,** tär-get-ēr', *n.* One armed with a target.

**Targum,** tär'gum, *n.* A Chaldee version of the Hebrew Scriptures.

**Tariff,** ta'rif, *n.* A list of goods with the duties to be paid; a list of charges generally.

**Tarlatan,** tär'la-tan, *n.* A thin cotton stuff resembling gauze.

**Tarn,** tärn, *n.* A small mountain lake.

**Tarnish,** tär'nish, *vt.* To sully; to dim.—*vi.* To lose luster.—*n.* A spot; soiled state.

**Tarpan,** tär'pan, *n.* The wild horse of Tartary.

**Tarpaulin, Tarpauling,** tä4r-pa̤'lin, tär-pa̤'ling, *n.* Canvas covered with tar.

**Tarpon, Tarpum,** tär'pon, tär'pum, *n.* A large, edible American sea-fish.

**Tarry,** ta'ri, *vi.* (tarrying, tarried). To stay; to delay.—*vt.* To wait for.

**Tarry,** tär'i, *a.* Consisting of tar, or like tar; covered or smeared with tar.

**Tarsia,** tär'si-a, *n.* A kind of Italian marquetry, representing landscapes, flowers, etc.

**Tarsus,** tär'sus, *n.*; pl. **-si.** The ankle or ankle-joint.

**Tart,** tärt, *a.* Sharp to the taste; sour; acid; severe; snappish.—*n.* A species of pastry, consisting of fruit baked in paste.

**Tartan,** tär'tan, *n.* Cloth woven in colors in a checkered pattern; a Mediterranean vessel somewhat resembling a sloop.—*a.* Consisting of or resembling tartan.

**Tartar,** tär'tar, *n.* A native of Tartary; a very irascible or rigorous person; a shrew; a reddish crust deposited by wine on casks; a concretion formed on the teeth.

**Tartarean, Tartareous,** tär-tā'rē-an, tär-tā'rē-us, *a.* Pertaining to Tartarus or the infernal regions; hellish.

**Tartly,** tärt'li, *adv.* In a tart manner; sharply; severely; with sourness of aspect.

**Task,** täsk, *n.* A piece of work imposed by another or requiring to be done; burdensome employment; toil.—*vt.* To impose a task upon.

**Task-master,** täsk'mäs-tėr, *n.* One who imposes a task, or burdens with labor.

**Tassel,** tas'el, *n.* An ornament consisting of a knob with hanging threads.—*vi.* (tasseling, tasseled). To put forth a tassel or flower, as maize.—*vt.* To adorn with tassels.

**Taste,** tāst, *vt.* (tasting, tasted). To test by the tongue and palate; to perceive the flavor of; to experience; to partake of.—*vi.* To make trial by the tongue and palate; to have a flavor; to have experience.—*n.* Act of tasting; sense of tasting; flavor; intellectual relish or discernment; manner or style.

**Tasteful,** tāst'ful, *a.* Having a high taste or relish; having good taste.

**Tasteless,** tāst'les, *a.* Having no taste; insipid; stale; flat; void of good taste.

**Taster,** tāst'ėr, *n.* One who tests provisions or liquors by tasting samples.

**Tastily,** tāst'i-li, *adv.* With good taste.

**Tasty,** tāst'i, *a.* Having or showing good taste; tasteful; palatable; nice; fine.

**Ta-ta,** ta'ta, *n.* and *interj.* A familiar form of salutation at parting; good-bye.

**Tatter,** tat'ėr, *n.* A rag or part torn and hanging to the thing.

**Tattered,** tat'ėrd, *p.a.* Showing tatters; torn; hanging in rags.

**Tatting,** tat'ing, *n.* A kind of crochet, made with a shuttle-shaped needle.

**Tattle,** tat'l, *vi.* (tattling, tattled). To talk idly; to gossip.—*n.* Prate; idle talk.

**Tattler,** tat'lėr, *n.* One who tattles; an idle talker; one who spreads idle gossip.

**Tattling,** tat'ling, *a.* Given to idle talk.

**Tattoo,** tat-tö', *n.* A beat of drum and bugle-call at night, calling soldiers to their quarters.—*vt.* and *i.* To prick the skin and stain the punctured spot with colors.

**Taunt,** tant, *vt.* To reproach with severe or sarcas-

tic words; to upbraid.—*n*. A bitter or sarcastic reproach.
**Taurine,** ta'rīn, *a*. Relating to or like a bull.
**Taurus,** tä'rus, *n*. The Bull, one of the twelve signs of the zodiac.
**Taut,** tat, *a*. Tight; not slack.
**Tautologic, Tautological,** ta-to-loj'ik, ta-to-loj'ik-al, *a*. Relating to or containing tautology; repeating the same thing.
**Tautology,** ta-tol'o-ji, *n*. Needless repetition of the same meaning in different words.
**Tavern,** ta'vėrn, *n*. A house where liquors are sold; an inn.
**Taw,** ta, *vt*. To make into white leather for gloves, etc., by treating skins with alum, salt, and other matters.—*n*. A marble to be played with; a game at marbles.
**Tawdry,** ta'dri, *a*. Tastelessly ornamental; cheap and showy.
**Tawery,** ta'ė-ri, *n*. A place where skins are tawed or treated with alum, etc.
**Tawny,** ta'ni, *a*. Of a yellowish-brown color, like things tanned.
**Tax,** taks, *n*. A contribution levied by authority; a rate, duty, or impost charged on income or property; a burdensome duty; an exaction.—*vt*. To impose a tax on; to put to a certain effort; to accuse.
**Taxable,** taks'a-bl, *a*. That may be taxed; liable by law to the assessment of taxes.
**Taxation,** taks-ā'shon, *n*. Act of levying taxes; the aggregate of taxes.
**Taxicab, Taxi,** tak'si-kab, tak'si, *n*. An automobile provided with a meter which shows distance run and fare due.
**Taxidermy,** tak'si-dėr-mi, *n*. The art of stuffing animals, or of preserving the skins.
**Taxology,** tak-sol'o-ji, *n*. *See* TAXONOMY.
**Taxonomy,** tak-son'o-mi, *n*. That department of natural history which treats of the laws and principles of classification.
**Tea,** tē, *n*. The dried leaves of plants cultivated in China, Assam, Ceylon, etc.; the plant itself; a decoction of tea leaves in boiling water; any decoction of vegetables.—*vi*. (teaing, teaed). To take tea.
**Teach,** tēch, *vt*. (teaching, taught). To instruct; to inform; to make familiar with.—*vi*. To practice giving instruction.
**Teachable,** tēch'a-bl, *a*. That may be taught; apt to learn; docile.
**Teacher,** tēch'ėr, *n*. One who teaches; an instructor; a preceptor; a schoolmaster.
**Teaching,** tēch'ing, *n*. Act or business of instructing; instruction.
**Tea-cup,** tē'kup, *n*. A small cup for drinking tea from.
**Teak,** tēk, *n*. An E. Indian tree which furnishes hard and valuable timber.
**Teal,** tēl, *n*. A small British duck found about fresh-water lakes.
**Team,** tēm, *n*. A brood; horses or other beasts harnessed together; a side in a game, match, etc.
**Teamster,** tēm'stėr, *n*. One who drives a team.
**Tea-pot,** tē'pot, *n*. A vessel in which tea is infused.
**Tear,** tēr, *n*. A drop of the watery fluid appearing in the eyes; any transparent drop.
**Tear,** tār, *vt*. (pret. tore, pp. torn). To pull in pieces; to rend; to wound; to drag; to pull with violence; to make by rending.—*vi*. To be rent or torn; to rage.—*n*. A rent.
**Tear-drop,** tēr'drop, *n*. A tear.
**Tearful,** tēr'ful, *a*. Abounding with tears; weeping; shedding tears.
**Tearless,** tēr'les, *a*. Shedding no tears; without tears; unfeeling.
**Tease,** tēz, *vt*. (teasing, teased). To pull apart the fibers of; to annoy; to torment.
**Teasel,** tē'zl, *n*. The fuller's thistle, used to raise the nap on woollen cloths.—*vt*. To raise a nap, as on cloth, by teasels.
**Tea-service,** tē'sėr-vis, *n*. A complete set of dishes or utensils for the tea-table.
**Tea-set,** tē'set, *n*. A tea-service.
**Teat,** tēt, *n*. The projecting part of the female breast; pap; nipple.
**Technical,** tek'ni-kal, *a*. Pertaining to an art, science, pofession, handicraft, etc.
**Technicality,** tek-ni-kal'i-ti, *n*. Quality or state of being technical.
**Technique,** tek-nēk', *n*. Method of manipulation in an art; artistic execution.
**Technological,** tek-no-loj'ik-al, *a*. Pertaining to technology.
**Technology,** tek-nol'o-ji, *n*. The science of the industrial arts.
**Tectonic,** tek-ton'ik, *a*. Pertaining to building or construction.
**Tectonics,** tek-ton'iks, *n*. The art of building or construction.
**Ted,** ted, *vt*. (tedding, tedded). To spread or turn, as new-mowed grass or hay.
**Tedious,** tē'di-us, *a*. Tiresome; wearisome; irksome; fatiguing; dilatory; tardy.
**Tediously,** tē'di-us-li, *adv*. Wearisomely.
**Tedium,** tē'di-um, *n*. Irksomeness.
**Tee,** tē, *n*. A point of aim or starting-point in certain games, as quoits and golf; a small cone of sand, rubber, etc., on which a golfer places his ball when driving off.—*vt*. To place (ball) on tee.
**Teem,** tēm, *vi*. To bring forth young; to be prolific.—*vt*. To bring forth.
**Teeming,** tēm'ing, *a*. Producing young; prolific; overflowing; exceedingly abundant.
**Teens,** tēnz, *n.pl*. The years of one's age having the termination *-teen*.
**Teeth,** tēth, *n.pl*. of *tooth*.
**Teethe,** tēTH, *vi*. (teething, teethed). To have the teeth growing or cutting the gums.
**Teething,** tēTH'ing, *n*. Operation, process, or period of the first growth of teeth.
**Teetotal,** tē'tō-tal, *a*. Totally abstaining from intoxicants.
**Teetotaler, Teetotaller,** tē'tō-tal-ėr, *n*. A total abstainer from intoxicants.
**Teetotalism,** tē'tō-tal-izm, *n*. The principles or practice of teetotalers.
**Tee-totum,** tē-to'tum, *n*. A small four-sided toy of the top kind.
**Tegular,** teg'ū-lėr, *a*. Resembling a tile; consisting of tiles.
**Tegument,** teg'ū-ment, *n*. A cover or covering; an integument.
**Tegumentary,** teg-ū-ment'a-ri, *a*. Pertaining to teguments.
**Teil,** tēl, *n*. The lime-tree or linden.
**Teind,** tēnd, *n*. In Scotland, a tithe.
**Telegram,** tel'e-gram, *n*. A communication sent by telegraph.
**Telegraph,** tel'e-graf, *n*. Any apparatus for transmitting messages to a distance; an apparatus for transmitting messages along a wire by electricity, but now also wireless.—*vt*. To convey or announce by telegraph.
**Telegraphic, Telegraphical,** tel-e-graf'ik, tel-e-graf'ik-al, *a*. Pertaining to the telegraph; communicated by a telegraph.
**Telegraphist,** tel'e-graf-ist or te-leg'ra-fist, *n*. One who works a telegraph.
**Telegraphy,** te-leg'ra-fi, *n*. The art or practice of communicating by a telegraph.
**Telemeter,** te-lem'et-ėr, *n*. A range-finder or similar instrument; an instrument to transmit variations marked by some physical instrument.
**Teleology,** tel-ē-ol'o-ji, *n*. The science or doctrine of final causes.
**Teleostean,** tel-ē-os'tē-an, *n*. One of an order of fishes having a well-ossified skeleton, and including most familiar food-fishes.
**Telepathic,** tel-e-path'ik, *a*. Pertaining to telepathy.
**Telepathy,** te-lep'a-thi or tel'e-path-i, *n*. Occult communication between persons at some distance.

T

**Telephone,** tel'e-fōn, *n.* An instrument transmitting sound to a distance by means of electricity and telegraph wires.—*vt.* (telephoning, telephoned). To transmit by means of the telephone.
**Telephonic,** tel-e-fon'ik, *a.* Relating to the telephone; communicated by the telephone.
**Telescope,** tel'e-skōp, *n.* An optical instrument for viewing distant objects.—*vt.* (telescoping, telescoped). To drive the parts of into each other, like the joints of a telescope.
**Telescopic,** tel-e-skop'ik, *a.* Pertaining to a telescope; seen only by a telescope.
**Television,** tel'e-vizh''un, *n.* Radio transmission of scenes or pictures so that they can be received at a distance (on a cathode ray tube screen).
**Telic,** tel'ik, *a.* Denoting end or purpose.
**Tell,** tel, *vt.* (telling, told). To number; to relate; to disclose; to explain; to distinguish; to inform; to bid.—*vi.* To give an account; to take effect.
**Teller,** tel'ėr, *n.* One who tells; an officer of a bank who receives and pays money; one appointed to count votes.
**Telling,** tel'ing, *p.a.* Having great effect.
**Tell-tale,** tel'tāl, *a.* Telling tales; blabbing; serving to betray; informative.—*n.* One who discloses private concerns, or what he should suppress.
**Tellurian,** tel-ū'ri-an, *a.* Pertaining to the earth.—*n.* An inhabitant of the earth.
**Telluric,** tel-ū'rik, *a.* Pertaining to the earth or to tellurium.
**Tellurium,** tel-ū'ri-um, *n.* A non-metallic element of a tin-white crystalline appearance.
**Telpherage,** tel'fėr-āj, *n.* A system of transporting goods on a kind of elevated railway by means of electricity.
**Temerarious,** tem-ē-rā'ri-us, *a.* Reckless.
**Temerity,** tē-me'ri-ti, *n.* Contempt of danger; extreme boldness; rashness.
**Temper,** tem'pėr, *vt.* To proportion duly; to moderate; to form to a proper hardness.—*n.* Due mixture; disposition of the mind; temperament; irritation; state of a metal as to its hardness; medium.
**Tempera,** tem'pe-ra, *n.* Distemper, in *painting*.
**Temperament,** tem'pėr-a-ment, *n.* Due mixture of qualities; combined mental and physical constitution; disposition.
**Temperance,** tem'pėr-ans, *n.* Moderation in indulgence of the natural appetities; sobriety; abstinence from intoxicants.
**Temperate,** tem'pėr-āt, *a.* Moderate; abstemious; free from ardent passion; calm; cool; measured; sober.
**Temperature,** tem'pėr-a-tūr, *n.* State with regard to heat or cold; climatic heat.
**Tempered,** tem'pėrd, *a.* Having a certain disposition or temper; disposed.
**Tempest,** tem'pest, *n.* A violent storm; hurricane; violent tumult or commotion.
**Tempestuous,** tem-pest'ū-us, *a.* Very stormy; turbulent; subject to storms of passion.
**Templar,** tem'plėr, *n.* One of a religious military order established to protect pilgrims to the Holy Land; a lawyer or student living in the Temple in London.—**Good Templars,** a modern teetotal society.
**Temple,** tem'pl, *n.* A place of worship; a church; part of the head between the forehead and the ear.
**Templet, Template,** tem'plet, tem'plāt, *n.* A board whose edge is shaped so as to serve as a guide in making an article with a corresponding contour.
**Tempo,** tem'pō, *n.* The time of a piece of music; musical time.
**Temporal,** tem'pō-ral, *a.* Pertaining to time; pertaining to this life; not spiritual or ecclesiastical, secular; pertaining to the temples of the head.—*n.* Anything temporal or secular; a temporality.
**Temporality,** tem-pō-ral'i-ti, *n.* State or quality of being temporal; a secular possession; *pl.* revenues of an ecclesiastic from lands, tithes, etc.
**Temporalty,** tem'pō-ral-ti, *n.* The laity; a secular possession; a temporality.
**Temporarily,** tem'pō-ra-ri-li, *adv.* For a time only; provisionally.
**Temporary,** tem'pō-ra-ri, *a.* Lasting but for a time; transient; provisional.
**Temporize,** tem'pō-rīz, *vi.* To comply with the time or occasion; to trim.
**Tempt,** temt, *vt.* To incite to an evil act; to provoke; to entice; to put to a test.
**Temptation,** tem-tā'shon, *n.* Act of tempting; state of being tempted; enticement to evil; an allurement.
**Tempter,** temt'ėr, *n.* One who tempts; the devil.
**Tempting,** temt'ing, *p.a.* Adapted to tempt; attractive; seductive.
**Temptress,** temt'res, *n.* A female who tempts.
**Temulence,** tem'ū-lens, *n.* Drunkenness.
**Temulent,** tem'ū-lent, *a.* Drunken.
**Ten,** ten, *a.* and *n.* Twice five; nine and one.
**Tenable,** te'na-bl, *a.* That may be held or maintained.
**Tenacious,** te-nā'shus, *a.* Holding fast; retentive; adhesive; stubborn.
**Tenaciously,** te-nā'shus-li, *adv.* Obstinately; with firm adherence; toughly.
**Tenacity,** te-nas'i-ti, *n.* State or quality of being tenacious; adhesiveness; glutinousness; toughness; cohesiveness.
**Tenancy,** te'nan-si, *n.* A holding lands or tenements as a tenant; tenure.
**Tenant,** te'nant, *n.* One who occupies lands or houses for which he pays rent.—*vt.* To hold as a tenant.—*vi.* To live as a tenant; to dwell.
**Tenantable,** te'nant-a-bl, *a.* In a state suitable for a tenant; fit to be rented.
**Tenantless,** te'nant-les, *a.* Having no tenant.
**Tenantry,** te'nant-ri, *n.* The body of tenants.
**Tench,** tensh, *n.* A European fresh-water fish of the carp family.
**Tend,** tend, *vi.* To move in or have a certain direction; to conduce; to attend.—*vt.* To attend; to guard; to take care of.
**Tendance,** ten'dans, *n.* Act of tending or attending; attendance.
**Tendency,** ten'den-si, *n.* Inclination; leaning; bent; proneness.
**Tender,** ten'dėr, *n.* One who attends; a small vessel employed to attend on a larger one; a carriage with fuel, etc., attached to a locomotive; an offer of money or service; an estimate; thing offered.—*vt.* To present for acceptance.—*a.* Fragile; delicate; compassionate; kind.
**Tenderly,** ten'dėr-li, *adv.* In a tender manner; with tenderness; mildly; fondly.
**Tendinous,** ten'din-us, *a.* Pertaining to a tendon; full of tendons; sinewy.
**Tendon,** ten'don, *n.* A sinew; a hard, insensible cord or bundle of fibers by which a muscle is attached to a bone.
**Tendril,** ten'dril, *n.* A slender, twining growth, by which a plant adheres to something.
**Tenebrosity,** te-nē-bros'i-ti, *n.* Darkness.
**Tenebrous, Tenebrose,** te'nē-brus, te'nē-brōs, *a.* Dark; gloomy.
**Tenement,** te'nē-ment, *n.* An abode; a habitation; a block of buildings divided into separate houses.
**Tenemental, Tenementary,** te-nē-ment'al, te-nē-ment'a-ri, *a.* Pertaining to a tenement; capable of being leased; held by tenants.
**Tenet,** te'net, *n.* A doctrine, opinion, principle, or dogma.
**Tenfold,** ten'fōld, *a.* Ten times more.
**Tenia,** tē'ni-a, *n.* The tape-worm; a fillet or band; a ligature.
**Tennis,** ten'is, *n.* A game in which a ball is driven against a wall, and caused to rebound; in ordinary use, lawn-tennis.
**Tenon,** ten'on, *n.* The specially shaped end of a piece of wood, etc., to be inserted into the mor-

tise to form a joint.
**Tenor,** ten'or, *n.* A prevailing course or direction; purport; substance, as of a discourse; the highest of the male adult chest voices; one who sings a tenor part.—*a.* Adapted for singing or playing the tenor.
**Tense,** tens, *n.* Inflection of a verb to express time.—*a.* Stretched; tight; strained to stiffness; rigid; not lax.
**Tensile,** tens'īl, *a.* Pertaining to tension; capable of tension.
**Tension,** ten'shon, *n.* Act of stretching; state of being stretched; tightness; strain; intensity; elastic force.
**Tensity,** tens'i-ti, *n.* State of being tense.
**Tensor,** ten'sor, *n.* A muscle that extends or stretches the part to which it is fixed.
**Tent,** tent, *n.* A portable shelter consisting of some flexible covering; a roll of lint, etc., to dilate a sore.—*vi.* To lodge in a tent.—*vt.* To supply with tents; to probe; to keep open with a tent, as a sore.
**Tentacle,** ten'ta-kl, *n. sing.* and *pl.* A filiform organ of various animals, used for prehension or as a feeler.
**Tentative,** ten'ta-tiv, *a.* Experimental; empirical.—*n.* An essay; a trial.
**Tentatively,** ten'ta-tiv-li, *adv.* By way of experiment or trial.
**Tenter,** ten'tėr, *n.* A machine for stretching cloth; a tenter-hook; a person in a manufactory who looks after machines.—*vt.* To hang or stretch on tenters.
**Tenter-hook,** ten'tėr-huk, *n.* A hook for stretching cloth on a tenter; anything that painfully strains, racks, or tortures.
**Tenth,** tenth, *a.* Next after the ninth.—*n.* One of ten equal parts.
**Tenuity,** ten-ū'i-ti, *n.* State of being thin or fine; thinness; slenderness; rarity.
**Tenuous,** ten'ū-us, *a.* Thin; slender.
**Tenure,** ten'ūr, *n.* A holding or manner of holding real estate; condition of occupancy; manner of possessing in general.
**Tepid,** te'pid, *a.* Moderately warm; lukewarm.
**Teraph,** te'raf, *n.*; pl. **-phim.** A household deity or image.
**Teratology,** ter-a-tol'o-ji, *n.* The science of monsters or malformations.
**Terce,** tėrs, *n.* A tierce; in *Scots law,* the right of a widow to a liferent or one-third of her deceased husband's heritage.
**Tercentenary,** tėr-sen'ten-a-ri, *a.* Comprising three hundred years.—*n.* The three-hundredth anniversary.
**Terebene,** ter'ē-bēn, *n.* A liquid hydrocarbon produced by treating oil of turpentine with sulphuric acid.
**Terebinth,** te'rē-binth, *n.* The turpentine-tree.
**Teredo,** te-rē'dō, *n.* A worm-like molluscous animal, the ship-worm, which perforates submerged wood.
**Terete,** te-rēt', *a.* Cylindrical and smooth; long and round.
**Tergal,** tėr'gal, *a.* Pertaining to the back.
**Term,** tėrm, *n.* A limit; boundary; time for which anything lasts; period of session, etc.; day on which rent or interest is paid; a word; a word having a technical meaning; *pl.* conditions; relative position or footing.—*vt.* To name; to call.
**Termagant,** tėr'ma-gant, *n.* A brawling woman; a shrew; a scold.—*a.* Quarrelsome; shrewish.
**Terminable,** tėr'min-a-bl, *a.* That may be terminated or bounded; limitable.
**Terminal,** tėr'min-al, *a.* Pertaining to or forming the end; terminating.—*n.* An extremity; the clamping screw at each end of a voltaic battery.
**Terminate,** tėr'min-āt, *vt.* and *i.* (terminating, terminated). To bound; to limit; to end.—*a.* Limited.
**Termination,** tėr-min-ā'shon, *n.* Act of terminating; close; extremity; ending of a word; conclusion; result.
**Terminology,** tėr-min-ol'o-ji, *n.* The science or theory of technical or other terms; terms used in any art, science, etc.
**Terminus,** tėr'mi-nus, *n.*; pl. **-ni.** A boundary; a limit; station at the end of a railway, etc.
**Termite,** tėr'mīt, *n.* A neuropterous insect commonly called the white ant.
**Termless,** tėrm'les, *a.* Boundless; nameless.
**Termly,** tėrm'li, *a.* and *adv.* At every term.
**Tern,** tėrn, *n.* A long-winged bird of the gull family.—*a.* Consisting of three.
**Ternary,** tėr'na-ri, *a.* Proceeding by threes; consisting of three.
**Ternate,** tėr'nāt, *a.* Arranged in threes.
**Terpsichorean,** tėrp'si-kō-rē''an, *a.* Relating to Terpsichore, the goddess of dancing.
**Terra,** ter'ra, *n.* Earth; the earth.—**Terra firma,** dry land.
**Terrace,** te'räs, *n.* A raised level bank of earth; a raised flat area; a row of houses; flat roof of a house.—*vt.* (terracing, terraced). To form into or furnish with a terrace.
**Terra-cotta,** ter'ra-kot-a, *n.* A kind of pottery, commonly of a reddish color; a work of art in terra-cotta.
**Terrapin,** te'ra-pin, *n.* A fresh-water tortoise.
**Terraqueous,** te-rak'wē-us, *a.* Consisting of land and water, as the globe or earth.
**Terrene,** te-rēn', *a.* Earthly; terrestrial.
**Terrestrial,** te-res'tri-al, *a.* Pertaining to the earth; mundane; pertaining to land.—*n.* An inhabitant of the earth.
**Terrible,** te'ri-bl, *a.* Adapted to arouse terror; dreadful; fearful; extraordinary.
**Terribly,** te'ri-bli, *adv.* In a terrible manner; dreadfully; excessively; very greatly.
**Terrier,** te'ri-ėr, *n.* A small variety of dog that creeps into holes in the earth, after animals that burrow.
**Terrific,** te-rif'ik, *a.* Terrifying; dreadful.
**Terrifically,** te-rif'ik-al-li, *adv.* In a terrific manner; terribly; frightfully.
**Terrify,** te'ri-fī, *vt.* (terrifying, terrified). To cause or produce terror in; to alarm.
**Terrigenous,** te-rij'en-us, *a.* Earth-born.
**Territorial,** te-ri-tō'ri-al, *a.* Pertaining to a territory; concerned with a certain district.
**Territory,** te'ri-to-ri, *n.* A definite piece of land under any distinct administration; a dominion; region; country.
**Terror,** te'ror, *n.* Such fear as agitates body and mind; dread; alarm; cause of fear.
**Terrorism,** te'ror-izm, *n.* A system of government by terror; intimidation.
**Terrorize,** te'ror-īz, *vt.* To impress with terror; to domineer over by means of terror.
**Terse,** tėrs, *a.* Free from superfluities of language; concise; forcible; pithy.
**Tersely,** tėrs'li, *adv.* Pithily; concisely.
**Tertian,** tėr'shan, *a.* Occurring or having its paroxysms every third day, as a fever.
**Tertiary,** tėr'shi-a-ri, *a.* Third; applied to the third great division of stratified rocks, resting on the chalk.—*n.* The tertiary system of rocks.
**Tessellar,** tes'se-lär, *a.* Formed in tesserae.
**Tessellate,** tes'se-lāt, *vt.* To form with tesserae; to lay with checkered work.
**Tessellation,** tes-se-lā'shon, *n.* Tessellated work, or the operation of making it.
**Tessera,** tes'e-ra, *n.*; pl. **-rae.** A small cube of marble, ivory, etc., used for mosaic work.
**Test,** test, *n.* A vessel used in trying or refining gold, etc.; a cupel; examination; means of trial; a standard; oath taken before admission to privileges; a hard outer covering.—*vt.* To put to a trial; to refine; to examine; to prove; to attest.
**Testacean,** tes-tā'shē-an, *n.* A testaceous animal; a mollusk with a shell.
**Testaceous,** tes-tā'shus, *a.* Having a molluskous shell; pertaining to shell-fish.
**Testacy,** tes'ta-si, *n.* The state of being testate.
**Testament,** tes'ta-ment, *n.* In *law,* a person's will; (with cap.) one of the two general divisions of the Scriptures.

**Testamental,** tes-ta-ment'al, *a.* Testamentary.
**Testamentary,** tes-ta-ment'a-ri, *a.* Pertaining to a will; bequeathed or done by will.
**Testate,** tes'tāt, *a.* Having left a will.
**Testator,** tes-tāt'or, *n.* A man who laves a will or testament at death.
**Testatrix,** tes-tāt'riks, *n.* A woman who leaves a will at death.
**Testicle,** tes'ti-kl, *n.* One of the two glands which secrete the seminal fluid in males.
**Testify,** tes'ti-fī, *vi.* (testifying, testified). To bear witness; to give evidence.—*vt.* To bear witness to.
**Testily,** tes'ti-li, *adv.* Irritably; peevishly.
**Testimonial,** tes-ti-m'ō'ni-al, *n.* A certificate of qualifications; a gift in token of appreciation or esteem.
**Testimony,** tes'ti-mo-ni, *n.* Witness; evidence; affirmation; attestation; profession; divine revelation; law of God.
**Testy,** tes'ti, *a.* Fretful; peevish; petulant.
**Tetantus,** tet'a-nus, *n.* Spasm with rigidity; lockjaw.
**Tête-à-tête,** tāt-ä-tāt, *adv.* Face to face; in private.—*n.* A private interview or talk.
**Tether,** teᴛʜ'ėr, *n.* A rope confining a grazing animal with certain limits; scope allowed.—*vt.* To confine with a tether.
**Tetragon,** tet'ra-gon, *n.* A plane figure having four angles; a quadrilateral.
**Tetrahedron,** te-tra-hē'dron, *n.* A solid body having four equal triangles as its faces.
**Tetralogy,** te-tral'o-ji, *n.* A group of four connected dramatic compositions.
**Tetrameter,** te-tram'et-ėr, *n.* A metrical verse of four feet.
**Tetrarch,** tet'rärk, *n.* A Roman governor of the fourth part of a province; a petty king.
**Tetrarchate, Tetrarchy,** tet'rärk-āt, tet'rärk-i, *n.* Office or jurisdiction of a tetrarch.
**Tetrasyllable,** tet'ra-si-la-bl, *n.* A word consisting of four syllables.
**Tetter,** tet'ėr, *n.* A cutaneous disease.
**Teuton,** tū'ton, *n.* A person of Germanic race in the widest sense of the term.
**Teutonic,** tū-ton'ik, *a.* Belonging to the Teutons and to the languages spoken by them.—*n.* The languages collectively of the Teutons.
**Text,** tekst, *n.* An author's own work as distinct from annotations; a passage of Scripture selected as the subject of a discourse; a topic; a large kind of handwriting; particular kind of lettering.
**Text-book,** tekst'buk, *n.* A book containing the leading principles of a science, etc., arranged for the use of students.
**Textile,** teks'tīl, *a.* Woven; capable of being woven.—*n.* A fabric made by weaving.
**Textorial,** teks-tō'ri-al,-*a.* Pertaining to weaving.
**Textual,** teks'tū-al, *a.* Contained in the text; pertaining to the text.
**Textualist,** teks'tū-al-ist, *n.* One who adheres to the text; one who can quote texts.
**Texture,** teks'tūr, *n.* A web; that which is woven; a fabric; manner in which constituent parts are connected; the grain or peculiar character of a solid.
**Thalamus,** thal'a-mus, *n.*; pl. **-mi.** A large ganglion in the brain; the receptacle of a flower, or part on which the carpels are placed.
**Thaler,** tä'lėr, *n.* A German coin.
**Thallogen, Thallophyte,** thal'ō-jen, thal'ō-fīt, *n.* A stemless plant consisting only of expansions of cellular tissue.
**Thallus,** thal'us, *n.* A solid mass of cells, forming the substance of the thallogens.
**Than,** ᴛʜan, *conj.* A particle used after certain adjectives and adverbs expressing compariosn or diversity, as *more, other,* etc.
**Thane,** thān, *n.* Among the Anglo-Saxons, a man of similar rank to a baron.
**Thanedom,** thān'dum, *n.* The district, office, or jurisdiction of a thane.
**Thank,** thangk, *n.* Expression of gratitude; an acknowledgment of favor or kindness; almost always in *pl.*—*vt.* To give thanks to; to express gratitude to for a favor.
**Thankful,** thangk'ful, *a.* Grateful; impressed with a sense of kindness received, and ready to acknowledge it.
**Thankfully,** thangk'ful-li, *adv.* In a thankful manner; gratefully.
**Thankless,** thangk'les, *a.* Ungrateful; not obtaining or likely to gain thanks.
**Thanksgiving,** thangks'giv-ing, *n.* Act of giving thanks; public celebration of divine goodness.
**That,** ᴛʜat, *a.* and *pron.*; pl. **Those,** ᴛʜōz. A pronominal adjective pointing to a person or thing mentioned or understood; a demonstrative pronoun; a relative pronoun equivalent to *who* or *which.*—*conj.* Introducing a reason, purpose, or result, a noun clause, or a wish.
**Thatch,** thach, *n.* Straw or rushes used to cover a building or stacks.—*vt.* To put thatch on.
**Thatcher,** thach'ėr, *n.* One who thatches.
**Thatching,** thach'ing, *n.* Act or art of covering buildings with thatch; material so used.
**Thaumaturgy,** tha'ma-tėr-ji, *n.* Miracle-working; magic; legerdemain.
**Thaw,** tha, *vi.* To melt, as ice or snow; to cease to freeze; to become genial.—*vt.* To melt; to make less cold or reserved.—*n.* The melting of ice or snow; warmth after frost.
**The,** ᴛʜē or ᴛʜi, *def. art.* Used before nouns with a specifying or limiting effect; used before adjectives and adverbs in the comparative degree it means by so much.
**Theanthropism,** thē-an'thro-pizm, *n.* The state of being God and man.
**Thearchy,** thē'är-ki, *n.* Government by God; theocracy.
**Theater,** thē'a-tėr, *n.* A house for the exhibition of dramatic performances; a place of action; a room for anatomical demonstrations, etc.
**Theatric, Theatrical,** thē-at'rik, thē-at'rik-al, *a.* Pertaining to a theater; calculated for display; artificial; false.
**Theatricals,** thē-at'rik-alz, *n.pl.* Dramatic performances, especially by amateurs.
**Theca,** thē'ka, *n.*; pl. **-cae.** The spore-case of ferns, mosses, and other cryptogams.
**Thee,** ᴛʜē, *pron.* The objective and dative case of *thou.*
**Theft,** theft, *n.* Act of stealing; unlawful taking of another's goods; thing stolen.
**Their,** ᴛʜār, *pronominal* or *possessive adj.* Pertaining or belonging to them.—**Theirs,** possessive case of *they,* used without a noun.
**Theism,** thē'izm, *n.* Acknowledgment of the existence of a God; belief in gods.
**Theist,** thē'ist, *n.* One who believes in the existence of a God.
**Theistic, Theistical,** thē-ist'ik, thē-ist'ik-al, *a.* Pertaining to theism or to a theist.
**Them,** ᴛʜem, *pron.* The dative and objective case of *they*; those persons or things.
**Theme,** thēm, *n.* A subject or topic; short dissertation by a student; leading subject in a musical composition.
**Then,** ᴛʜen, *adv.* At that time, past or future; soon afterwards.—*conj.* In that case; therefore.
**Thence,** ᴛʜens, *adv.* From that place or time; for that reason; elsewhere.
**Thenceforth,** ᴛʜens'fōrth, *adv.* From that time forward.
**Thenceforward,** ᴛʜens'for-wėrd, *adv.* From that time or place onward.
**Theocracy,** thē-ok'ra-si, *n.* Government by the immediate direction of God; the state thus governed.
**Theocrasy,** thē-ok'ra-si, *n.* Intimate union of the soul with God in contemplation.
**Theocratic, Theocratical,** thē-o-krat'ik, thē-o-krat'ik-al, *a.* Pertaining to a theocracy.
**Theodicy,** thē-od'i-si, *n.* A vindication of the ways of God in creation; a doctrine as to the provi-

dential government of God.
**Theodolite,** thē-od'o-līt, *n.* An instrument for measuring horizontal and vertical angles, used by surveyors.
**Theogony,** thē-og'o-ni, *n.* Doctrine as to the genealogy of pagan deities.
**Theologian,** thē-o-lō'ji-an, *n.* A person well versed in theology; a divine.
**Theologic, Theological,** thē-o-loj'ik, thē-o-loj'ik-al, *a.* Pertaining to theology.
**Theologist,** thē-ol'o-jis, *n.* A theologian.
**Theologize,** thē-ol'o-jīz, *vi.* To theorize on theological subjects.
**Theology,** thē-ol'o-ji, *n.* The science of God and divine things; divinity.
**Theomancy,** thē-om'an-si, *n.* Divination from the responses of oracles.
**Theophany,** thē-of'an-i, *n.* The actual appearing of God to man.
**Theorbo,** thē-or'bō, *n.* A musical instrument somewhat like a large lute.
**Theorem,** thē'ō-rem, *n.* A proposition to be proved by reasoning; a speculative truth.
**Theoretic, Theoretical,** thē-ō-ret'ik, thē-ō-ret'ik-al, *a.* Pertaining to theory; speculative; not practical.
**Theorist, Theorizer,** thē-'ō-rist, thē'ō-rīz-ėr, *n.* One who forms theories.
**Theorize,** thē'ō-rīz, *vi.* (theorizing, theorized). To form a theory or theories; to speculate.
**Theory,** thē'ō-ri, *n.* Speculation; hypothesis to explain something; rules or knowledge of an art as distinguished from practice.
**Therapeutic,** the-ra-pūt'ik, *a.* Pertaining to the healing art; curative.
**Therapeutics,** the-ra-pūt'iks, *n.* That part of medicine which deals with the application and operation of remedies.
**There,** ᴛʜār, *adv.* In or at that place; at that point; thither.
**Thereabout, Thereabouts,** ᴛʜār-a-bout', ᴛʜār-a-bouts', *adv.* About that; near that place; nearly.
**Thereafter,** ᴛʜār-aft'ėr, *adv.* After that; accordingly; afterward.
**Thereby,** ᴛʜār-bī', *adv.* By that; in consequence of that; near that place; nearly.
**Therefor,** ᴛʜār-for', *adv.* For that or this.
**Therefore,** ᴛʜār'for, *adv.* or *conj.* For that or this reason; consequently.
**Therein,** ᴛʜār-in', *adv.* In that or this place, time, thing, or respect.
**Thereof,** ᴛʜār-ov', *adv.* Of that or this.
**Thereon,** ᴛʜār-on', *adv.* On that or this.
**Thereto, Thereunto,** ᴛʜār-tö', ᴛʜār-un-tö', *adv.* To that or this.
**Thereupon,** ᴛʜār-up-on', *adv.* Upon that or this; in consequence of that; immediately.
**Therewith,** ᴛʜar-with', *adv.* With that or this.
**Theriotomy,** thē-ri-ot'o-mi, *n.* The anatomy of animals.
**Thermae,** thėr'mē, *n.pl.* Hot springs or hot baths.
**Thermal, Thermic,** thėr'mal, thėr'mik, *a.* Pertaining to heat; warm; hot.
**Thermograph, Thermometrograph,** thėr'mō-graf, thėr'mō-met-ro-graf, *n.* An instrument for recording variations of temperature.
**Thermometer,** thėr-mom'et-ėr, *n.* An instrument for measuring temperature.
**Thermometric, Thermometrical,** thėr'mō-met-rik, thėr'mō-met-rik-al, *a.* Pertaining to a thermometer.
**Thermotic,** thėr-mot'ik, *a.* Relating to heat; dependent on heat.
**Thermotics,** thėr-mot'iks, *n.* The science of heat.
**Thesaurus,** the-sa'rus, *n.* A treasury; a lexicon.
**These,** ᴛʜēz, *pronominal adj.* Pl. of this.
**Thesis,** thē'sis, *n.*; pl. **-ses.** A proposition which a person advances; a theme; an essay written by a candidate for a degree.
**Thespian,** thes'pi-an, *a.* Relating to dramatic acting.
**Theurgy,** thē'ėr-ji, *n.* The working of a divine agency in human affairs.
**Thewed,** thūd, *a.* Having thews or muscle.
**Thews,** thūz, *n.pl.* Muscles, sinews, strength.
**They,** ᴛʜā, *pron. pl.* The plural of *he, she,* or *it;* sometimes used indefinitely.
**Thick,** thik, *a.* Having extent measured through; dense; foggy; crowded; close; stupid; gross.—*n.* The thickest part.—*adv.* In close succession; fast or close together.
**Thicken,** thik'n, *vt.* To make thick or thicker.—*vi.* To become thick.
**Thickening,** thik'n-ing, *n.* Something put into a liquid or mass to make it more thick.
**Thicket,** thik'et, *n.* A wood or collection of trees or shrubs closely set.
**Thick-headed,** thik'hed-ed, *a.* Stupid.
**Thickly,** thik'li, *adv.* Densely; closely; in quick succession.
**Thickness,** thik'nes, *n.* Measure through and through; thick part; denseness.
**Thickset,** thik'set, *a.* Thickly planted; stout; stumpy.—*n.* A close hedge; dense underwood.
**Thick-skinned,** thik'skind, *a.* Having a thick skin or rind; callous; insensible.
**Thief,** thēf, *n.*; pl. **Thieves,** thēvz. A person who steals or is guilty of theft.
**Thieve,** thēv, *vi.* and *t.* (thieving, thieved). To practice theft; to steal.
**Thigh,** thī, *n.* The thick part of the leg above the knee; the femur.
**Thimble,** thim'bl, *n.* A metal cover for the finger in sewing.
**Thimble-rig,** thim'bl-rig, *n.* A sleight-of-hand trick with three thimbles and a pea.
**Thin,** thin, *a.* Not thick; rare; sparse; slim; lean; meager; faint or feeble.—*vt.* (thinning, thinned). To make thin.—*vi.* To become thin.
**Thine,** ᴛʜīn, *prominal, adj., poss.* of *thou.* Thy; belonging to thee.
**Thing,** thing, *n.* Whatever may be thought of or spoken of; any separate entity; a creature; matter, circumstance, event; *pl.* clothes, personal belongings, etc.
**Think,** thingk, *vi.* (thinking, thought). To have the mind occupied on some subject; to judge; to intend; to imagine; to consider.—*vt.* To imagine; to believe; to consider.
**Thinker,** thingk'ėr, *n.* One who thinks; one who writes on speculative subjects.
**Thinking,** thingk'ing, *p.a.* Having the faculty of thought; cogitative.—*n.* Act or state of one who thinks; thought.
**Thinly,** thin'li, *adv.* In a thin manner or condition; not thickly; slightly.
**Thin-skinned,** thin'skind, *a.* Having a thin skin; unduly sensitive; irritable.
**Third,** thėrd, *a.* The next after the second; being one of three equal parts.—*n.* The third part of anything.
**Thirst,** thėrst, *n.* The desire or distress occasioned by want of water; eager desire after anything.—*vi.* To feel thirst; to desire vehemently.
**Thirsty,** thėrst'i, *a.* Feeling thirst; having a vehement desire; dry; parched.
**Thirteen,** thėr'tēn, *a.* and *n.* Ten and three.
**Thirteenth,** thėr'tēnth, *a.* The third after the tenth.—One of thirteen equal parts.
**Thirtieth,** thėr'ti-eth, *a.* The next after the twenty-ninth.—*n.* One of thirty equal parts.
**Thirty,** thėr'ti, *a.* and *n.* Thrice ten.
**This,** ᴛʜis, *a.* and *pron.*; pl. **These,** ᴛʜēz. A demonstrative, used with or without a noun, referringto something present, near, or just ended.
**Thistle,** this'l, *n.* A prickly composite plant, the national emblem of Scotland.
**Thistle-down,** this'l-doun, *n.* The fine down attached to the seeds of thistles.
**Thistly,** this'li, *a.* Overgrown with thistles; like a thistle; prickly.
**Thole, Thole-pin,** thōl, thōl'pin, *n.* A pin in the gunwale of a boat to support an oar: also written *thowl.*
**Thong,** thong, *n.* A strap of leather, used for fas-

T

tening anything.
**Thorax,** thōraks, *n.*; pl. **-races.** That part of the human body which contains the lungs, heart, etc.; the chest.
**Thorn,** thorn, *n.* A tree or shrub armed with spines or prickles; a prickle; anything troublesome.
**Thorny,** thorn'i, *a.* Full of thorns or spines; prickly; troublesome; vexatious.
**Thorough,** thu'rō, *a.* Passing through or to the end; complete; perfect.
**Thorough-bred,** thu'rō-bred, *a.* Bred from pure and unmixed blood, as horses; completely bred or accomplished; high-spirited.—*n.* An animal of pure blood.
**Thoroughfare,** thu'rō-fār, *n.* A passage through; unobstructed way; power of passing.
**Thoroughly,** thu'rō-li, *adv.* In a thorough manner; fully; entirely; completely.
**Thorp, Thorpe,** thorp, *n.* A group of houses in the country; a hamlet; a village.
**Those,** THŌZ, *a.* and *pron.* Pl. of *that.*
**Thou,** THOU, *pron.* The second personal pronoun singular; in ordinary language supplanted by the plural form *you.*
**Though,** THŌ, *conj.* Granting it to be the fact that; notwithstanding that; if.—*adv.* However.
**Thought,** that, *n.* The power or act of thinking; idea; opinion; judgment; notion; purpose; contemplation; care; concern.
**Thoughtful,** that'ful, *a.* Full of thought; meditative; careful; considerate; anxious.
**Thoughtfully,** that'ful-li, *adv.* In a thoughtful manner; considerately.
**Thoughtless,** that'les, *a.* Free from thought or care; light-minded; heedless; careless.
**Thought-reading,** that'rēd-ing, *n.* A power by which it is claimed some persons are able tor read the thoughts of others.
**Thousand,** thou'zand, *a.* and *n.* Ten hundred; a great number indefinitely.
**Thousandth,** thou'zandth, *a.* Completing the number a thousand.—*n.* One of a thousand equal parts.
**Thraldom,** thral'dom, *n.* Bondage.
**Thrall,** thral, *n.* A slave; a bondsman.
**Thrash, Thresh,** thrash, thresh, *vt.* To beat out the grain or seeds from; to beat soundly; to drub.
**Thrasher, Thresher,** thrash'ėr, thresh'ėr, *n.* One who thrashes grain; a species of shark.
**Thrashing, Threshing,** thrash'ing, thresh'ing, *n.* Act of beating out grain; a sound drubbing.
**Thrasonical,** thra-son'ik-al, *a.* Given to bragging; boastful.
**Thread,** thred, *n.* A fine cord; any fine filament; prominent spiral part of a screw; continued course or tenor; general purpose.—*vt.* To pass a thread through; to pass or pierce through.
**Threadbare,** thred'bār, *a.* Having the nap worn off; worn out; trite; hackneyed.
**Threat,** thret, *n.* A menace; declaration of intention to punish or hurt.
**Threaten,** thret'n, *vt.* To use threats towards; to menace; to show to be impending.—*vi.* To use threats.
**Threatening,** thret'n-ing, *a.* Indicating a threat, or something impending.
**Three,** thrē, *a.* and *n.* Two and one.
**Threefold,** thrē'fōld, *a.* Consisting of three in one; triple.—*adv.* Trebly.
**Threepence,** thre'pens, thrip'ens, *n.* An old silver coin.
**Threepenny,** thrē'pen-i, thrip'en-i, *a.* Worth threepence; of little value; mean.—*n.* A threepence.
**Three-ply,** thrē'plī, *a.* Threefold; consisting of three strands, as cord, yarn, etc.
**Threescore,** thrē'skōr, *a.* Three times a score; sixty.
**Threne,** thrēn, *n.* A lamentation.
**Threnetic,** thren-et'ik, *a.* Mournful.
**Threnodist,** thren'o-dist, *n.* A writer of threnodies.
**Threnody,** thren'o-di, *n.* A song of lamentation; a dirge.
**Thresh,** thresh, *vt.* *See* THRASH.
**Threshold,** Thresh'ōld, *n.* The stone or piece of timber which lies under a door; a doorsill; entrance; outset.
**Thrice,** thrīs, *adv.* Three times.
**Thrift,** thrift, *n.* Frugality; economy; sea-pink.
**Thriftily,** thrift'i-li, *adv.* In a thrifty manner; frugally.
**Thriftless,** thrift'les, *a.* Having no thrift; wasteful; profuse; extravagant.
**Thrifty,** thrift'i, *a.* Characterized by thrift; frugal; economical.
**Thrill,** thril, *vt.* To send a quiver through; to affect with a keen tingling.—*vi.* To quiver; to move tremulously.—*n.* A warbling; thrilling sensation.
**Thrilling,** thril'ing, *p.a.* Serving to thrill; exciting.
**Thrips,** thrips, *n.* A minute insect, destructive to wheat.
**Thrive,** thrīv, *vi.* (thriving, pret. throve, pp. thriven). To prosper; to grow vigorously; to flourish.
**Thriving,** thriv'ing, *p.a.* Prosperous; successful; growing; flourishing.
**Thro',** thrö. A short spelling of *through.*
**Throat,** thrōt, *n.* The fore part of the neck of an animal; the opening downward at the back of the mouth.
**Throb,** throb, *vi.* (throbbing, throbbed). To beat, as the heart, with unusual force or rapidity; to palpitate.—*n.* A beat or strong pulsation.
**Throe,** thrō, *n.* Extreme pain; anguish of travail in childbirth.—*vi.* (throeing, throed). To struggle in extreme pain.
**Thrombosis,** throm'bō-sis, *n.* The obstruction of a blood-vessel by a clot of blood.
**Thrombus,** throm'bus, *n.* A clot of blood.
**Throne,** thrōn, *n.* The seat of a king or ruler; sovereign power and dignity.—*vt.* (throning, throned). To place on a royal seat; to enthrone; to exalt.
**Throng,** throng, *n.* A crowd; a great number.—*vi.* and *t.* To crowd or press together.
**Throttle,** throt'l, *n.* The windpipe or trachea; the throat; the gullet.—*vt.* (throttling, throttled). To choke; to strangle.
**Through,** thrö, *prep.* From end to end of; by means of; on account of; throughout.—*adv.* From end to end; to completion.—*a.* Going with little or no interruption from one place to another.
**Throughout,** thrö-out', *prep.* Quite through; in every part of.—*adv.* In every part.
**Throw,** thrō, *vt.* (pret. threw, pp. thrown). To fling or cast; to propel; to twist filaments of together; to venture at dice; to shed; to utter; to overturn.—*vi.* To cast; to case dice.—*n.* Act of one who throws; a cast; distance to which a thing is thrown; ventured.
**Throw-back,** thrō'bak, *n.* Reversion to an ancestral or earlier type; atavism.
**Thrum,** thrum, *n.* The end of weavers' threads cut off; any coarse yarn.—*vt.* (thrumming, thrummed). To make of or cover with thrums; to drum; to tap.—*vi.* To make a drumming noise.
**Thrush,** thrush, *n.* A singing bird; a disease affecting the lips and mouth; also a disease in the feet of the horse.
**Thrust,** thrust, *vt.* (pret. and pp. thrust). To push or drive with force; to shove; to stab; to obtrude (oneself).—*vi.* To make a push; to make a lunge with a weapon; to intrude.—*n.* A violent push; a stab; a horizontal outward pressure.
**Thud,** thud, *n.* The dull sound of a blow; a blow causing a dull sound.
**Thumb,** thum, *n.* The short thick finger of the hand.—*vt.* To soil or handle awkwardly with the fingers.

**Thumbkins,** thum'kinz, *n*. An instrument of torture for compressing the thumb.
**Thumb-screw,** thum'skrö, *n*. A screw to be turned by the fingers; the thumbkins.
**Thump,** thump, *n*. A dull, heavy blow; sound made by such a blow.—*vt*. and *i*. To strike with something thick or heavy.
**Thumping,** thump'ing, *a*. Heavy; strikingly large.
**Thunder,** thund'dėr, *n*. The sound which follows lightning; any loud noise.—*vi*. To emit the sound of thunder; to make a loud noise.—*vt*. To emit with noise and terror; to publish, as any denunciation.
**Thunderbolt,** thun'dėr-bōlt, *n*. A shaft of lightning; a daring hero; a fulmination.
**Thundering,** thun'dėr-ing, *a*. Producing or accompanied by a noise like thunder; extraordinary or excessive.
**Thunder-storm,** thun'dėr-storm, *n*. A storm accompanied with thunder.
**Thursday,** thėrz'dā, *n*. The fifth day of the week.
**Thus,** THus, *adv*. In this manner; to this degree or extent; accordingly.
**Thwack,** thwak, *vt*. To strike, bang, beat.—*n*. A heavy blow; a bang.
**Thwart,** thwart, *a*. Transverse; being across.—*vt*. To cross; tö frustrate or defeat.—*n*. The bench on which the rowers sit, athwart the boat.
**Thy,** THī, *pron. poss.* of *thou*. Belonging or pertaining to thee.
**Thyme,** tīm, *n*. A small aromatic shrub.
**Thymol,** tīm'ol, *n*. A crystalline substance obtained from oil of thyme, an antiseptic and disinfectant.
**Thyrsus,** thėr'sus, *n*.; pl. **-si.** A staff wreathed with ivy and vine branches.
**Thyself,** THī-self', *pron*. Used after *thou*, to express distinction with emphasis; also used without *thou*.
**Tiara,** tī-a'ra, *n*. An ornament worn on the head; the pope's triple crown.
**Tibia,** tib'i-a, *n*. A kind of ancient musical pipe; the shin-bone.
**Tibial,** tib'i-al, *a*. Pertaining to the tibia.
**Tic,** tik, *n*. Facial neuralgia.
**Tick,** tik, *vi*. To make a small noise by beating, etc.—*vt*. To mark with a tick or dot.—*n*. A small distinct noise; a small dot; a small parasitical mite; cover continaining the feathers, etc., of a bed; credit.
**Ticket,** tik'et, *n*. A label; a card or paper enabling one to enter a place, travel in a railway, etc.—*vt*. To put a ticket on; to label.
**Ticking,** tik'ing, *n*. A striped closely-woven cloth containing the feathers, etc., of beds.
**Tickle,** tik'l, *vt*. (tickling, tickled). To touch and cause a peculiar thrilling sensation in; to please; to flatter; to puzzle.
**Tickler,** tik'lėr, *n*. One who tickles or pleases; something that puzzles or perplexes.
**Ticklish,** tik'lish, *a*. Easily tickled; touchy; liable to be overthrown; difficult; critical.
**Tidal,** tīd'al, *a*. Pertaining to tides.
**Tide,** tīd, *n*. Time; season; the rising and falling of the sea; flow; current.—*vt*. or *i*. (tiding, tided). To drive with the tide.—**To tide over,** to surmount.
**Tideless,** tīd'les, *a*. Having no tide.
**Tide-table,** tīd'tā-bl, *n*. A table showing the time of high-water.
**Tide-Waiter,** tīd'wāt-ėr, *n*. An officer who watches the landing of goods, to secure the payment of customs duties.
**Tide-way,** tīd'wā, *n*. The channel in which the tide sets.
**Tidily,** tī'di-li, *adv*. Neatly.
**Tidings,** tī'dingz, *n.pl*. News; intelligence.
**Tidy,** tī'di, *a*. Clean and orderly; neat; trim; moderately large.—*vt*. (tidying, tidied). To make tidy.—*n*. A piece of fancy work to throw over a chair, etc.
**Tie,** tī, *vt*. (tying, tied). To bind; to fasten; to oblige; to constrain.—*n*. That which binds or fastens together; a fastening; a neck-tie; bond; obligation; an equality in numbers.
**Tie-beam,** tī'bēm, *n*. The beam which connects the bottom of a pair of rafters.
**Tier,** tēr, *n*. A row; a rank.
**Tierce,** tērs, *n*. A measure equal to one-third of a pipe, or 35 imperial gallons; a cask; in *fencing*, a position in which the wrists and nails are turned downwards.
**Tiercel, Tiercelet,** tēr'sel, tērs'let, *n*. A male hawk or falcon.
**Tie-wig,** tī'wig, *n*. A wig having a queue tied with a ribbon.
**Tiff,** tif, *n*. A fit of peevishness; a slight quarrel; small draft of liquor.—*vi*. To be in a pet.—*vt*. To sip.
**Tiffany,** tif'a-ni, *n*. A gauze or very thin silk.
**Tiger,** tī'gėr, *n*. An Asiatic carnivorous striped mammal of the cat family as large as the lion; a boy in livery.
**Tight,** tīt, *a*. Compact; well-knit; stanch not loose; fitting close or too close; taut; slightly intoxicated; difficult to obtain, as money.
**Tighten,** tīt'n, *vt*. To make tight or tighter.—*vi*. To become tight.
**Tightly,** tīt'li, *adv*. In a tight manner; closely. compactly.
**Tights,** tīts, *n.pl*. A tight-fitting covering for the legs or whole body.
**Tigress,** tī'gres, *n*. A female tiger.
**Tile,** tīl, *n*. A slab of baked clay for covering roofs, floors, walls, etc.—*vt*. (tiling, tiled). To cover with tiles; to guard against the entrance of the uninitiated.
**Till,** til, *n*. A money box or drawer for money in a shop, etc.—*prep*. To the time of; until.—*vt*. To cultivate; to plow and prepare for seed.
**Tillage,** til'āj, *n*. Act or operation of tilling; cultivation; agriculture.
**Tiller,** til'ėr, *n*. One who tills; the handle of a rudder; shoot of a plant springing from the root.—*vi*. To put forth shoots from the root.
**Tilt,** tilt, *vi*. To run or ride and thrust with a lance; to joust; to lean or slope; to heel over.—*vt*. To set in a sloping position; to cover with an awning.—*n*. Inclination forward; a military contest with lances on horseback; a tilt-hammer; an awning.
**Timber,** tim'bėr, *n*. Wood suitable for building purposes; trees yielding such wood; one of the main beams of a fabric.—*vt*. To furnish with timber.
**Timbering,** tim'bėr-ing, *n*. Timber materials; the timber in a structure.
**Timbre,** tim'br or tam'br, *n*. Characteristic quality of sound.
**Timbrel,** tim'brel, *n*. A kind of drum or tabor; a tambourine.
**Time,** tīm, *n*. The measure of duration; a particular part or point of duration; occasion; season; epoch; present life; leisure; rhythm' rate of movement.—*vt*. (timing, timed). To adapt to the time or occasion; to regulate or measure as to time.
**Time-fuse,** tīm'fūz, *n*. A fuse arranged so as to explode a charge at a certain time.
**Time-honored,** tīm'on-ėrd, *a*. Honored for a long time.
**Time-keeper,** tīm'kēp-ėr, *n*. A clock; one appointed to keep the workmen's time.
**Timeless,** tīm'les, *a*. Untimely; eternal.
**Timely,** tīm'li, *a*. Being in good time; opportune.—*adv*. Early; in good season.
**Time-piece,** tīm'pēs, *n*. A clock or watch.
**Time-table,** tīm'tā-bl, *n*. A table of the times of school classes, starting of trains, etc.
**Timid,** ti'mid, *a*. Fearful; timorous; wanting courage; faint-hearted; shy.
**Timidity,** ti-mid'i-ti, *n*. State or quality of being timid; habitual cowardice.
**Timorous,** ti'mor-us, *a*. Fearful of danger; timid.
**Timothy-grass,** tim'o-thi-gräs, *n*. A hard coarse pasture grass extensively cultivated.
**Tin,** tin, *n*. A malleable metal of a white color

tinged with gray; a dish made of tin.—*vt.* (tinning, tinned). To cover with tin; to put in a tin.
**Tincal,** ting'kal, *n.* Crude or unrefined borax.
**Tinctorial,** tingk-tō'ri-al, *a.* Relating to tinctures or dyes; coloring.
**Tincture,** tingk'tūr, *n.* A tinge, tint, or shade; slight quality added to anything; flavor; extract or solution of the active principles of some substance.—*vt.* (tincturing, tinctured). To tinge; to imbue.
**Tinder,** tin'dėr, *n.* An inflammable substance used for obtaining fire from a spark.
**Tine,** tīn, *n.* The tooth of a fork or harrow; a prong; point of a deer's horn.
**Tin-foil,** tin'foil, *n.* Tin, alloyed with a little lead, reduced to a thin leaf.
**Tinge,** tinj, *vt.* (tingeing, tinged). To give a certain hue or color to; to tint; to imbue,—*n.* A slight color; tint; tincture; smack.
**Tingle,** ting'gl, *vi.* (tingling, tingled) To feel a kind of thrilling sensation.—*vt.* To cause to give a sharp, ringing sound.
**Tinker,** ting'kėr, *n.* A mender of kettles, pans, etc.; a botcher.—*vt.* and *i.* To mend; to cobble; to botch.
**Tinkle,** ting'kl, *vi.* (tinkling, tinkled). To make small, sharp sounds; to tingle; to clink. —*vt.* To cause to clink.—*n.* A sharp, ringing noise.
**Tinkling,** ting'kling, *n.* A small, sharp, ringing sound.
**Tinning,** tin'ing, *n.* Act or process of covering with tin; covering of tin.
**Tinplate,** tin'plāt, *n.* Thin sheet-iron coated with tin.
**Tinsel,** tin'sel, *n.* Thin, glittering metallic sheets; cloth overlaid with foil; something superficially showy.—*a.* Consisting of tinsel; showy to excess.—*vt.* (tinselling, tinselled). To adorn with tinsel.
**Tinsmith,** tin'smith, *n.* A worker of tin.
**Tint,** tint, *n.* a tinge; a slight coloring; hue.—*vt.* To tinge.
**Tinting,** tint'ing, *n.* A forming of tints; a particular way of shading in engraving.
**Tintinnabular, Tintinnabulary,** tin-tin-nab'ū-lėr, tin-tin-nab'ū-lar-ri, *a.* Relating to bells or their sound.
**Tinware,** tin'wār, *n.* Articles made of tinned sheet-iron.
**Tiny,** tī'ni, *a.* Very small; little; puny.
**Tip,** tip, *n.* A small end or point; a tap; a small present in money.—*vt.* (tipping, tipped). To form the tip of; to cant up, as a cart; to give a small money-gift to.
**Tippet,** tip'et, *n.* A cape or covering for the neck and shoulders.
**Tipple,** tip'l, *vi.* (tippling, tippled) To drink spirituous liquors habitually.—*vt.* To drink or imbibe often.—*n.* Liquor.
**Tippler,** tip'lėr, *n.* A toper; a soaker.
**Tipsy,** tip'si, *a.* Fuddled; affected with strong drink; intoxicated.
**Tiptoe,** tip'tō, *n.* The tip or end of the toe.
**Tirade,** ti-rād', *n.* A violent declamation; an invective; a harangue.
**Tire,** tīr, *n.* A head-dress; a band or hoop round a wheel; attire.—*vt.* (tiring, tired). To fatigue; to weary; to adorn; to attire.—*vi.* To become weary.
**Tiresome,** tīr'sum, *a.* Wearisome; tedious.
**Tiro,** tīrō. *See* TYRO.
**'Tis,** tiz, a contraction of *it is.*
**Tissue,** ti'shū, *n.* Any woven stuff; a textile fabric; a primary layer of organic substance; a fabrication.
**Tissue-paper,** ti'shū-pā-pėr, *n.* A very thin paper, used for protecting or wrapping.
**Titan,** tī'tan, *n.* A giant deity in Greek mythology.
**Titanic,** tī-tan'ik, *a.* Pertaining to the Titans; gigantic; huge; pertaining to titanium.
**Titanium,** tī-tā'ni-um, *n.* A metallic element somewhat resembling tin.
**Tithe,** tīTH, *n.* The tenth part of anything; tenth part allotted to the clergy; any small part.—*vt.* (tithing, tithed). To levy a tithe on.—*vi.* To pay tithes.
**Tithing,** tīTH'ing, *n.* Act of levying tithes; a tithe.
**Tithonic,** ti'thon'ik, *a.* Pertaining to the chemical rays of light.
**Titillate,** ti'til-lāt, *vi.* To tickle.
**Titillation,** ti-til-lā'shon, *n.* Act of tickling; state of being tickled; any slight pleasure.
**Title,** tī'tl, *n.* An inscription put over anything; heading; name; appellation of dignity; a right; document which is evidence of a right.—*vt.* (titling, titled). To entitle; to name.
**Titled,** tī'tld, *a.* Having a title of nobility.
**Title-page,** tī'tl-pāj, *n.* The page of a book which contains its title.
**Title-role,** tī'tl-rōl, *n.* The part in a play which gives its name to it.
**Titmouse,** tit'mous, *n.*; pl. **-mice.** A small insessorial bird with shrill notes.
**Titrate,** tī'trāt, *vt.* (titrating, titrated). To submit to the process of titration.
**Titration,** tī-trā'shon, *n.* A process for ascertaining the quantity of a chemical constituent in a compound by means of a liquid of known strength.
**Titter,** tit'ėr, *vi.* To laugh with restraint.—*n.* A restrained laugh.
**Tittle,** tit'l, *n.* A small particle; a jot.
**Titular,** tit'ū-lėr, *a.* Holding a position by title or name only; nominal.
**To,** tu or tō, *prep.* Denoting motion towards; indicating a point reached, destination, addition, ratio, opposition, or contrast; marking an object; the sign of the infinitive mood.—*adv.* Forward; on.
**Toad,** tōd, *n.* A reptile resembling the frog, but not adapted for leaping.
**Toad-stool,** tōd'stöl, *n.* A fungus.
**Toady,** tō'di, *n.* A base sycophant; a flatterer.—*vt.* (toadying, toadied). To fawn upon.
**To-and-fro,** tö'and-frō', *a.* Backward and forward; reciprocal.
**Toast,** tōst, *vt.* To scorch by the heat of a fire; to warm thoroughly; to drink in honor of.—*n.* Bread scorched by the fire; anyone or anything honored in drinking; a sentiment proposed in drinking.
**Toaster,** tōst'ėr, *n.* One who toasts; an instrument for toasting bread or cheese.
**Tobacco,** tō-bak'ō, *n.* A narcotic plant of the potato family; its leaves prepared for smoking.
**Tobacconist,** tō-bak'ō-nist, *n.* A dealer in tobacco.
**Tobaggan, Tobogan,** tō-bog'an, *n.* A kind of sled used for sliding down snow-covered slopes.—*vi.* To use such a sled.
**Tocsin** tok'sin, *n.* An alarm-bell.
**Today,** tu-dā', *n.* The present day; also, on this day, adverbially.
**Toddle,** tod'l, *vi.* (toddling, toddled). To walk with short, tottering steps.—*n.* A little toddling walk.
**Toddy,** tod'i, *n.* A sweet juice extracted from palm-trees; a mixture of spirit and hot water sweetened.
**To-do,** tu-dö', *n.* Ado; bustle; commotion.
**Toe,** tō, *n.* One of the small members forming the extremity of the foot.—*vt.* (toeing, toed). To touch or reach with the toes.
**Toffy, Toffee,** tof'i, *n.* A sweetmeat composed of boiled sugar with butter.
**Toga,** tō'ga, *n.* A loose robe, the principal outer garment of the ancient Romans.
**Together,** tu-geTH'ėr, *adv.* In company; in concert; without intermission.
**Toil,** toil, *vi.* To labor; to work; to drudge. —*n.* Labor with fatigue; a string or web for taking prey.
**Toilet,** toi'let, *n.* A cloth over a table in a dressing room; a dressing-table; act or mode of dressing; attire.
**Toilsome,** toil'sum, *a.* Attended with toil; laborious; wearisome; fatiguing.
**Tokay,** tō-kā', *n.* A rich highly-prized wine pro-

duced at Tokay in Northern Hungary, made from white grapes.
**Token,** tō'kn, *n.* A mark; sign; indication; souvenir; keepsake; a piece of money current by sufferance, not coined by authority.
**Tolerable,** tol'ė-ra-bl, *a.* That may be tolerated; passable; middling.
**Tolerably,** tol'ė-ra-bli, *adv.* In a tolerable manner; moderately well; passably.
**Tolerance,** tol'ė-rans, *n.* The quality of being tolerant; toleration; endurance.
**Tolerant,** tol'ė-rant, *a.* Ready to tolerate; enduring; indulgent; favoring toleration.
**Tolerate,** tol'ė-rāt, *vt.* (tolerating, tolerated). To allow or permit; to treat with forbearance; to put up with; to allow religious freedom to.
**Toleration,** tol'ė-rā'shon, *n.* Act of tolerating; allowance given to that which is not wholly approved; recognition of the right of private judgment in religion.
**Toll,** tōl, *n.* A tax on travellers or vehicles passing along public roads, etc.; stroke of a bell.—*vi.* To pay or take toll; to sound, as a bell, with slow, measured strokes.—*vt.* To take toll from; to sound (a bell); to ring on account of.
**Toll-bar,** tōl'bär, *n.* A bar on a road, for stopping passengers till they pay toll.
**Tollbooth, Tolbooth,** tōl'bötн, *n.* The old Scottish name for a burgh jail.
**Toll-gate,** tōl'gāt, *n.* A gate where toll is taken.
**Toll-house,** tōl'hous, *n.* A house where a man who takes the toll is stationed.
**Tomahawk,** to'ma-hak, *n.* A hatchet used in war by the North American Indians—*vt.* To cut or kill with a tomahawk.
**Tomato,** tō-mä'tō, *n.*; pl. **-toes.** A tropical plant and its fruit, now widely cultivated.
**Tomb,** töm, *n.* A grave; a sepulchral structure,—*vt.* To bury; to entomb.
**Tombac, Tombak,** tom'bak, *n.* A kind of brass, or alloy of copper and zinc, used as an imitation of gold.
**Tombless,** töm'les, *a.* Destitue of a tomb or sepulchral monument.
**Tomboy,** tom'boi, *n.* A wild, romping girl.
**Tombstone,** töm'stōn, *n.* A stone erected over a grave; a sepulchral monument.
**Tom-cat,** tom'kat, *n.* A full-grown male cat.
**Tome,** tōm, *n.* A volume; a large book.
**Tomentose, Tomentous,** tō-men'tōs, tō-men'tus, *a.* Downy; nappy.
**Tomentum,** tō-men'tum, *n.* Pubescence; downy matter.
**Tomfoolery,** tom-föl'ė-ri, *n.* Foolishness; trifling; absurd knick-knacks.
**Tommy,** tom'i, *n.* A private soldier in the British Army.
**Tommy gun,** tom'i gun, *n.* An automatic rifle; The Thompson sub-machine-gun.
**Tomorrow,** tö-mo'rō, *n.* The day after the present; on the day after the present, adverbially.
**Ton,** tun, *n.* A weight equal to 20 hundred-weight or 2,240 pounds avoirdupois (the long ton used in Great Brittain); a weight equal to 2,000 pounds avoirdupois (the short ton used in the United States, Canada and South Africa).
**Tone,** tōn, *n.* Any sound in relation to its pitch, quality, or strength; sound as expressive of sentiment; timbre; healthy activity of animal organs; mood; tenor; prevailing character.—*vt.* (toning, toned). To give a certain tone to.—**To tone down,** to soften.
**Tongs,** tongz, *n.pl.* A metal instrument for taking hold of coals, heated metals, etc.
**Tongue,** tung, *n.* The fleshy movable organ in the mouth, of taste, speech, etc.; speech; a language; strip of land; a tapering flame; pin of a buckle.—*vt.* To utter; to scold; to modify with the tongue in playing, as in the flute.
**Tongue-tied,** tung'tid, tung'takt, *a.* Having an impediment in the speech; unable to speak freely.
**Tonic,** ton'ik, *a.* Increasing strength; restoring healthy functions; relating to tones or sounds.—*n.* A medicine that gives tone to the system; the key-note in mucic.
**Tonicity,** to-nis'i-ti, *n.* The elasticity of living parts, as muscles.
**Tonight,** tö-nīt', *n.* The present night; in the present or coming night, adverbially.
**Tonite,** tōn'it, *n.* A powerful explosive prepared from pulverized gun-cotton.
**Tonnage,** tun'āj, *n.* The number of tons carried by a ship; a duty on ships; ships estimated by their carrying capacity.
**Tonsil,** ton'sil, *n.* One of the two oblong glands on each side of the throat.
**Tonsilar, Tonsillar, Tonsilitic,** ton'sil-ėr, ton-si-lit'ik, *a.* Pertaining to the tonsils.
**Tonsile,** ton'sīl, *a.* That may be shorn.
**Tonsor,** ton'sor, *n.* A barber; one who shaves.
**Tonsorial,** ton-sō'ri-al, *a.* Pertaining to a barber or to shaving.
**Tonsure,** ton'sūr, *n.* The act of clipping the hair; the round bare place on the heads of the Roman Catholic priests.
**Tontine,** ton'tīn, *n.* An annuity shared by subscribers to a loan, and going wholly to the last survivor.
**Too,** tö, *adv.* Over; more than sufficiently; very; likewise; also; besides.
**Tool,** töl, *n.* Any instrument to be used by the hands; a person used as an instrument by another.—*vt.* To shape or mark with a tool.
**Tooling,** töl'ing, *n.* Skilled work with a tool; carving; ornamental marking.
**Toot,** töt, *vi.* To make a noise like that of a pipe or horn.—*vt.* To sound, as a horn.—*n.* A sound blown on a horn.
**Tooth,** töth, *n.*; pl. **Teeth,** tēth. A bony growth in the jaws for chewing; any projection resembling a tooth.—*vt.* To furnish with teeth; to indent.
**Toothache,** töth'āk, *n.* A pain in the teeth.
**Toothed,** tötht, *a.* Having teeth or cogs.
**Toothpick,** töth'pik, *n.* An instrument to pick out substances lodged among the teeth.
**Toothsome,** töth'sum, *a.* Grateful to the taste; palatable.
**Top,** top, *n.* The highest part of anything; highest rank; platform in ships surrounding the head of the lower masts; a whirling toy.—*a.* Being on the top; highest.—*vi.* (topping, topped). To rise aloft; to be eminent.—*vt.* To cap; to surmount; to rise to the top of.
**Topaz,** tō'paz, *n.* A transparent or translucent gem of various light colors.
**Top-boots,** top-böts, *n.pl.* Boots having tops of light-colored leather, used chiefly for riding.
**Top-coat,** top'kōt, *n.* An upper or over coat.
**Tope,** tōp, *n.* a fish of the shark kind; a Buddhist monument containing relics, etc.—*vi.* (toping, toped). To drink spirituous liquors to excess.
**Topgallant,** top'gal-ant, *a.* Being the third above the deck; above the topmast.
**Top-heavy,** top'he-vi, *a.* Having the top or upper part too heavy for the lower.
**Topiary,** tō'pi-a-ri, *a.* Shaped by clipping, pruning, or training.
**Topic,** to'pik, *n.* Subject of any discourse; matter treated of.
**Topical,** to'pik-al, *a.* Pertaining to a topic; local; pertaining to the topics of the day.
**Topically,** to'pik-al-li, *adv.* Locally; with application to a particular part.
**Top-knot,** top'not, *n.* A knot worn by females on the top of the head.
**Topmast,** top'mäst, *n.* The mast which is next above the lower mast.
**Topmost,** top'mōst, *a.* Highest; uppermost.
**Topographer, Topographist,** to-pog'raf-ėr, to-pog'raf-ist, *n.* One who deals with or is versed in topography.
**Topographic, Topographical,** to-po-graf'ik, to-po-graf'ik-al, *a.* Descriptive of a place.
**Topography,** to-pog'ra-fi, *n.* The description of a

T

particular place, tract of land, etc.
**Topple,** top'l, *vi.* (toppling, toppled). To fall, as with the top first.—*vt.* To throw forward.
**Top-sail,** top'sāl, *n.* The second sail above the deck on any mast.
**Topsy-turvy,** top'si-tėr-vi, *adv.* Upside down.
**Torch,** torch, *n.* A light to be carried in the hand; a flambeau.
**Toreador,** tor'e-a-dor'', *n.* A Spanish bull-fighter, especially one on horseback.
**Toreutic,** to-rū'tik, *a.* Pertaining to carved work.
**Torment,** tor'ment, *n.* Extreme pain; torture; that which gives pain.—*vt.* tor-ment'. To torture; to distress; to tease.
**Tormenter,** tor-ment'ėr, *n.* One who torments.
**Tormentil, Tormentilla,** tor'men-til, tor-men-til'a, *n.* A weed with small yellow flowers.
**Tormenting,** tor-ment'ing, *a.* Causing torment.
**Tormentor,** tor-ment'or, *n.* One who torments; a kind of harrow with wheels.
**Tornado,** tor-nā'dō, *n.*; pl. **-oes.** A violent whirling wind; a hurricane.
**Torpedo,** tor-pē'do, *n.*; pl. **-oes.** A fish allied to the rays; an explosive engine propelled under water.
**Torpedo-boat,** tor-pē'dō-bōt, *n.* A small swift boat intended to discharge torpedoes.
**Torpescence,** tor-pes'ens, *n.* A becoming torpid.
**Torpescent,** tor-pes'ent, *a.* Becoming torpid.
**Torpid,** tor'pid, *a.* Numb; stupefied; stupid; sluggish; inactive.
**Torpidity,** tor-pid'i-ti, *n.* State of being torpid; numbness; dullness; inactivity.
**Torpor,** tor'por, *n.* State of being torpid; numbness; loss of motion; sluggishness.
**Torrent,** to'rent, *n.* A violent rushing stream.
**Torrential, Torrentine,** to-ren'shal, to-ren'-tin, *a.* Pertaining to a torrent.
**Torrid,** to'rid, *a.* Parched; violently hot; burning or parching.
**Torsion,** tor'shon, *n.* The act of twisting; the force with which a body, such as a wire, resists a twist; the twisting of the cut end of an artery to stop the flow of blood.
**Torsk,** torsk, *n.* A fish of the cod tribe, caught and salted and dried as food.
**Torso,** tor'sō, *n.* The trunk of a statue deprived of its head and limbs.
**Tort,** tort, *n.* Wrong; injury.
**Tortile,** tor'til, *n.* Twisted; coiled.
**Tortious,** tor'shus, *a.* Of the nature of or implying tort or injury.
**Tortive,** tor'tiv, *a.* Twisted.
**Tortoise,** tor'tois or tor'tis, *n.* A reptile covered with a flattened shell; a turtle.
**Tortoise-shell,** tor'tois-shel, *n.* The shell of tortoises which inhabit tropical seas.
**Tortuous,** tor'tū-us, *a.* Twisted; circuitous and underhand; roundabout.
**Torture,** tor'tūr, *n.* Extreme pain; agony; torment.—*vt.* (torturing, tortured). To pain to extremity; to torment; to harass.
**Tory,** tō'ri, *n.* An ardent supporter of established institutions in politics; a Conservative.—*a.* Pertaining to Tories.
**Toryism,** tō'ri-izm, *n.* The principles or practices of the Tories.
**Toss,** tos, *vt.* To pitch; to fling; to jerk, as the head; to agitate.—*vi.* To roll and tumble; to be in violent commotion.—*n.* A throw; pitch; throw of the head.
**Toss-up,** tos'up, *n.* The throwing up of a coin to decide something; an even chance.
**Tot,** tot, *n.* Anything small or insignificant.—*vt.* (totting, totted). To sum (with *up*).
**Total,** tō'tal, *a.* Pertaining to the whole; complete.—*n.* The whole; an aggregate.
**Totalitarian,** tō-tal'it-ār''i-an, *a.* Applied to states under a highly centralized government which suppresses all rival political parties.
**Totality,** tō'tal'i-ti, *n.* Total amount.
**Totally,** tō'tal-li, *adv.* Wholly; completely.
**Totem,** tō'tem, *n.* A figure, as of an animal, plant, etc., used as a badge of a tribe or family among rude races.
**Totter,** tot'ėr, *vi.* To threaten to fall; to vaciliate; to shake; to reel.
**Tottery,** tot'ėr-i, *a.* Unsteady; shaking.
**Toucan,** tö'kan, *n.* A scansorial bird of tropical America having an enormous beak.
**Touch,** tuch, *vt.* To perceive by the sense of feeling; to come in contact with; to taste; to reach or arrive at; to refer to; to affect.—*vi.* To be in contact; to take effect; to make mention; to call when on a voyage.—*n.* Act of touching; contact; sense of feeling; a trait; a little; a stroke; distinctive handling; in football, etc., part of the field beyond the flags.
**Touch-hole,** tuch'hōl, *n.* The vent of a fire-arm communicating fire to the charge.
**Touching,** tuch'ing, *a.* Affecting; moving; pathetic.—*prep.* Concerning; with respect to.
**Touch-needle,** tuch'nē-dl, *n.* A small bar of an alloy of gold or silver, used with the touchstone to test articles of gold and silver.
**Touchstone,** tuch'stōn, *n.* A compact, dark-colored, siliceous stone used in testing gold and silver; a test or criterion.
**Touchwood,** tuch'wud, *n.* Soft decayed wood, serving the purpose of tinder.
**Touchy,** tuch'i, *a.* Irritable; irascible; apt to take offense.
**Tough,** tuf, *a.* Flexible and not brittle; tenacious; durable; viscous; stiff; stubborn.
**Toughen,** tuf'n, *vi.* To grow tough.—*vt.* To make tough.
**Toupee, Toupet,** tö-pē', tö'pē, *n.* A curl or artificial lock of hair; a small wig or upper part of wig.
**Tour,** tör, *n.* A journey; a lengthy jaunt or excursion.—*vi.* To make a tour.
**Tourist,** tör'ist, *n.* One who makes a tour.
**Tourmalin, Tourmaline,** tör'ma-lin, *n.* A mineral of various colors, possessing strong electrical properties.
**Tournament,** tör'na-ment, *n.* A martial sport performed by knights on horseback; contest in which a number take part.
**Tourney,** tör'ni, *n.* A tournament.—*vi.* To tilt; to engage in a tournament.
**Tourniquet,** tör'ni-ket, *n.* A bandage tightened by a screw to check a flow of blood.
**Touse,** touz, *vt.* (tousing, toused). To pull or drag; to tousle.
**Tousle,** tou'zl, *vt.* (tousling, tousled). To dishevel.
**Tout,** tout, *vi.* To ply or seek for customers.—*n.* One who plies for customers.
**Tow,** tō, *vt.* To drag, as a boat, by a rope.—*n.* Act of towing; state of being towed; coarse part of flax or hemp.
**Toward, Towards,** tō'ėrd, tō'ėrdz, *prep.* In the direction of; regarding; in aid of; for; about.—*adv.* At hand; going on.
**Towel,** tou'el, *n.* A cloth for drying the skin after washing, or for domestic purposes.
**Towelling,** tou'el-ing, *n.* Cloth for towels.
**Tower,** tou'ėr, *n.* A lofty narrow building; a citadel; a fortress.—*vi.* To soar; to be lofty; to stand sublime.
**Towering,** tou'ėr-ing, *a.* Very high; extreme; viiolent.
**Towing-path,** tō'ing-path, *n.* A path used in towing boats along a canal, etc.
**Tow-line,** tō'līn, *n.* A rope used in towing.
**Town,** toun, *n.* Any collection of houses larger than a village; a city; borough; inhabitants of a town; the metropolis.—*a.* Pertaining to a town.
**Town-clerk,** toun'klärk, *n.* An officer who acts as clerk to the council of a town.
**Town-council,** toun'koun-sil, *n.* The elective governing body in a town.
**Town-councillor,** toun'koun-sil-ėr, *n.* A member of a town-council.
**Town-hall,** toun'hal, *n.* A building belonging to a town in which the town-council ordinarily hold their meetings.

**Townsfolk,** tounz'fōk, *n.pl.* Townspeople.
**Township,** toun'ship, *n.* Territory of a town; division of certain parishes.
**Townspeople,** tounz'pē-pl, *n.pl.* The inhabitants of a town.
**Toxic, Toxical,** tok'sik, tok'sik-al, *a.* Pertaining to poisons; poisonous.
**Toxicant,** tok'si-kant, *n.* A poison of a stimulating, narcotic, or anesthetic nature.
**Toxicology,** toks-i-kol'o-ji, *n.* That branch of medicine which treats of poisons and their antidotes.
**Toxin,** toks'in, *n.* A poisonous substance generated in an animal body.
**Toxophilite,** tok-sof'i-līt, *n.* A lover of archery.—*a.* Pertaining to archery.
**Toy,** toi, *n.* A plaything; a bauble; a trifle.—*vi.* To dally; to trifle.
**Toyshop,** toi'shop, *n.* A shop where toys are sold.
**Trace,** trās, *n.* A mark left by anything; footstep; vestige; track; one of the straps by which a carriage, etc., is drawn.—*vt.* (tracing, traced). To track out; to follow by marks left; to draw or copy with lines or marks.
**Traceable,** trās'a-bl, *a.* That may be traced.
**Tracer bullet,** trās'ėr bul'et, *n.* One that leaves a trail of light marking its course.
**Tracery,** trās'ė-ri, *n.* A species of rich open work, seen in Gothic windows, etc.
**Trachea,** trā'kē-a, *n.* The wind-pipe.
**Tracheotomy,** trā-kē-ot'o-mi, *n.* The operation of cutting into the trachea, as in suffocation.
**Tracing,** trās'ing, *n.* Act of one who traces; copy of a design made by following its lines through a transparent medium.
**Tracing-paper,** trās'ing-pā-pėr, *n.* Transparent paper for making tracings of designs.
**Track,** trak, *n.* A footprint; rut made by a wheel; trace; beaten path; course.—*vt.* To trace; to follow step by step; to tow by a line from the shore.
**Tracker,** trak'ėr, *n.* One who hunts by following the track.
**Trackless,** trak'les, *a.* Having no track; untrodden; pathless.
**Track-road,** trak'rōd, *n.* A towing-path.
**Tract,** trakt, *n.* A region of indefinite extent; a short dissertation.
**Tractable,** trakt'a-bl, *a.* That may be easily managed; docile; manageable.
**Tractably,** trakt'a-bli, *adv.* In a tractable manner; with ready compliance.
**Tractate,** trak'tāt, *n.* A treatise; tract.
**Traction,** trak'shon, *n.* The act of drawing a body along a surface of land or water.
**Tractor,** trak'tor, *n.* A powerful motor-driven vehicle for pulling heavy loads, particularly farm machinery; a heavy truck used primarily for pulling cargo trailers, etc.
**Trade,** trād, *n.* Employment; commerce; traffic; those engaged in any trade.—*a.* Pertaining to trade.—*vi.* (trading, traded). To traffic; to carry on commerce; to have dealings.—*vt.* To sell or exchange in commerce.
**Trade-mark,** trād'märk, *n.* A distinctive mark put by a manufacturer on his goods.
**Trades-union,** trādz-ūn'yon, *n.* A combination of workmen in a trade to secure conditions most favorable for labor.
**Trades-unionism,** trādz-ūn'yon-izm, *n.* The principles or practices of trades-unions.
**Trade-wind,** trād'wind, *n.* A periodic wind blowing for six months in one direction.
**Trading,** trād'ing, *p.a.* Carrying on commerce; engaged in trade; venal.
**Tradition,** tra-di'shon, *n.* The handing down of opinions, stories, etc., from father to son, by oral communication; a statement so handed down.
**Traditional, Traditionary,** tra-di'shon-al, tra-di'shon-a-ri, *a.* Relating to or derived from tradition.
**Traditionalism,** tra-di'shon-al-izm, *n.* Adherence to or importance placed on tradition.
**Traditionally,** tra-di'shon-al-li, *adv.* In a traditional manner; by tradition.
**Traduce,** tra-dūs', *vt.* (traducing, traduced). To calumniate; to vilify; to defame.
**Traducer,** tra-dūs'ėr, *n.* One that traduces; a slanderer; a calumniator.
**Traducianism,** tra-du'si-an-izm, *n.* The doctrine that the souls of children as well as their bodies are begotten.
**Traffic,** traf'ik, *n.* An interchange of commodities; commerce; goods or persons passing along a road, railway, etc.; dealings.—*vi.* (trafficking, trafficked). To trade; to deal; to trade meanly or mercenarily.
**Tragacanth,** trag'a-kanth, *n.* A leguminous plant yielding a mucilaginous substance called gum-dragon.
**Tragedian,** tra-jē'di-an, *n.* A writer of tragedy; an actor of tragedy.
**Tragedy,** tra'je-di, *n.* A drama representing an important event generally having a fatal issue; a fatal and mournful event; a murderous or bloody deed.
**Tragic, Tragical,** tra'jik, tra'jik-al, *a.* Pertaining to tragedy; murderous; calamitous.
**Tragically,** tra'jik-al-li, *adv.* In a tragic manner.
**Tragi-comedy,** tra-ji-ko'me-di, *n.* A drama in which tragedy and comic scenes are blended.
**Tragopan,** trag'ō-pan, *n.* An Asiatic bird of the pheasant family with two fleshy horns on the head.
**Trail,** trāl, *n.* Something dragged behind; a train; the end of a field gun-carriage that rests on the ground in firing; a path; track followed by a hunter; the position of a rifle when carried horizontally at the full extent of the right arm.—*vt.* To draw behind or along the ground; to drag.—*vi.* To be dragged along a surface; to hang down loosely; to grow along the ground.
**Trailer,** trāl'ėr, *n.* One who trails; a plant which cannot grow upward without support; a carriage dragged by a motor vehicle; a series of excerpts advertising coming attractions at the cinema.
**Trail-net,** trāl'net, *n.* A net trailed behind a boat; a trawl-net.
**Train,** trān, *vt.* To draw; to entice; to rear and instruct; to drill; to bring into proper bodily condition; to shape; to bring to bear, as a gun.—*vi.* To undergo special drill.—*n.* A trail; that part of a gown which trails; tail; a series; course; retinue; line of carriages and an engine on a railway; line to conduct fire to a charge or mine.
**Train-bearer,** trān'bār-ėr, *n.*One who holds up a train, as of a robe or gown of state.
**Trained,** trānd, *p.a.* Formed by training; exercised; instructed; skilled by practice.
**Trainer,** trān'ėr, *n.* One who prepares men or horses for races, etc.
**Training,** trān'ing, *n.* Act of one who trains; education; drill.
**Training-ship** trān'ing-ship, *n.*A ship to train lads for the sea.
**Train-oil,** trān'oil, *n.* Oil from the blubber or fat of whales.
**Traipse,** trāps, *vi.* (traipsing, traipsed). To gad about in an idle way.
**Trait,** trāt or trā, *n.* A stroke; touch; feature; characteristic; peculiarity.
**Traitor,** trā'tor, *n.* One who betrays his trust or allegiance; one guilty of treason.
**Traitorous,** trā'tor-us, *a.* Guilty of treason; treacherous; treasonable.
**Trajectory,** tra-jek'to-ri, *n.* The path described by a body, as a planet, projectile, etc.
**Tram,** tram, *n.* One of the rails or tracks of a tramway; a tram-car; a tramway; a kind of silk thread.
**Trammel,** tram'el, *n.* A net for birds or fishes; shackles for regulating the motions of a horse; whatever hinders or confines; an iron hook.—*vt.* (trammelling, trammelled). To impede; to shackle.

**Tramontane,** tra-mon'tān, *a.* Being beyond the mountains; foreign; barbarous.
**Tramp,** tramp, *vt.* and *i.* To tread under foot; to travel on foot.—*n.* A tread; sound made by the feet in walking; journey on foot; a strolling beggar; a cargo steamer which makes irregular and usually short voyages.
**Trample,** tram'pl, *vt.* (trampling, trampled). To tread on heavily; to tread down; to treat with pride or insult.—*vi.* To treat in contempt; to tread with force.
**Tramp-pick,** tramp'pik, *n.* A kind of iron pick or lever which the foot helps to drive into the ground.
**Tramway,** tram'wā, *n.* A railway for passenger cars laid along a road or street.
**Trance,** trans, *n.* A state of insensibility; ecstasy; catalepsy.—*vt.* (trancing, tranced). To entrance; to enchant.
**Tranquil,** tran'kwil, *a.* Quiet; calm; undisturbed; peaceful.
**Tranquillity,** tran-kwil'i-ti, *n.* State of being tranquil; quietness; calmness; peace.
**Tranquillize,** tran'kwil-īz, *vt.* To render tranquil; to quiet;; to compose.
**Tranquilly,** tran'kwil—li, *adv.* Quietly.
**Transact,** trans-akt', *vt.* and *i.* To carry through; to perform; to manage.
**Transaction,** trans-ak'shon, *n.* The doing of any business; affair; proceeding; *pl.* reports of proceedings of societies.
**Transactor,** trans-ak'tor, *n.* One who transacts.
**Transalpine,** trans-al'pīn, *a.* Being beyond the Alps.
**Transatlantic,** trans-at-lan'tik, *a.* Being beyond or crossing the Atlantic.
**Transcend,** trans-send', *vt.* To rise above; to surpass; to outgo; to excel; to exceed.
**Transcendence, Transcendency,** trans-send'-ens, trans-send'en-si, *n.* Transcendent state; superior excellence.
**Transcendent,** trans-send'ent, *a.* Supreme in excellence; transcending human experience.
**Transcendental,** trans-send-ent'al, *a.* Transcendent; transcending knowledge acquired by experience; abstrusely speculative.
**Transcendentalism,** trans-send-ent'al-izm, *n.* A system of philosophy which claims to go deeper than experience can.
**Transcendently,** trans-send'ent-li, *adv.* In a transcendent manner; supereminently.
**Transcribe,** tran-skrīb', *vt.* (transcribing, transcribed). To write over again or in the same words; to copy.
**Transcript,** tran'skript, *n.* That which is transcribed; a copy; an imitation.
**Transcription,** tran-skrip'shon, *n.* Act of transcribing; a copy; transcript.
**Transept,** tran'sept, *n.* The transverse portion of a church built in form of a cross.
**Transfer,** trans-fėr', *vt.* (transferring, transferred). To convey from one place or person to another; to make over.—*n.* trans'fėr. Act of trarnsferring; removal of a thing from one place or person to another; something transferred.
**Transferable,** trans-fėr'a-bl or trans'fėr-a-bl, *a.* Capable of being transferred.
**Transferee,** trans-fėr-ē', *n.* The person to whom a transfer is made.
**Transference,** trans'fėr-ens, *n.* Act of transferring; passage of anything from one place to another.
**Transferrer,** trans-fėr'ėr, *n.* One who makes a transfer or conveyance.
**Transfiguration,** trans-fig'ūr-ā''shon, *n.* A change of form or figure; the supernatural change in the appearance of Christ on the mount; a Church feast held on the 6th of August, in commemoration of this change.
**Transfigure,** trans-fig'ūr, *vt.* To change in form or shape; to idealize.
**Transfix,** trans-fiks', *vt.* To pierce through; to cause to be immovable.
**Transfluent,** trans'flu-ent, *a.* Flowing or running across or through.
**Transform,** trans-form', *vt.* To change the form of; to change, as the natural disposition of.—*vi.* To be changed in form.
**Transformation,** trans-for-mā'shon, *n.* Act of transforming; an entire change in form, disposition, etc.
**Transfuse,** trans-fūz', *vt.* (transfusing, transfused). To transfer by pouring; to cause to pass from one to another.
**Transfusion,** trans-fū'zhon, *n.* Act of transfusing, as the blood of one animal into another.
**Transgress,** trans-gres', *vt.* To break or violate; to infringe.—*vi.* To do wrong; to sin.
**Transgression,** trans-gre'shon, *n.* Act of transgressing; a trespass; offense; crime.
**Transgressor,** trans-gres'or, *n.* One who transgresses; an offender; a criminal.
**Transience, Transiency,** tran'si-ens, tran'si-en-si, *n.* State or quality of being transient; evanescence.
**Transient,** tran'si-ent, *a.* Passing quickly; fleeting; momentary; fugitive.
**Transiently,** tran'si-ent-li, *adv.* In a transient manner; not with continuance.
**Transit,** tran'sit, *n.* Act of passing; passage; passage of a heavenly body over the disk of a larger one.
**Transition,** tran-zi'shon, *n.* Passage from one place, state, or topic to another.—*a.* Pertaining to passage from one state, etc., to another.
**Transitional, Transitionary,** tran-zi'shon-al, tran-zi'shon-a-ri, *a.* Containing or denoting transition.
**Transitive,** tran'sit-iv, *a.* In *grammar,* taking an object after it, as a verb.
**Transitively,** tran'sit-iv-li, *adv.* In a transitive manner; with a grammatical object.
**Transitory,** tran'si-to-ri, *a.* Passing away; fleeting; transient.
**Translate,** trans-lātu', *vt.* (translating, translated). To remove fröm one place to another; to transfer; to render into another language.
**Translation,** trans-lā'shon, *n.* Act of translating; removal; act of turning into another language; interpretation; a version.
**Translator,** trans-lāt'or, *n.* One who renders one language into another.
**Transliterate,** trans-lit'ėr-āt, *vt.* To write or spell in different characters intended to express the same sound.
**Translucence, Translucency,** trans-lū'sens, trans-lū'sens-i, *n.* Quality of being translucent.
**Translucent,** trans-lū'sent, *a.* Transmitting rays of light, but not so as to render objects distinctly visible; transparent; clear.
**Translunar, Translunary,** trans-lū'nėr, trans'lū-na-ri, *a.* Being beyond the moon.
**Transmarine,** trans-ma-rēn', *a.* Lying or being beyond the sea.
**Transmigrate,** trans'mi-grāt, *vi.* To pass from one country or body to another.
**Transmigration,** trans-mi-grā'shon, *n.* Act of transmigrating; the passing of a soul into another body after death.
**Transmigratory,** trans-mi'gra-to-ri, *a.* Passing from one place or state to another.
**Transmissible, Transmittable,** trans-mis'i-bl, trans-mit'i-bl, *a.* That may be transmitted.
**Transmission,** trans-mi'shon, *n.* Act of transmitting; transference; a passing through any body, as of light through glass, the gear box of an automobile by which engine power is transmitted to the wheels.
**Transmit,** trans-mit', *vt.* (transmitting, transmitted). To send from one person or place to another; to hand down; to allow to pass through.
**Transmittal, Transmittance,** trans-mit'al, trans-mit'ans, *n.* Transmission.
**Transmogrify,** trans-mog'ri-fī, *vt.* To transform; to change the appearance of.

**Transmutable,** trans-mūt'a-bl, *a.* Capable of being transmuted.
**Transmutation,** trans-mū-tā'shon, *n.* Act of transmuting; conversion into something different.
**Transmute,** trans-mūt', *vt.* (transmuting, transmuted). To change from one nature or substance into another.
**Transoceanic,** trans'ō-shē-an''ik, *a.* Beyond the ocean; crossing the ocean.
**Transom,** tran'sum, *n.* A strengthening horizontal beam; a cross-bar.
**Transparence,** trans-pā'rens, *n.* Transparency.
**Transparency,** trans-pā'ren-si, *n.* State or quality of being trans-pā'rent, a picture painted on transparent materials.
**Transparent,** trans-pā'rent, *a.* That can be seen through distinctly; not sufficient to hide underlying feelings.
**Transparently,** trans-pā'rent-li, *adv.* Clearly; so as to be seen through.
**Transpicuous,** trans-pik'ū-us, *a.* Transparentt pervious to the sight.
**Transpirable,** trans-pīr'a-bl, *a.* Capable of being transpired.
**Transpiration,** trans-pi-rā'shon, *n.* Act or process of transpiring; exhalation.
**Transpiratory,** trans-pīr'a-to-ri, *a.* Pertaining to transpiration; exhaling.
**Transpire,** trans-pīr, *vt.* (transpiring, transpired). To emit through the pores of the skin; to send off in vapor.—*vi.* To exhale; to escape from secrecy; to become public.
**Transplant,** trans-plant', *vt.* To remove and plant in another place.
**Transport,** trans-pōrt', *vt.* To carry from one place to another; to carry into banishment; to carry away by violence of passion; to ravish with pleasure.—*n.* trans'pōrt. Transportation; a ship employed to carry soldiers, warlike stores, etc.; passion; ecstasy.
**Transportable,** trans-pōrt'abl, *a.* That may be transported.
**Transportation,** trans-pōrt-ā'shon, *n.* Act of transporting; banishment to a penal settlement; transmission; conveyance.
**Transposal,** trans-pōz'al, *n.* Act of transposing; transposition.
**Transpose,** trans-pōz', *vt.* (transposing, transposed). To change the order of things by putting each in the other's place; to cause to change places.
**Transposition,** trans-pō-zi'shon, *n.* Act of transposing; state of being transposed; change of the order of words for effect.
**Transverberate,** trans-vėr'bėr-āt, *vt.* To beat or strike through.
**Transversal,** trans-vėrs'al, *a.* Transverse; running or lying across.
**Transverse,** trans'vėrs or trans-vėrs', *a.* Lying or being across or in a cross direction.
**Transversely,** trans'vėrs-li or trans-vėrs'li, *adv.* In a transverse manner or direction.
**Trap,** trap, *n.* A contrivance for catching unawares; an ambush; a contrivance in drains to prevent effluvia rising; a carriage of any kind, on springs; a kind of movable ladder; an igneous rock.—*vt.* (trapping, trapped). To catch in a trap; to insnare; to adorn.—*vi.* To set traps for game.
**Trap-door,** trap'dōr, *n.* A door in a floor or roof, with which when shut it is flush.
**Trape,** trāp, *vi.* (traping, traped). To traipse.
**Trapes, Traipse,** trāps, *n.* A slattern; an idle sluttish woman.—*vi.* To gad about in an idle way.
**Trapeze,** tra-pēz', *n.* A sort of swing, consisting of a cross-bar suspended by cords, for gymnastic exercises.
**Trapezium,** tra'pe'zi-um, *n.* A plane four-sided figure having no two sides parallel.
**Trapezoid,** tra'pe-zoid, *n.;* pl. **-ia** or **-iums.** A plane figure contained by four straight lines, two of them parallel; a bone of the wrist.
**Trappean, Trappy,** trap-ē'an, trap'i, *a.* Pertaining to the rock known as trap.
**Trapper,** trap'ėr, *n.* One who traps animals for their furs.
**Trappings,** trap'ingz, *n.pl.* Ornaments; dress; decorations; finery.
**Trappist,** trap'ist, *n.* A member of an ascetic order of the Roman Catholic Church.
**Traps,** traps, *n.pl.* Personal luggage.
**Trash,** trash, *n.* Loppings of trees; broken pieces; rubbish; refuse.—*vt.* To lop.
**Trashy,** trash'i, *a.* Worthless; useless.
**Trass,** tras, *n.* A volcanic production found in the Rhine valley, and used as a cement.
**Traumatic,** tra-mat'ik, *a.* Pertaining to wounds.—*n.* A medicine useful in the cure of wounds.
**Travail,** tra'vāl, *vi.* To labor; to toil; to suffer the pangs of childbirth.—*n.* Labor; severe toil; childbirth.
**Trave, Travis,** trāv, tra'vis, *n.* A cross beam; frame to confine a horse while shoeing.
**Travel,** tra'vel, *n.* Act of journeying; journey to a distant country; *pl.* account of occurrences during a journey.—*vi.* (travelling, travelled). To journey; to go to a distant country; to pass; to move.
**Travelled,** tra'veld, *p.a.* Having made many journeys; experienced from travelling.
**Traveller,** tra'vel-ėr, *n.* One who travels; one who travels from place to place to solicit orders for goods, etc.
**Travelling,** tra'vel-ing, *p.a.* Pertaining to, used in, or incurred by travel.
**Traverse,** tra'vėrs, *a.* Transverse.—*n.* Something that is transverse; something that thwarts; a denial.—*vt.* (traversing, traversed). To cross; to thwart; to cross in travelling; to deny.—*adv.* Athwart; crosswise.
**Traverse-table,** tra'vėrs-tā-bl, *n.* A table by means of which the dead-reckoning in navigation is worked out; a movable platform for shifting carriages, etc., from one line of rails to another.
**Traversing-platform,** tra'vėrs-ing-plat-form, *n.* A platform to support a gun and carriage, which can easily be turned round.
**Travertin,** tra'vėr-tin, *n.* A white limestone deposited from the water of springs holding carbonate of lime in solution.
**Travesty,** tra'ves-ti, *vt.* (travestying, travestied). To transform so as to have a ludicrous effect; to burlesque.—*n.* A burlesque treatment; parody.
**Trawl,** tral, *vi.* To fish with a trawl-net; to drag, as a net.—*n.* A trawl-net.
**Trawler,** tral'ėr, *n.* One who trawls; a fishing vessel which fishes with a trawl-net.
**Trawling,** tral'ing, *n.* The act of one who trawls; fishing with a trawl-net.
**Trawl-net,** tral'net, *n.* A long purse-shaped net for deep-sea fishing, dragged behind a vessel.
**Tray,** trā, *n.* A sort of waiter or salver, of wood, metal, etc., on which dishes and the like are presented.
**Treacherous,** trech'ėr-us, *a.* Guilty of treachery; faithless; traitorous; perfidious.
**Treacherously,** trech'ėr-us-li, *adv.* Traitorously; faithlessly; perfidiously.
**Treachery,** trech'ėr-ri, *n.* Violation of allegiance or of faith; perfidy; treason.
**Treacle,** trēkl, *n.* The uncrystallizable part of sugar obtained in refineries; molasses.
**Tread,** tred, *vi.* (pret. trod, pp. trod, trodden). To set the foot on the ground; to step; to walk with a measured step; to copulate, as fowls.—*vt.* To plant the foot on; to trample; to dance; to walk on in a formal manner; to copulate with, as a bird.—*n.* A step; gait; horizontal part of the step of a stair.
**Treadle, Treddle,** tred'l, *n.* The part of a loom or other machine moved by the foot.
**Treadmill,** tred'mil, *n.* A mill worked by persons or animals treading on movable steps.
**Treadwheel,** tred'whēl, *n.* A wheel with steps on its exterior surface, by treading on which the

T

wheel is turned.

**Treason**, trē'zon, *n*. A betrayal; breach of allegiance; treachery; disloyalty.

**Treasonable**, trē'zon-a-bl, *a*. Pertaining to, consisting of, or involving treason.

**Treasure**, tre'zhūr, *n*. Wealth accumulated; great abundance; something very much valued.—*vt*. (treasuring, treasured). To lay up or collect; to prize.

**Treasurer**, tre'zhūr-ėr, *n*. One who has the charge of a treasury or funds.

**Treasure-trove**, tre'zhūr-tōv, *n*. Money or bullion found hidden, the owner of which is not known.

**Treasury**, tre'zhū-ri, *n*. A place where treasure is laid up; department of government which controls the revenue; a book containing much valuable material.

**Treat**, trēt, *vt*. To handle; to act towards; to discourse on; to entertain; to manage.—*vi*. To handle; to discourse; to negotiate.—*n*. An entertainment given as a compliment; an unusual gratification.

**Treating**, trēt'ing, *n*. Act of one who treats; bribing voters with meat or drink.

**Treatise**, trē'tiz, *n*. A written composition on some particular subject; a dissertation.

**Treatment**, trēt'ment, *n*. Act or manner of treating; management; usage.

**Treaty**, trē'ti, *n*. Negotiation; agreement between two or more nations.

**Treble**, tre'bl, *a*. Threefold; triple; in *music*, pertaining to the highest sounds.—*n*. The highest part in a concerted piece of music; a soprano.—*vt*. and *i*. (trebling, trebled). To make or become thrice as much.

**Tree**, trē, *n*. A perennial plant having a woody trunk and branches; something resembling a tree; a cross; a wooden piece in machines, etc.—*vt*. (treeing, treed). To cause to take refuge in a tree.—*vi*. To take refuge in a tree.

**Treenail, Trenail**, trē'nāl, *n*. A long wooden pin, used to secure the planks of a ship's side, etc.

**Trefoil**, trē'foil, *n*. A three-leaved plant, as clover; an architectural ornament, consisting of three cusps.

**Trek**, trek, *vi*. (trekking, trekked). To travel by wagon.

**Trellis**, trel'is, *n*. A structure of cross-barred work or lattice-work.—*vt*. To furnish with a trellis; to form like a trellis.

**Trematode, Trematoid**, trem'a-tōd, trem'a-toid, *a*. A parasite worm living in the intestines of animals.

**Tremble**, trem'bl, *vi*. (trembling, trembled). To shake involuntarily; to quiver; to vibrate.—*n*. An involuntary shaking; a tremor.

**Trembling**, trem'bling, *n*. Act or state of shaking involuntarily; a tremor.

**Tremendous**, trē-men'dus, *a*. Such as may cause trembling; terrible; extraordinary.

**Tremendously**, trē-men'dus-li, *adv*. In a tremendous manner; astoundingly.

**Tremor**, tre'mor, *n*. An involuntary trembling; a shivering; vibration.

**Tremulous**, tre'mū-lus, *a*. Trembling; shaking; quivering; vibratory.

**Trench**, trensh, *vt*. To dig a ditch in; to turn over and mix, as soil.—*vi*. To cut a trench or trenches; to encroach (with *on* or *upon*).—*n*. A long narrow excavation; a deep ditch cut for defense.

**Trenchant**, tren'shant, *a*. Cutting; keen; severe.

**Trencher**, trensh'ėr, *n*. A wooden plate on which meat may be carved; food; pleasures of the table.

**Trencher-cap**, trensh'ėr-kap, *n*. A cap surmounted by a square flat piece.

**Trench mortar**, trensh mor'tār, *n*. A small portable mortar used for throwing bombs for short distances.

**Trend**, trend, *vi*. To extend in a particular direction.—*n*. Direction; tendency.

**Trental**, tren'tal, *n*. An office for the dead in the Roman Catholic service, consisting of thirty masses said on thirty successive days.

**Trepan**, trē-pan', *n*. A surgical saw for removing a portion of the skull.—*vt*. (trepanning, trepanned). To perforate with a trepan; to insnare.

**Trepang, Tripang**, trē-pang', *n*. The seaslug found in eastern seas, and used as a food in China.

**Trephine**, tre-fēn', *n*. An improved form of the trepan.—*vt*. (trephining, trephined). To perforate with a trephine.

**Trepidation**, tre-pid-ā'shon, *n*. Confused alarm; perturbation; involuntary trembling.

**Trespass**, tres'pas, *vi*. To enter unlawfully upon the land of another; to do wrong; to offend.—*n*. An offense; a sin; wrong done by entering on the land of another.

**Trespasser**, tres'pas-ėr, *n*. One who trespasses; a wrong-doer; a sinner.

**Tress**, tres, *n*. A braid, lock, or curl of hair.

**Trestle**, tres'l, *n*. A frame for supporting things; a frame with three or four legs attached to a horizontal piece.

**Trestle-bridge**, tres'l-brij, *n*. A bridge supported on trestles.

**Tret**, tret, *n*. An allowance to purchasers for waste.

**Trews**, tröz, *n.pl*. The tartan trousers of soldiers in Highland regiments.

**Triable**, trī'a-bl, *a*. That may be tried.

**Triad**, trī'ad, *n*. A union of three; a trinity.

**Trial**, trī'al, *n*. Act of trying; examination by a test; experience; probation; temptation; judicial examination.

**Triangle**, trī-ang'gl, *n*. A figure having three sides and angles.

**Triangular**, trī-ang'gū-lėr, *a*. Having three angles; having the form of a triangle.

**Triarchy**, trī'ärk-i, *n*. Government by three persons.

**Trias**, trī'as, *n*. In *geology*, the upper new red sandstone.

**Triassic**, trī-as'ik, *a*. Pertaining to the trias.

**Tribal**, trī'bal, *a*. Belonging to a tribe.

**Tribalism**, trī'bal-izm, *n*. The state of existence in separate tribes; tribal feeling.

**Tribe**, trīb, *n*. A division or class of people; a family or race; a class of animals or plants.

**Tribesman**, trībz'man, *n*. A member of a tribe.

**Tribrach**, trī'brak, *n*. A metrical foot of three short syllables.

**Tribulation**, tri-bū-lā'shon, *n*. Severe trouble or affliction; distress; trial; suffering.

**Tribunal**, trī-bū'nal, *n*. The seat of a judge; a court of justice.

**Tribune**, trī'būn, *n*. Among the ancient Romans, a magistrate chosen by the people, to protect them from the patricians; a platform; tribunal; throne of a bishop.

**Tribuneship, Tribunate**, trī'būn-ship, trī'būn-āt, *n*. The office of a tribune.

**Tribunician, Tribunitial**, trī-būn-i'shan, trī-būn-i'shal, *a*. Pertaining to tribunes.

**Tributary**, tri'bū-ta-ri, *a*. Paying tribute to another; subject; contributing.—*n*. One that pays tribute; a stream which falls into another.

**Tribute**, tri'būt, *n*. A sum paid by one prince or nation to another; personal contribution.

**Trice**, trīs, *n*. A very short time; an instant.—*vt*. (tricing, triced). To hoist by a rope.

**Tricennial**, trī-sen'ni-al, *a*. Belonging to the period of thirty years, or occurring once in that period.

**Tricentenary**, trī-sen'ten-a-ri, *n*. A period of three hundred years; the three hundredth anniversary.

**Trichina**, tri-kī'na, *n*.; pl. **-nae**. A minute nematoid worm, the larva of which causes disease in the flesh of mammals.

**Trichiniasis, Trichinosis**, trik-i-nī'a-sis, trik-i-nō'sis, *n*. The disease produced by trichinae.

**Trichord**, trī'kord, *n*. A musical instrument with three strings.—*a*. Having three strings; having

three strings for each note, as a piano.
**Trick,** trik, *n.* An artifice; a crafty device; fraud; a knack or art; a personal practice or habit; a prank; all the cards played in one round.—*vt.* To deceive; to impose on, to cheat; to draw in outline; to dress; to adorn (often with *out*).
**Trickery,** trik'ė-ri, *n.* Artifice; imposture.
**Trickle,** trik'l, *vi.* (trickling, trickled). To fall in drops; to flow gently.
**Trickster,** trik'ster, *n.* One who practices tricks.
**Tricky,** trik'i *a.* Trickish; mischievous.
**Tricolor,** trī'kul-ėr, *n.* The national French banner of blue, white, and red divided vertically.
**Tricostate,** trī-kos'tāt, *a.* Having three ribs or ridges.
**Tricuspid, Tricuspidate,** trī-kus'pid, trī-kus'pi-dāt, *a.* Having three cusps or points.
**Tricycle,** trī'si-kl, *n.* A cycle with three wheels.
**Trident,** trī'dent, *n.* Any instrument of the form of a fork with three prongs.
**Tried,** trīd, *p.a.* Tested by trial or experience; staunch; true.
**Triennial,** trī-en'ni-al, *a.* Continuing three years; happening every three years.
**Trifarious,** trī-fā'ri-us, *a.* Arranged in three rows; threefold.
**Trifid,** trī-fid, *a.* Divided into three parts.
**Trifle,** trī'fl, *n.* Something of no moment or value; a kind of fancy confection.—*vi.* (trifling, trifled). To act with levity; to play or toy; to finger lightly.—*vt.* To waste.
**Trifler,** trīf'lėr, *n.* One who trifles or acts with levity.
**Trifling,** trīf'ling, *a.* Apt to trifle; frivolous; trivial; insignificant.
**Trifoliate,** trī-fō'li-āt, *a.* Having three leaves.
**Triforium,** trī-fō'ri-um, *n.*; pl. **-ia.** A gallery above the arches of the nave of a church.
**Triform,** trī'form, *a.* Having a triple form or shape.
**Trifurcate,** trī-fer'kāt, *a.* Having three branches or forks.
**Trig,** trig, *vt.* (trigging, trigged). To stop or fasten, as a wheel.—*a.* Trim; spruce; neat.
**Trigamist,** tri'ga-mist, *n.* One who has three husbands or wives at the same time.
**Trigamy,** tri'ga-mi, *n.* The state of having three husbands or wives at the same time.
**Trigger,** trig'ėr, *n.* The catch which, on being pressed, liberates the striker of a gun.
**Triglyph,** trī-glif, *n.* A block in Doric friezes, repeated at equal intervals, with three perpendicular channels.
**Trigonometric, Trigonometrical,** tri'gon-o-met''rik, tri'gon-o-met''rik-al, *a.* Pertaining to trigonometry.
**Trigonometry,** tri-gon-om'et-ri, *n.* The science of determining the sides and angles of triangles; a geometrical method of calculation.
**Trigyn,** trī'jin, *n.* A plant having three styles of pistils.
**Trihedron,** trī-hē'dron, *n.* A solid figure having three equal sides.
**Trilateral,** trī-lat'ėr-al, *a.* Having three sides, as a triangle.
**Trilinear,** trī-lin'ē-ėr, *a.* Consisting of three lines.
**Trilingual,** trī-ling'gwal, *a.* Consisting of three languages.
**Triliteral,** trī-li'tėr-al, *a.* Consisting of three letters.
**Trilith, Trilithon,** trī'lith, trī'lith-on, *n.* Three large blocks of stone placed together like door-posts and a lintel, and standing by themselves, as in sundry ancient monuments.
**Trill,** tril, *n.* A shake of the voice in singing; a quavering sound.—*vt.* To sing with a quavering voice; to sing sweetly or clearly.—*vi.* To sound with tremulous vibrations; to pipe; to trickle.
**Trillion,** tril'yon, *n.* The product of a million multiplied twice by itself.
**Trilobate,** trī-lō'bāt, *n.* Having three lobes.
**Trilocular,** trī-lok'ū-lėr, *a.* Three-celled.
**Trilogy,** tril'o-ji, *n.* A series of three connected dramas, each complete in itself.
**Trim,** trim, *vt.* (trimming, trimmed). To put in order; to embellish; to clip or pare; to adjust.—*vi.* To hold a middle course between parties.—*a.* Set in good order; properly adjusted; neat; tidy.—*n.* Condition; order; mood; dress.
**Trimester,** trī-mes'tėr, *n.* A term or period of three months.
**Trimeter,** trim'et-ėr, *n.* and *a.* A line of poetry consisting of three measures.
**Trimly,** trim'li, *adv.* Neatly; smartly.
**Trine,** trīne, *a.* Threefold.—*n.* Postion of planets distant from each other 120 degrees.
**Tringle,** tring'gl, *n.* A curtain-rod, or similar rod on which rings run.
**Trinitarian,** tri-ni-tā'ri-an, *a.* Pertaining to the Trinity.—*n.* One who believes in the Trinity.
**Trinity,** tri'ni-ti, *n.* A union of three in one; the union of one Godhead of the Father, Son, and Holy Spirit.
**Trinket,** tring'ket, *n.* A small ornament; a trifle.—*vi.* To intrigue; to traffic.
**Trinketer,** tring'ket-ėr, *n.* One who traffics; an intriguer.
**Trinketry,** tring'ket-ri, *n.* Ornaments of dress; trinkets.
**Trinomial,** trī-nō'mi-al, *a.* Consisting of three terms connected by the signs + or −.
**Trio,** trī'ō or trē'ō, *n.* Three united; musical composition for three voices or instruments; performers of a trio.
**Triolet,** trī'o-let or trē'o-let, *n.* A stanza of eight lines the first being repeated as the fourth and seventh, and the second as the eighth.
**Trip,** trip, *vi.* (tripping, tripped). To run or step lightly; to skip; to stumble; to err.—*vt.* To cause to fall or stumble; to loose an anchor.—*n.* A stumble; a light short step; an excursion or jaunt; a mistake.
**Tripartite,** trip'ar-tit or trī-pärt'īt, *a.* Divided into three parts; made between three parties.
**Tripe,** trīp, *n.* The stomach of ruminating animals prepared for food.
**Tripedal,** trī-ped-al, *a.* Having three feet.
**Tripetalous,** trī-pe'tal-us, *a.* Having three petals.
**Triphthong,** trif'thong or trip'thong, *n.* A union of three vowels in one syllable, as in *adieu*.
**Triple,** tri'pl, *a.* Threefold; treble.—*vt.* (tripling, tripled). To treble.
**Triplet,** trip'let, *n.* Three of a kind: three lines of poetry rhyming together; one of three children born at a birth.
**Triplicate,** tri'pli-kāt, *a.* Threefold.—*n.* A third thing corresponding to two others.
**Triplication,** tri-pli-kā'shon, *n.* The act of trebling.
**Tripod,** trī'pod, *n.* A three-footed pot, seat, or stand.
**Tripper,** trip'ėr, *n.* One who trips, trips up, or walks nimbly; one who takes a jaunt.
**Triptych,** trip'tik, *n.* A picture or carving in three compartments side by side; a treatise in three sections.
**Trireme,** trī'rēm, *n.* A gallery or vessel with three ranks of oars on a side.
**Trisect,** trī-sekt', *vt.* To cut into three equal parts.
**Trisection,** trī-sek'shon, *n.* Act of trisecting; division of a thing into three equal parts.
**Tristichous,** trī'stik-us, *a.* In *botany,* arranged in three verticial rows.
**Trisulcate,** trī-sul'kāt, *a.* Having three furrows or grooves.
**Trisyllabic, Trisyllabical,** tri-sil-lab'ik, tri-sil-lab'ik-al, *a.* Consisting of three syllables.
**Trisyllable,** tri-sil'la-bl, *n.* A word consisting of three syllables.
**Trite,** trīt, *a.* Hackneyed; threadbare; stale.
**Tritheism,** trī'thē-izm, *n.* The opinion that the Father, Son, and Holy Spirit are three beings or gods.
**Triton,** trī'ton, *n.* A sea deity with fish-like lower extremities.
**Triturate,** tri'tū-rāt, *vt.* (triturating, triturated). To

T

rub or grind to a very fine powder.
**Triumph,** trī'umf, *n.* A magnificent procession in honor of a victorious Roman general; victory; achievement; joy for success.—*vi.* To rejoice for victory; to obtain victory; to exult insolently.
**Triumphal,** trī-umf'al, *a.* Pertaining to or used in a triumph.
**Triumphant,** trī-umf'ant, *a.* Feeling triumph; victorious; celebrating victory; expressing joy for success.
**Triumphantly,** trī-umf'ant-li, *adv.* In a triumphant manner; exultantly.
**Triumvir,** trī-um'vėr, *n.* One of three men united in office.
**Triumvirate,** trī-um'vėr-āt, *n.* A coalition of three men in office or authority.
**Trivalve,** trī'valv, *n.* A shell, etc., with three valves.
**Trivet,** tri'vet, *n.* Anything supported by three feet; an iron frame whereon to place vessels before or over a fire.
**Trivial,** tri'vi-al, *a.* Common; commonplace; trifling; insignificant.
**Triviality,** tri-vi-al'i-ti, *n.* State or quality of being trivial; a trifle.
**Trivially,** tri'vi-al-li, *adv.* In a trivial or trifling manner; lightly; insignificantly.
**Trochaic,** trō-kā'ik, *a.* Pertaining to or consisting of trochees.
**Troche ,** trōch or trosh, *n.* A small circular lozenge containing a drug.
**Trochee,** trō'kē, *n.* A metrical foot of two syllables, the first long and the second short.
**Trod, Trodden.** *See* TREAD.
**Troglodyte,** trō'glod-īt, *n.* A cave-dweller; one living in seclusion.
**Trogon,** trō'gon, *n.* A tropical bird with gorgeous plumage.
**Trojan,** trō'jan, *a.* Pertaining to ancient Troy.—*n.* An inhabitant of ancient Troy; a jolly fellow; a plucky determined fellow.
**Troll,** trōl, *vt.* To roll; to pass round; to sing in a full, jovial voice.—*vi.* To go round; to fish for pike by trolling.—*n.* A going round; a part-song; a reel on a fishing-rod; a dwarfish being in Scandinavian mythology, dwelling in caves and mounds.
**Trolley, Trolly,** trol'i, *n.* A kind of small truck; a small narrow cart.
**Trolling,** trōl'ing, *n.* Act of one who trolls; a method of rod-fishing for pike with a dead bait; trawling.
**Trollop,** trol'lop, *n.* A woman loosely dressed; a slattern; a drab.
**Trombone,** trom'bōn, *n.* A deep-toned instrument of the trumpet kind.
**Tromp,** tromp, *n.* A blowing-machine used in a process of smelting iron.
**Troop,** tröp, *n.* A collection of people; a company; a body of soldiers; *pl.* soldiers in general; a troupe.—*vi.* To collect in numbers; to march in a body.
**Trooper,** tröp'ėr, *n.* A horse-soldier.
**Troop-ship,** tröp'ship, *n.* A transport.
**Tropaeolum,** trō-pē'o-lum, *n.* A trailing or climbing plant of the geranium family.
**Trope,** trōp, *n.* A word used figuratively; a figure of speech.
**Trophy,** trō'fi, *n.* A memorial of some victory; an architectural ornament representing the stem of a tree, hung with military weapons.
**Tropic,** tro'pik, *n.* Either of two circles on the celestial sphere, limiting the sun's apparent annual path; either of two corresponding parallels of latitude including the torrid zone; *pl.* the regions between or near these.—*a.* Pertaining to the tropics.
**Tropical,** tro'pik-al, *a.* Pertaining to the tropics or to a trope.
**Trot,** trot, *vi.* (trotting, trotted). To run with small steps; to move fast.—*vt.* To cause to trot.—*n.* Pace of a horse more rapid than a walk.
**Trotter,** trot'ėr, *n.* One who trots; a trotting horse; foot of an animal.
**Troubador,** trö'ba-dör, *n.* one of a class of poets who flourished in S. Europe, especially in Provence, from the eleventh to the end of the thirteenth century.
**Trouble,** tru'bl, *vt.* (troubling, troubled). To disturb; to distress; to busy.—*n.* Distress; agitation; affliction; labor.
**Troublesome,** tru'bl-sum, *a.* Annoying; vexatious; burdensome; tiresome.
**Troublous,** tru'blus, *a.* Full of trouble or disorder; agitated; disquieting.
**Trough,** trof, *n.* A long vessel for holding water or food for animals; a depression between two waves.
**Trounce,** trouns, *vt.* (trouncing, trounced). To punish or to beat severely.
**Troupe,** tröp, *n.* A troop; a company of performers, as acrobats.
**Trousering,** trou'zėr-ing, *n.* Cloth for making trousers.
**Trousers,** trou'zėrz, *n.pl.* A garment for men; covering the lower part of the trunk and each leg separately.
**Trousseau,** trö-sō, *n.* The clothes and general outfit of a bride.
**Trout,** trout, *n.* A fresh-water fish of the salmon tribe.
**Troutlet, Troutling,** trout'let, trout'ling, *n.* A small trout.
**Trouvère,** trö'vär, *n.* One of a class of ancient poets of Northern France, who produced chiefly narrative poetry.
**Trover,** trō'vėr, *n.* The gaining possession of goods by finding them, or otherwise than by purchase.
**Trow,** trou or trō, *vi.* To believe; to suppose.
**Trowel,** trou'el, *n.* A hand-tool for lifting and dressing mortar and plaster, etc.; a gardener's tool.—*vt.* (trowelling, trowelled). To dress or form with a trowel.
**Troy, Troy-weight,** troi, troi'wāt, *n.* A weight used for gold and silver, divided into 12 ounces, each of 20 pennyweights, each of 24 grains, so that a pound troy = 5760 grains.
**Truant,** trö'ant, *n.* One who shirks duty; one who stays from school without leave.—*a.* Idle; wilfully absenting oneself.
**Truce,** trös, *n.* A temporary cessation of hostilities; armistice; short quiet.
**Truck,** truk, *vi.* and *t.* To barter.—*n.* Exchange of commodities; barter; payment of workmen's wages partly in goods; a small wheel; a barrow with two low wheels; an open railway wagon for goods; a motor driven vehicle used to carry heavy loads or general freight; the cap at the end of a flagstaff or topmast.
**Truckle,** truk'l, *n.* A small wheel or castor.—*vt.* (truckling, truckled). To move on rollers; to trundle.—*vi.* To yield obsequiously; to submit.
**Truculence, Truculency,** tru'kū-lens, tru'-kū-len-si, *n.* Ferocity; fierceness.
**Truculent,** tru'kū-lent, *a.* Terrible of aspect; fierce; wild; savage; fell.
**Trudge,** truj, *vi.* (trudging, trudged). To walk with labor or fatigue; to walk heavily.
**True,** trö, *a.* Conformable to fact; truthful; genuine; constant; faithful; loyal; honest; exact; correct; right.
**Trueblue,** trö'blö, *n.* A person of inflexible honesty or stanchness.—*a.* Stanch; inflexible.
**Trueborn,** trö'born, *a.* Of genuine birth; having a right by birth to any title.
**Truebred,** trö'bred, *a.* Of a genuine breed or education.
**Truehearted,** trö'härt-ed, *a.* Being of a true or faithful heart; honest; sincere.
**Truelove,** trö'luv, *n.* One truly loved or loving; a lover; a sweetheart.
**Truepenny,** trö'pen-i, *n.* A familiar phrase for an honest fellow.
**Truffle,** truf'l, *n.* An edible fungus growing beneath the surface of the ground.

**Truism,** trö'izm, *n.* A self-evident truth.
**Trull,** trul, *n.* A strumpet; a trollop.
**Truly,** trö'li, *adv.* In a true manner; according to the truth; honestly; justly.
**Trump,** trump, *n.* A winning card; one of a suit for the time being superior to the others; a person upon whom one can depend; a trumpet.—*vt.* To take with a trump card; to concoct or forge.
**Trumpery,** trum'pė-ri, *n.* Worthless finery; trifles; trash.—*a.* Worthless.
**Trumpet,** trum'pet, *n.* A metal wind-instrument of music; one who praises.—*vt.* To publish by sound of trumpet; to noise abroad; to sound the praises of.
**Trumpeter,** trum'pet-ėr, *n.* One who sounds a trumpet; one who proclaims; a variety of the domestic pigeon.
**Truncate,** trung'kāt, *vt.* To cut off; to lop.—*a.* Truncated.
**Truncated,** trung'kāt-ed, *p.a.* Cut short abruptly.
**Truncation,** trung-kā'shon, *n.* Act of truncating; state of being truncated.
**Truncheon,** trun'shon, *n.* A short staff; a club; a baton of authority; a tree the branches of which have been lopped off to produce rapid growth.—*vt.* To beat; to cudgel.
**Trundle** trun'dl, *vi.* (trundling, trundled). To roll, as on little wheels or as a bowl.—*vt.* To cause to roll.—*n.* A little wheel; a small truck.
**Trundle-bed,** trun'dl-bed, *n.* A truckle-bed.
**Trunk,** trungk, *n.* The woody stem of a tree; body of an animal without the limbs; main body; chest for containing clothes, etc.; a long wooden tube.
**Trunk-line,** trungk'līn, *n.* The main line of a railway, canal, etc.
**Trunnion,** trun'yon, *n.* A knob on each side of a gun, etc., serving to support it.
**Truss,** trus, *n.* A bundle, as of hay or straw; a bandage used in cases of rupture; a combination of timbers constituting an unyielding frame.—*vt.* To put in a bundle; to make tight or fast; to skewer.
**Trussing,** trus'ing, *n.* The timbers, etc., which form a truss.
**Trust,** trust, *n.* Reliance; confidence; hope; credit; that which is intrusted; safe-keeping; care; management.—*vt.* To rely on; to believe; to intrust; to sell to upon credit; to be confident.—*vi.* To have reliance; to confide readily.—*a.* Held in trust.
**Trustee,** trus-tē', *n.* One appointed to hold property for the benefit of those entitled to it.
**Trusteeship,** trus-tē'ship, *n.* The office or functions of a trustee.
**Trustworthy,** trust'wėr-ᴛʜi, *a.* Worthy of trust or confidence; faithful; reliable.
**Trusty,** trust'i, *a.* That may be trusted; trustworthy; that will not fail; strong.
**Truth,** tröth, *n.* Conformity to fact or reality; integrity; constancy; exactness; reality; verified fact.
**Truthful,** tröth'ful, *a.* Closely adhering to truth; veracious; correct; true.
**Truthfully,** tröth'ful-li, *adv.* In a truthful manner.
**Try,** trī, *vt.* (trying, tried). To test; to make trial of; to afflict; to examine judicially; to attempt.—*vi.* To endeavor.—*n.* The act of trying; a trial; experiment; in *Rugby football,* the right of trying to kick a goal, obtained by carrying the ball behind the opponents' goal-line and touching it down.
**Trying,** trī'ing, *a.* Severe; afflictive.
**Tryst,** trīst, *n.* An appointment to meet; a rendezvous.—*vi.* To agree to meet at any particular time or place.
**Tsar,** tsär. Same as *Czar.*
**Tsetse,** tset'se, *n.* An African fly whose bite is often fatal to horses and cattle.
**T-square,** tē'skwār, *n.* A sort of ruler shaped like a T, used in drawing straight or perpendicular lines.
**Tub,** tub, *n.* An open wooden vessel; a small cask; a clumsy boat; a vessel used as a bath.—*vt.* (tubbing, tubbed). To set in a tub.—*vi.* To make use of a bathing-tub.
**Tuba,** tū'ba, *n.* A large musical instrument of brass, low in pitch.
**Tubbing,** tub'ing, *n.* The lining of the shaft of a mine, etc., to prevent falling in of the sides.
**Tube,** tūb, *n.* A pipe; a hollow cylinder; the underground electric railway system in London.—*vt.* (tubing, tubed) To furnish with a tube.
**Tuber,** tū'bėr, *n.* An underground fleshy stem or root; a knot or swelling in any part.
**Tubercle,** tū'bėr-kl, *n.* A small tuber; a little projecting knob; a small mass of morbid matter developed in different parts of the body.
**Tubercular,** tū-bėr'kū-lėr, *a.* Pertaining to or affected with tubercles; consumptive. Also *Tuberculate, Tuberculose, Tuberculous.*
**Tuberculosis,** tū-bėr'kū-lō''sis, *n.* A disease due to the formation of tubercles; consumption.
**Tuberose, Tuberous,** tū-bėr-ōs, tū'bėr-us, *a.* Knobbed; having tubers; resembling a tuber.
**Tubing,** tūb'ing, *n.* Act of providing with tubes; a length of tube; series of tubes.
**Tubular,** tūb'ū-lėr, *a.* Having the form of a tube; consisting of tubes. Also *Tubulose, Tubulous.*
**Tubule,** tūb'ūl, *n.* A small tube or pipe.
**Tuck,** tuk, *vt.* To gather into a narrower compass; to fold in or under.—*n.* A horizontal fold in a garment to shorten it.
**Tucker,** tuk'ėr, *n.* One who tucks; a sort of frill round the top of a woman's dress.
**Tucket,** tuk'et, *n.* A flourish on a trumpet; a fanfare.
**Tuesday,** tūz'dā, *n.* The third day of the week.
**Tufa, Tuff,** tū'fa, tuf, *n.* A porous vesicular rock or stone.
**Tuft,** tuft, *n.* A cluster; clump; head of flowers.—*vt.* To adorn with tufts.
**Tug,** tug, *vt.* and *i.* (tugging, tugged). To pull with effort; to haul along; to drag by steam-tug.—*n.* A drawing or pulling with force; a tug-boat.
**Tug-boat,** tug'bōt, *n.* A powerful steam-boat used for towing other vessels.
**Tug-of-war,** tug'ov-war, *n.* A trial of strength between two parties of men tugging at opposite ends of a rope.
**Tuition,** tū-i'shon, *n.* Guardianship; instruction; business of teaching.
**Tulip,** tū'lip, *n.* A plant of the lily family with richly-colored flowers.
**Tulle,** tul, *n.* A thin silk fabric.
**Tumble,** tum'bl, *vi.* (tumbling, tumbled). To roll about; to lose footing and fall.—*vt.* To throw about; to rumple; to overturn.—*n.* A fall; a somersault.
**Tumbler,** tum'blėr, *n.* One who tumbles; an acrobat; a large drinking-glass; a variety of pigeon.
**Tumbrel, Tumbril,** tum'brel, tum'bril, *n.* A dung-cart; a covered military cart for tools, ammunition, etc.; a kind of ducking-stool for scolds.
**Tumefaction,** tū-me-fak'shon, *n.* Act of swelling; a tumor; a swelling.
**Tumefy,** tū'me-fi, *vt.* To cause to swell.—*vi.* To swell; to rise in a tumor.
**Tumid,** tū'mid, *a.* Swollen; distended; pompous; inflated; bombastic.
**Tumidity,** tū-mid'i-ti, *n.* A swelled state.
**Tumor,** tū'mor, *n.* A morbid swelling in some part of the body.
**Tumular,** tū'mū-lėr, *a.* Pertaining to a tumulus.
**Tumult,** tū'mult, *n.* A commotion or disturbance; uproar; high excitement.
**Tumultuous,** tū-mul'tū-us, *a.* Full of tumult; disorderly; turbulent; violent.
**Tumulus,** tū'mū-lus, *n.*; pl. **-li.** A mound or large heap of earth; a barrow.
**Tun,** tun, *n.* Any large cask; a vat; a measure of 4 hogsheads or 252 gallons.—*vt.* (tunning, tunned). To put into a tun.
**Tundra,** tun'dra, *n.* An immense stretch of flat boggy country in the arctic parts of Siberia.
**Tune,** tūn, *n.* A short air or melody; harmony; cor-

T

rect intonation; state of an instrument when it can give the proper sounds; frame of mind; mood.—*vt.* (tuning, tuned). To put into tune; to adapt.

**Tungsten,** tung'sten, *n.* A heavy metal of a grayish-white color.

**Tunic,** tū'nik, *n.* A garment of various kinds; an ecclesiastical vestment worn over the alb; a full-dress military coat; a covering membrane; an integument.

**Tuning,** tūn'ing, *n.* The art or operation of bringing musical instruments into tune.

**Tuning-fork,** tūn'ing-fork, *n.* A steel two-pronged instrument for regulating the pitch of voices or instruments.

**Tunnel,** tun'el, *n.* A tubular opening; a funnel; a subterranean passage cut through a hill, etc.—*vt.* (tunnelling, tunnelled). To form a tunnel through or under.

**Tunny,** tun'i, *n.* A large fish of the mackerel tribe.

**Tup,** tup, *n.* A ram.

**Turanian,** tū-rā'ni-an, *a.* Applied to the family of languages which includes the Turkish, Mongolian, etc.

**Turban,** tėr'ban, *n.* A head-dress worn by the Orientals, consisting of a fez and a sash wound round it; a kind of head-dress worn by ladies.

**Turbid,** tėr'bid, *a.* Muddy; having the sediment disturbed; not clear.

**Turbidity,** tėr-bid'i-ti, *n.* State of being turbid; muddiness.

**Turbinate,** tėr'bi-nāt, *a.* Shaped like a whipping-top; conical; spiral.

**Turbine,** tėr'bīn, *n.* A kind of water-wheel, usually horizontal, made to revolve under the influence of pressure derived from a fall of water; a similar contrivance driven by steam.

**Turbot,** tėr'bot, *n.* A species of large flat-fish.

**Turbulence, Turbulency,** tėr'bū-lens, tėr'bū-lensi, *n.* State of being turbulent; tumult; confusion; riotous behavior.

**Turbulent,** tėr'bū-lent, *a.* Being in violent commotion; refractory; disorderly.

**Tureen,** tu-rēn', *n.* A large and deep dish for holding soup at table.

**Turf,** tėrf, *n.* The grassy layer on the surface of the ground; a sod.—**The turf,** the race-course; the business of horse-racing.—*vt.* To cover with turf or sod.

**Turgent,** tėr'jent, *a.* Swelling; turgid.

**Turgescence,** tėr-jes'ens, *n.* State of becoming turgid; bombast.

**Turgescent,** tėr-jes'ent, *a.* Swelling.

**Turgid,** tėr'jid, *a.* Swelling; swollen; bloated; inflated; bombastic.

**Turgidity,** tėr-jid'i-ti, *n.* State of being turgid; bombast; inflation of style.

**Turk,** tėrk, *n.* A member of the ruling race of Turkey; a tyrannical man.

**Turkey,** tėr'ki, *n.* A large gallinaceous fowl.

**Turkey-red,** tėr'ki-red, *n.* A brilliant and durable red dye on cotton cloth.

**Turkey-stone, Turkey-hone,** tėr'ki-stōn, tėr'ki-hōn, *n.* A fine-grained siliceous stone used for sharpening instruments.

**Turkish,** tėr'kish, *a.* Pertaining to Turkey, or to the Turks, or to their language.—*n.* The language spoken by the Turks.—**Turkish bath,** *n.* A hot-air or steam bath, inducing copious perspiration, followed by shampooing and massage, etc.

**Turmeric,** tėr'mer-ik, *n.* An E. Indian plant of the ginger family yielding a condiment, a yellow dye, and a test for alkalies.

**Turmoil,** tėr'moil, *n.* Disturbance; trouble; disquiet.—*vt.* To harass.

**Turn,** tėrn, *vt.* To cause to move round; to shape by a lathe; to direct; to alter in course; to blunt; to reverse; to change.—*vi.* To revolve; to depend; to change position or course; to return; to have recourse; to become; to become sour; to reel; to become nauseated; to result.—*n.* Act of turning; a revolution; a bend; a short walk; an alteration of course; occasion; occasional act of kindness or malice; purpose; character; short spell, as a work; nervous shock.

**Turn-coat,** tėrn'kōt, *n.* One who meanly forsakes his party or principles.

**Turner,** tėrn'ėr, *n.* One who turns; one who forms things with a lathe.

**Turning,** tėrn'ing, *n.* A turn; bend; place where a road diverges from another; art or operation of shaping articles in a lathe.

**Turning-point,** tėrn'ing-point, *n.* The point on which or where a thing turns; the point at which a deciding change takes place.

**Turnip,** tėr'nip, *n.* A plant of the cabbage genus, cultivated for its bulbous esculent root.

**Turnkey,** tėrn'kē, *n.* A person who has charge of the keys of a prison.

**Turn-out,** tėrn'out, *n.* A coming forth; persons who have come out on some particular occasion; an equipage; the net quantity of produce yielded.

**Turn-over,** tėrn'ō-vėr, *n.* The amount of money turned over or drawn in a business.

**Turnpike,** tėrnpīk, *n.* A turnstile; a toll-bar or toll-gate.

**Turnsole, Turnsol,** tėrn'sōl, *n.* A plant whose flower turns toward the sun.

**Turnstile,** tėrn'stīl, *n.* A post at some passage surmounted by horizontal arms which move as a person pushes through.

**Turn-table,** tėrn'tā-bl, *n.* A revolving platform for reversing engines on a railway, or for shifting them from one line of rails to another.

**Turpentine,** tėr'pen-tīn, *n.* A resinous substance flowing from trees, as the pine, larch, fir, etc.; the oil distilled from this.

**Turpitude,** tėr-pi-tūd, *n.* Inherent baseness or vileness; moral depravity.

**Turps,** tėrps, *n.* The oil distilled from the resinous substance of pine-trees, etc.; oil or spirit of turpentine.

**Turquoise,** tėr'koiz, *n.* A greenish-blue or blue opaque precious stone.

**Turret,** tu'ret, *n.* A little tower on a larger building; a strong cylindrical iron structure on an iron-clad.

**Turret-ship,** tu'ret-ship, *n.* A man-of-war with one or more rotating armored turrets containing heavy guns.

**Turtle,** tėr'tl, *n.* A species of small pigeon; the sea-tortoise.

**Turtle-dove,** tėr'tl-duv, *n.* The European turtle or pigeon.

**Tuscan,** tus'kan, *a.* Pertaining to Tuscany in Italy; designating the unornamented, unfluted order of architecture.—*n.* An inhabitant of Tuscany; the Tuscan order; the Tuscan dialect of Italian.

**Tush,** tush, an *exclamation* indicating impatience or contempt.—*n.* A tusk; the canine tooth of a horse.

**Tusk,** tusk, *n.* A long prominent tooth of certain animals, as the elephant.

**Tusker,** tusk'ėr, *n.* An elephant that has its tusks developed.

**Tussle,** tus'l, *n.* A struggle; scuffle.

**Tussock,** tus'ok, *n.* A clump, tuft, or small hillock of growing grass.

**Tutelage,** tū'tel-āj, *n.* Guardianship; protection; state of being under a guardian.

**Tutelar, Tutelary,** tū'tel-ėr, tū'tel-a-ri, *a.* Guardian; protecting.

**Tutor,** tū'tor, *n.* A guardian; a private instructor; a fellow of an English college who superintends the studies of undergraduates.—*vt.* To instruct.

**Tutorage,** tū'tor-āj, *n.* Guardianship.

**Tutoress,** tū'tor-es, *n.* A female tutor.

**Tutorial,** tū-tō'ri-al, *a.* Belonging to or exercised by a tutor or instructor.

**Tuyere,** twi-yār' or tu-yār', *n.* The nozzle or the pipe that introduces the blast into a blast-furnace.

**Twaddle,** twod'l, *vi.* (twaddling, twaddled). To

prate; to chatter; to prose.—*n.* Empty, silly talk; gabble.
**Twaddler,** twod'lėr, *n.* One who twaddles.
**Twain,** twān, *a.* Two.—*n.* A pair.
**Twang,** twang, *vi.* To make the sound of a string which is stretched and suddenly pulled.—*vt.* To make to sound sharply.—*n.* A sharp vibrating sound; a nasal sound.
**'Twas,** twoz, a contraction of *It was.*
**Tweak,** twēk, *vt.* To twitch; to pinch and pull suddenly.—*n.* A sharp pinch or jerk.
**Tweed,** twēd, *n.* A twilled woollen fabric made in mixed colors.
**Tweezers,** twē'zėrz, *n.pl.* Small pincers to pluck out hairs, etc.; small forceps.
**Twelfth,** twelfth, *a.* The second after the tenth.—*n.* One of twelve equal parts.
**Twelfth-day,** twelfth'dā, *n.* The twelfth day after Christmas; festival of the Epiphany.
**Twelfth-night,** twelfth'nīt, *n.* The evening of the festival of the Epiphany.
**Twelve,** twelv, *a.* and *n.* Ten and two.
**Twelve-month,** twelv'munth, *n.* A year.
**Twentieth,** twen'ti-eth, *a.* The ordinal of twenty.—*n.* One of twenty equal parts.
**Twenty,** twen'ti, *a.* and *n.* Two tens, or twice ten.
**Twibill,** twī'bil, *n.* A kind of double axe or mattock.
**Twice,** twīs, *adv.* Two times; doubly.
**Twiddle,** twid'l, *vt.* and *i.* (twiddling, twiddled). To twirl in a small way; to fiddle with.
**Twig,** twig, *n.* A small shoot or branch.—*vt.* and *i.* (twigging, twigged). To observe; to understand.
**Twilight,** twī'līt, *n.* The faint light of the sun reflected after sunset and before sunrise; dubious view or conditon.—*a.* Faint; seen or done by twilight.
**Twill,** twil, *vt.* To weave so as to produce a kind of diagonal ribbed appearance.—*n.* A textile fabric with a kind of diagonal ribbed surface; surface of this kind.
**Twin,** twin, *n.* One of two born together; one of a pair or couple.—*a.* Being one of two born at a birth; very similar; two-fold.
**Twine,** twīn, *n.* A strong thread composed of two or three strands; a twist.—*vt.* and *i.* (twining, twined). To twist; to weave; to coil; to wrap closely about.
**Twinge,** twinj, *vt.* and *i.* (twinging, twinged). To affect with or have a sharp, sudden pain.—*n.* A sudden, sharp, darting pain.
**Twinkle,** twingk'l, *vi.* (twinkling, twinkled). To sparkle; to shine with a quivering light.—*n.* A gleam or sparkle.
**Twinkling,** twingk'ling, *n.* A quick movement of the eye; a wink; an instant; the scintillation of the stars.
**Twinling,** twin'ling, *n.* A twin lamb.
**Twin-screw,** twin'skrö, *n.* Any ship fitted with two propellers on separate shafts.
**Twirl,** twėrl, *vt.* and *i.* To turn round with rapidity; to spin.—*n.* A rapid whirl.
**Twist,** twist, *n.* Something twined, as a thread, etc.; roll of tobacco; a spiral; contortion; mental or moral bent.—*vt.* and *i.* To form into a cord; to twine; to contort; to insinuate; to pervert.
**Twit,** twit, *vt.* (twitting, twitted). To reproach; to taunt; to upbraid.
**Twitch,** twich, *vt.* To pull with a sudden jerk; to tug.—*vi.* To be suddenly contracted.—*n.* A sudden pull; short spasmodic contraction of a muscle.
**Twitter,** twit'ėr, *vi.* To utter small, tremulous notes, as birds; to chirp.—*n.* A chirp or continued chirping.
**'Twixt,** twikst, a contraction of *betwixt.*
**Two,** tö, *a.* and *n.* One and one together.
**Two-faced,** tö'fāst, *a.* Having two faces; insincere; given to double-dealing.
**Twofold,** tö'fōld, *a.* Double.—*adv.* Doubly; in a double degree.
**Two-handed,** tö'hand-ed, *a.* Having two hands; used or wielded by both hands.
**Tymbal,** tim'bal, *n.* A kettle-drum.
**Tympanum,** tim'pa-num, *n.*; pl. **-na.** The drum of the ear.
**Type,** tīp, *n.* A distinguishing mark; emblem; symbol; ideal representative; model; letter used in printing; such letters collectively.
**Typesetter,** tīp'set-ėr, *n.* One who sets up type; a compositor; a type-setting machine.
**Typewriter,** tīp'rīt-ėr, *n.* A machine used as a substitute for the pen, producing letters by inked types.
**Typhoid,** tī'foid, *n.* A fever characterized by abdominal pains and diarrhea; enteric fever.
**Typhoon,** tī-fön', *n.* A violent hurricane on the coasts of China and Japan.
**Typhous,** tī'fus, *a.* Relating to typhus.
**Typhus,** tī'fus, *n.* A contagious or epidemic fever characterized by a deep livid eruption.
**Typical,** tip'ik-al, *a.* Pertaining to a type; emblematic; symbolic; representative.
**Typically,** tip'ik-al-li, *adv.* In a typical manner; by way of image; symbolically.
**Typify,** tip'i-fī, *vt.* To serve as a type of; to represent; to exemplify.
**Typographic, Typographical,** tī-po-graf'ik, tī-po-graf'ik-al, *a.* Pertaining to typography or printing.
**Typography,** tī-pog'ra-fi, *n.* The art of printing; style of printing.
**Typology,** tī-pol'o-ji, *n.* A discourse on types; the doctrine of types in Scripture.
**Tyrannic, Tyrannical,** tī-ran'ik, tī-ran'ik-al, *a.* Pertaining to a tyrant; despotic; cruel.
**Tyrannize,** ti'ran-īz, *vi.* To act the tyrant; to rule with oppressive severity.
**Tyrannous,** ti'ran-us, *a.* Tyrannical; unjustly severe; oppressive.
**Tyranny,** ti'ran-i, *n.* Rule of a tyrant; despotic exercise of power; oppression.
**Tyrant,** tī'rant, *n.* A despot; a cruel sovereign or master; an oppressor.
**Tyrian,** ti'ri-an, *a.* Pertaining to Tyre, the ancient Phoenician city; of a purple color.
**Tyrolese,** ti' or tī'rol-ēz, *a.* Belonging to the Tyrol.—*n.* A native or natives of the Tyrol.
**Tzar, Tzarina,** tsär, tsä-rē'na. Same as *Czar, Czarina.*

# U

**Ubiety,** ū-bī'e-ti, *n.* The state of being somewhere.
**Ubiquitous,** ū-bi'kwi-tus, *a* Existing or being everywhere; omnipresent.
**Ubiquity,** ū-bi'kwi-ti, *n.* Existence everywhere at the same time; omnipresence.
**U-boat,** ū'bōt, *n.* A German submarine.
**Udder,** ud'ėr, *n.* The glandular organ of cows, etc., in which the milk is produced.
**Udometer,** ū-dom'et-ėr, *n.* A rain-gauge.
**Ugh,** u, an *exclamation* expressing horror or recoil, usually accompanied by a shudder.
**Ugly,** ug'li, *a.* Repulsive; disagreeable in appearance; hateful; ill-omened.
**Uhlan, Ulan,** ö'lan, *n.* A light cavalry soldier.
**Ukase,** ū-kās' *n.* An edict of the Russian government.
**Ukulele,** ū'ku-lā''lē, *n.* A small Hawaiian guitar.
**Ulcer,** ul'sėr, *n.* A sore that discharges pus.
**Ulcerate,** ul'sėr-āt, *vt.* To affect with an ulcer.—*vi.* To become ulcerous.
**Ulceration,** ul-sėr-ā'shon, *n.* The process of ulcerating; an ulcer.
**Ulcerous,** ul'sėr-us, *a.* Having the nature of an ulcer; affected with ulcers.
**Uliginous,** ū-li'ji-nus, *a.* Oozy; slimy.
**Ullage,** ul'āj, *n.* The quantity that a cask wants of being full.
**Ulna,** ul'na, *n.* The larger of the two bones of the forearm.
**Ulster,** ul'stėr, *n.* A long loose overcoat.
**Ulterior,** ul-tē'ri-or, *a.* Being beyond or on the far-

ther side; more remote; distant; not avowed; reserved.

**Ultimate,** ul'ti-māt, *a.* Farthest; last or final; extreme; arrived at as a final result.

**Ulltimately,** ul'ti-māt-li, *adv.* As an ultimate result; finally; at last.

**Ultimatum,** ul-ti-mā'tum, *n.*; pl. **-ta** or **-tums.** The last offer; a final proposition which being rejected may be followed by war.

**Ultimo,** ul'ti-mō, *a.* The last (month): usually contracted to *ult.*

**Ultra,** ul'tra, *prefix, a.* Beyond due limit; extreme.—*n.* An ultraist.

**Ultraist,** ul'tra-ist, *n.* One who advocates extreme measures; an extremist.

**Ultramarine,** ul'tra-ma-rēn'', *a.* Being beyond the sea.—*n.* A beautiful and durable sky-blue.

**Ultramontane,** ul-tra-mon'tān, *a.* Beyond the mountains.—*n.* One who belongs to the Italian party in the Church of Rome.

**Ultramontanism,** ul-tra-mon'tān-izm, *n.* The views of that party (the Italian) who exalt the power and influence of the pope.

**Ultramundane,** ul-tra-mun'dān, *a.* Being beyond the world.

**Ultra-violet,** ul'tra-vī''ō-let, *a.* Of the part of the spectrum beyond the violet end of the visible spectrum.

**Ultroneous,** ul-trō'nē-us, *a.* Spontaneous.

**Umbel,** um'bel, *n.* That mode of inflorescence which consists of a number of flower-stalks spreading from a common center, each bearing a single flower.

**Umbellate,** um'bel-āt, *a.* Bearing umbels; having the form of an umbel.

**Umbellifer,** um-bel'i-fėr, *n.* An umbelliferous plant.

**Umbelliferous,** um-bel-lif'ėr-us, *a.* Producing or bearing umbels.

**Umber,** um'bėr, *n.* A soft earthy pigment of an olive-brown color in its raw state, but redder when burnt.

**Umbilical, Umbilic,** um-bil'ik-al, um-bil'ik, *a.* Pertaining to the navel.

**Umbilicus,** um-bi-li'kus, *n.* The navel.

**Umbo,** um'bō, *n.* The boss of a shield; a boss or knob.

**Umbra,** um'bra, *n.* The total shadow of the earth or moon in an eclipse.

**Umbrage,** um'brāj, *n.* Shade; obscurity; jealousy; offense; resentment.

**Umbrageous,** um-brā'jus, *a.* Shady.

**Umbrella,** um-brel'la, *n.* A portable shade which opens and folds, for sheltering the person from the sun or rain.

**Umlaut,** um'lout, *n.* The change of a vowel in one syllablë through the influence of a different vowel in the syllable immediately following.

**Umpirage,** um'pīr-āj, *n.* The post or action of an umpire; arbitration.

**Umpire,** um'pīr, *n.* A person to whose decision a dispute is referred; a judge, arbiter, or referee.

**Unable,** un-ā'bl, *a.* Not able; not having sufficient ability; not equal for some task.

**Unacceptable,** un-ak-sept'a-bl, *a.* Not acceptable or pleasing; unwelcome.

**Unaccommodating,** un-ak-kom'mō-dāt-ing, *a.* Not ready to oblige; uncompliant.

**Unaccomplished,** un-ak-kom'plisht, *a.* Not performed completely; not having accomplishments.

**Unaccountable,** un-ak-kount'a-bl, *a.* Not to be accounted for; not responsible.

**Unaccustomed,** un-ak-kus'tumd, *a.* Not accustomed; not habituated; unusual.

**Unacquainted,** un-ak-kwānt'ed, *a.* Not acquainted; not having familiar knowledge.

**Unadorned,** un-a-dornd', *a.* Not adorned; not embellished.

**Unadvisable,** un-ad-vīz'a-bl, *a.* Not advisable; not expedient; not prudent.

**Unadvisedly,** un-ad-vīz'ed-li, *adv.* Imprudently; indiscreetly; rashly.

**Unaffected,** un-af-fekt'ed, *a.* Not affected; natural; simple; sincere; not moved.

**Unaided,** un-ād'ed, *a.* Without aid.

**Unalloyed,** un-al-loid'., *a.* Not alloyed; entire; perfect.

**Unalterable,** un-al'tėr-a-bl, *a.* Not alterable; unchangeable; immutable.

**Unamiable,** un-ā'mi-a-bl, *a.* Not amiable; not adapted to gain affection.

**Unanimity, ū-na-ni'mi-ti,** *n.* State of being unanimous; perfect concord.

**Unanimous,** ū-nan'i-mus, *a.* Being of one mind; agreeing in determination; formed by unanimity.

**Unanswerable,** un-an'sėr-a-bl, *a.* Not to be satisfactorily answered; irrefutable.

**Unappealable,** un-ap-pēl'a-bl, *a.* Not appealable; admitting no appeal; that cannot be carried to a higher court by appeal.

**Unappeasable,** un-ap-pēz'a-bl, *a.* Not to be appeased or pacified; not placable.

**Unappreciated,** un-ap-prē'shi-āt-ed, *a.* Not duly estimated or valued.

**Unapproachable,** un-ap-prōch'a-bl, *a.* That cannot be approached; inaccessible.

**Unappropriate,** un-ap-prō'pri-āt, *a.* Not appropriate; inappropriate.

**Unappropriated,** un-ap-prō'pri-āt-ed, *a.* Not appropriated; not applied to a specific object.

**Unarmed,** un-ärmd', *a.* Not having arms or armor; not equipped.

**Unaspiring,** un-as-pīr'ing, *a.* Not ambitious.

**Unassailable,** un-as-sāl'a-bl, *a.* Not assailable; that cannot be assaulted.

**Unassuming,** un-as-sūm'ing, *a.* Not assuming; retiring; modest.

**Unassured,** un-a-shörd', *a.* Not confident; not to be trusted; not insured.

**Unattended,** un-at-tend'ed, *a.* Having no attendants; not medically attended.

**Unattractive,** un-at-trakt'iv, *a.* Not attractive.

**Unauthorized,** un-a'thor-īzd, *a.* Not authorized; not warranted.

**Unavailable,** un-a-vāl'a-bl, *a.* Not available; vain; useless.

**Unavailing,** un-a-vāl'ing, *a.* Of no avail; ineffectual; useless.

**Unavoidable,** un-a-void'a-bl, *a.* Not to be shunned; inevitable.

**Unaware,** un-a-wār', *pred.a.* or *adv.* Not aware; unconscious; inattentive.

**Unawares,** un-a-wārz', *adv.* Unexpectedly; inadvertently; unconsciously.

**Unbearable,** un-bār'a-bl, *a.* Not to be endured; intolerable.

**Unbecoming,** un-bē-kum'ing, *a.* Not becoming; improper.

**Unbefitting,** un-bē-fit'ing, *a.* Unsuitable.

**Unbegot, Unbegotten,** un-bē-got', un-bē-got'n, *a.* Not begotten; not generated.

**Unbelief,** un-bē-lēf', *n.* Incredulity; infidelity; disbelief of the gospel.

**Unbridled,** un-brī'dld, *a.* Unrestrained.

**Unbroken,** un-brōk'n, *a.* Not broken; not tamed; not interrupted.

**Unbutton,** un-but'n, *vt.* To undo the buttons of.

**Uncalled,** un-kald', *a.* Not called; not summoned; not invited.

**Uncanny,** un-kan'i, *a.* Not canny; mysterious; of evil and supernatural character.

**Uncared,** un-kārd', *a.* Not regarded; not heeded; often with *for.*

**Unceasing,** un-sēs'ing, *a.* Not ceasing; continual.

**Uncertain,** un-sėr'tān, *a.* Not certain; doubtful; inconstant.

**Uncertainty,** un-sėr'tin-ti, *n.* Want of certainty; dubiety.

**Unchallenged,** un-chal'lenjd, *a.* Not objected to; not called in question.

**Unchanging,** un-chānj'ing, *a.* Not changing; suffering no change.

**Uncharitable,** un-cha'rit-a-bl, *a.* Not charitable; ready to think evil; harsh.

**Unchaste,** un-chāst', *a.* Not chaste; lewd.
**Unchristian,** un-kris'ti-an, *a.* Contrary to the spirit or laws of Christianity.
**Uncial,** un'shi-al, *n.* A letter of large size used in ancient Greek and Latin manuscripts.
**Unciform,** un'si-form, *a.* Having a curved or hooked form.
**Uncinate,** un'si-nāt, *a.* Hooked at the end; unciform.
**Uncivilized,** un-si'vil-īzd, *a.* Not civilized.
**Uncle,** ung'kl, *n.* The brother of one's father or mother.
**Unclean,** un-klēn' *a.* Not clean; foul; dirty; morally impure; lewd.
**Uncomfortable,** un-kum'fort-a-bl, *a.* Not comfortable; uneasy; ill at ease.
**Uncommon,** un-kom'mon, *a.* Not common; rare; strange; remarkable.
**Uncommunicative,** un-kom-mū'ni-kāt-iv, *a.* Not apt to communicate; reserved.
**Uncompromising,** un-kom'prō-mīz-ing, *a.* Not agreeing to terms; unyielding.
**Unconcern,** un-kon-sėrn', *n.* Want of concern; apathy; indifference.
**Unconcerned,** un-kon-sėrnd', *a.* Not concerned; not anxious; feeling no solicitude.
**Unconditional,** un-kon-di'shon-al, *a.* Not limited by conditions; absolute.
**Unconfined,** un-kon-fīnd', *a.* Not confined; free from restraint or control.
**Unconfirmed,** un-kon-fėrmd', *a.* Not confirmed; not firmly established.
**Unconnected,** un-kon-nekt'ed, *a.* Not connected; separate; incoherent; loose.
**Unconquerable,** un-kong'kėr-a-bl, *a.* Not conquerable; insuperable.
**Unconscious,** un-kon'shus, *a.* Not conscious; not perceiving; unaware.
**Unconstitutional,** un-kon'sti-tū''shon-al, *a.* Not agreeable to the constitution; against the law.
**Uncontrolable,** un-kon-trōl'a-bl, *a.* That cannot be controlled or restrained.
**Unconverted,** un-kon-vėrt'ed, *a.* Not converted; not regenerated.
**Uncork,** un-kork', *vt.* To draw the cork from.
**Uncorrected,** un-ko-rekt'ed, *a.* Not corrected; not revised; not reformed.
**Uncouple,** un-ku'pl, *vt.* To loose, as dogs coupled together; to disjoin.
**Uncourtly,** un-kōrt'li, *a.* Not courtly; blunt; uncivil; rude.
**Uncouth,** un-köth', *a.* Strange; odd in appearance; awkward.
**Uncover,** un-ku'vėr, *vt.* To divest of a cover; to disclose.—*vi.* To take off the hat.
**Unction,** ungk'shon, *n.* Act of anointing; an unguent; religious fervor; sham devotional fervor; oiliness.
**Unctuous,** ung'tū-us, *a.* Oily; greasy; nauseously emotional; oily; fawning.
**Uncultivated,** un-kul'ti-vāt-ed, *a.* Not cultivated; not tilled; boorish or rude.
**Uncut,** un-kut', *a.* Not cut.
**Undated,** un'dāt'ed, *a.* Wavy.
**Undated,** un-dāt'ed, *a.* Not dated.
**Undaunted,** un-dant'ed, *a.* Intrepid; fearless.
**Undecided,** un-dē-sīd'ed, *a.* Not decided; hesitating; irresolute.
**Undefinable,** un-dē-fīn'a-bl, *a.* Not definable; indefinable.
**Undefined,** un-dē-fīnd', *a.* Not defined; lacking in clearness or definiteness.
**Undeniable,** un-dē-nī'a-bl, *a.* incapable of being denied; indisputable.
**Under,** un'dėr, *prep.* Below; beneath; undergoing; affected by; subject to; inferior; during the time of; included in; in accordance with.—*adv.* In a lower condition or degree.—*a.* Lower; subject; subordinate.
**Undercarriage,** un'dėr-kar-ij, *n.* The landing apparatus of an aircraft.
**Undercharge,** un-dėr-chärj', *vt.* To charge insufficiently.—*n.* un'der-chärj. Too low a charge or price.
**Underclothes, Underclothing,** un'dėr-klōTHz, un'dėr-klōTH-ing, *n.* Clothes worn under others or next to the skin.
**Undercurrent,** un'dėr-ku-rent, *n.* A current below another; some movement or influence not apparent.
**Undergo,** un-dėr-gō, *vt.* To bear; to experience; to suffer.
**Undergraduate,** un-dėr-grad'ū-āt, *n.* A student who has not taken his first degree.
**Underground,** un'dėr-ground, *a.* and *adv.* Below the surface of the ground; operating in secret.
**Undergrowth,** un'dėr-grōth, *n.* Shrubs or small trees growing among large ones.
**Underhand,** un'dėr-hand, *a.* Working by stealth; secret; deceitful.—*adv.* In a clandestine manner.
**Underhung,** un'dėr-hung, *a.* Projecting beyond the upper jaw: said of the under jaw.
**Underlay,** un-dėr-lā', *vt.* To lay beneath; to support by something laid under.
**Underlie,** un-dėr-lī', *vt.* To lie beneath; to be at the basis of.
**Underline,** un-dėr-līn', *vt.* To mark with a line below the words.
**Underling,** un'dėr-ling, *n.* An inferior person or agent; a mean sorry fellow.
**Undermine,** un-dėr-mīn', *vt.* To sap; to injure by underhand means.
**Underneath,** un-dėr-nēth', *adv.* Beneath; below.—*prep.* Under; beneath.
**Underrate,** un-dėr-rāt', *vt.* To rate too low; to undervalue.
**Undershot,** un-dėr-shot', *a.* Moved by water passing under, as a wheel.
**Undershrub,** un'dėr-shrub, *n.* A low shrub, the branches of which decay yearly.
**Undersized,** un'dėr-sīzd, *a.* Being of a size or stature less than common; dwarfish.
**Understand,** un-dėr-stand', *vt.* To comprehend; to see through; to suppose to mean; to infer; to assume; to recognize as implied although not expressed.—*vi.* To comprehend; to learn.
**Understanding,** un-dėr-stand'ing, *a.* Intelligent.—*n.* Comprehension; discernment; knowledge; intellect; agreement of minds; anything agreed upon.
**Understate,** un-dėr-stāt', *vt.* To state too low or as less than actually.
**Undertake,** un'dėr-tāk, *vt.* To take in hand; to engage in; to attempt; to guarantee.—*vi.* To take upon oneself; to promise; to stand bound.
**Undertaker,** un'dėr-tāk-ėr, *n.* One who undertakes; one who manages funerals.
**Undertaking,** un'dėr-tāk-ing, *n.* That which is undertaken; enterprise; promise.
**Undertone,** un'dėr-tōn, *n.* A low tone.
**Under-tow,** un'dėr-tō, *n.* An undercurrent opposite to that at the surface; the backward flow of a wave breaking on a beach.
**Undervalue,** un-dėr-val'ū, *vt.* To value below the real worth; to esteem lightly.
**Underwear,** un'dėr-wār, *n.* Underclothes.
**Underworld,** un'dėr-wėrld, *n.* The lower world; this world; the antipodes; the place of departed souls; Hades.
**Underwrite,** un-dėr-rīt, *vt.* To write under; to subscribe one's name and become answerable for a certain amount.
**Underwriter,** un'dėr-rīt-ėr, *n.* One who underwrites or insures; an insurer.
**Underwriting,** un'dėr-rīt-ing, *n.* The business of an underwriter.
**Undesirable,** un-dē-zīr'a-bl, *a.* Not desirable.
**Undetermined,** un-dē-tėr'mind, *a.* Not determined; not decided, fixed, or settled.
**Undeterred,** un-dē-tėrd', *a.* Not restrained by fear or obstacles.
**Undigested,** un-di-jest'ed, *a.* Not digested; not properly prepared or arranged; crude.
**Undignified,** un-dig'ni-fīd, *a.* Not dignified; showing a want of dignity.

**Undine,** un'dīn, *n.* A female water-spirit.
**Undisguised,** un-dis-gīzd', *a.* Not disguised; open; candid; artless.
**Undisposed,** un-dis-pōzd', *a.* Not set apart; not allocated; not sold; with *of.*
**Undisputed,** un-dis-pūt'ed, *a.* Not disputed; not called in question; incontestable.
**Undistinguished,** un-dis-ting'gwisht, *a.* Not having any distinguishing mark; not famous; not possessing distinction.
**Undisturbed,** un-dis-tėrbd', *a.* Free from disturbance; calm; tranquil; not agitated.
**Undivided,** un-di-vīd'ed, *a.* Not divided; whole; entire.
**Undo,** un-dö', *vt.* To reverse what has been done; annul; to loose; to take to pieces; to ruin.
**Undoing,** un-dö'ing, *n.* Reversal; ruin.
**Undone,** un-dun', *pp.* Not done; untied or unfastened; reversed; ruined.
**Undoubtedly,** un-dout'ed-li, *adv.* Without doubt; without question; indubitably.
**Undress,** un-dres', *vt.* To divest of dress or clothes; to strip.—*n.* un'dres. A loose negligent dress; ordinary dress.
**Undue,** un-dū', *a.* Not due; not yet demandable by right; not right; inordinate.
**Undulate,** un'dū-lāt, *vi.* To have a wavy motion; to wave.—*vt.* To cause to wave.
**Undulation,** un-dū-lā'shon, *n.* Act of undulating; a waving motion; a wavy form; a gentle slope; a vibratory motion.
**Undulatory,** un'dū-la-to-ri, *a.* Having an undulating character; moving like waves.
**Unduly,** un-dū'li, *adv.* In an undue manner; unlawfully; unwarrantably; excessively.
**Undutiful,** un-dū'ti-ful, *a.* Not dutiful; not obedient; rebellious; irreverent.
**Undying,** un-dī'ing, *a.* Not dying; imperishable.
**Unearned,** un-ėrnd', *a.* Not merited by labor or services.—**Unearned increment,** the increase in the value of property not due to any expenditure on the part of the owner.
**Unearth,** un-ėrth', *vt.* To drive or bring from the earth; to uncover; to discover.
**Unearthly,** un-ėrth'li, *a.* Not earthly; weird.
**Uneasy,** un-ēz'i, *a.* Restless; disturbed; somewhat anxious; unquiet; stiff; not graceful; unpleasing; irksome.
**Uneducated,** un-ed'ū-kāt-ed, *a.* Not educated; illiterate; ignorant.
**Unemotional,** un-ē-mō'shon-al, *a.* Not emotional; impassive.
**Unemployed,** un-em-ploid', *a.* Not employed; having no work; not being in use.
**Unending,** un-end'ing, *a.* Not ending; perpetual; eternal.
**Unendurable,** un-en-dūr'a-bl, *a.* Intolerable.
**Unengaged,** un-en-gājd', *a.* Not engaged.
**Unenglish,** un-ing'glish, *a.* Not English.
**Unenlightened,** un-en-līt'nd, *a.* Not enlightened; not illuminated, mentally or morally.
**Unenterprising,** un-en'tėr-prīz-ing, *a.* Wanting in enterprise; not adventurous.
**Unenviable,** un-en'vi-a-bl, *a.* Not enviable; Not to be envied.
**Unequable,** un-ē'kwa-bl, *a.* Not equable; changeful; fitful.
**Unequal,** un-ē'kwal, *a.* Not equal; inadequate; insufficient; not equable.
**Unequalled,** un-ē'kwald, *a.* Not to be equalled; unrivalled.
**Unequivocal,** un-ē-kwiv'ō-kal, *a.* Not equivocal; not doubtful; clear; evident.
**Unerring,** un-er'ing, *a.* Not erring; incapable of error; certain.
**Unessential,** un-es-sen'shal, *a.* Not essential; not absolutely necessary.
**Uneven,** un-ē'vn, *a.* Not even or level; rough; crooked; not fair or just; odd.
**Unexcelled,** un-ek-seld', *a.* Not excelled.
**Unexceptionable,** un-ek-sep'shon-a-bl, *a.* Not liable to any exception; excellent.
**Unexpected,** un-eks-pekt'ed, *a.* Not expected; not looked for; sudden.
**Unexpired,** un-eks-pīrd', *a.* Not expired; not having come to the end of its term.
**Unexplored,** un-eks-plōrd', *a.* Not explored; not visited by any traveller.
**Unfading,** un-fād'ing, *a.* Not fading; not liable to wither or decay; ever fresh.
**Unfailing,** un-fāl'ing, *a.* Not liable to fail; that does not fail; certain.
**Unfair,** un-fār', *a.* Not honest or impartial; not just; inequitable; disingenuous.
**Unfaithful,** un-fāth'ful, *a.* Not faithful
**Unfamiliar,** un-fa-mil'i-ėr, *a.* Not familiar; not accustomed; strange.
**Unfashionable,** un-fa'shon-a-bl, *a.* Not fashionable or according to the fashion.
**Unfasten,** un-fäs'n, *vt.* To loose; to unfix.
**Unfathomable,** un-faᴛʜ'um-a-bl, *a.* That cannot be fathomed; incomprehensible.
**Unfavorable,** un-fā'vėr-a-bl, *a.* Not favorable; not propitious; discouraging.
**Unfeeling,** un-fēl'ing, *a.* Devoid of feeling; hard-hearted; harsh; brutal.
**Unfermented,** un-fer-ment'ed, *a.* Not having undergone fermentaiton.
**Unfetter,** un-fet'ėr, *vt.* To loose from fetters; to set at liberty.
**Unfinished,** un-fin'isht, *a.* Not finished.
**Unfit,** un-fit', *a.* Not fit; unsuitable; not competent.—*vt.* To make unfit.
**Unflinching,** un-flinsh'ing, *a.* Not flinching; not shrinking; resolute.
**Unfold,** un-fōld', *vt.* To open the folds of; to display.—*vi.* To open out.
**Unforeseen,** un-fōr-sēn', *a.* Not foreseen.
**Unforgiving,** un-for-giv'ing, *a.* Not forgiving; implacable.
**Unformed,** un-formd', *a.* Not formed or moulded into regular shape.
**Unfortunate,** un-for'tū-nāt, *a.* Not fortunate; unlucky; unhappy.—*n.* One who is unfortunate; a prostitute.
**Unfortunately,** un-for'tū-nāt-li, *adv.* In an unfortunate manner; by ill fortune.
**Unfounded,** un-found'ed, *a.* Having no real foundation; groundless; idle.
**Unfriendly,** un-frend'li, *a.* Not friendly.
**Unfrock,** un-frok', *vt.* To divest of a frock; to deprive of the character of a priest.
**Unfruitful,** un-fröt'ful, *a.* Not fruitful; barren.
**Unfunded,** un-fund'ëd, *a.* Not funded; having no permanent fund for the payment of its interest: said of government debt when it exists in the form of exchequer bills or the like.
**Unfurl,** un-fėrl', *vt.* To loose from a furled state; to expand to catch the wind.
**Unfurnished,** un-fėr'nisht, *a.* Not furnished; unsupplied; unprovided.
**Ungainly,** un-gān'li, *a.* Not handsome; uncouth; clumsy; awkward; ill-shaped.
**Ungentlemanly,** un-jen'tl-man-li, *a.* Not becoming a gentleman.
**Unglazed,** un-glāzd', *a.* Not glazed; not furnished with panes of glass.
**Ungodly,** un-god'li, *a.* Not godly; wicked.
**Ungovernable,** un-gu'vėrn-a-bl, *a.* That cannot be governed; wild; refractory.
**Ungraceful,** un-grās'ful, *a.* Not graceful.
**Ungracious,** un-grā'shus, *a.* Not gracious; uncivil; rude; impolite.
**Ungrateful,** un-grāt'ful, *a.* Not grateful; not thankful; unpleasing; harsh.
**Ungrounded,** un-ground'ed, *a.* Having no foundation or support; groundless.
**Ungrudging,** un-gruj'ing, *a.* Without a grudge; freely giving; hearty; liberal.
**Ungual,** ung'gwal, *a.* Pertaining to or having a nail, claw, or hoof.
**Unguarded,** un-gärd'ed, *a.* Not guarded; not cautious; negligent.
**Unguent,** un'gwent, *n.* An ointment.
**Unguiculate,** ung-gwik'ū-lāt, *a.* Having claws.
**Unguiform,** ung-gwik-form, *a.* Claw-shaped

**Ungulate,** ung'gū-lāt, *n*. A hoofed quadruped.—*a*. Hoof-shaped; having hoofs.
**Unhallowed,** un-hal'ōd, *a*. Not hallowed or sanctified; profane; unholy.
**Unhand,** un-hand', *vt*. To loose from the hand or hands; to lose hold of.
**Unhappily,** un-hap'i-li, *adv*. In an unhappy manner; unfortunately.
**Unhappy,** un-hap'i, *a*. Not happy; sad; unfortunate; unlucky; evil; ill-omened.
**Unharmed,** un-härmd', *a*. Not harmed.
**Unharness,** un-här'nes, *vt*. To strip of harness; to loose from harness; to disarm.
**Unhealthy,** un-helth'i, *a*. Not healthy; sickly; insalubrious; unwholesome.
**Unheard,** un-hėrd', *a*. Not heard; not admitted to audience; not known (with *of*).
**Unhesitating,** un-he'zi-tāt-ing, *a*. Not hesitating; not remaining in doubt; prompt.
**Unhinge,** un-hinj', *vt*. To take from the hinges; to unfix; to loosen; to derange.
**Unholy,** un-hō'li, *a*. Not holy; not sacred; unhallowed; profane; impious; wicked.
**Unicorn,** ū'ni-korn, *n*. A fabulous animal like a horse, with a long single horn on the forehead.
**Unicostate,** ū-ni-kos'tāt, *a*. Having one rib or ridge; in *botany*, having one large vein down the center, called the midrib.
**Unification,** ū'ni-fi-kā''shon, *n*. The act of unifying or uniting into one.
**Uniform,** ū'ni-form, *a*. Having always one and the same form; equable; invariable; consistent.—*n*. A distinctive dress worn by the members of the same body.
**Uniformity,** ū-ni-for'mi-ti, *n*. State or character of being uniform; conformity to one type; agreement; consistency.
**Uniformly,** ū'ni-form-li, *adv*. In a uniform manner; invariably.
**Unify,** ū'ni-fī, *vt*. To form into one.
**Unigenous,** ū-ni'jen-us, *a*. Of one kind; of the same genus.
**Unilluminated,** un-il-lūm'in-āt-ed, *a*. Not illuminated; dark; ignorant.
**Unimaginable,** un-im-aj'in-a-bl, *a*. Not imaginable; inconceivable.
**Unimpaired,** un-im-pārd', *a*. Not impaired; not diminished; uninjured.
**Unimpassioned,** un-im-pa'shond, *a*. Not impassioned; tranquil; not violent.
**Unimpeachable,** un-im-pēch'a-bl, *a*. Not impeachable; blameless; irreproachable.
**Unimportant,** un-im-pōr'tant, *a*. Not important; not of great moment.
**Unimproved,** un-im-prövd', *a*. Not improved; not cultivated.
**Uninhabited,** un-in-ha'bit-ed, *a*. Not inhabited by men; having no inhabitants.
**Uninstructed,** un-in-strukt'ed, *a*. Not instructed; not educated.
**Unintelligible,** un-in-tel'i-ji-bl, *a*. Not intelligible; meaningless.
**Unintentional,** un-in-ten'shon-al, *a*. Not intentional; done without design.
**Uninterested,** un-in'tėr-est-ed, *a*. Not interested; having no interest or concern.
**Uninteresting,** un-in'tėr-est-ing, *n*. Not interesting; dull; tame.
**Uninterrupted,** un-in'tėr-rupt''ed, *a*. Not interrupted; unintermitted; incessant.
**Uninviting,** un-in-vīt'ing, *a*. Not inviting; unattractive; rather repellent.
**Union,** ūn'yon, *n*. Act of joining; combination; agreement; harmony; marriage; confederacy; a trades-union; a mixed fabric of cotton, flax, jute, silk, or wool, etc.; a certain kind of flag.
**Unionist,** ūn'yon-ist, *n*. One who advocates union; a trades-unionist; one who upholds the union of the three kingdoms of Great Britain and Ireland.
**Union Jack,** ūn'yon-jak, *n*. The national flag of Great Britain and Northern Ireland, formed by the union of the cross of St. George, the saltire of St. Andrew, and the saltire of St. Patrick.
**Uniparous,** ū-nip'a-rus, *a*. Producing one at a birth.
**Unique,** ū-nēk', *a*. Without a like or equal; unmatched; unequalled.
**Unison,** ū-ni-son, *n*. Accordance; agreement; harmony; concord.
**Unisonant, Unisonous,** ū-ni'sō-nant, ū-ni'sō-nus, *a*. Being in unison; concordant.
**Unit,** ū'nit, *n*. A single thing or person; an individual; the number 1; a dimension or quantity assumed as a standard.
**Unitarian,** ū-ni-tā'ri-an, *n*. One who ascribes divinity to God only, and denies the Trinity.—*a*. Pertaining to Unitarians.
**Unitarianism,** ū-ni-tā'ri-an-izm, *n*. The doctrines of Unitarians.
**Unitary,** ū'ni-ta-ri, *a*. Of or relating to a unit.
**Unite,** ū-nīt', *vt*. (uniting, united). To combine; to connect; to associate.—*vi*. To become one; to combine; to concur.
**United,** ū-nīt'ed, *a*. Joined; combined together; made one.
**Unitedly,** ū-nīt'ed-li, *adv*. In a united manner; jointly; in combination.
**Unity,** ū'ni-ti, *n*. State of being one; concord; agreement; harmony; artistic harmony and symmetry.
**Univalve,** ū'ni-valv, *n*. A shell having one valve only.
**Universal,** ū-ni-vėrs'al, *a*. Pertaining to all; total; whole.—*n*. A general notion or idea.
**Universally,** ū-ni-vėrs'al-li, *adv*. With extension to the whole; without exception.
**Universe,** ū'ni-vėrs, *n*. The whole system of created things; the world.
**University,** ū-ni-vėrs'i-ti, *n*. An institution for instruction in science and literature, etc., and having the power of conferring degrees.
**Univocal,** ū-ni'vō-kal, *a*. Having one meaning only; having unison of sounds.—*n*. A word having only one meaning.
**Unjust,** un-just', *a*. Not just, upright, or equitable.
**Unjustifiable,** un-jus'ti-fī''a-bl, *a*. Not justifiable.
**Unjustly,** un-just'li, *adv*. Wrongfully.
**Unkempt,** un-kempt', *a*. Uncombed; rough.
**Unkind,** un-kīnd', *a*. Not kind; cruel.
**Unkindly,** un-kīnd'li, *a*. Unkind; ungracious.—*adv*. In an unkind manner.
**Unknowingly,** un-nō'ing-li, *adv*. Without knowledge or design; unwittingly.
**Unknown,** un-nōn', *a*. Not known; not discovered, found out, or ascertained.
**Unlace,** un-lās', *vt*. To loose the lacing or fastening of; to unfasten.
**Unlawful,** un-la'ful, *a*. Not lawful; illegal.
**Unlearned,** un-lėr'ned, *a*. Not learned or erudite; illiterate; (un-lėrnd') not known.
**Unless,** un-les', *conj*. If it be not that; if . . . not; except; excepting.
**Unlicensed,** un-lī'senst, *a*. Not having a license; done without due license.
**Unlike,** un-līk', *a*. Not like; dissimilar; having no resemblance; diverse.
**Unlikely,** un-līk'li, *a*. Not likely; improbable; likely to fail; unpromising.
**Unlimber,** un-lim'bėr, *vt*. To take off or detach the limbers from.
**Unlimited,** un-lim'it-ed, *a*. Not limited; boundless; indefinite.
**Unload,** un-lōd', *vt*. To take the load from; to discharge; to empty out.
**Unlock,** un-lok', *vt*. To unfasten; to open.
**Unlucky,** un-luk'i, *a*. Not lucky; unfortunate; not successful; ill-omened.
**Unmanageable,** un-man'āj-a-bl, *a*. Not manageable; beyond control.
**Unmannerly,** un-man'ėr-li, *a*. Not mannerly; rude; ill-bred.
**Unmask,** un-mask', *vt*. To strip of a mask; to expose.—*vi*. To put off a mask.
**Unmatched,** un-macht', *a*. Matchless.

**Unmeaning**, un-mēn'ing, *a*. Having no meaning; senseless; vacuous.
**Unmeasured**, un-me'zhūrd, *a*. Not measured; immense; infinite; excessive.
**Unmentionable**, un-men'shon-a-bl, *a*. Not mentionable.
**Unmerciful**, un-mėr'si-fụl, *a*. Not merciful; cruel; merciless.
**Unmerited**, un-mer'it-ed, *a*. Not deserved.
**Unmindful**, un-mīnd'fụl, *a*. Not mindful; regardless.
**Unmistakable, Unmistakeable**, un-mis-tāk'a-bl, *a*. Not capable of being mistaken; clear; obvious.
**Unmitigated**, un-mi'ti-gāt-ed, *a*. Not mitigated; thorough-paced.
**Unmotherly**, un-muᴛʜ'ėr-li, *a*. Not resembling or becoming a mother.
**Unmoved**, un-mövd', *a*. Not moved; firm; calm; cool.
**Unnamed**, un-nāmd', *a*. Not having received a name; not mentioned.
**Unnatural**, un-na'tūr-al, *a*. Not natural; contrary to nature; affected; artificial.
**Unnavigable**, un-na'vi-ga-bl, *a*. Not navigable; incapable of being navigated.
**Unnecessary**, un-ne'ses-sa-ri, *a*. Not necessary; needless.
**Unneighborly**, un-nā'bėr-li, *a*. Not neighborly; not kind and friendly.
**Unnerve**, un-nėrv', *vt*. To deprive of nerve, strength, or composure; to enfeeble.
**Unnoticed**, un-nōt'ist, *a*. Not observed.
**Unnumbered**, un-num'bėrd, *a*. Not numbered; innumerable; indefinitely numerous.
**Unobjectionable**, un-ob-jek'shon-a-bl, *a*. Not liable to objection; unexceptionable.
**Unobservant, Unobserving**, un-ob-zėrv'ant, un-ob-zėrv'ing, *a*. Not observant.
**Unobtrusive**, un-ob-trö'siv, *a*. Not obtrusive; not forward; modest; retiring.
**Unoccupied**, un-ok'kū-pīd, *a*. Not occupied; not possessed; at leisure.
**Unoffending**, un-of-fend'ing, *a*. Not giving offense; harmless; innocent; inoffensive.
**Unofficial**, un-of-fi'shal, *a*. Not official.
**Unopposed**, un-op-pōzd', *a*. Not opposed; not meeting with any obstruction.
**Unorthodox**, un-or'tho-doks, *a*. Not orthodox; heterodox.
**Unostentatious**, un-os'ten-tā''shus, *a*. Not ostentatious; not showy; modest.
**Unpack**, un-pak', *vt*. To take from a package; to unload.
**Unpaid**, un-pād', *a*. Not paid; remaining due; not receiving a salary.
**Unpalatable**, un-pa'lat-a-bl, *a*. Not palatable; disagreeable to the taste or feelings.
**Unparalleled**, un-pa'ral-eld, *a*. Having no parallel; unequalled; matchless.
**Unpardonable**, un-pär'dn-a-bl, *a*. Not to be forgiven; incapable of being pardoned.
**Unparliamentary**, un-pär'li-men''ta-ri, *a*. Contrary to the usages or rules of proceeding in parliament; unseemly, as language.
**Unpatriotic**, un-pā'tri-ot''ik, *a*. Not patriotic; wanting in patriotism.
**Unperceivable**, un-pėr-sēv'a-bl, *a*. Imperceptible.
**Unpin**, un-pin', *vt*. To loose from pins; to unfasten.
**Unpleasant**, un-ple'zant, *a*. Not pleasant.
**Unpleasing**, un-plēz'ing, *a*. Unpleasant.
**Unplumbed**, un-plumd', *a*. Not fathomed.
**Unpoetic, Unpoetical**, un-pō-et'ik, un-pō-et'ik-al, *a*. Not poetical.
**Unpolished**, un-po'lisht, *a*. Not polished; rude; plain.
**Unpopular**, un-po'pū-lėr, *a*. Not popular.
**Unpractical**, un-prak'ti-kal, *a*. Not practical.
**Unpracticed**, un-prak'tist, *a*. Not having been taught by practice; raw; unskillful.
**Unprecedented**, un-pre'sē-dent-ed, *a*. Having no precedent; unexampled.
**Unprejudiced**, un-pre'jū-dist, *a*. Not prejudiced; free from bias; impartial.
**Unpremeditated**, un-prē-me'di-tāt-ed, *a*. Not previously meditated; spontaneous.
**Unprepared**, un-prē-pārd', *a*. Not prepared.
**Unpretending**, un-prē-tend'ing, *a*. Not pretending to any distinction; unassuming.
**Unprincipled**, un-prin'si-pld, *a*. Not having settled principles; immoral.
**Unproductive**, un-prō-duk'tiv, *a*. Not productive; infertile; not returning a profit.
**Unprofessional**, un-prō-fe'shon-al, *a*. Contrary to the customs of a profession; not belonging to a profession.
**Unprofitable**, un-pro'fit-a-bl, *a*. Not profitable; useless; profitless.
**Unpromising**, un-pro'mis-ing, *a*. Not giving promise of success, etc.
**Unproved**, un-prövd', *a*. Not proved; not established as true by proof.
**Unpublished**, un-pub'lisht, *a*. Not published.
**Unpunctual**, un-pungk'tū-al, *a*. Not punctual; not exact as to time.
**Unqualified**, un-kwo'li-fīd, *a*. Not qualified; not having the requisite qualifications; not modified by conditions.
**Unquestionable**, un-kwest'yon-a-bl, *a*. Not to be called in question; indubitable.
**Unquiet**, un-kwī'et, *a*. Not quiet; disturbed.
**Unravel**, un-ra'vel, *vt*. To disentangle; to disengage or separate; to solve.
**Unread**, un-red', *a*. Not perused; illiterate.
**Unreadable**, un-rēd'a-bl, *a*. Incapable of being read; illegible; not worth reading.
**Unready**, un-re'di, *a*. Not ready; not prompt to act.
**Unreal**, un-rē'al, *a*. Not real; not substantial.
**Unreality**, un-rē-al'i-ti, *n*. Want of real existence; that which has no reality.
**Unreason**, un-rē'zn, *n*. Want of reason; folly; absurdity.
**Unreasonable**, un-rē'zn-a-bl, *a*. Not reasonable; immoderate.
**Unrecorded**, un-rē-kord'ed, *a*. Not recorded or registered; not kept in remembrance by documents or monuments.
**Unredeemed**, un-rē-dēmd', *a*. Not redeemed; not fulfilled; unmitigated.
**Unrefined**, un-rē-fīnd', *a*. Not refined or purified; not polished in manners, taste, etc.
**Unregenerate**, un-rē-jen'ė-rāt, *a*. Not regenerated or renewed in heart.
**Unregistered**, un-re'jis-tėrd, *a*. Not registered or entered in a register.
**Unrelated**, un-rē-lāt'ed, *a*. Not connected by blood; having no connection.
**Unrelenting**, un-rē-lent'ing, *a*. Not relenting; relentless; hard; pitiless.
**Unreliable**, un-rē-lī'a-bl, *a*. Not reliable; untrustworthy.
**Unrelieved**, un-rē-lēvd', *a*. Not relieved; monotonous.
**Unremitting**, un-rē-mit'ing, *a*. Not remitting or abating; incessant; continued.
**Unrepresented**, un-rep'rē-zent''ed, *a*. Not represented; not having a representative; not yet put on the stage.
**Unrequited**, un-rē-kwīt'ed, *a*. Not requited; not recompensed.
**Unreserved**, un-rē-zėrvd', *a*. Not reserved or restricted; full; free; open; frank.
**Unreservedly**, un-rē-zėrv'ed-li, *adv*. Without reservation; frankly.
**Unrest**, un-rest', *n*. Disquiet; uneasiness.
**Unresting**, un-rest'ing, *a*. Never resting.
**Unrestrained**, un-rē-strānd', *a*. Not restrained; licentious; loose.
**Unriddle**, un-rid'l, *vt*. To solve; to interpret.
**Unrighteous**, un-rīt'yus, *a*. Not righteous; not just; wicked.
**Unripe**, un-rīp', *a*. Not ripe; not mature; not fully prepared; not completed.

**Unrivaled,** un-rī'vald, *a.* Having no rival; incomparable.
**Unrobe,** un-rōb', *vt.* To strip of a robe; to undress.
**Unromantic,** un-rō-man'tik, *a.* Not romantic; not given to romantic fancies.
**Unruffled,** un-ruf'ld, *a.* Not ruffled; calm; tranquil; not agitated; not disturbed.
**Unruly,** un-rö'li, *a.* Disregarding rule; turbulent; ungovernable; disorderly.
**Unsafe,** un-sāf', *a.* Not safe; perilous.
**Unsaid,** un-sed', *a.* Not spoken.
**Unsatisfactory,** un-sa'tis-fak''to-ri, *a.* Not satisfactory; not satisfying.
**Unsavory,** un-sā'vo-ri, *a.* Not savory; insipid; unpleasing; offensive.
**Unscathed,** un-skāTHd', *a.* Not scathed; uninjured.
**Unscrew,** un-skrö', *vt.* To draw the screw from; to unfasten by screwing back.
**Unscrupulous,** un-skrö'pū-lus, *a.* Having no scruples; regardless of principle.
**Unseasonable,** un-sē'zn-a-bl, *a.* Not seasonable; ill-timed; untimely.
**Unseat,** un-sēt', *vt.* To remove from a seat; to depose from a seat in a legislature.
**Unseen,** un-sēn', *a.* Not seen; invisible.
**Unselfish,** un-sel'fish, *a.* Not selfish.
**Unsettle,** un-set'l, *vt.* To change from a settled state; to unhinge; to derange.
**Unsettled,** un-set'ld, *p.a.* Not settled; not calm or composed; having no fixed habitation; irregular; unpaid.
**Unshaken,** un-shā'kn, *a.* Not shaken; resolute; firm.
**Unshod,** un-shod', *a.* Having no shoes.
**Unshrinking,** un-shringk'ing, *a.* Not shrinking; not recoiling; fearless.
**Unsightly,** un-sīt'li, *a.* Not sightly; repulsive; ugly; deformed.
**Unsized,** un-sīzd', *a.* Not sized or stiffened; not made with size.
**Unskillful,** un-skil'ful, *a.* Not skillful; having no or little skill; wanting dexterity.
**Unsociable,** un-sō'shi-a-bl, *a.* Not sociable.
**Unsocial,** un-sō'shal, *a.* Not social; not caring to mix with one's fellows.
**Unsoiled,** un-soild', *a.* Not soiled; pure.
**Unsold,** un-sōld', *a.* Not sold.
**Unsolicited,** un-sō-lis'it-ed, *a.* Not asked.
**Unsophisticated,** un-sō-fist'ik-āt-ed, *a.* Pure; natural; artless; simple.
**Unsought,** un-sat', *a.* Not sought for.
**Unsound,** un-sound', *a.* Not sound; erroneous; not orthodox.
**Unsparing,** un-spār'ing, *a.* Not sparing; profuse; severe; rigorous.
**Unspeakable,** un-spēk'a-bl, *a.* Incapable of being spoken or uttered; unutterable.
**Unspoken,** un-spō'kn, *a.* Not spoken.
**Unspotted,** un-spot'ed, *a.* Free from spots; free from moral stain; pure.
**Unstable,** un-stā'bl, *a.* Not stable; inconstant; irresolute; wavering.
**Unstamped,** un-stampt', *a.* Not having a stamp impressed or affixed.
**Unsteady,** un-sted'i, *a.* Not steady; shaking; fickle; varying.
**Unstop,** un-stop', *vt.* To free from a stopper, as a bottle; to free from obstruction.
**Unstring,** un-string', *vt.* To deprive of strings; to relax; to loosen.
**Unstrung,** un-strung', *a.* Deprived of strings; having the nerves shaken.
**Unsubstantial,** un-sub-stan'shal, *a.* Not substantial; not real; not nutritive.
**Unsuccessful,** un-suk-ses'ful, *a.* Not successful; not fortunate in the result.
**Unsuitable,** un-sūt'a-bl, *a.* Not suitable; ill adapted; unfit.
**Unsuited,** un-sūt'ed, *a.* Not suited; unfit.
**Unsullied,** un-sul'id, *a.* Not sullied; pure.
**Unsung,** un-sung', *a.* Not sung; not celebrated in song or poetry.
**Unsurpassed,** un-sėr-past', *a.* Not surpassed, excelled, or outdone.
**Unsusceptible,** un-sus-sep'ti-bl, *a.* Not susceptible.
**Unsuspecting,** un-sus-pekt'ing, *a.* Not suspecting; free from suspicion.
**Unsuspicious,** un-sus-pi'shus, *a.* Not suspicious; unsuspecting.
**Unswerving,** un-swėrv'ing, *a.* Not swerving; unwavering; firm.
**Untainted,** un-tānt-ed, *a.* Not tainted.
**Untamable, Untameable,** un-tām'a-bl, *a.* Not capable of being tamed.
**Untasted,** un-tāst'ed, *a.* Not tasted; not experienced.
**Untaught,** un-tat', *a.* Not educated; unlettered; ignorant.
**Untenable,** un-ten'a-bl, *a.* Not to be maintained by argument; not defensible.
**Unthanked,** un-thangkt', *a.* Not repaid by thanks.
**Unthankful,** un-thangk'ful, *a.* Not thankful; ungrateful.
**Unthinkable,** un-thingk'a-bl, *a.* That cannot be made an object of thought.
**Unthinking,** un-thingk'ing, *a.* Not given to think; not heedful; inconsiderate.
**Unthought,** un-that', *a.* Not thought or conceived: often followed by *of.*
**Unthread,** un-thred', *vt.* To draw or take out a thread from.
**Unthrift,** un'thrift, *n.* Thriftlessness; a thriftless man; a prodigal.
**Unthrifty,** un-thrift'i, *a.* Not thrifty; prodigal; lavish; wasteful.
**Untidy,** un-tī'di, *a.* Not tidy; slovenly.
**Untie,** un-tī', *vt.* (untying, untied). To loosen, as a knot; to undo; to unfasten.
**Until,** un-til', *prep.* or *conj.* Till; to; till the time or point that.
**Untimely,** un-tīm'li, *a.* Not timely; ill timed; inopportune.—*adv.* Unseasonably.
**Untiring,** un-tīr'ing, *a.* Not tiring; unwearied.
**Untitled,** un-tī'tld, *a.* Not titled; having no title of rank or dignity.
**Unto,** un'tö, *prep.* To.
**Untold,** un-tōld', *a.* Not told; not revealed or counted.
**Untouched,** un-tucht', *a.* Not touched; uninjured; not affected.
**Untoward,** un-tō'wėrd, *a.* Not toward; froward; awkward; vexatious.
**Untraceable,** un-trās'a-bl, *a.* Incapable of being traced.
**Untractable,** un-trak'ta-bl, *a.* Not tractable; refractory.
**Untraveled,** un-tra'veld, *a.* Not trodden by passengers; not having traveled.
**Untried,** un-trīd', *a.* Not tried; not attempted; not yet experienced; not determined in law.
**Untrod, Untrodden,** un-trod', un-trod'n, *a.* Not having been trod; unfrequented.
**Untroubled,** un-tru'bld, *a.* Not troubled; not agitated or ruffled; not turbid.
**Untrue,** un-trö', *a.* Not true; false.
**Untrustworthy,** un-trust'wėr-THi, *a.* Not worthy of being trusted; unreliable.
**Untruth,** un-tröth', *n.* Falsehood.
**Untruthful,** un-tröth'ful, *a.* Not truthful.
**Unused,** un-ūzd', *a.* Not used; not put to use; not accustomed.
**Unusual,** un-ū'zhū-al, *a.* Not usual; rare.
**Unutterable,** un-ut'ėr-a-bl, *a.* That cannot be uttered; inexpressible.
**Unvarnished,** un-vär'nisht, *a.* Not varnished; not artfully embellished; plain.
**Unveil,** un-vāl', *vt.* To remove a veil from; to uncover; to disclose to view.
**Unwarranted,** un-wo'rant-ed, *a.* Not warranted; unjustifiable; not certain.
**Unwary,** un-wā'ri, *a.* Not cautious.
**Unwashed,** un-wosht', *a.* Not washed; dirty.
**Unwavering,** un-wā'vėr-ing, *a.* Not wavering;

U

steady; steadfast.
**Unwearied,** un-wē'rid, *a.* Not wearied or tired; indefatigable; assiduous.
**Unwed,** un-wed', *a.* Unmarried.
**Unwelcome,** un-wel'kum, *a.* Not welcome; not pleasing or grateful.
**Unwholesome,** un-hōl'sum, *a.* Not wholesome; insalubrious; causing sickness.
**Unwieldy,** un-wēl'di, *n.* Movable with difficulty; unmanageable.
**Unwilling,** un-wil'ing, *a.* Not willing; loath; disinclined; reluctant.
**Unwind,** un-wīnd', *vt.* To wind off.—*vi.* To admit of being unwound.
**Unwisdom,** un-wiz'dom, *n.* Want of wisdom; foolishness; folly.
**Unwise,** un-wīz', *a.* Not wise; injudicious.
**Unwitting,** un-wit'ing, *a.* Not knowing; unconscious; unaware.
**Unwomanly,** un-wu'man-li, *a.* Not womanly; unbecoming a woman.
**Unworldly,** un-wėrld'li, *a.* Not worldly; not influenced by worldly or sordid motives.
**Unworn,** un-wōrn', *a.* Not worn.
**Unworthy,** un-wėr'THi, *a.* Not worthy; worthless; base; not becoming or suitable.
**Unwrap,** un-rap', *vt.* To open or undo, as what is wrapped up.
**Unwritten,** un-rit'n, *a.* Not written; blank; understood though not expressed.
**Unyielding,** un-yēld'ing, *a.* Stiff; firm; obstinate.
**Up,** up, *adv.* Aloft; in or to a higher position; upright; above the horizon; out of bed; in a state of sedition; from the country to the metropolis; quite; to or at an end.—*prep.* To a higher place or point on; towards the interior of.
**Upas,** ū'pas, *n.* A poisonous tree of Java and the neighboring islands.
**Upbraid,** up-brād', *vt.* To reproach; to chide; to taunt.
**Upbringing,** up'bring-ing, *n.* Training; education; breeding.
**Upcast,** up'kast, *a.* Cast up.—*n.* The ventilating shaft of a mine.
**Upheaval,** up-hēv'al, *n.* Act of upheaving; lifting of a portion of the earth's crust.
**Upheave,** up-hēv', *vt.* To heave or lift up from beneath.
**Uphill,** up'hil, *a.* Leading or going up a rising ground; difficult; fatiguing.
**Uphold,** up-hōld', *vt.* To hold up; to keep erect; to support; to sustain.
**Upholder,** up-hōld'ėr, *n.* A supporter; defender.
**Upholster,** up-hōl'stėr, *vt.* To furnish with upholstery.
**Upholsterer,** up-hōl'stėr-ėr, *n.* One who furnishes houses with curtains, carpets, etc.
**Upholstery,** up-hōl'stė-ri, *n.* The articles supplied by upholsterers.
**Upkeep,** up'kēp, *n.* Maintenance.
**Upland,** up'land, *n.* Higher grounds; hillslopes.—*a.* Pertaining to uplands.
**Uplander,** up'land-ėr, *n.* An inhabitant of the uplands.
**Uplift,** up-lift', *vt.* To lift up.—*n.* up'lift. A raising; rise; exaltation.
**Up-line,** up'līn, *n.* A line of railway which leads to a main terminus from the provinces.
**Upmost,** up'mōst, *a.* Highest; uppermost.
**Upon,** up-on', *prep.* Up and on; resting on; on.
**Upper,** up'ėr, *a.* Higher in place or rank.—*n.* The upper part of a shoe.
**Upper-hand,** up'ėr-hand, *n.* Superiority.
**Uppermost,** up'ėr-mōst, *a. superl.* Highest in place, rank, or power.
**Uppish,** up'ish, *a.* Assuming lofty airs; arrogant.
**Upraise,** up-rāz', *vt.* To raise or lift up.
**Uprear,** up-rēr', *vt.* To rear up; to raise.
**Upright,** up'rīt, *a.* Straight up; erect; honest; just.—*n.* A vertical piece.
**Uprise,** up-rīz', *vi.* To rise up; to slope upwards.—*n.* up'rīz. Rise; elevation.
**Uprising,** up-rīz'ing, *n.* Rise; ascent or acclivity; a riot; a rebellion.
**Uproar,** up'rōr, *n.* A great tumult; violent disturbance; bustle and clamor.
**Uproarious,** up-rō'ri-us, *a.* Making an uproar or tumult; tumultuous.
**Uproot,** up-röt', *vt.* To tear up by the roots.
**Upset,** up-set', *vt.* To overturn; to discompose completely.—*n.* up'set. Act of upsetting.—*a.* Fixed; determined.—**Upset price,** the price at which anything is exposed to sale by auction.
**Upshot,** up'shot, *n.* Final issue; end.
**Upside,** up'sīd, *n.* The upper side.
**Upstairs,** up'stārz, *a.* or *adv.* Ascending the stairs; in or pertaining to the upper part of a house.
**Upstart,** up-stärt', *vi.* To start up suddenly.—*n.* up'stärt. A parvenu.
**Upthrow,** up-thrō', *vt.* To throw up.—*n.* up'thrō. A lifting up of a portion of the earth's crust; an upheaval.
**Upward,** up'wėrd, *a.* Directed to a higher place; ascending.—*adv.* Upwards.
**Upwards,** up'wėrdz, *adv.* To a higher place; above (with *of*).
**Uranium,** ū-rā'ni-um, *n.* A rare metal, colored like nickel or iron.
**Uranography,** ū-ra-nog'ra-fi, *n.* The description of the heavenly bodies, etc.
**Uranus,** ū'ra-nus, *n.* The most distant of all the planets except Neptune and Pluto.
**Urban,** ėr'ban, *a.* Of or belonging to a city or town.
**Urbane,** ėr-bān', *a.* Courteous; polite.
**Urbanity,** ėr-ban'i-ti, *n.* Politeness; courtesy.
**Urchin,** ėr'chin, *n.* A hedgehog; a sea-urchin; a child or small boy.
**Ureter,** ū-rē'tėr, *n.* The duct that conveys the urine from the kidney to the bladder.
**Urethra,** ū-rē'thra, *n.* The duct by which the urine is discharged from the bladder.
**Urge,** ėrj, *vt.* (urging, urged). To press to do something; to incite; to solicit; to insist on.—*vi.* To press forward.
**Urgency,** ėrj'en-si, *n.* Pressure of difficulty or necessity; importunity.
**Urgent,** ėrj'ent, *a.* That urges; pressing; importunate; vehement; eager.
**Urgently,** ėrj'ent-li, *adv.* In an urgent manner; with importunity; vehemently.
**Uric,** ū'rik, *a.* Pertaining to or obtained from urine.
**Urinal,** ū-rin-al, *n.* A convenience for persons requiring to pass urine.
**Urinary,** ū'ri-na-ri, *a.* Pertaining to urine.
**Urinate,** ū'ri-nāt, *vi.* To discharge urine.
**Urine,** ū'rin, *n.* An animal fluid secreted by the kidneys and stored in the bladder before being discharged.
**Urn,** ėrn, *n.* A vase swelling in the middle; a vessel for water.
**Ursine,** ėr'sīn, *a.* Pertaining to or resembling a bear.
**Urticate,** ėr'ti-kāt, *vt.* and *i.* To sting like a nettle.
**Urtication,** ėr-ti-kā'shon, *n.* The stinging of nettles; whipping with nettles to restore feeling.
**Us,** us, *pron.* The objective case of *we.*
**Usable,** ūz'a-bl, *a.* That may be used.
**Usage,** ūz'āj, *n.* Act or manner of using; treatment; practice; custom; use.
**Use,** ūs, *n.* Act of employing anything; employment; utility; need; practice; wont.—*vt.* ūz (using, used). To put to use; to employ; to accustom; to treat.—*vi.* To be accustomed.
**Useful,** ūs'ful, *a.* Valuable for use; serviceable; beneficial; advantageous.
**Useless,** ūs'les, *a.* Worthless; unavailing.
**User,** ūz'ėr, *n.* One who uses.
**Usher,** ush'ėr, *n.* A door-keeper; an officer who introduces strangers, etc.; a subordinate teacher.—*vt.* To give entrance to; to introduce.
**Usual,** ū'zhū-al, *a.* Customary; common; frequent; ordinary; general.
**Usually,** ū'zhū-al-li, *adv.* Customarily.

**Usufruct,** ū'zū-frukt, *n.* In *law*, the use and enjoyment of lands or tenements.
**Usurer,** ū'zhūr-ėr, *n.* One who takes exorbitant interest.
**Usurious,** ū-zhū'ri-us, *a.* Pertaining to usury.
**Usurp,** ū-zėrp', *vt.* To seize and hold without right; to appropriate wrongfully.
**Usurpation,** ū-zėrp-ā'zhon, *n.* Act of usurping; illegal seizure or possession.
**Usurper,** ū-zėrp'ėr, *n.* One who seizes power or possessions without right.
**Usury,** ū'zhū-ri, *n.* Extortionate interest for money; practice of taking exorbitant interest.
**Utensil,** ū-ten'sil, *n.* That which is used; an instrument; implement.
**Uterine,** ū'tėr-īn, *a.* Pertaining to the uterus.
**Uterus,** ū'tėr-us, *n.*; pl. **-ri.** The womb.
**Utilitarian,** ū-til'i-tā''ri-an, *a.* Pertaining to utility or utilitarianism.—*n.* One who holds the doctrine of utilitarianism.
**Utilitarianism,** ū-til'i-tā''ri-an-izm, *n.* The doctrine that utility is the sole standard of moral conduct; the doctrine of the greatest happiness of the greatest number.
**Utility,** ū-til'i-ti, *n.* State or quality of being useful; usefulness; a useful thing.
**Utilize,** ū'til-īz, *vt.* (utilizing, utilized). To render useful; to put to use; to make use of.
**Utmost,** ut'mōst, *a.* Being farthest out; uttermost; extreme.—*n.* The greatest power, degree, or effort.
**Utopia,** ū-tō'pi-a, *n.* A place or state of ideal perfection.
**Utopian,** ū-tō'pi-an, *a.* Ideally perfect.—*n.* An ardent but unpractical reformer.
**Utricle,** ū'tri-kl, *n.* A little sac, cell, or reservoir.
**Utter,** ut'ėr, *a.* Complete; total; absolute.—*vt.* To give vent to; to put into circulation; to declare; to speak.
**Utterable,** ut'ėr-a-bl, *a.* That may be uttered, pronounced, or expressed.
**Utterance,** ut'ėr-ans, *n.* Act of uttering; pronunciation; words uttered.
**Utterly,** ut'ėr-li, *adv.* Totally; absolutely.
**Uttermost,** ut'ėr-mōst, *a.* Being in the furthest or greatest degree; extreme.—*n.* The utmost power or degree.
**Uvula,** ū'vū-la, *n.* The small fleshy body which hangs over the root of the tongue.

# V

**Vacancy,** vā'kan-si, *n.* Empty space; vacuity; an interval of leisure; listlessness; a place or office not occupied.
**Vacant,** vā'kant, *a.* Empty; void; unoccupied; leisure; thoughtless; inane.
**Vacate,** va-kāt', *vt.* (vacating, vacated). To make vacant; to leave unoccupied; to annul.
**Vacation,** va-kā'shon, *n.* Act of vacating; intermission; recess; holidays.
**Vaccinate,** vak'si-nāt, *vt.* To inoculate with the cow-pox, in order to ward off small-pox.
**Vaccination,** vak-si-nā'shon, *n.* The act, art, or practice of vaccinating.
**Vaccine,** vak'sīn, *a.* Pertaining to cows or to cow-pox.
**Vacillate,** va'sil-lāt, *vi.* To sway; to waver; to fluctuate.
**Vacillating,** va'sil-lāt-ing, *p.a.* Inclined to vacillate; apt to waver; inconstant.
**Vacillation,** va-sil-lā'shon, *n.* A wavering; fluctuation of mind; unsteadiness.
**Vacuity,** va-kū'i-ti, *n.* Emptiness; vacancy; inanity; vacant expression.
**Vacuous,** va'kū-us, *a.* Empty; void; vacant; inane; inexpressive.
**Vacuum,** va'kū-um, *n.* Empty space; a void; an enclosed space void of air.—**Vacuum cleaner,** *n.* An apparatus used for removing dust from carpets, etc., by means of suction.
**Vagabond,** va'ga-bond, *a.* Wandering to and fro; pertaining to a vagrant.—*n.* A wanderer; a vagrant; a rascal.
**Vagary,** va-gā'ri, *n.* A wild freak; a whim.
**Vagina,** va-jī'na, *n.* A sheath; the canal in females leading inwards to the uterus.
**Vaginal,** va'ji-nal, *a.* Pertaining to or like a sheath; pertaining to the vagina.
**Vagrancy,** vā'gran-si, *n.* State or life of a vagrant.
**Vagrant,** vā'grant, *a.* Wandering; unsettled.—*n.* A wanderer; a vagabond; a sturdy beggar; a tramp.
**Vague,** vāg, *a.* Indefinite; hazy; uncertain.
**Vaguely,** vāg'li, *adv.* In a vague manner.
**Vail,** vāl, *vi.* To avail: *poetical*.—*n.* A tip or gratuity to a domestic; veil.
**Vain,** vān, *a.* Without real value; empty; worthless; ineffectual; light-minded; conceited.—**In vain,** to no purpose.
**Vainly,** vān'li, *adv.* In a vain manner; without effect; with vanity; idly.
**Vair,** vār, *n.* In *heraldry*, one of the furs represented by little shield-shaped pieces.
**Valance, Valence,** val'ans, val'ens, *n.* The drapery hanging round a bed, couch, etc.
**Vale,** vāl, *n.* A valley.
**Valediction,** va-lē-dik'shon, *n.* A farewell.
**Valedictory,** va-lē-dik'to-ri, *a.* Bidding farewell; pertaining to a leave-taking.
**Valence, Valency,** vā'lens, vā'len-si, *n.* The force which determines with how many atoms of an element an atom of another element will combine chemically.
**Valentine,** va'len-tīn, *n.* A sweetheart selected or got by lot on St. *Valentine's* Day, 14th February; a missive of an amatory or satirical kind, sent on this day.
**Valet,** va'let or va'lā, *n.* A man-servant.—*vt.* To attend on a gentleman's person.
**Valiant,** val'yant, *a.* Brave; courageous; intrepid; heroic.
**Valiantly,** val'yant-li, *adv.* Bravely; heroically.
**Valid,** va'lid, *a.* Well based or grounded; sound; just; good or sufficient in law.
**Validate,** va'lid-āt, *vt.* To make valid.
**Validity,** va-lid'i-ti, *n.* Justness; soundness; legal sufficiency.
**Valise,** va-lēs', *n.* A small traveling-bag.
**Valley,** val'i, *n.* A low tract of land between hills; a river-basin.
**Valor,** va'lor, *n.* Bravery; courage; intrepidity; prowess in war.
**Valorous,** va'lor-us, *a.* Brave; valiant.
**Valuable,** va'lū-a-bl, *a.* Of great worth; precious; worthy.—*n.* A thing of value; choice article of personal property; usually in *pl.*
**Valuation,** va-lū-ā'shon, *n.* Act or art of valuing; appraisement; estimated worth.
**Valuator,** va'lū-āt-or, *n.* One who sets a value; an appraiser.
**Value,** va'lū, *n.* Worth; utility; importance; import; precise signification.—*vt.* (valuing, valued). To rate at a certain price; to estimate; to esteem; to prize; to regard.
**Valueless,** va'lū-les, *a.* Worthless.
**Valve,** valv, *n.* A leaf of a folding door; a lid for an orifice, opening only one way and regulating the passage of fluid or air; a separable portion of the shell of a mollusk.
**Valvular,** valv'ū-lėr, *a.* Containing valves; having the character of or acting as a valve.
**Vamp,** vamp, *n.* The upper leather of a boot; a piece added for appearance sake.—*vt.* To repair; to furbish up; to patch.
**Vampire,** vam'pīr, *n.* A dead person believed to have an unnatural life so as to be able to leave the grave at night and suck the blood of living persons; an extortioner; a blood-sucker; a vampire-bat.
**Vampire-bat,** vam'pīr-bat, *n.* A blood-sucking bat of South America with long sharp teeth.
**Van,** van, *n.* The front of an army or fleet; foremost portion; a winnowing fan; a covered vehi-

cle for goods.
**Vanadium,** va-nā'di-um, *n.* A silvery brittle metal.
**Vandal,** van'dal, *n.* One who willfully or ignorantly destroys any work of art or the like.
**Vandalism,** van'dal-izm, *n.* Conduct of a vandal; hostility to art or literature.
**Vane,** vān, *n.* A weathercock; the broad part of a feather on either side of the shaft; blade of a windmill, etc.
**Vanguard,** van'gärd, *n.* The troops who march in the van of an army.
**Vanilla,** va-nil'a, *n.* A tropical orchid; a fragrant substance obtained from it, used for seasoning.
**Vanish,** va'nish, *vi.* To disappear; to pass away.
**Vanity,** va'ni-ti, *n.* Quality or state of being vain; worthlessness; vain pursuit; desire of indiscriminate admiration; conceit; a trifle.
**Vanquish,** vang'kwish, *vt.* To conquer; to overcome; to confute.
**Vanquisher,** vang'kwish-ėr, *n.* A conqueror.
**Vantage,** van'tāj, *n.* Advantage; vantage-ground; in lawn tennis, being in a position to win the game by winning the next point.
**Vapid,** va'pid, *a.* Spiritless; flat; dull.
**Vapidity,** va-pid'i-ti, *n.* Flatness; dullness; want of life or spirit.
**Vaporize,** vā-por-īz, *vt.* To convert into vapor.—*vi.* To pass off in vapor.
**Vaporous,** vā'por-us, *a.* Like vapor; full of vapors; unreal; whimsical.
**Vapor,** vā'por, *n.* An exhalation or fume; visible moisture or steam; hazy matter; a vain imagination; *pl.* a nervous hysterical affection; the blues.—*vi.* To boast; to bully.
**Variability,** vā-ri-a-bil'i-ti, *n.* State of being variable; liability to vary.
**Variable,** vā'ri-a-bl, *a.* That may vary or alter; changeable; fickle; unsteady.
**Variance,** vā'ri-ans, *n.* Variation; disagreement; dissension; discord.
**Variant,** vā'ri-ant, *a.* Varying; different.—*n.* Something the same, but with another form; a different version.
**Variation,** vā-ri-ā'shon, *n.* Act or process of varying; alteration; amount or rate of change; inflection; deviation.
**Varicose,** va'ri-kōs, *a.* Exhibiting a morbid enlargement or dilation, as the veins.
**Varied,** vā'rid, *p.a.* Characterized by variety; diverse; various.
**Variegate,** vā'ri-e-gāt, *vt.* (variegating, variegated). To diversify in appearance; to mark with different colors.
**Variegation,** vā'ri-e-gā''shon, *n.* State of being variegated; diversity of colors.
**Variety,** va-rī'e-ti, *n.* State or quality of being varied or various; diversity; a varied assortment; a sort; a kind.
**Variorum,** vā-ri-ō'rum, *a.* Applied to an edition of a work containing the notes of various editors.
**Various,** vā'ri-us, *a.* Different; several; changeable; uncertain; diverse.
**Varlet,** vär'let, *n.* A footman; a rascal.
**Varnish,** vär'nish, *n.* A clear solution of resinous matter, for coating surfaces and giving a gloss; outside show; gloss.—*vt.* To lay varnish on; to gloss over.
**Vary,** vā'ri, *vt.* (varying, varied). To change; to diversify.—*vi.* To alter; to change; to differ; to swerve; to disagree.
**Vascular,** vas'kū-lėr, *a.* Pertaining to those vessels that have to do with conveying blood, chyle, etc.
**Vasculum,** vas'kū-lum, *n.*; pl. **-la.** A botanist's case for carrying specimens.
**Vase,** väz, *n.* A vessel of some size and of various materials and forms, generally ornamental rather than useful.
**Vase-painting,** väz-pānt'ing, *n.* The embellishment of vases with pigments.
**Vassal,** vas'al, *n.* A feudal tenant; a subject; a retainer; a bondman.
**Vassalage,** vas'al-āj, *n.* Servitude; dependence.
**Vast,** väst, *a.* Of great extent; immense; mighty; great in importance or degree.—*n.* A boundless space; immensity.
**Vastly,** väst'li, *adv.* Very greatly; exceedingly.
**Vat,** vat, *n.* A large vessel for holding liquors; a tun; a wooden tank or cistern.—*vt.* (vatting, vatted). To put in a vat.
**Vatican,** vat'i-kan, *n.* The palace of the Pope at Rome; the papal power or government.
**Vaticinate,** vā-tis'i-nāt, *vi.* and *t.* To prophesy; to foretell.
**Vaudeville,** vōd'vēl, *n.* A light, gay song; a ballad; a dramatic piece with light or comic songs.
**Vault,** valt, *n.* An arched roof; a subterranean chamber; a cellar; a leap; a leap with the hand resting on something.—*vt.* To arch.—*vi.* To leap; to bound.
**Vaulted,** valt'ed, *p.a.* Arched; concave.
**Vaulting,** valt'ing, *n.* Vaulted work; vaults collectively.—*p.a.* Leaping.
**Vaunt,** vant, *vi.* To brag; to exult.—*vt.* To boast of; to make a vain display of.—*n.* A boast.
**Vauntingly,** vant'ing-li, *adv.* With vaunting; boastfully.
**Vaward,** vä'wėrd, *n.* The van or vanguard.—*a.* Being in the van or front.
**Veal,** vēl, *n.* The flesh of a calf.
**V-bomb,** vē'bom, *n.* A self-propelled bomb or rocket employed by the Germans in 1944 and 1945.
**Veda,** vā'dä or vē'da, *n.* The body of ancient Sanskrithymns on which Brahmanism is based.
**Vedette, Vidette,** vē-det', *n.* A mounted sentry; a picket or outpost.
**Veer,** vēr, *vi.* To change direction; to turn round.—*vt.* To direct to a different course.
**Vegetable,** ve'je-ta-bl, *a.* Belonging to or like plants.—*n.* A plant; a plant for culinary purposes.
**Vegetal,** ve'je-tal, *a.* Vegetable; pertaining to the vital phenomena common to plants and animals.
**Vegetarian,** ve-je-tā'ri-an, *n.* One who abstains from animal food and lives on vegetables.
**Vegetate,** ve'je-tāt, *vi.* (vegetating, vegetated). To grow as plants; to live a monotonous, useless life; to have a mere existence.
**Vegetation,** ve-je-tā'shon, *n.* The process of growing, as plants; plants in general.
**Vegetative,** ve'je-tāt-iv, *a.* Having the power of growing, as plants; having the power to produce growth in plants.
**Vehemence,** vē'he-mens, *n.* Ardor; violence; force; impetuosity; fury.
**Vehement,** vē'he-ment, *a.* Very eager or urgent; ardent; violent; furious.
**Vehemently,** vē'he-ment-li, *adv.* With vehemence; passionately; violently.
**Vehicle,** vē'hi-kl, *n.* Any kind of carriage moving on land; conveyance; medium.
**Vehicular, Vehiculary,** vē-hik'ū-lėr, vē-hik'ū-lėr-i, *a.* Pertaining to a vehicle.
**Veil,** vāl, *n.* A screen; an article of dress shading the face; a covering or disguise; the soft palate.—*vt.* To cover with a veil; to envelop; to disguise.
**Vein,** vān, *n.* A blood-vessel which returns impure blood to the heart and lungs; a blood-vessel; a sap tube in leaves; a crack in a rock, filled up by substances different from the rock; a streak; disposition; mood.—*vt.* To fill or variegate with veins.
**Veining,** vān'ing, *n.* Arrangement of veins; a streaked appearance as if from veins.
**Veiny,** vān'i, *a.* Full of veins.
**Veldt, Veld,** felt, *n.* A term in S. Africa for open unenclosed country.
**Velleity,** vel-lē'i-ti, *n.* Volition in the weakest form; mere inclination.
**Vellicate,** vel'i-kāt, *vt.* To twitch.
**Vellum,** vel'um, *n.* A fine parchment made of

calf's skin.
**Velocipede,** vē-los'i-pēd, *n.* A light vehicle propelled by the rider; bicycle, etc.
**Velocity,** vē-los'i-ti, *n.* Rate of motion; speed; rapidity.
**Velvet,** vel'vet, *n.* A rich silk stuff with a close, fine, soft pile.—*a.* Made of or like velvet.
**Velveteen,** vel-vet-ēn', *n.* A cloth made of cotton in imitation of velvet; cotton velvet.
**Venal,** vē'nal, *a.* Ready to accept a bribe; mercenary.
**Venality,** vē-nal'i-ti, *n.* State of being venal; prostitution of talents or services.
**Venation,** vē-nā'shon, *n.* The manner in which the veins of leaves are arranged.
**Vend,** vend, *vt.* To sell.
**Vendace,** ven'dās, *n.* A fish of the salmon family found only in a few British lakes and in Sweden.
**Vender,** ven'dėr, *n.* One who vends; a seller.
**Vendetta,** ven-det'ta, *n.* A blood-feud; the practice of the nearest of kin executing vengeance on a murderer.
**Vendible,** vend'i-bl, *a.* That may be vended or sold; saleable; marketable.
**Vendor,** ven'dor, *n.* A vender; a seller.
**Veneer,** ve-nēr', *n.* A thin facing of fine wood glued on a less valuable sort; any similar coating; fair outward show.—*vt.* To overlay with veneer; to put a fine superficial show on.
**Venerable,** ve'nė-ra-bl, *a.* Worthy of veneration; deserving respect from age, character, or associations.
**Venerate,** ve'nė-rāt, *vt.* (venerating, venerated). To reverence; to revere; to regard as sacred.
**Veneration,** ve-nė-rā'shon, *n.* The highest degree of respect and reverence; respect mingled with some degree of awe.
**Venereal,** ve-nē'rē-al, *a.* Pertaining to sexual intercourse.
**Venery,** ve'nė-ri, *n.* Hunting; sexual intercourse.
**Venesection,** ve-nē-sek'shon, *n.* Blood-letting; phlebotomy.
**Venetian,** vē-nē'shi-an, *a.* Belonging to Venice; denoting a window blind made of thin slats of wood.
**Vengeance,** venj'ans, *n.* Punishment in return for an injury; penal retribution.
**Vengeful,** venj'ful, *a.* Full of vengeance; vindictive; retributive; revengeful.
**Venial,** vē'ni-al, *a.* That may be pardoned or forgiven; excusable.
**Venison,** ven'zn or ven'i-zn, *n.* The flesh of deer.
**Venom,** ve'nom, *n.* Poison; spite; malice; malignity; virulency.
**Venomous,** ve'nom-us, *a.* Full of venom; poisonous; noxious; spiteful.
**Venose,** vē'nōz, *n.* Having numerous branched veins, as leaves.
**Venous,** vē'nus, *a.* Pertaining to a vein; contained in veins, as blood; venose.
**Vent,** vent, *n.* A small opening; flue or funnel; an outlet; the anus; utterance; expression; sale; market.—*vt.* To let out; to publish.
**Ventage,** vent'āj, *n.* A small hole, as of a musical instrument.
**Venter,** ven'tėr, *n.* The abdomen; in *law,* the uterus.
**Ventilate,** ven'ti-lāt, *vt.* (ventilating, ventilated). To winnow; to expose to the air; to supply with fresh air; to let be freely discussed.
**Ventilation,** ven-ti-lā'shon, *n.* Act of ventilating; replacement of vitiated air by fresh air, a bringing forward for discussion.
**Ventilator,** ven'ti-lāt-ėr, *n.* A contrivance for keeping the air fresh in any close space.
**Ventral,** ven'tral, *a.* Belonging to the belly; abdominal.
**Ventricle,** ven'tri-kl, *n.* A small cavity in an animal body; either of two cavities of the heart which propel the blood into the arteries.
**Ventricular,** ven-trik'ū-lėr, *a.* Pertaining to a ventricle; distended in the middle.
**Ventriloquism, Ventriloquy,** ven-tri'lo-kwizm, ven-tri'lo-kwi, *n.* The art of uttering sounds so that the voice appears to come not from the actual speaker.
**Ventriloquist,** ven-tri'lo-kwist, *n.* One who practices or is skilled in ventriloquism.
**Ventriloquize,** ven-tri'lo-kwīz, *vi.* To practice ventriloquism.
**Venture,** ven'tūr, *n.* An undertaking which involves hazard or danger; a commercial speculation; thing put to hazard; chance.—*vi.* (venturing, ventured). To make a venture; to dare.—*vt.* To risk.
**Venturesome,** ven'tūr-sum, *a.* Apt or inclined to venture; bold; hazardous.
**Venturous,** ven'tūr-us, *a.* Venturesome.
**Venue,** ven'ū, *n.* A thrust; the place where an action is laid or the trial of a cause takes place.
**Venus,** vē'nus, *n.* The Roman goddess of beauty and love; a planet.
**Veracious,** ve-rā'shus, *a.* Observant of truth; truthful; true.
**Veracity,** ve-ras'i-ti, *n.* Truthfulness; truth; that which is true.
**Veranda, Verandah,** ve-ran'da, *n.* An open portico or light gallery along the front of a building.
**Veratrin, Veratrine,** ve-rā'trin, *n.* A poisonous drug obtained from plants of the hellebore genus.
**Verb,** vėrb, *n.* The part of speech which signifies to be, to do, or to suffer.
**Verbal,** vėrb'al, *a.* Relating to words; spoken; literal; derived from a verb.—*n.* A noun derived from a verb.
**Verbalism,** vėrb'al-izm, *n.* Something expressed orally.
**Verbalist,** vėrb'al-ist, *n.* One who deals in words merely; a minute critic of words.
**Verbalize,** vėrb'al-īz, *vt.* To convert into or employ as a verb.
**Verbally,** vėrb'al-li, *adv.* In a verbal manner; by words uttered; word for word.
**Verbatim,** vėr-bā'tim, *adv.* Word for word; in the same words.
**Verbena,** vėr-bē'na, *n.* A genus of plants (and type of an order), some of which are cultivated for the beauty of their flowers.
**Verbiage,** vėr'bi-āj, *n.* Verbosity.
**Verbose,** vėr-bōs', *a.* Wordy; prolix.
**Verbosity,** vėr-bos'i-ti, *n.* Superabundance of words; wordiness; prolixity.
**Verdancy,** vėr'dan-si, *n.* Greenness; inexperience.
**Verdant,** vėr'dant, *a.* Green with herbage or foliage; simple and inexperienced.
**Verd-antique,** vėrd-an-tēk', *n.* A stone consisting of an aggregate of serpentine and lighter-colored stone having a greenish color; a green porphyry used as marble.
**Verderer, Verderor,** vėr'dėr-ėr, vėr'dėr-or, *n.* An official having charge of the trees, etc., in a royal forest.
**Verdict,** vėr'dikt, *n.* The answer of a jury; decision in general; opinion.
**Verdigris, Verdegris,** vėr'di-gris, vėr'de-gris, *n.* The rust of copper; a substance obtained by exposing copper to the air in contact with acetic acid.
**Verditer,** vėr'di-tėr, *n.* A blue or bluish-green pigment.
**Verdure,** vėr'dūr, *n.* Greenness; freshness of vegetation; green vegetation.
**Verdurous,** vėr'dūr-us, *a.* Verdant.
**Verge,** vėrj, *n.* A rod of office; a mace; a wand; brink; margin; compass; scope.—*vi.* (verging, verged). To incline; to tend; to border.
**Verger,** vėrj'ėr, *n.* A mace-bearer; an official who takes care of the interior of a church.
**Veridical,** ve-rid'ik-al, *a.* Veracious.
**Verifiable,** ve'ri-fī-a-bl, *a.* That may be verified.
**Verification,** ve'ri-fi-kā''shon, *n.* Act of verifying; confirmation.
**Verify,** ve'ri-fī, *vt.* (verifying, verified). To prove to

be true; to confirm; to fulfil.
**Verily,** ve'ri-li, *adv*. In truth; really; truly.
**Verisimilar,** ve-ri-si'mi-lėr, *a*. Having the appearance of truth; probable; likely.
**Verisimilitude,** ve'ri-si-mil''i-tūd, *n*. The appearance of truth; probability; likelihood.
**Veritable,** ve'ri-ta-bl, *a*. True; real; actual.
**Verity,** ve'ri-ti, *n*. Truth; reality; a truth.
**Verjuice,** vėr'jūs, *n*. An acid liquor expressed from fruit; sourness of temper, manner, etc.
**Vermeil,** vėr'mil, *n*. Vermilion; silver or bronze gilt.
**Vermicelli,** vėr-mi-chel'li, *n*. An Italian article of food made of flour, etc., in the form of long threads.
**Vermicide,** vėr'mi-sīd, *n*. A substance which destroys intestinal worms.
**Vermicular,** vėr-mik'ū-lėr, *a*. Pertaining to worms; like a worm; vermiculated.
**Vermiculate,** vėr-mik'ū-lāt, *vt*. To ornament so as to suggest worms or a worm-eaten surface.—*a*. Worm-like in appearance.
**Vermiculation,** vėr-mik'ū-lā''shon, *n*. A worm-like motion or ornamentation.
**Vermiculose, Vermiculous,** vėr-mik'ū-lōs, vėr-mik'ū-lus, *a*. Containing worms or grubs; like worms.
**Vermifuge,** vėr'mi-fūj, *n*. A medicine that expels intestinal worms.
**Vermilion,** vėr-mil'yon, *n*. Cinnabar or red sulphide of mercury; a beautiful red color.—*vt*. To color with vermilion.
**Vermin,** vėr'min, *n*. *sing*. and *pl*. A term for all sorts of small noxious mammals and insects.
**Verminate,** vėr'min-āt, *vi*. To breed vermin.
**Verminous,** vėr'min-us, *a*. Pertaining to vermin; like vermin; caused by vermin; infested by vermin.
**Vermivorous,** vėr-miv'o-rus, *a*. Devouring worms; feeding on worms.
**Vernacular,** vėr-nak'ū-lėr, *a*. Belonging to the country of one's birth or the everyday idiom of a place.—*n*. The native idiom of a place.
**Vernacularism,** vėr-nak'ū-lėr-izm, *n*. A vernacular idiom.
**Vernal,** vėr'nal, *a*. Pertaining to the spring; belonging to youth.
**Vernation,** vėr-nā'shon, *n*. The arrangement of the young leaves within the bud.
**Vernier,** vėr'ni-ėr, *n*. A small sliding scale, parallel to the fixed scale of a barometer, or other graduated instrument, and subdividing the divisions into more minute parts.
**Veronica,** ve-ron'i-ka, *n*. A genus of plants including the various species of speedwell.
**Verrucose, Verrucous,** ver'ū-kōs, ver'ū-kus, *a*. Warty.
**Versant,** vėr'sant, *n*. Part of a country sloping in one direction; slope of surface.
**Versatile,** vėrs'a-til, *a*. Readily turning; inconstant; having many accomplishments.
**Versatility,** vėrs-a-til'i-ti, *n*. Aptness to change; facility in taking up various intellectual pursuits.
**Verse,** vėrs, *n*. A line of poetry; meter; poetry; versification; a stanza; a short division of any composition.
**Versed,** vėrst, *a*. Conversant; practiced; skilled; with *in*.
**Versicle,** vėrs'i-kl, *n*. A little verse; a short verse in a church service, spoken or chanted.
**Versification,** vėrs'i-fi-kā''shon, *n*. Act or art of versifying; metrical composition.
**Versifier,** vėrs'i-fī-ėr, *n*. One who versifies; one who makes verses.
**Versify,** vėrs'i-fī, *vi*. (versifying, versified). To make verses.—*vt*. To form or turn into verse.
**Version,** vėr'shon, *n*. Act of translating; a translation; rendering; account.
**Verso,** vėr'sō, *n*. A left-hand page.
**Verst,** verst, *n*. A Russian measure of length, about two-thirds of an English mile.
**Versus,** vėr'sus, *prep*. Against.
**Vert,** vėrt, *n*. In *law*, growing wood, or the right to cut it; the heraldic name of green.
**Vertebra,** vėr'te-bra, *n*.; pl. **-rae.** One of the bones of the spine; *pl*. the spine.
**Vertebral,** bėr'te-bral, *a*. Pertaining to the vertebrae; consisting of vertebrae.
**Vertebrata,** vėr-te-brā'ta, *n.pl*. The highest division of animals, consisting of those which possess a backbone.
**Vertebrate,** vėr'te-brāt, *a*. Having a backbone.—*n*. One of the Vertebrata.
**Vertex,** vėr'teks, *n*.; pl. **-texes** or **-tices.** The highest point; top; apex; zenith.
**Vertical,** vėr'ti-kal, *a*. Pertaining to the vertex; directly over the head; perpendicular to the horizon; upright.
**Vertiginous,** vėr-ti'jin-us, *a*. Giddy or dizzy; affected with vertigo.
**Vertigo,** vėr-tī'gō or vėr'ti-gō, *n*. Dizziness or swimming of the head; giddiness.
**Vertu,** vėr'tu, *n*. Excellence in objects of art or curiosity; such objects collectively.
**Vervain,** vėr'vān, *n*. A plant once held in repute for its medicinal virtues.
**Verve,** verv, *n*. Spirit; energy.
**Very,** ve'ri, *a*. True; real; actual.—*adv*. Truly; in a great or high degree.
**Vesical,** ve'si-kal, *a*. Pertaining to the bladder.
**Vesicant,** ve'si-kant, *n*. A blistering application.
**Vesicate,** ve'si-kāt, *vt*. To blister.
**Vesication,** ve-si-kā'shon, *n*. The process of raising blisters on the skin.
**Vesicle,** ve'si-kl, *n*. A small bladder-like structure or cavity; a little sac or cyst.
**Vesicular,** ve-sik'ū-lėr, *a*. Pertaining to or consisting of or full of vesicles.
**Vesiculose, Vesiculous,** ve-sik'ū-lōs, ve-sik'ū-los, *a*. Vesicular.
**Vesper,** ves'pėr, *n*. The evening; the evening-star; *pl*. evening worship or service.—*a*. Relating to the evening or to vespers.
**Vespiary,** ves'pi-a-ri, *n*. A nest of wasps, hornets, etc.
**Vessel,** ves'el, *n*. A hollow utensil for holding liquids or solids; a ship; a tube or canal for blood or sap; a person.
**Vest,** vest, *n*. Undergarment for the upper part of the body; a waistcoat.—*vt*. To clothe; to endow; to invest.—*vi*. To descend to; to devolve; to take effect, as a title or right.
**Vesta,** ves'ta, *n*. The Roman goddess of hearth and home; a wax match.
**Vestal,** ves'tal, *a*. Pertaining to Vesta; virgin; chaste.—*n*. A virgin consecrated to Vesta; a woman of spotless chastity.
**Vested,** vest'ed, *a*. Clothed or habited; robed; well settled or established.
**Vestibule,** ves'ti-būl, *n*. A passage or hall inside the outer door of a house.
**Vestige,** ves'tij, *n*. Footprint; mark or trace of something; mark or remnant left.
**Vestment,** vest'ment, *n*. A garment; a special article of dress worn by clergymen when officiating.
**Vestry,** ves'tri, *n*. A room connected with a church, where the ecclesiastical vestments are kept; a body of ratepayers elected for the local government of a parish.
**Vesture,** ves'tūr, *n*. Dress; apparel; clothing.
**Vesuvian,** ve-sū'vi-an, *n*. A kind of match for lighting cigars, etc.
**Vetch,** vech, *n*. The popular name of plants allied to the bean, cultivated for fodder.
**Vetchy,** vech'i, *a*. Consisting of or abounding with vetches.
**Veteran,** ve'te-ran, *a*. Having been long exercised; long experienced in war.—*n*. An old soldier; a man of great experience.
**Veterinary,** ve'te-ri-na-ri, *a*. Pertaining to the art of healing the diseases of domestic animals.
**Veto,** vē'tō, *n*. The power or right of forbidding; any authoritative prohibition or refusal.—*vt*. (vetoing, vetoed). To forbid; to interdict.

**Vex,** veks, *vt.* To irritate; to torment; to annoy; to distress; to make sorrowful.
**Vexation,** veks-ā'shon, *n.* Irritation; annoyance; grief; affliction.
**Vexatious,** veks-ā'shus, *a.* Irritating; annoying; distressing; troublesome.
**Vexed,** vekst, *a.* Annoyed; troubled; much disputed or contested.
**Vexillum,** vek-sil'um, *n.*; pl. **-illa.** An ancient Roman military standard; an ecclesiastical banner.
**Via,** vī'a, *prep.* By way of.
**Viable,** vī'a-bl, *a.* Capable of living, applied to a new-born child.
**Viaduct,** vī'a-dukt, *n.* A long bridge for carrying a road or railway over a valley.
**Vial,** vī'al, *n.* A phial; a small glass bottle.
**Viand,** vī'and, *n.* Meat dressed; food; victuals: used chiefly in *pl.*
**Viaticum,** vī-at'i-kum, *n.* Provisions for a journey; the communion given to a dying person.
**Vibrant,** vī'brant, *a.* Vibrating; tremulous.
**Vibrate,** vī'brāt, *vi.* (vibrating, vibrated). To swing; to quiver; to be unstable.—*vt.* To wave to and fro; to cause to quiver.
**Vibration,** vī-brā'shon, *n.* Act of vibrating; a swing; a quivering motion.
**Vibratory,** vī'bra-to-ri, *a.* Causing to vibrate; vibrating.
**Vicar,** vi'kėr, *n.* A substitute in office; deputy; the priest of a parish in England who receives the smaller tithes, or a salary.
**Vicarage,** vi'kėr-āj, *n.* The benefice of a vicar; residence of a vicar.
**Vicarial,** vī-kā'ri-al, *a.* Pertaining to a vicar; delegated; vicarious.
**Vicariate,** vī-kā'ri-āt, *n.* Office of a vicar.—*a.* Vicarial.
**Vicarious,** vī-kā'ri-us, *a.* Pertaining to a substitute; deputed, substituted or suffered for or in the place of another.
**Vice,** vīs, *n.* A blemish; fault; moral failing; profligacy; a fault or bad trick in a horse; an iron instrument which holds fast anything worked upon; a prefix denoting position second in rank.
**Vice,** vī'sē, *prep.* In place of.
**Vice-admiral,** vīs-ad'mi-ral, *n.* A naval officer, the next in rank to an Admiral.
**Vice-chancellor,** vīs-chan'sel-lor, *n.* An officer acting as deputy for a chancellor.
**Vice-consul,** vīs-kon'sul, *n.* One who acts for a consul; a consul of subordinate rank.
**Vicegerent,** vīs-jē'rent, *n.* One who acts in the place of a superior; a substitute.
**Vicenary,** vis'e-na-ri, *a.* Belonging to or consisting of twenty.
**Vicennial,** vi-sen'ni-al, *a.* Lasting twenty years.
**Vice-president,** vīs-pre'zi-dent, *n.* An office-bearer next in rank below a president.
**Vice-regal,** vīs-rē'gal, *a.* Pertaining to a viceroy or viceroyalty.
**Viceroy,** vīs'roi, *n.* One who governs in place of a king or queen.
**Viceroyalty, Viceroyship,** vīs-roi'al-ti, vīs'roi-ship, *n.* The dignity, office, or jurisdiction of a viceroy.
**Vicinage,** vi'sin-āj, *n.* Neighborhood.
**Vicinity,** vi-sin'i-ti, *n.* Neighborhood; proximity.
**Vicious,** vi'shus, *a.* Characterized by vice; faulty; depraved; immoral; spiteful.
**Vicissitude,** vi-sis'i-tūd, *n.* Change or alternation; one of the ups and downs of life.
**Victim,** vik'tim, *n.* A living being sacrificed; a person or thing destroyed; a person who suffers; a gull.
**Victimize,** vik'tim-īz, *vt.* To make a victim of; to cheat; to deceive.
**Victor,** vik'tor, *n.* One who conquers; one who proves the winner.—*a.* Victorious.
**Victoria,** vik-tō'ri-a, *n.* A four-wheeled carriage, with a collapsible top, seated for two persons.—**Victoria Cross,** a British decoration granted for valor in battle.
**Victorious,** vik-tō'ri-us, *a.* Having gained victory; conquering; indicating victory.
**Victory,** vik'to-ri, *n.* Conquest; a gaining of the superiority in any contest.
**Victress,** vik'tres, *n.* A female that conquers.
**Victual,** vit'l, *n.* Food provided; provisions: generally in *pl.*—*vt.* (victualling, victualled). To supply with victuals or stores.
**Victualler,** vit'l-ėr, *n.* One who furnishes victuals; a tavern-keeper; a ship carrying provisions for other ships.
**Vicugna, Vicuña,** vi-kLon'ya, *n.* A South American animal yielding a wool used for delicate fabrics.
**Vide,** vī'dē, *vt.* See; refer to.
**Videlicet,** vī-del'i-set, *adv.* To wit; that is; namely: usually abbreviated to *viz.*
**Vidette,** vi-det', *n. See* VEDETTE.
**Vidimus,** vī'di-mus or vid', *n.* An examination, as of accounts; an abstract of contents.
**Viduity,** vi-dū'i-ti, *n.* Widowhood.
**Vie,** vī, *vi.* (vying, vied). To contend.
**Viennese,** vi-en-ēz', *n. sing.* and *pl.* A native of Vienna; natives of Vienna.
**View,** vū, *n.* A look; inspection; consideration; range of vision; power of perception; sight; scene; pictorial sketch; judgment; intention.—*vt.* To see; to survey; to consider.—*vi.* To look.
**Viewer,** vū'ėr, *n.* One who views, surveys, or examines; an inspector; an overseer.
**Viewless,** vū'les, *a.* Invisible.
**Viewy,** vū'i, *a.* Holding peculiar views; given to doctrinaire notions.
**Vigesimal,** vī-jes'i-mal, *a.* Twentieth.
**Vigil,** vi'jil, *n.* Act of keeping awake; a devotional watching; the eve or day preceding a church festival.
**Vigilance,** vi'ji-lans, *n.* Watchfulness.
**Vigilant,** vi'ji-lant, *a.* Watchful; circumspect; wary; on the outlook; alert.
**Vignette,** vin-yet' or vi-net', *n.* Flowers, head and tail pieces, etc., in books; a wood-cut without a definite border; a small photographic portrait; a small attractive picture.
**Vigorous,** vi'gor-us, *a.* Full of vigor; strong; lusty; powerful; energetic.
**Vigor,** vi'gor, *n.* Active force or strength; physical force; strength of mind.
**Viking,** vīk'ing, *n.* An ancient Scandinavian rover or sea-robber.
**Vile,** vīl, *a.* Morally worthless; despicable; depraved; bad.
**Vilely,** vīl'li, *adv.* Basely; meanly.
**Vilification,** vi'li-fi-kā''shon, *n.* The act of vilifying or defaming.
**Vilify,** vi'li-fī, *vt.* (vilifying, vilified). To defame; to traduce; to slander.
**Vilipend,** vi'li-pend, *vt.* To slander.
**Vill,** vil, *n.* A hamlet; a district of a parish.
**Villa,** vil'a, *n.* A country seat; a suburban house.
**Village,** vil'āj, *n.* A collection of houses, smaller than a town and larger than a hamlet.
**Villager,** vil'āj-ėr, *n.* An inhabitant of a village.
**Villain,** vil'an or vil'ān, *n.* A feudal serf; a peasant; a knave or scoundrel.
**Villainous,** vil'an-us, *a.* Base; vile; wicked; depraved; mean.
**Villainy,** vil'an-i, *n.* Depravity; wickedness; a crime.
**Villein,** vil'en, *n.* A feudal serf.
**Villeinage, Villenage,** vil'en-āj, *n.* The feudal tenure of lands and tenements by a villein; tenure at the will of a lord.
**Villi,** vil'lī, *n.pl.* Fine small fibers; soft hairs on certain fruits, flowers, etc.
**Villosity,** vil-los'i-ti, *n.* The state of being villous.
**Villous, Villose,** vil'lus, vil'lōs, *a.* Having a velvety, shaggy, or woolly surface.
**Vim,** vim, *n.* Vigor; energy.
**Vinaceous,** vī-nā'shus, *a.* Belonging to wine or grapes; of the color of wine.
**Vinaigrette,** vin-ā-gret, *n.* A small box, with per-

forations on the top, for holding smelling-salts.
**Vinaigrous,** vin'äg-rus, *a.* Sour like vinegar; crabbed; peevish.
**Vincible,** vin'si-bl, *a.* Conquerable.
**Vinculum,** ving'kū-lum, *n.*; pl. **-ia.** A bond of union; a bond or tie.
**Vindicate,** vin'di-kāt, *vt.* (vindicating, vindicated). To prove to be just or valid; to maintain the rights of; to defend; to justify.
**Vindication,** vin-di-kā'shon, *n.* Act of vindicating; a defense or justification.
**Vindicative,** vin'di-kāt-iv, *a.* Tending to vindicate.
**Vindicator,** vin'di-kāt-or, *n.* One who vindicates; one who defends.
**Vindicatory,** vin'di-ka-to-ri, *n.* Tending to vindicate; justificatory; punitory.
**Vindictive,** vin-dik'tiv, *a.* Revengeful.
**Vine,** vīn, *n.* A climbing plant producing grapes; the slender stem of any climbing plant.
**Vinegar,** vi'nē-gėr, *n.* Diluted and impure acetic acid, obtained from wine, beer, etc.; sourness of temper.
**Vinegarette,** vi'nē-gėr-et, *n.* A vinaigrette.
**Vinery,** vīn'ė-ri, *n.* A hot-house for vines.
**Vineyard,** vin'yärd, *n.* A plantation of vines producing grapes.
**Vinous, Vinose,** vīn'us, vīn'ōs, *a.* Having the qualities of wine; pertaining to wine.
**Vintage,** vint'āj, *n.* The gathering of the grape crop; the crop itself; the wine produced by the grapes of one season.
**Vintager,** vint'āj-ėr, *n.* One that gathers the vintage.
**Vintner,** vint'nėr, *n.* One who deals in wine; a wine-seller; a licensed victualler.
**Vintnery,** vint'nėr-i, *n.* The trade or occupation of a vintner.
**Viol,** vī'ol, *n.* An ancient musical instrument like the violin.
**Viola,** vī'ō-la, *n.* The violet, an extensive genus of plants.
**Viola,** vē-o'la, *n.* The tenor violin.
**Violable,** vī'ō-la-bl, *a.* That may be violated.
**Violate,** vī'ō-lāt, *vt.* (violating, violated). To injure; to outrage; to desecrate; to profane; to transgress.
**Violation,** vī-ō-lā'shon, *n.* Infringement; transgression; desecration; rape.
**Violator,** vī'ō-lāt-or, *n.* One who violates.
**Violence,** vī'ō-lens, *n.* Quality of being violent; vehemence; outrage; injury.
**Violent,** vī'ō-lent, *a.* Impetuous; furious; outrageous; fierce; severe.
**Violently,** vī'ō-lent-li, *adv.* With violence.
**Violet,** vī'ō-let, *n.* A genus of plants that includes the pansy, etc.; a plant having a bluish purple flower with a delicious smell; a rich bluish-purple.—*a.* Of a bluish-purple color.
**Violin,** vī-ō-lin', *n.* A musical instrument with four strings, played with a bow; a fiddle.
**Violinist,** vī-ō-lin'ist, *n.* A player on the violin.
**Violist,** vī'ō-list, *n.* A player on the viola.
**Violoncellist,** vī'ō-lon-sel''ist, *n.* A player on the violoncello.
**Violoncello,** vī'ō-lon-sel''lō or vē'ō-lon-chel''lō, *n.* A large and powerful bow instrument of the violin kind.
**Viper,** vī'pėr, *n.* A venomous serpent.
**Viperine,** vī'pėr-īn, *a.* Pertaining to a viper or to vipers.
**Viperish,** vī'pėr-ish, *a.* Inclining to the character of a viper.
**Viperous,** vī'pėr-us, *a.* Having the qualities of a viper.
**Virago,** vi-rā'gō, *n.* A man-like woman; a termagant.
**Virelay,** vi're-lā, *n.* A short poem, in short lines, with a refrain, and only two rhymes.
**Virescent,** vī-res'sent, *a.* Slightly green; beginning to be green.
**Virgilian,** vėr-jil'i-an, *a.* Pertaining to Virgil, or resembling his style.
**Virgin,** vėr'jin, *n.* A woman who has had no carnal knowledge of man; a maid; a sign of the zodiac.—*a.* Chaste; maidenly; unsullied.
**Virginal,** vėr'jin-al, *a.* Maidenly; virgin.—*n.* An ancient keyed musical instrument resembling the spinet.
**Virginity,** vėr-jin'i-ti, *n.* Maidenhood; perfect chastity.
**Virgo,** vėr'gō, *n.* The Virgin in the zodiac.
**Viridity,** vi-rid'i-ti, *n.* Greenness; verdure.
**Virile,** vi'rīl or vi'ril, *a.* Pertaining to a man; masculine; manly; strong.
**Virility,** vi-ril'i-ti, *n.* Manhood; the power of procreation; masculine action or vigor.
**Virose,** vī'rōs, *a.* Poisonous; emitting a fetid odor.
**Virtu,** vir-tö', *n.* *See* VERTU.
**Virtual,** vėr'tū-al, *a.* Being in essence or effect, not in name or fact.
**Virtually,** vėr'tū-al-li, *adv.* In efficacy or effect, though not really.
**Virtue,** vėr'tū, *n.* Moral goodness; rectitude; morality; chastity; merit; efficacy.
**Virtuoso,** vėr-tū-ō'sō, *n.*; pl. **-osos** or **-osi.** A man skilled in the fine arts, or antiquities, curiosities, etc.
**Virtuous,** vėr'tū-us, *a.* Marked by virtue; morally good; pure or chaste.
**Virtuously,** vėr'tū-us-li, *adv.* In a virtuous manner.
**Virulence,** vi'rū-lens, *n.* Acrimony; malignity; rancour.
**Virulent,** vi'rū-lent, *a.* Very poisonous or poxious; bitter in enmity; malignant.
**Virulently,** vi'rū-lent-li, *adv.* In a virulent manner; with malignant activity.
**Virus,** vī'rus, *n.* Contagious poisonous matter; extreme acrimony; malignity.
**Vis,** vis, *n.* Force; power; energy.
**Visage,** vi'zāj, *n.* The face or countenance.
**Visaged,** vi'zājd, *a.* Having a visage of this or that sort.
**Vis-à-vis,** vē-zä-vē, *adv.* Face to face.—*n.* One placed face to face with another; a light carriage for two persons sitting face to face.
**Viscera,** vis'e-ra, *n.pl.* The entrails.
**Visceral,** vis'e-ral, *a.* Pertaining to the viscera.
**Viscid,** vis'id, *a.* Sticky or adhesive; glutinous; tenacious.
**Viscidity,** vis-id'i-ti, *n.* Glutinousness.
**Viscosity,** vis-kos'i-ti, *n.* Viscidity.
**Viscount,** vī'kount, *n.* A nobleman of rank between an earl and baron.
**Viscountess,** vī'kount-es, *n.* The wife of a viscount.
**Viscous,** vis'kus, *a.* Glutinous; viscid.
**Visé,** vē-zā, *n.* An indorsation upon a passport denoting that it has been examined and found correct.
**Visibility,** vi-zi-bil'i-ti, *n.* State or quality of being visible.
**Visible,** vi'zi-bl, *a.* Perceivable by the eye; apparent; open; conspicuous.
**Visibly,** vi'zi-bli, *adv.* In a visible manner; manifestly; conspicuously; obviously.
**Vision,** vi'zhon, *n.* Act of seeing; sight; that which is seen; an apparition; a fanciful view.
**Visionary,** vi'zhon-a-ri, *a.* Pertaining to visions; imaginative; imaginary; not real.—*n.* One who is visionary; one who upholds impracticable schemes.
**Visit,** vi'zit, *vt.* To go or come to see; to view officially; to afflict.—*vi.* To practice going to see others; to make calls.—*n.* Act of visiting; a call.
**Visitant,** vi'zit-ant, *n.* A visitor.
**Visitation,** vi-zit-ā'shon, *n.* Act of visiting; a formal or official visit; special dispensation of divine favor or retribution.
**Visitor,** vi'zit-or, *n.* One who visits; a caller; an inspector.
**Visiting,** vi'zit-ing, *a.* Pertaining to visits; authorized to visit and inspect.—*n.* The act or practice of paying visits.
**Visiting-card,** vi'zit-ing-kärd, *n.* A small card bearing one's name, etc., to be left in paying

visits.
**Visor, Vizor,** vī'zor, *n.* The movable faceguard of a helmet; a mask.
**Vista,** vis'ta, *n.* A view through an avenue; trees, etc., that form the avenue; an extended view.
**Visual,** vi'zhū-al, *a.* Pertaining to sight or vision; used in seeing.
**Vital,** vī'tal, *a.* Pertaining to life; necessary to life; indispensable; essential.
**Vitalism,** vī'tal-izm, *a.* The doctrine that ascribes all organic functions to a vital principle distinct from chemical and other physical forces.
**Vitality,** vī-tal'i-ti, *n.* State or quality of having life; principle of life; animation.
**Vitalize,** vī'tal-īz, *vt.* To give life to; to furnish with the vital principle.
**Vitally,** vī'tal-li, *adv.* Essentially.
**Vitals,** vī'talz, *n.pl.* Parts essential to life.
**Vitamin,** vī'ta-min, *n.* One of several substances necessary for animal nutrition, and occurring in minute quantities in natural foods; numerous types have been distinguished, and designated by the letters of the alphabet.
**Vitiate,** vi'shi-āt, *vt.* (vitiating, vitiated). To make faulty; to impair; to corrupt; to invalidate.
**Vitiation,** vi-shi-ā'shon, *n.* Act of vitiating; depravation.
**Viticulture,** vit'i-kul-tūr, *n.* The culture of the vine.
**Vitreous,** vit'rē-us, *a.* Glassy; pertaining to glass; resembling glass.
**Vitrescence,** vi-tres'ens, *n.* Quality of being vitrescent; glassiness.
**Vitrescent,** vi-tres'ent, *a.* Tending to become glass or glassy.
**Vitric,** vit'rik, *a.* Vitreous.
**Vitrifaction, Vitrification,** vit-ri-fak'shon, vit'ri-fi-kā''shon, *n.* The act, process, or operation of converting into glass by heat.
**Vitrifacture,** vit-ri-fak'tūr, *n.* The manufacture of glass.
**Vitrify,** vit'ri-fī, *vt.* To convert into glass by heat.—*vi.* To become glass.
**Vitriol,** vit'ri-ol, *n.* Sulphuric acid or one of its compounds.
**Vitriolic,** vit'ri-ol'ik, *a.* Pertaining to vitriol; like vitriol; very biting or sarcastic.
**Vitriolize,** vit'ri-ol-īz, *vt.* To convert into vitriol; to treat with vitriol.
**Vitta,** vit'a, *n.*; pl. **-ae.** A head-band, fillet, or garland; a receptacle of oil in the fruits of umbelliferous plants.
**Vituline,** vit'ū-līn, *a.* Belonging to a calf, or to veal.
**Vituperate,** vī-tū'pe-rāt, *vt.* To abuse; to censure offensively; to rate.
**Vituperation,** vī-tū'pe-rā''shon, *n.* Act of vituperating; abuse; abusive language.
**Vituperative,** vī-tū'pe-rāt-iv, *a.* Containing vituperation; abusive; railing.
**Vivacious,** vī-vā'shus or vi-, *a.* Lively; brisk; sprightly; tenacious of life.
**Vivacity,** vī-vas'i-ti or vi-, *n.* Animation; spirit; liveliness; briskness.
**Vivandière,** vē-väng-di-ār, *n.* A female sutler.
**Vivarium,** vī-vā'ri-um, *n.*; pl. **-ia.** A place for keeping animals in their natural state.
**Viva voce,** vī'va vō'sē, *adv.* By word of mouth; orally: sometimes used adjectively.
**Vivid,** vi'vid, *a.* Bright, clear, or lively; forcible; striking; realistic.
**Vividly,** vi'vid-li, *adv.* In a vivid manner; with life; with striking truth.
**Vivify,** vi'vi-fī, *vt.* (vivifying, vivified). To make alive; to endure with life; to animate.
**Viviparous,** vī-vip'a-rus, *a.* Producing young in a living state.
**Vivisection,** vi-vi-sek'shon, *n.* Act of experimenting on a living animal.
**Vivisector,** vi'vi-sek-tėr, *n.* One who practices vivisection.
**Vixen,** viks'en, *n.* A she-fox; a snappish, bitter woman; a termagant.
**Vixenish,** viks'en-ish, *a.* Pertaining to a vixen.
**Vizier,** vi-zēr' or vi'zi-ėr, *n.* A high political officer in Turkey, etc.
**Vizor,** *n.* *See* VISOR.
**Vley, Vlei,** vlī or flī, *n.* In S. Africa, a swampy pool that dried up at certain seasons.
**Vocable,** vō'ka-bl, *n.* A word; a term.
**Vocabulary,** vō-kab'ū-la-ri, *n.* A list of words arranged alphabetically and explained briefly; range of expression.
**Vocal,** vō'kal, *a.* Pertaining to the voice; uttered by the voice; endowed with a voice; having a vowel character.
**Vocalic,** vō-kal'ik, *a.* Pertaining to vowel sound; having many vowels.
**Vocalist,** vō'kal-ist, *n.* A vocal musician; a public singer.
**Vocalize,** vō'kal-īz, *vt.* To form into voice; to make vocal.
**Vocally,** vō'kal-li, *adv.* With voice; with an audible sound; in words.
**Vocation,** vō-kā'shon, *n.* A calling; employment; profession; business.
**Vocative,** vo'ka-tiv, *a.* Relating to calling by name.—*n.* The vocative case.
**Vociferate,** vō-sif'ė-rāt, *vi.* and *t.* (vociferating; vociferated). To cry out with vehemence, to exclaim.
**Vociferation,** vō-sif'ė-rā''shon, *n.* A violent outcry; clamor.
**Vociferous,** vō-sif'ėr-us, *a.* Making a loud outcry; clamorous; noisy.
**Vodka,** vod'ka, *n.* An intoxicating spirit distilled from rye, much used in Russia.
**Vogue,** vōg, *n.* Temporary mode or fashion.
**Voice,** vois, *n.* The sound uttered by the mouth; articulate human utterance; state of vocal organs; speech; sound emitted; right of expressing an opinion; vote; a form of verb inflection.—*vt.* (voicing, voiced). To utter or express; to declare.
**Voiceless,** vois'les, *a.* Having no voice or vote.
**Void,** void, *a.* Empty; devoid; ineffectual; null.—*n.* An empty space.—*vt.* To make vacant; to quit; to nullify; to emit; to evacuate from the bowels.
**Voidance,** void'ans, *n.* Act of voiding; ejection from a benefice; vacancy.
**Volant,** vō'land, *a.* Flying; nimble; rapid.
**Volapuk,** vō'la-puk, *n.* An artificial language devised in 1879 and intended as an international medium of communication.
**Volatile,** vo-la-til, *a.* Readily diffusible in the atmosphere; flighty; airy; fickle; fugitive.
**Volatility,** vo-la-til'i-ti, *n.* Quality of being volatile; capability of evaporating; flightiness; fickleness; levity.
**Volatilize,** vo'la-til-īz, *vt.* To cause to exhale or evaporate.—*vi.* To become vaporous.
**Volcanic,** vol-kan'ik, *a.* Pertaining to volcanoes; produced by a volcano.
**Volcanism,** vol'kan-izm, *n.* Volcanic character or phenomena.
**Volcanist,** vol'kan-ist, *n.* One versed in volcanoes.
**Volcano,** vol-kā'no, *n.*; pl. **-oes.** A mountain emitting clouds of vapor, gases, showers of ashes, lava, etc.
**Vole,** vōl, *n.* A rodent animal resembling a rat or mouse; a deal at cards that draws all the tricks.
**Volition,** vō-li'shon, *n.* Act or power of willing; will.
**Volley,** vol'i, *n.* A discharge of a number of missile weapons, as small-arms; emission of many things at once.—*vt.* and *i.* To discharge or be discharged in a volley; to sound like a volley; to strike and return a ball (in lawn-tennis, etc.) before it touches the ground.
**Volt,** vōlt, *n.* A sudden movement in fencing to avoid a thrust; the unit of electromotive force.
**Voltage,** vōlt'āj, *n.* Electromotive force as measured in volts.
**Voltaic,** vol-tā'ik, *a.* Pertaining to voltaism.

**Voltaism**, vol'ta-izm, *n*. Electricity produced by chemical action; galvanism.
**Volubility**, vo-lū'bil'i-ti, *n*. Great readiness or fluency of speech.
**Voluble**, vo'lū-bl, *a*. Rolling round or revolving; glib in speech; over fluent.
**Volubly**, vo'lū-bli, *adv*. In a voluble or fluent manner; with volubility.
**Volume**, vo'lūm, *n*. Something rolled up; a book; a coil; a convolution; mass or bulk; quantity or strength.
**Volumeter**, vo-lū'me-tėr, *n*. An instrument for measuring the volumes of gases.
**Volumetric**, vo-lū-met'rik, *a*. Pertaining to the measurement of volumes or substances.
**Voluminous**, vō-lū'min-us, *a*. Bulky; being in many volumes; having written much; copious.
**Voluntarily**, vo'lun-ta-ri-li, *adv*. Spontaneously; of one's own free will.
**Voluntary**, vo'lun-ta-ri, *a*. Willing; free to act; spontaneous; regulated by the will.—*n*. A volunteer; a supporter of voluntaryism; an organ solo during a church service.
**Voluntaryism**, vo'lun-ta-ri-izm, *n*. The principle of supporting anything, especially religion, entirely by voluntary effort.
**Volunteer**, vo-lun-tēr', *n*. A person who enters into military or other service of his own free will.—*a*. Pertaining to volunteers.—*vt*. To offer or bestow voluntarily.—*vi*. To enter into any service voluntarily.
**Voluptuary**, vō-lup'tū-a-ri, *n*. One addicted to luxury; a sensualist.
**Voluptuous**, vō-lup'tū-us, *a*. Pertaining to sensual pleasure; luxurious.
**Voluptuously**, vō-lup'tū-us-li, *adv*. Luxuriously; sensually.
**Volute**, vō-lūt', *n*. A spiral scroll characteristic of Ionic and Corinthian capitals.
**Voluted**, vō-lūt'ed, *a*. Having a volute or volutes.
**Vomit**, vo'mit, *vi*. To eject the contents of the stomach by the mouth.—*vt*. To eject from the stomach; to belch forth.—*n*. Matter ejected from the stomach; an emetic.
**Vomitory**, vo'mi-to-ri, *a*. Causing vomiting.—*n*. An emetic.
**Voodoo**, vö-dö, *n*. A person among the American negroes who professes to be a sorcerer; sorcery; an evil spirit.
**Voracious**, vō-rā'shus, *a*. Eating or swallowing greedily; ravenous; rapacious.
**voracity**, vō-ras'i-ti, *n*. Quality of being voracious; greediness of appetite.
**Vortex**, vor'teks, *n*.; pl. **-tices** or **-texes.** A whirling motion in any fluid; a whirlpool or a whirlwind; an eddy.
**Vortical**, vor'tik-al, *a*. Pertaining to a vortex; whirling.
**Vorticose**, **Vortiginal**, vor'ti-kōs, vor-ti'jin-al, *a*. Vortical.
**Votaress**, vō'ta-res, *n*. A female votary.
**Votary**, vō'ta-ri, *n*. One who is bound by a vow; one devoted to some particular service, state of life, etc.
**Vote**, vōt, *n*. Act or power of expressing opinion or choice; a suffrage; thing conferred by vote; result of voting; votes collectively.—*vi*. (voting, voted). To give a vote.—*vt*. To choose or grant by vote.
**Voter**, vōt'ėr, *n*. One who vites; an elector.
**Votive**, vōt'iv, *a*. Pertaining to a vow; promised or given, in consequence of a vow.
**Vouch**, vouch, *vt*. To attest; to affirm; to answer for.—*vi*. To bear witness; to stand surety.
**Voucher**, vouch'ėr, *n*. One who vouches; a paper which serves to vouch the truth of accounts, or to confirm facts of any kind; a written evidence of the payment of money.
**Vouchsafe**, vouch-sāf', *vt*. (vouchsafing, vouchsafed). To condescend to grant; to concede.—*vi*. To deign.
**Voussoir**, vös'war, *n*. One of the wedgeshaped shones of an arch.
**Vow**, vou, *n*. A solemn promise; an oath; promise of fidelity.—*vt*. To promise solemnly; to dedicate, as to a divine power.—*vi*. To make vows.
**Vowel**, vou'el, *n*. A sound produced by opening the mouth and giving utterance to voice; the letter which represents such a sound.—*a*. Pertaining to a vowel; vocal.
**Voyage**, voi'āj, *n*. A journey by water to a distance.—*vi*. (voyaging, voyaged). To pass by water.
**Voyager**, voi'āj-ėr, *n*. One who voyages.
**Vulcanic**, vul-kan'ik, *a*. Volcanic.
**Vulcanism**, vul'kan-izm, *n*. The phenomena of volcanoes, hot springs, etc.
**Vulcanite**, vul'kan-īt, *n*. A superior vulcanized india-rubber; ebonite.
**Vulcanize**, vul'kan-īz, *vt*. To harden (india-rubber) by combining with sulphur, etc.
**Vulgar**, vul'gėr, *a*. Pertaining to the common people; vernacular; common; coarse.—**The vulgar**, the common people.
**Vulgarian**, vul-gā'ri-an, *n*. A vulgar person.
**Vulgarism**, vul'gėr-izm, *n*. A vulgar phrase or expression; vulgarity.
**Vulgarity**, vul-ga'ri-ti, *n*. Coarseness; an act of low manners.
**Vulgarize**, vul'gėr-īz, *vt*. To make vulgar.
**Vulgarly**, vul'gėr-li, *adv*. In a vulgar manner; commonly; coarsely.
**Vulgate**, vul'gāt, *n*. The Latin version of the Scriptures used by the R. Catholic church.
**Vulnerable**, vul'nėr-a-bl, *a*. That may be wounded; liable to injury.
**Vulnerary**, vul'nėr-a-ri, *a*. Useful in healing wounds.—*n*. A plant useful in the cure of wounds.
**Vulpine**, vul'pīn, *a*. Pertaining to the fox; cunning; crafty.
**Vulpinite**, vul'pin-īt, *n*. A variety of gypsum employed for small statues, etc.
**Vulture**, vul'tūr, *n*. A bird of prey which lives chiefly on carrion.
**Vulturine**, vul'tūr-īn, *a*. Belonging to or resembling the vulture.

# W

**Wabble**, wob'l, *vi*. (wabbling, wabbled). To vacillate; to wobble.—*n*. A rocking motion.
**Wacke**, wak'ē, *n*. A soft and earthy volcanic rock usually containing crystals.
**Wad**, wod, *n*. A soft mass of fibrous material, used for stuffing; material for stopping the charge in a gun.—*vt*. (wadding, wadded). To furnish with a wad or wadding.
**Wad**, **Wadd**, wod, *n*. An earthy ore of manganese.
**Wadding**, wod'ing, *n*. A soft fibrous stuff used for stuffing articles of dress; wad.
**Waddle**, wod'l, *vi*. (waddling, waddled). To walk with a rolling gait; to toddle.
**Waddy**, wad'i, *n*. A wooden club used by the Australian aborigines.
**Wade**, wād, *vi*. (wading, waded). To walk through a substance that hinders the lower limbs, as water; to move or pass with labor.—*vt*. To ford.
**Wader**, wād'ėr, *n*. One that wades; a wading or grallatorial bird.
**Wafer**, wā'fėr, *n*. A thin cake, as of bread; a thin disc of paste for fastening letters.—*vt*. To seal with a wafer.
**Waft**, wäft, *vt*. To impel through water or air.—*vi*. To sail or float.—*n*. A sweep, as with the arm; a breath of wind.
**Waftage**, wäft'āj, *n*. The act of wafting; state of being wafted.
**Wag**, wag, *vt*. and *i*. (wagging, wagged). To swing or sway; to wave; to nod.—*n*. A wit; a joker.
**Wage**, wāj, *vt*. (waging, waged). To carry on; to engage in, as in a contest.—*n*. Payment for work done; hire; recompense; generally in *pl*.

**Wager,** wā'jėr, *n.* A bet; stake laid; subject on which bets are laid.—*vt.* and *i.* To bet; to stake.
**Waggery,** wag'ė-ri, *n.* Merriment; jocular talk; pleasantry.
**Waggish,** wag'ish, *a.* Roguish in merriment; jocular; sportive.
**Waggle,** wag'l, *vi.* and *t.* (waggling, waggled). To sway; to wag with short movements.
**Wagon, Waggon,** wag'on, *n.* A four-wheeled vehicle for heavy loads.
**Wagonage,** wag'on-āj, *n.* Money paid for conveyance by wagon.
**Wagoner,** wag'on-ėr, *n.* One who drives a wagon.
**Wagonette,** wag-on-et', *n.* A four-wheeled pleasure vehicle with longitudinal seats.
**Wagtail,** wag'tāl, *n.* A small bird of several species; a pert person.
**Waif,** wāf, *n.* A stray article; a neglected, homeless wretch.
**Wail,** wāl, *vt.* To lament; to bewail.—*vi.* To weep.—*n.* A mournful cry or sound.
**Wailing,** wāl'ing, *n.* Loud weeping.
**Wain,** wān, *n.* A wagon.
**Wainscot,** wān'skot, *n.* The timber-work that lines the walls of a room.—*vt.* (wainscoting, wainscotted). To line with wainscot.
**Wainscotting,** wān'skot-ing, *n.* Wainscot, or the material used for it.
**Waist,** wāst, *n.* That part of the human body between the ribs and hips; middle part of a ship.
**Waistband,** wāst'band, *n.* The band of trousers, etc., which encompasses the waist.
**Waistcoat,** wāst'kōt, *n.* A short sleeveless garment worn under the coat; a vest.
**Wait,** wāt, *vi.* To stay in expectation; to continue in patience; to attend; to serve at table.—*vt.* To await.—*n.* Act of waiting; ambush; a musician who promenades in the night about Christmas time.
**Waiter,** wāt'ėr, *n.* One who waits; a male attendant; a small tray or salver.
**Waiting-maid, Waiting-woman,** wāt'ing-mād, wāt'ing-wu-man, *n.* A maid-servant who attends a lady.
**Waitress,** wāt'res, *n.* A female waiter.
**Waive,** wāv, *vt.* (waiving, waived). To relinquish; to forgo.
**Wake,** wāk, *vi.* (waking, woke or waked). To be awake; to awake; to become active.—*vt.* To rouse from sleep; to arouse.—*n.* The feast of the dedication of a parish church; a vigil; the watching of a dead body prior to burial; track left by a ship; track in general.
**Wakeful,** wāk'ful, *a.* Keeping awake in bed; indisposed to sleep; watchful; vigilant.
**Waken,** wāk'n, *vi.* To wake.—*vt.* To rouse from sleep; to rouse into action.
**Waldenses,** wal-den'sēz, *n.* A sect of reforming Christians in Northern Italy.
**Wale,** wāl, *n.* A streak produced by a whip on an animal's skin; a weal; a plank along a ship a little above the water-line.—*vt.* (waling, waled). To mark with wales.
**Walk,** wak, *vi.* To advance by steps without running; to go about; to behave.—*vt.* To pass over or through on foot; to lead about.—*n.* A short excursion on foot; gait; an avenue, promenade, etc.; sphere; way of living; tract of ground for grazing.
**Walker,** wak'ėr, *n.* One who walks; a pedestrian.
**Walking,** wak'ing, *n.* The act or practice of moving on the feet without running; practice of taking walks; pedestrianism.
**Walking-stick,** wak'ing-stik, *n.* A staff or stick carried in the hand in walking.
**Wall,** wal, *n.* A structure of stone or brick, enclosing a space, forming a division, supporting a weight, etc.; side of a building or room; means of protection.—*vt.* To enclose with a wall; to defend by walls.
**Wallet,** wol'et, *n.* A bag or knapsack; pack; bundle.
**Wall-eye,** wal'ī, *n.* An eye in which the iris is of a very light grey or whitish color.
**Wall-flower,** wal'flou-ėr, *n.* A plant with fragrant yellowish flowers.
**Walloon,** wo-lön', *n.* A people inhabiting part of Belgium and north-eastern France; their language, a French dialect.
**Wallop,** wol'op, *vt.* To beat; to drub; to thrash.
**Wallow,** wol'ō, *vi.* To tumble and roll in water or mire; to live in filth or gross vice.
**Walnut,** wal'nut, *n.* A valuable tree, a native of Persia; the edible nut of the tree.
**Walrus,** wol'rus, *n.* A hugh marine carnivorous mammal inhabiting the arctic seas.
**Waltz,** walts, *n.* A kind of dance for two persons; music for the dance.—*vi.* To dance a waltz.
**Waltzer,** walts'ėr, *n.* A person who waltzes.
**Wampum,** wom'pum, *n.* Small beads made of shells, used by the American Indians as money or ornaments.
**Wan,** won, *a.* Dark or gloomy; languid of look; pale.
**Wand,** wond, *n.* A long flexible stick; a rod; a staff of authority; a baton.
**Wander,** won'dėr, *vi.* To ramble here and there; to roam; to rove; to err; to be delirious.—*vt.* To traverse.
**Wanderer,** won'dėr-ėr, *n.* One who wanders; a rambler; one that goes astray.
**Wandering,** won'dėr-ing, *a.* Given to wander; unsettled.—*n.* A travelling without a settled course; aberration.
**Wane,** wān, *vt.* (waning, waned). To diminish; to grow less, as the moon; to fail; to decline.—*n.* Decline; decrease.
**Wannish,** won'ish, *a.* Somewhat wan.
**Want,** wont, *n.* State of not having; deficiency; lack; need; indigence.—*vt.* To be without; to lack; to require; to desire.—*vi.* To be deficient; to be in want.
**Wanton,** won'ton, *a.* Not kept in due restraint; unprovoked; lustful; frolicsome; rank.—*n.* A lewd person; a trifler.—*vi.* To revel unrestrainedly; to sport lasciviously.
**Wantonly,** won'ton-li, *adv.* Without restraint or provocation; sportively; lasciviously.
**Wapenshaw, Wapinshaw,** wä'pn-sha, wä'pin-sha, *n.* In Scotland, a review of persons under arms.
**Wapentake,** wä'pn-tāk, *n.* An old division of some of the northern shires of England.
**Wapiti,** wap'i-ti, *n.* The North American stag.
**War,** war, *n.* A contest between nations or parties carried on by force of arms; profession of arms; art of war; hostility; enmity.—*vi.* (warring, warred). To make or carry on war; to strive.
**Warble,** war'bl, *vt.* and *i.* (warbling, warbled). To utter musically in a quavering manner; to carol; to sing musically.—*n.* A quavering melodious sound; a song.
**Warbler,** war'bl-ėr, *n.* A singer; a song-bird.
**War-cry,** war'krī, *n.* A word, cry, motto, or phrase used in common by troops in battle.
**Ward,** ward, *vt.* To guard; to fend off; to turn aside.—*n.* Guard; a defensive motion or position in fencing; custody; guardianship; a minor who is under guardianship; a division of a town or county; apartment of an hospital; a piece in a lock.
**Warden,** war'den, *n.* A guardian; a keeper; head of a college; superior of a conventual church; member of organization for assistance of civil population in air-raids.
**Warder,** ward'ėr, *n.* A guard; a keeper.
**Wardrobe,** ward'rōb, *n.* A piece of furniture in which wearing apparel is kept; a person's wearing apparel collectively.
**Ward-room,** ward'röm, *n.* A room in a warship where the senior officers mess.
**Wardship,** ward'ship, *n.* Guardianship; also pupilage.
**Ware,** wār, *n.* Articles of merchandise; goods: generally in *pl.*; sea-weeds, employed as a manure, etc.—*a.* On one's guard; aware: *poet.*—*vt.*

To beware of: *poet.*

**Warehouse,** wār'hous, *n.* A storehouse for goods; a large shop.—*vt.* To deposit or secure in a warehouse.

**Warehouseman,** wā'hous-man, *n.* One who keeps or is employed in a warehouse.

**Warfare,** war'fā, *n.* Military service; war; contest; hostilities.

**Warily,** wā'ri-li, *adv.* Cautiously.

**Warlike,** wār'lik, *a.* Pertaining to war; military; fit for war; disposed for war.

**Warm,** warm, *a.* Having moderate heat; flushed; zealous; excitable; brisk; rich.—*vt.* To make warm; to animate; to interest.*vi.* To become warm or animated.

**Warmer,** war'ėr, *n.* One who or that which warms.

**Warm-hearted,** warm'hėrt-ed, *a.* Having warmth of heart; cördial; sincere; hearty.

**Warmly,** warm'li, *adv.* In a warm manner; with heat; hotly; eagerly; earnestly.

**Warmth,** warmth, *n.* Gentle heat; cordiality; ardour; animation; enthusiasm; slight anger or irritation.

**Warn,** warn, *vt.* To caution against; to admonish; to advise; to inform previously.

**Warning,** warn'ing, *n.* Act of one who warns; caution against danger, etc.; admonition; previous notice.

**War-office,** war'of-is, *n.* A public office or department managing military affairs.

**Warp,** warp, *vt.* and *i.* To turn or twist out of shape; to contort; to pervert; to move, as a ship, by a rope attached to something.—*n.* The threads extended lengthwise in a loom; a rope used in moving a ship; deposit of rich mud; twist of wood in drying.

**Warped,** warpt, *a.* Twisted by shrinking; perverted.

**Warrant,** wo'rant, *vt.* To guarantee; to authorize; to justify.—*n.* An act or instrument investing one with authority; guarantee; document authorizing an officer to seize an offender; authority; a voucher; right.

**Warrantable,** wo'rant-a-bl, *a.* Authorized; justifiable; defensible; lawful.

**Warranter,** wo'rant-ėr, *n.* One who gives authority; one who guarantees.

**Warrant-officer,** wo'rant-of-is-ėr, *n.* An officer ranking below a commissioned officer.

**Warrantor,** wo'rant-or, *n.* One who warrants.

**Warranty,** wo'ran-ti, *n.* Warrant; guarantee; authority; a legal deed of security.

**Warren,** wo'ren, *n.* Ground appropriated for rabbits; a preserve in a river for fish.

**Warrior,** wa'ri-or, *n.* A soldier; a brave or able soldier.

**War-ship,** war'ship, *n.* A ship constructed for engaging in warfare; a man-of-war.

**Wart,** wart, *n.* A hard dry growth on the skin.

**Warty,** wart'i, *a.* Full of or like warts; overgrown with warts.

**Wary,** wā'ri, *a.* Cautious; prudent.

**Was,** woz, *v.* The first and third person singular of the past tense of *to be.*

**Wash,** wosh, *vt.* To apply water, etc., to, to cleanse; to flow along or dash against; to remove by abultion; to tint lightly.—*vi.* To cleanse oneself by water; to stand the operation of washing; to stand the test.—*n.* Act of washing; clothes washed on one occasion; flow or dash of water; sound made by water; a shallow; swill; lotion; thin coat of color or metal.

**Wash-board,** wosh'bōrd, *n.* A board with a ribbed surface for washing clothes on; a board to prevent the sea from breaking over the gunwale of a boat; a skirting-board.

**Washer,** wosh'er, *n.* One who or that which washed; a ring of iron, leather, etc., used under a nut that is screwed on a bolt.

**Washerwoman,** wosh'ėr-wu-man, *n.* A woman that washed clothes for hire.

**Washhand-basin,** wosh'hand-bā-sn, *n.* A basin for washing the hands in.

**Washhand-stand,** wosh'hand-stand, *n.* A wash-stand.

**Wash-house, Washing-house,** wosh'house, wosh'ing-house, *n.* A building or an apartment for washing linen, etc.

**Washing,** wosh'ing, *n.* Act of cleansing with water; ablution; clothes washed.

**Wash-out,** wosh'out, *n.* A shot which misses the target, so a complete failure (used of persons and things).

**Wash-stand,** wosh'stand, *n.* A piece of bedroom furniture supporting a basin.

**Wash-tub,** wosh'tub, *n.* A tub in which clothes are washed.

**Washy,** wosh'i, *a.* Watery; highly diluted; thin; weak; feeble; worthless.

**Wasp,** wosp, *n.* An active, stinging, winged insect, resembling the bee.

**Waspish,** wosp'ish, *a.* Like a wasp; venomous; irritable; snappish.

**Wassail,** wos'el, *n.* A festive occasion with drinking of healths; a drinking bout; liquor used on such occasions.—*vi.* To hold a merry drinking meeting.

**Wast,** wost. The second person singular of *was.*

**Wastage,** wāst'āj, *n.* oss by use, leakage, etc.

**Waste,** wāst, *vt.* (wasting, wasted). To make desolate; to ravage; to wear away gradually; to squander.—*vi.* To decrease gradually.—*a.* Desolate; spoiled; refuse.—*n.* Act of wasting; prodigality; refuse matter; gradual decrease; a desert region.

**Wasteful,** wāst'ful, *a.* Causing waste; destructive; ruinous; lavish; prodigal.

**Waste-pipe,** wāst'pip, *n.* A pipe for carrying off waste water, etc.

**Waster,** wāst'ė, *n.* One who wastes; a prodigal; a squanderer.

**Wasting,** wāst'ing, *a.* Such as to waste; desolating; enfeebling.

**Watch,** woch, *n.* A keeping awake to guard, etc.; vigilance; a guard; time during which a person is on guard or duty; a small pocket timepiece.—*vi.* To keep awake; to give heed; to act as a guard, etc.; to wait.—*vt.* To look with close attention at or on; to tend; to guard.

**Watch-dog,** woch'dog, *n.* A dog kept to guard premises and property.

**Watcher,** woch'ėr, *n.* One who watches.

**Watch-fire,** woch'fir, *n.* A fire kept up in the night as a signal or for the use of a guard.

**Watchful,** woch'ful, *a.* Keeping on the watch; vigilant; attentive; cautious.

**Watch-house,** woch'hous, *n.* A guard-house; a lock-up.

**Watch-maker,** woch'māk-ėr, *n.* One who makes or repairs watches.

**Watchman,** woch'man, *n.* A guard; a caretaker on duty at night.

**Watch-tower,** woch'tou-ėr, *n.* A tower on which a sentinel is placed to watch.

**Watchword,** woch'wėrd, *n.* A word by which sentinels distinguish a friend from an enemy; a motto.

**Water,** wā'tėr, *n.* A transparent fluid; a fluid consisting of hydrogen and oxygen; the sea; rain; saliva; urine; color or luster of a diamond, etc.—*vt.* To wet or supply with water; to give a wavy appearance to, as silk.—*vi.* To shed liquid matter; to take in water; to gather saliva; to have a longing desire.

**Water-bailiff,** wa'tėr-bā-lif, *n.* A customhouse officer for searching ships; one who watches a river to prevent poaching.

**Water-bed,** wa'tėr-bed, *n.* An india-rubber bed or mattress filled with water.

**Water-cart,** wa'tėr-kärt, *n.* A cart carrying water for sale, watering streets, etc.

**Water-closet,** wa'tėr-kloz-et, *n.* A privy in which the discharges are carried away by water.

**Water-color,** watėr-kul-ėr, *n.* A pigment ground up with water and isinglass or other mucilage in-

stead of oil.
**Water-course,** wa'tėr-kōrs, *n.* A stream of water; a channel for water.
**Watered,** wa'tėrd, *a.* Having a wavy and shiny appearance on the surface.
**Waterfall,** wa'tėr-fal, *n.* A fall or steep descent in a stream; a cascade.
**Water-frame,** wa'tėr-frām, *n.* A frame for spinning cotton, at first driven by water.
**Water-gas,** wa'tėr-gas, *n.* An illuminating gas obtained by decomposing water.
**Watering,** wa'tėr-ing, *n.* Act of one who waters; ornamentation giving a wavy lustre.
**Watering-place,** wa'tėr-ing-plās, *n.* A place to which people resort for mineral waters, or for bathing, etc.
**Water-level,** wa'tėr-le-vel, *n.* The level at which water stands; a levelling instrument in which water is employed.
**Water-line,** wa'tėr-līn, *n.* The line formed by the surface of water, as on ships.
**Water-logged,** wa'tėr-logd, *a.* Floating but full of water, as a ship.
**Waterman,** wa'tėr-man, *n.* A boatman.
**Water-mark,** wa'tėr-märk, *n.* A mark indicating the rise and fall of water; a mark made in paper during manufacture.
**Water-mill,** wa'tėr-mil, *n.* A mill whose machinery is driven by means of water.
**Water-polo,** wa'tėr-pō''lō, *n.* A ball-game played by swimmers, who try to throw the ball into their opponents' goal.
**Water-power,** wa'tėr-pou-ėr, *n.* The power of water employed to drive machinery.
**Waterproof,** wa'tėr-prüf, *a.* So compact as not to admit water.—*n.* Cloth made waterproof; a garment of such cloth.—*vt.* To render impervious to water.
**Watershed,** wa'tėr-shed, *n.* A rise of land from which rivers, etc., naturally flow in opposite directions.
**Water-spout,** wa'tėr-spout, *n.* A column of spray or water drawn up from the sea or a lake by a violent whirlwind.
**Water-tight,** wa'tėr-tīt, *a.* So tight as to retain or not to admit water; stanch.
**Water-way,** wa'tėr-wā, *n.* That part of a river, the sea, etc., through which vessels sail.
**Water-wheel,** wa'tėr-whēl, *n.* A wheel for raising water, or moved by water.
**Water-works,** wa'tėr-wėrks, *n.pl.* The works and appliances for the distribution of water to communities; ornamental fountains.
**Watery,** wa'tėr-i, *a.* Pertaining to or like water; thin; moist; tasteless; insipid.
**Wattle,** wot'l, *n.* A hurdle of interlaced rods. —*vt.* (wattling, wattled). To interlace (twigs or branches); to plat.
**Watt,** wot, *n.* The practical unit of power, or rate of conveying energy, used in electricity.
**Waul,** wal, *vi.* To cry as a cat.
**Wave,** wāv, *vi.* and *i.* (waving, waved). To sway or play loosely; to undulate; to brandish; to becon.—*n.* A swell or ridge on moving water; anything resembling a wave; an undulation; a signal made by waving the hand, a flag, etc.
**Wave,** wāv, *vt.* To waive. *See.* Waive.
**Waved,** wāvd, *a.* Undulating; wavy.
**Wavelet,** wāv'let, *n.* A small wave.
**Waver,** wā'vėr, *vi.* To wave gently; to fluctuate; to be undertermined.
**Waverer,** wā'vėr-ėr, *n.* One who wavers.
**Wavy,** wāv'i, *a.* Rising or swelling in waves; full of waves; undulating.
**Wax,** waks, *n.* A tenacious substance excreted by bees or in the ear; any similar substance; sealing-wax.—*vt.* To smear or rub with wax.—*vi.* To increase; to grow; to become.
**Wax-cloth,** waks'kloth, *n.* Cloth covered with a waxy coating; floor-cloth.
**Waxen,** waks'en, *a.* Made of wax.
**Wax-work,** waks'wėrk, *n.* Work in wax; figures of persons in wax as near reality as possible.
**Waxy,** waks'i, *a.* Resembling wax; made of wax; abounding in wax.
**Way,** wā, *n.* A track, path, or road of any kind; distance traversed; progress; direction; line of business; condition; device; method; course; *pl.* the timbers on which a ship is launched.
**Way-bill,** wā'bil, *n.* A list of passengers or goods carried by a public conveyance.
**Wayfarer,** wāfār-ėr, *n.* One who fares or travels; a traveller; a foot-passenger.
**Wayfaring,** wā'fār-ing, *a.* Travelling; passing; being on a journey.
**Waylay,** wā-lā', *vt.* To lay oneself in the way of; to beset in ambush.
**Wayside,** wā'sid, *n.* The side of a road.—*a.* Growing, situated, etc., by sides of roads.
**Wayward,** wā'wėrd, *a.* Full of troublesome whims; forward; peevish; perverse.
**Waywardly,** wā'wėrd-li, *adv.* Perversely.
**Wayworn,** wā'wōrn, *a.* Worn or wearied by travelling.
**We,** wē, *pron.* Plural of I.
**Weak,** wēk, *a.* Not strong; feeble; infirm; frail; silly; vaillating; wanting resolution; wanting moral courage; ineffective; denoting verbs inflected by adding a letter or syllable.
**Weaken,** wēk'n, *vt.* To make weak or weaker.—*vi.* To become weak or weaker.
**Weakling,** wēk'ling, *n.* A weak creature.
**Weakly,** wēk'li, *adv.* Feebly; not forcibly; injudiciously.—*a.* Infirm.
**Weakness,** wēk'nes, *n.* The state or quality of being weak; irresoltuion; want of validity; a failing.
**Weal,** wēl, *n.* Welfare; prosperity; happiness; mark of a strip; wale.
**Weald,** wēld, *n.* A piece of open forest land; a wold.
**Wealth,** welth, *n.* Riches; affluence; opulence; abundance.
**Wealthy,** welth'i, *a.* Possessing wealth; rich; opulent; abundant; ample.
**Wean,** wēn, *vt.* To accustom to do without the mother's milk; to alienate; to disengage from any habit.
**Weanling,** ē'ling, *n.* A child or animal newly weaned.
**Weapon,** we'pon, *n.* Any instrument of offence or defence.
**Wear,** wār, *vt.* (pret. wore, pp. worn). To carry as belonging to dress; to have on; to waste by rubbing; to destroy by degrees; to produce by rubbing; to exhibit.—*vi.* To last well or ill; to waste gradually; to make gradual progress.—Act of wearing; diminution by friction, use, time, etc.; fashion.
**Wear,** wār, *vt.* (pret. & pp. wore). To bring on the other tack by turning the ship round, stern towards the wind.
**Wearer,** wār'ėr, *n.* One who wears.
**Wearily,** wē'ri-li, *adv.* In a weary manner; like one fatigued.
**Wearing,** wār'ing, *a.* Used by being worn; such as to wear; exhausting.
**Wearisome,** wē'ri-sum, *a.* Causing weariness; tiresome; fatiguing; monotonous.
**Weary,** wē'ri, *a.* Having the strength or patience exhausted; tired; disgusted; tiresome.—*vt.* (wearying, wearied). To make weary; to tire.—*vi.* To become weary.
**Weasand, Weazand,** wē'zand, *n.* The windpipe.
**Weasel,** wē'zl, *n.* A small carnivorous animal akin to the ferret, etec.
**Weather,** weᴛʜ'er, *n.* The general atmospheric conditions at any particular time. *a.* Turned towards the wind; windward.—*vt.* To affect by the weather; to sail to the windward of; to bear up against and overcome.
**Weather-beaten,** weᴛʜ'ėr-bēt-n, *a.* Beaten by the weather; hardened by exposure.
**Weather-cock,** weᴛʜ'ėr-kok, *n.* Something in the shape of a cock, etc., for showing the direction of the wind; a vane; a fickle person.

**Weather-gage,** weᴛʜ'ėr-gāj, *n.* Advantage of the wind obtained by a ship in maneuvring; advantage of position.

**Weather-glass,** weᴛʜ'ėr-glās, *n.* A barometer.

**Weatherly,** weᴛʜ'ėr-li, *a.* Applied to a ship that makes very little leeway.

**Weathermost,** weᴛʜ'ėr-mōst, *a.* Being farthest to the windward.

**Weather-wise,** weᴛʜ'ėr-wīz, *a.* Wise or skilful in forecasting the weather.

**Weather-worn,** weᴛʜ'ėr-wōrn, *a.* Worn by the action of the weather.

**Weave,** wēv, *vt.* (weaving, pret. wove, pp. woven). To form by interlacing thread, yard, etc.; to form a tissue with; to work up; to contrive. *vi.* To practise weaving; to be woven.

**Weaver,** wēv'ėr, *n.* One who weaves; one whose occupation is to weave.

**Weaving,** wēv'ing, *n.* Act or art of producing cloth or other textile fabrics.

**Weazen,** wē'zn, *n.* Thin; lean; wizened.

**Web,** web, *n.* The whole piece of cloth woven in a loom; a large roll of paper; membrance which unites the toes of water-fowl; the threads which a spider spins; a cobweb; anything carefully contrived.

**Webbed,** webd, *a.* Having the toes united by a membrance or web.

**Webbing,** web'ing, *n.* A strong fabric of hemp, two or three inches wide.

**Webby,** web'i, *a.* Relating to or like a web.

**Weber,** vā'ber, *n.* The electric unit of magnetic quantity.

**Web-foot,** web'fut, *n.* A foot whose toes are united by a membrane.

**Web-footed,** web'fu-ed, *a.* Having the toes united by a membrane.

**Wed,** wed, *vt.* and *i.* (wedding, wedded and wed). To marry; to unite closely.

**Wedded,** wed'ed, *a.* Pertaining to matrimony; intimately united.

**Wedding,** wed'ing, *n.* Marriage; nuptials.

**Wedge,** wej, *n.* A body sloping to a thin edge at one end.—*vt.* (wedging, wedged). To drive as a wedge is driven; to crowd or compress; to fasten or split with a wedge.

**Wedlock,** wed'lok, *n.* The wedded state; marriage.

**Wednesday,** wenz'dā, *n.* The fourth day of the week.

**Wee,** wē, *a.* Small; little.

**Weed,** wēd, *n.* Any plant regarded as useless or troublesome; a sorry, worthless animal; a cigar; *pl.* mourning dressof a widow or female.—*vt.* To free from weeds or anything offensive.

**Weeder,** wēd'ėr, *n.* One that weeds; a tool for weeding.

**Weedy,** wēd'i, *a.* Consisting of weeds; abounding with weeds; worthless.

**Week,** wēk, *n.* The space of seven days; space from one Sunday to another.

**Week-day, wēk'dā,** *n.* Any day of the week except Sunday.

**Weekly,** wēk'li, *a.* Coming or done once a week; lasting for a week.—*n.* A periodical appearing once a week.—*adv.* Once a week.

**Ween,** wēm. *vi.* To think; to fancy.

**Weep,** wēp, *vi.* (pret. and pp. wept). To manifest grief, etc., by shedding tears; to drip; to droop.—*vt.* To lament; to shed or drop, as tears; to get rid of by weeping.

**Weeper,** wēp'ėr, *n.* One who weeps; a sort of white linen cuff on a mourning dress.

**Weeping,** wēp'ing, *n.* Lamenting; the shedding of tears.

**Weever,** wē'vėr, *n.* A spined edible fish.

**Weevil,** wē'vil, *n.* An insect of the beetle family, destructive to grain, fruit, etc.

**Weft,** weft, *n.* The woof of cloth.

**Weigh,** wā, *vt.* To raise; to find the heaviness of; to allot or take by weight; to consider; to balance; to burthen.—*vi.* To have weight; to amount to in weight; to bear heavily.

**Weigh-bridge,** wā'brij, *n.* A machine for weighing carts, wagons, etc., with their load.

**Weigh-house,** wā'hous, *n.* A public building at or in which goods are weighed.

**Weight,** wāt, *n.* Heaviness; gravity; the amount which anything weighs; a metal standard for weighing; a heavy mass; pressure; burden; importance; moment.—*vt.* To add to the heaviness of.

**Weighty,** wāt'i, *a.* Heavy; important; momentous; cogent.

**Weir,** wēr,l *n.* A dam across a stream for supplying water to a mill, irrigation, etc.; a fence of twigs in a stream for catching fish.

**Weird,** wērd, *n.* Destiny; **fate**.—*a.* Connected with fate; unearthly.

**Welcome,** wel'kum,*a.* Received with gladness; grateful; pleasing.—*n.* Greeting or kind reception.—*vt.* (welcoming, welcomed). To receive kindly and hospitably.

**Weld,** weld, *vt.* To melt together, as heated iron; to unite closely.—*n.* A junction by fusion of heated metals; a species of migonette used as a yellow dye.

**Welfare,** wel'fār, *n.* Well-being; prosperity; happiness.

**Welkin,** wel'kin, *n.* The sky; the heavens; the firmament.

**Well,** wel, *n.* A spring; a pit sunk for water; perpendicular space in a building in which stairs or a hoist is place.—*vi.* To bubble up; to issue forth.

**Well,** wel, *adv.* In a proper manner; rightly; commendably; considerably.—*a.* Being in health; comfortable; fortunate; convenient; proper.

**Welladay,** wel'a-dā, *interj.* Welaway! alas! lackaday!

**Well-being,** wel'bē-ing, *n.* State of being well; prosperity; happinessl welfdare.

**Well-born,** wel'born, *a.* Born of a good family; of good descent.

**Well-bred,** wel'bred, *a.* Of good breeding; polite; refined.

**Wellington,** wel'ing-ton, *n.* A kind of long boot worn by men; a long-legged rubber boot made in one piece.

**Wellingtonia,** wel-ing-tō'ni-a, *n.* A genus of large coniferous trees.

**Well-meaning,** wel'mēn-ing, *a.* Having a good intention.

**Well-spoken,** wel'ōk-n, *a.* Spoken well; speaking well; civil; courteous.

**Well-spring,** wel'spring, *n.* A fountain; a source of continual supply.

**Well-timed,** wel-tīmd, *a.* Done at a proper time; opportune.

**Well-to-do,** wel'tö-dö, *a.* Being in easy circumstances; well-off; prosperous.

**Welsh,** welsh, *a.* Pertaining to Wales or to its people.—*n.* The language of Wales; *pl.* the inhabitants of Wales.

**Welt,** welt, *n.* A border of edging; a strip of leather sewed round the upper of a boot to which the sole is fastened.—*vt.* To furnish with a welt; to beat severly.

**Welter,** welt'ėr, *vi.* To roll; to tumble about; to wallow.—A turmoil.—*a.* Said of a horse race in which extra heavy weights are laid on some horses.

**Wen,** wen, *n.* A harmless fatty tumor.

**Wench,** wensh, *n.* A young woman; a woman of loose character.—*vi.* To frequent the company of women of ill-fame.

**Wend,** wend, *vt.* To go; to direct.—*vi.* To go; to travel.

**Went,** went. Used as the pret. of go.

**Were,** wer, *v.* The past tense plural indicative and the past subjunctive of *be*.

**Werewolf,** wēr'wulf, *n.* A werwolf.

**Wert,** wėrt, The sëcond person singular of *was* or *were*.

**Werwolf,** wėr'wulf, *n.* A man transformed into a wolf.

**Wesleyan,** wes'li-an, *a.* Pertaining to the religious body established by John Wesley.—*n.* A Methodist.
**West,** west, *n.* The point where the sun sets, opposite to the east.—*a.* Being in or towards the west; coming from the west.—*adv.* To the west.
**Westerly,** west'ėr-li, *a.* Tending or being towards the west; coming from the west.
**Western,** west'ėrn. *a.* Being in or moving toward the west; coming from the west.
**Westernmost,** westėrn-mōst, *a.* Farthest to the west.
**Westing,** west'ing, *n.* Space or distance westward.
**Westmost,** west'mōst, *a.* Farthest to the west.
**Westward,** west'wėrd, *adv.* Toward the west.
**Westwardly,** west'wėrd-li, *adv.* In a direction toward the west.
**Westwards,** west'wėrdz, *adv.* Westward.
**Wet,**wet, *a.* Covered or soaked with water; moist; rainy.—*n.* Water; moisture; rain.—*vt.* (wetting, wetted). To make wet; to soak in liquor.
**Wether,** weTH'ėr, *n.* A ram castrated.
**Wet-nurse,** wet'nėrs, *n.* A nurse engaged to suckle an infant.
**Wettish,** wet'ish, *a.* Somewhat wet.
**Wey,** wā, *n.* A certain weight or measure; of wool, 182 lbs; of wheat, 5 quarters; of cheese, 224 lbs., etc.
**Whack,** whak, *vt.* and *i.* To thwack; to give a resonding blow to.—*n.* A resounding blow; a thwack.
**Whale,** whāl, *n.* The largest of sea animals, a mammal.
**Whalebone,** whāl'bōn, *n.* An elastic horny substance obtained from the upper jaw of certain whales; baleen.
**Whaler,** whāl'ėr, *n.* A person or ship employed in the whale-fishery.
**Wharf,** wharf, *n.*; pl. **-fs or -ves**. A quay for loading or unloading ships.
**Wharfage,** *wharf'āj, n.* The fee for using a wharf; accommodations at a wharf; wharfs collectively.
**Wharfinger,** whar'in-jėr, *n.* A person who owns or has the charge of a wharf.
**What,** whot, *pron.* An interrogative pronoun used chiefly of things; employed adjectively as equivalent to how great, remarkable, etc.; substantively as equivalent to the thing (or things) which.
**Whatever,** whot-ev'ėr, *pron.* Used as substantive, anything that; all that; used as an adj, of any kind.
**What-not,** whot'not, *n.* A piece of household furniture with shelves for books, etc.
**Whatsoever, Whatsoe'er,** whot-sō-ev'ėr, whot-sō-ār', *pron.* Whatever (emphatic).
**Wheat,** whēt, *n.* A cereal plant; its seeds, which yield a white nutritious flour.
**Wheatear,** whēt'ėr, *n.* A bird akin to the stone-chat.
**Wheat-ear,** whēt'ēr, *n.* An ear of wheat.
**Wheaten,** whēt'n, *a.* Pertaining to wheat; made of wheat.
**Wheedle,** whē'dl, *vt.* and *i.* (wheedling, wheedled). To flatter; to cajole; to coax.
**Wheel,** whēl, *n.* A circular frame turning on an axis; an old instrument of torture; a revolution; a cycle.—*vt.* To cause to turn round.—*vi.* to revolve; to roll forward.
**Wheel-barrow,** whēl'ba-rē, *n.* A barrow with one wheel.
**Wheeled,** whēld, *a.* Having wheels.
**Wheeler,** whēl'ėr, *n.* One who wheels; a maker of wheels; horse next a carriage.
**Wheel-wright,** whēl-rī, *n.* A wright whose occupation is to make wheels.
**Wheeze,** whēz, *vi.* (wheezing, wheezed). To breathe hard and audibly, as persons affected with asthma.
**Wheezy,** whēz'i, *a.* Affected with wheezing.
**Whelk,** whelk, *n.* A shell-fish, a species of periwinkle or mollusc; a pustule.
**Whelm,** whelm, *vt.* To engulf; to swallow up; to ruin or devastate.
**Whelp,** whelp, *n.* A puppy; a cub; a young man.—*vi.* To bring forth whelps.—*vt.* To bring forth; to originate.
**When,** when, *adv.* and *conj.* At what or which time;p while; whereas; used substantively with *since* or *till*.
**Whence,** whens, *adv.* and *conj.* From what place, source, etc.; how.
**Whencesoever,** whens-sō-ev'ėr, *adv.* From whatever place, cause, or source.
**Whene'er, Whenever,** when-ār', when-ev'ė, *adv.* At whatever time.
**Whensoever,** when-sō-ev'ėr, *adv.* From whatever place, cause, or source.
**Where,** whār, *adv.* and *conj.* At or in what place; at the place in which; whither.
**Whereabout,** whār'a-bout, *adv.* and *conj.* About what place; concerning which.
**Whereabouts,** whār'a-bouts, *adv.* and *conj.* Near what or which place; whereabout; often used substantively.
**Whereas,** Whār-az' *conj.* Things being so; when really or in fact.
**Whereat,** whā-at', *adv.* and *conj.* At which or what.
**Whereby,** whār-bi', *adv.* and *conj.* By which or what.
**Wherefore,** whār'for, *adv.* and *conj.* For which reason; consequently; why.
**Wherein,** whār-in', *adv.* and *conj.* In which; in which thing, time, respect, etc.
**Whereinto,** whār-in-tö', *adv.* and *conj.* Into which or what.
**Whereof,** whār-ov', *adv.* and *conj.* Of which or what.
**Whereon,** whār-on', *adv.* and *conj.* On which or on what.
**Wheresoever, Wheresoe'er,** whār-sō-ev'ėr, whār'sō-ār, *adv.* In whatever place.
**Whereto,** whār-tö', *adv.* and *conj.* To which or what; to what end.
**Whereupon,** whār-up-on', *adv.* Upon which or what; in consequence of which.
**Wherever, Where'er,** whār-ev'ėr, whār-ār, *adv.* At whatever place.
**Wherewith, Wherewithal,** whār-with', whār-with-al', *adv.* and *conj.* With which or what.—*n.* Means or money.
**Wherry,** whe'ri, *n.* A light river boat for passengers.
**Whet,** whet, *vi.* (whetting, whetted or whet). To rub to sharpen; to edge; to excite; to stimulate.—*n.* Act of sharpening; something that stimulates the appetite.
**Whether,** whTH'ėr, *pron.* Which of two.—*conj.* and *adv.* Which of two or more, introducing alternative clauses.
**Whetstone,** whet'stōn, *n.* A stone used for sharpening instruments by friction.
**Whew,** whū, *exclam.* A sound made with the lips, expressing astonishment or contempt.—*n.* The sound thus uttered.
**Whey,** whā, *n.* The thin part of milk, from which the curd, etc., have been separated.
**Which,** which, *pron.* An interrogative pronoun, used adjectively or substantively; a relative pronoun, the neuter of *who*; an indefinite pronoun, any one which.
**Whichever, Whichsoever,** which-ev'ėr, which-sō-ev'ėr, *pron.* No matter which; anyone.
**Whiff,** whif, *n.* A puff of air; a puff conveying a small.—*vt.* and *i.* To puff; to throw out whiffs; to smoke.
**Whiffle,** whif'l, *vi.* (whiffling, whiffled). To veer about; to be fickle; to prevaricate.
**Whig,** whig, *n.* Formerly a member of the political party in Britain, opposed to the *Tories*; one of the more conservative section of the Liberal party, opposed to the *Radicals*.—*a.* Belonging to or composed of Whigs.

**Whiggery, Whiggism,** whig'ėr-i, whig'izm, *n.* The principles of the Whigs.
**Whiggish,** whig'ish, *a.* Pertaining to Whigs or their principles.
**While,** whīl, *n.* A time; short space of time.—*conj.* During the time that; though.—*vt.* whiling, whiled). To cause to pass pleasantly: usually with *away*.
**Whilom,** whī'lom, *a.* Former; quondam.
**Whilst,** whīlst, *adv.* While.
**Whim,** *n.* A sudden fancy; a caprice.
**Whimbrel,** whim'brel, *n.* A British bird closely allied to the curlew.
**Whimper,** whim'pėr, *vi.* To express grief with a whining voice.—*vt.* To utter in a low, whining tone.—*n.* A peevish cry.
**Whimsical,** whim'zik-al, *a.* Full of whims; capricious; odd; fantastic.
**Whimsy, Whimsey,** whim'zi, *n.* A whim; a caprice; a capricious notion.
**Whin,** whin, *n.* Gorse; furze.
**Whin-chat,** whin'chat, *n.* A British chat commonly found among broom and furze.
**Whine,** whīn, *vi.* (whinning, whined). To express distress by a plaintive drawling cry.—*n.* A drawling plaintive tone; mean or affected complaint.
**Whinny,** whin'i, *vi.* (whinnying, whinnied). To neigh, especially in a low tone.—*n.* Neigh of a horse.—*a.* Abounding in whins.
**Whinstone,** whin'ston, *n.* A hard or tough unstratified rock.
**Whip,** whip, *vt.* (whipping, whipped). To put or snatch with a sudden motion; to flog; to drive with lashes; to beat into a froth.—*vi.* To start suddenly and run.—*n.* A lash; the driver of a carriage; a member of parliament who looks after the attendance of his party; the summons he sends out.
**Whip-hand,** whip'hand, *n.* The hand that holds the whip; control.
**Whipper-snapper,** whip'ėr-snap-ėr, *n.* A diminutive, insignificant person.
**Whipping,** whip'ing, *n.* Act of striking with a whip; flagellation.
**Whipster,** whip'stėr, *n.* A nimble little fellow; a sharp shallow fellow.
**Whir,** whėr, *vi.* (whirring, whirred). To fly, revolve, etc., with a whizzing or buzzing sound; to whiz.—*n.* A buzzing sound.
**Whirl,** whėrl, *vt.* and *i.* To turn round rapidly; to move quickly.—*n.* A rapid turning.
**Whirl-bone,** whėrl-bōn, *n.* The knee-pan.
**Whirligig,** whėrl-i-gig, *n.* A toy which children spin or whirl round.
**Whirlpool,** whėrl'pöl, *n.* An eddy or gulf where the water moves round in a circle.
**Whirlwig,** whėrl'wig, *n.* A beetle which circles round rapidly on the surface of ponds, etc.
**Whirlwind,** whėrl'wind, *n.* A whirling wind; a violent wind moving as if round an axis, this axis at the same time progressing.
**Whisk,** whisk, *vt.* To sweep or agitate with a light rapid motion.—*vi.* To move nimbly.—*n.* A rapid, sweeping motion; a small besom; an instrument for frothing cream, eggs, etc.
**Whisker,** whis'kėr, *n.* Long hair growing on the cheek.
**Whiskified, Whiskeyfied,** whis'ki-fīd, *a.* Affected with whisky; intoxicated.
**Whisky, Whiskey,** *n.* An ardent spirit distilled generally from barley; a light one-horse chaise.
**Whisper,** whis'pėr, *vt.* To speak with a low sibilant voice; to converse secretly.—*vt.* To utter in a whisper.—*n.* A low soft sibilant voice; a faint utterance.
**Whispering,** whis'pėr-ing, *a.* Speaking in a whisper; having or giving a soft sibilant sound.—*n.* Act of one who whispers; talebearing.
**Whist,** whist, *interj.* Silence! hush!—*a.* Silent.—*n.* A game at cards, played by four persons.
**Whistle,** whis'l, *vi.* (whistling, whistled). To utter a clear shrill sound by forcing the breath through the lips; to warble; to sound shrilly.—*vt.* To utter or signal by whistling.—*n.* Sound produced by one who whistles; any similar sound; a small pipe blown with the breath; instrument sounded by steam.
**Whit,** whit, *n.* The smallest particle; tittle.
**White,** whīt, *a.* Being of the color of pure snow; pale; pallid; pure and unsulled.—*n.* The color of snow; a white pigment; white of an egg, eye, etc., —*vt.* (whiting, whited). To make white.
**White-bait,** whī'bāt, *n.* The fry or young of the herring and sprat.
**White-friar,** whīt'frī-ėr, *n.* A friar of the Carmelite order, from their white cloaks.
**White-iron,** whīt'i-ėrn, *n.* Thin sheet-iron covered with a coating of tin; tinplate.
**White-lead,** whīt'led, *n.* A carbonate of lead much used in painting; ceruse.
**White-livered,** whīt-liv-ėrd, *a.* Cowardly.
**Whiten,** whīt'n, *vt.* To make white; to bleach; to blanch. —*vi.* To grow white.
**White-smith,** whīt'smith, *n.* A tinsmith; a worker in iron who finishes or polishes.
**Whitewash,** whīt'wosh, *n.* A composition of lime or whiting water, for whitening walls, etc. —*vt.* To cover with whitewash; to restore the reputation of.
**Whither,** whiᴛʜ'ėr, *adv.* To what or which place; where.
**Whitersoever,** whiᴛʜ'ėr-sō-ev-ėr.*adv.* To whatever place.
**Whiting,** whi+īt'ing, *n.* A small fish of the cod tribe; pulverized chalk used in whitewashing, for cleaning plate, etc.
**Whitish,** whī'ish, *conj.* Somewhat white.
**Whitlow,** whit'lō, *n.* A swelling about the small bones of the fingers, generally terminating in an abscess.
**Whit-Monday,** whit'mun-dā, *n.* The Monday following Whitsunday.
**Whitsun,** whit'sun, *a.* Pertaining to Whitsuntide.
**Whitsunday,** whit'sun-dā, *n.* The seventh Sunday after Easter.
**Whitsuntide,** whit'sun-tīd, *n.* The season of Pentecost.
**Whittle,** whit'l, *n.* A large knife.—*vt.* (whittling, whittled). To cut or pare with a knife.
**Whiz,** whiz, *vi.* whizzing, whizzed). To make a humnming or hissing sound.—*n.* A hissing and humming sound.
**Who,** hö, *pron.*; possessive *Whose*, höz; objective *Whom*, hm̈. A relative and interrogative pronoun always used substantively and with reference to persons.
**Whoever,** hö-ev'ėr, *pron.* Any one without exception; any person whatever.
**Whole,** hōl, *a.* Sound; healthy; healed; intact; entire.—*n.* An entire thing; total assemblage of parts.
**Whole-length,** hōl'length, *n.* A picture or statue exhibiting the whole figure.
**Wholesale,** hōl'sāl, *n.* Sale of goods by the entire piece or in large quantities.—*a.* Pertaining to trade in large quantities; extensive and indiscriminate.
**Wholesome,** hōl'sum, *a.* Tending to promote health; salubrious; useful; salutary.
**Wholly,** hōl'li, *adv.* As a whole; entirely.
**Whoop,** whöp or höp, *vi.* To shout loudly; to hoot.—*vt.* To shout at; to hoot; to insult with shouts.—*n.* A shout; a loud clear call.
**Whooping-cough,** *n.* *See.* HOOPING-COUGH.
**Whop,** whop, *vt.* (whopping, whopped). To beat.
**Whopper,** whop'ėr, *n.* Anything uncommonly large; a manifest lie.
**Whore,** (hōr, *n.* A prostitute; a harlot.—*vi.* (whoring, whored). To have to do with prostitutes.
**Whoredom,** hōr'dum, *n.* Lewdness; fornication; prostitution.
**Whoremonger,** hōr'mung-gėr, *n.* One who practises whoring; a fornicator.
**Whoreson,** hōr'sun, *n.* A bastard.

**Whorl,** whorl or wherl, *n.* A ring of leaves, etc., of a plant all on the same plane.
**Whortleberry,** whort'l-be-ri, *n.* The bilberry and its fruit.
**Whose,** höz, *pron.* The possessive case of *who* or *which*.
**Whoso,** hö'sō, *pron.* Whosoever; whoever.
**Whosoever,** hö-sō-ev'ėr, *pron.* Any person whatever; any one.
**Why,** whī, *adv.* and *conj.* For what reason; wherefore.
**Wick,** wik, *n.* The loose spongy string or band in candles or lamps.
**Wicked,** wik'ed, *a.* Evil in principle or practice; sinful; immoral; bad; roguish.
**Wickedly,** wik'ed-li, *adv.* In a wicked manner; viciously; immorally.
**Wickedness,** wik'ed-nes, *n.* Immorality; depravity; sin; a wicked act.
**Wicker,** *n.* A small pliable twig; work made of such twigs.—*a.* Made of plaited twigs.
**Wicket,** wik'et, *n.* A small gate; in *cricket*, the three upright rods and the balls which rest on them at which the bowler aims.
**Wide,** wīd, *a.* Having a great extent each way; broad; extensive; liberal; remote from anything.—*adv.* At or to a distance; far from; astray.
**Wide-awake,** wīd'a-wāk, *a.* On the alert.—*n.* A soft felt hat with a broad brim.
**Widely,** wīd'li, *adv.* Extensively; far.
**Widen,** wīd'n, *vt.* To make wide or wider.—*vi.* To grow wide or wider.
**Widgeon, Wigeon,** wi'jon, *n.* A migratory waterfowl of the duck group.
**Widow,** wi'dō, *n.* A woman whose husband is dead.—*vt.* To bereave of a husband.
**Widower,** wi'dō-ėr, *n.* A man whose wife is dead.
**Widowhood,** wi'dō-hud, *n.* The condition of being a widow or widower.
**Width** width, *n.* Breadth; extent from side to side.
**Wield,** wēld, *vt.* To manage freely in the hands; to sway; to exercise.
**Wieldable,** wēld'a-bl, *a.* Capable of being wielded.
**Wielder,** wēld'ėr, *n.* One who wields.
**Wieldy,** wēld'i, *a.* Manageable.
**Wife,** wif, *n.*; pl. *Wives*, wīvz. A married woman.
**Wifelike,** wif'lik, *a.* Resembling or pertaining to a wife or woman.
**Wifely,** wīf'li, *a.* Like or becoming a wife.
**Wig,** wig, *n.* An artificial covering of hair for the head.
**Wigging,** wig'ing, *n.* A rating; a scolding.
**Wight,** wīt, *n.* A human being; a person.—*a.* Strong and active; of warlike prowess.
**Wigwam,** wig'wam, *n.* A tent or hut of the North American Indians.
**Wild,** wild, *a.* Living in a state of nature; not tame; not cultivated; desert; stormy; furious; frolicsome; rash; extravagant; excited.—*n.* An uncultivated tract.
**Wilder,** wil'dėr, *vt.* To bewilder.
**Wilderness,** wil'dėr-nes, *n.* A desert; waste; irregular collection of things.
**Wildfire,** wīld'fir, *n.* A kind of lightning unaccompanied by thunder; erysipelas.
**Wilding,** wīld'ing, *n.* A young tree that grows without cultivation.
**Wildish,** wīld'ish, *a.* Somewhat wild.
**Wildly,** wīld'li, *adv.* In a wild state or manner; irrationally; savagely.
**Wile,** wīl, *n.* An artifice; stratagem; trick.—*vt.* wiling, wiled. To entice; to while.
**Wileful,** wīl'ful, *a.* Wily; tricky.
**Wilful,** wil'ful, *a.* Under the influence of self-will; obstinate; wayward; intentional.
**Wilfully,** wil''ful-li, *adv.* In a wilful manner; obstinately; with set purpose.
**Wiliness,** wī'li-nes, *n.* Cunning; guile.
**Will,** wil, *v. aux.* (past, would), expresses futurity in the second and third persons, and willingness, etc., or determination in the first.—*vt.* and *i.* To determine by choice; to wish; to bequeath.—*n.* Wish; choice; determination; purpose; legal declaration of a person as to what is to be done after his death with his property; faculty by which we determine to do or not to do something; volition.
**Willing,** wil'ling, *a.* Ready; desirous; spontaneous; voluntary; prompt.
**Willingly,** wil'ing-li, *adv.* In a willing manner; cheerfully; readily; gladly.
**Wil-o'the-wisp,** wil'o-THi-wisp. *n.* The ignis-fatuus.
**Willow,** wil'ō, *n.* A tree or shrub, valuable for basket-making, etc.
**Willowy,** wil'o-i, *a.* Abounding with willows; slender and graceful.
**Willy-nilly,** wil'i-nil-i, *adv.* Willing or unwilling.
**Wilt,** wilt, *vi.* To fade; to wither or droop.
**Wily,** wi'li, *a.* Using wiles; cunning; sly.
**Wimble,** wim'bl, *n.* An instrument for boring holes.—*vt.* (wimbling, wimbled). To bore, as with a wimble.
**Wimple,** wim'pl, *n.* A female head-dress still worn by nuns.—*vt.* (wimpling, wimpled). To cover with a wimple; to hoodwink.—*vi.* To ripple; to undulate.
**Win,** win, *vt.* (winning, won). To gain; to be victorious in; to allure; to reach; to attain.—*vi.* To gain the victory.
**Wince,** wins, *vi.* (wincing, winced). To shrink, as from pain; to start back.—*n.* A start, as from pain.
**Wincey,** winsh, *n.* The bent handle for turning a wheel, etc.; a kind of windlass turned by a crank handle.
**Wind,** wind, in poetry often wīnd, *n.* Air in motion; a current of air; breath; power of respiration; empty words; flatulence.—*vt.* wind (pret. & pp. wound, sometimes winded). To blow, as a horn.—*vt.* wind (pret. pp. winded). To follow by the scent; to render scant of wind; to let rest and recover wind.
**Wind,** wīnd, *vt.* (pret. & pp. wound). To bend or turn; to twist; to coil.—*vi.* To twine or twist; to crook; to bend; to meander.
**Windage,** wind'āj, *n.* The difference between the diameter of a gun and that of the shell; influence of the wind in deflecting a missle; extent of deflection.
**Wind-bag,** wind'bag, *n.* A bag filled with wind; a man of mere words; a noisy pretender.
**Wind-bound,** wind'bound, *a.* Prevented from sailing by a contrary wind.
**Winder,** wīnd'ėr, *n.* One who or that which winds; an instrument for winding yarn, etc.
**Windfall,** wind'fal, *n.* Fruit blown down; an unexpected legacy or advantage.
**Windgall,** wind'gal, *n.* A soft tumor on the fetlock-joints of a horse.
**Winding,** wind'ing, *a.* Bending; twisting; spiral.—*n.* A turn or turning; a bend.
**Winding-sheet,** wīnd'ing-shēt, *n.* A sheet in which a corpse is wrapped.
**Wind-instrument,** wind'in-stru-ment, *n.* An instrument of music played by wind or breath, as an organ, flute, etc.
**Windlass,** wind'las, *n.* A revolving cylinder on which a rope is wound, used for raising weights, etc., by hand or other power.
**Windlestraw,** win'dl-stra, *n.* A kind of grass; a stalk of grass.
**Windmill,** wind'mil, *n.* A mill driven by the wind.
**Window,** win'dō, *n.* An opening in a wall for the admission of light or air; the frame (usually fitted with glass) in this opening.
**Window-sash,** win'dōl-sash, *n.* The light frame in which glass is set in windows.
**Windpipe,** wind'pip, *n.* The cartilaginous pipe or passage for the breath; the trachea.
**Wind-sail,** wind'sāl, *n.* A wide tube or funnel of canvas, used to convey air into the lower apartments of a ship.
**Wind-up,** wīnd-up, *n.* The conclusion or final set-

W

tlement of any matter; the close.
**Windward,** wīnd'wėrd, *n.* The point from which the wind blows.—*a.* and *adv.* Towards the wind.
**Windy,** wind'i, *a.* Boisterous; exposed to the wind; empty; flatulent.
**Wine,** wīn, *n.* An intoxicating liquor obtained from the fermented juice of grapes, etc.
**Wine-cellar,** wīn'sel-ėr, *n.* An apartment or cellar for storing wine.
**Wine-fat,** wīn'fat, *n.* The vat into which the liquor flows from the wine-press.
**Wine-glass,** wīn'gläs, *n.* A small glass in which wine is drunk.
**Wine-press,** wīn'pres, *n.* An apparatus in which the juice is pressed out of grapes.
**Wine-taster,** wīn'tāst-ėr, *n.* A person employed to judge of wine for purchasers.
**Wing,** wing, *n.* One of the anterior limbs in birds; organ of flight; flight; a lateral extension; side; side division of an army, etc.—*vt.* To furnish with wings; to fly; to traverse by flying; to wound in the wing.
**Wing-case,** wing'kās, *n.* The hard case which covers the wings of beetles, etc.
**Wing-commander,** wing-kom-mand'ėr. *n.* Officer in the Royal Air Force corresponding in rank to a commander in the navy or a lieutenant-colonel in the army.
**Winged,** wingd, *a.* Having wings; swift.
**Winglet,** wing'let, *n.* A little wing.
**Wink,** wingk, *vi.* To shut and open the eyelids; to give a hint by the eyelids; to connive; to be wilfully blind (with *at*).—*n.* Act of shutting and opening the eyelids rapidly; a twinkling; a hint given by means of the eye.
**Winner,** win'ėr, *n.* One who wins.
**Winning,** win'ing, *a.* Attractive; charming.—*n.* The sum won by success in competition; chiefly in *pl.*
**Winnow,** win'ō, *vt.* To separate the chaff from by wind; to fan; to sift; to scrutinize.—*vi.* To separate chaff from corn.
**Winsey,** win'si, *n.* Same as *Wincey.*
**Winsome,** win'sum, *a.* Attractive; winning.
**Winter,** win'tėr, *n.* The cold season of the year; a year; any cheerless situation.—*a.* Belonging to winter—*vi.* To pass the winter.—*vt.* To keep or feed during winter.
**Winterly,** win'tėr-li, *a.* Wintry.
**Wintry, Wintery,** win'tri, win'tėr-i, *a.* Pertaining or suitable to winter; cold; stormy.
**Winy,** wīn'i, *a.* Like wine.
**Winze,** winz, *n.* A small shaft in a mine.
**Wipe,** wīp, *vt.* (wiping, wiped). To clean by gentle rubbing; to strike gently; to efface.—*n.* A rub for the purpose of cleaning; a gibe.
**Wire,** wīr, *n.* A thread of metal; a telegraph wire; the telegraph.—*vt.* (wiring, wired). To bind with wire; to put a wire on; to send by telegraph.—*vi.* To communicate by telegraph.
**Wire-draw,** wīr'dra, *vt.* To draw into wire; to spin out at length; to protract.
**Wireless,** wir'les, *n.* Wireless telegraphy or telephony; communication between distant places by means of electromagnetic waves, without the use of wires.
**Wire-puller,** wīr'pul-ėr, *n.* One who pulls the wires of puppets; one who secretly controls the actions of others; an intriguer.
**Wire-pulling,** wīr-pul-ing, *n.* The procedure of a wire-puller.
**Wire-worm,** wīr'wėrm, *n.* A name for hard, wiry larvae or grubs.
**Wiry,** wīr'i, *a.* Made of or like wire; tough; lean and sinewy.
**Wisdom,** wiz'dom, *n.* Sound judgment and sagacity; prudence; learning or erudition.
**Wisdom-tooth,** wiz'dom-töth, *n.* A large back double tooth, the last to come.
**Wise,** wiz, *a.* Having wisdom; sagacious; judicious; skilled; sage.—*n.* Manner; mode.
**Wiseacre,** wīz'ā-kėr, *n.* A pretender to wisdom; a dunce who poses as a wise man.
**Wisely,** wīz'li, *adv.* Sensibly; judiciously.
**Wish,** wish, *vi.* To have a desire; to long; with *for.*—*vt.* To desire; to long for; to invoke.—*n.* A desire; the thing desired.
**Wishful,** wish'ful, *a.* Desirous; eager; earnest.
**Wishy-washy,** wish'i-wosh'i, *a.* Very thin and weak; diluted; feeble.
**Wisp,** wisp, *n.* A small bundle of straw, etc.
**Wistful,** wist'ful, *a.* Thoughtful; attentive; earnest; pensive; longing.
**Wistfully,** wist'ful-li, *adv.* In a wistful manner; attentively; pensively; longingly.
**Wit,** wit, *vt.* and *i.* (pres. tense, wot, pret. wist, pres. part. witting and wotting). To know; to be aware.—*To wit,* namely; that is to say.—*n.* Understanding; sense; wisdom; intelligence; faculty of associating ideas cleverly and in apt language; a person possessing this faculty; cleverness.
**Witch,** wich, *n.* A woman who practises sorcery.—*vt.* To betwitch.
**Witchcraft,** wich'kraft, *n.* Sorcery; enchantment; fascination.
**Witch-elm.** *See.* WYCH-ELM.
**Witchery,** wich'ėr-ri, *n.* Witchcraft; fascination.
**Witch-hazel,** *See.* WYCH-HAZEL.
**Witching,** wich'ing, *a. a.* Bewitching.
**Witenagemot,** wit'en-a-ge-mot'', *n.* The Anglo-Saxon national council.
**With,** WITH, *prep.* Against; in the company of; among; showing; marked by; immediately after; through; by.—*n.* With or with. A withe.
**Withal,** WITH-al', *adv.* Moreover; likewise; at the same time.—*prep.* With: used after relatives at the end of a clause.
**Withdraw,** WITH-dra, *vt.* To draw back or away; to retract; to cause to retire.—*vi.* To retire; to secede.
**Withdrawal,** WITH-dra'al, *n.* Act of withdrawing or taking back; a recalling.
**Withe,** with or with, *n.* A willow twig; any flexible twig used to bind something.
**Wither,** WITH'ėr, *vi.* To fade or shrivel; to become dry and wrinkled; to decline.—*vt.* To cause to fade; to prove fatal to.
**Withering,** WITH'ėr-ing, *a.* Such as to wither, blast, or fatally affect.
**Withers,** WITH'ėrz, *n.pl.* The junction of the shoulder-bones of a horse, forming the highest part of the back.
**Withhold,** WITH-hōld,'*vt.* To hold back; to restrain; to retain; not to grant.
**Within,** WITH-in',*prep.* In the interior of; in the compass of.—*adv.* In the inner part; inwardly; indoors; at home.
**Without,** WITH-out',*prep.* On the outside of; out of; beyond; not having.—*adv.* On the outside; outwardly; out-of-doors.
**Withstand,** WITH-stand', *vt.*and *interj.* To oppose; to resist.
**Withy,** wi'thi, *n.* A withe.
**Witless,** wit'les, *a.* Destitute of wit; thoughtless; indiscreet; silly.
**Witness,** wit'nes, *n.* Testimony; attestation of a fact or event; one who knows or sees anything; one who gives evidence in a trial. —*vt.* To attest; to see the execution of a legal instrument, and subscribe it.—*vi.* To bear testimony.
**Witted,** wit'ed, *a* Having wit.
**Witticism,** wit'i-sizm, *n.* A witty remark.
**Wittily,** wit'i-li, *adv.* With wit.
**Wittingly,** wit'ing-li, *adv.* Knowingly; by design.
**Witty,** wit'i, *a.* Possessed of wit; full of wit; keenly or brillantly humorous; facetious.
**Wive,** wiv, *vt.* and *i.* (wiving, wived). To provide with or take a wife.
**Wivern.** *See.* WYVERN.
**Wives,** wivz, pl. of *wife.*
**Wizard,** wiz'ard, *n.* A wise man or sage; a sorcerer; a magician; a conjurer.
**Wizen, Wizened,** wiz'n, wiz'nd, *a.* Hard, dry, and shrivelled; withered; weazen.
**Woad,** wōd, *n.* A plant, the leaves of which yield a

blue dye.
**Wobble,** wob'l, *vi.*. (wobbling, wobbled). To move unsteadily in rotating; to rock.
**Woe, Wo,** wō, *n.* Grief; misery; affliction.
**Woebegone,** wōbē-gon, *a.* Overwhelmed with woe; sorrowful; melancholy.
**Woeful, Woful,** wōfl, *a.* Full of woe; sorrowful; afflicted; wretched; pitiful.
**Woefullyi, Wofully,** wōful-li, *adv.* In a woeful manner; wretchedly; extremely.
**Wold,** wōld, *n.* A tract of open country; a low hill; a down.
**Wolf,** wulf, *n.*; pl. **Wolves,** wulvz. A carnivorous quadrüped akin to the dog, crafty and rapacious; a cruel or cunning person.
**Wolf Cub,** wulf kub, *n.* A junior Boy Scout, between the ages of 8 and 11.
**Wolfish,** wulf'ish, *a.* Like a wolf.
**Wolfram,** wul'fram, *n.* An ore of the metal tungsten; the metal itself. +
**Wolf's-bane,** wufs'ban,*n.* The plant monk's-hood or aconite.
**Woman,** wu'man, *n.*; pl. **Women,** wi'men. The female of the human race; the female sex; an adult female.
**Womanhood,** wu'man-hud, *n.* The state, character, or qualities of a woman.
**Womanish,** wu'man-hud, *n.* Women collectively; the female sex.
**Womankind,** wuman-kīnd, *n.* Women collectively; the female sex.
**Womanlike,** wuman-līk, *a.* Like a woman.
**Womanly,** wuman-li, *a.* Becoming a woman; feminine in a praiseworthy sense.
**Womb,** wöm,*n.* The uterus; place where anything is produced; any deep cavity.
**Wombat,** wom'bat, *n.* A marsupial mammal about the size of a badger.
**Won,** wun, pret. and pp. of *win*.
**Wonder,** wun'dėr, *n.* Something very strange; a prodigy or marvel; feeling excited by something strange.—*vi.* To be struck with wonder; to marvel; to entertain some doubt and curiosity.
**Wonderful,** wun'dėr-ful, *a.* Marvellous; surprising; strange; astonishing.
**Wonderfully,** wun'dėr-ful-li, *adv.* In a wonderful manner; surprisingly; very.
**Wonderment,** wun'dėr-ment, *n.* Wonder; surprise; astonishment.
**Wondrous,** wun'drus, *a.* Wonderful; strange.—*adv.* Remarkably.
**Wondrously,** wun'drus-li, *adv.* In a wondrous or wonderful manner or degree.
**Won't,** wōnt. A contraction for *will not*.
**Wont,** wōnt or wunt, *a.* Accustomed.—*n.*. Custom; habit; use.—*vi.* (pret. & pp. wont, sometimes wonted). To be accustomed to use.
**Wonted,** wōnt'ed or wunt'ed, *a.* Accustomed; usual.
**Woo,** wö, *vt.*and *i.* (wooing, wooed). To make love to ; to solicit in love; to court.
**Wood,** wud, *n.* A large collection of growing trees; the hard or solid substance of trees; timber.—*vi.* To take in or get supplies of wood.*vt.* To supply with wood.
**Woodbine, Woodbind,** wu'bin, wu'bind, *n.* The wild honeysuckle.
**Woodcock,** wud-kok, *n.* A bird allied to the snipe, esteemed for the tablle.
**Wood-cut,** wud'kut, *n.* An engraving on wood, or a print from such engraving.
**Wood-cutting,** wud'kut-ing, *n.* Act of cutting wood; wood-engraving.
**Wooded,** wud'ed, *a.* Abounding in or covered with wood or growing timber.
**Wooden,** wud'n, *a.* Made of wood; clumsy; awkward, dull.
**Wood-engraving,** wud'en-grāv-ing, *n.* The art of producing designs in relief on the surface of a block of wood; an impression from such a block.
**Woodland,** wud'land, *n.* Land covered with wood.—*a.* Relating to woods; sylvan.
**Woodman,** wud'man, *n.* A forester.
**Woodpecker,** wud'pek-ėr, *n.* A climbing bird which feeds on insects and their larvae on trees.
**Wood-pigeon,** wud'pi-jon, *n.* The ring-dove or cushat.
**Woodruff, Woodroof,** wud'ruf, wud,ruf, *n.* A plant of the madder family.
**Wood-sorrel,** wud'so-rel, *n.* A common British wild flower.
**Wood-work,** wud'wėrk, *n.* The part of any structure that is made of wood.
**Woody,** wud'i, *a.* Abounding with wood; wooded; consisting of wood; like wood.
**Wooer,** wu'ėr, *n.* One who woos.
**Woof,** wöf, *n.* The threads that cross the warp in weaving; the weft; texture in general.
**Wool,** wul, *n.* That soft species of hair on sheep; any fleecy substance resembling wool.
**Wool-gathering,** wul'gaTH-ėr-ing. *n.* Act of gatering wool; indulgence of idle fancies; a foolish or fruitless pursuit.
**Wool-grower,** wul'-grō-ėr, *n.* A person who raises sheep for the production wool.
**Woollen,** wul'en, *a.* Made of or pertaining to wool.—*n.* Cloth made of wool.
**Woolly,** wu'i, *a.* Consisting of wool; resembling wool; clothed with wool.
**Woolpack,** wul'pak, *n.* A bag of wool; a bundle or bale weighing 240 lbs.
**Woolsack,** wul'sak, *n.* A sack of wool; seat of the lord-chancellor in House of Lords.
**Wool-stapler,** wul'stā-pl-ėr, *n.* A dealer in wool; a sorter of wool.
**Wootz,** wuts, *n.* A very superior kind of steel imported from the East Indies.
**Word,** wėrd, *n.* An articulate sound expressing an idea; a term; information; a saying; motto; order; assertion or promise; in *pl.*, talk; wrangle.—*vi.* To express in words.
**Word-book,** wėrd'buk, *n.* A vocabulary; a dictionary.
**Wording,** wėrd'ing,*n.* The mode of expressing in words; form of stating.
**Wordy,** wėrd'ng, *a.* Using many words; verbose.
**Wore,** wōr, pret. of *wear*.
**Work,** wėrk, *n.* Effort; labor; employment; a task; achievement; a literary or artistic performance; some extensive structure; establishment where labor of some kind is carried on; result of force acting.—*vi.* (pret. and pp. worked or wrought). To put forth effort; to labor; to take effect; to tend or conduce; to seethe; to ferment.—*vt.* To bestow labor upon; to bring about; to keep at work; to influence; to achieve; to fashion; to embroider; to cause to ferment.
**Workable,** wėrk'a-bl, *a.* That can be worked, or that is worth working.
**Workaday,** wėrk'a-dā, *a.* Working-day; everyday; toiling.
**Worker,** wėrk'ėr, *n.* One that works; a toiler; a laborer; a working bee.
**Workhouse,** wėrk'hous, *n.* A house in which able-bodied paupers work; a pauper asylum.
**Working,** wėrk''ing, *a.* Engaged in bodily toil; industrious.—*n.* Act of laboring; movement; operation; fermentation; *pl.* portions of a mine, etc., worked.
**Working-class,** wėrk'ing-klas, *n.* Those who earn their bread by manual labor.
**Working-day,** wėrk'ing-dā, *n.* A day on which labor is performed.—*a.* Relating to such days; laborious.
**Workman,** wėrkman, *n.* An artisan; mechanic' laborer; worker.
**Workmanlike,** wėrk'man-līk, *a.* Like a proper workman; skilful; well performed.
**Workmanly,** wėrk'man-li, *a.* Workmanlike.
**Workmanship,** wėrk'man-ship, *n.* Skill or art of a workman; style or character of execution; art; dexterity; handicraft.
**Workshop,** wėrk'shop, *n.* A shop or building where any craft or work is carried on.

**World,** wėrld, *n*. The whole creation; the earth; any celestial orb; a large portion of our globe; sphere of existence; a domain or realm; mankind; the public; great degree or quantity.
**Wordling,** wėrld'ling, *n*. One devoted exclusively to workdly pleasures.
**Wordly,** wėrld'li, *a*. Relating to this world or this life; secular; carnal; sordid.
**World-wide,** wėrld'wid, *a*. Wide as the world; extending over all the world.
**Worm,** wėrm, *n*. A small creeping animal; an intestinal parasite; *pl*. the disease caused by such parasites; something spiral.—*vi*. To wriggle; to work gradually and secretly.—*vt*. To effect by stealthy means; *refi*. to insinuate oneself; to extract cunningly.
**Worm-eaten,** wērm'ėt-n, *a*. Gnawed by worms; having cavities made by worms.
**Wormling,** wėrm'lling, *n*. A minute worm.
**Wormwood,** wėrm'wud, *n*. A plant with bitter, tonic, and stimulating qualities.
**Wormy,** wėrm'i, *a*. Abounding with worms; eaten by worms; groveling; earthy.
**Worn,** wōrn, *pp. of wear*.
**Worn-out,** wōrn'out, *a*. Useless from being much worn; wearied; exhausted.
**Worry,** wu'ri, *vt*.(worrying, worried). To tear with the teeth, as dogs; to harass; to annoy.—*vi*. To trouble oneself; to fret.—*n*. Trouble; care; anxiety.
**Worse,**wėrs, *a*. Bad or ill in a greater degree; inferior; more unwell; more ill off.—The worse, defeat; disadvantage.—*adv*. In a manner or degree more evil or bad.
**Worsen,** wėr'sn, *vi* and *t*.. To grow or make worse.
**Worser,** wėrs'ėr, *a* and *adv*. A redundant comparative of *worse*.
**Worship,**wėrship, *n*. Dignity; honor; a title of honor; religious service; adoration; reverence.—*vt*. (worshipping, worshipped). To adore; to pay divine honors to; to idolize.—*vi*. To perform religious service.
**Worshipful,** wėr'ship-ful, *a*. Worthy of honor or high respect; honorable.
**Worshipper,** wėr'ship-er, *n*. One who worships.
**Worst,** wėrst, *a*. Bad or evil in the highest degree.—*n*. The most evil state or action.—*adv*. Most extremely.—*vt*. To defeat.
**Worsted,** wust'ed, *n*. Yarn spun from wool, and used in knitting.—*a*. Made of worsted.
**Wort,** wėrt, *n*. The infusion of malt before it becomes beer by fermentation; an herb.
**Worth,** wėrth, *a*. Equal in value or price to; deserving of; possessing.—*n*. Value; price; merit; excellence.—*vi*. To be; to betide.
**Worthily,** wėr'TH-li, *adv*. In a worthy manner; suitably; deservedly; justly.
**Worthless,** wėrth'les, *a*. Having no worth; valueless; contemptible; not deserving.
**Worthy,** wėrTHi, *a*. Possessing worth; estimable; virtuous; deserving; fitting.—*n*. A man of eminent worth; a local celebrity.
**Wot, wot.** *See* WIT.
**Would,** wud, Pret. of *will*, mainly used in subjunctive or conditional senses.
**Would-be,** wud'bē, *a*. Wishing to be; vainly pretending to be.—*n*. A vain pretender.
**Wound,** wönd, *n*. A cut or stab, etc.; injury; hurt or pain to the feelings; damage.—*vt*. or *i*. To inflict a wound on; to pain.
**Wove,** wuv, pret. and sometimes pp. of *weave*.
**Wrack,** räk, *n*. Sea-weed generally; wreck; a thin flying cloud.
**Wraith,** räth, *n*. An apparition of a person about to die or newly dead.
**Wrangle,** rang'gl, *vi*. (wrangling, wrangled). To dispute angrily; to argue.—*n*. A dispute.
**Wrangler,** rang'glėr, *n*. One who wrangles; in Cambridge University, one who attains a first class in the final examination for honors in mathematics.
**Wrap,** rap, *vt*. (wrapping, wrapped or wrapt). To fold or roll; to cover by something wound; to envelop.—*n*. An outer article of dress for warmth.
**Wrapper,** rap'ėr, *n*. One that wraps; a cover; a loose upper garment.
**Wrapping,**rap'ing, *a*. Used or designed to wrap.—*n*. A cover; a wrapper.
**Wrath,** räth or rath, *n*. Violent anger; rage; fury.
**Wrathful,** räth'fül or rath'ful, *a*. Full of wrath; furious; wroth.
**Wreak,** rēk, *vt*. To revenge or avenge; to inflict; to gratify by punishment.
**Wreath,** rēth, *n*. Something twisted or curled; a garland; a chaplet; a snow-drift.
**Wreathe,** rēTH, *vt*. (wreathing, wreathed). To twist into a wreath; to entwine; to encircle; to dress in a garland.—*vi*. To be entwined.
**Wreathy,** rēth'i, *a*. Forming a wreath; spral.
**Wreck,** rek, *n*. Ruin; overthrow; a ruin; destruction of a vessel at sea.—*vt*. To cause to become a wreck; to ruin.
**Wreckage,** rek'āj, *a*. Act of wrecking; remains of a ship or cargo that has been wrecked.
**Wrecker,** rek'ėr, *n*. One who causesshipwrecks or plunders wrecks; one who recovers goods from wrecked vessels.
**Wren,** ren, *n*. A name of various small birds; a small song-bird; a member of the Women's Royal Naval Service (W.R.N.S.).
**Wrench,** rensh, *n*. A violent twist; injury by twisting; an instrument for screwing a bolt or nut.—*vt*. To pull with a twist; to distort.
**Wrest,** rest, *vt*. To twist; to take or force by violence; to distort.—*n*. Act of wresting; a wrench; an implement to tune stringed instruments with.
**Wrestle,** res'l, *vi*. (wrestling, wrestled). To contend with in wrestling.—*n*. A bout at wrestling.
**Wrestler,** res'lėr, *a*. One who wrestles.
**Wretch,** rech, *n*. A miserable person; a mean, base, or vile creaeture.
**Wretched,** rech'ed, *a*. Very miserable; distressing; worthless; despicable.
**Wretchedly,** rech'ed-li, *adv*. In a wretched manner; most miserably; contemptibly.
**Wriggle,** rig'l, *vi*. and *t*. (wriggling, wriggled). To move with writhing or twisting.—*n*. A quick twisting motion.
**Wright,** rit, *n*. An artisan or artificer; a worker in wood; a carpenter.
**Wring,** ring, *vt*. (wringing, wrung). To twist with the hands; to twist and compress; to torture; to extort.—*vi*. To writhe.
**Wringer,** ring'ėr, *n*. One who wrings; an apparatus for forcing water from clothes.
**Wrinkle,** ring'kl, *n*. A small ridge or furrow; a crease; a hint; a notion.—*vt*. and *i*. (wrinkling, wrinkled). To form into wrinkles; to contract into furrows; to crease.
**Wrinkly,** ring'kl-i, *a*. Somewhat wrinkled; puckered.
**Wrist,** rist, *n*. The joint by which the hand is united to the arm.
**Wristband,** rist'band, *n*. The band of a sleeve covering the wrist.
**Wristlet,** rist'let, *n*. Some small object worn round the wrist; a bracelet.
**Writ,** rit, *n*. That which is written; the Scriptures; a legal document commanding a person to do some act.
**Write** rit, *vt*. (writing, pret. wrote, pp. written). To form by a pen, etc.; to set down in letters or words; to cover with letters; to send in writing; to compose.—*vi*. To trace characters with a pen, etc.; to be engaged in literary work; to conduct correspondence.
**Writer,** rit'ėr, *n*. One who writes; an author; a clerk; in Scotland, a law agent.
**Writhe,** rīTH, *vt*. (writhing, writhed). To twist or distort, as the body or limbs.—*vi*. To twist and turn; to be distorted, as from agony.
**Writing,** rit'ing, *n*. Act of one who writes; a book, manuscript, or document; style.

**Written,** rit'n, *a.* Expressed in writing.
**Wrong,** rong, *a.* Not right; not fit; not what ought to be; erroneous.—*n.* What is not right; an injustice; injury.—*adv.* In a wrong manner.—*vt.* To do wrong to; to treat with injustice.
**Wrong-doer,** rong'dö-ėr, *n.* One who does wrong.
**Wrongful,** rong'ful, *a.* Injurious; unjust.
**Wrong-headed,** rong'hed-ed, *a.* Obstinately or perversely wrong; stubborn.
**Wrongly,** rong'li, *adv.* In a wrong manner; mistakenly; erroneously; unjustly.
**Wrongous,** rong'us, *a.* In *Scots law*, unjust.
**Wroth,** roth, *a.* Very angry; indignant.
**Wrought,** rat, pret. and pp. of *work.*
**Wry,** ri, *a.* Crooked; twisted; askew.
**Wryneck,** ri'nek, *n.* A twisted neck; a small European bird allied to the woodpeckers.
**Wych-elm,** wich'elm, *n.* An elm with large leaves and pendulous branches.
**Wych-hazel,** wich'hā-zel, *n.* An American shrub with yellow flowers.
**Wyund,** wind, *n.* A narrow alley, a lane.
**Wyvern,** wī'vėrn, *n.* An heraldic monster, a sort of dragon, with two wings, two eagle's legs, and a tapering body.

# X

**Xanthic,** zan'thik, *a.* Yellowish.
**Xanthin, Xanthine,** zan'thin, *n.* A yellow coloring matter.
**Xanthous,** zan'thus, *a.* Fair-haired.
**Xebec,** zē'bek or ze-bek', *n.* A three-masted vessel used in the Mediterranean.
**Xerotes,** zē'ro-tėz, *n.* A dry habit of the body.
**Xiphold,** zēf'old, *a.* Shaped like a sword.
**X-rays,** eks'raz, or roentgen rays, runt'gen, *n.* Electro-magnetic waves of high frequency, which penitrate most sutstances and enable photo graphs to be taken of these in the living body.
**Xylem,** *n.* Woody vegetable tissue.
**Xylograph,** zi'lo-graf, *n.* A wood-engraving.
**Xylography,** zi-log'ra-fi, *n.* Wood-engraving; a process of decorative painting on wood.
**Xyloid,** zī'loid, *a.* Having the nature of wood; resembling wood.
**Xylonite,** zī'lī-nīt, *n.* Celluloid.
**Xylophagous,** zī-lof'a-gus, *a.* Wood-eating.
**Xylophone,** zī-lo-fōn, *n.* A musical instrument in which the notes are given by pieces of wood struck with hammers.
**Xyst, Xystus,** zist, zis'tus, *n.* A covered portico or open court for athletic exercises.
**Xyster,**zis'tėr, *n.* A surgeon's instrument for scraping bones.

# Y

**Yacht,** yot, *n.* A light vessel used for racing, pleasure, etc.,—*vi.* To sail in a yacht.
**Yachter,** yot'ėr, *n.* A yachtsman.
**Yachiting,** yot'ing, *a.* Belonging to a yacht.—*n.* Act of sailing a yacht.
**Yachtsman,** yots',man, *n.* One who keeps or sails a yacht.
**Yahoo,** yä'hö, *n.* A rude, boorish person.
**Yak,** yak, *n.* A wild ox with long silky hair.
**Yam,** yam, *n.* A climbing plant, cultivated in tropical climates for its large roots.
**Yankee,** yang'kē, *n.* A citizen of New England; a native of the United States.
**Yap,** yap, *vi.* (yapping, yapped). To yelp; to bark,—*n.* Cry of a dog; yelp.
**Yard,** yärd, *n.* A standard measure of 3 feet; a long beam slung crosswise to a mast and supporting a sail; piece of enclosed ground.
**Yard-arm,** yärd'ärm, *n.* Either end of a ship's yard.
**Yard-stick,** yärd'stik, *n.* A stick 3 feet in length.
**Yare,** yār, *a.* Ready; desterous.
**Yarn,** yärn, *n.* Thread prepared from wool or flax for weaving; a story.
**Yarrow,** ya'rō, *n.* Milfoil.
**Yataghan,** yat'a-gan, *n.* A dagger-like saber about 2 feet long.
**Yaw,** ya, *vi.* To swerve suddenly inb sailing.—*n.* The sudden temporary deviation of a ship.
**Yawl,** yal, *n.* A small ship's boat, usually rowed by four or six oars; a small two-masted yacht.—*vi.* To howl; to yell.
**Yawn,** yan, *vi.* To have the mouth open involuntarily while a deep breath is taken; to gape.—*n.* A gaping; act of yawning; a chasm.
**Ye,** yē, *pron.* The nominative and objective plural of the second personal pronoun.
**Yea,** yā, *adv.* Yes; the opposite of *nay.*
**Yean,** yēn, *vi.* and *i.* To bring forth young, as a goat or sheep.
**Yeanling,** yēn'ling, *n.* A lamb.
**Year,** yēr, *n.* The period of time during which the earth makes one revolution in its orbit; twelve months; *pl.* old age; time of life.
**Year-book,** yēr-buk, *n.* A book published every year giving fresh information regarding matters that change.
**Yearling,** yēr'ling, *n.* A young beast one year old.—*a.* Being a year old.
**Yearly,** yēr'li, *a.* Annual; happening every year.—*adv.* Once a year.
**Yearn,** yėrn, *vi.* To feel uneasiness of mind from longing or pity; to long.
**Yearning,** *yėrn'ing, a.* Longing.—*n.* A feeling of longing desire.
**Yeast,** yēst, *n.* A yellowish substance produced in alcoholic fermentation; barm.
**Yeasty,** yēst'i, *n.* Like or containing yeast.
**Yell,** yel, *vi.* To cry out with a loud piercing noise; to scream.—*n.* A loud, piercing outcry.
**Yellow,** yel'ō, *a.* Being of a bright golden color.—*n.* A bright golden color.
**Yellow-fever,** yel'ō-fē-vėr, *n.* A malignant fever of warm climates, attended with yellow-ness of the skin.
**Yellow-hammer,Yellow-ammer,** yel'ō-ham-ėr, yel'ō-am-ėr, *n.* A species of bunting, with much yellow in its plumage.
**Yellowish,** yel'ō-ish, *a.* Somewhat yellow.
**Yelp,** yelp, *vi.* To utter a sharp bark or cry, as a dog.—*n.* A sharp cry of a dog.
**Yeoman,** yō'man, *n.*; pl. **-men.** A man who owns a small estate in land; a gentleman farmer; one of the yeomanry.
**Yeomanly,** yō'man-li, *a.* Pertaining to a yeoman.—*adv.* Like ayeoman; bravely.
**Yeomanry,** yō'man-ri, *n.* The collective body of yeomen; a volunteer cavalry force.
**Yes,** yes, *adv.* Even so; expressing affirmation or consent; opposed to *no.*
**Yester,** yes'tėr, *a.* Pertaining to the day before the present; last.
**Yesterday,** yes'tėr-dāā, *n.* The day before the present.—*adv.* On the day last past.
**Yestereve, Yestereven,** yes'tėr-ėv, yes'tėr-ē-vn, *n.* The evening last past.
**Yestermorn, Yestermorning,** yes'tėr-morn, yes-tėr-mor'ning, *n.* The morn or morning last past.
**Yesternight,** yes'tėr-nīt, *n.* The night last past.
**Yet,** yet, *adv.* In addition; still; hitherto; nevertheless.—*conj.* Nevertheless, however.
**Yew,** yū, *n.* An evergreen tree, with poisonous leaves, and yielding a hard durable timber.
**Yield,** yēld, *vt.* To produce in return for labor, etc.; to afford; to grant; to give up.—*vi.* To submit; to comply; to produce.—*n.* Amount yielded; product; return.
**Yielding,** yēld'ing, *a.* Inclined to yield; accommodating; compliant; facile.
**Yodel, Yodle,** yō'dl, *vt.* and *i.* (yodelling, yodling; yodelled, yodled). To sing like the Swiss and Tyrolese mountaineers by changing suddenly from the natural voice to the falsetto.

**Yoke,** yōk, *n.* Gear connecting draught animals by passing across their necks; a pair of draught animals; something resembling a yoke; shoulder-piece of a garment supporting the rest; servitude; burden; a bond; a tie.—*vt.* (yoking, yoked). To put a yoke on; to couple; to enslave.
**Yoke-fellow, Yoke-mate,** yōk'fel-ō, yōk'-māt, *n.* An associate; a partner.
**Yokel,** yō'kl, *n.* A rustic; an ignorant peasant; a country bumpkin.
**Yolk,** yōk, *n.* The yellow part of an egg.
**Yon,** yon, *a.* That; those; yonder.
**Yonder,** yon'dėr *a.* That or those away there.—*adv.* At or in that place there.
**Yore,** yōr, *adv.* Long ago; in old time: now used only in the phrase *of yore.*
**You,** yö, *pron.* The nominative and objective plural of *thou*: commonly used when a single person is addressed.
**Young,** yung, *a.* Being in the early stage of life; youthful.—*n.* The offspring of an animal.
**Youngish,** yung'ish, *a.* Somewhat young.
**Youngling,** yung'ling, *n.* Any animal in the first part of life; a young person.
**Youngster,** yung'stėr, *n.* A young person.
**Younker,** yung'kėr, *n.* A youngster.
**Your,** yör, possessive corresponding to *ye, you.* Pertaining or belonging to you.
**Yours,** yörz, *poss. pron.* That or those which belong to you. **Yourself,** Yör-self' *pron.*; pl. **-selves.** You, used distinctively or reflexively.
**Youth,** yöth, *n.* State or quality of being young; period during which one is young; a young man; young persons collectively.
**Youthful,** yöth'ful, *a.* Young; pertaining to youth; fresh or vigorous, as in youth.
**Yowl,** youl, *vi.* To give a long distressful or mournful cry, as a dog.—*n.* A mournful cry.
**Yule,** yöl, *n.* Christmas.

# Z

**Zaffre,** zaf'ėr, *n.* A substance obtained from cobalt, used by enamellers as a blue color.
**Zany,** zā'ni, *n.* A buffoon or merry-andrew.
**Zareba.** Same as *Zereba.*
**Zax,** zaks, *n.* An instrument used for cutting and dressing slates.
**Zeal,** zēl, *n.* Eagerness; passionate ardour; enthusiasm.
**Zealot,** ze'lot, *n.* One who is zealous; a fanatical partisan; a bigot.
**Zealotry,** ze'lot-ri, *n.* Behavior of a zealot; excessive zeal; fanaticism.
**Zealous,** ze'lus, *a.* Inspired with zeal; fervent; eager; earnest.
**Zealously,** ze'lus-li, *adv.* In a zealous manner; ardently; eagerly; fervently.
**Zebec, Zebeck,** zē'bek, *n.* Same as *Xebec.*
**Zebra,** zē'bra, *n.* A striped South African animal allied to the horse and ass.
**Zebu,** zē'bū, *n.* The humped ox of India.
**Zemindar,** zem-in-där, *n.* In India, a landholder or landed proprietor.
**Zenana,** ze-nä'na, *n.* The portion of a Hindu's house devoted to females.
**Zend,** zend, *n.* An ancient Iranian or Persian language, closely allied to Sanskrit.
**Zenith,** zē'nith or zen'ith, *n.* The point of the heavens right above a spectator's head; highest point.
**Zephyr,** zef'ėr, *n.* The west wind; any soft, mild, gentle breeze.
**Zeppelin,** zep'el-in, *n.* A German air-ship.
**Zereba,** ze-rē'ba, *n.* In the Sudan, a temporary camp guarded by a fence of bushes, etc.
**Zero,** zē'rō, *n.* Number or quantity diminished to nothing: a cipher; lowest point.
**Zest,** zest, *n.* Orange or lemon peel, used to flavor liquor; relish; charm; gusto.
**Zigzag,** zig'zag, *n.* Something in the form of straight lines with sharp turns.—*a.* Having sharp turns or bends.—*vi.* (zigzagging, zigzagged). To move in a zigzag fashion; to form zigzags.
**Zigzaggy,** zig'zag-i, *a.* Zigzag.
**Zinc,** zingk, *n.* A metal of bluish-white color, used for roofing, to form alloys, etc.
**Zincky, Zinky,** zingk'i, *a.* Pertaining to or like zinc; containing zinc.
**Zincode,** zingk'ōd, *n.* The positive pole of a galvanic battery.
**Zincography,** zing-kog'ra-fi, *n.* A mode of printing similar to lithography, a plate of zinc taking the place of the stone.
**Zincoid,** zingk'oid, *a.* Zincky.
**Zip-fastener,** zip-fas'n-ėr, *n.* A kind of fastener, pulled open or shut by a tag, and joining two edges together, used on purses, tobacco-pouches, golf-bags, etc.
**Zircon,** zėr'kon, *n.* A hard lustrous mineral, one of the gems called also jargon.
**Zither, Zithern,** zith'ėr, zith'ėrn, *n.* A flat musical instrument with from twenty-nine to forty-two strings, played with the fingers.
**Zodiac,** zō'di-ak, *n.* An imaginary belt or zone in the heavens, within which the apparent motions of the sun, moon, and principal planets are confined, divided into twelve equal parts or signs.
**Zodiacal,** zō-dī'ak-al, *a.* Pertaining to the zodiac.
**Zoetrope,** zō'ē-trōp, *n.* An optical contrivance by which, when the instrument revolves, certain painted figures inside appear to move in a life-like manner.
**Zone,** zōn, *n.* A girdle or belt; one of the five great divisions of the earth, bounded by circles parallel to the equator; any well-defined belt.
**Zonule,** zōn'ūl, *n.* A little zone.
**Zoogony, Zoogeny,** zō-og'o-ni, zō-oj'e-ni, *n.* The doctrine of the origin of life.
**Zoography,** zō-og'ra-fi, *n.* The description of animals.
**Zooid,** zō'oid, *a.* Resembling or pertaining to an animal.—*n.* An organism, in some respects resembling a distinct animal.
**Zoolite,** zō'ol-līt, *n.* An animal substance petrified or fossil.
**Zoological,** zō-o-loj'ik-al, *a.* Pertaining to zoology.
**Zoologist,** zō-ol'o-jist, *n.* One who is versed in zoology.
**Zoology,** zō-ol'o-ji, *n.* The science of the natural history of animals.
**Zoon,** zō'on, *n.* An animal.
**Zoonomy,** zō-on'o-mi, *n.* The laws of animal life, or the science which treats of it.
**Zoophagous,** zō-of'a-gus, *a.* Feeding on animals; carnivorous.
**Zoophyte,** zō'o-fīt, *n.* A name applied to many plant-like animals, as sponges.
**Zoroastrian,** zor-o-as'tri-an, *a.* Pertaining to Zoroaster or Zoroastrianism.—*n.* A believer in this religion.
**Zoroastrianism,** zor-o-as'tri-an-izm, *n.* The ancient Persian religion founded by Zoroaster, one feature of which was a belief in a good and an evil power perpetually at strife; the religion of the Parsees; fire-worship.
**Zouave,** zwäv, *n.* A French infantry soldier dressed after the Turkish fashion.
**Zulu,** zö'lö, *n.* A member of a branch of the Kaffir race in South Africa.
**Zymic,** zim'ik, *a.* Pertaining to fermentation.
**Zymology,** zi-mol'o-ji, *n.* The doctrine of ferments and fermentation.
**Zymotic,** zi-mot'ik, *a.* Pertaining to fermentation; applied to epidemic and contagious diseases, supposed to be produced by germs acting like a ferment.

# NOTES

# NOTES